Doyice J. Cotten & John T. Wolohan
Sport Risk Consulting   *Syracuse University*

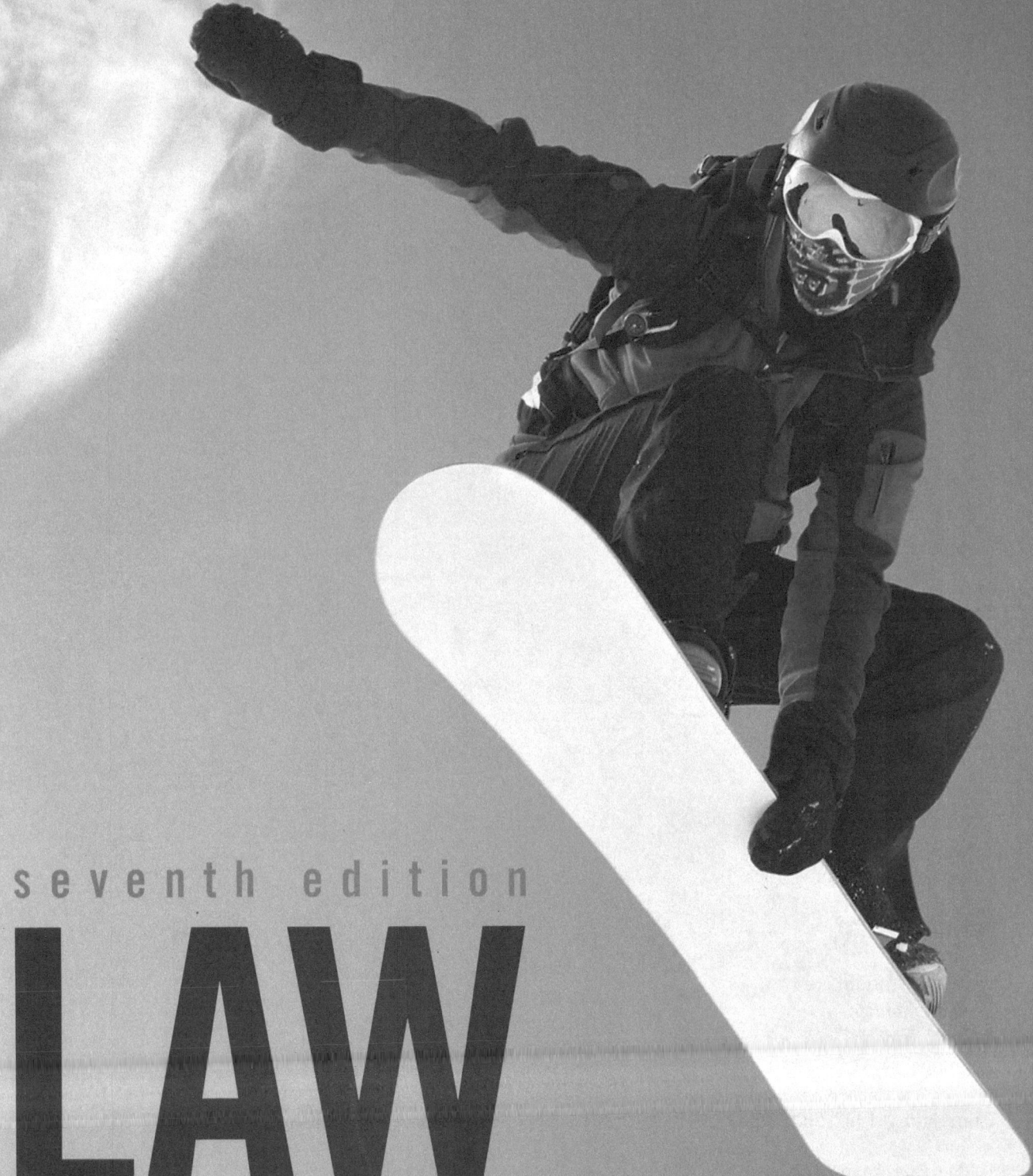

seventh edition

LAW

for recreation & sport managers

Kendall Hunt
publishing company

Cover image © Shutterstock, Inc.

Kendall Hunt
publishing company

www.kendallhunt.com
Send all inquiries to:
4050 Westmark Drive
Dubuque, IA 52004-1840

Copyright © 1997, 2001, 2003, 2007, 2010, 2013, 2017 by Kendall Hunt Publishing Company

ISBN 978-1-5249-0268-1

All rights reserved. No part of this publication may be reproduced, stored in a retrieval system, or transmitted, in any form or by any means, electronic, mechanical, photocopying, recording, or otherwise, without the prior written permission of the copyright owner.

Printed in the United States of America

Dedication

*This 7th edition is dedicated to **Lynne Gaskin**, a friend and colleague for many years. Lynne was one of the original contributing authors of this book and has played an important role in its success, both as a contributing author and as a valued advisor. Lynne has been a leader in the fields of physical education and sport law, receiving Honor Awards from the North Carolina AHPERD, the Georgia AHPERD, and the Sport and Recreation Law Association. She is Professor Emerita from the University of West Georgia and is now enjoying her retirement in Georgia.*

BRIEF CONTENTS

1.00 INTRODUCTION TO SPORT LAW

1.10	The Legal System	2
1.20	Legal Research	15
1.30	Business Structure and Legal Authority	29

2.00 NEGLIGENCE LAW

2.10	Negligence Theory	40
2.20	Defenses	75
2.30	Recreation and Sport Management Applications	129

3.00 INTENTIONAL TORTS AND CRIMINAL ACTS

3.10	Intentional Tort Applications	214
3.20	Sport-Related Crimes	247

4.00 RISK MANAGEMENT

4.10	Risk Management Theory	274
4.20	Recreation and Sport Management Applications	286

5.00 CONTRACT LAW

5.10	Contract Essentials	360
5.20	Recreation and Sport Management Applications	373
5.30	Alternative Dispute Resolution	394

6.00 CONSTITUTIONAL LAW

6.10	Concepts	404
6.20	Recreation and Sport Management Applications	467

7.00 SPORT AND LEGISLATION

7.10	Federal Statutes and Discrimination	522
7.20	Intellectual Property Law	591
7.30	Antitrust and Labor Law	626
7.40	Sport Agent Legislation	660

CONTENTS

Preface viii
Acknowledgments ix
About the Authors x
Contributing Authors xi

1.00 INTRODUCTION TO SPORT LAW

1.10	The Legal System *Kristi L. Schoepfer Bochicchio*	2
1.20	Legal Research *Anita M. Moorman*	15
1.30	Business Structure and Legal Authority *John T. Wolohan*	29

2.00 NEGLIGENCE LAW

2.10	**Negligence Theory**	40
	2.11 Negligence *Doyice J. Cotten*	40
	2.12 Which Parties are Liable? *Doyice J. Cotten*	52
	2.13 Liability of Sports Participants, Instructors, and Officials *Doyice J. Cotten*	63
2.20	**Defenses**	75
	2.21 Defenses against Negligence *Doyice J. Cotten*	75
	2.22 Immunity *Doyice J. Cotten*	88
	2.23 Waivers and Releases *Doyice J. Cotten*	105
	2.24 Agreements Related to the Inherent Risk *Doyice J. Cotten*	116
2.30	**Recreation and Sport Management Applications**	129
	2.31 Premises Liability *John Grady*	129
	2.32 Property Law *Sarah J. Young*	139
	2.33 Emergency Care *Kristi L. Schoepfer Bochicchio*	149
	2.34 Supervision *Paul J. Batista, Andrew T. Pittman, & Lynne P. Gaskin*	165
	2.35 Transportation *Paul J. Batista & Andrew T. Pittman*	178
	2.36 Products Liability *Rebecca J. Mowrey*	190
	2.37 Hospitality and Tourism Law *Sarah J. Young*	200

3.00 INTENTIONAL TORTS AND CRIMINAL ACTS

3.10	**Intentional Tort Applications**	214
	3.11 Assault and Battery *Curt Hamakawa*	214
	3.12 Defamation *Anita M. Moorman*	225
	3.13 Other Intentional Torts: *Gary Rushing*	236
3.20	**Sport-Related Crimes**	247
	3.21 Criminal Law and Sport *Kristi L. Schoepfer Bochicchio*	247
	3.22 Hazing *Ellen J. Staurowsky*	258

4.00 RISK MANAGEMENT

4.10	**Risk Management Theory**	274
	4.11 Risk Management Process *Robin Ammon*	274
4.20	**Recreation and Sport Management Applications**	286
	4.21 Standards of Practice *Joann M. Eickhoff-Shemek*	286
	4.22 Audits in Risk Management *Todd L. Seidler*	296
	4.23 Crisis Management *Daniel Connaughton & Thomas A. Baker, III*	313
	4.24 Crowd Management *Robin Ammon, Jr. & Nita Unruh*	327

	4.25	Managing Risk through Insurance *Doyice J. Cotten*	340
	4.26	Workers' Compensation *John T. Wolohan*	348

5.00 CONTRACT LAW

5.10	Contract Essentials *Bridget Niland*	360
5.20	Recreation and Sport Management Applications	373
	5.21 Employment Contracts *Rodney L. Caughron*	373
	5.22 Game, Event, and Sponsorship Contracts *Bridget Niland*	385
5.30	Alternative Dispute Resolution *Rebecca J. Mowrey*	394

6.00 CONSTITUTIONAL LAW

6.10	Concepts	404
	6.11 Judicial Review, Standing, and Injunctions *Jim Masteralexis & Lisa Pike Masteralexis*	404
	6.12 State Action *John Wolohan*	416
	6.13 Due Process *John T. Wolohan*	426
	6.14 Equal Protection *Sarah K. Fields*	435
	6.15 Search and Seizure/Right to Privacy *Margaret E. Ciccolella*	446
	6.16 First Amendment *John T. Wolohan*	455
6.20	Recreation and Sport Management Applications	467
	6.21 Voluntary Associations and Eligibility Issues *Colleen Colles*	467
	6.22 Conduct Issues *W.S. Bill Miller*	479
	6.23 Drug Testing *John T. Wolohan*	490
	6.24 Participants with Disabilities *John T. Wolohan*	501
	6.25 Private Clubs in Sport and Recreation *Anne DeMartini & Mark Dodds*	513

7.00 SPORT AND LEGISLATION

7.10	Federal Statutes and Discrimination	522
	7.11 Gender Equity: Opportunities to Participate *Linda Jean Carpenter*	522
	7.12 Gender Equity: Coaching and Administration *Barbara Osborne*	532
	7.13 Title VII of the Civil Rights Act of 1964 *Stephanie A. Tryce & Lisa Pike Masteralexis*	543
	7.14 Sexual Harassment *Barbara Osborne*	556
	7.15 Age Discrimination in Employment *Anne DeMartini*	569
	7.16 Title I of the Americans with Disabilities Act *Mary A. Hums*	581
7.20	Intellectual Property Law	591
	7.21 Copyright and Patent Law *Merry Moiseichik*	592
	7.22 Principles of Trademark Law *Paul M. Anderson*	602
	7.23 Image Rights *John T. Wolohan*	613
7.30	Antitrust and Labor Law	630
	7.31 Antitrust Law: Professional Sport Applications *Lisa Pike Masteralexis*	626
	7.32 Antitrust Law: Amateur Sport Applications *John T. Wolohan*	637
	7.33 Labor Law: Professional Sport Applications *Lisa Pike Masteralexis*	647
7.40	Sport Agent Legislation *John T. Wolohan*	660

Case Index	671
Subject Index	687

PREFACE

It has been 20 years since the publication of the first edition of this textbook in 1996. Much has changed since that first edition: the original title, **Sport Law for Sport Managers**, was changed for the second edition; chapters have been removed; other chapters added; some authors have left; others have joined us; and interestingly, we began with 57 chapters and we have 57 chapters in this 7th edition. Two things, however, have not changed. First, the text immediately became the most popular sport law text available, and it remains the most popular today. Second, the commitment of the editors and contributing authors has remained the same through seven editions – to provide students and professionals with the best, most comprehensive and most up-to-date sport and recreation law text available.

In this Seventh Edition, John, Doyice, and the contributing authors have worked hard to provide

1. **An easy-to-read, user-friendly text** of accurate legal information appropriate for recreation majors, sport management majors, and recreation and sport managers in the field. And yet, each short chapter is crammed full of crucial information on the topic.

2. A recreation and sport law text that contains information that is **current, up-to-date, and accurate**. One author could not keep a book of this size up to date every three years. However, since more than 30 authors are involved in writing the book, this text remains the most current of the sport law texts available.

3. A text that can be effective with both **undergraduate and graduate students**. The chapters are easily understanable by undergraduates and, at the same time, provide enough depth to challenge graduate students. Also, the online cases make in-depth, graduate study more convenient.

4. A total of **57 chapters** covering such topic areas as negligence law, intentional torts, risk management, contract law, constitutional law, and more. This enables each professor to pick and choose the chapters that meet the professor's goals for the class.

5. A book that a student can keep to serve as a **reference book** for future use.

Change in the law is constant and the same is true for *Law for Recreation and Sport Managers*. In this edition, we welcome back Andy Pittman, who was a contributing author for the first four editions; and we say a reluctant goodbye to a few authors including Lynne Gaskin, who was one of the original authors and has been with us through the six previous editions.

All chapters have undergone changes ranging from major rewrites, to substantial revisions, to minor updates. We think that the user will appreciate the changes and be able to see that they are getting the latest information on the subject.

It is our hope that professors adopting the text and students using the text will find it even more helpful than previous editions. We welcome any comments or suggestions that would make the text more useful to you.

Doyice and John

ACKNOWLEDGMENTS

Many persons deserve credit for the success of this 7th edition of **Law for Recreation and Sport Managers**.

First, thanks go to the diligent efforts of the **chapter authors and co-authors**. Their writing and research are major factors in making this the most widely-used text in the area of sport and recreation law.

Thanks, too, to an often unrecognized contributor to a book – **the user** – the professors who adopt the text and the students who use it. We would like to thank you for your loyalty and especially thank those of you who have offered suggestions for improvement. This text is always changing (just like the law) and we try to address as many of your recommendations as possible. While some suggestions do not fit with the goals of the text, you will see many changes in the book. In the 5th edition, we added the Supplemental CD containing cases relating to each chapter; in the 6th edition, the number of cases was increased to five or more per chapter and the cases were made available online. We have continued this with this new edition. For the first time, we have made no changes in the lineup of chapters; however, all have been updated – many with major revisions and updates. We hope each of you will share your input with us!

Also, we want to thank **Sarah Young**, Associate Professor at the University of Indiana, and **Allison Fletcher**, Ph.D. student at the University of Indiana, for their diligent work in preparing, expanding, and updating the Test Bank and the Chapter Power Points.

And special thanks go to Kendall-Hunt's **Lynne Rogers and Sudheer Purushothaman** who have been so helpful in making this 7th edition the best edition yet. Thanks, also, to the many behind-the-scenes professionals at Kendall-Hunt who helped to make this edition successful.

And finally, thanks to **our wives and families**: to Doyice's wife, Mary, for her support and invaluable assistance in the editing process; and to John's wife and family, Nicole, J.T. and Katie, for their love and support.

Doyice & John

ABOUT THE AUTHORS

DOYICE J. COTTEN

Doyice J. Cotten is an emeritus professor of sport management at Georgia Southern University where he taught graduate and undergraduate courses in sport law and risk management. He manages his own writing and risk management consulting business, Sport Risk Consulting.

Dr. Cotten's major area of interest is liability waivers. He speaks on waivers at conferences such as the Athletic Business Conference, the American College of Sports Medicine (ACSM), and the National Equine Law Conference. He also writes waivers for all types of sport and recreation businesses.

Dr. Cotten has published more than 150 articles on legal liability and risk management. He has collected and analyzed over 1,400 sport- and recreation-related waiver cases and has co-authored two books on the subject, including *Waivers & Releases of Liability* (9th ed., 2016).

Readers are invited to visit Dr. Cotten's website, www.sportwaiver.com. The site features current information regarding both risk management and liability waivers and contains more than 250 articles by Dr. Cotten and many other authorities in the fields of liability waivers and risk management.

JOHN T. WOLOHAN

Attorney John Wolohan is a professor of Sports Law in the Department of Sport Management in the David B. Falk College of Sport and Human Dynamics at Syracuse University as well as in the Syracuse College of Law at Syracuse University. Professor Wolohan, who is a member of the Massachusetts Bar Associations, received his B.A. from the University of Massachusetts-Amherst, and his J.D. from Western New England University School of Law.

In addition to being the author of the "Sports Law Report" a monthly article that appears in *Athletic Business*, Professor Wolohan has also published numerous articles and book chapters in the areas of doping, intellectual property and antitrust issues in sport in such journals as the *Marquette Sports Law Journal*, *Seton Hall Journal of Sports Law, Villanova Sports & Entertainment Law Journal, University of Missouri-Kansas City Law Review, Educational Law Reporter, International Sports Law Journal, Journal of the Legal Aspects of Sport and the Journal of Sport Management*. Professor Wolohan has also made numerous presentations in the area of sports law to such organizations as the American Bar Association, International Sports Lawyers Association, Athletic Business, US Sport Congress, US Indoor Sports Association, the Sport and Recreation Law Association, the North American Society of Sport Management, the European Association for Sport Management and the Asser Sports Law Institute.

CONTRIBUTING AUTHORS

Robin Ammon Jr.

Dr. Ammon graduated with an EdD in Sport Administration from the University of Northern Colorado and his areas of research include: legal liabilities in sport, recreation and physical education, risk management in sport and athletics, and premises liability. Currently he is the Chair of the Division of Kinesiology & Sport Science at the University of South Dakota. Prior to that, he was the Chair of the Sport Management Department at Slippery Rock University in Slippery Rock, Pennsylvania, for over 16 years. Dr. Ammon has written extensively in refereed journals, chapters in Sport Management books, and multiple textbooks. He has presented over 80 times at local, regional, national and international conferences on a variety of topics including facility, legal, crowd management and security issues. For the past thirteen years Dr. Ammon has served as an "expert witness" in various court cases regarding several of these issues. Before entering the academic arena, he was involved in intercollegiate athletics for ten years as a coach and administrator. In addition he has been associated with special events as a practitioner since 1976. Dr. Ammon has worked for himself and for two national crowd management companies (Contemporary Services Corporation & Landmark Event Staff Services) as a supervisor, manager and consultant. This experience has included various Super Bowls, the 2011 Winter Classic, professional and collegiate athletic events and hundreds of concerts all across North America. In 2002, Dr. Ammon was elected as the 17th President of the North American Society for Sport Management (NASSM). In 2009 he was selected as a trainer for the delivery of the Department of Homeland Security (DHS) Risk Management Training for Sports Event Security Management.

Paul Anderson

Paul M. Anderson is the Director of the Sports Law program and National Sports Law Institute and an Adjunct Professor of Law at Marquette University Law School. Professor Anderson teaches the advanced legal research—sports law, legal and business issues in collegiate athletics, legal issues in youth, high school and recreational sports, selected topics in sports law, entertainment law, and sections of sports venues, economics of sports, and athlete agent courses. He coordinates all recruiting, events, internships, competitions, and the Sports Law Certificate program within Marquette's Sports Law program, the nation's most comprehensive Sports Law program. He also coordinates all events, publications, and activities of the National Sports Law Institute. He is the author or editor of several books and numerous chapters and articles. Professor Anderson is former Editor-in-Chief and current faculty co-advisor to the Marquette Sports Law Review, former Editor of the Journal of Legal Aspects of Sport, and former Managing Editor of the Journal of Sport and Social Issues. A member of the Case-law Committee of the International Association of Sports Law, the Sports Lawyers Association, the ABA's Forum on Entertainment and Sports Industries, and an Observer for the Uniform Law Commission's Drafting Committee on the Uniform Athlete Agents Act, he is also Past Chair of the Sports and Entertainment Law Section of the State Bar of Wisconsin. He earned his B.A. in economics and philosophy, cum laude and Phi Beta Kappa, and his J.D. from Marquette University where he also was the first recipient of the Joseph E. O'Neill scholarship for sports ethics.

Thomas A. Baker, III

Dr. Baker is an Assistant Professor at the Sport Management and Policy program at the University of Georgia. He conducts research in sport management that primarily focuses on the application of the law to sport. Within that focus he specializes in how commercial laws influence and affect the sport industry. Additionally, he conducts risk management research focused on: (a) preventing sexual abuse in youth sports, and (b) terrorism management at sports facilities. Dr. Baker received his Ph.D. from the University of Florida in Sport Management where he was a Dr. Charles W. LaPradd Ph.D. Fellow, earned the Clifford A. Boyd Graduate Scholarship Award, and the Norma M. Leavitt Scholarship. He earned his J.D. from Loyola University New Orleans School of Law where he graduated in the top 10% of his class (cum laude) earning the distinction of William L. Crowe, Cr. Scholar.

Paul Batista

Paul J. Batista, J.D., is an Associate Professor in the Sport Management Division at Texas A&M University. He received his law degree from Baylor University Law School in 1976, and his B. S. in Business Administration from Trinity University in 1973. He continued his education by earning a Certificate of Advanced Studies in European Sports Law and Policy from the Faculty of Law at the University of Leuven, Belgium in 2013. He is admitted to practice before the United States Supreme Court, is licensed to appear in all Texas courts, is a certified Mediator and Arbitrator, and is a former Judge in Burleson County, Texas. Prof. Batista has taught graduate and undergraduate courses involving the legal aspects of sport in the Sport Management program at Texas A&M since 1991. He has received the Association of Former Students Distinguished Achievement Award in Teaching, the Student Lead Award for Teaching Excellence, and has been named a Montague Center for Teaching Excellence Scholar. In 2015 the George H.W. Bush Presidential Library Foundation presented him with the Texas A&M Bush Excellence Award for Faculty in International Teaching based on his study abroad programs focusing on the International Business of Sport and Sport Governance. He is a member and Past President of the Sport and Recreation Law Association, which has named him a Research Fellow. His primary research interest is sports related liability issues in school settings, with particular emphasis on First Amendment religion and free speech issues. He has delivered research presentations at numerous conferences throughout the United States, as well as in Canada, China, Germany, Ireland, Slovenia and South Korea.

Kristi Schoepfer Bochicchio

Kristi L. Schoepfer Bochicchio is an Associate Professor in the Department of Physical Education, Sport and Human Performance at Winthrop University in Rock Hill, South Carolina. She currently serves as Program Director for the undergraduate Sport Management Program and teaches Legal Issues in Sport courses at the undergraduate and graduate level. Additionally, she teaches Sport Marketing, Sport Public Relations and Introduction to Sport Management at the undergraduate level. She received a B.S. in Secondary Education from the University of Dayton and a J.D. from Marquette University. Additionally, she earned a certificate in Sport Law from the National Sport Law Institute. Prior to assuming her current position, she taught for five years at the University of Wisconsin-Parkside in Kenosha, Wisconsin.

Linda Jean Carpenter

Linda Jean Carpenter, Ph.D., J.D., Professor Emerita of Physical Education and Exercise Science at Brooklyn College of the City University of New York, is also a member of the New York State and United States Supreme Court Bars. She has published numerous books and articles as well as speaking at many national and international professional meetings. Her research, including the national longitudinal study on the status of women in sport, coauthored with Vivian Acosta and now in its 37th year, is frequently cited in scholarly writing as well as the lay press and has been used often in Senate and Congressional hearings on Title IX and equity in sport. She holds the B.S. and M.S. from Brigham Young University, the Ph.D. from the University of Southern California and the J.D. from Fordham Law School.

Rodney L. Caughron

Rod Caughron, Ph.D., received both his B.A. in Political Science and M.S. in Exercise Physiology from Iowa State University and his Ph.D. from The University of Iowa in Athletic Administration. Previous to his current position, Caughron served as Coordinator of Fitness for the Saudi Air Force and worked in the Student Services and ticket office at The University of Iowa. Professor Caughron currently teaches graduate courses in sport law and sport management and sport leadership.

Margaret Ciccolella

Margaret E. Ciccolella is a Professor in the Department of Health, Exercise, and Sport Sciences at the University of the Pacific. She received her doctorate in exercise physiology from Brigham Young University and her law degree from Humphreys College. Dr. Ciccolella's research focuses on the integration of law and science, and in recent years has published primarily in the area of disability law. At the University of the Pacific, she teaches graduate and undergraduate courses in sports law and higher education law.

Colleen Colles

Colleen Colles is a Professor in the Sport Industry Operations program at Metropolitan State College of Denver. She received her bachelor's degree in Health and Fitness Management from Northern Michigan University, her master's degree in Physical Education from Eastern Kentucky University and her doctorate in Sport Administration from the University of Northern Colorado. She has experience as a collegiate volleyball coach, event manager and employee wellness director. She is an active member of SRLA and NASSM and currently serves on the COSMA Board of Commissioners. Her primary research interests include gender equity in sport and sport management pedagogy.

Dan Connaughton

Daniel P. Connaughton, EdD, is a professor in the sport management program and an associate dean in the College of Health and Human Performance at the University of Florida. His teaching and research are focused on the study of law, policy, and risk management in sport and physical activity programs. A frequent conference presenter and author of many publications, Connaughton has received several teaching and research awards. The American Heart Association has funded his research investigating implementation constraints and risk management practices related to automated external defibrillators in sport and recreation programs. Since 2008 he has served as the principal investigator of the Bicycle Safety and Risk Management Project, which is funded by the Florida Department of Transportation Safety Office. Connaughton is a research fellow with the Sport and Recreation Law Association and Research Consortium of SHAPE America. With an educational background in exercise and sport sciences, Connaughton also holds advanced degrees in recreation administration (University of Florida), physical education (Bridgewater State College), and sport management (Florida State University). Connaughton has held management positions in campus and public recreation departments, aquatic facilities, and health and fitness programs. He holds several professional certifications and frequently serves as a consultant and expert witness in sport and physical activity–related lawsuits.

Anne DeMartini

Anne L. DeMartini is an Associate Professor of Sport Management at Flagler College where she teaches Sport Law, Sport Ethics, Sport Sociology and Recreation and Fitness Management. She received her undergraduate degree in political science and physical education and exercise science from the University of North Carolina—Chapel Hill. She received a Master's degree in sports studies and juris doctorate from the University of Georgia. Her research interests include discrimination in sport, CrossFit's litigation, and characteristics of successful sport management students. She is an active member in the Sport and Recreation Law Association and a certified Level 2 Crossfit Trainer.

Mark Dodds

Mark Dodds is an Associate Professor teaching sport law and sport marketing at the State University of New York, College at Cortland. He holds a J.D. from Marquette University Law School, a M.B.A. with a sport management concentration from Robert Morris University and a B.S. in marketing management from Syracuse University. While at MULS, he earned a Sport Law Certificate from the National Sport Law Institute. His research area is focused on legal issues of sport, the use of sport in civic engagement, sponsorship activation and sport brand equity creation. He was an editor for The Encyclopedia of Sport Management and Marketing, and has published articles in journals such as: Marquette Sports Law Review, The Journal of Physical Education, Recreation, and Dance, Journal of Sponsorship, International Journal of Sport Management and Marketing and College Athletics and the Law.

JoAnn Eickhoff-Shemek

JoAnn Eickhoff-Shemek is a Professor in the Exercise Science program at the University of South Florida in Tampa. She is the lead author of a comprehensive textbook entitled *Risk Management for Health/Fitness Professionals: Legal Issues and Strategies* and a co-author of *The Australian Fitness Industry Risk Management Manual*. Dr. Eickhoff-Shemek served as an associate editor and the legal columnist for *ACSM's Health & Fitness Journal* from 2001-2010. She also is the President and Founder of the Fitness Law Academy, a company devoted to advancing the fitness profession by providing educational programs to help enhance fitness safety and minimize legal liability. Dr. Eickhoff-Shemek is a Fellow of the American College of Sports Medicine and the Association for Worksite Health Promotion. She received her Ph.D. from the University of Nebraska-Lincoln in 1995.

Sarah K. Fields

Sarah K. Fields is an Associate Dean in the College of Liberal Arts and Sciences and an associate professor of communication at the University of Colorado Denver. She received her undergraduate degree from Yale University, her juris doctorate from Washington University in St. Louis, her master's degree from Washington State University, and her doctorate in American Studies from the University of Iowa. She is the author of *Female Gladiators: Gender, Law, and Contact Sport in America* (2005), co-editor of *Sport and the Law: Historical and Cultural intersections* (2014), and author of *Game Faces: Sport Celebrity and the Laws of Reputation* (2016). She has also published more than fifty articles in scholarly journals such as the *Journal of Sport History*, the *Journal of College and University Law*, the *American Journal of Sports Medicine*, and *JAMA: Pediatrics*.

Lynne P. Gaskin

Lynne Gaskin, Associate Dean of the College of Education and Professor Emerita of Physical Education at the University of West Georgia (UWG), received her B.S. degree from Wesleyan College and her M.S. and Ed.D. degrees from the University of North Carolina at Greensboro (UNCG). Dr. Gaskin has taught courses in sport law, marketing, and facility management at UNCG and UWG at the undergraduate and graduate levels; published extensively at the national and international levels in the area of sport law; and provided numerous research presentations at conferences, conventions, and college and university colloquia. In addition to numerous other awards, she received the Honor Award and Meritorious Service Award from the Sport and Recreation Law Association.

John Grady

John Grady is an Associate Professor in the Department of Sport & Entertainment Management at the University of South Carolina. He received a B.S. in Management with Honors in Finance from Penn State University. Both his law degree and Ph.D. are from Florida State University. Dr. Grady's research interests focus primarily on the legal aspects of the business of sport. This includes concentrations in the implementation of the Americans with Disabilities Act by the sport venue industry as well as intellectual property protection by professional, collegiate, and Olympic sport properties. He is president of the Sport and Recreation Law Association. At the University of South Carolina, he teaches graduate and undergraduate courses in the areas of sport law and risk management.

Curt Hamakawa

Curt Hamakawa is associate professor of sport management at Western New England University, where he also serves as director of the Center for International Sport Business (CISB), a forum for the study of the business of sport, as well as director of the College of Business (COB) Honors Program and director of the COB's Sophomore Experience Abroad Program.

Prof. Hamakawa teaches courses in sport management, sport law, business law, human resources law, in addition to a freshman seminar for sport management majors.

Prof. Hamakawa earned his B.A. degree from the University of Hawaii, his M.Ed. degree from Springfield College, and his J.D. degree from Western New England University.

Prior to joining the Western New England University faculty, Prof. Hamakawa worked for the United States Olympic Committee from 1990-2006; first as associate general counsel, then as director of athlete services, and finally as director of international relations. Prior to that, Prof. Hamakawa worked for the NCAA in its compliance and enforcement department from 1987–1990.

Mary A. Hums

Mary A. Hums, PhD, is a Professor of Sport Administration at the University of Louisville. In addition to being the 2014 NASSM Diversity Award recipient, the 2009 NASSM Earle F. Zeigler Lecturer, and a 2008 Erasmus Mundus Fellow in Belgium, Hums is a past President of SRLA. She was a co-contributor to the United Nations Convention on the Rights of Persons with Disabilities, and has co-authored or co-edited five sport management textbooks. She is a member of the International Olympic Academy Participants Association as well as NASSM and SRLA, and has worked at four Paralympic Games and the Para-Pan American Games. She is also a member of the Indiana ASA Softball Hall of Fame

Jim Masteralexis

Jim Masteralexis is an Associate Professor of Sport Law at Western New England University's College of Business in Springfield, Massachusetts. His research focuses on professional baseball, and labor and employment issues in sport. He is a graduate of the University of New Hampshire and Suffolk University Law School. He is a partner in a professional athlete management firm.

Lisa Pike Masteralexis

Lisa P. Masteralexis is an Associate Dean for Administration and an Associate Professor of Sport Law in the Isenberg School of Management at the University of Massachusetts, Amherst. She earned a J.D. at Suffolk University School of Law and a B.S. in Sport Management at the University of Massachusetts. Professor Masteralexis' research interests are in sport law and labor relations in sport. In addition to her academic articles, Professor Masteralexis is lead editor of *Principles and Practice of Sport Management*. A member of the Massachusetts and U.S. Supreme Court Bars, she co-authored an amicus brief to the U.S. Supreme Court on behalf of professional golfer Casey Martin. She is a certified agent with the Major League Baseball Players Association. Professor Masteralexis has served on the Boards of the Women's Sports Foundation and the National Sports Law Institute.

W.S. "Bill" Miller

Bill Miller is an Associate Professor and Chairperson for the Health, Exercise Science and Sport Management Department at the University of Wisconsin-Parkside. He received his B.A. from Ripon College and a J.D. from Marquette University Law School. Prior to joining UWP, Miller spent seven years as a consultant to numerous major and minor league franchises, private entities and governmental bodies on a variety of sports business issues. He has authored or co-authored multiple books and articles related to sports facility development and leases, naming rights, sports ownership and assorted sports law issues. Miller is also a former Chair of the Entertainment and Sports Law Section of the State Bar of Wisconsin.

Merry Moiseichik

Merry Moiseichik is currently a Full Professor at the University of Arkansas in Recreation and Sport Management. She received her doctorate from Indiana University in Recreation Administration and Bachelors and Masters from SUNY Cortland in Recreation, and a Juris Doctorate from the University of Arkansas. Dr. Moiseichik has worked in recreation administration in central New York, Her research interests are in community development and legal aspects both as they affect recreation and sport. She teaches courses in Legal Aspects of Sport and Recreation Services, Sport and Recreation Risk Management as well as other recreation and sport administration courses.

Anita M. Moorman

Anita M. Moorman, J.D., is a Professor in Sport Administration at the University of Louisville where she teaches sport law and legal aspects of sport. She has a law degree from Southern Methodist University and, prior to her academic pursuits, practiced law in Oklahoma City in the areas of commercial and corporate litigation for 10 years. She also holds an M.S. degree in sport management from the University of Oklahoma and a B.S. in political science from Oklahoma State University. Moorman was admitted to practice before the United States Supreme Court in 2000 when she served as co-counsel for nine disability sport organizations and prepared an amicus curiae brief in the landmark Americans with Disabilities Act case involving the disabled professional golfer, Casey Martin and the PGA Tour (*Martin v. PGA Tour, Inc.*).

Moorman has served on the editorial board of Journal of Sport Management, Journal of Legal Aspects of Sport, and Sport Marketing Quarterly, and is co-editor of a feature column in Sport Marketing Quarterly entitled "Sport Marketing and the Law". Moorman also actively participates in the North American Society for Sport Management, Sport & Recreation Law Association, and the Academy of Legal Studies in Business. Professor Moorman is a Research Fellow with the Institute for Human Centered Design and an active policy advisor on legal issues impacting rights of persons with disabilities. She has published more than 40 articles in peer-reviewed/academic journals, including the Journal of Sport Management, Sport Management Review, Sport Marketing Quarterly, Journal of Legal Aspects of Sport, JOPERD, Leisure Science, International Sport Journal, Journal of Sport and Social Issues, Journal of the Academy of Marketing Science, and ACSM's Health and Fitness Journal, and has given more than 75 presentations at national and international conferences.

Rebecca J. Mowrey

Rebecca Mowrey is a Professor of Sport Management and Director of Graduate Sport Management programs at Millersville University of Pennsylvania. She has worked as an administrator in both intercollegiate athletics and intercollegiate campus recreation. Her teaching focus includes graduate and undergraduate sport law and risk management. Dr. Mowrey is a past President of both the Sport and Recreation Law Association (SRLA) and the Safety and Risk Management Council. She served on the Executive Board and as President of the Sport Management Council of the National Association for Sport and Physical Education (NASPE) when this organization, working in partnership with the North American Society for Sport Management (NASSM), initiated formation of the Commission of Sport Management Accreditation (COSMA) and the Sport Management Education Journal (SMEJ). She served as President of the Coaching Council of NASPE when this organization initiated formation of the National Committee for Accreditation of Coaching Education (NCACE). Dr. Mowrey has served or is currently serving on the Editorial Boards of the *Journal of Legal Aspects of Sport*, the *Sport Management Education Journal*, and the *Recreational Sports Journal*.

Bridget Niland

Bridget Niland is an Associate Professor of Business Administration at Daemen College in Amherst, New York. She currently serves as Coordinator of the Sport Management Specialization and teaches courses in Sport Law, Sport Management, Labor Relations and Business Law. She earned a B.S. in History, Political Science and Legal Studies and an M.Ed. in Higher Education Administration from the State University of New York at Buffalo, and a J.D. from the University of Buffalo School of Law. Prior to joining the Daemen faculty, she served as a trial attorney for the United States Department of Justice in Washington, D.C. and was an Associate Director of Legislative Services at the National Collegiate Athletic Association. Her research focuses on legal issues in inter-collegiate athletics.

Barbara Osborne

Barbara Osborne is an Associate Professor in Exercise and Sport Science with a joint appoint in the School of Law at the University of North Carolina at Chapel Hill. She has earned degrees in Communications (University of Wisconsin-Parkside), Sport Management (Boston University) and Law (Boston College Law School) and worked for 14 years as an administrator in intercollegiate athletics. She practiced law with Ice Miller LLP in the Collegiate Sports practice group, served as Counsel for the National Association for Collegiate Women Athletics Administrators, and has also had experience as a coach, public relations coordinator, television sports commentator, publisher and sports information director. Barbara is licensed to practice law in North Carolina and Massachusetts. Her current academic research focuses on legal issues in intercollegiate athletics, Title IX, and women's issues in sport.

Andy Pittman

Andrew T. Pittman, PhD, is a clinical associate professor in the HLKN Department at Texas A&M University where he is coordinator of the Sport Management Master's Resident Program. At Baylor and Texas A&M, he has taught classes in Sport Law, Sport Finance, Sport Management, Facility Management, Risk Management, Event Management, Sport Marketing, and Sport Sociology. Dr. Pittman has authored/co-authored four books as well as eight chapters in books and numerous articles in refereed journals. In addition, he is a frequent presenter at conferences ranging from the local to the international level on topics related to sport law. Dr. Pittman has a Bachelor of Science in Physical Education from Baylor University; Master of Education in Sports Administration from Ohio University; Certificate in Accounting and a Master of Science in Taxation from the University of Baltimore; Doctor of Philosophy, Higher Education Administration from Texas A&M University; and completed some Post-Doctoral studies in Law at the Baylor University Law School.

Dr. Pittman is a member of many organizations, including the Society of Health and Physical Educators (formerly AAHPERD); the Sports Lawyers Association; and the Sport and Recreation Law Association. Dr. Pittman taught at Baylor for 28 years where he retired in 2009 and was designated Professor Emeritus. He has received numerous awards for his work in higher education and has served in leadership positions for many organizations.

Gary Rushing

Garold Rushing, Full Professor, received his Ed.D. from the University of Northern Colorado, his B.S. and M.S. from the University of Arizona. Currently he is the Human Performance Department Chair at Minnesota State University, Mankato. His research and teaching areas include a variety of sport management courses such as Sport Law and Facility Design and Management. He has published in several law reporters and coaching journals and has over twenty-five years of experience in athletics as a coach and administrator.

Todd L. Seidler

Todd Seidler is currently Professor and Chair of the Department of Health, Exercise and Sports Sciences at the University of New Mexico. He is also a member of the faculty of the Sport Administration program, one of only a few programs that offer both the Master's and Doctorate in Sport Administration. Dr. Seidler received his Bachelor's degree in Physical Education from San Diego State University and then taught and coached in high school. He then went on to graduate school and earned his Master's and Ph.D. in Sports Administration from the University of New Mexico.

Prior to returning to U.N.M., Dr. Seidler spent six years as the coordinator of the graduate Sports Administration program at Wayne State University and then was the coordinator of the undergraduate Sport Management Program at Guilford College in North Carolina.

Dr. Seidler is currently Executive Director and a former President of the Sport and Recreation Law Association, a professional organization for those interested in teaching Sport Law and Risk Management. He also served on the Executive Board and as Chair of both the Sport Management Council and the Council on Facilities and Equipment within the American Alliance for Health, Physical Education, Recreation and Dance (AAHPERD) and is an active member of the North American Society for Sport Management (NASSM). Dr. Seidler is also a Certified Strength and Conditioning Specialist (C.S.C.S., 1987) through the National Strength and Conditioning Association (N.S.C.A.).

Dr. Seidler's primary areas of interest include risk management and legal issues in sport and in planning and managing sports facilities. He is active as a consultant on facility planning and risk management for sport and recreation and frequently presents, publishes, and teaches classes such as Risk Management in Sport, Sport Facility Planning and Design, Facility and Event Management, and Legal Aspects of Sport.

Ellen Staurowsky

Dr. Staurowsky is a professor in the Department of Sport Management and interim associate director for the Center of Hospitality and Sport Management at Drexel University. She is internationally recognized as an expert on social justice issues in sport including college athletes rights and the exploitation of college athletes, gender equity and Title IX, and the misappropriation of American Indian imagery in sport. She is co-author of the book, *College Athletes for Hire: The Evolution and Legacy of the NCAA Amateur Myth*, editor of the forthcoming *Women in Sport: Continuing a Journey of Liberation and Celebration*. Dr. Staurowsky served as a witness on behalf of the plaintiff in *O'Bannon v. NCAA*. She is lead author on the Women's Sports Foundation's 2015 report *Her Life Depends on It III: Sport and Physical Activity in the Lives of American Girls and Women* and co-author on a forthcoming report from the WSF on workplace climate for women working in college sport.

Stephanie Tryce

Stephanie A. Tryce, J.D. is an Assistant Professor of Sports Marketing at Saint Joseph's University. Professor Tryce began her teaching career as a full-time lecturer at the Mark H. McCormack Sport Management Department of the Isenberg School of Business at the University of Massachusetts-Amherst. Upon returning to her native Philadelphia, Professor Tryce practiced law in the areas of civil rights and local business tax, while teaching as an Affiliated Faculty member in the Legal Studies and Business Ethics Department of The Wharton School of the University of Pennsylvania and Adjunct Faculty in the Sport Management Department at the University of Delaware.

Professor Tryce has presented at annual conferences for the North American Society for the Sociology of Sport, the Sport and Recreation Law Association, Sports Marketing Association and the Alliance for Sport Business. Her research interests are at the intersection of law, sports and marketing, with a particular focus on social justice. Some of her scholarly work includes: co-authorship of "Black Women and Title IX: Ain't I a Woman," in the Special Issue of the *Journal of the Study of Sports and Athletics in Education*. Professor Tryce was the lead author of, "Mock Debate on the Washington Redskins Brand – Fostering Critical Thinking and Cultural Sensitivity in Sport Business Students," published in the Spring 2015 edition of *Sport Management Education Journal*. Most recently, Professor Tryce published a book chapter titled, "Using Sports' History to Develop Cultural Competence in Millennial Marketers: Teaching Title IX, NFL's Rooney Rule and Post-Apartheid Rugby in South Africa" for the book titled, *Global Perspectives on Contemporary Marketing Education*. Professor Tryce serves on the executive committee of the Alliance for Sport Business.

Nita Unruh

Nita Unruh is currently a Professor, the Department Chair of KSS and Degree Coordinator for the Sports Management program in the Kinesiology and Sport Sciences Department at the University of Nebraska Kearney. She received her Ed.D. from the University of Arkansas, an M.S. from Florida State University and her B.S. from Henderson State University. She enjoys helping students become familiar with and interested in the areas of Risk Management and Legal Issues in Sport and Recreation.

Sara J. Young

Sarah J. Young, PhD, is an associate professor in the Department of Recreation, Park and Tourism Studies at Indiana University, where she coordinates the Public, Non-Profit, and Community Recreation curriculum at both the graduate and undergraduate levels. She has 11 years of experience administering and programming campus intramural sport programs and teaches legal aspects courses to undergraduate and graduate students in sport and recreation. Dr. Young has published over 55 journal articles and book chapters in sport and recreation publications, and has given more than 65 presentations at professional conferences. She is co-author of *Case Studies in Sport Law* published by Human Kinetics. She is a member of the Sport and Recreation Law Association, the National Intramural Recreational Sport Association, and the National Recreation and Park Association.

INTRODUCTION TO SPORT LAW

1.00

In today's litigious society, it is important that sport and recreation administrators have a sound understanding of the law. The following *Introduction to Sport Law* section consists of three chapters covering a wide range of legal areas intended to provide administrators with a basic introduction to legal principles as they apply to the sport and recreation industry.

Chapter 1.10 *The Legal System* is intended to help the reader understand how the legal system functions and prepare the reader for effectively using this book.

The second chapter, Chapter 1.20 *Legal Research*, introduces the reader to the tools that are available for conducting legal research. Additionally, the author provides guidance to the reader regarding the basic steps to be used in conducting legal research.

The third chapter, Chapter 1.30 *Business Structure and Legal Authority*, provides an overview of the business structures available to the recreation and sport manager. Guidance is given regarding the type of protection provided by a number of popular business structures.

1.10 THE LEGAL SYSTEM

Kristi L. Schoepfer Bochicchio | Winthrop University

The United States has become an increasingly litigious society; annually, millions of lawsuits are filed by citizens seeking legal remedy to problems they have encountered in the course of their personal or professional lives. As such, recreation and sport managers are likely to encounter legal issues related to the administration of their organizations and programs. Specifically, legal concerns are present in recreation and sport in many different areas, such as negligence (tort law), risk management, contract law, constitutional law, and federal legislation regarding gender equity, employment discrimination and intellectual property. However, before these and other specific legal concerns can be presented, recreation and sport managers must understand the basic components of the complex United States legal system, including origins of the law, the legal system, and the legal process.

FUNDAMENTAL CONCEPTS

Origins of the Law

The **law** is a collection of rules and regulations that govern the affairs of a community and are enforced by a legal authority. There are multiple sources of law including Constitutional law and laws enacted, enforced, and interpreted by the three branches of government.

A **constitution** is a document that sets forth the basic principles of government, including limits on government power. The federal government, as well as all 50 states, has a constitution; each constitution provides citizens many protections. Additionally, the federal and state governments each have three branches that exist as a source of law: the legislative branch, which is responsible for enacting new laws and amending existing laws through federal or state legislatures; the executive branch, which enforces existing laws through elected officials or administrative agencies; and, the judicial branch which interprets constitutions or other existing laws through the federal and state court systems. At both the federal and state level, constitutions and all three branches of government have a specific and important role in establishing the law.

Legislative Branch

A Congress (or legislature), either state or federal, is the legislative branch of the government, comprised of elected officials in the Senate and in the House of Representatives.[1] This legislative branch of government is responsible for enacting and amending statutory laws. Statutory laws, or **statutes**, are written laws adopted by legislatures at all levels including federal, state, city, county and municipal (statutes at the local level are typically called ordinances). Statutes are only valid in the area governed by the authoring legislature; in other words, South Carolina statutes are only valid in South Carolina. Any individual in South Carolina, either a South Carolina citizen or visitor, must abide by South Carolina statutes; however, South Carolina statutes do not have any legal significance in any other state.

For example, the South Carolina legislature has enacted statutory law that both defines bungee jumping and prohibits certain acts related to bungee jumping. Specifically, South Carolina statute §52-19-20 reads:

> "For purposes of this chapter, the term "bungee jumping" includes and refers to the sport, activity, or practice of jumping, stepping out, dropping, or otherwise being released into the air while attached or fastened to a cord made of rubber, latex, or other elastic type material, whether natural or synthetic, whereby the cord, stops the fall, lengthens and shortens, allows the person to bounce up and down, and is intended to finally bring the person to a stop at a point above the surface."

---

[1] Every state has a bicameral legislature that consists of two houses except for Nebraska; the Nebraska Legislature is unicameral. Additionally, states use varying names to identify the two legislative branches of government within the state.

Further, South Carolina statute §52-19-30 reads:

(A) The practice of bungee jumping from a device other than a fixed platform is prohibited in this State.
(B) The practice of bungee jumping using an ankle harness is prohibited in this State.
(C) The practice of pre stretching and releasing bungee cords for the purpose of catapulting jumpers is prohibited in this State.
(D) The practice of bungee jumping over water, sand, or any surface other than a safety air bag is prohibited in this State.
(E) The practice of tandem or multiple bungee jumping is prohibited in this State.
(F) The practice of sandbagging is prohibited in this State. For purposes of this chapter, "sandbagging" means the practice of holding onto any object (including another person) while bungee jumping, for the purpose of exerting more force on the bungee cord in order to stretch it further, and then releasing the object during the jump causing the jumper to rebound with more force than could be created by the jumper's weight alone.
(G) The use of any mechanical lifting device in conjunction with bungee jumping is prohibited.

This statute may be subject to interpretation if it were ever part of a lawsuit (see subsequent section on the Judicial branch); however, by writing this statute the South Carolina legislature has provided the law in the state regarding bungee jumping. That is the function of statutes; to create the law within a particular area.

Executive Branch
Often times, statutes require further explanation to be applied to real-life scenarios. This guidance typically comes in the form of regulations created by the executive branch, or an administrative agency created by the executive branch. **Regulations** are "rules and administrative codes issued by governmental agencies at all levels, municipal, county, state and federal. Although they are not laws, regulations have the force of law, since they are adopted under authority granted by statutes, and often include penalties for violations." For example, the National Labor Relations Act is federal statutory law. While the law itself is guiding, many of the provisions have been further interpreted through regulations enacted by the National Labor Relations Board ("NLRB"), a federal agency given this charge. Although the NLRB provisions are not laws, they have the force of law; thus, the executive branch plays a role in creating law.

Judicial Branch
Whether the source of law is a constitution, a statute, or a regulation, the judicial branch is charged with interpreting and applying the law by adjudicating legal claims. When a court makes a decision in a legal case, and authors a written opinion, the decision is referred to as **case law**; the collective body of case law is called **common law**.

The collective body of common law is exceptionally important because it establishes precedent for future cases. **Precedent** exists when a prior reported opinion of an appeals court establishes the legal rule for future cases involving the same legal question. Further, there are two types of precedent: Binding precedent and persuasive precedent. **Binding precedent** exists within a specific court system and must be followed by all courts within that system at the same or lower level. For example, if the Wisconsin Supreme Court decides a case on a particular legal issue, all future cases on that same issue in the Wisconsin court system will be bound by the decision (meaning the courts must follow the precedent and make the same decision). In contrast, **persuasive precedent** can come from any court system. For example, if the Idaho Court of Appeals makes a decision that supports a legal claim in Texas, the lawyer arguing the case in Texas can present the Idaho decision as persuasive precedent. The court in Texas may choose to allow the Idaho decision to influence its own decision, but the Texas court is not required to do so; thus, any precedential value the Idaho case may have is only persuasive. When you are reading the Significant Cases in each chapter of the textbook, you will frequently encounter precedent, both binding and persuasive.

The Court System

Once laws are created, they must be interpreted and applied to particular circumstances; as discussed above, this interpretation/application occurs in the judiciary, or court systems. A **court system** is a structured collection of individual courts, each court being an "organized body with defined powers, meeting at certain times and places for the hearing and decision of causes and other matters brought before it" (Black's, 1990). There are multiple court systems that can apply the laws; three primary court systems must be discussed, as well as how an individual decides which court system is appropriate in any given case.

Federal Court System

The federal court system uses a hierarchal approach, meaning that cases originate in lower courts, and when appropriate, may be appealed to higher level courts (see Figure 1.10.1). The lowest tier in the federal hierarchy is the District Court level; **District Courts** are the courts of origin in the federal court system. If a lawsuit is filed in the federal court system, a District Court will be the first to hear the case. There are 94 District Courts in the United States. Each state has at least one federal District Court within its boundaries (although these courts are not part of the state court system), and some larger states, such as California, have multiple District Courts. An individual or corporation wishing to use the federal court system for its lawsuit will access a federal District Court within its state.

If a party to the lawsuit does not feel the law was properly interpreted or applied in the District Court, he or she may **appeal** the case on the basis of legal error; in other words, ask a higher level court to review the case for mistakes of law. The middle tier in the federal hierarchy is known as the **Circuit Courts**. This appellate level is divided into 11 geographic circuits, and a separate circuit for the District of Columbia (see Figure 1.10.2).[2] The geographic location of the original district court determines which of the 12 appellate circuits will hear the case on appeal.

Lastly, a party may choose to again appeal his or her case to the highest tier in the federal court system, the **United States Supreme Court** (USSC). To appeal a case to this highest level, the party must request **certiorari** by filing a petition asking the USSC to hear the case; the USSC will either grant or deny this request.[3] The USSC is very selective about the cases it chooses to hear; each year, the USSC accepts less than 5% of the certiorari requests.

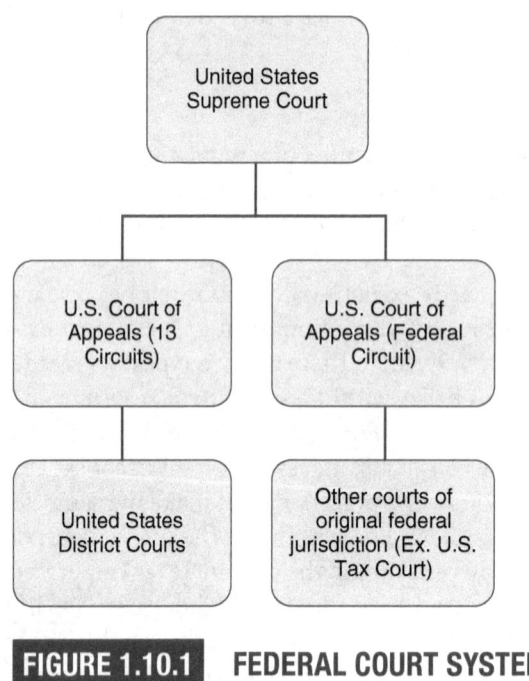

FIGURE 1.10.1 FEDERAL COURT SYSTEM

---

[2] There is also an additional federal appellate court called the United States Court of Appeals for the Federal Circuit. This court hears appeals from all district courts in patent law cases, as well as appeals from the U.S. Court of Federal Claims and the Court of International Trade.

[3] Certiorari is "an order of a higher court to a lower court to send all the documents in a case to it so the higher court can review the lower court's decision." If the USSC grants certiorari, they are accepting the case for review.

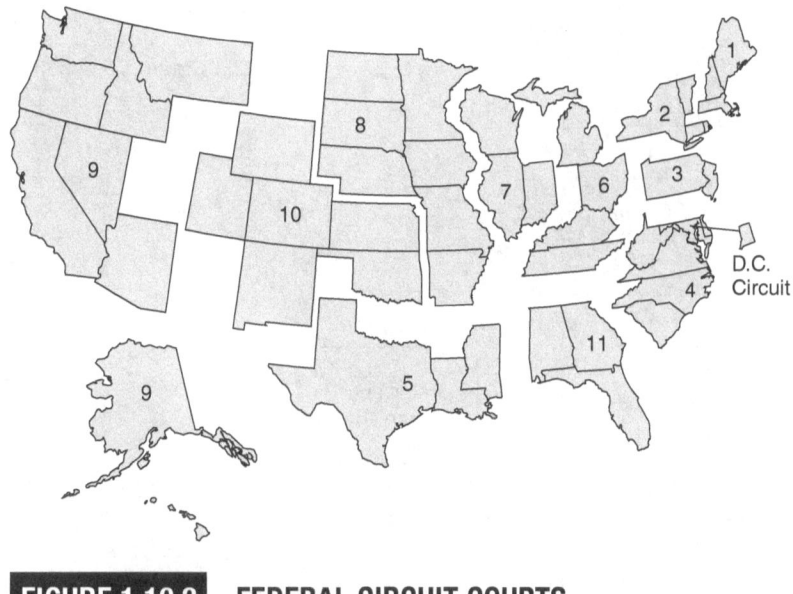

FIGURE 1.10.2 FEDERAL CIRCUIT COURTS

Source: www.thehrspecialist.com

State Court System

Each state has its own court system. Similar to the federal court system, most states also use the hierarchal approach, separating the courts into three levels. Most states have *trial courts* of either limited or general jurisdiction (see subsequent discussion on jurisdiction), *appellate courts*, and a *supreme court*. However, there are many variances among state court systems; not all states use the same court names or structure.

For example, in Colorado the trial court level is divided into separate courts (see Figure 1.10.2). The County Courts hear a variety of cases, including those with alleged damages under $15,000; the District Courts hear civil cases in any amount (and uniquely, serve as an appellate court for the County Courts). The Colorado Court of Appeals is the appellate court for the District Courts and also reviews state administrative agencies. The Colorado Supreme Court, the state's highest court, hears appeals from the Court of Appeals.

In Maryland, the hierarchal approach is similar, but the trial courts and appellate courts use different names (see Figure 1.10.3). There are two types of courts classified as trial courts, District Courts and Circuit Courts. District Courts do not have juries; rather, trials are by judges only and cover civil claims up to $30,000, as well as other civil and criminal matters. The Circuit Courts handle major civil cases, along with more serious criminal matters, and do allow for trial by jury. In the appellate courts, the Court of Special Appeals serves as the intermediate appellate court, reviewing cases from the trial courts; the Court of Appeals (commonly called the Supreme Court in other states) is the highest court in the state and hears cases almost exclusively based on certiorari.

Some states, Montana for instance, have only trial courts and a supreme court with no intermediate appellate review (see Figure 1.10.3). Regarding court names, the New York court system is vastly different from most other states using the name Supreme Court to identify its trial courts (see Figure 1.10.3). The intermediate appellate courts are called Appellate Divisions of the Supreme Court and the Court of Appeals is the highest court of the state.

These examples demonstrate that while state court systems are similar in their hierarchal approach, the similarities end there. All 50 states have their own unique variances that impact the progression of a case through the respective state court system.

Administrative Court System

The vast majority of recreation and sport lawsuits are filed in state or federal courts; however, the administrative court system is still noteworthy. As discussed, the executive branch of government includes administrative agencies that create regulations, or rules to operationalize statutes created by legislatures. Administrative courts sit as fact-finding bodies that apply these regulations. When disputes arise regarding the implementation of the regulations, evidence is presented to an administrative law judge, who will make a decision.

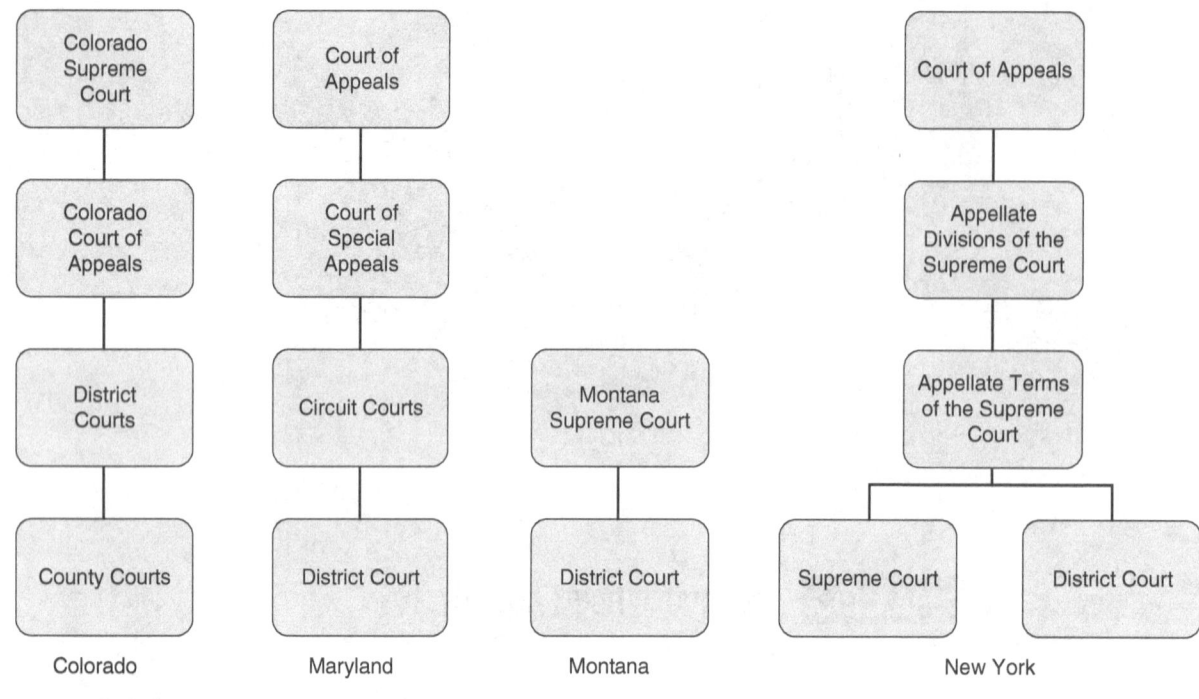

FIGURE 1.10.3 STATE COURT SYSTEMS

At the state level, administrative court procedures again vary by state. For example, in Montana, all workers' compensation claims are heard in Workers' Compensation Court, which has the limited ability to review only that type claim. In this administrative court, there are no jury trials; rather, the judge decides how the regulations should be applied in each individual case. When federal regulations are in question, a federal administrative law judge will render a decision; any appeal of the administrative law judge's findings will go to the federal appellate level, or Circuit Courts. Although these appeals can be heard in any circuit, most appeals from federal agencies are heard in the District of Columbia Circuit.

Jurisdiction

Given that more than one court system exists, it is necessary to understand when it is appropriate to use each one. Selecting the proper court system requires a determination of which court has **jurisdiction**; a court's ability to hear a case and provide remedy. A court must have both **personal jurisdiction**, which is power over the parties in the case, and **subject matter jurisdiction**, the power to hear the type of case (see Figure 1.10.4). When filing a lawsuit, a party must be certain that jurisdiction is correct, or the case may be dismissed.

In the federal court system, a District Court determines whether personal jurisdiction exists by using the procedural rules of the state in which it is located. For example, a federal district court located in Michigan will follow Michigan procedural rules governing personal jurisdiction. To determine if personal jurisdiction exists, the court will consider such factors as location of the parties, location of property or consent to personal jurisdiction by the defendant. To obtain federal subject matter jurisdiction, one of the following criteria must be met: (1) the claim must arise from federal statutes or the U.S. Constitution (**federal question jurisdiction**); (2) the claim must be filed by (or against) the federal government; or (3) the amount in controversy exceeds $75,000, and all opposing parties live in different states (**diversity of citizenship jurisdiction**). Federal courts also have exclusive subject matter jurisdiction over lawsuits between states, federal criminal cases, bankruptcy cases, patent, trademark and copyright cases, antitrust cases, maritime cases, and cases arising out of federal statutes.

In the state court systems, a court has personal jurisdiction over parties that reside in the state, conduct business in the state, consent to jurisdiction (typically through court appearance) or have sufficient "minimum contact" with the state (a court determines if a party has enough contact with the state to make jurisdiction appropriate). Subject matter jurisdiction exists for any event or activity that occurred within the state. Within

FIGURE 1.10.4 — SUBJECT MATTER JURISDICTION OF FEDERAL AND/OR STATE COURTS

State Courts	Federal Courts	State or Federal Courts
Crimes under state legislation.	Crimes under statutes enacted by congress.	Crimes punishable under both federal and state law.
State constitutional issues and cases involving state laws or regulations.	Most cases involving federal laws or regulations (for example: tax, Social Security, broadcasting, civil rights)	Federal constitutional issues.
Family law issues.	Matters involving interstate and international commerce, including airline and railroad regulation.	Certain civil rights claims.
Real property issues.	Cases involving securities and commodities regulation, including takeover of publicly held corporations.	"Class action" cases.
Most private contract disputes (except those resolved under bankruptcy law).	Admiralty cases.	Environmental regulations.
Most issues involving the regulation of trades and professions.	International trade law matters.	Certain disputes involving federal law.
Most professional malpractice issues.	Patent, copyright, and other intellectual property issues.	
Most issues involving the internal governance of business associations such as partnerships and corporations.	Cases involving rights under treaties, foreign states, and foreign nationals.	
Most personal injury lawsuits.	State law disputes when "diversity of citizenship" exists.	
Most workers' injury claims.	Bankruptcy matters.	
Probate and inheritance matters.	Disputes between states.	
Most traffic violations and registration of motor vehicles.	Habeas corpus actions.	
	Traffic violations and other misdemeanors occurring on certain federal property.	

Source: http://www.uscourts.gov/EducationalResources/FederalCourtBasics/CourtStructure/JurisdictionOfStateAndFederalCourts.aspx

the state trial courts, some courts have limited subject matter jurisdiction, and can only hear specific claims; areas of limited subject matter jurisdiction may include family law, probate law, juvenile court, etc. Other trial level courts have general subject matter jurisdiction and can hear claims related to any area of law, so long as the case involves an event or activity that occurred within the state.

Finally, **concurrent jurisdiction** must be addressed; that is when one case qualifies for both federal and state jurisdiction. For example, if a Minnesota Vikings fan, who is a Minnesota resident, attends a Green Bay Packers game in Green Bay, WI, and accidentally injures a local Packers fan, the Packers fan (plaintiff, see Trial Phase later) will need to decide where to file the claim. The plaintiff may file the lawsuit in federal or state court based on his or her preference; the case may be filed in the jurisdiction where the defendant lives or the jurisdiction where the cause of action arose. The plaintiff can chose a court system based on preference regarding procedure, choice of law, or other factors related to legal procedure. However, if the case is filed in state court, the defendant may opt to have the case removed to federal court (changing from state jurisdiction to federal jurisdiction based on diversity of citizenship).

State courts also have concurrent jurisdiction regarding federal questions; any state court may interpret the U.S. Constitution or a federal statute if the applicable provision has a direct bearing on a case brought in state court under a state law.

The Legal Process

Cases must be filed in accordance with a well established legal process. There are many steps involved in this process, often referred to as civil procedure (or criminal procedure for criminal cases; this chapter only addresses civil law). The following discussion is not intended to cover completely all procedural elements of a legal case; rather, the selected elements are highlighted to help you understand subsequent Significant Cases in the textbook. Each element will be discussed and, when appropriate, you will find a definition, an example from an actual case, and an explanation of the example that highlights the particular element. Also, the discussion is separated into two separate phases: the trial phase, which is the where a case originates, and the appellate phase, which only occurs if a party to the case appeals the original decision based on legal error.

Trial Phase

Standing. The legal right to file a lawsuit is called **standing**. To establish standing, a plaintiff (see next section) must establish that he or she sustained a harm, that the court has the power to provide a remedy, and that the plaintiff has an interest in the outcome of a case. Typically, the issue of standing is raised by the defendant (see next section); the plaintiff does not need to prove that standing exists unless it is challenged.

Parties to the Lawsuit. The **plaintiff(s)** is the party filing the lawsuit; this is the individual or group that has allegedly suffered harm and seeks legal remedy from the court. The **defendant(s)** is the party against whom the claim is filed. In many cases, there are multiple defendants; often, more than one person or group may have been responsible for a harm occurring. Also, some cases are filed as **class action** lawsuits, meaning that a large group of people are filing a lawsuit collectively against a defendant.

Case Example #1: This case demonstrates that parties to a case can vary in number; multiple plaintiffs and defendants are common.

IAIN FRASER; STEVE TRITTSCHUH; SEAN BOWERS; MARK SEMIOLI; RHETT HARTY; DAVID SCOTT VAUDREUIL; MARK DODD; and MARK DOUGHERTY, Plaintiffs v. MAJOR LEAGUE SOCCER, L.L.C.; KRAFT SOCCER, L.P.; ANSCHUTZ SOCCER, INC.; ANSCHUTZ CHICAGO SOCCER, INC.; SOUTH FLORIDA SOCCER, L.L.C., TEAM COLUMBUS SOCCER, L.L.C.; TEAM KANSAS CITY SOCCER, L.L.C.; LOS ANGELES SOCCER PARTNERS, L.P.; EMPIRE SOCCER CLUB, L.P.; WASHINGTON SOCCER, L.P.; and UNITED STATES SOCCER FEDERATION, INC., Defendants
2000 U.S. Dist. LEXIS 5434

MEMORANDUM AND ORDER
April 19, 2000

The individual **plaintiffs** are the representatives of the **certified class** of professional soccer players who are or who have been employed by the **defendant** Major League Soccer, L.L.C. ("MLS"). MLS is a limited liability company ("LLC") organized under Delaware law. The **defendant** United States Soccer Federation, Inc. ("USSF") is the national governing body for professional and amateur soccer in the United States. **All the other defendants** are investors in MLS, each a capital-contributing member of MLS that has contracted with MLS to operate one or more of MLS's teams.

Explanation

Often times, the plaintiff(s) and defendant(s) can be determined from looking at the case name; however, most court opinions also offer further explanation of the parties in the first paragraph. In this case, the named plaintiffs represent a larger group who have filed a class action lawsuit against the defendants. Major League Soccer, the respective MLS teams, and the United States Soccer Federation are the defendants in this case.

Jurisdiction. The preceding section of this chapter presents a complete discussion of jurisdiction; however, Case Example #2 further clarifies the importance of identifying the appropriate jurisdiction before filing a lawsuit.

Filing the Complaint. After the plaintiff has identified the appropriate jurisdiction to file the lawsuit, he or she will formally commence the legal process by filing a complaint. A **complaint** is a formal pleading to the court that must state both the factual and legal basis for the claim. Also, a complaint must follow specific statutory requirements regarding form. For example, a complaint must follow a specific format, name both the party making the claim and all defendants, and state what result (damages or performance, see subsequent discussion) the plaintiff is requesting. When a complaint is filed, the court will issue a **summons**, which gives the name and file number of the lawsuit and instructs the defendant to file an answer or other response. A copy of the complaint and the summons must be served on a defendant before a response is required.

Prior to filing a complaint, a plaintiff must be aware of the statute of limitations in the selected jurisdiction regarding the claim. A **statute of limitations** is the maximum amount of time a potential plaintiff can wait before filing a legal claim; these statutes vary by court system, both state and federal, jurisdiction, and subject matter. For example, in Connecticut, "no action founded upon a tort shall be brought but within three years from the date of the act or omission complained of" (Conn. Gen. Stat. § 52-577 (2015)). In other words, plaintiff wishing to file a personal injury lawsuit based on tort law must do so within three years of the cause of action occurring. Alternatively, in Minnesota, a plaintiff has six years to file a personal injury claim (Minn. Stat. § 541.01 (2015)). In most states, the statute of limitations will differ for cases filed under contract law, tort law (personal injury) or property law (see Chapter 2.21, *Defenses against Negligence*).

Filing the Answer. After a complaint is filed, and summons issued, a defendant has a specific period of time, typically 30 or 60 days, in which to file an answer with the court. An **answer** is a pleading to the court, filed by a defendant, which responds to each allegation in the complaint. A defendant may deny the claims, admit the claims, or do either in part. The answer may also include affirmative defenses, such as comparative negligence (see Chapter 2.21 *Defenses against Negligence*), allegations which contradict the complaint, or allegations which are intended to derail the claims in the complaint. Similar to the complaint, the format of the answer must follow specific rules established within each jurisdiction.

Discovery and Motions. After the defendant files an answer, both parties to the lawsuit enter the discovery and motions phase. **Discovery** is the period of time during which both parties gather facts and information to be used as evidence in a trial. Discovery includes requests for documents, requests to admit facts into evidence (declarations), and depositions (statements given by parties to the case under oath). Opposing counsel has the right to discover any material reasonably related to the case.

Motions are formal requests made to the court seeking a specific action or decision. Various motions are common in the legal process; they can be made both before and after discovery. Some common motions include: (1) a **motion for judgment on the pleadings**, which asserts that no cause of action exists even if everything in the complaint were true; (2) a **motion to dismiss**, often based on expiration of the statute of limitations or filing in the wrong jurisdiction; and (3) a **motion for summary judgment**, which is filed when one party believes that no questions of fact are present in the case, and the legal issue can be decided as a matter of law. Both parties ascertain the facts of the case during discovery; if either party feels that the facts are not in dispute, and do not need to be substantiated by a fact-finding body (a jury), they will file a motion for summary judgment. A motion for summary judgment is very common in the legal process; these motions eliminate the need for a jury to determine the facts based on evidence, since the facts are not in question. The party moving for summary judgment must initially establish that there is no genuine issue of material fact and that he or she is entitled to judgment as a matter of law. Therefore, when a motion for summary judgment is filed, if the facts of the case are not in dispute, the judge will consider the facts, apply the law in question to those facts, and render a judgment. Generally, a motion for summary judgment is not made until all discovery has been completed (see Case Example #3).

Case Example #2: This case incorporates many examples from the previous sections; specifically, the issue in the case is jurisdiction, but the court also discusses matters related to the complaint, motions, and discovery.

MARLON BRANDO ROMAN, a Minor, etc., Plaintiff and Appellant, v. LIBERTY UNIVERSITY, INC., et al., Defendants and Respondents. 2008 Cal. App. LEXIS 636

A. Plaintiff's Complaint: **Plaintiff . . . filed an action for personal injury damages against defendants in the Superior Court of the State of California, County of San Bernardino.**
The **complaint** alleged that Liberty's recruiting coordinator had come to Rialto, California, before June 5, 2003, to recruit plaintiff to play football for Liberty in Virginia . . . Plaintiff executed Liberty's 2003–2004 Athletic Scholarship/Grant-in-Aid Agreement at his home in Rialto on June 8, 2003, and executed a revised agreement in Rialto on July 19, 2003. Thereafter, plaintiff attended Liberty and played first string defensive back for its football team.

The **complaint** alleged that, while at Liberty, plaintiff's roommate, Lancaster [(also a defendant and also from Virginia)], played football for Liberty's team. Plaintiff and Lancaster had a history of leaving campus to consume alcohol after curfew . . . On April 21, 2004, plaintiff and Lancaster went out drinking. During the evening, Lancaster physically assaulted plaintiff. Plaintiff started to walk back to campus and fell from a train trestle. He sustained catastrophic brain injuries.

B. Liberty's Motion: **Liberty filed a motion to quash service of summons for lack of personal jurisdiction**.

Jerry Falwell, Jr., the vice chancellor and general counsel for Liberty, **provided a declaration** . . . stating that Liberty is incorporated in Virginia and maintains its principal place of business in Virginia. Liberty has no employees in California, does not have an office or mailing address in California, does not own or lease any real property in California, is not registered or otherwise qualified to do business in California, and does not have an agent for service of process in California. Liberty does not pay any income, property, or use taxes to the state of California. Liberty does not manufacture any product that could find its way through the stream of commerce into California. **Falwell's declaration further states** that coach Pete Sundheim, who had direct personal contact with plaintiff, lives and works in Virginia. Coach Ed Gomes, the director of spiritual development for Liberty's football team, also had personal contact with plaintiff and also lives and works in Virginia.

The Court of Appeal affirmed the trial court's orders. The court concluded that the **trial court properly granted the university's motion to quash for lack of personal jurisdiction.** The university did not purposely avail itself of the benefits of doing business in California such that it could expect to be subject to the jurisdiction of California courts. The only conduct plaintiff established was that the university's recruiting coordinator visited him in California to recruit him to play football for the university, and thereafter, the university mailed plaintiff a scholarship agreement and amended scholarship agreement that plaintiff executed in California. The nexus between the university's activities in California and the injury plaintiff suffered in Virginia was so attenuated as to be virtually nonexistent.

Explanation

The legal issue in this case is whether the California state court system has personal jurisdiction over Liberty University. The court's opinion sets forth the arguments the plaintiff used in attempt to substantiate minimum contacts with California, as well as arguments made by Liberty University to defeat a finding a personal jurisdiction. The court concludes that the California court system does not have personal jurisdiction over Liberty University, and thus the California state court system lacks jurisdiction to hear the case.

Case Example #3: This case focuses primarily on a motion for summary judgment. This case is on appeal, meaning it is a review of the trial court decision. The discussion of the legal issues has been omitted, but the appellate court concludes that the motion for summary judgment is appropriate, meaning the case has reached its conclusion.

JOSH SANDERS, Plaintiff-Appellant, v. KUNA JOINT SCHOOL DISTRICT and MR. "JOHN DOE" EMERY, Defendants-Respondents. 876 P.2d 154 (1994)

FACTS AND PROCEDURE

The underlying facts of this lawsuit are generally agreed upon by all of the parties. On May 15, 1990, Josh Sanders, a student at Kuna High School, attempted to slide into first base during a softball game and broke his ankle. Sanders had been enrolled in a specialized physical education class which provided instruction in weight lifting. On the date of the incident, the instructor, respondent Ron Emry[4], decided to have the class play softball outside instead of weight lifting. The students were not informed of this decision until after they appeared in the school's weight room. According to Sanders, on that particular day he was wearing a pair of "Saucony Shadows," a shoe designed specifically for running. Once on the softball field, Emry did not give instruction in the game of softball and supervised the game from behind a backstop.

---

[4]The court spelled defendant Emery's name incorrectly throughout the case.

> During one particular sequence of play, Sanders attempted to slide into first base in order to avoid being tagged out. During the slide, Sanders broke his ankle.
>
> Following proper notice as required by I.C. §§ 6-901 et seq., Sanders filed suit against Emry and the school district as Emry's employer. Sanders claimed that Emry had been negligent by requiring the students to play softball, by failing to adequately supervise the students, including inspecting their footwear, and by failing to properly instruct the students on how to play softball.
>
> **After initial discovery was completed, the respondents filed a motion for summary judgment on grounds that, accepting the truth of Sanders' evidence, it did not prove a claim of negligence as a matter of fact.** The district court granted the respondents' motion. Sanders now appeals to this Court, claiming that the district court improperly granted the summary judgment.
>
> * * * *
>
> CONCLUSION
>
> **The respondents in this case properly carried their burden on their motion for summary judgment by showing that Sanders was unable to present sufficient evidence on the causal connection between the alleged negligence and the injury.** The burden then shifted to Sanders to show that a genuine issue did exist. Sanders failed to meet this burden and therefore the **summary judgment was properly granted**.

Explanation
As noted by the court, the facts of this case were not disputed by either party; thus the defendants filed a motion for summary judgment. The defendants argued that the facts presented by the plaintiff were insufficient to establish the claim; because the facts were agreed upon by both parties, and no additional facts would be determined by a jury, the judge in the case should decide the case as a matter of law. After consideration of the facts presented, the court concluded that summary judgment was appropriate.

Settlement, Alternative Dispute Resolution, or Trial. After the motion and discovery phase is complete, the parties in the case will proceed towards a final resolution, which can be reached in many ways. First, the parties may settle the case; this occurs as a result of negotiations between the parties to reach a result that both sides agree with. A **settlement** is carried out using formal contractual agreements that are filed with the court; often times, settlement agreements are not made public and only the parties to the case know the final result. Another option is to seek resolution using a form of **alternative dispute resolution** ("ADR") such as **arbitration** or **mediation**. These formalized resolution processes are intended to reach an outcome, yet avoid litigation. Both arbitration and mediation are discussed completely in Chapter 5.30, *Alternative Dispute Resolution*. Lastly, the parties may opt not to settle or use ADR and proceed to trial seeking adjudication. A trial is a part of the legal process that has its own specific rules and procedure which will not be discussed; however, in a civil case, a trial will most often result in a either a finding of liability on behalf of the defendant (victory for the plaintiff) or a finding of non-liability (victory for the defendant). This is a generalized way of discussing the potential outcome, because shared liability is possible as well; for a full discussion, see Chapter 2.21, *Defenses against Negligence*.

Damages. If the defendant is found liable, damages will likely be awarded to the plaintiff (although this is not always the case). As discussed in Chapter 2.11, *Negligence*, **damages** is the monetary compensation awarded as a remedy for defendant liability. Damages can be compensatory (intended to compensate for harm) or punitive (intended to punish the wrongdoer and deter similar future acts), and vary based on the specific claim and individual outcome of each trial.

Appellate Phase

After a trial court adjudicates a claim, either party has the opportunity to file a **notice of appeal**, requesting that the appropriate appellate court review the case. As noted earlier, appeals are requested based on legal error; a misinterpretation or misapplication of the law. Neither party has the right to appeal simply because they disagree with the trial court outcome; the appeals process is intended to correct legal error, not give the parties a second chance at their claim. All 50 states and the federal court system have very specific rules regarding appellate procedure; they are as complex, if not more so, than the trial process. While the full appellate process will not be discussed in this chapter, it is important to discuss the role of an appellate court generally.

On appeal, the reviewing court will use the facts of the case established at the trial court level; the appellate court is not a fact-finding court. Using those facts, the appellate court will determine whether the decision reached by the trial court was correct in totality (**affirmed**), correct in part (**affirmed in part**), incorrect in totality (**reversed**), or incorrect in part (**reversed in part**). Often times, when the appellate court affirms or reverses a decision in part, it will also **remand** the case back to the trial court for further proceedings consistent with the appellate decision, which means the appellate court will ask the court of origin to hear parts of the case a second time.

Most of the Significant Cases you will read in this textbook are authored by appellate courts; thus, the opinion you read will likely summarize the finding and decisions at the trial court level, and then proceed with the appellate review. Any precedential value that the case has (binding or persuasive, see earlier discussion) will come from the appellate court decision.

> **Case Example #4:** This case highlights a majority of the procedural elements discussed in the Legal Process section. Note that the Factual and Procedural Background section is a summary of the trial court level case, written by the appellate court (who authored this opinion). The discussion of the legal issues at the appellate level is omitted; however, the appellate court's disposition (decision) is included.

> MARIO SOLIS et al., Plaintiffs and Appellants, v. KIRKWOOD RESORT COMPANY, Defendant and Respondent. 114 Cal. Rptr. 2d 265 (2001)
>
> OPINION
>
> Mario (**plaintiff**) and Janelle Solis sued Kirkwood Resort Company (**defendant**, the true name of which is Kirkwood Mountain Resort, LLC), after a ski accident. The **trial** court granted defendant's motion for summary judgment, finding plaintiff signed a release of negligence liability which embraced this accident, and that defendant owed no duty to plaintiff under the primary assumption of the risk rule. **Plaintiff filed a timely notice of appeal from the ensuing judgment**.
>
> We conclude plaintiff established an ambiguity in the release and a jury could find it was not intended to cover this accident. Moreover, there is a critical factual question regarding whether defendant increased the risk of harm to skiers beyond that inherent in the sport. **We reverse**.
>
> STANDARD OF REVIEW
>
> Summary judgment is properly granted to a defendant who shows without refutation that a plaintiff cannot establish an essential element of his cause of action or that there is an affirmative defense which bars recovery: Our review is de novo.
>
> FACTUAL AND PROCEDURAL BACKGROUND
>
> The **complaint** alleges Mario Solis was skiing at defendant's resort when, without warning, he entered an area of the resort that had recently been altered to accommodate a ski race. This area now consisted of hazardous man-made jumps, which increased the risk of harm to skiers and caused him to fall down. **The complaint raised theories of negligence and premises liability, with a pendent loss of consortium claim for plaintiff's wife, Janelle.**
>
> **The answer generally denied the allegations and asserted a number of defenses, including a release of liability signed by plaintiff, and primary assumption of the risk.**
>
> The undisputed facts show the accident occurred on Sunday, March 28, 1999. Earlier that ski season, plaintiff bought a midweek season pass from defendant, entitled "Season Pass & Liability Release Agreement." This allowed him to use defendant's facilities Monday through Friday for the entire season, except for designated holiday dates. Part of the application for the season pass consists of a release of liability form, the terms of which will be recited in a moment. The entire application is reproduced as an appendix to this opinion. Although a checked box indicates plaintiff bought a "Midweek Plus Season Pass," the parties agree he paid for and obtained the "Midweek Season Pass." In part this states "Pass is only valid Monday through Friday," with certain exceptions not relevant to this case. Because his season pass did not allow weekend usage, in order to ski the Sunday of the accident, plaintiff had to buy a day pass. Defendant does not require purchasers of day passes to sign a release or at least did not require plaintiff to do so.

> **Defendant produced declarations of two ski patrollers who helped plaintiff after the accident, and supporting documentation including photographs and reports prepared by the ski patrol.** The gist of this evidence was that plaintiff, through inattention or for a thrill, skied past a line of crossed bamboo poles, which closed the jumps off from the run plaintiff was using. Defendant acknowledged that that part of the mountain had been turned into a racing start for a special event scheduled for later that day. **Defendant also produced portions of plaintiff's deposition, where he described himself as an expert skier.** Plaintiff had claimed a mound or "berm" of snow "kicked me into the air."
>
> Plaintiff argued defendant "created a temporary hazard that caused the injury." **According to declarations submitted by plaintiff and by his skiing partner that day**, the bamboo warning poles were not erected until after the accident. Plaintiff argued the release contained in his season pass application was temporally delimited by the scope of the pass itself, that is, the release was operative only Monday through Friday.
>
> **The trial court granted summary judgment**, as follows: "Kirkwood's evidence establishes that plaintiff Mario Solis executed a valid, binding, and enforceable contract when he signed the 'Season Pass & Liability Release Agreement.' The court finds that the contract is clear and unambiguous on it[s] face, and specifically finds that the Liability Release contained within the contract is not limited by the type of pass that a skier purchases. The clear intent of the contract is that the Liability Release bars all claims by all season pass holders, regardless of the type of pass purchased.
>
> "Plaintiffs do not dispute that the Release is inherently valid and enforceable; instead **plaintiff argues that because the accident occurred on a day on which his particular pass was not valid, the Release was also not valid. The Court finds this argument unpersuasive**. The Release is not a part of, subordinate to, or governed by the season pass; both are encompassed by the 'Season Pass & Liability Release Agreement.' The obvious intent of that document is that one release shall bind all claims by all pass holders.
>
> "The agreement is devoid of language which suggests that the Release's applicability is dependent upon the type of pass. Nor does the language support an interpretation that the Release is only valid on days when the pass is also valid. Such a conclusion contradicts the simple and clear language on the face of the document. The court finds that plaintiff entered the contract without mistake of fact.
>
> "The court finds that plaintiffs' claims are also barred by the doctrine of primary assumption of risk. Plaintiff's descriptions of the terrain feature on which he lost control are inconsistent. Based upon the evidence presented, the court is unable to rule whether the terrain feature is [natural] or man-made. **In either event, plaintiffs' evidence does not establish that the terrain feature on which plaintiff lost control increased the risks inherent in the sport.** Whether the object was natural or man-made, the evidence supports a finding that it posed a risk inherent in the sport of skiing. **Plaintiff's deposition testimony establishes that he was familiar with such risks, and understood that skiers assume the dangers posed thereby.** The plaintiffs' claims are, therefore, also barred under the doctrine of primary assumption of risk."
>
> **A judgment was entered accordingly and plaintiff filed a timely notice of appeal therefrom.**
>
> DISCUSSION: Omitted
>
> DISPOSITION:
> The **trial court judgment is reversed with directions to vacate the order granting summary judgment and enter an order denying the motion**. Defendant is to pay plaintiff's costs of this appeal.

Explanation
*This case demonstrates the complexity of the legal process, highlighting many of the important steps along the way. The plaintiff initiated the case by filing a complaint with the appropriate trial court in the California state court system; the defendant then filed an answer. Both parties conducted discovery, obtaining declarations and depositions. After discovery, the defendant filed a motion for summary judgment, which was granted by the trial court. The plaintiff appealed that finding to the Court of Appeal of California, who reversed the decision and entered judgment for the plaintiff denying the motion for summary judgment. **It is important to note** what this means procedurally; this does not mean that the plaintiff has won the case or will receive damages; rather, this means that the plaintiff can proceed with the original complaint in trial court and continue to a trial if he so desires. Other options for the plaintiff include settlement or ADR.*

QUESTIONS YOU SHOULD BE ABLE TO ANSWER

1. What is the difference between common law and statutory law?

2. What is precedent? How is it created? What forms of precedent exist?

3. Describe the difference between the federal and state court systems.

4. What is a motion for summary judgment? When/Why is it typically filed?

5. What is the role of the appellate courts in the legal process?

REFERENCES

Cases
Fraser v. Major League Soccer, 2000 U.S. Dist. LEXIS 5434
Roman v. Liberty University, et. al., 2008 Cal. App. LEXIS 636
Sanders v. Kuna Joint School District, 876 P.2d 154 (1994)
Solis v. Kirkwood Resort Company, 114 Cal. Rptr. 2d 265 (2001)

Publications
Black, H. C. (1990). Black's Law Dictionary, (6th Ed.) St. Paul: West Publishing Co.
Colorado State Court System. Available at: http://www.courts.state.co.us/Courts/Index.cfm
Hill, G. and Hill, K. Online Legal Dictionary. Available at: http://dictionary.law.com/
Maryland's Judicial System. Available at: http://www.courts.state.md.us/overview.html
Montana Judicial System. Available at http://home.mcn.net/~montanabw/judsys.html
New York State Unified Court System. Available at http://www.courts.state.ny.us/courts/structure.shtml

Legislation
Conn. Gen. Stat. § 52-577 (2015)
Minn. Stat. § 541.01 (2015)
S.C. Code Ann. §52-19-20 (2014)

LEGAL RESEARCH

Anita M. Moorman | University of Louisville

Many sport organizations have legal counsel on staff or have ready access to outside legal counsel who can certainly assist as legal issues arise. However, recreation and sport managers should also have the ability to perform and analyze legal research for themselves either in an effort to proactively anticipate legal issues or to respond to a legal issue once it has arisen. In addition, the ability to conduct legal research will allow the recreation and sport manager to obtain information about current and emerging legal developments. A meaningful understanding of current legal developments is as critical to the recreation and sport manager as is a firm understanding of current developments in communication, marketing, finance, sponsorship, ethics, and many other areas. This chapter will introduce future and current recreation and sport managers to the variety of legal resources available in the traditional law library as well as from electronic and Internet sources.

Locating legal information is much easier if the researcher has a comfortable understanding of how the legal system works. Thus, it is imperative for the recreation and sport manager to understand that the U.S. judicial system is divided into distinctly separate federal and state systems. Thus, legal information is also separated based on whether a legal issue involved a state law or a federal law. For example, the court decision in *National Football League Management Council v. NFLPA* (2015) (which vacated Tom Brady's four game suspension penalty imposed by Roger Goodell as part of the Deflategate scandal) was made by a federal court because it involved a question of federal law related to federal labor law. The "law" can mean different things to different people, but for the purposes of conducting legal research "the law" refers to a source that actually establishes a legal standard, principle, or mandate. For example, to govern a democratic society such as the United States, that society typically will create a governing document that will define how it will govern itself. Typically, this governing document is called a Constitution and it will define the powers and authority of the various branches of the government as well as limitations on governmental powers and authority. Thus both the United States Constitution and the various state constitutions are examples of primary sources of law. Another example of the law can be found in legislation or statutes. Legislation or statutes are enacted by the state and federal legislatures which in turn rely on state and federal agencies to enforce the statutes. Thus administrative agencies tend to be primarily responsible for writing or promulgating rules and regulations to enforce the statutes. Lastly, the courts must interpret the statutes or rules and fill any gaps left by the legislatures or administrative agencies. Thus, **Constitutions**, **Statutes**, **Administrative Regulations/Rules**, and **Court Decisions** make up the four primary sources of law. All the activities described above are recorded, cataloged, stored, indexed, and housed in thousands of volumes. And while the sheer volume of this legal information can appear daunting to a beginning researcher, because it is cataloged and indexed so thoroughly, a well-planned research project can be managed effectively.

The purpose of this chapter is to help the reader understand legal research. First, we will look at the legal resources available to the researcher. These include the four **primary sources** listed above (the actual law), **secondary sources** (explanations/definitions/summaries of the law), and certain **research tools** (digests, electronic databases, computerized legal research). Then we will look at two important techniques to use in conducting legal research. These are **Developing the Research Plan** and **Summarizing Cases**.

LEGAL RESOURCES

Primary Legal Resources

Primary legal sources include constitutions, statutes, rules and regulations, and court decisions. Primary legal sources represent the actual law, whether it is a decision of the U.S. Supreme Court or a state statute enacted by the State of Oklahoma. *Regardless of the type of legal research being conducted, ultimately only primary legal sources can be relied on in determining what the law is and what the law requires.*

Constitutions/Statutes/Rules/Regulations

The U.S. Constitution is the supreme law of the land. It both authorizes and restricts conduct of the federal and state governments, as well as conduct of private citizens. Each of the fifty states will similarly have a state constitution governing conduct of the state government and citizens of that state. The U.S. Congress and fifty state legislatures enact laws known as statutes addressing issues ranging from the enforceability of contracts, to sport lotteries, to registration of trademarks. The federal statutes are codified (or published) in a series of volumes known as the *United States Code* (U.S.C.). Each of the fifty states also codifies its state statutes, which are called civil codes, public laws, session laws, or revised statutes. Both the *United States Code* and the state statutes are published in both official print and electronic formats and are also available using a variety of web-based legal research sources. For example, the Legal Information Institute at Cornell University provides web-based access to the entire United States Code making it easily accessible for lawyers and practitioners alike. However, one benefit of using the official codes available in print form or electronically from LexisNexis or Westlaw is access to **annotations** that categorize court decisions, law review articles, and legal treatises interpreting the statute in question. These annotations are similar to an index and will assist the researcher in locating specific court decisions and understanding how the statute has been interpreted and applied by the courts. For example, if you were trying to determine whether a federal district court in your state had ruled in a case involving the *Olympic and Amateur Sports Act* (this is the act that created and empowered the U.S. Olympic Committee), you could use the annotations to locate specific cases decided by courts in your state.

Congress and the state legislatures also create regulatory bodies such as the Federal Aviation Administration, Environmental Protection Agency, Equal Employment Opportunity Commission, and many others. These regulatory bodies often are required to create rules and regulations to fulfill their assigned purpose. These rules and regulations for federal agencies are codified in the *Code of Federal Regulations* (C.F.R.) and can be a useful resource for research related to a particular agency's activities. Most state and federal agencies also maintain up to date information concerning rules, regulations, and policies on the Internet to permit easy access to this information. A partial list of constitutional and statutory resources is as follows:

U.S. Constitution	State Constitutions
Treaties	Federal Statutes (the *U.S. Code* [U.S.C.])
State Statutes	Municipal Ordinances
Rules of Court	Executive Orders and Promulgations
Rules/Regulations of Federal Administrative Agencies (C.F.R.)	
Rules/Regulations of State Administrative Agencies	
Attorney General Opinions—federal and state	

Court Decisions

A court decision results from a jury verdict or court order that resolves a case or an issue in a case. For example, suppose Cam Newton sued John Brown Company based on the company's unauthorized use of Cam Newton's name in an advertisement. Newton's lawsuit or case will probably include several different legal claims such as trademark infringement, violation of the right of publicity, and misappropriation of goodwill. It is possible that John Brown would file a motion for summary judgment (remember this was discussed in the previous chapter) asking the court to dismiss Newton's trademark infringement claim. When the court either grants or denies the motion for summary judgment, it will enter an order to that effect. This order represents a court decision. Ultimately, if the case goes to trial, another court decision may be entered reflecting the outcome of the trial. Either or both of these court decisions may be published. Thus, if we want to be able to find and read this decision, we must understand when and where these court decisions are published.

Understanding the court system (which was covered in the previous chapter) aids us in locating these decisions. You may recall that court systems are hierarchical in structure, that is, that some courts are superior to others. The highest court is usually a supreme or superior court, followed by an intermediate appellate court, and ending with a district or trial court at the bottom. Most cases will originate at the trial or district court level and work their way *up* through the court system. This process can take years for a case to move through all levels of the court system. Any number of court decisions may be entered in a case as it winds its way through the court system to its ultimate conclusion, so to find court decisions, you need to understand how those decisions are reported. First, we will explore the federal court system and then the state court system.

Federal Courts

In the federal court system, the vast majority of federal cases originate in the U.S. District Court. The U.S. District Court is the federal trial court and the first level within the federal court system. Any appeal from a U.S. District Court decision would be made to the appropriate U.S. Court of Appeals. Any party to the district court action may appeal to the U.S. Court of Appeals. The U.S. Courts of Appeals represent the second level or the intermediate appellate level in the federal court system. As explained in the previous chapter, the court of appeals only exercises appellate jurisdiction. That means cases do not originate in the court of appeals; instead, a case would only reach the court of appeals after a decision has been made in a lower court (such as the district court) and a party appeals from that decision. That appeal requests the appellate court to review a portion of the lower court's decision to determine whether the lower court made a mistake. After the U.S. Court of Appeals renders its decision, a party can still request another appellate review by the U.S. Supreme Court. However, the U.S. Supreme Court is not required to hear these appeals. The appellate jurisdiction of the U.S. Supreme Court is considered discretionary and, as such, requests for appeal (known as petitions for *certiorari*) are rarely granted. The U.S. Supreme Court is the highest court in the land, and its decisions are considered the supreme law of the land, which must be followed by all lower federal and state courts. As the federal courts make these decisions regarding cases, they are published or reported in the reporters listed following.

U.S. District Courts

Federal Supplement and *Federal Supplement Second Series* (cited F. Supp., or F. Supp. 2d). (Note: These reporters are a continuing series of cases reported by the U.S. District Courts from 1932 to the present date. This reporter is in its second series or edition now).

Sample Citation: *Hoopla Sports and Entertainment, Inc. v. Nike, Inc.*, 947 F. Supp. 347 (N.D. Ill. 1996). This citation tells us that this court decision can be located in volume 947 at page 347 in the Federal Supplement. It further tells us that the decision was made by the U.S. District Court for the Northern District of Illinois in 1996.

U.S. Courts of Appeals

Federal Reporter, Federal Reporter Second Series, Federal Reporter Third Series (cited F., F.2d, or F.3d). (Note: These reporters are a continuing series of cases reported by the U.S. Courts of Appeals from 1880 to the present date. This reporter is in its third series or edition now).

Sample Citation: *National Basketball Association v. Motorola, Inc.*, 105 F.3d 841 (2nd Cir. 1997). This citation tells us that this court decision can be found in volume 105 at page 841 in the Federal Reporter Third Series. It further tells us that the decision was made by the U.S. Court of Appeals for the Second Circuit in 1997.

U.S. Supreme Court

U.S. Supreme Court Reports (cited U.S.); Supreme Court Reporter (cited S. Ct.); Lawyer's Edition (cited L.Ed.2d). (Note: These three reporters all report the same Supreme Court cases. *U.S. Supreme Court Reports* is the official Supreme Court reporter, but *Supreme Court Reporter* is most commonly used and user friendly).

Sample Citation: *PGA Tour, Inc. v. Martin*, 532 U.S. 661, 121 S. Ct. 1879, 149 L. Ed. 2d 904 (2001). You will often see all three reporters cited, this is called a string cite. The first part of the string is the citation to the U.S. Supreme Court Reports (532 U.S. 661), followed by the citation to the Supreme Court Reporter (121 S. Ct. 1879), and ending with the citation to the Lawyer's Edition (149 L. Ed. 2d 904). You may also see a Supreme Court case cited with only one of these three possible citations, such as *PGA Tour, Inc. v. Martin*, 121 S. Ct. 1879 (2001). This citation tells us that this decision can be found at volume 121 at page 1879 in the Supreme Court Reporter. It further tells us that this decision of the U.S. Supreme Court was made in 2001.

State Courts

The state court systems are organized in a similar fashion to the federal courts. Most states will have several trial or district courts located in the various counties in the state. Most cases will originate in the trial or district courts and then follow a similar path as federal cases with appeals going to an intermediate appellate court or directly to the state supreme court. Typically, only decisions made by a state's Supreme Court are selected for publication in the **state reporters**. These decisions, once published, are organized in a reporter system in two different ways. Each state's decisions can be found in its separate state reporter such as the *California Reporter*. However, many law libraries only carry the individual state reporter for the state in which they are located. For all other states' court decisions, the library will likely have the **regional reporter** that publishes the same state court decisions but grouped together in a specific region. The regional reporters are broken down following.

Atlantic Reporter (cited A. and A.2d)
[Pennsylvania, Vermont, New Hampshire, Maine, Rhode Island, Connecticut, New Jersey, Delaware, and Maryland]
North Eastern Reporter (cited N.E. and N.E.2d)
[New York, Massachusetts, Ohio, Indiana, and Illinois]
North Western Reporter (cited N.W. and N.W.2d)
[North Dakota, South Dakota, Minnesota, Wisconsin, Michigan, Nebraska, and Iowa]
Pacific Reporter (cited P. and P.2d)
[Kansas, Oklahoma, New Mexico, Colorado, Wyoming, Montana, Arizona, Utah, Idaho, Nevada, Washington, Oregon, California, Hawaii, and Alaska]
South Eastern Reporter (cited S.E. and S.E.2d)
[West Virginia, Virginia, North Carolina, South Carolina, and Georgia]
Southern Reporter (cited So. and So.2d)
[Louisiana, Mississippi, Alabama, and Florida]
South Western Reporter (cited S.W. and S.W.2d)
[Kentucky, Tennessee, Missouri, Arkansas, and Texas]

The following sample citations to state reporters follow a similar format to those we examined in the federal courts:

Maisonave v. Newark Bears Professional Baseball Club, 881 A.2d 700 (N.J. 2005). This case can be found in volume 881 at page 700 in the Atlantic Reporter, Second Series. This is a 2005 decision of the New Jersey Supreme Court.

Rowe v. Pinellas Sports Auth., 461 So. 2d 72 (Fla. 1984). This case can be found in volume 461 at page 72 in the Southern Reporter, Second Series and is a 1984 decision of the Florida Supreme Court.

Crespin v. Albuquerque Baseball Club, 216 P.3d 827 (N.M. App. 2009). This case can be found in volume 216 at page 827 of the Pacific Reporter, Third Series; and it is a 2009 decision of the Court of Appeals of New Mexico. This is one of those instances where an intermediate appellate court decision was published and the use of the term "App." or "Ct. App." in the parenthesis with the date is how you can distinguish between decisions of the court of appeals and those of the various state supreme courts. If the citation does not contain "App" or "Ct. App," but instead just the state abbreviation as in the first two sample citations, this usually means the decision was made by the state's highest court (either a supreme court or superior court).

Secondary Resources

Secondary resources include articles, journals, papers, and other written sources that summarize, explain, interpret, or analyze certain issues or topics of the law. In addition to making a scholarly contribution to the understanding of legal issues and topics, they provide the sport or recreation manager with an overview or insight into a particular area. Secondary resources also can be a valuable source for locating additional or related primary sources; however, only primary resources represent the actual law. *Thus, secondary resources should never be solely relied on as legal authority.* Following is a listing of several secondary resources by type and description.

Legal Dictionaries: *Black's Law Dictionary* provides definitions of legal terms. It is a must for studying and researching law. Many paperback, condensed versions are available.

Lawyer Directories: Martindale-Hubbell is useful for locating attorneys in any state in the United States.

Annotated Law Reports (A.L.R.): A.L.R. contains commentary and summary on areas of law. It covers both state and federal courts. The annotation usually includes a case summary together with commentary about the case and how it may or does affect other cases or the current status of the law. A.L.R. is very useful if you have a specific case for which you wish to study the impact it has had on the law.

Legal Encyclopedias: *Corpus Juris Secundum* and *American Jurisprudence* (Am. Jur.). A legal encyclopedia functions like a standard encyclopedia and includes topical summaries of numerous legal issues. The summary will also include supporting references to cases, statutes, and other primary and secondary resources. This is a good place to start if you know little or nothing about a topic and want a jumping-off point. These will not provide much analysis and may not contain the latest developments.

Restatement of Law (Torts, contracts, etc.): Restatements are comprehensive surveys of a specific and major category of law. For example, the **Restatement of Contracts** summarizes the origin, development, and current application of contract law in the United States noting differences among individual states, majority positions, and the general rule of law for all issues related to contracts. These can be useful to develop a better understanding of the principle and theory of law if the reader has some familiarity with the law already.

Treatises (Textbooks, Casebooks, and Hornbooks): Treatises are written by scholars and experts on a particular legal issue or topic. These resources are usually very comprehensive and provide an in-depth examination of the issue or topic. Note, however, that a treatise represents the author's interpretation of the law—a treatise is not the actual law. Treatises can provide the reader with substantial references and resources on a specific topic. Most law libraries have extensive collections of treatises. The preeminent publication in the field is the three-volume set by Betty van der Smissen entitled *Legal Liability and Risk Management for Public and Private Entities*. Some sport law treatises include: *Torts and Sports: Legal Liability in Professional and Amateur Athletics* by Raymond L. Yasser; *Sports and Law: Contemporary Issues* by Herb Appenzeller.

Shepard's Citations: Shepard's Citations is a publication that allows the researcher to track a court decision or statute through a citation index. The citation index lists court decisions that have cited previous court decisions and court decisions interpreting specific statutory sections. This resource is useful to locate additional cases once the research has located a major or dispositive case. But more importantly, this index tracks any "treatment" of a particular case. Thus, the index identifies if a case the researcher is relying on has been questioned, criticized, followed, reversed, or otherwise interpreted by later court decisions. This is extremely important to ensure that court decisions relied on are indeed still representative of the current legal standard.

Legal Indexes *(Index to Legal Periodicals* (ILP)): The ILP allows the researcher to locate law review articles by topic and/or author. The ILP is available both in the traditional book form and electronically. The researcher can conduct a topical electronic search and will be provided with citation and location information for law review articles on that topic.

Law Review Articles: Published primarily by law schools or professional law associations throughout the United States. To date there are numerous law reviews/journals regularly addressing sport law issues. Some of these include: *Marquette Sports Law Review*; *Villanova Sports & Entertainment Law Journal*; *Univ. Miami Entertainment & Sports Law Review*; *Seton Hall Journal of Sport Law*; *American Bar Association Entertainment & Sports Lawyer*; and *Sports Lawyers Journal*.

Academic Legal Journals: Several academic associations publish journals focused on legal issues. In sport, the Sport and Recreation Law Association publishes the *Journal of Legal Aspects of Sport* containing scholarly papers related to legal issues in sport and recreation. Other scholarly publications include *From the Gym to the Jury*; *Sports in the Courts*; *Sports, Parks and Recreation Law Reporter*; and *The Exercise, Sports and Sports Medicine Standards & Malpractice Reporter*.

Business or Academic Journals: Many current legal issues related to sport may be covered in business and academic journals. Many academic business journals also contain special sections for legal developments. For example, the *Sport Marketing Quarterly* has a column entitled Marketing and the Law featured in each issue. *Journal of Marketing & Public Policy* also has a similar feature.

Business Magazines and Newspapers: The sport industry is often the subject of articles in business magazines and daily newspapers. Often current developments in the sport industry have a legal impact. For example, the filing of a case will often be reported in major newspapers both in their print and electronic versions. Street and Smith's *SportsBusiness Journal* and *Athletic Business* often report on recent legal developments and issues. These articles can help sport and recreation managers identify the issues and stay current with legal developments in the sport and recreation industries.

Electronic and Web-based Research Tools
The availability and efficiency of electronic and Web-based research tools has enabled almost all legal research to be conducted via computer. Both secondary and primary sources are readily available in a variety of electronic formats.

Electronic Search Engines and Databases
Many law schools provide students with access to electronic databases known as **WESTLAW** and **LEXIS**, which allow the researcher to search topically or for a specific case or statute. Some law libraries restrict access to these databases to law students. In that case, **LexisNexis Academic Universe**, available through most college and university libraries, is also a valuable research tool and provides for searching top news; general news topics; company, industry, and market news; legal news; company financial information; law reviews; federal case law; *U.S. Code*; and state legal research. In the event that your library does not have or allow access to any of these resources, there are several additional Web-based research sites.

In addition to using electronic databases, we also have many electronic subscription services available to keep us abreast of current legal developments specific to the sport industry. Many of these services are free, such as the *FindLaw* Website, which offers a free subscription to a weekly e-mail listing current developments in sport law. An excellent paid subscription is available from *Sports Litigation Alerts*. Students are offered reduced subscription rates and will receive a bi-weekly, detailed summary of recent sport law developments. A listing and description of several other excellent electronic resources is contained at the end of the chapter.

Legal Blogs and Internet Searches
Thanks to Google and Yahoo and other Internet-based search engines, legal information often times can be accessed with just a click of the mouse. For example, if you enter the search term "sport law" into Google, Google's search engine will return more than 230,000 results from your search if you happened to put "sport law" in parenthesis to limit the number of hits. If you did not put "sport law" in parentheses, Google will actually return more than 199,000,000 hits in just a few seconds. This capability can be both a benefit and a detriment. The speed and ease of such a search is a great benefit, but obviously, it could take days or even weeks to sort through 230,000 results, and tackling almost two hundred million results is nearly impossible. So for maximum effectiveness, our searches need to be as specific and detailed as possible.

Google and other search engines can also be used very effectively to locate current relevant developments in sport law. For example, assume you are a sport or recreation manager and have been following a pending lawsuit. In the past, it could take days or even weeks after a final decision was made in that pending case for you to be able to learn of the decision and access a copy of the court's order or opinion. Today, often times the notification of the final decision is made almost simultaneously with the decision itself and the actual written decision or order is available within just a few minutes or hours. Almost every major news outlet delivers the news via the Internet and enables you to receive instant notifications of breaking news stories.

A good example of just how useful these services are to a sport or recreation manager can be found related in the New York attorney general's decision to enjoin Draft Kings and Fan Duel from operating in the State of New York based on the AG's decision that daily fantasy sports were illegal gambling activities. This case was watched closely by sport managers beyond the obvious New York state gambling law issues presented. These developments in New York also prompted several other states to examine the nature of daily fantasy sports raising several questions about the future of daily fantasy sports and the impact on professional sport leagues which had been actively involved in the expansion of the fantasy sport industry. If you had been following this situation, and followed any one of the dozens of sport law Twitter based news outlets, you would have been notified immediately when the Attorney General announced the injunction. In addition, within just a few hours a great deal of legal commentary was also available interpreting and analyzing the Attorney General's decision. This kind of immediate information concerning legal developments can be very useful to a sport or recreation manager to identify business risks, threats, and opportunities.

In addition to the search engines and news alerts, a number of legal blogs and social media outlets also exist that can be a valuable resource for practitioners. **Blogs** (which is short for weblogs) originally began as websites where individuals posted commentary or personal diaries. In the past, a blog was not a very useful research source, particularly for legal research because it primarily represented the personal opinion of the blogger and contained anonymous and/or random comments by the blog's readers. Like Google searches, not every post on a blog is credible, particularly when one is conducting legal research. Legal research must lead to verifiable and credible conclusions. Thus, while blogs generally should still be viewed with some skepticism when conducting legal research, a number of "credible legal authorities" provide their opinions, commentary, and legal analysis via weblogs. These legal blogs, such as the Sports Law Blog are a useful legal resource for tracking current legal developments, reviewing credible commentary concerning legal issues, and linking to additional resources related to legal developments.

Social media is a tremendous source of current information and instantaneous access to information. Hundreds of legal scholars and sport law news outlets maintain a highly active presence on social media platforms such as Twitter. Students in sport and recreation law courses as well as sport managers should select six to ten of some of the leading contributors in the sport law field and follow them on Twitter as a highly effective way to stay up to date on current industry trends and events. A list of several leading legal scholars and commentators on Twitter is provided later in this chapter.

The researcher still should exercise caution when citing to these sources unless he or she is able to satisfy himself or herself that the information is credible and reasonable to rely upon to support his or her conclusions. And if the researcher is going to rely upon these sources, he or she needs to take care to cite the sources properly to assure that the reader understands that a particular statement or conclusion is based upon a *secondary source* (not a primary source) and represents the opinion or analysis of an another, not necessarily the opinion or analysis of a court or legal expert or authority. If used cautiously and properly though, legal blogs are quite effective research tools.

Electronic and Internet Resources
Provided below are a number of Websites, search engines, electronic resources, sport and recreation law blogs, and leading scholars on Twitter that should help you rapidly locate current developments in sport law as well as conduct more in-depth research.

General Legal Research
Searchable databases that cover a broad range of topics including general federal and state law information, federal and state court decisions:

> FindLaw Search Database: www.findlaw.com/
> Internet Reference Desk Website: www.refdesk.com
> Law Library Resource Xchange: www.llrx.com
> Law Journal EXTRA! Federal Courts: http://lawonline.ljx.com/federal/
> Where to Find Court Opinions: www.legalonline.com/courts.htm
> National Center for State Courts: www.ncsc.dni.us/
> The 'Lectric Law Lexicon: www.lectlaw.com//ref.html
> American Law Source On-Line: www.lawsource.com/also/

Government Research Sources : Websites, some searchable, that provide information about government agencies, governmental functions, Congress, and general information:

> United States Patent and Trademark Office: http://trademarks.uspto.gov/
> United States Geological Survey: http://mapping.usgs.gov/www.gnis

State and Local Government on the Net: www.piperinfo.com/state/states.html
United States Federal Trade Commission: www.ftc.gov
United States Department of Labor: www.dol.gov.
United States Congress: www.congress.org.
United States Library of Congress: http://thomas.loc.gov/
United States Supreme Court: http://www.supremecourtus.gov/

University Sponsored Research Sites

Searchable databases and links that include general research of state and federal court decisions, the Constitution, and state and federal statutes as well as Websites focused on a single topic, such as Title IX and hazing:

The Legal Information Institute of Cornell Law School: www.law.cornell.edu
University of Iowa Gender Equity in Sports Project: http://bailiwick.lib.uiowa.edu/ge/
The Legal Education Network at the University of Pittsburgh: http://jurist.law.pitt.edu/
Indiana State University Sport Law Links: http://library.indstate.edu/level1.dir/lio.dir/sportslaw.htm#Sports

Law Journals and Associations Sites

Websites with sport law links and general information about sport law studies and research:

Emory Law School: www.law.emory.edu/FEDCTS/
Marquette Law School: www.marquette.edu/law/sports/links.html
National Sport Law Institute publications: http://law.marquette.edu/cgi-bin/site.pl?2130&pageID=463#YMTC
Sport and Recreation Law Association: www.srlaweb.org

Miscellaneous Private Sites

Dozens of individuals and companies offer sport law information and links:

Mark's Sports Law News: www.sportslawnews.com/
Insurance Information Website: www.insure.com
Waiver/Risk Management Website: www.sportwaiver.com
Court TV Glossary of Legal Terms: www.courttv.com/legalterms/glossary.html
Sport Law Blogs
http://www.sportslawblog.com
http://thesportslawprofessor.blogspot.com/
http://blog.willamette.edu/wucl/journals/sportslaw/
http://abajournal.com/blawgs/entertainment+sports+law
http://ctsportslaw.com/
http://athleteagent.blogspot.com/
http://www.sportsagentblog.com/
http://recreation-law.com/
www.http://defendingsportsblog.com/

Recommended Twitter Accounts

Michael McCann: @McCannSportsLaw
Marc Edelman: @MarcEdelman
Eric Macramalla: @EricOnSportsLaw
Law In Sport: @LawinSport
Kristi Dosh: @SportsBizMiss
The Sports Law Blog: @InsideSportsLaw
Lex Sportiva: @AMELIAsportLAW

Warren K. Zola: @WarrenKZola
World Sports Law Report: @sport_law
Asser Sports Law: @Sportslaw_Asser

RESEARCH TECHNIQUES

Developing the Research Plan

Once the researcher is comfortable with the court system and how legal information is codified and reported, it is time to begin the actual research. Having a clearly defined research plan is vital to locating legal information efficiently. Otherwise, the researcher could spend countless hours in the law library with little to show for it. The following six steps represent a good approach to conducting legal research.

Step One: Identify the Problem or Issue Using Secondary Sources

Step One is by far the most important step in the research process. If the issue or problem is not clearly identified, it will be impossible to narrow your search enough to produce meaningful results. A clearly defined issue will also help to discover key words, phrases, and terms that may facilitate the research. However, before you can identify the legal issue involved, you must search current business and professional literature to stay on top of industry activities. For example, when the State of Maryland passed legislation exempting fantasy sports from state gambling prohibitions, interest increased regarding which other states either already permitted fee-based fantasy sports contests or where such contests may be legally permissible (Rosenwald, 2012). Under that new exemption, individuals who participate in fee-based fantasy sports leagues in Maryland could legally collect the prize money that comes along with winning a fantasy sports league. However, this subsequently led to the proliferation of daily fantasy sports games which has led a number of legal scholars to comment on this development and publish law review articles on the legality of daily fantasy sports as opposed to the traditional league long fantasy game(Edelman, 2012). These scholarly contributions could be easily located by sport industry professionals to help them understand the legislation as well as its implications for the gaming industry.

Several good sources of recent developments in the sport industry are available. The *Chronicle of Higher Education* has sections on college athletics, which report recent educational, administrative, business, and legal developments. Several industry publications such as Street and Smith's *SportsBusiness Journal* also will report emerging business and legal issues. In addition, any current news source will be a good place to locate current trends and issues. Once the general issue has been identified, it then becomes easier to identify the legal issues. However, if instead of a specific recent development, a familiar topic or subject in the sport industry is to be the focus of our research, such as Title IX (Gender Equity), then the *Index to Legal Periodicals* and **LexisNexis Academic Universe** are helpful to track down previous law review articles on the subject. Also, remember electronic sources such as **www.findlaw.com** and **www.law.com** have subject sections available with links to numerous other information sources.

Step Two: Read and Summarize Cases

Cases identified in Step Two need to be read thoroughly and then summarized according to their importance and relevance to the issue. A sample summary for a key case is provided at the end of this chapter. Any relevant literature such as law review articles, business journal articles, or other literature must be summarized to help frame the importance of the issue to the sport industry.

Step Three: Locate Additional Cases and Shepardize

Once a few key cases are located, locating more recent or relevant cases is fairly simple. For this task the **West's Key Number System** together with the **digests** is critical. Each case published in the West's Reporter System will contain several short summaries indexed by topic and key number throughout the West's Digest System. Basically, once you have found a major case relevant to your problem, finding other similar cases from the same jurisdiction or from other states or federal cases is easy to accomplish using the West's Digest. **Shepard's**

Citations is the most available updating service. Shepard's Citations will also help to locate additional cases and verify whether the cases the researcher is relying on are still good law. This process is usually referred to as "Shepardizing." If the cases you are relying on have been reversed, overruled, or somehow disregarded by later courts, your position can be severely weakened. Although the service is a bit cumbersome to use, it is important to make the effort. Most law librarians will demonstrate how to use the service once you have a particular case citation that you would like to update.

Step Four: Determine Any Constitutional or Statutory Connections

Not every problem or issue requires an examination of constitutional and statutory law; however, if a particular article of a constitution or a statute, state or federal, is implicated, it needs to be located and thoroughly read and updated. It is not uncommon for Congress or state legislatures to frequently amend and modify existing statutory laws; thus, the researcher must find the most current version of any statutory provisions. Always be sure to consult the "pocket part" of any statutory volume for the latest amendments or modifications.

Step Five: Organize Your Information

Organizing all the general information, cases, and statutes can be a daunting task, but it is critical to effectively answer your question or problem identified in Step One. It is recommended that you summarize every case, define and redefine your issue as you gain a better understanding of the issue, search other jurisdictions for similar or dissimilar cases, and then locate any relevant statutory laws. After that, you will be able to integrate all the information together. For example, if your issue deals with gender equity in sports, you will soon learn that not only is there a specific federal statute to consider (Title IX), but numerous court decisions have also been published that help to interpret and understand the statute. Also, you will find that some rules or regulations issued by the Office of Civil Rights help in understanding the scope and impact of Title IX. In addition, scholars are frequently writing treatises and law review articles on this subject. A researcher could literally find hundreds of pages of information about Title IX.

So how does a researcher organize hundreds of pages of information? Simple, look back to the original problem or question. Limit or narrow the inquiry to only those bits of information that actually provide an answer to the original problem or question. Once that is completed, it is recommended that you then organize the information as follows:

> **Statement of Facts:** Identify the facts or circumstances that created the need to study the problem.
> **Statement of the Issue/Problem:** State the actual issue, question, or problem that will be answered.
> **Identification of the Relevant Law:** Identify the cases, statutes, or other information needed to understand this issue. This should include a brief summary of relevant cases, relevant statutory language, and other information needed to understand the law.
> **Application of the Law:** This section should include a detailed analysis of the law identified in the *Identification of the Relevant Law* section and how it applies to the *Statement of Facts* section to answer the question identified in the *Statement of the Issue/Problem* section.
> **Conclusion:** Discuss the anticipated effect of your analysis in the *Application of the Law* section. How are recreation and sport managers or the industry affected by this legal issue?

SUMMARIZING CASES

As mentioned earlier, planning and organization are critical to the research plan. Court decisions must be read, summarized, and applied to answer the original research question. Following is an excerpt of a tort case involving an injury received by a fan at a wrestling match.

Illustrative Case

This case presents a good opportunity to demonstrate how to condense a case into its most important elements: citation, key facts, issues to be decided, decision of the court, and reasoning of the court. If every important case revealed during your research is summarized in this fashion, you will be able to quickly and efficiently incorporate this information into any report or written findings.

McGue v. Kingdom Sports Center, Inc.
2015 U.S. Dist. LEXIS 40668 (S.D. Ohio, 2015).

This case arises from an incident that occurred during a basketball game at Defendant's indoor sports facility. Plaintiff alleges that he was severely injured when he accelerated toward the basketball goal, made a lay-up, and landed on the goal's support structure. Plaintiff claims that Defendant negligently maintained its premises in a manner that allowed the goal's support structure to be positioned too close to the baseline of the court, rendering the court dangerous for play. Defendant now moves for summary judgment on this claim.

UNDISPUTED FACTS

1. Kingdom Sports Center, Inc. ("KSP") is a privately-owned multi-sport indoor sports facility located in Franklin, Ohio.
2. KSP is not a member of the Amateur Athletic Union ("AAU").
3. KSP is not a member of the National Federation of High School Sports ("NFHSS").
4. KSP is not a member of the Ohio High School Athletic Association.
5. Plaintiff injured his leg at KSP while playing in a basketball game on April 30, 2011.
6. Plaintiff was seventeen years old at the time of his injury.
7. Plaintiff's injury occurred when he was attempting a fast-break lay-up.
8. KSP purchased the basketball goal in question from a private seller.
9. KSP was advised by the seller that these were "collegiate basketball goals."
10. Prior to Plaintiff's injury, KSP was never advised by any person or entity that its use of these basketball goals was improper at the KSP facility.
11. KSP purchased the basketball goals at issue in 2004.
12. The basketball goals at issue were utilized for at least six basketball seasons prior to Plaintiff's accident, and approximately 1,000 games were played with these goals per year.
13. In the six or more basketball seasons prior to Plaintiff's accident, there were no other injuries reported to KSP as occurring due to the use of these basketball goals.
14. In the six or more basketball seasons prior to Plaintiff's accident, there were no other complaints reported to KSP regarding the use of these basketball goals.
15. Neither Plaintiff nor any of his coaches or teammates registered any complaint or concern to KSP regarding the basketball goals at issue, prior to engaging in play on the basketball court in question on the day of Plaintiff's injury.
16. Prior to the accident at KSP, Plaintiff had played basketball for three years for his high school team at Lloyd High School in Northern Kentucky and overall had played basketball for approximately ten years, including his elementary school years.
17. On the day of Plaintiff's accident, Plaintiff's team did a shoot-around, but its initial game was forfeited because the other team did not show. Plaintiff and others then sat on the sidelines and watched another game, before retaking the court for warm-ups and the game where the injury occurred.
18. On the day of Plaintiff's accident, the basketball goals were open to view, with no barriers or visual obstructions to them.

NEGLIGENCE CLAIM

To recover on a negligence claim, the plaintiff is required to prove the traditional tort elements of duty, breach, and proximate causation. *Bennison v. Stillpass Transit Co.*, 5 Ohio St.2d 122, 214 N.E.2d 213 (1966). In a premises liability case, the defendant's duty to the plaintiff depends on the plaintiff's status—invitee, licensee, or trespasser. *Gladon v. Greater Cleveland Regional Transit Auth.*, 75 Ohio St.3d 312, 315, 1996 Ohio 137, 662 N.E.2d 287 (1996). The owner of a business is owes its business invitees a duty of ordinary care to maintain the premises in a reasonably safe condition and to warn invitees of latent or hidden dangers. *Uddin v. Embassy Suites Hotel*, 165 Ohio App. 3d 699, 2005-Ohio-6613, 848 N.E.2d 519 (10th Dist.) Here, Defendant does not dispute that Plaintiff was a business invitee.

OPEN-AND-OBVIOUS DOCTRINE

The open-and-obvious doctrine relates to the threshold question of whether the defendant owes a duty of care to the plaintiff. "Where a danger is open and obvious, a landowner *owes no duty of care* to individuals lawfully on the premises." *Armstrong v. Best Buy Co.*, 99 Ohio St.

3d 79, 79, 2003-Ohio-2573, 788 N.E.2d 1088 (syllabus) (emphasis added). The rationale behind the doctrine is "that the open and obvious nature of the hazard itself serves as a warning." "Thus, the owner or occupier may reasonably expect that persons entering the premises will discover those dangers and take appropriate measures to protect themselves." *Id*.

While an open-and-obvious hazard is one that an invitee may reasonably be expected to discover, the invitee does not necessarily have to see the hazard for it to be open and obvious. Where the open-and-obvious doctrine applies, it operates as a complete bar to negligence claims. Whether a danger is open and obvious may present a question of law. *E.g. id*. However, Ohio courts have held that, where reasonable minds could differ with respect to whether a danger is open and obvious, the obviousness of the risk is an issue for the jury to determine.

Plaintiff argues that he could not have known the danger posed by the improperly sized goal because it was not *obvious* to the reasonable person. It is undisputed that, on the day of the Plaintiff's accident, the basketball goals were open to view, with no barriers or visual obstructions to them.

Plaintiff cites *Carpenter* for the proposition that the obviousness of the risk is an issue for the jury. In *Carpenter*, the Plaintiff tripped over a wooden pallet that protruded approximately six inches from the end of a merchandise display aisle. The court denied summary judgment because it found that the plaintiff's "view had been blocked by a movable display rack filled with merchandise, and her attention had been distracted by goods on display." *Carpenter*, 124 Ohio App.3d 236, 240, 705 N.E.2d 1281. The court found that reasonable minds could differ as to whether the display pallet was open and obvious. *Id*.

Here, Plaintiff was aware of the location and nature of the goals. His team did a shoot-around session prior to his first scheduled game, and then, after the game was forfeited by the other team, Plaintiff sat and watched another entire game. After that, Plaintiff's team went through a warm-up prior to the game in which the injury occurred. The hazard was observable by the reasonable person, and Plaintiff has failed to set forth specific facts showing that the basketball hoop was not an open-and-obvious hazard. Accordingly, the Court finds that the goal presented an open-and-obvious danger and, accordingly, Plaintiff's negligence claim is barred.

***

Illustrative Case Summary

McGue v. Kingdom Sports Center, Inc.
2015 U.S. Dist. LEXIS 40668 (S.D. Ohio, 2015).

KEY FACTS

Teaching Note: In this section, you should select only those facts that directly relate to the court's final decision. Which facts were relevant to the court in reaching its conclusion?

Plaintiff injured his leg at KSP's indoor sport facility when he accelerated toward the basketball goal, made a lay-up, and landed on the goal's support structure. Neither he nor his coaches complained or expressed concerns about the basketball goals. Prior to his game, he participated in a shoot around on the court, and also watched another game from the sidelines. The goals were open to view with no visual obstructions.

ISSUES TO BE DECIDED

Teaching Note: In this section, you should identify the specific legal question that the court is being asked to decide. It should be stated in the form of a question and should incorporate enough of the facts involved in the case so that it is distinctive. This question will be answered in the next section.

Whether the defendant owed a duty of care to the plaintiff to protect him from the risks associated with using the basketball goal which is open to view but positioned too close to the baseline of the court.

DECISION OF THE COURT

Teaching Note: In this section, you should simply answer the question posed in the previous section. Your answer should be an affirmative or negative restatement of the question posed above.

No, the defendant did not owe a duty of care to warn the plaintiff of the risks associated with using a basketball goal which is open to view but positioned too close to the baseline of the court.

REASONING OF THE COURT

Teaching Note: This section summarized the reasoning or rationale of the court. It answers the "why" question. Why did the court answer the legal question in the way that it did? This section is critical to being able to apply the decision of case to future cases and vital to an in-depth understanding of the legal question and outcome.

A good way to organize the court's reasoning is to follow the Rule – Application – Conclusion formula. What Rule has the court identified should be applied to resolve this case? How did the court Apply the Rule to the Facts of the case? What Conclusion did the court reach based on its Application of the Rule.

Rule: While a business normally owes a duty of ordinary care to its business invitees to maintain the premises in a reasonably safe condition and to warn of any latent or hidden dangers, the open and obvious doctrine eliminates that duty with regard to dangers that a reasonable person would observe or discover.

Application: Since the plaintiff had played on the court and watched one entire game from the sidelines, he should have been aware of the positioning and nature of the goal and its support structure.

Conclusion: Thus, the hazard posed by the goal's positioning was open and obvious.

QUESTIONS YOU SHOULD BE ABLE TO ANSWER

1. Explain the difference between primary legal sources and secondary legal sources.
2. Identify and provide an example of each of the four primary legal sources.
3. Summarize the steps in the research process.
4. Why should researchers exercise caution when relying on secondary legal sources, especially Internet-based sources or blogs?
5. What is the legal "issue" and "rationale of the court" in a court decision and why is it important to be able to properly identify the legal issue and the court's reasoning in a court decision?

REFERENCES

Cases
National Football League Management Council v. NFLPA, 2015 U.S. Dist. LEXIS 117662 (S.D.N.Y. 2015).

Sources
Edelman, M. (2012, January). A short treatise on fantasy sports and the law: How America regulates its new national pastime. *Harvard Journal of Sports & Entertainment Law, 3*, 1–53. Retrieved at: http://papers.ssrn.com/sol3/papers.cfm?abstract_id=1907272&download=yes

Larsen, S., & Bourdeau, J. (1997). *Legal research for beginners.* Hauppauge, NY: Barron's Educational Series, Inc.

Rosenwald, M.S. (2012, April 10). Md. Legislature in chaos, but it did legalize fantasy football. *The Washington Post.* Retrieved at: http://www.washingtonpost.com/blogs/rosenwald-md/post/md-legislature-in-chaos-but-it-did-legalize-fantasy-football/2012/04/10/gIQAmwKE8S_blog.html

West Publishing Co. (1991). *Sample pages* (3rd ed.). St. Paul, MN: West Publishing Co.

Useful Books on Legal Research

Delaney, S. (2002). *Electronic legal research: An integrated approach*. Albany, NY: West/Thomson Learning.

Elias, S., & Levinkind, S. (2002). *Legal research: How to find and understand the law*. Berkeley, CA: Nolo.

Journal of International Law & Economics. (2002). *Guide to international legal research*. Newark, NJ: LexisNexis/Matthew Bender.

Manz, W. H. (2002). *Guide to state legislative and administrative materials*. Buffalo, NY: William S. Hein.

Redfield, S. E. (2002). *Thinking like a lawyer: An educator's guide to legal analysis and research*. Durham, NC: Carolina Academic Press.

BUSINESS STRUCTURE AND LEGAL AUTHORITY

John T. Wolohan | Syracuse University

One of the first, and perhaps most important, decisions a sport or recreation business owner must make is how to organize or structure the new business. For example, should the new sport and recreation organization use one of the traditional common business structures, such as a sole proprietorship, partnership, or corporation, or one like a limited liability corporation (LLC). Although each business structure has some distinct advantages and disadvantages, such as federal, state, and local taxes, duration of the business, control, as well as the limited legal liability of the business owners, the type of structure a new sport and recreation organization chooses should depend in large part on the nature of the business. This section examines the legal issues surrounding new businesses, and identifies some of the advantages and disadvantages of the different business structures used in the sport and recreation industry.

FUNDAMENTAL CONCEPTS

Three of the most common business structures in sport and recreation include sole proprietorships, partnerships, and corporations. In selecting the business structure or form that is appropriate for your business, sport and recreation administrators should be aware of the following factors: limited legal liability; federal, state, and local tax laws; flexibility; access to capital; cost and ease of formation; and transferability of ownership in the business (Hamilton, 2001).

Sole Proprietorships

The most common business structure in the United States, and the easiest one for an individual to start and maintain, is the sole proprietorship. A sole proprietorship is an unincorporated business, owned by one individual, which has no legal existence apart from the owner (Eisenberg, 2005). While most sole proprietorships are small mom and pop businesses, it is important to note that size does not dictate the business structure. Sole proprietorships do not have to be small, but can be as large and complex as needed. The courts will automatically view the business as a sole proprietorship, unless the individual starting the business files articles of incorporation with the secretary of state in the state in which the business is located.

The sole proprietorship is one of the most popular business structures in the sport and recreation industry because of the low costs and ease involved in its formation. The cost of formation is low because there are no legal papers to file, thus eliminating the need and expense of a lawyer. The sole proprietorship or owner also has unlimited control over business and personnel issues. In addition, because the income and expenses of the business are attributed to the owner, there are no business or corporate taxes to be paid or additional tax forms to file.

The sole proprietorship does have some disadvantage over other business forms, however. First, because the business has no legal existence apart from the owner, the owner has unlimited personal liability for all the financial and legal risks of the business. For example, if the business is sued over a slip and fall accident, the victim can seek damages from both the business and the individual owner. Another disadvantage is that the life of the business is limited to the life of the owner; when he or she dies, the business ends. In addition, the business's ability to raise large amounts of capital is limited to the owner's assets or borrowing power (Miller, 1997).

Partnerships

Another common form of business in the sport and recreation industry is the general partnership. A partnership is created when two or more people, each contributing one or more of: money, property, labor, or skill, enter into a business with the expectation that each will share proportionally in the profits and losses (*Crane & Bromberg*, 1968). Because a partnership is basically a creation of contract law, no formal written agreement is necessary to create a valid partnership. However, like any good contract, to help avoid future disagreements, it is important that there be a formal written partnership agreement so that all partners understand their rights and obligations, and how profits and losses will be shared (Hamilton, 2001). For example, unless otherwise stated in a partnership agreement, the partners will share in the profits and losses of the business equally.

Partnerships enjoy many of the same benefits of the sole proprietorship, such as low costs, ease of formation, and single taxation. Partnerships have conduit or pass-through taxation, in that income or loss of the partnership is passed on to personal income taxes of the partners. While the IRS requires the partnership to file an annual informational tax return to document profits and losses among the partners, the partnership pays no tax (Crane & Bromberg, 1968).

The major disadvantage of the partnership over other forms of business is that each partner has a fiduciary duty toward the other partners, through which they are legally bound by each other's actions. As a result of this fiduciary duty, each of the partners has unlimited joint and several liability for the acts of each of the other general partners, regardless of whether the partner consented or had notice of such acts (Miller, 1997). Therefore, it is essential that partners trust each other and are aware of each other's activities. Another disadvantage of the partnership is that, because it is created by contract, partners are prohibited from selling or transferring their share in the partnership, even with the consent of the other partners. In order for one to sell or transfer their share in the partnership, the partners must dissolve the first partnership and create a second separate partnership (Miller, 1997).

Limited Partnerships

"There was nothing more limited than being a limited partner of [George] Steinbrenner's."
John McMullen limited partner of the New York Yankees in 1979

The only real difference between a limited partnership and a general partnership is that the limited partner(s) enjoys limited legal and financial liability for the debts and legal obligations of the partnership. To receive this limited liability, however, the limited partner must give up any control or involvement in the day-to-day operations of the business (Hamilton, 2001). All control in the business is vested in the general partner, who is usually someone with an expertise in the business. The limited partner, therefore, is usually only involved as an investor. If however a limited partner does become involved in the management of the business, he or she forfeits their status as a limited partner and becomes a general partner, assuming unlimited joint and several liability for the acts of the partnerships (Crane & Bromberg, 1968). Limited partnerships are generally governed by the Uniform Limited Partnership Act (ULPA) or the Revised Uniform Limited Partnership Act (RULPA) (Allen, Kraakman and Subramanian, 2009).

Limited Liability Partnership (LLP)

Since 1991, when Texas became the first state to adopt the unincorporated business structure Limited Liability Partnership (LLP), every other state has followed and passed their own form of LLP. The LLP is basically the same as a general partnership; however, under a LLP all the partners receive limited liability with respect to the partnership's liabilities stemming from the negligence, misconduct or malpractice of another partner. Some states, New York and Minnesota, extend partnership limited liability protection to include contract debt as well as torts liability (Allen, Kraakman and Subramanian, 2009). In exchange for this protection, the states do require that the LLP keep certain minimum capitalization or insurance to insure that the LLP has the funds available to meet their legal obligations in the effect of a lawsuit (Allen, Kraakman and Subramanian, 2009).

Limited Liability Company (LLC)

Another unincorporated business structure is the Limited Liability Company (LLC). The LLC structure is attractive to businesses because it provides greater flexibility in management of the business and has less-restrictive ownership requirements, by combining the best aspects of both the partnership and the corporation forms (Soderquist, 2005). For example, like a partnership, the LLC usually qualifies for pass-through taxation. In other words, the LLC's profits pass through to the company's members, who report their share of the profits on their personal federal tax returns. The company itself does not pay a federal tax before the money is distributed to the members, as in the case of C corporations (see the following page). However, as a separate legal entity, like a corporation, the LLC provides all the members with limited liability protection from business debts (Callison & Sullivan, 2008).

In addition, like corporations, LLCs provide limited liability against damages. Another advantage of the LLC is that, unlike S corporations (see below), there can be an unlimited number of members, and membership is not limited to individuals, but may include partnerships, corporations, other LLCs and foreign entities. Most states also permit "single member" LLCs, those having only one owner. Finally, because it is designed as a single entity, the LLC also provides the business with important protection from federal antitrust law. (For more information on single entities and antitrust law see Section 7.31, *Antitrust Law: Professional Applications*). In fact, the LLC is so attractive as a new business form that Major League Soccer established themselves as an LLC.

The sports or recreation business may be managed either by its members or by a designated group of managers, who may or may not be members of the company. If the members, as in a partnership, manage the business, each of the members has the same ability as in a partnership to bind the entire business through their acts. However, as mentioned earlier, the LLC provides each member limited liability. If a Designated group, as in a corporation, manages the business, members do not have the ability to bind the entire business unless they are in the designated group managing the business (Soderquist, 2005).

Corporations

Although there are a number of different types of corporations, all corporations share some basic characteristics. First, to do business as a corporation, the business must file "Articles of Incorporation" with the secretary of state in the state of incorporation. The state of incorporation is usually the state in which the business is located. A business, however, can incorporate in any state it chooses. Once the Articles of Incorporation are filed, the laws of the state of incorporation govern the corporation. Second, all corporations are treated as separate legal entities, with many of the same legal rights as an individual. For example, corporations can sue or be sued, carry on business activities, enter into contracts, and own property and other tangible and intangible assets (Eisenberg, 2005). Third, because a corporation is a separate legal entity, the business can be sold or transferred through the sale of stock, making changes in ownership simple. Fourth, the life of a corporation is unlimited. Because a corporation is a separate legal entity, the life of the business extends beyond the illness or death of the owners, individual officers, managers, or shareholders. Finally, and most importantly, all corporations provide the owner or shareholders with limited liability for corporate obligations. In other words, because corporations are treated as individual entities, separate from the owner or shareholders, the only legal and financial liability of the owner or shareholder is the money they invested into the company (Eisenberg, 2005).

In addition to the preceding benefits of corporations, there are a number of disadvantages involved in incorporating; these include the cost, the formal legal requirements, state and federal rules and regulations, and double taxation. First, because to form a corporation, an individual must file articles of incorporation with the secretary of state, a corporation requires more paperwork and record-keeping than other business forms. Also, unlike other forms of business, corporations must pay taxes on the income of the business, rather than passing it through to the owner's personal income tax (Hamilton, 2001). In addition, individual shareholders must also pay taxes on any dividends the corporation distributes. As a result, the corporation's profits are taxed twice, once at the corporate rate and again at the individual shareholder's rate (Hamilton, 2001). Finally, because an attorney is needed to help file all the necessary forms and meet all the requirements and formalities, there is a higher cost associated with the formation of a corporation.

Due to the inherent physical risks associated with most sports and recreation activities, it might seem that the advantages of limited liability are so great that all businesses in the sports and recreation industry should be conducted as corporations (Hamilton, 2001). However, the nature of the business is only one factor that a new business should consider when selecting a business form. For example, you should also consider the tax consequences, cost of formation, the formal requirements, flexibility, and simplicity.

Although all corporations share some of the same characteristics; Congress has created certain tax benefits or other advantages that distinguish different corporations. The following section examines some of the differences among corporate forms.

C Corporations

C corporations are the most common form of corporation. C corporations get their name because the tax rate these corporations use is found in subchapter C of the Internal Revenue Code. C corporations may have an unlimited number of shareholders, and may issue more than one class of stock (Hamilton, 2001). In deciding whether to form a new business as a C corporation, it is important to understand that all corporate income that is distributed to shareholders under C corporations is subject to double taxation. For example, as indicated previously, if at the end of the year the business has taxable income, the corporation must pay a corporate income tax. If any income is distributed to the shareholders, each individual shareholder must declare the income on his or her individual tax return and pay a second tax on the same money.

S Corporations

Instead of electing to be taxed under subchapter C of the Internal Revenue Code, a corporation can elect to be taxed under subchapter S; therefore, the choice is more of a tax election. Corporations making this selection are called S corporations. To be eligible for S corporation status, corporations must have fewer than seventy-five shareholders, may not have shareholders who are nonresident aliens, and may only issue one class of stock (Hamilton, 2001). Although S corporations have the same basic features as C corporations, S corporations have the benefit of allowing shareholders to elect to be taxed under a conduit or pass-through taxation approach that is similar to a partnership or proprietorship (Lind, Schwarz, Lathrope & Rosenberg, 2008).

Publicly Traded Corporations

The main reason for "going public" with your business is financial. For example, in 1998, the Cleveland Indians raised $55 million by selling four million shares of stock in the team. However, besides the financial benefit, there are a number of other issues to consider. First, the organization must comply with all Security and Exchange Commission (SEC) rules and regulations. Second, the corporation must make full financial disclosures concerning profits and losses. Third, because common shareholders are owners of the corporation, they have certain rights, such as voting on the makeup of the board of directors and attending annual meetings. Therefore, there are more legal formalities, and organizations have less control. Finally, there are the added costs to the organization. The corporation must have annual board of director meetings, create and mail annual financial reports, assign staff for investor relations, and incur added legal costs (Eisenberg, 2005).

Nonprofit Corporations

Some organizations, due to their special nature or mission, are nonprofit corporations. The major difference between a nonprofit and a regular for-profit corporation is that, unlike regular corporations, nonprofit corporations do not have shareholders or owners of any kind (Soderquist, 2005). Instead, nonprofit corporations are run by the members of the organization or people in the community (van der Smissen, 1999). No matter who is running the nonprofit corporation, the members or the people in the community, none of the income or property generated by the nonprofit can be distributed as a dividend (Soderquist, 2005). It should be noted, however, that this does not mean that nonprofit corporations cannot make a profit. It only means that none of the profits can be distributed to the members.

An example of a nonprofit, publicly owned corporation is the Green Bay Packers. Incorporated and publicly owned since August 18, 1923, the Packers have sold over 5 million shares, to about 380,000 stockholders none of whom receives any dividend on the initial investment. In 2011, the Green Bay Packers sold more than 268,000 shares in their fifth stock offering in team history, raising $67million. (Tkach, March 2, 2012) The corporation is governed by a board of directors and a seven member executive committee. To protect against an individual taking control of the team, the articles of incorporation prohibit any person from owning more than 200,000 shares.

There are generally two types of nonprofit corporations: **eleemosynary** (or charitable) and **mutual benefit**. In distinguishing the two types, the courts look at whether the purpose of the corporation is to benefit its members or to benefit some other group (Soderquist, 2005). Private schools and universities are generally classified as eleemosynary, whereas private clubs would generally be considered mutual benefit nonprofit corporations. The trustees of the eleemosynary corporation are analogous to directors and stockholders in a business corporation, in that their duty is the administration of the charitable trust or corporation. (*Gilbert v. McLeod Infirmary*, 1951)

No matter which type of nonprofit corporation (eleemosynary or mutual benefit) the business is classified as, because nonprofit corporations serve a public purpose, they receive a number of benefits or privileges not available to other types of corporations. Some of these benefits include being exempt from most federal and state taxes, special postage rates, and exemption from certain labor law requirements (van der Smissen, 1999). At the federal level, nonprofit corporations are known as having 501 (c)(3) tax status. Even if a corporation is nonprofit, however, it is also important to note that any profits that arise from essentially commercial activities will be taxable in the same manner they would be in a business corporation (Soderquist, 2005).

For a business to be recognized as a nonprofit corporation, it must file the required forms and meet the established legal requirements. Currently every state has legislation establishing nonprofit corporations, and the incorporation process usually follows the same procedure as business corporations.

Public Corporations

Another type of corporation that is involved in providing sports and recreational activities is a public corporation. Public corporations are usually municipalities such as cities, towns, and villages (Soderquist, 2005). In addition to municipalities, public corporations are sometimes formed by special legislative acts to perform some special purpose. For example, the National Park Service was formed by Congress and has administrative control over all national parks and forests. In forming a public corporation, like the National Park Service, Congress hopes to take the organization, operation, and finances of the organization from the governmental sphere of influence and place them in a more businesslike structure (Soderquist, 2005).

SIGNIFICANT CASE

The following case examines the decision of Major League Soccer to organize as a limited liability company and whether the league is a single entity for antitrust purposes.

FRASER V. MAJOR LEAGUE SOCCER
United States District Court for the District of Massachusetts
97 F. Supp. 130 (2000)

MEMORANDUM AND ORDER

The individual plaintiffs are the representatives of the certified class of professional soccer players who are or who have been employed by the defendant Major League Soccer, L.L.C. ("MLS"). MLS is a limited liability company ("LLC") organized under Delaware law. The defendant United States Soccer Federation, Inc. ("USSF") is the national governing body for professional and amateur soccer in the United States.

The plaintiffs assert a number of antitrust claims. In Count I, they allege that MLS and several of its investors who operate MLS teams (hereafter "operator-investors" or "operators") have unlawfully combined to restrain trade or commerce in violation to § 1 of the Sherman Anti-Trust Act, 15 U.S.C. § 1, by contracting for player services centrally through MLS, effectively eliminating the competition for those services that would take place if each MLS team were free to bid for and sign players directly. . .. Count III alleges that all defendants have jointly exercised monopoly power in violation of § 2 of the Sherman Act, 15 U.S.C. § 2. In Count IV, the plaintiffs allege that the transaction which brought MLS into existence violated § 7 of the Clayton Act, 15 U.S.C. § 18.

* * *

The plaintiffs have moved for summary judgment as to the defendants' so-called "single entity" defense. The gist of their argument is that although MLS appears to be a single business entity, so that its method of hiring players centrally can be characterized as the act of a single economic actor for antitrust purposes, the organizational form is really just a sham that should be considered ineffective to insulate from condemnation what are in substance illegal horizontal restraints on the hiring of players resulting from the unlawful concerted behavior of the several MLS team operators. . ..

I. RELEVANT FACTS

At the time MLS was formed, no "Division I" or "premiere" professional outdoor soccer league operated in the United States. The last premiere soccer league to operate in this country had been the North American Soccer League ("NASL"), which led a turbulent existence from 1968 until the mid-1980s, when it collapsed. In 1988, Federation Internationale de Football Association ("FIFA") awarded to the United States the right to host the 1994 World Cup, soccer's illustrious international competition. In consideration for that award, the organizers of the event promised to resurrect premiere professional soccer in the United States.

In the early 1990s, Alan Rothenberg, the President of USSF and of World Cup USA 1994, with assistance from others began developing plans for a Division I professional outdoor soccer league in the United States. Rothenberg and others at the USSF consulted extensively with potential investors in an effort to understand what type of league structure and business plan they might find attractive. He also consulted antitrust counsel in the hope of avoiding the antitrust problems that which other sports leagues such as the National Football League ("NFL") had encountered. Eventually the planners settled on the concept of organizing a limited liability company to run the league, and in 1995 MLS was formed.

The structure and mode of operation of MLS is governed by its Limited Liability Company Agreement ("MLS Agreement" or "Agreement"). The MLS Agreement establishes a Management Committee consisting of representatives of each of the investors. The Management Committee has authority to manage the business and affairs of MLS. Several of the investors have signed Operating Agreements with MLS which, subject to certain conditions and obligations, give them the right to operate specific MLS teams. There are also passive investors in MLS who do not operate teams. None of the passive investors is a defendant here.

Operator-investors do not hire players for their respective teams directly. Rather, players are hired by MLS as employees of the league itself and then are assigned to the various teams. Each player's employment contract is between the player and MLS, not between the player and the operator of the team to which the player is assigned. MLS centrally establishes and administers rules for the acquisition, assignment, and drafting of players, and all player assignments are subject to guidelines set by the Management Committee. Among other things, the guidelines limit the aggregate salaries that the league may pay its players.

Under applicable player assignment policies, MLS centrally allocates the top or "marquee" players among the teams, aiming to prevent talent imbalances and assure a degree of comparability of team strength in order to promote competitive soccer matches. These assignments are effective unless disapproved by a two-thirds vote of a subcommittee of the Management Committee. Most of the rest of the players—the non-"marquee" players—are selected for teams by the individual operator-investors through player drafts and the like. The league allows player trades between teams, but MLS's central league office must approve (and routinely does approve) such trades. Team operators are not permitted to trade players in exchange for cash compensation.

MLS distributes profits (and losses) to its investors in a manner consistent with its charter as a limited liability company, not unlike the distribution of dividends to shareholders in a corporation. Revenues generated by league operations belong directly to MLS. MLS owns and controls all trademarks, copyrights, and other intellectual property rights that relate in any way either to the league or to any of its teams. MLS owns all tickets to MLS games and receives the revenues from ticket sales. There are central league regulations regarding ticket policies, even including limits on the number of complimentary tickets any team may give away. Team operators do retain the ability to negotiate some purely local matters, including local sponsorship agreements with respect to a limited array of products and services and local broadcast agreements, but they do so as agents of MLS.

Under the Operating Agreement, each team operator receives from MLS a management fee. As of the time this action was filed, the management fee consisted of (a) 100% of the first $1.24 million, and 30% of the excess over $1.24 million, of local television broadcast and sponsorship revenues, the latter percentage subject to some specified annual increase; (b) 50% of ticket revenues from home games, increasing to 55% in year six of the league's operation; and (c) 50% of stadium revenues from concessions and other sources.

Expenses are allocated in a way similar to the allocation of revenues. MLS is responsible for most expenses associated with league operations. For example, MLS pays all player acquisition costs, player salaries, and player benefits. It also pays the salaries of all league personnel (including referees), game-related travel expenses for each team, workers' compensation insurance, fees and expenses of foreign teams playing in exhibition games promoted by MLS within the U.S., league-wide marketing expenses, and 50% of each individual team's stadium rental expense.

The team operators are responsible for the other half of their stadium rents, costs of approved local marketing, licensing, and promotion, and general team administration, including salaries of the team's management and coaching staff.

Passive investors do not pay any team operating expenses or receive any management fee. They share in the general distribution of profits (and losses) resulting from league operations.

Team operators cannot transfer their MLS interests or operational rights without the consent of the Management Committee. That consent may be withheld without cause, but the league is required to repurchase the team operator's interest at its fair market value if approval is withheld. Team operators derive whatever rights they may have exclusively from MLS, and the league may terminate these rights if a team operator violates these provisions or fails to act in the best interest of the league.

* * *

III. THE OPERATION OF MLS

Section 1 of the Sherman Act forbids contracts, combinations, and conspiracies in restraint of trade or commerce. See 15 U.S.C. § 1. Agreements between separate economic actors that have the effect of substantially and unreasonably reducing competition in a particular market violate § 1. The plaintiffs argue that MLS player policies constitute an unlawful agreement among the various team operators to limit or eliminate competition in the market for players' services.

Though the language of § 1 is sweeping, there are some limits to its reach. One critical limitation for the purposes of this case is that the statute does not prohibit single economic entities from acting unilaterally in ways that may, in some manner, decrease competition. . . . Because it is directed against contracts, combinations or conspiracies, § 1 only prohibits collective activity by plural economic actors, which unreasonably restrains competition. See *Copperweld Corp. v. Independence Tube Corp.*, 467 U.S. 752 (1984). The MLS defendants contend that MLS is a "single entity" and that even if its policies and practices have the effect of substantially reducing competition for players' salaries, they do not—*cannot* as a matter of law—violate § 1.

MLS is a limited liability company organized under Delaware law. An LLC is a form of statutory business organization that combines some of the advantages of a partnership with some of the advantages of a corporation. Under Delaware law, an LLC is a separate legal entity distinct from its members. Del. Code Ann. tit. 6, § 18-201(b). As in a corporation, investors (shareholders in a corporation, members in an LLC) have limited liability (*Id.*, § 18-303), own undivided interests in the company's property (§ 18-701), are bound by the terms of their Agreement (like the corporate Articles), and share in the overall profits and losses ratably according to their investment or as otherwise provided by the organizing Agreement (§ 18-503). The Federal Trade Commission has treated LLCs like corporations. . . . In the present context, there is little reason to treat an LLC such as MLS differently from a corporation.

MLS's operations should therefore be analyzed as the operations of a single corporation would be, with its operator-investors treated essentially as officers and shareholders. There can be no § 1 claim based on concerted action among a corporation and its officers, nor among officers themselves, so long as the officers are not acting to promote an interest, from which they would directly benefit, that is independent from the corporation's success. . . . If an LLC should be considered like a corporation for these purposes, as I conclude it should, then there can be no § 1 violation by reason of concerted action between the LLC as an entity and its members, or between the individual members themselves, unless the members are acting not in the interest of the entity, but rather in their own separate self-interest. The "independent personal stake" exception has not yet been squarely addressed in this Circuit; recognizing the risk that this exception, if left unchecked, might swallow the rule, courts that employ it have done so conservatively.

* * *

The plaintiffs argue that even if MLS is deemed a single entity, the divergent self-interests of the operator-investors provides sufficient cause to invoke the independent personal stake exception. The plaintiffs base this argument largely on their assertion that the operator-investors do not truly share in MLS's profits and losses. Instead of owning undivided interests in the league that are not attached to the operation of any given team, they pay certain operating expenses individually and receive management fees from MLS that are calculated in large part according to their local team-generated revenues. Also, they are able to harvest the value of the particular teams they operate by selling their operational rights or, if the Management Committee vetoes the sale, by requiring the league to pay them the fair market value of their investment.

The management fee arrangement exists in addition to, not in place of, the overall profit and loss sharing specified in the Agreement. Indeed, the fact that there are passive investors in MLS is strong evidence that the payment of management fees and assignment of local expenses do not account for all economic risks and benefits associated with the league's operation.

Furthermore, successful local operation of a team benefits the entire league. The league's net revenues, not just the local operator's management fees, increase when more local revenues are generated.

A similar effect is foreseeable in the market for operator-investor shares. Admittedly, unlike undifferentiated shares of stock, the market value of a team operator's investment will not simply reflect an aliquot share of the whole enterprise, but will also reflect in certain respects the success of the local operation. Nonetheless, unlike competition in most markets, where the value of an enterprise would usually be enhanced if its competitors grew weaker, the value of the right to operate an MLS team would be diminished, not enhanced, by the weaknesses of other teams, their operators, and the league as a whole. Management fees and operational rights notwithstanding, every operator-investor has a strong incentive to make the league—and the other operator-investors—as robust as possible. Each operator-investor's personal stake is not independent of the success of MLS as a whole enterprise.

The plaintiffs point to other ways in which the operator-investors compete on and off the field. That teams (and, by extension, their operators) compete playing soccer, and that operators directly hire certain staff, such as coaches, to make teams more capable of on-field heroics, does nothing to assist the plaintiffs. Exciting on-field competition between teams is what makes MLS games worth watching. *Chicago Prof 'l Sports*, 95 F.3d at 598-99 ("a league with one team would be like one hand clapping"). Game competition, without doubt, is part of the league's entertainment product, not an indicator of divergent economic interests among operators.

On balance, the business organization of MLS is quite centralized. The league owns the teams themselves; disgruntled operators may not simply "take their ball and go home" by withdrawing the teams they operate and forming or joining a rival league. MLS also owns all intellectual property related to the teams. It contracts for local-level services through its operators, who act on its behalf as agents. Operators risk losing their rights to operate their teams if they breach the governing Agreement. The Management Committee exercises supervisory authority over most of the league's activities. It may reject, without cause, any operator's individual attempt to assign the rights to operate a team.

It is true that MLS is run by a Management Committee that can be controlled by the operator-investors, who constitute the majority of the members of the Committee. It is not remarkable that principal investors can collectively control the governing board of an LLC (or of a corporation). That fact hardly proves that the investors are pursuing economic interests separate from the interests of the firm. The notion that the members of the Management Committee of a single firm violate the antitrust laws when they vote together to maximize the price or minimize the cost of the firm's product is easily rejected.

As a factual matter, therefore, there is insufficient basis in the record for concluding that operators have divergent economic interests within MLS's structure. Even if one draws the most favorable inference on the plaintiffs' behalf, there is no reasonable basis for imposing § 1 liability.

MLS's player policies, in particular, do not call for application of the independent personal stake exception. The operator-investors benefit from those policies because centralized contracting for player services results in lower salaries. However, that benefit is, in the MLS structure, a derivative one. No operator has an individual player payroll to worry about; the league pays the salaries. Moreover, the MLS investor gets the lower-cost benefit in exchange for having surrendered the degree of autonomy that team owners in "plural entity" leagues typically enjoy. The reason an individual team owner in one of those other leagues is willing to bid up players' salaries to get the particular players it wants is because by paying high salaries to get desirable players, the owner can achieve other substantial benefits, such as increased sales of tickets and promotional goods, media revenues, and the like. The MLS operator-investors have largely yielded that opportunity to the central league office. Plainly, there are trade-offs in the different approaches. The MLS members have calculated that the surrender of autonomy, together with the attendant benefit of lower and more controlled player payrolls and greater parity in talent among teams, will help MLS to succeed where others, notably NASL, failed. That is a calculation made on behalf of the entity, and it does not serve only the ulterior interests of the individual investors standing on their own. It is not an occasion for application of the independent personal stake exception to the general single-entity rule described in *Copperweld*.

The plaintiffs also argue that the structure of MLS is a sham designed to allow what is actually an illegal combination of plural actors to masquerade as the business conduct of a single entity. The plaintiffs do not argue that the structure of MLS as established by the its organizing Agreement is legally defective so that it should not be recognized as a lawful entity under Delaware law. Rather, they say that even if MLS is a legitimate LLC—a legitimate single entity for state law purposes—a court should disregard that legal form in evaluating under antitrust principles whether the operator—investors are engaged in a horizontal restraint in the market for players' services. To make the argument, the plaintiffs put a reverse spin on the *Copperweld* holding.

Copperweld held that a corporation could not conspire with its wholly owned subsidiary in violation of § 1 because, though the parent and subsidiary were distinct legal entities, the economic reality was that they functioned as a single business enterprise. Cases following *Copperweld* have mainly addressed the question whether to disregard formal distinctions among entities in order to find economic singularity for the purposes of § 1.

See, e.g., *Sullivan v. NFL*, 34 F.3d 1091, 1099 (1st Cir. 1994) (NFL, composed of separately owned clubs, not a single entity in the market for ownership of teams); *Chicago Prof 'l Sports Ltd. Partnership v. NBA*, 95 F.3d 593, 597-600 (7th Cir. 1996) (characterizing NBA, composed of separately owned clubs, as a single entity for the purpose of league-wide limitations on locally televising games through "superstations," though expressly withholding judgment as to whether NBA was single entity in other markets, such as player contracting). . . .

The plaintiffs propose that the "economic reality" test should be applied not only to *ignore* formal legal distinctions between separate corporations as the court did in *Copperweld*, but conversely to *envision* distinctions in what is formally a single legal entity when doing so would accurately describe how the business of the entity actually operates. The argument may have some superficial appeal, but on close examination it appears that it rests on a misconception of the scope of the *Copperweld* principle.

It was noted above that the courts have not given the sweeping language of § 1 its broadest possible effect. The "rule of reason" is an obvious example of a limitation on the literal scope of the statutory language. . . .

The *Copperweld* rule similarly limits the reach of the statute's broad language. While concerted action between two separate corporations, one the parent and the other a subsidiary, could literally be described as a "combination" that restrains trade, the Supreme Court concluded that it was not the kind of combination that § 1 was intended to forbid. Like the coordination between a corporation and its unincorporated division, an agreement between a parent and its subsidiary did not represent "a sudden joining of two independent sources of economic power previously pursuing separate interests." *Copperweld*, 467 U.S. at 770. The plaintiffs are correct that the Court was looking to substance, not merely form.

But that does not mean that form is irrelevant. Copperweld does not support the proposition that a business organized as a single legal entity should have its form ignored, or its "veil" pierced, so that courts could examine whether participants in the firm have conducted concerted activity that would violate § 1. Merely posing that proposition suggests how troublesome it would be as a practical matter. It would permit the atomization of firms into their constituent parts, then to have the relationships of those parts examined to see if they produced anti-competitive effects that, had they been brought about by independent economic actors, would have violated § 1. The number of companies that could be vulnerable to examination of internal business decisions under such an approach would be mind-boggling. No case has suggested that it would be appropriate to deconstruct a corporate entity in that way.

Practical objections aside, the theory is also fundamentally incompatible with the axiom the *Copperweld* Court's analysis started with—that coordination of business activities within a single firm is not subject to scrutiny under § 1. *Copperweld* cannot be understood to authorize an "economic reality" analysis that would require rejection of the very premise the holding of the case depended on. Moreover, the plaintiffs' proposition would plainly interfere with the objective of the antitrust laws. "Subjecting a single firm's every action to judicial scrutiny for reasonableness would threaten to discourage the competitive enthusiasm that the antitrust laws seek to promote." *Copperweld*, 467 U.S. at 775.

In sum, the plaintiffs' deconstruction efforts are unavailing. MLS is what it is. As a single entity, it cannot conspire or combine with its investors in violation of § 1, and its investors do not combine or conspire with each other in pursuing the economic interests of the entity. MLS's policy of contracting centrally for player services is unilateral activity of a single firm. Since § 1 does not apply to unilateral activity—even unilateral activity that tends to restrain trade—the claim set forth in Count I cannot succeed as a matter of law.

IV. THE FORMATION OF MLS

In addition to the claim that the player policies of MLS are an unlawful horizontal restraint of trade, the plaintiffs also claim that the very formation of MLS in the first place violated § 7 of the Clayton Act, which prohibits acquisitions or mergers the effect of which "may be substantially to lessen competition, or to tend to create a monopoly" in any line of commerce or activity affecting commerce, 15 U.S.C. § 18, as well as § 1 of the Sherman Act. The two theories are related.

* * *

2. Existing Market

. . . There can be no § 7 liability because the formation of MLS did not involve the acquisition or merger of existing business enterprises, but rather the formation of an entirely new entity which itself represented the creation of an entirely new market. The relevant test under § 7 looks to whether competition in *existing* markets has been reduced. . . . Where there is no existing market, there can be no reduction in the level of competition. There are no negative numbers in this math; there is nothing lower than zero. Competition that does not exist cannot be decreased. The creation of MLS did not reduce competition in an existing market because when the company was formed there was no active market for Division I professional soccer in the United States.

* * *

B. The Sherman Act Claim

In addition to the Clayton Act theory, the plaintiffs urge that the formation of MLS, by which multiple operator-investors combined to create the single entity, also violated the Sherman Act's prohibition of contracts, combinations or conspiracies in restraint of trade.

It is generally held that a coming together that does not violate § 7 of the Clayton Act does not violate § 1 of the Sherman Act either. See *White Consol. Indus. v. Whirlpool Corp.*, 781 F.2d 1224, 1228 (6th Cir. 1986) (failure to show Clayton § 7 violation precluded Sherman § 1 violation for same conduct). A merger of market participants that does not lessen competition and thus does not offend § 7 ordinarily would not constitute a combination in restraint of trade in violation of § 1. Though the statutory provisions present slightly different modes of analysis, when those modes are applied to the same constellation of facts, the answer will ordinarily be the same.

Here, the pertinent facts are that the founding investors of MLS created both a new company and simultaneously a new market, in effect increasing the number of competitors from zero to one. As explained above, that did not represent a lessening of actual or potential competition in an existing market. Similarly, it did not represent a "sudden joining of . . . independent sources of economic power previously pursuing separate interests," see *Copperweld*, 467 U.S. at 770, which is what is forbidden by § 1.

V. CONCLUSION AND ORDER

For all the reasons set forth above, the defendants' motion for summary judgment in their favor under Counts I and IV of the Amended Complaint is GRANTED. It follows that the plaintiffs' motion for summary judgment on the defendants' "single entity" defense is DENIED.

IT IS SO ORDERED.

QUESTIONS YOU SHOULD BE ABLE TO ANSWER

1. What are the advantages of forming a corporation rather than a partnership?
2. What are the disadvantages of forming a corporation rather than a partnership?
3. What happens when a limited partner becomes active in managing the business?
4. For sport organizations, what are some of the major benefits of a LLC?
5. Since publicly traded businesses are able to generate additional revenue by selling stock, why are there not more publicly traded sports organizations?

REFERENCES

Cases
Fraser v. Major League Soccer, 97 F. Supp. 130 (2000).
Gilbert v. McLeod Infirmary, 219 S.C. 174 (S.C. 1951).

Publications
Allen, W. Kraakman, R. & Subramanian, G. (2009). *Commentaries and Cases on the Law of Business Organization* (3rd Ed.). New York, NY: Wolters Kluwer.
Callison, J. W., & Sullivan, M. A. (2008). *Limited Liability Companies: A State-By-State Guide to Law and Practice*. Eagan, MN: Thomson/West Publishing.
Crane, J. A., & Bromberg, A. R. (1968). *Law of Partnership*. St. Paul, MN: West Publishing.
Eisenberg, M. A. (2005). *Corporations and other Business Organizations* (9th ed.). New York, NY: Foundation Press.
Hamilton, R. W. (2001). *Corporations: Including partnerships and limited partnerships* (7th ed.). St. Paul, MN: West Publishing.
Lind, S. A., Schwarz, S., Lathrope, D. J., & Rosenberg, J. D. (2008). *Fundamentals of Corporate Taxation* (7th ed.). New York, NY: Foundation Press.
Miller, L. K. (1997). *Sport business management*. Gaithersburg, MD: Aspen Publishers.
Soderquist, L. B. et al. (2005). *Corporations and other business organizations* (6th ed.). Newark, NJ: LexisNexis Publishing Group.
John Tkach, F1's Barrichello to race in IndyCar, USA TODAY, March 2, 2012, at 9C
Van der Smissen, B. et al. (1999) *Management of park and recreation agencies*. Ashburn, VA: National Recreation and Park Association.

NEGLIGENCE LAW 2.00

Negligence law is that law which deals with unintentional torts committed by individuals or organizations. *Negligence* is an unintentional tort that injures an individual in person, property, or reputation. Negligence Law is divided into three sections. The first section, 2.10 *Negligence Theory* examines both the elements of negligence and which parties are liable. This section serves as a foundation for each of the two succeeding sections.

It is important that the recreation or sport manager understand that being sued for negligence does not necessarily mean that one will lose that suit. Section 2.20 *Defenses* addresses many of the defenses available to recreation and sport providers. Some of these defenses are based in common law, some in contract law, and some in statutory law.

Section 2.30 *Recreation and Sport Management Applications* addresses some of the many recreation and sport management applications of negligence theory. This section includes seven comprehensive chapters illustrating the application of negligence theory in various settings.

* * *

This reader is cautioned, however, regarding a limitation of this or any other text. **Negligence law is primarily state law and, as such, will vary considerably from state to state. It is impossible to cover all of the quirks and variations in the various laws and court rulings for each state. It is, therefore, necessary to utilize generalizations or "general rules" when discussing most topics. The reader must understand that these generalizations are not necessarily true in every state and that certain exceptions may exist**

NEGLIGENCE

Doyice J. Cotten | Sport Risk Consulting

In every state, case law is replete with legal actions against sport, recreation, and fitness service providers. Defendants include a diversity of providers such as universities, public schools, professional sports teams, recreation departments, state and national parks, vehicle racing providers, ski resorts, country clubs, equine activity providers, adventure outfitters, bowling alleys, personal trainers, and health clubs.

The majority of these lawsuits involve injuries to a participant (plaintiff) who alleges negligence on the part of the service provider (defendant). **Negligence** is an unintentional tort that causes injury to a person in the form of physical injury, property loss, or reputation. In negligence, there is no intent to cause injury or harm. Negligence may be in the form of an **act of omission** (something one should have done, but did not do) or in the form of an **act of commission** (something that one did, but should not have done).

Authorities have defined negligence in many ways. Black's Law Dictionary (1990) offers the following definitions that help one understand the concept:

- Negligence is the failure to use such care as a reasonably prudent and careful person would use under similar circumstances; it is the doing of some act which a person of ordinary prudence would not have done under similar circumstances or failure to do what a person of ordinary prudence would have done under similar circumstances.
- Conduct which falls below the standard established by law for the protection of others against unreasonable risk of harm.
- The term refers only to that legal delinquency which results whenever a man fails to exhibit the care which he ought to exhibit, whether it be slight, ordinary, or great. (p. 1032)

There are four elements of negligence. To prove negligence against the service provider, the plaintiff must show that all four of the elements are present. *If all four of the elements are present, there is negligence—and subsequent liability. If any one of the elements is not met, there is no negligence* and the service provider is not liable. The elements are:

1. **Duty.** The service provider must owe a duty (created by a special relationship between the service provider and the participant) to protect the participant from unreasonable risk of harm.
2. **Breach of Duty.** The service provider must breach its duty to protect the participant from unreasonable risk of harm.
3. **Damage or Injury.** The participant must suffer physical damage to person or property, or emotional damage.
4. **Proximate Cause.** The breach of duty must have been the proximate cause (reason) the injury occurred.

FUNDAMENTAL CONCEPTS

Duty

The first requirement for liability is that one must have owed the plaintiff a legal duty of care. According to van der Smissen (1990, Part A, pp. 2–3), **duty** (as an element of negligence) refers to a responsibility toward others (arising from a relationship between parties) **to protect them from unreasonable risk of injury**.

van der Smissen frequently distinguished between the term *duty* (the first element of negligence) and what she often referred to as **obligations** to parties to whom a duty is owed. These obligations are the means by which one fulfills the duty to protect them from unreasonable risk of injury. In fact, she frequently stressed that calling these obligations "duties" (e.g., duty to warn, duty to inspect, duty to supervise) is a misnomer; they should be referred to as "obligation" to warn, "obligation" to inspect, and "obligation" to supervise. Additionally, van der Smissen pointed out that there is no duty to inspect, duty to warn, or duty to supervise unless one first has a duty based on a status or special relationship to others (1990, Part A, pp. 2–3).

Courts traditionally have imposed certain obligations (often referred to as duties) on those who have a duty to protect others from unreasonable risk of injury. The particular obligations required in any specific situation vary depending upon such factors as the nature of the activity, nature of the participants, nature of the facility, and location of the activity. Examples of obligations include:

Obligation to warn	Obligation to inspect facilities and equipment
Obligation to supervise	Obligation to provide a safe environment
Obligation to instruct	Obligation to provide safe vehicles
Obligation to match competitors	Obligation to provide safety equipment
Obligation to hire qualified staff	Obligation to provide first aid & emergency care
Obligation to provide "fit" staff	Obligation to evaluate for injury or incapacity

For any specific situation, a service provider might have additional obligations not listed here; conversely, many of these obligations might not apply in some situations. For example, a health club might have no obligation to match competitors or to provide safe vehicles, but it might have an obligation to screen participants for certain health problems. *It is important to remember that if the provider has no duty to protect participants from unreasonable risk of injury, the provider has no obligations.*

To illustrate, suppose Happy Holiday Stables rents a horse to a novice rider for a trail ride. Due to their relationship of equine provider and client, Happy Holiday has the duty to protect the rider from unreasonable risk of injury. To fulfill this duty, the stable has many obligations to the novice rider. Some obligations required to fulfill the provider's duty to protect might include providing a properly trained horse, matching the rider to the appropriate horse, providing proper tack, correctly saddling the horse, warning the rider of the inherent risks, providing basic instruction if needed, and providing a competent, qualified employee to supervise and lead the ride. If the stable met all of its obligations and the client fell from the horse and broke a leg when the horse was startled by a nearby lightning strike (an inherent risk of a trail ride), Happy Holiday would not be liable because (1) it fulfilled its duty to protect the rider from the unreasonable risk of injury and (2) the stable is not required to protect the rider from the inherent risks of the activity if the rider is aware of the inherent risks (hence the warning of the risks by the provider).

Sources of Duty

There are three sources or origins of *duty as an element of negligence*. They are (1) from a relationship inherent in the situation, (2) from the voluntary assumption of a duty, and (3) from duties mandated by statutes.

Inherent Relationship. A duty arises when one has an inherent relationship with another party. Examples of such a relationship include that of a parent and child, coach and athlete, health club and patrons, school and students, scoutmaster and scouts, bus driver and passengers, and service provider and users of the service. The general duty owed is to protect others from exposure to unreasonable risks that may cause injury; however, the specific duties (or obligations) owed depend upon many factors (van der Smissen, 2007).

For example, a vacationer casually walking down the beach has no *legal* duty to rescue a stranger in the water who is shouting for help because there is no special relationship between them. On the other hand, the lifeguard on duty at the time does have a legal duty to do all that he or she can to rescue the drowning party because of the lifeguard-swimmer relationship.

Voluntary Assumption. There are occasions when one has no duty, but voluntarily assumes such a duty. When one voluntarily assumes a duty, a special relationship is established, bestowing an obligation to perform the act with the appropriate standard of care. For example, if the vacationer walking on the beach, hears the shouts for help from the swimmer in distress, rushes into the water, swims out, and tries to rescue the swimmer, he or she voluntarily assumes the duty of rescue and an obligation to do all that he or she can to rescue the drowning party.

Voluntary assumption of a duty often is associated with a decision to aid one in need (e.g., a passerby administering CPR, rescuing a swimmer in difficulty, or assisting at an automobile accident). In such cases, there might be a moral duty to rescue or assist, but there is generally no legal duty. A few states have very limited "duty to rescue" statutes, but they often carry insignificant penalties and are seldom enforced.

The voluntary assumption of a duty is not limited to one administering emergency care. A parent who volunteers to serve as a little league coach creates a relationship with the team members and assumes the duty to protect them from unreasonable risk of injury. As the coach, he then has the responsibility to act as a reasonable, prudent coach and perform the obligations of such a coach (e.g., to instruct, supervise, inspect, warn, etc.). Other examples of individuals who voluntarily assume a duty include one who volunteers to direct traffic before a game, a physician who volunteers to be the team doctor, a teacher who volunteers to sponsor a club, and a sport management major who volunteers time to work with a professional team.

Statutes. Statutes or laws often specify duties of one party to another. If the state legislature passes a statute requiring that an ambulance and a physician are present at every high school football game, an athletic director failing to provide both might be found to have breached his statutory duty. West Virginia has a statute that specifies that whitewater guides and ski operators owe their patrons a duty of ordinary care (W.Va.C. 20-38-1 to 8). Since this duty is a statutory duty, operators may not shield themselves from liability for negligent conduct by using a liability waiver.

Violations of statutes and ordinances frequently are associated with negligence *per se*. **Negligence *per se*** has been described as negligence attached to acts that are deemed negligent without having to prove negligence or investigate the reasonableness of the conduct (van der Smissen, 1990). The act is so opposed to common prudence that it is obvious that no reasonable person would have done it. However, violation of a statute or ordinance does not always constitute negligence *per se*. The law varies greatly among states but, generally, one must show that a statute was broken, that it was a safety statute, and that the violation of the statute was the actual proximate cause of the injury. According to Prosser and Keeton (1984, p. 227), a defendant may become liable in some cases simply by violating a statute; and neither ignorance nor any excuse will avoid liability. In these cases, the statute falls under strict liability, yet often is referred to as negligence *per se*.

Foreseeability

Foreseeability involves one's ability to predict what will occur as a result of his or her action (commission) or inaction (omission). Since no conduct can be considered to be unreasonable when there is no foreseeable risk, the scope of liability is governed by whether the risk of injury is foreseeable. The question then becomes "what is foreseeable?" Foreseeability is established by showing that a person of ordinary intelligence and circumspection reasonably should have been able to predict the consequences of an action or a failure to act. van der Smissen (1990) concluded that when negative results of an act cannot be reasonably anticipated by reasonable people, it cannot be said that the result was foreseeable; therefore, there is no duty to protect against it. It is important, then, to understand that although one has a special relationship and owes a duty to protect, there is no liability for an injury caused by an unforeseeable risk.

Another situation where no proactive action to protect is necessary in spite of a duty created by a special relationship is when there is an "open and obvious" environmental hazard. Since the hazard is open and obvious, it generally is not foreseeable that an individual would ignore the hazard and continue the activity. So, in spite of the special relationship, one generally has no duty to protect (van der Smissen, 2007). An exception occurs with young children; it might well be foreseeable that a seven-year-old would ignore an open and obvious hazard and continue play in spite of the hazard.

The key to foreseeability is foresight and the reasonable, prudent professional must be able to anticipate or foresee dangers or risks faced by the participant. *One is not required to be able to foresee the exact nature of the accident or of the injury—one need only to foresee that injury is likely.* Of course, reasonable people can disagree as to what is, or should have been, foreseeable. When reasonable people disagree, it is the job of the jury to resolve the question.

Breach of Duty

The second requirement for liability is that the defendant must have breached his duty to the plaintiff. Black (1990) described breach of duty as "any violation or omission of a legal or moral duty. More particularly, [it is] the neglect or failure to fulfill in a just and proper manner the duties of an office or fiduciary employment" (p. 189).

> In the Happy Holiday Stables illustration, the business relationship between Happy Holidays and the novice rider imposes the duty to protect the rider from unreasonable risk of injury. Two obligations of the stable include the provision of good tack and proper saddling of the horse. If the novice rider falls and breaks a leg because worn and faulty tack breaks or because the Happy Holiday employee failed to tighten the saddle adequately resulting in the saddle slipping, Happy Holiday could be liable for negligence because the stable failed to meet its obligations and breached its duty to protect the rider from unreasonable risk of injury.

There are three components used to determine if the duty has been breached. These three components may be addressed by asking the questions: What are the types of risk? What is reasonable care? Was the risk foreseeable?

What are the Types of Risks?

The first question asked to determine whether there is a breach of duty is "What type of risk caused the injury?" Risks may be placed into three categories. They are risks arising from (1) inherent risks, (2) ordinary negligence, and (3) aggravated negligence (extreme behavior that goes beyond ordinary negligence [e.g., gross negligence, reckless misconduct, and willful and wanton misconduct]). Generally, the service provider has no duty to protect one from the inherent risks of an activity provided the participant was aware of the inherent risks. The provider does have a duty, however, to protect participants from unreasonable risks of injury that include risks created by both negligent behavior and aggravated negligence.

Risks Arising from Inherent Risks. Inherent risks are those risks that are integral to the activity; risks that if removed would essentially alter the nature of the sport or activity (van der Smissen, 2007). *The provider of an activity generally has no duty to protect one from the inherent risks of the activity.* Examples of inherent risks include a softball player pulling a hamstring while running the bases, a college football player suffering an ACL injury when tackled, a raft striking a rock and capsizing during a whitewater rafting expedition, a hiker in the mountains encountering a dangerous animal, and one's horse being spooked by thunder or lightning while on a trail ride. These risks are inherent to the activity and cannot be eliminated. In fact, if whitewater rafting were done on a stream with no rocks or rapids, it is no longer "whitewater" rafting and loses much of its excitement and appeal.

Under the doctrine of primary assumption of risk (see Chapter 2.21 *Defenses Against Negligence*), a participant generally assumes the inherent risks of the activity. Thus, *"[T]here is no liability for injury that occurs due to inherent risks of which the injured participant is knowledgeable or should have been knowledgeable"* (van der Smissen, 2007, p. 38). In *Harting v. Dayton Dragons Professional Baseball Club, LLC (2007)*, Roxane Harting was struck in the head by a foul ball and knocked unconscious while she was distracted by the San Diego Chicken. She argued that the mascot was not an inherent risk of a baseball game, but the court ruled that it was perfectly reasonable for a spectator at a baseball game to observe mascots, such as the Chicken, during the course of the game.

van der Smissen (2007) emphasized the importance of a participant being knowledgeable of inherent risks to which he or she is exposed. Therefore, in the whitewater rafting example above, it is important that the provider adequately warn the participant of the inherent risks of whitewater rafting or the provider may be found liable for injury resulting from inherent risks unknown to the participant. One may inform participants of the risks through (1) oral instructions; (2) detailed risk information in documents such as applications, assumption of risk agreements, or liability waivers; and (3) detailed printed risk information in brochures, handouts, and signs. The information regarding the inherent risks must provide the participant with adequate information so that he or she will know, understand, and appreciate the inherent risks of the activity (van der Smissen, personal communication, March 6, 1996).

Risks Arising from Ordinary Negligence. Negligent acts fall below the required standard of care and constitute a breach of the duty to protect others from unreasonable risk of injury. The California Supreme Court stated, "[A]lthough defendants generally have no legal duty to eliminate (or protect a plaintiff against) risks inherent in the sport itself, it is well established that defendants generally *do have a duty to use due care not to increase the risks to a participant over and above those inherent in the sport*" (*Knight v. Jewett*, 1992, p. 14). When a provider increases the risks by negligent actions, these risks are not assumed by the participant and the provider can be found liable for any resulting injuries.

Two cases illustrate acts of ordinary negligence. A girl suffered injury when she collided with an unpadded metal pole that supported a basketball backboard. The school district was found negligent because the school increased the risk by allowing students to play basketball around poles that they knew were dangerous (*Gill v. Tamalpais Union High School District*, 2008). In *Sisino v. Island Motocross of N.Y., Inc.* (2007), motorcyclist Sisino was injured when his motorcycle was struck by an all-terrain vehicle (ATV). The court said that the owners of the track were negligent by allowing ATV riders to use the track at the same time as motorcyclists since they increased the risk of injury beyond those risks inherent in the sport.

Risks Arising from Aggravated Negligence. There are at least two schools of thought regarding negligence and aggravated negligence. One school holds that there are no degrees of negligence (Keeton, 1984). Those who hold this view suggest **that the standard of care required for reasonable conduct** must vary with the apparent risk faced in the activity—accordingly, as the danger increases, the caution or care required of the provider increases commensurately. The level of care required for the conduct of a very dangerous activity is very high and the threshold for negligence is low (e.g., when operating a bungee jump, where the danger is great, even slight faults or mistakes might be considered unreasonable, and thereby, constitute negligence due to the potential consequences of a mistake). However, the level of care required for reasonable conduct of a relatively safe, low-risk activity is less and the threshold for negligence is higher (e.g., when operating a water slide, where the risk of serious injury is slight, faults that might result in minor injuries might be considered reasonable and not trigger negligence). In other words, the standard of care for reasonable conduct varies depending upon the risk of the activity. Consequently, according to this school of thought, the creation of degrees of negligence is not necessary. Jurisdictions adopting this approach recognize only reasonable care (no negligence) and negligence.

Another school of thought regarding degrees of negligence advocates that there are distinct degrees of negligence (Keeton, 1984). Supporters of this approach propose that there are both small and large departures from reasonable care or conduct—these departures are most commonly identified as ordinary negligence, gross negligence, reckless misconduct, and willful and wanton misconduct. Gross negligence, reckless misconduct, and willful and wanton misconduct are considered more extreme departures from reasonable care than ordinary negligence and are sometimes referred to as **aggravated negligence**.

Those who attempt to distinguish among the degrees of aggravated negligence encounter a number of challenges. First, one finds that defining the concepts that commonly constitute aggravated negligence is problematic. For instance, when Black's definitions of gross negligence, reckless misconduct, and willful and wanton misconduct are examined carefully, there appears to be considerably more similarities than differences among the concepts.[1,2] Second, the situation is complicated further by the fact that jurisdictions using the same term frequently define the term differently. Therefore, when one encounters the terms *gross*

---

[1]Black (1990, p. 1033) defined **gross negligence** as "The intentional failure to perform a manifest duty in reckless disregard of the consequences as affecting the life or property of another." He defined **reckless misconduct** as a situation in which "... the actor intentionally does an act or fails to do an act which it is his duty to another to do, knowing or having reason to know of facts which would lead a reasonable man to conclude such conduct creates an unreasonable risk of bodily harm ..." (p. 1271). He defined **willful and wanton misconduct** as "Conduct which is either intentional or committed under the circumstances exhibiting a reckless disregard for the safety of others ..." (p. 1600).

[2]For example, California courts defined *gross negligence* as "a want of even scant care" or "an extreme departure from the ordinary standard of conduct" (*City of Santa Barbara v. Superior Court*, 2007 p. 6), while the Wisconsin Jury Instruction 1006 defined *gross negligence* as conduct "which shows either a willful intent to injury or reckless and wanton disregard of the rights [or] safety" of another person. Similarly, a Michigan court defined both *reckless misconduct* and *willful and wanton conduct* as conduct by a person who may have no intent to harm, but who intentionally acts while knowing harm is highly probable (*Lamp v. Reynolds*, 2002). A California court defined reckless misconduct as an act where one is aware

negligence, reckless misconduct, and willful and wanton conduct, he or she should be aware that while the same term might be used, the actual definition of the term will vary from jurisdiction to jurisdiction. Third, one finds that while courts in most jurisdictions are consistent in employing the term "ordinary negligence," terms used to describe degrees of aggravated negligence vary greatly among jurisdictions.[3] And finally, one finds that, in light of the lack of a common, discriminating definition and consistent application of the terms in all jurisdictions, it is impossible to draw clear lines of demarcation among the recognized degrees of aggravated negligence.

While distinguishing among the three degrees of aggravated negligence may seem futile, legislatures (in statutes) and courts (in case law) in most jurisdictions have endeavored to define and recognize one or more degrees of aggravated negligence. Generally gross negligence is considered the least outrageous of the three and is considered to be less extreme than willful and wanton misconduct. In fact, there appears to be an unofficial hierarchy from gross negligence to reckless misconduct to willful and wanton misconduct.

In light of these critical variations in state law, *it is essential that the recreation and sport manager ascertain both the degrees of aggravated negligence recognized in his or her state and how each is defined by the courts in that particular state.*

Importance of Distinguishing among the Degrees of Negligence. In spite of the numerous problems associated with degrees of negligence, it is necessary to address them. Distinguishing among the degrees of departure from reasonable care is important for at least five reasons.

First, the **immunity** provided by legislation (e.g., governmental immunity, state tort claims acts, recreational user statutes, Good Samaritan statutes, AED statutes, volunteer statutes, and sport immunity statutes) depends upon compliance with the standard of care required in the statute. Some statutes protect when the service provider is negligent and some only when the service provider exercised ordinary care. Few apply when the service provider has committed gross negligence, reckless conduct or willful and wanton acts (see Chapter 2.21 *Defenses Against Negligence* and Chapter 2.22 *Immunity*).

Second, while **liability waivers** protect providers from liability for ordinary negligence in most states, they protect against liability resulting from gross negligence or reckless misconduct in only four and two states, respectively. Further, no waivers in any state have been found that protect against liability for willful and wanton actions or intentional acts (see Chapter 2.23 *Waivers and Releases*).

Third, although the law regarding **exemplary** or **punitive damages** varies by state, generally such damages are not awarded for injury unless gross negligence, reckless conduct, or willful and wanton actions are involved. The degree required for such awards varies with state law (see the Damage section later in this chapter).

Fourth, the general rule in most jurisdictions is that a **participant** is not liable for injuries to a **co-participant** that result from ordinary negligence. Participants generally are liable if the act is reckless or willful and wanton, but usually are not liable for ordinary negligence except in a few jurisdictions and under select circumstances (*Pfister v. Shusta* [Ill. 1995]; see also Chapter 2.13 *Liability of Sports Participants, Sports Instructors, and Sports Officials*). In some states, courts have ruled that a sports instructor or coach is not liable for ordinary negligence in certain circumstances. In *Kahn v. East Side Union School District* (2003), the California Supreme Court stated in a case alleging that a sports instructor required an athlete to perform beyond his capacity, the plaintiff must show

> that the instructor acted with intent to cause a student's injury or that the instructor acted recklessly in the sense that the instructor's conduct was "totally outside the range of the ordinary activity" involved in teaching or coaching the sport. (p. 43)

Fifth, the degree of negligence can affect the liability of the service provider for the actions of its employees. The doctrine of *respondeat superior* (vicarious liability) holds that the negligence of the employee is imputed to

---

that one's conduct is likely to cause injury, yet proceeds to act heedlessly, willfully, and wantonly (*City of Santa Barbara v. Superior Court*, 2007, p. 6).

[3]Some jurisdictions use only one of these terms to describe aggravated negligence, in effect, establishing two degrees of negligence (e.g., ordinary and gross; ordinary and reckless; or ordinary and willful/wanton). Other jurisdictions employ two or more terms to distinguish among degrees of aggravated negligence (e.g., ordinary, gross, and reckless; ordinary, gross, reckless, and willful/wanton), thereby, establishing three or more degrees of negligence. The terms utilized and their definitions are employed in the jurisdiction's statutory law and case law.

the corporate entity if the employee is acting within the scope of the employee's responsibility and authority, and if the act is not grossly negligent, willful/wanton, and does not involve malfeasance (van der Smissen, 1990). Therefore, if the act is aggravated negligence, the employee generally stands alone and the employer is often not liable.

What Is Reasonable Care?

The second component of breach of duty can be evaluated only after determining what constitutes reasonable care. The **standard of care** is determined by the reasonable and prudent person concept (*i.e.*, one is required to act as a reasonable and prudent person would act under the circumstances). *One should note, however, that when an individual is a professional in a field (e.g., sport management, coaching, recreation, athletic training), it is not enough to act as the imaginary reasonable and prudent "person;" but as a **reasonable and prudent "professional"** would act under the given circumstances* (van der Smissen, 1990).

A service provider is not required to be an insurer of the safety of its patrons, but is expected to provide reasonably safe premises and conditions for the activity. In a Maine case involving the standard of care required of an athletic trainer, the court held that the defendant trainer "has the duty to conform to the standard of care required of an ordinary, careful trainer" (*Searles v. Trustees of St. Joseph College*, 1997). Likewise, in *Cerny v. Cedar Bluffs Junior/Senior High* (2004), the Nebraska Supreme Court ruled that a football coach allowing a football player to participate after an injury is held to the standard of conduct of a reasonably prudent person holding a Nebraska teaching certificate with a coaching endorsement.

A Single Standard of Care. Since the required standard of care is that of a reasonable and prudent professional, an inexperienced physical educator, sport manager, or park ranger is held to the same standard of care required of an experienced, reasonable, and prudent physical educator, sport manager, or park ranger. In other words, there is only one standard of care for a given situation. van der Smissen (1990) stressed that "*the standard is not that of a person with the actual qualification of the individual, but of a person competent for the position for which the individual holds oneself to be qualified*" (Part A, p. 43).

Was the Risk Foreseeable?

The third component of breach of duty is to determine whether the risk was foreseeable by a reasonable and prudent professional. As discussed in the Duty section of this chapter, there is liability only if the risk was foreseeable. The reasonable and prudent professional needs only to have foreseen that an injury was likely and need not have been able to foresee the exact nature of the incident or of the injury.

Proximate Cause

The third requirement for liability is that the injured party must show that the breach of duty was the cause-in-fact of the injury (*i.e.*, the proximate cause). Black [1990] defined **proximate cause** or **cause-in-fact** as "[T]hat particular cause which produces an event and without which the event would not have occurred" (p. 221). In other words, proximate cause refers to an act from which an injury is the natural, direct, and uninterrupted consequence.

> Returning to the Happy Holiday Stables illustration, one of the obligations of the stable is to consider the ability and experience of the rider when assigning a horse. If the stable employee fails to assign a disciplined, easy-to-handle horse to a novice rider, the undisciplined horse is too headstrong for the novice rider to control, and the novice falls from the horse breaking a leg, Happy Holiday may be liable for negligence. On the other hand, suppose the employee fails to match the horse to the rider properly and the horse bolts when struck by a snake, causing the rider to be thrown and break a leg, Happy Holiday would not be liable because the breach of duty had nothing to do with the injury because even a properly matched horse would have bolted under the circumstances. Happy Holiday would not be liable because the breach of duty was not the proximate cause of the injury.

Southwest Key Program, Inc. v. Gil-Perez (2000) illustrates an instance in which a negligent act was the proximate cause of the injury (see the Supplemental Website). Gil-Perez was injured when employees of the Southwest Key Program allowed the boys to play tackle football without pads, instruction, or supervision. On the other hand, *Rutecki v. CSX Hotels* (2007) is a case in which the negligent act was not determined to be the proximate cause of injury. In *Rutecki*, the resort operator conducted a horseback ride and violated a statute by failing to determine the riding skill of the plaintiff. During the ride, the guide's horse misbehaved and fell, startling the plaintiff's horse, and causing the plaintiff to fall. The court ruled that the violation of the statute was not causally related to the injury and ruled for the defendant.

Many states use the **probable consequences rule** that holds the defendant liable for injuries that are the natural and probable consequences of one's negligent act. A Texas court stated that the elements of proximate cause may be inferred from the circumstances of the event and that the jury should be allowed latitude in determining proximate cause. Other jurisdictions have adopted the **substantial factor test**. Under this theory, the law does not require that a negligent act be the only causal factor, but may be a substantial factor among several factors that cause the injury. In a Kentucky case (*Figure World v. Farley*, 1984), a bar sold alcohol to six minors in violation of a state statute. The boys drank most of the alcohol, went swimming in a pond, and one of the boys drowned. The court ruled that a jury could find that injury was foreseeable and that the sale of the alcohol to the minors was a substantial factor in the death and remanded the case for trial.

Many plaintiffs name **failure to supervise** as the proximate cause of an injury. Most jurisdictions, however, require that supervision must be the actual proximate cause (i.e., show that the injury was a consequence of the lack of supervision and would not have occurred had there been adequate supervision.)

When two parties commit two separate negligent acts prior to an injury, the court must determine which of the acts constituted the proximate cause. *Cirillo v. City of Milwaukee* (1967) illustrates such a situation. When a teacher left an unsupervised physical education class of 49 adolescent boys shooting baskets, the boys (including the plaintiff) soon began participating in roughhousing and rowdy behavior. After 25 minutes, Cirillo was injured and his parents subsequently sued alleging negligence on the part of the teacher. In this case, both the action of the teacher and the rowdy behavior of the plaintiff were instrumental in causing the injury. The question was which act constituted the proximate cause of the injury—the failure to supervise, which allowed the roughhousing, or the intervening act of roughhousing indulged in by the student.

When a negligent act is followed by a second unforeseeable and independent negligent act by another party, the second negligent act can be deemed the proximate cause—thereby intervening and averting liability from the doer of the first negligent act. Such an act is called an **intervening act** or **intervening cause**. The intervening act must be independent of the original act, must be capable in itself of creating the injury, and must not have been foreseeable by the party committing the first act.

Damage

The fourth element of negligence is damage. If there is no damage, then there is no negligence and, therefore, no compensation. **Damage** is "injury, loss, or deterioration caused by the negligence, design, or accident of one person to another in respect to the latter's person or property" (Black, 1996, p. 389). Although the damage that is compensable varies from state to state, it commonly includes (1) economic losses, (2) physical pain and suffering, (3) emotional distress, and (4) physical impairment (van der Smissen, 1990).

Economic loss may include medical expenses, lost wages, rehabilitation expenses, custodial care, and much more. The court determines the economic loss based upon actual expenses and projected expenses by expert witnesses. Monetary award for **pain and suffering** is determined by the jury. The amount of such awards depends on many factors such as the credibility of witnesses, whether the plaintiff's actions are consistent with one in pain, pre-existing injuries, whether the plaintiff can do what he or she could do in everyday life, the plaintiff's pain tolerance, the plaintiff's occupation, whether the plaintiff makes a sympathetic witness, and the skill of the attorney (http://injury-law.freeadvice.com). **Emotional distress** is not always compensable in negligence cases. In states that allow awards for emotional distress, the distress generally is in the form of fright, anxiety, humiliation, and loss of being able to enjoy a normal life. **Physical impairments** may constitute damage and may be considered in lieu of emotional distress. The award may be given for temporary and permanent impairments as well as for partial or total impairments (van der Smissen, 1990).

Damages

Damage and damages are sometimes confused. Whereas damage is the actual element of negligence (injury or loss), **damages** is the monetary compensation sought or awarded as a remedy for a tortious act. There are two major types of damages—compensatory and punitive. **Compensatory damages** denote a monetary award intended to compensate the injured party for injury or loss caused by the wrong. The award is intended to restore the injured party to his or her position prior to the injury. **Punitive** or **exemplary damages** entail an award beyond the compensatory damages, generally where the action involves violence, oppression, malice, fraud, or wanton conduct by the defendant. This award is intended (1) to punish the wrongdoer for outrageous conduct and (2) to deter such acts in the future.

Punitive or exemplary damages vary greatly from state to state. Some states do not permit them, while others limit the amount of the award. Generally, these awards are made only when the negligent party acts from a wrongful motive or knowing indifference for the safety and rights of others. Thus, these awards generally are available when the act is gross negligence (rarely), reckless misconduct, or willful and wanton acts (varying by state), and usually are at the discretion of the jury (van der Smissen, 1990).

In *Borne v. Haverhill Golf and Country Club, Inc.* (2003), Borne and eight other women sued the club alleging that the club, a place of public accommodation, discriminated unfairly against them on the basis of their sex. The trial judge instructed the jury that punitive damages could be awarded only if there had been extraordinary misconduct by the defendant—". . . for malicious, wanton or oppressive conduct done in reckless disregard of the plaintiff's rights or in callous indifference to the plaintiff" (p. 28). After a 22-day trial, the court ruled in favor of the plaintiffs and awarded $1,967,400 in damages including $1,430,000 in punitive damages. The appellate court affirmed the trial court verdict.

Finally, in the Happy Holiday Stables illustration, the novice rider suffered a broken leg due to the fall from the horse. A physical injury such as this constitutes damage and creates the possibility of monetary recovery if a negligent act by the Happy Holidays was the proximate cause of the injury. In the event of negligence, the court can award compensatory damages—*e.g.*, medical expenses, pain and suffering, and lost wages (in the case of a working adult). The plaintiff would not be eligible for punitive damages because the conduct of the stables was ordinary negligence and involved no outrageous conduct. If the injury resulted from an inherent risk of horseback riding (e.g., horse bolting because of a snake or nearby lightning strike), Happy Holidays would not be liable and there would be no damages awarded.

SIGNIFICANT CASE

The question of whether the City of New York and the school district were negligent revolves around the first of the four requirements for negligence – duty. It is interesting that the incident at issue took place when a student was assaulted after school hours and not on the school premises. Note what factors were examined in determining if there was a duty to the student.

PINERO V. THE CITY OF NEW YORK

Supreme Court of New York, Bronx County
2012 N.Y. Misc. LEXIS 6404; 2012 NY Slip Op 33452(U)

OPINION BY:

Mary Ann Brigantti-Hughes

* * *

I. Factual History

At relevant times, Plaintiff was a student at defendant Lehman High School. On January 13, 2005, Plaintiff alleges he was assaulted while on his way home from school approximately 15 minutes after school had ended, and while he was no longer on school property. The incident occurred at Westchester Square, approximately one quarter mile from the school. Plaintiff was walking with friends, when a female friend got into a verbal altercation and subsequent physical altercation with an unknown boy. Plaintiff attempted to break up the fight. Plaintiff alleged that gang members nearby threw Plaintiff against a fence and assaulted him with their fists. Plaintiff and his friend managed to escape briefly, but the gang caught up to them and continued the assault with their fists. Plaintiff was rendered unconscious. He was later helped to his feet by a NYPD officer and returned to school. The assistant principal at the time refused to send Plaintiff home in a cab, as per Plaintiff's mother's request, and called an ambulance to take Plaintiff to Jacobi hospital. Plaintiff did not identify his assailants and no arrests were made.

Defendants argue they owed no duty to Plaintiff as the alleged incident occurred after school hours and off school property. There can be no actionable breach of a school's duty where the injury occurs off of school premises, since the duty extends only to the boundaries of school property. Plaintiff was on a public sidewalk here separated from school property by a chainlink fence. Defendants also allege that they owed no duty to Plaintiff since the incident occurred outside of normal school hours. The incident allegedly occurred at 3:00PM, when the school day ended at 2:46 PM.

Even if the incident did take place on school property, and during school hours, Defendants argue that they had no duty to protect Plaintiff as no liability may arise from attacks from third parties absent a special duty of protection. Finally, Defendants assert that the alleged incident was spontaneous in nature and more supervision, therefore, could not have prevented it. They allege that schools are not insurers of a student's safety, for they cannot reasonably be expected to supervise continuously all students' movements and daily activities, much less "guard against all of the sudden, spontaneous acts that take place among students daily."

In opposition, Plaintiff argues that Defendants had notice of gang related violent propensities of fellow students. Plaintiff submits a newspaper article detailing gang around the School from 1999, and a police incident report stemming from this incident which notes that "fights happen every day" where the incident occurred. The assailant was a student of the same school as Plaintiff, according to Plaintiff's testimony. Moreover, Plaintiff argues that the incident occurred within school boundaries. According to the testimony of Scott Arbuse and Giusseppi Di Maio, former and current assistant principles of security and administration for the school, respectively, a "safe corridor," or a designated route established by the school with the NYPD to provide a safe exit to the students, was purposefully established to afford protection to students exiting the high school. Mr. DiMaio testified that the corridor "encompasses one side of the school all the way to the other side of the school, Exit 6 is the one corner of the school and White Castle is where the football field would end. We provide a safe corridor in that whole area of the school." Mr. Arbuse concurred with "safe corridor" definition. Plaintiff testified that this incident occurred near the football fields.

Plaintiff also argues that Defendant owes a duty during class dismissal times. This incident occurred 13 minutes following the [*5] conclusion of Plaintiff's final class for the day. Finally, Plaintiff argues that a "special duty of protection" did indeed exist between Defendant and Plaintiff, obligating Defendant to protect Plaintiff from third-party attacks. Here, Plaintiff alleges (1) defendants affirmatively took action to prevent attacks against students after dismissal; (2) defendants knew inaction could lead to harm; (3) there was direct contact between Plaintiff and Defendant principal; and (4) Plaintiff justifiably relied on the school's affirmative undertaking.

* * *

III. Analysis

It is well settled that an action for negligence does not lie unless there exists a duty on the part of the defendant and a corresponding right in the plaintiff. A school district's duty of care is "coextensive with, and concomitant to, its physical custody and control over a child". Thus, the duty of care owed to the students is present while they are in the school's physical custody or orbit of authority, or when a specific statutory duty has been imposed.

In this case, there are factual issues surrounding whether, at the time of the incident, Plaintiff was still in Defendant's "orbit of control" thus giving rise to a custodial duty of care. * * * Plaintiff testified that this incident occurred in front of the School's football fields. The above testimony presents factual issues as to whether the incident thus occurred within Defendant's area of authority and control.

Further, the mere fact that this incident occurred 13 minutes following the end of Plaintiff's last class of the day does not automatically release Defendant from a custodial duty. Indeed, it has been held that dismissal times are when fights amongst a congregation of students is most likely to occur. Moreover, the incident report prepared in this matter stated that the incident occurred during school hours. The report was confirmed by Mr. DiMaio at his deposition. He also testified that the report was unclear as to the location of the incident.

Defendants assert that, nevertheless, they are entitled to judgment as they owed no duty of care and cannot be liable for negligent supervision.

It is well established that "a municipality's duty to provide police protection is ordinarily one owed to the public at large and not to any particular individual or class of individuals" and that, absent a "special relationship" which creates a "special duty", a claim grounded in the lack of such protection is legally insufficient and must be dismissed. A special relationship is comprised of the following elements (1) an assumption by the municipality, through promises or actions, of an affirmative duty to act on behalf of the party who was injured; (2) knowledge on the part of the municipality's agents that inaction could lead to harm; (3) some form of direct contact between the municipality's agents and the injured; and (4) the party's justifiable reliance on the municipality's affirmative undertaken. If the aforementioned elements are not established, a plaintiff cannot sustain an action against a municipality for failure to provide police or school guard protection. Logan.

However, separate and distinct from a municipality's provision of police or school guard protection, is a duty of supervision owed by a school to its students, which "stems from the fact of its physical custody over them" thus depriving custody of the child's parent or guardian. Therefore, the actor who takes custody of a child is properly required to give him the protection which the custody or manner in which it is taken has deprived him. Schools are under a duty to adequately supervise the students in their charge and they will be held liable for foreseeable injuries proximately related to the absence of adequate supervision. In determining whether the duty to provide adequate supervision has been breached in the context of injuries caused by the acts of fellow students, it must be established that school authorities had sufficiently specific knowledge or notice of the dangerous conduct which caused injury, or that the conduct could reasonably have been anticipated. Such actual or constructive notice to the school of prior similar conduct is generally required because school personnel cannot reasonably be expected to guard against all of the sudden, spontaneous acts that take place among students daily.

An injury caused by the impulsive, unanticipated act of a fellow student ordinarily will not give rise to a finding of negligence absent proof of prior conduct that would have put a reasonable person on notice to protect against the injury-causing act. The test to be applied is whether under all the circumstances the chain of events that followed the negligent act or omission was a normal or foreseeable consequence of the situation created by the school's negligence. To this point, Defendants argue that this incident was spontaneous and unforeseeable.

In Logan, a student was raped by fellow students while on school premises. * * * "While a school is not an insurer of student safety, it will be held liable in damages for a foreseeable injury proximately related to the absence of supervision."

In this matter, Plaintiff testified that gang members got involved when he tried to break up a fight between two Lehman High students. He testified at deposition that he had seen the gang members at the School before and testified that they attended the School. While the newspaper article and incident report submitted by Plaintiff constitute inadmissible hearsay evidence, there is sufficient evidence on the motion record to raise a triable issue of fact as to whether this incident was foreseeable. Plaintiff testified that fights would occur with the gangs surrounding the school prior to this incident, although he could not recall specifics. The School had worked with the NYPD to instill "safe corridor" around the school grounds in order to provide the students safe egress following dismissal from classes. One of these alleged safe corridors was the path from the School to a White Castle restaurant in nearby Westchester Square, abutting the School's football field, where the incident allegedly occurred. Accordingly, it appears that the School had established careful security measures to prevent incidents like this one from occurring. There is therefore a factual issue as to whether Defendants had actual or constructive notice that their students were at risk of attack when traveling along the boundaries of the school grounds following dismissal for the day. Moreover, questions of notice, foreseeability of danger, necessity for an adequacy of supervision, and causation are, generally, for the jury.

IV. Conclusion

Accordingly, it is hereby ORDERED, that Defendants' motion to renew their previously filed motion to dismiss pursuant to CPLR 3211 or for summary judgment pursuant to CPLR 3212 is granted, and upon renewal, it is hereby ORDERED, that Defendants' motion for dismissal and/or summary judgment is denied.

This constitutes the Decision and Order of this Court.
Dated: February 22, 2012
/s/ Mary Ann Brigantti-Hughes
Hon. Mary Ann Brigantti-Hughes, J.S.C.

CASES ON THE SUPPLEMENTAL WEBSITE

Craig v. Amateur Softball Association of America, 2008 PA Super 123; 951 A.2d 372; 2008 Pa. Super. LEXIS 1108. The primary issue in this case is whether or not a duty was owed.

Spotlite Skating Rink, Inc. v. Barnes, 988 So. 2d 364; 2008 Miss. LEXIS 322. This case illustrates the need for the plaintiff to show a duty, a breach of duty, and causation. Notice that there is conflicting testimony regarding the facts of the case so the jury or judge must judge who is telling the truth.

Southwest Key Program v. Gil-Perez, 2000 Tex. App. LEXIS 7851; 79 S.W.3d 571. The court established that a duty was owed to the plaintiff, that the duty was breached, and that the breach was the proximate cause of injury. Further, they found that the injury was foreseeable.

Howard v. Missouri Bone and Joint Center, Inc., 2010 U.S. App. LEXIS 16699. The major point to focus on in this case is causation.

Zavras v. Capeway Rovers Motorcycle Club, Inc., 1997 Mass. App. LEXIS 248. This case has an interesting discussion distinguishing between gross and ordinary negligence. The court also discusses gross negligence in relation to negligent hire and gross negligence by an employee.

QUESTIONS YOU SHOULD BE ABLE TO ANSWER

1. What is forseeability and how does it relate to liability?
2. Compare the duty of a person who has an inherent relationship (e.g., a teacher to his or her student) to the duty of a person who volunteers to perform a task (e.g., coach a little league team or administer first aid).
3. What are three reasons why the distinction between ordinary negligence and gross negligence is important?
4. Compare the standard of care owed by a first year coach, a coach with 10 years of experience, and a coach with 30 years of experience.
5. Explain proximate cause and the effect of an intervening act. Give a clear example.

REFERENCES
Cases
Barnes v. New Hampshire Karting Association, 1991 La. App. LEXIS 158.
Borne v. Haverhill Golf and Country Club, 2003 Mass App. LEXIS 642.
Cerny v. Cedar Bluff's Junior/Senior Public School, 679 N.W.2d. 198 (Neb. 2004).
Cirillo v. City of Milwaukee, 1967 Wisc. LEXIS 1123.
City of Santa Barbara v. Superior Court, 2007 Cal. LEXIS 7603.
Durrell v. Parachutes Are Fun, 1987 Del. Super. LEXIS 1321.
Figure World v. Farley, 680 S.W.2d 33 (Tex. App. 1984).
Gill v. Tamalpais Union High School District, 2008 Cal. App. Unpub. LEXIS 3928.
Gouger v. Hardtke, 1992 Wisc. LEXIS 183.
Cincinnati Ins. Co. v. Oancea, 2004 Ohio App. LEXIS 3891.
Harting v. Dayton Dragons Professional Baseball Club, LLC, 2007 Ohio App LEXIS 1956.
Hatch v. V.P. Fair Foundation, Inc., 990 S.W.2d 126 (Mo. App. 1999).
Hawkins v. Peart, 2001 Utah LEXIS 177.
Kahn v. East Side Union High School District, 2003 Cal. LEXIS 6373.
Knight v. Jewett, 3 Cal.4th 296; 834 P.2d 696 (1992).
Lamp v. Reynolds, 2002 Mich. App. LEXIS 123.
Milne v. USA Cycling Inc., 2007 U.S. Dist. LEXIS 42579.
Pfister v. Shusta, 1995 Ill. LEXIS 201.
Rodriguez v. City of Moses Lake, 2010 Wash. App. LEXIS 2682.
Rutecki v. CSX Hotels, Inc., 2007 U.S. Dist. LEXIS 3181.
Searles v. Trustees of St. Joseph College, 695 A2d. 1206 (Me 1997).
Sisino v. Island Motocross of N.Y., Inc., 2007 WL 1629958 (N.Y. App. Div. June 5, 2007).
Southwest Key Program v. Gil-Perez, 2000 Tex. App. LEXIS 7851; 79 S.W.3d 571.
Sparks v. Starks, 2006 Ill. App. LEXIS 881.
Wagner v. SFX Motor Sports, Inc., 2006 U.S. Dist. LEXIS 79099.
Wolfgang v. Mid-America Sports, Inc., 1997 U.S. App. LEXIS 8817.
Zavras v. Capeway Rovers Motorcycle Club, Inc., 1997 Mass. App. LEXIS 248.

Publications
Black, H.C. (1990). Black's Law Dictionary, (6th Ed.) St. Paul: West Publishing Co.
Keeton, W.P. (1984). *Prosser and Keeton on the law of torts* (5th ed.). St. Paul, MN: West Publishing Co.
van der Smissen, B. (2007). Elements of Negligence. In Cotten, D.J. and Wolohan. J.T. Law for recreation and Sport Managers (4th Ed.) Dubuque, Iowa: Kendall/Hunt Publishing Co.
van der Smissen, B. (1996). Tort Liability and Risk Management. In Parkhouse, B.L. The Management of Sport (2nd Ed.) St. Louis: C.V.Mosby Company.
van der Smissen, B. (1990). Legal Liability and Risk Management for Public and Private Entities. Cincinnati: Anderson Publishing Company.

Websites
http://injury-law.freeadvice.com/injury-law/pain_and_suffering_factors.htm

Legislation
W.Va.C. 20-38-1 to 8.

2.12 WHICH PARTIES ARE LIABLE?

Doyice J. Cotten | Sport Risk Consulting

Recreation and sport law students often ask, "Why did they sue the school system or the recreation department when it was the teacher or the employee who was negligent?" or "If I am the supervisor, will I be liable if someone in my charge is negligent?" These questions represent just two of the many issues to be considered in answering the question of which parties may be liable when an injury occurs. Whereas in the past, the party sued was usually the corporate entity or the "deep pocket," today the trend is to sue everyone associated with the incident leading to the injury. For instance, suppose an aerobics instructor employed by a health club conducts an aerobics class in a room where speakers have been placed very near the participants. A participant loses his or her balance, falls into the speaker, and suffers injury. The participant might well name as individual defendants not only the aerobics instructor, but the manager of the health club, the program director, the person responsible for room setup and maintenance, the owner of the health club, as well as the health club corporate entity.

The question to be addressed in this chapter is: Who is liable when a negligent act results in an injury? The reader should remember, however, that since the laws regarding liability in such situations differ somewhat from state to state, the discussion will be general in nature. State law in any one state may differ somewhat from these general concepts.

FUNDAMENTAL CONCEPTS

There are three categories of parties that may be liable in any given situation. The first category consists of the **employee** or **service personnel** involved. This is usually the person who committed the negligent act. This category includes persons who generally have actual contact with the participants (e.g., teacher, coach, weight room attendant, referee, aerobics instructor, scout master). Also included in this category are the maintenance personnel or custodians who are often in direct contact with the participant.

The second category is the **administrative or supervisory personnel**. These are generally individuals who have some sort of administrative or supervisory authority over the service personnel. Examples include a director of recreation and intramurals, city recreation director, a principal, a head coach, a school superintendent, a manager of a health club, or a general manager of a professional baseball club. It is important to remember, however, that the classification of this individual can vary with the act being performed. For instance, the department head would be categorized as service personnel when teaching a class, but as administrative when performing scheduling duties.

The third category is the **corporate entity**. This category includes the governing body of the organization. Examples include the county school board, the municipal recreation board, the university board of regents, the corporation board of directors, the owner of a business, or the local health club corporation.

Who Is Liable?

The liability of three categories or groups is addressed here—employees or service personnel, administrative/supervisory personnel, and the corporate entity. In general, both employees and administrative/supervisory personnel are liable for their own negligence. In addition, under the doctrine of *respondeat superior*, the employer or corporate entity is liable for injury to person or property when the injury results from the negligent acts of the employee—so long as the injury occurs while the employee is acting within the scope of his or her authority. While each can be liable under certain circumstances, state immunity statutes (intended to help protect providers and employees from liability in certain situations) affect that liability.

Immunity. Sovereign or governmental immunity, still in effect in some states, generally protects the public corporate entity but not its employees. However, officials of public bodies are generally immune from liability for discretionary acts performed within the scope of their authority (see Chapter 2.21 *Defenses against Negligence* and Chapter 2.22 *Immunity*) and a few states do provide the employee with immunity from liability for any act as long as it is in performance of the employee's duties and is not willful and wanton (van der Smissen, 1990). In addition, many states have passed limited liability statutes that provide immunity to certain individuals under selected circumstances. These statutes include recreational use statutes (landowners), Good Samaritan statutes (those who come to the aid of the injured), various sport volunteer statutes (volunteer coaches and officials), and assumption of risk statutes for specific activities, for general activities, and for hazardous recreational activities (providers of recreational activities and sports). Most states also have passed laws which allow either for the indemnification of a public employee or for liability insurance coverage of the employee (see Chapter 2.21 *Defenses against Negligence* and Chapter 4.25 *Managing Risk Through Insurance*).

Employees/Service Personnel

In the absence of immunity, *employees are individually liable for their own negligent conduct*. The employee who performed the negligent act is generally the person in close contact with the participant (e.g., a teacher, a lifeguard, a camp counselor, an assistant coach, an athletic trainer, or a maintenance person). If the employee has a duty, breaches that duty by failing to meet the required standard of care, and that breach is the proximate cause of injury to the plaintiff, the employee is negligent and may be legally liable. Sometimes employees think they are not liable because they have insurance coverage. Insurance does not prevent or bar liability; however, it may pay the damages in the event of an award.

The aerobics instructor in the example at the beginning of this chapter would fall into the employee/service personnel category. If the instructor breaches a duty to the aerobics class by allowing participation too close to a hazard (e.g., the speaker), and that breach is shown to be the proximate cause of the injury, then the instructor is negligent and may be legally liable for damages.

Administrative/Supervisory Personnel

Whereas the question regarding liability of service personnel is relatively simple, the question of liability of the administrative or supervisory personnel for the negligence of subordinates is much more complex. *When there is no immunity, the general rule is that administrative/supervisory personnel are individually liable for their own negligent conduct, but are not liable for the negligence of subordinates. The administrator/supervisor is liable, however, if the administrator owes a duty and acts (or omissions) of the administrator enhanced the likelihood of injury* (van der Smissen, 1990).

Administrative duties fall into five categories (van der Smissen, 1990). These duties are to:

1. Employ competent personnel and discharge those unfit;
2. Provide proper supervision and to have a supervisory plan;
3. Direct the services or program in a proper manner;
4. Establish safety rules and regulations and to comply with policy and statutory requirements;
5. Remedy dangerous conditions and defective equipment or to warn users of dangers involved.

In the example involving the aerobics instructor, the health club manager would fall into the administrative/supervisory personnel category. Normally the manager is not liable for the negligence of the aerobics instructor unless the manager did something that enhanced the likelihood of injury. The health club manager hired a qualified, certified instructor, supervised the program adequately, and the aerobics program was conducted according to standards suggested by a national association. The manager may have breached an administrative/supervisory duty, however, by failing to establish or enforce safety rules regarding hazards on the floor or minimal clear space requirements, or by failing to identify and remedy or warn of dangerous conditions. On the other hand, if the presence of the speaker on the floor was a one-time occurrence and the manager had safety rules regarding hazards and space and regularly enforced them, then the manager would likely not be liable since the manager breached no duty and did not increase the likelihood of injury.

However, the administrative or supervisory personnel can be liable for human resources law violations (see *Respondeat Superior* in Human Resources Law later in this chapter). Human resources law includes three major areas of concern: (1) The employment process (including recruitment, selection, hiring, and firing of employees); (2) The workplace environment (including hostile work environment, sexual harassment, and employee protection laws; and (3) Employee behaviors (addressing employment process negligence, negligent supervision, negligent hire, and negligent retention) (van der Smissen, 2007).

The Corporate Entity

The next question regards the liability of the business or corporate entity for the negligence of an employee, whether that employee is classified as service personnel or administrative/supervisory personnel. The answer to this question is governed by the **doctrine of *respondeat superior*** (also referred to as **vicarious liability**) which states that *the negligence of an employee is imputed to the corporate entity if the employee was acting within the scope of the employee's responsibility and authority and if the act was not grossly negligent, willful/wanton, and did not involve malfeasance* (van der Smissen, 1990). So, according to this doctrine, if an employee commits ordinary negligence while engaged in the furtherance of the employer's enterprise, the employer as well as the employee can be liable.

In the foregoing example, the aerobics instructor instructing the class was acting within the scope of responsibility and authority and was engaged in the furtherance of the employer's enterprise. If it is shown that allowing activity too near the speakers constituted negligence, then not only is the instructor liable, but liability is also imputed to the health club corporate entity.

Ultra Vires Acts. Acts that are beyond the scope of responsibility and authority of the employee are considered ***ultra vires* acts** and, generally, such an act relieves the corporate entity of liability via *respondeat superior*. The city in *Myricks v. Lynnwood Unified School District* (1999) was not liable for an accident transporting a team since the trip was not within the scope of the driver's responsibility. Exceptions to this rule occur when the corporate entity benefited from, had notice of, or condoned the act.

Respondeat Superior* in Human Resources Law.** When employment torts are concerned, the corporate entity is liable for the intentional torts and criminal acts of its employees. Traditionally, under the doctrine of *respondeat superior*, an employer is liable for injuries to the person or property of third persons resulting from actions by an employee that were within the scope of employment, but the employer carried no liability for unauthorized acts by employees including willful acts to injure another. In recent years, however, many jurisdictions have extended the **doctrine of *respondeat superior to include workplace torts (i.e., the wrongdoing of those in positions of authority), sexual assaults, sexual harassment, and abuse by a party in a position of authority over children (Carter, 1995; van der Smissen, 1996; *Williams v. Butler*, 1991). The concept of "acting within the scope of authority" continues to apply, but is more broadly interpreted to mean any activities which carry out the objectives of the employer (van der Smissen, 1996) and those during which the employer was or could have been exercising control of the activities of the employee (*Longin v. Kelly*, 1995).

The employer may also be held liable for acts of the employee in cases of **employment process negligence** (i.e., when the employer in the employment process negligently allows the assignment of an unfit employee or fails to use reasonable care to discover the unfitness of an employee). Liability of the employer can result from negligent hiring, negligent supervision, negligent training, negligent retention, and negligent referral of an employee that is unfit (van der Smissen, 1996; Carter, 1995).

Board Members. *Board members are not individually liable for the actions of the board or for the negligence of employees of the organization.* Board members are, however, individually liable for (1) collective acts of the board or individual acts that are outside the scope of authority; (2) breaches of statutory duty or violation of participant/employee Constitutional rights; and (3) intentional torts (e.g., assault and battery, slander, libel) (Kaiser & Robinson, 1999).

Intentional Torts or Willful Acts by an Employee. Many employers believe that they are not liable for intentional acts committed by their employees. This commonly held belief is not always true. In fact, courts generally look at whether there is social justification for holding the employer liable rather than at whether the conduct of the employee was intentional or negligent. So whether the employer is vicariously liable for an intentional act by the employee depends upon whether the action was (1) within the scope of employment (required by or was incidental to employment) or (2) reasonably foreseeable by the employer. If either prong of the test is met, the employer can be held liable even if the employee's act was willful or malicious.

Three cases in which an employee assaulted a patron while on duty resulted in rulings in favor of the victim (*Glucksman v. Walters*, 1995; *Rogers v. Fred R. Hiller Company of GA., Inc.*, 1994; *Pelletier v. Bilbiles*, 1967). Each court stated that a master is liable for the willful torts of his servant if the tort was committed within the scope of the servant's employment and in furtherance of his master's business. The *Glucksman* court further stated that the fact that the specific method employed to accomplish the master's orders is not authorized does not relieve the master of liability. One fact that employers should remember is that the court determines what falls "within the scope of employment" and there is little consistency among courts.

Furthermore, employers can be found liable in some cases even when the employee's action was not within the scope of employment if the employer ratifies the employee's action. Ratification may be either express or implied and can include such factors as failing to investigate the complaint, failing to redress the harm done, and failing to discharge the employee.

So there is no simple rule of thumb that the employer is not liable for intentional or willful acts of an employee. Each case is different and the result will turn on the facts of the particular case.

Volunteers, Trainees, and Interns. The question often arises as to whether the acts of a **volunteer**, a **trainee**, or an **intern** fall under the doctrine of *respondeat superior*. In general, volunteers, trainees, and interns are liable individually for their own negligence. If they were under the control of the corporate entity and were acting within the scope of "employment," authority, and responsibility, the corporate entity is liable under the doctrine of *respondeat superior*. Volunteers of public or nonprofit organizations are immune from liability for their own negligence if they qualify under the federal Volunteer Protection Act of 1997 or a state volunteer immunity statute (see Chapter 2.21 *Defenses against Negligence* and Chapter 2.22 *Immunity*). In those instances, the corporate entity is usually still liable for the negligence of the volunteer (van der Smissen, 1990; Manley, 1995). It is worth noting that the volunteer, trainee, or intern *is held to the same standard of care as that of an experienced, competent professional*.

University Athletes. An issue that sometimes arises is whether a university is liable under *respondeat superior* for the negligent acts of a university varsity athlete (*Townsend v. The State of California*, 1987; *Hanson v. Kynast*, 1986; *Brown v. Day*, 1990). Courts have ruled the applicability of the doctrine requires an individualized determination of whether a master-servant relationship exists between the tortfeasor and the university. The *Townsend* court concluded that whether on scholarship or not, the athlete is not an employee and the university is not vicariously liable for the athlete's negligent acts.

Joint and Several Liability and Uniform Contribution among Joint Tortfeasors. The **joint and several liability doctrine** holds that one defendant can be held liable for the total damages even though other defendants were also at fault. If more than one party is found liable, the court does not limit the injured party's recovery against each to a proportionate share of fault. A classic example of this can be found in *Walt Disney World Co. v. Wood* (1987) where Disney was found 1 percent at fault, plaintiff was 14 percent at fault, and other defendants were 85 percent at fault. Under joint and several liability, Disney was ordered to pay the entire 86 percent of damages. In the 1980s, however, most states enacted statutes that provide for **uniform contribution among joint tortfeasors** in equitable portions, but not necessarily equal portions. When one tortfeasor has paid a disproportionate share of damages, that tortfeasor can file suit against the other tortfeasor in a separate action.

In *Universal Gym Equipment, Inc. v. Vic Tanny International, Inc.* (1994), the plaintiff was injured while working on a Universal machine. She had signed a waiver that protected Tanny from litigation, so she sued Universal and obtained a settlement of $225,000. Universal then commenced action against Tanny alleging failure to maintain safe premises and that Tanny had an obligation to indemnify or contribute to any settlement between the injured plaintiff and Universal. Michigan law allowed Tanny to use any defense that would have been valid against liability for the injury to exonerate it from liability for contribution. Thus, the waiver signed by the injured party protected Tanny from liability for contribution to Universal. The court remanded the case to determine if Tanny was grossly negligent—in which case, the waiver would not protect Tanny from liability for the injury or from liability for the contribution.

Limiting Corporate Liability by Contract

Corporate entities frequently limit their liability through the use of various types of contractual arrangements. The following are four ways in which contracts are used to protect the corporate entity.

Facility Leases

The use of sport and recreational facilities by another group or organization is a common practice. The details of these transactions can range from free use by oral agreement to a formal lease with a rental charge. In any case, the question is: What is the liability of the owner of the premises when an injury occurs on the premises while being used by another organization? To determine such liability, one must first determine whether the injury was premise-related (resulting from unsafe premises) or activity-related (resulting from the conduct of the activity) (van der Smissen, 1990). Unless specified in the contract, the owner generally remains liable for premise-related injuries. Second, if the injury is activity-related, one must determine if the owner retained *control* over the activity or the use of the premises. Essentially, the liability for activity-related injury generally lies with the party that had control over the activity. Thus, if a university leases an arena to a promoter of an ice skating event and retains no control over how the activity is conducted, the university would not be liable for activity-related injuries, but might be liable if the injury resulted from an unsafe facility.

Facility owners generally require that the leasing party provide a certificate of insurance showing adequate liability insurance for the event. Many require that the owners be named as a co-insured on the policy (see Chapter 2.21 *Defenses against Negligence* and Chapter 2.31 *Premises Liability*).

Independent Contractors

An **independent contractor** is an individual or a company that contracts to perform a particular task using his own methods and is subject to the employer's control only as to end product or final result of his work (Black's Law Dictionary, 1990). Examples of persons that are often classified as independent contractors include referees for a contest, an aerobics specialist at a health club, a team physician, or a diving business that teaches scuba diving for a municipal recreation department.

A major reason that corporations use independent contractors is to reduce the amount of liability faced by the service provider. *The general rule is that if an injury results from the negligence of the independent contractor, the liability for negligence is shifted from the corporate entity to the independent contractor* (see Figure 2.21.1 in Chapter 2.21 *Defenses Against Negligence*). Thus, the *corporate entity* avoids much of the potential liability posed by offering the activity. However, the *corporate entity* does retain some responsibilities. The *corporate entity* is responsible (1) for using reasonable care in selecting a competent independent contractor and for inspection after completion; (2) for keeping the premises reasonably safe for invitees and employees; and (3) for "inherently dangerous activities" (e.g., activities presenting substantial harm unless precautions are taken such as fireworks displays, keeping of dangerous animals, ultra hazardous activities).

In *Hatch v. V.P. Fair Foundation, Inc.* (1999), a patron was injured when an independent contractor at a fair failed to attach the bungee cord to the platform prior to the jump. The court ruled that a landowner who hires an independent contractor to perform an "inherently dangerous activity" has a non-delegable duty to take special precautions to prevent injury from the activity. The landowner remains liable for the torts of the contractor even though the landowner was not negligent.

Often, whether one is an employee or an independent contractor is at issue. Courts generally rule that one is an **employee** if one is hired, paid a set wage or salary, is often trained by the employer, works on an ongoing basis, must perform the work as directed by the employer, and is paid by the hour, week, or month. An **independent contractor** is one who is generally engaged for a specific project, usually for a set sum, often paid at the end of the project, may do the job in one's own way, often furnishes one's own equipment, is subject to minimal restrictions, and is responsible only for the satisfactory completion of the job (*Jaeger v. Western Rivers Fly Fisher*, 1994). The distinction is important from a financial standpoint because the classification can affect the amount owed for (1) unemployment contributions, (2) workers' compensation, (3) FICA, and (4) federal and state income tax withholding. The IRS and other relevant agencies can levy heavy fines for failure to pay sufficient taxes or fees when companies have been improperly classified as independent contractors.

Unfortunately, there is no specific number of these conditions that must be met and no magic formula for weighting these conditions to determine if, indeed, one is an independent contractor. A review board or court may determine that failure, to some degree, to meet any one of the conditions is sufficient to invalidate the claim for independent contractor status. The difficulty in determining whether the person is properly classified as an employee or an independent contractor is illustrated in a case involving fitness instructors. Fitness Plus provided fitness classes for corporate clients on the premises of the client (*In the Matter of Fitness*

Plus, Inc., 2002). Fitness Plus would assess the needs of the client, contact one of about 30 instructors, negotiate a fee, bill the client, pay the instructor regardless of profit or loss, pay the instructor every two weeks, and report their income on a 1099 form. Most of these procedures fit the conditions for an independent contractor. In selecting the instructors, Fitness Plus conducted interviews, checked background, training, certification, and experience, and usually observed them in a class—seemingly meeting the requirement that they select qualified contractors. Instructors worked generally one to six hours weekly and signed an agreement that their status was that of an independent contractor. The court determined that there was sufficient evidence that Fitness Plus exercised sufficient direction and control over the services of the instructors to support the Unemployment Insurance Appeal Board ruling that they were employees.

Indemnification

An **indemnification agreement** is an agreement by which one party agrees to indemnify, reimburse, or restore a loss of another upon the occurrence of an anticipated loss. They are sometimes referred to as **hold harmless agreements** or **save harmless agreements**. Indemnification agreements can be very effective when one business indemnifies another business against loss; however, they are not always enforceable when used as a waiver of liability in which the user of the service must agree to indemnify the service provider for loss resulting from the negligence of the provider (see also Chapter 2.21 *Defenses Against Negligence*).

A perfect example of a business entity requiring that another associated business entity indemnify it from liability is illustrated in *Southwick v. City of Rutland* (2011). In this case (included on the Supplemental Website), the City of Rutland required the Vermont Swim Association (VSA) to indemnify the city for any loss the city might incur as a result of VSA holding a swim meet on city facilities. A child was injured on the adjoining city playground and sued the city. VSA claimed that the agreement did not cover injury resulting from the negligence of the city. The appellate court ruled that the indemnification agreement signed by VSA was clear and unambiguous. The court upheld the lower court award to the city.

For more information on indemnification, see Chapter 2.21 *Defenses against Negligence* and Chapter 2.23 *Waivers and Releases*.

Waivers

The corporate entity may protect itself and its employees from liability by use of waivers of liability in which the participant or service user contractually releases the business from liability for negligence by the corporate entity or its employees (see also Chapter 2.23 *Waivers and Releases*).

Corporate Liability in Other Situations

Corporations often have relationships with various types of events that involve sport and recreational activities. The corporate liability in such relationships varies depending upon the nature of the relationship.

Financial Sponsorship

Many organizations provide financial sponsorship for recreational activities or teams. **Financial sponsorship** exists when the sponsoring organization provides financial support, but exercises no control over the activity. An example of this type of sponsorship would be civic clubs or private businesses sponsoring recreation department softball teams. Financial sponsorship of this sort generally carries with it no liability. Whether the sponsoring organization is liable for injuries that occur due to negligence depends upon several things: (1) was the person in charge an agent of the organization?; (2) did the organization have control over the activity?; and (3) was a duty owed to the participant? (van der Smissen, 1990).

In *Wilson v. United States of America* (1993), the issue was whether an agency relationship existed between the Boy Scouts of America and adult volunteers of a troop so as to provide for vicarious liability for the negligence of the adult troop leaders. The court stated that liability based upon *respondeat superior* requires evidence of a master-servant relationship. In this case, there was no liability since the national organization exerts no direct control over the leaders or the activities of individual troops. In an older case, Boy Scouts of America was found liable for the negligence of an adult volunteer at a Scout-o-Rama controlled by the regional council. The key difference was control (*Riker v. Boy Scouts of America*, 1959). In *Fazzinga v. Westchester Track Club* (2008),

PepsiCo was named in a negligence suit involving a death in a 5K run. The court ruled that PepsiCo was not liable because it did not supervise or control the event and was a "mere sponsor" of the race. By way of contrast, in *Williams v. City of Albany* (2000) the defendant Capital District Flag Football, Inc. claimed to be only a sponsor of a flag football game in which Williams was injured. The court rejected this contention because the organization organized the league in question, arranged for the use of six fields, provided referees for league play, and acquired insurance for its protection.

Program Sponsorship and Joint Programming

Program sponsorship exists when an organization or entity organizes an event or maintains control over an event. An example would be when a recreation department organizes and conducts a Fourth of July slate of special activities. In *Stevens v. Payne* (2015), a spectator at an auto race fell from the bleachers lacking side railings and filed suit against the race sponsor. Summary judgment was granted the sponsor because the sponsor's role was limited to running and officiating the races in that event; he had no control over the bleachers and no duty to maintain them.

Joint programming is when more than one entity is involved in program sponsorship. Examples of such sponsorship or programming include an NCAA championship event, a high school game under the auspices of the state high school athletic association, and an event sponsored and conducted by the University of Georgia and the Southeastern Conference.

When leagues or athletic associations exert control over the conduct of the game and the eligibility of the participants, duties are created and liability for negligence emerges. When two organizations are involved in joint programming or joint sponsorship of an activity, each is responsible and liable for injuries resulting from negligence.

Governing Organization Sponsorship

Governing organizations of sports or other activities often sponsor events or lend their name to such events. If the organization has no hand in the actual conduct of the event, it owes no duty to the participants. Of course, there is no liability when there is no duty.

In *Lautieri v. Bai v. USA Triathlon, Inc.* (2003), the liability of a governing organization was at issue. The governing organization was USA Triathlon, Inc. (USAT), the program sponsor was William Fiske d/b/a Fiske Independent Race Management. Fiske was found to be grossly negligent, however, the court held that for USAT to be liable, it must be established that USAT owed a duty of care to the plaintiff. To accomplish this, the plaintiff would have to show that such a duty has a source (1) existing in social values and customs or that (2) USAT voluntarily, or for consideration, assumed a duty of care to the plaintiff. Evidence indicated that USAT's only involvement was its approval of the application of the organizer of the event. There was no evidence to indicate that USAT was obligated to or was expected to participate in the planning, operation, or supervision of the race.

Joint Ventures

A **joint venture** is "an agreement between two or more persons, ordinarily, but not necessarily limited to a single transaction for the purpose of making a profit" (*Jaeger v. Western Rivers Fly Fisher*, 1994, p. 1224). Some essential elements for a joint venture include combining of property, money, efforts, skill, labor, knowledge, and a sharing of losses and profits. A group of college students who wanted to go whitewater rafting, put up notices informing other students of the proposed trip, met, planned the trip, shared resources, and went on the trip would form a joint venture. It would not be a joint venture if the campus recreation department conceived the idea of the trip, publicized the proposed trip, helped them plan the trip, and supplied equipment for the trip. In the latter case, the university would be a sponsor of the activity and would be liable in the event of negligence. In a true joint venture, there is no group sponsorship and, hence, no liability for the corporation.

Apparent Authority

Apparent authority is a legal doctrine that describes a situation in which the principal (a person or organization) treats a second party in such as way as to lead a third party to think that the second party is an agent of the principal or has the authority to bind the principal. Under agency law, the principal is responsible for or liable for the acts of a second party that the principal allows to appear to have authority. Those in the recreation and tourism industries, in particular, need to take steps to insure that the relationship between the organization and independent contractors creates no confusion that might cause the client to rely on the appearance of an agency relationship between the principal and the apparent agent.

In a 2004 case (*Cash v. Six Continents Hotels*), two tourists were injured while climbing Dunn's River Falls in Jamaica. While the tour was provided by Harmony Tours (which had a desk in the hotel lobby), the plaintiffs had booked the tour through their hotel. They claimed the hotel was liable for Harmony Tours' negligence under the doctrine of apparent authority since the hotel allowed it to appear that the company was an agent of the hotel. The court found for the hotel since the hotel did not make representations of an affiliation, had a large sign stating "Harmony Tours" near the desk, and included a statement on the ticket informing that the company was an independent contractor and that the hotel was not responsible.

In *Santoro v. Unique Vacations Inc.* (2014), the plaintiff purchased a vacation package from Unique Vacations that included time at a Sandals resort and transportation to the resort. At the airport in St. Lucia, Santoro was given a taxi voucher. On the way to the resort the taxi driver fell asleep and was involved in an accident injuring Santoro. Santoro filed suit against Unique arguing, among other things, agency and apparent authority. The court stated that apparent authority must be based on actions of the principal – not those of the alleged agent. Summary judgment was granted Unique Vacations on the issue.

SIGNIFICANT CASE

This Significant Case was chosen because it illustrates an instance in which the corporate entity (in this case, two corporate entities) is sued because of the negligence of an employee. Under respondeat superior, the corporations would probably have been found liable absent a Ski Statute protecting ski operators from liability for accidents resulting from inherent risks of skiing.

HANUS. V. LOON MOUNTAIN RECREATION CORP.
United States District Court for the District of New Hampshire
2014 U.S. Dist. LEXIS 52778

OPINION BY:

Joseph N. Laplante

MEMORANDUM ORDER

Every winter, thousands of skiers and snowboarders journey to the slopes of New Hampshire's ski areas from locations both far and near. Like many states with a robust ski industry, New Hampshire has enacted a statute—the "Skiers, Ski Area and Passenger Tramway Safety" law, N.H. Rev. Stat. Ann. § 225-A:1 et seq. (the "Ski Statute") that limits those areas' liability to their visitors. In particular, the Ski Statute provides that "[e]ach person who participates in the sport of skiing . . . accepts as a matter of law, the dangers inherent in the sport, and to that extent may not maintain an action against [a ski area] operator for any injuries which result from such inherent risks, dangers, or hazards." * * * The question presented in this case is the extent to which this provision immunizes ski areas from liability for skier-to-skier collisions caused by their employees.

Plaintiffs Susan and Michael Hanus have sued Loon Mountain Recreation Corporation ("LMRC") and Boyne USA, Inc., the operators of one of New Hampshire's ski areas, Loon Mountain Resort, for injuries the plaintiffs' minor son suffered while skiing. Those injuries arose from an on-trail collision between the boy and a Loon Mountain employee who, the plaintiffs allege, "ducked under a rope marking a permanently closed section of the trail" immediately before the collision. LMRC and Boyne have moved to dismiss the plaintiffs' claims against them, arguing that § 225-A:24, I—which expressly identifies "collisions with other skiers or other persons" as one of the "inherent risks, dangers, or hazards" of skiing—bars those claims.

* * *

The plaintiffs have gamely attempted to pry this suit from the clutches of the Ski Statute's ski area immunity provision by arguing that the provision does not apply where, as here, the suit arises out of injuries caused by a ski area employee who fails to observe the responsibilities the Ski Statute imposes on skiers. This argument, however, cannot be reconciled with the broad language of the statute itself, nor with the case law interpreting it. Plaintiffs' claims against LMRC and Boyne must be dismissed.

* * *

II. Background

On February 3, 2011, the plaintiffs' thirteen-year-old son, "M.H.", was participating in a ski racing program at Loon Mountain. Accompanied by his younger sister, "J.H.", and the head coach for the program, M.H. had skied down the Rampasture trail and was headed, via a crossing trail, to the Coolidge Street trail, where he had helped set up a race course. At the same time, Scott Patterson, a ski instructor employed at Loon Mountain, was snowboarding down the Upper Northstar trail, which intersects with the crossing trail on which M.H. was skiing.

As he approached the area where the two trails intersect, Patterson, without stopping, ducked under a rope closing off a section of the Upper Northstar trail and jumped a lip between the trails. While Susan Hanus watched from her seat on a chair lift above, Patterson struck M.H. in close proximity to J.H. As a result of the collision, M.H. suffered severe injuries, including a concussion and fractured bones in his right arm and leg.

The plaintiffs filed this action against LMRC and Patterson, and shortly thereafter, amended their complaint to add Boyne as a defendant. As amended, the complaint alleges claims against LMRC and Boyne for negligent supervision, negligent operation of a ski area, gross negligence, and respondeat superior; claims against Patterson for negligence and gross negligence; and a claim against all three defendants for negligent infliction of emotional distress. LMRC and Boyne, after answering the complaint, filed the motion at bar. (Patterson has not yet filed any motion seeking to dispose of the claims against him.)

III. Analysis

The Ski Statute "recogniz[es] that the sport of skiing and other ski area activities involve risks and hazards which must be assumed as a matter of law by those engaging in such activities, regardless of all safety measures taken by the ski area operators." Accordingly, the statute—as noted at the outset—contains an immunity provision for ski area operators, providing that:

> Each person who participates in the sport of skiing . . . accepts as a matter of law, the dangers inherent in the sport, * * * include but are not limited to . . . collisions with other skiers or other persons . . . .

As interpreted by the New Hampshire Supreme Court, this provision "mean[s] that a ski area operator owes its patrons no duty to protect them from inherent risks of skiing," and, "[t]o the extent that a skier's injury is caused by an inherent risk of skiing, the skier may not recover from the ski area operator."

* * *

LMRC and Boyne argue that, because the plaintiffs seek to recover for injuries resulting from a collision with another "skier," specifically identified by the statute as one of the inherent risks of skiing, this action falls squarely within the provision—irrespective of Patterson's status as a Loon Mountain employee—and is therefore barred. The plaintiffs, for their part, concede that "under ordinary circumstances," a skier-to-skier collision would constitute an inherent risk of skiing for which they could not recover. * * * They argue, however, that Patterson's collision with M.H. "was not an inherent risk of skiing because Patterson violated the Ski Statute by ducking under a rope and traversing across a delineated, closed-off trail boundary." * * * LMRC and Boyne have the better argument.

Insofar as the Ski Statute provides ski area operators with an immunity limiting plaintiffs' common-law rights, it must be "strictly construed." * * * Here, the "plain and ordinary meaning" of the ski area immunity provision could hardly be clearer: it identifies "collisions with other skiers or other persons" as one of the "risks, dangers, or hazards which the skier . . . assumes as a matter of law." It makes no exception for collisions with skiers who are violating the Ski Statute, nor does it except collisions with ski area employees, even when those employees are themselves violating the Ski Statute or otherwise conducting themselves in a negligent or reckless fashion.

* * *

In an effort to escape this conclusion, the plaintiffs point to case law holding that the Ski Statute does not grant immunity "to ski area operators who breach a statutorily imposed safety responsibility." Section 225-A:24, the plaintiffs note, imposes several safety responsibilities on skiers, which, they say, Patterson breached by his conduct:

- § 225-A:24, III provides that "[e]ach skier . . . shall conduct himself or herself, within the limits of his or her own ability, maintain control of his or her speed and course at all times both on the ground and in the air, while skiing, snowboarding, snow tubing, and snowshoeing heed all posted warnings, and refrain from acting in a manner which may cause or contribute to the injury of himself, herself, or others";
- § 225-A:24, V(c) provides that no skier shall "[e]ngage in any type of conduct which will contribute to cause injury to any other person"; and
- § 225-A:24, V(g) provides that no skier shall "[s]ki or otherwise access terrain outside open and designated ski trails and slopes or beyond ski area boundaries without written permission of said operator or designee."

The plaintiffs maintain that because (in their view) Patterson breached these responsibilities during the scope of his employment at Loon Mountain, LMRC and Boyne may be held vicariously liable for his breaches under the rule noted in the Nutbrown line of cases.

* * *

In arguing that LMRC and Boyne may be held liable for Patterson's breach of those responsibilities, then, the plaintiffs are inviting the court to recognize a basis for liability that finds no footing in either the language of the Ski Statute or the case law interpreting it—and which is, in fact, contrary to the plain language of the statute. As another judge of this court observed when urged to recognize a novel exception to the Ski Statute's ski area immunity provision, "plaintiffs who select a federal forum in preference to an available state forum may not expect the federal court to steer state law into unprecedented configurations."

* * *

For the foregoing reasons, the court concludes that M.H.'s collision with Patterson was an "inherent risk, danger, or hazard" of skiing, despite Patterson's alleged violation of the responsibilities set forth in § 225-A:24. The court is sympathetic to the plaintiffs and their son; the collision was unfortunate and undoubtedly frustrating in that it was caused by a Loon Mountain employee. Because the plaintiffs' injuries resulted from an inherent risk of skiing, however, they "may not maintain an action against" LMRC or Boyne to recover for those injuries.

IV. Conclusion

For the reasons set forth above, the defendants' motion to dismiss the plaintiffs' claims against them is GRANTED. The plaintiffs' claims against Patterson remain pending, as do the counterclaims against the plaintiffs by LMRC and Boyne.
SO ORDERED.
Joseph N. Laplante, United States District Judge
Dated: April 16, 2014

CASES ON THE SUPPLEMENTAL WEBSITE

Rostai v. Neste Enterprises, 2006 Cal. App. LEXIS 476. In this case, both the club and the independent contractor personal trainer were sued for the alleged negligence of the trainer.

Avenoso v. Mangan, 2006 Conn. Super. LEXIS 489. Under agency theory, the agency (the soccer club) is not liable if the agent (the coach) is not negligent. Why, then, didn't the court rule that the soccer club was not liable?

Eastman v. Yutzy, 2001 Mass. Super. LEXIS 157. Note the number of defendants, their positions in the camp, and what the court says about their duties.

B.R. v. Little League Baseball, Inc., 2009 Cal. App. Unpub. LEXIS 7652. Little League Baseball was sued because a minor was molested by a registered sex offender employed by a local little league organization. Discover why Little League Baseball, Inc. was not liable.

Southwick v. City of Rutland, 2011 Vt. LEXIS 51. This case clearly illustrates how liability can be shifted from one business entity to another by an indemnification agreement.

QUESTIONS YOU SHOULD BE ABLE TO ANSWER

1. Under what circumstances is the administrator or supervisor liable for the negligence of employees whom they supervise?

2. When is the corporate entity liable for willful acts by employees?

3. Why is it necessary to determine if a party is an independent contractor or an employee?

4. When an injury results from negligence at an event, which is most likely to be held liable, a financial sponsor, the program sponsor, or a national governing organization? Why?

5. When a teacher is negligent, who is liable, the teacher, the immediate superior of the teacher, or the school district? Explain.

REFERENCES
Cases
Cash v. Six Continents Hotels, 2004 U.S. Dist. LEXIS 2901.
Doe v. Taylor Independent School District, 15 F.3d 443 (Texas 1994).
Glucksman v. Walters, 659 A.2d 1217 (Conn. 1995).
Hanson v. Kynast, 494 N.E.2d 1091 (Ohio 1986).
Hatch v. V.P. Fair Foundation, Inc., 1999 MO. App. LEXIS 315.
In the Matter of Fitness Plus, Inc., 2002 N.Y. App. Div. LEXIS 3830.
Jaeger v. Western Rivers Fly Fisher, 855 F. Supp. 1217 (Utah 1994).
Lautieri v. Bai v. USA Triathlon, Inc., 2003 Mass. Super. LEXIS 290.
Longin v. Kelly, 875 F. Supp. 196 (NY 1995).
Myricks v. Lynnwood Unified School District, 87 Cal. Rptr. 2d 734 (Cal. App. 2 Dist. 1999).
Pelletier v. Bilbiles, 227 A.2d 251 (Conn. 1967).
Riker v. Boy Scouts of America, 183 N.Y.S.2d 484 (1959).
Rogers v. Fred R. Hiller Company of Georgia, Inc., 448 S.E.2d 46 (Ga. 1994).
Santoro v. Unique Vacations Inc., 2015 U.S. Dist. LEXIS 4101.
Southwick v. City of Rutland, 2011 Vt. LEXIS 51.
Stevens v. Payne, 2015 N.Y. Misc. LEXIS 1298.
Townsend v. The State of California, 237 Cal. Rptr. 146 (Cal. 1987).
Universal Gym Equipment, Inc. v. Vic Tanny International, Inc., 526 N.W.2d 5 (Mich. 1994).
Walt Disney World Co. v. Wood, 489 So.2d 61 (1986); 515 So.2d 198 (Fla. 1987).
Williams v. Butler, 577 So.2d 1113 (La. App. 1 Cir. 1991).
Wilson v. United States of America, 989 F.2d 953 (Mo. 1993)

Publications
Carter, P. (1995). Employer's Liability for Assault, Theft, or Similar Intentional Wrong Committed by Employee at Home or Business of Customer, 13 A.L.R.5th 217.
Creason, J. and Dunlap L. Evaluating Employers' Liability for Intentional Torts of Employees. http://www.creasonandaarvig.com/CM/Articles/Articles2.asp
Kaiser, R., & Robinson, K. (1999). Risk Management. In van der Smissen, B., Moiseichik, M., Hartenburg, V., & Twardgik, L. (Eds.). *Management of park and recreation agencies* (pp. 713–741). Ashuba, VA: National Recreation and Parks Association.
Manley, A. (1995). Liability of Charitable Organization Under *Respondeat Superior* Doctrine for Tort of Unpaid Volunteer, 82 *A.L.R.* 3d 1213.
van der Smissen, B. (1990). *Legal liability and risk management for public and private entities*. Cincinnati: Anderson Publishing Co.
van der Smissen, B. (1996). *Legal liability and risk management for public and private entities*. Cincinnati: Anderson Publishing Co. (Prepublication supplement)
van der Smissen, B. (2007). Human Resources Law in Cotten, D. and Wolohan, J. (Eds.) *Law for Recreation and Sport Managers* (4th ed.) Dubuque, Iowa: Kendall-Hunt Publishing Company.

LIABILITY OF SPORTS PARTICIPANTS, INSTRUCTORS, AND OFFICIALS

Doyice J. Cotten | Sport Risk Consulting

Under tort law, when a person is injured due to the negligence or carelessness of another person, the injured party may file a claim for compensation for the injury. If a person slips and falls because of a puddle inside a grocery store, the business may be found liable for damages. If a driver drives carelessly and causes an accident and injury, the driver may be found liable. In other words, under tort law, one may be found liable for one's harmful behavior (see Chapter 2.11 *Negligence*).

In sports activities, however, actions that would be found to be unlawful in daily life may be perfectly acceptable. Examples of this are abundant in sport—ranging from throwing a baseball at a batter or a base runner colliding with the catcher to dislodge the ball to hitting the quarterback long after he has thrown the football. Sometimes the actions are within the rules or are considered part of the game (*Avila v. Citrus Community College District*, 2006). On the other hand, the action is sometimes a violation of the rules and a penalty is prescribed by the rules of the sport. (e.g., hitting the quarterback late incurs a 15 yard penalty).

When the actions of sports participants, sports instructors, and sports officials result in an injury to a sport participant, legal action is sometimes taken by the injured party. Whether the actor is liable for the injury depends upon several factors—the circumstances, the nature of the activity, and the issue to be examined in this chapter – the standard of care the participant, instructor, or official owes the injured party in that state.

The recreation and sport manager should understand that this chapter examines state law and that not only does the required standard of care vary by state, but that within many states the required standard varies by sport or type of activity.[1] The states and cases discussed and listed here provide an explanation of the concepts and how the law differs in various jurisdictions; however, no effort has been made to address the law in every state or for every sport or activity. Therefore, it is important that the recreation and sport manager learn the required standard of care for sports participants, sports instructors, and sports officials in his or her particular state.

FUNDAMENTAL CONCEPTS

Standards of Care

The most common standards of care that determine liability in sports situations are the negligence standard and the recklessness standard. It is important that the recreation and sport manager understand the difference between these two standards.

The **negligence standard** is the standard of care described in Chapter 2.11. This standard requires that the actor (i.e., sports participant, sports instructor, or sports official) protect the participant from unreasonable risk of harm. Under this standard, the actor is held liable for actions reaching the level of ordinary negligence.

---

[1] This variation in state law is illustrated best in the case of golf. In several states, when a golf participant is injured due to the negligence of a co-participant, courts hold the co-participant liable for the injury. However, in a number of other states, the co-participant is not held liable unless the injury resulted from grossly negligent, reckless, or wanton and willful actions of the co-participant. More details regarding liability involving golf participants will be discussed later in this chapter.

This concept is exemplified in an Illinois case (*Novak v. Virene*, 1991) in which a skier struck and injured another skier. The court found that 1) Virene owed his fellow skier a duty of reasonable care; 2) Virene breached that duty by failing to control his momentum while skiing; 3) Novak suffered injury in the collision; and 4) the breach of duty was the cause of the injury. The court ruled that there is no reason to exempt downhill skiers from liability if they negligently collide with other skiers. The court went on to say that many activities in life are fraught with danger, and absent a specific assumption of risk, one may obtain damages when injured by another's negligence.

The other standard of care is the **recklessness standard**. This standard maintains that the actor (i.e., sports participant, sports instructor, or sports official) is not liable for injuries resulting from his or her negligent actions, but is liable only if the injury results from actions that go beyond the scope of ordinary negligence—hence, the term "recklessness standard." Note that while this concept is commonly referred to as the "recklessness standard" in the literature and case law, it would be more accurate to say that the act must exceed ordinary negligence (i.e., gross negligence, recklessness, willful-wanton actions or intentional acts). Refer to the discussion of *Aggravated Negligence* in Chapter 2.11 *Negligence*.

The application of this standard is illustrated in *Mark v. Moser* (2001), an Indiana triathlon case in which Mr. Moser maneuvered his bicycle carelessly and caused a collision of bicycles. Ms. Mark was seriously injured, but was unable to recover damages because the court ruled sports participants assume the risks and recover only if the other participant either intentionally caused the injury or his conduct was so reckless as to be totally outside the range of ordinary activity associated with the sport.

PARTICIPANTS AND CO-PARTICIPANTS

The first issue to be addressed is the standard of care required of participants to co-participants. Under the theory of primary assumption of risk (see Chapter 2.21 *Defenses against Negligence*), a voluntary participant in a sport or recreational activity assumes the risks inherent in the particular activity and, generally, may not recover damages from injuries resulting from those risks. However, when the injury results from risks other than the inherent risks [ordinary negligence or aggravated negligence (recklessness) by a co-participant], liability may attach—depending upon the nature of the sport or activity and the standard of care required in that jurisdiction.

Recklessness Standard for Participants

Most jurisdictions have adopted the **recklessness standard** *for at least some types of activities; this means that a participant is not liable to a co-participant unless he or she was reckless or intended to cause injury.* This standard was first established in Illinois in a case in which a young soccer player recklessly kicked another player in the head (*Nabozny v. Barnhill*, 1975). That court stated that a player is liable if his conduct is either deliberate, willful, or demonstrates a reckless disregard for the safety of a co-participant; this was subsequently referred to as the **contact sports exception** to the negligence rule requiring ordinary care.

Contact Sports, Team Sports, and Competitive Sports

The theory that sports participants in contact, team, and competitive sports (e.g., basketball, football, hockey, lacrosse, karate, softball, horse races, foot races, bicycle races, and others) should be held to the recklessness standard was based on three rationales. 1) First, the heat of competition and the desire to win result in play involving a very high level of intensity. 2) There is the belief that participants in bodily contact and competitive games willingly assume greater risks that do participants in non-physical contact sports – thus justifying a different standard of care depending on the nature of the activity. 3) Finally, it was felt that provisions in the rules of the sport often provide penalties such as ejection from the game, yardage penalties, foul shots, free kicks, yellow cards, and penalty boxes – penalties that might be more appropriate than legal solutions in most instances.

After *Nabozny*, other Illinois courts expanded the contact sports exception to include team practices (*Savino v. Robertson*, 1995), basketball games (*Oswald v. Township High School District No. 214, (1980)* and to unorganized, informal, and sometimes spontaneous sports-related activities such as kick-the-can and killerball (*Pfister v. Shusta*, 1995; *Azzano v. Catholic Bishops of Chicago*, 1999).

Some other jurisdictions applying the recklessness standard include: courts in Louisiana, Missouri, Idaho, Rhode Island, and Virginia to softball (*Picou v. Hartford Ins. Co*, 1990; *Ross v. Clouser*, 1982; *Galloway v. Walker*, 2004: *Kiley v. Patterson*, 2000; *Stephenson v. Redd*, 1990); an Illinois court to a horserace (*Lang v. Silva*, 1999); California, New Mexico, and Nebraska courts to touch football and pick-up football (*Knight v. Jewett*, 1992; *Kabella v. Bouschelle*, 1983; *Dotzler v. Tuttle*, 1990); a Texas court to a polo match (*Connell v. Payne*, 1991); two Connecticut courts to a coed indoor soccer game and to an indoor hockey game in a physical education class (*Jaworski v. Kiernan*, 1997; *Rubbo v. Guilford Board of Education*, 2011); a New Jersey court to karate (*Rosania v. Carmona*, 1998); and a Michigan court to a hockey fight (*Overall v. Kadella*, 1984).

Additionally, a New Jersey court applied the reckless standard in a lacrosse game when the defendant was an 11-year-old competitor (*C.J.R. v. G.A.*, 2011). The Wisconsin Legislature passed a statute (**W.S. 895.525, 4(m)(a)**) requiring the recklessness standard for recreational activities that involve physical contact; that standard was enforced in a subsequent cheerleader case (*Noffke v Bakke*, 2008).

Informal Recreational Activities, Individual Sports, and Non-Contact Sports

In time, a number of states have extended the recklessness standard to include some **informal recreational activities** and some **individual sports and non-contact sports**. The rationale is based on the belief that: 1) the negligence standard would have a chilling effect on participation; 2) the courts may not have the ability to discern what constitutes reasonable conduct in informal sports activity – but egregious conduct would be easily identified; 3) the negligence standard would spur a flood of litigation; and 4) while contact may not be intended, it does often occur.

The New Jersey Supreme Court held that recreational players owe the recklessness standard of care to co-participants in recreational sporting contexts (*Schick v. Ferolito*, 2001). Subsequently, in a New Jersey snowboard injury case, the court held that the recklessness standard generally applied even when the activity involves no direct contact between participants (*Angland v. Mountain Creek Resort, Inc.*, 2011). Additionally, the Iowa Supreme Court and courts in Oklahoma and Texas applied the recklessness standard to paintball and in some, to BB guns (*Leonard v. Behrens*, 1999; *Taylor v. Hesser*, 1998; *Reddell v. Johnson*, 1997; *Moore v. Phi Delta Theta Co.*, 1998). Other examples include: an Ohio court to skiing (*Horvath v. Ish*, 2012); a Michigan court to ice skating (*Ritchie-Gamester v. City of Berkley*, 1999); a New Jersey court to roller skating (*Calhanas v. South Amboy Roller Rink*, 1996); an Iowa court and a Texas court to softball (*Feld v. Borkowski*, 2010; *Dunagan v. Coleman*, 2014).

Although physical contact in golf and tennis is rare, the recklessness standard is sometimes applied. The Ohio Supreme Court was one of the first to apply the recklessness standard to golf (*Thompson v. McNeill*, 1990). Since then other states, including California (*Dilger v. Moyles*, 1997), Texas (*Allen v. Donath*, 1994); Indiana (*Gyuriak v. Millice*, 2002); and Massachusetts (*Mangone v. Pickering*, 1997) have also applied the recklessness standard to golf. Courts in at least two states have applied the recklessness standard to tennis – Kentucky and New Jersey (*Hoke v. Cullinan*, 1995; *Schick v. Ferolito*, 1999). California courts used the standard for sailing and figure skating (*Stimson v. Carlson*, 1992; *Staten v. Superior Court*, 1996).

Courts in the various states have sound rationales for their decisions to apply the recklessness standard. Nevertheless, a seemingly reasonable argument against that standard is that it leaves the injured participant unable to recover for the negligent or careless actions of a co-participant. The recklessness standard provides the co-participant with less incentive to take care in his or her contact with others.

Effect of Negligence as an Inherent Risk. Courts in some jurisdictions have ruled that certain "negligent acts" (or actions generally considered negligent actions) are an "inherent risk" in some activities. The California Supreme Court (*Knight v. Jewett*, 1992) examined a case in which a number of acquaintances at a Super Bowl party played an informal game of touch football during halftime. A young woman was injured when a man jumped for a ball and came down on her causing injury. The court stated that participants have "a duty to use due care not to increase the risks to a participant over and above those inherent in the sport." The court went on to say that *careless conduct of others is sometimes treated as an inherent risk of the activity* and bars recovery (p. 315–316). *In other words, some negligent actions by participants in sports and recreational activities can be considered an inherent risk*—resulting in no participant liability. The court ruled in favor of the defendant stating that a participant in an active sport breaches his or her duty to co-participants only if the participant intentionally injures the co-participant or engages in reckless conduct that is outside the range of the ordinary activity of the sport (i.e., the recklessness standard).

The ruling in a West Virginia horseracing case clearly illustrates participant error can be an inherent risk of activity (*Santiago v. Clark*, 1978). Santiago cut his horse in front of Clark's horse causing a fall. The court stated that horseracing is a perilous sport marked by a 100 pound jockey attempting to maneuver a 1000 pound horse through traffic at full speed. The court went on to say that jockey error is commonplace and is an inherent risk in the sport, ruling that there can be no recovery for "jockey error" and "careless riding" (negligence) in horseracing.

Negligence Standard for Participants

While the recklessness standard has been adopted for at least some activities in most states, the negligence standard is still supported to some extent in a number of jurisdictions. Courts in those jurisdictions feel that participants, like others, owe co-participants a duty of reasonable care.

Negligence Standard for all Activities

While a number of jurisdictions apply the negligence standard to one or more sports, at least five states seem to apply the standard to participants in all sport and recreational activities. The Nevada Supreme Court, in a case in which the defendant's horse kicked and injured the plaintiff, established the negligence standard for all recreational injury cases stating:

> The negligence standard is sufficiently flexible to accommodate liability issues underlying all recreational injury cases. There is no reduction in the defendant's standard of care (e.g., reckless or intentional), nor is there any fictitious undertaking that the defendant does not owe a duty to the plaintiff (*Auckenthaler v. Grundmeyer*, 1994, p. 16).

The court stated that "Within the factual climate of recreational activities or even sporting events, the question posed is whether the defendant participated in a reasonable manner and within the rules of the game or in accordance with the ordinary scope of the activity." (p. 16)

A Tennessee appellate court (*Becksfort v. Jackson*, 1996) examined the issue of the required standard of care that a participant owed a co-participant in a tennis case. The court disagreed with the reasoning in *Knight* that use of the negligence standard would stifle competition and result in more lawsuits. The court thought that the public would recognize that the reasonableness of one's conduct will be measured differently on the playing field than in non-sport situations. The court further stated that a different standard of care for each sport is not needed because Tennessee courts will recognize that the reasonable conduct standard of care should be determined in context with the sport.

An Arizona appellate court (*Estes v. Tripson*, 1997) declined to vary from the general negligence standard. The case involved a softball base runner stepping on the leg of a catcher. The court held that the base runner did not breach a duty to the catcher and was not negligent.

Likewise, the Supreme Court of New Hampshire (*Allen v. Dover*, 2002) refused to adopt the recklessness standard in a coed slow-pitch softball case. The court applied the negligence standard stating "We believe that the negligence standard, properly understood and applied, is suitable for recreational athletic activities because" participant conduct is measured against the conduct of a reasonable participant, under similar circumstances. (p. 21)

Both South Dakota courts and legislature have acted to establish the negligence standard. The legislature has enacted **SDCL § 20-9-1** mandating the negligence standard; courts have rejected attempts to lessen the standard to recklessness in a skiing case (*Rantapaa v. Black Hills Chair Lift Co.*, 2001).

Negligence Standard for Non-competitive, Non-contact Recreational Activities

Courts in some jurisdictions have held that the recklessness standard should not apply to some **non-competitive, non-contact recreational activities** (e.g., skiing, badminton, fishing, bowling), reasoning that the assumed risks in those activities are not created by participant negligence, but by the nature of the activity. In this type of activity, the possibility of a lawsuit for participant negligence would not place a damper on participation (*Cruz v. Gloss*, 2002).

The following is a sample of states that have adopted the negligence standard for a selected activity or activities. In a Colorado case, the U.S. Court of Appeals applied the negligence standard when the activity was skiing (*LaVine v. Clear Creek Skiing Corp*, 1977). In addition, the **Colorado Ski Safety Act 33-44-109(2)** provides that the skier has a duty to avoid collisions; a collision with another skier is not an inherent or assumed risk. Negligence was also the standard in skiing cases in New York, Illinois, and Utah (*Duncan v. Kelly*, 1998; *Novak v. Virene*, 1991; *Ricci v. Schoultz*, 1998). Likewise, courts in Illinois, Massachusetts, and New York applied the negligence standard in golf cases (*Zurla v. Hydel*, 1997; *Orth v. Novelli*, 1997; *Jackson v. Livingston Country Club, Inc.*, 1977). Also regarding golf, the Virginia Supreme Court held that "the basic rule of law applicable to golfers is that a player upon a golf course must exercise reasonable care in playing the game to prevent injury to others" (*Thurston Metals & Supply Co. v. Taylor*, 1986, p. 3).

The negligence standard was also applied to the following activities: a Missouri court to bowling (*Gamble v. Bost*, 1995); a Michigan court to fishing (*Williams v. Wood*, 1932); and a New Mexico court to roughhousing (*Yount v. Johnson*, 1996). Motorized activities have also been held to the negligence standard: an Indiana court to jet skiing (*Davis v. LeCuyer*, 2006) and a Michigan court to watercraft, snowmobiles, and all-terrain vehicles (*Allred v Broekuis*, 2007).

SPORTS INSTRUCTORS AND SPORTS OFFICIALS

Injuries to sports participants sometimes result from actions of sports instructors (e.g., coaches, teachers, personal trainers, aerobics instructors, tennis pros, trip leaders) or actions by the sports officials (e.g., referees, umpires) handling the contest. Sports instructors and officials have a number of duties or obligations to the participant (e.g., supervision, provide safety equipment, to provide a relatively safe environment) (see Chapter 2.34 *Supervision* and Chapter 2.31 *Premises Liability*).

Negligence Standard

For these types of duties or obligations, sports instructors and sports officials generally owe a duty of reasonable care to those whom they teach, coach, or officiate. Both the sports instructor and the sports official can be legally liable if he or she breaches a duty or obligation and that breach results in an injury. For example, a gymnastics coach can be unfocused and fail to adequately spot an athlete; a fist fight resulting in injury may occur when an instructor leaves the class unsupervised; or a football referee may contribute to an injury by failing to curb violent acts. Each of these might be found negligent in the event of a lawsuit.

In *Everett v. Warren* (1978), the coach supplied a player with a defective helmet. In 1997, a school and its coaches were sued when a pole vaulter was injured in an unsafe pit while using a pole that was too light for his weight (*Moose v. Massachusetts Institute of Technology*). In *Lautieri v. Bae* (2003), triathlon organizers were sued alleging negligent course layout, signage, and supervision. In each of these cases, the negligence standard was applied and the coaches and schools were held liable.

A New York appellate court case (*Parisi v. Harpursville Central School District*, 1990) illustrates coach liability for failure to provide reasonable care. The coach, with two catcher's masks available, failed to suggest or require a second baseman to wear a mask when she volunteered to catch a pitcher considered to be an expert in high-velocity pitching. A handbook issued by the State Public High School Athletic Association governing interscholastic modified sports programs required that any player warming up a pitcher, on or off the fields, wear protective equipment. Plaintiff sued alleging negligence by the coach in failing to use reasonable care in supervision and in failing to provide protective equipment. The court upheld the lower court ruling denying summary judgment and remanded the case for trial to determine negligence.

The law is quite clear and consistent among states regarding sports instructor and sports official liability when he or she has breached a duty or obligation. However, the law regarding the liability of sports instructors and sports officials varies from state to state when the situation involves errors in judgment by the instructor or official. At issue is whether the instructor or official should be held to the negligence standard or to the recklessness standard.

Recklessness Standard (for judgment errors)

In the course of instructing, leading a group, coaching, or officiating, sports instructors and sports officials sometimes make errors in judgment. A guide leading a wilderness hike can misjudge the environmental conditions, the terrain to be covered, or the fitness of the participants; a coach can err in evaluating the capability of a participant and urge or "push" a participant to exert greater effort to improve performance or continue the activity. These errors can result in injury to the participant. In some jurisdictions, courts would construe these actions to constitute negligence on the part of the guide or coach; in other jurisdictions, these same acts are considered inherent risks of the activity and the instructor or coach is not liable. In effect, these latter jurisdictions are applying the recklessness standard to these judgment-related errors

As mentioned above, California courts were the ground-breakers in defining actions involving errors in judgment by sports instructors and officials as an inherent risk (*Knight*, 1992). The California Supreme Court said that one typically has a duty to use due care to avoid injury to others, but that in sport, actions that would usually be deemed as dangerous are often an integral part of the sport itself. Hence, *Knight* says it is important to consider the nature of the sport when defining the duty of care owed. *Knight* states that defendants generally have no duty to eliminate risks inherent in the sport, but *do have a duty to not increase the risks above those inherent in the sport*. Since instructor or official misjudgment of conditions or capacity of the participant is considered an inherent risk of some activities—and the instructor or coach has no duty to eliminate inherent risks—no liability is incurred for such judgment errors by the instructor or coach in those activities.

In *Bushnell v. Japanese-American Religious and Cultural Center* (1996), the court stated that sport instruction often involves challenging or "pushing" the athlete to attempt new and more difficult tasks. It went on to say *that the athlete's failure to meet the challenge is an inherent risk in learning a sport and to impose a duty to mitigate the inherent risks could have a chilling effect on teaching a sport*. Subsequently, in a California case involving ski instruction (*Kane v. National Ski Patrol System, Inc.*, 2001), a California appellate court held that *instructor errors, whether judging skill level or difficulty of conditions, are within the range of ordinary activity involved in a sport*. In *Kahn v. East Side Union High School Dist.* (2003), the California Supreme court expanded its prior ruling in *Knight* stating that "... *the risks associated with learning a sport may themselves be inherent risks of the sport*, and that an instructor or coach generally does not increase the risk of harm inherent in learning the sport simply by urging the student to strive to excel or to reach a new level of competence." (p.115) [Emphasis added] The court went on to conclude

> ... a sports instructor may be found to have breached a duty of care to a student or athlete only if the instructor intentionally injures the student or engages in conduct that is reckless in the sense that it is 'totally outside the range of the ordinary activity' involved in teaching or coaching the sport. (p.107)

Other California court rulings holding to this recklessness standard include: A tae kwon do drill in *Rodrigo v. Koryo Martial Arts* (2002); using a wild pitcher at twilight in *Balthazor v. Little League Baseball, Inc.* (1988); and urging aggressive play at football practice in *Fortier v. Los Rios Community College Dist.* (1996). A court in Maryland supported the concept that errors can be inherent risks in a negligent coaching claim (*Kelly v. McCarrick*, 2004). The recklessness standard was also applied in a horseback riding case under Wyoming law (*Cooperman v. David*, 2000). Cooperman was injured and sued alleging wrangler error (ordinary negligence) in failing to adequately tighten the cinch. The court relied on the Wyoming Sport Safety Act **W.S.A 1-1-123(b)** which provides that a loose cinch is an inherent risk of horseback riding because cinching a horse is a matter of judgment and the horse will sometimes be cinched incorrectly (negligently).

The Ohio Supreme Court ruled that "... before a party may proceed with a cause of action involving injury resulting from a recreational or sports activity, reckless or intentional conduct must exist" (*Marchetti v. Kalish*, 1990. (p. 99–100) An Ohio appellate court subsequently applied the recklessness standard for a soccer referee who was sued following an injury caused by one player kicking another (*Kline v. OID Assocs., Inc.*, 1992).

Courts in two states, Massachusetts and Connecticut, ruled in favor of the recklessness standard regarding allegations that the coaches failed in preventing dangerous conduct by their players. In *Kavanaugh v. Trustees of Boston University* (2003), the plaintiff claimed the coach was negligent in failing to take steps to prevent his player from punching the plaintiff. In *Trujillo v. Yeager* (2009), the plaintiff alleged that the coach failed to educate or train his player to participate in a match after a relatively inexperienced player caused an injury.

The *Geiersbach v. Frieje* (2004) court defined *"participant" to include all participants in the sporting event or practice, including players, coaches, and players who are on the bench* [emphasis added]. The court went on to say that the participant should not be able to recover from the player, team, or stadium without proving recklessness or intent. So "participant" would include coaches, and probably officials as well. In determining the law in your state, it would be important to first determine how the courts define "participant" in a sport activity. It may well be that many more states classify sports instructors and sports officials as participants.

Immunity Statutes

Another factor that affects the required standard of care is state immunity statutes. For instance, almost every state legislature has enacted legislation to help protect selected recreation and sport providers from liability for injuries resulting from the inherent risks and/or the ordinary negligence of the provider. Many of these raise the standard of care to recklessness. Statutes relating to equestrian activities, skating, and skiing are the most common, but some states have statutes relating to activities such as motor sports, fishing, outfitters, sport shooting, and snowmobiling (see Chapter 2.22 *Immunity*).

In addition, more than 20 state legislatures have enacted volunteer immunity statutes specifically for coaches and sports officials in amateur sports (see Chapter 2.22 *Immunity*). While these statutes vary somewhat, they generally provide protection from liability for ordinary negligence—thus, in effect, requiring the recklessness standard. Some states with these statutes include: Arkansas, Colorado, Delaware, Georgia, Hawaii, Indiana, Illinois, Kansas, Louisiana, Maryland, Massachusetts, Minnesota, Mississippi, Nevada, New Hampshire, New Jersey, New Mexico, North Dakota, Oklahoma, Pennsylvania, Rhode Island, Tennessee, and Texas.

It is important to note that these statutes vary in wording, effectiveness, and in which parties are protected, but most do provide some protection for the coach and official in amateur sport.

Negligence Standard (for judgment errors)

While California and a number of other jurisdictions hold sports instructors and sports officials to the recklessness standard in certain circumstances, many states continue to apply the negligence standard—holding instructors and officials liable for injuries to sports participants resulting from negligence by an instructor or official.

New York's highest court, The Court of Appeals, ruled that the board of education and its employees (which would include coaches and referees) must exercise ordinary reasonable care to protect student athletes in extracurricular activities "from unassumed, concealed, or unreasonably increased risks" (*Benitez v. New York City Board of Education*, 1989).

The New Hampshire Supreme Court failed to grant coaches and referees discretionary immunity on decisions made during a contest (*Hacking v. Town of Belmont*, 1999). The court stated that forcing an individual to bear the loss caused by the negligence of a municipal employee is against the basic principles of equality and ordinary justice. Both coaches and referees were held to the negligence standard.

A South Dakota gymnast sued her coach when injured after attempting a move 30 times in one practice session (*Wilson v. O'Gorman High School*, 2008). The court ruled that to succeed, she had to show that the coach failed to use reasonable care. The court ruled that there was no reason to adopt a different standard from the negligence standard set forth by statute (**S.D. § 20-9-1**).

A Massachusetts court, in a case in which the field hockey coach was alleged to have failed to have the girl evaluated after a head injury, ruled that a coach is held to the negligence standard (*Dugan v. Thayer Academy*, 2015). The court stated that a coach has to exercise the standard of care of a reasonably prudent coach.

Carabba v. Anacortes School District, No. 103 (1967), in Washington State, involved a case in which a serious injury occurred while the wrestling referee was momentarily distracted. The appellate court adhered to the negligence standard.

In *Hearon v. May* (1995), the Nebraska Supreme Court examined an injury that occurred when a participant was injured while wrestling with a referee who was coaching the plaintiff in a wrestling move. The court affirmed the recklessness standard for participant to co-participant injuries, but held that

> ... instructors, teachers, and coaches are liable for injuries sustained by an instructee if such injuries are received by the instructee while the instructor, teacher, or coach engages in physical contact with the instructee and the instructee's injuries are the proximate result of the ordinary negligence of the instructor, teacher, or coach. p. 15

The court held ordinary negligence to be the proper cause of action when negligent supervision or negligent instruction is involved in a sporting activity. In a subsequent case involving actions taken following an injury, the Nebraska Supreme Court stated that the standard of care required of coaches is that of the reasonably prudent person holding a Nebraska teaching certificate with a coaching endorsement (*Cerny v. Cedar Bluffs Junior/Senior Public School*, 2001).

Those advocating the negligence standard hold that the sports instructor or official has a duty to participants to act reasonably; and if a failure to do so results in injury, he/she should be held liable. They feel that in the case of a charge of negligence against the instructor or official, the law will determine if the instructor or official acted as a reasonable and prudent person would have acted in similar circumstances.

SIGNIFICANT CASE

The injured athlete (Trujillo) filed suit against the opposing athlete (Yeager) who caused the injury, the coach of the opposing athlete (Pilger), and the school of the opposing athlete (Trinity College). This Connecticut case quickly establishes that the standard of care one athlete owes another is the recklessness standard. The focus, however, is the determination of the standard of care owed to athletes by their coaches. The reader should note the importance of precedent from the Connecticut Supreme Court as well as from decisions of the sister state of Massachusetts.

TRUJILLO V. YEAGER
United States District Court for the District of Connecticut
642 F. Supp. 2d 86; 2009 U.S. Dist. LEXIS 111055

OPINION BY:

Janet C. Hall

Plaintiff Kevin Trujillo brings this action against defendants Philip Yeager a/k/a Phil Yeager, Trinity College, and Michael Pilger. Trujillo alleges that he was severely injured during an NCAA Division III men's varsity soccer match between his team, Coast Guard Academy, and Trinity College. He alleges that Yeager, acting with negligence and recklessness, caused him severe injury during the course of the game. He alleges that Pilger, Yeager's coach, and Trinity College, where Yeager was a student and Pilger was employed, acted with negligence in failing to train or educate Yeager and in allowing an inadequately trained and educated player to participate in the match when defendants reasonably should have known that injury to other players would result. Pending before the court is defendant Yeager's Motion to Dismiss Count One, and defendants Pilger and Trinity College's Motion to Dismiss Count Three.

I. STANDARD OF REVIEW
* * *

II. FACTUAL BACKGROUND
* * *

On or about September 12, 2006, Trujillo and Yeager were playing in a soccer match between the Coast Guard Academy and Trinity College. During the game, Trujillo was struck in the head by Yeager. According to Trujillo's allegations, Yeager was careless and negligent, as well as reckless, in using force against Trujillo. Trujillo also alleges that Trinity College and Pilger were negligent in failing to properly train and educate Yeager, and in allowing an inadequately trained and educated player to participate in the soccer match when they knew or reasonably should have known that injury to other players would result.

As a result of defendants' negligence, and defendant Yeager's recklessness, Trujillo suffered serious and debilitating injuries, some or all of which may be permanent.

Trujillo has incurred medical expenses and may incur similar expenditures in the future. Trujillo has suffered lost wages and an impairment of his ability to earn income.

III. DISCUSSION

A. Yeager's Motion to Dismiss Count One

Yeager has moved to dismiss Count One on the grounds that he cannot be held liable in negligence for injuries caused in the course of a competitive contact sport. Yeager relies on the Connecticut Supreme Court's decision in Jaworski v. Kiernan, 241 Conn. 399, 696 A.2d 332 (1997). Trujillo has not filed an opposition to Yeager's Motion.

In Jaworski, the Connecticut Supreme Court analyzed the duty owed among adult coparticipants in team contact sports. Id. Jaworski, like the instant case, involved an adult soccer match. In analyzing the facts of that case, the court engaged in an extensive policy discussion about the tension between promoting vigorous athletic competition and protecting those who participate. It noted that the vast majority of states have adopted an intentional or reckless standard of care for injuries occurring during athletic contests. Ultimately, the court concluded that "a participant in an athletic contest [may] . . . maintain an action against a coparticipant only for reckless or intentional conduct and not for merely negligent conduct."

Trujillo's Count One is a negligence count against Yeager, Trujillo's coparticipant in the adult soccer match. Jaworski squarely forecloses Trujillo's ability to recover from Yeager merely upon proof of negligence. Accordingly, Yeager's Motion to Dismiss is GRANTED, and Count One, Trujillo's negligence count against Yeager, is DISMISSED.

B. Pilger and Trinity College's Motion to Dismiss Count Three

Defendants Pilger and Trinity College (hereinafter "the Trinity defendants") have moved to dismiss Count Three on the grounds that they cannot be held liable in negligence for injuries sustained by Trujillo. The Trinity defendants acknowledge that Connecticut courts have not explicitly addressed the issue of whether a negligence cause of action is available to injured players against non-participants such as coaches, but contend that Jaworski's reasoning and logic is equally applicable to claims against non-participants. They also rely upon cases from other jurisdictions, particularly the Massachusetts case of Kavanagh v. Trustees of Boston University, 440 Mass. 195, 795 N.E.2d 1170 (2003), which have held that a plaintiff injured while playing a competitive contact sport must allege reckless or intentional conduct to hold a non-participant defendant liable. The facts of Kavanagh are quite similar to this case. In Kavanagh, the plaintiff alleged that the university and its coach were negligent in not taking steps to prevent the plaintiff from being punched by an opposing player during a scuffle during an intercollegiate basketball game.

* * *

Restatement (2d) of Torts § 442B; Stewart, 234 Conn. at 607-08. Trujillo contends that, under this rule, the coach may be held liable in negligence for Yeager's intentional act, provided that the injury is reasonably foreseeable in relation to the coach's conduct. That is, Trujillo contends that he need only adequately plead that Yeager's conduct was of the type that would naturally flow from a failure to properly train and supervise him.

Trujillo also seeks to distinguish Kavanagh. Trujillo notes that the assault in that case occurred outside the course of ordinary play, and that special training need not be provided to keep players from punching an opponent in a scuffle, because such behavior is obviously not permitted. He seeks to distinguish that assault from dangerous play within the course of the game, the avoidance of which may be aided by proper coaching. Second, and relatedly, Trujillo contends that criminal conduct in the course of collegiate basketball play (the punch) is not within the scope of foreseeability, as distinguished from the dangerous play resulting from the failure to train players to abide by the NCAA rules on safe play.

This court's task is to determine whether the Connecticut Supreme Court would extend Jaworski to encompass the facts of Trujillo's claims against the Trinity defendants. In doing so, this court must apply the standards set out in Jaworski itself for determining whether a duty arises in this situation.

In Jaworski, in analyzing duty, the Connecticut Supreme Court first conducted a threshold inquiry of whether the harm to the plaintiff was foreseeable. Concluding that it was, the court then considered four factors in determining the extent of a co-participant's responsibility:

(1) the normal expectations of participants in the sport in which the plaintiff and the defendant were engaged; (2) the public policy of encouraging continued vigorous participation in recreational sporting activities while weighing the safety of the participants; (3) the avoidance of increased litigation; and (4) the decisions of other jurisdictions.

This court, similarly, first turns to the foreseeability inquiry. Determining foreseeability requires analyzing whether "a reasonable person in the defendant's position, knowing what he knew or should have known, would have anticipated the harm that resulted from his actions." Certainly the injury could have been anticipated. * * * Although the defendants in Count Three are a coach and college rather than the opposing player, a coach can reasonably foresee that negligent training of player might result in injuries of the type that occurred in this case. On the facts pled, the court concludes that the injury was foreseeable.

As to the factors beyond the foreseeability inquiry, the Connecticut Supreme Court made clear in <u>Jaworski</u> that the normal and reasonable expectations of participants in contact team sports include the potential for injuries, that utilizing simple negligence as the standard of care for athletic contests would lead to a flood of undesirable litigation, and that a majority of other jurisdictions have adopted a reckless or negligence standard of care for athletic contests. It expressed its concern that liability for simple negligence would have the effect of dampening enthusiasm for competition or participation in sporting activities for fear of liability. Similar concerns are present in Count Three against the Trinity defendants. Trujillo, like the plaintiff in Jaworski, had a normal and reasonable expectation that injuries might occur. Holding coaches liable for negligence in training athletes under their care who recklessly or intentionally injure other individuals could dampen coaches' willingness to aggressively coach their athletes. At the level of organized, intercollegiate sports conducted under the auspices of the NCAA, a system of rules and discipline exists to control the behavior of coaches and players alike. To impose an overlay of liability in tort for simple negligence over this internal system of regulation would run the risk of undermining that system and creating the flood of unwarranted litigation that the Connecticut Supreme Court was eager to avoid.

Furthermore, as Jaworski's fourth factor makes clear, the Connecticut Supreme Court has specifically looked in this context to the decisions of other jurisdictions. In other situations, as well, that court has looked to the decisions of the Massachusetts Supreme Judicial Court. Therefore, the Supreme Judicial Court's precedent in Kavanagh, while not binding, is highly persuasive on how the Connecticut Supreme Court might rule on the issue of coaches' liability.

* * *

Trujillo has alleged that Pilger failed to properly train and educate Yeager, and that Pilger allowed Yeager, an inadequately trained and educated player, to participate in the soccer match. While not identical to an allegation that Pilger encouraged Yeager to play aggressively, the court finds Trujillo's efforts to distinguish Kavanagh unconvincing. Both the injuries in Kavanagh and in the instant case occurred at the hand of an opposing player during the heat of the game, and in both cases, the injured parties sought to hold the coach of the opposing player and that coach's employer liable. Whether the injury was inflicted by an opposing player during an in-game fight "outside the course of ordinary play," as opposed to the negligent behavior of an opposing player during the heat of competition, holding coaches liable in negligence, particularly to players on a different college's team, would unreasonably threaten to chill competitive play. Moreover, as the Kavanagh court points out, "[u]nder the rules of any sport, fouls or other violations carry their own penalties, and it is up to the officials refereeing the competition to enforce those rules and impose those penalties." The obligation is not on the coaches. This is particularly true in the context of intercollegiate or professional competition, which employ a professional staff of referees, as compared with the recreational competition at issue in Jaworski.

Lastly, the court must address plaintiff's contention that the Connecticut Supreme Court would apply Stewart to find a cause of action in this case. This court concludes that, with regard to injuries sustained in athletic competition, the Connecticut Supreme Court would look to its precedent in Jaworski and the decisions of other states regarding injuries sustained in athletic contests, rather than applying the more generic Restatement standard. Given that Jaworski, and the decisions of sister states, militate strongly against permitting negligence claims to redress injuries sustained by participants in adult contact sports, this court concludes that the Connecticut Supreme Court would find that the appropriate standard of care to be imposed on coaches for injuries caused by their players is one of reckless or intentional conduct.

As to Trinity College, Trujillo seeks to hold it liable as the employer of Pilger and for its own failure to train and educate Yeager. The allegations against Trinity College are identical to those against Pilger and fail for the same reasons. Because the college acts, in effect, through the coach in training or educating players, allowing negligence claims against colleges for a coach's failure to adequately train or educate a player would allow plaintiffs to evade the policy of not allowing negligence claims against coaches for injuries caused by their players. Accordingly, Pilger and Trinity College's Motion to Dismiss is GRANTED, and Count Three is DISMISSED.

SO ORDERED.

Dated this 19th day of May, 2009, at Bridgeport, Connecticut.

/s/ Janet C. Hall
Janet C. Hall
United [**17] States District Judge

CASES ON THE SUPPLEMENTAL WEBSITE

Kline v. OID Associates, Inc., 1992 Ohio App. LEXIS 2371. The Ohio court ruled that participant liability is possible only if there is reckless or intentional misconduct; and applied this rule to non-participants involved in the game (coaches, officials).

Kahn v. East Side Union High School District, 2003 Cal. LEXIS 6373. Look particularly at the duty of the sports instructor and under what circumstance the instructor is liable for injuries to students.

Thompson v. McNeill, 1990 Ohio LEXIS 341. In this case, the Ohio Supreme Court expresses reasoning to justify the application of the recklessness standard to a non-contact sport.

Auckenthaler v. Grundmeyer, 1994 Nev. LEXIS 87. The Nevada Supreme Court adopted the negligence standard in this ruling stating that the negligence standard is sufficiently flexible to accommodate liability issues underlying all recreational injury cases.

Karas v. Strevell, 2008 Ill.LEXIS 284. The Illinois Supreme Court applied the contact sports exception in a recent ice hockey contest.

QUESTIONS YOU SHOULD BE ABLE TO ANSWER

1. Explain the difference between "negligence standard" and "recklessness standard."
2. What is meant by the term "contact sports exception?"
3. What is the rationale for having a different standard for contact sports and non-contact sports?
4. Under what circumstances might a coach not be liable for his or her ordinary negligence?
5. In the Significant Case, what standard of care was applied for participants? For coaches? For schools?

REFERENCES
Cases

Allen v. Donath, 1994 Tex. App. LEXIS 816.
Allen v. Dover, 2002 N.H. LEXIS 145.
Allred v Broekuis, 2007 U.S. Dist. LEXIS 77457.
Angland v. Mountain Creek Resort, Inc., 2013 N.J. LEXIS 570.
Auckenthaler v. Grundmeyer, 1994 Nev. LEXIS 87.
Avila v. Citrus Community College District, 131 P.3d 383 (2006).
Azzano v. Catholic Bishop of Chicago, 1999 Ill. App. LEXIS 195.
Balthazor v. Little League Baseball, Inc., 1998 Cal. App. LEXIS 194.
Barry v. Ishpeming-Nice Community Schools, 2005 Mich. App. LEXIS 2818.
Becksfort v. Jackson, 1996 Tenn. App. LEXIS 257.
Benitez v. New York City Board of Education, 1989 N.Y. LEXIS 662.
Bushnell v. Japanese-American Religious and Cultural Center, 1996 Cal. App. LEXIS 216.
Calhanas v. South Amboy Roller Rink, 1996 N.J. Super. LEXIS 306.
Carabba v. Anacortes School District, 1967 Wash. LEXIS 880.
Cerney v. Cedar Bluffs Junior/Senior Public School, 2004 Neb. LEXIS 80.
C.J.R. v. G.A., 2014 N.J. Super. LEXIS 165
Connell v. Payne, 1991 Tex. App. LEXIS 2347.
Cooperman v. David, 214 F.3d 1162.
Cruz v. Gloss, 2002 Pa. Dist. & Cnty. Dec. LEXIS 140.
Davis v. LeCuyer, 2006 Ind. App. LEXIS 1203.
Dilger v. Moyles, 1997 Cal. App. LEXIS 380.
Dotzler v. Tuttle, 1990 Neb. LEXIS 1.
Dugan v. Thayer Academy, 2015 Mass. Super. LEXIS 59.
Dunagan v. Coleman, 2014 Tex. App. LEXIS 3712.
Duncan v. Kelly, 1998 N.Y. App. Div. LEXIS 4515.
Estes v. Tripson, 1997 Ariz. App. LEXIS 24.
Everett v. Warren, 1978 Mass. LEXIS 1123.
Feld v. Borkowski, 2010 Iowa Sup. LEXIS 102.
Fortier v. Los Rios Community College Dist., 1996 Cal. App. LEXIS 441.
Galloway v. Walker, 2004 Ida. App. LEXIS 89.
Gamble v. Bost, 1995 Mo. App. LEXIS 789.
Geiersbach v. Frieje, 2004 Ind. App. LEXIS 757.
Gyuriak v. Millice, 2002 Ind. App. LEXIS 1586.
Hacking v. Town of Belmont, 1999 N.H. LEXIS 42.
Hearon v. May, 1995 Neb. LEXIS 229.
Hoke v. Cullinan, 1995 Ky. LEXIS 140.
Horvath v. Ish, 2012 Ohio LEXIS 2872.

Jackson v. Livingston Country Club, Inc., 1977 N.Y. App. Div. LEXIS 10401.
Jaworski v. Kiernan, 1997 Conn. LEXIS 182.
Kabella v. Bouschelle, 1983 N.M. App. LEXIS 791.
Kahn v. East Side Union High School Dist., 2003 Cal. LEXIS 6373.
Kane v. National Ski Patrol System, 2001 Cal. App. LEXIS 254.
Kavanaugh v. Trustees of Boston University, 795 NE 2d 1170, (2003).
Kelly v. McCarrick, 2004 Md. App. LEXIS 13.
Kiley v. Patterson, 2000 R.I. LEXIS 246.
Kline v. OID Assocs., Inc., 1992 Ohio App. LEXIS 2371.
Knight v. Jewett, 1992 Cal. LEXIS 3969.
Lang v. Silva, 1999 Ill. App. LEXIS 543.
Lautieri v. Bae, 2003 Mass. Super. LEXIS 290.
Leonard v. Behrens, 1999 Iowa Sup. LEXIS 255.
LaVine v. Clear Creek Skiing Corp., 1977 U.S. App. LEXIS 12808.
Mangone v. Pickering, 1997 Mass. Super. LEXIS 458.
Marchetti v. Kalish, 1990 Ohio LEXIS 342.
Mark v. Moser, 2001 Ind. App. LEXIS 671.
Moore v. Phi DeltaTheta Co., 1998 Tex. App. LEXIS 2676.
Moose v. Massachusetts Institute of Technology, 1997 Mass. App. LEXIS 189.
Nabozny v. Barnhill, 1975 Ill. App. LEXIS 2772.
Noffke v. Bakke, 2009 Wisc. LEXIS 5.
Novak v. Virene, 1991 Ill. App. LEXIS 2194.
Orth v. Novelli, 1997 Mass. Super. LEXIS 119.
Oswald v. Township, 1980 Ill. App. LEXIS 2962.
Overall v. Kadella, 1984 Mich. App. LEXIS 3019.
Parisi v. Harpursville Central School District, 1990 N.Y. App. Div. LEXIS 3756.
Pfister v. Shusta, 1995 Ill. LEXIS 201.
Picou v. Hartford Ins. Co., 1990 La. App. LEXIS 663.
Rantapaa v. Black Hills Chair Lift Co., 633 N.W.2d 196 (S.D. 2001).
Reddell v. Johnson, 1997 Okla. LEXIS 82.
Ricci v. Schoultz, 1998 Utah App. LEXIS 57.
Ritchie-Gamester v. City of Berkley, 1999 Mich. LEXIS 2060
Rodrigo v. Koryo Martial Arts, 2002 Cal. App. LEXIS 4462.
Rosania v. Carmona, 1998 N.J. Super. LEXIS 93.
Ross v. Clouser, 1982 Mo. LEXIS 403.
Rubbo v. Guilford Board of Education, 2011 Conn. Super. LEXIS 1811.
Santiago v. Clark, 1978 U.S. Dist. LEXIS 20322.
Savino v. Robertson, 1995 Ill. App. LEXIS 480.
Schick v. Ferolito, 2001 N.J. LEXIS 186.
Staten v. Superior Court, 1996 Cal. App. LEXIS 498.
Stephenson v. Redd, 1990 Va. Cir. LEXIS 466.
Stimson v. Carlson, 1992 Cal. App. LEXIS 1469
Taylor v. Hesser, 1998 Okla. Civ. App. LEXIS 120.
Thompson v. McNeill, 1990 Ohio LEXIS 341.
Trujillo v. Yeager, 2009 U.S. Dist. LEXIS 111055.
Thurston Metals & Supply Co. v. Taylor, 1986 Va. LEXIS 149.
Williams v. Woods, 1932 Mich. LEXIS 1121.
Wilson v. O'Gorman High School, 2008 U.S. Dist. LEXIS 49489.
Yount v. Johnson, 1996 N.M. App. LEXIS 23.
Zurla v. Hydel, 1997 Ill. App. LEXIS 387.

DEFENSES AGAINST NEGLIGENCE

Doyice J. Cotten | Sport Risk Consulting

In today's litigious society, lawsuits following injuries during recreational and sports events or activities have become commonplace. The fact that a recreation or sport business is sued, however, does not necessarily mean that loss of the suit is inevitable. There are many effective defenses that may be used by the defendant. Many of these defenses are described in this and the three subsequent chapters (see Chapter 2.22 *Immunity*, Chapter 2.23 *Waivers and Releases*, and Chapter 2.24 *Agreements Related to the Inherent Risks*).

There are essentially two types of risks—inherent risks and negligence risks. The **inherent risks** are those that are a normal, integral part of the activity—risks that cannot normally be eliminated without changing the nature of the activity itself. Such injuries as an athlete pulling a hamstring while running wind sprints, a hiker spraining an ankle while hiking over rough terrain, a rider falling from a horse, or a football player breaking his collarbone while throwing a block exemplify injuries due to the inherent risks of the activity. On the other hand, some injuries result from the **negligence** of the service provider or its employees. Some examples of injuries which might have been due to negligence are a tumbler injured because of an inattentive spotter; a novice karate student injured when matched against a larger, more experienced individual; a golfer struck by a ball hit by someone in a trailing foursome; or a basketball player injured in sustained rough play while the teacher left the class unsupervised (see Chapter 2.11 *Elements of Negligence*).

Both inherent risks and negligence risks can have an impact upon the recreation and sport provider, but the provider is not generally liable for injuries resulting from inherent risks – though there are exceptions to this rule. Negligence risks, however, can pose great physical risk to the participant and significant financial risk to the provider. One or more of the following defenses can usually provide at least some degree of protection to the provider against the impact of these risks.

FUNDAMENTAL CONCEPTS

All of these defenses come from one of three sources—common law, contract law, and statutory law. **Common law** is that body of principles and rules of action that derive their authority solely from the prior judgments and decrees of the courts. It is the body of law that develops and derives through judicial decisions—as distinguished from legislative enactments. **Contract law** is that body of law that governs the rules regarding binding agreements between parties. Several means by which risk can be allocated derive from this body of law. **Statutory law** is that body of law that is created by acts of a legislative body. Such law requiring or prohibiting specific acts or actions may apply to individuals, public recreation and sport entities, or private recreation and sport entities—depending upon the intent and wording of the legislation. *The reader is cautioned that this presentation must be general in nature because of sometimes significant differences among state laws. The details regarding some of the defenses differ from one state to the next. In addition, not all of the defenses apply in every state.*

The reader is directed to Figure 2.21.1, which outlines the more than 20 types of defenses in terms of (1) to whom the risk is allocated, (2) who is eligible for the defense, (3) which risks are allocated, (4) the effect upon the standard of care required, and (5) the impact on the liability of the service provider. To use the Figure effectively, the reader should keep in mind two points: first, state law in the reader's state may differ from the Figure, and second, the effectiveness of any defense depends upon the facts of any given situation.

Regarding how the facts of the situation affect the effectiveness of a defense, consider a situation in which a skateboarder is injured (due in part to provider negligence) in a skateboard competition in Texas. Whether the *primary assumption of risk defense* will protect depends upon the facts: his participation was voluntary, he was experienced, and he knew the inherent risks. In this scenario, the defense still would not protect because the defense does not protect against negligence risks. What about the *waiver of liability defense*? The facts are that Texas law enforces waivers and he signed a waiver prior to competition agreeing to release the provider from liability for negligence – the defense would protect against negligence liability. BUT, let's add a couple more facts: the skater was a minor and Texas law will not enforce waivers for minor clients – so the waiver does not protect and the provider is liable.

Defenses Based on Common Law
Elements of Ordinary Negligence Not Proven
Perhaps the best defense against a claim of negligence is that one or more of the elements required for negligence is not present. As discussed in Chapter 2.11 *Negligence*, to be liable, one must have a legal duty to the plaintiff, must breach that duty, and the breach of duty must be the proximate cause of an injury to the plaintiff. If one of these elements is missing (duty, breach, proximate cause, or injury), then no other defense is necessary—no negligence, no liability.

Primary Assumption of Risk[1]
Primary assumption of risk is a legal theory by which a plaintiff may not recover for an injury received when the plaintiff voluntarily exposes himself or herself to a known and appreciated danger. In other words, when one knows the inherent dangers involved and voluntarily participates, one assumes those risks inherent in the activity and the service provider is not liable for injuries resulting from those inherent risks.

Prior to the advent of comparative negligence in the 1970's (discussed later in this chapter), primary assumption of risk was an affirmative defense protecting service providers from liability. Since that time, many states have abolished the defense by statute; in other states, it has been subsumed into the comparative negligence doctrine; and in some states, it remains an effective defense – unaffected by comparative negligence statutes. The concept of primary assumption of risk remains important to the service provider both in the states where it remains an affirmative defense as well as in the states that have adopted comparative negligence. The reader should read the Significant Case (*Layden v. Plante*, 2012) for an informative discussion of assumption of risk. Contrast the views of the majority with those of the dissenting judges.

An individual can assume the risks of an activity in one of two ways. First, the risks may be assumed from the *conduct* of the individual; the assumption is never stated aloud or communicated in written form. By the act of participating in the activity, the participant is assuming the risks. This is called **implied assumption of risk**. For example, suppose, a man is at a party and takes part in a pick-up basketball game. He knows there is a risk of injury when playing basketball, but still participates. In doing so, he has impliedly assumed the risk even though he has not agreed to accept the risks either verbally or in writing.

Second, the individual can assume the risk of an activity by explicitly stating that he is assuming the risks, or he or she can assume the risks by signing a written agreement to accept the risk. Each is considered to be an **express assumption of risk**. This agreement limits the risks assumed to the inherent risks of the activity; more often, however, this agreement, when written, is worded to include an assumption of both inherent risks and the risks of ordinary negligence. In other words, the agreement releases the provider not only from liability for the inherent risks, but also from liability for ordinary negligence and is, in essence, a waiver of liability. Waivers will be addressed in detail in Chapter 2.23 *Waivers & Releases*.

Implied assumption of risk acts as a defense in that it relieves the defendant of a duty that might otherwise be owed to the plaintiff. The organizer of an event has a duty to produce a reasonably safe event and is required to use ordinary care not to increase the risk beyond what is inherent in the activity. For example, if a man attends a YMCA, knows and appreciates the risks involved in weight lifting, chooses to lift weights, and injures his back, the YMCA has no duty and bears no responsibility, absent negligence on its part, because of primary assumption of risk (or more specifically, implied assumption of risk).

---

[1] The author must re-emphasize to the recreation or sport manager that these defenses differ significantly from state to state. This is particularly important when examining primary assumption of risk because its availability and effectiveness have changed greatly over the years. Most states have abolished contributory negligence and gone to a form of comparative fault (discussed later in the chapter). With the adoption of comparative fault, many states have eliminated primary assumption of risk as a complete defense and treat it as a factor that may reduce any recovery due the plaintiff.

FIGURE 2.21.1 DEFENSES AND THE ALLOCATION OF RISK[1,2]

Authority and Defenses	To Whom Risk is Allocated	Eligibility for Defense	Which Risks Are Allocated	Effect on Standard of Care Owed	Impact on Liability of Provider
COMMON LAW					
Elements of Negligence Not Proven	participant	any service provider	injuries not due to provider negligence	none	provider not liable
Primary Assumption of Risk	participant	consent/voluntary; inherent risks; know, understand, & appreciate risks	inherent risks	none	provider not liable for inherent risks
Secondary Assumption of Risk	participant	fault-related conduct; understands dangers; usually age 6 or older	participant fault that enhances chance of injury	none	bars or reduces award
Sovereign & Government Immunity	participant	public entity only	all risks related to governmental function	reduces duty to willful/wanton	bars provider from liability for ordinary or gross negligence.
Ultra Vires Acts	employee	action outside scope of responsibility or authority	ordinary negligence	none	liability shifts from employer to employee
CONTRACT LAW					
Waivers	participant	participant of majority age	ordinary negligence	reduces duty to gross negligence	not liable for ordinary negligence
Inherent Risk Agreements Informed Consent	participant or subject	adequately informed of treatment risk; majority age or parental signature	treatment risks	none	stronger primary & secondary assumption of risk defenses
Agreement to Participate (Including A of R)	participant	adequately informed of activity risks and behavioral expectations	inherent risks	none	stronger primary & secondary assumption of risk defenses
Facility Lease Agreements	lessee	authorization for lease by corporate entity; lessee of majority age	activity risks to lessee; facility risks to lessee & lessor	none	not liable for activity risks; lessee & provider share facility risk as per contract
Equipment Rental Agreements	user (renter)	user of majority age	inherent risks; risks from equip. misuse or user conduct; provider retains risk of equip. failure	none	not liable for inherent risks or risks from misuse or misconduct
Indemnity Agreements	indemnitor	appropriate relationship	financial loss of indemnitee	none	indemnitee losses pass to indemnitor
Independent Contractor	independent contractors	authorization of entity; check contractor credentials	all risks of provider except for "inherently dangerous" activities	none	all liability to independent contractor (except "inherently dangerous" activities)

---

[1] Figure was adapted with the permission and assistance of Dr. Betty van der Smissen from a chart on allocation of risk in a handout entitled "How to Defend Yourself and Your Program," SSLASPA, 1997.

[2] The reader is cautioned that a Figure is simply an outline of the subject and that it is impossible to include all elements of the subject or all exceptions. This Figure is meant as an overview of Allocation of Risk and the reader is directed to this chapter as well as Chapter 2.22 *Immunity*, Chapter 2.23 *Waivers and Releases*, and Chapter 2.24 *Agreements Related to the Inherent Risks* for more detail regarding the subject.

(Continued)

FIGURE 2.21.1 DEFENSES AND THE ALLOCATION OF RISK[1,2] (CONTINUED)

Authority and Defenses	To Whom Risk is Allocated	Eligibility for Defense	Which Risks Are Allocated	Effect on Standard of Care Owed	Impact on Liability of Provider
STATUTORY LAW					
Comparative Fault	shared based on % fault	fault-related conduct; participant age 6 or older; all providers eligible	damages risk shared based on % of fault	none	reduces damages by % participant at fault
Legislation-Based & Charitable Immunity	participant	charitable, educational, and religious organizations	ordinary negligence	reduces duty to gross negligence	not liable for ordinary negligence
Tort Claims Acts	participant	public entities qualified by specific state statutes	discretionary acts; negligence except dangerous physical conditions usually	reduced to w/w; retain duty for dangerous conditions	provider liable for dangerous physical conditions and for willful/wanton acts
Recreational User Immunity	user	owners of natural, undeveloped area; no fee for use of land; specified by state statute	open & obvious premise risks & all activity risks; retain ultra hazardous environmental risks	only duty: to warn of ultra-hazardous & of known, hidden hazards	no liability except for ultra-hazardous; retains liability for willful/malicious (sometimes gross)
Volunteer Immunity (State)	participant	charitable & educational organization volunteers; safety training in some states	ordinary negligence in most states	volunteer to gross negligence	no effect on liability of provider
Federal Volunteer Protection Act	participant	Certified volunteers of public and non-profit organizations within scope of responsibility	ordinary negligence	volunteer to gross negligence	no effect on liability of provider
Good Samaritan Immunity	injured party	In good faith; gratuitous	usually ordinary negligence	caregiver to gross negligence	not available to provider
Good Samaritan (AED) Immunity	injured party	in good faith, gratuitous aid; training in some states	usually ordinary negligence	caregiver to gross negligence	immunity in many states
Specific Activity Laws for Rec/Spt Immunity	inherent to participant; often neglig.	usually all providers & participants in specified activities	inherent activity risk to participant; not operational, facility & premise risks	inherent risks to participant; often negligence risks	not liable for inherent activity risks; often not liable for negligence
General Rec & Sport Statutes (numerous sports)	inherent to participant	all providers & participants in specified activities	inherent activity risk to participant; not operational, facility & premise risks	none; participant assumes inherent risks	not liable for inherent activity-related risks; liable for negligence
Hazardous Recreational Activity (many activities)	participant	public entities & employees w/o fee for activity	inherent risks & secondary A of R to participant; provider must warn and maintain premises	reduces activity duty to gross; no effect on duty to warn & maintain	not liable for inherent risk or activity negligence; liable for operational, facility, & premise risks & no warning
Statute of Limitations	participant	all providers	all risks	none	Removes liability if filing date is not met
Notice of Claim (Tort Claims Act)	participant	only public entities	all risks	none	Removes liability if filing date is not met

Required Elements. Courts have ruled that three elements must exist for a successful primary assumption of risk defense. They are: *(1) the risk must be inherent to the sport or activity; (2) the participant must voluntarily consent to be exposed to the risk; and (3) the participant must know, understand, and appreciate the inherent risks of the activity*. However, this varies somewhat from state to state (e.g., under Missouri law, a skier assumes the inherent risks of or incidental to skiing, regardless of his or her subjective knowledge of those risks [*Bennett v. Hidden Valley Golf and Ski, Inc.*, 2003]).

In examining the first requirement for primary assumption of risk, it is important that the recreation or sport manager understand that the participant assumes only the risks that are **inherent** to the sport or activity. The participant does not normally assume risks incurred as a result of the **negligence** of the service provider (unless an express assumption of risks is worded to include a waiver of negligence).

A person who is playing recreation league softball, someone in a pickup basketball game, or a member on the varsity football team is participating by choice and thus meets the second requirement for primary assumption of risk—**voluntary consent**. Voluntary consent is sometimes at issue in cases regarding injuries in required physical education classes. If the plaintiff is a student in a required class where gymnastics is a required activity and is injured performing a mandatory back handspring, the voluntary consent requirement would be difficult to meet. On the other hand, if the student elected from among several choices to take gymnastics to meet the physical education requirement, there might be a degree of voluntary participation.

Thirdly, one cannot assume a risk of which one has no **knowledge, understanding, or appreciation**. Courts have ruled that one must not only know of the facts creating the danger, but also must comprehend and appreciate the nature of the danger to be confronted. Whether one is held to know, understand, and appreciate the risks usually depends upon the plaintiff's age, experience, and opportunity to become aware of the risks. Courts have held that it is not necessary that the injured plaintiff foresee the exact manner in which his or her injury occurred (*Tremblay v. West Experience Inc.*, 2002). In Maryland (and other jurisdictions), however, knowledge and appreciation are measured by an objective test and can be determined by law when "any person of normal intelligence in [the plaintiff's] position must have understood the danger" (*Leakas v. Columbia Country Club*, 1993).

One way to strengthen the primary assumption of risk defense is to ensure that participants know, understand, and appreciate the risks of the activity. Some recreation and sport providers (e.g., whitewater rafting, sky diving, trampoline centers) have attempted to do this by requiring the participant to view a short video showing the activity. Another act that helps to inform the participant of the risks is through the use of pre-participation agreements such as agreements to participate or assumption of risk agreements that provide a representative list of inherent risks (see Chapter 2.24 *Agreements Related to Inherent Risks*). The inherent risks may (and should) also be included in liability waivers – doing this moves the assumption of risk from implied assumption of risk to express assumption of risk (see Chapter 2.23 *Waivers and Releases*).

Secondary Assumption of Risk

Frequently in recreation and sport activities, actions taken by the participant lead to or contribute to an injury to the participant. The participant, like the provider, has a duty to act as a reasonable person; when the participant fails to do so and an injury results, the participant may be deemed to have contributed to the injury. Such contributory fault (more commonly referred to today as **secondary assumption of risk**) involves the voluntary choice or conduct of the participant to encounter a known or obvious risk created by the *negligent conduct of the service provider*, or to *fail to follow rules or heed warnings* set down by the provider (*Riddle v. Universal Sport Camp*, 1990). There are three types of situations in which secondary assumption of risk (contributory fault) may occur.

In the *first*, the participant voluntarily participates when there is a substantial risk that the defendant will act in a negligent manner (e.g., going up in a plane with someone who has a reputation for wild or careless acts). The *second* is when the service provider has already been negligent and the participant takes part anyway (e.g., playing softball in an outfield that has obvious rocks and holes scattered about). The *third* is when the participant fails to follow rules or heed warnings (e.g. refuses to wear safety equipment or violates safety rules). In each case, the conduct of the participant (electing to participate) falls below the standard to which one is required to conform for one's own protection. Consequently, the participant fault (negligence) can be a contributing factor to the subsequent injury.

Contributory fault law provides that the participant may not recover for damages suffered if there is *any* contributing fault by the participant — regardless of the extent of fault or negligence attributable to the provider. At one time this law was pervasive; however, the harshness of this law led to its elimination in most states. Today contributory fault is still the law in only four states and the District of Columbia (see Figure 2.21.2). Most states today use a type of **comparative negligence** or **comparative fault** in apportioning damages based on weighing the provider negligence against the participant negligence. (see Comparative Fault later in this chapter).

Sovereign and Governmental Immunity
Sovereign and governmental immunity are judicial doctrines that prevent one from filing suit against the government and its political subdivisions without their consent (see Chapter 2.22 *Immunity*).

Ultra Vires Act
A defense that can be very helpful to the corporate entity is the defense that the act by the employee was an *ultra vires* act—one that is not within the authority or scope of responsibility of the employee. Normally under the doctrine of *respondeat superior*, the employer is liable for the negligent acts of the employee (see Chapter 2.12 *Which Parties Are Liable?*). A major exception to this rule, however, is when the employee had no authority or responsibility to perform the act in question. In such a case, generally only the employee is liable for the negligent act.

If a coach injured a youngster while administering corporal punishment when the school had a strict rule prohibiting corporal punishment, the act might be outside the authority of the coach and the school system might escape liability. The coach would still be liable for the act. Note, however, that if the school is aware of the fact that the coach uses corporal punishment and has failed to act upon this knowledge, the school will also be liable for the action. In essence, by not taking action after knowing of the coach's behavior, the school is in fact condoning the act and may be liable.

Defenses Based on Contract Law
Waivers
A **waiver** is a contract in which the participant or user of a service agrees to relieve the provider of the duty of ordinary care. The signer relinquishes the right to pursue legal action against the service provider in the event that the *negligence* of the provider results in an injury to the participant (see Chapter 2.23 *Waivers and Releases*).

Informed Consent
An **informed consent agreement** is a formal contract used to protect the provider from liability for the informed treatment risks of a treatment or program to which the signer is subjected. The agreement is designed to provide full disclosure to the individual regarding both the known risks and the anticipated outcome or benefits of the treatment, thereby enabling the participant to make an informed decision regarding acceptance of the treatment. *By signing the agreement, the signer is agreeing to assume the treatment risks of which he or she is informed. The signer is not agreeing to relieve the entity from liability for injury resulting from negligent acts of the entity or its employees* (see Chapter 2.24 *Agreements Related to the Inherent Risks*).

Agreement to Participate
The **agreement to participate**, while technically not a contractual agreement, is a document which helps to protect by informing participants in recreation, sport, or educational activities of (1) the nature of the activity, (2) the risks to be encountered through participation in the activity, and (3) the behaviors expected of the participant. It is designed to help protect the provider from liability for injuries resulting from the inherent risks of the activity, but is informative rather than contractual in nature. An assumption of risk agreement is usually included within the agreement to participate. The **assumption of risk agreement** is a statement whereby the signer (1) explicitly asserts that the signer knows the nature of the activity, understands the physical and skill demands of the activity, and appreciates the types of injuries that may result from participation;

(2) asserts that participation is voluntary; and (3) agrees to assume those risks that are inherent to the activity (see Chapter 2.24 *Agreements Related to the Inherent Risks*).

Facility Lease Agreements

Owners of facilities often permit groups or other businesses to make use of their facilities. A recreational softball team might sign up for a field to conduct a team practice; a facility owner might lease an arena to a promoter for a concert; or a facility owner might lease the entire facility or a part of the facility for a matter of months or years (e. g. a university might lease its dressing facilities and practice fields to a professional football team for several months for preseason practice). When an injury occurs at the facility, it is not unlikely that the facility owner will be named as a defendant in a lawsuit regarding the injury. A defense against such litigation may be provided to owners of property/lessors by virtue of their status as lessors or by contractual provisions.

To determine the extent of the liability of the facility owner, one must determine if the injury was **activity-related** or **premise-related**. Generally, injuries that are activity-related are the responsibility of the lessee. When injuries are premise-related, liability may rest on both the entity conducting the activity and the facility owner. Generally, the facility owner is responsible for structural type problems and the entity conducting the activity is often responsible for maintenance type problems. In the instance of the softball team using the field, the facility owner would retain liability. In the case of the football team leasing the facility for preseason practice, the responsibility would probably be shared by lessor and lessee depending on the nature of the hazard unless the lease contract includes provisions that assign sole responsibility for certain types of hazards to the lessee football team (see Chapter 2.31 *Premises Liability*).

It is common practice for lessors of property to include an indemnification clause within the lease agreement (see the Indemnification Agreements section below).

Equipment Rental Agreements

When individuals rent equipment, rental agreements are often used to help protect the lessor or renter (owner of equipment or property). Rental agreements often include a waiver of liability signed by the lessee (user or party acquiring the use of equipment) of the equipment as well as an indemnification agreement. By including a waiver in the rental agreement, the provider is passing the liability for a negligence-related injury on to the lessee. An indemnification agreement is usually included to have the lessee agree to repay the provider for loss of or damage to equipment and loss due to litigation resulting from accidents to the lessee or to a third party (see the next section).

Rental agreements can also function much like an agreement to participate (see also Chapter 2.24 *Agreements Related to Inherent Risks*) in that they can inform the lessee of behavior expected and his/her responsibility for third-party injuries, and gain affirmation that the lessee is knowledgeable regarding the use of the equipment. The renter then passes along much of the responsibility for injury to the lessee and enhances the position of the renter when comparative negligence is determined. The renter, however, usually retains liability for injury relating to defective equipment.

Indemnification Agreements

An **indemnification agreement** is an agreement by which one party agrees to indemnify or reimburse another upon the occurrence of an anticipated loss. The agreement creates a contractual right under which the loss is generally shifted from a tortfeasor (e.g., facility lessor, facility owner) who is passively at fault to one that is actively responsible (e.g., facility lessee, facility user). Indemnification agreements are commonly included in facility leases to protect the property owner from loss resulting from litigation by the lessee or by a third party patron naming the owner as a defendant. For instance, a municipality leasing an arena to a wrestling promoter for an event would generally include within the lease a provision by which the promoter agrees to indemnify or reimburse the municipality for any loss resulting from the event (e.g., an injured wrestler or spectator, facility damage from a riot). Then if an injury occurs and the municipality is named as a co-defendant or if there is property damage, the promoter is responsible for the municipality's legal fees, any award, and any other related expenses. In *Auburn School District No. 408 v. King County* (1999), the school district agreed to indemnify the county for loss due to the district's use of the county swimming pool. A student injured in the pool sued both the county and the school district. The school district was ordered to reimburse the county for its financial loss. This defense is summarized in Figure 2.21.1 (see also Chapter 2.23 *Waivers and Releases* and Chapter 2.12 *Which Parties Are Liable?*).

The law regarding the enforcement of indemnification agreements is more exacting in some states than in others. For instance, in Georgia the public policy is reluctant to cast the burden for negligent actions upon one who is not actually at fault. Unless a contract for indemnification explicitly and expressly states that the negligence of the indemnitee is covered, courts will not enforce the contract against the indemnitor. In *Pride Park Atlanta v. City of Atlanta* (2000), the agreement was not enforced because the agreement said ". . . agrees to protect and hold harmless . . . from any and all claims . . ." and did not explicitly refer to negligence by the indemnitee.

While most indemnity agreements involve two corporate entities, some involve a corporate entity and an individual. Some courts have held that indemnification agreements used with consumers and intended to perform much like a waiver are not enforceable, but indemnification law varies from state to state. A rafting company (*Madsen v. Wyoming River Trips, Inc.*, 1999) required that a father agree to indemnify the company on behalf of himself and his family. When the wife was injured due to negligence of the rafting company, the Wyoming court refused to enforce the agreement stating that such contracts are not enforced in a consumer services context. The court ruled that the agreement, which sought to hold an innocent party liable for the negligence of the indemnitee, was void as against public policy.

In *Yang v. Voyagaire Houseboats, Inc.* (2005), Voyagaire had rented a houseboat to Yang and required that Yang sign an indemnity agreement. After six members of Yang's party suffered injury from carbon monoxide poisoning, Yang and others filed suit against Voyagaire; however, Voyagaire claimed protection by the waiver and indemnity agreement signed by Yang. The Supreme Court of Minnesota ruled that the waiver and indemnity agreement were against public policy since Voyagaire was, in effect, a resort providing a public service by furnishing sleeping accommodations to the public. It also stated that the indemnity clause was unenforceable because it did not contain language that (1) specifically refers to negligence, (2) expressly state that the renter will indemnify Voyagaire for Voyagaire's negligence, or (3) clearly indicate that the renter would indemnify Voyagaire for negligence occurring before the renter took possession of the houseboat. This ruling suggests that parties relying on indemnity agreements take care to clearly state the intent of the clause.

On the other hand, courts in some states have upheld such agreements (*Beaver v. Foamcraft, Inc.*, 2002). In a 2005 Wisconsin case, a man was injured during a tractor pull contest after signing a waiver and indemnification agreement. The waiver protected against the plaintiff's claims, but did not protect against a loss of consortium claim by the wife. The indemnity language within the document stated clearly and without ambiguity that the plaintiff agreed to indemnify the provider for all claims—thus the indemnity agreement protected the provider from the loss of consortium claim (*Walsh v. Luedtke*, 2005).

In several cases, corporate entities (in an effort to bypass the law in some states that disallows liability waivers signed by parents on behalf of minors) have attempted to gain liability protection by having parents sign indemnity agreements in order for the child to be able to participate in an activity. Some courts have said that such agreements are enforceable because they involve a contract between two adults (*Eastman v. Yutzy*, 2001). Other courts have ruled such an agreement invalid as against public policy since it is inconsistent with the parent's duty to the child (*Hawkins v. Peart*, 2001; *Cooper v. The Aspen Skiing Company*, 2002).

Independent Contract for Services

An independent contract for services involves an agreement between the corporate entity and an individual or a company that contracts to perform a service for the corporate entity (see Chapter 2.12 *Which Parties Are Liable?*). When one contracts with an independent contractor, the corporate entity generally avoids liability for injuries resulting from the negligence of the independent contractor. However, the employer retains the responsibility: (1) to use reasonable care in selecting a competent independent contractor and to inspect after completion of the project; (2) to keep the premises reasonably safe for invitees and employees; and (3) for "inherently dangerous activities" (e.g., fireworks displays, keeping of dangerous animals, and ultra hazardous activities) (see Chapter 2.12 *Which Parties Are Liable?*).

Defenses Based on Statutory Law
Comparative Fault
Comparative fault is not a true defense against liability for negligence. More precisely, **comparative fault** is a method for apportioning damages awarded based on the fault or blame or the relative degree of responsibility for the injury. The jury compares the fault of each party (i.e., the plaintiff and the defendant) and generally allocates the fault by percentage.[2] Any fault allotted to the plaintiff reduces the award to the plaintiff based upon the percentage of fault resulting from the plaintiff's own negligence.

Comparative fault has two forms, pure and modified. **Pure comparative fault** has been adopted by a number of states (see Figure 2.21.2). In this form, the award to the plaintiff is reduced by the percentage of fault assigned to the plaintiff. For example, suppose the award is $100,000 and the fault is apportioned 75 percent to the plaintiff and 25 percent to the defendant. Since the plaintiff is 75 percent to blame, the plaintiff's award would be reduced by 75 percent and the plaintiff would receive $25,000. **Modified comparative fault** operates on the theory that the plaintiff is not entitled to recovery if the plaintiff is substantially at fault. There are three types of modified comparative fault laws. The first, *Modified Comparative Fault – 50% Bar*, allows proportional recovery if the fault of the plaintiff is between 0% and 49%. So plaintiff is barred from recovery if plaintiff and defendant fault are equal. The second category, *Modified Comparative Fault – 51% Bar*, allows proportional recovery if the fault of the plaintiff is between 0% and 50%. The third category, *Slight/Gross Negligence Comparative Fault*, is a variation employed only in South Dakota. Comparative fault is employed only when the negligence of the plaintiff is "slight" and the negligence of the defendant is "gross." A major problem with this concept lies in the lack of exact standards as to what constitutes "slight" and "gross" negligence.

FIGURE 2.21.2 CONTRIBUTORY FAULT/COMPARATIVE FAULT LAWS IN THE UNITED STATES[3]

Contributory Fault	Pure Comparative Fault	Modified Comparative Fault 50% Bar	Modified Comparative Fault 51% Bar		Slight/Gross Negligence Comparative Fault
Alabama Washington D.C. Maryland North Carolina Virginia	Alaska Arizona California Florida Kentucky Louisiana Mississippi Missouri New Mexico New York Rhode Island Washington	Arkansas Colorado Georgia Idaho Kansas Maine Nebraska North Dakota Tennessee Utah West Virginia	Connecticut Delaware Hawaii Illinois Indiana Iowa Massachusetts Michigan Minnesota Montana Nevada	New Hampshire New Jersey Ohio Oklahoma Oregon Pennsylvania South Carolina Texas Vermont Wisconsin Wyoming	South Dakota

---

[2]**Contributory fault** (formerly called contributory negligence) exists when the conduct of the plaintiff in any way helps to cause or aggravate the plaintiff's injury. In the past, this was a major defense against negligence claims because in states adhering to the contributory fault doctrine, any contributory fault by the plaintiff, regardless of how slight, served as a complete bar to recovery. Now, however, only four states and the District of Columbia hold to this doctrine (see Figure 2.21.2). In **comparative fault** states, contributory fault serves to reduce the award to the plaintiff by the proportion of fault allotted to the plaintiff; even under the comparative fault theory, however, most states bar recovery if the fault of the plaintiff is 50 percent or greater.

Regarding age, the general rule has been that children over the age of fourteen are capable of negligence and children under seven are incapable of negligence. Those between seven and fourteen are judged capable of negligence in certain circumstances. These lines of demarcation seem to be weakening in recent years as cases in various jurisdictions have begun to allocate contributory fault to children six years of age and under (*Grace v. Kumalaa*, 1963; *Lash v. Cutts*, 1991; *Robertson v. Travis*, 1980).

[3]"Contributory Negligence/Comparative Fault Laws in all 50 States," https://www.mwl-law.com/wp-content/uploads/2013/03/contributory-negligence-comparative-fault-laws-in-all-50-states.pdf, 2015.

Legislation-based Immunity

There are several forms of legislation-based immunity that affect recreation and sport managers as well as the business entity. **Charitable immunity** is a doctrine that relieves or immunizes charitable organizations from liability for tort. Most states have abolished this defense; however it is still strong in a few states. **Federal and state tort claims acts** rescinded sovereign/governmental immunity and enumerated the areas or acts for which immunity was retained. **Recreational user immunity** was passed to protect certain landowners who gratuitously allow others to use their property for recreational purposes. **Volunteer immunity** was enacted to aid in the recruitment of volunteers for public, charitable, and nonprofit entities. **AED statutes** and **Good Samaritan statutes** protect those utilizing AEDs and rendering aid to victims in cases of medical emergency. **Shared responsibility and statutory assumption of risk statutes** are intended to help protect providers of recreation and sport activities from liability for injuries resulting from the inherent risks (and negligence in some statutes) of the activity or sport. These are discussed in detail in Chapter 2.22 *Immunity*.

Procedural Noncompliance

A **statute of limitations** is a restriction on the length of time an injured party has in which to file suit. The law differs from state to state and also with the nature of the claim. In tort claims, states usually allow one to four years in which to file suit with most allowing two or three years. When minors are involved, the statute of limitations does not begin running until the minor has reached the age of majority. So, if a child is injured at age 11 due to the negligence of an employee at a recreation department, the youngster would have one to four years (the length of the statute of limitations in that state) after reaching the age of 18 (in most states) in which to file suit.

Notice of claim statutes relate usually to tort claim statutes and provide that the plaintiff must provide the defendant *public entity* with a notice of intent to file suit. This notice must be filed within a period of time (ranging from 90 days to 2 years, depending on the state) following the accident or the right to sue is lost. In essence, the notice of claim is a form of statute of limitations with a similar effect. In a 2010 Arizona case (*Little v. State of Arizona*), failure to file a notice of claim within the 180 day time limit was at issue. A member of the University of Arizona's women's basketball team died as a result of medical misconduct; however, the claim was dismissed because plaintiff failed to comply with the notice of claim requirement. Not all states have a notice of claim provision in their tort law statutes and the notice of claim requirements apply only when the defendant is a public entity.

SIGNIFICANT CASE

This case features an informative discussion of assumption of risk. Examine how voluntary participation, commonly appreciated risks, and prior experience relate to assumption of risk. Most importantly, compare the concept as perceived by the majority with the concept as seen by the dissenting judges.

LAYDEN V. PLANTE

Supreme Court of New York, Appellate Division, Third Department
101 A.D.3d 1540; 957 N.Y.S.2d 458; 2012 N.Y. App. Div. LEXIS 9109
JUDGES: Mercure, J.P., Malone Jr., Kavanagh, Stein and Garry, JJ. Kavanagh and Stein, JJ., concur. Mercure, J.P. dissenting. Malone Jr., J., concurs.

OPINION BY:

Garry

Plaintiff Dianne A. Layden (hereinafter plaintiff) participated in a training session with defendant Angela Plante, a certified personal trainer, at No Limits Fitness, a fitness center owned by defendant Deborah W. Greenfield. Plaintiff advised the trainer before the session that she had a history of back problems and a herniated disc. The trainer then instructed plaintiff in a program of weightlifting moves that plaintiff performed under her supervision. Two days later, plaintiff used the trainer's written instructions to repeat the program without supervision. While performing a maneuver called a Smith squat, plaintiff experienced lower back pain, and ultimately thereafter underwent surgery to correct two herniated discs with fragments. Plaintiff and her husband, derivatively, commenced this personal injury action alleging that the injury to her back was caused by the trainer's improper supervision and instruction, by Greenfield's negligence in failing to provide a safe place and properly trained staff, and also upon the doctrine of respondeat superior based on the trainer's acts as an agent or employee. Defendants each moved for summary judgment. Supreme Court granted the motions and dismissed the complaint, based upon plaintiff's assumption of the risk. Plaintiffs appeal.

The doctrine of assumption of risk provides that a person who voluntarily participates in recreational or athletic activities is deemed to consent to the "commonly appreciated risk[s]" inherent in that activity. However, a participant does not assume risks resulting from "a dangerous condition over and above the usual dangers inherent in the activity". As application of the doctrine undermines the principles of comparative causation, it "must be closely circumscribed" and has therefore been limited to apply only "in the context of pursuits both unusually risky and beneficial that the defendant has in some nonculpable way enabled".

Initially, noting that assumption of risk has been applied to the use of exercise apparatus, we reject plaintiffs' contention that the doctrine does not apply to the noncompetitive fitness activity in which plaintiff was engaged. Further, plaintiff's own testimony established that she had previously participated in weight-lifting exercise programs—including a prior program designed by the trainer—and that she knew that back injuries are an inherent risk of such activities. Accordingly, we find that defendants met their initial burden on summary judgment to establish on a prima facie basis that plaintiff knew of the risks, appreciated their nature and voluntarily assumed them.

However, noting that "[t]he application of the doctrine of assumption of risk is generally a question of fact to be resolved by a jury," we find triable issues of fact presented as to whether the trainer's actions "unreasonably heightened the risks to which [plaintiff] was exposed" beyond those usually inherent in weight-lifting. Plaintiffs presented the affidavits of two personal training experts who opined that the Smith squat, even when properly performed, is contraindicated for a person with a herniated disc as it causes "direct vertical loading of the spinal column" and places "extreme stress" on the lower back, and thus should not have been recommended for plaintiff. The experts further averred that safe performance of the maneuver requires keeping the back straight, and that the trainer erred in instructing plaintiff to "stick her butt out" during the exercise. The trainer acknowledged that she gave plaintiff this instruction but explained that she meant that plaintiff should move her body backward while keeping her back straight. The trainer further testified that whether the Smith squat is dangerous for a person with a back injury "depends on the form" used by the exerciser and acknowledged that, although she knew plaintiff had a herniated disc, she did not warn plaintiff that the exercise posed any risk to her back. Based on this testimony, plaintiffs raised triable issues of fact as to whether the trainer's direction to perform the Smith squat, her allegedly improper instructions, or both, served to unreasonably increase the risk to which plaintiff was exposed.

As an alternate ground for affirmance, Greenfield contends that there is no evidence that she breached a duty that proximately caused plaintiff's injury. Plaintiffs do not assert that plaintiff's injury resulted from faulty equipment or any other property defect at the fitness center, and although one of plaintiffs' experts described multiple alleged inadequacies in the fitness center's safety procedures, there was no showing that these caused or contributed to plaintiff's injury. Instead, both experts averred without equivocation that the trainer caused the injury by instructing plaintiff to perform the Smith squat despite her back condition. Thus, no direct negligence was shown, and Greenfield may be held liable only if the trainer's negligence may be imputed under a theory of respondeat superior. As to this doctrine, Greenfield contends that there is no derivative liability because the trainer was an independent contractor rather than an employee. This determination requires analysis of the extent of the fitness center's power to regulate the manner in which the trainer performed her work, and the parties' conflicting evidence poses factual questions as to this issue, barring summary determination.

Finally, we find the release that Greenfield proffers to be unenforceable. An agreement that seeks to release a defendant from the consequences of his or her own negligence must "plainly and precisely" state that it extends this far. The release at issue here makes no unequivocal reference to any negligence or fault of the fitness center employees or agents, but merely enumerates activities on plaintiff's part that will not lead to liability, and then provides in general terms that the fitness center is not liable for "any claims, demands, injuries, damages or actions" resulting from use of the facility. This release does not bar plaintiffs' claim.

Kavanagh and Stein, JJ., concur.

DISSENT BY: MERCURE

Mercure, J.P. (dissenting). Because we conclude that plaintiff Dianne A. Layden (hereinafter plaintiff) assumed the risk of aggravating her prior back injury while weightlifting at a gym, we respectfully dissent. The doctrine of primary assumption of risk provides that a voluntary participant "engaging in a sport or recreational activity . . . consents to those commonly appreciated risks which are inherent in and arise out of the nature of the sport generally and flow from such participation." The doctrine limits the scope of the duty owed to a voluntary participant—"[u]nder this theory, a plaintiff who freely accepts a known risk 'commensurately negates any duty on the part of the defendant to safeguard him or her from the risk'. While "participants are not deemed to have assumed risks resulting from the reckless or intentional conduct of others, or risks that are concealed or unreasonably enhanced," the duty of care that is owed is simply "'to make the conditions as safe as they appear to be'".

As we have previously acknowledged, "'[e]xtensive and unrestricted application of the doctrine of primary assumption of the risk to tort cases generally represents a throwback to the former doctrine of contributory negligence' "abolished by CPLR 1411. Thus, the primary assumption of risk "doctrine 'must be closely circumscribed if it is not seriously to undermine and displace the principles of comparative causation' ". Nevertheless, the doctrine is not limited to organized sporting events or competitions, as plaintiffs assert; rather, the doctrine, if otherwise applicable, encompasses noncompetitive fitness or exercise activity. Most recently, the Court of Appeals has explained that "application of assumption of the risk should be limited to cases appropriate for absolution of duty"—i.e., "'case[s] in which the defendant[s] solely by reason of having sponsored or otherwise supported some risk-laden but socially valuable voluntary activity ha[ve] been called to account in damages' ". The Court noted that in its prior cases applying the doctrine, the defendant "sponsored or otherwise supported" the activity, or it "occurred in a designated athletic or recreational venue". Among those prior cases were two in which students were injured while attending martial arts classes. As in this case, the plaintiffs' noncompetitive, non-contact exercise activity took place at designated venues and the plaintiffs challenged the adequacy of the supervision—in one case, a 15-year old student was left in charge of the class—as well as the quality of the instruction and the particular exercises that they were directed to perform. Nevertheless, the Court of Appeals concluded that the plaintiffs had assumed the risk of falling while tumbling and performing floor exercises. In explaining the justification for application of the doctrine, the Court explained that "[t]he primary means of improving one's sporting prowess and the inherent motivation behind participation in sports is to improve one's skills by undertaking and overcoming new challenges and obstacles".

Here, plaintiff was experienced with weight-lifting and had been a member of No Limits Fitness, the fitness center owned by defendant Deborah W. Greenfield, for nine months prior to the accident. She first hired defendant Angela Plante, a certified personal trainer, to design an exercise program in March 2007, and then performed the exercise program on her own for three months. Thereafter, plaintiff requested that Plante teach her a new program "because [plaintiff] was getting tired of doing the same exercises for three months. [She] wanted to learn new exercises." Plaintiff performed the new exercise program during a single training session with Plante without experiencing any discomfort, but experienced mild back pain shortly afterwards and for the next day. Although plaintiff had a history of back problems and was aware that she had a herniated disc, she nevertheless returned to perform the program by herself and felt back pain while performing a Smith squat. Plaintiff acknowledged that her discomfort was apparent from the first squat, but she continued to do 14 more.

In our view, plaintiff—who was a registered nurse and well aware both of her preexisting back condition and that weight-lifting could further injure her back—assumed this commonly appreciated risk. Given plaintiff's admitted awareness of the risk, any assertion that Plante's exercise program unreasonably enhanced the risk is meritless inasmuch as plaintiff's reliance on Plante to negate the danger of further injury was not justifiable. Despite the parties' dispute over whether Plante told plaintiff to stop any exercise that caused her pain and whether the Smith squat was contraindicated for anyone with a herniated disc, there is no evidence that Plante or anyone else either urged plaintiff to continue with that exercise or reassured her that performing it was safe despite her discomfort. Nor is there any evidence that plaintiff was encouraged to stop performing the previous program that Plante had designed and that plaintiff had safely used for three months. Rather, plaintiff simply grew "tired" of the previous program and, despite her awareness of the risk, sought to "improve [her weight-lifting] skills by undertaking and overcoming new challenges and obstacles". Under these circumstances, the doctrine of primary assumption of risk bars recovery as a matter of law.

Malone Jr., J., concurs. Ordered that the order is modified, on the law, without costs, by reversing so much thereof as granted defendants' motions for summary judgment; motions denied; and, as so modified, affirmed.

CASES ON THE SUPPLEMENTAL WEBSITE

Knight v. Jewett, 3 Cal.4th 296 [1992]. This is the seminal case concerning the doctrine of assumption of risk, in which the California Supreme Court considered the application of assumption of risk in light of the adoption of comparative fault principles. Note the distinction made between "primary assumption of risk" and "secondary assumption of risk."

Ribaudo v. La Salle Institute, 2007 NY Slip Op 8431; 45 A.D.3d 556; 2007 N.Y. App. Div. LEXIS 11249. The court emphasized that the doctrine of primary assumption of the risk will not serve as a bar to liability if the risk is unassumed, concealed, or unreasonably increased.

Cicconi v. Bedford Central School District, 2005 N.Y. App. Div. LEXIS 8484. Note the reasoning why the court ruled that the doctrine of assumption of risk protected the school district.

Bartell v. Mesa Soccer Club, Inc., 2010 Ariz. App. Unpub. LEXIS 882. The issue of whether a volunteer is an agent of the club or is an independent contractor is addressed. Liability of the club rides on the issue.

Cohen v. Five Brooks Stable, 2008 Cal. App. LEXIS 222. The defendants claim assumption of risk and waiver of risks as defenses.

QUESTIONS YOU SHOULD BE ABLE TO ANSWER

1. What is meant by an inherent risk? Give an example.
2. Explain the concept of primary assumption of risk. In the Significant Case, why do the dissenting judges disagree with the majority decision?
3. What is secondary assumption of risk? Give an example.
4. What is meant by comparative fault?
5. Explain the role of an indemnification agreement in a facility lease agreement.

REFERENCES
Cases
Auburn School District No. 408 v. King County, 1999 Wash. App. LEXIS 1748.
Beaver v. Foamcraft, Inc., 2002 U.S. Dist. LEXIS 4651.
Bennett v. Hidden Valley Golf and Ski, Inc., 2003 U.S. App. LEXIS 1658.
Cooper v. The Aspen Skiing Company, 2002 Colo. LEXIS 528.
Daigle v. West Mountain 2001 N.Y. App. Div. LEXIS 12326
Eastman v. Yutzy, 2001 Mass. Super. LEXIS 157.
El-Halees v. Chauser, 2002 Cal. App. Unpub. LEXIS 8124.
Grace v. Kumalaa, 387 P.2d 872 (Hawaii 1963).
Hawkins v. Peart, 2001 Utah LEXIS 177.
Home v. North Kitsap School District, 965 P.2d 1112; 1998 Wash. App. LEXIS 1405.
Knight v. Jewett, 3 Cal.4th 296; 11 Cal. Rptr. 2d, 834 P.2d 696 (1992).
Leakas v. Columbia Country Club, 831 F. Supp. 1231 (Md. 1993).
Little v. State of Arizona, 2010 Ariz. App. LEXIS 158.
Madsen v. Wyoming River Trips, Inc., 1999 U.S. Dist. LEXIS 77.
Pride Park Atlanta v. City of Atlanta, 2000 Ga. App. LEXIS 1330.
Riddle v. Universal Sport Camp, 786 P.2d 641 (Kan. 1990).
Robertson v. Travis, 393 So.2d 304 (La. 1980).
Saffro v. Elite Racing, Inc., 2002 Cal. App. LEXIS 2076 at 1
Tremblay v. West Experience Inc., 2002 N.Y. App. Div. LEXIS 7591.
Truett v. Fell, 68 N.Y.2d 432.
Walsh v. Luedtke, 2005 Wisc. App. LEXIS 744.
Yang v. Voyagaire Houseboats, Inc., 2005 Minn. LEXIS 465.

Publications and Presentations
"Contributory Negligence/Comparative Fault Laws In All 50 States," https://www.mwl-law.com/wp-content/uploads/2013/03/contributory-negligence-comparative-fault-laws-in-all-50-states.pdf, 2015.
Gregg, C.R. (2000). "Inherent Risks," SSLASPA Conference, Albuquerque.
van der Smissen, B. (1990). *Legal liability and risk management for public and private entities*. Cincinnati: Anderson. Publishing Co.
van der Smissen, B. (1997) How to Defend Yourself and Your Program. Unpublished handout at an SSLASPA Conference.
Volunteer Protection Act of 1997, PL 105-19 (S543) June 18, 1997.

2.22 IMMUNITY

Doyice J. Cotten | Sport Risk Consulting

A major category of defense for individuals and service providers in the fields of recreation and sport is immunity from liability. **Immunity** is the state of being exempt from or protected against civil liability under certain circumstances. In this chapter, several types of immunity that apply to recreation and sport managers will be presented—ranging from sovereign immunity to sport-related statutes pertaining to the recreational user, sport volunteers, Good Samaritan acts, statutory assumption of risk, and shared responsibility. Since it is not possible to spell out the law in each state regarding each type of immunity, the reader is encouraged to use Table 2.22.1 to research the law in his or her state. Moreover, the reader should consult Table 2.21.1 in Chapter 2.21 *Defenses against Negligence* for a summary of each of these defenses.

Many types of immunity are available to those in the fields of recreation and sport. Each has been designed to provide shelter from liability to one or more protected classes of people or entities. Statutes are aimed at providing protection for public entity service providers (tort claims acts, sovereign immunity, hazardous recreation statutes), private service providers (shared responsibility statutes, statutory assumption of risk statutes), nonprofit and charitable providers (charitable immunity), and property owners (recreational user statutes). Volunteer statutes are enacted to encourage volunteers (Volunteer Protection Act, state volunteer statutes), sport volunteers (sport volunteer statutes), and medical emergency volunteers (Good Samaritan statutes, AED Good Samaritan statutes). There is also immunity designed to protect public employees (hazardous recreation statutes, tort claims acts, discretionary act immunity) and private employees (AED Good Samaritan statutes).

FUNDAMENTAL CONCEPTS

Sovereign/Governmental Immunity

Sovereign immunity refers to "the immunity of the state and its agencies, departments, boards, institutions, et al." (van der Smissen, 1990, p. 148). **Governmental immunity**, on the other hand, "is the protection afforded local governing entities, such as municipalities (cities, towns, villages) and schools." (van der Smissen, 1990, p. 148). It is important to understand that while many states distinguish between the two concepts, the terms sovereign immunity and governmental immunity are often used interchangeably. In this chapter, the term "sovereign/governmental immunity" will be used to refer to both concepts.

There are two major limitations to sovereign/governmental immunity. First, *it applies only to governmental entities* and second, *it does not extend to the officers, agents, or employees of the governing entity* (except when the statute specifically provides for it). This doctrine of sovereign/governmental immunity was the commanding approach to immunity until the 1950s. However, during the last half of the twentieth century most states abolished or significantly weakened and restricted this immunity so that it no longer has the dominant impact that it once did. The rationale for the change was that the immunity was unfair to the innocent victim of negligent actions by the governmental entity or its employees. Common law regarding immunity has been collected and arranged more systematically, or codified, in the tort claims acts. These acts, to be discussed below, extend immunity to government officers, agents, and employees in many states.

Tort Claims Acts

Congress passed the **Federal Tort Claims Act** (28 U.S.C. 2671–2680 [1976]) with the intent of waiving sovereign/governmental immunity, thereby allowing liability exposure for the federal government comparable to that of the private sector. The statute removed the power of the federal government to claim immunity from a lawsuit for damages due to negligent or intentional injury by a federal employee in the scope of his/her work for the government. While the Federal Tort Claims Act allows suit of the government in certain instances, unlike sovereign/governmental immunity, *it provides immunity for federal officials performing discretionary acts within the scope of their responsibilities.*

Individual states began to follow suit, passing their own **state tort claims acts** to enable individuals harmed by torts, including negligence, to file suit under certain conditions. *In essence, what these acts did was (1) to rescind sovereign/governmental immunity at the state level in those states and (2) to enumerate those areas or acts for which immunity was retained.*

Discretionary/Ministerial Function

One major change at this time was movement from that of governmental/proprietary function to the discretionary/ministerial doctrine. The **governmental/proprietary doctrine** classified the functions of public entities as either a fundamental **governmental function** (e.g., police, fire, and education), for which immunity was granted, or as a **proprietary function** (e.g., water works, electrical power, selling game refreshments, and other for-profit activities), for which no immunity was granted. The governmental/proprietary doctrine *provided immunity based upon the nature of the function* provided by the governmental entity. Immunity was provided if the action was a "public good" function of the entity; but not for proprietary or money-making functions of the entity.

Replacing the governmental/proprietary doctrine was the **discretionary/ministerial doctrine** which grants immunity for discretionary acts, but, for the most part, not for ministerial acts. **Discretionary acts** are those that involve deliberation, planning, decision making, policy making, and most often involve managerial level personnel such as the athletic director or head of the recreation department. **Ministerial acts** are more likely to involve operational acts, obedience of orders, performance of a duty, implementation of decisions or policies, and lower echelon employees such as assistant coaches and instructors. Under this doctrine, the classification is not based upon who performed the act, but upon the nature of the act. The rationale behind this immunity is to free the governing body charged with making policy decisions regarding public welfare from suits that might restrain them from performing their duties. The big problem, however, is that making the distinction between discretionary and ministerial acts is difficult at best. In addition, it has been growing increasingly so as the courts in some states have persisted in blurring the lines of distinction, often interpreting even trivial decisions as discretionary. By classifying most acts as discretionary, the courts, in effect, strengthen the immunity of the employee and the entity.

The discretionary/ministerial doctrine provides immunity *based on the act of the employee*—not the function or job title. Thus an employee might be immune for actions deemed discretionary (policy-related planning for a 5K Run) but not immune for actions ruled ministerial (carrying out the policies for a 5K Run). A university activity center director might receive immunity for staffing decisions, but might not be immune for actions taken when teaching a fitness class – it is the act of the employee, not the job title that counts.

In *Feagins v. Waddy* (2007), a girl on the track team suffered injury when she was assigned to compete in the high jump in a meet without prior instruction. The court held that the coach had immunity as a state agent because the selection of participants for events involves an exercise of judgment and is, therefore, a discretionary duty. In the past, such a decision would likely have been classified as ministerial; the decision as to whether to have a track team would be discretionary. This is just one example of courts blurring the distinction between discretionary and ministerial acts.

Charitable Immunity

During the first half of the twentieth century, charitable immunity provided substantial liability protection to charitable, educational, and religious organizations. **Charitable immunity** is a doctrine that relieves or immunizes charitable organizations from liability for tort. The doctrine is based upon four premises: (1) public policy encourages charitable organizations since they benefit the public; (2) money possessed by such organizations was donated for other purposes and is held in trust; (3) since the recipient of the charity receives benefits, he or she, in turn, accepts the risks of negligence; and (4) there is no *respondeat superior* since the charity does not benefit from the actions of employees.

Charitable immunity, which focused on the protection of the agency or institution, has been repealed in most states. In most of the few states that retain some semblance of charitable immunity, the immunity has been emasculated to the point where its effectiveness is very limited.[1] Today volunteer protection acts do provide some protection for the nonprofit or charitable institution volunteer. In addition, a few states still protect those gratuitously serving such institutions as a member, director, trustee, or board member.

Recreational User Statutes[2]

In order to encourage private owners of natural, rural areas to allow others to use their property for recreational purposes, state legislatures began passing recreational user statutes in the 1960s. The **recreational user statute** is a law designed to provide protection for the private property-owner against lawsuits by parties injured while on the landowner's property for recreational purposes. Originally, the immunity laws applied when four conditions were met: (1) private landowners; (2) no fee charged; (3) unimproved, undeveloped land for recreational use; and (4) owner fulfilled his or her obligation to provide a warning for any known, concealed danger that would not be apparent to the recreational user.

Today, all states have enacted some type of recreational user statute. While differences exist among the statutes, they were enacted with comparable intent. Statutes generally (1) are intended to encourage landowners to make their property available to the public for recreational use; (2) stipulate that no fee is charged for the use of the land; (3) declare that the owner owes no duty of care to keep the land safe for use for recreational purpose nor to warn of a dangerous condition; (4) state that the landowner extends no assurance that the land is safe for any purpose and does not confer on the user the legal status of invitee or licensee; and (5) say that the landowner does not assume responsibility for or incur liability for any injury, death, or loss to any person or property caused by an act or omission of the landowner.

Resultant of the immunity provided by most such statutes, the provider's only duty is to warn of ultra hazardous situations and of known hidden hazards. In most states, the provider has no liability except for willful or malicious acts and for ultra hazardous situations. The immunity generally applies to all activity risks and all open and obvious premise risks.

While most recreational user statutes were adopted for the same purpose (encouraging property owners to open their land for recreational use), courts in some states have significantly broadened their application. Courts in those states have expanded the immunity provided by the statutes by interpreting them liberally (e.g., by applying the statutes in cases where the injury occurred on a tennis court or when a fee was paid). The reader is encouraged to read an excellent presentation on the subject in Chapter 2.32 *Property Law*. The specific statutes for each state may be found in Table 2.22.1 of this chapter and a summary of recreational user immunity may be found in Table 2.21.1 in Chapter 2.21 *Defenses against Negligence*.

Volunteer Immunity Statutes

Prior to the decade of the 1980s, lawsuits against volunteers in recreation and sport activities were rare. In that decade, insurance coverage became both expensive and difficult to obtain, some coverage was unavailable, more exclusions were added to policies, many agencies discontinued or reduced insurance coverage, volunteer lawsuits began to increase in frequency, and volunteer recruitment became more difficult. This predicament prompted a number of states to pass legislation aimed at protecting certain volunteers in recreational and sport activities (see Table 2.22.1 in this chapter).

State Volunteer Immunity Statutes

In the late 1980s, state legislatures were encouraged to pass a model act designed to protect volunteers working with certain nonprofit organizations and governmental entities from liability for injuries resulting from the ordinary or gross negligence of the volunteers. The Model State Act called for immunity from civil liability for

---

[1]Charitable immunity is still strong in New Jersey (*Gilbert v. Seton Hall University*, 2003) and Virginia (*Chrisman v. Brown*, 2007; *Kuykendall v. Young Life*, 2006). Some states that still retain very limited immunity include Arkansas, Georgia, Maine, Maryland, Massachusetts, Tennessee, Utah, and Wyoming (Non-Profit Risk Management Center, 2009).

[2]Convenient access to the complete recreational user statutes in every state is available on the Internet thanks to the work of Holly Rudolph, J.D. Access the Equine Land Conservation Resource website for links to the statutes for each state: https://elcr.org/statestatutes/.

TABLE 2.22.1 STATE RECREATION- AND SPORT-RELATED IMMUNITY LEGISLATION

State	Recreational User Statutes	Rec/Sport Volunteer Statutes	Good Samaritan Statutes	Good Samaritan Statutes (AED)	Equine Immunity Statutes	Ski Operator Immunity Statutes	Skating Immunity Statutes	Other Sport & Recreation Statutes	General Sport & Recreation Statutes	Hazardous Recreational Activity Statutes
U.S.		PL. 105-19 42 U.S.C.S. 14,501-14,505		PL. 107-188 42 U.S.C.S. 238q						
AL	AC 35-15- (1-28)		AC 6-5-332	AC 6-5-332	AC 6-5-337		AC 6-5-342 Skateboard Parks			
AK	AS 09.65.200 AS 34.17.055		AS 09-65-090	AS 09.65.090	None	AS 05.45.010 to .210			AS 09.65. 290 (2009)	
AZ	ARS 33-1551		ARS 32-1471 ARS 32-1472 ARS 36.21.1	ARS 36-2261-2264	ARS 12-553	ARS 5-701 - 707		ARS 12-554 Baseball ARS 12-556 Motor Sports		
AR	ARS 18-11- 301 to 307	ARS 16-120-102	ARS 17-95-101	ARS 20-13-1305 ARS 20-13-1306	ARS 16-120-201 to 202					
CA	CCC 846, 846.1		CCHSC 1799.102	ACC 1714.21 HSC 1797.190 SB 911 of 1999	None	5 county ordinances	CGC 831.7 (Hazardous Rec. Act. Statute)			CGC 831.7
CO	CRS 33-41- 101 to106	CRS 13-21-116	CRS 13-21-15.5	CRS 13-21-108.1	CRS 13-21-119	CRS 33-44-101 to 114		CRS 13-21-111.8(1) and 25-12-109 Sport Shooting CRS 13-21-120 Baseball CRS 12-55-103 to 118 Outfitters & Guides		
CT	CGSA 52-557f-k		CGSA 52-557B	CGSA 52-57b	CGSA 52-557p	CGSA 29-201 to 214				
DE	7 DCA 5901-5907	16 DCA 6835 16 DCA 6836	16 DCA 6801	DCA 6801	10 DCA 8140					
FL	FS 375.251		FS 768.13	FS 768.1325	FS 773.01 to .05		FS 316.0085 Skateboard Parks, Inline skating	549.09 Motorsports 316.0085 biking, paintball 790.333 & 823.16 Sport Shooting		FS 316.0085
GA	OCGA 51-3-20 to 26; OCGA 27-3-1	OCGA 51-1-20.1	OCGA 51-1-230 OCGA 768.135	OCGA 31-11-53.1 OCGA 51-1-29.3	OCGA 4-12-1 to 5	OCGA § 43-43A 1-8	OCGA51-1-43 Roller Skating	OCGA 27-4-280 to 283 Fishing		
HI	HRS 520-1 to 8	HRS 662D - 4	HI 663-1.5	HRS 663-1.5	HRS 663B-1 to 2		HRS 662-19, HRS 46-72.5, HRS 662D-4 Skateboarding		HRS 663-1.54	

(Continued)

TABLE 2.22.1 STATE RECREATION- AND SPORT-RELATED IMMUNITY LEGISLATION (continued)

State	Recreational User Statutes	Rec/Sport Volunteer Statutes	Good Samaritan Statutes	Good Samaritan Statutes (AED)	Equine Immunity Statutes	Ski Operator Immunity Statutes	Skating Immunity Statutes	Other Sport & Recreation Statutes	General Sport & Recreation Statutes	Hazardous Recreational Activity Statutes
ID	IC 36-1604		IC 5-330	IC 5-337	IC 6-1801 to 1802	IC 6-1101-1109		IC 6-1201 to 1206 Outfitters & Guides IC 6-2701 to 2702 Sport Shooting		
IL	745 ILCS 65/1 to 7	745 ILCS 80/1	745 ILCS 49/12	410 ILCS 4/30 745 ILCS 49/12	745 ILCS 47/1 to 47/999		745 ILCS 72/1 to 30 Roller Skating	745 ILCS 52/1 to /99 Hockey Facilities		745 ILCS 10/3-109
IN	ICA 14-22-10-2 to 2.5	ICA 34-30-4-2 ICA 34-30-19-3 to 4	ICA 34-30-12-1	ICA 16-31-6.2 ICA 34-30-12-1	ICA 34-6-2-40 to 43, 69, 95, 103; ICA 34-31-5-1 to 5		ICA 34-31-6-1 to 4 Roller Skating			
IA	ICA 461C.1 to .7		ICA 115.3 ICA 915.3	ICA 147A.10	ICA 673.1 to 4		ICA 670.4 Skateboard Parks			
KS	KSA 58-3201 to 3207	KSA 60-3607	KSA 65-2891	KSA 65-6149a	KSA 60-4001 to 4004					
KY	KRS 150.645 KRS 411.190		KRS 411.148 KRS 411.150	KRS 311.668	KRS 247.401 to 4029					
LA	LRS 9:2791, 2795	LRS 9:2798	LRS 9:2793	LRS 40:1236. 11 to .14 LRS 9:2793	LRS 9: 2795.1					
ME	14 MRSA 159-A		14 MRSA 164	22 MRSA 2150-C	7 MRSA 4101-4104A	26 MRSA 471 - 490-G 32 MRSA 15201 to 15227	8 MRSA 23-601-608 Roller Skating, 8 MRSA 24- 621-626 Ice Skating	8 MRSA 801-806 Amuse Rides; 32 MRSA 15219 Hang Gliding		
MD	MCA 5-1101 to1109	MCA 5-607 MCA 5-802	MCA 5-603	MCA 13-517	None					
MA	21 MGL 17C	231 MGL 85V	71 ALM 55A 111C ALM 20	112 ALM 12V1/2	128 MGL 2D	143 MGL 71H to 71S				
MI	MCLA 324.73301		MCLA 691.1501 MCLA 691.1507 MCLA 333.20965	MCLA 333.20965	MCLA 691.1661 to 1667	MCLA 408.321 to .344 or MSA 13A.82126	MCLA 445.1721 to .1726 Roller Skating	MCLA 681. 1541 to .1544 MCLA 691.1544 Sport Shooting; MCLA 342.82126 Snowmobiling		
MN	MSA 604A.20 to 27	MSA 604A.11	MSA 604A.01	MSA 604A.01	MSA 604A.12					

State	Recreational User Statutes	Rec/Sport Volunteer Statutes	Good Samaritan Statutes	Good Samaritan Statutes (AED)	Equine Immunity Statutes	Ski Operator Immunity Statutes	Skating Immunity Statutes	Other Sport & Recreation Statutes	General Sport & Recreation Statutes	Hazardous Recreational Activity Statutes
MS	MCA 89-2-1 to 27	MCA 95-9-3	MCA 63-3-405 MCA 73-25-37	MCA 41-60-33	MCA 95-11-1 to 7					
MO	MAS 537.345 to .348		RSM 537.037	RSM 190.092	MAS 537.325			RSMO 537.327 Outfitters, Paddlesports (canoe, raft, kayak, tubing)		
MT	MCA 70-16-301 to 302		MCA 27-1-714	MCA 50-6-505	MCA 27-1-725 to 728	MCA 23-2-732 to -736		MCA 23-2-651 to 656 Snowmobiling MCA 27-1-733 Rodeos		
NE	NRS 37-729 to 736		NRS 25-21, 186	NRS 71-51, 102	NRS 25-21.249 to .253		NRS 13-910 (2009) Skateparks, inline skating, Skateboarding, Bicycle Motocross Parks, Bicycling,	NRS 13-910 (2009) Bicycle Motocross Parks, Bicycling,		
NV	NRS 41.510	NRS 41.630	NRS 41.5000	NRS 41.500	None	NRS 455A.010 to -.190	NRS 455B.200 to 300 Skateboard Parks	NRS 455B.010 to 455B.100 Amusement Rides		
NH	NHSA 212:34, NHSA 231-A:1 to 8	NHSA 508.17	RSA 508:12	RSA 153-A:31	NHSA 508:19	NHSA 225-A:1 to :26	NHSA 507 - B:11 Skateboard Parks			NHSA 507 B-11
NJ	NJS 13:1B-15. 134 to 142 NJS 2A:42A-2 to 10	NJS 2A:62A-6	NJS 2A:62A-1 NJS 26:2K-29	NJS 2A:62A-25	NJ S 5:15-1 to 12	NJS 34:4A-1; NJS 5:13-1 to 11	NJS 5:14-1 to 7 Roller Skating			
NM	NMSA 17-4-7	NMSA 41-12-1 NMSA 41-12-2	NMSA 24-10-3	NMSA 34-10B-4	NMSA 42-13-2 to 5	NMSA 24-15-1-14				
NY	NY GOL 9-103		NYCLSPH 3000-a	NYCLSPH 3000-a NYCLSPH 3000-b	None	NY GOL 18-101 to -108 NYLL 865 to 868				
NC	NCGS 38A-1 to 4		NCGS 20-166 NCGS 90-21.14	NCGS 90-21.15	NCGS 99E-1 to 3	NCGS 99C-1 to 5	NCGS 99E-10 to 14 Roller Skating	NCGS 14-409.46 Sport Shooting		NCGS Art 99E – 21-25
ND	NDCC 53-08-01 to 06	NDCC 32-3-46	NDCC 32-03.1-02	NDCC 32-03.1-02.3	NDCC 53-10-01 to 02	NDCC 53-09-01 to 11				
OH	ORCA 1533.18 ORCA 1533.181		ORCA 2305.23	ORCA 2305.235	ORCA 2305.321	ORCA 4169.01 to .99	ORCA 4171.01 to .10 Roller Skating			

(*Continued*)

TABLE 2.22.1 STATE RECREATION- AND SPORT-RELATED IMMUNITY LEGISLATION (continued)

State	Recreational User Statutes	Rec/Sport Volunteer Statutes	Good Samaritan Statutes	Good Samaritan Statutes (AED)	Equine Immunity Statutes	Ski Operator Immunity Statutes	Skating Immunity Statutes	Other Sport & Recreation Statutes	General Sport & Recreation Statutes	Hazardous Recreational Activity Statutes
OK	2 OS 1301-315 76 OS 5, 11 OS 76-10 to 15	76 OS 31	OS 76.5	76 OS 5A	OS 76 50.1 to -4					
OR	ORS 105.670 to .700		ORS 30.800 ORS 433.830	ORS 30.802	ORS 30.687 – .697	ORS 30.970 to .990				
PA	68 PCSA 477-1 to 7	42 PCSA 8332.1	42 PCSA 8332	42 PCSA 8331.2	PCSA 2005 SB 618	42 PCSA 7102 or 40 PCSA 2051				
RI	RIGL 32-6-1 to 7	RIGL 9-1-48	RIGL 9-1-27.1 RIGL 9-1-34	RIGL 9-1-34	RIGL 4-21-1 to 4	RIGL 41-8-1 to 4		RIGL 9-20-5 Snow Mobiles & ATVs		
SC	SCCA 27-3-10 to 70		SCCA 15-1-310	SCCA 4-76-40	SCCA 47-9-710 to 730		SCCA 52-21-10 to 60 Ice Skating and Roller Skating			
SD	SDCLA 20-9-12 to 18		SDCLA 32034-3 SDCLA 20-9-3	SDCLA 20-9-4.1	SDCLA 42-11-1 to 5			SDCLA 32-20A-21 to 22 Snowmobiling	SDCLA 20-9-12 to 18 25 plus outdoor sports	
TN	TCA 11-10-101 to 105 TCA 70-7-101 to 105	TCA 62-50-201-203	TCA 63-6-218	TCA 63-6-218	TCA 44-20-101 to 105	TCA 68-114-102 to 107		TCA 70-7-201-204 Whitewater rafting		
TX	TCPRC 4- 75.001 to .004	TCPRC 84.0001 to 008	VTCA 74.001-/003	TCPRC 74.001	TCPRC 87.001 to .005		759.001 to .005 Roller Skating 760.001 to .006 Ice Skating	TCPRC 4-75.001 Hockey, hunting, fishing, water skiing, more.		
UT	UCA 57-14-1 to 7		UCA 78-11-22	UCA 28-8-7.5 or 75	UCA 78-27b-101 to 103	UCA 78-27-51 to 54	See Gen Rec & Sport Statutes for Skateboard Parks	UCA 47-3-1 to 3 Sport Shooting; UCA 78-27-61 Amuse Rides; UCA 78-27-62 Hockey Facilities	UCA 78-27-63	
VT	12 VSA 5791-5795			12 VSA 519	12 VSA 1039	12 VSA 1036 to 1038	See Genl Rec & Sport Statutes for Skateboard Parks	10 VSA 5227 Sport Shooting	12 VSA 1037	
VA	VCA 29.1-509		VCA 8.00-225	VCA 8.01-225	VCA 3.1-796.130 to .133					

State	Recreational User Statutes	Rec/Sport Volunteer Statutes	Good Samaritan Statutes	Good Samaritan Statutes (AED)	Equine Immunity Statutes	Ski Operator Immunity Statutes	Skating Immunity Statutes	Other Sport & Recreation Statutes	General Sport & Recreation Statutes	Hazardous Recreational Activity Statutes
WA	RCW 4.24.200 to 210		RCW 4.24.300	RCW 70.54.310	RCW 4.24.530 to .540	RCW 70.117.010 to .040; RCW 79A.45.010 to .060	RCW 4.24.210 Skateboarding (among others)		RCW 4.24.210 More than 20 activities	
WV	WVC 19-25-1 to 7		WVC 55-7-15	WVC 16-4D-3 to 4	WVC 20-4-1 to 7	WVC 20-3A-1 to 8		WVC 20-3B-1 to 5 Outfitter/Guides WVC 20-15 ATV	WVC 20-16 Non-profit Youth Organiz.	
WI	WSA 895.52 to .525)		WSA 895.48	WSA 895.48	WSA 895.481-895.481 3 (e)	WSA 895.525	See Gen Rec & Sport Statutes for Skateboard Parks	WSA 875.527 Sport Shooting	WSA 895.525	
WY	WYO STAT 34-19-101 to 106		WYO STAT 1-1-120	WYO STAT 35-26-102 to 103	WYO STAT 1-1-121 to 123	WYO.STAT. 1-1-121 to 123		WYO.STAT. 1-1-118 Rodeos 23-2-401 to 418 Outfitters and Guides	WYO STAT 1-1-121 to 123	

any act or omission of the volunteer that resulted in damage or injury if the volunteer was acting in good faith and within the scope of duty for a nonprofit organization or governmental entity—so long as the injury was not caused by wanton and willful misconduct and did not involve the operation of a motor vehicle. The model act, however, intended no protection for the nonprofit or governmental agency for which the volunteer worked.

Subsequently, all states now have either (1) a general volunteer liability statute (often modeled after the Model State Act) designed to provide protection for volunteers, or (2) a statute intended to protect certain volunteers in recreation and sports activities (*e.g.*, coaches, referees), or (3) both types of statutes. The general volunteer statutes vary greatly from state to state. Many of the states protect only directors or officers in the organization and all have exceptions to immunity. Common exceptions include the motor vehicle exception, action based on federal law, action that constitutes gross negligence, willful and wanton acts, and, in a few states, ordinary negligence. Many of these general state statutes are worded such that they should provide immunity for recreation and sport volunteers. Additionally, in 1997 the volunteer was provided with even more protection when Congress enacted the Volunteer Protection Act (discussed in detail below).

Recreation and Sport Volunteer Immunity Statutes

Twenty states have passed some type of volunteer statute for volunteer sport coaches and officials.[3] In addition, a Hawaii statute protects volunteers at public skateboard parks and youth sport volunteers are specifically mentioned in the Oklahoma and Texas general volunteer immunity statutes.

There are ten points that are frequently addressed in recreation and sport volunteer immunity statutes.

1. The volunteer must be **unpaid**. Some statutes specify that officials (e.g., referees, umpires) may receive a small stipend and retain their immunity.
2. The volunteer must act in **good faith**.
3. The volunteer must act within the **scope** of his or her duties.
4. **Protected parties** are usually specified and may include any or all of athletic coach, assistant coach, manager, assistant manager, instructor, official, referee, umpire, leader, league official, athletic trainer, and physician or other healthcare provider. The law in Arkansas, Kansas, and Mississippi restricts eligibility for immunity to sports officials who officiate at any level of competition.
5. Additionally, most statutes define the **type organization** (e.g., nonprofit, charitable, educational) whose volunteers qualify.
6. Some states stipulate that protected parties must undergo an approved **training program**, usually relating to safety or first aid.
7. Some states specify that immunity does not protect when activities are **unsupervised**.
8. Most, but not all, exclude public and private **school coaches** from immunity.
9. It is the **nature of the act** that is protected. Most include immunity for ordinary negligence, but several include gross negligence, excluding only wanton and willful acts or intentional acts. Pennsylvania and New Mexico statutes specify immunity unless the conduct is substantially below the generally accepted level.
10. Almost all exclude negligence in the operation of a **motor vehicle** from immunity.

Heard v. City of Villa Rica (2010) illustrates the function of these statutes. A boy was injured when training for the long jump under the instruction of a volunteer coach. The coach claimed immunity while the plaintiff claimed that immunity did not apply when the coach was grossly negligent. The court held that there was no gross negligence and held that the defendant was immune under the statute.

Volunteer Protection Act (VPA)

The **Volunteer Protection Act** (VPA) was signed into law in 1997 (Public Law 105-19). This federal statute preempts state laws (except for those that provide for more volunteer protection than the VPA) and is intended to provide broad protection to volunteers nationwide under the following conditions:

---

[3] Arkansas, Colorado, Delaware, Georgia, Illinois, Indiana, Kansas, Louisiana, Maryland, Massachusetts, Minnesota, Mississippi, Nevada, New Hampshire, New Jersey, New Mexico, North Dakota, Pennsylvania, Tennessee, and Rhode Island. Volunteer recreation and sport statutes may be found in Table 2.22.1 in this chapter.

- The volunteer was acting within the scope of the volunteer's responsibilities in the nonprofit organization or governmental entity at the time of the act or omission;
- If appropriate or required, the volunteer was properly licensed, certified or authorized by the appropriate authorities for the activities or practice in the state;
- The harm was not caused by willful or criminal misconduct, gross negligence, reckless misconduct, or a conscious, flagrant indifference to the rights or safety of the individual harmed by the volunteer;
- The harm was not caused by the volunteer operating a motor vehicle . . . for which the State requires . . . an operator's license; or . . . insurance.

Of particular interest is the second condition—that the immunity applies only if the volunteer is licensed, certified or authorized when such empowerments are relevant. *It is important to note that the act does not affect the liability of any nonprofit or governmental entity—but rather protects only individuals from liability.* In *Avenoso v. Mangan* (2006), Mangan, a volunteer soccer coach, caused injury to Avenoso when he ran too close to him. The court granted summary judgment on the basis of the VPA, but ruled that the co-defendant soccer club did not qualify for immunity under the act.

Acts that are not encompassed by the statute include (1) crimes of violence or terrorism, (2) hate crimes, (3) sexual offense convictions, (4) violation of federal or state civil rights law, and (5) those committed while under the influence of drugs or alcohol. Punitive damages can be awarded only if the volunteer's actions constituted willful or criminal misconduct or a conscious flagrant indifference to the rights and safety of the injured party. For losses due to physical or emotional pain, the volunteer will be liable only to the extent of his or her percentage of responsibility.

First Aid Statutes (Good Samaritan)

Every state has some form of Good Samaritan statute which is intended to provide immunity from liability for certain parties who voluntarily and gratuitously come to the aid of injured persons. Good Samaritan laws were developed to encourage both physicians and laymen to help others in emergency situations.

There is no general legal duty to assist or rescue injured parties in most states. An exception is Vermont, which requires a person who knows that another is exposed to grave physical harm to give reasonable assistance to the exposed person if he can do so without danger or peril to himself. Penalty for violation, however, is only $100. Mississippi, North Carolina, and South Dakota require that the driver of a vehicle involved in an accident assist injured parties if needed if assisting presents no danger to the one assisting. Most then provide immunity for the driver. Georgia has a duty to assist and rescue in the event of watercraft accidents.

There are six elements that are common to most Good Samaritan statutes. The first is the stipulation of **who is protected** by the statute. The most common designation is any person who comes to the aid of another in an emergency situation. More than 40 states offer protection for any individual who assists in an emergency situation. Some states, however, restrict the immunity to healthcare personnel (physicians, surgeons, nurses, EMS personnel, physical therapists, and/or others) or those with first aid training. Many states exclude healthcare professionals from protection if the action is within the scope of the duty of the healthcare professional.

The second and third elements are that the parties must act in **good faith** and without expectation of **remuneration**. Almost every state specifies one or the other and most list both. Fourth, almost all of the statutes specify that the action must occur in an **emergency situation** away from a medical facility. There are also many states that have statutes specific to assisting those choking on food in restaurants. A few statutes limit coverage to more specific situations (e.g., choking, crime victims, cardiopulmonary rescues, life-threatening situations, athletic events) and some apply to volunteer team physicians. Fifth, the statutes almost always stipulate that the care must be done **at the scene** of the accident. A number also add protection during transport to the hospital.

Finally, virtually all of the statutes specify a **standard of care required**. Unfortunately, that standard varies by state. A few states, including Arkansas, Florida, and Mississippi require that the acts of the volunteer be those of a reasonable and prudent person. In these states, and possibly a few others, the "Good Samaritan" is **not** protected against liability for negligence. Most states protect the volunteer from liability when the act is negligent, but not if the rescuer is grossly negligent, reckless, or willful and wanton. Statutes in a few states specify that there is immunity unless there is reckless or willful and wanton conduct.

While "Good Samaritan" laws differ considerably among states, the typical statute asserts that *any person who, in good faith, gratuitously renders emergency care at the scene of an accident cannot be held liable for injury resulting from acts and omissions unless the conduct constitutes gross negligence or willful/wanton conduct*. It is, however, prudent for one to know the law in one's own state. Good Samaritan legislation in each state may be found in Table 2.22.1 in this chapter and is summarized in Table 2.21.1 in Chapter 2.21 *Defenses against Negligence*.

In a 2008 California Supreme Court ruling (*Van Horn v. Watson*), the court held that the California Good Samaritan statute applied only to the rendering of care at the scene of a medical emergency and did not encompass rescue or extrication. Injuries incurred during a rescue or while transporting the injured party to medical aid (e.g., after an accident in a wilderness area) may subject the rescuer/transporter to civil liability. A number of other states have similar provisions in their statute so Californians are not the only ones who may be affected in this situation.

AED Statutes

The development of the automated external defibrillator (AED) in the 1990s provided a major technological advance in the fight against sudden cardiac arrest deaths in the United States. The **AED** is a medical device which (1) recognizes the presence or absence of ventricular fibrillation; (2) is capable of determining if defibrillation should be performed; (3) can automatically charge and request delivery of an electrical impulse; and (4) can deliver an appropriate impulse upon action by the operator. While it has been estimated that more than half of the 250,000 plus sudden cardiac arrest deaths annually in the nation could be prevented by timely use of an AED, its widespread use has been hampered by the lack of laws enabling its use by non-medical personnel.

With the intent of encouraging the extensive use of the AED, some states began passing Good Samaritan legislation specifically aimed at AED usage while others added the AED to existing Good Samaritan statutes. While all states have now passed some type of AED legislation, that legislation differs significantly from state to state in terms of (1) who is protected, (2) requirements for immunity, and (3) what acts are immunized. AED legislation in each state may be found in Table 2.22.1 in this chapter and the immunity is summarized in Table 2.21.1 in Chapter 2.21 *Defenses against Negligence*.

Parties protected may include any or all of the following, varying by state: (1) trained users, (2) any user in a perceived emergency, (3) the entity that acquires the device, (4) the prescribing physician, (5) parties who train others to use the AED, or (6) certified healthcare professionals. A major difference involves the requirements for immunity. Many states offer immunity for **any user** who acts gratuitously and in good faith in a perceived medical emergency to render emergency care. Many other states provide the same immunity, but only to **trained users**. The definition of trained also differs considerably. Some states require that expected users (or employees) be trained, but that a "Good Samaritan" passerby is immune regardless of training. Legislation in a few states seems to legalize the use of the device, but provides no immunity.

There is also great variance in what acts are immunized by the law. At least one provides immunity only where the user acted as an ordinary reasonably prudent person would have acted—seemingly providing no immunity from negligence. Most specify no immunity protection for grossly negligent actions or willful or wanton misconduct—thereby providing immunity for negligence. Several exclude only willful and wanton actions from immunity—thus apparently creating immunity for grossly negligent acts. Several also seem to provide blanket immunity, specifying no restrictions on the immunity of an AED user.

AED Requirements. A number of states (Arkansas, California, Connecticut, Illinois, Indiana, Iowa, Louisiana, Maryland, Massachusetts, Michigan, New Jersey, New York, Oregon, Pennsylvania, Rhode Island, and Washington D.C.) have passed statutes requiring AED availability in health clubs and/or recreational facilities.

A number of states now require or encourage AEDs in schools – though the degree of implementation varies greatly. Alabama, Arkansas, Colorado, Connecticut, Florida, Georgia, Illinois, Iowa, Kentucky, Louisiana, Maine, Maryland, Massachusetts, Michigan, Nevada, New Jersey, New York, North Dakota, Ohio, Pennsylvania, South Carolina, Tennessee, Texas, Virginia, and Wisconsin require devices in at least some schools. Oregon and Hawaii, however, require AEDs in all public schools, all private schools, and in all colleges. One point to remember, however, is that because a device is mandated does not always mean the mandate is enforced.

Requiring availability of AEDs, however, does not always insure that available AEDs will be utilized. In a New York case (*Deguilio v. Gran, Inc.*, 2009), a client collapsed in a health club. An AED was available, but was not used because employees thought it was locked up. After the client died, suit was filed alleging negligence in failing to make the AED easily accessible and/or failing to advise its employees that the cabinet housing it was unlocked. The court ruled that the club had no duty to use a defibrillator because the client had assumed the risk of cardiac arrest by walking on the treadmill. The club was not found liable because it complied with the statute to maintain an accessible defibrillator on the premises.

More recently in *Miglino v. Bally Total Fitness of Greater New York, Inc.* (2013), Miglino suffered a heart attack at the club. The club had an AED and a employee qualified to operate it, but the club failed to utilize the instrument and Miglino died. The executor sued the health club for failing to use an AED contending that **Public Health Law § 3000-b (4)** (which provides that health clubs with 500 or more members must have an AED available and have a trained employee on hand to administer it) creates an affirmative duty for clubs to use the AED in the event of a cardiac emergency. The court disagreed; it pointed out that both statutes requiring AEDs in clubs use the words "volunteer" and "voluntarily." The court felt this was convincing evidence that the legislature's intent was to protect health clubs and their employees from the risk of liability for ordinary negligence with respect to AEDs. The court ruled that the statutes do not create a duty on the facility to use the AED. See Chapter 2.33 *Emergency Care* for more information regarding AEDs.

Cardiac Arrest Survival Act (CASA)

In an effort to further combat sudden cardiac arrest deaths, Congress passed the **Cardiac Arrest Survival Act** (2002) (42 *USCS* 238q [2002]). The legislation, like the state legislation preceding it, is designed to accelerate the widespread use of automated external defibrillators by providing Good Samaritan immunity in those states not having such protection. The legislation was intended to augment existing state "Good Samaritan" laws by providing federal liability protection for both users and purchasers of AEDs.

The law specifies that "**any person who uses** or attempts to use an AED device on a victim of a perceived medical emergency is immune from civil liability for any harm resulting from the use or attempted use of such device," including healthcare professionals outside the scope of their license or certification. This immunity to the Good Samaritan user applies regardless of training and protects the user from liability for ordinary negligence. **Any person who acquires the device** is also immune from such liability provided the harm was not due to failure of the acquirer to notify appropriate local entities of the placement of the device, to properly maintain and test the device, or to provide appropriate training to employees using the device.

CASA preempts state law only where the state statute does not provide protection for a user or acquirer. Thus, CASA fills in the immunity gaps left by some state legislation since all users and acquirers are covered by state law (if state statute provides immunity) or by federal law (if immunity is not provided for by state law). When state law fails to protect either the user or the acquirer, CASA provides that protection.

Immunity is not provided by CASA: (1) for willful or criminal misconduct, gross negligence, reckless misconduct or a conscious, flagrant indifference to the rights or safety of the victim who was harmed; (2) for licensed health professionals operating within the scope of their employment; or (3) for certain healthcare providers or lessors of AEDs.

Shared Responsibility and Statutory Assumption of Risk Statutes

Legislation has been enacted in most states to help protect selected recreation and sport providers from liability for injuries resulting from the inherent risks of particular activities, or in many cases, from certain types of ordinary negligence by the provider. Some of these acts are in the form of shared responsibility statutes while others are more accurately designated as statutory assumption of risk statutes. These acts, originally called **sport safety acts**, usually seek to provide some liability protections for recreation and sport businesses that make certain activities available to the public.

Shared responsibility statutes generally have four distinguishing features. They enumerate the **duties of the recreation or sport provider**. Failure to satisfy these duties constitutes negligence and makes the statute inapplicable. Duties enumerated in such statutes have been deemed to establish a statutory standard of care. The second earmark of these statutes is that they specify **duties of the participant**. Common duties listed include the responsibility to read and obey signs and to stay within the limits of his or her ability. Failure to perform the required participant duties could constitute secondary assumption of risk. Secondary assumption of risk (formerly called contributory negligence) would serve to decrease situations in which recovery for participants is possible and may, at the same time, increase liability of the participant to other participants. Shared responsibility statutes usually contain certain **provisions that preclude recovery**. Most specify that recovery is not permitted when the injury resulted from inherent risks. Many statutes specifically define the inherent risks of the activity or sport, prompting many courts to grant summary judgment based upon the statute. The final feature of these statutes is that **some type of immunity is provided**—or perhaps, more accurately, they reassert that there is *no liability* for injuries resulting from the inherent risks. Some, however, provide that there is no liability unless the provider failed to comply with the specified duties; others provide immunity from liability for certain types of negligence.

Some statutes are more accurately classified as **statutory assumption of risk statutes** since the major provision of the statute is to make clear that the participant is assuming the inherent risks of the activity. These statutes usually do not include duties of the participant. Notwithstanding the differences between these two types of statutes, the characteristic they have in common is that they usually are intended to protect the service provider from liability for injury resulting from the inherent risks of the activity, and in many cases, from liability for injuries resulting from ordinary negligence.

These two types of statutes have been grouped into six categories: (1) equine liability statutes; (2) skiing statutes; (3) skating statutes [*i.e.*, roller skating, ice skating, skateboarding, in-line skating, skate parks]; (4) statutes pertaining to other activities; (5) general recreation and sport statutes; and (6) hazardous recreational activity statutes.

Equine Liability Statutes[4]

State legislatures have enacted equine liability statutes in 45 states; the only states without an equine statute are Alaska, California, Maryland, New York, and Nevada. Equine acts usually include horses, ponies, donkeys, mules, hinnies, and in some states, llamas. The laws are designed to protect owners, sponsors, and organizers of named equine activities from liability for equine-related accidents resulting from the inherent risks of the activity, and in many cases from ordinary negligence. Most may be closer to statutory assumption of risk statutes than to shared responsibility statutes since they generally do not specify responsibilities or duties of the participant. While the statutes differ somewhat from state to state, most equine statutes *immunize equine owners from liability for injuries resulting from the inherent risks of equine activities except when the provider*

1. provided faulty equipment or tack that caused the injury;
2. failed to make reasonable and prudent efforts to determine the ability of the participant to engage safely in the activity or determine the ability of the participant to safely manage the particular equine;
3. failed to post warning of known dangerous latent conditions on the facilities; or
4. commits an act or omission that is below the required level of care. The minimum level described varies by state, but includes ordinary negligence, gross negligence, reckless conduct, and willful and wanton conduct.

In general, these statutes do not provide the same protection as that provided by the immunity statutes described in previous sections of this chapter since under most equine statutes the provider remains liable for injuries resulting from some or all negligent acts. Statutes generally define the equine activities covered by the law, the categories of providers protected, the immunity provided, the exceptions, signage requirements, and the inherent risks of equine activities. Usually included in the inherent risks are (1) equine behavior propensities, (2) unpredictability of animal reactions, (3) hazards such as surface and subsurface conditions, (4) collisions with other equines and objects, and (5) the potential of a participant to act in a negligent manner that may cause injury. Equine legislation in each state may be found in Table 2.22.1 in this chapter.

Ski Operator Immunity Statutes

Ski operator statutes were among the first shared-responsibility statutes—*intended to clarify the duties of the ski operator and the skier and to reduce litigation arising from injuries due to the inherent risks of skiing*. At least 29 state legislatures have enacted some type of shared responsibility ski statute. While these statutes differ

---

[4]Convenient access to the equine liability statutes in every state is available on the Internet thanks to the work of Holly Rudolph, J.D. Access the Equine Land Conservation Resource website for links to the statutes for each state: https://elcr.org/statestatutes/.

considerably, they generally include duties of the ski operator, duties of the skier, a listing of the inherent risks of skiing, and the affirmation that the skier assumes the inherent risks of the activity and that the ski operator is not liable for injuries resulting from the inherent risks. Lists of operator and skier duties are generally extensive. These acts generally include no immunity for ordinary negligence; however, in some states, negligence is limited to the failure to perform specified duties.

States approach inherent risks in various ways. Some states (e.g., Tennessee, New Mexico, and Idaho) express that any injury not caused by a violation of the ski operator duties is an inherent risk of the activity and that subsequent legal action is barred. Colorado, North Carolina, and Alaska statutes specify that a violation of the statute by either operator or skier constitutes negligence. Other states require a jury to determine if the risk was inherent. Ski legislation in each state may be found in Table 2.22.1 in this chapter.

Skating Statutes

About twenty states have enacted roller-skating, ice skating, inline skating, and/or skateboarding statutes of some kind. These statutes generally contain four critical sections: (1) duties of the operator—usually including posting of notices regarding duties of skaters and inherent risks of skating; (2) duties of the skater—usually including skating within the range of one's ability, maintaining control of the skater's speed and course at all times, and heeding safety warnings; (3) some of the inherent dangers of skating; and (4) a declaration that the skater assumes the inherent risks and a statement that a skater or operator who violates duties set forth is liable to an injured person in a civil action. Skating legislation in each state may be found in Table 2.22.1 in this chapter. In addition, a number of states have adopted omnibus legislation (discussed later) or recreational user statutes that provide some liability protection for providers of certain types of skating.

Skateboard Parks. Popular types of skating emerging in recent years have included skateboarding, rollerblading, roller skiing, and in-line skating. Several state legislatures have passed legislation protecting providers of facilities for such activities as well as for stunt or freestyle biking.

The Nevada legislature passed a shared-responsibility statute that provides limited protection for an agency or political subdivision of the state that provides skateboard parks for public use. Iowa passed an assumption of risk statute that immunizes municipalities and their employees from liability for injuries resulting from the inherent risks of skateboarding or in-line skating on public property. The injured person must have known or reasonably should have known that the activity created a substantial risk of injury. Likewise, the Utah and Vermont legislatures established statutory assumption of risk statutes providing protection from liability for inherent risks of skating and skateboard-type activities. The Vermont statute encompassed all providers of all sports and the Utah statute included county and municipalities providing facilities for bike riding, biking, skateboarding, roller skating, and in-line skating (see *General Recreation and Sport Immunity Statutes* below). *These statutes have granted protection to governmental providers (except Vermont which included all sport providers) and their employees from liability for injuries resulting from the* **inherent risks** *of the activities.*

California, Florida, and New Hampshire have enacted hazardous recreational activity legislation that includes skateboard parks (see *Hazardous Recreational Activity Immunity Statutes* below). *This legislation grants protection from liability for some types of* ordinary negligence *to governmental entities (and employees) that provide these activities.*

Statutes Pertaining to Other Activities

Immunity statutes affecting other recreation and sport activities have also been enacted. Statutes were found in eight states for sport shooting, five states for outfitters and guides, and four states for snow-mobile operators. Acts for these sports vary significantly by activity and by state. For instance, **sport shooting** statutes designate that the participant (and spectator in Colorado) assumes the inherent risks of the activity. In Utah, the statute names the risks and specifies that the risks that are obvious and inherent are assumed. Utah and Michigan statutes declare that operators are generally not civilly or criminally liable for noise and limit claims of nuisance. However, the Idaho statute protects the operator for liability for injuries incurred because of operator ordinary negligence. **Outfitter and Guide** statutes, usually true shared-responsibility statutes, designate duties of both operators and participants and limit the liability of the outfitter to those specified duties. They usually specify that operators are liable only in the event of negligence. **Snowmobile statutes** usually announce that the operator is not liable for the inherent risks. In some states the immunity is extended to ordinary negligence. They, like the other statutes included in this paragraph, are shared-responsibility statutes as they prescribe duties of participants and operators. Interestingly, in South Dakota, providers renting snowmobiles are liable only if they are grossly negligent.

Statutes found less frequently include **amusement rides**, **baseball**, **bicycling**, **hockey**, **paddle sports**, **rodeo**, **fishing**, **ATVs**, and **hang gliding**.

These statutes are as varied as the activities to which they relate. Some are true **shared-responsibility statutes**, while others are more accurately labeled **statutory assumption of risk statutes** as they simply declare that the participant assumes the inherent risks. However, regardless of the differences among these statutes, *the common link is that they are all intended to protect the provider from liability for injuries resulting from the inherent risks (and in some cases, ordinary negligence) of the activity*. Legislation relating to these activities may be found in Table 2.22.1 in this chapter.

General Recreation and Sport Immunity Statutes

Six states have enacted laws sometimes referred to as **omnibus legislation** (Spengler & Burket, 2001) that is intended to encompass a large number of activities and sports rather than one or two. The intent is to enact one law that will give immunity from liability for injuries resulting from the inherent risks to the service providers of a number of different sports. These states are Alaska, Hawaii, Utah, Vermont, Wisconsin, and Wyoming. The Vermont statute is the most inclusive, including all sports and all providers and the Utah statute is the least inclusive—protecting only counties and municipalities from liability for rodeo, bike riding, biking, equestrian, skateboarding, roller skating, and in-line skating. Wisconsin and Wyoming protect all providers of more than 20 recreational and sport activities while Alaska lists more than 30 activities. *In each of these states, providers are immune from liability for inherent risks, but retain liability for the negligence of the entity or its employees*. Some of these statutes prescribe duties of the participant and the provider, and thus, could be classified as shared responsibility statutes. In addition, the recreational user statutes in both South Dakota and Washington list more than 25 outdoor activities and serve essentially the same function as the omnibus statutes (see Table 2.22.1 for the statutes). A 2015 statute is **WVC § 20-16-1 to 8**, entitled the Nonprofit Adventure and Recreational Activity Responsibility Act. The purpose of this West Virginia act is to define the duties and liability of non-profit organizations and the owners of extremely large properties on which the organizations offer activities (thought to be written specifically for Boy Scouts of America and owners allowing use of their property). The act includes literally dozens of covered sports and recreational activities.

Hazardous Recreational Activity Immunity Statutes

Legislatures in two states, California and Illinois, have passed statutes similar to the omnibus legislation just mentioned—except for two major differences. First, *the laws protect only public entities and their employees*. Secondly, the statutes protect the service provider and its employees from liability *for at least some types of ordinary negligence*. Protection is not provided (1) for failure to guard or warn of a known dangerous condition, (2) when a fee is charged for participation in the activity (a fee may be charged for entrance into the park), (3) for failure to properly construct or maintain recreational equipment or machinery, (4) when the entity recklessly or with gross negligence promoted the participation, or (5) when the injury resulted from gross negligence or reckless conduct of the entity or its employees. Thus, the entity and its employees are not liable for ordinary negligence except for failure to guard or warn of a dangerous condition and for failure to properly construct or maintain recreational equipment and machinery. In each state, more than 30 sports and activities are included within the protection. California has passed subsequent legislation specifically listing skateboarding as a hazardous recreational activity.

Three other states, Florida, New Hampshire, and North Carolina, have passed similar legislation affecting fewer activities. The Florida and North Carolina statutes protect governmental entities and their employees from liability for ordinary negligence (except the failure to warn of dangerous conditions of which the participant cannot reasonably expect to have notice) for three hazardous activities—skateboarding, in-line skating, and freestyle bicycling. New Hampshire provides immunity from liability for ordinary negligence for municipalities and school districts that without charge provide facilities for skateboarding, rollerblading, stunt biking, or roller skiing (see Table 2.22.1 for the statutes).

SIGNIFICANT CASE

In the interest of space, the student is referred to the Significant Case in Chapter 2.21 Defenses against Negligence. The case, Hanus v. Loon Mountain Recreation Corp. (2014), examines the extent to which this New Hampshire Ski Statute immunizes ski areas from liability for skier-to-skier collisions caused by their employees.

CASES ON THE SUPPLEMENTAL WEBSITE

Fowler v. Tyler Independent School District, (2007 Tex. App. LEXIS 6433,*;232 S.W.3d 335). Because it is a governmental unit, a school district is immune from suit under the doctrine of sovereign/governmental immunity. Here, the Fowlers claim that since TISD was renting its stadium to the two high schools, TISD was acting in a proprietary capacity at the time of Bridget Fowler's injury, and therefore was not protected by sovereign/governmental immunity from suit.

Mounts v. Van Beeste, (2004 Mich. App. LEXIS 2062). This is a case in which the court addresses the issue of whether the equine immunity statute applies.

Thompson v. Rochester Community Schools, (2006 Mich. App. LEXIS 3233). This is an interesting case involving sovereign/governmental immunity of a school, a number of employees, and the lack of emergency care administered to an unconscious student. There is a very informative discussion of gross negligence and proximate cause.

Vaughn v. Barton, 2010 Ill. App. LEXIS 694. In this youth baseball case, the coach claims immunity based on the Recreational User Statute and the Sport Volunteer Immunity Act.

Yeater v. Board of Education, Labrae School District, 2010 Ohio App. LEXIS 3139. An injury to a student results in a suit alleging negligence by a student, a teacher, and the school district. Read carefully to learn why the immunity defense failed.

QUESTIONS YOU SHOULD BE ABLE TO ANSWER

1. Explain the intended function of the Federal Tort Claims Act and the state tort claims acts.
2. Give an example that illustrates how a school can lose immunity because of a proprietary act.
3. What are the restrictions placed on qualification for Good Samaritan immunity?
4. What are the main differences between the shared responsibility acts and the statutory assumption of risk laws?
5. List the types of immunity that might help to protect the owner of a private business.

REFERENCES

Cases
Avenoso v. Mangan, 2006 Conn. Super. LEXIS 489.
Chrisman v. Brown, 2007 Tex. App. LEXIS 7745.
Deguilio v. Gran, Inc., 2009 N.Y. Misc. LEXIS 2962.
Feagins v. Waddy, 978 So.2d 712 (Ala. 2007).
Gilbert v. Seton Hall University, 2003 U.S. App. LEXIS 11722.
Heard v. City of Villa Rica, 2010 Ga. App. LEXIS 924.
Kuykendall v. Young Life, 2006 U.S.Dist. LEXIS 81380.
Miglino v. Bally Total Fitness of Greater New York, Inc., 2013 N.Y. LEXIS 111.
Ola v. YMCA, 2005Va. LEXIS 93.
Van Horn v. Watson, 2008 Cal. LEXIS 14589.

Publications

Brown, J. (1997). Legislators strike out: Volunteer little league coaches should not be immune from tort liability. *Seton Hall J. Sports L., 7*, 559.

Carter-Yamauchi, C.A. (1996). Volunteerism—A risky business? Honolulu: Legislative Reference Bureau.

Centner, T. J. (2000). Tort liability for sports and recreational activities: Expanding statutory immunity for protected classes and activities. *J. Legis, 26*, 1.

Centner, T. J. (2001). Simplifying sports liability law through a shared responsibility chapter. 1 *Va. Sports & Ent. L. J., 1*, 54.

Chalat, J. H. (2000). Survey of ski law in the United States. Vail, CO: CLE International Ski Liability Conference.

Dawson, R. O. (1999). Equine activity statutes: Part I—IV. Online, Internet. www.law.utexas.edu/dawson/horselaw/update1.htm

Jordan, B. (2001). What is the Good Samaritan law? Online, Internet. http://pa.essortment.com/goodsamaritanl_redg.htm

Non-Profit Risk Management Center (2009). State Liability Laws for Charitable Organizations and Volunteers. http://www.nonprofitrisk.org/downloads/state-liability.pdf.

Ridolfi, K. M. (2000). Law, ethics, and the Good Samaritan: Should there be a duty to rescue? *Santa Clara L. Rev., 40*, 957.

Rudolph, H. Recreational User Statutes. https://elcr.org/statestatutes/.

Rudolph, H. Equine Liability Statutes. https://elcr.org/statestatutes/.

Runquist, L. A., & Zybach, J. F. (1997). Volunteer Protection Act of 1997—an imperfect solution. Online, Internet. www.runquist.com/article_vol_protect.htm

Slank, N. L. (1999). A symposium on tort and sport: Leveling the playing field. *Washburn L. J., 38*, 847.

Spengler, J. O., & Burket, B. P. (2001). Sport safety statutes and inherent risk: A comparison study of sport specific legislation. *Journal of Legal Aspects of Sport, 11*(2), 135.

van der Smissen, B. (1990). *Legal liability and risk management for public and private entities*. Cincinnati: Anderson Publishing Company.

WAIVERS AND RELEASES

Doyice J. Cotten | Sport Risk Consulting

2.23

A **waiver** of liability in the recreation or sport setting is a contract in which the participant, in exchange for the right to participate, agrees to relinquish the right to pursue legal action against the service provider in the event that the ordinary negligence of the provider results in an injury to the participant. In essence, the signer relieves the provider of its duty of ordinary care – so the service provider is not liable for injuries resulting from the ordinary negligence of the provider or its employees. The term **"release"** is used synonymously with waiver; however, it can be confusing because *release* often refers to a settlement agreement signed after the injury. **Exculpatory agreement** and **covenant not to sue** are also tantamount to waivers; there are some differences, but each is intended to relieve the provider of liability for its own negligence.

The following three terms are often confused with waivers, but differ in important ways. A **disclaimer** is a statement by which the provider proclaims that the provider is not liable for injury. It is often found on a ticket or on a sign, is not signed by the patron, and is usually ineffective. An **informed consent** is a contract by which a provider informs the signer of the risks and benefits of a *treatment or training program* and secures participant's consent to participate and assume the informed risks. Many erroneously use the term synonymously with waiver; however, it provides no protection from liability for negligence. A **parental permission form**, often used in lieu of a waiver, grants permission for the youngster to participate, but it, too, provides no protection from liability for negligence.

Sport and recreation providers know that injuries are unavoidable in physical activities; therefore, they often rely on waivers of liability to protect themselves from financial loss. Injuries in sport and recreation result from one of three causes: (1) inherent risks of the activity (common accidents where no one is at fault), (2) negligent acts (careless acts by the service provider, its employees, the participant, or others), and (3) more extreme or aggravated acts (by the service provider, its employees, the participant, or others). Aggravated acts can include gross negligence, reckless conduct, willful/wanton acts, and intentional acts (see Chapter 2.11 *Negligence*).

The **primary function of the waiver** is to protect the service provider from liability for injuries resulting from the *ordinary negligence* of the service provider and its employees. The document can also be written to include protection against liability for the inherent risks of the activity; to do this, a section should explain the inherent risks of the activity and include a statement by which the signer assumes those *inherent risks*. The provider is then protected from liability for injuries caused by two of the three causes of injury. The waiver, however, cannot generally provide protection against liability for *gross negligence and the other extreme actions*.[1]

FUNDAMENTAL CONCEPTS

Public Policy, Contract Law, and Waivers

Courts in most states declare that waivers are not favored by law and must be strictly construed against the relying party; nevertheless, courts in most states enforce well-written waivers provided they do not violate public policy. **Public policy** differs from state to state, but has been defined as "that principle of law under which freedom of contract or private dealings is restricted for the good of the community" (*Merten v. Nathan*, 1982).

---

[1] Courts in only four states (Florida, Illinois, Kentucky, and Pennsylvania) and in the Virgin Islands either indicated 1) they have enforced or 2) that they will enforce waivers meant to protect providers from liability for gross negligence. In addition, courts in Florida and West Virginia have indicated that they will enforce waivers protecting against liability for reckless conduct.

Waivers are often considered to be against public policy and unenforceable: (1) when an activity involves an essential service or public interest; (2) when the waiver conflicts with a statutory duty; (3) when the waiver is ambiguous and not understood by the signer; (4) when the contract is between parties with unequal bargaining power (e.g., employer/employee); and (5) when the waiver is too broad in scope (e.g., includes gross negligence, reckless conduct). Keep in mind, however, that the legislature and/or courts in each state determine and define what constitutes public policy in that particular state – and often, a factor that violates public policy in one state may not violate public policy in a neighboring state.

Courts in most jurisdictions hold that sport and recreational activity providers do not provide an essential public service; for that reason, waivers involving sport and recreational activities are generally not against public policy. Courts in some states mandate very strict requirements and enforce waivers with reluctance while courts in other states maintain lenient standards enabling more waivers to be enforced. The law in only two states currently clearly forbids all personal injury waivers – Louisiana and Virginia.

Waivers are governed by **contract law**; to be enforceable and valid in the event they are challenged, they must contain certain elements. Those elements are mutual assent, consideration, capacity, and legality. These are presented in detail in Chapter 5.10 *Contract Essentials* so only a few brief points relating the application to liability waivers will be emphasized here. First, assent is shown by a voluntary signature following a clearly worded agreement. Second, courts approach unanimity in declaring that the opportunity to participate constitutes consideration. Third, parties not having capacity would include persons lacking mental capacity, those unduly influenced by drugs or alcohol, and persons who have not reached the age of majority (18 years in all but two states). And finally, lack of legality applies to contracts involving illegal actions or actions that violate public policy.

Waiver Law by State or Jurisdiction

Although waivers are commonly used by more sport- and recreation-related businesses than ever before, many service providers are still under the erroneous impression that waivers are worthless and offer no protection to the service provider. Cotten and Cotten (2016) have estimated the *likelihood of enforcement of a well-written waiver* by courts in each of 54 jurisdictions (the 50 states, admiralty law, Washington, D.C., Puerto Rico, and the Virgin Islands) and placed each in one of four categories. Listed in Figure 2.23.1 are the jurisdictions in each category. Nine fall in the category of *Excellent* likelihood and the likelihood in 29 others is estimated to be *Good*. The probability in nine other states is *Fair*; but, chance of enforcement in seven states is considered to be *Poor*. Keep in mind that this does not mean that a waiver in a state categorized as *Excellent* will always be enforced; likewise, it doesn't mean a waiver in a *Poor* state will always fail. One can say, however, that a well-written waiver is more likely to be enforced than a poorly written waiver, regardless of how the state is classified.

The classification system shown in Figure 2.23.1 represents a change from the system of classification used in previous editions; the former system used a classification based on how strict or lenient courts in each state were in the requirements for a valid waiver. The authors felt that providers using waivers were not really interested in how strict the courts were; they were more interested in the chance that their waiver would be enforced if challenged in court.

Thus, in at least 47 of the 54 jurisdictions (the 50 states, admiralty law, Puerto Rico, the Virgin Islands, and Washington D.C.) a well-written, properly administered waiver, voluntarily signed by an adult, has a reasonable chance of protecting the recreation or sport business from liability for ordinary negligence by the business or its employees.

Waivers and Admiralty Law

Admiralty law (also called maritime law) is federal law that applies to activities on any navigable waterway (e.g., lakes, rivers, canals, seashores, bays, and oceans). Admiralty law is important because it supersedes state law, including state waiver law; however, if admiralty law does not address an issue, state law can often apply. Admiralty law has been applied to recreational activities that include swimming, body surfing, wakeboarding, snorkeling, snuba, scuba, jet skis, sailing, charter fishing, pleasure boating, powerboat riding, parasailing, and recreational activities on cruise ships.

While admiralty law has traditionally disfavored waivers, today *liability waivers, disclaimers, and exculpatory clauses are not against public policy and are usually deemed to be enforceable so long as they are not overreaching*. The rationale for upholding such clauses is that businessmen must be free to bargain over which party is to bear the risk of damage. This enables the businessman to be able to provide a risky activity at a more reasonable price.

FIGURE 2.23.1 LIKELIHOOD OF COURTS TO ENFORCE A LIABILITY WAIVER FOR ADULT PARTICIPANTS[2]

Poor	Fair	Good		Excellent
Alaska	Arkansas	Alabama	New York[3]	Admiralty Law
Arizona	Delaware	Florida	North Carolina	California
Connecticut	Maine	Idaho	Oklahoma	Colorado
Hawaii	Mississippi	Illinois	Pennsylvania	District of Columbia
Louisiana	Nevada	Indiana	Puerto Rico	Georgia
Virginia	New Hampshire	Kansas	South Carolina	Iowa
Wisconsin	Oregon	Kentucky	South Dakota	Michigan
	Rhode Island	Maryland	Tennessee	North Dakota
	West Virginia	Massachusetts	Texas	Ohio
		Minnesota	Utah	
		Missouri	Vermont	
		Montana	Virgin Islands	
		Nebraska	Washington	
		New Jersey	Wyoming	
		New Mexico		

Public policy, however, does put some restrictions on waivers to which admiralty law is applied. Some examples of prohibitions include: waivers required of employees by employers; waivers involving critical public services; those allowing violation of safety statutes; those where one party has a far superior bargaining position; and waivers intended to protect providers from gross negligence, reckless conduct, willful or wanton acts and acts intended to harm. Further, the intent of the waiver must be clearly and unambiguous expressed – though it is not required that waivers contain the word "negligence."

Owners of recreational vessels and providers of recreational activities are free to use written waivers to disclaim liability for recreational activities in navigable waters so long as the waiver is clear, unambiguous, and does not violate federal public policy. Under admiralty law a waiver for recreational sporting activities is not adhesionary because recreational activities are not essential services (*Charnis v. Watersport Pro LLC*, 2009).

Cruise Line Exception. Cruise lines, like other common carriers, are held to a standard of reasonable care. Federal statute **46 U.S.C. § 30509** prohibits limitations of liability for any vessel transporting passengers between U.S. ports or to a foreign port. It expressly voids any contract provision purporting to limit the liability of a cruise line for injuries resulting from its own negligence. Therefore, use of disclaimers and liability waivers to protect the cruise line from liability for its own negligence is prohibited by admiralty law. This prohibition applies to waivers protecting the cruise line from negligence liability for recreational activities aboard the ship, in the water, and on shore excursions. Admiralty courts have held that *recreational boats, whose primary purpose is to provide recreation rather than transportation between ports, are not subject to this statute.*

Waiver Law and Minors

As mentioned in the Public Policy, Contract Law, and Waivers section, certain classes of individuals are not generally bound by contracts. The general rule has long been *that a waiver is a contract and that a minor cannot be bound by a contract that is signed only by the minor*. Consequently, while the service provider contracting with a minor is bound by the contract, the minor is not. Thus the waiver will not prevent the minor from taking legal action against a negligent service provider. This general rule is well-supported. In *Dilallo v. Riding Safely*

---

[2]This figure is taken from Cotten, D.J. and Cotten, M.B. (2016). **Waivers & Releases of Liability**. 9th ed. Sport Risk Consulting: www.createspace.com.

[3]Likelihood of enforcement is poor if G.O.L. 5-326 applies. The statute forbids enforcement of waivers for places of amusement or recreation or similar establishments for which the owner or operator receives a fee or other compensation for the use.

Inc. (1997), a 14-year-old Florida girl signed a waiver absolving a stable of liability. The court held that "a minor child injured because of a defendant's negligence is not bound by her contractual waiver of her right to file a lawsuit." In a Pennsylvania case (*Emerick v. Fox Raceway*, 2004), the court did not enforce a waiver signed by a 16-year-old boy who misrepresented his age in order to enter a motocross race.

Since waivers signed solely by the minor are ineffective, providers have relied heavily upon the strategy of requiring that the parent or legal guardian sign the waiver on behalf of the minor client (thereby releasing the provider of liability for negligence). This waiver is referred to as a **parental waiver**.

Parental Waivers and State Law

In the past, parental waivers have not been effective. For example, a 10-year-old girl was injured when another child jumped into a swimming pool on top of her. The girl's mother signed a post-injury release in exchange for a $3275 settlement. Eight years after the accident, upon reaching the age of majority, the girl filed suit against the YMCA. The court stated that "It is well settled in Michigan that, in order to protect the rights of minors, a parent has no authority, merely by virtue of being a parent, to waive, release, or compromise claims by or against the parent's child" and ruled that the YMCA was not protected by the release signed by the mother (*Smith v. YMCA of Benton Harbor/St. Joseph*, 1996). The Michigan Supreme Court reinforced this ruling in *Woodman v. Kera* in 2010.

In recent years, however, courts in a number of states have begun to enforce waivers and indemnity agreements signed by parents on behalf of their minor children (see Figure 2.23.2); the rationale is that parents will

FIGURE 2.23.2 PARENTAL WAIVER LAW BY STATE[4]

Courts Do Not Enforce Parental Waivers	Insufficient Information to Predict Enforcement of Parental Waivers	Courts Enforce Parental Waivers under Some or All Circumstances		
		Specific Activity Named by Statute	Non-Profit School-Community Recreation	Enforces Waivers by Either Commercial Entities or by Both Commercial and Non-Profit School-Community Recreation Entities
AL AR CT FL[5] HI IA IL LA ME MI MS NJ NY OK OR PA RI TN TX UT VA WA WV WI	ADM AZ[6] DC GA ID KS KY MO MT NE NV NH NM PR SC SD VT VI WY	AZ[7] GA[9] FL[11] HI[12] IL[14] IN[16] KY[17] MN[18] UT[19] VA[20]	CT[8] FL[10] ND NY[13] NC	AK DE CA CO IN MD MA MN OH WI[15]

---

[4]This figure is taken from Cotten, D.J. and Cotten, M.B. (2016). **Waivers & Releases of Liability**. 9th ed. Sport Risk Consulting: www.createspace.com.

[5]**Florida** Supreme Court has ruled that parental waivers used by commercial recreation entities are unenforceable.

[6]The Arizona Supreme Court has interpreted the **Arizona** Constitution to mean that all assumption of risk questions are a matter for the jury and not to be decided by summary judgment.

[7]**A.R.S 12 – 553 A.2** equine statute allows owners to use parental waivers for liability protection.

[8]Supreme Court rulings in **Connecticut** and **Wisconsin** seem to indicate that any sport- or recreation-related waivers are unenforceable in those states.

[9]OCGA § 4-12-4 equine statute allows parental waivers.

[10]Parental waivers for school- or community-based activities are still enforced by appellate courts in some **Florida** jurisdictions.

[11]The Motorsport Non-Spectator Liability Release statute (**F.S. 549.09**) provides that parental waivers are enforceable for minor competitors in certain motorsport events in **Florida**.

[12]**Hawaii** statute §663-10.95 allows the enforcement of parental waivers for motorsports participants (with a witness).

[13]A federal court enforced a parental waiver, but similar rulings by **New York** courts are questionable.

[14]Equine Statute **745 ILCS 47/1-25** allows the enforcement of parental waivers for equine activities.

act in the best interest of the minor and the parent makes other life decisions for the minor (e.g., religious training, medical decisions). California courts were the first to enforce parental waivers. In 1990, *Hohe v. San Diego Unified Sch. Dist.* made it clear that while minors are free to disaffirm contracts signed only by the minor, they cannot disaffirm contracts made by the parent or guardian of the minor. Since that time, numerous California courts have ruled similarly. The Supreme Court of Ohio also ruled waivers signed by parents in favor of non-profit, public service providers are enforceable against the minor child (*Zivich v. Mentor Soccer Club*, 1998). Trumping a Colorado Supreme Court ruling parental waivers unenforceable, the legislature passed a statute allowing their enforcement.

From Figure 2.23.2, one can see that courts or legislatures in 24 jurisdictions have held that parental waivers are not enforceable and that courts from 19 jurisdictions have not addressed the issue – so, we do not really know whether parental waivers will be enforced in these states or not. In the section of the figure titled Courts Enforce Parental Waivers under Some or All Circumstances, one first finds 10 states listed that, by statute, allow parental waivers for one particular activity. Then five states are listed in which at least one parental waiver (for a non-profit, school-community recreation activity) has been enforced. Whether parental waivers for commercial entities will be enforced in those states is unknown. In the final section, jurisdictions that have enforced a parental waiver for a commercial entity and jurisdictions that have enforced parental waivers from both commercial and non-profit entities are grouped together (on the rationale that a jurisdiction enforcing a commercial entity waiver would certainly enforce one from a non-profit entity). The reader should read the footnotes to obtain a more complete understanding of the status of parental waivers.

Parental Waivers and Admiralty Law

It is not clear whether parental waivers are valid and enforceable in admiralty law. One case indicates that they might be enforceable for non-profit entities, but not for commercial enterprises (*In re: The Complaint of Royal Caribbean Cruises, LTD.*, 2006). It could be, however, that the validity might depend upon the law of the state in which the incident occurs. The father signed the waiver on behalf of his minor son in order for the boy to ride a jet ski.

Parental Indemnity Agreements & Parental Arbitration Agreements

As one can see above, parental waivers are not effective in many states. A second tactic that has also met with limited success is to require the parent to indemnify the provider (agree to repay the provider for any loss suffered due to the participation of the minor, e.g., monetary award by the court). This agreement is called a **parental indemnity agreement**. Courts in at least four states, Connecticut, Massachusetts, Maine, and Missouri have upheld parental indemnity agreements. In contrast, courts in Illinois, New York, New Jersey, Tennessee, Utah, and West Virginia have indicated that parental indemnity agreements were unenforceable.

A third tactic to reduce exposure to liability is to require the parent to sign a mediation/arbitration agreement by which the parent agrees to submit any claim to mediation and/or arbitration rather than filing a lawsuit. This agreement is referred to as a **parental arbitration agreement**. Courts in California, Florida, Hawaii, Louisiana, New Jersey, and Ohio have upheld agreements by which parents agreed to submit any claims of the minor to arbitration. While courts in Idaho, Pennsylvania, and Texas have ruled that minors are not bound by parental arbitration agreements, this tactic would seem to hold promise since the rights of the minor are not threatened – the issue is simply addressed in a different forum.

---

[15] See the **Connecticut** footnote above.
[16] **I.C. 34-28-3** Partial Emancipation for Minors to Participate in Automobile and Motorcycle Racing Act allows waivers and indemnity agreements by certain minors and their parents for participation in professional racing events in **Indiana**.
[17] **Kentucky** statute (**KRS 247.4027(2)a**) provides that parental waivers with a required warning can protect equine providers from liability for inherent risks, but not for negligence.
[18] Minnesota statute **MN ST § 604.055** allow enforcement of parental equine waivers.
[19] The Limitations on Liability for Equine and Livestock Activities Act (**Utah Code Ann. 78B-4-203(2)b**) specifies that a release for a minor participant signed by the minor's legal guardian shall be sufficient if it includes the definition of inherent risk in Section **78B-4-201** and states that the sponsor is not liable for those inherent risks.
[20] Virginia Statute **VCA §3.2-6202** allows enforcement of parental equine waivers.

It is also important to understand that the enforceability of parental waivers, indemnity agreements, and arbitration agreements has not been addressed by the courts in most states; for this reason, they may be enforced in a number of those states as well. Consequently, providers in all states might consider the use of such agreements when dealing with minor participants. However, in doing so, the provider should remember two things: (1) always have the parents sign the document and (2) use liability protection (e.g., insurance) in addition to the waiver, indemnity agreement, or mediation/arbitration agreement.

Format of the Waiver

Waivers are generally found in one of four formats. The first is as a **stand-alone document**—one in which the only function of the document is to provide liability protection for the service provider. The patron is asked to sign a sheet of paper (or an electronic version) containing only a waiver and related exculpatory material. The second format is the **waiver within another document** such as a membership agreement, an entry form, or a rental agreement (see the example in the Significant Case). The third format is a **group waiver**—which generally includes a waiver at the top of a sheet on which several parties sign (e.g., a team roster, a sign-in sheet at a health club). Both the waiver within another document and the group waiver can be effective when carefully worded and properly administered; however, many courts, and this author, have encouraged providers to use the stand-alone waiver since it reduces the likelihood of ambiguity and can provide much more protection than the shorter agreements. The fourth format is the **disclaimer** of liability, often found on the back of tickets and sometimes in the form of posted signage. A disclaimer is a statement asserting that the provider is not responsible for injuries. The disclaimer is not signed, provides no evidence that the participant agreed to it, and, with a few exceptions, is ineffective (certainly less likely to be effective). There is no harm in including such disclaimers on the back of a ticket, but generally they will only be enforced if the provider has conclusive evidence that the party was aware of the disclaimer. Such evidence is difficult to obtain without a signature by the party. Consequently, the service provider should operate on the assumption that the disclaimer will not effectively protect the business.

Participant Agreement

Since many courts recommend the use of a stand-alone document, that format will be emphasized in this chapter. A relatively new concept in liability protection is the **participant agreement**, a stand-alone document that combines the waiver of ordinary negligence with both an assumption of inherent risks and an indemnity agreement – thereby providing protection against liability for both injury due to provider negligence and the inherent risks of the activity. In addition, the document (1) is designed to improve the rapport and understanding between the provider and the participant; (2) increases the participant's understanding of the rewards and risks of participating in the activity; (3) serves as an exchange of information between the parties; (4) prepares the participant psychologically for any discomforts, making legal action less likely; (5) allows the participant to make more a informed decision as to participation; and (6) acquires certain agreements and permissions (including emergency actions) from the signer. The participant agreement provides much broader protection than any of the previously mentioned formats and should be used by any provider wanting maximum protection.

The contents of the participant agreement can include the following items:

1. Material which informs the participant of the **nature of the activity** and helps him or her understand and appreciate the risks involved.
2. A statement by which the signer **assumes the inherent risks** of the activity.
3. A statement by which the **signer releases the provider from liability for injuries resulting from the ordinary negligence** of the provider or its employees.
4. A statement by which the **signer agrees to indemnify** (reimburse any loss) the provider for losses suffered by the provider as a result of the actions of or participation of the participant.
5. Five selected clauses which help to protect the provider from loss: 1) a **severability clause** (provides that if any part of the document is void, the rest remains in effect), 2) a **mediation and/or arbitration clause** (provides that any resultant claims will be submitted to mediation and binding arbitration rather than

entering the court system) [see Chapter 5.30 *Alternative Dispute Resolution*], 3) a clause specifying **venue and jurisdiction** (spells out where legal action must occur and what law applies), 4) a **covenant not to sue** (a clause by which one contracts not to sue to enforce a right of action), and 5) an **integration clause** (a clause by which the signer asserts that this is the entire agreement and supersedes any previous oral or written agreements.)

6. Authorizations, assertions, and agreements regarding **health status**, **emergency care**, and **rules and safety** (informs provider of serious health problems, gives permission for emergency care, signer agrees to follow the rules, and more).
7. **Final acknowledgements and signatures of parties** (summarizes the agreement; signer acknowledges having read, understanding of, and concurrence with the agreement; and includes spaces for the signature of the participant (and parents or legal guardians if participant is a minor) and date.

The scope of this book does not allow the presentation of further detail. For a complete discussion of waivers and participant agreements, including the waiver law in each state and more than 50 guidelines for writing and preparing waivers and participant agreements, the reader is referred to Cotten and Cotten (2016).

Guidelines for Your Waiver

When Writing or Evaluating your Waiver. Out of hundreds of possible guidelines and tips for waivers, the following may serve as a good foundation. Your waiver should be written specifically for your business – not found on the Internet, in a book, or borrowed from a friend. Do not make promises of safe participation or assurances of participant well-being – accidents will happen. Address both assumption of inherent risks and release of liability for provider negligence – but do not merge them together; separate by paragraphs and headings. Make certain the language CLEARLY waives the liability for provider negligence – and best practice calls for the use of the term "negligence." Take care to carefully identify all releasing parties, all protected parties,[21] and what aspects of the operation are meant to be protected – and don't forget to specify the duration of the waiver. Finally, the judge in *Cohen v. Five Brooks Stable* (2008) gave what may be the most thought-provoking and insightful statement yet.

> While it is true, as we have seen, that California courts hold releases of liability to a high standard of clarity, it does not in our view require Olympian efforts to meet the standard. **An effective release is hard to draft only if the party for whom it is prepared desires to hide the ball, which is what the law is designed to prevent**. A release that forthrightly makes clear to a person untrained in the law that the releasor gives up any claim against the releasee for the latter's own negligence . . . or that the releasee cannot be held liable for *any and all risks* the releasor encounters while on the former's premises or using its facilities . . ., ordinarily passes muster (*Cohen v. Five Brooks Stable*, 2008, pp. 27–28). [Emphasis added.]

When Administering your Waiver. Many waivers fail to protect the provider from liability because of flaws in the administration process. A few critical guidelines are noted here. Educate your staff to be straightforward in explaining what the waiver is and what it is intended to do – not minimizing its role or its importance. Provide conditions conducive to reading and allow time for reading and questions – in fact, provide readers for non-readers (and interpreters if necessary). Require that **all** participants must sign the waiver in order to participate – enforce a no-exception policy. Institute a system for preserving signed waivers indefinitely and for retrieving them promptly – a waiver that can't be found is unlikely to be enforced.

---

[21] A common mistake made by writers of waivers is the failure to adequately identify the parties affected by the contract. The party relinquishing rights is obviously the signer of the document. However, the spouse or heirs often file suit against the service provider when the signer is seriously injured or killed; thus, a phrase by which the signer relinquishes the right of others to recover for injury or death should be included in the waiver (e.g., on behalf of self, spouse, heirs, estate, and assigns). Providers should be aware, however, that such phrases are not enforceable in all states. The waiver also must specify the parties protected by the agreement. Parties for which protection is often sought (e.g., corporation, management, employees, sponsors, volunteers, agents, equipment suppliers) should be listed. One is safer to list all protected parties, at least by category, than to rely on some inclusive phrase such as ". . . and all others who are involved."

SIGNIFICANT CASE

Stokes v. Bally's Pacwest, Inc. provides an excellent, straightforward example of the value of liability waivers in protecting against liability for negligence in the recreation or sport setting. The case illustrates very clearly the need to make sure the waiver is conspicuous and that the document plainly provides for protection against liability for negligence. When read carefully, one can see that Stokes specifically releases Bally's from liability for Bally's negligence. While the recommended waiver format is the stand-alone waiver, this waiver within another document is better than average and provided effective liability protection to Bally's. Observe, also, that the fact Stokes did not read the waiver is irrelevant.

STOKES V. BALLY'S PACWEST, INC.

Court of Appeals of Washington, Division One
113 Wn. App. 442; 54 P.3d 161; 2002 Wash. App. LEXIS 2233
September 16, 2002, Filed

Opinion: Cox, A.C.J.

Persons may expressly agree in advance of an accident that one has no duty of care to the other, and shall not be liable for ordinary negligence (Chauvlier v. Booth Creek Ski Holdings, Inc., 109 Wn. App. 334, 339, 35 P.3d 383 (2001)). Such exculpatory agreements are generally enforceable, subject to three exceptions. Because the "waiver and release" language at issue here was conspicuously stated in the agreement that Michael Stokes signed, we reverse both summary judgment orders and direct entry of summary judgment in favor of Bally's Pacwest Total Fitness Center on remand.

Stokes joined Bally's, a health club. He signed a retail installment contract that evidenced the terms and conditions of membership. The contract contained the waiver and release provisions at issue in this appeal. Several months after signing the agreement, Stokes slipped on a round metallic plate placed in a wooden floor at the club while playing basketball. He injured his knee and shoulder. Stokes sued Bally's, alleging that the health club's negligence caused him serious, painful, and permanent injuries. Bally's moved for summary judgment, which the trial court denied. According to the trial court, there were "material questions of fact whether the 'Waiver and Release' provisions set forth in the Retail Installment Contract [that Stokes signed], were sufficiently conspicuous or knowingly consented to by [him]."

We granted discretionary review of that decision. Pursuant to RAP 7.2, we also granted Bally's permission to renew its summary judgment motion in the trial court in order to allow that court to consider this court's then recent decision in Chauvlier. Following Bally's renewed motion, the trial court again denied summary judgment for the same reason that it did before.

* * *

We now focus our attention on the two orders before us. To prevail on his ordinary negligence claim against Bally's, Stokes must establish that the health club owed him a duty. Whether such a duty exists is a question of law. As we recently noted in Chauvlier, our Supreme Court has recognized the right of parties, subject to certain exceptions, to expressly agree in advance that one party is under no obligation of care to the other, and shall not be held liable for ordinary negligence.

The general rule in Washington is that such exculpatory clauses are enforceable unless (1) they violate public policy; (2) the negligent act falls greatly below the standard established by law for protection of others; or (3) they are inconspicuous (Scott v. Pacific West Mountain Resort, 119 Wn.2d 484, 492, 834 P.2d 6 (1992). Neither of the first two of these exceptions is at issue here. The trial court expressly relied on only the third exception in making its rulings, denying summary judgment on the ground that a genuine issue of material fact existed whether the waiver and release clause was inconspicuous.

This court will not uphold an exculpatory agreement if "the releasing language is so inconspicuous that reasonable persons could reach different conclusions as to whether the document was unwittingly signed" (Chauvlier, at 341). Conversely, where reasonable persons could only reach the conclusion that the release language is conspicuous, there is no question of the document having been unwittingly signed. Whether Stokes subjectively unwittingly signed the form is not at issue. Rather, the question is whether, objectively, the waiver provision was so inconspicuous that it is unenforceable.

As we stated in Chauvlier, a person who signs an agreement without reading it is generally bound by its terms as long as there was ample opportunity to examine the contract and the person failed to do so for personal reasons. Here, Stokes admitted that he did not remember reading the waiver and release provision of the contract.

But this admission does not end our review. We must still determine whether the waiver and release language is inconspicuous so as to invalidate Stokes' release of Bally's from any duty to him for its alleged ordinary negligence.

We most recently considered whether a release was inconspicuous and unwittingly signed in Chauvlier. The release in that case was printed on a ski pass application. Comparing the release to those considered in Baker and Hewitt v. Miller, n16 we held that the release was sufficiently conspicuous to be enforceable. We noted that the release was not hidden within part of a larger agreement, and that it was clearly entitled "LIABILITY RELEASE & PROMISE NOT TO SUE. PLEASE READ CAREFULLY!." We also noted that the words "RELEASE" and "HOLD HARMLESS AND INDEMNIFY" were set off in capital letters throughout the agreement, and that the release contained the language, just above the signature line, "Please Read and Sign: I have read, understood, and accepted the conditions of the Liability Release printed above."

At the other end of the spectrum of reported cases is Baker (Baker, 79 Wn.2d at 202). There, our Supreme Court held that a disclaimer in a golf cart rental agreement, consisting of several lines of release language printed in the middle of a paragraph discussing other information, was so inconspicuous that enforcement of the release would be unconscionable.

In McCorkle, another division of this court held that a trial court erred in granting summary judgment on McCorkle's negligence claims against a fitness club. The holding was that there were genuine issues of material fact whether a liability statement contained in a membership application McCorkle signed was sufficiently conspicuous.

The provision at issue in that case had as a heading "LIABILITY STATEMENT." In the first few sentences, the provision declared that the member accepted liability for damages that the member or the member's guests caused. The last sentence of the provision stated that the member waived any claim for damages as a result of any act of a Club employee or agent. And nothing in the document alerted the reader to the shift in the liability discussion from liability of the member to waiver of liability for claims against the Club.

The parties now before us cite to other cases, Hewitt and Conradt v. Four Star Promotions (Hewitt, 11 Wn. App. at 78-80; Conradt, 45 Wn. App. at 850). Both are factually distinguishable. In each of those cases, the waiver and release form was in a separate document, not a separate provision in one document

Here, the release is more like that in Chauvlier and unlike that in Baker or McCorkle. In our view, reasonable minds could not differ regarding whether the waiver and release provisions in this retail installment sales contract were so inconspicuous that it was unwittingly signed. The language is conspicuous, as a matter of law, and it was not unwittingly signed.

The release provision in this retail installment contract, which Stokes signed, must be read in context. Several lines above Stokes' signature is a section in bold type, which states:

NOTICE TO BUYER: (a) Do not sign this Contract before you read it or if any of the spaces intended for the agreed terms, except as to unavailable information, are blank. . ..

THIS IS A RETAIL INSTALLMENT CONTRACT, THE RECEIPT OF AN EXECUTED COPY OF WHICH, AS WELL AS A COPY OF THE CLUB RULES AND REGULATIONS AND A WRITTEN DESCRIPTION OF THE SERVICES AND EQUIPMENT TO BE PROVIDED, IS HEREBY ACKNOWLEDGED BY THE BUYER.

Immediately following Stokes' signature is a line, starting in bold and capital letters, stating: "WAIVER AND RELEASE: This contract contains a WAIVER AND RELEASE in Paragraph 10 to which you will be bound."

Paragraph 10, which is expressly referenced in the line directly below Stokes' signature, is entitled "WAIVER AND RELEASE." It states as follows:

You (Buyer, each Member and all guests) agree that if you engage in any physical exercise or activity or use any club facility on the premises, you do so at your own risk. This includes, without limitation, your use of the locker room, pool, whirlpool, sauna, steamroom, parking area, sidewalk or any equipment in the health club and your participation in any activity, class, program or instruction. You agree that you are voluntarily participating in these activities and using these facilities and premises and assume all risk of injury to you or the contraction of any illness or medical condition that might result, or any damage, loss or theft of any personal property. You agree on behalf of yourself (and your personal representatives, heirs, executors, administrators, agents and assigns) to release and discharge us (and our affiliates, employees, agents, representatives, successors and assigns) from any and all claims or causes of action (known or unknown) arising out of our negligence. This Waiver and Release of liability includes, without limitation, injuries which may occur as a result of (a) your use of any exercise equipment or facilities which may malfunction or break, (b) our improper maintenance of any exercise equipment or facilities, (c) our negligent instruction or supervision, and (d) you slipping and falling while in the health club or on the premises. You acknowledge that you have carefully read this Waiver and Release and fully understand that it is a release of liability. You are waiving any right that you may have to bring a legal action to assert a claim against us for our negligence.

Unlike the waiver provisions in Baker and McCorkle, this paragraph discusses only Stokes' agreement to release Bally's from liability for its negligence. Stokes' argument that he believed that the paragraph somehow related to release from liability for his financial obligations under the retail installment sale agreement is wholly unpersuasive. As our Supreme Court stated in National Bank, it "would be impossible for a person of ordinary intelligence, much less a person of the intelligence and ability of appellant, to have misunderstood the contents of this instrument upon a casual reading thereof . . ." The same principle applies here. Reasonable persons could not disagree that the content of paragraph 10 is quite clearly a waiver and release of liability for negligence, not financial obligations. Likewise, reasonable persons could not disagree that the waiver and release provisions of the paragraph are conspicuously displayed within the larger document.

Stokes also argues that an exculpatory provision may be placed in a document separate from the retail installment sales agreement, but concedes that this is not required. Bally's counters that RCW 63.14.020 and other laws require that the exculpatory clauses and financial terms and conditions between a health club and its members all must be within one document.

We need not decide in this case whether Bally's' argument is correct. It is sufficient to state that no authority supports the proposition that an exculpatory clause must be contained in a separate document to be enforceable. Rather, what is required is that the release language in a document be conspicuous.

The language at issue in this case is conspicuous and enforceable. Bally's owes no duty to Stokes for his injuries. Summary judgment in favor of Bally's is required.

We reverse both summary judgment orders, and direct entry of summary judgment in favor of Bally's on remand.

WE CONCUR.

CASES ON THE SUPPLEMENTAL WEBSITE

BJ'S Wholesale Club, Inc. v. Rosen, 2013 Md. LEXIS 897. With this ruling from Maryland's highest court, the state joins the ranks of the states in which a parental waiver is enforceable. Pay particular attention to the extremely strong argument made in favor of parental waivers.

Moore v. Waller (2007 D.C. App. LEXIS 476). Examine the discussion regarding unequal bargaining power and adhesion contracts. Also of interest is the section regarding the necessity of using the word "negligence." Finally, read and evaluate the waiver used in this case.

Cohen v. Five Brooks Stable (2008 Cal. App. LEXIS 222). Study carefully the court's discussion regarding ambiguity and the use of the term "negligence."

Bailey v. Palladino, 2006 N.J. Super. Unpub. LEXIS 1774. The most interesting points in this waiver case involving a martial arts student are the lack of supervision and the fact that the martial arts business was not named as a protected party in the waiver.

Johnson v. Ubar, LLC, 2009 Wash. App. LEXIS 710. In this case, a lady is injured while working with a personal trainer in a health club. The waiver, found within the membership contract, was not enforced, in part because it was inconspicuous.

Belliconish v. Fun Slides Carpet Skate Park and Party Center, LLC (2014 Pa. Super. Unpub. LEXIS 349). The skate park used one waiver for adults and another for minor clients. The adult plaintiff in this case was inadvertently given and signed a minor waiver rather than an adult waiver. The main issue was the validity of the waiver in light of the error. Pennsylvania waiver law, including its attitude toward adhesionary waivers, is explained.

Supplemental Case from another Chapter

Chapter 4.21 *Jiminez v. 24 Hour Fitness USA, Inc.*, 2015 Cal. App. LEXIS 494. This case is included in the Supplemental Cases for Chapter 4.21 Standards of Practice. Pay particular attention to the way in which the waiver was administered to a client who neither read nor spoke English and how the procedure used led to a case of fraud. The case suggests that care should be taken to ensure that non-readers understand what they are signing.

QUESTIONS YOU SHOULD BE ABLE TO ANSWER

1. Explain what is meant by the term *public policy* and explain why recreation- and sport-related waivers are generally not against public policy.

2. Contrast the rationale for enforcing parental waivers with that against such enforcement.

3. Other than the waiver of negligence section of the participant agreement, what is the most important component? Defend your answer.

4. In *Stokes v. Bally's Pacwest*, how was the waiver made conspicuous? Why was it important that it be conspicuous?

5. Some people feel that a waiver is "bad" or unethical. Defend the use of waivers by a recreation- or sport-related business.

REFERENCES
Cases
Atkins v. Swimwest Family Fitness Center, 2005 Wisc. LEXIS 2.
BJ'S Wholesale Club, Inc. v. Rosen, 2013 Md. LEXIS 897.
Belliconish v. Fun Slides Carpet Skate Park and Party Center, LLC, 2014 Pa. Super. Unpub. LEXIS 349.
Bothell v. Two Point Acres, Inc., 1998 Ariz.App. LEXIS 32.
Cohen v. Five Brooks Stable, 2008 Cal. App. LEXIS 222.
Coughlin v. T.M.H. International Attractions, Inc., 1995 U.S. Dist. LEXIS 12499 (Ky).
Craig v. Lakeshore Athletic Club, Inc., 1997 Wash. App. LEXIS 907.
Davis v. Sun Valley Ski Education Foundation, Inc., 1997 Ida. LEXIS 82.
Dilallo v. Riding Safely Inc., 687 S o.2d 353 [Fla. 4th Dist. 1997].
Hanks v. Powder Ridge Restaurant Corporation, 2005 Conn. LEXIS 500.
Hohe v. San Diego Unified Sch. Dist., 274 Cal.Rptr. 647 (1990).
Hong v. Hockessin Athletic Club, 2012 Del. Super. LEXIS 340.
Huffman v. Monroe County Community School, 564 N.E.2d 961 (Ind., 1991).
Jiminez v. 24 Hour Fitness USA, Inc., 2015 Cal. App. LEXIS 494.
Lantz v. Iron Horse Saloon, Inc., 717 So.2d 590 [Fla. 5th Dist. 1998].
Mahoney v. USA Hockey, Inc., 1999 U.S. Dist. LEXIS 19359.
Maurer v. Cerkvenik-Anderson Travel, Inc., 165 Ariz. Adv. Rep. 51 (1994).
Merten v. Nathan, 321 N.W.2d 173, quoting *Higgins v. McFarland*, 86 S.E.2d 168 at 172 (Va., 1955).
Murphy v. North American River Runners, Inc., 412 S.E.2d. 504 (1991).
Pena v, The Rolladium, 2002 Cal. App. Unpub. LEXIS 1466.
Phelps v. Firebird Raceway, Inc., 2005 Ariz. LEXIS 53.
Quinn v. Mississippi State University, 1998 Miss. LEXIS 328 59.
Reardon v. Windswept Farm LLC., 2006 Conn. LEXIS 330.
Rosen v. BJ's Wholesale Club, Inc., 2012 Md. App. LEXIS 100.
Smith v. YMCA of Benton Harbor/St. Joseph, 550 N.W.2d 262 [Mich. 1996].
Swierkosz v. Starved Rock Stables, 607 N.E. 2d 280 (Ill., 1993).
Wabash County YMCA v. Thompson, 2012 Ind. App. LEXIS 428.
Woodman v. Kera, Mich. LEXIS 1125.
Zivich v. Mentor Soccer Club, 1997 Ohio App. LEXIS 1577.

Publications
Cotten, D. J. and Cotten, M. B. (2016). *Waivers & Releases of Liability*. 9th ed. Sport Risk Consulting: www.createspace.com.
van der Smissen, B. (1990). *Legal liability and risk management for public and private entities*. Cincinnati: Anderson Publishing Co.

2.24 AGREEMENTS RELATED TO THE INHERENT RISKS

Doyice J. Cotten | Sport Risk Consulting

This chapter presents three additional documents that can strengthen defenses for the service provider—the informed consent agreement, the agreement to participate, and the assumption of risk agreement. Each addresses either the inherent risks of the activity or the informed risks of a training program/treatment and helps to produce a stronger assumption of risk defense.

INFORMED CONSENT AGREEMENTS

The **informed consent** agreement is a document used to protect the provider from liability for the informed, treatment risks of a treatment, program, or regimen to which the signer is subjected. The factor that makes the informed consent unique is that **something is done to the participant** by another party with the consent of the participant. It may be in the form of medical treatment, rehabilitation, therapy, fitness testing, or a training program (e.g., when one is to be treated for an injury by an athletic trainer; when a participant is to undergo a training program developed by a personal trainer). The document informs the signer of the risks, thereby enabling the signer to make an educated, informed decision. The informed consent is based in contract law, thus the signing parties must be of age. The informed consent offers little or no protection against liability for injuries resulting from negligence.

The doctrine of informed consent derives from two principles: (1) a person's inherent right to control what happens to his or her body and (2) the physician's fiduciary duty to the patient—to warn the patient of risks and make certain the patient knows enough to make an informed decision regarding his or her care. It is an ethical, moral, and legal concept that is ingrained in American culture.

There are two separate, but related, components of informed consent—**disclosure** and **consent** (Nolan-Haley, 1999). The doctrine requires that those who consent be competent (i.e., of legal age, intellectually capable of consent), sufficiently informed about the treatment to enable an educated decision, and consent voluntarily with no duress (Koeberle & Herbert, 1998).

Medicine

Informed consents originated with and have been primarily used in conjunction with the medical profession. The first cases defining informed consent appeared in the late 1950s and were based on the tort of **battery**—the intentional, unpermitted, unprivileged, and offensive touching (physical contact) of the person of one individual by another. Today most medical cases are based on **negligence** since consent is obtained and the issue is whether the consent was adequately "informed." Informed consent is more than simply getting a patient to sign a written consent form—it is a communication process by which the physician provides relevant information to enable the patient to make an educated, informed decision (American Medical Association, 1998). While state law regarding informed consent varies from state to state, generally physicians are required to inform regarding the nature of the proposed treatment, foreseeable risk and discomforts, anticipated benefits, alternative procedures, and instructions regarding food, drink, or lifestyles.

Human Subject Research

A major application of the informed consent has been in the area of human subject research. The American College of Sports Medicine (1999) stated that:

By law, any experimental subject or clinical patient who is exposed to possible physical, psychological, or social injury must give informed consent prior to participating in a proposed project. (p. vi)

The Office of Human Subjects Research of the National Institutes of Health outlines requirements for such research. The consent should (1) be obtained in writing, (2) be understandable, (3) be obtained in non-coercive circumstances, and (4) contain no language suggesting a relinquishment of rights.

Some of the elements that should be included in the consent are: (1) purpose and duration of the research, (2) description of the procedures, risks, and discomforts involved, (3) benefits and compensation to the subject, (4) alternative procedures, (5) confidentiality policies, (6) compensation and treatment available in the event of injury, 7) whom to contact for questions, and (8) a statement of voluntary participation. They specify that the document should be written at a level below that of a high school graduate—making liberal use of subheads, avoiding multi-syllable words when possible, and keeping sentences short and understandable (Office of Human Subjects Research, 2000).

Sport and Fitness

In recent years, informed consents have been used more frequently in sport and fitness. Service providers are becoming more aware of the necessity of utilizing informed consents for participants in certain types of programs. Injury rehabilitation programs, fitness testing, and fitness regimens directed by personal trainers are three examples of situations in which the use of informed consents is standard practice.

Koeberle and Herbert (1998) describe the informed consent in the fitness setting as "a voluntary agreement from a client who has been informed of, appreciates, and understands the material and relevant risks associated with participation in the activity or range of activities involved in exercise testing and activity provided through prescription." (p. 52) Since having a client undergo an exercise prescription or fitness test can be construed as either **actual** or **constructive contact**, they stress that an informed consent is necessary to gain the client's permission for contact. Without the informed consent, the fitness professional is risking action for civil or criminal battery. Koeberle and Herbert suggest that informed consents in personal fitness settings do not require consent forms in the same detail as those required of physicians. The trainer is not held to a standard as high as that of the physician since activity programs contain a very low incidence of risk when compared to even the safest medical procedures.

The following guidelines for the content and administration of the informed consent for sport, recreation, and fitness activities are drawn from four sources (Herbert & Herbert, 2002[1]; Independent Review Consulting, Inc., 2000; Koeberle & Herbert, 1998; Olivier & Olivier, 2001).

Content
The content of the informed consent for the recreation, sport, and fitness setting should:

- Be in writing on a preprinted form;
- Be written in plain, understandable language;
- State the purpose of the exercise program, test, or prescribed action;
- Include a general description of the exercise program, test, or prescribed action;
- List any likely discomforts that might be associated with the program, test, or activity;
- List the potential risks and potential benefits of the exercise program, test, or activity;
- Be worded to allow all staff members to have physical contact or interact with the participant;
- Have participant acknowledge voluntary participation;
- Have participant acknowledge that consent was not signed under duress;
- Have participant acknowledge an opportunity to ask questions and have them answered to his or her satisfaction;
- Have participant acknowledge that the participant read and understood the informed consent document.

---

[1] Consult this publication for an in-depth look at the concept of the informed consent.

FIGURE 2.24.1 ILLUSTRATIVE INFORMED CONSENT FOR PERSONAL TRAINERS

CONSENT FOR PHYSICAL FITNESS TRAINING PROGRAM

Program Objectives

I understand that my physical fitness program is individually tailored to meet the goals and objectives agreed upon by my personal trainer and myself.

Description of the Exercise Program

I understand that my exercise program can involve participation in a number of types of fitness activities. These activities will vary depending upon the objectives that my personal trainer and I establish, but can include: (1) aerobic activities including, but not limited to, the use of treadmills, stationary bicycles, step machines, rowing machines, and running track; (2) muscular endurance and strength building exercises including, but not limited to, the use of free weights, weight machines, calisthenics, and exercise apparatus; (3) nutrition and weight control activities; and (4) selected physical fitness and body composition tests, including but not limited to strength tests, cardiovascular fitness tests, and body composition tests.

Description of Potential Risks

I understand that my personal trainer cannot guarantee my personal safety because all exercise programs have inherent risks regardless of the care taken by a personal trainer. **I will initial the types of activities (including their risks) that my trainer and I have selected for my program to acknowledge that I understand the potential risks of my training program.**

_____ **Aerobic Activities**: I realize that participation in any cardiovascular activity may involve sustained, vigorous exertion which places stress on the muscles, joints, and cardiovascular system, sometimes resulting in injuries ranging from minor injuries (e.g., muscle soreness, pulled muscles, and musculo-skeletal strains and sprains) to the infrequent serious injury (e.g., torn ligaments, heart attack, and stroke) to the rare catastrophic incident (e.g., death, paralysis).

_____ **Muscular Endurance & Strength**: I realize that participation in muscular endurance and strength building activities involves repetitive exertions and maximal exertions which can result in stress-related injuries ranging from minor injuries (e.g., muscle soreness, muscle strains, and ligament injuries) to the infrequent serious injury (e.g., torn rotator cuffs, herniated disks or other back injuries, crushed fingers, and heart attack) to the rare catastrophic incident (e.g., death, paralysis).

_____ **Nutrition and Weight Control**: I realize that the nutrition and weight control program may involve a dietary change, selected nutritional supplements, and regular exercise. I also understand that no nutrition and weight control program is without risk and that some of the risks range from minor concerns (e.g., failure to achieve my goals, muscle soreness, and strains) to the infrequent serious injury (e.g., physical reaction to food supplements or nutrition products, adverse body reaction to weight loss, or heart attack) to the rare catastrophic incident (e.g., death, paralysis).

_____ **Fitness and Body Composition Tests**: I realize that participation in tests can result in injuries ranging from minor injuries (e.g., muscle soreness, pulled muscles, and sprains) to the infrequent serious injury (e.g., torn ligaments, back injuries, and heart attack) to the rare catastrophic incident (e.g., death, paralysis).

Description of Potential Benefits

I understand that a regular exercise program has been shown to have definite benefits to general health and well-being. **I will initial the types of activities (including their benefits) that my trainer and I have selected for my program to acknowledge that I understand the potential benefits of my training program**.

_____ **Aerobic Activities**: loss of weight, reduction of body fat, improvement of blood lipids, lowering of blood pressure, improvement in cardiovascular function, reduction in risk of heart disease, increased muscular endurance, improved posture, and improved flexibility.

_____ **Muscular Endurance & Strength**: loss of weight, reduction of body fat, increased muscle mass, improvement of blood lipids, lowering of blood pressure, improved strength and muscular endurance, improved posture.

_____ **Nutrition and Weight Control**: loss of weight, reduction of body fat, improvement of blood lipids, lowering of blood pressure, improvement in cardiovascular function, reduction in risk of heart disease.

_____ **Fitness and Body Composition Tests**: learn current status and gain information regarding areas needing improvement.

Participant Responsibilities

I understand that it is my responsibility to (1) fully disclose any health issues or medications that are relevant to participation in a strenuous exercise program; (2) cease exercise and report promptly any unusual feelings (e.g., chest discomfort, nausea, difficulty breathing, apparent injury) during the exercise program; and (3) clear my participation with my physician.

Participant Acknowledgments

In agreeing to this exercise program:

- I acknowledge that my participation is completely voluntary.
- I understand the potential physical risks and believe that the potential benefits outweigh those risks.
- I give consent to certain physical touching that may be necessary to ensure proper technique and body alignment.
- I understand that the achievement of health or fitness goals cannot be guaranteed.
- I have had a voice in planning and approving the activities selected for my exercise program.
- I have been able to ask questions regarding any concerns, and have had those questions answered to my satisfaction.
- I am in good physical condition, have no disability that might prevent my participation in such activities, and have been advised to consult a physician prior to beginning this program.
- I have been advised to cease exercise immediately if I experience unusual discomfort and feel the need to stop.

I have read and understand the above agreement; I have been able to ask questions regarding any concerns I might have; I have had those questions answered to my satisfaction; and I am freely signing this agreement.

_____	_____	_____	_____	_____
Signature of Participant	Name of Participant (Print)	Date	Signature of Trainer	Date

_____	_____	_____
Signature of Parent/Guardian (If Participant is a Minor)	Name of Parent/Guardian (Print)	Date

_____	_____	_____
Signature of Parent/Guardian (If Participant is a Minor)	Name of Parent/Guardian (Print)	Date

Administration

The administrative procedures relating to the obtaining and handling of the informed consent can make a difference in the effectiveness of the agreement.

- A separate form should be used for each type of activity (e.g., exercise program, test, rehabilitation, fitness activity).
- The professional should explain the content of the informed consent and give the participant an opportunity to ask and have his or her questions answered satisfactorily.

- The consent form should be signed by the participant and professional, and dated.
- A copy of the consent should be provided to the participant.
- The signed and dated consent should be placed in the participant's file.

If the participant is a **minor**:

- It is imperative that one or both parents sign the agreement;
- The provider should use an informed consent form written specifically for parents of minors;
- The consent should contain language directed to the parent by which the parent gives permission for the activity, acknowledges an understanding of the risks, and signs the agreement.

An illustrative informed consent for personal trainers is presented in Figure 2.24.1. This form is for illustrative purposes only and the reader is cautioned to consult a competent attorney for legal advice regarding such a form.

It is important that the recreation or sport manager understand that the informed consent is important in avoiding liability for injuries resulting from the inherent risks of the activity. It is equally important that the recreation or sport manager remember two things about the informed consent: (1) that the informed consent is contractual in nature, thus requiring the signature of a parent or guardian when the client is a minor, and (2) that the consent provides no protection against liability for injuries resulting from the negligence of the service provider, its employees, or its agents. For such protection, a waiver should be utilized (see Chapter 2.23 *Waivers and Releases*).

Documentation

Herbert and Herbert (2002) stress the importance of documentation and record-keeping when working with individuals who have consented to programs. Just as physicians now must keep detailed notes on patient visits (e.g., complaints, treatments, responses to treatment, instructions), personal trainers, therapists, and other providers utilizing informed consents should do the same. While the extent of documentation required might not be the same, all documentation and notes can serve as evidence and can help the provider recollect the facts if called upon to testify in the event of litigation—sometimes years later. Development and use of a standardized form that includes spaces for the date, signature, and notes is suggested.

AGREEMENTS TO PARTICIPATE

The **agreement to participate** (not to be confused with the participant agreement in Chapter 2.23) is a document intended to strengthen the defenses against liability for injuries resulting from the inherent risks of the activity. The agreement to participate is a document by which the signer is (1) made aware of and acknowledges knowledge of the inherent risks of the activity and (2) is informed of the rules of the activity and behavioral expectations and agrees to abide by them (van der Smissen, 1990). The agreement to participate is often used when persons are about to participate in an activity, sport, or class (e.g., extreme sport participants, physical education class members, participants in intramural or recreational programs). The agreement is based in tort law and does not constitute a formal contract; therefore it is an ideal instrument for dealing with minor participants. The agreement differs from the informed consent in that it is not a contract and nothing is *done to* the participant. Rather, the participant is **seeking to participate**.

The agreement to participate, unlike the informed consent, is not a contract. It is simply an agreement by which the participant is informed of the inherent risks and behavioral expectations of participants and affirms his or her assumption of the inherent risks of participation in the activity. However, in order to assume the inherent risks, like the informed consent, the signer (1) must have knowledge of the nature of the activity, (2) must understand the activity in terms of his or her own condition and skill, and (3) must appreciate the type of injuries that may occur. It is important to the provider that the participant understands these inherent risks and the provider, by requiring an agreement to participate, is taking steps (e.g., the agreement to participate) to insure this understanding. Since the agreement is merely informative in nature, it can be used when the participant or client is an adult or is a minor. For a minor, the signature of a parent is desirable from a public relations standpoint, but is not mandated.

The agreement to participate has two main functions. First, it informs the participant of the inherent risks (which the participant assumes); thereby, the agreement strengthens the primary assumption of risk defense. Second, it informs the participant of the rules of the activity or entity (which the participant consents to obey); in so doing, the agreement strengthens the secondary assumption of risk defense (contributory negligence). By establishing that the participant was aware of the conduct expected, any conduct contrary to expected participant behaviors might be a factor in causing the injury to the participant. For instance, suppose a member of a racquetball class, after instruction prohibiting more than four players on a court at the same time, is injured while playing with five players on the court. His negligent act could be considered a contributing factor to the injury, thereby preventing recovery in contributory negligence states and reducing recovery in comparative negligence states. This, in effect, would either eliminate or reduce any liability by the teacher or provider. The agreement does not protect against liability for negligence unless an exculpatory clause is added – then, the signature of a parent or guardian is required for minor participants.

It is important to understand that the agreement to participate is not merely a parental permission slip. A **permission slip** is just that and no more; it informs the entity that the parent grants permission for the youngster to participate – nothing else. It does not protect against liability for injuries resulting from inherent risks or from provider negligence. In *Sweeney v. City of Bettendorf* (2009), the parent gave permission for her daughter to attend a minor league baseball game; she was injured by a bat that flew into the stands. The permission slip read:

> I hereby give permission for my child Tara M. Sweeney to attend the Bettendorf Park Board field trip to John O'Donnell Stadium with the Playgrounds Program on Monday, June 30, 2003. *I realize that the Bettendorf Park Board is not responsible or liable for any accidents or injuries that may occur while on this special occasion.* Failure to sign this release as is without amendment or alteration is grounds for denial of participation. [Italics added.]

Most permission slips do not include language such as the italicized sentence; but even with this attempt to eliminate liability, the permission slip provided no protection. The court ruled that "The language at issue here refers only to "accidents" generally and contains nothing specifically indicating that a parent would be waiving potential claims for the City's negligence."

Contents

There are no "magic phrases" that are either legally required or even universally useful in the construction of agreements to participate. There also is no ironclad format that is required. However, certain information should be in any agreement to participate and the following would serve as a logical order for inclusion (Cotten & Cotten, 2016).

Nature of the Activity

It is important that the activity be described in some detail. The description should be specific to the activity and not generic in nature. It should include a description of what the activity is like, remembering that the less familiar the participant is with the activity, the more detail required in the description. Include negative or unpleasant aspects that the participant should expect, how much physical stress is involved, and the intensity level of the activity. Each section of the agreement to participate is illustrated in Figure 2.24.2.

Possible Consequences of Injury

Two areas should be covered in this section. First, the participant should be made aware of the types of accidents that may occur in the specific sport involved. Here one should list some insignificant accidents that are common to the sport (being struck by the ball in racquetball), as well as some serious accidents that occur occasionally (falling and striking one's head on the floor in racquetball). Second, include some of the injuries that can occur in the sport. List some minor injuries that are common to the sport (e.g., bruises, strains, sprains in racquetball), some more serious injuries (e.g., loss of vision, broken bones, concussions), as well as catastrophic injuries (e.g., paralysis and death). Use phrases such as "some of the...," "injuries such as...," and "including, but not limited to..." in listing both accidents and injuries.

FIGURE 2.24.2 ILLUSTRATIVE AGREEMENT TO PARTICIPATE FOR MINORS

AGREEMENT TO PARTICIPATE AND LIABILITY WAIVER FOR MINORS

Participating in the *Annual 5k Fun Run*

All physical activities involve certain inherent risks making it impossible to ensure the safety of all participants. The *5K Fun Run* is a vigorous, cardiovascular activity requiring *sustained running endurance, coordination, and running skill*. While the *Club* is using care in conducting the event, it is unable to eliminate all risk from the activity.

It is possible for *runners* to suffer common injuries such as *cramps, muscle strains, and sprains*. More serious, but less frequent, injuries such as *broken bones, cuts, concussions, heart attacks, strokes, paralysis, and death* may also occur. These injuries, and others, may result from such incidents as (but not limited to) *slips and falls, tripping, colliding with another runner, imperfections in the street surfaces, heat-related illnesses, and stress placed on the cardiovascular system*.

All *runners* are expected to follow these safety guidelines:

1. *Wear proper footwear.*
2. *Be alert for unanticipated hazards on the course.*
3. *Do not crowd other runners.*
4. *Consume adequate liquids during the run.*
5. *Follow all announced or posted rules.*

I agree to follow the preceding safety rules, all posted safety rules, and all rules common to *running*. Further, I agree to report any unsafe practices, conditions, or equipment to the *race* management.

I certify that (1) I possess a sufficient degree of physical fitness to safely participate in *the 5K Fun Run*, (2) I understand that I am to discontinue *running* at any time I feel undue discomfort or stress, and (3) I will indicate below any health-related conditions that might affect my ability to safely *complete the run* and I will verbally inform activity management immediately.

Circle: Diabetes   Heart Problems   Seizures   Asthma   Other _____

I have read the preceding information and my questions have been answered. **I know, understand, and appreciate the risks associated with *distance runs* and I am voluntarily participating in the activity. In doing so, I am assuming all of the inherent risks of the sport**. I further understand that in the event of a medical emergency, *management will call EMS to render assistance and that I will be financially responsible for any expenses involved*.

Signature of Participant	Date	Name of Participant (Please Print)
Signature of Parent	Date	Name of Parent (Please Print)
Signature of Parent	Date	Name of Parent (Please Print)

Waiver of Liability: In consideration of being permitted to run in the *5K Fun Run*, on behalf of myself, my family, my heirs, and my assigns, **the undersigned Participant and Parent or Guardian hereby release the club from liability for injury, loss, or death** to the minor, while *participating in the run or while in any way associated with participating in the event now or in the future*, **resulting from the ordinary negligence of the *club*, its agents, or employees**.

Signature of Participant	Date	Name of Participant (Please Print)
Signature of Parent	Date	Name of Parent (Please Print)
Signature of Parent	Date	Name of Parent (Please Print)

Behavioral Expectations of the Participant
The major purpose of this section is to transfer some of the responsibility for the participant's safety from the recreation or sport business to the participant. One might list several very important rules to which the participant is expected to adhere. An example in racquetball might be that participants are required to wear eye protection at all times. If there are few rules, they might be listed on the front of the agreement. If there are numerous rules, the participant might be referred to the back of the sheet where they are listed. In either case, giving the participant a copy of these rules would be desirable. Once again, one should not attempt to make the list all-inclusive.

Condition of the Participant
The participant should affirm that he or she possesses the physical condition and required competencies to participate in the activity safely. The required level, which will vary with the activity, should be described in Section I of the agreement. The participant will also affirm that the participant has no physical conditions that would preclude participation in the activity and will identify any conditions of which the recreation or sport business should be aware (e.g., heart problems, seizures, asthma). Particularly for vigorous activities, a statement that the participant should discontinue the activity if undue discomfort or stress occurs should be included. Participant affirmation of condition is generally adequate for activities such as 5K runs, health club memberships, and between-inning promotions at baseball games. Other situations might require more confirmation of condition. For example, residential camps usually require health histories and schools generally demand pre-participatory physical exams prior to varsity competition.

Concluding Statement
This concluding section should contain six items. They are: (1) a statement by which the participant affirms knowledge, understanding, and appreciation of the inherent risks of the activity; (2) affirmation that participation is voluntary, if that is the case; (3) an assumption of risk statement; (4) notice of the procedures to be followed in the event of an emergency and the financial responsibility of the participant for emergency actions; (5) insurance requirements; and (6) a space for the signature of the participant (and the parent if the participant is a minor) at the bottom of the agreement. The critical signature is that of the minor; however, the parent's signature is important for public relations purposes.

Optional Sections
Waiver. This is an optional section that may be used with agreements to participate (see Chapter 2.23 *Waivers and Releases*). This section should follow the signature section of the agreement to participate and provide space for a second signature by the participant (and parent, if the participant is a minor) relating specifically to the exculpatory clause (an illustrative agreement to participate including the critical information is given in Figure 2.24.2).

Parental Permission Form (Slip). This optional section merely gives permission for a minor to participate in the activity—strengthening neither the primary nor secondary assumption of risk defense. The form has some public relations value in informing the parent of the activity in which the child will be participating and can be used to gain permission for emergency medical treatment, to assign financial responsibility for such treatment, and to obtain permission for the use of the participant's name and photograph. It may be convenient to include it as a component of the agreement to participate when the participant is a minor.

Using the Agreement to Participate
Some guidelines regarding the use of the agreement to participate can help to insure the effectiveness of the agreement in strengthening the assumption of risk and the contributory negligence defenses. First, presentation of the agreement should be accompanied by a verbal explanation of the risks participants will encounter through participation and of their responsibility for their own safety. Second, it is important to provide an opportunity for the signer to ask questions and gain clarification. Third, stress the participants' duty to inform

you of any dangerous practices, hazardous conditions, or faulty equipment of which they may become aware while participating. This, however, in no way reduces or relieves the recreation or sport business of its duty to inspect the facility, examine the equipment, or supervise the activity. In addition, the language used in both the agreement and the verbal explanation should be appropriate to the age and maturity of the participant.

Finally, keep in mind that the agreement to participate can serve as important evidence in the event of a lawsuit. These records should be safely stored so that they may be retrieved when needed. The time during which a person may file a timely suit varies from one to four years after the injury, depending upon the state. However, keep in mind that a minor who is injured can generally file a suit until one to four years after reaching the age of majority. So in the event of an injury, it would be helpful to make and carefully store a file on that individual which would include the agreement to participate along with all other pertinent documentation (e.g., accident report, written statements by witnesses, parental permission slips).

ASSUMPTION OF RISK AGREEMENTS

The assumption of risk agreement is quite similar to the agreement to participate. They both are intended to have the participant acknowledge the assumption of the inherent risks of the activity; the assumption of risk agreement, however, is most often brief (often a single paragraph) while the agreement to participate usually includes a listing of the inherent risks and is a full page, stand alone document. The **assumption of risk agreement** is a pact by which the participant or client may be informed of the inherent risks of the activity and attests that participant or client assumes the inherent risks of the activity. The participant or client further confirms that he or she (1) has been informed of the nature of the activity and its inherent risks, (2) understands the activity in terms of its demands on the participant's own physical condition and skill level, and (3) appreciates the type of injuries that may occur and the consequences of such injuries. Finally, the participant or client should verify that his or her participation is voluntary and that he or she assumes the inherent risks of the activity.

As with the informed consent and the agreement to participate, the assumption of risk agreement may contain a written characterization of the nature of the activity and a listing of the inherent risks involved. The listing of the risks should not attempt to be all-inclusive, but should include the likely minor injuries, the unlikely major injuries, and the highly unlikely catastrophic injuries or death. One should not shy away from presenting the possibility of serious injuries. The assumption of risk agreement (labeled as "Acknowledgment of Risk") in the *Fairchild v. Amundson* Significant Case below is an example of an agreement that protects only against liability for inherent risks; fortunately for the provider, the plaintiff was unable to show negligence on the part of the provider.

The agreement can be used prior to participation in recreation and sport activities, prior to internships, or in almost any situation in which the service provider wants documentation that the participant understood and assumed the inherent risks of the activity. The assumption of risk agreement can be a stand-alone document, but is more often included as part of a liability waiver. Traditionally the assumption of risk agreement in a waiver has not included a list of the risks of the activity. Today, however, courts in many states mandate the inclusion of inherent risks for a waiver to be enforceable.

The assumption of risk agreement used in conjunction with a liability waiver helps to provide more protection for the service provider. The waiver protects against liability for negligence while the assumption of risk statement helps to protect against liability for injuries resulting from the inherent risks of the activity.

King v. University of Indianapolis (2002) illustrates one of the limitations of an assumption of risk agreement. King signed an agreement prior to his death while practicing for varsity football. The agreement would have protected the university from liability had his death been due to the inherent risks, but offered no protection against the allegation of negligence. The case was remanded for trial. On the other hand, the court in *Stowers v. Clinton Central School Corporation* (2006) admitted an acknowledgement and release form into evidence which neither contained the word "negligence" nor relieved the defendant of liability for negligence. The court said the form was relevant to the defense of incurred risk since it provided evidence that the plaintiff knew and appreciated the risks involved and voluntarily accepted those risks.

Interestingly, some service providers use an assumption of risk clause while under the impression that it is a waiver of liability for negligence. In a health club case in California (*Zipusch v. LA Workout*, 2007), LA Workout included an assumption of risk agreement within its membership agreement. At the end of the assumption of risk, the club included the sentence "The member or guest will defend and indemnify LA Workout for any negligence EXCEPT the sole negligence of the club." The club learned that the agreement offered no protection against its negligence.

In conclusion, it is critical that the reader understand two things regarding assumption of risk agreements. First, the assumption of risk agreement applies to assumption of the inherent risks and offers no protection against liability for provider negligence. Second, assumption of risk agreements should include a representative (but not comprehensive) list of the inherent risks.

SIGNIFICANT CASE

This case illustrates perfectly the value of the assumption of risk agreement. Observe in reading the case four different facts that help to establish that Fairchild was aware of the inherent risks of whitewater rafting. It is also important to understand that the assumption of risk document protects Amundson from liability for an injury resulting from the inherent risks of the activity as contrasted with the waiver case in Chapter 2.23 in which the waiver protects the provider from liability for negligence. Note that in this case, negligence was not at issue before the trial court and was, therefore, not considered by the appellate court.

FAIRCHILD V. AMUNDSON
Court of Appeals of Washington, Division One
2001 Wash. App. LEXIS 149

Opinion By: Ronald E. Cox

At issue is whether Wild Water River Tours owed a duty to its customer, Thomas Fairchild, for injuries that he suffered during a rafting trip on the Toutle River. Because the doctrine of implied primary assumption of risk bars Fairchild's claim, we affirm the summary dismissal of this action.

In April 1995, Tom Fairchild participated in a whitewater rafting trip on the Toutle River. Rodney Amundson, d/b/a Wild Water River Tours (WWRT), guided the commercial rafting trip. Fairchild had been on whitewater rafting trips before, and knew that one of the dangers inherent in rafting was the possibility that rafters would fall out into the water. He also read brochures of WWRT that described certain dangers of river rafting.

On the day of the rafting trip, Fairchild and his church group assembled near the river under the supervision of WWRT. Fairchild donned a wetsuit, helmet, and life vest issued by WWRT. The rafters all signed an "Acknowledgement of Risk" form. WWRT guides then instructed them on paddling techniques and safety measures. The safety measures included instructions on maneuvering the raft near logs, rocks, and reversals. They also included instructions on swimming in the event rafters are in the water, pulling a swimmer back into the raft, and escaping from underneath a capsized raft.

River rapids are classified on a scale from class I (easiest) to class VI (most difficult). The Toutle River has two class IV rapids, one of which is known as Hollywood Gorge (Gorge). The Gorge also contains a "reversal," a point in the river subject to strong downward pressure that may cause a raft to overturn.

As they approached the Gorge, all the rafts stopped, and Amundson and other WWRT guides got out of the rafts and scouted the Gorge. After everyone returned to their rafts and re-entered the river, Amundson's raft successfully navigated through the Gorge to an eddy just beyond the reversal. Amundson then waited for the other rafts.

As Fairchild's raft entered the Gorge, it was sucked into a reversal, and all the occupants were thrown into the water. Amundson observed this from his raft and immediately paddled out of the eddy and into the river's current to retrieve Fairchild. Amundson and others administered CPR to Fairchild, who had been floating face down in the river, and resuscitated him. Thereafter, Fairchild went to a hospital, where he was treated and released the next day.

Fairchild sued. The trial court granted WWRT's motion for summary judgment.

Fairchild appeals.

Implied Assumption of Risk

Fairchild argues that material factual issues exist as to whether the doctrine of implied primary assumption of risk bars his recovery. We disagree.

We may affirm an order granting summary judgment if there are no genuine issues of material fact and the moving party is entitled to judgment as a matter of law. We consider all facts and reasonable inferences in the light most favorable to the nonmoving party. We review questions of law de novo.

The moving party bears the initial burden of showing the absence of a genuine issue of material fact. Once that burden is met, the burden shifts to the party with the burden of proof at trial to make a showing sufficient to establish the existence of an element essential to that party's case. If the claimant fails to meet that burden, the trial court should grant the motion because there can be no genuine issue of material fact given that a complete failure of proof concerning an essential element of the nonmoving party's case necessarily renders all other facts immaterial.

WWRT asserts that the doctrine of assumption of risk bars recovery. That doctrine has four facets: (1) express assumption of risk, (2) implied primary assumption of risk, (3) implied reasonable assumption of risk, and (4) implied unreasonable assumption of risk. Implied primary assumption of risk is at issue here. It occurs where the plaintiff impliedly has consented to relieve the defendant of an obligation or duty to act. With implied primary assumption of risk, the plaintiff engages in conduct from which consent is then implied. If implied primary assumption of risk is established, it bars any recovery.

At summary judgment, WWRT was required to show that (a) Fairchild had full subjective understanding of the nature and presence of a specific risk, and (b) he voluntarily chose to encounter the risk. Knowledge of and appreciation of the specific risk of danger, and voluntariness are questions of fact for the jury, except when reasonable minds could not differ.

Here, WWRT established both elements of implied primary assumption of risk. First, the evidence shows that Fairchild subjectively knew and understood the specific risk of falling into the water and drowning. Prior to the rafting trip, Fairchild read WWRT's brochures describing whitewater rafting on the Toutle River. The brochures listed the Toutle River as a class IV river and described rafting on that river as "fast & furious" and "[y]ou'll never know when you're going to hit crushing waves and bottomless holes." Fairchild testified in his deposition that he had been rafting on a slower river before and wanted a more exciting whitewater rafting trip when he signed up with WWRT. Prior to boarding the rafts, WWRT outfitted Fairchild with a wetsuit, helmet, and vest. It also instructed him on swimming techniques. Moreover, Fairchild admitted in his deposition that getting thrown from the raft into a rushing river was a danger inherent to whitewater rafting on the Toutle River. Reasonable minds could not differ in deciding that Fairchild knew of and appreciated the specific risk of falling into the water and possibly drowning. Likewise, reasonable minds could not differ that Fairchild was aware of the above specific risks when he signed the "acknowledgment of risk" form which states that:

> *I am aware that participating in this raft trip arranged by Wildwater River Tours, its agents or associates, that I face certain risks, dangers, and personal property damage. This may include but not be limited to the hazards of traveling down rivers in inflatable rafts, accident or illness in remote places without medical facilities, forces of nature and travel by automobile or other conveyance. In consideration of, and as part payment for the right to participate in this trip and the services and food arranged for me by Wildwater River Tours, and its agents or associates, I do hereby acknowledge all of the above risks. The terms hereof shall serve as my acknowledgment of risk for my heirs, executors and administrators and for all members of my family . . . I have carefully read this agreement and fully understand its contents.* (Italics ours)

The above facts all establish that Fairchild knew of the nature and presence of the specific risk of falling into the river and possibly drowning. It also shows that he voluntarily assumed those risks.

Fairchild attempts to establish that a genuine issue of material fact exists as to his subjective knowledge or understanding of the risk of being thrown into the water. We reject this argument.

"When a party has given clear answers to unambiguous [deposition] questions which negate the existence of any genuine issue of material fact, that party cannot thereafter create such an issue with an affidavit that merely contradicts, without explanation, previously given clear testimony." In his declaration, Fairchild stated that he was not aware of the risk of being thrown into the water at the time he signed the "acknowledgment of risk" form. But this contradicts, without explanation, Fairchild's prior deposition testimony in which he admitted that he knew of that specific risk. Thus, Fairchild has failed to establish a genuine issue of material fact on the issue of whether he subjectively knew the presence and nature of the risk of being thrown into the water.

Fairchild also attempts to show that a genuine issue of material fact exists as to whether he voluntarily chose to encounter the risk of being thrown into the water. He contends that because there were no reasonable alternatives available to him to assuming the inherent risks of river rafting, he did not voluntarily choose to assume those risks. We disagree.

Whether a plaintiff decides voluntarily to encounter a risk depends on whether he or she elects to encounter it despite knowing of a reasonable alternative course of action. In other words, the plaintiff must have had a reasonable opportunity to act differently or proceed on an alternate course that would have avoided the danger in order for assumption of risk to bar recovery.

Here, Fairchild chose to encounter the risk of being thrown into the water despite having numerous reasonable alternatives. He could have chosen to take a slower rafting trip. He could have elected to forego whitewater rafting altogether. He could have chosen not to continue with the trip once he reached the starting point or gotten out when his raft stopped and WRRT guides walked on the bank to scout the Gorge. In sum, Fairchild fails to establish a genuine issue of fact as to whether he voluntarily encountered the risk.

Fairchild also argues that he did not assume the risk of WWRT's alleged negligence in operating the raft because he knew that he might fall out of the raft and into the river. This was not an argument that Fairchild made below. Thus, we need not consider it for the first time on appeal. In any event, there is nothing in this record that establishes that any action or omission of WWRT was outside the scope of the risks that are inherent in the sport of river rafting.

We need not address Fairchild's contention that by signing the "acknowledgment of risk" form, he did not expressly assume the risk of falling into the water. WWRT does not argue that express assumption of risk applies to bar Fairchild's recovery. Rather, the issue is whether implied assumption of risk applies. We hold that it does.

Fairchild also asserts that the trial court improperly placed the burden of proof on him "to show that there was negligence rather than [placing] the burden on [WWRT] to show that no reasonable jury could find negligence from the material facts submitted in the record." There was no improper shifting of burden here. WWRT moved for summary judgment based on implied primary assumption of risk. It was then Fairchild's burden to show whether a genuine issue of material fact exists as to the doctrine. He simply failed to do so.

We affirm the order granting defendants' motion for summary judgment.

CASES ON THE SUPPLEMENTAL WEBSITE

McDermott v. Carie (2005 MT 293; 329 Mont. 295; 124 P.3d 168; 2005 Mont. LEXIS 480). No cases involving agreements to participate have been found, however, this case illustrates the value of listing a selection of inherent risks on a waiver. In this Montana case (where waivers are not enforced) the document was admitted with the waiver language redacted to show the plaintiff understood the inherent risks.

Vaughan v. Nielson (2008 Tex. App. LEXIS 6608). This case illustrates failure to obtain an informed consent in a medical situation.

King v. CJM Country Stables (2004 U.S. Dist. LEXIS 7511). This case includes the Hawaii statute which says waivers are enforceable to protect against liability for inherent risks providing there is full disclosure of the inherent risks associated with the activity.

Crase v. Kent State University, 2009 Ohio App. LEXIS 5785. The cheerleader, who was injured by a fall from a pyramid, sued. The defendant university sought protection from an informed consent agreement, but that agreement protected against informed activity risks, not negligence.

King v. University of Indianapolis, 2002 U.S. Dist. LEXIS 19070. A college football player signed an assumption of risk agreement prior to participation and subsequently died in football practice. The university sought protection from the assumption of risk agreement, but the agreement provided no protection from liability for negligence.

Sweeney v. City of Bettendorf, 2009 Iowa Sup. LEXIS 26. The court examines a parental permission slip in this case and evaluates its exculpatory value. Learn why the court ruled that the slip did not protect the school from liability for negligence.

QUESTIONS YOU SHOULD BE ABLE TO ANSWER

1. What is the primary difference between an informed consent agreement and an agreement to participate?

2. Which of the three agreements in this chapter requires the signature of a parent? Why?

3. Explain the difference in the consent granted in a parental permission slip and the consent in an informed consent agreement for an experimental training program.

4. Explain how an agreement to participate might reduce or eliminate a service provider's liability for negligence.

5. What role did the Wild Water River Tours brochures and their "acknowledgement of risk" form play in the court's verdict in the Significant Case?

REFERENCES

Cases
Fairchild v. Amundson, 2001 Wash. App. LEXIS 149.
King v. University of Indianapolis, 2002 U.S. Dist LEXIS 19070.
Stokes v. Bally's Pacwest, Inc., 54 P.3d 161 (2002).
Stowers v. Clinton Central School Corporation, 2006 Ind. App. LEXIS 2151.
Sweeney v. City of Bettendorf, 2009 Iowa Sup. LEXIS 26.
Zipusch v. LA Workout, 2007 Cal. App. LEXIS 1652.

Publications
American College of Sports Medicine. (1999). Policy statement regarding the use of human subjects and informed consent. *Medicine and Science in Sports and Exercise, 31* (7), vi.

American Medical Association. (1998). *Informed consent*. Online, Internet. www.ama-assn.org/ama/pub/category/4608.html.

Cotten, Doyice J. and Cotten, Mary B. (2016). *Waivers & Releases of Liability*. 9th ed. Sport Risk Consulting: www.createsspace.com.

Herbert, D. L., & Herbert, W. G. *Legal aspects of preventive, rehabilitative and recreational exercise programs*. (4th ed.). Canton, OH: PRC Publishing, Inc.

Independent Review Consulting, Inc. (2000). *Post-approval requirements: informed consent*. Corte Madera, CA.

Koeberle, B. E., & Herbert, D. L. (1998). *Legal aspects of personal fitness training*, (2nd ed.). Canton, OH: PRC Publishing, Inc.

Nolan-Haley, J. M. (1999). Informed consent in mediation: A guiding principle for truly educated decision making. *Notre Dame L. Rev.*, 74, 775.

Office of Human Subjects Research (OHSR) National Institutes of Health. (2000). *Guidelines for writing informed-consent documents*. Online, Internet. http://ohsr.od.nih.gov/info_6.php3

Olivier, S. & Olivier, A. (2001). Informed consent in sport science. *Sportscience*. Online, Internet. www.sportsci.org/jour/0101/so.htm

van der Smissen, B. (1990). *Legal liability and risk management for public and private entities*. Cincinnati, OH: Anderson Publishing.

PREMISES LIABILITY

John Grady | University of South Carolina

"[T]he operator of a commercial recreational [or sport] facility, like the operator of any other business, has a general duty to exercise reasonable care for the safety of its patrons" (*Schneider v. American Hockey and Ice Skating Center, Inc.*, 2001, p. 534).

Premises liability is the body of law which makes the person who is in possession of land or premises responsible for certain injuries suffered by persons who are present on the premises (American Lawyer Directory, n.d.). Black's Law Dictionary (2014) defines premises liability as "a landowner's or landholder's tort liability for conditions or activities on the premises" (p. 1371). It is expected that the owner or operator of a sport or recreation business will provide a reasonably safe environment for all who enter the premises (Seidler, 2005).

FUNDAMENTAL CONCEPTS

Duty of Care

A landowner "owes a duty of reasonable care to guard against any dangerous conditions on his or her property that the owner either knows about or should have discovered" (Restatement (Second) of Torts § 343 (1969)). The specific legal duties owed by the sport or recreation business to its patrons arise not only because the patrons provide the business with an economic benefit and should, therefore, be entitled to protection from harm while on the premises but also because "the operator is in the best position to know of risks, or to discover risks, that threaten customers" (Maloy & Higgins, 2000, p. 35).

The legal duty that a landowner owes to individuals entering his or her premises depends upon the status of the entrant (62 AM. JUR. 2D Premises Liability § 68 [2012]). In most states, persons entering the land are classified into three groups, each of which incurs a different level of care depending on the entrant's relationship with the landowner. The landowner's duty to the entrant varies depending on whether the entrant was an invitee, licensee, or trespasser.

Invitee

"An invitee is a person who has an express or implied invitation to enter or use another's premise," such as a customer to a store (Black's Law Dictionary, 2014, p. 955). *Invitees are owed the greatest level of protection. The landowner is required to maintain his or her premises in a reasonably safe condition under the circumstances. The duty owed to an invitee also extends to warning about known dangers, inspecting the land for hidden dangers, and not exposing the invitee to an unreasonable risk.*

Patrons of sport and recreation businesses would typically be classified as **business invitees** because they are expressly invited onto the land and their presence also provides the business with some economic benefit. For example, spectators at a sporting event or participants in a commercial white water rafting trip would be classified as business invitees. Where the land is open to the public, such as a community park, the visitor would be classified as a **public invitee** since the visitor is invited to enter and remain on the property for a purpose for which the property is held open to the public (Black's Law Dictionary, 2014). A public invitee is owed the same legal obligations by the premise owner as a business invitee.

In *Creely v. Corpus Christi Football Team, Inc.* (2007), Creely was the owner of a cheerleading gym. Pursuant to a contract with the local football team, the Hammerheads, Creely became an official sponsor of the Hammerheads Cheerleaders and Shark Attack Rowdy Squad. In exchange for various types of advertising, she agreed to organize half-time performances by the cheerleading and tumbling camp participants. During a football game, Creely was getting ready for a half-time performance and was standing 25 to 30 feet into what she describes as a "tunnel," located at the end of the stadium next to the stage. A football from the field flew into the tunnel and hit her, injuring her left thumb. The injury required surgery.

Creely sued the Hammerheads for failing to exercise reasonable care in ensuring her safety during the football event. Creely attached a copy of the agreement she entered into with the Hammerheads. The court found that, by virtue of the agreement, Creely was an invitee on the premises. *The general rule is that an owner or occupier of land has a duty to use reasonable care to keep the premises under his control in a safe condition and to use reasonable care to protect an invitee from reasonably foreseeable injuries.* As the duty of reasonable care applies to stadium owners, the court found that the evidence was sufficient to establish that the Hammerheads owed her a duty of reasonable care.

Licensee

A **licensee** is "one who has permission to enter or use another's premises, but only for one's own purposes and not for the occupier's benefit" (Black's Law Dictionary, 2014, p. 1061). *Social guests of the landowner are often classified as licensees.* For example, a landowner inviting neighbors over to swim in a private swimming pool in the landowner's backyard would be a licensee situation. Licensees are owed the same duties as invitees with one exception, *the licensee is to be warned or protected only from harms of which the possessor of the land is aware; there is no duty to inspect the land for hidden dangers.* When compared to the duty owed to invitees, the lower standard of care owed to licensees is justified if one compares the social guest to a member of the landowner's family. "The guest understands when he comes that he is to be placed on the same footing as one of the family, and must take the premises as the occupier himself uses them, without any preparations made for his safety . . ." (Prosser, 1942, p. 604).

Trespasser

A **trespasser** is one "one who intentionally and without consent or privilege enters another's property" (Black's Law Dictionary, 2014, p. 1735). *Trespassers are owed the least amount of protection, sometimes referred to as "zero duty."* In cases involving a trespasser, the landowner is only required to avoid **willful and wanton misconduct** (see Chapter 2.11 *Negligence*) and to refrain from making the premises more dangerous than the trespasser would ordinarily expect. For example, the landowner cannot set a trap whereby the trespasser would be injured upon entering the land.

Attractive nuisance is an exception to the general liability standard for trespassers. Attractive nuisance is defined as "a dangerous condition that may attract children onto land, thereby causing a risk to their safety" (Black's Law Dictionary, 2014, p. 1234). The landowner can be held responsible for creating the dangerous condition because the landowner is obliged to realize that the condition is sufficient to lure persons, particularly children, onto the land. Attractive nuisance can also be applied where the person injured was a trespasser because the landowner should realize that the situation present on his/her land would be both attractive and dangerous. *Attractive nuisance may also apply to adults if the injury or death was the result of an attempt to rescue the child from danger on the land.*

A frequently occurring risk that many landowners may not even think about, but which definitely could give rise to an attractive nuisance claim, is an unguarded trampoline in a homeowner's backyard. The probability of a trampoline luring neighborhood children onto the land is high and this type of recreational equipment can cause serious bodily injury if used improperly, particularly when used at night. Sport and recreation managers must also be vigilant about safeguarding active construction areas on their premises due to the potential for children to be lured into the construction area and become injured by climbing onto heavy-duty construction equipment or a pile of sand or gravel. In the recreation context, it is important to recognize that a body of standing water, such as a lake or pond or flowing water, such as a creek, would not be considered an attractive nuisance in the absence of hidden inherent dangers because the danger of drowning is an apparent open danger (*City of Mangum v. Powell*, 1946).

Recreational User

A recreational user is someone who enters upon land for the purpose of engaging in a recreational activity covered under their state's recreational user statute and is recreating on land suitable for the activity and covered under the statute. For example, Arkansas's recreational user statute defines recreational purposes to include hunting, fishing, swimming, boating, camping, picnicking, and hiking, among others (A.C.A. § 18-11-302). Recreational user statutes, in effect, serve as an affirmative defense to claims of negligence by those engaged in recreational activities on the landowner's property (Clark, 1998).

Currently, all 50 states have a type of tort immunity legislation commonly referred to as recreational user statutes (Spengler, Carroll, Connaughton, & Evenson, 2010). "The basic intent of these statutes is to limit landowner liability when allowing people to utilize their land for recreational purposes" (Carroll, Connaughton, & Spengler, 2007). In *Johnson v. Gibson and Stillson* (2013), Johnson filed a negligence claim against two city employees for injuries she sustained when she stepped into a hole while jogging in a city-owned park. The hole was created by one of the two defendants, both of whom were responsible for maintenance and repair of the sprinkler system in the park. Jogging had been identified as a recreational activity for the purposes of Oregon's recreational user statute (Or. Rev. Stat. § 105.682). There was no dispute the park is land covered by the act or that Johnson was not charged for her use of the park. The only question before the court was whether defendants qualify as "owners" for the purposes of the act. The court found the city employees fell within the scope of the definition of "owner" as defined in the Act and were entitled to immunity. The rationale for shielding property owners from liability through recreational user statutes is explained in *Conant v. Stroup (2002)*. The court explained that if landowners "will make their lands available to the general public for recreational purposes, the state will 'trade' that public access for immunity from liability that might result from the use of the property" (p. 275–276). (For additional discussion of the legal benefits that recreational user statutes can offer the recreation or sport provider, see Chapter 2.32 *Property Law* and Chapter 2.22 *Immunity*).

Trend toward the Reasonable Care Standard
The extent of the duty owed by landowners depends upon state law and varies from state to state. While the status of the visitor is still retained in most states, the legislatures or courts in many states have adopted a different standard of care for property owners. Eight states (Alaska, California, Hawaii, Louisiana, Montana, Nevada, New York, and Tennessee) have abolished the distinctions of invitee, licensee, and trespasser for purposes of premises liability (Daller, 2010). They now state that a *landowner owes a duty to act as a reasonable person in maintaining his property in a reasonably safe condition under the circumstances.*

Fifteen states (Delaware, Illinois, Iowa, Kansas, Maine, Massachusetts, Michigan, Nebraska, New Mexico, North Carolina, North Dakota, Rhode Island, West Virginia, Wisconsin, and Wyoming) and the District of Columbia have abolished the distinction between invitee and licensee and have determined that *owners and occupiers of land owe a duty to exercise reasonable care under the circumstances to any person that is lawfully on his or her property* (Daller, 2010). New Hampshire law is less clear. While in the past, the traditional three-pronged classification of entrants on land was in effect for determining the obligations of landowners, landowners now must use reasonable care in the maintenance or operation of their property. However, the court has ruled that the character of and circumstances surrounding the entry is relevant and important in determining the standard of care owed to the entrant (*Ouellette v. Blanchard*, 1976).

Given the variations in state law, it is important for landowners to recognize whether their state retains the legal distinctions for entrants of invitee, licensee, and trespasser. As a practical matter, however, a landowner who maintains a duty of reasonable care, the highest standard of care owed to invitees, should, in theory, always be protected from liability regardless of the status of the entrant.

Factors Affecting Liability
Several factors affect potential liability of premises owners and operators. Several of the most important are discussed here.

Foreseeability
Premises liability law imposes a duty upon landowners to only protect invitees from foreseeable dangers. In *McPherson v. Tennessee Football Incorporated* (2007), New Orleans Saints player Adrian McPherson participated in a preseason football game between the Saints and the Tennessee Titans in Nashville. Before the start

of the second half, McPherson alleges that he was catching punts from the Saints' punter and that while doing so, T-Rac, the Titans' mascot, drove a golf cart in his area and struck and injured him. The court found that Tennessee law imposes a duty upon owners and operators of business premises to protect its customers from probable or foreseeable dangers and noted that this duty has been extended to supervision of athletic events.

Actual vs. Constructive Notice

While the landowner has a duty to protect invitees from foreseeable dangers, the landowner (or invitor) is not the insurer of the invitee's safety (*Hammond v. Allegretti*, 1974). Before liability may be imposed, the premise owner must have actual or constructive notice of the danger. **Actual notice** refers to situations when the premise owner becomes aware of a problem or defect on the land. For example, an arena manager may discover that a pipe is leaking by discovering water on the floor during a periodic inspection of the restroom. There are a number of other ways for the premise owner to obtain actual notice of a danger. These include being told about it by an employee or patron or, in the worst case, discovering the problem when someone is injured as a result of it.

Constructive notice, on the other hand, arises in situations where the facility manager should have discovered the danger during the course of prudent facility management, including routine facility inspections. If the facility manager would have been aware of the condition by being reasonably attentive, the manager has constructive notice (*Sall vs. T's*, 2006). Establishing that the facility manager had constructive notice may require the use of an expert witness to establish the legal standard of care and to detail what a reasonably prudent facility manager would have done under similar circumstances. For example, in evaluating what is a reasonable time for repair of a broken stadium seat, the expert witness's testimony could establish the reasonableness of the facility manager's actions and whether what was done complied with industry standards. "The determination of what constitutes a reasonable time period between inspections will necessarily vary according to the particular circumstances" (*Zipusch v. LA Workout*, 2007, p. 1293).

In *Stadt v. United Center Joint Venture* (2005), Gary Stadt was injured when he slipped and fell on a puddle of water in the "Standing Room Only" section of the United Center which was hosting a Chicago Black Hawks hockey game. Upon further inspection of the area where Stadt fell, a beer cup was discovered next to the puddle. Stadt sued for negligence asserting that the defendants, including the facility, the team, and the facility maintenance company, were negligent for failing to maintain the premises in a reasonably safe condition. The defendants argued that they did not know of the spilled liquid on which the Stadt allegedly slipped and therefore could not be held liable for his injuries.

Stadt did not argue that the defendants actually knew about the liquid, so the issue before the court was whether the facility had constructive notice of liquid on the floor. "Constructive notice can be established under two alternative theories: (1) the dangerous condition existed for a sufficient amount of time so that it would have been discovered by the exercise of ordinary care, or (2) the dangerous condition was part of a pattern of conduct or a recurring incident" (*Culli v. Marathon Petroleum Co.*, 1988, p. 123). Because Stadt could not show when the spill occurred, he had to rely upon the **recurring incident theory**. Applying this theory, the court found that the spilling of liquids may be characterized as recurring incidents since patrons oftentimes spill drinks in the stadium, including the standing room only section where plaintiff fell. The court held that a dangerous condition that frequently occurs may establish constructive notice because the recurrence of the condition provides opportunities to take measures and rectify or prevent the condition.

"Open and Obvious" Dangers

A premises owner's duty to protect the invitee from an unreasonable risk of harm caused by a dangerous condition on the land generally does not encompass a duty to protect an invitee from **"open and obvious" dangers** (Marks, 2005). For example, a pothole in a stadium parking lot, snow and ice accumulating on an outdoor surface, or a puddle of water on a rainy day would all be considered "open and obvious" dangers because the conditions themselves serve as adequate notice of the danger.

In *McGue v. Kingdom Sports Center* (2015), 17 year old Dalton McGue was injured while playing basketball at an indoor multi-sport facility. McGue accelerated toward the basketball goal, made a lay-up, and landed on the goal's support structure. While it was not disputed that McGue was a business invitee of the sports center, defendants claimed that the support structure was an "open and obvious" risk well known to him. The court found the plaintiff was well aware of the goals through a shoot around session, watching another team's game and then in the game where the injury occurred. The court found that the hazard was observable by the reasonable person and plaintiff has failed to set forth specific facts showing that the basketball hoop was not an open-and-obvious hazard. Therefore, the goal presented an open and obvious danger, thus barring his claim for negligence.

However, if there are "special aspects" of a condition that make even an "open and obvious" danger "unreasonably dangerous," the landowner still is obligated to undertake reasonable precautions to protect invitees from the danger. In *Mann v. Shusteric Enterprises* (2004), a case involving an intoxicated bar patron who slipped and fell on ice and snow that had accumulated in the bar's parking lot during a blizzard, the court stated that "special aspects" are defined by whether an otherwise "open and obvious" danger is "effectively unavoidable" or "impose[s] an unreasonably high risk of severe harm" to the invitee (*Mann*, 2004, p. 579). Moreover, the court noted that the fact-finder must consider the condition of the premises, not the condition of the plaintiff. A typical open and obvious danger, such as a pothole, would not give rise to these "special aspects" because the condition does not involve an especially high likelihood of injury, a reasonable person would typically be able to see the pothole and avoid it, and there is little risk of severe harm.

While premise owners have a duty to protect invitees from *unreasonable* risks of harm, *they are not absolute insurers of the safety of their invitees. Therefore, where a danger is "open and obvious," the premise owner cannot be held liable for a failure to warn the invitee of the danger.* However, practically speaking, this should not discourage premise owners from warning participants and patrons of any dangerous conditions, including dangers that might not presently exist but frequently occur (Carroll & Baker, 2006, p. 9).

There is one well-known exception to the duty to warn about "open and obvious" dangers. The **distraction exception** applies where the person would be distracted from noticing the "open and obvious" danger and, because of the distraction, fail to take reasonable precautions to avoid the risk of danger. In *Menough v. Woodfield Gardens* (1998), a young man was injured while playing a pick-up game of basketball at the apartment complex owned by the defendant. The basketball court at the complex consisted of a single pole anchored inside a concrete-filled tire. During the course of play, the plaintiff made a "lay-up shot" at the net. When his foot came down, it landed on the tire, snapping plaintiff's ankle. The plaintiff testified that he had not played on the basketball court at the Woodfield Gardens apartment complex prior to the date he was injured. He stated that he first became aware of the tire under the basketball net when he fell on it.

The apartment complex argued that the risk of harm posed by a tire which anchored the pole holding a backboard and net was open and obvious and therefore it owed no duty to remedy that condition. The court found the distraction theory to be applicable in this case because it was reasonably foreseeable that he would have been distracted and fail to see the tire. Therefore, the apartment complex owed a duty of reasonable care to warn the ball player about the presence of the tire.

Limited Duty Rule

An exception to general negligence principles which applies to sport and recreation facilities, notably baseball stadiums and hockey arenas, is the **limited duty rule**. A sports facility operator's limited duty of care has two components: first, the operator must provide protected seating sufficient for those spectators who may be reasonably anticipated to desire protected seats on an ordinary occasion, and second, the operator must provide protection for spectators in the most dangerous section of the stands (*Akins v. Glens Falls City Sch. Dist., 1981*). The second component of this limited duty ordinarily may be satisfied by the operator providing screened seats behind home plate in baseball and behind the goals in hockey (*Akins v. Glens Falls City Sch. Dist.*, 1981).

Edward C. v. City of Albuquerque (2010) illustrates the application of the limited duty rule. In the case, a child was injured by a baseball during pre-game batting practice at Isotopes stadium in Albuquerque, New Mexico. The child was seated in the picnic area beyond the left field wall when, without warning, pre-game batting practice began and a batted baseball went over the wall, struck him, and fractured his skull. On appeal, the New Mexico Supreme Court had to consider what duty owner/occupants of commercial baseball stadiums have to protect spectators from projectiles leaving the field of play. The court also had to decide whether New Mexico should recognize a limited duty for owner/occupants of commercial baseball stadiums. The court held that an owner and/or occupant of a commercial baseball stadium owed a duty that was symmetrical to the duty of the spectator. Spectators had to exercise ordinary care to protect them from the inherent risk of being hit by a projectile that leaves the field of play and the owner/occupant was required to exercise ordinary care not to increase that inherent risk. Factually significant, the court acknowledged that it was alleged that the injured child was not in an area dedicated solely to viewing the game, but was in the picnic area with tables positioned perpendicular to the field of play, described as a multi-purpose area. Given the scope of the duty outlined by the court, summary judgment for defendants based on the limited duty rule was not appropriate and the case was remanded for further proceedings.

Projectiles leaving the playing field has now even been extended to take into consideration flying hot dogs! *Coomer v. Kansas City Royals* (2014) involved a mascot wildly throwing hot dogs wrapped in tin foil during a hot dog "launch." The Missouri Supreme Court had to decide if such activity was a risk that Coomer assumed, given his past experiences at the ballpark; and whether a flying hot dog was analogous to a fly ball or flying bat, with the latter being requirements to play the game of baseball. Ultimately, the Missouri Supreme Court stated that, "In the past, this Court has held that spectators cannot sue a baseball team for injuries caused when a ball or bat enters the stands. Such risks are an unavoidable – even desirable – part of the joy that comes with being close enough to the Great American Pastime . . . . The risk of being injured by Sluggerrr's hotdog toss, on the other hand, is not an unavoidable part of watching the Royals play baseball." The case was remanded back to the lower court for further proceedings. A Missouri jury later found neither party at fault (Draper, 2015).

Legal Obligations of Sport and Recreation Facility Managers

The sport or recreation manager's duty to use reasonable care to keep the premises under his/her control in a safe condition can be further delineated in terms of five obligations (Seidler, 2005).

Keep the Premises in Safe Repair
Routine maintenance by the facility management and staff is necessary to keep patrons safe while they are engaged in sport or recreation, either as a participant or spectator. For example, a fitness center would have an obligation to re-surface a swimming pool deck where the slip-resistant surface had worn off and an obligation to maintain exercise equipment used by patrons. In *Zipusch v. LA Workout* (2007), a health club member alleged that the club negligently maintained its exercise equipment. This resulted in a sticky substance remaining on a treadmill, causing Zipusch to lose her balance when her foot became stuck to it. In considering whether the health club kept the exercise equipment in working order, the court stated that, "unlike those who run outside on cracked sidewalks speckled with gum, [the plaintiff] and other health club members pay dues in exchange for access to a safe and well-maintained exercise environment" (p. 1292).

Inspect the Premises to Discover Obvious and Hidden Hazards
Periodic inspections are a necessary and expected obligation of facility managers. Through the use of inspection checklists, the facility is able to document that they have taken reasonable steps to discover hazards on the premises and remedy them. In addition to the claims for negligent maintenance, the court in *Zipusch v. LA Workout* (2007), discussed above, also considered whether LA Workout negligently failed to inspect the equipment. The court held that the health club had an obligation to inspect and maintain the equipment. Based on Zipusch's own observations, no staff member inspected or cleaned the equipment in the 85 minute time period prior to the accident. Because of the fact that numerous individuals are engaging in vigorous physical activity at the health club, a reasonable argument could be made that inspection of the premises was especially important, and that the time period between inspections was unreasonably long (*Zipusch*, 2007). Evidence that the facility manager failed to periodically inspect the premises before an accident is normally sufficient to infer that the risk existed long enough for the property owner, in the exercise of due care, to have discovered and removed it (*Ortega v. Kmart Corp.*, 2001).

Remove the Hazards or Warn Others of Their Presence
Once a dangerous condition is discovered on the premises, the facility manager has the obligation to either remove it or warn patrons of its presence. For example, consider college basketball patrons bringing wet umbrellas into an arena and causing the floor to be slippery. This would be a typical situation where the facility manager has an obligation to try to keep the floor dry. In addition, the facility manager would have an

obligation to use "Wet Floor" signs near the entrance to warn patrons about the dangerous condition in the entry way. Other commonly occurring hazards in sport or recreation facilities include uneven surfaces or deteriorated materials or equipment.

For a hazard that cannot be removed, such as the threat of lightning on a golf course, the premise owner still has the obligation to warn participants about the danger that is present. While the golf course in the *Sall* case obviously could not remove the threat of lightning or other weather-related risks, the golf course's warning procedure was to blow an air horn as a signal to return to the clubhouse in the event of dangerous weather. The golf course's policies or procedures for inclement weather also called for the manager on duty to monitor the local television stations, radar images on the Internet, and visually inspect the weather by stepping outside and to monitor conditions using a weather radio.

Anticipate Foreseeable Uses and Take Reasonable Precautions to Protect

This obligation of the facility owner/operator to **anticipate foreseeable uses** and activities by invitees and take reasonable precautions to protect the invitees from foreseeable dangers takes into consideration the normal uses of the facility and frequently occurring incidents or activities by patrons (e.g., tailgating prior to a football game). In *Hayden v. University of Notre Dame* (1999), a season ticket holder at a Notre Dame football game was injured when, after the football was kicked into the stands, several people from the crowd lunged for the ball in an effort to retrieve it. Hayden claimed that Notre Dame was negligent in failing to protect her. Notre Dame argued that it owed no duty to protect her from a third party's criminal act (arguably a battery). Notre Dame contended that the third party's action was unforeseeable, and that it therefore owed no duty to anticipate it and protect her. Given evidence that there were many prior incidents of people being jostled or injured by efforts of fans to retrieve the ball, the court found that the totality of the circumstances established that Notre Dame should have foreseen that injury would likely result from the actions of a third party. As a result, it owed a duty to Hayden to protect her from such injury.

In the context of premises liability, the **"totality of the circumstances" test** "requires landowners to take reasonable precautions to prevent foreseeable criminal actions against invitees" (*Delta Tau Delta v. Johnson*, 1999, p. 973). "Under the totality of the circumstances test, a court considers all of the circumstances surrounding an event, including the nature, condition, and location of the land, as well as prior similar incidents, to determine whether a criminal act was foreseeable" (p. 972). "A substantial factor in the determination is the number, nature, and location of prior similar incidents, but the lack of prior similar incidents will not preclude a claim where the landowner knew or should have known that the criminal act was foreseeable" (p. 973). The totality of the circumstances test is the most widely adopted approach for determining the duty of a business owner. This test is broader than others and places a lesser evidentiary burden on plaintiffs seeking to prove foreseeability of harm in negligence claims against land or business owners (*Delta Tau Delta v. Johnson*, 1999).

In *Pfenning v. Lineman* (2010), a sixteen year old volunteer was driving a beverage cart during a golf tournament when she was struck in the mouth by an errant ball. The beverage cart did not contain a canopy or a windshield to provide her with some measure of protection from being struck by a flying golf ball. Pfenning contends that the sponsor of the tournament (Whitey's, a local bar) and the Elks, as the owner/operator of the golf course, breached a duty of reasonable care owed to her under the theory of premises liability. Applying the "totality of the circumstances" test to determine if the defendants breached a duty of care owed to her, the court ruled that "Pfenning does not assert that a third party's criminal act caused her injury; that the act was foreseeable; or that there had been similar prior incidents" (p. 56). Thus, the Elks and Whitey's did not have a duty to protect her from the danger of an errant golf ball while operating a beverage cart.

Conduct Operations on the Premises with Reasonable Care for the Safety of All

No matter if the sport or recreation business consists of providing amusement at a water park or providing recreational opportunities on intramural fields, the facility manager must conduct operations on the premises in such a way that provides that anyone who comes onto the land will be safe. The golf lightning cases illustrate the point that when a golf course has taken steps to protect golfers from lightning strikes, it owes them a duty of reasonable care to implement its safety precautions properly (*Maussner v. Atlantic City Country Club, Inc.*, 1997). If a golf course builds shelters on the course for golfers who get stranded on the course during inclement weather, it must build lightning-proof shelters (*Maussner*, 1997). Similarly, if a golf course has an evacuation plan, the evacuation plan must be reasonable and must be posted (*Maussner*, 1997). Depending on the industry, there may be an industry standard or customary practice for how best to protect patrons from specific dangers common to that industry, such as lightning strikes on golf courses or how to protect skiers from colliding into snow making equipment on ski slopes.

SIGNIFICANT CASE

The case below illustrates several of the concepts in the chapter, including actual and constructive notice and alleged failures to cure defective conditions. All are commonly raised issues in sport and recreation premise liability actions.

RIDDER V. TENNIS ENTERPRISES, LTD ET AL.
Superior Court of Connecticut, Judicial District of Hartford at Hartford
2014 Conn. Super. LEXIS 3093 December 15, 2014, Decided December 15, 2014, Filed

Opinion

The plaintiff, a minor, brought this action through his father to recover damages for an injury he allegedly sustained while participating in a lacrosse event being held at the indoor tennis courts of the Farmington Farms Tennis & Athletic Club. In the first and second counts, which are at issue in the pending motion for summary judgment, the plaintiff asserts premises liability claims against Tennis Enterprises, Ltd., and Farmington Farms Tennis & Athletic Club, Inc. (collectively, "Farmington Farms"), as the alleged owner and operator of the facility, respectively. Farmington Farms has moved for summary judgment on the ground that the plaintiff has no evidence that these defendants had any actual or constructive notice of the alleged defect—a hook that was part of a tennis net post and was bent outward into the area in which the lacrosse play took place—on which the plaintiff allegedly injured his leg. The plaintiff objected to the motion for summary judgment.

The standard for summary judgment is well established. "Practice Book §17-49 provides that summary judgment 'shall be rendered forthwith if the pleadings, affidavits and any other proof submitted show that there is no genuine issue as to any material fact and that the moving party is entitled to judgment as a matter of law.'" *LaFlamme v. Dallessio*, 261 Conn. 247, 250, 802 A.2d 63 (2002). "In deciding a motion for summary judgment, the trial court must view the evidence in the light most favorable to the nonmoving party . . . The test is whether a party would be entitled to a directed verdict on the same facts." (Citation omitted; internal quotation marks omitted.) *Sherwood v. Danbury Hospital*, 252 Conn. 193, 201, 746 A.2d 730 (2000). Furthermore, on summary judgment all inferences from the facts must be construed in the light most favorable to the party opposing the motion. *Buell Industries, Inc. v. Greater New York Mutual Ins. Co.*, 259 Conn. 527, 558, 791 A.2d 489 (2002).

* * *

Under applicable principles of law, the plaintiff is required to prove that the defendants had actual or constructive knowledge of the defective condition that allegedly caused the injury for a sufficient period of time to remedy it. See *Meek v. Wal-Mart Stores, Inc.*, 72 Conn. App. 467, 474, 806 A.2d 546, cert. denied, 262 Conn. 912, 810 A.2d 278 (2002); *Cruz v. Drezek*, 175 Conn. 230, 235-39, 397 A.2d 1335 (1978). A plaintiff may present circumstantial evidence as to the question of notice. *Cruz v. Drezek, supra*, 175 Conn. 238-39.

In support of the motion for summary judgment, Farmington Farms relies on affidavits by Frederick Timme and Joel Taylor, who are, respectively, president and secretary of the Farmington Farms Tennis & Athletic Club, Inc., and co-owners of Tennis Enterprises, Ltd. Both Timme and Taylor aver that prior to the date of the plaintiff's alleged injury, they "had no personal knowledge of a bent hook condition on one of the net posts alleged to have caused the plaintiff, Daniel Rider, to become injured." They further aver that they are not aware of any "board member, agent, servant and/or employee of Farmington Farms Tennis & Athletic Club, Inc., or Tennis Enterprises, Ltd." who had personal knowledge of such a bent hook condition prior to the date of the plaintiff's alleged injury, and that neither "Farmington Farms Tennis & Athletic Club, Inc., or Tennis Enterprises, Ltd. received any written or verbal notice of a bent hook condition" prior to the date of the plaintiff's alleged injury. The defendants further rely on the plaintiff's responses to requests for admission, in which the plaintiff admits that, at the time of his responses, he was not aware of any evidence showing that either defendant had actual knowledge of the specific bent hook at issue. The plaintiff qualified his response to each request, however, with the following statement: "Admitted at this time, however, discovery is not complete and therefore this answer is subject to change." The plaintiff also admitted that he was not aware of any evidence establishing how long the hook at issue had been bent and elongated prior to the plaintiff's accident. His response, however, was similarly qualified by his reservation that discovery was not complete and the answer was subject to change.

Even without considering the plaintiff's submissions in opposition to summary judgment, the defendants' submissions do not establish that they are entitled to summary judgment because they do not address at all the issue of constructive knowledge. At most, the defendants' submissions establish that neither owner had personal knowledge of the alleged defect, that they were not aware of any employee or agent of the defendants who had personal knowledge of the defect, and that the corporate defendants had not received written notice of the defect. The plaintiff's admissions that he did not know how long the defect had existed were qualified by his statement that discovery was not yet complete.

In opposition to the motion for summary judgment, the plaintiff argues that both affidavits leave open the possibility that the bent and elongated hook remained in place for an extended period of time and was simply not discovered by the defendants. The plaintiff submitted deposition excerpts in which Joel Taylor testified that Farmington Farms had between 50 and 80 employees at various times of the year; that it was not anyone's job in particular to inspect the net post hooks; that he had no idea when the defendants had last inspected the hook that lacerated the plaintiff's thigh; and that if an employee had noticed that the hook was bent before the accident, it would not have been regarded as defective because it was holding the tennis net in place. Taylor also admitted that "prior to and at the time of the incident . . . in 2010 Farmington Farms had-allowed the tennis net and hook to remain in the condition" that was allegedly defective. Finally, he also admitted that Farmington Farms did not ordinarily rent out the space for sports other than tennis, and that the rental to the lacrosse organization at issue was the first time the facility had been rented for that purpose.

As the plaintiff argues, the evidence presented by the defendants does not exclude the possibility that a reasonable jury could find that the defective condition had existed for a sufficient period of time that the defendants should have discovered it in the exercise of reasonable care. This is particularly true in light of the fact that the facility was being used for a purpose for which it was not designed—that is, lacrosse rather than tennis—apparently without a specific inspection to determine whether it was safe for such use. Moreover, even if the evidence submitted by the defendants had been sufficient to shift the burden of responding to the plaintiff, the plaintiff's evidence, as summarized above, is sufficient to create a triable issue of fact as to whether the defendants, in the exercise of reasonable care, should have known of the defective condition of the hook prior to the plaintiff's accident and with sufficient time to remedy it. Accordingly, the motion for summary judgment is denied.

CASES ON THE SUPPLEMENTAL WEBSITE

Bearman v. Notre Dame, 453 N.E.2d 1196 (Ind. Ct. App. 1983). Pay particular attention to the discussion of duty owed and the foreseeability of harm given prior similar tailgating incidents.

Coomer v. Kansas City Royals Baseball Corporation, Case 437 S.W.3d 184 (Mo. 2014) (en banc). How does the court's decision impact the future of the limited duty rule, particularly when the injuries involve mascots?

Maheshwari v. City of New York, 810 N.E.2d 894 (N.Y. App. 2004). Focus on what factors the court analyzed in determining whether the landowner had a duty to protect the plaintiff from the criminal acts of third parties.

Young v. New Southgate Lanes, et al., 2007 Ohio App. LEXIS 2700 (Ohio Ct. Appeals 2007). What evidence was the plaintiff able to use to try to establish that a negligent act or omission on the part of the business caused her to slip and fall?

QUESTIONS YOU SHOULD BE ABLE TO ANSWER

1. From a policy perspective, why are business invitees owed the highest duty of care?

2. How and why does the court's willingness to expand the application of recreational user statutes provide additional protection from liability for sport and recreation businesses?

3. If a danger is "open and obvious," how does this fact alter the premise owner's duty to warn?

4. In applying the "totality of the circumstances" test to determine the foreseeability of criminal acts by third parties in a case for negligent security at a sport or recreation facility, what factors might be dispositive?

5. How does the limited duty rule differ from the business invitee rule in terms of the sport facility's duty to protect patrons from the risk of flying objects?

REFERENCES

Cases

Akins v. Glens Falls City Sch. Dist, 424 N.E.2d 531 (Ct. App. N.Y. 1981).
City of Mangum v. Powell, 165 P.2d 136 (Okla. 1946).
Coomer v. Kansas City Royals, 437 S.W.3d 184; 2014 Mo. LEXIS 154.
Conant v. Stroup, 51 P.3d 1263 (Ct. App. OR 2002).
Creely v. Corpus Christ Football Team, Inc. d/b/a Corpus Christi Hammerheads, 2007 Tex. App. LEXIS 6769 (Ct. App. T.X., Thirteenth Dist. 2007).
Culli v. Marathon Petroleum Co., 862 F.2d 119 (7th Cir. 1988).
Delta Tau Delta v. Johnson, 712 N.E.2d 968 (Ind. 1999)
Edward C. v. City of Albuquerque, 241 P.3d 1086 (N.M. 2010).
Hammond v. Allegretti, 311 N.E.2d 821 (Ind. 1974).
Hayden v. University of Notre Dame, 716 N.E.2d 603 (Ind. Ct. App. 1999).
Johnson v. Gibson and Stillson, 918 F. Supp. 2d 1075 (D. Or. 2013).
Mann v. Shusteric Enters., 683 N.W.2d 573 (Mich. 2004).
Maussner v. Atlantic City Country Club, Inc., 691 A.2d 826 (N.J. App.Div. 1997).
McGue v. Kingdom Sports Center, 2015 U.S. Dist. LEXIS 40668 (S. Dist. Oh. 2015).
McPherson v. Tennessee Football Incorporated, 2007 U.S. Dist. LEXIS 39595 (M.D. Tenn. 2007).
Miller v. Dunham's Discount Sports, 2010 Mich. App. LEXIS 2424 (Mich. Ct. App. 2010).
Menough v. Woodfield Gardens, 694 N.E.2d 1038 (Ill. Ct. App. 1998).
Ortega v. Kmart Corp., 36 P.3d 11 (Cal. 2001).
Ouellette v. Blanchard, 364 A.2d 631 (N.H. 1976).
Pfenning v. Lineman, et al, 922 N.E.2d 45 (Ind. Ct. App. 2010).
Saffro v. Elite Racing, Inc. 98 Cal.App.4th 173 (Cal. App. 4th Dist. 2002).
Sall vs. Smiley's Golf Complex, (136 P.3d 471 (Kan. 2006).
Schneider v. American Hockey and Ice Skating Center, 777 A.2d 380 (N.J. App.Div. 2001)).
Stadt v. United Center Joint Venture, 2005 U.S. Dist. LEXIS 9580 (N.D. Ill. 2005)
Zipusch v. LA Workout, Inc., 155 Cal.App.4th 1281 (Cal. Ct. App. 2007).

Publications

62 Am. Jur. 2d Premises Liability § 68 (2012).
Carroll, M.S. & Baker, T.A. (2006). The use of constructive notice in slip and fall cases in sport facilities. *JOPERD, 77*(8), 8–9.
Carroll, M.S., Connaughton, D.P, & Spengler, J.O. (2007). Recreational user statutes and landowner immunity: a comparison study of state legislation, *Journal of Legal Aspects of Sport, 17*(2), 163–182.
Clark, P.F. (1998). Into the wild: A review of the recreational use statute. *New York State Bar Journal, 70*(5), 22–26.
Connolly, M.J., Black, H.C., Nolan-Haley, J.M., & Nolan, J.R. (2014). *Black's law dictionary*, 10th ed. St. Paul, Minn: West Publ.
Daller, M.F. (2010) Tort Law Desk Reference. New York: Aspen Publishers.
Draper, B. (2015, June 17). Jury: Neither Royals, man hurt by flying hot dog at fault. *Yahoo! Sports*. Retrieved from http://sports.yahoo.com/news/royals-mascot-face-civil-case-hot-dog-injury-151956869—mlb.html.
Fitzpatrick, B. (2015). Broken bats and broken bones: Holding stadium owners accountable for alcohol-fueled fan-on-fan violence, *Jeffrey S. Moorad Sports Law Journal*, 22, 663-689.
Lewis, J. (1991). Recreational use Statutes: Ambiguous laws yield conflicting results, 27 *Trial, 27*, 68.
Maloy & Higgins. (2000). *No Excuses Risk Management*. Carmel, IN: Cooper Publishing Group.
Marks, J.H. (2005). The limit to premises liability for harms caused by "known or obvious" dangers: Will it trip and fall over the duty-breach framework emerging in the Restatement (Third) of Torts? *Texas Tech Law Review, 38*, 1–71.
Prosser, W.L. (1942). Business visitors and invitees, *Minnesota Law Review, 26*, 573.
Restatement (Second) of Torts (1969).
Sall v. T's, 136 P.3d 471 (Kan., 2006).
Seidler, T. (2005). Conducting a facility risk review. In H. Appenzeller, *Risk management in sport: Issues and Strategies* (2nd ed.), 317–328. Durham, NC: Carolina Academic Press.
Spengler, J.O., Carroll, M.S., Connaughton, D.P., & Evenson, K.R. (2010). Policies to promote the community use of schools. *American Journal of Preventive Medicine, 39*, 81–88.
Statelawyers.com. (n.d.). Premise liability. Retrieved February1, 2016 from http://www.statelawyers.com/Practice/Practice_Detail.cfm/PracticeTypeID:77

Legislation

Ark. Code Ann.§18-11-302 (2012).
Or. Rev. Stat. § 105.682 (2009).

PROPERTY LAW

Sarah J. Young | Indiana University

It is important that recreation and sport managers possess a basic understanding of property law because they are responsible for land areas containing sport facilities, parks, walking/biking trails, and natural attractions, such as lakes, rivers, climbing areas and ski slopes. This chapter will examine property law as it pertains to recreation and sport management with specific focus on real property, recreational use statutes, and nuisance actions.

FUNDAMENTAL CONCEPTS

Real Property

Real property is land and generally any structure that is affixed to, erected on, or growing on the land. Sport facilities are constructed and maintained on real property. It is essential that the recreation or sport manager possess a sound understanding of the legal aspects of acquisition and control of property.

Rights of Real Property

To gain a basic understanding of property law as it relates to recreation and sport, it is important to first identify the rights an organization has under different modes of acquisition. There are basically two types of rights in real property: fee simple absolute and less than fee simple. **Fee simple absolute** is the term used to describe a landowner who has complete control of the property. Swanson, Arnold and Rasmussen (2005) described fee simple absolute as a control that includes "the right to exclude others, to sell or contract away one or more rights, and to make any use of the property not restricted by law" (p. 207). A fee simple title means that the legal holder of the title has the authority to do whatever he desires to the property within the limits of the law.

Less than fee simple describes the use of property that is generally based on a contract. Examples of less than fee simple titles include easements, leases, use permits, and joint use or cooperative agreements (Swanson et al., 2005). The existence of less than fee simple titles is common in recreation, sport, and leisure services. For example, a community sports program conducted by a private association on a school-owned sports complex illustrates a joint use agreement. Additionally, pedestrian access strips across private oceanfront property enabling public access to the beach are easements and examples of less than fee simple rights in real property. It is essential that rights to the easement are clearly articulated in property deeds as illustrated by *Konneker v. Romano* (2010). In a dispute over whether plaintiffs' easement granted riparian rights (i.e., access to waterway or body of water), the court ruled the language of the deed containing the easement was ambiguous.

Modes of Acquisition

A number of modes of property acquisition are available to the recreation or sport manager. The most common one is **purchase** of a parcel of land or a facility. Acquisition of property through purchasing falls under the fee simple absolute category of rights. Typically, when one purchases a piece of property, total control of that land would be assumed. The purchase of property is usually based on a fair market value on which both the buyer and seller agree. However, there are a number of variations that both the buyer and seller may use to make the deal better from each of their perspectives. Buyers may choose to enter into an option to buy with the seller, thereby purchasing the right to buy the property with no other competition until a mutually agreed on date. Sellers may add restrictive covenants into the purchase that dictate how the property may be used. For example, a private off-road club may desire to purchase an open parcel of land from a municipality to be used for dirt bike and ATV trails. However, before purchasing, the buyer notices a noise restriction contained in the purchase agreement. This type of restrictive covenant would be detrimental to the purpose for which the land was to be used by the off-road club. As a result, buyers must be particularly aware of any restrictions in the title.

Gifts are another type of acquisition under the fee simple rights of real property that many recreation, sport, and leisure services agencies can use to their advantage. Property gifts can be made outright by the donor, as part of an annuity plan, or as the result of an individual's will. Although a gift of property is usually considered an asset to an organization, the manager should be aware of possible restrictions or requirements of the gift agreement. This is especially true if the title is not given in fee simple. For example, if a parcel of land is given to an entity, yet the gift is contingent on the performance of some function or service by the recipient, then the entity may want to carefully consider whether the gift is feasible to accept.

Dedication of land is yet another mode of acquisition in real property. This type of acquisition typically corresponds with the fee simple absolute rights. Mandatory or statutory, dedication of land requires land developers to set aside a portion of their development for public use purposes. Because development generally decreases open space, it increases the demand on remaining open spaces or existing park and recreation facilities. This provides the rationale for this type of acquisition (Swanson et al., 2005). Dedication of property can also be a voluntary act whereby a landowner dedicates land for public use. Typically two elements are necessary for a complete dedication: (1) the intention of the owner to dedicate, and (2) acceptance by the public. An example of a voluntary act of dedication is found in a Washington case where in 1899 a private landowner allowed the city to build a road across his property to the beach. The landowner dedicated the right-of-way to the City of Bainbridge Island. In the more than 100 years since this transaction, the property had been subdivided and developed into lots, with several lot owners challenging the public's use of the right-of-way to gain access to the beach area. In an attempt to prevent public access, several lot owners erected a fence and a locked gate barring passage on the road. The court ruled that although the exact property boundary was not known, the intent of the original landowner had been to dedicate the road on his property to the city, the public had accepted the dedication, and the current lot owners were on notice as to the public nature of the area when they purchased their properties (*City of Bainbridge Island v. Brennan*, 2005).

When the owner of property is unwilling to sell his or her land, another mode of acquisition that can be implemented is known as **eminent domain** or **condemnation**. Under the U.S. Constitution, the taking of private property for public use cannot occur without just and fair compensation to the owner. Eminent domain is the power of the government to take private property, whereas condemnation is the vehicle through which this power is generally exercised. Condemnation of private property is appropriate only when the use of the property will be public, the public interests require it, and the property being condemned is necessary to accomplish a public purpose. In recent years a number of states have supported the use of eminent domain and condemnation for the construction of professional sport venues (Hubbard, 2008). This phenomenon is illustrated in *Goldstein v. Pataki* (2008) where a group of Brooklyn, New York, property owners challenged an eminent domain taking for the purpose of building the Barclays Center at Atlantic Yards, a multi-use urban arena for the Brooklyn Nets NBA basketball team and the New York Islanders NHL hockey team. In the taking of another's property it is critical that the government agency adhere to the aforementioned criteria and the specific language of state statutes or local ordinances as is illustrated in *In Re: Condemnation Proceedings of Montgomery Township* (2012). In this case, the township wanted to take 50 acres of condemnee's property for public open space. Yet the township code only authorized the government to take property to create specific recreational facilities like playgrounds, swimming pools, playfields, etc. As a result, the court ruled that the township had to submit a specific plan for the taking illustrating how the property would be used for recreational purposes.

Related to the taking of property is **adverse possession**—the transfer of property ownership over time in an actual, hostile, open, continuous, and exclusive manner. Dating back to ancient English common law, adverse possession has been used to clarify title to land as well as to discourage property owners from "sleeping on their rights" by neglecting to take the appropriate legal steps to maintain their property. One who claims title by adverse possession cannot simply stretch "one's boundaries to include property beyond one's deed" (*Moore v. Stills*, 2010, p. 72), but must provide clear evidence of actual, continuous, exclusive, visible, and distinct possession usually over a specified period of time. For example in the State of Connecticut, the time period for possession is 15 years (*Aramony. v. District of Chapman Beach*, 2013). An example of adverse possession is found in *Hillsmere Shores Improvement Association v. Singleton* (2008), where several residents of a subdivision sought declaration for gaining title by adverse possession of a community beach situated between their lots and a river. For over 20 years, the residents maintained the property, built bulkheads along the waterfront, and were even assessed taxes on the property. The court ruled the residents had fully demonstrated to have acquired title to the property through adverse possession.

Modes of acquisition falling under the less than fee simple rights of real property include easements, leases, and cooperative agreements. These modes of acquisition most often correspond with less than fee simple rights and refer to acquiring the use of property rather than ownership. An **easement** is defined as extending to certain individuals the right to use the land of another for a specific purpose. Affirmative and negative easements are most commonly recognized. An **affirmative easement** allows the right of use over the property of another such as allowing access to an adjacent property owner for her commercial guests to use a zip line erected on her property (*Wykidal v. Bain*, 2015). A **negative easement**, on the other hand, restricts use in a particular manner. For example, a scenic easement may restrict the construction of facilities to protect a beautiful vista (Swanson et al., 2005). **Leases** are used extensively in sport and recreation situations and are considered a common method of acquiring the use of land or buildings for a specified length of time. Finally, **cooperative agreements** are frequently used to allow two organizations to share the same facilities.

Land Use Controls

In addition to the acquisition of property, the recreation or sport manager must have a basic knowledge of the legal aspects of controlling the use of land under their supervision. A common law device of controlling land use is the public trust doctrine. **The public trust doctrine** provides that submerged and submersible lands are preserved for public use in navigation, fishing, and recreation. "Historically, the doctrine was applied primarily to water and submerged lands under navigable waters" (van der Smissen, 1990, p. 75); however, the doctrine has evolved to apply to dry lands as well. The main purpose of the public trust doctrine is the idea that certain natural resources belong to the public and should be preserved for the good of society. Management and control over the property held in trust cannot be relinquished by transfer of property (Garcia & Baltodano, 2005). Further, it is the responsibility of public agencies to control the use of these natural resources and areas so they can be enjoyed by current and future generations. A New Jersey case concerning whether the public has a right to use the area of the beach above the mean high water mark of ocean front property illustrates the application of the public trust doctrine. Defendant landowners attempted to prevent plaintiff from sitting on their private beach. Yet, the court ruled the property line of an owner of oceanfront property only extends to the high water mark with all property below that line considered as public. The public had a right to use oceanfront property held in trust for recreational activities such as sunbathing and swimming (*Bubis v. Kassin*, 2008).

Another type of land use control commonly implemented in recreation is **zoning**, defined as dividing "a municipality into geographical districts or zones and then regulating the nature and use of land in the various zones" (van der Smissen, 1990, p. 78). The regulation extends not only to the development of the land, but also to the structures on the land and the activities conducted thereon. Further, van der Smissen explained "zoning is primarily a legislative function of the municipality and represents judgment of the elected governing body as to how land should be utilized within its jurisdiction" (p. 79). In California, a private nonprofit water ski club purchased an island designated as open space and zoned as agricultural. The county's zoning ordinances allowed no more than one single-family residence per five-acre parcel of land. Over 35 years, however, the water ski club built 28 residential units and docks on the five-acre island. Because the water ski club had knowingly violated the county's zoning ordinance and land use requirement, the court ruled in favor of the county demolishing all but one structure on the island (*Golden Gate Water Ski Club v. County of Contra Costa*, 2008).

The **control of activities** and the use of property are central to the issue of zoning. Zoning regulations generally correspond with a governmental agency's comprehensive plan to avoid claims of arbitrary or unreasonable zoning ordinances. This also ensures the proper use and development of property for current and future public needs. In New Hampshire, a private landowner who owned and operated a Christmas tree farm in an area zoned as agricultural, brought suit after the town planner informed him that operating a wedding reception facility on his farm was not permitted under zoning ordinances. The ordinance listed accessory uses were permitted but limited to home/business retail and bed and breakfast homes. **Accessory uses** are defined as a secondary use of real property that occurs occasionally and is related to the primary purpose of the property. While plaintiff argued that conducting commercial weddings and similar events on his farm qualified under the accessory uses exemption of the ordinance, the Supreme Court of New Hampshire disagreed, ruling that such events were not permitted in the farm's zoning district (*Forster v. Town of Henniker*, 2015).

Recreational User Statutes

Recreational user statutes are legislative acts that are established in all states for the purpose of protecting landowners from liability if they permit the public to use their property for recreation at no cost to the user (see Chapter 2.22, *Immunity*). In 1965, the Council of State Governments addressed a growing need in the United States for more recreational land by recommending that states pass an act known as the Model Act encouraging private landowners to open their property to the public for recreational enjoyment and use. Legislation of this type was eventually adopted by all 50 states but with a great deal of variation by state. As a result, one should be familiar with the aspects of the statute for a specific state. Yet, the overall essence of the statute is that landowners owe no duty to recreational users of their property (*Matheny v. United States*, 2006) creating a defense against ordinary negligence claims, but not claims for willful and wanton conduct (*Webb v. City of Richland*, 2011). A listing by state, a link to each entire statute, and summary of each state recreational user statute is provided by Holly Rudolph in one convenient location (Rudolph, 2010)[1].

General Characteristics

Although each state has its own variation of the recreational user statute and interpretations through case law, there are several characteristics of the statute common to most states presented below.

The first of these characteristics is that the statute only applies to the **owner of the land**. In some states, the immunity protection provided by the statute is targeted toward private landowners, whereas in other states owners of public lands (i.e., local, state, and federal government agencies) are also afforded immunity. The original intent of the Model Act was to encourage private landowners to open their property to others who were using the land for recreational use. For example, private landowners, David and Heather Blackston, relied on the Ohio recreational use statute as a defense to a negligence claim of their neighbors, the Drury's, after they volunteered to babysit the Drury children. While under the Blackston's supervision, four-year-old James Drury entered defendant's backyard pool without his "'arm floaties' which he needed to be able to swim" (*Drury v. Blackston*, 2015, p. 2) whereupon he ingested pool water. His parents sued defendants for negligence. The Ohio appellate court ruled that the state's recreational activity doctrine barred plaintiff's claim. A number of states have broadened their interpretation from the private landowner to any property owner, lessees, tenants, occupants, or persons controlling the premises. As a result, many public agencies now look to recreational use statutes as an alternative source of immunity. For example in *Yagle v. United States* (2009) plaintiff was operating his ATV at Steele Peak in California on property owned by the federal government through the Bureau of Land Management (BLM). While riding his ATV, plaintiff fell into an abandoned mineshaft and was injured. To reach the mineshaft, plaintiff had traveled off-road, uphill, and off designated trails. There were signs in the area advising riders to stay on trails and to not climb the hills as the terrain was uneven and covered in heavy vegetation. Plaintiff sued for the extent of his injuries he alleged were negligently caused by BLM. Under the California recreational use statute, plaintiff's claim was barred because landowners are not liable for negligence to individuals using their lands for recreational purposes. In another case, a municipality in Rhode Island was protected by the state's recreational use statute after plaintiff was injured on a wooden jungle gym in a city park (*Symonds v. City of Pawtucket*, 2015).

The broad interpretation of qualified property owners by many states has led to the practice of school districts also seeking protection under recreational user statutes. In *Moore v. Fargo Public School District 1* (2010), the North Dakota court specifically addressed the issue of whether a school district could seek protection under the statute. Although the recreational user statute did not apply in the *Moore* case, a number of school districts have successfully defended themselves from liability for negligence using their state's statute (*Kahler v. Town of Middleboro*, 2011; *Hayes v. City of Plummer*, 2015).

---

[1] Thanks to Holly Rudolph, J.D., convenient access to the complete recreational user statutes in every state is available on the Internet. Rudolph, H. Directory of Equine Activity and Recreational Use Statutes for Horsemen and Landowners. https://elcr.org/statestatutes/.

A second characteristic of the recreational user statute is that the landowner **cannot charge a fee** for individuals to use the premises. Although most state statutes have provided that immunity will not apply if a fee is charged, there is some variation among the states as to how "fee" is interpreted. Most courts have maintained immunity for landowners except where an actual fee has been charged for entry onto the land. This type of charge is a narrow interpretation of the law, which requires an explicit quid pro quo arrangement of payment in exchange for admission onto the premises. For example, in *Albertson v. Fremont County* (2011) plaintiff was killed when his snowmobile trail located on national forest lands intersected with a state highway and he was struck by a vehicle. In the negligence suit that followed, plaintiff's family argued that warning signs or traffic control signals should have been placed at the intersection to warn both snowmobile operators and motorists. The National Forest Service argued immunity under the Idaho Recreational Use statute even though plaintiff had been required to pay a $31 fee to register his snowmobile prior to using the trails. While plaintiffs argued this constituted a fee, the court ruled the fee was not charged for entry onto the public land, thereby allowing defendant immunity under the Idaho state statute. Illustrating another perspective of the quid pro quo arrangement, the Oregon Supreme Court ruled the recreational use statute did not apply to a state park where plaintiff was injured while riding his bike. The state park had charged plaintiff a fee to camp at the park, and as campers, plaintiff and his wife were entitled to use all park facilities including the bike trails. The court ruled that when the fee was charged for permission to use the land, even if plaintiff was not engaged in camping, he was engaged in a recreational pursuit, and defendant forfeited its immunity (*Coleman v. Oregon Parks & Recreation Dept.*, 2009).

A third characteristic of the recreational user statute is that land is being used for a **recreational purpose**. The interpretation of this characteristic varies widely from state to state with a number of states applying the statute to developed recreational facilities such as ball fields, playgrounds, and swimming pools. For example, in California, a court ruled that the statute provided defendant immunity after plaintiff fell while exploring unguarded mine shafts in the Dumont Dunes area of the southern part of the state (*Schafer v. United States of America*, 2011). In *Scott v. United States* (2011) plaintiff was attending a private party in the Officer's Club at the Naval Station in Newport, Rhode Island when she slipped and fell on wet stairs. Partying and social events fell within the broad definition of recreational activity resulting in defendant successfully seeking immunity under the state's recreational use statute.

A final general characteristic of the recreational user statute involves **obligations of the landowner**. The owner's only obligation under the statute is to provide a warning for any known concealed danger that would not be apparent to the recreational user. Owners have no duty to warn of open and obvious hazards, nor do they have a duty to warn of conditions that are unknown to them. A Texas case involving a man-made beach and public park area on a coastal peninsula illustrates this characteristic. The plaintiff in this case claimed the city was negligent for failing to post signs warning of the perilous conditions created by the interaction between the beach and the coastal waters which were not obvious to swimmers. Plaintiff's husband and nine-year-old twin daughters drowned off the shore after a strong current caused the girls to be swept into deep water after they had been wading in knee-deep water along the shore. The Texas Supreme Court considered whether the city owner of the area had a duty to warn recreational users about the conditions. After a thorough review of the evidence, the court ruled the city had no actual, subjective awareness of the combined effect of the man-made beach and the natural water conditions, nor did they realize "the gravity of the danger created" (p. 637). Therefore, the court ruled the city had immunity under the state's recreational use statute (*Suarez v. City of Texas City*, 2015). Another case illustrating the obligations of landowners involved a cyclist riding a bike trail through a city park. While crossing a bridge at a moderate speed, plaintiff encountered two protruding wooden planks on the far side of the arched bridge. Attempting to jump his bike over the planks, plaintiff was thrown from his bike. In his negligence claim against the city, the court ruled the planks were clearly obvious to anyone using the bridge and the city had no notice of the hazard because it was created by heavy rains over the weekend. As a result, the state's recreational use statute protected the city from liability (*City of Dallas v. Hughes*, 2011)

A Two-Pronged Analysis of Applicability

Many states use a two-pronged analysis to determine whether the recreational user statute applies and the defendant is entitled to immunity. The first analysis is whether the activity is a recreational activity. The determination of what constitutes a recreational activity has been the focus of a number of cases. In *Reed v. City of*

Portsmouth (2013), the court ruled that plaintiff walking through a park to examine a statue more closely was a recreational activity and that because an activity is not expressly listed in a state's statute does not mean it cannot be considered as a recreational activity. A majority of states use the phrase "included, but not limited to" (van der Smissen, 1990, p. 213) in providing a list of recreational activities. In an Ohio case, being a participant/spectator of the discus throw at a junior high school track meet was considered a recreational activity. The plaintiff who was hit in the face with a discus thrown by a teammate was not able to collect for damages because the school district was entitled to immunity under the recreational user statute (*Mason v. Bristol*, 2006). Conversely, a Texas court ruled even though plaintiff was watching her daughter play in a soccer game that activity was not considered recreational under the state statute (*University of Texas at Arlington v. Williams*, 2015).

The second prong of the analysis is whether the plaintiff is recreating on land suitable for the activity. In *McCarthy v. New York State Canal Corp.* (1998) the court ruled that a concrete seawall on the Mohawk River was an area suitable for the recreational activity of fishing. Once again, there is some variation in the manner in which each state interprets the suitability of the land for recreational activity. In Hawaii, the proper focus is on the landowner's intent (*Howard v. United States of America*, 1999). In other words, if a landowner has opened up lands for recreational use without a fee, then it is not significant that a person coming onto the property may have a non-recreational or commercial purpose in mind. In a California case, the court determined recreational use through "consideration of the totality of facts and circumstances" (*Armstrong v. United States*, 2008, p. 8). Plaintiff argued the recreational use statute did not apply to the Golden Gate National Recreation Area because he was riding his bicycle in a parking lot rather than on the bike trail. The court ruled that although he was in a parking lot when he hit a pothole causing him to fall, he was riding for a recreational purpose allowing defendant to prevail under the statute.

Nuisance Law

Nuisance is an area of property law dealing with activity or use of one's property that produces material annoyance, inconvenience, and discomfort for those around the property. The law of nuisance is fairly comprehensive and includes that which endangers life and health, gives offense to the senses, violates laws of decency, or obstructs reasonable use of property. Nuisances are typically classified as public or private. **Public nuisances** are acts that obstruct the enjoyment or use of common property or cause inconvenience or damage to the public. More specifically, a public nuisance exists if the following criteria are supported by the evidence: 1) the condition complained of has a natural tendency to create danger or inflict injury on person or property; 2) the danger created is a continuing one; 3) the use of the land is unreasonable or unlawful; and 4) the condition interferes with a right common to the general public (*Spiegelhalter v. Town of Hamden*, 2014, p. 19). For example, plaintiff suffered catastrophic injury in a bicycle motocross (BMX) accident in a public park in Hamden, Connecticut. The area of the park where plaintiff was injured was informally known as the bike park but had not been officially created nor maintained by the city parks and recreation department. Plaintiff claimed the bike park was a public nuisance and that the town should be liable for his injuries by maintaining a nuisance. In applying the criteria for a public nuisance to the facts of the case, the court ruled that use of a public park is a common right of the general public, the bike park had existed for over five years, and the city had exercised control over the bike park yet had not taken specific measures to reduce the dangerous hazards found there. As a result, the city was held liable for maintaining a public nuisance on which plaintiff was injured (*Spiegelhalter, 2014*).

Private nuisance is defined as a non trespassory invasion of another's interest in the use or enjoyment of one's own property. In a private nuisance claim courts are usually expecting plaintiffs to present evidence showing an injury specific to the use and enjoyment of his or her land (*Tally Bissell Neighbors, Inc. v. Eyrie Shotgun Ranch, LLC*, 2010). The primary factors to be considered in a private nuisance claim are the gravity of the harm to the plaintiff, the value of the defendant's activity to the community, the burden that will be placed on the defendant if a particular remedy is granted, and whether the defendant's activity was in progress when the plaintiff arrived at the locality. *Hot Rod Hill Motor Park v. Triolo* (2008) provides a good example of a private nuisance. Plaintiff claimed racing activities on defendant landowner's track was deafening, loud, excessive, and disturbing. The noise from race cars would cause neighbors' windows and light fixtures to shake, and prevent them from sleeping, watching television, or spending time outdoors during the evenings when the track was operating. The court ruled that while defendant had taken steps to reduce the noise, the track was a private nuisance that seriously interfered with his neighbors use and enjoyment of their property.

Related to a private nuisance is the **statute of repose** which prevents a cause of action from an unsafe condition of real property occurring more than 20 years after the date of improvement to the property (*Mitchell v. WSG Bay Hills IV*, 2013). A statute of repose precludes liability for latent defects in design, construction, or maintenance of real property after the specified time period (i.e., 20 years). In the *Mitchell* case, the plaintiff was hit in the parking lot of her condominium by a golf ball from an adjacent golf course. The statute of repose was deemed an appropriate defense because plaintiff had known about the golf balls flying into the parking lot for years, yet never filed a nuisance claim against the golf course.

Attractive nuisance is another dimension of nuisance law that is focused on children entering property because they are attracted by a unique, artificial condition such as a swimming pool *(Bennett v. Stanley, 2001)*, a trampoline (*Kopczynski v. Barger, 2008*), or abandoned state-owned buildings which were allegedly haunted (*Burton v. State of Rhode Island*, 2012). For the doctrine of attractive nuisance to apply, the landowner of the artificial condition should know or have reason to know that children are likely to trespass the premises. Additionally, the landowner should know or have reason to know that the condition will involve an unreasonable risk to trespassing children, and the children, because of their youth and inexperience, will not realize this danger. Finally, the burden of eliminating the condition is minimal to the landowner, yet, he or she fails to protect children from the condition. Attractive nuisance was the claim in *Butler v. Newark Country Club* (2005), when plaintiff's 8-year-old son fell through the ice and drowned in a pond located on a golf course while on his way to the local community center. The boy was accompanied by his 11-year-old sister and 13-year-old cousin, who had tested the ice by stomping on it prior to them playing on the pond. Although the pond was artificial in that it was man-made and contained a large spillway pipe, it was determined that was not the quality that had attracted the children to it. The court ruled that attractive nuisance doctrine did not apply because it was the natural properties (i.e., the frozen pond) that lured the children to venture onto the ice. Generally, park, recreation, and sport facilities are not nuisances, but may become such if not properly planned, located, or managed according to recognized standards.

SIGNIFICANT CASE

This case from the Connecticut state court system provides a great illustration of the general characteristics of recreational use statutes discussed in the chapter.

ALEXSON V. WHITE MEMORIAL FOUNDATION, INC.
Superior Court of Connecticut, Judicial District of Litchfield at Litchfield
2008 Conn. Super. LEXIS 567
March 5, 2008, Decided
March 5, 2008, Filed

Opinion By: Judge Richard M. Marano

On June 6, 2007 the plaintiff, Thomas Alexson, Jr., commenced this action by service of process against the defendant, White Memorial Foundation. The plaintiff filed a single-count complaint in which he alleges the following facts. At some time prior to July 24, 2006, workmen for the defendant were notified that a tree had fallen across a roadway on the defendant's property. The workmen subsequently attended to the obstruction and began to cut up fallen tree, but failed to complete the task prior to the date on which the defendant collided with the obstruction. On July 24, 2006, the plaintiff was riding his bicycle on the defendant's property and, after seeing the portion of the tree which still blocked the roadway, decided that he could push the obstruction aside as he passed. The plaintiff alleges that the collision with the branch while on his bicycle resulted in serious injury to his person. The plaintiff alleges that the defendant was careless and negligent in only partially removing the branch from a portion of roadway on the defendant's property and that the failure of the defendant to warn or guard against the obstruction was wilful and intentional.

The defendant filed a motion for summary judgment on December 12, 2007 and simultaneously filed a memorandum of law in support. The plaintiff filed a memorandum in opposition on January 9, 2008.

Discussion

* * *

The defendant moves for summary judgment on the ground that there are no genuine issues of material fact and it is entitled to judgment as a matter of law because the defendant is immune from liability pursuant to General Statutes §52-557g(a) otherwise known as the Recreational Use Act. The defendant argues that it is undisputed that the defendant is: (1) the owner of the land in question; (2) that the defendant made all or part of the land where the plaintiff was injured available for use to the public free of charge; and (3) that the plaintiff, at the time that he was injured, was using the land for a recreational purpose.

In support of its motion for summary judgment, the defendant submits the following evidence: (1) the signed and sworn affidavit of Keith Cudworth, executive director of the White Memorial Foundation; (2) the deposition testimony of the plaintiff; and (3) the deposition of the plaintiff's companion, Ray Messenger, who witnessed the plaintiff's injuries.

The plaintiff argues that there is a genuine issue of material fact as to whether the defendant made the land available to the public free of charge, as required by §52-557g. In addition, the plaintiff argues that there is a genuine issue of material fact as to whether the exception to the recreational land use immunity statute, codified in §52-557h, applies to the defendant because, as alleged by the plaintiff, the defendant wilfully and maliciously failed to warn against a dangerous and defective condition.

In support of his memorandum in opposition the plaintiff submits the following evidence: (1) a printed version of information from the defendant's website, indicating the services that the defendant provides; (2) the signed, sworn affidavit of Thomas Alexson, Jr.; and (3) the signed, sworn affidavit of Stephen Alexson, the plaintiff's uncle who witnessed the accident.

In order to fall within the purview of §52-557g(a), the defendant . . . must establish only that it is the possessor of the fee interest in land available to the public without charge for recreational purposes. In essence, three separate prongs must be proven in order for a defendant to qualify for immunity under §52-557g(a); the defendant must: (1) qualify as an owner; and (2) all or part of the land must be available to the public free of charge; and (3) the land must be available for recreational purposes.

The first prong of the statute requires the defendant to be the owner of the land in question. Pursuant to §52-557f(3), "owner" means, *inter alia*, the possessor of a fee interest . . . or [a] person in control of the premises. In the present case, it is undisputed that the defendant was the owner of the land in question. Therefore, the defendant satisfies the first prong of the statute.

The second prong of the statute requires that the defendant make all or part of the land where the plaintiff was injured, available for use by the public, free of charge. Pursuant to §52-557f(1), "[c]harge" means the admission price or fee asked in return for invitation or permission to enter or go upon the land. The defendant has submitted the affidavit of Keith Cudworth, the executive director of the White Memorial Foundation, wherein he states that the land on which the plaintiff was injured was always available for recreational use to the public, without charge. The plaintiff does not dispute that on the day he was injured, he was not charged by the defendant. In addition, the plaintiff indicates, in his deposition testimony, that the only time he has been charged a fee was when he was admitted into the museum. The plaintiff admits he was never charged to ride his bicycle on the land surrounding the museum. There is no genuine issue of material fact as to the defendant making the land upon which the plaintiff was injured available, free of charge, to the public. Thus, the defendant satisfies the second prong of the test.

The last prong of the statute requires that the land be available for recreational purposes. Section 52-557f(4) provides: 'recreational purpose' includes, but is not limited to, any of the following, or any combination thereof: Hunting, fishing, swimming, boating, camping, picnicking, hiking, pleasure driving, nature study, water skiing, snow skiing, ice skating, sledding, hang gliding, sport parachuting, hot air ballooning and viewing or enjoying historical, archaeological, scenic or scientific sites. It is noted, however, that, this statute clearly states that [r]ecreational purpose includes, but is *not limited to*, any of the following . . . It is evident that the enumerated activities set forth in the statute are not exclusive. Riding a bicycle falls within the penumbra of activities that are considered "recreational" for the purpose of §52-557g(a). Therefore the defendant satisfies the third prong of the statute. Thus, the defendant is entitled to statutory immunity, unless the exception in General Statutes §52-557h applies.

Section 52-557h states Nothing in sections 52-557f to 52-557i, inclusive, limits in any way the liability of any owner of land which otherwise exists: (1) For wilful or malicious failure to guard or warn against a dangerous condition, use, structure or activity; (2) for injury suffered in any case where the owner of land charges the person or persons who enter or go on the land for the recreational use thereof, except that, in the case of land leased to the state or a subdivision thereof, any consideration received by the owner for the lease shall not be deemed a charge within the meaning of this section.

The courts have not yet interpreted 'wilful or malicious' failure to warn with respect to §52-557h. However, the phrase 'wilful or malicious,' has been interpreted under a companion recreational immunity statute, §52-557j, to mean conduct which 'must encompass both the physical act proscribed by the statute and its injurious consequences.' . . . Additionally, Connecticut law is replete with interpretations of the phrase 'wilful misconduct' in other contexts . . . Wilful misconduct has been defined as intentional conduct designed to injure for which there is no just cause or excuse. Its characteristic element is the design to injure either actually entertained or to be implied from the conduct and circumstances. Not only the action producing the injury but the resulting injury also must be intentional.

A party's conclusory statements, in the affidavit and elsewhere . . . do not constitute evidence sufficient to establish the existence of disputed material facts. In the present case, the plaintiff alleges that on or about July 24, 2006, the workmen of the defendant began cutting a tree; failed to complete the job; and left the tree in the road without any warning. The plaintiff argues that this constitutes a wilful failure to guard or warn against a danger sufficient to fall within the purview of 52-557h.

The plaintiff's conclusory statements in his complaint, coupled with the conclusory statements in the affidavit of Stephen Alexson (the admissibility of which are dubious at best) do not raise a genuine issue of material fact. The complaint is bereft of the factual predicate necessary to lead a reasonable person to infer that the workmen intended to injure passers by, and this plaintiff in particular, by their actions.

Conclusion

For the foregoing reasons, the evidence submitted by both parties shows that there is no genuine issue of material fact and that the defendant is entitled to statutory immunity under §52-557g(a). Therefore the defendant's motion for summary judgment is GRANTED.

CASES ON THE SUPPLEMENTAL WEBSITE

Goldstein v. Pataki (516 F.3d 50, 2008). The reader should note the court's opinion that once a valid public use has been discerned, it makes no difference that the property will be transferred to private developers. Also of interest is to identify at what point is the public use requirement satisfied?

Mitchell v. WSG Bay Hills IV, LLC (2013 U.S. Dist. LEXIS 173596). This case illustrates how the statute of repose helped the defendant golf course to shield itself from a lawsuit claiming negligence and private nuisance.

McAfee MX v. Foster (2008 Tex. App. LEXIS 968). The reader should note the discussion of balancing the equities that courts must consider in determining an appropriate remedy for a nuisance claim.

Webb v. City of Richland (2011 U.S. Dist. LEXIS 71857). This case illustrates how the Washington recreational use statute did not provide defendant immunity because there was a question of wanton misconduct.

Tally Bissell Neighbors, Inc. v. Eyrie Shotgun Ranch, LLC (228 P.3d 1134, 2010). The reader should note this case involves claims of public, private and attractive nuisance all involving the defendant's shooting range.

QUESTIONS YOU SHOULD BE ABLE TO ANSWER

1. Explain the difference between fee simple absolute and less than fee simple absolute types of real property. What are examples of each?

2. What are the pros and cons of taking private property for professional sport venues?

3. What is the primary purpose of the recreational use statute? Identify the characteristics common to recreational use statutes.

4. Explain the two-prong analysis used by courts to determine whether the recreational use statute might apply to a situation.

5. What are the factors the court will consider in determining whether property contains an attractive nuisance?

REFERENCES

Cases

Albertson v. Fremont County, Idaho, 2011 U.S. Dist. LEXIS 139645
Alexson v. White Memorial Foundation, Inc., 2008 Conn. Super. LEXIS 567
Aramony v. District of Chapman Beach, 72 A.3d 1252 (2013).
Armstrong v. United States of America, 2008 U.S. Dist. LEXIS 95578
Bennett v. Stanley, 748 N.E.2d 41 (2001).

Bubis v. Kassin, 960 A.2d 779 (2008).
Burton v. State of Rhode Island, 2012 R.I. Super. LEXIS 26
Butler v. Newark Country Club, 2005 Del. Super. LEXIS 301 (2005).
City of Bainbridge Island v. Brennan, 2005 Wash. App. LEXIS 1744 (2005).
City of Dallas v. Hughes, 344 S.W.3d 549 (2011).
Coleman v. Oregon Parks & Recreation Department, 217 P.3d 61 (2009).
Drury v. Blackston, 2015 Ohio App. LEXIS 4604
Forster v. Town of Henniker, 118 A.3d 1016 (2015).
Golden Gate Water Ski Club v. County of Contra Costa, 165 Cal. App. 4th 249 (2008).
Goldstein v. Pataki, 516 F.3d 50 (2008).
Hayes v. City of Plummer, 357 P.3d 1276 (2015).
Hillsmere Shores Improvement Association v. Singleton, 959 A.2d 130 (2008).
Howard v. United States of America, 181 F.3d 1064 (1999).
Hot Rod Hill Motor Park v. Triolo, 2008 Tex. App. LEXIS 9040 (2008).
In Re: Condemnation Proceedings of Montgomery Township, 56 A.3d 710 (2012).
Kahler v. Town of Middleboro, 2011 Mass. App. Unpub. LEXIS 929
Konneker v. Romano, 785 N.W.2d 432 (2010).
Kopczynski v. Barger, 887 N.E.2d 928 (2008).
Mason v. Bristol, 2006 Ohio App. LEXIS 5126 (2006)
Matheny v. United States of America, 469 F.3d 1093 (2006).
McAfee v. Foster, 2008 Tex. App. LEXIS 968 (2008).
McCarthy v. New York State Canal Corp., 244 A.D.2d 57 (1998).
Mitchell v. WSG Bay Hills IV, LLC et al., 2013 U.S. Dist. LEXIS 173596
Moore v Fargo Public School District 1, 783 N.W.2d 806 (2010).
Moore v. Stills, 307 S.W.3d 71 (2010).
Recreation Land Corporation v. Hartzfeld, 947 A.2d 771 (2008).
Reed v. City of Portsmouth, 2013 U.S. Dist. LEXIS 48959
Reed v. National Council of the Boy Scouts of America, Inc., 706 F.Supp. 2d 180 (2010).
Schafer v. United States of America, 2011 U.S. Dist. LEXIS 83748
Scott v. United States of America, 2011 U.S. Dist. LEXIS 135695
Spiegelhalter v. Town of Hamden, 2014 Conn. Super. LEXIS 1370
Suarez v. City of Texas, 465 S.W.3d 623 (2015).
Symonds v. City of Pawtucket et al., 126 A.3d 421 (2015).
Tally Bissell Neighbors, Inc. v. Eyrie Shotgun Ranch, LLC, 228 P.3d 1134 (2010).
University of Texas at Arlington v. Williams, 459 S.W.3d 48 (2015).
Webb v. City of Richland, 2011 U.S. Dist. LEXIS 71857
Woods v. Louisville/Jefferson County Metro Government, 2005 Ky. App. LEXIS 106 (2005).
Wykidal v. Bain, 2015 Cal. App. Unpub. LEXIS 1148
Yagle v. United States of America, 2009 U.S. Dist. LEXIS 75783

Publications

Garcia, R., & Baltodano, E. F. (2005). Free the beach! Public access, equal justice, and the California coast. *Stanford Journal of Civil Rights and Civil Liberties, 2*, 143–208.

Hubbard, T. E. (2008). For the public's use? Eminent domain in stadium construction. *Sports Lawyers Journal, 15*, 173–193.

Rudolph, H.C. (2010). Directory of Equine Activity and Recreational Use Statutes for Horsemen and Landowners. https://elcr.org/statestatutes/.

Swanson, T., Arnold, R. C., Rasmussen, G. A. (2005). Physical resource planning. In B. van der Smissen, M. Moiseichik, & V. J. Hartenburg (Eds.), *Management of park and recreation agencies* (2nd ed., pp. 205–242). Ashburn, VA: National Recreation and Park Association.

van der Smissen, B. (1990). *Legal liability and risk management for public and private entities* (Vol. I & II). Cincinnati, OH: Anderson Publishing Company.

EMERGENCY CARE

Kristi L. Schoepfer Bochicchio | Winthrop University

According to the Centers for Disease Control Injury Center (CDC), more than 10,000 people are treated in emergency departments each day for injuries sustained in sport, recreation, and exercise activities. In recent years, Americans made an estimated 1.5 million emergency department visits for injuries sustained while playing basketball, baseball, softball, football, or soccer. More specifically, over "7,100 children ages 0-19 were treated in hospital emergency departments for sports and recreation-related injuries each day in 2009; that works out to 2.6 million children a year" (CDC, 2013). Also, "between 2009 and 2014, 1,053,370 injuries occurred among student athletes participating in 25 different NCAA sports – an average of more than 210,000 a year" (Dall, 2015). Further, approximately 715,000 sports and recreation injuries occur each year in school settings alone (CDC, 2006). Due to the heightened risk of injury in recreation and sport activities, ranging from minor to catastrophic harms, recreation and sport managers must understand the responsibility to plan for and provide emergency care. **Emergency care** can be defined as the provision of medical assistance to an injured person in an urgent, immediate, or unexpected circumstance. When injuries occur, recreation and sport managers (or staff) have a duty to provide competent medical assistance or summon such assistance in a timely manner. Also, emergency care includes planning for the various emergencies that are likely to occur in a recreation or sport setting.

FUNDAMENTAL CONCEPTS

Origins of the Duty

The responsibility to plan for and provide emergency care stems from a special relationship that exists between recreation and/or sport business and its participants/patrons. As defined in Chapter 2.11 *Negligence*, this special relationship creates a duty that gives rise to an obligation to protect the individual from an unreasonable risk of harm. Previous chapters have outlined the various origins of this relationship, including inherent relationships, voluntary assumption, and relationships created by statute (*see* Chapter 2.11 *Negligence*). Further, Chapter 2.31 *Premises Liability* outlined relationships that exist between premise owners/operators and visitors.

Inherent Relationship

An inherent relationship is one that is obvious or inseparable; it is essential to the activity. Such a relationship exists in many recreation and sport contexts, such as an activity director/participant or coach/player (see Chapter 2.11 *Negligence*). Regarding emergency care, an inherent relationship gives rise to the duty to plan for and provide emergency care. A participant or patron in the recreation or sport setting with an inherent relationship to the provider must be able to rely upon that provider for emergency care. For example, in the Significant Case (*Kleinknecht v. Gettysburg College*, 1993), the court provides a lengthy discussion of the relationship that existed between the college and the student athlete. This relationship, in addition to other considerations, resulted in a finding that the college had a duty to provide emergency care.

Voluntary Assumption

A duty is voluntarily assumed when an individual chooses to engage in an activity that creates a special relationship. For example, if an individual volunteers to coach a youth soccer team, he or she has voluntarily created a special relationship between himself or herself and the players on the team. In this situation, the voluntary relationship results in a duty to provide emergency care (among others).

Individuals may assume a relationship by voluntarily rendering aid in an emergency circumstance. When volunteers provide emergency care, they have a duty to act as the reasonable person would in the same or similar circumstance; however, absent gross negligence or willful and wanton conduct, an individual who voluntarily renders aid may be covered by a Good Samaritan statute should a harm occur (see Chapter 2.22 *Immunity*).

Statute

A statute is a law passed by a legislative body that mandates or regulates conduct. Many states have statutes that require specific emergency equipment, services, or responsibilities. For example, 14 states require health and fitness facilities to have automatic external defibrillators (AEDs) on site (this topic will be discussed later in this chapter). Other examples include the following. In North Carolina, the Gfeller-Waller Concussion Awareness Act requires public schools offering interscholastic sports to create an emergency action plan specific to head injuries (2011 N.C. ALS 147). A city ordinance in Fairfield, Alabama, requires an ambulance to be on site at all varsity high school games and college games in the city (Norris, 2011). In Texas, each athletic coach must participate in AED instruction, and maintain certification from the American Red Cross or American Heart Association [Tex. Educ. Code § 22.902 (2015)].

Premises Liability

As discussed in Chapter 2.31 *Premises Liability*, premise owners and operators owe a duty to invitees to keep a facility reasonably safe. This includes an obligation to respond to medical emergencies in a prompt and competent manner. Regardless of whether an individual is an activity participant or a spectator, those persons classified as invitees have a reasonable expectation of emergency care.

Elements of Emergency Care

Recreation and sport managers that have a duty to provide adequate emergency care must carefully consider four distinct elements. These include: (1) Emergency planning; (2) Appropriate personnel/injury assessment; (3) Adequate equipment/certifications; and (4) Implementation of emergency procedures. All four elements are essential to adequately fulfill the duty to provide emergency care.

Emergency Planning

Once a duty to provide emergency care is established, recreation and sport organizations must participate in emergency planning in order to adequately prepare for future emergencies. While no emergency can be anticipated with absolute certainty, many emergency circumstances in recreation and sport are reasonably foreseeable (see Chapter 2.11 *Negligence*). Emergency planning includes reviewing each foreseeable emergency separately, and developing an **Emergency Response Plan** (ERP) according to the needs of individual emergency situations. According to the Risk Management Manual published by the National Intramural-Recreational Sports Association (NIRSA), an **ERP** is a "predetermined plan to deal with an emergency in an organized and efficient manner." General planning is not adequate; rather, specific emergencies must be planned for.[1]

In planning for specific emergencies, sport and recreation managers should be aware of research relating to possible injuries. For example, recent data and research demonstrate that head injuries are foreseeable within sport and recreation. Specifically, estimates indicate that in the United States, 3.8 million sport and recreation related concussions occur each year (Majerske, 2008); further, the CDC projects that a minimum of 96,000 youth, aged 5–18, experience sports-related concussions annually (Diehl, 2010). In contrast to the decline of other serious injuries over the past ten years, the incidence of concussions has doubled (Diehl, 2010). Given the foreseeability of such occurrences, all sport and recreation service providers should specifically plan for head injury response and management. Further, state law mandates this planning. Currently, all 50 states

---

[1] Many organizations offer activity specific guides to emergency planning on their respective websites. See American College of Sports Medicine (www.acsm.org); U.S. Department of Education (www.ed.gov); American Heart Association (www.americanheart.org); American Red Cross (www.redcross.org); and National Athletic Trainers Association (www.nata.org).

have passed youth concussion laws, also referred to as **Lystedt laws**[2] (Lowery, 2015). While these laws vary by jurisdiction, most prescribe head injury protocols and contain specific "return to play" requirements.

The importance of emergency planning for head injuries is further substantiated through case law. In recent years, there have been many lawsuits filed where plaintiffs claimed that response to a sustained head injury was inadequate. For example, in 2015, a Massachusetts Superior Court determined that a coach and school district could be held liable for failing to provide adequate post-concussion care. Specifically, Amy Dugan was a high-school junior and member of the varsity field hockey team. In October, 2011, she was struck in the head by a field hockey ball and suffered a head injury or concussion. Her coach, who saw the ball hit Dugan, "did not attempt to determine whether Amy had suffered a concussion or other injury as a result and did not remove Amy from the game" (*Dugan v. Thayer*, 2015). Additionally, at no time during or after the game did [the coach] ask Dugan if she had any symptoms related to the head injury or communicate the nature of the injury to a school nurse or medical professional. Less than one week later, the team played another game and the coach allowed Dugan to play despite the fact that she "had not been evaluated by, or received clearance from, a medical professional." During the game, Dugan was struck in the head after colliding with an opposing player. The coach witnessed this injury, too, but again did not try to determine whether Dugan had suffered injury and did not remove Dugan from the game. The two injuries together resulted in serious injuries to Dugan. Additionally, in 2012, Three Forks High School in Montana was sued by the parents of a football player who sustained repeated concussions during football practice. The parents alleged that their son was allowed to return to practice prematurely, where he sustained additional concussions. Further, the lawsuit alleged that "despite being knocked unconscious and receiving an obvious second concussion, the coaches did not call 911, did not contact the school nurse and did not contact [the students] parents. Instead, they merely sat him on the sidelines and sent him home after practice." These cases, however, are only two of many similar examples (See *Pinson v. State of Tennessee*, 1995; *Plevretes v. La Salle University*, PA 2005 [settlement for $7.5M]; *Dougherty v. Montclair High School*, NJ 2008 [case pending]; *Lystedt v. Tahoma School District*, WA 2009 [settlement for $14.6M]; *Gault v. Sequin School District* [case pending]; *Frith v. Lafayette County School District*, MO 2009 [settlement for $3M]; *Sellers v. Rudert, et al*, 918 N.E.2d 586 [2009]).

Beyond head injuries, emergency planning must consider other types of emergencies which are foreseeable in sport and recreation such as over-exertion, heat related illness, cardiac arrest, or other medical situations. According to the NIRSA Manual, the primary concern for medical emergencies is "dealing with the ill/injured person by ensuring that the plan covers immediate attention to the medical condition, coupled with an effective system to get professional assistance." Lastly, emergency planning should also encompass non-medical foreseeable emergencies, such as those related to a fire or chemical spill.

Appropriate Personnel/Injury Assessment

A well-written ERP will designate appropriate personnel to respond in a given emergency. These designations must be based on which staff members are best suited to respond quickly and competently in an emergency situation.

In determining staff roles and responsibilities, a recreation or sport manager must consider staff assignments; specifically, are there enough personnel available at any given time? Does each staff member know his or her role during a medical emergency? Is there a clear chain of command in place? According to the NIRSA Manual, there are three clear roles during an emergency: (1) the **Charge person**, who assumes the overall responsibility and has specific training; (2) the **Call person**, who calls and meets summoned emergency personnel; and (3) the **Control person**, who is responsible for keeping people away from the scene. Recreation and sport managers must designate appropriate personnel to fill these roles.

In addition, when designating which staff members will respond in an emergency, and which roles they will play, a recreation or sport manager must consider each staff member's ability to assess injury. Injuries must be assessed immediately so that proper treatment can be administered. In *Ashburn v. Bowling Green*

---

[2]These laws are named for Zachary Lystedt, a middle school football player who suffered a brain injury after returning to a football game with a concussion. His parents, physicians, and community partners lobbied the Washington state legislature to pass a youth concussion law to protect young athletes. Since passage of the Lystedt law in 2009, the NFL and NCAA have successfully lobbied other states to pass similar laws (NFL Health and Safety, 2012).

State Univ. (2011), a Bowling Green University football player died at his first football practice from a full-blown sickle cell anemia episode that resulted in cardiac arrest. During the practice, the player complained of leg cramps; his cramps intensified so severely that he discontinued practice. Assuming he was faking injury, a coach ordered him off the field, sending only a student athletic trainer to monitor him. Shortly thereafter, the cramping impacted his whole body, at which point 911 was called. The player stopped breathing after 911 was summoned, and was not resuscitated. In finding for the University, the court relied on expert medical testimony to determine that the player died from a unique set of metabolic abnormalities, and that faster emergency medical care would not have changed the outcome. However, the facts of this case demonstrate that timely access to injury assessment should be part of an ERP. Minimally, key personnel in the recreation and sport industry should be certified in first aid and should be competent to assess various injury types. However, the staff member with highest level of certification, and most knowledge regarding injury assessment, should generally be designated in the *Charge* role discussed earlier.

Adequate Certifications/Equipment

Recreation and sport managers must ensure that staff members have both the necessary certifications and medical equipment to respond in a medical emergency. While many emergencies require the prompt attention of professional emergency medical technicians, recreation and sport staff may need to care for the injured individual until professional care arrives. Requiring personnel to maintain appropriate certifications and having proper equipment in place will facilitate this interim care.

Mandatory certifications can vary depending on factors such as the specific activity involved, and the age of the participants. There are many professional organizations that provide published standards of practice to guide management decisions in recreation and sport. Examples of such organizations are listed in Chapter 4.21 *Standards of Practice*. While specific mandates vary depending on the activity, most published standards indicate that all personnel should maintain certifications in basic first aid, cardio pulmonary resuscitation (CPR) and automated external defibrillation.

Regarding adequate medical equipment, all recreation and sport organizations should minimally be equipped with a first aid kit including items such as adhesive bandages, Save-A-Tooth, slings, finger splints, and ace wraps. These medical devices are often required to treat minor or moderate injuries. However, in a catastrophic situation such as sudden cardiac arrest, an **automated external defibrillator** (AED) is desirable. An **AED** is a portable electronic device that can be used by non-medical personnel to treat a person in cardiac arrest. Per the American Heart Association (AHA), more than 294,000 Americans experience sudden cardiac arrest (SCA) outside of a hospital each year. While only 7.9 % of SCA victims survive, on average, CPR and early defibrillation with an AED more than double a victim's chance of survival.

Automated External Defibrillators (AED). There are two primary legal issues surrounding the use of AEDs. First, which facilities are required by law to have AEDs? Second, is immunity granted to those individuals using an AED in a medical emergency?

AED Required by Law. There is currently no legal mandate requiring AEDs in all facilities offering recreation and/or sport services. However, several states have adopted legislation that mandates AEDs in certain facilities, such as school buildings, health/fitness clubs, state parks and state buildings.

In Alabama, Arkansas, Colorado, Florida, Georgia, Illinois, Louisiana, Maine, Maryland, Nevada, New Hampshire, New Mexico, New York, North Dakota, Ohio, Oklahoma, Oregon, Pennsylvania, Rhode Island, South Carolina, Tennessee, Texas, and West Virginia AEDs are required or encouraged in some schools, although the extent varies. For example, in Maryland, each school board is required to develop an AED program to ensure an AED is present at every school site; further, the statute requires that a person trained in the operation and use of an AED is present at every high-school sponsored athletic event [Md. Educ. Code Ann. § 7-425 (2013)]. Similarly, in Florida, "each public school that is a member of the Florida High School Athletic Association must have an operational automated external defibrillator on the school grounds" [Fla. Stat. §1006.165 (2015)]. In Nevada, the Board of Regents of the University of Nevada must ensure that at least two automated external defibrillators are placed in central locations at each of: (1) The largest indoor sporting arena or events center controlled by the University in a county whose population is 100,000 or more but less than 700,000; and (2) The largest indoor sporting arena or events center controlled by the University in a county whose population is 700,000 or more. [Nev. Rev. Stat. Ann. § 450B.600 (2015)]. However, some states only "encourage" AEDs. For example, New Hampshire encourages "all schools to obtain and maintain automated external defibrillators at appropriate school locations for the safety and protection of students and others participating in or attending school athletic and related activities" [RSA 153-A:28 (2015)]. In Tennessee, schools "are encouraged, within existing budgetary limits, to place automated external defibrillator (AED) devices in schools" [Tenn. Code Ann. § 49-2-122 (2015)].

For health and fitness facilities, Arkansas, California, Connecticut, Illinois, Indiana, Iowa, Maryland, Massachusetts, Michigan, New Jersey, New York, Pennsylvania, Oregon and Rhode Island and the District of Columbia require AEDs. In addition to requiring the presence of an AED, some statutes also dictate proper use requirements. For example, the Arkansas statute states specific requirements for the number, placement and use of AEDs in both staffed and unstaffed situations.

A recent trend is statutes mandating AEDs in state buildings or state parks. For example, Florida now encourages AEDs in state parks, along with proper training for park employees and registration of the AED with the appropriate medical emergency services director [Fla. Stat. § 258.0165 (2015)]. Also, Arizona, California, and New Jersey make this distinction, requiring AEDs in all state owned, operated, or constructed facilities.

However, it is important to note that just because a state law may require a certain sport or recreation facility to have an AED on its premises, the law **may not require** the service provider to actually use the AED in an emergency situation. In *Miglino v. Bally Total Fitness* (2013), a Bally's member collapsed and suffered cardiac arrest while working out. A Bally's employee obtained the AED, but opted not to use it because the patron was breathing and had a faint pulse. The patron died, and the family subsequently filed a lawsuit alleging Bally's was negligent for failure to use the AED. A New York court held in favor of Bally's, stating that NY General Business Law § 627-a requires fitness facilities to "have on premises at least one [AED] and [to] have in attendance, at all times during staffed business hours, at least one individual performing employment or individual acting as an authorized volunteer who holds a valid certification of completion of a course in the study of the operation of AEDs and a valid certification of the completion of a course in the training of [CPR] provided by a nationally recognized organization or association." However, the court also held that the law does not create a duty from a health club to its members to use an AED in the event of an emergency. Similarly, in *Limones v. School District of Lee County* (2013), a high school soccer player collapsed and suffered cardiac arrest. The school did have an AED present on the field, but none of the emergency responders chose to use it. The family of the athlete sued the school district for negligence; a Florida Court held that although "each public school that is a member of the Florida High School Athletic Association must have an operational automated external defibrillator on the school grounds" [Fla. Stat. §1006.165 (2015)], the only requirement imposed by the statute is to have an operational AED on school grounds, to register its location, and to provide appropriate training. The court was unwilling to create a private cause of action for negligence based on the AED requirement statute (See Chapter 2.22, *Immunity*).

It also must be noted that not all states have statutory requirements; and in these states, case law does not support a duty to maintain an AED. In *Rutnik v. Colonie Center Club, Inc.* (1998), *Atcovitz v. Gulph Mills Tennis Club, Inc.* (2002) and *Salte v. YMCA* (2004) defendants were found not to have a duty to defibrillate patrons who suffered cardiac arrest. Further, even when facilities do have an AED on site, the duty to notify patrons of the AED's location may be questioned. In *Rotolo v. San Jose Sport and Entertainment, LLC* (2007), parents of the deceased alleged that the defendant owner/operator of an ice skating rink had a duty to notify users of the existence and location of an AED at the facility. In affirming the trial court's holding, the California Court of Appeals disagreed stating "the duty the parents sought to impose was not supported by the statutes or the principles developed in California common law."

Immunity for AED Use. All states and the U.S. federal government have enacted legislation that provides some form of immunity to AED users. Most provide protection to those non-medical persons who use an AED in a medical emergency (See Chapter 2.22, *Immunity*). Without these statutes, some recreation and sport managers might be hesitant to purchase and utilize AEDs due to the risk of alleged negligence for AED misuse. AED immunity statutes seemingly allow recreation and sport managers to create ERPs that include the use of AEDs in an emergency without fear of increased liability.

Most important to note is that the extent of the immunity provided, and to whom it applies, varies in each state. Prior to creating an ERP that includes an AED, a recreation or sport manager should thoroughly investigate the laws in the individual state, making certain to comply with any necessary training, maintenance, or supervisory provisions. Operating an AED outside of these legislative provisions may disqualify an individual from the immunity protection.

Implementation of Emergency Procedures

Even after the above considerations are made, recreation and sport managers must properly train staff and personnel regarding implementation of the ERP. A manager can never assume that personnel will be able to execute the plan in a given emergency situation.

Consider the facts in *Carter v. City of Cleveland*, (1998). Carter, a twelve year old boy, nearly drowned at the Alexander Hamilton indoor swimming pool. When Carter's body was discovered in the pool, emergency care was not summoned promptly. As a consequence of the near drowning, he developed acute bronchial pneumonia and was declared brain dead four days later. Lifeguards had not been instructed on the use of 911 nor told that it was necessary to first dial a nine to get an outside line. When asked about the lack of training, the pool manager testified that he just assumed that the guards had been briefed how to get an outside line to dial 911. The court stated, "the city, in its admitted failure to train its employees on the use of 911, left them without the knowledge necessary to handle the emergency as it arose." This case clearly illustrates the need to train all recreation and sport staff on how to implement the Emergency Response Plan to ensure actual execution of proper emergency procedures.

Specific Sport and Recreation Applications

As noted, the duty to provide emergency care requires recreation and sport mangers to address the specific concerns present in varying participation and spectator opportunities. The following analysis is intended to identify some of the legal obligations that recreation and sport providers have in meeting the duty to provide emergency care to clients in various sport and recreation settings.

Sport Participation

School-based Sport. Emergency care for student athletes must be an important consideration in any school setting. Athletic administrators, coaches, and athletic trainers have a responsibility to ensure that student athletes with injuries or symptoms of medical distress (e.g., head injury, heat-related illness, diabetic coma, etc.) receive prompt and competent emergency care.

There is ample case law to support this fact. First, in *Kleinknecht v. Gettysburg College* (1993), the U.S. Court of Appeals for the Third Circuit found that a college owes a duty of emergency care to student athletes that are recruited by the university (see the Significant Case). Also, in *Mogabgab v. Orleans Parish School Board* (1970) the Louisiana Court of Appeals found that sport coaches owe participants a legal duty to recognize when emergency care is needed and promptly summon competent medical attention. Further, the court held that attempted first aid procedures should stabilize the situation until emergency medical personnel arrive; and, any attempted first aid should not take the place of prompt medical care (see the Supplemental Website for Chapter 4.23). Also, in *Pinson v. State* (1995) and *Halper v. Vayo* (1991) the courts found that coaches or activity instructors must employ proper post-injury procedures so as to not aggravate the injury.

However, case law does not confirm a duty to provide emergency care in every situation. In *Kennedy v. Syracuse University* (1995), the court found that failure to have an athletic trainer present to render first aid was not the cause of an injured gymnast's injury, nor did it exacerbate the injury. In *Yatsko v. Berezwick* (2008), a female basketball player with a head injury was intentionally kept from trainers so she could remain in the game; she consequently suffered severe brain injuries. The court found that the coaches' actions did not "shock the conscience" and dismissed the claims. Lastly, in *Avila v. Citrus Cmty. Coll. Dist.*, (2006) a baseball player was hit in the head with a pitch and suffered serious injuries. Avila claimed the college was negligent when it failed to provide medical care; however, the court found that the college was not liable because it was protected by the assumption of risk doctrine.

Youth Sport Programs. Similar to school-based programs, emergency care must be carefully considered in youth sport programs. This can be particularly challenging given the nature of youth sport and the prevalence of volunteer staff. While many programs are organized and offered through organizations such as the

YMCA or community recreation centers, coaches and other supervisory staff are often volunteers. This poses a problem relative to the four considerations regarding emergency care. While organizations may be able to conduct emergency planning, it may not always be possible to identify adequate personnel with appropriate certifications. Depending on the local situation, volunteer coaches and others assisting may or may not be required to maintain certifications such as First Aid and CPR. Further, having appropriate emergency equipment available at all youth sport events is unlikely given the varied facilities in which youth sport take place. Lastly, properly communicating and actually implementing an ERP may be difficult for youth sport organizations that use volunteers. In spite of the logistical challenges regarding emergency care, youth sport organizations still must undertake emergency care planning.

The Estate of Deshaun Newton, et al. v. Wes Grandstaff, et. al (2011) provides a recent example of why youth sport organizations must carefully consider emergency care planning prior to hosting events. In 2008, Newton was participating in a 128 team basketball tournament at a YMCA facility in Dallas, Texas. The tournament was sponsored by Grandstaff as owner of Next Level Ballers, a youth basketball organization. After playing in the first half of a game, Newton was seated on the bench when he suddenly went into cardiac arrest. The coach attempted CPR, but no one else came to his aid. Emergency medical personnel were ultimately dispatched, but could not enter the facility quickly; no professional care was available for 30 minutes. The Estate claimed that Grandstaff failed to "hire or arrange for any medical personnel, or trainers certified in administering CPR, to provide first aid to injured players in need of medical attention; provide for any emergency medical equipment, such as a defibrillator to be available in the event of a medical emergency; and provide effective ingress and egress to the facility that would have allowed emergency medical personnel to access quickly the premises and render immediate and necessary medical aid." In a subsequent 2013 decision in this case, the court ultimately found in favor of the defendants; however, that finding was based on a procedural mistake the plaintiffs made. The facts of the case still serve as an important reminder that careful emergency planning is necessary at all youth sport events (See Supplemental Website).

Other case law exists that further demonstrates the difficulties present in emergency care planning in youth sport. In *Lasseigne v. American Legion, Nicholson Post #38* (1990), a youth baseball player was hit on the head with a ball thrown by a team member. Although a fill-in coach examined the player and ordered him to sit down, the player resumed play shortly thereafter; he required head surgery 24 hours later. The family filed a lawsuit alleging that the fill-in coach "did not render such aid and assistance as would be expected from ordinary prudent persons in a like position." The court held for the defendants, finding that the coach "acted reasonably under the circumstances." In *Kelly, et al. vs. The Catholic Archdiocese of Washington D.C. et al.* (2004) a seventh grade CYO softball player severely injured her ankle (see the Supplemental Website). Her parents sued alleging, among other claims, that the defendants failed to ensure coaches and volunteers were trained to handle emergencies involving injuries. Specifically, the parents contended that transporting the injured off the field and into her mother's care was improper. The parents stated she should have been left on the field until emergency technicians arrived. The court held that there was no delay in treatment attributable to the manner in which she left the field, nor was there a lack of emergency care training. Also, in *Myers v. Friends of Shenendehowa Crew, Inc.* (2006) a 14 year old, who trained in rowing with defendant at a YMCA, fainted during practice. The supervisor took the child to the YMCA front desk and asked for a nurse; however, the child was left unattended after the request was made. The child subsequently fainted, hit her head, and had multiple seizures. In denying the defendants' motion for summary judgment, the court held that a question of fact existed as to whether leaving the child unattended after an injury was negligent.

Recreation/Fitness Participants

Campus Recreation Centers. Participation rates in intramural and other recreational collegiate activities have increased significantly in recent decades. Along with this growth comes a rise in the number of accidents and injuries that occur in the campus recreational setting (Steir and Kampf, 2008).

With such a variety of intramural activities now offered, including non-traditional sports such as rock climbing, water polo, kayaking, skiing, and boxing, the emergency care planning process has become a more significant undertaking. Best practice requires campus recreation managers to create an ERP for each individual activity, carefully considering personnel, equipment and implementation. In *Spiegler v. State of Arizona* (1996) a female student working out in the campus weight room at the University of Arizona suffered a cardiac arrest. The ERP in place required the supervising student staff member to administer CPR as necessary; however, this was not done. The supervising student employee did call 911, but the impaired student suffered permanent brain damage. The jury found for the plaintiff stating that she had not been given the standard of care required by the campus policies for emergency care. Additional examples are found in *Lemoine v. Cornell University* (2003) where a student was injured when she fell from a rock climbing wall during a rock climbing class and *Kyriazis v. University of West Virginia* (1994) where a male rugby participant was injured while playing intramural rugby.

Aquatics. Recreation and sport facilities with aquatic components such as swimming pools or lakes must carefully consider emergency care. All states have specific regulatory codes that dictate what aquatic facilities must maintain regarding safety equipment, personnel, and certifications. However, even though many of the required elements of an ERP are mandated in an aquatics facility, managers of these areas still must carefully consider additional elements of emergency planning.

Cases that have considered emergency care in aquatics facilities also often consider whether supervision was adequate (see Chapter 2.34 *Supervision*). In *Robinson v. Chicago Park District* (2001), a swimmer at a county pool was spotted at the bottom of the deep end. Lifeguards on duty were alleged to have hesitated in retrieving the deceased, thus causing a delay in emergency care. Even though allegations existed that the deceased should have been resuscitated much sooner, the defendants were not liable pursuant to the Illinois Tort Immunity Act. Similarly, in *Trotter v. School District* (2000) a member of a freshman swim class died after struggling, and subsequently drowning, in the deep end of the school pool. The instructor hired to teach the freshman swimming class did not have water safety or lifeguarding certifications; also, there were problems accessing emergency lifesaving equipment. Although the Illinois Appellate court granted the school district's motion for summary judgment regarding immunity, the case was remanded to consider the question of whether the instructor was adequately skilled to provide supervision and/or first aid to a swim class. Lastly, in *Walker v. Daniels* (1991), a student at Fort Valley State College drowned during a recreational swim session that did not have the approval of campus administration. The lifeguards present were alleged to be inattentive; further, medical evidence demonstrated that the student had been underwater for at least four to six minutes before he was discovered, and additional time elapsed before emergency care was administered. The college was assessed damages of 1.5 million dollars based on these breaches of duty.

Health Clubs and Spas. Fitness facilities and health clubs are highly susceptible to claims of negligence regarding inadequate emergency care. Failure to provide First Aid/CPR (*Lewin v. Fitworks of Cincinnati, LLC*, 2005); failure to summon emergency medical services (*Chai v. Sport and Fitness Clubs of America*, 2005); failure to do more than summon emergency medical services (*Brown v. Atlas-Kona Kai*, 2009); and, in some states failure to have and/or use an AED are all potential areas of risk for health/fitness facility operators (*Rotolo v. San Jose Sports and Entertainment, LLC*, 2007). In *L.A. Fitness International v. Mayer* (2008), the daughter of Alessio Tringali filed a wrongful death action against the club after her father died as a result of cardiac arrest suffered while using a step machine. Among other claims, Mayer asserted that L.A. Fitness failed to administer CPR; failed to have an AED on its premises; and failed to train its employees and agents to handle medical emergencies. Noting that the issue of the duty owed by a health club owner to an injured patron was one of first impression in Florida, the Florida Court of Appeals held that L.A. Fitness satisfied its duty to render assistance when it summoned emergency medical assistance. Further, the court held that in Florida, there is no common law or statutory duty for a health club to have an AED on its premises (see the Supplemental Website).

Additionally, many fitness and health clubs require patrons to sign a waiver and/or release of liability (see Chapter 2.23 *Waivers and Releases*). However, a waiver may not be enforceable regarding the failure to provide emergency care. In *Brown v. Bally Total Fitness Corporation* (2003), a patron experienced heart problems while on the treadmill. The plaintiff alleged "that defendant's employees failed to check decedent's pulse, failed to administer cardio-pulmonary resuscitation (CPR), and prevented a Good Samaritan, off-duty police officer, from attempting lifesaving procedures. In addition, plaintiffs alleged that defendant knew or should have known that its employees were not qualified, nor able, to provide emergency medical services, including CPR."

After careful analysis of the waiver, the court reversed summary judgment for Bally's indicating that the waiver of liability did not apply to negligence in rendering emergency care.

Other Participant Activities. Court cases provide examples of other recreation and sport activities where emergency care was an issue.

Skating Rinks. In *Spotlite Skating Rink Inc. v. Barnes* (2008), a 10 year-old died after falling and hitting her head on the ice rink operated by the defendant. The Supreme Court of Mississippi held that the skate rink had a duty to provide appropriate medical treatment to the patron, and that there was sufficient evidence to support a finding that the rink breached its duty of care to render aid (see the Supplemental Website).

Road Races/Fitness Challenges. In *Gehling v. St. George's University School of Medicine* (1989), a medical student participated in a 2.5 mile road race sponsored by the University. After completing the race, Earl Gehling collapsed, suffering from heat stroke, and died a short time later. After reviewing the emergency care measures in place such as water on the course, trained medical staff, and a person trailing the race to aid injured runners, the Court found in favor of the defendant.

Adult Recreation/Sport Activities. In *Colon v. Chelsea Piers Mgmt.* (2006), the decedent suffered cardiac arrest and died while playing in an adult basketball league at Chelsea Piers. The plaintiff alleged that the defendant had a duty to provide staff adequately trained in medical care, as well as maintain emergency equipment, such as a resuscitation device, on the premises. The court held that the operator of the basketball league did not have this duty and granted summary judgment for the defendant. Also, in *Carter v. Baldwin*, (2009), an off-road racer suffered injuries in a collision with another car and claimed the injuries were exacerbated due to a lack of adequate emergency medical care at the track. On appeal of the trial court's decision to dismiss the gross negligence claim, the court affirmed, holding the promoters did not breach any duty they owed to Carter because he assumed the risk of injury from the risks inherent in the sport. While the court noted that the alleged lack of proper medical care may have increased the severity of the injury, the court did not address whether the promoters had a duty to provide reasonable medical care on the premises.

Golf. Although no case law was found specifically addressing the duty to provide emergency care on a golf course, injuries in golf are common and range from moderate, such as a ball strike (*Yoneda v. Tom*, 2006; *Sullivan-Coughlin v. Palos Country Club, Inc.*, 2004) to severe, such as a lightning strike (*Hames v. State*, 1991; *Maussner v. Atlantic City Country Club*, 1997). Further, according to the American Heart Association, golf courses rank in the top five most common public places for sudden cardiac arrest to occur. As such, golf course owner/operators should have an ERP that adequately considers these common golf injuries, as well as the necessity for and availability of an AED.

Professional Sport Teams. All athletes risk injury, even professional ones. Take, for example, Korey Stringer of the Minnesota Vikings who died from heat stroke during football practice (*Stringer v. Minnesota Vikings Football Club, L.L.C.*, 2004); or take Carl Phelps, a professional racecar driver who suffered severe burns at Firebird Raceway when his car erupted into flames. (*Phelps v. Firebird Raceway, Inc.*, 2005). Allegations of inadequate medical care after the injury were made in both of these cases, however the *Stringer* Court ruled that the plaintiff received emergency care. In *Phelps*, the appellate court did not specifically address the issue of emergency care since the primary issue was the validity of a waiver. However, both cases demonstrate the importance of emergency care in professional sport.

Sport Spectators

Stadia. While the duty to provide emergency care is clearly a concern regarding participant injuries, sport spectators are also entitled to emergency care. Based on premises liability law, and the classification of sport patrons as invitees, stadium owners have a duty to provide a reasonably safe premise for spectators at sporting events. Sport and recreation facility managers must be concerned with the safety of attendees, spectators and patrons (Madden, 1998). Specific considerations regarding emergency care for spectators and patrons are discussed in Chapter 4.22 *Audits in Risk Management*; Chapter 4.23 *Crisis Management*; and Chapter 4.24 *Crowd Management*.

SIGNIFICANT CASE

The following case is one of the most significant regarding the duty to provide emergency care. The court provides a clear and thorough discussion of the origin of the duty; most notably, the court discusses the special relationship between the college and the athlete, as well as the foreseeability of the harm. When reading this case, take note of these two discussions, as well as the facts leading up to the allegation of negligence. This case clearly supports a need for emergency care planning, identification of appropriate personnel, equipment and certifications, as well as implementation of the ERP.

KLEINKNECHT V. GETTYSBURG COLLEGE
United States Court Of Appeals For The Third Circuit
989 F.2d 1360 (1993)

II. FACTUAL HISTORY

In September 1988, Drew Kleinknecht was a sophomore student at the College, which had recruited him for its Division III intercollegiate lacrosse team. The College is a private, four-year liberal arts school. In 1988, it * * * * supported twenty-one intercollegiate sports teams involving approximately 525 male and female athletes. * * *

Lacrosse players can typically suffer a variety of injuries. * * * * Before Drew died, however, no athlete at the College had experienced cardiac arrest while playing lacrosse or any other sport.

In September 1988, the College employed two full-time athletic trainers, Joseph Donolli and Gareth Biser. Both men were certified by the National Athletic Trainers Association, which requires, *inter alia*, current certification in both cardio-pulmonary resuscitation ("CPR") and standard first aid. In addition, twelve student trainers participated in the College's sports program. * * *

Because lacrosse is a spring sport, daily practices were held during the spring semester in order to prepare for competition. Student trainers were assigned to cover both spring practices and games. Fall practice was held only for the players to learn "skills and drills," and to become acquainted with the other team members. No student trainers were assigned to the fall practices.

Drew participated in a fall lacrosse practice on the afternoon of September 16, 1988. Coaches Janczyk and Anderson attended and supervised this practice. It was held on the softball fields outside Musselman Stadium. No trainers or student trainers were present. Neither coach had certification in CPR. Neither coach had a radio on the practice field. The nearest telephone was inside the training room at Musselman Stadium, roughly 200–250 yards away. The shortest route to this telephone required scaling an eight-foot high cyclone fence surrounding the stadium. According to Coach Janczyk, he and Coach Anderson had never discussed how they would handle an emergency during fall lacrosse practice.

[At] the September 16, 1988 practice * * * * Drew was a defenseman and was participating in one of the drills when he suffered a cardiac arrest. According to a teammate, Drew simply stepped away from the play and dropped to the ground. Another teammate stated that no person or object struck Drew prior to his collapse.

After Drew fell, his teammates and Coach Janczyk ran to his side. Coach Janczyk and some of the players noticed that Drew was lying so that his head appeared to be in an awkward position. No one knew precisely what had happened at that time, and at least some of those present suspected a spinal injury. Team captain Daniel Polizzotti testified that he heard a continuous "funny" "gurgling" noise coming from Drew, and knew from what he observed that something "major" was wrong. Other teammates testified that Drew's skin began quickly to change colors. One team member testified that by the time the coaches had arrived, "[Drew] was really blue."

According to the College, Coach Janczyk acted in accordance with the school's emergency plan by first assessing Drew's condition, then dispatching players to get a trainer and call for an ambulance. Coach Janczyk himself then began to run toward Musselman Stadium to summon help.

The Kleinknechts dispute the College's version of the facts. They note that although Coach Janczyk claims to have told two players to run to Apple Hall, a nearby dormitory, for help, Coach Anderson did not recall Coach Janczyk's sending anyone for help. Even if Coach Janczyk did send the two players to Apple Hall, the Kleinknechts maintain, his action was inappropriate because Apple Hall was not the location of the nearest telephone. It is undisputed that two other team members ran for help, but the Kleinknechts contend that the team members did this on their own accord, without instruction from either coach.

The parties do not dispute that Polizzotti, the team captain, ran toward the stadium, where he knew a training room was located and a student trainer could be found. In doing so, Polizzotti scaled a chain link fence that surrounded the stadium and ran across the field, encountering student trainer Traci Moore outside the door to the training room. He told her that a lacrosse player was down and needed help. She ran toward the football stadium's main gate, managed to squeeze through a gap between one side of the locked gate and the brick pillar forming its support, and continued on to the practice field by foot until flagging a ride from a passing car. In the meantime, Polizzotti continued into the training room where he told the student trainers there what had happened. One of them phoned Plank Gymnasium and told Head Trainer Donolli about the emergency.

Contemporaneously with Polizzotti's dash to the stadium, Dave Kerney, another team member, ran toward the stadium for assistance. Upon seeing that Polizzotti was going to beat him there, Kerney concluded that it was pointless for both of them to arrive at the same destination and changed his course toward the College Union Building. He told the student at the front desk of the emergency on the practice field. The student called his supervisor on duty in the building, and she immediately telephoned for an ambulance.

Student trainer Moore was first to reach Drew. She saw Drew's breathing was labored, and the color of his complexion changed as she watched. Because Drew was breathing, she did not attempt CPR or any other first aid technique, but only monitored his condition, observing no visible bruises or lacerations.

By this time, Coach Janczyk had entered the stadium training room and learned that Donolli had been notified and an ambulance called. Coach Janczyk returned to the practice field at the same time Donolli arrived in a golf cart. Donolli saw that Drew was not breathing, and turned him on his back to begin CPR with the help of a student band member who was certified as an emergency medical technician and had by chance arrived on the scene. The two of them performed CPR until two ambulances arrived at approximately 4:15 p.m. Drew was defibrillated and drugs were administered to strengthen his heart. He was placed in an ambulance and taken to the hospital, but despite repeated resuscitation efforts, Drew could not be revived. He was pronounced dead at 4:58 p.m.

As the district court observed, the parties vigorously dispute the amount of time that elapsed in connection with the events following Drew's collapse. The College maintains that "Coach Janczyk immediately ran to Drew's side, followed closely by assistant coach, Anderson. Team captain Polizzotti estimated that it took him no more than thirty seconds to get from the practice field to the training room. The College contends that it took Moore no more than two minutes to get from the training room to Drew's side. In fact, the College maintains, the lacrosse team was practicing on this particular field because of its close proximity to the training room and the student trainers. The College estimates that an ambulance was present within eight to ten minutes after Drew's collapse.

The Kleinknechts, on the other hand, assert that as much as a minute to a minute and a half passed before Coach Janczyk arrived at Drew's side. * * * * They estimate that it took Polizzotti a minute and a half to arrive at the stadium training room from the practice field, advise someone on duty, and have that person notify Donolli. The Kleinknechts also estimate that it took Kerney two minutes and thirteen seconds to arrive at the College Union Building, speak to the student at the desk, and then have the secretary telephone for an ambulance. They point to Donolli's deposition testimony indicating that it took him approximately three minutes and fifteen seconds to arrive at the scene. The Kleinknechts further maintain, and the College does not dispute, that at least five minutes elapsed from the time that Drew was first observed on the ground until Head Trainer Donolli began administering CPR. Thus, the Kleinknechts contend that * * * * as long as twelve minutes elapsed before CPR was administered. They also estimate that roughly ten more minutes passed before the first ambulance arrived on the scene.

Prior to his collapse, Drew had no medical history of heart problems. * * * * In January 1988, a College physician had examined Drew to determine his fitness to participate in sports and found him to be in excellent health. The Kleinknecht's family physician had also examined Drew in August 1987 and found him healthy and able to participate in physical activity.

Medical evidence indicated Drew died of cardiac arrest after a fatal attack of cardiac arrhythmia.

* * * *

III. ISSUES ON APPEAL

The Kleinknechts present three general issues on appeal: (1) the district court erred in determining that the College had no legal duty to implement preventive measures assuring prompt assistance and treatment in the event one of its student athletes suffered cardiac arrest while engaged in school-supervised intercollegiate athletic activity; (2) the district court erred in determining that the actions of school employees following Drew's collapse were reasonable and that the College therefore did not breach any duty of care; and (3) the district court erred in determining that both Traci Moore and the College were entitled to immunity under the Pennsylvania Good Samaritan Act. [discussion omitted]

IV. ANALYSIS
1. The Duty of Care Issue

Whether a defendant owes a duty of care to a plaintiff is a question of law . . . In order to prevail on a cause of action in negligence under Pennsylvania law, a plaintiff must establish: (1) a duty or obligation recognized by the law, requiring the actor to conform to a certain standard of conduct; (2) a failure to conform to the standard required; (3) a causal connection between the conduct and the resulting injury; and (4) actual loss or damage resulting to the interests of another. . .

The Kleinknechts assert three different theories upon which they predicate the College's duty to establish preventive measures capable of providing treatment to student athletes in the event of a medical emergency such as Drew's cardiac arrest: (1) existence of a special relationship between the College and its student athletes; (2) foreseeability that a student athlete may suffer cardiac arrest while engaged in athletic activity; and (3) public policy [discussion omitted].

* * * *

a. Special Relationship

The Kleinknechts argue that the College had a duty of care to Drew by virtue of his status as a member of an intercollegiate athletic team. The Supreme Court of Pennsylvania has stated that "duty, in any given situation, is predicated on the relationship existing between the parties at the relevant time . . .." *Morena*, 462 A.2d at 684. The Kleinknechts argue that although the Supreme Court has not addressed this precise issue, it would conclude that a college or university owes a duty to its intercollegiate athletes to provide preventive measures in the event of a medical emergency.

In support of their argument, the Kleinknechts cite the case of *Hanson v. Kynast*, No. CA-828 (Ohio Ct. App. June 3, 1985), *rev'd on other grounds*, 494 N.E.2d 1091 (Ohio 1986). In *Hanson* an intercollegiate, recruited lacrosse player was seriously injured while playing in a lacrosse game against another college. The plaintiff alleged that his university breached its legal duty to have an ambulance present during the lacrosse game. The trial court granted the defendant's motion for summary judgment based on its holding, *inter alia*, that

> *There is no duty as a matter of law for the Defendant College or other sponsor of athletic events to have ambulances, emergency vehicles, trained help or doctors present during the playing of a lacrosse game or other athletic events, and the failure to do so does not constitute negligence as a matter of law.*

The court of appeals reversed, concluding, "It is a question of fact for the jury to determine whether or not appellee University acted reasonably in failing to have an ambulance present at the field or to provide quick access to the field in the event of an emergency." *Id.* at 6. By directing the trial court to submit the case to a jury, the court of appeals implicitly held that the university owed a duty of care to the plaintiff.

Although the *Hanson* court did not specify the theory on which it predicated this duty, we think it reached the correct result, and we predict that the Supreme Court of Pennsylvania would conclude that a similar a duty exists on the facts of this case. Like the lacrosse student in *Hanson*, Drew chose to attend Gettysburg College because he was persuaded it had a good lacrosse program, a sport in which he wanted to participate at the intercollegiate level. Head Trainer Donolli actively recruited Drew to play lacrosse at the College. At the time he was stricken, Drew was not engaged in his own private affairs as a student at Gettysburg College. Instead, he was participating in a scheduled athletic practice for an intercollegiate team sponsored by the College under the supervision of College employees. On these facts we believe that the Supreme Court of Pennsylvania would hold that a special relationship existed between the College and Drew that was sufficient to impose a duty of reasonable care on the College.

* * * *

Drew was not acting in his capacity as a private student when he collapsed. Indeed, the Kleinknechts concede that if he had been, they would have no recourse against the College. There is a distinction between a student injured while participating as an intercollegiate athlete in a sport for which he was recruited and a student injured at a college while pursuing his private interests, scholastic or otherwise. This distinction serves to limit the class of students to whom a college owes the duty of care that arises here. Had Drew been participating in a fraternity football game, for example, the College might not have owed him the same duty or perhaps any duty at all. There is, however, no need for us to reach or decide the duty question either in that context or in the context of whether a college would owe a duty towards students participating in intramural sports. On the other hand, the fact that Drew's cardiac arrest occurred during an athletic event involving an intercollegiate team of which he was a member does impose a duty of due care on a college that actively sought his participation in that sport. We cannot help but think that the College recruited Drew for its own benefit, probably thinking that his skill at lacrosse would bring favorable attention and so aid the College in attracting other students.

* * * *

In conclusion, we predict that the Supreme Court of Pennsylvania would hold that the College owed Drew a duty of care in his capacity as an intercollegiate athlete engaged in school-sponsored intercollegiate athletic activity for which he had been recruited.

b. Foreseeability

This does not end our inquiry, however. The determination that the College owes a duty of care to its intercollegiate athletes could merely define the class of persons to whom the duty extends, without determining the nature of the duty or demands it makes on the College. Because it is foreseeable that student athletes may sustain severe and even life-threatening injuries while engaged in athletic activity, the Kleinknechts argue that the College's duty of care required it to be ready to respond swiftly and adequately to a medical emergency. . . .

* * * *

The type of foreseeability that determines a duty of care, as opposed to proximate cause, is not dependent on the foreseeability of a specific event . . . Instead, in the context of duty, "the concept of foreseeability means the likelihood of the occurrence of a general type of risk rather than the likelihood of the occurrence of the precise chain of events leading to the injury." *Suchomajcz v. Hummel Chem. Co.*, 524 F.2d 19, 28 n.8 (3d Cir. 1975) (citing Harper & James, The Law of Torts § 18.2, at 1026, § 20.5, at 1147-49 (1956)). . . . Only when even the general likelihood of some broadly definable class of events, of which the particular event that caused the plaintiff's injury is a subclass, is unforeseeable can a court hold as a matter of law that the defendant did not have a duty to the plaintiff to guard against that broad general class of risks within which the particular harm the plaintiff suffered befell. . . .

* * * *

Although the district court correctly determined that the Kleinknechts had presented evidence establishing that the occurrence of severe and life-threatening injuries is not out of the ordinary during contact sports, it held that the College had no duty because the cardiac arrest suffered by Drew, a twenty-year old athlete with no history of any severe medical problems, was not reasonably foreseeable. Its definition of foreseeability is too narrow. Although it is true that a defendant is not required to guard against every possible risk, he must take reasonable steps to guard against hazards which are generally foreseeable. . . Though the specific risk that a person like Drew would suffer a cardiac arrest may be unforeseeable, the Kleinknechts produced ample evidence that a life-threatening injury occurring during participation in an athletic event like lacrosse was reasonably foreseeable. In addition to the testimony of numerous medical and athletic experts, Coach Janczyk, Head Trainer Donolli, and student trainer Moore all testified that they were aware of instances in which athletes had died during athletic competitions. The foreseeability of a life-threatening injury to Drew was not hidden from the College's view. Therefore, the College did owe Drew a duty to take reasonable precautions against the risk of death while Drew was taking part in the College's intercollegiate lacrosse program.

* * * *

Our holding is narrow. It predicts only that a court applying Pennsylvania law would conclude that the College had a duty to provide prompt and adequate emergency medical services to Drew, one of its intercollegiate athletes, while he was engaged in a school-sponsored athletic activity for which he had been recruited. Whether the College breached that duty is a question of fact. . . .

* * *

2. The Reasonableness of the College's Actions

On the duty question, it remains only for us to address the district court's second holding that the conduct of the College's agents in providing Drew with medical assistance and treatment following his cardiac arrest was reasonable. . . . The question of breach must be reconsidered on remand in light of this Court's holding that the College did owe Drew a duty of care to provide prompt and adequate emergency medical assistance to Drew while participating as one of its intercollegiate athletes in a school-sponsored athletic activity.

* * *

V. CONCLUSION

The district court's holding that the College's duty of care to Drew as an intercollegiate athlete did not include, prior to his collapse, a duty to provide prompt emergency medical service while he was engaged in school-sponsored athletic activity will be reversed. . . .We will remand this matter to the district court for further proceedings consistent with this opinion. . . .

CASES ON THE SUPPLEMENTAL WEBSITE

Estate of Newton v. Grandstaff, (2011 U.S. Dist. LEXIS 73897). The reader should note the court's implied finding that youth sport organizations have a duty to provide emergency care to participants.

L.A. Fitness International v. Mayer (2008 Fla. App. LEXIS 5893). The reader should note the court's holding that summoning professional emergency assistance satisfies the duty to provide emergency care.

Limones v. School District of Lee County (111 So.3d 901 (2013)). The reader should note that although schools who are members of the Florida State High School Athletic Association are required to have AEDs at all sport events, the court would not imply a duty to actually use the AED.

Mogabgab v. Orleans Parish School Board (1970 La. LEXIS 3455). This classic case illustrates the duty owed by sport coaches to recognize when emergency care is needed and summon prompt medical attention.

Spotlite Skating Rink, Inc. v. Barnes (2008 Miss. LEXIS 322). The reader should note the court's interpretation of the duty to provide emergency care, and consider possible implications for service providers.

QUESTIONS YOU SHOULD BE ABLE TO ANSWER

1. Describe the four elements of emergency care.
2. As a manager of a health/fitness facility, should you advocate purchasing an AED? Why or why not?
3. What certifications should be held by all staff employed in recreation and sport?
4. How would you best communicate an ERP to your staff? How would you insure they read and understand the requirements?
5. Select a facility or activity at your school. What do you need to consider regarding the four elements of emergency care?

REFERENCES
Cases
Ashburn v. Bowling Green State Univ., No. 10AP-716, 2011 Ohio App. LEXIS 1297
Atcovitz v. Gulph Mills Tennis Club, Inc., 812 A.2d 1218 (2002)
Avila v. Citrus Cmty. Coll. Dist., 131 P.3d 383 (2006)
Brown v. Atlas-Kona Kai, 2009 Cal. App. Unpub. LEXIS 2108
Brown v. Bally Total Fitness, 2003 Cal. App. Unpub. LEXIS 8245
Carter v. Baldwin, 2009 Cal. App. Unpub. LEXIS 529
Carter v. City of Cleveland, 83 Ohio St. 3d (1998)
Chai v. Sport and Fitness Clubs of America (2005)
Colon v. Chelsea Piers Mgmt., 2006 N.Y. Misc. LEXIS 2831
Dugan et. al v. Thayer et. al, 32 Mass. L. Rep. 657 (2015)
Estate of Newton v. Grandstaff, 2011 U.S. Dist. LEXIS 73897
Estate of Newton v. Grandstaff, 2013 U.S. Dist. LEXIS 8236.
Gehling v. St. George's University School of Medicine, Ltd., 705 F.Supp 761 (E.D.N.Y. 1989)
Halper v. Vayo, 568 N.E.2d 914 (1991)
Hames v. State, 1990 Tenn. App. LEXIS 53
Kelly et al. vs. Catholic Archdiocese of Washington D.C. et al., 841 A.2d 869 (2004)
Kennedy v. Syracuse University, 1995 U.S. Dist. LEXIS 13539
Kleinknecht v. Gettysburg College, 989 F.2d 1360 (1993)
Kyriazis v. University of West Virginia, 450 S.E.2d 649 (1994)
L.A. Fitness International v. Mayer, 980 So.2d 550 (2008)
Lasseigne v. American Legion, 588 So.2d 614 (1990)
Lemoine v. Cornell University, 2003 N.Y. App. LEXIS 13209
Lewin v. Fitworks of Cincinnati (2005)
Limones v. School District of Lee County, 111 So.3d 901 (2013).
Maussner v. Atlantic City Country Club, Inc., 691 A.2d 826 (1997)
Miglino v. Bally Total Fitness of Greater New York, 2013 N.Y. App. Div. LEXIS 9478
Mogabgab v. Orleans Parish School Board, 239 So.2d 456 (1970)
Myers v. Friends of Shenendehowa Crew, Inc., 31 A.D.3d 853 (2006)
Phelps v. Firebird Raceway, 83 P.3d 1090 (2004)
Pinson v. State, 1995 Tenn. App. LEXIS 807
Robinson v. Chicago Park Dist., 757 N.E.2d 565 (2001)
Rotolo v. San Jose Sports and Entertainment, 2007 Cal. App. LEXIS 843
Rutnik v. Colonie Center Club, Inc., 672 N.Y.S.2d 451 (1998)
Salte v. YMCA of Metroploitan Chicago Foundation, 814 N.E.2d 610 (2004)
Sellers v. Rudert, et al, 918 N.E.2d 586 (2009)
Spiegler v. State of Arizona, Maricopa County Supreme Ct., Case No. CV92-13608
Spotlite Skating Rink, Inc., v. Barnes, 988 So. 2d 364 (2008)
Stringer v. Minnesota Vikings Football Club, L.L.C., 686 N.W.2d 545 (2004)
Sullivan-Coughlin v. Palos Country Club, Inc., 812 N.E.2d 496 (2004)
Trotter v. School Dist., 733 N.E.2d 363 (2000)
Walker v. Daniels, 407 S.E.2d 70 (1991)
Yatsko v. Berezwick, 2008 U.S. Dist. LEXIS 47280
Yoneda v. Tom, 133 P.3d 796 (2006)

Publications

American Heart Association. *Heart Disease and Stroke Statistics–2009 Update. Circulation*; 2008. Available at: http://circ.ahajournals.org/cgi/reprint/CIRCULATIONAHA.108.191261.

Carrabis, A.B. (2011). *Head hunters: The rise of neurological concussions in American football and its legal implications.* 2 Harvard Journal of Sport & Ent. Law 371.

Center for Disease Control (2006), *Injury Research Agenda.* Available at http://www.cdc.gov/ncipc/pub-res/research_agenda/05_sports.htm

Center for Disease Control (2013), *A National Action Plan for Child Injury Prevention: Reducing Sports and Recreation-Related Injuries in Children.* Available at http://www.cdc.gov/safechild/pdf/NAP_Sports_Rec_Injuries-a.pdf

Connaughton, D.P, Spengler, J.O. & Zhang, J.J. (2007). *An analysis of automated defibrillator implementation and related risk management practices in health/fitness clubs.* 17 Legal Aspects of Sport, 81–106.

Dall, C. (2015). Sprains, strains and fractures: CDC issues report on college sports injuries. Available at http://www.uhc.com/bmtn-categories/bmtn-news/2015/12/15/sprains-strains-and-fractures-cdc-issues-report-on-college-sports-injuries

Diehl, E.A. (2010). *Note: What's all the headache?; Reform needed to cope with the effects of concussions in football.* 23 J.L. & Health 83.

Dworkin, G.M. (1993). *The standard of care in lifeguarding*, in American lifeguard magazine. Available at http://www.lifesaving.com/issues/articles/standard_of_care.html

Eickhoff-Shemek, J.M., Herbert, D.L., & Connaughton, D.P. (2009). *Risk management for health/fitness professionals: legal issues and strategies.* Baltimore, MD: Lippincott, Williams & Wilkins.

Glassman, S.J. & Holt, B.D. (2011). *Concussions and student athletes: Medical-legal issues in concussion care and physician and school system risks.* 52 N.H.B.J. 26.

Hausen, J. (2012). Former Three Forks football player suing school for head injuries. Available at: http://www.bozemandailychronicle.com/news/crime/article_5152ae26-881c-11e1-a1c0-001a4bcf887a.html

Lowery, K. M. (2015). State laws addressing youth sports-related traumatic brain injury and the future of concussion law and policy. 10 Journal of Business and Technology Law, 61, 61.

Madden, T. D. (1998). *Risk management and facility insurance.* In T. D. Madden (Ed.), Public assembly facility law (pp. 199–230). Irving, TX: International Association of Assembly Managers.

Majerske, C. W. et al. (2008). *Concussion is sports: Postconcussive activity levels, symptoms, and neurocognitive performance.* 43 Journal of Athletic Training 265, 265.

McGregor, I., MacDonald, J. (1990). *Risk management manual for sport and recreation organizations.* Corvallis, OR: NIRSA

NFL Health and Safety: Lystedt Law Overview. Available at http://nflhealthandsafety.com/zackery-lystedt-law/lystedt-law-overview/

Norris, T. (2011). *New Fairfield ordinance requires ambulances on site for high school, college games in the city.* Available at http://blog.al.com/birmingham-news-stories/2011/10/new_fairfield_ordinance_requir.html

Prentice, W.E. (2006). *Athletic training: an introduction to professional practice.* New York, NY: McGraw Hill.

Shamberg, J.E. et. al (2009). *Football Concussion Results in $3 Million Settlement with High School Coaches and Administrators in Brain Injury Case,* Available at http://www.sjblaw.com/CM/Newsletters/2009-spring.pdf.

Spengler, J.O., Connaughton, D.P., & Pittman, A.T. (2006). *Risk management in sport and recreation.* Champaign, IL: Human Kinetics.

Steir, W.F, Schneider, R.C., Kampf, S. et. al (2008). *Selected risk management policies, practices, and procedures for intramural activities at NIRSA institutions*, in Recreational Sport Journal, 32, 28–44.

Weisfeldt, M.L., Kerber, R.E., McGoldrick, R.P. et al. (1995) *A statement for healthcare professionals from the American Heart Association task force on automatic external defibrillation.*

Wood, S. (2009). *La Salle to Pay Brain Injured Footballer $7.5 Million.* Available at http://articles.philly.com/2009-11-30/news/24988280_1_second-impact-syndrome-braininjuries-concussion.

Young, S.J., Fields, S.K. & Powell, G.M. (2007). *Risk perceptions versus legal realities in campus recreational sport programs*, in Recreational Sports Journal, 31, 131–145.

Legislation

Code of Ala. § 16-1-45 (2015)
A.C.A. § 6-10-122 (2015)
A.C.A. § 20-13-1306 (2015)
A.R.S. § 34-401 (2015)
Cal Health & Saf Code § 104113 (2014)
C.R.S. 22-1-125 (2015)
Fla. Stat. § 258.0165 (2015)
Fla. Stat. § 1006.165 (2015)
O.C.G.A. § 20-2-775 (2014)
105 ILCS 110/3 (2015)
210 ILCS 74/15 (2015)
Burns Ind. Code Ann. § 24-4-15-5 (2015)

La. R.S. 40:1236.11 (2014)
La. R.S. 40:1236.13 (2014)
20-A M.R.S. § 6304 (2015)
MCLS § 333.26312 (2015)
Md. Educ.Code Ann. § 7-425 (2013)
Nev. Rev. Stat. Ann. § 450B.600 (2015)
RSA 153-A:28 (2015)
N.M. Stat. Ann. § 24-10C-1 (2015)
NY CLS Gen Bus § 627-a (2015)
NY CLS Educ. § 917 (2015)
N.J. Stat. § 2A:62A-31 (2015)
2011 N.C. ALS 147
N.D. Cent. Code, § 15.1-07-31 (2015)
ORS § 327.365 (2013)
ORS § 431.680 (2013)
70 Okl. St. § 1210.200 (2015)
ORC Ann. 3313.717 (2015)
24 P.S. § 14-1423 (2014)
R.I. Gen. Laws § 5-50-12 (2015)
R.I. Gen. Laws § 23-6.2-2 (2015)
S.C. Code Ann. § 59-17-155 (2014)
Tenn. Code Ann. § 49-2-122 (2015)
Tex. Educ. Code § 22.902 (2015)
Tex. Educ. Code § 38.017 (2015)
W. Va. Code § 16-4D-1 (2014)

SUPERVISION

Paul J. Batista | Texas A & M University
Andrew T. Pittman | Texas A & M University
Lynne P. Gaskin | University of West Georgia

Most lawsuits filed against recreation and sport organizations for injuries sustained during activities allege not only negligence, but include the more specific complaint regarding inadequate supervision. In fact, van der Smissen (1990) estimated that approximately 80 percent of cases involving programmatic situations allege **lack of supervision** or **improper supervision**.

Supervision is a broad term denoting responsibility for an area and for the activities that take place in that area (Kaiser, 1986) and includes coordinating, directing, overseeing, implementing, managing, superintending, and regulating (*Longfellow v. Corey*, 1997). The courts have provided direction in defining non-negligent supervision.

For example, in *Toller v. Plainfield School District 202* (1991), the court determined that a teacher used reasonable care by teaching the rules of wrestling; demonstrating wrestling maneuvers; matching students according to height, weight, and size; and closely supervising them. Similarly, when learning an activity, students should receive proper instruction and preparation including basic rules and procedures, suggestions for proper performance, and identification of risks (*Scott v. Rapides Parish School Board*, 1999). In addition to an instructor's explaining how to use athletic equipment and demonstrating proper techniques, the importance of observing the participant's use of the equipment also has been emphasized (*David v. County of Suffolk*, 2003). The significant case in the chapter, *Kahn v. East Side Union High School District* (2003), emphasizes the importance of providing consistent, progressive instruction concerning safe performance of a skill and not coercing participants through threats.

FUNDAMENTAL CONCEPTS

Duty to Supervise

According to van der Smissen (1990), the **duty to supervise** arises from three sources: (a) a duty inherent in the situation, (b) a voluntary assumption of a duty, or (c) a duty mandated by law (see Chapter 2.11, *Elements of Negligence*). "The basis of the duty is whether or not there is a special relationship between plaintiff and defendant which requires that the defendant take affirmative action to provide a reasonably safe environment" (van der Smissen, 1990, p. 164).

When sponsoring an activity, certain organizational relationships such as school/students, fitness club/clients, and recreation department/participants, constitute **special relationships** and require the defendant organization to exercise reasonable care for the protection of participants under its supervision. Individual supervisors also have a duty to supervise that arises from the relationships inherent in the situation. These may include teacher/student, coach/player, recreation leader/participant, and supervisor/facility user. Negligence on the part of these individuals may result in both individual liability and liability for the organization (see Chapter 2.12, *Which Parties Are Liable?*).

In certain situations, there may be no duty to supervise, such as the immunity provided in numerous **recreational user statutes** (see Chapter 2.22, *Immunity*). Other examples include playgrounds at a recreation center, school grounds after hours, public beaches, and a nature trail in a public park (for a listing of individual state statutes, see Table 2.22.1 in Chapter 2.22, *Immunity*). However, the owner of the land, recreation department, school, or other sport or recreation organization can **voluntarily assume** a duty to supervise. If the decision is made to provide supervision (e.g., by having lifeguards supervise a beach and adjacent ocean at an unimproved city beach), such supervision must be non-negligent or the organization will be liable (*Fleuhr v. City of Cape May*, 1999).

In many cases, state legislatures impose a **statutory duty** to supervise various activities. For example, an Indiana statute requires roller-skating rink operators to have at least one floor supervisor for each 175 skaters, maintain the skating surface in proper and reasonably safe condition, clean and inspect the skating surface before each skating session, and maintain the rental skates in good mechanical conditions, among other duties. (Ind. Code § 34-31-6, *et seq.*, 2009). In *St. Margaret Mercy Healthcare Centers, Inc. v. Poland* (2005), the plaintiff was injured while skating when she was knocked to the floor by a skater who was skating very fast and aggressively. Although the defendant asserted that the plaintiff had assumed the inherent risks of skating (see Chapter 2.21 *Defenses against Negligence*), including being knocked down by another skater, the court held the operator liable for not supervising properly according to the requirements imposed by the statute.

When a duty to supervise exists, the individual in the supervisory role also has a duty not to increase the risks inherent in learning, practicing, or participating in the activity or sport (*Lilley v. Elk Grove Unified School Dist.*, 1998).

Foreseeability and Causation Factors

When filing suit alleging improper supervision, plaintiffs must establish both that the injury was **reasonably foreseeable** under the circumstances, and that the defendant's negligent behavior was the **proximate cause** of the injury. Although supervisors are expected to be on site and in reasonable proximity to the activity they are supervising, failure to be present when an injury occurs does not necessarily mean that the supervisor is automatically liable. The plaintiff still must show that the failure to supervise was the proximate cause of the injury. In other words, no liability exists if the injury would have occurred notwithstanding the supervisor's absence (see Chapter 2.11, *Negligence*).

When the plaintiff alleges that the supervisor's absence was the proximate cause of the injury, the plaintiff must prove that the supervisor's presence would have prevented the injury. A number of cases, however, demonstrate that there are situations in which no amount of supervision would have prevented an injury. For example, a roller skater being struck by another skater (*Blashka v. South Shore Skating, Inc.*, 1993), basketball players bumping heads while jumping for the ball (*Kaufman v. City of New York*, 1961), a player running head first and colliding with a catcher who was blocking home plate (*Passantino v. Board of Educ.*, 1976), and a child falling down at a day care center while running in a grassy area of the playground (*Ward v. Mount Calvary Lutheran Church*, 1994).

Non-negligent supervision entails supervisors taking action to prevent reasonably foreseeable injuries to participants. For example, an injured plaintiff prevailed in a case in which he alleged negligent supervision since it was reasonably foreseeable that a catcher chasing a foul ball would trip over spectators who were allowed to congregate close to the base line. The supervisors had stopped the game twice prior to the injury to move the spectators back away from the third-base line and against the fence. The court found the defendants negligent for failing to control the crowd and found that the plaintiff was not guilty of contributory negligence (*Domino v. Mercurio*, 1963). In *Sheehan v. St. Peter's Catholic School* (1971), the court held that it was reasonably foreseeable that unattended students would throw rocks at each other, resulting in blindness in one of the children. Similarly, in *Dailey v. Los Angeles Unified School District* (1970), a boy died as a result of a head injury incurred during a slap-boxing incident. The person on duty at the time was in his office eating lunch rather than supervising the students. Because the injury to the boy was foreseeable and proper supervision would have prevented the injury, the court found that Dailey was liable for negligent supervision. Although *Ferguson v. DeSoto Parish School Board* (1985) involved an incident at a school, the principles established by the court should apply to all sport and recreation organizations:

> School teachers charged with the duty of superintending children in the school must exercise reasonable supervision over them, commensurate with the age of the children and the attendant circumstances. A greater degree of care must be exercised if the student is required to use or to come in contact with an inherently dangerous object, or to engage in an activity where it is reasonably foreseeable that an accident or injury may occur. The teacher is not liable in damages unless it is shown that he or she, by exercising the degree of supervision required by the circumstances, might have prevented the act which caused the damage, and did not do so. It also is essential to recovery that there be proof of negligence in failing to provide the required supervision and proof of a causal connection between that lack of supervision and the accident.

In summary, if the potential for injury is foreseeable and the presence of the supervisor would have prevented the injury, there is a likelihood the defendant will be found liable. If, however, the injury was not reasonably foreseeable or would have occurred even if the supervisor had been there, there can be no liability. Supervisors cannot ensure the safety of participants and cannot be expected to prevent all injuries that might occur during the course of normal play or sporting activities.

Types of Supervision

Supervision, which may be general, specific, or transitional, should be predicated on the age, skill, experience, judgment, and physical condition of participants and the activity involved. **General supervision** is overseeing individuals or groups involved in an activity that does not require constant, unremitting scrutiny of the activity or facility. General supervision should be used to observe participants and activities on the playground, in the gymnasium, in the weight room, on a baseball field, or in the swimming pool, when the supervisor is not expected to have every individual under constant supervision (*Fagan v. Summers*, 1972; *Herring v. Bossier Parish School Board*, 1994; *Partin v. Vernon Parish School Board*, 1977; *Stevens v. Chesteen*, 1990). General supervision includes knowing what and how to observe, where to stand, how to move around the area, when to respond, and what action to take if a problem occurs.

Specific supervision is constant and continuous, the type of supervision that is more appropriate for individuals or small groups receiving instruction, involved in high-risk activities, or using areas that have the potential for serious injury. For example, participants who are learning an activity or skill need specific, direct supervision. Similarly, participants who are not able to perform a skill adequately need specific supervision. Specific supervision also is mandated when participants behave, or would be expected to behave, in ways that may injure themselves or others. Specific supervision also implies proximity; that is, how close the supervisor needs to be to the participants or activity to be effective. The more dangerous the activity, the more closely it should be supervised.

According to van der Smissen (1990), supervision cannot be categorized simply as general or specific, but is frequently **transitional** in nature. For example, supervision may change from specific, to general, then back to specific, depending on such factors as the participants' need for instruction, their ability to perform certain activities, their use of equipment, their involvement with others, and their use of the facility. As the potential for harm increases, the degree of supervision should increase proportionally. Specific supervision is appropriate when the supervisor perceives a situation as dangerous. Whether involved in general or specific supervision, or moving from one to the other, supervisors are expected to identify dangerous activities and intervene to stop the activity or facilitate its continuing safely.

Attributes of Proper Supervision

Qualifications of Supervisors

Organizations should hire only supervisors who have exhibited competence in properly supervising the participants involved, activities conducted, and facilities utilized. Whenever possible, supervisors should be regular, full-time employees who have appropriate qualifications and undergo regular staff development to improve their skill and knowledge. Requiring that employees hold all mandated qualifications and certifications can help protect the organization in the event of employee negligence. However, possession of required certifications and qualifications by the supervisor does not protect the supervisor from liability for his or her negligence. For example, if a supervisor is negligent (e.g., failure to enforce a "no diving" rule in the shallow end of the pool results in injury), the supervisor having certificates and qualifications helps to protect the organization from liability, but does not provide protection for the supervisor.

Individuals in supervisory positions should have the appropriate qualifications, certification, experience, and training necessary for the job. An example of standards regarding qualifications in the health and fitness industry is found in the benchmarks developed by the American College of Sports Medicine (ACSM). Notably, one of the six standards explicitly addresses supervision of youth services and programs, and another addresses competencies of those responsible for program supervision (American College of Sports Medicine, 1997). The standard of care imposed on a supervisor is not dependent on his or her qualifications, but is the degree of care that a person of ordinary prudence, charged with comparable duties, would exercise under the same circumstances.

In a joint endeavor with the American Heart Association, ACSM advocated more stringent standards and guidelines for health and fitness facilities for cardiovascular screening, staffing (supervision), and emergency policies and procedures (ACSM & American Heart Association [AHA], 1998). Both of these efforts have been recognized for their importance in assisting health and fitness facilities with standard of care issues (Herbert, 1997, 1998). Supervisors will be measured against these guidelines in determining whether they acted as reasonably prudent health and fitness practitioners.

Number of Supervisors
The number of persons required to provide reasonable supervision depends on the participants and the nature of the activity. Moreover, when plaintiffs allege negligence due to an insufficient number of supervisors, they must show that inadequate supervision was the proximate cause of the injury and that additional supervisors would have prevented the injury (*Kaczmarcsyk v. City & County of Honolulu*, 1982). Except for swimming pool and school playground cases, however, the courts generally have not imposed liability when there has been at least one supervisor present (Gaskin, 2003). Instead of focusing on the number of supervisors, the courts generally have examined whether the supervision was reasonable in light of the age, maturity, and experience of the participants and the circumstances that existed at the time of the accident. As the court said in *Glankler v. Rapides Parish School Board* (1993), "in considering a defendant's duty to a particular person, consideration should be given to the person's age, maturity, experience, familiarity with the premises and its dangers, and other factors which might increase or decrease the risk of harm to that person."

Not only must supervisors warn of dangers, they also must make sure the participants comply with the warnings and expected behavior. In *Rollins v. Concordia Parish School Board* (1985), a teacher warned very young students to slow down a merry-go-round because it was going too fast. When a dispute over a basketball arose between other students, her attention was drawn away from the children on the merry-go-round, and one of the children was hurt. The teacher and school were held liable for injuries to the student based on failure to supervise properly. Another teacher was available to be on the playground at the time, but instead she was allowed to take a break during the period rather than help supervise.

Established Standards of Conduct
To properly organize and manage an event, a supervisor must be familiar with any standards of conduct or practice that establish criteria for proper handling of the event. *Black's Law Dictionary* (Garner, 2004) defines a **standard** as "a model accepted as correct by custom, consent, or authority" and "a criterion for measuring acceptability, quality, or accuracy." Failure to adhere to recognized standards of practice can leave the supervisor subject to liability (see Chapter 4.21, *Standards of Practice*).

Primary Duties of Supervision
Although there are numerous legal duties associated with proper supervision of recreation and sporting activities, authors differ on the number and description of those duties (McCaskey & Biedzynski, 1996; Nygaard & Boone, 1985). These commonly recognized duties can be condensed to six primary general duties, each requiring that the prudent supervisor undertake various specific actions. The six duties are (1) effective planning, (2) proper instruction, (3) warning of risks, (4) providing a safe environment, (5) evaluating the physical and mental condition of participants, and (6) providing emergency care.

Effective Planning
Effective planning is the first, and most important, element of proper supervision. Just as successful coaches prepare game plans for upcoming games, the prudent recreation or sport manager will organize every activity or event in advance by taking into account all foreseeable dangers or risks of potential injury to the participants. Recreation and sport managers need to develop, implement, and evaluate a supervision plan for facilities, activities and individuals on the premises. Although many of the elements of proper supervision overlap, effective planning precedes all of them. Regardless of the situation, a systematic procedure should be developed

to document specifically each component to be addressed in supervision: **who**, **what**, **when**, **where**, **how**, and **why**. There should be both a master plan (including all the facilities, when they will be used, by whom, for what, and who will be supervising) and a detailed supervision plan for each area and activity. The prudent supervisor will ask, "What is the worst thing that could happen here, and how do we avoid it?"

Several cases support the necessity of having adequate supervision plans. In *Dailey v. Los Angeles Unified School Dist.* (1970), negligent supervision was at issue when the supervision plan did not provide for a formal supervision schedule, and allowed too much discretion on the part of subordinates. In *Broward County School Board v. Ruiz* (1986), the supervision plan failed to provide for supervision in an after-school waiting area. Due to inadequate supervision plans, negligence was found in each of these cases. Other cases where supervisors have created liability for themselves or their organizations include failure to prepare a plan (*Landers v. School District No. 203*, 1978), deviating from an approved plan (*Keesee v. Board of Education of the City of New York*, 1962), failing to follow an approved plan (*Brahatcek v. Millard School District No. 17*, 1979), and creating a hazardous plan (*DeGooyer v. Harkness*, 1944).

An effective supervision plan requires detailed planning, development, implementation, evaluation, and revision. Everyone involved in the activity should be involved in developing supervision plans, evaluating them, and revising them with primary emphasis on maintaining the safety of participants in a safe environment. Although the framework for a supervision plan may vary, the plan should be in writing, be specific, and be evaluated on a regular schedule to assess its effectiveness.

Proper Instruction

The standard of care imposed on supervisors is the degree of care that persons of ordinary prudence, charged with comparable duties, would exercise under the same circumstances (*Dailey v. Los Angeles Unified School District*, 1970). In *Green v. Orleans Parish School Board (1978)*, a 16-year-old male was permanently paralyzed by injuries sustained while performing a wrestling drill in a required physical education class. While addressing the issue of whether the teacher's method of conducting the class was so substandard as to create an unreasonable risk of injury to students, the court described some of the attributes of **proper instruction**. The court included the following factors: an explanation of basic rules and procedures, suggestions for proper performance (of wrestling moves), identification of risks (including the extent of physical conditioning), the difficulty and inherent dangerousness of the activity, and the age and experience of the students. In *Scott v. Rapides Parish School Board* (1999), an 18-year-old student successfully sued for a knee injury sustained when the track coach gave him a tryout for the long jump without instructions on proper technique.

Proper instruction includes the requirement that participants be trained in the proper use of the premises and equipment involved in the activity. Supervisors and all staff members should make sure that all participants are instructed in the safe use of equipment and facilities; are observed to ensure that they are using the equipment and facility properly; and are informed of the risks and possible injuries associated with the equipment, facility, and activity (*Corrigan v. Musclemakers, Inc.*, 1999). In *Thomas v. Sport City, Inc.* (1999), a health club member was injured after he did not properly secure a squat machine that he had used. The court confirmed that the health and fitness facility owed a duty of reasonable care to protect members from injury while they are on the premises, and that the duty includes insuring that the members know how to use the exercise equipment properly.

Proper instruction also should be clear, age appropriate, in logical sequence, repeated as many times as necessary for the participants to understand the activity, and include sufficient time for feedback (including questions and answers) for the instructor to be satisfied that the participants have grasped the directions.

Warnings of Risks

Supervisors of activities have a **duty to warn** of all inherent risks associated with the activity. **Inherent risks** are those that are foreseeable and customary risks of the sport or recreational activity (*Barakat v. Pordash*, 2005). Although most courts have concluded that participants assume the inherent risks of the activities in competitive sporting events, the rule may be different for other activities. When dangerous conditions exist or when there is an **elevated risk** of injury in conducting the activity, courts have found activity supervisors liable for failure to adequately warn of the risks or dangers involved. In *Corrigan v. Musclemakers, Inc.* (1999), despite the fact that the 49-year-old health club patron had never used a treadmill, her personal trainer placed her on the treadmill, left her unattended, and failed to instruct her how to adjust the speed, stop the belt, or operate the control panel. The court rejected the defendant's argument that plaintiff had assumed the risk, finding that the risks were not obvious to an untrained patron. The prudent supervisor will warn of all risks associated with any activity, assuming that the courts will scrutinize whether or not the participant was aware of all the risks, both inherent and otherwise.

Many states have passed various **immunity statutes** requiring that written warnings be posted for the proprietor or operator to benefit from limited liability. An example of such statutes is the equine statutes passed in virtually every state. These statutes generally require that the operator post a sign advising participants that taking part in the activity subjects them to assumption of all inherent risks of the activity, thereby relieving the operator from any liability for injury caused by such risks. *St. Margaret Mercy Healthcare Centers, Inc. v. Poland* (2005) discusses a similar statute for roller-skating (see Chapter 2.22, *Immunity* [especially Table 2.22.1], Chapter 2.21, *Defenses against Negligence*, and Chapter 2.32, *Property Law*).

Providing a Safe Environment

Courts often declare that supervisors are not **guarantors** that participants will not be hurt or injured. Stated another way, supervisors are not charged with a legal duty to protect participants from the inherent risks of the activity, or to eliminate all risks of taking part in the activity (*Kahn v. East Side Union High School District*, 2003; *Kelly v. McCarrick*, 2002). However, supervisors have a duty not to increase the risk of harm beyond that which is inherent in the activity or to expose participants to risks that are concealed (*Benitez v. New York City Board of Education*, 1989).

Courts have established different standards for compulsory participation (such as required school physical education courses) and purely voluntary activities (such as extracurricular interscholastic school sports). In the latter, courts consistently hold that the participant assumes the inherent risks of the activity provided the participant is aware of the risks. Hurst and Knight (2003) summarized the difficulty in establishing liability against the coach and school in such cases by indicating that a successful plaintiff must prove "serious misconduct" amounting to "serious inattention, ignorance and indifference." In the compulsory participation circumstance, the defense of assumption of risk may not be a protection from liability when the injured party is compelled to participate by a superior (*Benitez v. New York City Board of Education*, 1989). The court's rationale is that participation and assumption of the risks are no longer voluntarily undertaken by the participant.

Providing a safe environment includes the obligation to provide **safe facilities** for participants by properly maintaining equipment, buildings, playgrounds, and other facilities. Although this duty is charged to the owner or operator, supervisors who work for the owners or operators continually must inspect the facility, repair or eliminate dangerous conditions, and warn users of concealed or hidden hazards (see Chapter 2.31, *Premises Liability*).

Another aspect of a safe environment is the proper use of equipment, particularly safety equipment. Courts discussed liability relating to equipment use in the following cases: failure to require that a previously injured football player wear a neck roll according to doctor's instructions (*Harvey v. Ouachita Parish School Board*, 1996); reversal of a summary judgment for the school when a football player was injured after running into a blocking sled that was stored on the sidelines of the practice field (*Cruz v. City of New York*, 2001); reversal and remand of a case in which the school was held not liable for failing to furnish eye goggles that were necessary for the safety of the player (*Palmer v. Mount Vernon Township High School District 201*, 1995); and furnishing a football uniform, but not furnishing a knee brace to a recently injured player (*Lowe v. Texas Tech University*, 1975).

Evaluating the Physical and Mental Condition of Participants

The responsibility to supervise varies with the age and experience of participants, their mental condition, and the nature of the activity in which they are engaged.

Young Children. Supervisors observing young children have a heightened duty of care (*Ferguson v. DeSoto Parish School Bd.*, 1985). Ordinarily, it is necessary to exercise greater caution for the protection and safety of a young child than for an adult who possesses normal physical and mental faculties. A supervisor dealing with children must anticipate the ordinary behavior of children. Children usually do not use the same degree of caution for their own safety as adults do, and they often are thoughtless and impulsive. It is precisely this lack of mature judgment that necessitates a higher degree of supervision. (*Calandri v. Ione Unified School Dist.*, 1963).

Youth. Even older high school volleyball players who are left unsupervised may engage in horseplay and incur debilitating injuries (*Barretto v. City of New York*, 1997). However, at least one court rejected the theory that a lower standard of care is warranted when supervising high school (as opposed to elementary school) students (*Beckett v. Clinton Prairie School Corp.*, 1987).

Adults. In comparison with children, adults participating in activity generally require less supervision. Just as when dealing with children, however, supervisors must be alert to adults who may be involved in horseplay and be prepared to intervene as necessary.

Novices. The reasonableness of supervision is also related to the abilities of participants. Novice participants (adult or children) require close supervision because it is foreseeable that they may be injured primarily because they are unfamiliar with, and inexperienced in, the activity (*Brahatcek v. Millard School District*, 1979).

Disabled Participants. Generally, greater caution is required for participants with disabling conditions, and the courts have provided sound direction for supervising children with disabling conditions. For example, in *Foster v. Houston General Insurance Co.* (1982), when a Special Olympics team was walking three blocks from campus to a gymnasium to practice basketball, a developmentally disabled child unexpectedly ran into the street and was run over, resulting in his death. The court noted that the teachers' duty was to protect the child from his own impulsive acts, and held that the teachers were negligent for failing to provide an adequate number of supervisory personnel, and for failing to select the safest route for the walk, particularly given the mental abilities of the students.

Dangerous Activities. Participants involved in dangerous activities mandate a higher degree of supervision than others do. If an activity is dangerous or has the potential to be dangerous, it is essential that supervisors provide participants with detailed instructions, familiarize them with basic rules and procedures necessary for executing skills, and warn them of reasonably foreseeable dangers before they attempt the skill or engage in the activity. Both *Green v. Orleans Parish School Board* (1978) and *Carabba v. Anacortes School District No. 103* (1967) involved wrestling. Both courts held that continuous and constant supervision is required.

Mismatching. Mismatching is a situation in which a smaller, younger, less-skillful, and/or less-experienced participant is injured while participating with a larger, older, more skillful, and/or more experienced participant. Many mismatching cases involve a situation where one participant is an inexperienced, smaller member of a junior varsity team who is pitted against a larger, advanced skill-level player (*Tepper v. City of New Rochelle School District*, 1988). Allegations of mismatching also have been made where the defendant supervisor (teacher, coach, or leader) breached the standard of care by failing to fulfill his or her duties to provide non-negligent supervision by becoming a participant in the activity. Some courts have found the defendant supervisor at fault while others have ruled that participating while supervising did not constitute a breach of duty. Examples include a wrestling case in which the referee-instructor injured a high school wrestler while attempting to show him the fireman's carry (*Hearon v. May*, 1995), a tag game in an after-school child care program in which the adult-leader participated (*Longfellow v. Corey*, 1997), a touch football game in which the teacher participated during lunch recess (*Hamill v. Town of Southampton*, 1999), and an after-school Big Buddy Program in which a child was injured in a basketball game in which the coach participated (*Prejean v. East Baton Rouge Sch. Brd.*, 1999).

Although supervision often includes directing, teaching, and demonstrating techniques, it does not encompass prolonged, active participation that rises to the level of intense one-on-one competition that has a winner and a loser. Under such circumstances, the teacher, coach, or leader may be abandoning the role of supervisor and becoming an equal competitor with the participant(s).

Supervisors who use **coercion** or **threats** to induce participants to perform some activity raise the potential of liability in the event the participant is injured. It is not unusual for participants to make excuses why they should not perform the activity assigned by the supervisor. At that point, the supervisor is placed in the position of both doctor and psychiatrist, trying to determine whether the reluctance is legitimate or not. Caution should be used before coercing participants to continue with the activity. In *Kahn v. East Side Union High School District* (2003), this chapter's significant case, the inexperienced swimmer had "a deep-seated fear that she would suffer a traumatic head injury from diving into shallow water" and had so informed her coaches. They ignored her fear and required her to dive, resulting in a broken neck. Although the court in this case did not find the coach responsible for negligent supervision, it did remand the case to the trial court for such a determination. In *Koch v. Billings School Dist. No. 2* (1992), a junior high student was encouraged by his teacher to squat-press 360 pounds against the plaintiff's protests. The plaintiff sustained significant injuries when he could not sustain the weight. Although the case was decided on sovereign immunity issues, the court remanded the case to determine whether the teacher was negligent in pushing the student to lift the weight. Supervisors must be very cautious to find the delicate balance between appropriately pushing participants to a higher level of performance, and coercing or threatening them unreasonably, thereby increasing the risk of injury.

Providing Emergency Care
In the event that a participant is injured during the conduct of the activity, a supervisor has a duty to provide adequate emergency care (see Chapter 2.33, *Emergency Care*).

Adhering to Policies or Standards in Manuals
Knowledge of and adherence to policies in staff manuals have become increasingly important in helping supervisors demonstrate that they know what is expected of them and that they have followed these policies or standards in carrying out their responsibilities. In *Kahn v. East Side Union High School District* (2003), the Red Cross manual for swimming coaches, which the coach indicated that he followed, contained specific recommendations about the progression coaches should use in helping swimmers learn a racing dive. The coach failed to instruct the plaintiff how to perform a shallow-water racing dive before she was asked to do so in a competitive swim meet, resulting in her injury. Failure to follow the Red Cross standard was one of the pivotal factors in the court's decision to reverse and remand the case for further proceedings.

If the defendant fails to follow policies or standards in a manual that have been adopted, developed, and shared by the organization, association, or program, the individual may be accused of negligent supervision. Although having a policy manual demonstrates that there are standards employees are expected to follow, it is equally important that these policies are shared, discussed, and practiced. When policies are clear, well-understood, and valued, employees have a sense of confidence in being up-to-date in adhering to standards of practice that reflect strong professional competency (see Chapter 5.21, *Standards of Practice*).

SIGNIFICANT CASE

The California Supreme Court case of Kahn v. East Side Union High School District is a treasure-trove of legal principles that includes discussion of many of the subjects covered in this and other chapters. Among the issues discussed in this case are proper supervision, proximate cause, primary assumption of risk, inherent risks, duty not to increase the risks inherent in the activity, coercion to perform by an authority figure (coach), effect of applicable standards or guidelines established by professional associations, and use or nonuse of safety training manuals. The case was reversed and remanded for trial to determine whether the coach's actions in teaching and coaching the plaintiff were reckless, and were the proximate cause of plaintiff's injuries. The case presented here has been significantly condensed to save space. The full opinion also includes discussions of premises liability, summary judgment review, proximate cause and intervening acts, and the weight to be given to expert witness testimony.

KAHN V. EAST SIDE UNION HIGH SCHOOL DISTRICT
Supreme Court of California
49 P.3d 349 (2003)

This case presents a question concerning the proper application of the doctrine of primary assumption of risk. At the time of her injury, plaintiff was a 14-year-old novice member of defendant school district's junior varsity [high school] swim team. She was participating in a competitive swim meet when she executed a practice dive into a shallow racing pool that was located on defendant school district's property and broke her neck. She alleged that the injury was caused in part by the failure of her coach, a district employee, to provide her with any instruction in how to safely dive into a shallow racing pool. She also alleged lack of adequate supervision and further that the coach breached the duty of care owed to her by insisting that she dive at the swim meet despite her objections, her lack of expertise, her fear of diving, and the coach's previous promise to exempt her from diving.

* * * In the present case, we recognize that the relationship of a sports instructor or coach to a student or athlete is different from the relationship between coparticipants in a sport. But because a significant part of an instructor's or coach's role is to challenge or "push" a student or athlete to advance in his or her skill level and to undertake more difficult tasks, and because the fulfillment of such a role could be improperly chilled by too stringent a standard of potential legal liability, we conclude that the same general standard should apply in cases in which an instructor's alleged liability rests primarily on a claim that he or she challenged the player to perform beyond his or her capacity or failed to provide adequate instruction or supervision before directing or permitting a student to perform a particular maneuver that has resulted in injury to the student. A sports instructor may be found to have breached a duty of care to a student or athlete only if the instructor intentionally injures the student or engages in conduct that is reckless in the sense that it is "totally outside the range of the ordinary activity" involved in teaching or coaching the sport.

Applying this standard to the present case, we conclude that, on the basis of the declarations and deposition testimony filed in support of and in opposition to defendants' motion for summary judgment, the Court of Appeal majority erred in determining that the doctrine of primary assumption of risk warranted entry of summary judgment in defendants' favor. We conclude that the totality of the circumstances precludes the grant of defendants' motion for summary judgment. Specifically, we refer to evidence of defendant coach's failure to provide plaintiff with training in shallow-water diving, his awareness of plaintiff's intense fear of diving into shallow water, his conduct in lulling plaintiff into a false sense of security by promising that she would not be required to dive at competitions, his last-minute breach of this promise in the heat of a competition, and his threat to remove her from competition or at least from the meet if she refused to dive. Plaintiff's evidence supports the conclusion that the maneuver of diving into a shallow racing pool, if not done correctly, poses a significant risk of extremely serious injury, and that there is a well-established mode of instruction for teaching a student to perform this maneuver safely. The declarations before the trial court raise a disputed issue of fact as to whether defendant coach provided any instruction at all to plaintiff with regard to the safe performance of such a maneuver, as well as to the existence and nature of the coach's promises and threats. Under these circumstances, the question whether the coach's conduct was reckless in that it fell totally outside the range of ordinary activity involved in teaching or coaching this sport cannot properly be resolved on summary judgment. Accordingly, the judgment of the Court of Appeal is reversed.

* * *

Plaintiff did not have prior experience as a competitive swimmer, but she was a competent swimmer and had executed dives into deep water on a recreational basis. She recalled that during a team practice session, Coach McKay directed other team members to help her practice diving off the deck of the diving pool into deep water. Coach Chiaramonte-Tracy observed her dives, plaintiff asserted, and stated that plaintiff needed more practice. Teammates remarked that plaintiff had gone in too deep. Plaintiff had a deep-seated fear that she would suffer a traumatic head injury from diving into shallow water, and had so informed the two coaches when she joined the team in September. She alleged that during the few weeks between the commencement of the swim season and the accident, the coaches failed to offer her any instruction or training in shallow-water racing diving, nor, prior to the date of her accident, did she receive such instruction from her teammates. McKay assured her that, although three out of the four team members who participate in a relay must dive into the pool, plaintiff would not be required to dive at meets. Rather, she would be the team member who started from inside the pool. At the two or three meets that preceded the occasion on which plaintiff was injured, McKay directed plaintiff to execute the first leg of the relay race, which caused her to start in the water rather than from the deck of the pool.

Plaintiff asserted that McKay informed her, minutes before the meet was to begin * * * that this time he would not permit her to start her relay from inside the pool. She panicked and begged him to change the rotation so she could start in the water. She reiterated that she was afraid to dive into the shallow pool, that she did not know how to perform a racing dive, and that she never had performed one. McKay, she claimed, informed her that unless she dove off the starting block, he would not permit her to participate. (She could not recall whether he said she could not participate in the meet or could not be on the team.) She claimed that he did not give her the option of diving from the deck of the pool. Two teammates offered to show plaintiff how to perform the racing dive, and without any coach's supervision she began to practice diving from the starting block into the shallow racing pool. Plaintiff asserted that the coaches had not directed her to refrain from practicing unless they were present. Plaintiff could see coach McKay in her peripheral vision. On her third practice dive, she broke her neck.

In support of her opposition to defendants' motion for summary judgment, plaintiff offered a Red Cross safety training manual for swim coaches, a manual whose recommendations McKay stated that he followed. The manual notes that diving into water less than five feet deep is dangerous and that 95 percent of swimming injuries occur in water five feet deep or less. The manual states: "Even an experienced diver can be seriously injured by diving improperly . . . or diving from starting blocks without proper training and supervision." The manual also states that "[i]t is important that swim coaches take all reasonable precautions to prevent accidents in shallow water entries." Coaches should require persons learning the racing dive to perform adequate shallow dives from the deck into the deep pool on a consistent basis, then require students to perform a shallow dive from a starting block into the deep pool. This is important, the manual declares, "because of the increased velocity the swimmer achieves from entering the water from an increased height." Then, "[w]hen the swimmer's skill level has been consistently established from the starting block in deep water and the swimmer is able to maintain his or her racing start depth at two to two and a half feet, the swimmer may proceed to the shallow end. The coach then takes the swimmer through the same steps, beginning with shallow dives from the deck and then moving up to the block."

Plaintiff's expert, Stanley Shulman, had been a certified water safety instructor for 40 years, had coached junior and senior high school swimming for 17 years, and had published a number of studies of swimming injuries. He stated that diving into three and a half feet of water from the deck of a pool or from a starting block is extremely dangerous, and is ultrahazardous if done by a swimmer without adequate training. The sequence of instruction laid out in the Red Cross manual should be strictly followed, he declared, and "[b]efore an inexperienced diver attempts a racing dive into a shallow pool, [he or she] should perfect the same dive off starting blocks in the deep pool. [¶] The dive should be consistently done in the deep pool at a depth not exceeding two to two and a half feet before attempting it in shallow water."

On January 14, 2000, the trial court granted summary judgment in favor of defendants. It found that, under the doctrine of primary assumption of risk, defendants could not be liable unless they had elevated the risks inherent in competitive swimming or had behaved recklessly. Viewing the evidence in the light most favorable to plaintiff, the trial court determined that defendants were entitled to judgment as a matter of law and entered judgment in their favor. Plaintiff's motion for new trial was denied, and she appealed.

In February 2002, the Court of Appeal affirmed the grant of summary judgment on the theory that the doctrine of primary assumption of risk barred plaintiff's claim. In a split decision, the court concluded that shallow-water diving is a fundamental part of competitive swimming and that such diving presents a danger that is an inherent risk of the sport.

In reaching its decision, the court considered whether defendants should be liable for plaintiff's injury because they "pushed plaintiff beyond her capabilities or because they increased her risk in some other way." The majority determined that, assuming coach McKay required plaintiff to compete at a level beyond her existing skill level, coaches who merely challenge their students to move beyond their current level of performance have not breached a duty of care.

* * *

Although persons generally owe a duty of due care not to cause an unreasonable risk of harm to others (Civ. Code, § 1714, subd. (a)), some activities—and, specifically, many sports—are inherently dangerous. Imposing a duty to mitigate those inherent dangers could alter the nature of the activity or inhibit vigorous participation. In a game of touch football, for example, there is an inherent risk that players will collide; to impose a general duty on coparticipants to avoid the risk of harm arising from a collision would work a basic alteration—or cause abandonment—of the sport.

* * *

But the question of duty depends not only on the nature of the sport, but also on the "role of the defendant whose conduct is at issue in a given case." [Knight v. Jewett (1992) 3 Cal.4th 296] Duties with respect to the same risk may vary according to the *role* played by particular defendants involved in the sport.

* * *

We had occasion to comment in passing on an instructor's duty * * * Citing Court of Appeal cases that had been decided subsequent to our decision in *Knight*, * * * we explained that "there are circumstances in which the relationship between defendant and plaintiff gives rise to a duty on the part of the defendant to use due care not to increase the risks inherent in the plaintiff's activity. For example, a purveyor of recreational activities owes a duty to a patron not to increase the risks inherent in the activity in which the patron has paid to engage. [Citations.] Likewise, *a coach or sport instructor owes a duty to a student not to increase the risks inherent in the learning process undertaken by the student.* * * *

The general proposition that a sports instructor or coach owes a duty of due care not to increase the risk of harm inherent in learning an active sport is consistent with a growing line of Court of Appeal opinions that have applied the *Knight* analysis to claims against such defendants. In these cases, the reviewing courts examined the particular circumstances of the sport, its inherent risks, and the relationship of the parties to the sport and to each other. Most also examined the question whether imposing broader liability on coaches and instructors would harm the sport or cause it to be changed or abandoned. In each instance, the Courts of Appeal have agreed that although the coach or athletic instructor did not have a duty to eliminate the risks presented by a sport, he or she did have a duty to the student not to increase the risk inherent in learning, practicing, or performing in the sport. * * *

Subsequent decisions have clarified that the risks associated with *learning* a sport may themselves be inherent risks of the sport, and that an instructor or coach generally does not increase the risk of harm inherent in learning the sport simply by urging the student to strive to excel or to reach a new level of competence. This line of cases analyzes and articulates an important and appropriate limitation on the duty of a sports instructor. The cases point out that instruction in a sport frequently entails challenging or "pushing" a student to attempt new or more difficult feats, and that "liability should not be imposed simply because an instructor asked the student to take action beyond what, with hindsight, is found to have been the student's abilities." * * * As a general matter, although the nature of the sport and the relationship of the parties to it and to each other remain relevant, a student's inability to meet an instructor's legitimate challenge is a risk that is inherent in learning a sport. To impose a duty to mitigate the inherent risks of learning a sport by refraining from challenging a student, as these cases explain, could have a chilling effect on the enterprise of teaching and learning skills that are necessary to the sport. At a competitive level, especially, this chilling effect is undesirable.

* * *

We agree that the object to be served by the doctrine of primary assumption of risk in the sports setting is to avoid recognizing a duty of care when to do so would tend to alter the nature of an active sport or chill vigorous participation in the activity. This concern applies to the process of learning to become competent or competitive in such a sport. Novices and children need instruction if they are to participate and compete, and we agree with the many Court of Appeal decisions that have refused to define a duty of care in terms that would inhibit adequate instruction and learning or eventually alter the nature of the sport. Accordingly, we believe that the standard set forth in *Knight*, * * * as it applies to coparticipants, generally should apply to sports instructors, keeping in mind, of course, that different facts are of significance in each setting. In order to support a cause of action in cases in which it is alleged that a sports instructor has required a student to perform beyond the student's capacity or without providing adequate instruction, it must be alleged and proved that the instructor acted with intent to cause a student's injury or that the instructor acted recklessly in the sense that the instructor's conduct was "totally outside the range of the ordinary activity" (*Knight, supra*, 3 Cal.4th at p. 318,) involved in teaching or coaching the sport.

The Court of Appeal majority in the present case concluded that in light of plaintiff's allegations and supporting evidence, coach McKay merely challenged her to go beyond her current level of competence. We believe that this takes an unduly narrow view of plaintiff's claim and her evidence, which went far beyond a claim that the coach made an ordinary error of judgment in determining that she was ready to perform the shallow-water dive.

As noted above, the Red Cross teaching manual submitted by plaintiff acknowledged that the principal danger faced by persons learning to compete in swimming is the shallow-water dive. The risk presented is not simply that the swimmer might suffer bruises or even break an arm; the risk is that the student may sustain serious head and spinal cord injuries by striking the bottom of the pool. Plaintiff presented evidence, both documentary and expert, that a settled progression of instruction in the dive is considered essential to a student's safety. Her own declaration and deposition testimony was that she had not received any instruction at all from her coaches or teammates on the performance of the shallow-water dive.

She also claimed that she had expressed a mortal fear of performing the shallow-water dive and that she had been assured by the coach that she would not be required to perform it. Her evidence was that the coach made a last-minute demand that she take a position in the relay race that would require her to dive, threatening that if she did not comply, either she would be dropped from the team or she would not be permitted to compete that day.

Defendant McKay did not challenge the sequence of instruction prescribed by the Red Cross manual, but said in his declaration and deposition testimony that he generally followed it.

* * *

We agree that the following factors indicated a triable issue with respect to whether the coach's behavior was reckless: the lack of training in the shallow-water dive disclosed by plaintiff's evidence, especially in the face of the sequenced training recommended in the Red Cross manual submitted by plaintiff; the coach's awareness of plaintiff's deep-seated fear of such diving; his conduct in lulling her into a false sense of security through a promise that she would not be required to dive, thereby eliminating any motivation on her part to learn to dive safely; his last-minute breach of that promise under the pressure of a competitive meet; and his threat to remove her from the team or at least the meet if she refused to dive.

Clearly, a disputed issue of fact exists as to whether the coach provided any instruction at all on shallow-water diving, and the nature of the coach's promises and threats to plaintiff also are in dispute. If a jury were to find that defendant coach directed plaintiff (a novice on the swim team) to perform a shallow racing dive in competition without providing any instruction, that he ignored her overwhelming fears and made a last-minute demand that she dive during competition, in breach of a previous promise that she would not be required to dive, we believe the trier of fact properly could determine that such conduct was reckless in that it was totally outside the range of the ordinary activity involved in teaching or coaching the sport of competitive swimming. Accordingly, on this record, we conclude that the trial court erred in granting summary judgment in favor of defendants and that the Court of Appeal erred in affirming that determination.

* * *

Keeping in mind that ultimately it will be plaintiff's obligation to establish the elements of her cause of action before the trier of fact by a preponderance of the evidence, we believe that triable issues of material fact exist regarding the question whether coach McKay breached a duty of care owed to plaintiff, thereby causing her injury, by engaging in conduct that was reckless in that it was totally outside the range of ordinary activity involved in teaching or coaching the sport of competitive swimming.

For the foregoing reasons, the judgment of the Court of Appeal is reversed and the matter is remanded for further proceedings consistent with this opinion.

CASES ON THE SUPPLEMENTAL WEBSITE

Brahatcek v. Millard School Dist., 202 Neb. 86, 273 N.W.2d 680 (Neb. 1979). Plaintiff alleged lack of supervision as the proximate cause of the 14-year-old student's death when he was struck by a golf club in a physical education class. The court discussed heightened supervision required for a young and inexperienced student.

Green v. Orleans Parish School Bd., 365 So.2d 834 (La.App., 1978). A 16-year-old student was injured while wrestling in a required physical education class. The court recognized that the teacher had the legal duty to conduct classes in such a way that students were not exposed to an unreasonable risk of injury. The court also acknowledged that students should receive proper instruction, basic rules, suggestions for proper performance, and recognition of risks involved.

Mirand v. City of New York, 84 N.Y.2d 44 (N.Y. 1994). Even though this case does not involve sport or recreation, it is instructive on the requirements for proper supervision of students who might injure other students. When the school is aware of potential danger and reasonably could have anticipated one student injuring another, failure to adequately supervise students could make the school liable. The court in this case acknowledged that while schools are not the insurer of students' safety, they are charged with providing adequate supervision.

St. Margaret Mercy Healthcare Centers, Inc. v. Poland, 828 N.E.2d 396 (Ind. Ct. App. 2005). An injured roller skater alleged that the roller rink operator was guilty of negligent supervision. Indiana has a statute that places a legal duty on rink operators to ". . . use reasonable care in supervising roller skaters." The court reviewed the facts of the case to determine whether the rink had discharged its obligations under the statute. The court analyzed the four elements of negligence in resolving the negligent supervision issue. The court also discussed the application of assumption of risk as a complete defense, and comparative fault in order to apportion damages.

Zipusch v. LA Workout, Inc., 155 Cal. App. 4th 1281, 66 Cal. Rptr. 3d 704 (Cal. App. 2 Dist., 2007). Plaintiff alleged the health club was negligent for failing to inspect and maintain its exercise equipment when a sticky substance on a treadmill caused her fall, resulting in an injury.

QUESTIONS YOU SHOULD BE ABLE TO ANSWER

1. Identify the three sources from which the duty to supervise arises and briefly discuss the important aspects of each.

2. A participant is injured and alleges negligence on the part of the supervisor. Describe how the concepts of foreseeability and causation apply, specifically, concerning the presence or absence of the supervisor.

3. Identify and briefly describe the appropriateness of the three types of supervision as they relate to the age, skill, experience, judgment, and physical condition of participants and the activity involved.

4. When teaching or coaching, what are the most important concepts for one to consider in planning, instructing, and warning of risks involved in the activity?

5. What are the major concerns one should consider when supervising young children, high school students, adults, and individuals with varying abilities?

REFERENCES

Cases
Baltierra v, Corona-Norco Unified School District, 2006 WL 1233026 (Cal. App. 4 Dist., Div. 2, 2006).
Barakat v. Pordash, 842 N.E.2d 120, 2005 WL 3074729 (Ohio App. 8 Dist., 2005).
Barretto v. City of New York, 229 A.D.2d 214; 655 N.Y.S.2d 484 (1997).
Beckett v. Clinton Prairie School. Corp., 504 N.E.2d 552 (Ind. 1987).
Benitez v. New York City Board of Education, 541 N.E.2d 29 (NY 1989).
Blashka v. South Shore Skating, Inc., 598 N.Y.S.2d 74 (App. Div. 2d Dept. 1993).
Brahatcek v. Millard School Dist., 202 Neb. 86, 273 N.W.2d 680 (Neb. 1979).
Broward County School Board v. Ruiz, 493 So.2d 474 (Fla. App. 1986).

Calandri v. Ione Unified School Dist., 219 Cal. App.2d 542, 33 Cal.Rptr. 333 (1963).
Carabba v. Anacortes School District No. 103, 72 Wash.2d 939, 435 P.2d 936 (Wash. 1967).
Corrigan v. Musclemakers, Inc., 258 A.D.2d 861, 686 N.Y.S.2d 143 (1999).
Cruz v. City of New York, 288 A.D.2d 250 (N. Y. App. Div. 2001).
David v. County of Suffolk, 1 N.Y. 3d 525 (2003).
Dailey v. Los Angeles Unified School District, 470 P.2d 360 (Cal. 1970).
DeGooyer v. Harkness, 13 N.W. 2d 815 (SD, 1944).
Domino v. Mercurio, 17 A.D.2d 342, 234 N.Y.S.2d 1011 (1962), *aff'd*, 13 N.Y.S.2d 922, 193 N.E.2d 893, 244 N.Y.S.2d 69 (1963).
Fagan v. Summers, 498 P.2d 1227 (Wyo. 1972).
Ferguson v. DeSoto Parish School Bd., 467 So.2d 1257 (La. 1985).
Fluehr v. City of Cape May, 732 A.2d 1035 (N.J. 1999).
Foster v. Houston General Insurance Co., 407 So.2d 759 (La. Ct. App. 1982).
Glankler v. Rapides Parish School Board, 610 So.2d 1020 (La. App. 1993).
Green v. Orleans Parish School Board, 365 So.2d 834 (La. Ct. App. 1978).
Hamill v. Town of Southampton, 261 A.D.2d 361, 689 N.Y.S.2d 196 (App. Div. 1999).
Harvey v. Ouachita Parish School Board, 674 So.2d 372 (La. App. 2 Cir. 1996).
Hearon v. May, 248 Neb. 887, 540 N.W.2d 124 (1995).
Herring v. Bossier Parish School Board, 632 So.2d 920 (La. Ct. App. 1994).
Kaczmarcsyk v. City & County of Honolulu, 63 Hawaii 612, 656 P.2d 89 (Hawaii 1982).
Kahn v. East Side Union High School District, 75 P. 3d 30 (Cal. 2003).
Kaufman v. City of New York, 30 Misc.2d 285, 214 N.Y.S.2d 767 (1961).
Keesee v. Board of Education of the City of New York, 235 N.Y.S. 2d 300 (N. Y. Sup. Ct. 1962).
Kelly v. McCarrick, 841 A.2d 869 (Md. Ct. Spec. App. 2002).
Landers v. School District No. 203, O'Fallon, 383 N.E.2d 645 (Ill. App. Ct. — 5th Dist. 1978).
Lilley v. Elk Grove Unified School Dist., 68 Cal. App.4th 939, 80 Cal. Rptr.2d 638 (1998).
Longfellow v. Corey, 286 Ill. App.3d 366, 368, 675 N.E.2d 1386 (1997).
Lowe v. Texas Tech University, 540 S.W.2d 297 (Tex. 1976).
Mirand v. City of New York, 84 N.Y.2d 44 (N.Y. 1994).
Palmer v. Mount Vernon Township High School District 201, 647 N.E.2d 1043 (Ill. App. Ct. 1995).
Partin v. Vernon Parish School Board, 343 So.2d 417 (La. App. 1977).
Prejean v. East Baton Rouge Sch. Brd., 729 So.2d 686 (La. 1999).
Rollins v. Concordia Parish School Board, 465 So.2d 213 (La. App. 1985).
Scott v. Rapides Parish School Board, 732 So.2d 749 (La. App. 1999).
Sheehan v. St. Peter's Catholic School, 29 Minn. 1, 188 N.W.2d 868 (1971).
Stevens v. Chesteen, 561 So.2d 1100 (Ala. 1990).
St. Margaret Mercy Healthcare Centers, Inc. v. Poland, 828 N.E.2d 396 (Ind. Ct. App. 2005).
Tepper v. City of New Rochelle School District, 531 N.Y.S.2d 367 (N. Y. Sup. Ct. 1988).
Thomas v. Sport City, Inc., 738 So.2d 1153 (La. App. 2nd Cir. 1999).
Toller v. Plainfield School District 202, 582 N.E.2d 237 (Ill. App. 1991).
Zipusch v. LA Workout, Inc., 155 Cal. App. 4th 1281, 66 Cal. Rptr. 3d 704 (Cal. App. 2 Dist., 2007).

Publications

American College of Sports Medicine. (1997). *ACSM's health/fitness facility standards & guidelines* (2nd ed.). Champaign, IL: Human Kinetics.

American College of Sports Medicine & American Heart Association. (1998). Recommendations for cardiovascular screening, staffing, and emergency policies at health/fitness facilities. *Medicine & Science in Sports & Exercise, 30*(6), 1009–1018.

Gaskin, L. P. (2003). Supervision of Participants. In D. J. Cotten & J. T. Wolohan (Eds.), *Law for recreation and sport managers* (pp. 138–148). Dubuque, IA: Kendall/Hunt.

Garner, B. A. (Ed.). (2004). *Black's law dictionary* (8th ed.). St. Paul, MN: Thomson/West.

Herbert, D. L. (1997). A review of ACSM's standards & guidelines for health & fitness facilities. *The Sports, Parks & Recreation Law Reporter, 11*(2), 23–24.

Herbert, D. L. (1998). New standards for health and fitness facilities from the American Heart Association (AHA) and the American College of Sports Medicine (ACSM). *The Sports, Parks & Recreation Law Reporter*, 12(2), 30–31.

Hurst, T. R., & Knight, J. M. (2003). Coaches' liability for athletes' injuries and deaths. *Seton Hall Journal of Sport Law, 13*, 27–51.

Kaiser, R. A. (1986). *Liability and law in recreation, parks, and sports*. Englewood Cliffs, NJ: Prentice Hall.

McCaskey, A. S., & Biedzynski, K. W. (1996). A guide to the legal liability of coaches for a sports participant's injuries. *Seton Hall Journal of Sport Law, 6*, 7–125.

Nygaard, G., & Boone, T. H. (1985). *Coaches guide to sport law*. Champaign, IL: Human Kinetics.

van der Smissen, B. (1990). *Legal liability and risk management for public and private entities*. Cincinnati, OH: Anderson.

Legislation

Limited Liability for Operators of Roller Skating Rinks, Ind. Code Ann. § 34-31-6, et seq. (2009).
Volunteer Protection Act of 1997, 42 U. S. C. § 14501, et. seq. (2009).

2.35 TRANSPORTATION

Paul J. Batista | Texas A&M University
Andrew T. Pittman | Texas A&M University

Participants' safety and welfare should be the primary concern for those organizations that transport participants involved in recreation or sport activities. Both public and private entities, as well as individuals, must be aware of the duty of care required by law when providing transportation. The potential for liability extends not only to transporting them to and from events, but also to the use of vehicles in completing special tasks associated with the event (such as transporting injured persons to a hospital), and to supervisory concerns before, during, and after transport (see Chapter 2.34 *Supervision*).

FUNDAMENTAL CONCEPTS

Duty to Provide Transportation

As a general rule, organizations are under no legal duty to provide transportation to and from events or activities. However, in the event that an organization elects to provide transportation, the organization assumes the legal duty to use ordinary care, and act as a reasonably prudent person.

If the organization chooses to provide transportation, then it must be provided in a safe manner regardless of the mode of travel. The duty to provide transportation usually begins at the point of departure and continues until those using the transportation have been returned to the original departure point. Liability exists regardless of whether the participants meet at the designated place and are then assigned a particular vehicle, or they are picked up by the driver at their homes or elsewhere. It may be possible to avoid liability by establishing a policy that no transportation will be provided for anyone for a particular event. In that case, participants are instructed to convene at the site of the event. However, this policy may not be practical if the event is located far away, large numbers of people are involved, or participants do not have access to an alternative form of transportation. The organization must also establish a policy governing the conditions under which a participant may leave an event by transportation other than that provided by the organization. For minors, parental permission should be required, with each child being "signed out" by the responsible parent or guardian. The supervisor should create a specific policy, and insure that everyone involved in transportation is aware of, and conforms to, the policy. Do not allow any exceptions to the policy. Allowing a parent or participant to avoid the policy requirement by making exceptions will increase the potential for liability.

Duty of Care

When an organization provides transportation, it owes a duty of care with respect to such transportation. Generally, reasonable and ordinary care under the circumstances is the appropriate standard of care. However, there is authority that indicates that the operators of school buses are in the same general position as common carriers, requiring the highest degree of care consistent with the practical operation of the bus. The standard of care required of the drivers is determined by the particular circumstances. Some factors that may be considered in determining the standard of care include the age, knowledge, judgment, and experience of both the driver and passengers.

In a situation where a driver or organization has violated a specific statute enacted for the protection of the passengers, and that violation is the proximate cause of an injury, the standard of care is irrelevant. In that instance, the organization would be held absolutely liable.

Jurisdictions differ as to the duty required concerning supervision. In some jurisdictions the duty of care includes a duty to provide a location where participants can wait for the transportation with reasonable safety, and a duty to select a discharge point that does not needlessly expose them to any unreasonable or significant safety hazards. The duty to provide a reasonably safe location may also impose a duty upon the organization to provide proper supervision (see Chapter 2.34 *Supervision*). In contrast, courts in other jurisdictions have ruled that the duty of an organization toward participants under its control applies only during the period they are transported to and from the event, beginning when the participant enters the vehicle and continuing until they have been safely discharged. Likewise, absent the existence of a special duty, this duty may not extend to situations where the participant is no longer under the organization's authority or is no longer under its physical custody. In order to decrease the potential of liability and insure the safety of participants, the best policy in every state would include providing appropriate supervision from the time the participant arrives at the pick-up point at the beginning of the trip until the participant leaves the discharge point at the end of the excursion.

Transportation Options

The transportation of participants to and from recreation or sport events and activities can be accomplished in one of three ways: (a) through an independent contractor, (b) by using an organization-owned vehicle, or (c) by privately owned vehicles (owned either by the employee or by a non-employee third person, such as a participant's parent). The potential for liability varies from situation to situation with the least potential for liability existing where independent contractors are used, and the greatest potential where private vehicles are used. The risk of liability is not as high when an organization uses an independent contractor because most of the risk is transferred to the contractor. The risk of liability is greatest when non-employee vehicles are used because the organization has the least control. The keys to the determination of liability are the ownership of the vehicle and the relationship of the driver to the entity responsible for the participants.

Independent Contractor

If an organization can afford it, using an independent contractor for transportation is the best legal option, since the contract for service shifts liability to the contractor. The independent contractor may be of two types: common or private carrier. A **common carrier** is one that is in the business of transporting goods or persons for hire. A **private carrier**, on the other hand, only hires out to deliver goods or persons in particular cases. With regard to the qualifications of the driver and the condition of the vehicle, a common carrier is typically held to a higher standard of care than a private carrier or a noncommercial driver.

An organization may delegate its duty of safe transportation to third party independent contractors, but the organization must use due diligence to select a contractor with a proven safety record. In most cases, the primary issue for the court is whether the third party is truly an **independent contractor**. This determination is made based on several factors, including who has the right to control the manner in which the work (in this case, the transportation) is conducted, the method of payment, the right to hire and fire employees, the skill required, and who furnishes the tools, equipment, or materials needed to accomplish the work. With respect to transportation, if factors such as the use of specific vehicles, the driver, the route, the intermediate stops, and the manner of driving are all within the control of the transportation company and its employees, then it is likely the relationship is that of an independent contractor (see Chapter 2.12 *Which Parties Are Liable?* and Chapter 2.21 *Defenses Against Negligence*). This is an area fraught with danger, so consultation with an attorney prior to hiring an independent contractor is essential.

Be aware that an organization may not be able to avoid liability if the organization is negligent in its selection of an independent contractor. Therefore, it is always good administrative practice to investigate independent contractors carefully prior to entering into a contract with them. A recent analysis of Division 1 schools revealed that at least 85 used charter bus companies that had one or more deficiencies on federal government safety scores (Lavigne, 2009). The article highlights numerous actual and potential hazards when hiring charter bus companies, and includes suggested questions as well as links to government records to verify company safety records. Additionally, the Federal Motor Carrier Safety Administration (FMCSA) has issued a guide to hiring charter transportation that contains questions to ask and links to other safety information (FMCSA, n.d.). When researching a company for potential hire, secure a **certificate of insurance** verifying the company has sufficient liability insurance for the company and each vehicle, and the company's U.S. Department of Transportation number, which can be used to access the company's latest safety report at www.safer.fmcsa.dot.gov.

Transportation policy became a central theme in the National Transportation Safety Board (NTSB) report regarding the crash of an aircraft transporting members of the Oklahoma State University (OSU) basketball team and other team personnel (NTSB, 2003). Although it was determined that the pilot's spatial disorientations and failure to maintain positive manual control was the major cause of the accident, the NTSB concluded, "OSU did not provide any significant oversight for the accident flight."

OSU policy required charter flights and university airplane flights to be coordinated through the OSU flight department. However, since this specific flight was donated by someone outside the University, it was not coordinated through the flight department. Therefore, OSU had no records on file regarding the pilots or the plane as required by its flight department. OSU has since adopted a comprehensive transportation management system in an attempt to ensure necessary oversight. This comprehensive policy provides an outstanding model for transportation issues facing all organizations, and may be accessed at http://sidearm.sites.s3.amazonaws.com/okstate.com/documents/2015/10/29/Team_Travel.pdf.

As a result of the OSU accident, the NTSB recommended that collegiate athletic associations review athletic team travel policies and develop a model transportation policy that could be implemented by member schools. In response, the NCAA and the American Council on Education (ACE) produced a transportation manual titled Safety in Student Transportation: A Resource Guide for Colleges and Universities, which contains comprehensive information and recommendations. It is available on the Internet at: http://s3.amazonaws.com/zanran_storage/www.hsutx.edu/ContentPages/44538022.pdf.

Ironically, and tragically, on November 19, 2011, shortly after the 10 year anniversary of the OSU accident, the OSU's women's head basketball coach Kurt Budke and assistant coach Miranda Serna were killed in an airplane crash while on a recruiting trip. The plane was privately owned, and piloted by an 82 year old former Oklahoma State Senator and OSU booster. The University reported that the University travel policy relating to flights did not apply to coaches on recruiting trips, but that the policy would be reviewed once again (Associated Press, 2011).

Organization-Owned Vehicles

For some organizations or entities, the use of an independent contractor is not a viable option due to the cost involved. Organization-owned vehicles are the most common means of transporting participants, and provide the next best transportation option. Since the organization owns the vehicles, it has the legal responsibility for the safe transportation of the participants. The organization has a duty to see that the vehicles are in safe operating condition and to see that the drivers are properly qualified. In the event of legal action, written policies, checklists, and maintenance records provide documentation that these duties have been fulfilled (see Chapter 4.11 *Risk Management Process* and Chapter 4.22 *Audits in Risk Management*).

Driver. Both the driver and the organization could be liable for the driver's negligence. In order to protect itself, the organization should require that the driver meet established qualifications that may include age, experience, special licenses, training, and verification of driving record. The organization should also use due diligence to determine that the driver complies with its transportation policies.

If an employee is acting in the course and scope of his/her employment when the accident occurs, both the driver and organization will be held liable for the driver's negligence. In *Foster v. Board of Trustees* (1991) (the significant case in this chapter), the Kansas court defined **course and scope of employment** as the employee "performing services for which he has been employed, or when he is doing anything which is reasonably incidental to his employment." However, when the driver commits an ***ultra vires*** **act** (i.e., an act that is outside the course and scope of employment), the negligence of the driver is not assigned to the organization. Examples of *ultra vires* acts include exceeding the speed limit, running a red light or stop sign, and deviating from the designated route. In *Smith v. Gardner* (1998), the court held that a baseball coach who, after an away game, drove the school van to purchase some tobacco products and decided to sightsee rather than returning to the hotel, was not acting within the course and scope of his employment. It is important to emphasize to drivers that they should not deviate from the scheduled route and itinerary without approval. In *Myricks v. Lynwood Unified School District* (1999), neither the school nor the city (which paid some of the expenses of the traveling summer basketball team) was liable for a driver's negligence. In this case, the driver was not acting within the scope of employment since this was a summer team not affiliated with the school.

Vehicle. Being able to establish the roadworthiness of the vehicle is of utmost importance to the organization. With all organization-owned vehicles, the organization is responsible for maintenance, and failure to maintain the vehicle in a safe condition leaves the organization liable. All vehicles need to be maintained by competent maintenance personnel in accordance with the owner's manual and vehicle specifications. Any vehicle with maintenance problems (e.g., defective lights, worn tires) should not be used until the condition is corrected and documented. Complete documentation of all maintenance should be stored in a safe, accessible manner.

Prior to each trip, each vehicle needs to be inspected by a competent authorized maintenance person. After each trip, a similar inspection should be performed and the driver should report any problems encountered on the trip. Pre-trip and post-trip vehicle inspection forms and checklists need to be developed for this purpose. Emergency equipment (e.g., first aid kit, flares, flashers, spare tires, and jack) should also be included on these forms and in these inspections.

Policies. Prior to the trip, an administrator or another authorized individual must be informed of and authorize travel plans. A trip request form should be utilized which includes the purpose of the trip, the destination, lodging arrangements, route, contact phone numbers, a list of those traveling, the person in charge, and the driver. Irrespective of the mode of travel (e.g., car, van, bus, plane), policies need to be established that address who can travel, maximum distances, traveling at night, disciplinary action, emergency procedures, driver qualifications, maximum driving hours in a 24 hour period, and oversight of the drivers.

Schools. State laws control the right to use a vehicle owned by a school to transport students to activities other than classes. Some states have no restrictions while others limit the use of school buses to providing transportation to and from classes. Other states restrict use depending upon the source of operating funds, which may be a critical factor in the application of governmental immunity.

In the past, state sovereign immunity statues provided liability protection for cities or schools when their employees were negligent. **Sovereign immunity** is the legal theory that a person cannot sue a governmental body without its permission. Now, however, most states have enacted **tort claims acts** that waive sovereign immunity and create liability for governmental entities under certain circumstances. Typically, these statutes make the governmental body liable for injuries caused by the operation of motor vehicles, but limit the amount of financial liability of the governmental institutions. The potential of liability for public colleges and universities, public secondary schools, school boards and districts, and other public agencies such as recreation departments, must be considered in light of these statutes (see Chapter 2.22 *Immunity*).

Privately Owned Vehicles

In some cases, organizations may find it convenient or necessary to use privately owned vehicles for transportation. The vehicles could be owned either by employees or by non-employees (e.g., parents, volunteers, and participants). In either case, liability for negligence is generally retained by the organization.

Before authorizing and approving use of private vehicles, risk management policies should be established to verify that both vehicles and drivers conform to adequate safety standards. These policies should require a physical inspection of the vehicle, review of maintenance records, and current insurance and registration on the vehicle. Policies should also ensure that the driver is properly licensed, has a good driving reputation, has a violation-free driving record, and has no impairments that would preclude driving.

Employee Vehicles. When an employee, as a part of his/her employment, uses a personal vehicle for transporting students or patrons, a **principal-agent relationship** is established. An organization is **vicariously liable** for employee negligence committed within the course and scope of employment. This will hold true even in the situation of an employee driving another employee's vehicle as in the case of *Murray v. Zarger* (1994). Richard Zarger was a volunteer diving coach for Cory Area (Pennsylvania) High School and was compensated with a small salary by the school district. While driving Cherese Murray, a member of the diving team, and three others in the head coach's car, Zarger was involved in an accident that resulted in Murray's death. Murray's estate filed suit for damages allegedly caused by the negligence of the school district, the car owner, and Zarger. The school district argued that Zarger was not an employee of the district on the following grounds: they had no control over the manner in which he performed; Zarger was not responsible for the swim team's performance; there was no agreement between Zarger and the school district; Zarger was used for his special diving skills only; and Zarger was an employee of two other companies. In holding that Zarger was an employee of the school district, the court stated that the definition of "employee" in the applicable state statute did not require that an employee be compensated or possess a formal employment contract with the government unit, but only that the person act in the government's interests (see Chapter 2.12 *Which Parties are Liable?*).

In this chapter's significant case, *Foster v. Board of Trustees* (1991), Christopher Foster was a basketball player making a recruiting visit to Butler County Community College. At the request of the head basketball coach, volunteer driver George Johnson picked Foster up at the airport, after which Foster was injured in a collision on the way to the campus. The issue in the case was Johnson's status as either an employee or a volunteer. The court examined the requirements for Johnson to be an employee (even though he was unpaid), found that he was an employee, and that his actions were negligent, thereby making the College vicariously liable for Johnson's negligence.

Use of privately owned vehicles increases the risks to the organization; therefore, the establishment and enforcement of **risk management policies** regarding the driver and the vehicle are essential (see Chapter 4.22 *Audits in Risk Management*). If the employee uses his or her privately owned vehicle as a service to the organization and in accordance with organization policy, most jurisdictions require that the driver exercise reasonable and ordinary care. The employee will be personally liable for negligent operation of the vehicle, in addition to the vicarious liability of the organization.

Non-employee Vehicles. When an organization has a duty to provide transportation and uses a private vehicle provided by someone who is not an employee, a principal-agent relationship is created just as it is when a privately owned employee vehicle is used. The organization is liable for the negligence of the driver. Because an organization has the least control when non-employee vehicles are used, this category creates the greatest risk of liability to the organization. It is imperative that the organization institute and enforce the risk management policies suggested at the beginning of the section, *Privately Owned Vehicles*.

Other Transportation Issues

State Codes

State legislatures enact laws that are related to transportation. However, sometimes it is not clear which part of the Code may apply. At issue in *Barnhart v. Cabrillo Community College* (1999) was whether or not an intercollegiate match was a field trip as defined under Title 5, California Code of Regulations, section 5545. The court of appeals ruled that since school-related athletic activities necessarily include extracurricular sport programs, the trip was a field trip and would fall under the immunity granted in the Code.

Although most states, and the U.S. Congress, have passed volunteer protection statutes providing **immunity** or **limited liability** for volunteers under certain circumstances, virtually all of those statutes contain exceptions for operation of motor vehicles. For example, the federal Volunteer Protection Act (42 U. S. C. § 14501, et. seq.) provides a defense for volunteers meeting the statutory criteria, but exempts from immunity a "volunteer operating a motor vehicle, vessel, aircraft, or other vehicle for which the State requires the operator or the owner of the vehicle, craft, or vessel to (A) possess an operator's license; or (B) maintain insurance." A typical state statute, the Texas Charitable Immunity and Liability Act of 1987 (Texas Civil Practice and Remedies Code § 84.001 et. seq.), creates volunteer liability for "the operation or use of any motor-driven equipment," but limits damages to the extent to which insurance coverage is required and exists, thereby protecting the volunteer who has secured the required insurance. Additional information on state volunteer driver laws may be found on the National Conference of State Legislatures website located at http://www.ncsl.org/research/transportation/information-for-state-volunteer-driver-liability-l.aspx (see Chapter 2.22 *Immunity*). The sport or recreation manager should have the organization's attorney review the state Codes that are applicable to transportation. Knowledge of the Codes is a valuable tool in the policy-making process and can serve to minimize litigation.

Many states are considering banning driving while using electronic communications devices such as cell phones, text messaging, etc. Clearly, a reasonably prudent person would not be doing those things while driving students or participants. The organization should adopt a strict policy that requires leaving the roadway and stopping the vehicle in order to use a cell phone or similar device, except in cases of emergency.

Workers' Compensation

If an individual is injured in an automobile accident while within his/her scope of employment and the business required the employee to be where the accident occurred as part of his/her job responsibilities, workers' compensation may be applicable. In *Bolton v. Tulane University* (1997), Bolton was an assistant basketball coach returning from a recruiting trip, and was a passenger in an automobile driven by another assistant coach. She was injured when the driver fell asleep and the car ended up in a ravine. Tulane provided workers' compensation benefits and paid most of her medical bills, but Bolton sued the University for negligence, seeking additional damages. In deciding the workers' compensation claim, the Court of Appeals held that Bolton was in the course and scope of her employment, and workers' compensation was her exclusive remedy.

School Buses and Vans

School buses are one of the safest forms of transportation in the United States. Every year approximately 485,500 school buses travel approximately 4.2 billion miles to transport 23 million children to and from school and school-related activities. The school bus occupant fatality rate of 0.23 fatalities per 100 million vehicle miles traveled is nearly 6 times lower than the rates for passenger cars. The National Academy of Sciences estimates that an average of 19 school-age children die in school-related traffic crashes each year; 5 are occupants of school buses and 14 are pedestrians near the loading zone of the school bus. Based on these statistics, the National Highway Safety Administration has denied the petition for installation of three-point seat belts for all seating positions (Federal Motor Vehicle Safety Standards; Denial of Petition for Rulemaking; School Buses) but does require such belts on all large buses (greater than 26,000 pounds). The effective date of this final rule is November 28, 2016. Optional early compliance is permitted. Data from NHTSA's Fatal Analysis Reporting System (FARS) shows that over the 10-year period between 2000 and 2009 that 83 percent of the fatalities in buses were in large buses.

Vans vs. School Buses. While most states require the use of school buses to transport children to and from school and school-related events, some states do not. Many states have statutes that address whether vans may be used to transport school children to school and extracurricular activities. The prudent sport and recreation manager should be aware of his/her state laws governing such transportation issues. State laws regarding 12 and 15 passenger vans can be found at: http://www.nasdpts.org/documents/vanssurveyfeb04.pdf.

Van Accidents. According to the National Highway Traffic Safety Administration (NHTSA), between 1997 and 2006 there were 1,374 15-passenger vans involved in fatal crashes that resulted in 1,090 fatalities to occupants of such vans. Eighty-three percent of people who died in single vehicle rollovers of these vehicles were not wearing safety belts. (NHTSA, 2008a).

15-Passenger Vans. Recent research conducted by the NHTSA (NHTSA 2008a) found that the risk of a rollover crash is greatly increased when ten or more individuals ride in a 15-passenger van. The risk of a rollover is increased because the center of gravity of the vehicle is raised when more passengers are transported. Placing any load on the roof also raises the center of gravity and increases the likelihood of a rollover. The result is less resistance to rollover and increased difficulty in steering. The NHTSA identified three major situations that can lead to a rollover in the 15-passenger vans: (1) The van goes off a rural road, striking a ditch, or soft shoulder; (2) the driver is fatigued or driving too fast, and; (3) the driver overcorrects. Further, 80% of people killed in 15-passenger vans were not wearing seat belts, and NHTSA estimates that people wearing seat belts are 75% less likely to be killed in a rollover crash. Organizations should create a policy requiring each person to wear a seat belt, and carefully adhere to the policy. Drivers should check compliance before beginning the trip. Other problems noted were the vans being driven by individuals under 22 years of age (lack of experience) and excessive speed. (NHTSA, n.d.)

On August 10, 2005, Congress passed the Safe, Accountable, Flexible, Efficient Transportation Equity Act: A Legacy for Users (23 U.S.C. § 101). Section 10309, 15-Passenger Van Safety, addresses new safety standards related to the use of 15-passenger vans. The Act defines a 15-passenger van as a vehicle that seats 10 to 14 passengers, not including the driver. The Act prohibits a school or school system from purchasing or leasing a new 15-pasenger van if it will be used significantly by, or on behalf of, the school or school system to transport preprimary, primary, or secondary school students to or from school or an event related to school, unless the 15-passenger van complies with the motor vehicle standards prescribed for school buses and multifunction school activity buses under this title.

Team travel by van has created a problem that does not have an easy solution. Budget restrictions and squad size are major considerations when choosing to use vans or other modes of transportation. If the organization chooses to use a 15-passenger van, Hawes (2000), LaVetter (2005) and McGregor (2000) have made the following policy recommendations that parallel the identified causes of van accidents:

- Eliminate 15-passenger vans, if possible, and travel more frequently by bus
- Eliminate coaches driving any vehicles, and enforce stricter driver qualifications
- Limit the number of passengers in vans to fewer than 10, remove the rear seats from 15-passenger vans, and place passengers and equipment forward of the van's rear axle
- Limit to 300 miles or five hours the number of hours or mileage driven by each driver per day, and avoid travel between midnight and 6 a.m.
- Check the van's tire pressure frequently—and before and after every trip
- Confer with your organization's insurance company or risk-management consultants.
- Schedule competition to permit travel by different teams sharing the same bus.
- Set age limits for the driver, hire outside drivers, and give extensive driver training.
- Require seat belts to be worn at all times
- Stress the importance of adhering to speed limits and the possible need to adjust speed due to weather conditions
- Monitor weather conditions and establish policies that permit the person in charge to decide when to spend the night in a hotel rather than continuing driving in hazardous conditions
- Review vehicle maintenance policies

Volunteer Drivers

Volunteer drivers can present a level of risk that needs to be addressed. (Nonprofit Risk Management Center, 2008). Most non-profit organizations' insurance policies cover volunteer drivers who, with permission, drive the non-profit's vehicles. In addition, some policies may also cover vehicles that are not owned by the non-profit such as those vehicles leased by the non-profit or personal vehicles driven on the nonprofit's behalf. For-profit organizations must check their policies to see if they have similar coverage. It is important to remember that volunteers will be covered initially by their insurance policies. An organization must check to insure that volunteers have at least the minimum coverage required in their state. Some risk management steps that the Center recommends are: (1) a driving program supervisor or coordinator should be identified; (2) volunteer drivers should be screened; (3) conduct guidelines should be created; (4) volunteers should be required to sign a pledge form; and (5) volunteers should be trained in emergency procedures.

Policy Recommendations

Every organization should have written travel policies, and should ensure that everyone adheres to them. Prudent administrators should ask and answer the following questions before approving any travel: (a) What is the purpose of the trip, (b) who is travelling, (c) who is in charge, (d) who is allowed to drive, and (e) are emergency procedures in place? The links earlier in this chapter would be a good starting point for developing such a policy. The policy should also require the following documentation: (a) a passenger checklist, (b) a key contact checklist provided to everyone involved in the travel decision, (c) emergency procedures for breakdowns and accidents, (d) accident report forms, if needed, and (e) pre- and post-trip vehicle inspection checklists. (McGregor, 2000).

The NCAA has developed an extensive resource guide "designed for anyone who cares about the safe transportation of college and university students." (NCAA, 2006) It is a comprehensive report, and should be required reading for any sport or recreation manager involved in transporting participants to and from events.

SIGNIFICANT CASE

Christopher Foster was a high school senior basketball player making a recruiting visit to Butler County Community College (BCCC). George Johnson, a volunteer driver acting on behalf of the BCCC coach, picked Foster up at the airport. Returning to the school, Johnson was involved in an accident that killed him, and severely injured Foster. Foster filed suit for injuries claiming negligence by both Johnson and BCCC. The primary issue in the case was whether Johnson was an "employee" of BCCC, thereby creating vicarious liability for the College. Among other legal issues involved in the case are negligence, damages, sufficiency of the evidence, vicarious liability through respondeat superior, comparative negligence, and course and scope of employment.

FOSTER V. BOARD OF TRUSTEES OF BUTLER COUNTY
Community College, Et Al.
United States District Court for the District of Kansas
771 F. Supp. 1122, 1991 U.S. Dist. LEXIS 11003

FRANK G. THEIS, UNITED STATES DISTRICT JUDGE

* * *

This case arose out of a motor vehicle collision occurring at the intersection of Airport/Yoder Road and U.S. Highway 50 in Reno County, Kansas on March 22, 1987. Plaintiff Christopher Foster was a passenger in a car driven by George Johnson. Johnson was travelling south on Airport Road. Plaintiff Gregory Clark was travelling east on Highway 50. Johnson failed to stop at the stop sign on Airport Road and collided with the tractor-trailer rig driven by plaintiff Clark. Johnson died as a result of the injuries he received in the accident. Foster and Clark were injured.

Foster, a native of Ohio, was a high school senior at the time of the accident. He was visiting Kansas on a recruiting visit at the request of defendant Randy Smithson, the head coach of the BCCC basketball team. Johnson picked Foster up at the Wichita airport at Smithson's request. Smithson had previously taken several other recruits to Hutchinson for the National Junior College Basketball Tournament. Contrary to the instructions given by Smithson, Johnson took Foster to Hutchinson to watch the game. Johnson telephoned Smithson from Hutchinson just prior to the collision. Smithson told Johnson to bring Foster to El Dorado. Johnson was en route to El Dorado when the collision occurred. * * *

At the close of the evidence, the court directed a verdict in favor of the plaintiffs on the issue of respondeat superior, ruling that Johnson was the servant or employee of the BCCC defendants and was acting within the scope of his authority at the time of the accident. On February 27, 1991 the jury returned a verdict finding plaintiff Clark 10% at fault and defendants 90% at fault. Damages in the amount of $ 2,257,000 were awarded to plaintiff Foster and in the amount of $ 302,000 to plaintiff Clark. After reducing the judgment by Clark's 10% fault, the court entered judgment in the amount of $ 2,031,300 in favor of Foster and $ 271,800 in favor of Clark. These motions for new trial followed.

* * *

The BCCC defendants raise the following issues: (1) the verdict is contrary to the evidence; (2) the amount of damages awarded is so excessive as to appear to have been based on passion and prejudice; (3) the court improperly allowed the jury to consider testimony regarding Johnson's lack of liability insurance coverage and evidence regarding the proof of insurance that must be provided by a student who is operating his own automobile in connection with a school function; (4) the court improperly refused to submit to the jury the questions of whether Johnson was the employee of BCCC and whether Johnson was operating within the scope of his employment at the time of the accident; (5) the court improperly refused to submit the issue of plaintiff Foster's comparative negligence to the jury; (6) the court improperly refused to allow testimony concerning plaintiff Clark's opinion that he considered the intersection where the accident occurred to be a dangerous one. * * *

* * *

* * * It was stipulated that Johnson ran the stop sign at the intersection of Airport Road and Highway 50. This fact alone would have been sufficient to support a finding that Johnson was 100% at fault, notwithstanding the defendants' accident reconstructionist who opined that Clark committed several driving errors. The evidence certainly was sufficient to support a finding that defendants were 90% at fault for the accident. * * * [T]he evidence was sufficient to support the damages awarded. The verdict was not clearly against the weight of the evidence.

* * *

B. Excessiveness of Verdict

* * *

As with all of its functions as trier of fact, the jury has wide discretion in determining the amount of damages that will fairly compensate the aggrieved party. * * *

> Absent an award so excessive as to shock the judicial conscience and to raise an irresistible inference that passion, prejudice, corruption or other improper cause invaded the trial, the jury's determination of the damages is considered inviolate. Such bias, prejudice or passion can be inferred from excessiveness. However, a verdict will not be set aside on this basis unless it is so plainly excessive as to suggest that it was the product of such passion or prejudice on the part of the jury.

* * *

The damage award to Clark is not so excessive as to shock the judicial conscience. The damages in this case included the normal personal injury damage components of past and future medical expenses, lost past and future income, pain and suffering and aggravation of pre-existing condition. The court also instructed the jury on loss of enjoyment of life as a component of the award for pain, suffering, disabilities, and disfigurement. * * *

* * *

C. Evidentiary Rulings

* * *

At trial, plaintiffs introduced evidence that the BCCC defendants were negligent in selecting Johnson as a gratuitous employee. An employer may be liable for injuries to a third person which are a direct result of the incompetence or unfitness of his employee when the employer was negligent in employing the employee or in retaining him in employment when the employer knew or should have known of such incompetence or unfitness. *Plains Resources, Inc. v. Gable*, 235 Kan. 580, 591, 682 P.2d 653 (1984). Johnson was unfit to drive a basketball recruit since he lacked a driver's license and liability insurance and his vehicle was not registered. The BCCC defendants could have discovered Johnson's unfitness for the task had any investigation been conducted. The evidence introduced by the plaintiffs was relevant to show the BCCC defendants' negligence. The evidence of Johnson's lack of liability insurance was relevant to show that the BCCC defendants failed to use due care in selecting Johnson to perform the task of transporting Foster.

* * *

2. *BCCC transportation and vehicle policies*

In connection with the direct negligence claim and the evidence of Johnson's lack of insurance, the plaintiffs offered evidence of BCCC policies regarding use of college and personal vehicles. The BCCC Policies and Procedures Manual provides in pertinent part:

College Vehicle Policy

College vehicles. All persons, included students, employees, and noncollege personnel, must have a driving record review and clearance. Requests for students and noncollege employees to drive college vehicles must be approved by the Director of Buildings and Grounds. These requests must be in writing and forwarded through the Business Office.

Personal vehicles. In cases when a college vehicle has been officially requested and is not available, the person making the request may be reimbursed for mileage if using a personal vehicle. In cases when an instructor or sponsor is not able to drive a college vehicle, a student with proof of current liability insurance may be permitted to use his/her car and be reimbursed for mileage with prior approval from the Director of Buildings and Grounds.

* * * The BCCC Athletic Policies and Procedures Manual provides that "School transportation must be used whenever possible. Private cars should be used only with permission of the athletic director." * * *

While these policies were not directly applicable since Johnson was not officially a coach, they indicated a general school policy of requiring an inquiry before allowing a teacher or coach to drive a BCCC vehicle and proof of liability insurance before allowing a student to use a personal vehicle for BCCC business. It was undisputed that Smithson did not obtain the permission of the athletic director before arranging for Johnson to transport Foster. This evidence was relevant to plaintiffs' claim that the BCCC defendants were directly negligent in appointing Johnson as a gratuitous employee charged with the duty of transporting Foster.

* * *

D. Directed Verdict on Respondeat Superior

At the close of the evidence, the court directed a verdict on two issues: that Johnson was the servant or employee of BCCC and that Johnson was acting within the scope of his authority at the time of the accident. The BCCC defendants challenge this ruling.

* * *

* * * Under Kansas law, the controlling test in determining the existence of agency, so that the doctrine of respondeat superior would apply, is the right to control the purported employee. *Hendrix*, 203 Kan. at 155; see also *Hughes v. Jones*, 206 Kan. 82, 88, 476 P.2d 588

(1970). When agency relationship is in issue, the party relying on the existence of an agency relationship to establish his claim has the burden of establishing the existence of the relationship by clear and satisfactory evidence. *Highland Lumber Co.*, 219 Kan. at 370.

An employer is not liable for a tortious act committed by his employee, unless the act is done by authority of the employer, either express or implied, or unless the act is done by the employee in the course or within the scope of his employment. *Beggerly v. Walker*, 194 Kan. 61, 64, 397 P.2d 395 (1964). Under Kansas law,

> An employee is acting within the scope of his authority when he is performing services for which he has been employed, or when he is doing anything which is reasonably incidental to his employment. The test is not necessarily whether the specific conduct was expressly authorized or forbidden by the employer, but whether such conduct should have been fairly foreseen from the nature of the employment and the duties relating to it.

Williams v. Community Drive-in Theater, Inc., 214 Kan. 359, 364, 520 P.2d 1296 (1974) (quoting PIK 7.04); *Hollinger v. Jane C. Stormont Hospital and Training School for Nurses*, 2 Kan. App. 2d 302, 311, 578 P.2d 1121 (1978). Whether an act is within the employee's scope of employment ordinarily presents a question to be determined by the jury. *Williams*, 214 Kan. at 365 (quoting 53 Am. Jur. 2d, *Master and Servant* § 427). The liability of the employer for the acts of the employee depends upon whether the employee, when he did the wrong, was acting in the prosecution of the employer's business and within the scope of his authority or whether he had stepped aside from the business and had done an individual wrong. *Hollinger*, 2 Kan. App. 2d at 311.

The determination of whether an employee was acting within the scope of his employment involves a consideration of the individual factual setting of each case, including objective as well as subjective considerations. *Focke v. United States*, 597 F. Supp. 1325, 1339 (D. Kan. 1982). Several factors are relevant to the determination of scope of employment. First, the key consideration in determining whether an employee is acting within the scope of employment is the purpose of the employee's act rather than the method of performance. This calls for consideration of the objective circumstances of the incident as well as the subjective thoughts of the employee. *Id.* at 1340-41. Second, the court must examine whether the employee has express or implied authority to do the acts in question, although in certain situations, an employer may be liable for the acts of the employee, even if the acts are done in excess of the authority conferred. *Id.* at 1341. Third, the determination of whether an employee's acts are incidental to his employment involves a consideration of whether the employee's acts were reasonably foreseeable by the employer. Finally, the time at which the agent commits the alleged wrongful act is a factor to be considered, although it is not accorded great weight. *Id.*

Defendants have not argued that Smithson lacked the authority to hire Johnson to assist in Smithson's recruiting duties. Johnson could be an employee or servant even though no compensation was paid or expected. Whether compensation was paid or not paid is not determinative.

The evidence that Johnson was acting as the employee of Smithson and was acting within the scope of his authority came from the testimony of defendant Smithson. Smithson had the right to control and indeed exercised significant control over Johnson. Smithson testified that he instructed Johnson on what to do that evening. Smithson testified that he instructed Johnson to pick up Foster from the airport, get him something to eat, take him to the motel in El Dorado and await Smithson's return from Hutchinson. Smithson gave Johnson twenty dollars to pay for dinner. Smithson further testified that when Johnson called late that evening from Hutchinson, Smithson told Johnson to bring Foster back to El Dorado as quickly and as safely as possible. Smithson gave Johnson directions on the two routes available from Hutchinson to El Dorado, via Highway 96 or via Airport Road/Highway 50. Smithson indicated that he used the Airport Road/Highway 50 route. Smithson told Johnson to ask for directions to Airport Road from where Johnson was located.

* * *

Construing the evidence in the light most favorable to the BCCC defendants, the evidence points only one way. There were no conflicts in the evidence. There was no evidence from which a reasonable mind could conclude that Johnson either was not the employee of BCCC or was not acting within the scope of his authority at the time of the collision. There was no evidence upon which the jury could properly find for the BCCC defendants on the issue of employment and scope. Defendants have pointed to no such evidence in the record.

* * *

IT IS BY THE COURT THEREFORE ORDERED that defendant Pringle's motion for a new trial (Doc. 152) is hereby denied as to plaintiff Clark and is moot as to plaintiff Foster.

IT IS FURTHER ORDERED that defendants Board of Trustees of Butler County Community College, Butler County Community College, and Randy Smithson's motion for a new trial (Doc. 153) is hereby denied as to plaintiff Clark and is moot as to plaintiff Foster.

CASES ON THE SUPPLEMENTAL WEBSITE

Clement v. Griffin (634 So. 2d 412, La.App. 4 Cir. 1994). This court discusses the duty owed by the defendant Community College to (1) maintain the vehicle, (2) select a qualified driver, and (3) properly train the driver. The court also discussed the defendant's vicarious duty to insure the driver properly operated the vehicle. In terms of transportation risk management, this case serves as a model course in "how *not* to do it."

Dixon v. Whitfield, 654 So. 2d 1230 (Fla. Dist. Ct. App., 1st Dist.). This Florida case affirms that schools have "a duty of reasonable care in providing (students) with safe transportation," but also verifies that schools have authority to hire independent contractors to operate the school buses. The defendants were found to be independent contractors rather than employees. By hiring independent contractors, the school avoided liability for the student's death.

Federal Insurance Company v. Executive Coach Luxury Travel, Inc., 944 N.E.2d 215 (2010-Ohio-6300). This case involved the deaths of five members of the Bluffton University baseball team on a spring break road trip. The issue before the court was whether the driver was covered by the University's insurance policy since he worked for an independent contractor. The Court held that under the terms of the policy, the driver was a covered insured. The case points out the necessity to determine whether or not a driver is covered under the Insured's policy.

Myricks v. Lynwood Unified School District, 87 Cal. Rptr. 2d 734 (Cal. App. 2 Dist. 1999). A girls' summer basketball team made up of players from their high school team, and coached by their high school coach, took an out-of-state trip to play in summer basketball tournaments. After suffering injuries in an accident, team members sued the school as well as the city (which provided some financial support). The court held this was not a school-sponsored activity, so the school was not liable. The court also found that the city was not liable since the city provided only financial support.

QUESTIONS YOU SHOULD BE ABLE TO ANSWER

1. Name numerous specific duties related to providing safe transportation.
2. What are the benefits of using an independent contractor as opposed to other means of transportation?
3. What are the criteria courts use to determine whether a company is an independent contractor?
4. Discuss the relative merits of travelling in organization-owned, employee-owned, or non-employed owned vehicles, buses or 15-passenger vans.
5. Prepare a basic transportation policy for your organization, including specific rules and regulations relating to transporting participants to an activity 200 miles from your normal meeting place.

REFERENCES

Cases
Barnhart v. Cabrillo Community College, 90 Cal. Rptr. 2d 709 (Cal. App. 6 Dist. 1999).
Bolton v. Tulane University of Louisiana, 692 So.2d 1113 (La. App. 4 Cir. 1997).
Foster v. Board of Trustees of Butler County Community College, 771 F. Supp. 1122 (D. Kan. 1991).
Murray v. Zarger, 642 A.2d 575 (Pa. Cmwlth. 1994).
Myricks v. Lynwood Unified School District, 87 Cal. Rptr. 2d 734 (Cal. App. 2 Dist. 1999).
Smith v. Gardner, 998 F. Supp. 708 (S.D. Miss. 1998).

Publications
Associated Press (2014, Sep 27). 4 College Softball Players Killed and 11 Others Are Injured in Oklahoma Crash. *The Oklahoman*. Retrieved February 15, 2016 from http://newsok.com/article/5346357
Associated Press (2014, Dec 2). 2 children, adult killed in Tenn. school bus crash. *Knoxville News Sentinel*. Retrieved February 10, 2016 from http://www.knoxnews.com/news/local/two-children-one-adult-killed-in-crash-between-two-school-buses-27-injured-ep-807986302-353850071.html

Associated Press (2011, Nov. 20). Oklahoma State plane crash: travel rules to be examined by University after deaths. *Huffington Post*. Retrieved Feb. 11, 2011 from http://www.huffingtonpost.com/2011/11/21/oklahoma-state-plane-crash-travel-rules_n_1104558.html.

Federal Motor Carrier Safety Administration (n.d.). *Keeping Kids Safe–A guide to hiring charter transportation*. Retrieved February 9, 2016 from http://www.ntassoc.com/uploads/FileLinks/cf5316da789b43b7a8f4fb3f26775515/Guide%20to%20Hiring%20Charter%20Transportation.pdf

Hawes, K. (2000, August 28). Warning: Road Risks Ahead. Precautions Reduce Dangers of Van-related Travel. *National Collegiate Athletic Association*.

LaVetter, D. (2005, December 5). Safety Must Drive Decisions in Van Use. *National Collegiate Athletic Association*

Lavigne, P. (2009, March 31). Bus Safety an Issue for Colleges. *ESPN*, retrieved February 11, 2012, from http://sports.espn.go.com/espn/otl/news/story?id=3997988&userid=63b283733d372ce0b01b1146c9fca4d4&messageid=308.

McGregor, I. (2000, February). Travel Trouble: Developing Transportation Policies and Procedures. *Athletic Business*, Retrieved February 9, 2016, from http://www.athleticbusiness.com/rules-regulations/developing-transportation-policies-and-procedures.html

National Collegiate Athletic Association (2006). Safety in Student Transportation: A Resource Guide for Colleges and Universities. Retrieved February 9, 2016 from http://s3.amazonaws.com/zanran_storage/www.hsutx.edu/ContentPages/44538022.pdf

National Collegiate Athletic Association (2006, July 3). Student transportation safety guide caps cooperative effort to limit risk. Retrieved February 9, 2016 from http://fs.ncaa.org/Docs/NCAANewsArchive/2006/Association-wide/student+transportation+safety+guide+caps+cooperative+effort+to+limit+risk+-+7-3-06+ncaa+news.html

National Conference of State Legislatures (2006). Information for State Volunteer Driver Liability Laws. Retrieved Feb. 9, 2016 from http://www.ncsl.org/research/transportation/information-for-state-volunteer-driver-liability-l.aspx

National Highway Traffic Safety Administration (NHTSA) (2008a). *Fatalities to Occupants of 15-Passenger Vans, 1997–2006*. Retrieved Feb. 11, 2012 from http://www-nrd.nhtsa.dot.gov/Pubs/810947.PDF.

National Highway Traffic Safety Administration (NHTSA) (n.d.) *Reducing the Risk of Rollover Crashes in 15-Passenger Vans*. Retrieved February 9, 2016 from http://www.mississippi.edu/rm/downloads/safety_resources/rollover_vans.pdf

National Transportation Safety Board (NTSB) (January 23, 2003). *Spatial Disorientation Cited in Crash of Airplane Carrying Oklahoma State University Athletes*. Retrieved February 9, 2016 from http://www.ntsb.gov/news/press-releases/Pages/Spatial_Disorientation_Cited_in_Crash_of_Airplane_Carrying_Oklahoma_State_University_Athletes.aspx

Nonprofit Risk Management Center (May/June, 2008). Retrieved February 10, 2016 from http://www.nonprofitrisk.org/library/articles/auto050608.shtml.

Oklahoma State University (2015). Retrieved February 9, 2016 from http://sidearm.sites.s3.amazonaws.com/okstate.com/documents/2015/10/29/Team_Travel.pdf.

School bus crash kills 2 students, seriously injures 3. *The Eagle*. Retrieved February 9, 2016 from http://www.readingeagle.com/ap/article/school-bus-crash-kills-2-students-seriously-injures-3.

Scott, J. (2015, August). Weekend Incidents Put Spotlight on Team Travel Safety. Athletic Business, retrieved February 9, 2016 from http://www.athleticbusiness.com/athlete-safety/two-killed-16-hurt-when-volleyball-team-s-bus-hits-car.html.

2.36 PRODUCTS LIABILITY

Rebecca J. Mowrey | Millersville University of Pennsylvania

Products liability cases typically represent an area of negligence resulting from a recreation or sporting good. Managers of sport and recreation are frequently responsible for the selection, purchase, installation, use, and maintenance of products utilized within their facilities and programs. Imagine a local fitness center without equipment; an indoor climbing facility minus a climbing wall or safety harnesses; a track and field team without starting blocks, hurdles, or any jumping or throwing apparatus. Without their equipment, the first two businesses would merely be empty buildings, and the track and field team would not be very competitive. These examples make us acutely aware of how dependent the sport and recreation industries are upon specialized products.

Products liability relates primarily to the negligent action of a manufacturer or seller who produces a defective product; hence the product is unreasonably dangerous to the user. While it is true that most professionals working in sport and recreation are not manufacturing or selling products, claims of products liability may provide recourse against liable parties involved *throughout* the chain of production and distribution of products. Therefore, sport and recreation professionals may be deemed as suppliers, included among those who loan, rent, or assign equipment to others, and can be liable if defective equipment is issued and the supplier should have known about the defect.

A case example that illustrates this point is found in *Everett v. Bucky Warren*, (1978). The court held that the coach, acting as a supplier, negligently selected for and supplied to his team defective and dangerous hockey helmets. In contrast to the decision in *Everett*, more recently in *Fischer v. Olde Towne Tours, LLC* (2011), the court held that the defendant was not in the supply chain and therefore not liable for product defects. While enjoying a cruise of the Panama Canal, Jennifer Fisher and her husband elected to participate in a snorkeling excursion. Transportation to the snorkeling site involved a five mile trip in a two—person inflatable dinghy. During the ride to the snorkeling location a large wave struck the boat and Fisher grabbed the mooring line as instructed, but the line failed. She fell backward, striking her back against a fiberglass bench, sustaining injuries to her lumbar vertebrae which required surgery.

The trial court granted summary judgment to Olde Towne on the negligence claims as the signed liability waiver was in order. The products liability charges failed as a matter of law when the court determined that the tour operator was only an end user of the dinghy. The plaintiff claimed that Olde Towne Tours was liable for the defective condition of the dinghy because it either assembled the dinghy incorrectly or modified it by removing the grab holds. During the trial Olde Towne Tours provided evidence that the dinghy in which Fisher was injured was not equipped with grab holds for passengers but that the dinghy arrived from the manufacturer fully assembled. Furthermore, Old Towne argued that they did not design, manufacture, distribute, test, or assemble the dinghy. If the plaintiff had claimed liability due to Olde Towne Tours providing defective equipment, this case may have had a different outcome.

The contrast between the *Everett* decision in 1978 and the *Fischer* decision in 2011 is worthy of further consideration. Section 20 of the Third Restatement (1997) identifies the scope of liability when one "provides a combination of products and services." In *Fisher* the court held that Old Towne merely furnished services to the public; in this case directions and a mode of transportation, but not products *and* services, thus placing the tour company outside the "chain of distribution". Therefore, while a sport or recreation management professional may be involved in products liability cases as one who selects, purchases, receives, installs, maintains, and uses products; the role of others who only *use* products to provide services may be deemed as being outside the "chain of distribution". Furthermore, sport and recreation managers who do not assemble nor modify equipment may be identified as end users and not responsible for using equipment received in a defective state directly from the manufacturer.

FUNDAMENTAL CONCEPTS

Categories of Product Defects

In this section we will examine the three categories of product defects commonly recognized by the courts and classified by the Restatement (third) of Torts (1997); namely, **design defects, manufacturing defects, and marketing defects**. Manufacturers make many decisions regarding products, including design, material selection, and construction. At each stage of a product's life, the product may fail or be defective, thereby rendering the product to be unreasonably dangerous. We will first examine how things might go wrong with a product from its very inception, the design stage.

Design defects occur in products that cause harm as a result of issues related to the faulty design of a product. Lots of good ideas do not hold up well to the requirements or demands of actual usage. We have an example of a design defect in *Brett v. Hillerich & Bradsby Co.* (2001). The Hillerich and Bradsby Company manufactured baseball bats. Designers working with Hillerich and Bradsby discovered ways to make use of new aluminum materials resulting in improved performance by batters. High school pitcher and plaintiff Jeremy Brett, was seriously injured when hit by a ball coming off of one of these newly designed bats. He alleged that the Air Attack 2, an aluminum composite bat designed by Hillerich & Bradsby Co., had a design defect because it allowed batted balls to reach dangerous speeds, exceeding the reaction time needed for pitchers to protect themselves. The decision in this case was in favor of Brett, resulting in several states banning the use of Air Attack 2 and other similarly designed aluminum bats.

Manufacturing defects refer to production errors that result in flaws to an otherwise defect-free product, design, and manufacturing process. In *Diversified Products Corp. v. Faxon* (1987) Faxon purchased a weight machine manufactured by Diversified Products Corporation. He assembled the machine according to the manufacturer's instructions. While he was performing a standing curl, an eyebolt on the curl bar broke, causing him to fall backward. The eyebolt was a factory-assembled piece of the machine and Faxon had not altered this bar nor tampered with the eyebolt. Faxon's fall resulted in serious injuries to his spine. The court decided in favor of Faxon, finding sufficient evidence to support the plaintiff's claim that the eyebolt was defective while it was still in the possession of Diversified Products Corporation, and that this was a manufacturing defect that the Corporation should have detected prior to selling the machine to Faxon.

Marketing defects occur when the warnings or instructions accompanying a product are inadequate, rendering the product not reasonably safe. Warnings must address both foreseeable misuses of a product (van der Smissen, 1990; *Whitacre v. Halo Optical Products, Inc.*, 1987) as well as dangers inherent in the normal use of the product. In some jurisdictions, even if there is an absence of design and manufacturing defect, failure to warn may stand alone as a cause of action (*Garrett v. Nissen*, 1972; *Pavlides v. Galveston Yacht Basin*, 1984). We see an example of marketing defect in *Sullivan v. Nissen Trampoline Company* (1967). Sullivan was using a mini–trampoline called an Aqua Diver. This product consisted of a mini–trampoline that people could bounce on and then dive into a pool or lake. As Sullivan bounced on the Aqua Diver, her foot became caught in the webbing that connected the trampoline to the base. The Nissen Trampoline Company did not provide any warning labels alerting users to this potential risk even though their own pre-market testing had shown this to be a risk.

We see another example of marketing defect in *Dudley Sports Co. v. Schmitt* (1972). Schmitt, a high school student, was simply sweeping the storage room floor where a baseball pitching machine was located. As he was sweeping the floor, the throwing arm of the unplugged and inactive pitching machine suddenly and unexpectedly snapped forward causing severe facial injuries to Schmitt. The court ruled that the manufacturer was negligent in designing the machine without a protective guard around the throwing arm mechanism. The court also concluded that Dudley Sports Co. failed to provide an adequate warning about the specific risks associated with their pitching machines, namely that the machine's throwing arm could be triggered when unplugged. According to the court, the warning label only implied that the machine could be dangerous when in use. It is not uncommon for plaintiffs to state more than one category of product defect as we see in *Covell v. Bell Sports, Inc.* (2011), which includes allegations of both design defect and marketing defect (see the Significant Case in this chapter).

With the increasing attention directed towards sport and recreation related post-concussive syndrome (PCS), products designed for head protection may be the focus of increasing litigation (theconcussionblog.com). Products designed for protection will also need to keep up with improving athletic performances including speed and strength. We see this illustrated in *Wolf v. Rawlings Sporting Goods Co.* (2010), where the plaintiff's skull was fractured after he was struck in the head by a pitch. Wolf sought damages based upon strict products liability, negligence, and breach of warranty; claiming that the helmet was only made to withstand a sixty-mile-per-hour pitch.

Now that we are familiar with the three categories of defects that might make one liable for harm associated with products, we will examine the three legal causes of action associated with products liability as well as the defenses for each.

Causes of Action and Defenses

In Chapter 2.10 you read about negligence and strict liability. To review, **negligence** is an unintentional tort that injures an individual in person, property, or reputation. **Strict liability** means that a defendant can be held liable without fault. In the context of products liability, strict liability would apply when there is nothing wrong with the design, manufacturing, or warning. You might be wondering how that is possible. Courts have held that some products are just too dangerous to exist. Therefore, if a manufacturer decided to design, manufacture and market such a product, an injured party could claim, under strict liability, that the product could not possibly be made safe and should not have been produced in the first place. **Breach of warranty** occurs when a product fails to fulfill either the expressed or implied warranty.

In Figure 2.36.1 you will examine the three causes of action under which recovery for products liability may be sought and the defenses to each cause of action.

Strict Liability Considerations

Now that we have the basics of products liability covered, we will examine some issues related to strict liability a bit further. Typically only manufacturers and sellers are subject to strict liability for defective products. In *Escola v. Coca-Cola Bottling Co. of Fresno* (1944), Justice Traynor summarizes the burden strict liability places upon manufacturers to resist bringing to market products that are hazardous to life and health.

> Even if there is no negligence, however, public policy demands that responsibility be fixed wherever it will most effectively reduce the hazards to life and health inherent in defective products that reach the market. It is evident that the manufacturer can anticipate some hazards and guard against the recurrence of others, as the public cannot.

So how does one determine if a product is **unreasonably dangerous**? Without a consistent gauge for measuring or determining what is "reasonable" and "unreasonable," product manufacturers may place themselves in jeopardy of strict liability. One solution may be the use of a **risk-utility balancing test** (Restatement (third) of Torts (1997)) to determine whether or not a product design is unreasonably dangerous. Under this test, a product is considered unreasonably dangerous if the dangers outweigh the social utility of the product. The factors commonly considered in risk-utility balancing are as follows:

1. The gravity of the danger
2. The likelihood of injury
3. The obviousness of the danger
4. The feasibility and expense of an alternate design
5. The common knowledge of consumers
6. The adequacy of warnings
7. The usefulness and desirability of the product as designed

By examining a product against the seven factors of the risk-utility balancing test, those associated with product design and development are better situated to defend against strict liability. For example, if the dangers presented by a product are great but there is high demand from consumers for the product and the dangers and

FIGURE 2.36.1   COMMON CAUSES OF ACTION AND DEFENSES UNDER PRODUCTS LIABILITY LAW

Negligence	Strict Liability	Breach of Warranty
A manufacturer, supplier, or seller may be sued for negligence in design, testing, manufacturing, inspecting, packaging, labeling or distribution of a defective product, or for failure to warn (failure to warn users of the non-obvious risks presented by the product, including the dangers of misusing the product).	This cause of action may prevail when a product is deemed to be so inherently and unreasonably dangerous that it cannot truly be made safe; regardless of the amount of care given to the design, construction, labeling, and inspection. For example, a jury may conclude that street luge is inherently dangerous and should not occur, thus finding those who manufacture street luge equipment liable using the theory of strict liability. No defense to strict liability is available if • the product is determined to be unreasonably dangerous, • a defect existed at the time of the sale, and • the product was used properly and was the cause of harm.	When a product fails to perform in a way that is promised (warranted), whether this warranty is expressed or implied, a breach of warranty has occurred. Product liability law is concerned with three types of warranties: • express warranty; • implied warranty of merchantability; and • implied warranty of fitness for a particular purpose (See remainder of chapter for discussion of these three types of warranties).
Defenses for Negligence	**Defenses for Strict Liability**	**Defenses for Breach of Warranty**
No evidence of duty, breach, proximate cause, or harm. Specifically: 1. Product defect is unproven. 2. Product defect is not the cause of the harm. 3. Evidence that an adequate warning of non–obvious risk was provided and assumed. 4. The danger/risk were open and obvious. 5. The failure to warn was not the cause of the harm. 6. The actions of the plaintiff contributed to the harm. 7. Reasonable care was used by the manufacturer, supplier, or seller; however, the defect was not detectable via reasonable care.	1. Product was altered following purchase or misused in an unforeseeable manner by the plaintiff. 2. An adequate warning was provided and/or secondary assumption of risk applied to the plaintiff. 3. Wear and tear of the product, due to use and age of the product, was appropriate and predictable. 4. The actions of the plaintiff contributed to the harm. 5. See discussion of the risk–utility balancing test below.	1. The product was altered. 2. The product was mis-used. 3. The product was not properly installed. 4. The user failed to properly maintain the product. 5. The actions of the plaintiff contributed to the harm. 6. An adequate warning was provided and/or secondary assumption of risk applied to the plaintiff.

warnings are clear and commonly known, the balancing test may be useful in defending against strict liability. The potential use of this balancing test is perhaps most notable when considering consumers' avid pursuit of extreme sport and recreation activities and the increasing demand for products to satisfy these pursuits. Similarly, when the risk of using a product is high but the cost of redesigning the product and thereby making it safer is low, a product designer and developer may feel challenged to do so. We will now turn our attention toward special considerations associated with breach of warranty as a cause of action in products liability cases.

Breach of Warranty Considerations and Warranty Liability

There are several issues related to product warranty with which sport and recreation managers should be familiar. The traditional common law rule regarding warranties is that the plaintiff must have entered into a contractual relationship, or **privity of contract**,[1] with the defendant to claim breach of warranty as a cause of action. For example, under the privity of contract doctrine, a seller could be liable to the buyer, but the seller would not be liable to others because they were not in privity of contract, or direct contact, with the seller. More

---

[1] "**Privity of contract** is one of the most basic rules of the common law of contract and one of the defining tests for the validity of any contract. This doctrine essentially determines who is a party to contract and who may rely upon the rights granted under the contract to sue another" (Lim, 2008). The privity of contract doctrine dictates that only persons who are parties to a contract are entitled to take action to enforce it.

recently; however, states are abandoning the privity of contract doctrine, as claims of breach of warranty are now codified and primarily governed by the **Uniform Commercial Code (UCC)**.

The UCC reflects the expanding liability of manufacturers and sellers, including the expectation that the seller, not the consumer, should bear the burden of determining that products are safe and conform to established standards. For example, in Alternative A of the UCC, the version adopted by the most jurisdictions, the seller is liable for the personal injuries to the "buyer, members of the buyer's family, and guests in the buyer's home." Perhaps this expectation for product sellers is broader in scope than what you presumed. Under Alternative A of the UCC, a seller sending athletic equipment home with a purchaser would need to provide guidance regarding where and how it should be stored and secured so siblings or other family members or house guests would not be injured by the equipment. As you can imagine, the increased liability for sellers and manufacturers has resulted in a proliferation of product warnings and warranty conditions.

Implied Warranty. Under the UCC, implied warranties must accompany products at the time of selling / purchasing. These warranties must include the **implied warranty of merchantability**, promising that a product is "of fair average quality," and the **implied warranty of fitness**, promising that a product is "fit for the ordinary purposes for which such goods are used." (U.C.C. 2-314). More specifically, the implied warranty of fitness addresses the product warranty promise extended to the buyer/user that is relying on the seller's expertise to provide an appropriate product fit for his/her particular purpose. We see this illustrated in *Filler v. Rayex Corp.* (1970), where Filler, a high school baseball coach had purchased sunglasses from the Rayex Corporation based upon their marketing guarantees featuring "instant eye protection." The Rayex advertisements and product packaging specifically identified baseball players as an ideal user group for the Rayex product, as the players would benefit by using these "scientific lenses." Filler lost his right eye when a baseball hit the Rayex lens and it shattered. As explained by the court of appeals "Since they lacked the safety features of plastic or shatterproof glass, the sunglasses were in truth not fit for baseball playing, the particular purpose for which they were sold" (*Filler v. Rayex Corp.*, 1970, p. 338).

Express Warranty. Under the UCC, a seller's **express warranty** may be provided in several ways. An express warranty is an oral or written statement of fact, promise, description, or model that a buyer relies upon when purchasing products. As you make a decision about which baseball pitching machine to purchase, you know you are considering the machine that best meets your needs due to the express warranty (product facts; description; photo; model, etc.). However, you want to know if the height of the pitch can be varied and the seller says "absolutely", but upon delivery you discover that the height cannot be varied. Under the UCC, the court would say that the verbal "absolutely" resulted in an express warranty as this information helped to form the basis of your decision to purchase that particular pitching machine.

Another consideration related to breach of warranty is **misrepresentation of warranty**. This occurs when claims are made, primarily in the marketing or selling phase of a product's life, which are untrue or misleading. When the user's actions are based upon the misrepresentation of warranty and he/she is harmed or property is harmed, the claim to products liability may be misrepresentation of warranty. As an example of misrepresentation of warranty, we will examine *Hauter v. Zogarts* (1975). Louise Hauter purchased a "Golfing Gizmo" for Fred, her 13-year-old son. The Gizmo consisted of a golf ball attached to an elasticized cord that was secured to the ground with metal pegs. Zogarts, the defendant and manufacturer of the Golfing Gizmo, marketed the product as a device that would improve one's swing with this claim: "COMPLETELY SAFE BALL WILL NOT HIT PLAYER." Fred Hauter suffered permanent brain damage after the cord wrapped around his golf club and the ball hit his head with great force. The Hauter's successfully sued, alleging misrepresentation of warranty and breach of expressed and implied liability.

They also successfully sued under strict liability as the court found that the Golfing Gizmo was too dangerous to exist. Although the Hauter case was decided before the Risk-Utility Balancing Test was established, it is easy to see that the Golfing Gizmo would likely fail on all seven factors of the Risk-Utility Balancing Test. In Hauter, the court ruled in favor of the plaintiff on all four causes of action. Regarding the charge of misinformation, the court found that the defendant breached the implied warranty of merchantability as the golf training device, intended for use by novices, would likely injure novice users.

Please note that the marketing on the package encouraged the user to "drive the ball with full power." The combination of this encouragement and the "COMPLETELY SAFE" promotion, according to the court, served to significantly misrepresent the risk to the user. It is virtually impossible to ever claim that a product is "100 percent" anything; "completely safe"; or even "safe" or "foolproof." It is best not to make such claims as part of programs or activities associated with sport or recreation.

In summary, design defects, manufacturing defects, or marketing defects resulting in property damage or personal injury to a user or bystander may lead to products liability for a manufacturer, seller, distributor, or supervisor. The causes of action used by plaintiffs in products liability cases will be negligence, strict liability, and/or breach of warranty. As mentioned earlier in the *Wolf v. Rawlings Sporting Goods Co.*, in some cases the plaintiff will use all of these causes of action.

Although some products are simply too dangerous to exist (such as the previously discussed Golfing Gizmo), other useful and quality products also disappear as a result of products liability claims. Sport and recreation professionals are wise to protect against these products liability cases as cost containment and free enterprise issues, in addition to and secondary to the desire to keep constituents as safe as possible. What is our connection to cost containment and free enterprise? When a manufacturer is successfully sued for design, manufacturing, or marketing defects; that corporation may be hampered financially to the point of bankruptcy, or the corporation may elect to no longer participate in the segment of the industry in which it has been sued. The result of these corporate decisions has a palpable impact upon sport and recreation professionals, resulting in less choice for consumers seeking products, and less competitive pricing. Alternatively, in many cases design improvements are the outcome of products liability cases. For example, sport and recreation management has seen significant design changes in helmets to accommodate growing concerns regarding concussive syndrome.

As you read the following case, consider all that you have learned from reading this chapter. The introduction to the Significant Case provides questions for you to respond to as you read through this design defect case.

SIGNIFICANT CASE

This case will provide you with the opportunity to do some critical thinking, problem—solving, and apply your knowledge regarding products liability while you read the arguments and decision. The importance of industrial standards such as those established by the United States Consumer Product Safety Commission (CPSC) is of paramount importance to many products liability cases and is well documented within Covell v. Bell. Also at issue within this case is the use of Restatement (Second) of Torts and Restatement (Third) of Torts.

COVELL V. BELL SPORTS, INC.
United States Court of Appeals, Third Circuit.
651 F.3d 357 (2011)

ALDISERT, UNITED STATES CIRCUIT JUDGE.

David W. Covell and Margaret Covell, who are plenary guardians of their adult son David F. Covell, appeal from a jury's verdict for the defendant in their products liability suit against Easton-Bell Sports, Inc. They urge us to order a new trial on the ground that the District Court erred by admitting evidence and charging the jury pursuant to sections 1 and 2 of the Restatement (Third) of Torts (1998), rather than section 402A of the Restatement (Second) of Torts (1965). Having held in *Berrier v. Simplicity Manufacturing, Inc.*, 563 F.3d 38 (3d Cir.2009), cert. denied, U.S, 130 S.Ct. 553, 175 L.Ed.2d 383 (2009), that federal district courts applying Pennsylvania law to products liability cases should look to sections 1 and 2 of the Restatement (Third) of Torts, and seeing no reason to reverse course now, we will affirm.

David F. Covell, a 36 year-old schoolteacher, sustained serious brain injuries when he was struck by a car while bicycling to work in 2007. Tragically, he is now so disabled that his parents (the "Covells") have been appointed his legal guardians. In that capacity, they filed this products liability suit against Easton-Bell Sports, Inc. ("Bell"), which manufactured the "Giro Monza" bicycle helmet their son wore during the collision.

* * *

At trial, and over the Covells' strident objections, the District Court permitted Bell to introduce expert testimony that was based in part upon the United States

Consumer Product Safety Commission's Safety Standard for Bicycle Helmets (the "CPSC Standard").

* * *

The Covells offered their own expert testimony regarding the CPSC Standard. Ultimately, experts for both sides agreed that the CPSC Standard forms the starting point for any bicycle helmet design, and that the Giro Monza helmet satisfied the CPSC Standard in all respects. At the trial's conclusion, the District Court instructed the jury pursuant to sections 1 and 2 of the Restatement (Third) of 360*360 Torts. The Court also instructed the jury that, in determining whether the Giro Monza helmet was or was not defective, it could consider evidence of standards or customs in the bicycle helmet industry, including the CPSC Standard. The jury returned a verdict for the defense, finding that the helmet was not defective. The Covells timely filed this appeal.

* * *

In past products liability cases, the Supreme Court of Pennsylvania has looked to section 402A of the Restatement (Second) of Torts. *E.g., Webb v. Zern*, 422 Pa. 424, 220 A.2d 853, 854 (1966) ("We hereby adopt the foregoing language [of § 402A] as the law of Pennsylvania."). Section 402A makes sellers liable for harm caused to consumers by unreasonably dangerous products, even if the seller exercised reasonable care.

* * *

Restatement (Second) of Torts § 402A (1965). Section 402A thus creates a strict liability regime by insulating products liability cases from negligence concepts. See id. § 402A(2)(a); *Azzarello v. Black Bros. Co.*, 480 Pa. 547, 391 A.2d 1020, 1025-1026 (1978) (charging courts to avoid negligence concepts when instructing a jury pursuant to § 402A.).

* * *

The Supreme Court of Pennsylvania has repeatedly addressed confusion arising from a core conflict in the structure of section 402A itself: Section 402A instructs courts to ignore evidence that the seller "exercised all possible care in the preparation and sale of his product," § 402A(2)(a), yet imposes liability only for products that are "unreasonably dangerous," § 402A(1). In many cases it is difficult or impossible to determine whether a product is "unreasonably dangerous" to consumers without reference to evidence that the seller did or did not exercise "care in the preparation" of the product. *See Schmidt v. Boardman Co.*, 11 A.3d 924, 940 (Pa.2011) ("This no-negligence-in-strict-liability rubric has resulted in material ambiguities and inconsistencies in Pennsylvania's procedure."); *see also Phillips v. Cricket Lighters*, 576 Pa. 644, 841 A.2d 1000, 1015-1016 (2003) (Saylor, J., dissenting).

* * *

Nonetheless, the Supreme Court of Pennsylvania has endeavored to segregate strict liability's "product-oriented" analysis from the "conduct-oriented" analysis of negligence. *Phillips*, 841 A.2d at 1006 ("[W]e have remained steadfast in our proclamations that negligence concepts should not be imported into strict liability law . . ."). In so doing, Pennsylvania's high court has stated repeatedly that negligence concepts have no place in products liability. *E.g., id.; Azzarello*, 391 A.2d at 1025-1026. That endeavor has not always been successful, *see Davis v. Berwind Corp.*, 547 Pa. 260, 690 A.2d 186, 190 (1997) (holding that if a "product has reached the user or consumer with substantial change," liability depends upon "whether the manufacturer could have reasonably expected or foreseen such an alteration of its product.") (emphasis added), nor has it been uniformly embraced by the Justices of that Court, *see Schmidt*, 11 A.3d at 940 (disapproving of Pennsylvania's "almost unfathomable approach to products litigation") (quotation omitted).

* * *

The District Court followed *Berrier*. In so doing it admitted evidence of the CPSC 363*363 Standard as relevant to the amount of care Bell exercised, and it instructed the jury according to the framework set forth in sections 1 and 2 of the Restatement (Third) of Torts. The Covells contend that these decisions by the District Court were erroneous, because they would be improper under section 402A of the Restatement (Second) of Torts. They maintain that section 402A "has been the law in Pennsylvania since it was adopted in *Webb v. Zern*, [422 Pa. 424, 220 A.2d 853 (1966)]" and that "[n]o decision of the Pennsylvania Supreme Court has changed this." If the District Court had applied the Restatement (Second) of Torts, it would not have permitted Bell to admit evidence of the CPSC Standard (because due care is irrelevant under the Restatement (Second) of Torts), and it would not have instructed the jury to consider whether the Giro Monza helmet was "unreasonably" dangerous (because the only relevant inquiry under the Restatement (Second) of Torts is whether the product itself was defective). The Covells maintain that each of these decisions by the District Court violated the doctrine of *Erie Railroad Co. v. Tompkins*, 304 U.S. 64, 58 S.Ct. 817, 82 L.Ed. 1188 (1938), as set forth in *Van Dusen v. Barrack*, 376 U.S. 612, 84 S.Ct. 805, 11 L.Ed.2d 945 (1964), which requires federal courts sitting in diversity to apply state substantive law. 376 U.S. at 638, 84 S.Ct. 805.

* * *

We will affirm the District Court's application of sections 1 and 2 of the Restatement (Third) of Torts. Much of the briefing from the parties, and all of the briefing from the amici, is devoted to which Restatement of Torts is best as a matter of policy, and which most logically extends the decisions of the Supreme Court of Pennsylvania—all of which are issues we waded through and resolved only two years ago when we decided *Berrier*.

* * *

We conclude that the state of the law in Pennsylvania is exactly as it was when we decided *Berrier*. Absent a change in Pennsylvania's law, we see no reason to upset our precedent. Applying *Berrier*, we hold that the District Court did not err in using the Restatement (Third) of Torts to guide its decisions to admit evidence, and to frame its jury instructions.

* * *

The Covells' fallback contention is that even if sections 1 and 2 of the Restatement (Third) of Torts were the law of Pennsylvania (i.e., even if the jury instructions in this case were correct), the District Court nonetheless erred by admitting evidence of the CPSC Standard. The Covells point out that the CPSC Standard is an "industry regulation" as described in section 4 of the Restatement (Third) of Torts, which—unlike sections 1 and 2—has365*365 not been cited or discussed by the Supreme Court of Pennsylvania. *Cf.Berrier,* 563 F.3d at 40 (holding only that the Supreme Court of Pennsylvania would apply sections 1 and 2 of the Restatement (Third) of Torts to products liability cases), The Covells maintain that if we affirm the District Court on this point we will apply section 4 before the Supreme Court of Pennsylvania does so—something to be avoided in a diversity case. *Cf.Van Dusen,* 376 U.S. at 638, 84 S.Ct. 805. We conclude that we need break no new ground today; we will affirm the District Court without resort to section 4 of the Restatement (Third) of Torts because the CPSC Standard was admissible pursuant to section 2.

The Covells are correct that most jurisdictions applying the Restatement (Third) of Torts to products liability cases hold that evidence of compliance with product regulations is admissible to prove whether or not a product is defective. *E.g., Doyle v. Volkswagenwerk Aktiengesellschaft,* 267 Ga. 574, 481 S.E.2d 518, 521 (1997).

* * *

In connection with liability for defective design or inadequate instructions or warnings: (a) a product's noncompliance with an applicable product safety statute or administrative regulation renders the product defective with respect to the risk sought to be reduced by the statute or regulation; and(b) a product's compliance with an applicable product safety standard or administrative regulation is properly considered in determining whether the product is defective with respect to the risks sought to be reduced by the statute or regulation, but such compliance does not preclude as a matter of law a finding of a product defect.

The District Court admitted such evidence in this case. It permitted Bell to demonstrate its compliance with the CPSC Standard, 16 C.F.R. § 1203.1, as evidence that its helmet was not "defective," under section 2 of the Restatement (Third) of Torts. The Covells contend that this was reversible error because section 4, not section 2, of the Restatement (Third) of Torts deals with governmental regulations, and—setting aside all debate over the validity of our holding in *Berrier*—there has been no indication from the Supreme Court of Pennsylvania that it would apply section 4. Because section 4 is not in play, they contend, there was no basis upon which the District Court could have admitted evidence of Bell's compliance with the CPSC Standard, regardless of which version of the Restatement it applied. For support, they rely upon *Lewis v. Coffing Hoist Division, Duff-Norton, Co.,* 515 Pa. 334, 528 A.2d 590, 594 (1987).

* * *

Whether the District Court erred in admitting evidence of the CPSC Standard thus depends not on pre-*Berrier* decisions like *Lewis*, but upon the post-*Berrier* legal framework that controls Pennsylvania products liability cases. In our view, it is highly unlikely that the Supreme Court of Pennsylvania would apply sections 1 and 2 of the Restatement (Third) of Torts (allowing negligence concepts), but not section 4 (providing for relevant industry regulation). We have difficulty imagining a negligence-friendly products liability regime that ignores compliance or non-compliance with pertinent state and federal regulations. At any rate, we need not determine whether the Supreme Court of Pennsylvania would adopt section 4 because we agree with Bell that evidence of its compliance with the CPSC Standard was relevant to section 2 of the Restatement (Third) of Torts as applied in *Berrier*, and was admissible pursuant to the Federal Rules of Evidence. The relevancy provisions of the Federal Rules of Evidence control in this case because they are "arguably procedural." *See Kelly v. Crown Equip. Co.,* 970 F.2d 1273, 1278 (3d Cir. 1992) (Federal Rules of Evidence that are "arguably procedural" control in diversity actions, "notwithstanding Pennsylvania law to the contrary."). Under the Federal Rules of Evidence, "[r]elevant evidence' means evidence having any tendency to make the existence of any fact that is of consequence to the determination of the action more probable or less probable than it would be without the evidence," Rule 401, and "[a]ll relevant evidence is admissible, except as otherwise provided by the Constitution of the United States, by Act of Congress, by these rules, or by other rules prescribed by the Supreme Court pursuant to statutory authority," Rule 402.

Applying this standard, we conclude that evidence of Bell's compliance with the CPSC Standard was relevant to the jury's inquiry because it went to at least two facts of consequence under section 2 of the Restatement (Third) of Torts, section 2. First, the CPSC Standard sets forth detailed rules for impact resistance and testing, and for labels and warning—both on the helmet and its sales packaging. Evidence that Bell complied with the CPSC Standard's requirement for impact resistance testing makes it "more probable," Rule 401, that "all possible care was exercised in the preparation and marketing of the product," Restatement (Third) of Torts § 2(a). Second, evidence that Bell complied with the CPSC Standard makes it "less probable," Rule 401, that "the foreseeable risks of harm posed by the product could have been reduced or avoided by the provision of reasonable instructions or warnings," Restatement (Third) of Torts § 2(c). Of course, such evidence was not conclusive on these points, but it was relevant and therefore presumptively admissible under the Federal Rules.

Our conclusion in this respect—i.e., that industry standards and government regulations are relevant to facts of consequence in this case—is also in line with the Commentary 367*367 to section 2 of the Restatement (Third) of Torts. Comment (b) explicitly states that industry regulations may be relevant to a plaintiff's case under section 2, irrespective of section 4.

* * *

Further, comment (d) states that defendants may admit evidence of industry practice to show that an alternative design would not have made their product safer: The defendant is thus allowed to introduce evidence with regard to industry practice that bears on whether the omission of an alternative design rendered the product not reasonably safe. While such evidence is admissible, it is not necessarily dispositive. *Id.* § 2 comment (d). The commentary to section 2 of the Restatement (Third) of Torts thus buttresses our conclusion that evidence related to the CPSC Standard was properly admitted in this case. In sum, we conclude that we need not consider whether evidence of the CPSC Standard was admissible pursuant to section 4 of the Restatement (Third) of Torts because in this case the evidence was admissible pursuant to section 2, as applied in *Berrier*. We will therefore affirm the District Court.

* * * *

We have considered all of the arguments advanced by the parties and conclude that no further discussion is necessary. The judgment of the District Court will be AFFIRMED. Honorable Jane A. Restani, Judge of the United States Court of International Trade, sitting by designation.

* * * * * *

We have considered all of the arguments advanced by the parties and conclude that no further discussion is necessary. The judgment of the District Court will be AFFIRMED. Honorable Jane A. Restani, Judge of the United States Court of International Trade, sitting by designation.

CASES ON THE SUPPLEMENTAL WEBSITE

Bouillon v. Harry Gill Company (1973 Ill. App. LEXIS 1604). From *Bouillon* we learn about a plaintiff severely injured while pole vaulting. As you read the case, note the cause of action brought against Gill, the athletic equipment manufacturing giant.

Muller v. Jackson Hole Mt. Resort (2006 U.S. App. LEXIS 32098). *Muller* will lead you to consider the role of the service provider and the importance of documenting maintenance in products liability cases. Describe what impact, if any, the risk-utility balancing test has in this case.

Sanders v. Laurel Highlands River Tours, Inc., (1992 U.S. App. LEXIS 15094). While reading *Sanders*, consider if the UCC applies to this case, and if so, in what ways?

Traub v. Cornell University (1998 U.S. Dist. LEXIS 5530). Identify all three products liability causes of action. Make note of the potential liability of different types of defendants, including the manufacturer, retail distributor, and general contractor for the basketball court.

Wissell v. Ohio High School Athletic Association, (1992 Ohio App. LEXIS 904). In *Wissell* we learn about a football player who was rendered a quadriplegic during a high school game. As you read this case, identify the grounds on which the plaintiffs appealed as well as the original products liability causes of action.

QUESTIONS YOU SHOULD BE ABLE TO ANSWER

1. Compare and contrast the three common causes of action in products liability cases.

2. Discuss how manufacturers might use the risk-utility balancing test.

3. Research the Hillerich & Bradsby Company on line and discover what changes they have made to their product line as a result of being named as a defendant in multiple products liability cases.

4. What are the three categories of product defects identified in the Restatement (third) Tort law?

5. What is meant by the Implied Warranty of Fitness?

REFERENCES

Cases
Anthony Pools, Inc. v. Sheehan, 455 A.2d 434 (Md. 1983).
Arnold v. Riddell, Inc., 882 F. Supp. 979 (D. Kan. 1995).
Back v. Wickes Corp., 378 N.E.2d 964 (Mass. 1978).
Bhardwaj v. 24 Hour Fitness, Inc., 2002 Cal. App. Unpub. LEXIS 3288 (Cal. App. 2002).
Brett v. Hillerich & Bradsby Co., 2001 U.S. Dist. LEXIS 26319.
Byrns v. Riddell, Inc., 550 P.2d 1065 (Ariz. 1976).
Covell v. Bell Sports, Inc., 651 F.3d 357; 2011 U.S. App. LEXIS 14252.
Curtis v. Hoosier Racing Tire Corp., 299 F. Supp. 2d 777 (N.D. Ohio 2004).
Diversified Products Corp. v. Faxon, 514 So.2d 1161 (Fla. App. 1987).
Dudley Sports Co. v. Schmitt, 279 N.E.2d 266 (Ind. App. 1972).
Escola v. Coca-Cola Bottling Co. of Fresno, 150 P.2d 436 (1944).
Everett v. Bucky Warren, Inc., 376 Mass. 280, 380 N.E.2d 653 (1978).
Filler v. Rayex Corp., 435 F.2d 336 (1970).
Fisher v. Olde Towne Tours, LLC, 2011 Cal. App. Unpub. LEXIS 5856.
Garrett v. Nissen, 498 P.2d 1359 (N. Mex. 1972).
Gentile v. MacGregor Mfg. Co., 493 A.2d 647 (N.J. Super. L. 1985).
Green v. BDI Pharmaceuticals, 2001 La. App. LEXIS 2390 (La. App. 2001).
Hauter v. Zogarts, 120 Cal. Rptr. 681, 534 P.2d 377 (1975).
Hurley v. Larry's Water Ski School, 762 F.2d 925 (11th Cir. 1985). http://theconcussionblog.com
Levey v. Yamaha Motor Corp., 825 A.2d 554 (N.J. Super. 2003).
Mohney v. USA Hockey, Inc., 2001 U.S. App. LEXIS 3584 (6th Cir. 2001)
Mohney v. USA Hockey, Inc., 2005 U.S. App. LEXIS 14373 (6th Cir. 2005).
Pavlides v. Galveston Yacht Basin, 727 F.2d 330 (5th Cir. 1984).
Perton v. Motel Properties, Inc., 497 S.E.2d 29 (Ga. App. 1998).
Rodriguez v. Riddell Sports, Inc., 242 F.3d 567 (5th Cir. 2001).
Traub v. Cornell University, 1998 U.S. Dist. LEXIS 5530 (N.D.N.Y. 1998).
Sullivan v. Nissen Trampoline Company, 1967 Ill. App. LEXIS 938, (1967).
Vantour v. Body Masters Sports Industries, Inc. 147 N. H. 150; 784 A. 2d 1178 (N.H. Supreme C. 2001).
Whitacre v. Halo Optical Products, Inc., 501 So.2d 994 (La. App. 2 Cir. 1987).
Wolf v. Rawlings Sporting Goods Co., 2010 U. S. Dist. 116294.

Publications
Garrett, M. C. (1972). Allowance of punitive damages in products liability claims. *Georgia Law Review, 6*(3), 613–630.
Lim, R. (2008). The Doctrine of Privity of Contract. Http://www.articlealley.com/article_655389_18.html.
Nader, R. (1972). *Unsafe at any speed: The designed-in dangers of the American automobile*. New York: Grossman.
Plant, M. L. (1957). Strict liability of manufacturers for injuries caused by defects in products: An opposing view. *Tennessee Law Review, 24*(7), 938–951.
tulane.baseball.arbitration@gmail.com (The Baseball Arbitration Competition)
van der Smissen, B. (1990). *Legal liability and risk management for public and private entities*. Cincinnati, OH: Anderson Publishing Company.

Legislation
Restatement (Second) of Torts §402A (1965).
Restatement (Third) of Torts §2 and related comments (1997).

2.37 HOSPITALITY AND TOURISM LAW

Sarah J. Young | Indiana University

Imagine for a moment that you are traveling to an exotic island beach resort in the Caribbean where your travel agent booked reservations for you at a four-star hotel right on the beach. Your departure day finds you waiting for a flight delay that extends into hours causing you to miss your connecting flight and arrive one day late for your vacation. Upon check-in at the hotel, you discover they have overbooked and, because you are a day late, have switched your reservation to a three-star hotel two miles inland. The hotel shuttle is involved in a minor traffic accident en route to your new accommodations, causing you to crack your head on the window. Woozy, you finally get to your hotel, only to find that a family of mice has already taken up residence in your room. You inform the front desk that you must have another room (a clean one!) and go to the restaurant for a bite to eat while the hotel straightens out the room situation. At the restaurant, you eat some bad seafood, which resurrects itself at 3 o'clock in the morning. While you lay curled up on your bed watching the television because your stomach hurts, you learn there is a category-four hurricane headed straight for your location, and authorities are mandating evacuation of the island immediately.

Sound like a tourist's worst nightmare? This might lead one to think about the legal duties and responsibilities of travel agents, airlines, hotels, and restaurants to tourists. Although many of the legal concepts and principles discussed in other chapters of this text apply to tourism settings, there are unique legal aspects that arise because of the very nature of tourism. Barth (2009) recognized the interconnectivity of travel and hospitality as one phenomenon that makes legal issues in tourism unique. For example, vacation packages often include transportation, lodging, meals, and recreation activities. When something goes wrong, and the tourist does not receive what was promised, which service provider should be held liable? It is the reliance of one or more service providers on others for quality performance that makes the area of tourism law more complex. Jurisdiction issues, differences in how travel terms are perceived, identity of the actual service provider, weather, civil unrest, and disease are all factors that can create problems for travelers, tourists, and hotel guests, as well as result in litigation. These factors are phenomena over which hotel and restaurant managers, travel agents, and tour operators may or may not have control. Yet, no one in the travel supply chain is immune from legal action. Therefore, what follows is an overview of legal issues unique to managers in the hospitality and travel industries.

FUNDAMENTAL CONCEPTS

Hotels

Dating back to English common law, innkeepers and hotel operators had a duty to receive travelers who registered as guests. Today, common law and statutory law identify hotels, motels, and other establishments providing lodging as places of public accommodation and continue to obligate hotel operators to receive all guests. There are circumstances, however, under which the hotel manager may refuse to register an individual as a guest. Typically, if a person is intoxicated, drunk or disorderly, suffers from an obvious contagious disease, brings property into the hotel that could pose a hazard to other guests (e.g., firearms, explosives, animals), or cannot pay for the price of the room, the manager has the right to refuse accommodation (Jeffries, 1995).

For a person visiting a hotel's property to qualify as a guest, the visit must be for the primary purpose for which the hotel operates—the rental of rooms suitable for overnight stay. The duty owed a guest by a hotel is the same as that owed to an invitee. In other words, the hotel owes a guest a reasonably clean and safe accommodation. An example of this duty is provided in *Minass v. HHC TRS Portsmouth, LLC* (2014) where plaintiff was bitten by bedbugs while staying one night at defendant's hotel. When plaintiff went to sleep she did not have any bug bites, but when she awoke she experienced pain, itchiness, and discomfort from hundreds of bedbug bites. The discovery process revealed defendant's hotel had approximately 25 to 30 complaints of bedbugs on their property in the previous 21 months, but only two cases of bedbugs had been confirmed. The legal duty of a hotel to provide reasonably safe accommodations extends to its parking lot as well. This legal principle is illustrated by *Spahr v. Ferber Resorts* (2011) where plaintiff, a registered guest, fell six feet into a ditch from the parking lot in the dark. The court ruled that the hotel knew or should have known about the ditch and realized the unreasonable risk of harm it posed to guests. Both of these cases demonstrate the hotel breaching its duty to provide reasonable (i.e., clean and safe) accommodations.

In another example of the hotel's duty to its guests, plaintiff who was wheelchair bound, fell and sustained significant injuries when she attempted to transfer herself from the hotel's shower seat to her wheelchair (*Bray v. Marriott International*, 2016). Plaintiff claimed the hotel was negligent in failing to provide accessible accommodations in violation of the Americans with Disabilities Act.

Overbooking

General contract law is enacted every time a potential guest inquires with the hotel as to the availability of a room for a definite period of time at a specified price. Once agreed upon, either verbally or in writing, a breach of this agreement by either the prospective guest or the hotel can result in liability for damages. The hotel reservation, once made and confirmed, constitutes a contract and binds the hotel to provide accommodations as well as the guest to stay there. Yet, many hotels overbook their rooms because of the persistent problem of no-show guests. History and experience prove that a certain percentage of guests will not use their reservations. As a result, some hotels overbook by the expected attrition rate, and then are not able to accommodate all their reservations when the expected no-show guests do actually appear. *Onyx Acceptance Corp. v. Trump Hotel & Casino Resorts, Inc.* (2008) showcases a classic example of the liability that can occur from intentional overbooking. Plaintiff planned a holiday party as a reward for its most valued customers at the Trump Taj Mahal Casino Resort in Atlantic City. Onyx prepaid for a banquet and 60 guest rooms at a cost of approximately $29,000. The hotel represented that those room reservations were guaranteed. On the arrival date, 26 guests were not accommodated because the front desk staff informed them that the hotel was sold out and had overbooked. Onyx sued defendants for breach of contract for which the court awarded them treble (i.e., triple) damages of the prepaid amount.

Protecting Guest Property

Guests bring a variety of personal property with them during their stays on hotel premises (*Whittemore v. Country Inn & Suites*, 2014). Typically guests bring money, clothing, jewelry, computers, sports equipment, and perhaps, a vehicle. What is the legal responsibility of the hotel to their guests for this personal property? Historically, this responsibility is based on a rule of absolute liability holding the innkeeper liable for any loss of guest property that was "*infra hospitium*, or within the inn" (Garner, 2009, p. 850). This doctrine emanated from the time when not every innkeeper was honest and often was the culprit of missing guest property. There were exceptions, however, to the absolute liability rule. Loss of property because of an act of God (e.g., tornadoes, floods, earthquakes) and loss of property by a public enemy (e.g., terrorists or acts of war) were two exceptions for which the innkeeper was not held liable. A third exception was the negligence of the guest, such as leaving bags unattended in a hotel lobby, sidewalk, hallway, or public area.

Today most states have enacted statutes limiting liability for guest property loss. If a hotel adheres to the statutes it will be liable for the loss only up to an established maximum amount (e.g., $1,000). This is the case even if a guest's property is worth far more than the maximum amount. Although each state's statutes vary in the details, there are common provisions that hotels must generally follow:

1. The hotel must provide a safe available for guest property.
2. The hotel must post notices communicating the availability of safes.
3. The hotel must communicate to guests that their liability for lost or stolen property is limited.
4. The hotel must communicate the maximum recovery amount allowed.

The availability of limited liability provides an incentive for hotel managers to comply with the strict interpretation of these statutes. Without evidence of compliance, the hotel becomes liable under common law for the full amount of the lost or stolen property. Hotels can be held liable beyond the limits of the statute when theft occurs from the safe provided to guests. As illustrated in *Liberty Mutual v. Zurich Insurance* (2010), the hotel guests of a Ritz-Carlton hotel placed jewelry and cash in their guest room wall safe while touring the sites of Chicago. Upon their return they discovered their valuables missing from the safe. Defendants paid the guests $1 million in compensation for their loss.

Within the hospitality industry there are times when a hotel or restaurant manager may be entrusted with a guest's property that is covered under a type of contract law other than the limited liability statute. The theory of bailment is often used by hotels and restaurants for valet parking, coat checks, laundry services, and luggage storage. A **bailment** is defined as the delivery of goods or personal property by one to another with the expectation the property will be returned in the same condition it was received (Garner, 2009). When one hands over possession of his/her personal property for safekeeping by another and the party knowingly has exclusive control over the property, a bailment is established. The individual who gives his/her property to another is known as the **bailor**, whereas the individual who accepts responsibility for the property is known as the **bailee**. Morris, Marshall, and Cournoyer (2008) identified the essential elements of a bailment as personal property, delivery of possession, acceptance of possession by bailee, and a bailment agreement, either implicit or express. Bailments only involve tangible, personal property like cars, clothing, and sports equipment.

The *Arguello v. Sunset Station* (2011) case provides not only an example of a bailment, but also an attempt of the hotel to apply the limited liability statute. Plaintiff left his car keys with the valet at Sunset Station Casino located in Henderson, Nevada, and received a claim ticket. When he was ready to leave the resort property it was discovered his car had been stolen from the valet parking lot. Upon recovering his car the following day in a stripped condition, plaintiff filed a lawsuit against the hotel for breach of a bailment contract. The hotel argued it was shielded by Nevada's limited liability statute and only owed plaintiff a maximum of $750 to which the district court agreed. The appellate court reversed the lower court's ruling by stating the intent of the statute was to limit liability for loss of personal property within a vehicle, not for the vehicle itself and that the hotel had breached the bailment agreement.

Guest Privacy

A registered hotel guest has the right to privacy and peaceful possession of his/her room without disruption from hotel personnel. Morris et al. (2008) identified five exceptions to this right of hotel guests. An innkeeper is authorized to enter a guest's room for normal maintenance, to warn of imminent danger, for nonpayment of the room, when requested to enter by the guest, and upon expiration of the rental period. Unless there is a legal basis for entry, hotel staff and non-guests are not permitted to enter a guest's room at will as illustrated by *State of Ohio v. Wright* (2013). Police were called to a hotel for a disturbance call sometime after midnight. Upon arrival they found defendant naked, sweating profusely, and foaming at the mouth after ingesting PCP. He had been pounding on the doors of other guest rooms and had damaged the hotel hallway. After Wright was transported to the hospital, hotel staff asked police officers to check his room for damages. Without a warrant or Wright's permission to enter his room, a police officer discovered not only damage to Wright's room but also a bag of crack cocaine and a PCP vial. When Wright was indicted for drug possession and trafficking, he claimed the search of his hotel room was unconstitutional under the Fourth Amendment. Both the trial and appellate courts agreed by stating unless a guest is evicted from his hotel room, he maintains an expectation of privacy from unreasonable searches and seizures. However, sometimes guests do engage in illegal activity in their hotel rooms. If evidence of illegal activity is discovered by a hotel employee who is legally in the guest's room, the hotel has an obligation to report their findings to the police. This was the case in *State of Minnesota v. Yang* (2014) where housekeeping staff making up the guest's room discovered a glass pipe used to smoke narcotics partially sticking out from underneath a bed pillow. Additionally, hotel security found plastic bags containing a large amount of white crystal-like substance that appeared to be methamphetamine, a digital scale, numerous small baggies, and several small paper scoops.

Another dimension of guest privacy was deliberated in the U. S. Supreme Court in 2015. In Los Angeles, California, the Municipal Code compels every hotel operator to keep a record containing personal information of every guest for up to 90 days and to make this information available to any LA police officer on demand. The penalty for failing to do so is arrest of the hotel operator. A group of hotel operators challenged the constitutionality of this local ordinance under the Fourth Amendment claiming these business records were the private property of the hotel. The U. S. Supreme Court ruled the ordinance was unconstitutional because it was penalizing hotel operators who declined to turn over their records without affording them an opportunity for judicial review prior to compliance (*City of Los Angeles v. Patel*, 2015).

Recreational Facilities

Often hotels provide additional services and facilities such as spas, swimming pools, workout rooms, trails, putting greens, and other specialized facilities for their guests' enjoyment. In most states, the general standard for hotels is to exercise reasonable care in preventing injury to a guest who uses these activity areas. Whether reasonable care is exercised depends on the facts and circumstances in each case. In *Lovett v. Omni Hotels Management Corp.* (2015), plaintiff filed tort claims after she was injured by a Xering resistance band which was part of a Get Fit Kit which was a benefit for Omni's Select Guest Loyalty Program. Summary judgment for the hotel was denied because instructions or warnings about how to use the Xering band were not provided with the kit.

Because they are attractive to guests, especially children, most hotels have aquatics facilities on their property, yet aquatics facilities represent a potential liability to the hotel operator. Most hotels provide signage around the pool area indicating that no lifeguard is on duty and that guests should swim at their own risk (*Yi v. Pleasant Travel Service*, 2011). However, the duty to maintain a reasonably safe pool area for hotel guests is emphasized in *Krueger v. La Quinta Inn* (2014). Here, the appellate court reversed and remanded the trial court's dismissal when plaintiff stepped on broken glass in the hotel's pool severely cutting his foot. The court ruled that the hotel had constructive notice of the pool's defective condition.

Because hotel guests have access to recreational activity areas does not always mean the area is within the hotel's **sphere of control**. *Fabend v. Rosewood Hotels and Resorts* (2004) illustrates this concept. Plaintiff sued the Rosewood Hotel and the National Park Service (NPS) after he was injured bodysurfing in the Virgin Islands. He claimed the hotel failed to warn him of a dangerous shorebreak condition on the beach, which created a forceful wave driving him into the sand and leaving him a quadriplegic. Although the hotel advertised the white, sandy beaches in their promotional materials, the NPS maintained physical control over all the beaches. Additionally, NPS provided signs and brochures warning visitors of the dangerous conditions of the park. The court ruled that because the beach was not in the hotel's sphere of control, it did not have a legal duty to warn swimmers of the shorebreak danger.

Travel and Tourism

Jurisdiction

Most plaintiffs expect to pursue their filed claim in their local courts, yet when travel is involved, and the defendant resides in a different state, the plaintiff's local court must have jurisdiction over both plaintiff and defendant in order for the claim to move forward. Travel, by its very nature, creates issues that call into question the authority of a court to rule on legal matters. For example, a resident of Pennsylvania was injured while on vacation at a beachfront hotel in San Juan, Puerto Rico. The injured party sued the hotel for negligence after she tripped and fell on a concealed and buried rope (*Spear v. Marriott Hotel Services, Inc.*, 2016). At issue was the jurisdiction of the court, Pennsylvania or Puerto Rico, to hear the case. **Jurisdiction** is defined as the authority of the court to decide a matter of controversy (Garner, 2009) as well as maintain control over the subject matter and parties to the dispute. In most states, jurisdiction over corporate defendants is determined by the amount and frequency of business defendants conduct in a given state. Generally, "doing business" depends on factors such as the existence of an office in the state, the solicitation of business, the presence of bank accounts or property in the state, and the presence of employees.

The importance of establishing jurisdiction is illustrated in *McCrann v. Riu Hotels* (2010) where plaintiffs fell while horseback riding on a tour arranged by an Aruban enterprise that promoted its services in the defendant's hotel. Because defendant's primary offices were located in Spain and Florida, plaintiffs had to show that their home state of New York had jurisdiction. Because defendant had no bank accounts, property, or employees in New York, plaintiffs were unable to produce evidence showing defendant "engaged in any systematic or continuous business solicitation in New York" (p. 7). The court therefore ruled that a New York court did not have jurisdiction over defendant. Another issue related to jurisdiction is whether a hospitality service provider purposefully avails itself of the privilege of conducting activities within a state (*Gutman v. Allegro Resorts Marketing Corp.*, 2015). In order to establish **purposeful availment** the service provider must first have direct, relevant contact with the state. Second, those contacts must be purposeful rather than random, and thirdly, the service provider must seek some benefit or profit by availing itself to the jurisdiction. For more information regarding jurisdiction, see Chapter 1.10 *The Legal System*.

Internet Sales. The sale of travel and vacation packages via the Internet affects the jurisdiction of legal claims. Many courts have adopted a sliding scale analysis categorizing websites as passive to interactive for the purpose of determining whether specific jurisdiction exists. A **passive website** containing information about the hotel or travel destination available to the general public, but not providing a way to take reservations, is viewed as an insufficient basis for establishing jurisdiction. In *Cervantes v. Ramparts, Inc.* (2003), a California plaintiff filed suit against the Luxor Hotel located in Las Vegas, Nevada, after he slipped and fell in the hotel's restroom. Plaintiff tried to establish that California courts would have jurisdiction over the defendant because defendant maintained a website accessible in California. The court disagreed, noting the hotel's website was passive and only provided information about the Luxor. On the other end of the scale, an **interactive website** is generally characterized by information, e-mail communication, detailed descriptions of goods and services, and online sales. *Conley v. MLT, Inc.* (2012) illustrates this type of web site. Plaintiff, a Michigan resident, sought relief for negligence from OccidentalHotels.com after suffering a serious head injury at a hotel resort in Cozumel, Mexico. Defendant provided to the general public a fully interactive website through which customers and travel agents made reservations and booked stays at Occidental's resorts. Furthermore, defendants had actively solicited business on its website and allowed consumers to enter into legal contracts based upon services advertised, resulting in defendants effectively placing their business and its services into the stream of commerce of the state of Michigan. However, in *Martino-Valdes v. Renaissance Hotel* (2011) the court ruled the mere presence of an interactive website, on its own, was not enough to establish general jurisdiction, especially if it was not used to make a reservation.

Forum Non Conveniens. Related to issues of jurisdiction is ***forum non conveniens***, which refers to the discretionary power of the court to "divest itself of jurisdiction" when convenience of the parties and justice would be better served if the case was brought forth in another forum (Garner, 2009, p. 726). In determining whether a different venue would be more convenient for the parties involved in a case, the court typically considers three factors (*Fallhowe v. Hilton Worldwide, Inc.*, 2015).

First, the court must determine whether an alternative forum exists. For example, a New York couple was the guest of the Sandals Grande St. Lucian Resort when the wife was injured from a mirror falling from the wall in their hotel room and landing on her foot. Saint Lucia, an independent island country in the Caribbean, was deemed an adequate alternative forum because its legal system is based on that of the United Kingdom and recognized negligence claims (*Muraco v. Sandals Resort International*, 2015).

Secondly, the court must determine the private interest of the litigant including the relative ease of access to sources of proof, availability of compulsory processes to obtain unwilling witnesses' attendance in court, cost of obtaining attendance of witnesses, the possibility of viewing the premises, and any other practical considerations that make the hearing of a case more expedient and less expensive. As an example, the court in *Ellis v. Marriott International* (2011) ruled it was more reasonable and convenient for the court proceedings to be moved from Pennsylvania to Hawaii where plaintiff's injury occurred.

The third and final consideration balances public interest factors such as court congestion, the burden of jury duty on the people of the community who have no relation to the litigation, and the appropriateness of trying a case in a forum familiar with the governing law of the case. A good illustration of how *forum non conveniens* works is found in *Goldstein v. Hard Rock Café International, Inc.* (2013). Plaintiff slipped and fell injuring his knee on a walkway at the Hard Rock Hotel in the Dominican Republic. Plaintiff filed suit for negligence in Florida district court, yet defendant moved to dismiss the case on the basis of *forum non conveniens*. The U. S. Court of Appeals (11th Cir.) determined the Dominican Republic was an available and adequate alternative forum, the two Dominican physicians who treated plaintiff's injuries could not be compelled to testify in U. S. Court, and Dominican law would be most appropriate to determine an injury which occurred in the Dominican Republic.

Forum Selection Clauses. Often tourist destinations and common carriers will include a **forum selection clause** in the agreement between agency and tourist citing any litigation must be brought forth in the court where the agency is headquartered. Dickerson (2004) explained that hospitality and travel providers institute forum selection clauses as a way to discourage guests or travelers from prosecuting their legal claims.

Historically and traditionally the courts have held firm in the enforcement of forum selection clauses once the terms and conditions of a contract have been reasonably communicated (*Starkey v. G. Adventures, Inc.*, 2015). For example in *McArthur v. Kerzner International Limited* (2015), the contract plaintiffs signed with their travel agent for an Atlantis Resort vacation in the Bahamas specifically and clearly stated that any legal disputes had to be litigated by the Supreme Court of the Bahamas.

The U. S. Supreme Court in *Carnival Cruise Lines, Inc. v. Shute* (1991) also noted the forum selection clause must be deemed fundamentally fair. Similarly, in *Gonzalez-Martinez v. Royal Caribbean Cruises LTD.*, (2015), the court ruled the forum selection clause was fair and enforceable, primarily because plaintiff had plenty of time to review her ticket, and the explicitly stated terms contained within.

Although the majority of forum selection clause cases favor defendants, this is not always the case. *Stobaugh v. Norwegian Cruise Line* (1999) provides a good example of when a travel service provider's forum selection clause was deemed fundamentally unfair. Plaintiffs, residents of Texas, had contracted with the cruise line to take a seven-day cruise to Bermuda departing August 31. They received their passenger tickets with all the terms of the agreement, including the forum selection clause, on August 8. A few days before their departure, plaintiffs learned of several tropical storm systems in the Atlantic Ocean. On inquiring with Norwegian about refunds if they decided to cancel on account of the weather, they were told they should proceed with the trip and trust the judgment of the ship's captain. Plaintiffs did as suggested, and defendant's ship sailed into Hurricane Eduardo, which allegedly resulted in physical and emotional injuries to many passengers on board. Plaintiffs filed a class action lawsuit in Texas court against Norwegian Cruise Lines, who asserted their forum selection clause (based in Florida) as a basis to dismiss the case. The court ruled against the cruise line stating that because their forum selection clause was not clearly communicated to passengers until after they paid in full for the cruise, the clause was not fair nor enforceable.

Transportation

Transportation is another major dimension of the travel and tourism industry with airplanes, cruise ships, buses, tour buses, trains, and taxis serving as common carriers. A **common carrier** is one who takes on the responsibility to transport from place to place any person who chooses to employ it for hire (Garner, 2009). *A common carrier owes its passengers the highest degree of care* with the passenger–carrier relationship continuing until the passenger has had a reasonable opportunity to reach a place of safety. Furthermore, *common carriers are vicariously liable for their employees' intentional and negligent torts, even when they are committed outside the scope of employment* (*Twardy v. Northwest Airlines, Inc.*, 2001).

Airlines. Air travel is the method of choice for long-distance travel for many tourists. The contract between an airline and its passengers is known as a **tariff** and outlines the terms to which the passenger agrees when purchasing a ticket. The terms of the tariff affect how passengers are treated and vary among the major carriers. For example, not all airlines have the same policy regarding flight delays and how passengers whose flights are delayed are handled. The terms of handling flight delays are contained in the tariff, or ticket information. On the other hand, federal regulations require all airlines to provide a standard compensation to passengers who are bumped from their flights due to overbooking. Although most passengers accept the airlines' compensation, there are some who choose to claim damages for breach of contract of the tariff. A bumped passenger claiming contract damages may sue for costs of alternate transportation, meals, and compensation for inconvenience caused by the bump. Illustrated in *Stone v. Continental Airlines* (2005), plaintiff and his thirteen-year-old daughter were bumped on Christmas day from their flight from New York City to Telluride, Colorado, for a ski trip. Plaintiff was awarded damages totaling $3,110 for unrecoverable lodging accommodations, lost baggage, and inconvenience of missing the scheduled holiday vacation trip.

For airlines operating international flights, liability for personal injury, damaged or lost baggage, and damages caused by delays is limited by the Montreal Convention. The Montreal Convention, enacted in 2003 replacing the Warsaw Convention, is an international treaty to which the United States is a party, governing and limiting the liability of air carriers transporting passengers and cargo on international flights. For example, in *Vumbaca v. Terminal One Group Assn.* (2012) plaintiff filed her mental distress claim in a New York state court for being kept on board an aircraft arriving from Rome at JFK airport in New York City. An unexpected snowstorm had dropped a foot of snow on the ground closing the airport therefore making it impossible for passengers to disembark their aircraft. Because the U.S. is a signatory to the convention [which allows recovery only for physical injury], her suit failed.

Recovery under the convention is limited to an accident that occurs either on board the aircraft or in the course of any operations of embarking or disembarking. In *Boyd v. Lufthansa* (2015) plaintiff sued defendant airline for recovery under the Montreal Convention after she fell and broke her hip while walking to the U. S. Customs area of a Houston airport. Lufthansa successfully argued that plaintiff was not under their direction or control as she was clearly inside the airport and therefore her claim was outside the scope of the Montreal Convention.

Cruise Lines. Vacations aboard luxury cruise ships have increased in popularity with nearly 24 million passengers expected to sail in 2016 which is a dramatic increase from 15 million just 10 years ago (Cruise Lines International Association, 2016). Modern-day cruise ships are essentially floating hotels (Barth, 2009; Dickerson, 2004) with amenities including ice-skating rinks, rock-climbing walls, golf simulators, water slides, private pools, spas, and planetariums. As a result, many of the legal issues of guest safety, security, and liability are similar to those faced by land-based hospitality managers. Furthermore, like all common carriers, those operating cruise ships are subject to a wide array of local, state, federal, and international laws.

Yet, in addition to these legal principles, cruise ships and their passengers are subject to **maritime law**, a system of law relating to navigable waters. In *Smith v. Royal Caribbean Cruises LTD.* (2015), plaintiff willingly entered a pool on Royal's Liberty of the Seas cruise ship with water that looked green, cloudy, and murky. While swimming under water he hit his head on the side of the pool which caused him neck pain and rendered his right arm limp. Plaintiff claimed Royal was negligent in its maintenance and operation of the pool water and for failing to warn of the dangers of swimming in opaque pool water. The court found in favor of defendant because under maritime law plaintiff's claims were invalidated as the duty to warn only extends to dangers which are not open and obvious.

Furthermore, liability waivers used to protect cruise lines from liability for injuries aboard ship are not enforceable. Federal statute 46 USCS § 30509a states:

(a) Prohibition.—

(1) In general.—The owner, master, manager, or agent of a vessel transporting passengers between ports in the United States, or between a port in the United States and a port in a foreign country, may not include in a regulation or contract a provision limiting—

(A) the liability of the owner, master, or agent for personal injury or death caused by the negligence or fault of the owner or the owner's employees or agents; or

(B) the right of a claimant for personal injury or death to a trial by court of competent jurisdiction.

Similar to the limits on liability provided for international air travel, the **Athens Convention** limits liability of cruise ships to passengers aboard cruises not touching a U.S. port. Although the United States is not a signatory to the Athens Convention, many of the cruise lines serving U.S. passengers are owned by companies located in countries that do abide by the terms of the convention. For example, in *Henson v. Seabourn Cruise Line Limited, Inc.* (2005), defendant sought limits on liability from negligence claims by the plaintiff. Defendant cruise line was flagged as a vessel of the Bahamas, which is party to the treaty, and the Athens Convention was included as a term in the ticket contract with the plaintiff. The court ruled, however, that because the cruise was scheduled to make several stops at U.S. ports, U.S. federal law prevailed over the liability limitations of the Athens Convention.

Agency Law

Inherent to understanding legal liability in the travel and tourism industry is **agency law**, an area of law governed by a combination of contract law and tort law (Cheeseman, 2015). At the heart of agency law is the principal–agent relationship. A party employing another to act on its behalf is known as the **principal**, whereas the **agent** becomes the party agreeing to act on another's behalf. The **principal–agent relationship** is created when both parties agree that the agent has the authority to represent the principal and can enter into contracts on the principal's behalf. This principal–agent relationship is illustrated in *Belik v. Carlson Travel Group* (2011) where plaintiff embarked on a cruise purchased from defendant Carlson who touted itself as the largest singles cruise operator in the U.S. Plaintiff was seriously injured in a diving accident and sued both the cruise line and Carlson through which he had booked his vacation. Plaintiff claimed that because the actions of the operator mirrored those of an agent for its principal that both defendants were liable. The court agreed when the evidence clearly showed the cruise line acknowledged the defendant would act on its behalf thereby making it an actual agency relationship.

Formation of the agency relationship can occur through an express agreement, an implied agreement, or an apparent agency. The express agreement involves either an oral or written contract, whereas the implied agreement is inferred by the conduct of both parties. An **apparent agent** is one whom the principal allows others to believe is acting as its agent, regardless of whether or not the principal has actually conferred that authority (Garner, 2009, p. 72). This concept is illustrated in *Bridgewater v. Carnival Corp.* (2011) where plaintiff, a ticketed passenger on a Carnival cruise, participated in an excursion involving a watersport. While on the excursion, plaintiff was struck by lightning as she held onto a metal cable on the excursion boat. Plaintiff claimed the excursion operator was an apparent agent of Carnival because at no time did the cruise line company state the excursion operator was not an agent or employed by Carnival. The court ruled that just because Carnival failed to disavow an agency relationship did not mean they had engaged in an agency relationship with the excursion operator.

Travel Agents. Many people making travel plans use the services of a travel agent whose job is to provide customers travel information, organize travel packages, and sell travel services such as airline tickets, cruise vacations, hotel rooms, and excursion trips. Travel agents work on commission from airlines, hotels, tour operators, and other types of travel services, making them legal representatives (agents) of the service provider (principal). Although travel agents are viewed as legal representatives of different travel services, they also have a duty to their customers to act with skill, care, and diligence in rendering the kind of services that can reasonably be expected. Travel agents owe a *fiduciary duty* to their clients. For example, a travel agent has a legal duty to select appropriate travel providers and conduct reasonable investigations of the travel providers they book. This was the case in *Giampietro v. Viator, Inc.* (2015) where plaintiff booked a Vespa tour of Florence, Italy on defendant's recommendation. The travel agent characterized the tour as no larger than 10 people with travel on quiet and scenic roads after a 30-minute orientation on how to ride the scooter safely. Plaintiff claimed defendant negligently misrepresented the tour because it "was not as advertised in terms of the number of people on the tour, the safety briefing and Vespa orientation, and the condition of the roads to be travelled by the scooter" (p. 8-9).

Travel agents are not insurers or guarantors of customers' travel safety as illustrated in *Giuffra v. Vantage Travel Service, Inc.* (2015); however, they do have a duty to disclose. When a travel agent has knowledge of safety factors or quality issues, he/she has a duty to inform the customer of those facts. For example, in *Hallman v. Unique Vacations* (2010) plaintiffs claimed negligence against their travel agency after resort hotel personnel providing a scuba diving activity left them stranded on the open ocean for more than two hours. Plaintiffs alleged Unique Vacations "breached its duty to warn of the dangerous operation" (p. 2) as evidence of similar prior occurrences of the hotel leaving divers stranded emerged from discovery.

Likewise, websites providing online users with travel related products and services are often viewed as 21st century travel agents; however, this is not true of all travel websites (*Kelly v. Priceline.com, Inc.*, 2012). For those websites viewed as virtual travel agents such as Expedia.com, the same legal duty applies as in the case of a live travel agent. For example in *Hofer v. Gap, Inc.* (2007) plaintiff booked her travel and accommodations to Jamaica through Expedia.com [which was also a defendant in the lawsuit]. Upon arrival at the resort hotel, plaintiff discovered the stairs leading up to the lobby of the hotel were dimly lit and did not have a handrail. During her stay plaintiff lost her balance at the top of those stairs and fell into an adjacent turtle pond, severely cutting her leg on sharp rocks in the pond. Plaintiff alleged Expedia breached its duty to warn her that the resort hotel's stairway was dimly lit and lacked a handrail. Yet, the court held that a travel agent [Expedia] cannot be held responsible for conditions at a hotel if the agent exercises no control over the facilities. Although the Expedia.com website contained a promise that their "travel specialists visit thousands of hotels across the globe to ensure our descriptions are accurate and up-to-date" (p. 168), there was no evidence that Expedia exercised any control over the resort property where plaintiff was injured.

When customers rely on the expertise of travel agents for information about third-party suppliers (such as tour operators), the travel agent has a duty to provide accurate information and take reasonable care in investigating these travel suppliers. The role of the travel agent in terms of third-party suppliers is illustrated in *Wolf v. Tico Travel* (2011). Plaintiffs traveled to Costa Rica for a fishing expedition. Defendants booked all the necessary arrangements with a local fishing guide company with which they had planned previous excursions. The fishing guide took plaintiffs out on the ocean to fish even though the Coast Guard had issued a warning that day against doing so due to the turbulent and choppy nature of the seas. The boat capsized, and while one plaintiff was able to swim to shore his travel companion drowned. There was no evidence presented showing that defendant "failed to exercise good faith or reasonable skill, care, or diligence in making travel plans" (p. 14) for plaintiffs. The court ruled that travel agents are not liable for the acts or omissions of independent suppliers of services because they have no control over such entities.

Tour Operators. Tour operators are distinguished from travel agents in that operators are usually in a position to actually provide a travel service, such as excursions, guided tours, and trips. Tour operators are often considered the primary provider of the service, whereas the travel agent is a representative of their services. Tour operators can be held liable for their own negligent actions that result in injuries to tourists. A bicycle tour company could be held liable for providing bicycles with faulty brakes (*Steinfield v. EmPG Int'l, LLC*, 2015). Likewise, a St. Maartens tour operator involved in a bus crash while transporting passengers to the tour site could be liable for injuries to the passengers (*Ash v. Royal Caribbean Cruises LTD*, 2014). However, like the travel agent, if a tour operator is contracting with another third-party travel supplier, then they are not liable for the negligence of that third-party supplier provided they exercised care in the selection of the supplier. For example, a Massachusetts-based tour operator was not held liable for a client's negligence claim because they had contracted with a third-party to handle a horseback riding excursion for a South American tour on which plaintiff was a party (*Shridhar v. Vantage Travel Service, Inc.*, 2016).

When a travel agent accepts the additional role of tour operator, the agent assumes the duties and responsibilities of the principal, or the actual service provider. An Arizona travel agency organized, promoted, sold, and operated student vacation tours to Mazatlan, Mexico, which plaintiff's eighteen-year old-daughter, Molly, had purchased. Part of the tour was a train ride called the party train, from which Molly fell when walking from one train car to another (*Maurer v. Cerkvenik-Anderson Travel*, 1994). The travel agency, relying on its role of agent, claimed it had no duty to control the train to make it safe, nor did it have knowledge of the specific condition causing Molly's death. The court disagreed and ruled that because of defendant's dual role as both agent and principal, the travel agency had a duty to warn of dangers of which they were aware, or should have been aware. In another illustration of a travel agent taking on the role of tour operator, a Chicago independent travel agent made arrangements for a private school's eighth-grade graduation trip to Six Flags near St. Louis, Missouri (*Lewis v. Elsin*, 2002). Additionally, the travel agent agreed to serve as the group's tour guide and accompanied them on the trip. Upon check-in at the hotel where the group was staying overnight, defendant left the group and went out for the evening. While absent from the group, one of the students drowned in the hotel's swimming pool. The travel agent/tour guide was sued because he had neglected his role as tour guide and failed to provide for appropriate supervision of the pool area for the group.

Tour operators can gain some protection by using liability waivers and disclaimers as illustrated in *Wolf v. Celebrity Cruises, Inc.* (2015). Plaintiff, a cruise ship passenger, purchased a ticket for a shore excursion in Costa Rica provided by a third party tour operator, Original Canopy Tours. He was injured when he crashed into the receiving platform at a high rate of speed on the final leg of a zip line. The guest ticket contract entered into by the parties precluded liability for conduct of the third-party tour operator, and was also successful in protecting the cruise line from plaintiff's negligence claim.

SIGNIFICANT CASE

Any entity within the travel supply chain can be sued for a variety of claims. This case illustrates the importance of plaintiff's establishing jurisdiction. Additionally, this case provides an explanation of purposeful availment as well as alter egos which is related to the interconnectivity of the travel industry.

GUTMAN V. ALLEGRO RESORTS MARKETING CORP.
United State District Court for the Eastern District of Michigan, Southern Division
2015 U.S. Dist. LEXIS 166647
December 14, 2015, Decided

OPINION BY: JUDGE LAWSON

I.

The underlying facts, as relevant to the disposition of the present motion, are essentially undisputed by the parties. The plaintiffs allege that Karen Gutman was injured while a guest at the defendants' Occidental Grand XCaret Hotel and Resort near Playa Riviera, Mexico, on February 1, 2014. According to the complaint, at around 8:30 p.m., Gutman walked out of the resort's restaurant after dinner, "misstepped over an un- or poorly-marked three-to-four-inch change in elevation," fell, and broke her ankle. Her injury required surgery and installation of stabilizing hardware. Gutman contends that she suffers from impaired mobility and continuing pain, and her husband alleges that as a result of her injuries he has been deprived of the enjoyment of his wife's companionship.

The defendant admits that Allegro Resorts Marketing Corporation is a Florida corporation with its principal place of business in Florida. Allegro concedes that its business is limited solely to advertising, marketing and otherwise soliciting business in the United States on behalf of 'Occidental' branded hotels and resorts, all of which are located outside of the United States. Allegro contends that it did not have any contact with the plaintiffs relating to their stay at the Occidental property in Mexico, and that Allegro itself does not own or control that property. However, Allegro does not appear to contest seriously any of the basic factual conclusions reached by the district court in another case against Allegro and Occidental, where the court found that that Allegro and the Occidental Defendants are the same companies for personal jurisdiction purposes, and found that Allegro and Occidental shared common ownership, governing boards, and control, and that despite separate corporate identities, Allegro essentially served as Occidental's marketing department.

According to the complaint, Occidental Hoteles Management, S.L. is a Spanish corporation with its principal place of business in Madrid. Allegro does not appear to contest the allegations that Occidental owns the hotel property in Mexico where the Gutmans took their February 2014 vacation, or that Allegro is a wholly owned subsidiary of Occidental.

Allegro points out, however, that the plaintiffs do not allege in their complaint, and they do not suggest in their briefing, any particular facts regarding how they booked or conducted their trip to Mexico or their stay at Occidental's hotel. Nor do the plaintiffs assert that they used that website to book their stay at the hotel. They do contend that Allegro markets Occidental properties to Michigan residents through various means, including contacts with Michigan travel agents. But they do not offer any specific facts to explain how and when, if at all, they were exposed to any of Allegro's marketing efforts.

For its part, Allegro affirmatively asserts that the plaintiffs did not book their hotel stay through Occidental's website. Allegro further asserts that it never sent any materials to the plaintiffs in Michigan, does not maintain any place of business or contacts in the state, does not sell any goods or services here, and does not derive substantial revenue within Michigan.

The plaintiffs filed their complaint on August 4, 2015, raising state law claims for premises liability (count I), negligence (count II), and loss of consortium (count III). Allegro filed its motion to dismiss for lack of personal jurisdiction on August 25, 2015.

II.

* * *

In a case where subject matter jurisdiction is based on diversity of citizenship, federal courts look to state law to determine personal jurisdiction. If a Michigan court would have jurisdiction over a defendant, so would a federal district court sitting in this state. * * * Michigan interprets its

Long Arm Statute to allow personal jurisdiction to extend to the limits imposed by the federal constitution.

* * *

For a State to exercise jurisdiction consistent with due process, the defendant's suit-related conduct must create a substantial connection with the forum State. Thus, in order to determine whether the [Court is] authorized to exercise jurisdiction over [the defendant], we ask whether the exercise of jurisdiction 'comports with the limits imposed by federal due process' on the [forum state]. Although a nonresident's physical presence within the territorial jurisdiction of the court is not required, the nonresident generally must have certain minimum contacts such that the maintenance of the suit does not offend traditional notions of fair play and substantial justice. The Sixth Circuit historically has applied three criteria to guide the minimum contacts analysis:

> First, the defendant must purposefully avail himself of the privilege of acting in the forum state or causing a consequence in the forum state. Second, the cause of action must arise from the defendant's activities there. Finally, the acts of the defendant or consequences caused by the defendant must have a substantial enough connection with the forum state to make the exercise of jurisdiction over the defendant reasonable.

A. Purposeful Availment

The Sixth Circuit views the purposeful availment prong * * * as essential to a finding of personal jurisdiction. Purposeful availment occurs when the defendant's contacts with the forum state proximately result from actions by the defendant himself that create a substantial connection with the forum State.

Physical presence within the state is not required to create such a connection. The Supreme Court has consistently rejected the notion that an absence of physical contacts can defeat personal jurisdiction there. The defendant's maintenance of its fully interactive website, which allows Michigan residents to enter into booking contracts with the defendants, easily satisfies this requirement. The facts discussed fortify this conclusion: from 2007 to 2010, 155 guests with Michigan addresses booked hotel or resort reservations through Defendants' website. . . . Defendants entered into contracts with Michigan residents using their website. Allegro does not dispute these facts. And it follows logically that Allegro should have had reason to foresee being 'haled before' a Michigan court.

B. Cause of Action Arising From Local Activities

It is this second requirement that causes the plaintiffs to stumble here. The plaintiffs argue without elaboration that the defendants' marketing activities in Michigan are somehow intertwined with the defective premises in Mexico. That connection, however, is not self-evident. And the Sixth Circuit has emphasized that [i]t is not enough that there be some connection between the in-state activity and the cause of action — that connection must be *substantial*, and [t]he defendant's contacts with the forum state must relate to the operative facts and nature of the controversy.

One might posit that without the marketing efforts, the plaintiffs may not have learned of the defendants' resort and would not have booked their trip to Mexico there. And absent the booking, the accident would not have occurred. However, the Sixth Circuit explained recently in *Beydoun v. Wataniya Restaurants Holding, Q.S.C.*, 768 F.3d 499 (6th Cir. 2014), that the type of mere but-for association relied upon by the plaintiffs is not sufficient to support the exercise of limited personal jurisdiction.

* * *

The asserted basis of liability in this case is premises liability, which by definition infers that the claim arose where the "premises" are located. The claim did not — could not — arise from the defendants' advertising contacts in Michigan.

That point was made well a few years ago by the Eleventh Circuit, which concluded on similar facts that there is no substantial or proximate factual relationship between advertising of vacation accommodations and an alleged on-site personal injury that occurs at the defendant's remote hotel property, where none of the allegedly negligent acts occurred within the forum state.

* * *

The plaintiffs appear to argue that Allegro's marketing and advertising activity fall within the corporate sphere of Occidental's worldwide activities, which includes reaching into Michigan to solicit customers to come to its resorts. * * * More importantly, however, the argument fails here because there is nothing in the record that would make Michigan "home" to either Allegro or Occidental, and the plaintiffs still must connect the advertising activity to the tortious conduct to prevail on their case-specific personal jurisdiction theory, which they have failed to do.

* * *

Because the plaintiff is relying on the *alter ego* identity between Allegro and Occidental Hoteles to pursue its case in this district against that premises owner, personal jurisdiction over the latter must fail as well, since it is based on the Internet conduct of the former. Although Occidental Hoteles has not been served with process yet, the Court can see no basis for maintaining the case against it in this forum. No supporting facts appear in the complaint. That does not leave the plaintiff without a remedy, as it appears that general personal jurisdiction likely exists in Florida over Allegro and, by extension, its *alter ego*. The case here, however, must be dismissed for want of personal jurisdiction.

III.

The plaintiff has not established a *prima facie* case for limited personal jurisdiction over the defendants that can satisfy the Due Process Clause.

CASES ON THE SUPPLEMENTAL WEBSITE

Arguello v. Sunset Station, Inc. (252 P.3d 206, 2011). This case is a good example of a breach of bailment contract as well as a failed attempt of the defendant hotel to apply the Nevada statute of limited liability as a defense for stolen property in the hotel's possession.

Belik v. Carlson Travel Group, Inc. (2011 U.S. Dist. LEXIS 60337). This case illustrates negligence, agency and contract issues. It also provides the reader with a good distinction between actual and apparent agency.

*Fallhowe v. Hilton Worldwide, Inc. (*2015 U.S. Dist. LEXIS 114640). The reader should note the consideration of all factors in determining the best court venue for this case (i.e., *forum non conveniens*).

Starkey v. G Adventures, Inc. (796 F.3d 193, 2015). The reader should identify how effective the forum selection clause was in defending the service provider against plaintiff's claim.

Yi v. Pleasant Travel Service, Inc., (2011 U.S. Dist. LEXIS 137924). In this near drowning case, the reader should note how the hotel was not held liable for two reasons: 1) the pool had a "No Lifeguard On Duty" sign, and 2) the pool was viewed as an open and obvious risk.

QUESTIONS YOU SHOULD BE ABLE TO ANSWER

1. What is a hotel's legal responsibility to their guests for guest's personal property?
2. Explain the essential elements that must occur for the theory of bailment to apply.
3. How is jurisdiction determined when one uses the Internet to transact travel arrangements?
4. Explain the factors to consider when a claim of *forum non conveniens* is made.
5. What is the legal duty of travel agents to their clients?

REFERENCES

Cases

Arguello v. Sunset Station, Inc., 252 P.3d 206 (2011)
Ash v. Royal Caribbean Cruises LTD., 2014 U.S. Dist. LEXIS 164691
Belik v. Carlson Travel Group, Inc., 2011 U.S. Dist. LEXIS 60337
Boyd v. Lufthansa German Airlines, 2015 U.S. Dist. LEXIS 72482
Bray v. Marriott International, 2016 U. S. Dist. LEXIS 9232
Bridgewater v. Carnival Corporation, 2011 U.S. Dist. LEXIS 20626
Carnival Cruise Lines, Inc. v. Shute, 111 S. Ct. 1522 (1991)
Cervantes v. Ramparts, Inc., 2003 Cal. App. Unpub. LEXIS 1283
City of Los Angeles, California v. Patel, 135 S. Ct. 2443 (2015)
Conley v. MLT, Inc., 2012 U.S. Dist. LEXIS 71821
Ellis v. Marriott International, 2011 U.S. Dist. LEXIS 145417
Fabend v. Rosewood Hotels and Resorts, L.L.C., 381 F.3d 152 (2004)
Fallhowe v. Hilton Worldwide, Inc., 2015 U. S. Dist. LEXIS 114640
Giampietro v. Viator, Inc., 2015 U.S. Dist. LEXIS 132225
Gonzalez-Martinez v. Royal Caribbean Cruises LTD., 94 F.Supp.3d 147 (2015)
Goldstein v. Hard Rock Café International, Inc., 519 Fed. Appx. 653 (2013)
Giuffra v. Vantage Travel Service, Inc., 2015 U.S. Dist. LEXIS 70331
Gutman v. Allegro Resorts Marketing Corp., 2015 U.S. Dist. LEXIS 166647
Hallman v. Unique Vacations, Inc., 2010 U.S. Dist. LEXIS 138919
Henson v. Seabourn Cruise Line Limited, Inc., 2005 U.S. Dist. LEXIS 26221
Hofer v. Gap, Inc., 516 F.Supp.2d 161 (2007)
Kelly v. Priceline.com Inc., 2012 U.S. Dist. LEXIS 45285
Krueger v. La Quinta Inn & Suites, 2014 La. App. Unpub. LEXIS 404

Lewis v. Elsin, 2002 Mo. App. LEXIS 435
Liberty Mutual v. Zurich Insurance Company, 930 N.E.2d 573 (2010)
Lovett v. Omni Hotels Management Corporation, 2015 U.S. Dist. LEXIS 138464
Martino-Valdes v. Renaissance Hotel Management Company LLC, 2011 U.S. Dist. LEXIS 127487
Maurer v. Cerkvenik-Anderson Travel, Inc., 890 P.2d 69 (1994)
McArthur v. Kerzner International Bahamas Limited, 607 Fed. Appx. 845 (2015)
McCrann v. Riu Hotels, 2010 U.S. Dist. LEXIS 129194
Minass v. HHC TRS Portsmouth, LLC, 2014 U.S. Dist. LEXIS 115668
Muraco v. Sandals Resorts International, 2015 U.S. Dist. LEXIS 172156
Onyx Acceptance Corporation v. Trump Hotel & Casino Resorts, Inc., 2008 N.J. Super. Unpub. LEXIS 1095
Shridhar v. Vantage Travel Service, Inc., 2016 U.S. Dist. LEXIS 6184
Smith v. Royal Caribbean Cruises, LTD., 620 Fed. Appx. 727 (2015)
Spahr v. Ferber Resorts, LLC, 419 Fed. Appx. 796 (2011)
Spear v. Marriott Hotel Services, Inc., 2016 U.S. Dist. LEXIS 5461
Starkey v. G Adventures, Inc., 796 F.3d 193 (2015)
State of Minnesota v. Yang, 2014 Minn. App. Unpub. LEXIS 1350
State of Ohio v. Wright, 2013 Ohio App. LEXIS 4703
Steinfield v. EmPG Int'l, LLC, 2015 U.S. Dist. LEXIS 101881
Stobaugh v. Norwegian Cruise Line Limited, 5 S.W.3d 232 (1999)
Stone v. Continental Airlines, 804 N.Y.S.2d 652 (2005)
Twardy v. Northwest Airlines, Inc., 2001 U.S. Dist. LEXIS 2112
Vumbaca v. Terminal One Group Association L.P., 859 F. Supp.2d 343 (2012)
Whittemore v. Country Inn & Suites by Carlson, Inc., 2014 U.S. Dist. LEXIS 178075
Wolf v. Celebrity Cruises, Inc., 101 F.Supp.3d 1298 (2015)
Wolf v. Tico Travel, 2011 U.S. Dist. LEXIS 136024
Yi v. Pleasant Travel Service, Inc., 2011 U.S. Dist. LEXIS 137942

Publications

Barth, S. (2009). *Hospitality law* (3rd ed.). Hoboken, NJ: John Wiley & Sons.
Cheeseman, H. R. (2015). *Business law* (9th ed.). Upper Saddle River, NJ: Prentice Hall.
Cruise Lines International Association. (2016, January). Continued evolution of cruise travel drives growth. *Cruise News*. Retrieved from http://www.msiak.net/aca/290/index.html
Dickerson, T. A. (2004). Recent development: The cruise passenger's dilemma: Twenty-first-century ships, nineteenth-century rights. *Tulane Maritime Law Journal, 28*, 447–465.
Garner, B. A. (Ed.) (2009). *Black's law dictionary* (9th ed.). St. Paul, MN: Thomson Reuters.
Jeffries, J. P. (1995). *Understanding hospitality law* (3rd ed.). East Lansing, MI: Educational Institute of the American Hotel and Motel Association.
Morris, K. L., Marshall, A. G., & Cournoyer, N. G. (2008). *Hotel, restaurant, and travel law: A preventive approach* (7th ed.). Clifton Park, NY: Thomson Delmar Learning.

Legislation

46 USCS § 30509a (2016)

INTENTIONAL TORTS AND CRIMINAL ACTS

3.00

Some actions go beyond the level of the unintentional tort-negligence. Two such actions included in this section are intentional torts and criminal acts. An *intentional tort* is a tort, or wrong, in which the actor possessed intent or purpose to injure. An intention tort contains three elements: (1) there must be an injury, (2) the act is the proximate cause of an injury, and (3) there must be intent to bring about the injury. Legal action must be instituted by the victim or plaintiff and in civil suits punishment generally takes the form of a monetary award to the victim.

Intentional Torts and Criminal Acts addresses a number of actions that are a concern for the recreation and sport manager. Section 3.10 *Intentional Tort Applications* addresses several intentional torts that are of particular interest to the recreation or sport manager. They are assault and battery, defamation, invasion of privacy, breach of fiduciary duty, tortious interference with contract, and intentional infliction of emotional distress.

Recreation and sport managers are becoming more concerned with the effects of crimes on their programs. **Criminal law** is that body of law made up of state and federal statutes that define certain offenses against persons, against public welfare, and against the government. The punishment for crimes can range from fines to long-term prison sentences, depending upon the nature of the crime. The state must institute the action and there is generally no remuneration to the victim.

Section 3.20 *Sport-Related Criminal Acts* includes two chapters. The first addresses a number of sport-related crimes and the second deals with hazing — sometimes considered a crime and sometimes an intentional tort.

3.11 ASSAULT AND BATTERY

Curt Hamakawa | Western New England University

Suppose that you, as a sport or recreation manager, just heard from one of your employees that "There's a fight out front and a guy is bleeding all over the place!" Your first reaction might be to respond quickly to the scene to try to break up the scuffle and render first aid. But after stabilizing the situation and returning to your office, you realize that the physical altercation resulting in injuries might lead to legal liability. Questions swirl through your head: What would be the **cause of action**? Who would be liable; just the aggressor or both combatants? Could you, as the manager, and the organization you work for, be liable as well? Might criminal charges be filed in addition to a civil lawsuit, as a result of the fight? And most importantly, what can you do to minimize risks of harm and legal liability to you and your organization?

Sport and recreation managers must be familiar with actions in **tort** that constitute intentional harms,[1] because as the manager in the above example may discover, liability for assault and battery could extend to management as well. **Assault** and **battery** generally involve either the threat of bodily harm or an unlawful touching of another person without justification or excuse. Both are torts as well as crimes (Black's Law Dictionary, 2004) and will be defined in more detail later in this chapter. You may be aware that it is not uncommon in the sport or recreation environment for a person to be harmed as a result of another's intentional conduct, both on and off the "field of play." One need only tune in to the news to learn about the latest and most sensational assault and battery cases involving professional athletes or other celebrity figures. In 2014, a jaw-dropping video from an elevator surveillance camera caught Baltimore Ravens running back Ray Rice cold-cocking his then-fiancee, Janay Palmer, at an Atlantic City hotel, who was then seen dragging her unconscious body out of the elevator door to the floor. Also in 2014, Minnesota Vikings running back Adrian Peterson was charged with child abuse over his methods of disciplining his four-year-old son. While both of these cases involved domestic incidents, they are nonetheless illustrative of violence in sport that may very well result in legal consequences.

It should be noted that these increasingly outlandish incidents are not confined to sport's highest levels. In 2015, two high school football players from John Jay High School in San Antonio, Texas, appeared to intentionally blindside an umpire during a play, with the first player tackling the official from behind while the second player dives on the downed official helmet first. Video of this sensational scene went viral, and viewers reacted with utter disbelief of what they saw. The official, who suffered a concussion from the incident, said he was uncertain whether he will officiate again. In December, 2011, cross-town basketball rivals Xavier and Cincinnati made the national news following a televised game that featured a bench-clearing brawl. Several players were injured necessitating the game being called with nine seconds remaining. Only after meeting with both teams' coaches and being convinced that the aggressors would be severely disciplined, did the prosecutor decide against filing criminal charges. Another highly publicized incident was the "Malice at the Palace" or "Basketbrawl" that took place on November 19, 2004, at the Palace of Auburn between the NBA Detroit Pistons and Indiana Pacers. Near the end of the highly charged game, Piston forward/center Ben Wallace was fouled by Pacer forward Ron Artest, and after a shove back by Wallace, several players from both teams joined in the fray. After a spectator threw a cup at Artest near the scorer's table, Artest charged the stands and a melee broke out between several spectators and Pacers. In addition to NBA suspensions handed down to players on both teams, five Pacers and seven Pistons fans were criminally charged with assault and battery.

In addition to well-publicized allegations of criminal and/or civil assault and battery involving high-profile athletes (*e.g.*, Vancouver Canuck Todd Bertuzzi's career-ending sucker punch on Colorado Avalanche player

---

[1] Note that while intentional torts and negligence fall within the same family and classification as "civil wrongs," intentional torts are separate and distinct from negligence, which is addressed in Chapter 2.11 *Negligence*.

Steve Moore in a game during the NHL's 2004 season; NBA's Kobe Bryant's 2003 sexual assault of a 19-year-old woman at a Vail, Colorado, resort; Los Angeles Laker Kermit Washington's infamous punch out of the Houston Rockets' Rudy Tomjanovich in 1977; and Golden State Warrior Latrell Sprewell's choking take down of coach P.J. Carlesimo at a practice in 1997), local media are replete with reports that can and do give rise to liability for assault and battery.

Unfortunately, such liability is not limited to athletes-as-combatants. At a youth football game in September, 2011, in Sarasota, Florida, a referee was attacked by three coaches and tackled by a 14-year-old player, resulting in charges of felony battery. In addition, the offending team and coaches were suspended and expelled from the conference. Thus, recreation and sport managers should be aware that their organizations are not immune from incidents involving participants, parents and other spectators, coaches and officials, security personnel, and anyone else who might find occasion to become engaged in behavior that meets the threshold requirements for assault and battery.

Although the conduct giving rise to assault and battery can result both in civil lawsuits and criminal charges, this chapter addresses only *civil* assault and battery (see Chapter 3.21 *Criminal Law and Sport* for a discussion of criminal assault and battery). It is worth reiterating that in the sport and recreation context, parties to assault and battery could involve athletes, coaches, officials, spectators (including parents), club patrons, and any variety of "innocent" bystanders. Furthermore, while most sport- and recreation-related assaults and batteries never make the national headlines, it should not escape anyone's notice that such incidents occur with regularity. Consequently, sport and recreation managers must be educated about the potential risks posed by the intentional torts of assault and battery, and remain vigilant to these threats by devising measures to prevent or mitigate their occurrence.

FUNDAMENTAL CONCEPTS

While most people know—from their television and movie viewing habits, as well as from media reports—that assault and battery are types of crimes, probably fewer are aware that they also constitute torts, which are *civil* wrongs (Black's Law Dictionary, 2004). Thus, a person's conduct constituting assault and battery is actionable in both criminal and civil law. In other words, an individual who is accused of assault and battery can be charged by the police and prosecuted by the public prosecutor (referred to in the states variously as the district attorney, state's attorney, or prosecuting attorney, and in the federal system as the U.S. attorney) in criminal court, and be subject to criminal punishment (*e.g.*, incarceration, probation, and/or fines), and/or be sued by the injured party for **damages** (*i.e.*, monetary award to the plaintiff) in civil court (see Chapter 2.11 *Negligence*). Thus, depending on the circumstances, a person's actions arising out of a single event can result in both a criminal prosecution and a civil lawsuit. The reason that a person can be subjected to *both* civil lawsuit and criminal prosecutions and not run afoul of **constitutional** provisions is because the **Fifth Amendment** prohibition against **double jeopardy**[2] applies only to crimes, and not civil actions. You may recall that O.J. Simpson, who was found **not guilty** by the jury in his criminal trial for the murders of his ex-wife Nicole Brown Simpson and her friend, Ronald Goldman, subsequently was held **liable** for their **wrongful deaths** in the civil trial. In the sport and recreation environment, criminal prosecutions for assault and battery occur far less frequently than civil suits for several reasons.

First, the culture of sport is averse to the idea that someone should be held criminally responsible for causing harm to another person in an organized sporting or recreational activity, where harsh and even violent physical contacts are deemed "part of the game." Second, the **standard of proof** in a criminal case is a much higher burden than in a civil case[3], thus making criminal prosecutions more difficult to win (which in part explains the differing **verdicts** in the O.J. Simpson cases mentioned above). And third, there is a societal reluctance to prosecute—never mind convict—a class of people who pursue the ideal of an active and healthy lifestyle and who are often venerated for their on-field achievements. Assault and battery cases that involve

---

[2] Legal concept that protects an individual from being subjected to prosecution more than once for the same alleged crime.
[3] In a criminal case, the government must prove all the elements of a crime **beyond a reasonable doubt**, while in a civil case, a plaintiff need only prove his/her case by a **preponderance of the evidence**.

non-competitors (*e.g.*, parents or spectators) or that involve athletes and occur off the field of competition (*e.g.* domestic abuse, bar fights) are entirely situation dependent. Perhaps as many people believe that athletes-as-celebrities receive favorable treatment when it comes to criminal prosecution, as defendant-athletes believe they are unfairly singled out for prosecution *because* they are famous.

Thus, a district attorney's decision to prosecute a criminal defendant on behalf of the public and an aggrieved private party's decision to sue the same person for civil remedies arising out of the same set of facts are based on independent variables. An important distinction between criminal prosecutions and civil lawsuits is that a criminal conviction can result in the defendant's forfeiture of life, liberty or property, including incarceration and/or payment of fines; while a defendant who is found liable in a civil case most often will be ordered to pay **damages**, or a sum of money, to the plaintiff. Ordinarily, fines imposed on convicted criminals as part of their sentence are not paid to their victims, unless the court specifically orders that **restitution** be paid for the harm caused to the victims. Without a doubt, decisions *not* to prosecute or sue for assault and battery far outnumber decisions to bring legal action. Two prominent examples of havoc in the field of battle that did *not* result in either criminal charges or lawsuits include heavyweight boxer Mike Tyson's biting off part of Evander Holyfield's ear in a 1997 bout, and France's Zinedine Zidane's horrific head butt of Italy's Marco Materazzi near the end of the 2006 World Cup Final. The remainder of this chapter focuses on *civil* assault and battery, while *criminal* assault and battery are addressed elsewhere (see Chapter 3.21, *Criminal Law and Sport*).

Torts of Assault and Battery

While the terms "assault and battery" commonly are used in concert, they are actually separate and distinct torts. Thus, in seeking redress for harms caused by an intentional tort, a **plaintiff's** lawsuit against a **defendant** for assault, battery, or both, will be dictated by the facts and circumstances of the case. By definition, assault and battery are intentional torts, meaning that the **tortfeasor** desired "to bring about [a] result that will invade [the] interests of another" (*Wager v. Pro*, 1979), as distinguished from **negligence**, which is characterized by "inadvertence, thoughtlessness, inattention, and the like" (Black's Law Dictionary, 2004). It is worth noting, however, that assault and battery are defined variously by state law, and that the precise elements of what constitutes assault and battery in one state might differ from another state. For example, some states do not distinguish between assault and battery, and treat both as one and the same, while other states give assault a broader meaning, thereby encompassing the technical definition of battery of other jurisdictions. This is an example of the nuances of law; that is, law is rarely absolute and clear cut. Instead, law is often drawn in shades of grey, making it subject to interpretation. As noted above, law also varies from state to state, so it is important for recreation and sport managers to understand these nuances and to consult legal experts as appropriate. For our purposes, we have taken the classical approach in treating – and defining – assault and battery as separate and mutually exclusive torts.

Assault

Assault is any willful attempt or threat to inflict injury upon the person of another, when coupled with an apparent present ability to do so and giving the victim reason to fear or expect immediate bodily harm (*State v. Murphy*, 1972). In fact, the Louisiana Criminal Code defines assault as "an attempt to commit a battery, or the intentional placing of another in reasonable apprehension of receiving a battery" (LA-R.S. 14:36). Put another way, assault is an attempt or threat to cause offensive contact with another person, coupled with the victim's reasonable apprehension of immediate bodily harm. Even more succinctly, it is putting someone in fear of receiving a battery (Kinsella, 1996). Thus, the tort of assault can be committed without actually touching, striking, or doing bodily harm to the victim (*State v. Murphy*, 1972). Still, words alone—regardless how insulting, provocative, or threatening—without the requisite elements (capability of doing harm and immediacy of the harm), do not constitute assault.

Elements of Assault. In order for an assault to occur, the following elements must be present:

- an intentional act by the defendant
- that causes reasonable apprehension on the part of the plaintiff
- of imminent harmful or offensive contact

For example, a coach's statement to a player that he will "ring his bell" if the player messes up the play again would not constitute assault, because mere words unaccompanied by any act to cause apprehension of imminent injury do not satisfy the elemental requirements. However, an ominous approach by a just-fouled pickup basketball player with a clenched fist and cocked arm, accompanied by some unflattering name calling and his threat to "get even" would likely constitute assault if the second player feared that he was about to be struck by the fouled player. Importantly, the tortfeasor must have intended to cause a harmful or offensive contact with the plaintiff (American Law Institute, 2009), and the plaintiff's apprehension of fear cannot be derived from the defendant's **negligent** or **reckless** conduct.

Because assault requires apprehension of harm on the part of the victim, no assault can occur where the victim is not aware that he or she is about to be struck. Thus, for example, a field hockey player who is blindsided and intentionally taken down by an opposing player cannot sue for assault (although she could sue for battery!). Finally, the harmful or offensive contact must be imminent and likely to occur momentarily; as opposed to the more distant threat of a sports bookie to "break your legs" if he does not receive the amount owed him on losing bets within 24 hours of the event's outcome.

Battery

If assault can be characterized in a loose and general way as attempted battery, then the completion of the threat or act culminating in actual physical contact, without consent, is battery. Put another way, battery is the consummation of an assault (*People v. Solak*, 1985). The classic definition of **battery** is the "intentional and wrongful physical contact with a person without his or her consent that entails some injury or offensive touching" (*Mason v. Cohn*, 1981). Prosser and Keeton (1984) stated that the freedom from intentional and unpermitted contacts with an individual's person "extends to any part of the body, or to anything which is attached to it and practically identified with it." Thus, an untoward and unwelcomed contact with a person's clothing, handbag, backpack, or even a held object could be grounds for a suit in battery. Also, a baseball pitcher who intentionally throws a fast ball at a heckling fan in the stands and injures him would be liable for battery even though the pitcher was not in the immediate physical presence of the fan.

Elements of Battery. In order for there to be a battery, the following elements must be present:

- intentional conduct by defendant
- causing harmful or offensive contact to plaintiff
- without consent

As with assault, battery is an intentional tort that requires a willful act on the part of the perpetrator. Unlike assault, however—which has no necessity of physical contact—battery (as the term implies) requires a "battering" or otherwise unwelcome or unpermitted touching. To be sure, there need not be any grievous injury; all that is required is a physical touching, however slight, as the law does not discriminate between degrees of force (*Steele v. State*, 1989). Thus, a jubilant fan who gets caught up in the excitement of his team's victory and spontaneously turns to kiss an unknowing spectator might be liable for battery (provided the gesture was unwelcomed and nonconsensual). The requirement of the tortfeasor's intent for battery applies to the resulting harmful or offensive contact to the victim, and not to the willful commitment to do the act. For example, in a case for battery against a golfer whose tee shot struck a resident who was standing outside her condominium bordering the fairway, the court said that the mere fact that the golfer *intended to hit the ball* was insufficient. What was required for battery was the golfer's intent to cause "an offensive contact with or unconsented touching of, or trauma upon [the plaintiff]" (*Hennessey v. Pyne, 1979*). An important distinction from assault is that battery does not require that the victim be aware of the harmful or offensive contact. There is no requirement that the plaintiff have an apprehension of the impending physical contact for battery to occur.

Consent

Consent, or rather the absence thereof, is an essential element in proving battery, and many cases will hinge on whether the plaintiff could be construed to have given his or her consent to participate in the activity that resulted in the allegation of battery. In a suit for battery brought by a high school basketball player against his coach, a question arose whether the physical contact at a pre-practice altercation involving wrestling techniques was consensual, since the coach disputed the player's assertions that he twice told the coach to release his arm. The coach characterized the incident instead as "playfully antagonistic" (*Goff v. Clarke*, 2003). This, of course, is a question of fact for the jury to determine, but it also raises the issue of consent in the realm of horseplay. One person might be enjoying the jovial, good-natured roughhousing activity, while another person is feeling abused and victimized. In *Clayton v. New Dreamland Roller Skating Rink* (1951), a woman who was skating at a roller skating rink injured her arm in a fall and was taken to the rink's first aid room, where a rink employee proceeded to manipulate the woman's arm. The employee was not a medical doctor and not authorized to perform physical manipulation treatments. Yet in the face of protestations by the woman, he continued to work on the woman's arm by applying traction. Subsequently, the woman was taken to a hospital, where x-rays revealed a fracture. This case reaffirms the rule that, absent consent, even a do-gooder's unwanted physical intervention on the person of another would subject him to liability for assault and battery, regardless of noble intentions.

In a classic case of an injury sustained in the course of a game (*Cunico v. Miller*, 2002), a high school soccer goalie sued an opposing player, her parents, and the opposing player's coach after being kicked by the opposing player. In rejecting the battery claim, the court said that as a matter of law, plaintiff "consented to the inherent risks of soccer from the undisputed fact of her voluntary participation in the soccer game." Such consent negates one of the elements of a battery claim because "the act of stepping onto the field of play may be described as 'consent to the inherent risks of the activity' " (*Ritchie-Gamester v. City of Berkley*, 1999). In another case involving a game-related injury (*Overall v. Kadella*, 1984), the court held that while consent (to bodily contacts that are permitted by the rules of the game) is manifested by a player' participation in a hockey game, an intentional act causing injury that goes beyond what is ordinarily permissible is actionable in tort (see the Supplemental Website).

Defenses to Assault and Battery

Since winning a case of assault or battery requires the plaintiff to prove the elements of the tort by a preponderance of the evidence, any defense would be predicated on the **absence of one or more of the requisite elements**. A defendant could also claim self defense or defense of another, in which the alleged assault and/or battery were justifiable in order to protect oneself or a third party from harm. Thus, in a heated exchange between a baseball manager and umpire who are nose-to-nose with one another, if the manager was readying to spew a wad of spit at the umpire's face, the umpire could raise his arms to protect himself, even if he brushes the manager's face or pushes him away in the process.

Express or Implied Consent. In the sport and recreation context, however, perhaps the most common defense against assault and/or battery is that the alleged victim either expressly or impliedly consented to the harms visited upon him or her. The reason is that where no public interest is implicated, the law does not seek to intervene by protecting against one's own folly (Prosser and Keeton, 1984). In other words, if in undertaking to enter a martial arts competition an athlete consents to any and all physical harms caused by an opponent in the ordinary course of the competition, the consent negates not only the opponent's otherwise wrongful conduct, but also the very existence of the tort. The concept of a person's consent to expose oneself to the inherent risks in sport applies whether the activity is ultimate fighting or table tennis.

For example, in the combative sports of boxing, ultimate fighting, wrestling, karate, judo, taekwondo, and the like, the object of the game is to physically beat or subdue the opposing player/athlete, just as the rules of certain team sports condone blocking, tackling, and body checking, and otherwise encourage harsh physical play. As noted previously, conduct that would readily result in criminal action or civil lawsuits off the field of play is given closer scrutiny within the confines of organized sport, under the guise that the injured participant is deemed to have consented to the contact and attendant risk of harm. Again, a player's consent implies acceptance of the risks inherent in sport, and does not extend to intentional contacts that are not usually and ordinarily a part of the game or activity. In *Esshaki v. Millman* (2009), the Michigan Court of Appeals said that "Even assuming that soccer includes a degree of intentional—and potentially harmful—contact, we conclude that, as a matter of law, a participant's consent to the risks inherent to participating in a soccer match does not include consent to be attacked by a co-participant." Thus in the right circumstances, an aggrieved party might still press for criminal prosecution and/or civil remedies. In *Brokaw v. Winfield-Mt. Union Community School*

District (2010), a court found a high school basketball player liable for striking an opposing player in the head with his elbow, and awarded damages of $13,000 for medical expenses, and $10,000 for pain and suffering (see also Chapter 2.13 *Liability of Sport Participants* and Chapter 3.21 *Criminal Law and Sport* relating to liability for negligent and criminal actions).

In a highly publicized incident involving former Florida State University standout quarterback Jameis Winston, a female FSU student accused the 2013 Heisman Trophy winner and the first overall pick in the 2015 NFL Draft of rape at an off-campus apartment in December 2012. After the Florida State Attorney's investigation concluded that there was insufficient evidence in which prosecute Winston, the victim, Erica Kinsman, sued Winston for sexual battery in federal court. Kinsman was featured in CNN's 2015 documentary, "The Hunting Ground," which purports to expose institutional ineptitude, if not nonfeasance, in response to students' claims of sexual assault within the university setting. The outcome of Kinsman's lawsuit, as in many allegations of sexual assault, will hinge on the issue of consent. It is important to note that Winston, who was neither charged with a crime nor disciplined by FSU after his student code of conduct hearing, has maintained that his sexual encounter with Kinsman was consensual. The case, Kinsman v. Winston, Case No. 6:15-cv-00696 (M.D.C. Fla., 2015), was pending at the time of publication.

Privilege. Another defense to intentional torts is that of privilege, which is in the realm of excuse or justification. An action that might otherwise result in liability is **privileged** if the defendant acted in furtherance of an interest of such social importance that it is entitled to legal protection, even though the plaintiff suffered harm (Prosser and Keeton, 1984). In essence, the tortfeasor is shielded from liability because circumstances and social policy permit or require it, as in the case of self defense. In the sport and recreation context, a coach or trainer might be entitled to such privilege in demonstrating a skill or technique to a participant.

Immunity. Related, but different, is the concept of **immunity**, which prevents even the initiation of a lawsuit or prosecution. An example of immunity would be the acts of law enforcement personnel acting in their official capacities as peace officers. Thus, police officers who physically accost a criminal suspect in the performance of their duties would be immune from suit or criminal prosecution for assault and battery.

Insurance. In response to the rash of high-profile assaults and batteries in sport in recent years, some insurance companies have sought to limit coverage of their general liability policies by writing exclusions for assault and battery. In other words, if you in your capacity as a coach or athletics director sought to prevent or break up a fight involving your school's student-athletes, which necessitated that you physically shove or restrain players on the sideline, your school's insurance policy might not protect you against a suit for assault and battery as a result of your intervention, no matter how noble your intentions. While this movement to exclude coverage for assault and battery is by no means widespread, it is yet another piece of evidence whereby insurance companies are seeking to curtail their exposure for actions of "rogue" actors in scuffles between players, coaches, officials, and even spectators.

Tort Remedies

Typically, the remedies available to plaintiffs who prevail in suits in tort (including assault and battery) are **damages**, or the award of a sum of money to the plaintiff. **Compensatory damages** (also referred to as **actual damages**) are those which compensate the plaintiff for the injury sustained; the rationale being that such damages would restore the injured party to the position he or she would be in but for the injury (*Northwestern Nat. Cas. Co. v. McNulty*, 1962). In general, if the injury is slight or there is no substantial loss, the damages will be nominal, since the purpose of compensatory damages is not to provide the prevailing party with a windfall. On the other hand, **punitive damages** (also referred to as **exemplary damages**), may be awarded in cases of particularly grievous circumstances where the plaintiff suffered extreme anguish, or to punish the perpetrator for horrific or heinous behavior and to make an example of him (Black's Law Dictionary, 2004), as well as to deter others from engaging in similar conduct in the future. Punitive damages can amount to large sums of money, and are often criticized as a financial windfall by defendants because they reward the plaintiff above and beyond the extent of his or her injuries (see discussion of damages in Chapter 2.11 *Negligence*). It should be noted, however, that punitive damages are less commonly awarded, because courts must first be persuaded that the requisite extenuating circumstances exist to merit this extraordinary remedy.

Plaintiffs can also seek **equitable** relief, which takes the form of an **injunction** or **specific performance**. These are essentially court orders that command or prohibit an act. For example, in the wake of the infamous spectator-infused donnybrook at the Detroit Pistons-Indiana Pacers NBA game in 2004, Pacer Ron Artest obtained a **restraining order** against John Green, the Pistons fan who threw a cup at Artest that fueled the melee in the stands.

Vicarious Liability

Recreation and sport managers should be aware that supervisors and organizations can be held liable for the intentional torts committed by their employees under the employer-employee doctrine of ***respondeat superior*** (see Chapter 2.12 *Which Parties Are Liable?*). A significant, and practical, reason for naming parties in addition to the actual tortfeasor as defendants in a suit is that oftentimes the perpetrator is **judgment proof**, meaning that he or she does not have the assets with which to satisfy the plaintiff's award for damages. In order to attach liability to the employer, the tort must have been committed by an employee within the course and scope of employment. For example, under this theory, if security personnel at an event or a bouncer at a club wrongfully manhandles a patron resulting in injury, the patron could bring suit against the assailant's employer. On the other hand, if the employee committed an assault and/or battery in a capacity that was unrelated to the performance of his job (*e.g.*, carrying out a personal grudge), then the employer would not be liable to the injured party. Thus, recreation and sport managers should be aware of this potential liability and take steps to ensure that their employees—particularly those employees whose duties contemplate the likelihood of physical contact with others—are properly trained in the appropriate use of force.

Toone v. Adams (1964) involved a suit by a minor league umpire against a baseball manager and his club for injuries sustained in a punch from a fan after a particularly contentious game. The umpire alleged that the manager's on-field protests of the umpire's calls incited the fan to commit the assault. The court, however, concluded that the manager and club were not liable because the manager's conduct was not directly related to the ensuing assault. In this case, the nexus between the manager's antics and fan's violent act was not sufficiently drawn for one to be a natural and proximate result of the other.

In *Godfrey v. Iverson* (2009), nightclub patron Marlin Godfrey was battered by NBA player Allen Iverson's bodyguard and suffered injuries that required hospital emergency room attention. Even though Iverson was not personally involved in the scuffle, he was present and watched the fight from the VIP section of the nightclub. The appellate court said that "negligent supervision arises when an employer knew or should have known that its employee behaved in a dangerous or otherwise incompetent manner, and that the employer, armed with that knowledge, failed to adequately supervise its employee," and upheld the trial court's verdict against Iverson and award of $260,000 for Godfrey. (For other cases involving assault and battery and naming the assailants' employer as an additional defendant under the doctrine of vicarious liability, see *Hackbart v. Cincinnati Bengals* [1979] and *Manning v. Grimsley* [1981] on the Supplemental Website.)

For an excellent discussion and to obtain a better understanding of an employer's liability for intentional torts committed by an employee, see *Baumeister v. Plunkett* (1996), where the court held that defendant Humana Hospital was not liable for the assault committed by a nursing supervisor on a nurse technician, because even though the assault occurred during the supervisor's course of employment (*i.e.*, during working hours and at the hospital's premises), the act of violence was neither primarily employment rooted nor reasonably incidental to the performance of the supervisor's duties.

SIGNIFICANT CASE

The following case involves an injury sustained by an age-group football player in practice as a result of his being the subject in a tackling demonstration conducted by a coach. It raises the issue of consent and whether the scope of this consent extends to his participation in direct physical contact with participants beyond his age and experience. Note the court's analysis of assault and battery, and its conclusion that the plaintiff's apprehension of imminent harm—a requisite element of assault—was wanting in this case. Note also the court's admonishment on remand that the plaintiff could pursue its claim for punitive damages. The dissenting opinion that immediately follows the court's opinion is provided to illustrate the nuanced views of the law.

KOFFMAN V. GARNETT
Supreme Court of Virginia
265 Va. 12, 574 S.E.2d 258
Jan. 10, 2003

Opinion by Justice Elizabeth B. Lacy

In this case we consider whether the trial court properly dismissed the plaintiffs' second amended motion for judgment for failure to state causes of action for gross negligence, assault, and battery.

* * *

In the fall of 2000, Andrew W. Koffman, a 13-year old middle school student at a public school in Botetourt County, began participating on the school's football team. It was Andy's first season playing organized football, and he was positioned as a third-string defensive player. James Garnett was employed by the Botetourt County School Board as an assistant coach for the football team and was responsible for the supervision, training, and instruction of the team's defensive players.

The team lost its first game of the season. Garnett was upset by the defensive players' inadequate tackling in that game and became further displeased by what he perceived as inadequate tackling during the first practice following the loss.

Garnett ordered Andy to hold a football and "stand upright and motionless" so that Garnett could explain the proper tackling technique to the defensive players. Then Garnett, without further warning, thrust his arms around Andy's body, lifted him "off his feet by two feet or more," and "slamm[ed]" him to the ground. Andy weighed 144 pounds, while Garnett weighed approximately 260 pounds. The force of the tackle broke the humerus bone in Andy's left arm. During prior practices, no coach had used physical force to instruct players on rules or techniques of playing football.

In his second amended motion for judgment, Andy, by his father and next friend, Richard Koffman, and Andy's parents, Richard and Rebecca Koffman, individually, (collectively "the Koffmans") alleged that Andy was injured as a result of Garnett's simple and gross negligence and intentional acts of assault and battery. Garnett filed a demurrer and plea of sovereign immunity, asserting that the second amended motion for judgment did not allege sufficient facts to support a lack of consent to the tackling demonstration and, therefore, did not plead causes of action for either gross negligence, assault, or battery. The trial court dismissed the action, finding that Garnett, as a school board employee, was entitled to sovereign immunity for acts of simple negligence and that the facts alleged were insufficient to state causes of action for gross negligence, assault, or battery because the instruction and playing of football are "inherently dangerous and always potentially violent." In this appeal, the Koffmans do not challenge the trial court's ruling on Garnett's plea of sovereign immunity but do assert that they pled sufficient facts in their second amended motion for judgment to sustain their claims of gross negligence, assault, and battery.

* * *

The disparity in size between Garnett and Andy was obvious to Garnett. Because of his authority as a coach, Garnett must have anticipated that Andy would comply with his instructions to stand in a non-defensive, upright, and motionless position. Under these circumstances, Garnett proceeded to aggressively tackle the much smaller, inexperienced student football player, by lifting him more than two feet from the ground and slamming him into the turf. According to the Koffmans' allegations, no coach had tackled any player previously so there was no reason for Andy to expect to be tackled by Garnett, nor was Andy warned of the impending tackle or of the force Garnett would use.

As the trial court observed, receiving an injury while participating in a tackling demonstration may be part of the sport. The facts alleged in this case, however, go beyond the circumstances of simply being tackled in the course of participating in organized football. Here Garnett's knowledge of his greater size and experience, his instruction implying that Andy was not to take any action to defend himself from the force of a tackle, the force he used during the tackle, and Garnett's previous practice of not personally using force to demonstrate or teach football technique could lead a reasonable person to conclude that, in this instance, Garnett's actions were imprudent and were taken in utter disregard for the safety of the player involved. Because reasonable persons could disagree on this issue, a jury issue was presented, and the trial court erred in holding that, as a matter of law, the second amended motion for judgment was inadequate to state a claim for gross negligence.

* * *

The trial court held that the second amended motion for judgment was insufficient as a matter of law to establish causes of action for the torts of assault and battery. We begin by identifying the elements of these two independent torts. See Charles E. Friend, Personal Injury Law in Virginia 6.2.1 (2d ed. 1998).

The tort of assault consists of an act intended to cause either harmful or offensive contact with another person or apprehension of such contact, and that creates in that other person's mind a reasonable apprehension of an imminent battery. Restatement (Second) of Torts 21 (1965); Friend 6.3.1 at 226; Fowler V. Harper, et al., The Law of Torts 3.5 at 3:18-:19 (3d ed. Cum. Supp. 2003).

The tort of battery is an unwanted touching which is neither consented to, excused, nor justified. See Washburn v. Klara, 263 Va. 586, 561 S.E.2d 682 (2002); Woodbury v. Courtney, 239 Va. 651, 391 S.E.2d 293 (1990). Although these two torts "go together like ham and eggs," the difference between them is "that between physical contact and the mere apprehension of it. One may exist without the other." W. Page Keeton, Prosser and Keeton on Torts 10 at 46; see also Friend 6.3.

The Koffmans' second amended motion for judgment does not include an allegation that Andy had any apprehension of an immediate battery. This allegation cannot be supplied by inference because any inference of Andy's apprehension is discredited by the affirmative allegations that Andy had no warning of an imminent forceful tackle by Garnett. The Koffmans argue that a reasonable inference of apprehension can be found "in the very short period of time that it took the coach to lift Andy into the air and throw him violently to the ground." At this point, however, the battery alleged by the Koffmans was in progress. Accordingly, we find that the pleadings were insufficient as a matter of law to establish a cause of action for civil assault.

The second amended motion for judgment is sufficient, however, to establish a cause of action for the tort of battery. The Koffmans pled that Andy consented to physical contact with players "of like age and experience" and that neither Andy nor his parents expected or consented to his "participation in aggressive contact tackling by the adult coaches." Further, the Koffmans pled that, in the past, coaches had not tackled players as a method of instruction. Garnett asserts that, by consenting to play football, Andy consented to be tackled, by either other football players or by the coaches. Whether Andy consented to be tackled by Garnett in the manner alleged was a matter of fact. Based on the allegations in the Koffmans' second amended motion for judgment, reasonable persons could disagree on whether Andy gave such consent. Thus, we find that the trial court erred in holding that the Koffmans' second amended motion for judgment was insufficient as a matter of law to establish a claim for battery.

For the above reasons, we will reverse the trial court's judgment that the Koffmans' second amended motion for judgment was insufficient as a matter of law to establish the causes of actions for gross negligence and battery and remand the case for further proceedings consistent with this opinion.*

Reversed and remanded.

JUSTICE KINSER, concurring in part and dissenting in part.

I agree with the majority opinion except with regard to the issue of consent as it pertains to the intentional tort of battery. In my view, the second amended motion for judgment filed by the plaintiffs, Andrew W. Koffman, by his father and next friend, and Richard Koffman and Rebecca Koffman, individually, was insufficient as a matter of law to state a claim for battery.**

Absent fraud, consent is generally a defense to an alleged battery. See Banovitch v. Commonwealth, 196 Va. 210, 219, 83 S.E.2d 369, 375 (1954); Perkins v. Commonwealth, 31 Va. App. 326, 330, 523 S.E.2d 512, 513 (2000); People ex rel. Arvada v. Nissen, 650 P.2d 547, 551 (Colo. 1982); Bergman v. Anderson, 411 N.W.2d 336, 339 (Neb. 1987); Willey v. Carpenter, 23 A. 630, 631 (Vt. 1891); Restatement (Second) of Torts 13, cmt. d (1965). In the context of this case, "[t]aking part in a game manifests a willingness to submit to such bodily contacts or restrictions of liberty as are permitted by its rules or usages." Restatement (Second) of Torts 50, cmt. b (1965), quoted in Thompson v. McNeill, 559 N.E.2d 705, 708 (Ohio 1990); see also Kabella v. Bouschelle, 672 P.2d 290, 292 (N.M. Ct. App. 1983). However, participating in a particular sport "does not

---

*Because we have concluded that a cause of action for an intentional tort was sufficiently pled, on remand, the Koffmans may pursue their claim for punitive damages.

**Although the circuit court sustained the demurrer with regard to the alleged battery on the basis that an intention to batter and inflict injury on Andy could not be inferred from the alleged facts, the majority does not address that holding. Since the majority discusses only the issue of consent, I confine my dissent to that question.

manifest consent to contacts which are prohibited by rules or usages of the game if such rules or usages are designed to protect the participants and not merely to secure the better playing of the game as a test of skill." Restatement (Second) of Torts 50, cmt. b (1965) quoted in Thompson, 559 N.E.2d at 708; see also Kabella, 672 P.2d at 292.

The thrust of the plaintiffs' allegations is that they did not consent to "Andy's participation in aggressive contact tackling by the adult coaches" but that they consented only to Andy's engaging "in a contact sport with other children of like age and experience." They further alleged that the coaches had not previously tackled the players when instructing them about the rules and techniques of football.

It is notable, in my opinion, that the plaintiffs admitted in their pleading that Andy's coach was "responsible . . . for the supervision, training and instruction of the defensive players." It cannot be disputed that one responsibility of a football coach is to minimize the possibility that players will sustain "something more than slight injury" while playing the sport. Vendrell v. School District No. 26C, Malheur County, 376 P.2d 406, 413 (Ore. 1962). A football coach cannot be expected "to extract from the game the body clashes that cause bruises, jolts and hard falls." Id. Instead, a coach should ensure that players are able to "withstand the shocks, blows and other rough treatment with which they would meet in actual play" by making certain that players are in "sound physical condition," are issued proper protective equipment, and are "taught and shown how to handle [themselves] while in play." Id. The instruction on how to handle themselves during a game should include demonstrations of proper tackling techniques. Id. By voluntarily participating in football, Andy and his parents necessarily consented to instruction by the coach on such techniques. The alleged battery occurred during that instruction.

The plaintiffs alleged that they were not aware that Andy's coach would use physical force to instruct on the rules and techniques of football since neither he nor the other coaches had done so in the past. Surely, the plaintiffs are not claiming that the scope of their consent changed from day to day depending on the coaches' instruction methods during prior practices. Moreover, they did not allege that they were told that the coaches would not use physical demonstrations to instruct the players.

Additionally, the plaintiffs did not allege that the tackle itself violated any rule or usage of the sport of football. Nor did they plead that Andy could not have been tackled by a larger, physically stronger, and more experienced player either during a game or practice. Tackling and instruction on proper tackling techniques are aspects of the sport of football to which a player consents when making a decision to participate in the sport.

In sum, I conclude that the plaintiffs did not sufficiently plead a claim for battery. We must remember that acts that might give rise to a battery on a city street will not do so in the context of the sport of football. See Thompson, 559 N.E.2d at 707. We must also not blur the lines between gross negligence and battery because the latter is an intentional tort. I agree fully that the plaintiffs alleged sufficient facts to proceed with their claim for gross negligence.

For these reasons, I respectfully concur, in part, and dissent, in part, and would affirm the judgment of the circuit court sustaining the demurrer with regard to the claim for battery.

CASES ON THE SUPPLEMENTAL WEBSITE

Archibald v. Kemble, 971 A.2d 513 (Pa. Super. 2009), appeal denied, 989 A.2d 914 (Pa. 2010). Note the court's application of the reckless—versus intentional—conduct standard in the situation of an adult, no-check hockey game, where injury was sustained as a result of an illegal check.

Hackbart v. Cincinnati Bengals, Inc., 601 F.2d 516 (10th Cir. 1979), cert. denied, 444 U.S. 931 (1979). Stands for the proposition that even in professional football, a player may be held responsible for injuring an opponent if he acts with reckless disregard for the opponent's safety.

Overall v. Kadella, 361 N.W.2d 352, 138 Mich.App. 351 (1985). Pay heed to the proposition that while a hockey player's participation in a game manifests his consent to bodily contacts that are permitted by the rules of the game, a player is liable for intentional acts resulting in injury that go beyond what is ordinarily permissible.

Manning v. Grimsley, 643 F.2d 20 (First Cir. 1981). Examines the issue of vicarious liability, and how an employer can be held liable for damages for injuries attributable to an employee's assault of a patron.

Regina v. Cey, 48 C.C.C. 3d 480 (Sask. Ct. App. 1989). Consider this Canadian court's guidelines in determining whether an ice hockey player's violent conduct exceeds the bounds of normality.

QUESTIONS YOU SHOULD BE ABLE TO ANSWER

1. What are the elements necessary to prove a case for assault? Battery?

2. Since assault and battery are crimes as well as torts, is it possible for a person to be prosecuted in criminal court and sued in civil court for committing the same acts? Why or why not?

3. How is negligence distinguishable from assault and battery?

4. What are the legal remedies available to a victim of civil assault and battery?

5. In the sport and recreation environment, how can managers insulate themselves and their organizations from liability for assault and battery?

REFERENCES

Cases
Baumeister v. Plunkett, 673 S.2d 994 (La. 1996).
Brokaw v. Winfield-Mt. Union Community School District, 788 N.W.2d 386 (Ia. 2010).
Claytonv. New Dreamland Roller Skating Rink, 82 A.2d 458 (N.J. Super. 1951).
Cunico v. Miller, 2002 WL 339385 (Cal.App. 2 Dist.).
Esshaki v. Millman, 2009 Mich. App. Lexis 582.
Godfrey v. Iverson, No. 07-7151 (D.C. Cir. 2009).
Goff v. Clarke, 302 A.D.2d 725, 755 N.Y.S.2d 493 (NY App.Div. 2003).
Hennessey v. Pyne, 694 A.2d 691 (R.I. 1979).
Mason v. Cohn, 438 N.Y.S.2d 462 (Sup. Ct. 1981).
Northwestern Nat. Cas. Co. v. McNulty, 307 F.2d 432 (5th Cir. 1962).
People v. Solak, 382 NW2d 495 (Mich.App. 1985).
Ritchie-Gamester v. City of Berkeley, 461 Mich. 73, 597 N.W.2d 517 (1999).
State v. Murphy, 500 P.2d 1276 (1972).
Steele v. State, 778 P.2d 929 (Ok.Cr.App. 1989).
Toone v. Adams, 262 N.C. 403, 137 S.E.2d 132 (1964).
Wager v. Pro, 603 F.2d 1005 (D.C. Cir. 1979).

Publications
American Law Institute, (2009), Restatement (Second) of Torts.
FindLaw, http://injury.findlaw.com/assault-and-battery/elements-of-assault.html, accessed March 16, 2009.
Garner, B.A., ed. (2004), Black's Law Dictionary, 8th edition, Thomson West.
http://hoopedia.nba.com/index.php?title=Pacers-Pistons_Brawl, accessed March 15, 2009.
Keeton, W.P., Dobbs, D.B., Keeton, R.E., Owen, D.G. (1984), Prosser and Keeton on Torts, 5th ed., West Publishing Co., St. Paul, MN.
Kinsella, N.S. (1996), "Punishment and Proportionality: The Estoppel Approach," Journal of Libertarian Studies, 12:1.
Legal Information Institute, http://topics.law.cornell.edu/wex/asault, accessed December 17, 2008.
McCarthy, M., "Fan Who Ignited Brawl Forever Banned from Pistons' Homes Games," USA Today, November 17, 2006.

Legislation
LA-R.S. 14:36 (Louisiana Criminal Code), definition of assault.

DEFAMATION
Anita M. Moorman | University of Louisville

The tort of defamation dates back to early sixteenth-century common law. Defamation law provides recourse for false, insidious, or irresponsible statements that damage an individual's reputation. As defined by *Black's Law Dictionary* (Black, 1990), **defamation** is "that which tends to injure reputation; to diminish the esteem, respect, goodwill or confidence in which the plaintiff is held, or to excite adverse, derogatory or unpleasant feelings or opinions against him" (p. 417).

FUNDAMENTAL CONCEPTS

In the sport industry, defamation claims are raised in a variety of settings that may include statements made by an athletic director about reasons for terminating a coach; statements made by a coach about one of his assistant coaches; statements made by a professional athlete about his agent; statements published by a newspaper about an athlete; statements published on an Internet discussion board about an athlete, coach, or owner of a professional sport team; or statements made during a television sports program comparing an athlete to another person convicted of numerous crimes. All of these examples, depending on the substance and truthfulness of the statements made, could easily form the basis of a defamation action. For example, in 2013, former St. Louis Cardinal and current Los Angeles Angels of Anaheim first baseman Albert Pujols filed a defamation lawsuit against retired player turned radio personality Jack Clark after Clark claimed during a radio show that Pujols used performance enhancing drugs. Pujols, in the complaint, alleged that Clark lied and that his comments damaged Pujols' reputation, causing him to suffer "personal humiliation, mental anguish and anxiety" (DiGiovanna, 2013). Clark eventually issued a retraction and Pujols dropped the lawsuit (Axisa, 2014).

Elements of a Defamation Claim

The tort of defamation is a state law claim, which means each state will define the essential elements of the claim. Most states follow elements very similar to those included in the Restatement (Second) of Torts § 558, which requires the following four elements to establish a defamation claim:

1. a false and defamatory statement of fact,
2. publication to a third party,
3. fault or negligence of the publisher, and
4. damage or actual injury.

The plaintiff bears the burden of proof in a defamation action (Restatement [Second] of Torts). Under common law defamation, the standard for proving negligence or fault varies depending upon whether the person about whom the statement is made is a **public** or **private figure**. For example, in order for a sport celebrity or other public figure, such as Tom Brady of the New England Patriots, to prove negligence or fault (the third element identified above), he would have to demonstrate that the person making the statement did so with actual malice. To show **actual malice**, it must be shown that the speaker knew the statement was false or published it with a total disregard for whether it was true or false. A private person would only have to prove that the statement was published negligently, which means that the speaker failed to exercise reasonable care to determine whether the statement was true or false. This is a much lower burden of proof for the private individual. Although private figures are not required to show actual malice in order to recover for defamation, they must prove actual injury. As defined by the Supreme Court in *Gertz v. Robert Welch, Inc.* (1974), actual injury includes "impairment of reputation and standing in the community, personal humiliation, and mental anguish and suffering" (p. 350). The distinction between the burden of proof for public figures as opposed to a private individual, such as spectator or security guard, is further explained in the Defamation and the First Amendment section.

Franklin & Rabin (1996, p. 880) also observed that "no liability exists if a third person unexpectedly overhears a private conversation between plaintiff and defendant." Further, publications that are merely embarrassing do not qualify as defamatory. Rather, publications must truly reflect "sharp criticism" that damages reputation (Franklin & Rabin, 1996). Regardless, when ascertaining whether a defendant is liable for defamation, the entire publication (e.g., title, punctuation, paragraphing, full article) will be considered versus one particular phrase or statement.

Types of Defamation: Slander and Libel

The tort of defamation includes both slander and libel. Defamatory comments made verbally, such as those heard on television, exemplify **slander**. **Libel** is a broader category of communication. Written comments, photographs, and cartoons, such as those appearing in newspapers, on the Internet, and in other written or tangible forms, are examples of libel. A verbal comment is slanderous *per se* (which means inherently defamatory) and a written comment is libel *per se* if it falls into one of the following categories: (1) accuses the plaintiff of criminal conduct; (2) accuses the plaintiff of having a loathsome disease; (3) accuses the female plaintiff of being unchaste; (4) accuses the plaintiff of misconduct in public office; or (5) injures the plaintiff's profession, business, or trade. If a statement falls into one of these categories, it is presumed as a matter of law that the reputation of the individual about whom the false statement was made will be injured. For example, false comments accusing someone of embezzling funds from a community youth sports organization, having sex with an entire lacrosse team, or engaging in illegal student athlete recruiting practices could be construed as slanderous *per se* (Carpenter, 1995). No reasonable person could ever interpret such statements as reflecting positively upon the person about whom they were spoken. As explained by the court in *Romaine v. Kallinger* (1988), if a published statement is susceptible of one meaning only, and that meaning is defamatory, the statement is libelous as a matter of law. This can be an important distinction since statements that are considered defamatory *per se* do not require the plaintiff to prove special damages because the damage is presumed since the statements are *per se* (inherently) harmful. The Significant Case at the end of the chapter applies these concepts to statements made by an athletic director about a coach. Recall this distinction between defamation and defamation *per se* as you read through that case.

Slander and libel were originally recognized as two distinct types of defamation. Libel, written defamatory statements, was thought to be more damaging because, at the time the distinction arose, few persons could read or write. Therefore, anything which was written would carry a louder ring of purported truth (*Matherson v. Marchello*, 1984). In addition, a written defamation could be disseminated more widely and carried a degree of permanence. For example, newspapers and magazines could be retained for weeks while statements made on television vanished within seconds. Technology now secures media statements in a tangible form and most jurisdictions refer to the two terms (i.e., slander and libel) interchangeably as simply defamation (Pember, 1990).

Defamation and the First Amendment

The tort of defamation, like most tort theories, evolved as a matter of state law. However, unlike other torts, the law of defamation has been influenced significantly by First Amendment considerations since the mid-1960s (Franklin & Rabin, 1996). Allowing one person to sue another person because of what that person said or wrote often collides with First Amendment freedom of speech and freedom of the press. Thus, the interests of the state in protecting its citizens from defamatory statements is often weighed against the interests preserved in the First Amendment insuring an open forum for all ideas.

Elaborating on the importance of defamation law to an individual, Justice Stewart said, "The right of a man to the protection of his own reputation from unjustified invasion and wrongful hurt reflects no more than our basic concept of the essential dignity and worth of every human being . . ." (*Rosenblatt v. Baer*, 1966, p. 92). Conversely, critics say defamation law stifles individual commentary which contributes to the marketplace of ideas. As stated earlier, the judicial system attempts to balance the right to preserve one's reputation with individual Constitutional rights.

To promote balance between plaintiff and defendant, Supreme Court decisions have recognized that certain persons enjoy greater protection from damaging statements than do other persons. For example, we have a right to know, ask, and talk about the past financial dealings of our elected officials in a public forum because it may affect their ability to perform and our confidence in them. However, we certainly have no right to know, ask, or talk about the past financial dealings of our next door neighbor or a coworker in a public forum. Simply put, some people, such as a celebrity, professional athlete, or sports broadcaster must tolerate more intrusive or hurtful comments made publicly about them based upon their position or actions in our society. Thus, three categories have emerged from Supreme Court decisions to help correctly balance individual interests against First Amendment rights. These three categories are: public officials, public figures, and private figures.

The Public Official

Defamation law changed drastically in the mid-1960s from earlier sixteenth-century interpretations which considered attacks on public officials as seditious libels that could be treated as criminal (Franklin & Rabin, 1996). The 1964 Supreme Court decision in *New York Times Co. v. Sullivan* (hereinafter "*New York Times*") revolutionized the way the judiciary interpreted and applied defamation law. As stated by Pember (1990), "This is one of the most important First Amendment cases ever decided..." (p. 129). In *New York Times*, the Supreme Court prohibited *public officials* from recovering damages for defamatory comments relating to official conduct unless the plaintiff could prove with convincing clarity that the statement was made with *actual malice*. Communication made with **actual malice** was defined by the Court as communication made "with knowledge that it was false or with reckless disregard of whether it was false or not" (*New York Times*, 1964, p. 380).

The Supreme Court believed that the public had a right to know and evaluate for themselves how leaders governed. Further, open debate, although at times caustic and unpleasant, assured the exchange of ideas necessary to bring about political and social change desired by the people (*New York Times*, 1964). Further, the freedom of the people to criticize freely and without actual malice better balances the absolute privilege enjoyed by the public official.

Pember (1990) succinctly defines a **public official** as "someone who works for a government and draws a salary from the public payroll" (p. 133). The Supreme Court also attempted to define the public official. In *Rosenblatt v. Baer* (1966) the Court questioned whether all individuals employed by the state are public officials or just those employed in "high-powered" positions. As stated by Justice Douglas in a concurring opinion, "anyone on the public payroll" qualifies as a public official (p. 89).

It would appear from the above decisions that subsequent court decisions would classify all teachers, coaches, and recreation supervisors as public officials. However, a contrary decision was issued by the Supreme Court of Kentucky in *Warford v. Lexington Herald* in 1980. As decided by this court, an assistant basketball recruiting coach at the University of Pittsburgh was not classified as either a public official or a public or limited-purpose public figure (see the section below dealing with the public figure and limited-purpose public figure).

The Public Figure

In a subsequent landmark case, *Curtis Publishing Co. v. Butts* (1967), the Supreme Court extended the constitutional protection given to statements about public officials in *New York Times* to public figures as well. Celebrities, television personalities, and highly successful business/industry leaders (i.e., public figures) often had as much societal influence as government officials, hence the similar constitutional protection afforded to those communicating about these individuals. Similar to the standard of proof established in *New York Times*, the *Curtis* court stated that individuals falling into the status of a public figure must prove actual malice to recover for damages. The determination of whether a person is a public figure is a matter of law. Public figure status does not depend on the desires of the individual. A plaintiff may not escape public figure status if he voluntarily engages in a course of conduct that invites attention and comment. Indeed, the distinction between public and private figures is based upon two considerations: the plaintiff's access to the media, and the extent to which the plaintiff, by virtue of his position in the community or involvement in a particular matter of public concern, can be said to invite public comment and attention.

As explained by the Supreme Court in *Curtis Publishing Co. v. Butts* (1967), a **public figure** is an individual who has, because of his or her activities, "commanded sufficient continuing public interest" (p. 155). The Supreme Court recognized the Athletic Director of the University of Georgia (Wally Butts), as a public figure. To date, *Butts* is the only Supreme Court case to apply the public figure test to a sports figure; since then many other courts have treated athletic directors, coaches, and athletes as public figures in a variety of settings from professional sports to high school athletics. In *Waldbaum v. Fairchild Publications, Inc.* (1980) the district court observed that "many well-known athletes, entertainers, and other personages endorse commercial products... This phenomenon, regardless of whether it is justified, indicates that famous persons may be able to transfer their recognition and influence from one field to another" (p. 1294). Athletes, like politicians, can sway individual thinking. Consequently, their individual actions are open to public debate and scrutiny.

The *Curtis* court further provided two reasons for its extension of the actual malice standard to public figures as well as public officials. First, the plaintiff–public figure voluntarily "thrusts" himself or herself into the "vortex" of "important public controversies" (*Curtis Publishing Co. v. Butts*, 1967). If society chooses to direct massive public attention to a particular sphere of activity, those who enter that sphere invite such attention and must overcome the *Times* [actual malice] standard (*Chuy v. Philadelphia Eagles Football Club*, 1979, p. 267). Second, like public officials, public figures had "sufficient access to the means of counter argument" via the media. Certainly most, if not all, persons classified as public figures have ready access to the media and public forums in which they can defend themselves or respond to criticism or controversial statements. David Beckham's libel and slander lawsuit against In Touch magazine over a story claiming he had cheated on his wife with a prostitute was dismissed because the federal district judge concluded Beckham hadn't shown any evidence that the story had been published with malice. The court also stated that the allegations of infidelity by Beckham would be of interest to the public because of his status as a public figure (CBSNews, 2015).

The Limited-Purpose Public Person

Persons with instant national recognition and constant national media exposure such as Jay Leno, Peyton Manning, Dick Vitale, and Diane Sawyer are considered all-purpose public figures (Barron & Dienes, 1979). However, the 1974 Supreme Court decision in *Gertz v. Robert Welch, Inc.* introduced the concept of a **limited purpose public person** as "... an individual [who] voluntarily injects himself or is drawn into a particular public controversy and thereby becomes a public figure for a limited range of issues" (p. 351). The limited-purpose public figure has instant *local* recognition and constant media coverage on a *local* level. A limited purpose public figure is a person who becomes a public figure for a specific range of issues by being drawn into or voluntarily injecting himself into a specific public controversy.

To determine whether a person is a limited purpose public figure we must examine that person's participation in the controversy from which the alleged defamation arose, and whether he has attained a general notoriety in the community by reason of that participation (*Daubenmire v. Sommers*, 2004). A three-part test is used to make this determination: The court must determine that (1) there is a public controversy; (2) the plaintiff played a sufficiently central role in that controversy; and (3) the alleged defamation was germane to the plaintiff's involvement in the controversy (*Daubenmire v. Sommers*, 2004).

For example, if your community is considering building a multimillion dollar sports stadium, and a local university professor who is an expert in stadium finance appears on a local radio talk show and actively participates in the public debate on the funding initiative, she may qualify as a limited-purpose public figure, even though in any other context she would have most certainly been a private person. Most sport figures (e.g., coaches, athletes, sport broadcasters) tend to be classified as limited-purpose public figures. For example, in *Bell v. the Associated Press* (1984), a wide receiver for the Tampa Bay Buccaneers, whose notorious career includes a litany of misdeeds, was found to be a limited purpose public figure. The court held, "with respect to professional athletes ... charges of criminal misconduct are a subject of public controversy and those who are the subject of such charges are public figures for that limited purpose."

Further, many jobs "produce at least limited-purpose public figure status by virtue of the associations it entails" (Franklin & Rabin, 1996, p. 991). To recover in a defamation action, a public figure, including a limited purpose public figure, must show by clear and convincing evidence that the statements were made with actual malice, that is, with knowledge that the statements were false or with reckless disregard of whether they were false or not. Sufficient evidence must exist to permit the conclusion that the defendant in fact had serious doubt as to the truth of the statements (*Daubenmire v. Sommers*, 2004).

The Private Figure
The "private figure" classification refers to individual citizens who are not involved in public issues or employed as a public official. Distinguishing between a public versus private figure is a critical issue for a plaintiff. Classification as a private person is important as private figures need only prove that an alleged defamatory statement was negligently made rather than made with actual malice as discussed above. Negligence is the failure to exercise "reasonable care." This is a much lower standard of proof than that required for public officials, public figures, or limited-purpose public figures.

The difficulty comes in ascertaining who qualifies as a "private figure." Defendants allege that private citizens involved in matters of interest to the public constitute limited-purpose public figures and are subject to the actual malice standard of proof required by *New York Times*. According to the Supreme Court's plurality decision in *Rosenbloom v. Metromedia, Inc.* (1971), all publication regarding matters of general interest or public concern should be protected by requiring plaintiffs to prove actual malice. Subsequent courts, concerned about the improper balance between competing interests, repudiated the "public interest" or "subject matter" standard established in the 1971 *Rosenbloom* case.

Two dominant reasons explain why the Court preserved the private person status granting individuals a lower standard of proof. First, it is assumed that private individuals do not have the same ability to access the media as public officials and public figures. Access to the media provides public officials and public figures with an opportunity to refute defamatory statements. The value of media access is illustrated by the Iowa Libel Research Project. According to this research project, almost 75 percent of defamed plaintiffs indicated they would have found adequate recourse if "the news medium would have published or broadcast a correction, retraction or apology" (Pember, 1990). Second, it is said that public figures and public officials relinquish rights when they voluntarily become entangled in an issue of public concern. Private individuals, in comparison, are not attempting to influence society and are not desirous of media attention.

Statements of Fact v. Expressions of Opinion
Early common law protected statements of opinion from defamatory allegations. The Supreme Court affirmed this sentiment in the *Gertz* case in 1974. As stated by the Supreme Court, "Under the First Amendment there is no such thing as a false idea" (*Gertz v. Robert Welch, Inc.*, 1974, p. 339). However, statements based upon false facts, or undisclosed facts, are actionable. In other words, if an opinion is stated, then all the facts that were used in deriving the opinion should be disclosed. This enables an individual to read the facts and then draw his or her own conclusion (i.e., opinion), which may differ from that of the writer or publisher. The decision as to whether a statement constitutes fact or opinion is a question of law for the court to decide.

The Supreme Court in *Milkovich v. Lorain Journal Co.* (1990) further narrowed the protection given to statements of opinion. As explained by the Court, merely prefacing a statement with "In my opinion . . ." does not insulate an individual from defamation liability. More specifically, the Court stated

> "Even if the speaker states the facts upon which he bases his opinion, if those facts are either incorrect or incomplete, or if his assessment of them is erroneous, the statement may still imply a false assertion of fact. Simply couching such statements in terms of opinion does not dispel these implications . . ." (p. 2706).

Statements made or included on websites, discussion boards, and chat rooms all have the potential to raise questions regarding defamation. While most statements in an Internet chat room would be considered statements of opinion, often statements of opinion are cloaked with statements of fact (See *Diebella v. Hopkins* (2002) included in the Supplemental Website) and as mentioned previously could form the basis of a defamation action when posted to Facebook or Twitter.

In *Stepien v. Franklin* (1988) the Court of Appeals of Ohio held an assortment of disparaging adjectives to be constitutionally protected opinion. The adjectives included the following: "Stupid," "dumb," "buffoon," "nincompoop," "scum," "a cancer," "an obscenity," "gutless liar," "unmitigated liar," "pathological liar," "egomaniac," "nuts," "crazy," "irrational," "suicidal," "lunatic" (p. 1327). As illustrated above, the specific language used by the defendant is overtly injurious. However, the syllabus by the court, justifying its action, stated, "The area of sports is a traditional haven for cajoling, invective, and hyperbole . . ." (p. 1326).

Society commonly accepts rowdy behavior as "part of the game." Even during the 1960s, the era of individual rights, the heckling involved in sport was viewed as commonplace. As explained by the Supreme Court of North Carolina in *Toone v. Adams* (1964), "For present day fans, a goodly part of the sport in a baseball game is goading and denouncing the umpire when they do not concur in his decisions, and most feel that, without one or more rhubarbs, they have not received their money" (p. 136).

The Supreme Court of Ohio (*Scott v. News-Herald*, 1986) concluded that most information conveyed in the sports section of a newspaper is "constitutionally protected." The *Scott* court's decision, although of limited precedential value, is precarious because it suggests that comments about a sport-related figure, regardless of their veracity or the publisher's degree of fault, are constitutionally protected.

Defenses to Defamation Claims

Truth is an absolute defense to all claims of defamation. Even if the actual facts turn out to be different than those contained in the statement, a defense of truthfulness may still apply. The statements do not necessarily have to be completely accurate, only substantively correct or truthful for the Truth defense to shield them. For example, truth would still serve as a viable defense in the situation where a personal trainer was charged with selling $250,000 worth of steroids to players when in actuality he only sold $125,000. In one case, a statement that a boxer tested positive for cocaine, when actually he had tested positive for marijuana was considered substantially true (*Cobb v. Time Inc.*, 1995). The significant case at the end of the chapter will help to further illustrate substantial truth as a defense to defamation.

Privilege, a second defense, refers to "a particular and peculiar benefit or advantage enjoyed by a person, company, or class, beyond the common advantages of other citizens" (Black, 1990, p. 1197). Privileged statements made without malice are immune from defamation liability (*Iacco v. Bohannon*, 1976; *Institute of Athletic Motivation v. Univ. of Ill.*, 1982). Common types of privilege include absolute privilege, qualified privilege, and fair comment.

Absolute privilege is enjoyed by those in: (1) a legislative forum (e.g., congressmen, congresswomen, senators, city council members); (2) the judicial forum (e.g., judges, lawyers, plaintiffs, defendants); and (3) administrative and executive branches of government (e.g., presidents, mayors, department heads). Persons occupying these roles have **"absolute" privilege**, i.e., there can be no liability for statements regardless of their falsity or disregard for the truth. This privilege exists to avoid censorship of desired communication that could otherwise possibly benefit society. The media is also protected from liability if during the broadcast or publication of statements during a public debate, defamatory comments are made by individuals who are protected by absolute privilege (Franklin & Rabin, 1996).

Qualified or conditional privilege represents a defense available to other defendants. Similar to absolute privilege, some situations demand the protection of communication to benefit society at large. As explained by Carpenter (1995), **qualified privilege** applies to statements made: (1) without knowledge of falsity, (2) by a person with reason to communicate the statement, and (3) communicated only to a person with a "justifiable interest in knowing." Individual managers often have qualified privilege, for example, when discussing employee behaviors with superiors and when providing employee references.

Fair comment represents a defense commonly used by media defendants. As explained by Black (1990), **fair comment** is a "form of qualified privilege applied to news media publications relating to discussion of matters which are of legitimate concern to the community as a whole because they materially affect the interests of all the community" (p. 596). There typically is no liability if the media publishes defamatory information so long as their report represents a fair and accurate summary or restatement of communication available to the public upon which they are relying. The fair comment defense is only appropriate when comments are made without malice and statements are based on true facts (Black, 1990; *Cohen v. Cowles Publishing Co.*, 1954; *Conkwright v. Globe News Publishing Company*, 1965).

Neutral reportage represents another defense similar in concept to fair reporting that is available to media defendants in certain circuits. Based upon the U.S. Court of Appeals landmark decision in *Edwards v. National Audubon Society* (1977), media defendants can publish statements made by responsible or prominent organizations even though the publisher doubts the veracity of the statements.

Defamation and the Internet

The growth of Internet-based information and news sources and social media has triggered a new wave of online defamation claims which raise several interesting questions. First, issues of jurisdiction arise since typically a defamation case should be filed in the state in which the defamation occurs (i.e. the statement is made). However, when the statement is made via social media such as Facebook and Twitter, the person making the statement is mobile and the statement itself is disseminated immediately to hundreds and possibly thousands of third parties simultaneously. The first Twitter defamation case brought by a landlord against a tenant making disparaging remarks about her apartment was dismissed and the judge ruled that a "tweet was nonactionable as a matter of law" (Bennett, 2010). Since that time however, a highly visible case against Courtney Love by a fashion designer resulted in a $430,000 settlement. Love had intended to use the "it's just a tweet defense" which seemed successful in the landlord/tenant case, but the California trial court refused to dismiss the case (Gardner, 2009). Love settled before trial started.

Potentially defamatory statements may take place in Internet chat rooms, message boards, or social media such as Twitter and Facebook. Internet-based defamation also creates the additional issue of anonymity, as a person making the defamatory comment may do so using an alias or pseudonym, thus making it more difficult to identify the defendant. Actor James Woods filed a $10 million defamation lawsuit against an anonymous Twitter user who suggested in a tweet that Woods was a drug addict (Simmons, 2015).

Many jurisdictions require the plaintiff to prove its case before a court will issue an order that an Internet service provider unveil the identity of the anonymous poster (*Dendrite International v. Doe*, 2001; *Doe v. Cahill*, 2005). Several sports-figures have sued for defamation based on anonymous comments. Professional golfer Phil Mickelson received a court order to compel an Internet service provider to unveil the identities of two anonymous bloggers who had claimed Mickelson had an illegitimate child (Vlessing, 2012). National Hockey League executive Brian Burke won the right to serve multiple message board users through non-traditional means who had speculated that Burke was fired from his positon of Toronto Maple Leafs General Manager due to an alleged extramarital affair (Rush, 2013). The court allowed Burke to serve multiple defendants by posting on various message boards where the defendants made their allegedly defamatory comments. These examples illustrate the unique issues that arise when defamation occurs in the Internet, thus requiring the cooperation of Internet service providers.

Damages

Defamation law encompasses two types of damages (*Matherson v. Marchello*, 1984). First, special damages reflect "actual pecuniary losses that the plaintiff can prove he or she sustained" as a direct result of the defendant's comments (Franklin & Rabin, 1996, p. 895; *Liberman v. Gelstein*, 1992). Lost wages or the loss of identified business customers, for example, are quantifiable and reflect special damages. Second, general damages, on the other hand, reflect nonquantifiable damages such as the presumed damage to one's reputation. Plaintiffs suing for slander must prove special damages unless the cause of action is slander *per se*.

Although an anomaly in tort law, the tort of defamation does not always require proof of damage. For example, in some states, plaintiffs suing for libel are not required to prove special damages (Franklin & Rabin, 1996). Rather, the existence of damage is *presumed* as a result of the publication itself (*Matherson v. Marchello*, 1984).

SIGNIFICANT CASE

The significant case presented below not only outlines the elements of a defamation action very well, but also addresses the concepts of special damages and the defense of qualified privilege. This case is also particularly helpful for current study since the allegedly offending statements were made in connection with employment termination. An increasing number of lawsuits involving wrongful termination and/or discrimination claims also include allegations of defamation. This emphasizes the importance of taking care in discussing employee performance and systematically evaluating employee performance consistent with established policies and practices.

TANNERITE SPORTS, LLC V. NBC UNIVERSAL MEDIA LLC
2015 U.S Dist. LEXIS 134862 (S.D.N.Y. 2015).

Tannerite Sports, LLC ("Tannerite") seeks injunctive and monetary relief for economic and reputational injuries that it allegedly suffered as result of statements made by Defendants in broadcast and Internet news reports published between March 23 and March 24, 2015. NBCU moves to dismiss the Amended Complaint for failure to state a claim under Rule 12(b)(6).

Facts
Tannerite is an Oregon-based company that "manufacturers, sells, and distributes Tannerite-brand binary (two-component) exploding rifle targets." Marketed for use at shooting ranges, Tannerite targets are designed to detonate upon the impact of a bullet fired from high-powered, center-fire rifles. Tannerite binary exploding targets result from the mixture of ammonium nitrate and aluminum powder, which the company sells as "kits" containing the chemicals in two separate and sealed packages. *** As designed, when the mixture meets the impact of a bullet fired from a high-power rifle, an explosion ensues. In its Product Guide, Tannerite provides detailed instructions for the safe use of its products and cautions that the dangers of misuse include serious injury and death. The company also urges target purchasers to "mix the targets at the range and shoot them immediately," and not to "transport, store, or sell the mixed composition" unless certified to do so. *** In addition, the Product Guide *** acknowledges that "there are, however, users doing unwise things with these targets" and warns that "[c]ontinued misuse of these targets may result in restrictions in their use." ***

NBCU's Allegedly Defamatory Statements
On March 23, 2015, NBC News aired a report on the "Today" show about the potential dangers of exploding rifle targets. In the lead-in to the NBCU Report, reporter Jeff Rossen is shown holding two explosive rifle targets while stating: "right now I am basically holding a bomb in my hand." Rossen then introduces a series of video clips capturing unusually explosive detonations, explaining that "you're about to see what can happen when this gets in the wrong hands." In one video, a refrigerator explodes and causes a bystander, Jennifer Plank-Greer, to lose a hand due to resulting shrapnel. The NBCU Report further discusses the use of ammonium nitrate — one of the two components of Tannerite targets — by terrorists in the Oklahoma City bombing and in attacks on American soldiers in Afghanistan. The NBCU Report also includes a graphic of an FBI bulletin warning that exploding targets have "potential use as explosives in IEDs," and shows an NBC News reporter purchasing Tannerite targets in bulk. Travis Bond, a firearms expert, expresses his opposition to the unregulated sale of exploding targets despite his strong support of the Second Amendment. Rossen then comments that "Tannerite is getting around the law on a technicality — separating the two ingredients even though they are sold together." The NBCU Report also displays and narrates Tannerite's statement that "no additional regulations are needed beyond current laws because the product is safe when used correctly." The segment concludes with Rossen reassuring the show's hosts that the targets in the studio are not dangerous without the "catalyst." In conjunction with the NBCU Report, NBCU published an Internet Article ("NBCU Internet Article") titled "Bombs for Sale: Targets containing dangerous explosives being sold legally." The Internet Article covers the same subjects and interviews as the NBCU Report, and links to a video of that broadcast.

Analysis
"Defamation is the invasion of an interest in reputation and good name." Whereas slander pertains to claims of allegedly defamatory words that are spoken and heard, libel concerns statements that are written and read. "To state a claim for defamation under New York Law, the plaintiff must allege: (1) a false statement about the plaintiff; (2) published to a third party without authorization or privilege; (3) through fault amounting to at least negligence on [the] part of the publisher; (4) that either constitutes defamation per se or caused 'special damages.'"

"Defamation by implication is premised not on direct statements but on false suggestions, impressions and implications arising from otherwise truthful statements" In New York, "[t]o survive a motion to dismiss a claim for defamation by implication where the factual statements are substantially true, the plaintiff must make a rigorous showing that the language of the communication as a whole can be reasonably read both to impart a defamatory inference and to affirmatively suggest that the author intended or endorsed that inference."

"[T]ruth or falsity is determined by the common law standard of substantial truth." Thus, a court may dismiss a complaint alleging defamation where it finds the complained of statements to be substantially true and therefore not reasonably susceptible to defamatory connotations. A statement is substantially true and not actionable "if the published statement could have produced no worse an effect on the mind of a reader than the truth pertinent to the allegation." Further, "[t]he accuracy of the report should be assessed on the publication as a whole, not isolated portions of it [and a] defendant is held only to a standard of substantial, not literal, accuracy." Indeed, "[i]t is only necessary that the gist or substance of the challenged statements be true." In addition, "[w]ords that are imprecise, whose meanings are 'debatable, loose and varying,' are 'insusceptible to proof of truth or falsity.'"

* * *

NBCU moves to dismiss under Rule 12(b)(6) for failure to state a claim. Tannerite alleges primarily that the NBCU Report and NBCU Internet Article contained defamatory statements that were harmful and made with malice. Tannerite takes particular issue with reporter Jeff Rossen's statement that, "right now I am basically holding a bomb," made while he held two exploding rifle targets, as well as with the title of the NBCU Internet Article which reads, "Bombs for Sale: Targets containing dangerous explosives being sold legally." Tannerite's claim for defamation rests on its assertion that its exploding targets are not bombs, which it defines as "destructive devices that are strictly regulated by the federal and state governments" that are "capable of exploding with few or no additional components." Tannerite further alleges that "the gist of NBCU's report was that Tannerite-brand targets are dangerous as sold, which is false," and that NBCU falsely implied that: (1) "a Tannerite-brand target was used to cause injury to Jennifer Plank-Greer;" (2) "firearms expert, Mr. Travis Bond, opposes the sale of Tannerite-brand targets as 'unacceptable'; and (3) "Tannerite Sports is in cahoots with overseas terrorists." NBCU responds that these statements were either substantially true or too imprecise to be provably false, and that Tannerite failed to make a rigorous showing of defamation by implication, as required to survive a motion to dismiss.

* * *

There is no question that "Tannerite-brand binary *exploding* rifle targets" explode. That is their purpose. Indeed, Tannerite's Product Guide details the explosive nature of the targets and provides a multitude of warnings for their safe and proper use. As a result, the statements in the NBCU Report and NBCU Internet Article characterizing the exploding targets as bombs were substantially true, and therefore not provably false.

This does not mean that NBCU's uses of the word "bomb" met the precise definition of the word. Rather, "the gist or substance of the challenged statements" were true in light of the many meanings that reasonable audiences associate with the word. In addition, neither the NBCU Report nor NBCU Internet Article suggested that Tannerite's exploding rifle targets are dangerous before the component ingredients are mixed, or that proper use of the products causes destruction or injury. Rather, the focus of the NBCU Report was that Tannerite and others were able to sell exploding targets legally, which is of concern given the dangers associated with their misuse.

As the NBCU Report explained, Tannerite sells the targets with the component ingredients separated. The NBCU Report included a full demonstration of how to mix the component ingredients and detonate the resulting target with a bullet, further conveying to a reasonable viewer that the products are not explosive or dangerous in their inert form "as they appear to customers on the shelf of a store, or as they would arrive to the consumer by mail through an online purchase." It is also significant that Rossen stated in the NBCU Report that the targets in the studio were not dangerous without the catalyst. The NBCU Internet Article repeats much of the NBCU Report's substance, including the statements by Bond, the firearms expert, about how Tannerite legally sells targets by separating the two ingredients, but that "*once it's mixed*, it's classified as an explosive."

The NBCU Report makes clear that fireballs and exploding objects do not result from proper use of the Tannerite targets. For example, when introducing the montage of explosions, Rossen states, "you are about to see what can happen when this gets into the *wrong* hands." The NBCU Report also includes Tannerite's statement that "the only injuries that have ever happened were results from the shooter misusing the products."

Because no viewer could conclude that the explosions featured in the NBCU Report resulted from the proper use of Tannerite products, Tannerite has failed to make "a rigorous showing that the communication as a whole can be reasonably read to impart a defamatory inference." For similar reasons, no defamatory inference can be drawn from the video of Ms. Plank-Greer's injury, which clearly resulted from a reckless and improper use of an exploding target, or from the text of the NBCU Internet Article.

Based on Tannerite's failure to *** present proof of falsity with respect to NBCU's statements in the NBCU Report and NBCU Internet Article, *** defendants' respective motions to dismiss are GRANTED.

CASES ON THE SUPPLEMENTAL WEBSITE

Barry v. Time, Inc., 584 F. Supp. 1110 (N.D. Cal. 1984). This case further illustrates the public controversy requirement of *Gertz* in determining whether a person is a limited purpose public figure.

Brewer v. Rogers, 439 S.E.2d 77 (Ga. App. 1993). This case illustrates how the public figure and limited purpose public figure standards were applied to a high school coach. This is a good case to compare to cases involving college and professional coaches.

Bull v. Ball State University, 2011 U.S. Dist. LEXIS 147774 (S.D. Ind. 2011). This case provides a good discussion of defamation under Indiana law and the application of immunity principles when individual state employees make statements in their official capacity as state employees.

Clemens v. McNamee, 615 F.3d 374 (5th Cir. 2011). This case involves Roger Clemens defamation claims against his former trainer. It addresses the jurisdictional issues that are common in defamation claims which will continue to be of greater importance with the rise of defamation claims based on online statements.

Diebella v. Hopkins, 187 F. Supp.2d 192 (S.D.N.Y. 2002). This case outlines the elements of a libel action and addresses how to determine whether a statement is an expression of opinion or fact. This is a good case to compare and contrast with the Significant Case above.

QUESTIONS YOU SHOULD BE ABLE TO ANSWER

1. What is the difference between libel and slander?
2. What makes a statement libel "*per se*" or slander "*per se*"; and why is that designation important?
3. What are the elements of a defamation claim?
4. What is actual malice and why are public figures required to prove actual malice in order to prevail in a defamation case?
5. What are three common defenses to a defamation action?

REFERENCES

Cases

Bell v. the Associated Press, 584 F. Supp. 128 (D.D.C. 1984)
Brooks v. Paige, 773 P.2d 1098 (Colo. App. 1988).
Cepeda v. Cowles Magazines and Broadcasting, Inc., 392 F.2d 417 (9th Cir. 1968).
Chuy v. Philadelphia Eagles Football Club, 595 F.2d 1265 (3rd Cir. 1979).
Cobb v. Time Inc. 24 Media L. Rep. 585 (M.D. Tenn 1995).
Cohen v. Cowles Publishing Co., 273 P.2d 893.
Conkwright v. Globe News Publishing Company, 398 S.W. 385 (1965).
Curtis Publishing Co. v. Butts, 388 U.S. 130 (1967).
Daubenmire v. Sommers, 805 N.E.2d 571 (Ohio App. 2004).
Dendrite International, Inc. v. Doe, 775 A.2d 756 (N.J. Super. Ct. App. Div. 2001).
Doe v. Cahill, 884 A.2d 451 (Del. 2005).
Edwards v. National Audubon Society, 556 F.2d 113 (2nd Cir.), *cert. denied*, 434 U.S. 1002 (1977).
Garrison v. Louisiana, 379 U.S. 64 (1964).
Gertz v. Robert Welch, Inc., 418 U.S. 323 (1974).
Gomez v. Murdoch, 475 A.2d 622 (N.J. Super. A.D. 1984).
Hotchner v. Castillo-Puche, 551 F.2d 910 (2nd Cir. 1977).
Iacco v. Bohannon, 245 N.W.2d 791 (Mich. 1976).
Institute of Athletic Motivation v. Univ. of Ill., 170 Cal. Rptr. 411 (Cal. App. 1982).
Liberman v. Gelstein, 605 N.E.2d 344 (1992).
Masson v. New Yorker Magazine, Inc., 960 F.2d 896 (9th Cir. 1991).

Matherson v. *Marchello*, 473 N.Y.S.2d 998 (1984).
Milkovich v. Lorain Journal Co., 497 U.S. 1 (1990).
Montefusco v. ESPN, Inc., 2002 U.S. App. LEXIS 19740; 30 Media L. Rep. 2311 (3rd Cir. 2002).
New York Times Co. v. Sullivan, 376 U.S. 254 (1964).
Ollman v. Evans, 750 F.2d 970 (D.C. Cir.), *cert. denied*, 471 U.S. 1127 (1985).
Philadelphia Newspapers, Inc. et al. v. Hepps et al., 475 U.S. 767 (1986).
Romaine v. Kallinger, 537 A.2d 284 (1988).
Rosenbloom v. Metromedia, Inc., 403 U.S. 29 (1971).
St. Amant v. Thompson, 390 U.S. 727 (1968).
Stepien v. Franklin, 528 N.E.2d 1324 (Ohio App. 1988).
Toone v. Adams, 137 S.E.2d 132 (1964).
Waldbaum v. Fairchild Publications, Inc., 637 F.2d 1287 (D.C. Cir.), *cert. denied*, 449 U.S. 898 (1980).
Warford v. Lexington Herald, 170 Cal. Rptr. 411 (1990).
Washington v. Smith, 893 F. Supp. 60 (D.D.C. 1995).
Weismann v. Riverhead Union Free School District, 2010 N.Y. Misc. LEXIS 4592 (Sup. Ct. N.Y. 2010).
Wolston v. Reader's Digest Ass'n, 443 U.S. 157 (1979).

Publications

Anderson, D. (1984). Reputation, compensation, and proof. *William & Mary Law Review, 25*(5), 747.
Anderson, D. A. (1991). Is libel law worth reforming? *University of Pennsylvania Law Review, 140*(2), 487–554.
Anderson Publications, Inc. (2002, August). Focus on: Pending litigation. *Legal Issues in Collegiate Athletics, 3*(10), 4.
Axisa, M. (2014, February 10). Albert Pujols, Jack Clark reach resolution in PED allegations lawsuit. *CBS Sports*. Retrieved at http://www.cbssports.com/mlb/eye-on-baseball/24438922/albert-pujols-jack-clark-reach-resolution-in-ped-allegations-lawsuit.
Barron, J., & Dienes, C. T. (1979). *Handbook of free speech and free press*. Boston: Little, Brown.
Bennett, N.K. (2011, February 8). Did Courtney Love make a good decision to settle her Twitter case. *Connecticut Business Litigation*. Retrieved at http://www.connecticutbusinesslitigation.com/2011/02/articles/technology-1/did-courtney-love-make-a-good-decision-to-settle-her-twitter-case/
Black, H. C. (1990). *Black's law dictionary* (6th ed.). St. Paul, MN: West Publishing Co.
Carpenter, L. J. (1995). *Legal concepts in sport: A primer*. Reston, VA: AAHPERD.
CBSNews. (2011, February 14). Judge tosses Beckham libel suit against magazine. CBSNews.com. Retrieved at http://www.cbsnews.com/news/judge-tosses-beckham-libel-suit-against-magazine/.
DiGiovanna, M. (2013, October 4). Albert Pujols files defamation lawsuit against Jack Clark. *Los Angeles Times*. Retrieved at http://articles.latimes.com/2013/oct/04/sports/la-sp-pujols-clark-20131005.
Franklin, M. A., & Rabin, R. L. (1996). *Tort law and alternatives: Cases and materials* (6th ed.). Westbury, NY: The Foundation Press.
Gardner, E. (2009, October 27). Courtney Love loses motion to dismiss Twitter defamation case. *Entertainment and Media Law*. Retrieved at: http://www.entmedialaw.com/defamation/lawsuit/privacy/.
Highlight case. (2002, February). *Legal Issues in Collegiate Athletics, 3*(4), 3.
Mayer, M. F. (1987). *The libel revolution: A new look at defamation and privacy*. Chelsea, MI: BookCrafters.
Pember, D. R. (1990). *Mass media law* (5th ed.). Dubuque, IA: Wm. C. Brown Publishers.
Ransom, E. (1995). The ex-public figure: A libel plaintiff without a class. *Seton Hall Journal of Sport Law, 5*(2), 389–417.
Restatement (Second) of Torts § 558.
Rush, C. (2013, May 29). Brian Burke lawsuit: B.C. court grants him permission to sue online. *Toronto Star*. Retrieved at http://www.thestar.com/sports/hockey/2013/05/29/brian_burke_lawsuit_bc_court_grants_him_permission_to_sue_online.html.
Simmons, A. (2015, July 30). How can James Woods sue an anonymous Twitter user? *Los Angeles Times*. Retrieved at http://www.latimes.com/local/lanow/la-me-ln-james-woods-twitter-lawsuit-20150730-htmlstory.html.
Smolla, R. A. (1983). Let the author beware: The rejuvenation of the American law of libel. *University of Pennsylvania Law Review, 132*(1), 1–94.
Soocher, S. (2002, October). Bit parts. *Entertainment Law & Finance, 18*(7), 10.
Vlessing, E. (2012, February 6). Phil Mickelson wins Quebec lawsuit to unmask online heckler. *Hollywood Reporter*. Retrieved at http://www.hollywoodreporter.com/news/phil-mickelson-wins-quebec-lawsuit-287272.

3.13 OTHER INTENTIONAL TORTS

Invasion of Privacy,

Breach of Fiduciary Duty,

Tortious Interference with Contract,

Intentional Infliction of Emotional Distress

Gary Rushing | Minnesota State University, Mankato

Intentional torts are deliberate wrongs done to others that cause harm. This type of tort differs from negligence torts in that lack of due care or engaging in abnormally dangerous activity is immaterial. Liability for intentional torts is predicated on the tortfeasor purposely causing harm to another person or engaging in an activity that is substantially certain to harm another (Restatement of Torts, 1965). This chapter discusses four "off the field" intentional torts that occasionally occur in sport and recreation settings. They are invasion of privacy, breach of fiduciary duty, tortious interference with contract, and intentional infliction of emotional distress (IIED). Although not an intentional tort, negligent infliction of emotional distress is also included in this chapter as it relates very closely to IIED.

INVASION OF PRIVACY

Privacy, as defined by the courts, is "the right to be left alone; to live one's life as one chooses free from assault, intrusion, or invasion except as they can be justified by the clear needs of the community under a government of law" (*Rosenbloom v. Metromedia, Inc.*, 1971). The legal principles that serve as the bases for privacy protection are found primarily in three sources of the law—the Fourteenth Amendment, the Constitution, and tort law. The Fourteenth Amendment and the Constitution are concerned with the rights claims against any of the various governmental entities. Tort law is devoted to providing relief to persons who have suffered harm from the wrongful acts of others (Miller & Cross, 2016). Further, most states recognize the right of privacy either by means of common law case decisions or by applicable statutes and state constitutions (McKinsey & Burke, 2015).

Right of privacy, as found in tort law, involves four distinct theories or ways in which one's privacy can be invaded. Keeton, Dobbs, Keeton, Prosser, and Owen (1984) explained that these theories do not concern one tort, but a complex of four kinds of invasion. They have little in common except that each represents intrusion upon an individual's reasonable expectation "to be let alone," which is at the center of all wrongful invasion suits. The four types of invasion are (1) unreasonable intrusion on the seclusion of another, (2) appropriation of another's name or likeness, (3) unreasonable disclosure of private facts, and (4) publicity that unreasonably places the other in a false light before the public. Because each type of "invasion" is notably different, only one of the torts, not all four, must be proven for a successful claim of invasion of privacy (Franklin, Cardin, & Green, 2008).

Unreasonable Intrusion on Seclusion

The first form or theory is straightforward and concerned with the invasion of one's home or illegally searching someone's personal belongings or documents. Usually, the intrusion takes the form of window peeking, eavesdropping, excessive surveillance, or constant annoyance (Yasser, McCurdy, Goplerud, & Weston, 2011). However, the courts have extended this tort to include eavesdropping by wiretap, unauthorized examining of a bank account, compulsory blood testing window peeping, and computer hacking (Clarkson, Cross & Miller, 2015). Although there are few cases to date, it appears that this tort also applies to the scanning of cellular phones (http://www.justice.gov/sites/default/files/criminal-ccips/legacy/2015/01/14/ssmanual2009.pdf).

In addition to the actual intrusion, any information obtained in these or similar ways that is made public is also invasion of privacy. This is true even if the information obtained is truthful and it serves the publics right to know (Schubert, Smith, & Trentadue, 1986). The requisite question is: Was the intrusion offensive or objectionable to a reasonable person? (Keeton et al., 1984). If so, then it is an illegal invasion of one's privacy.

A court case that illustrates this point is *Bilney v. Evening Star Newspaper Co.* (1979). In this dispute, the question was addressed as to how the reporters obtained athlete's academic information they had published. The court determined that they had obtained the information from an anonymous source and that there was no evidence that the defendant news reporters had learned of the players' academic problems from confidential records or by any acts of invasion or intrusion. However, had the information been obtained through wiretaps, computer hacking, or some other offensive manner, the court may have considered this to be invasion of privacy.

In a more recent example of an invasion of privacy intrusion case, ESPN sport reporter Erin Andrews sued several hotel chains for negligence; infliction of emotional distress and invasion of privacy after a stalker was given her room number. The stalker set up the adjacent room door peephole to videotaped her while she was "getting dressed". He then posted the videos on the Internet. She claimed the hotels were negligent for revealing where she was staying, and for failing to discover that he had altered the peepholes in her rooms. The perpetrator pleaded guilty to charges including the intent to harass or cause emotional distress and was sentenced to a little more than two years in prison. The lawsuit against Nashville Marriott, and Marriott International, Inc. was for 75 million; the jury awarded her 55 million. She was successful in this case because she was able to demonstrate that the intrusion was done in an objectionable manner. (http://www.foxnews.com/entertainment/2016/03/08/jury-awards-erin-andrews-55m-in-lawsuit-over-nude-video/) In a similar case, Hulk Hogan was awarded 115 million for "invasion of privacy." See (http://money.cnn.com/2016/03/18/media/hulk-hogan-gawker-jury-deliberations/index.html Jurors in Hulk Hogan-Gawker Case Defend Wrestler's Right to Privacy)

Appropriation

The second form of invasion of privacy involves the **unauthorized use of a person's name or likeness** for commercial purposes such as advertising or trade. The protection provided by this law is especially important to sport figures because it gives them some control over the extent to which their name and likeness can be commercially exploited. Without this control, an athlete would lose a significant source of income from commercial endorsements, trading cards, and other enterprises. It is a very common "privacy" complaint of athletes

Although sport figures can prohibit most unauthorized use of their names and likenesses, courts have upheld unauthorized uses for editorial purposes as well as when reused by publishers or broadcasters for campaigns to increase circulation or broadcasting audiences. According to the Citizen's Media Project when used in this manner, it is considered to be protected incidental use. (http://www.citmedialaw.org/legal-guide/using-name-or-likeness-another, 2016). For more information on the "incidental use" exception, see Chapter 7.23, *Image Rights*.

In a classic case that illustrates the salient issues in this area, Joe Namath sued *Sports Illustrated* (*Namath v. Sports Illustrated*, 1975) for the unauthorized use of his photo to promote subscription sales. He contended that this use was commercial and violated his **right to privacy**. Further, because he was in the business of endorsing products and selling the use of his name and likeness, it interfered with his right to profit from such sale. The photograph had originally been used without objection from Namath, in conjunction with a 1969 Super Bowl article. However, because it was reprinted to promote subscription sales, he felt he should be compensated for its use. In siding with *Sports Illustrated*, the court noted that the use of the photo was merely "incidental" advertising because it was used to illustrate the quality and content of the periodical in which it originally appeared.

In a similar invasion of privacy case (*Montana v. San Jose Mercury News, Inc.*, 1995), Joe Montana brought action against the *San Jose Mercury News* for misappropriation of his name, photograph, and likeness. At issue was the reproduction of Montana's photograph that originally appeared in conjunction with a 1990 Super Bowl victory for the San Francisco 49ers. His photo had been reproduced in poster form. Some of the posters were sold for five dollars each, and the rest were donated to charity organizations. The court reached a decision similar to that of the *Namath* case and found in favor of *San Jose Mercury News* for two reasons. First, the original newspaper account and the subsequent photograph constituted matters in the public interest. Second, the posters were sold to advertise the quality and content of its newspaper. They contained no additional information and they did not convey Montana's endorsement.

In another case, *Palmer v. Schonhorn Enterprises, Inc.* (1967), a toy manufacturing company appropriated the names and career profiles of golfers Arnold Palmer, Gary Player, Doug Sanders, and Jack Nicklaus for use in a game. In this situation, the court sided with the plaintiffs because the commercial use of their names and profiles was done without their permission and without compensation.

The appropriation theory of invasion of privacy generated the **right of publicity** cause of legal action (Breaux & Breaux, P., 2010). The major difference between the two concepts is that redress in a right of privacy (misappropriation) dispute is based on the mental duress resulting from "not being left alone," whereas the focus of redress in a right of publicity case is the financial loss caused by the appropriation of an individual's identity for commercial exploitation (see *Doe v. TCI Cablevision*, 2003, on the Supplemental Website for an expanded explanation of the differences).

Celebrities, including athletes, have had a difficult task in demonstrating to the courts that public exposure caused them mental duress in that "they sought such attention and profited from it" (Stapleton & McMurphy, 1999). For this reason, more and more states are adopting the right of publicity, which provides celebrities with stronger legal leverage for preventing the use of their name or image (Stapleton & McMurphy, 1999). It is an evolving doctrine and a state-based right, which means there could be variation from state to state (Faber, J. (2014) To better understand this subject, read the Significant Case in Chapter 7.23, *Image Rights*.

Unreasonable Disclosure of Private Facts

A third type of invasion of privacy involves public disclosure of private facts about an individual that an ordinary person would find objectionable. Public disclosure suits are sometimes referred to as embarrassment suits because they arise from objections to publicity of embarrassing private information (Dill, 1992). At the center of this type of suit is the balance between the public's right to know and the extent of the intrusion into one's private life. Although secondary issues must be satisfied to prevail in an embarrassment suit (Keeton et al., 1984, pp. 856–857), where public figures such as sport personalities are concerned, there are two major issues that the courts will address. They are (1) whether the disclosed information was **truly private** or was it public, and (2) if the disclosed information was **highly offensive** to an ordinary person.

Private v. Public Facts

For a plaintiff to succeed in a public disclosure suit, it must be shown that the disclosed publicity was a situation in which there was a legitimate expectancy of privacy. In other words, the disclosure must have involved truly private matters. What constitutes truly private for the average citizen, in terms of publicity, is different from that of a sport figure. Sports personalities, especially the highly paid athletes, have little privacy protection due to their public figure status. A **public figure** is someone who by "his [or her] accomplishments, fame, or mode of living, or by adopting a profession or calling which gives the public a legitimate interest in his doings, his affairs, and his character, has become a public personage" (Keeton et al., 1984, p. 859). (For an in-depth discussion of public figure status, see Chapter 3.12 *Defamation*.) By way of this notion, the Constitution allows the press to report matters that have become public interest.

The justification for this loss of privacy protection is the result of three considerations about public figures. First, public figures have, to a certain extent, sought publicity and have consented to it. Second, their personalities and affairs have become public and are no longer private business. Third, the press has a right to inform the public about those who have become matters of public interest (Prosser, 1960).

Whether or not college athletes are considered public figures is sometimes at issue. In the previously mentioned case of *Bilney v. Evening Star Newspaper Co.* (1979), because there was no evidence that the defendant news reporters had learned of the players' academic problems through improper methods, the court examined the issue of "public figure" status of the six players. The court reasoned that college basketball is a "big-time" sport and generates a great deal of public interest and excitement throughout the country. The court further stated that the players had "achieved the status of public figures . . . by virtue of their membership on the basketball team (and) . . . having sought . . . the limelight. . . . It's clear at least in this court that college athletes in big time sports are 'public figures'" (p. 574).

As for high school athletes, it remains unclear as to whether or not they would be considered public figures. A leading case on the subject suggests that most high school athletes will not be considered public figures regardless of their notoriety or the public interest (*Wilson v. Daily Gazette Co.*, 2003). Deem (2006), Long (2009), and, Poorman (2013), however, suggest that courts prefer to find "much publicized" high school athletes to be limited-purpose public figures as opposed to all purpose public figures (see Chapter 3.12 *Defamation*, for discussion of limited-purpose public figures).

In addition to the preceding issues dealing with private information, it should be noted that information that has been previously reported, or that has already been made accessible to the public through public records or other documentation, or that is newsworthy is not considered to be purely private in nature and therefore is discloseable (Wong, 2011).

Highly Offensive

Even though some facts may be newsworthy and therefore non-private, they may not be publishable if they can be viewed as highly offensive to the average person. For example, publication of a person's sexual orientation, HIV status, or financial troubles could lead to liability for publication of offensive private facts. However, because community norms vary from jurisdiction to jurisdiction, courts may have mixed decisions regarding what is permissible disclosure. Therefore, where public figures are concerned, even conservative courts will allow most private truthful facts, although embarrassing, to be disclosed unless they are " unredeemably offensive and not even remotely in the 'public interest' " (Dill, 1986, p. 137).

False Light Intrusion

Under this theory, an invasion of privacy occurs when publicity places the plaintiff in a **false light** in the public eye (i.e., a large audience, not just a few individuals). For example, in a sport setting, this could occur if someone in the media uses a photograph or makes a statement about a sport figure that gives a false impression to the public This false impression could emanate in several ways including "misleading descriptions, confusion of the person's identity with another, fictionalization of actual events, or photographs taken out of context" (Bussian & Levine, http://www.floridabar.org/, 2005)

However, for sport figures to prevail in a false light suit, they must not only show that the published information was false, but also that the disclosure was done by one knowing it was false or who had reckless disregard for the truth. This standard was established in *Time, Inc. v. Hill* (1967), which held that the First Amendment protects reports of newsworthy matters.

False light action is different from libel in that the publicity does not have to be defamatory. The depiction in question could be either complimentary or defamatory. Although most false light cases involve unflattering portrayals, the central issue is "being let alone" from the *effects* of a false reputation or false publicity (Samar, 1991). Both false light and libel complaints are permitted in some states; however, other states do not recognize false light claims and permit only libel suits.

An example of false light invasion occurred in the case of *Spahn v. Messner, Inc.* (1967). This case centered on an unauthorized biography written about Warren Spahn, a celebrated pitcher for the Milwaukee Braves. The author used "invented dialogue, and imaginary incidents" which he knew to be false and knew to present an untruthful depiction of Spahn. Spahn objected to this portrayal even though parts of the story were complimentary. The court awarded Spahn $10,000 in damages and enjoined further publication of the book. Of the four privacy torts, "false light" is the most frequently criticized and the least widely recognized (Findlaw Website: http://injury.findlaw.com/torts-and-personal-injuries/invasion-of-privacy--false-light.html)

BREACH OF FIDUCIARY DUTY

Another intentional tort is breach of fiduciary duty or responsibility. Miller and Cross, (2016) define a **fiduciary** as "[a] person having duty, created by her or his undertaking, to act primarily for another's benefit in matters connected with the undertaking." As an adjective, it means ". . . relating to or founded upon a trust and confidence" (p. 463). Carper et al. (2008) clarified this by adding that a fiduciary relationship is one involving a person in a position of trust who undertakes to act for the benefit of another. Examples of fiduciary relationships include lawyer–client, parent–child, and coach–athlete.

In the sport setting, the fiduciary relationship that is most troublesome is the association between a professional athlete and his or her agent (Ehrhardt & Rodgers, 1988; Powers, 1994). An agent can be responsible for managing many of the athlete's financial concerns such as tax planning, financial planning, money management, investments, estate planning, income tax preparation, incorporating the client, endorsements, sports medicine consultation, physical health consultation, post-career development, career and personal development and counseling, legal consultation, and insurance matters (Davis, 2006). Because many of these dealings are legally binding to the represented athlete, the law imposes a high obligation of trustworthiness on the agent. If an agent violates this trust and the athlete is harmed as a result, the agent is guilty of tortious conduct and may have to make restitution (Restatement (Second) of Torts #874, 1984, p. 300).

A fiduciary duty requires that the sport agent act with complete honesty in all dealings with athlete–clients. In addition, the agent must avoid any personal **conflicts of interest**. In other words, the interests of the athlete must come before those of the agent. Also, an agent must not represent two adverse parties in the same transaction. For example an agent cannot represent two or more athletes vying for the same endorsement contract nor represent both an athlete and the company with which he is negotiating for a contract. Finally, an agent must not receive hidden compensation or profits from third parties for transacting the player's business and must not take advantage of any business opportunity that rightfully belongs to the athlete (Thornton, 2010). An agent can avoid liability in this area by fully disclosing any possible conflicts of interest or other potentially improper conduct and obtaining the athlete's prior consent to the action.

Detroit Lions, Inc. v. Jerry Argovitz (1984) offers an instructional example of breach of fiduciary duty. In this case, Billy Sims' agent, Jerry Argovitz, engaged in a series of unethical practices with the intent of inducing Sims to sign a contract with the Houston Gamblers of the United States Football League. After the Gamblers made an offer to Sims, Argovitz failed to give the Detroit Lions an opportunity to match the bid. Sims signed with the Gamblers believing theirs to be the best offer. After it was revealed Argovitz was a substantial owner in the Gamblers' franchise and that he had withheld information that might have swayed Sims' decision, the court allowed Sims to rescind his contract and sign with the Detroit Lions. Sims was unaware of the extent of Argovitz's association with the Gamblers.

Dominion Sports Services, Inc. v. Bredehoft (2006) illustrates the necessity of having a valid fiduciary relationship established in order to have a successful claim of breach of fiduciary duty. Hockey North America (HNA) started an adult men's novice hockey league in Minnesota. Bradford Bredehoft, an independent contractor, was hired as the local administrator of the league. His contract had a restrictive covenant that prohibited him from starting a competing league in the area. After HNA encountered financial difficulties and owed money to many creditors, Dominion Sports Services purchased its assets but retained the HNA league name. As the purchase was being negotiated, Bredehoft met with the players and informed them of HNA's financial problems. This discussion ultimately prompted them to organize their own competing league. Dominion filed suit against Bredehoft and others for breach of contract, breach of fiduciary duty, and tortious interference with contractual relations. The court ruled against HNA on all claims. HNA did not have a valid breach of contract or tortious interference claim against Bredehoft because he did not have a contract with the new management. Dominion's purchase agreement explicitly stated that it would not assume the employment contracts of the former management employees. Without a valid contract, Bredehoft was never an agent of the new HNA, therefore, a breach of fiduciary duty claim could not be upheld.

TORTIOUS (WRONGFUL) INTERFERENCE WITH CONTRACT

This intentional tort involves the intentional inducement of another to breach one's contractual obligations (Gleason, 2008). **Tampering** is an alternate term sometimes used to describe when one team attempts to lure a player who is clearly under contract to another team. It is the equivalent of tortious interference with contract (Epstein, 2012). Because contracts play a vital role in sport, this is a significant area of concern. Inducement to break contracts has been alleged in situations that involve teams competing for talented players (*Cincinnati Bengals v. William Bergey, et al.*, 1974), boxing promoters arguing over promotion rights (*Don King Productions v. James "Buster" Douglas, et al.*, 1990), agents interfering with a college player's eligibility (Gray, 2006) and sport shoe companies vying for an endorsement contract (*Official Brands, Inc.* v. Roc *Nation Sports*, 2015).

There are three elements necessary to prove the existence of a wrongful interference tort:

1. A valid, enforceable contract must exist between two parties.
2. The defendant must have known of the contract's existence.
3. The defendant must have *intentionally* induced either of the two parties to breach the contract. (Cross & Miller, 2015)

The Significant Case in this chapter, *Official Brands v. Roc Nation Sports (2015)*, although not completely resolved at the time of this publication, serves to illustrate a tortious interference cause of action and is instructive in the three above elements of a tortious interference situation. The central issue in this case was a contract dispute between two shoe companies, which were competing "to utilize [professional football player] Dez Bryant's name, nickname, initials, autograph, facsimile signature, photograph, likeness, video, and/or endorsement in connection with the advertisement, marketing, promotion, and sale of" Bryant's brand, called "Throw up the X." According to the complaint, Roc Nation Sports "embarked upon a scheme to . . . unlawfully induce Dez Bryant to terminate [the] . . . contract with" Official Brands. Roc Nation's alleged plan included "unsolicited contact" with Bryant, "false and disparaging statements" about Official Brands, and "improper enticements to induce" him to cancel his contract and move all of his business to Roc Nation.

The first and the most pivotal issue in a tortious interference with contract case is whether or not a valid contract exists. In this case, there was a two-year agreement between Official Brands and Bryant that authorized the use of Bryant's likeness, etc. to develop the "Throw up the X" brand. Secondly, Roc Nation was aware of this contract, as their representative had requested copies of it on several occasions. Thirdly, Bryant, according to the complaint, was induced to break his agreement and this was done through "unsolicited contact," false and disparaging remarks, and "improper enticements." If these issues are sustained, Officials Brands may win the suit.

INTENTIONAL INFLICTION OF EMOTIONAL (MENTAL) DISTRESS

Intentional infliction of emotional or mental distress (IIED) is a tort claim for intentional conduct that results in extreme emotional distress (Miller & Cross, 2016) and is meant to protect a person's emotional tranquility (Wong, 2011). Although seldom successful due to its rigorous criteria, it has become a fairly common complaint in sport and recreation tort-related lawsuits. In some jurisdictions it is referred to as the tort of "outrage" due to its standard that requires the conduct in question be such that it would cause a reasonable person to respond with outrage (Huffaker, 2001).

Elements of Intentional Infliction of Emotional Distress

In order to prove a claim of IIED, the plaintiff must demonstrate that: (1) the defendant acted *intentionally* or with *reckless* disregard of the probability of causing emotional distress, (2) the defendant's action must have been *extreme* and *outrageous*, and (3) the action must have caused *severe* emotional distress. It should be noted that mere insults, indignities, threats, annoyances, petty oppressions, or other trivialities would not sustain an IIED claim. The conduct in question has to be so *extreme* and *outrageous* "as to go beyond all possible bounds of decency, and to be regarded as atrocious, and utterly intolerable in a civilized community" (Prosser, 1964, pp. 46-47; Rest. 2d Torts, 46). Whether or not the conduct is illegal does not determine whether it meets this standard. Additionally, "The emotional distress must in fact exist, and it must be severe" (Prosser, p. 51; Rest. 2d Torts, 46).

Measuring severe distress poses a problem. Many jurisdictions require that the emotional distress manifest itself in some physical symptom or illness or some documented emotional disturbance (See *Bojko v. Lima* on the Supplemental Website to examine exactly how the courts apply these criteria.).

Claims of IIED have arisen frequently and in a wide variety of situations in sport and recreation. These claims have included circumstances such as forcing an athlete to do "bear crawls" on hot asphalt for being late to practice (*Gorthy v. Clovis Unified Sch. Dist., 2006*); a swimmer being forced to sit on a hot deck chair (*Kelly v. N. Highlands Recreation & Park Dist., 2006*); failure of an official to inform players in a timely manner of their next game thus causing them to be eliminated from a tournament (*Warren v. United States Specialty Sports Ass'n,* 2006); a high school athlete who was distressed because he failed to make the varsity baseball team (*Cronk v. Suffern Senior High School,* 2005); a Pop Warner football coach who uttered insulting and humiliating remarks to a young player (*PPA v. The Pop Warner Football Team of Shelton, Inc.,* 2012) (see the Supplemental Website); and in the *Bojko* case, a mother who embarked on an e-mail campaign against a teacher in which she repeatedly referred to the teacher as a "pedophile" and alleged that the teacher had "abused" her daughter (*Bojko v. Lima,* 2009).

For various reasons, the *Bojko* case was the only one of the above-mentioned IIED lawsuits that was successful. As mentioned earlier, IIED cases are rarely successful due to the stringent requirements needed to prove *extreme* or *outrageous* conduct and *severe* emotional stress. *Chuy v. Philadelphia Eagles Football Club* (1979) is an oft-cited case that is exemplary in how to satisfy the high standards needed to succeed in an IIED claim. Don Chuy, an Eagles lineman, was subjected to severe emotional distress because a team doctor erroneously reported to the news media that he had a life threatening disease. When Chuy, who had no previous knowledge of the existence of the condition, heard of the statement he reportedly "panicked and his mind just snapped." In court, he was able to show that during a six-month period in which he had anticipated his death, he suffered extreme emotional anguish and torment, he became a mental wreck, lost his marriage, and suffered serious emotional stress. The court held that the doctor's conduct was sufficiently outrageous and stated:

> If you intentionally make a statement the material and probable consequences of which it will be known to the person and cause him or her emotional distress and if the making of that statement is shocking and outrageous and exceeds the bounds of decency with respect to its natural and probable impact, then a case of intentional infliction of emotional distress is made out. (*Chuy v. Philadelphia Eagles Football Club,* 1979, p. 10)

Wong (2011), in referring to the above case, recommended that sport and recreation personnel be very cautious when they are making statements to the media about a participant's playing ability, a coach's employment tenure, or an athlete's injury status.

Negligent Infliction of Emotional Distress

Although *not* an intentional tort, a cause of action that is closely aligned with IIED is *negligent infliction of emotional distress*. The obvious difference between the two is that IIED is caused by an intentional act which the defendant knew or should have known would cause severe emotional distress; whereas, NIED is the result of an act that negligently (unintentionally) causes severe emotional distress and resultant damage. In NIED, the plaintiff is relieved of the burden of proving that the defendant intended to cause severe emotional distress.

The requirements for proving NIED vary significantly from state to state, but the requirements typically parallel the four elements necessary to prove negligence (see Chapter 2.11 *Negligence*). To establish a claim for NIED in most states, the plaintiff must demonstrate that: (1) the defendant owed a duty to the plaintiff not to create a foreseeable risk of inflicting emotional distress; it may be a general duty or one created by statute; (2) the defendant breached that duty by engaging in behavior that the defendant should have realized involved an unreasonable risk of causing emotional distress that might result in illness or bodily injury; (3) the plaintiff suffered injury in the form of extreme emotional distress; and (4) the breach of the duty was the proximate cause of the injury (Clinton & McKain, 2015). If these elements can be sustained then NIED has been proven.

In *Turner v. Mandalay Sports Entm't, LLC* (2008), a fan was struck in the face by a foul ball while sitting in an unprotected area near a concession stand. She sued the team for negligence and NIED. The plaintiff was aware of stadium warnings regarding foul balls and that the team was not responsible for resultant injuries. The Supreme Court of Nevada determined that the woman's negligence claim failed to survive summary judgment under the limited duty rule (see Chapter 2.31 *Premises Liability* for a description of the limited duty rule). Because she could not establish that there was a breached duty of care, she was not able to establish her NIED claim either (see the *Bojko* case).

SIGNIFICANT CASE

This recent case, although currently in the "discovery" process, provides a definitive example of the elements necessary to sustain the intentional tort of "tortious interference with contract." It involves professional football player Dez Bryant who was persuaded to sign an endorsement contract while under contract with another company.

OFFICIAL BRANDS, INC. V. ROC NATION SPORTS, LLC
2015 U.S. Dist. LEXIS 167320 (2015)
(N.D. Tex., Dec. 8, 2015)

Overview

This 2014 case involved Official Brands, Inc. ("Official Brands") which signed a contract with Dez I Enterprises, Inc. ("Dez I"), a corporation owned by Dallas Cowboys wide receiver Dez Bryant ("Bryant"). The contract gave permission to Official Brands "to utilize Dez Bryant's name, nickname, initials, autograph, facsimile signature, photograph, likeness, video, and/or endorsement in connection with the advertisement, marketing, promotion, and sale of" Bryant's brand, called "Throw up the X." This arrangement expected to run from July 1, 2014 until June 30, 2016, but it was stopped short when Bryant prematurely terminated the contract on February 24, 2015. According to Official Brands, Bryant did this because Defendant Roc Nation, LLC ("Roc Nation"), along with Roc Nation Sports, LLC ("RNS") "embarked upon a scheme to . . . unlawfully induce Dez Bryant to terminate [the] . . . contract with" Official Brands. Roc Nation's and RNS' alleged game plan included "unsolicited contact" with Bryant, "false and disparaging statements" about Official Brands, and "improper enticements to induce" him to cancel the contract.

The reason for this conduct, Official Brands asserts, was to cause Bryant to "move all of his off-field business" to Roc Nation and RNS. According to the Original Petition, Bryant signed a standard representation agreement with both Defendants in November 2014, after which the alleged interference with Official Brands' contract began. For example, Official Brands states that Kimberly Miale, who allegedly works for Defendants, "reached out to [Official Brand's] officers on multiple occasions seeking a copy of the contract" between Official Brands and Dez I. Roc Nation challenges this, arguing that it has never had a contractual relationship with Bryant and that Miale is "not an agent, employee, or representative" of Roc Nation,

* * *

Tortious Interference With Contractual Relations

To prevail on a claim for tortious interference with an existing contract, a plaintiff must show "(1) an existing contract subject to interference, (2) a willful and intentional act of interference with the contract, (3) that proximately caused the plaintiff's injury, and (4) caused actual damages or loss." The alleged interference generally must have induced a breach of the contract to be actionable. ("Ordinarily, merely inducing a contract obligor to do what it has a right to do is not actionable interference."). The fact that a contract is terminable at will, however, "is no defense to an action for tortious interference with its performance."

Roc Nation argues that Official Brands' allegations are conclusory, and that it has failed altogether to allege intent on the part of Roc Nation's employees to interfere tortiously with Official Brands' contract. Official Brands responds that its allegations are sufficient to survive a motion to dismiss under Rule 12(b)(6).

Existing contract

Official Brands has alleged the existence of a contract subject to interference. The Original Petition describes a two-year agreement between Official Brands and Dez I that authorized the former to use Bryant's likeness, to grow the "Throw up the X" brand. This is sufficient to establish the first element of the claim.

Willful and intentional interference

"To show tortious interference, a plaintiff is not required to prove intent to injure, but rather 'only that the actor desires to cause the consequences of his act, or that he believes that the consequences are substantially certain to result from it. [T]he interfering party must have 'actual knowledge of the contract or business relation in question, or knowledge of facts and circumstances that would lead a reasonable person to believe in the existence of the contract or business relationship.'"

Official Brands' allegations are more than sufficient to meet this standard. Roc Nation clearly knew of the contract, as Miale—its employee—requested a copy of it "on multiple occasions." The Original Petition further alleges that Roc Nation provided Bryant with "numerous improper enticements *in order to induce . . . [him] to terminate the contract*" and to convince him to shift his business to Roc Nation. These assertions, taken as true, demonstrate that Roc Nation "desire[d] to cause the consequences of [its] act," and thus are sufficient to establish the second element of the claim.

The allegations in this case resemble those in *Hambric Sports Management, LLC v. Team AK, Inc.*, There, the plaintiff was a sports agency that had represented golfer Anthony Kim, and one of the defendants was a rival management company that had allegedly attempted to lure Kim away from the plaintiff. The court found that this element was fulfilled on the basis of allegations that the defendant (1) "possessed [and reviewed] copies" of the plaintiff's contract with Kim; (2) "entertained the prospect of entering into an agency agreement with Kim"; and (3) "research[ed] Kim's marketability with potential endorsement companies while the Agreement was in effect." 2010 U.S. Dist. LEXIS 65491. Here, Roc Nation allegedly (1) requested a copy of the contract between Official Brands and Dez I; (2) actually entered into a representation agreement with Bryant; and (3) blocked endorsement agreements that Official Brands sought to negotiate. Accordingly, the Court concludes that this activity, if true, would constitute intentional and willful interference.

Proximate cause

Establishing proximate cause requires a plaintiff to show that "the defendant took an active part in persuading a party to a contract to breach it." It is unclear whether Dez I's termination of the contract with Official Brands was a breach. As explained above, though, the termination of an at-will contract can give rise to a tortious interference claim, even if that termination was not a breach. It follows logically, then, that proximate cause is shown in a case such as this when a plaintiff alleges that the defendant actively persuaded a party to an at-will contract to terminate it.

* * *

Official Brands has made this showing. It asserts that Roc Nation initiated "unsolicited contact" with Bryant, made "false and disparaging statements" about Official Brands, and provided Bryant "with numerous improper enticements," all to incentivize Bryant to terminate the contract with Official Brands These allegations suffice to show active persuasion on Roc Nation's part. The third element is therefore fulfilled.

Actual damages or loss

Official Brands has also adequately alleged this element, as it asserts that Roc Nation's interference resulted in the termination of the contract and the accompanying revocation of Official Brands' ability to use and promote "Throw up " constitutes actual damages or loss. (denying motion to dismiss where plaintiff alleged that defendant's tortious interference resulted in the loss of a sale to which the plaintiff was otherwise contractually entitled).

The Original Petition thus contains satisfactory allegations of all four elements of tortious interference with an existing contract. Accordingly, Roc Nation is not entitled to dismissal of this claim.

* * *

The Court has determined that Official Brands has successfully stated a claim for tortious interference with contractual relations, and therefore believes that a more definite statement as to that claim is not necessary.

* * *

SO ORDERED.SIGNED:
December 15, 2015.
JANE J. BOYLE, UNITED STATES DISTRICT JUDGE

CASES ON THE SUPPLEMENTAL WEBSITE

Cassie v. Walled Lake Consolidated Schools (2006 Mich. App. Lexis 497) This case provides instructive examples of claims of IIED and Public Disclosure of Embarrassing Private Facts: Invasion of Privacy.

Bojko v. Lima (2009 Conn. Super. LEXIS 1359). This case provides an example of "extreme and outrageous" conduct that resulted in a rare, successful IIED claim by the plaintiff. The case also provides insight into a successful "false light" invasion of privacy claim

PPA v. Pop Warner Football, (2012 Conn. Super. LEXIS 2265) This IIED case involves coaches who used racial slurs, and profanity in an effort to motivate their young athletes.

Montana v. San Jose Mercury News (1995 Cal. App. LEXIS 411). Examine the section dealing with "The Posters Reported on Newsworthy Events" and "A Newspaper Has a Constitutional Right to Promote Itself by Reproducing Its News Stories." They present the central reasons used to justify appropriation of Montana's image.

Doe v. TCI Cablevision, 110 S.W.3d 363(Mo.2003). Please note the discussion in the "Head-notes" that addresses the difference between Invasion of Privacy: Appropriation (right of privacy) and the Right of Publicity. This section provides clarification as to the differences between the two.

Significant Cases from Other Chapters:
Chapter 7.23 *Image Rights. Vanna White v. Samsung Electronics America* (1992).

QUESTIONS YOU SHOULD BE ABLE TO ANSWER

1. What is "privacy" as defined by the courts?

2. List and explain the distinct ways in which one's privacy can be invaded.

3. Provide an example of a "fiduciary duty" and explain how it can be breached

4. How does false light invasion of privacy differ from defamation? Give examples of each.

5. Please list and briefly explain the elements necessary to sustained a "tortious interference with contract".

REFERENCES

Cases

Bilney v. Evening Star Newspaper Co., 43 Md. App. 560; 406 A.2d. 652 (Md. App. 1979).
Bojko v. Lima, 2009 Conn. Super. LEXIS 1359
Cassie v. Walled Lake Consolidated Schools, 2006 Mich. App. Lexis 497.
Central Sports Army Club v. Arena Association, Inc., 952 F. Supp. 181 (S.D.N.Y. 1997).
Chuy v. Philadelphia Eagles Football Club, U.S. App. LEXIS 16338 (1979).
Cincinnati Bengals v. William Bergey, et al., 453 F. Supp. 129 (1974).
Cronk v. Suffern Senior High School, 2005 N.Y. Misc. LEXIS 2820 (2005).
Detroit Lions, Inc. v. Jerry Argovitz, 580 F. Supp. 542 (1984).
Doe v. TCI Cablevision, 110 S.W.3d 363 (Mo.2003)
Dominion Sports Services Inc. v. Bredehoft, 2006 Minn. LEXIS 132 (Minn., Mar. 14, 2006).
Don King Productions v. James "Buster" Douglas, et al., 735 F. Supp. 522 (1990).
Gorthy v. Clovis Unified Sch. District, 2006 WL 236939 (E.D. Cal. 2006).
Holt v. Cox Enterprises, 590 F. Supp. 408 (N.D. Ga. 1984).
Kelly v. N. Highlands Recreation & Park Dist., 2006 U.S. Dist. LEXIS 39785 (E.D. Cal. 2006).
Montana v. San Jose Mercury News, Inc., 34 Cal. App.4th 790 (1995).
Namath v. Sports Illustrated, 48 A.D.2d 487; 371 N.Y.S.2d 10 (1975).
Official Brands, Inc. v. Roc Nation Sports, LLC and Roc Nation, 2015 U.S.Dist.Lexis16736.
Palmer v. Schonhorn Enterprises, Inc., 323 A.2d 458 (1967).
PPA v. The Pop Warner Football Team of Shelton, Inc. 2010 Conn. Super. LEXIS 3122 (2010)
Rosenbloom v. Metromedia, Inc., 403 U.S. 29; 29 L.Ed.2d 296 (1971).
Spahn v. Messner, Inc., 18 N.Y.2d 324; 274 N.Y.S.2d 877; 221 N.E.2d 543; *vacated* 387 U.S. 239; 18 L.Ed.2d 744 (1967).
St. Louis Convention & Visitors Commission v. National Football League, 154 F.3d 851 (8th Cir. 1998).
Time, Inc. v. Hill, 385 U.S. 374 (1967).
Turner v. Mandalay Sports Entm't, LLC, 180 P.3d 1172 (Nevada 2008).
Warren v. United States Specialty Sports Ass'n., Ok Civ. App 78 (Okla. Civ. App. 2006).
Wilson v. Daily Gazette Co., 588 S.E.2d 200 (2003).

Publications

Black, H. C. (2014). *Black's law dictionary* (10th ed.). St. Paul, MN: West Publishing Co.
Breaux, P., Brooks, A. & Breaux, P., (2009). *Introduction to sports law and business* (9th). Kendall Hunt Publishing.
Byrd, L. L. (1988). Privacy rights of entertainers and other celebrities: A need for change. *Entertainment and Sports Law Reporter*, 5(95), 95–116.
Clarkson, K. W., Miller, R. L., & Cross, F. B. (2015). *Business law* (13th ed.). Mason, OH: West Legal Studies in Business. Thompson Learning.
Cross, F. B., & Miller, R. L. (2015). *The legal environment of business*. (9th Ed.). Mason, OH: South-Western Cengage Learning. 2015
Davis, T. (2006). Regulating the athlete-agent industry: Intended and unintended consequences. *Willamette L. Rev.* 42, 781–791.
Deem, J. (2006). Student work: Freedom of the press: Classifying school athletes under the Gertz Public Figure Doctrine. *West Virginia Law Review*, 108, 799–839.
Dill, B. (1986). *The journalist's handbook on libel and privacy*. New York: The Free Press.
Ehrhardt, C. W., & Rodgers, J. M. (1988). Tightening the defense against offensive sports agents. *Florida State University Law Review, 16*, 634–674.
Epstein, A. (2012). *Sports law*. South-Western
Franklin, M. A., Cardi, W. J., & Green, M. D. (2008) *Torts*. (24th Ed.). Chicago, IL: Thomson/West.
Gleason, J. P. (2008). Comment: From Russian with love : The legal repercussion of the recruitment and contracting of foreign players in the National Hockey League. *Buffalo Law Review*, 599–654.

Gray, J. (2006). Sports agent's liability after Sparta. *Va. Sports & Ent. L. J.* 6, 141–162.

Huffaker, M. L. (2001). Recovery for infliction of emotional distress: A comment on the mental anguish accompanying such a claim in Alabama. *Alabama Law Review, 52*, 1003–1043.

Keeton, W. P., Dobbs, D. B., Keeton, R. E., Prosser, W. L., & Owen, D. G. (1984). *Prosser and Keeton on torts* (5th ed.). St. Paul, MN: West Publishing Co.

Long J. G. (2009). High Standards for High School Athletes: Defamation Law and Tomorrow's Stars. *Sports Law. Journal*,16, 255–275.

McKinsey, J. & Burke, D.D. (2015). *Carper's Understanding the Law* (7th). Cengage Learning. Stamford, CT.

Miller, R.L. & Cross (2016). *The Legal Environment Today* (8th). Centage Learning. Stamford CT.

Poorman, M. (2013) Get with the times: Why Defamation Law Must be Reformed in Order Protect Athletes and Celebrities from Media Attacks. *Texas Review of Entertainment & Sports Law*. Fall, 2013. 5 Tex. Rev. Ent. & Sports L. 67

Powers, A. (1994). The need to regulate sports agents. *Seton Hall Journal of Sport Law, 4*, 253–274.

Prosser, W. L. (1960). Privacy. *Cal. L. Rev., 48*, 383–398.

Prosser, W. L. (1964). *Handbook of the law of torts*. (3rd ed.). St. Paul, MN: West Publishing Co.

Samar, V. J. (1991). *The right to privacy*. Philadelphia: Temple University Press.

Schubert, G., Smith, R. K., & Trentadue, J. C. (1986). *Sports law*. St. Paul, MN: West Publishing Co.

Stapleton, L. L., & McMurphy, M. (1999). The professional athlete's right of publicity. *Marquette Sports Law Journal,10*, 23-68.

Thornton, P. K. (2010). *Sports law*. Sudbury, MA. Jones and Barlett Publishers, LLC.

Warren, S., & Brandeis, L. (1890). The right to privacy. *Harvard Law Review, 4*, 193.

Weistart, J. C., & Lowell, C. H. (1979). *Law and sports*. Charlottesville, VA: Michie/Bobbs Co.

Wong, G. (2011). *Essentials of sports law*. Denver, Co.: Praeger Publishers.

Yasser, R., McCurdy, J. R., Goplerud, C. P., & Weston, M. A. (2011). *Sport law*: Cases and materials. San Francisco, CA. Matthew/Bender. LexisNexis.

Legislation

Restatement (Third) of the Law of Unfair Competition (1995).
Restatement of Torts, Second, Torts 8A (1965).
Restatement of Torts, Second § 46, com.

Websites

Bussian, J. A., & Levine, P. J. Invasion of Privacy and the Media: The Right "To Be Let Alone. (2005). Retrieved January 20, 2016 from http://www.floridabar.org/

Clinton, M., & McKain, B. (2015). *Intentional infliction of emotional distress. Retrieved* Dec. 20, 2015 from http://www.lawguys.com/Negligent_Infliction_of_Emotional_Distress.htm

Faber, J. (2014). *Right of publicity..* retrieved January 25 2016, from Right of Publicity Website: http://www.rightofpublicity.com#sthash.we46pYcE.dpuf

Kinsey, J. (2015, October 15). Erin Andrews Wants $75 Million From Peephole Case. Retrieved January 28, 2016, from http://bustedcoverage.com/2015/10/15/erin-andrews-peephole-case-75-million-video-court-lawsuit/

http://www.foxnews.com/entertainment/2016/03/08/jury-awards-erin-andrews-55m-in-lawsuit-over-nude-video/

http://money.cnn.com/2016/03/18/media/hulk-hogan-gawker-jury-deliberations/index.htmlJurors in Hulk Hogan-Gawker Case Defend Wrestler's Right to Privacy

CRIMINAL LAW AND SPORT

Kristi L. Schoepfer Bochicchio | Winthrop University

The intersection of criminal law and sport has increased in recent years. While many lawsuits involving sport and recreation managers and participants are filed in civil courts (see Chapter 2.13, *Liability of Sports Participants, Sports Instructors, and Sports Officials*), sport and recreation managers must be aware of the evolving criminal law landscape. In recent years, many more athletes, coaches, and recreation participants have been charged criminally for acts occurring during an athletic event; in fact, some scholars claim sport violence, and subsequently sport crime, is an "epidemic plaguing our nation" (Harary, 2002). Further, crimes such as hazing, point shaving, and ticket scalping continue to impact sport and recreation managers. While all professionals in the sport and recreation industry hope to avoid sport or recreation related crime, the recent trends mandate that managers have the requisite knowledge to prevent or respond to such a circumstance.

FUNDAMENTAL CONCEPTS

Criminal Law Origins

Federal, state, and local legislative bodies deem certain conduct criminal, meaning the conduct is punishable by fines or imprisonment, or both. **Criminal statutes** define criminal conduct and dictate possible punishments; the statutes are written by legislatures in each jurisdiction to control conduct that is deemed harmful to citizens or to the government. All 50 states and the federal government have criminal statutes, but no jurisdiction is bound by a different jurisdiction's statute or interpretation (Kaplan, et. al., 1996). In virtually all states, criminal law is statutory in origin, meaning that "conduct is not criminally punishable unless it has been proscribed by statute" (Kaplan, et. al., 1996).

Aside from statutory origin, there are other important considerations regarding criminal law. Before criminal law can be considered as it impacts sport and recreation, additional foundations of criminal law must be established. Two of these of specific importance are the distinction between civil law and criminal law and the elements of a crime.

Criminal Law v. Civil Law

The American legal system allows for both civil law cases and criminal law cases; however, the two are quite different. In **civil law**, the plaintiff files a lawsuit against the defendant on his or her own behalf seeking monetary damages, or specific performance, to remedy or compensate for an incurred loss. However, in **criminal law**, the plaintiff is a government representative prosecuting an offense against the state; the victim does not prosecute his or her own case. Although the victim is the person or organization that incurred the harm, criminal law mandates that the government prosecute on behalf of the victim, because all crimes are considered crimes against society. Also distinguishable is the standard of proof required to succeed with the lawsuit (see Chapter 1.10, *The Legal System*). In a civil case, a plaintiff only needs to prove a "**preponderance of the evidence**" to support his or her claim; however, in a criminal case, the government (plaintiff) must prove that the defendant is guilty of the crime "**beyond a reasonable doubt**." The criminal law standard presents a more significant burden; this heightened standard exists because criminal punishments are more severe, and government is "far more willing to tolerate erroneous acquittal than erroneous convictions" (Kaplan, et. al., 1996). Lastly, civil cases are often adjudicated by only a judge, whereas in criminal law, trial by jury is much more common.

Elements of a Crime

For each alleged crime that is committed, the state must prove two things; *actus reus* and *mens rea*. *Actus reus* (guilty act) requires proof that the defendant committed an act in violation of a state or federal statute. An act is defined as "an outward manifestation of behavior or bodily movement, caused by a person's own will and volition" (Model

Penal Code § 2.01). ***Mens rea*** (guilty mind) requires proof that the defendant had the intent to commit the act. Intent is defined as committing the act "purposely, knowingly, recklessly or negligently, as the law may require, with respect to each material element of the offense" (Model Penal Code, § 2.02). These required elements are essential in criminal law; determining what the defendant was thinking when the crime was committed, as well as what the defendant intended, will impact the outcome of any criminal case. Also, note that the Model Penal Code provides the standard definitions; however, each state jurisdiction has its own interpretation. Specific state criminal statutes are influenced by the Model Penal Code, but most states include their own variations of these required elements.

Classifications of Crime

Crimes are most often thought of as harmful acts against individuals; however, criminal acts have a much broader scope. Some crimes that are committed are not against a person, but rather against the best interest of society, or the government itself. To best identify the varying crimes that are possible in recreation and sport, crime should be classified as (1) Crimes against Persons; (2) Crimes against Public Welfare; and (3) Crimes against Government (Epstein, 2009).

Crimes against Persons

This classification is appropriate when the victim is an individual person (or persons). Crimes against persons are most likely to be prosecuted because these crimes typically receive the most investigative resources and perpetrators are often easy to identify (Kaplan, et. al 1996). Athletes, coaches and recreation participants may all potentially commit a crime against a person during an athletic contest; specifically, these crimes may include assault and/or battery, criminal negligence, reckless endangerment or homicide, and hazing.[1]

Assault and Battery

As discussed in Chapter 3.11 *Assault and Battery*, assault and/or battery that occurs as part of an athletic contest is most often remedied in civil courts. Historically, individuals have not been accused of criminal liability for imposing injuries during athletic contests; however, there is a growing trend to prosecute these acts as crimes in many jurisdictions.

Assault is defined as "the threat or use of force on another that causes that person to have a reasonable apprehension of imminent harmful or offensive contact; the act of putting another person in reasonable fear or apprehension of an immediate battery by means of an act amounting to an attempt or threat to commit a battery (Black's, 2009). Further, the Model Penal Code distinguishes between two types of assault: simple assault and aggravated assault; the later involving a more severe degree of harm (Model Penal Code § 211.1). Also, although assault and battery are often thought of as one act, they are in fact two distinguishable crimes. **Battery** is defined as "the use of force against another, resulting in harmful or offensive contact" (Black's, 2009). Most important to note is that each state jurisdiction has its own statute, and specific statutory definitions do vary from state to state.

Criminal Negligence, Recklessness, or Homicide

As discussed in Chapter 2.11, *Negligence*, an individual's conduct can deviate from the reasonable person standard to varying degrees. When conduct is so unreasonable that it transcends the standards required for civil liability, an individual may also face liability for criminal negligence or recklessness. **Criminal negligence** or **recklessness** refer to criminal activity in which the defendant did not intend to commit the crime, but was not careful enough with his or her actions to avoid a crime occurring; in other words, the conduct was so unreasonable that it may be considered criminal. The difference between negligence and recklessness is a matter of degree; recklessness is the higher level of guilt. In 2009, a high school football coach was charged with reckless homicide for the heat-related death of a student athlete at practice. While the coach was also alleged to be liable in civil court, his actions (or omissions) were so unreasonable that he was charged criminally for his behavior (this case will be discussed more completely later in this chapter).

Many jurisdictions use the Model Penal Code as a directive when creating criminal statutes. The Code defines criminal negligence as "acts committed with such a blatant breach of duty that courts can assume the defendant acted with intent to injure" (§ 2.02). Crimes most commonly committed through criminal negligence

---

[1] Criminal activity among sport spectators is also prevalent; however, recreation and sport managers are best served by discussion of criminal law as it applies to athletes, coaches and recreation participants.

or recklessness are involuntary manslaughter (conscious disregard of a substantial and unjustifiable risk that would cause death [Model Penal Code § 210.3]; criminally negligent homicide (inadvertent homicide [Model Penal Code, § 210.4]); and reckless endangerment (conscious disregard for a substantial and unjustifiable risk that endangers another [Model Penal Code § 2.02.2c]). However, the exact terminology and language used to identify and define each crime varies from state to state.

Hazing

Hazing encompasses a broad range of behaviors; the definition of hazing varies significantly from state to state. However, in many jurisdictions, activities that require a subordinate person to endure some type of mental or physical threat will be considered **hazing** and classified as a crime. For a full discussion of hazing, including criminal hazing, see Chapter 3.22, *Hazing*.

Likelihood of Occurrence

Athletes/Recreation Participants. There is no shortage of overtly violent acts in sport. Athletes and participants at all levels of sport experience pressure to win; winning at all costs is a common mentality. This mindset often results in violent acts among athletes, resulting from aggressive play. Many of these potential assaults and batteries would certainly be considered criminal if they occurred away from the game; however, when they happen during a sport contest, they are often considered part of the game. Prosecutorial restraint has likely limited the cases involving recreation participants and athletes as defendants. Even so, there is no shortage of case law citing athletes who were charged criminally for an injury they caused while participating in athletics. For example, in *State v. Forbes* (1975), an NHL player was prosecuted for committing aggravated assault with a hockey stick; in *People v. Freer* (1976), a football player was convicted of assault after punching a ball carrier while tackling him; in *State v. Floyd* (1990), the basketball player was convicted of assault after delivering a hard foul. Similarly, in *State of Washington v. Shelley* (1997), Shelley struck another player during a basketball game and broke his jaw in three places. He was convicted of assault in the second degree (see Supplemental Website). In 2001, a basketball player in Texas was sentenced to 5 years in prison for aggravated assault with serious bodily injury (see *State v. Limon*, 2000). In *State v. Guidugli* (2004), a collegiate athlete was convicted of assault for punching an opponent in the eye during an intramural basketball game. More recently, a high school wrestler in Minnesota was convicted of fifth-degree assault and adjudicated delinquent for striking an opponent in the face during a high-school wrestling match (*In the Matter of the Welfare of J.S.I.*, 2009, see Supplemental Website). Most notable is the 2009 conviction of Sean Sanders, a recreational softball player found guilty of negligent homicide and third degree assault for punching an opposing player in the head after a contentious recreational softball game. As in common in recreational sport, the game was heated and included trash talking and verbal taunts; however, Sanders assaulted the opposing player from behind as the game concluded (Quinlan, 2009). Sanders served two years in prison before being paroled in 2011.

When athletes and participants are alleged to have committed a crime during the course of play, an automatic assumption of guilt is inappropriate. In most cases, athletes or participants assert consent of the participant as a defense against criminal liability. Multiple variations of the "consent defense" have been argued by defendant athletes and participants; these will be discussed in a subsequent section of this chapter.

Coaches. In recent years, coaches have increasingly been investigated for, or formally accused of, criminal conduct. For example, in 2009, Mike Leach, the former head coach of Texas Tech football, was investigated for mistreatment of a player whom he allegedly isolated in a dark electrical closet after the player refused to practice with a concussion (Johnson, 2009); in 2010, two Middletown, CT, football coaches were charged with reckless endangerment after a student-athlete collapsed while working out on a hot day (Fitzgerald, 2010); in 2011, former Pennsylvania State University assistant football coach Jerry Sandusky was accused of inappropriate sexual relationships with minors (Viera & Becker, 2011); similarly, Bernie Fine, an assistant basketball coach at Syracuse University was investigated for sexual misconduct with minor ball boys in the same year (Schwarz & Berko, 2011).[2] And, in 2012, police launched a criminal investigation against a high school football coach in Pennsylvania for allowing players to return to play despite having concussions (Toporek, 2012).

---

[2]Sexual misconduct by coaches has received significant recent attention due to the two high profile cases listed. While all administrators and coaches should be aware of criminal statutes regarding sexual misconduct, this chapter will not focus specifically on this area.

Similarly, a notable allegation of criminal conduct by a coach resulted from the heatstroke death of a high school football player in Kentucky. As noted above, in 2009, Jason Stinson, former head football coach at Pleasure Ridge High School in Louisville, KY, was charged with reckless homicide and wanton endangerment for the death of Max Gilpin, a lineman on the team. The charges stemmed from a summer practice, on a day with a heat index of 94 degrees, in which players were required to run sprints up and down the field, after already practicing for three hours. The team sprinted 12 times before Gilpin collapsed (he was the second player to collapse), and witnesses reported that Stinson denied the players water breaks. When Gilpin reached the hospital, he was suffering heat stroke with a body temperature of 107 degrees; Gilpin died three days later (McCann, 2009). The prosecutors in the case attempted to show that Stinson committed reckless homicide, which under Kentucky law is defined as the reckless causing of another person's death. Specifically, prosecutors attempted to demonstrate that Stinson: "(1) failed to perceive a substantial and unjustifiable risk of such a nature and degree that his failure constituted gross deviation from a reasonable standard of care; and (2) his failure resulted in Gilpin's death" (McCann, 2009). Regarding the wanton endangerment charge, prosecutors attempted to show that Stinson manifested an extreme indifference to the value of Gilpin's life. After Stinson pleaded not guilty, and a three week jury trial, Stinson was not convicted of either charge;[3] however, this case caused many coaches to re-examine their conduct, especially when it comes to players who are showing signs of fatigue and injury during practice or in a game. The shift from civil negligence to criminal negligence occurs across a fine line; all recreation and sport administrators should be cognizant of their susceptibility to criminal conduct.

Defenses

As noted, the most common defense used in criminal cases by athletes and others in sport and recreation is the consent defense; in other words, that the victim consented to the harm incurred by virtue of participation in the athletic event. While victim consent is not a defense allowed under traditional criminal law applications, the Model Penal Code creates an exception to this rule specifically for sport (Model Penal Code § 2.11.2(b)). Understandably, athletes and recreation participants must consent to some amount of physical contact, and possible harm, especially in contact sports. Some acts that may be perceived as assault or battery in non-sport settings are acceptable in sport given the nature, and expectation, of vigorous play. The line, however, between what acts are consented to and what acts are beyond consent has been vigorously discussed by the courts. The three approaches taken by the courts regarding the consent defense are: (1) Athletes only consent to those acts within a game that are reasonably foreseeable; (2) Athletes can only consent to those acts which are within the rules of the game; and (3) Athletes consent to any act in-connection to the athletic event.

Reasonably Foreseeable. In *State v. Guidugli* (2004), the court noted that the reasonably foreseeable test was most appropriate in determining whether a victim had consented to a harm incurred in an athletic event; victims can only consent to those harms that are reasonably foreseeable. Relying on *People v. Greer* (1976), *State v. Floyd* (1990), and *State of Washington v. Shelley* (1997), the court reasoned that there is a line between physical aggression that is reasonably foreseeable within the context of game play, and violence that takes place "after play has stopped, or is purely retaliatory, or exceeds in brutality or degree of injury anything that the player might have otherwise agreed to." The issue with this test is determining what actions within an athletic contest are reasonably foreseeable. This determination becomes even more challenging when individual sports are considered. Certainly, the amount of harm that is reasonably foreseeable will vary among sports. Take baseball for example; in *Avila v. Citrus Cmty. Coll. Dist.*, (2006), a civil case, the court decided that pitches thrown at a batter's head are part of the game of baseball. Although determined in a civil case, this could be used to substantiate the consent defense for a pitcher accused criminally for harm to a batter. Similar questions could be asked in each sport. As in civil law, determining reasonable foreseeability requires a case-by-case analysis. The same is true when applying the reasonably foreseeable test to the consent defense in criminal law.

Rules of the Game. While limited in application, this test was also discussed in *State of Washington v. Shelley* (1997). The trial court reasoned that the consent defense was unavailable to the defendant because the defendant's conduct exceeded what is permissible within the rules of basketball; the court stated that "consent is to contact that is contemplated within the rules of the game." However, the appellate court rejected this theory, arguing that fouls outside the rules of the game occur in almost all athletic contests; to hold that an athlete can only consent to actions within the rules of any game is far too narrow an application. Specifically, the court stated that in any athletic contest, "it may be ordinary and expected for minor assaults to occur" outside the rules of the game.

---

[3] The civil lawsuit filed by Max Gilpin's parents against the Jefferson County Public School District was settled for $1.75M.

In-Connection Standard. A New York court followed a third approach in *People v. Shacker* (1998) (see Supplemental Website). In a hockey game, the defendant skated up behind the victim, who was standing near the goal, and struck the victim on the back of the neck with his hand. The victim's head hit the crossbar, causing a concussion and other minor injuries. The court reasoned the victim had consented to all harms "in-connection" with the hockey game; thus the defendant's assault was excused. While the rules of the game test presented an application that was too narrow, the "in-connection" standard presents one that is too broad; by holding that athletes consent to all harm "in-connection" with an athletic contest, the court gives athletes far too much latitude for permissible sport violence (Standen, 2009).

Crimes against Public Health, Safety, and Welfare
Crimes where there is generally no single victim have been categorized as crimes against public health, safety, and welfare.

Point Shaving
Conspiracy to commit sports bribery is a federal crime [18 U.S.C.S § 224 (2015)]. One example of such a conspiracy is point-shaving. In the past 60 years nearly every bribery-related college betting scandal has involved point-shaving (*Gustky*, 2001; McCarthy, 2007).[4] **Point-shaving** is defined as deliberately limiting the number of points scored by one's team in an athletic contest, in return for a payment from gamblers to ensure winnings. Typically, point shaving is collaboration among athletes and gamblers to commit criminal sports wagering by manipulating the scores of sporting events. Athletes are bribed to manipulate the scores between teams so that the point margin is less than the point spread estimated by odds makers.

Recently, there have been an alarming number of point shaving allegations. In 2009, the University of Toledo was rocked by such a scandal; seven former athletes, three football players and four basketball players, were indicted by federal authorities on charges of conspiracy to commit sports bribery (Gilbert & Silka, 2009). Specifically, the players were accused of regularly discussing point spreads with a local gambler, purposefully manipulating the score of games, and receiving a payoff if the gambler won his bet (White, 2011). All seven players were sentenced to probation terms spanning one to three years, and all received monetary fines as well (Moore, 2015). In 2011, two University of San Diego (USD) basketball players and a USD assistant basketball coach were indicted for conspiracy to commit sports bribery and operating an illegal sports bookmaking service. The indictment alleged that one of the players took a bribe to influence the outcome of a game and solicited an individual to affect the outcome of USD basketball games. The other player and the assistant coach were alleged to have each solicited an individual to affect the outcome of a college basketball game. The three defendants each pleaded not guilty, however the assistant coach was sentenced to a year in prison, and one of the players was sentenced to six months in prison (Nguyen, 2015). Each of these examples illustrate the importance of educating student athletes about the potential perils of any conspiracy to commit sports bribery.

Sport Agent Crimes
Athlete agents may be found criminally liable under both state and federal law for inappropriate conduct with respect to student athletes. The Sport Agent Responsibility and Trust Act is a federal law that governs the athlete-agent relationship (15 U.S.C. §7801 et seq. (2015); the Uniform Athlete Agent Act is a model law that has been adopted in 40 states (www.ncaa.org, 2012). While these laws are discussed fully in Chapter 7.40, *Sport Agent Legislation*, it is important to note the recent trend of imposing harsh criminal penalties for illegal athlete agent conduct. Specifically, recent legislation in Texas renders agent misconduct a third degree felony, imposing a possible 10-year prison sentence [Tex. Occ. Code §2051.501 (2015)]; similarly, Arkansas also now considers agent misconduct as a felony offense, raising the maximum fine from $50,000 to $250,000 [A.C.A. §17-16-115 (2015)].

Crimes Against Government
Crimes against government include crimes that are in violation of government statutes. These include crimes such as ticket scalping and gambling.

---
[4] Among the most notable scandals are the 1951 point shaving scandal at City College of New York; a 1979 men's basketball point shaving scheme at Boston College [see *U.S. v. Burke, et. al.*, (1983)]; a 1985 scandal at Tulane University; a 1994 scandal at Arizona State University, in which basketball player Stevin Smith served nearly a year in prison for shaving points in four basketball games; and a 1995 scandal at Northwestern University.

Ticket Scalping

The resale of event tickets for above face value, also called **ticket scalping** or **ticket resale**, is a criminal activity in many jurisdictions; however, in-person resale and private party transactions occur for almost every sporting event. Further, ticket scalping also occurs in the online market. In 2006, websites such as eBay, StubHub, and RazorGator estimated annual ticket sales of approximately $3 billion; 2012 projections show an increase to $4.5 billion (Kirkman, 2009). The growing ticket resale market must be analyzed in two ways: (1) Statutory Regulation; and (2) Relevant Case law.

Statutory Regulation. According to Dodds, et. al., (2012), there is little consistency among the state laws that regulate ticket resale. Some jurisdictions prescribe specific requirements for resale, some jurisdictions prohibit any form of resale, and some jurisdictions have no prohibitions at all. For example, Rhode Island prohibits resale over face value, except for a service charge up to $3 or 10% over its face value (R. I. Gen Law § 5-22-26; 2014); New York allows resale by registered resellers without percentage over face value restrictions, but prohibits resale on the street within 1,500 feet of a venue with a seating capacity of more than 5,000 (N.Y. Arts & Cult. Aff. § 25.08 and § 25.13; 2014); and, Minnesota allows resale generally, but prohibits use of software to circumvent a ticket security or access control measure (Minn. Stat. 245 § 609. 806; 2014). Regardless of the jurisdiction or statute involved, state level regulation presents many challenges. First, many transactions take place using the Internet, and often across state lines; thus, personal jurisdiction and choice of law concerns arise. Second, enforcement of a statute in cyberspace is virtually impossible. For example, if a reseller in Rhode Island were to use Craigslist.com to post tickets for sale at 25% above face value, accept payment online via PayPal, and ship the buyer the tickets, there is no reasonable method to enforce the statute. For this reason, several states, such as Virginia, have recently modified prior prohibitive legislation and currently allow Internet transactions (Va. Code Ann. § 15. 2-969; 2014).

Relevant Case Law. Many parties, including fans, sport organizations, and ticket brokers, have attempted to control the ticket resale through litigation. Specifically, in *Cavoto v. Chicago National Baseball Club* (1993), a class action group of Cubs fans sued the Chicago Cubs (Cubs) after the team created Wrigley Field Premium Ticket Services (Premium). The class action fans alleged that the Cubs sold choice seat locations at face value to Premium, who then sold them at above face value to fans, allowing the Cubs to capitalize on revenues generated by the secondary market. The lawsuit alleged that this practice violated the Illinois anti-scalping statute. The trial court ruled that the statute did not prohibit the Cubs' parent company from establishing a ticket brokerage entity; thus, the Cubs did not violate the statute. On appeal, this decision was affirmed. In *New England Patriots, L.P. v. Stubhub, Inc.*, (2007) roles were reversed, with the sport organization filing the lawsuit against a resale broker. The New England Patriots sued StubHub, seeking access to the names, addresses, and phone numbers of season ticket holders who resold their tickets on StubHub's website. The Patriots alleged that StubHub was encouraging resale in violation of Massachusetts anti-scalping laws. StubHub countered the claim with allegations that the Patriots were trying to monopolize control of the secondary market for Patriot games; however, court held that StubHub needed to release the names to the Patriots (*See* Supplemental Website). Lastly, in *Ticketmaster, L.L.C. v. RMG Technologies, Inc.*, (2007), the ticket broker Ticketmaster filed a complaint against RMG Technologies alleging that RMG produced and sold software that allowed users to circumvent Ticketmaster security and quantity access measures, aiding in mass ticket procurement. The court ruled in favor of Ticketmaster on the grounds of copyright infringement and the Digital Millennium Copyright Act, awarding Ticketmaster over $18 million. Interestingly, since this decision, some jurisdictions, such as Minnesota (as noted above), have amended ticket resale statutes to specifically prohibit use of these software applications.

Gambling

Criminal activities related to gambling have the most relevance for a recreation or sport manager when they potentially impact the integrity of the game, as discussed in the section on point shaving and bribery. Further integrity issues may involve student athlete ineligibility for participating in gambling, or other NCAA rule violations relating to gambling within an athletic department. However, other than these unique concerns, gambling is a crime against government that does not have a direct impact on recreation and sport managers. While the federal and state governments have criminal statutes regulating gambling, violation of such statutes by an individual gambler will likely not impact a sport organization.[5]

---

[5] Federal laws that serve to regulate gambling include: Wire Communications Act of 1961; Racketeer Influenced and Corrupt Organizations Act of 1970; Professional and Amateur Sports Protection Act of 1992; and the Unlawful Internet Gambling Enforcement Act of 2006. Additionally, 49 states have laws that criminalize sports gambling.

SIGNIFICANT CASE

The following case is an example of an athlete's attempt to use the consent defense after being charged criminally as the result of violent acts in a recreational basketball game. Of important note is the philosophical discussion the court provides regarding the appropriateness of charging athletes in criminal court for on-court aggression. While the appellate court applies the reasonably foreseeable test, and finds no legal ground on which to overturn the trial court decision, the appellate court clearly states that prosecuting athletes for criminal conduct in connection with a game is a misapplication of criminal law.

STATE V. GUIDUGLI
Court of Appeals of Ohio
157 Ohio App. 3d 383 (2004)

Gorman, Judge.

Viewed narrowly, this appeal presents a simple question: whether the trial court erred by convicting the defendant-appellant, Gino Guidugli, of misdemeanor assault, in violation of R.C. 2903.13(A), for his role in a scuffle that broke out between members of opposing teams after a hard foul in a closely contested intramural basketball game at the University of Cincinnati. Viewed broadly, this appeal presents a far more complex social issue involving the wisdom of strictly applying the criminal law to physical altercations that arise within the context of sports contests, especially those contests that are already subject to league regulation and internal discipline—and particularly where the bodily injury to the alleged victim is not serious.

Unfortunately, the larger social question is not directly addressed by the legal issues presented on appeal, which concern only the sufficiency of the evidence and the competency of counsel in presenting Guidugli's unsuccessful claim of self-defense. Although questioning the necessity of prosecuting as a criminal offense what may have been dealt with internally by the University, and the harshness of the sentence imposed by the trial court, we are unable to find any reversible legal error. As a court of law, not of social policy, we affirm.

A Hard Foul Ignites a Fight

On March 9, 2003, Guidugli, the starting quarterback for the University of Cincinnati football team, was playing in an organized student intramural basketball game at the Armory Field House on the University of Cincinnati campus. When Guidugli's teammate protested a foul called by the referee, his teammate and an opposing player exchanged heated words, and the opposing player grabbed his teammate by the shirt. Both benches emptied as players took to the floor.

There was conflicting testimony regarding the nature of the ensuing scuffle. Keith Steineman, the intramural supervisor, described it as a "fracas" involving "pushing and shoving." He stated that supervisors were trained to "let players like work it out themselves so we don't get involved and get hit." Steineman testified, though, that the only punch he saw thrown was that by Guidugli. But one of Guidugli's teammates, Doug Monaghan, testified that the pushing and shoving quickly escalated into a donnybrook. In his words, "fists were flying."

According to Steinman, he witnessed Guidugli enter the fracas, and it was his opinion that Guidugli was, initially at least, "trying to break up [the] scuffle." But he then saw Guidugli knock over one of the opposing players, Levi Harris, and "punch him with a full swing" around the eye. Chris Brunswick, who was acting as scorekeeper, testified that he thought Harris was already on the ground when Guidugli ran onto the court and punched him. Guidugli, however, testified that he was one of the players on the floor and had taken a position along the foul lane, getting ready for the foul shots, when the fight broke out. He stated that he saw another teammate of his, Kevin Hazel, punch Harris, and that he was pulling someone off Monaghan when he saw a punch coming in his direction out of the corner of his eye. He stated that when he turned around, he recognized the person attempting to throw the punch as Harris and he "just defended himself."

Whatever the degree of the fight, Steineman testified that afterward the teams "worked it out" and order was restored. Guidugli's team was told, apparently by Steineman, that they had forfeited the game and should leave the gym, which they did.

The university police were called after Steineman reported the "group fight" by radio to the main office. Officer Kevin Manz arrived two minutes after being dispatched, but some thirty to forty-five minutes after the incident. Although Guidugli and his team had left, Harris and his team had remained because they had another game. Officer Manz spoke to Harris, who was holding a wet cloth to the area around his left eye. Officer Mainz took photographs of Harris's face. Harris then signed a complaint charging Guidugli with criminal assault. Harris's affidavit accompanying the complaint stated, "As I was walking away I was hit with two punches, one from the side and one from the back. I was unaware who hit me."

The trial court, upon hearing all the various versions of the fight and punch, rejected Guidugli's claim of self-defense, stating that the evidence showed that he had punched Harris in retaliation rather than to protect himself. The court thus convicted Guidugli of misdemeanor assault. After listening to arguments in favor of mitigation made by Guidugli's trial counsel, the court imposed a 180-day jail sentence, which it then suspended in favor of one year's probation with the conditions that Guidugli undergo 60 days of home incarceration using an electronic monitoring unit, and that he participate in any treatment or counseling, including anger management, recommended by the probation department. Further, Guidugli was required to pay a $100 fine and court costs.

On July 3, 2003, Guidugli, represented by new counsel, filed a written motion to mitigate, requesting the court to reconsider its sentence. In his motion, Guidugli asked the court to sentence him to community service only, asserting that the incident that had led to his conviction was an isolated event in which he had allowed his competitive nature to interfere with his better judgment. He claimed that he deeply regretted his behavior and had learned a valuable lesson that would preclude him from ever committing a similar offense. In support of his character, he pointed out that he had been a law-abiding citizen for the first twenty years of his young life and had maintained a grade point average of 3.27 as a business-management major at the University of Cincinnati while maintaining the rigorous schedule of a college athlete. He also pointed out that he had been an active member of CPAWS, a student-athlete group that took part in service projects throughout the greater Cincinnati area, and that he had voluntarily spoken at numerous fundraisers and had traveled to Mississippi Gulf Coast Community College to work as a camp counselor for disadvantaged children. He also observed that the sentence as imposed by the trial court had forced him to cancel plans to attend the Peyton Manning Sports Camp, and that it threatened his participation in certain media events important in garnering awards during the college football season, as well as his presence at a team training camp considered integral in preparation for the first game of the season.

On July 7, 2003, the trial court denied the motion. On August 14, 2003, the trial court granted Guidugli's motion to stay further execution of the sentence pending this appeal.

Other Available Defenses—Sports Violence and the Criminal Law

In mitigation, in other words after the trial court's finding of guilt, defense counsel raised the argument for the first time that such fights were typical of hard fought athletic contests, particularly among young college-aged men eager to test their manhood. As defense counsel pointed out, "You don't have to go any further than Riverfront Stadium to see athletes in altercations." Defense counsel asked that the trial court take into consideration that "this young man [Guidugli], like all the other guys who are out there that night, were competitors and in a game. And the game got a little out of control at a point. And it escalated into this * * *."

This argument brings into focus the larger question alluded to at the outset of this opinion: whether physical altercations arising in sports contests that are already subject to some form of internal regulation and discipline should necessarily result in criminal charges, at least where there are no serious physical injuries as a result. Legal scholars have questioned the strict application of the criminal law to sports contests in which, contrary to real-world norms that generally condemn such behavior, a premium is placed upon physical aggression, intimidation, and enforcement. See, e.g., Clarke, Law and Order on the Courts: The Application of Criminal Liability for Intentional Fouls During Sporting Events (2000), 32 Ariz. St.L.J. 1149; Harary, Aggressive Play or Criminal Assault? An In Depth Look at Sports Violence and Criminal Liability (2002), 25 Colum. J.L. & Arts 197.

"From an early age, athletes are taught to intimidate opponents and to precipitate physical altercations rather than to avoid them. Athletes learn that they need to be tough to get noticed and to excel in higher levels of competition." Clarke, supra, at 1157–1158. "Violence in sports can be attributed to many factors, including: the interplay between competition, frustration, and aggression; the 'game reasoning' or 'sport reasoning' that supplements—or, at times, replaces—ordinary moral reasoning during sporting events; the degree of 'sport socialization' that leads players to perceive sports violence as legitimate; *the sports norm of reciprocity for acts of aggression by opposing players*; and the significance placed upon winning at all costs. It is the confluence of these factors that create the curious world which is sports—a world in which real world behavioral models have no place." Id. at 1155–1156 (emphasis supplied).

Given the unique social dynamic involved in sports, "criminal prosecution of sports participants for conduct that occurs with the playing of the game is rare." Id. at 1168, citing Yasser, Mcurdy, and Goperlud, Sports Law (1990) 378. Most prosecutions, not surprisingly, have involved hockey games. See Calvert-Hanson and Dernis, Revisitng Excessive Violence in the Professional Sports Arena: Changes in the Past Twenty Years? (1996), 6 Seton Hall L.Rev. 127, 138. Perhaps saying something about the American competitive nature, prosecutors in the United States have shown far less zeal in punishing sports violence than their Canadian counterparts, who have been observed to use the criminal law much more frequently. See White, Sports Violence as Criminal Assault: Development of the Doctrine by Canadian Courts (1986), 1986 Duke L.J. 1030, 1034.

One stated rational for prosecutorial restraint is the inherent safeguards of league play, with its system of in-game punishment and suspension. As one commentator has written, "It is inevitable that players' passions will at times be aroused, but game officials and coaches are vested with the authority to impose sanctions for misconduct during the game. The penalties imposed by referees or umpires may seem minor when compared to those imposed on perpetrators of the same conduct outside the sport context, but those punishments are quick and certain, and are thought by some criminologists to be more effective in deterring undesirable behavior than the imposition of more severe penalties." Clarke, supra, at 1192.

* * * *

Canadian courts were among the first to establish the implied-consent doctrine of sports in criminal cases, see *Regina v. Green* (Ont. Provincial Ct. 1970), 2 C.C.C.2d 442, and *Regina v. Maki* (Ont. Provincial Ct. 1970), 1 C.C.C.2d 333, but, interestingly, the American Law Institute had earlier adopted the doctrine in its 1962 Official Draft of the Model Penal Code. Section 2.11(2) of the code provides that consent can be an absolute defense to bodily harm if "the conduct and the harm are a reasonably foreseeable hazard of joint participation in a lawful athletic competition or competitive sport * * *."

The Model Penal Code section has no analog in the Ohio Revised Code. As a matter of decisional law, the doctrine, although acknowledged, has found limited application in American courts. See *State v. Floyd* (Iowa App.1990), 466 N.W.2d 919, 922; *People v. Freer* (1976), 86 Misc. 2d 280, 381 N.Y.S.2d 976, 979: and *State v. Shelley* (Wash.App. 1997), 85 Wn. App. 24, 929 P.2d 489, 493. Courts have appeared to draw the line between physical aggression that can be reasonably foreseen within the context of game play, and thus, by inference, consented to by the player, and violence that takes place after play has stopped, or is purely retaliatory, or exceeds in brutality or degree of injury anything that the player might have otherwise agreed to. For example, in *Floyd* the court refused to apply the doctrine to a recreational basketball game in which the defendant assaulted players resting on the sideline during a timeout. In *Freer*, the court held the doctrine inapplicable to a punch thrown by a football player in retaliation for a punch thrown by the complainant in the midst of a game tackle. And in *Shelly* the court refused to allow the doctrine to justify a punch thrown by another recreational basketball player who felt the blow justified after the complainant had scratched him across the face during play.

Our research has not disclosed any Ohio cases involving application of the implied-consent doctrine in a criminal prosecution for sports violence. In *State v. Dunham* (1997), 118 Ohio App. 3d 724, 693 N.E.2d 1175, this court rejected application of the doctrine of mutual consent to a prosecution for felonious assault arising out a street fight. In *Dunham*, we noted that the doctrine of mutual consent arose out of the ancient maxim *volenti non fit injuria* (no legal wrong is done to him who consents) that forms the basis in civil law of the doctrine of assumption of the risk. Notwithstanding the survival of the Roman principle in the area of torts, we nonetheless concluded that, except for professional or amateur boxing exhibitions held pursuant to R.C. 3773.31, "fighting must be held to be illegal in this state because each combatant may be guilty of an assault in law as well as the battery which might follow as a consequence of the exchange of blows or, at least, by the demonstration of the ability to do harm. The fact that street fighters agree to engage in a public brawl to settle old or current differences cannot and does not negate the penal consequences." *Id.* at 729, 693 N.E.2d 1175.

Given its limited application, and our holding in *Dunham*, we cannot say that Guidugli's trial counsel was ineffective for not advancing the doctrine of implied consent as another affirmative defense. As noted, trial counsel appears to have argued the doctrine, in principle at least, during mitigation following the verdict, but not before. Even if we were to assume that the doctrine exists in Ohio, it is unlikely that the trial court would have found the doctrine applicable in this case. To have successfully argued the doctrine, Guidugli would have had to have persuaded the trial court that the punch he threw was a foreseeable part of the game and one to which Harris impliedly consented. Although it is specious to suggest that basketball remains today a non-contact sport, it is quite a stretch to argue that retaliatory punches during a pause in play are to be accepted as the unavoidable cost of playing the sport at the intramural level. It bears emphasis in this regard that the punch, as described by the state's witnesses, was entirely outside the scope of play and did not arise, for example, as a result of a scuffle under the basket or in a fight for a rebound.

Official's Time Out

Finally, we observed earlier that the trial court imposed a 180-day suspended jail sentence, 60 days of home incarceration/electronic monitoring in lieu of the suspended sentence, one year of probation, anger management counseling as recommended by the probation department, a $100 fine, and court costs—all for a minor welt in a basketball game suffered by a complainant who could not leave work to attend the trial. Later, the trial court denied a motion to reconsider its sentence despite several cogent arguments advanced by new counsel. Although the sentence may appear harsh, it has not been challenged on appeal and is not in any case subject to review. Guidugli, as the starting quarterback on the University of Cincinnati football team, can now serve the balance of his sentence before fall practice and the upcoming season begins. As Clarke notes, "Accountability among athletes is avoided by the simple expedient of ignoring anything but the on-court consequences of behavior." Clarke, supra, at 1156. At the very least, it seems, among the lessons learned from this case is that while sports norms may be very different from real-world norms, conduct on the court may still have very serious real-world consequences off the court.

The judgment of the trial court is affirmed.

CASES ON THE SUPPLEMENTAL WEBSITE

In the Matter of the Welfare of J.S.I., 2009 Minn. App. Unpub. LEXIS 140. This case demonstrates that even minors may be adjudicated delinquent if harm inflicted in an athletic contest is considered criminal.

NPS, LLC. v. StubHub, Inc., 22 Mass. L. Rptr 717 (2007). This case illustrates a professional football team's attempt to use anti-scalping laws to limit resale of tickets by a third party vendor.

People of the State of Colorado v. Hall, 999 P.2d 207 (2000). This case details a skier who was acquitted of reckless manslaughter after killing another skier in a skiing accident. While the text provides examples of recreation participants that were found criminally liable, this case details a finding in favor of the defendant.

People of the State of New York v. Shacker, 670 N.Y.S.2d 308 (1998). This case provides discussion of the consent defense and highlights the overly broad "in-connection" theory.

State of Washington v. Shelley, 929 P.2d 489 (1997). This case discusses both the rules of the game test and the reasonably foreseeable test; further, the case offers reasoning for upholding a criminal conviction for conduct stemming from a recreational basketball game.

QUESTIONS YOU SHOULD BE ABLE TO ANSWER

1. Describe the required elements of a crime.
2. What is the primary difference between civil negligence and criminal negligence?
3. What practical advice should you give recreational participants, athletes and coaches regarding potential criminal liability?
4. How would you best educate student athletes regarding the perils of point shaving?
5. How can the state anti-scalping laws benefit a sport organization?

REFERENCES

Cases

Avila v. Citrus Cmty. Coll. Dist., 131 P.3d 383 (2006)
Cavoto v. Chicago National League Ball Club, Inc., 222 Ill.2d 569 (2006)
In the Matter of the Welfare of J.S.I., 2009 Minn. App. Unpub. LEXIS 140
New England Patriots, L.P. v. Stubhub, Inc., 22 Mass. L. Rptr 717 (2007)
People of the State of New York v. Shacker, 670 N.Y.S.2d 308 (1998)
People v. Freer, 381 N.Y.S.2d 976 (1976).
State of Washington v. Shelley, 929 P.2d 489 (1997)
State v. Forbes, No. 63280 Minn. Dist. Ct. (1975)
State v. Floyd, 466 N.W.2d 919 (1990).
State v. Guidugli, 157 Ohio App. 3d 383 (2004)
State v. Limon, No. 1999-CR-2892 Dist. Ct. Texas (2000).
Ticketmaster, L.L.C. v. RMG Technologies, Inc., 507 F. Supp. 2d 1096 (2007)
U.S. v. Burke, et. al, 700 F.2d 70 (1983)

Publications

Black, H. C. (1990). Black's Law Dictionary, (6th Ed.) St. Paul: West Publishing Co.
Epstein, A. (2009) *Incorporating the Criminal Law in Sport Studies*. 12 The Sport Journal 3. Available at: http://www.thesportjournal.org/article/incorporating-criminal-law-sport-studies
Fitzgerald, D. (2010). *Friday night rights: Arrest of Middletown coaches evokes lessons of Stinson case*. Available at: http://ctsportslaw.com/2010/07/13/friday-night-rights-arrest-of-middletown-coaches-evokes-lessons-of-stinson-case/
Gilbert, M. & Silka, Z. (2009). *6 former University of Toledo athletes charged in point shaving scheme*. Available at: http://www.toledoblade.com/UT/2009/05/07/6-former-University-of-Toledo-athletes-charged-in-point-shaving-scheme.html

Gustky, E. (2001). *The problem still hasn't been fixed*. Available at: http://articles.latimes.com/2001/mar/30/sports/sp-44540

Harary, C. (2002). *Aggressive play or criminal assault? An in-depth look at sports violence and criminal liability.* 25 Colum. J.L. & Arts 197.

Johnson, G. (2009) *Isolation for concussed athlete scandal get worse.* Available at http://www.subtlebraininjury.com/blog/tag/texas-tech-coach-mike-leach-suspended-for-concussion-isolation-of-adam-james

Kaplan, J. et. al. (1996). *Criminal law: Cases and materials.* Boston, MA. Little, Brown and Company.

Kirkman, C. P. (2009). *Note: Who needs tickets? Examining problems in the growing online ticket resale industry.* Federal Communications Law Journal, 61, 739–763.

McCann, M. (2009). *Kentucky trial of high school coach has wide implications.* Available at : http://sportsillustrated.cnn.com/2009/writers/michael_mccann/08/26/kentucky.coach/index.html

McCarthy, M. (2007). *Point-shaving remains a concern in college athletics.* Available at: http://www.usatoday.com/sports/college/2007-05-08-point-shaving-cover_N.htm

Model Penal Code § 2.01 (2001).

Model Penal Code § 2.02 (2001).

Model Penal Code § 2.02.2(c) (2001).

Model Penal Code § 210.3–4 (2001).

Model Penal Code § 211.1 (2001).

Model Penal Code § 2.11.2(b) (2001).

Moore, M. (2015). Seven former Toledo athletes sentenced in point-shaving scheme. Available at:http://www.hustlebelt.com/2015/4/7/8367403/toledo-rockets-seven-sentenced-point-shaving-scheme-triplett-payne

Nguyen, A. (2015). USD fires coach Bill Grier after scandal tainted basketball career. Available at:http://timesofsandiego.com/sports/2015/03/16/usd-fires-basketball-coach-bill-grier-after-8-seasons/

Quinlan, L. (2009) *Irondequoit man convicted of homicide in softball player's death*. Available at: http://www.mpnnow.com/towns/irondequoit/x1098985647/Irondequoit-man-convicted-of-homicide-in-softball-players-death

Schwarz, M. & Berko, A. (2011). *Syracuse's Bernie Fine placed on leave.* Available at: http://espn.go.com/espn/otl/story/_/id/7248184/syracuse-police-investigating-bernie-fine-molesting-boy-1980s

Standen, J. (2009). *The manly sports: The problematic use of criminal law to regulate sports violence.* 99 J. of Crim. Law & Criminology 3.

Toporek, B. (2012). *Police open investigation into H.S. coach's concussion management.* Available at: http://blogs.edweek.org/edweek/schooled_in_sports/2012/01/police_open_investigation_into_hs_coachs_concussion_management.html

Viera, M & Becker, J. (2011). *Ex-coach denies charges amid new allegations.* Available at: http://www.nytimes.com/2011/11/15/sports/ncaafootball/jack-raykovitz-chief-of-second-mile-resigns-amid-penn-state-scandal.html

White, E. (2007). *Cuomo guilty in point-shaving scheme.* Available at: http://www.foxtoledo.com/dpp/news/local/Cuomo-guilty-in-point-shaving-scheme

Legislation

A.C.A. § 17-16-115 (2015)

Minn. Stat. 245 § 609. 806 (2014)

N.Y. Arts & Cult. Aff. § 25.08 and § 25.13 (2014)

R. I. Gen Law § 5-22-26 (2014)

Tex. Occ. Code § 2051.501 (2015)

Va. Code Ann. § 15. 2-969 (2014)

15 U.S.C. §7801 et seq. (2015)

18 U.S.C.S § 224 (2015)

3.22 HAZING

Ellen J. Staurowsky | Drexel University

On an October day in 1881, seven upper class students assaulted a Bowdoin College freshman in his dorm room as part of a hazing ritual (*Strout v. Packard*, 1884). The case offers a vivid description of escalating events not unfamiliar to us today. There was an invasion of an unsuspecting student's room, a beating, and general mayhem as more than one assailant threw "missiles" at the student. The issue raised in this case was whether a conspiracy existed among Strout's seven attackers and subsequently, who was liable for the harm done to Strout, who suffered, among other things, a serious eye injury after being hit with a thrown object. In ruling that there was not sufficient evidence to determine that a conspiracy existed, and culpability for the injury could be assigned only to the person from whose hand the object had been thrown, the judges of the Supreme Judicial Court of Maine raised considerations that resonate today about what constitutes hazing and who is responsible. Although the rights of the defendants were upheld in this case, there is a palpable sense in reading the opinion that the judges were aware that justice had not been served by so narrow a reading of the defendants' collective contribution to the events that occurred.

Over 125 years later, hazing endures and with it the attendant questions of accountability and culpability. As a case in point, a parental complaint to the Office of University Compliance and Integrity about alleged sexual harassment by members of the Ohio State Marching Band in May of 2014 led to a prompt Title IX investigation, revealing pervasive practices and traditions that were sexualized in nature. The two key findings from the University's Title IX investigation, based on a preponderance of the evidence standard, included a determination that "The Marching Band's culture facilitated acts of sexual harassment, creating a hostile environment for students" and that the band director had failed to "eliminate the sexual harassment, prevent its recurrence, and address its effects" (Office of University Compliance and Integrity, 2014). A subsequent task force investigation into the culture of the Band, which is an academic class at Ohio State, revealed that traditions such as the production of "row videos" (videos made to introduce band members in an initiation) "... contained some level of "disturbingly inappropriate behavior" including "... alcohol use and abuse and sexually inappropriate references and themes" (The OSU Marching Band Culture Task Force, 2014).

Despite the efforts of educators, administrators, public policy makers, and others to create awareness about the negative consequences of hazing and develop prevention programs, much remains unknown about the magnitude and degree of hazing as it occurs in school or professional sport and recreational settings. Conflicting perspectives regarding what constitutes hazing continue to be issues for parents and teachers, school officials and local law enforcement, students and athletes.

Three cases that occurred during the 2015-2016 academic year illustrate this point. In the aftermath of an incident that occurred while participating in a holiday tournament in December of 2015, three Ooltewah (TN) high school basketball players were charged with aggravated rape and aggravated assault. The alleged victim, a 15-year old first year player, required emergency surgery to repair internal injuries resulting from teammates restraining him while another prodded him with a pool cue. The 17-year old believed to have violated the alleged victim described the event as "horseplay" that devolved into the "accidental" use of too much force. Testifying in court about what had happened, the investigating police officer said that the case was "much smaller than what it's been blown up to be" and that it was just "something stupid that kids do". He went on to say, "... it wasn't done for sexual gratification ... It was an assault, really. It just happened that the end result fit the definition of aggravated rape" (Barr, 2016).

In contrast, the boys' basketball program at Strasburg High School (VA) was suspended indefinitely in January of 2016 pending an investigation into an alleged incident of misconduct on a team bus. Based on local law enforcement reports, a 16-year old boy may have been sexually assaulted by other team members on the trip (Associated Press, 2016; Bult, 2016). An attorney for one of the senior boys on the team who was suspended from school a few weeks after the incident was reported characterized the event as "kids roughhousing". As a defense, he argued that the African-American plaintiff may have been subjected to "racially loaded language" as a consequence of team members engaging in something called "the lynching game", but nothing in the behavior of his client could be defined as sexual misconduct. While school administrators explained that the suspensions were due to the need to prioritize the health and well-being of players on the team and students in the school, the treatment of the alleged perpetrators was challenged on the basis of due process (Frampton, 2016).

In the third case, a 20-year old softball player who had been a member of the St. Joseph's University (PA) team alleged in May, 2015, that an atmosphere of sexualized hazing involving excessive alcohol use and simulated sex acts was difficult to handle. She alleged in a lawsuit against the University and the softball coach that, after news of hazing on the softball team surfaced, there was an assumption that she was the source and she experienced retaliation as a result, leading to her giving up her athletic scholarship and leaving the school (*Jane Doe v. St. Joseph's University*, 2015). A second player, Jane Doe II, also filed a complaint, recounting that she, too, left the team after being accused of leaking the story about hazing on the team to the local news (*Jane Doe II v. St. Joseph University*, 2015). Both cases were settled in September, 2015, a day before the University was to file responses to the suits (Passarella, 2015). Results of an internal Title IX investigation by St. Joseph's released in July, 2015, concluded that members of the coaching staff had not violated University policy pertaining to discrimination, harassment, and retaliation (SJU Athletic Communications, 2015).

It is unclear if the adoption of hazing laws at the state level has served to deter the frequency of such behavior or diminish its magnitude. Numerous accounts of hazing incidents that impact the lives of athletes, coaches, families, and communities are reported in media sources around the United States nearly on a daily basis. In September, 2015, six of seven Sayreville (NJ) high school football players, after being accused of hazing and sexually assaulting four other teammates (NBCnewyork.com, 2015) were placed on probation after the case was heard in family court. Four out of the six pleaded to hazing and child endangerment and were spared being registered as sex offenders. In Norman, OK, teenage wrestlers aged 18, 17, and 16 were charged with three counts of raping by instrumentation during a hazing incident on the team bus. One of the alleged victims in that case was 12 years old (FoxNews.com, 2016).

Hazing incidents have increasingly resulted in one or more of the affected parties leaving the institution or being suspended for a period of time. In Mississippi, two 15-year-old boys transferred from Picayune Memorial High School to another school after suffering verbal abuse and being hospitalized for beatings. Due to Mississippi High School Athletic Association (MHSAA) regulations which prohibit students from switching schools to play sports, the two boys have been deemed ineligible. Despite parental claims that the transfers were made in order to protect the safety of the boys, the MHSAA ruled that they could not determine that a hardship warranting an exception to the transfer rules could be determined (Wall, 2012). In a different scenario, the three-week suspension of long-time Kennedy High School (CA) baseball coach, Manny Alvarado, by school officials after an alleged hazing incident led parents to march outside of the school expressing outrage over the decision based on their belief that hazing between players had not occurred (Sondheimer, 2012).

To complicate the issue further, Crow and MacIntosh (2009) point out that many definitions of hazing begin with an assumption that in order for hazing to occur, students seek membership in groups such as fraternities and sororities. As a threshold matter, definitions that address hazing in fraternities or sororities may not be adequate to address hazing in sport teams. They point out that while hazing may be a part of the process used to become a member of a fraternity, coaches determine membership on athletic teams. Thus, hazing in sport contexts speaks to issues associated with group acceptance and power structure rather than membership *per se*. They conclude that definitions of hazing should be redrafted to acknowledge this distinction.

Whereas individual instances provide rich examples of behavior that falls within the scope of hazing definitions, research findings provide some measures of magnitude. Studies reveal that hazing occurs among students in grades 6 through college at rates ranging from just over 17% to 79% (Allan & Madden, 2008; Campo, Poulos, & Sipple, 2005; Crandall, 2003; Gershel, Katz-Sidlow, Small, & Zandieh, 2003; Hoover, 1999, 2000; Waldron, 2015). In a study of members of marching bands at National Collegiate Athletic Association (NCAA) schools (N=1,215) using an online questionnaire, nearly 30% indicated that they had witnessed some form of hazing and were hesitant to report because of concerns about social retaliation or perceptions that no real harm or offense occurred (Silveira & Hudson, 2015). The general trends as documented in the research as well as individual instances show that recreation and sport managers must be proactive in their response to hazing by (1) anticipating that hazing will occur on teams and within student organizations; (2) questioning and monitoring the initiation activities of athletes, students, and employees; (3) working within existing organizational structures to formulate anti-hazing policies; (4) developing anti-hazing education programs. They must also be informed about policies that exist within their organizations and be knowledgeable about the local, state, and national laws that apply to hazing.

FUNDAMENTAL CONCEPTS

Definition and Scope

Definitions of hazing range from the succinct to the comprehensive. For example, in the state of Ohio, **hazing** "means doing an act or coercing another, including the victim, to do any act of initiation into any student or other organization that causes or creates a substantial risk of causing mental or physical harm to any person" (Ohio Revised Code 2903.31). In contrast, Florida law defines hazing to mean

> any action or situation which recklessly or intentionally endangers the mental or physical health or safety of a student for the purpose of initiation or admission into or affiliation with any organization operating under the sanction of a postsecondary institution. Such term includes, but is not limited to, any brutality of a physical nature, such as whipping, beating, branding, forced calisthenics, exposure to the elements, forced consumption of any food, liquor, drug, or other substance, or other forced physical activity which could adversely affect the physical health or safety of the student, and also includes any activity which would subject the student to extreme mental stress, such as sleep deprivation, forced exclusion from social contact, forced conduct which could result in extreme embarrassment, or other forced activity which could adversely affect the mental health or dignity of the student. (Florida State Code 240.1325)

Whereas the statutory definition of hazing is important, so too is the interpretation of the meaning of the term "student organization." In *Duitch v. Canton City Schools* (2004), a freshmen high school student alleged that on "Freshman Friday," he was beaten in a restroom by eight to ten juniors and seniors. Both the trial and appellate courts found that "the actions of the students did not constitute initiation into any student or other organization" and that "the attack was merely due to the appellant's status as a freshman." Initiation into the entire student body rather than into a specific student organization prevented the appellant from finding relief under the existing hazing law in the state of Ohio (see Cases on the Supplemental Website).

The Court of Appeals of Ohio in Clermont County reached a similar determination in *Golden v. Milford Exempted Village School District Board of Education* (2011). In *Golden*, the family of a high school basketball player sought relief after their son was wrestled to the ground, punched, and held there while another player exposed his penis, rubbing it on their son's face, and attempting to force it into their son's mouth. Affirming an earlier decision by the trial court granting summary judgment regarding the civil claim of hazing, the Court noted that the reported actions to which Golden's son was subjected did not meet the statutory requirements of hazing under Ohio law because the acts were not designed to initiate their son into the team but to drive him away. The language of the opinion, however, points to Ohio bullying law as an area of relief. As stated in the opinion, ". . . the incident in the vestibule was the culmination of disturbing acts of bullying by T. toward R." (n.p.). (see Cases on Supplemental Website).

The vast majority of hazing laws create a link between hazing and student welfare, thus limiting the applicability of the law to manifestations of hazing that may occur in other groups, like professional sport teams or athletic teams sponsored by national sport governing bodies (e.g., U.S. Olympic team). The New York statute reflects consideration for this possibility as seen in the language of the statute, which reads in part, "A person is guilty of hazing in the first degree when, in the course of another person's initiation into or affiliation with any organization . . ." (New York 120.16).

Civil Litigation

This section explores the legal basis on which a hazing victim may establish a cause of action in a civil suit. In a civil case, a hazing victim may be awarded monetary damages. Several challenges exist in establishing who is accountable and can be held liable in hazing cases. First, at the college and university level, negligence hinges on the ability to argue that a special relationship exists between the victim and the institution. In the absence of a **special relationship**, there is no **duty of care**. Second, in determining whether both parties (perpetrator and victim) may bear responsibility for hazing, the mere fact that an athlete agreed to participate on a team, by itself, does not provide a supportable rationale to establish **comparative negligence**. Third, coaches and school administrators may be **immune** from civil liability if their actions fall within the realm of professional discretion. Fourth, **parents** may be held negligent for not exercising appropriate supervision of their children.

Negligence. Within the past twenty years, as the number of hazing cases has risen, victims have increasingly sought redress in the courts alleging negligence on the part of athletes who haze as well as coaches, school administrators, and the institutions they represent.

At one time, college officials under the doctrine of *in loco parentis* could be held liable for hazing because administrators had a duty to care for their students much the same as parents had a duty to care for their children. Changing societal views of college students as young adults rather than dependent children shifted the burden of responsibility for student misbehavior from college officials to students. This does not mean, however, that there is no basis for an institutional or professional duty of care. Under the **landowner-invitee theory**, landlords owe a duty of reasonable care to those who are invited onto their property. Through offers of admission and assessment of fees, a similar relationship exists between institutions of higher education and their students (Crow & Rosner, 2002).

In *Knoll v. Board of Regents of the University of Nebraska* (1999), the Nebraska Supreme Court used this theory to reason that the university had an obligation to take steps to protect a student against reasonably foreseeable acts of hazing, which included abduction from his dorm room on campus, transport to a fraternity house off campus, and harm that accrued as a result of his attempt to escape. The implications of this case point to the necessity for school administrators and employers to acknowledge the history of hazing in athletics and to take proactive measures in the form of anti-hazing policies and education or risk failing in their duty to protect students and other persons associated with their organization (Crow & Rosner, 2002).

In *Siesto v. Bethpage Union Free School District* (1999), the Nassau County Supreme Court (NY) awarded summary judgment to the plaintiff, a member of the football team, who sustained a serious head wound as a result of a hazing incident that occurred in the locker room just a short distance from the coach's office. In dismissing the affirmative defenses of comparative negligence and assumption of risk asserted by the school district, the trial court determined that athletes who voluntarily participate in athletics do not assume the risk of injury resulting from being hazed.

Coach accountability and culpability are receiving increased scrutiny as well. In August of 2008, two baseball coaches from Wilson High School in Western New York were charged with endangering the welfare of a child and failure to prevent alleged sex-related attacks on players during a team bus ride the previous spring (Besecker, 2008). In the spring of 2009, an Anderson County High School softball coach resigned her position after authorizing an event in which upper class players arranged for first year teammates to stand in a hotel swimming pool wearing only one article of clothing, an event that violated the school's rules as well as Florida state law (Fowler, 2009). Also in the spring of 2009, five officials of the Las Vegas City Schools (the superintendent, athletic director, and three coaches) were accused of failing to report sexual assaults that younger players were subjected to during a pre-season football camp prior to the start of the academic year (Medina, 2009).

Immunity is a common defense in hazing cases. Immunity can free educational institutions and their employees from liability for negligence (Crow & Rosner, 2002). In *Caldwell v. Griffin Spalding County Board of Education, et al.* (1998), a first-year football player was attacked, beaten, and knocked unconscious in his dorm room during preseason. In a civil suit brought by the player against school officials, the Georgia Court of Appeals upheld a lower court ruling granting summary dismissal on the grounds that the principal, coach, and school board members were immune from civil liability.

In *Elbaz v. Beverly Hills Unified School District* (2007), a member of the BHUSD soccer team was severely beaten by several teammates while on a trip to play in a summer tournament. Attempting to assert three causes of action for negligence, the Court of Appeals of California upheld a lower court ruling granting a demurrer on the grounds that the school district was immune from liability because the trip to the tournament constituted a "field trip" or "excursion" rather than a "school sponsored activity." Whereas a "school sponsored activity" would have provided a basis for the complaint to proceed, under California law, students participating in "excursions" waive all claims against a school district for injury that occurs during such a trip. Further, according to California law, the beating itself did not fall under the definition of hazing in the California Penal Code because the student was already a member of the team.

Constitutional Rights—Students. Among the many avenues that students have pursued in seeking redress for harms endured as a result of hazing is protection under the First and Fourteenth Amendments. In 1993, a high school football player was accosted by teammates while leaving the showers, forcibly restrained, and bound to a towel rack with athletic tape. His former girlfriend was then led into the locker room to see him hanging there (*Seamons v. Snow*, 2000). Upon Seamon's release from the team because of his refusal to apologize for reporting the incident, he filed suit claiming that his First Amendment rights to free speech had been violated by the coach and the school district (*Seamons v. Snow*, 1994). After the district court granted summary judgment in favor of the defendants in 1998, the appellate court reversed that decision sending the case to trial—asserting for a second time that the coach was not entitled to qualified immunity for suspending Seamons from the team (*Seamons v. Snow*, 2000; see *Significant Case* later in this chapter).

In 2000, the Centennial Area School District (PA) settled a lawsuit brought forward by a former high school wrestler so as to avert a court decision regarding its liability. The wrestler alleged his Fourteenth Amendment right to protection of his own bodily integrity had been violated after the school failed to prevent his hazing, despite knowledge of the activity (*Nice v. Centennial Area School District*, 2000). However, in *Meeker v. Edmunson* (2005), the U.S. Court of Appeals for the Fourth Circuit determined that a wrestling coach who had authorized physical attacks on rookies by other members of his team was not protected by qualified immunity. The court determined that the action of a school official to cause a student to be beaten is contrary to the constitutional rights of a student under the Fourteenth Amendment.

In *Perkins, et al. v. Alamo Heights Independent School District* (2002), two high school cheerleaders were stripped of their eligibility to try out for future teams by school authorities because of their involvement in a party where underage drinking and hazing occurred. They sought an injunction claiming their rights under Title IX and the equal protection clause of the U.S. Constitution had been violated because school officials had not provided an adequate hearing prior to taking action and had engaged in disparate treatment of female students. In rejecting their request, the court determined that the "lengthy history of problematic behavior" exhibited by the team and advance warnings about inappropriate behavior served as adequate notice and concluded that the evidence to show disparate treatment was unpersuasive (see Cases on the Supplemental Website).

These cases highlight two issues pertaining to the protection of student rights for coaches and administrators. In the *Seamons v. Snow* case, Coach Snow potentially violated Brian's First Amendment right to free speech by punishing him for breaking the silence that surrounds hazing. In contrast, the Alamo Heights school officials were successful in defending against allegations of failure to provide due process because they had given appropriate notice and acted preemptively to reduce liability prior to the hazing event occurring.

Constitutional Rights—School Officials. School administrators, coaches, and teachers who believed they were wrongly disciplined or dismissed for the manner in which they handled hazing incidents have sometimes asserted that their constitutional rights were violated. In *Cioffi v. Averill Park Central School District* (2006), a high school athletic director appealed the ruling from the U.S. District Court for the Northern District of New York granting summary judgment to the defendants. It was the assertion of the athletic director that the school district's decision to reorganize administrative staffing leading to the abolishment of his position as athletic director was the result of retaliation for complaints he made about the football coach's approach to student health and welfare. In the aftermath of a student filing a criminal charge for sexual assault which allegedly occurred during a football team hazing incident, the athletic director made public comments regarding threats to student safety and potential district liability. In taking issue with the lower court's findings, the U.S. Court of Appeals for the Second Circuit found that statements made by the athletic director about the assault were of public concern and that as an employee, the athletic director's comments should not be deprived of First Amendment protection. Further, the short time between the public statements made by the athletic director and the school district's decision to abolish his position was sufficient to raise a triable issue on causation (see Cases on the Supplemental Website).

In contrast to this case, a softball coach at Brewer School Department, challenged the non-renewal of her contract in violation of the Maine Human Rights Act. According to the plaintiff, the superintendent did not rehire her because of her sexual orientation. The school district, in turn, took the position that the plaintiff should not be rehired because of a history of hazing that had developed during the time that she was coaching the team. In the final analysis, the court granted summary judgment in favor of the defendant (*Cookson v. Brewer School Department*, 2007).

Former Ohio State band director, Jonathan Waters, sought to get his job back after he was terminated for knowing, or he should have known, that hazing was happening in that program and he failed to put an end to it. Seeking relief under Title IX, Waters asserted that the University disciplined him in a harsher manner than a similarly situated female employee. Comparing his situation to that of a female cheerleading coach, who was also the subject of a Title IX investigation that alleged sexualized behavior on that team. Instead of terminating her employment, Ohio State gave the female coach an opportunity to address the issues identified in the investigation. Waters argues that he was given no such opportunity and as a result, the University acted in violation of Title IX (*Waters v. Michael Drake et al, 2015*).

Other Civil Charges. School administrators who show deliberate indifference in cases of peer-to-peer harassment may be subject to liability for the resulting damages (*Davis v. Monroe County Board of Education*, 1999). The case of *Snelling & Snelling v. Fall Mountain Regional School District, et al.* (2001) tested this theory. Derek and Joel Snelling, members of the basketball team, claimed they were targets of persistent verbal and physical abuse by teammates, and, on occasion, by the coach. Although the district court granted summary judgment to Fall Mountain dismissing Section 1983 claims made by the plaintiffs that the harassment violated their Fourteenth Amendment rights to substantive due process and equal protection, District Judge Joseph DiClerico also found a pattern of harassment that presented a trial-worthy issue for action under Title IX and raised an issue as to whether the defendants were deliberately indifferent to the treatment of the brothers (*Snelling & Snelling v. Fall Mountain Regional School District, et al.*, 2001).

While many hazing cases focus on the misbehavior of adolescents and young adults and the conduct of school employees, less attention has been directed toward the role that parents or other adults play in fostering a climate that supports hazing. Following the worldwide distribution of videotaped evidence documenting the violent hazing of girls from Glenbrook (IL) North High School, questions were raised regarding the culpability of adults who had supplied alcohol to the underage participants in the event.

Signaling what may be increasing attempts to hold parents accountable for the behavior of their children, four former coaches at Mepham High School, who lost their sport-related job assignments following a well-publicized football hazing scandal, sued the parents of three of the students involved in the physical and sexual assaults of younger players, seeking $20 million in damages. The attorney for the coaches reasoned that the parents knew or had reason to know that their sons were prone to violence and did not use care to restrain them ("Ex-coaches sue," 2004).

Hazing and Sex Crimes

In September of 2003, at a camp in the Pocono Mountains of Pennsylvania, Mepham High School varsity football players lured younger players into a cabin under the pretense that they would be subjected to some form of mild initiation. From that day forward until the end of camp, the new members of the team were sodomized, beaten, subjected to painful and humiliating treatment, and required to haze other players (Wencelblat, 2004). According to accounts, by the end of camp, the entire team knew what had happened but they all remained silent (Wayne County Grand Jury, 2004). There is strong evidence to suggest that, if not for the fact that two of the victims required medical treatment for their injuries, the incidents would not have been reported. Ultimately, four identified perpetrators were tried as juveniles rather than adult offenders and charged with involuntary deviate sexual intercourse, aggravated assault, and kidnapping (Wencelblat, 2004). Two pleaded guilty to felony charges and began serving time in a juvenile facility, a third pleaded guilty to felony charges and received a sentence of probation, and a fourth pleaded guilty to a misdemeanor charge.

Once notified that hazing had occurred at the camp, Mepham school officials cancelled the 2003 football season, reassigned the head football coach and one of the assistants who were tenured teachers to another school in the district, and elected not to reappoint them to their coaching positions the next year. The former coaches alleged they were improperly reassigned without explanation and denied due process to discuss the reasons for their reassignment (*McElroy & Canestero v. Bellmore-Merrick School District*, 2004). Although McElroy and Canestero were unsuccessful in their suit, this case illustrates the difficulties faced in balancing the interests and rights of students and teachers/coaches. The behavior of the coaches had been the subject of a Wayne County (PA) Grand Jury, who considered whether their conduct during the camp constituted crimes of endangering the welfare of children and recklessly endangering another person. The Grand Jury determined that by legal definition the coaches had not acted criminally, although there was "clear evidence that the coaches displayed a lack of common sense accountability". Given a history of previous hazing incidents in the program and in light of this finding, school administrators would have risked allegations of deliberate indifference if they had not acted in the manner they did. At the same time, Mr. McElroy has asserted that the burden of responsibility should have fallen on the players who committed the crimes because they were bound by Mepham High School's student code of conduct (Jones, 2003).

Given that the Mepham High School case is not an isolated one, it behooves school administrators, coaches, and teachers to be aware of hazing and sex abuse reporting laws within their states. They should also be vigilant for treatment that, if ignored, constitutes endangering the welfare of children.

Criminal Hazing

In contrast to the civil justice system, where hazing victims personally seek relief for the harms done to them, in the criminal justice system, a state entity, such as a county prosecutor, will bring charges against alleged perpetrators for the purpose of determining whether they are guilty or innocent of a criminal act.

Anti-hazing Statutes. The number of states that have adopted anti-hazing statutes has increased dramatically from 25 in 1990 to 44 in 2016. While the number of athletes charged criminally for their participation in hazing activities has increased as well during that span of time, substantial barriers to the enforcement and prosecution of anti-hazing laws remain due to the lack of uniformity in the laws from state to state and the modest penalties that go along with them (Crow & Rosner, 2002; Sussberg, 2003). An analysis of current state statutes, which appears in Table 3.22.1, reveals the following information.

TABLE 3.22.1 STATE ANTI-HAZING LAWS

State	State Hazing Statute	Classification of Crime	Is Failure to Notify a Crime?	Is Anti-hazing Policy Required in Schools?	Is Victim's Willing-ness a Defense?	Public/Private Status of School; Educational Level
AL	16-1-23	Class C misdemeanor	Yes	No	No	Any school
AK	§ 6-5-201.	Class B misdemeanor	Yes			Any school
AZ	15-2301		No	Yes	No	Public
AR	6-5-201	Class B misdemeanor	Yes	No	Yes	Any school
CA	32050-1	Misdemeanor or Felony	No	No	No	Any school
CO	18-9-124	Class 3 misdemeanor	No	No	Yes	Any school
CT	53-23(a)		No	No	No	Higher education
DE	9301-04	Class B misdemeanor	No	Yes	No	Each institution
FL	1006.63	1st degree misdemeanor, 3rd degree felony	No	Yes	No	Postsecondary Public & Private
GA	16-5-61	High and aggravated misdemeanor	No	No	No	Any school
HI	WCHR 0-9			Yes		Statewide system of Public education
ID	18-917	Misdemeanor	No	No	Yes	College or university
IL	720 ILCS 120	Class A misdemeanor, Class 4 felony	No	Yes	Yes	Any school
IN	IC 35-4-2-2	Class A or B misdemeanor, Class C or D felony	No	No	No	Not restricted to school settings; any person
IO	708.10	Serious or simple misdemeanor	No	No	No	Any school
KS	21-3434	Class B misdemeanor	No	No	Yes	Any social or fraternal organization—not limited to schools
KY	164.375		No	Yes	Yes	State colleges & universities
LA	17:1801		No	Yes	No	Only fraternities in any educational institution receiving state funds: Public elementary & secondary schools

State	State Hazing Statute	Classification of Crime	Is Failure to Notify a Crime?	Is Anti-hazing Policy Required in Schools?	Is Victim's Willing-ness a Defense?	Public/Private Status of School; Educational Level
ME	20-AMRS		Yes	Yes	Yes	Public school; postsecondary institution incorporated or chartered by the state
MD	27-268H	Misdemeanor	No	No	No	Any school, college, or university
MA	269-17		Yes	Yes	No	Any student or other person on public or private property Postsecondary schools
MI	7504411	Misdemeanor, Felony	No		No	Educational Institution
MN	127.465 135A-155		No	Yes		Each school board; student or staff hazing; state colleges and universities, private postsecondary
MS	97-3-105	Misdemeanor	No	No	Yes	Not specific to schools; any organization
MI	578.365	Class A misdemeanor, Class C felony	No	Yes	No	Public or private college or university
MT						
NE	28-311.06	Class II misdemeanor	No	No	No	Postsecondary institution
NV	200.605	Misdemeanor, Gross misdemeanor	No	No	No	High school, college, or university in the state
NH	631.7	Class B misdemeanor	Yes	No	No	Any school
NJ	2c:40-3	4th Degree crime	No	No	No	
NM	6.12.7.7					
NY	120.16	Class A misdemeanor	No	No		Not specific to schools or students
NC	9:14:35-38	Class 2 misdemeanor	Yes	No		Any school or college
ND	12.1-17-08	Class A Misdemeanor Class B Misdemeanor	No	No	No	Not limited to schools
OH	2307.44; 2903.31	Misdemeanor	No	No	No	Any school
OK	21-1190	Misdemeanor	No	Yes	No	Any school
OR	163.197	Misdemeanor	No	No		College or university
PA	5352	3rd Degree misdemeanor	No	Yes	No	Institution of higher education; associate degree or higher
RI	11-21-1	Misdemeanor	No	No	Yes	Any school
SC	59-101-200	Misdemeanor	Yes	No	No	Institution of higher learning
SD	None					
TN	49-7-123		No	Yes	No	Higher education
TX	37.152	Misdemeanor or Felony	Yes	Yes	No	Any school
UT	76-5-107.5	Misdemeanor or felony	No	Yes	No (< 21)	High school level
VT	76		No	Yes	No	All educational institutions
VA	18.2056	Class I misdemeanor	No	No	Yes	Any school
WA	28B.10.901	Misdemeanor	Yes	No	No	Any school
WV	18-2.33	Misdemeanor	No	Yes	No	Public Schools
WI	948.51	Class A misdemeanor, Class H & G felony	No	No	Yes	School, college & university
WY	None					

Source: Lexis Nexis Academic Search State Statutes

- Thirty-five of the 45 state codes (77%) classify hazing as a misdemeanor, whereas ten states expressly provide that hazing resulting in serious bodily harm and/or death is classified as a felony. The classification of hazing as a crime does not supersede or change penalties covered by other criminal statutes (see *Classification of Crime* column).
- Ten anti-hazing statutes (22%) specify that it is a crime to fail to report an incident to authorities (see *Is Failure to Notify a Crime?* column).
- Of the existing anti-hazing statutes, nearly 35% (16 of 45) require schools to either develop anti-hazing policies and penalties or devise specific means to educate students, teachers/faculty, and other employees about the state's anti-hazing laws (see *Is Anti-hazing Policy Required in School?* column). However, there is considerable variability with regard to the level and type of school to which statutes apply. For example, 62 percent (28 of 45) include any school or other institution, whether private or public, while two are restricted solely to public schools. Additionally, 11 percent of the codes (5 of 45) pertain solely to higher education institutions (see *Public/Private Status of School; Educational Level* column).
- Sixty-four percent (29 of 45) of the codes provide that implied or express consent on the part of the victim, or a willingness on the part of the person hazed to participate in their own hazing, is not an available defense (see *Is Victim's Willingness a Defense?* column).
- A further limitation is the lack of conformity across hazing laws regarding the mental harm associated with hazing (Sussberg, 2003).

Bills passed by legislators in Montana and New Mexico have included hazing as a behavior broadly defined under the umbrella of bullying (Goare, 2015; The Associated Press, 2015). Numerous improvements to existing anti-hazing laws have been proposed, including the adoption of a federal anti-hazing statute and the imposition of a duty for school personnel to act on these issues (Edelman, 2004; Sussberg, 2003). Additionally, as Ball (2004) pointed out, the Federal Educational Rights and Privacy Act (FERPA), which prohibits the disclosure of student records, may be in conflict with the Campus Security Act (CSA), which requires colleges and universities to make full reports of crimes committed on their campuses. Given the secretiveness surrounding hazing, the protections afforded students may be contributing to schools maintaining silence when these incidents occur. Some argue that rather than more legislation at the state or federal level, another way to bring uniformity to the system would be for the NCAA to adopt a uniform policy regarding athlete misconduct, with hazing being one of the behaviors included in the policy (Gutshall, 2008).

Whereas the evolution of anti-hazing law reflects a growing awareness that behavior assumed to be harmless may, in fact, be criminal, the definitional issues that remain to be resolved along with the meager penalties associated with hazing deserve consideration. As Table 3.22.2 shows, those convicted of hazing crimes are subject to modest fines that range between $10 and $10,000, imprisonment for as little as ten days to a maximum not to exceed one year, or a combination of both. As the Texas statute reveals, even when death results from hazing, the perpetrator may receive no more than two years in prison.

Bullying Laws

Increasingly, the terms hazing and bullying are appearing together in cases of sport team misconduct. Emblematic of that trend, in November of 2011, two members of the Andover High School boys basketball team were expelled and five students suspended for an unspecified amount of time and barred from playing varsity sports for the remainder of the year after an investigation resulted in a finding that an incident occurring at a summer camp five months previous violated the school's anti-bullying and anti-hazing policies. In this case, it was found that older students on the team forced two younger students to play a sex game that resulted in the loser having to eat a semen-covered cookie (Putnam & Messenger, 2011).

The catalyst for the enactment of anti-bullying legislation in the United States was the 1999 Columbine High School shooting incident. Since that time, "Bullying in schools has become widely viewed as an urgent social, health, and education concern that has moved to the forefront of public debate on school legislation and policy" (Stuart-Cassel, Bell, & Springer, 2011, p. ix). As of the fall of 2011, forty-six states have bullying laws (three of these prohibit bullying but do not define it).

TABLE 3.22.2 PENALTIES FOR HAZING

State	Minimum School Penalty	Fine	Sentence	Both Fine & Sentence
AL[1]				
AK	Expulsion			
AZ[2]				
CA	Suspension Expulsion	$100 to $5,000	Not more than one year	Possible
CT	Appropriate penalty Individual	not more than $1,000		
	Group	not more than $1,500 & suspension for no less than one year		
DE	Class B misdemeanor	$1,150	up to 6 months	Possible
FL		$5,000		
LA	Expulsion	$10 to $100	10 to 30 days	Possible
MD		$500	6 months	Possible
MA		$3,000	12 months	Possible
MS		$1000–$2,000	6 months	Possible
MI[3]		$1000 to $10,000		
NE		$10,000		
NC	Expulsion	$500	6 months	Possible
OK		$1500	3 months	Possible
OR		$1,000		
PA	Withhold diploma, other punishment			
RI[4]		$500	30 days to 12 months	Possible
SC	Dismissal, Expulsion			
TX[5]		$500 to $5,000	180 days to 12 months	Possible
VT		$5,000		
WA	forfeit state-funded grants, scholarships, or awards			
WV		$100 to $1,000	9 months	Possible

Source: Lexis Nexis Academic Search State Statutes

[1] In Alabama, state funding for scholarships and awards may be forfeited;
[2] In Arizona, an organization's permission to operate may be revoked and employees face disciplinary action.
[3] In Michigan, a $10,000 penalty in cases where hazing results in death.
[4] In Rhode Island, penalty for (Delete "penalty for") school official allowing hazing to go on can receive a monetary penalty between $10 to $100 per year.
[5] According to the Texas statute, "Any other offense under this section which causes the death of another is a misdemeanor punishable by a fine of not less than $5,000 nor more than $10,000, confinement in county jail for not less than one year nor more than two years, or both such fine and confinement." In convictions where the violation did not result in death, the judge may substitute community service for imprisonment.

SIGNIFICANT CASE

In this case, the court considered whether a high school football coach was liable for violating a player's free speech rights after dismissing the player from the team for refusing to apologize for reporting to authorities that he had been hazed by his teammates. The court also addressed whether the coach was entitled to qualified immunity.

SEAMONS V. SNOW
206 F.3d 1021 (2000)

High school football player who was assaulted by his teammates brought §1983 action against school district, football coach, and school's principal, alleging that player's free speech rights under First Amendment were violated when he was suspended and later dismissed from football team because he refused to apologize for reporting assault to police and school authorities. After summary judgment was granted for all defendants, 864 F.Supp. 1111, that judgment was reversed and remanded, 84 F.3d 1226. Upon remand, the United States District Court for the District of Utah, Dee V. Benson, J., again granted summary judgment for all defendants, 15 F.Supp.2d 1150. Player appealed. The Court of Appeals, Seymour, Chief Judge, held that: (1) if proven, coach's alleged actions could subject him to liability; (2) school district could be liable for coach's alleged conduct; (3) principal's lack of prior knowledge of or involvement in relevant events precluded his liability; and (4) coach was not entitled to qualified immunity.

Affirmed in part, reversed in part, and remanded.

* * *

Seymour, Chief Judge.

This case arises out of the locker-room assault of a high school football player, Brian Seamons, by several of his teammates. Brian filed this action under 42 U.S.C. § 1983 against the school's football coach and principal, as well as the school district. * * *

In the fall of 1993, Brian Seamons was a student at Sky View High School in Smithfield, Utah, and a member of the school's football team. On Monday, October 11 of that year, Brian was assaulted in the locker room by a group of his teammates. As Brian emerged from the showers, four teammates grabbed him, forcibly restrained him, and then bound him to a towel rack with highly adhesive athletic tape. Another teammate brought a girl Brian had dated into the locker room so that she could see what had been done to him.

Brian and his parents reported this incident to the police and to school authorities, including Myron Benson, Sky View's principal, and Doug Snow, the football coach. Two days after the assault, Brian and his parents met with Principal Benson and Coach Snow to discuss whether Brian would press criminal charges against the team members who assaulted him and whether Coach Snow would take any disciplinary action against them. Coach Snow stated he did not plan to remove any of the assailants from the team. Brian indicated that, in light of this, he would need to think about whether he wanted to remain on the team.

On Friday, October 15, the football team was scheduled to play an away game at Logan High School. That afternoon Brian informed Coach Snow that he wanted to remain on the team, and the two attended the traditional pre-game team-only spaghetti dinner in the school cafeteria. Coach Snow told Principal Benson that Brian was back on the team and everything had been worked out. In the meantime, Brian went home to get his uniform so he could dress for the game. When he returned to the school, Coach Snow asked Brian to meet with the four team captains, two of whom had participated in the assault. The purpose of this meeting, at which the Coach was present, was to allow the boys to clear up any residual hard feelings prior to the game.

During this meeting, a confrontation occurred between Brian and Dan Ward, a captain who had also been one of the assailants, over whether Brian should have to apologize to the team for reporting the assault to the police and school authorities. Specifically, Dan stated that he thought Brian had "betrayed the team" by reporting the assault and that Brian should not be allowed to play with the team until he apologized. Aplt.App., tab 14 at 376, 379. At this point, Coach Snow intervened and told Brian he needed to "forgive and forget and apologize" to the team captains. Id. at 359. When Brian refused, Coach Snow told him to "take the weekend and think about this," because without an apology he couldn't play with the team. Id. at 326. This ended the meeting.

Brian did not play in the game that night. He went home and told his parents he wasn't allowed to play because he had refused to apologize to the team. Brian's father, Sherwin Seamons, called the principal and angrily told him what had transpired at the meeting. Principal Benson, surprised to hear that Brian wasn't going to attend the game, drove to Logan High School and discussed the matter with Coach Snow.

The following Tuesday, Brian confronted Coach Snow in school, telling him he wasn't going to apologize to the team and he still wanted to play football. At this point, Coach Snow told Brian that he was "sick of [his] attitude, sick of [his] father's attitude," and that he was off of the team. Aplt.App., tab 15 at 432–33. The following day the remainder of Sky View's football season was canceled.

* * *

A. First Amendment Claim

In ruling on the motion for summary judgment, the district court determined that Coach Snow did not ask Brian to apologize for reporting the assault, and that Brian's ultimate failure to be involved with the football team was unrelated to his speech or refusal to speak. See Seamons III, 15 F.Supp.2d at 1155, 1157. Given the conflicting testimony presented at the evidentiary hearing and contained in the depositions, we fail to see how the district court could reach these conclusions without resolving factual disputes—something it cannot do at this stage of the proceedings. See, e.g., MacLean, 247 F.Supp. at 190 ("The Court's role in summary judgment proceedings is not to resolve issues of fact, but merely to pinpoint those facts which are not at issue."). We note in particular that the district court devoted a large portion of its opinion to a discussion of the differing accounts of the captains' meeting offered by Brian, Coach Snow, and Dan Ward during the evidentiary hearing. See Seamons III, 15 F.Supp.2d at 1156–57.

1. Whether Coach Snow asked Brian to apologize to the team captains

The district court found that Brian was not asked to apologize for reporting the hazing incident. In his deposition and at the evidentiary hearing, Brian testified to the following: during the captains' meeting Dan Ward told him he had betrayed the team by reporting the assault and demanded an apology; when Brian refused, Coach Snow said he would need to "forgive and forget and apologize" in order to remain playing on the team; Coach Snow further stated, "we would need an apology before we let you back on the team." Coach Snow admits to making statements of this nature, although he denies ever directly telling Brian to apologize. If we credit Brian's version, and we must at this stage, there is clearly a disputed issue of fact as to whether Coach Snow asked Brian to apologize to the team captains.

2. **The intended scope of this apology**

The district court found that, even if Coach Snow used the word "apologize," he was not asking Brian to apologize for reporting the assault. Instead, the court concluded that "[t]he request for an 'apology' was not a demand, or a request, for Brian to say he was wrong for reporting the hazing incident; it was rather a request for a mutual reconciliation among Brian and his teammates to allow the boys to function together as friends and teammates." *Seamons III*, 15 F.Supp.2d at 1157. Brian testified that Coach Snow's statements regarding the apology came in response to a heated discussion between Brian and Dan Ward, wherein Dan insisted that Brian not be allowed to play unless he apologized for reporting the assault. Coach Snow interrupted the exchange and expressed his desire that Brian apologize in order to remain on the team. Coach Snow further stated that the team would need an apology before Brian could return. When these remarks are taken in context, it is reasonable to infer that Coach Snow was telling Brian he could not return to the team unless he apologized for reporting the assault. In any event, that is how Brian interpreted the statement, and a jury could properly do the same. Thus, the intended scope of the apology is also a matter of dispute.

One difficulty presented here is the fact that the scope of the requested apology is dependent in part on Coach Snow's intent in asking for it. The Coach's purpose in making these statements to Brian is not easily ascertained and requires inferences drawn from the Coach's behavior throughout the meeting and the broader controversy. This is precisely why summary judgment is not appropriate at this stage. * * *

3. **Whether Brian's failure to apologize was a significant factor in his dismissal from the team**

The district court found that Brian had failed to produce facts showing a "legal causal connection between his speech and his ultimate failure to be involved with the football team." *Seamons III*, 15 F.Supp.2d at 1155. We disagree. There are ample facts in the record to indicate that Brian's suspension and dismissal from the football team were directly related to his failure to apologize for reporting the assault.

Brian testified that when Coach Snow told him to "take the weekend and think about it," he understood he was being told not to participate in that night's game. Aplt.App., tab 14 at 337, 350–52. Coach Snow testified that by making this statement he was telling Brian he couldn't participate in that night's game. *Id.* at 402, 405.

Presumably, had Brian offered the apology at the captains' meeting he would have been allowed to suit up for the game. He was at school and ready to play on Friday. There was no indication that he didn't want to play or would be prevented from playing in the Logan game. The only thing that happened to alter this situation was the captains' meeting at which Brian was asked, and refused, to apologize. Thus, there is evidence that Brian's refusal to apologize was directly related to the fact that he couldn't play in the Friday game, which was, in effect, a temporary suspension from the team.

A few days later when Brian told Coach Snow he was not going to apologize, he did not think he needed to apologize, and he still wanted to play football, Coach Snow stated that he was "sick of [his] attitude" and took him off the team for good. Aplt.App., tab 15 at 472. It can clearly be inferred that this final confrontation, which resulted in Brian's dismissal from the team, was a product of Brian's refusal to apologize. * * *

In this case, the record indicates that Coach Snow, and only Coach Snow, was vested by the school district with the authority to make final decisions regarding membership on the Sky View football team. Aplt.App., tab 18 at 434, 436, 492. Because of this delegation of authority, the school district can be held liable for Coach Snow's actions on team membership. *See Pembaur*, 475 U.S. at 483, 106 S.Ct. 1292 ("Authority to make municipal policy . . . may be delegated by an official who possesses such authority . . .") * * *

B. Qualified Immunity

The district court alternatively found that even if the evidence supported a First Amendment claim, defendant officials were entitled to qualified immunity because "Brian has failed to show *any law* sufficiently well established in 1993 to support the proposition" that under the circumstances of the case he is entitled to relief. *Seamons III*, 15 F.Supp.2d at 1159 (emphasis added). "We review the district court's grant of summary judgment based on qualified immunity de novo, applying the same standard used by the district court." *Roberts v. Kling*, 144 F.3d 710, 711 (10th Cir.1998) (per curiam) (citation omitted).

When the case was last before us, we held that Brian's complaint stated a claim that defendants violated clearly established law and that they therefore were not entitled to qualified immunity. *See Seamons II*, 84 F.3d at 1238–39. We went on to note that defendants could reassert their entitlement to qualified immunity at summary judgment, but only if "Brian's allegations in the complaint prove to be unfounded." *Id.* at 1238. The district court's conclusion that the law was not clear in 1993 is inconsistent with our mandate and relevant case law.

* * *

Coach Snow was the person most directly involved with Brian's suspension and dismissal from the football team. It was his responsibility to determine who played on the team and to make disciplinary decisions. He orchestrated the captains' meeting, instructed Brian not to attend the Logan game when Brian refused to apologize, and arguably dismissed Brian from the team when Brian again expressed an unwillingness to apologize. "[A] reasonably competent public official should know the law governing his conduct." *Chapman v. Nichols*, 989 F.2d 393, 397 (10th Cir. 1993) (quotation omitted). A "precise factual correlation between the then-existing law and the case at-hand is not required." *Patrick v. Miller*, 953 F.2d 1240, 1249 (10th Cir. 1992) (quotation omitted). Coach Snow is not entitled to qualified immunity for his actions with respect to Brian's suspension and removal from the Sky View football team.

In the proceedings below, the district court expressed a belief that this case had gone on for too long, spawned an inordinate amount of controversy, and was not significant enough to warrant time in the federal courts. While this sentiment by a busy judge may be understandable, it cannot justify summary disposition in the face of genuine issues of material fact . . . Brian has asked for his day in court. Because he meets the requirements for stating a claim and alleging material facts in dispute, he is entitled to a trial.

CASES ON THE SUPPLEMENTAL WEBSITE

Cioffi v. Averill Park Central School District Board of Education et al. (2006 U.S. App. LEXIS 814). As you read this case, consider whether a school employee loses a right to publicly express concern about the health and safety of students in programs offered in the Averill Park School District.

Duitch v. Canton City Schools (2004) Ohio App. LEXIS 1878). As you read this case, note the court's ruling regarding the term "hazing" as defined by Ohio state law.

Hunt v. Radwanski et al. (2014). Case No. 2014-CP39-997. The plaintiff in this case alleges twelve causes of action. Out of those twelve, which one is the strongest and which one is the weakest?

Marcantonio v. Dudzinski et al. (2015 U.S. Dist. LEXIS 168721). Consider as you review this case why the plaintiff was unable to successfully argue that his treatment constituted tortious interference with contractual relations, intentional infliction of emotional distress, and statutory conspiracy. On what grounds on counts of assault, battery, false imprisonment, hazing, and negligence were those maintained as pending against all other defendants but dismissed for Defendant Papendick.

Perkins & Phillips v. Alamo Heights Independent School District et al. (204 F. Supp.2d 991). (2002). In this case, were female cheerleaders treated differently than male athletes by being disciplined differently for their involvement in hazing? Was their treatment a violation of Title IX?

The Estate of Jon Thomas Carmichael, By and Through Jon Timothy and Tami Carmichael, Individually and Upon Behalf of His Heirs, Plaintiffs, v. Ronnie Galbraith, et al., Defendants. 2012 U.S. Dist. LEXIS 857. In this case, what would the plaintiffs need to do in order to successfully argue a plausible claim to establish that Joshua Independent School District officials violated Carmichael's rights under the Equal Protection Clause of the Fourteenth Amendment?

QUESTIONS YOU SHOULD BE ABLE TO ANSWER

1. Identify the range of behaviors that may constitute hazing.

2. What does it mean that consent is not a defense in a hazing case?

3. How might an athlete who has been hazed make a negligence claim against a school district or college? What grounds might they seek to establish in order for a negligence claim to be argued?

4. In *Cioffi v. Averill Park School District*, what was the issue related to the athletic director's right to express his concerns regarding the health and safety of athletes?

5. Under what circumstances may parents be held accountable for the actions of their children in hazing cases?

REFERENCES

Cases
Caldwell v. Griffin Spalding County Board of Education et al., 22 Ga. App. 892 (1998).
Cookson v. Brewer School Department et al., 2007 Me. Super. LEXIS 232.

Davis v. Monroe County Board of Education, 526 U.S. 629; 119 S. Ct. 1661; 143 L. Ed.2d 839 (1999).
Duitch v. Canton City Schools, et al., 157 Ohio App. 3d 80; 2004 Ohio 2173; 809 N.E. 2d 62 (2004)
Elbaz v. Beverly Hills Unified School District, 2007 Cal. App. Unpub. LEXIS 4318
Golden v. Milford Exempted Village School District Board of Education, 2011 Ohio 5355; 2011 Ohio App. LEXIS 4384
Jane Doe v. St. Joseph's University. Case No. 2:15-cv-02799-MSG (2015). Online. Internet. http://ia600309.us.archive.org/3/items/gov.uscourts.paed.504905/gov.uscourts.paed.504905.1.0.pdf
Jane Doe II v. St. Joseph's University. Case No. 2:2015cv03123 (2015).
Knoll v. Board of Regents of the University of Nebraska, 601 N.W.2d 757 (1999).
McElroy and Canestro v. Board of Education of the Bellmore-Merrick Central High School District, 5 Misc. 3d 321; 783 N.S.S.2d 781 (2004).
Meeker v. Edmunson et al., 415 F. 3d 317 (2005).
Nice v. Centennial Area School District, 98 F. Supp.2d 665 (2000).
Perkins & Phillips v. Alamo Heights Independent School District et al., 204 F. Supp.2d 991 (2002).
Seamons v. Snow, 864 F. Supp. 1111 (D. Utah 1994).
Seamons v. Snow, 206 F.3d 1021 (2000).
Siesto v. Bethpage Union Free School District, QDS: 72701944 (*New York Law Journal*, December 30, 1999).
Snelling & Snelling v. Fall Mountain Regional School District et al., 2001 DNH 57 (2001).
Strout v. Packard, 76 Me. 148 (1884)
The Estate of Jon Thomas Carmichael, by and through Jon Timothy and Tami Carmichael, Individually, and Upon Behalf of His Heirs, Plaintiffs v. Ronnie Galbraith, et al., Defendants, 2012 U.S. Dist. LEXIS 857
Waters v. Michael Drake et al. (2015). Online. Internet. http://www.dispatch.com/content/downloads/2015/04/Waters_v._Drake_et_al.pdf

Publications

Allen, E. J., & Madden, M. (2008). Hazing in view: College students at risk. Initial findings from the national study of student hazing. Orono, ME: University of Orono. Online. Internet. http://www.umaine.edu/hazingstudy/hazinginview1.htm

Associated Press. (2016, January 16). Strasburg High program suspended amid sexual misconduct allegation. *ESPN.com*. Online. Internet. http://espn.go.com/espn/story/_/id/14575266/strasburg-high-school-boys-basketball-program-suspended-amid-sex-misconduct-allegation

Barr, J. (2016, February 15). Coaches, AD charged for failing to report child sex abuse case. *ESPN.com*. Online. Internet.

Besecker, A. (2008, August 9). New allegations made in Wilson hazing case. *The Buffalo News*.

Bult, L. (2016, January 16). Four Virginia high school basketball players suspended over alleged sexual assault on a team bus, authorities say. *New York Daily News*. Online. Internet. http://www.nydailynews.com/news/national/va-hs-students-suspended-alleged-sexual-assault-article-1.2499083

Campo, S., Poulos, G., & Sipple, J. W. (2005). Prevalence and profiling: Hazing among college students and points of intervention. *American Journal of Health Behavior, 29* (2), p. 37–149.

Cook, B. (2012, February 6). Parents protest hazing-related suspension of longtime L.A. high school baseball Coach. *Forbes*. Online. Internet. http://www.forbes.com/sites/bobcook/2012/02/06/parents-protest-hazing-related-suspension-of-longtime-l-a-high-school-baseball-coach/

Crow, B., & MacIntosh, E. W. (2009, December). Conceptualizing a meaningful definition of hazing in sport. *European Sport Management Quarterly 9* (4), 433–451.

Crow, B., & Rosner, S. R. (2002, Winter). Institutional and organizational liability for hazing in intercollegiate and professional team sports. *St. John's Law Review*, 76.

Del Rosso, A. (2012, February 15). Hazing investigation underway at Bellaire high school. Online. Internet. http://www.wtov9.com

"Ex-coaches sue over students' behavior." (2004, August 4). *New York Law Journal, 24*, p. 2.

FAMU (2012, February 9). FAMU announces a new anti-hazing committee. Press release. Online. Internet. http://www.famu.edu/index.cfm?a=headlines&p=display&news=2539

Flock, J. (2003, May 22). Two adults charged in violent hazing incident. *CNN.com*. Online. Internet. http://articles.cnn.com/2003-05-21/justice/hazing.charges_1_glenbrook-north-high-school-hazing-school-board?_s=PM:LAW

Frampton, C. (2016, January 15). New details: Strasburg boys basketball program investigated for alleged sexual assault. *WHSV.com*. Online. Internet. http://www.whsv.com/content/news/Sheriffs-Office-Investigating-Strasburg-Boys-Basketball-Team-365333781.html

Gershel, J. C., Katz-Sidlow, R. J., Small, E., & Zandieh, S. (2003). Hazing of suburban middle school and high school athletes. *Society for Adolescent Medicine, 32* (5), p. 333–335.

Goare, A. (2015, April). Bullock expected to sign Montana school anti-bullying bill. MTN News. Online. Internet. http://www.hanknuwer.com/montana-may-become-the-45th-state-with-a-hazing-law-kxlh-report/

Gutshall, B. (2008, Spring). A new uniform: NCAA policy and student-athlete misconduct. *University of Missouri-Kansas City Law Review, 76.*

Hoover, N. O. (principal investigator). National survey: Initiation rites and athletes for NCAA sports teams. Alfred University (August 30, 1999). Online. Internet. www.alfred.edu/news/html/hazing_study.html

Hoover, N. O., & Pollard, N. J. Initiation rites in American high schools: A national survey. Alfred University (2000). Online, Internet. www.alfred.edu/news/html/hazing_study.html

Jones, L. (2003, October 14). Hazing in schools: Allegations highlight the challenge of ensuring safety. *New York Law Journal*, p. 16.

Medina, M. (2009, April 7). Adults charged in Robertson High hazing. KRQU.com. Online. Internet. http://www.krqu.com/

Middleton, B. (2011, December 2). Four FAMU students expelled after band members death. *BET.com*. Online. Internet.http://www.bet.com/news/national/2011/12/01/four-famu-students-expelled-after-band-member-s-death.htm

Monroe, I. (2012, January 27). Robert Champion death: Hazing or hate crime? *Huffington Post*. Online. Internet. http://www.huffingtonpost.com/irene-monroe/robert-champion-death_b_1232089.html

Office of University Compliance and Integrity. (2014, July 22). *Investigative report: Complaint against Jonathan Waters, Director of the OSU Marching Band*. Online. Internet. https://www.osu.edu/assets/pdf/Investigation-Report.pdf

Passarella, G. (2015, September 9). Saint Joseph's settles softball hazing suits. *The Legal Intelligencer*. Online. Internet. http://www.thelegalintelligencer.com/id=1202736656264/Saint-Josephs-University-Settles-Softball-Hazing-Suits?slreturn=20160128124259

Putnam, G. M., & Messneger, B. (2011, December 1). Expulsions, suspensions meted out in Andover hazing case. Eagle Tribune. Online. Internet. http://www.eagletribune.com/local/x910011623/Expulsions-suspensions-meted-out-in-Andover-hazing-case

Report of the Wayne County Investigative Grand Jury pursuant to 42 Pa. C.S. Section 4552 Investigation #4. No. 26-2003-Crminal Misc. (2004, February 24). Published by *Newsday* on March 10, 2004. Online. Internet. http://www.newsday.com/

Schneider, M. (2012, January 10). FAMU hazing: Robert Champion's family plans to sue owner of bus where student died. *Huffington Post*. Online. Internet. http://www.huffingtonpost.com/2012/01/10/family-to-sue-owner-of-bu_0_n_1196317.html

Schultz, T. A. (2012, February 15). Former Munster swim team member claims in lawsuit he was hazed. *Post Tribune*. Online. Internet. http://posttrib.suntimes.com/news/lake/10643112-418/former-munster-swim-team-member-claims-in-lawsuit-he-was-hazed.html

Silveira, J. M., & Hudson, M. W. (2015). Hazing in the college marching band. *Journal of Research in Music Education*, 1–23.

SJU Athletic Communications. (2015, July 6). University statement regarding softball program. Press release. Online. Internet. http://www.sjuhawks.com/ViewArticle.dbml?DB_OEM_ID=31200&ATCLID=210184894

Sondheimer, E. (2012, February 5). Suspension of Manny Alvarado for hazing riles parents. *Los Angeles Times*. Online. Internet. http://articles.latimes.com/2012/feb/05/sports/la-sp-0206-sondheimer-column-20120206

Staff. (2012, February 14). Plea deal reached Wisconsin Rapids wrestlers' hazing case. *Greenbay Press Gazette*. Online. Internet. http://www.greenbaypressgazette.com/article/20120214/GPG0101/302150009/Plea-deal-reached-Wisconsin-Rapids-wrestlers-hazing-case

Staskey, S. (2012, February 15). Bellaire school district deals with hazing issues. *Times Leader*. Online. Internet. http://www.timesleaderonline.com.

Stuart-Cassell, V., Bell, A., & Springer, J. F. (2011). *Analysis of state bullying laws and policies*. Report prepared for the U.S. Department of Education Office of Planning, Evaluation and Policy Development Policy and Program Studies Service. Online. Internet. http://www2.ed.gov/rschstat/eval/bullying/state-bullying-laws/state-bullying-laws.pdf

Sussberg, J. (2003). Shattered dreams: Hazing in college athletes. *Cordozo Law Review 24*.

The OSU Marching Band Culture Task Force. (2014, November 18). *OSU Marching Band cultural assessment & administrative oversight review*. Columbus, OH: The Ohio State University. Online. Internet. https://www.osu.edu/bandculturetaskforce

The Associated Press. (2015, September 3). Bill cracking down on bullying approved. *KRQE.com*. Online. Internet. http://krqe.com/2015/03/03/bill-cracking-down-on-bullying-approved/

Thompson, P. (2012, January 25). 'It's tradition': High school hockey coach fired for 'hazing' after players paraded through a bar in women's lingerie. *The Daily Mail*. Online. Internet. http://www.dailymail.co.uk/news/article-2091425/Its-tradition-High-school-hockey-coach-fired-hazing-players-paraded-bar-womens-lingerie.html?ito=feeds-newsxm

Waldron, J. (2015, November). Predictors of mild hazing, severe hazing, and positive initiation rituals in sport. *International Journal of Sports Science & Coaching 10* (6), 1089–1101.

Wall, J. (2012, February 15). Hazed students not allowed to play sports after switching schools. *Yahoo Sports*. Online. Internet. http://sports.yahoo.com/blogs/highschool-prep-rally/hazed-students-not-allowed-play-sports-switching-schools-160736540.html

Legislation
Florida State Code 240.1325
Minnesota State Code 127.465
Ohio Revised Code 2903.31
New York State Code 120.16

RISK MANAGEMENT 4.00

The primary purpose of a risk management plan is not the avoidance of legal liability. Rather, it is the maintenance of a quality program; that is, one which deals reasonably and fairly with its clients or students and their families. A program that delivers what is says it will deliver, and does so in the context of reasonable management of the risks, is not assured of "safety" or freedom from lawsuits. But generally, if such a level of performance is achieved, legal liability issues are minimized and take care of themselves. (Charles R. Gregg. Staying in the Field and Out of the Courthouse. 2002)

Many recreation and sport managers erroneously look upon risk management as safety or accident prevention. *Risk management* is much more than just safety or preventing accidents – it is an organized plan by which a recreation or sport business can manage or control both the programmatic risks and the financial risks facing the organization. Risk management involves not only *what to do* to control risks, but also involves *why to do it* – thus a sound risk management program is based upon the fundamental legal concepts discussed in Sections 2.10 *Negligence Theory*, 2.20 *Defenses*, and 2.30 *Recreation and Sport Management Applications*.

Section 4.00 is divided into two major parts. They are Section 4.10 *Risk Management Theory* and 4.20 *Recreation and Sport Management Applications*. *Risk Management Theory* discusses the fundamental concepts and foundations comprising risk management. Section 4.20 *Recreation and Sport Management Applications* looks closely at a number of crucial aspects of risk management – standards of practice, risk management audits, crisis management, crowd management, and insurance protection and requirements.

4.11 RISK MANAGEMENT PROCESS
Robin Ammon | University of South Dakota

The number of sport venues has increased worldwide, and the sport and entertainment events scheduled in them have produced global interest. Some of these events include both the Summer and Winter Olympics, Wimbledon, the National Collegiate Athletic Association's (NCAA) Bowl Championship Series, the Masters, major concert tours, and conventions. Media attention for these events has grown exponentially, resulting in increased event attendance. Each of these events and thousands like them has its own unique risks that result in the need of a comprehensive risk management plan.

Identification of the risks involved in recreation and sport did not become a serious concern until 30-35 years ago. While the concept of risk management had been extensively used by private business for some time, the recreation and sport industries' interest in managing risks came only after primary assumption of risk became less accepted as a complete defense in some jurisdictions and governmental immunity began to erode. As a result, litigation related to sport and recreation began to rise. While the focus of risk management in business is often primarily financial, a much broader focus becomes a necessity when risk management concepts are applied to the recreation and sport industries.

Some researchers believe that, while risk management literature suggested the concept was necessary to limit legal liability, others perceive risk management as a hindrance (Sharp, Moorman, and Claussen, 2007). Obviously, in light of the litigious nature of our society, risk management has become a necessity. Therefore, recreation and sport managers should become aware of the potential for injury and loss and learn to effectively manage the numerous risks that exist in their professions. The process of managing and controlling these risks has, over the last two or three decades, resulted in the field of risk management. The purpose of this chapter is to introduce students interested in recreation or sport management to the basics involved in a risk management process.

FUNDAMENTAL CONCEPTS

One of the first definitions of risk management, as it applied to sport and recreation, was developed in 1993. At that time Ammon defined **risk management** as controlling the financial and personal injury losses from sudden, unforeseen, unusual accidents and intentional torts (Ammon, 1993). In 2002, Corbett described risk management as "managing financial and human resources wisely, governing effectively, making decisions soundly, and projecting a positive image towards sponsors, government funders and the community" (¶. 4). A more recent definition (Spengler, Anderson, Connaughton & Baker, 2009) defined risk management as a "course of action designed to reduce the risk (probability or likelihood) and loss to sport participants, spectators, employees, management, and organizations" (p. 46). Finally, risk management has been defined as a proactive process that involves assessing all possible risks associated with the event and its stakeholders by strategically anticipating, preventing, minimizing, and planning responses to mitigate those identified risks (Leopkey & Parent, 2009).

Regardless of the definition, the "loss" resulting from the risk can be physical or financial in nature. For example, city parks and recreation administrators must continually attempt to reduce risks that cause physical injury to their clientele. In addition, financial losses may occur at high school, university or professional stadiums/arenas due to incidents such as vandalism, poorly written contracts, stolen equipment, and accidents in the venue's parking lot due to poor lighting. Risk management, however, doesn't seek to eliminate *all* risks, but rather it creates an environment where the inherent and negligence risks within activities and services provided by an organization are minimized without producing a change in the activity itself.

The D.I.M. Process

The **D.I.M. process** was developed as a tool to establish an effective risk management program. When used as an anticipatory technique rather than as a reactionary procedure, the D.I.M. process will assist recreation and sport organizations in decreasing the chance of litigation. This process involves three basic components: (1) D*eveloping* the risk management plan; (2) I*mplementing* the risk management plan; and (3) M*anaging* the risk management plan. Every group will have risks specific to its organization. Therefore each sport or recreation business, no matter the size, should have a current risk management plan that should be specifically developed for the particular business. For example, due to the specific risks, a risk management plan that works for an ice rink will not be the same as one used at a disc golf venue (Ammon, Southall & Nagel, 2016). Components used in creating this plan, however, will be similar no matter what type of organization or activity. Thus, managers at golf courses, aquatic centers, ski areas, skateboard parks, or park and recreation departments will utilize the same basic principles.

Developing the Risk Management Plan (the "D" of the D.I.M. Process)

Developing a risk management plan consists of three separate stages: (1) identifying the risks, (2) classifying those risks, and (3) selecting methods of treatment for each of the identified risks.

Identification Stage

The **identification stage** is one of the key aspects of developing a successful risk management program. If the recreation or sport manager wants to control risks in the program, he or she must first identify those risks. Risks are present in every sport and recreation program or event including privately or municipally owned buildings, professional or intercollegiate entertainment facilities, and outdoor or indoor recreational settings. Each event or activity is different and has its own unique risks or areas of potential loss. Identifying these risks, therefore, needs to be specific, constant, and ongoing.

An effective step to identify risk is to create categories of risk and then list risks within each category. There are several approaches that can be used to **categorize risk**.

van der Smissen (1990) indicated that risks should be categorized into four distinct groups (1) public liability caused by negligence in program services, (2) public liability [excluding negligence], (3) business operations, and (4) property exposures.

Recreation and sport managers often focus on bodily injuries resulting from **public liability caused by negligence**. Injuries may include death, quadriplegia or other paralysis, brain damage, loss of limbs, loss of senses, injury to internal organs, strains, sprains, fractures, ligament damage, cuts, punctures, and abrasions. These types of risks typically relate to the specific activities or services offered by an organization and often occur when a member of the organization is negligent in performing his or her duties. However, if risk identification is limited to only bodily injuries, many potential financial risks that could impact the organization may be overlooked.

Risks categorized under **public liability (excluding negligence)** include components such as malpractice by personnel, product liability, intentional torts, employment practices, sexual harassment, and civil liberty violations. Recreation and sport managers should note that the management of risk relating to employment law issues specifically regarding gender has become a great concern to many in the recreation and sport industries. While many of these cases use Title IX as their cause of action, individual state Equal Rights amendments and the 14th Amendment's Equal Protection clause have also been utilized. Individuals involved with an organization's human resource department must be aware that risks lurk within their purview as well. Typical cases in this category might relate to sexual harassment, gender or racial discrimination, equal pay disputes, and wrongful termination claims. Tools that can be used to identify risks include **questionnaires** and **discussions and interaction with employees** relating to employment practices. Also, it is helpful to **read the literature** published by professional organizations (e.g., The National Recreation and Park Association) and consult with colleagues regarding potential risks relating to employment practices of which the manager might not be aware.

Child abuse has been well documented in the field of sport and recreation. Many cases have pertained to the abuse between a coach and athlete. One of the child molestation incidents receiving national media attention involved ex-Penn State coach Jerry Sandusky. During the trial it became apparent there was a failure to have an established policy of reporting potential child abuse. Other incidents involving coaches sexually abusing their young athletes have been reported and they all illustrate the need for both an established policy and effective channels for reporting child abuse allegations. In addition, the existence of a policy is only worthwhile if employees know the policy and the steps involved to report an incident. A 2011 study indicated that 48 percent of 7-12 grade student respondents experienced some form of sexual harassment during the 2010-11 school year. An additional 30% were harassed via electronic means (texts, e-mails, Facebook, or other electronic means). The authors mentioned that many of the students who had been harassed through traditional methods were also harassed via cyberspace (AAUW, 2011). Since many sport and recreation participants are children, recreation and sport managers need to pay particular attention to devising strategies to control the risk of child abuse.

Property exposures are financial risks related to the ownership of real and personal property. Loss may occur as a result of fire, weather-related elements like lightning and floods, vandalism, and theft. Recreation and sport managers should rely on the help of various **insurance professionals** in identifying potential risks related to property exposures. For example, an insurance agent should be contacted to insure that the organization has adequate property insurance. The 2011 spring floods along the Missouri River forced the Sioux City, Iowa, YMCA to relocate across the river to a section of the Tyson Events Center. Having flood insurance enabled the YMCA to move back into their original facility once the waters subsided. In addition, a good agent can also help in identifying a multitude of additional risks.

Recreation and sport managers can also be exposed to risks via their organization's **business operations**. These risks are financial risks that result from business interruption, embezzlement and theft, the medical condition of employees, the health of key personnel, and employee accidents and injuries. To identify risks associated with business operations, a recreation or sport manager should examine the organization's operational **policies and procedures** to determine if the policies and procedures expose the organization to loss. Also, the manager should **observe** his or her employees at work to identify any activities that may lead to sickness, accidents, or disability.

The methods used to look for potential risks will vary depending upon the nature and size of the organization or business. Every entity, however, must establish a systematic procedure to assure that a complete risk assessment occurs (van der Smissen, 1990).

Classification Stage

Once the potential risks have been identified, the second stage in developing the plan is to **classify the risk**. The purpose of the classification stage is to determine how often (**frequency**) the risk may occur and the degree (**severity**) of the potential loss arising from the risk. Once the various risks have been identified, the risk manager takes each of the identified risks and evaluates them in terms of frequency and severity. The *frequency* of the risk is dependent on the number of times the risk or loss is likely to occur. The risk manager will view each identified risk and assign a frequency of "high," "medium," or "low." The *severity* of the risk is determined by the intensity of the potential injury and/or the degree of the threat to the financial stability of the organization. The severity is classified as "catastrophic," "critical," "moderate," or "low." The level of severity and the frequency are determined by the risk manager, based on his/her expertise derived from experience and training.

Regardless of the terminology, once the risks have been classified a matrix can be created that allows a consistent approach to the classification process. A matrix provides a risk manager with a method to classify all identified risks on the basis of frequency and extent of potential loss. Table 4.11.1 is a **risk category matrix** listing a few of the risks from a female high school volleyball tournament placed into their proper categories. *All identified risks should be appropriately placed in the matrix, indicating the specific frequency and severity of each risk.* By placing the identified risks in the matrix, the risk manager will have successfully completed the classification stage. However, it should be noted that risk assessment and classification is an ongoing process. Risks are constantly changing therefore their identification and classifications are consistently morphing as well.

TABLE 4.11.1 — RISK CATEGORY MATRIX (FOR A HIGH SCHOOL VOLLEYBALL TOURNAMENT)

	Severity of Injury or Financial Impact (Volleyball Games)			
	Catastrophic Loss	**Critical Loss**	**Moderate Loss**	**Low Loss**
High Frequency	None	None	• Fan suffers hip injury when she trips in poorly lighted area in or about premises. • Player injures knee due to uneven playing surface or wet spot on the court	• Spectators evade admission fee • Spectator in bleachers suffers gouge from protruding screw
Medium Frequency	None	None	• Vandalism of the gym • Player twists ankle on piece of ice thrown from the bleachers	• Incorrect change given to spectators at the concession stand • Fans suffer nausea from poorly prepared food at concession stands
Low Frequency	• Player breaks neck running into unpadded volleyball post • Domestic incident results in active shooter situation	• Spectator suffers facial laceration during altercation in bleachers • Poor crowd management leads to scuffle between teams	• Player sustains eye injury after being hit in face by spiked ball • Spectator suffers concussion from player diving into crowd after loose ball due to inadequate buffer zone	• Program seller gives away programs • Players' purses are stolen from the locker room

Treatment of Risk Stage

The final stage in developing a comprehensive risk management plan is to determine a **treatment** for each identified and classified risk. A treatment is a method used to reduce, control, manage, or eliminate financial risks and bodily injuries. There are **four basic treatments** available to the risk manager: 1) *avoidance* (or elimination) of the risk, 2) *transfer* of the risk to another party, 3) *retention* of the risk by the recreation or sport organization, and 4) *reduction* of the risk (Spengler et al., 2009).

The type of treatment a risk manager uses for the identified and classified risks depends on the nature of the risk and the likelihood of the risk occurring. Although it is sometimes difficult to determine the appropriate treatment, the use of a **risk treatment matrix** (Table 4.11.2) can assist in this task. After having identified and classified the risks in the risk category matrix (Table 4.11.1), the manager should then refer to a **Risk Treatment Matrix** for direction in selecting the appropriate treatment. *Note: While the contents of Risk Category Matrix (Table 4.11.1) will vary greatly from activity to activity, the contents of the subsequent Risk Treatment Matrix (Table 4.11.2), once established by the philosophy and the finances of the organization, remains the same for all activities.*

TABLE 4.11.2 — RISK TREATMENT MATRIX (FOR ANY ACTIVITY)

	Severity of Injury or Financial Impact			
	Catastrophic Loss	**Critical Loss**	**Moderate Loss**	**Low Loss**
High Frequency	Avoidance	Avoidance	Transfer & Reduction	Transfer/Retain & Reduction
Medium Frequency	Transfer/Avoidance & Reduction	Transfer/Avoidance & Reduction	Transfer & Reduction	Retain & Reduction
Low Frequency	Transfer & Reduction	Transfer & Reduction	Transfer/Retain & Reduction	Retain & Reduction

Avoidance/Elimination. This treatment requires that specific activities should not be included within the content of a program (avoidance) or they should be discontinued if they are presently being offered (elimination). Risks should be avoided or eliminated when they could cause a catastrophic or critical loss with medium or high frequency. In other words, an activity should not be included in the program if the severity of the incident would be critical or catastrophic and risk management is unable to reduce or control the frequency. Ideally, a risk manager should identify these risks before accidents occur and avoid them completely. For example, if a high-risk activity such as cheerleading has a history of causing moderate to critical injuries, the school or athletic program may wish to eliminate the activity if the risks cannot be controlled (*Noffke v Bakke, 2008*).

In most situations, eliminating activities offered by recreation and sport organizations is not an attractive option. Therefore elimination should not be the first choice for a risk manager. In the previously mentioned cheerleading situation, the decision to eliminate cheerleading might be unnecessary if strict policies regarding cheerleader supervisors, supervision, facility, progression of moves, and approved stunts are implemented. Avoidance or elimination of an activity should only be implemented as a last resort when risk is substantial and likelihood of injury is significant. An example of avoidance occurred about 40 years ago; the use of trampolines was a standard fixture in most physical education programs, but most school districts eliminated the equipment due to the large number (frequency) of injuries and their severity.

Transfer. Transfer is the shifting of the liability or responsibility for loss from the service provider to another party. This risk treatment occurs when two conditions exist: (1) the risk of loss is not substantial enough to warrant the avoidance of the activity, and (2) the risk is greater than the organization can assume on its own.

An important means of transfer is through the purchase of sufficient **insurance** coverage (see also Chapter 4.25 *Managing Risk Through Insurance* and Chapter 4.26 *Workers' Compensation*). Property insurance and personal injury liability insurance are often selected to provide protection from potential risks. It is important to understand the insurance company will only cover the policyholder up to the limits of the policy. For example, if a defendant has a $1 million liability policy and loses a $3 million judgment, the insurance company will *only* cover the first $1 million (Cotten, 2013).

Another important means of transfer is by **contract**. Examples of these contracts include liability waivers, indemnification clauses, and the use of independent contractors. A **waiver** is a contract by which a person voluntarily gives up the right to sue another party (e.g., the service provider) for its negligence. The signer of the waiver (normally the participant) agrees to accept the risks of harm caused by the negligent actions of the other party (usually the service provider). However, a waiver generally does not protect a service provider from liability for gross negligence or reckless misconduct and waivers signed by parents on behalf of minor participants are likely to be enforced in only a few states (see Chapter 2.23 *Waivers and Releases*).

Indemnification clauses are clauses in a contract that provide for one party to indemnify or reimburse the other for a specific loss. These clauses are generally included in equipment and facility rental contracts. For instance, an organization leasing a facility generally agrees contractually to indemnify the facility owners against any loss or litigation resulting from the event. These clauses, sometimes called **hold harmless** agreements, require the organization to be compensated by the individuals renting the facility if any damage occurs during the event or if someone is injured and files suit against the facility owner. Thus the risks during the event are *transferred* to the outside organization (see also Chapter 2.12 *Which Parties Are Liable?* and Chapter 2.21 *Defenses Against Negligence*).

An **independent contractor** is a person or business that contracts to perform a specific task for a service provider. Independent contractors provide expertise and are generally free to perform tasks as they see fit. The independent contractor is not an employee of the organization. Depending on the organization, some personnel (e.g., team doctors, referees, personal trainers, and aerobics instructors) may function as independent contractors. These individuals are responsible for providing their own unemployment and liability insurance and are generally solely responsible for their negligent actions. Many organizations use independent contractors to provide adventure activities (such as whitewater rafting, scuba, ropes courses, and rock climbing). A landowner is often immune from the contractor's negligence when hiring an independent contractor. The risk is transferred from the landowner to the independent party. However, a landowner is not always shielded from liability. If a landowner hires a contractor to perform an inherently dangerous activity, he or she then is responsible for supervising the actions of the contractor. A landowner must ensure the activity is being performed as safely as possible and that the contractor is taking the appropriate safety measures. This is known as the *inherently dangerous activity exception*. It should be noted that a landowner is not liable if a contractor's negligence is unusual in nature. However, a landowner *is* liable when the negligence of the contractor should have been initially considered by the landowner. The *inherently dangerous activity exception* is illustrated in *Hatch v. V.P. Fair Foundation and Northstar Entertainment* (1999). The plaintiff was injured while attempting a bungee jump operated by the Fair Foundation. Northstar Entertainment, the independent contractor, violated several of its own safety policies including: number of staff present, age of the jump master, and failure to conduct a daily safety inspection. The jump master failed to attach the bungee cord to the crane, resulting in a 170-foot fall and serious injuries to the back, legs, and shoulders of the plaintiff. Due to the inherently dangerous activity exception the jury found that both the Fair Foundation and the contractor were liable and awarded the plaintiff $5 million (see Chapter 2.12 *Which Parties Are Liable?* and Chapter 2.21 *Defenses Against Negligence*).

A combination of these transfer methods is usually preferable. For example, if a recreation center wishes to offer rock climbing and realizes the risk involved is too great for the organization, the provider may seek to transfer the risk. In this situation, the risk manager would pay an insurance company a premium to cover any physical or financial damages that may occur (Ammon et al., 2016). In addition, the manager can require that participants sign an assumption of risk document or waiver which helps to reduce or eliminate the service provider's liability. In doing so the provider has endeavored to transfer the risk to the insurance company and the participant. If the risk is substantial, as in rock climbing, and cannot be adequately transferred, the activity should be avoided.

Retention. The third treatment, **retention**, means that the organization keeps the risk and assumes financial responsibility for certain injuries or financial losses that may occur. Retention is often utilized with minor or inexpensive risks. Retaining these risks is often less expensive than buying insurance to cover them.

Sometimes retention is termed **self-insurance**. In essence, the sport or recreation organization is simply paying a premium to itself. But this is not as easy as it sounds. If utilized, the organization must include retention as a line item in the budget and accumulate a reserve or "pool" of revenue to pay for such injuries (Ammon et al., 2016). Looking at the risk treatment matrix (see Table 4.11.2), the risks to be retained are those that have a low potential for loss and occur with low to medium frequency. An organization can accept these risks due to the fact that there is very little chance of incurring substantial financial losses. This, of course, is assuming that once the risk manager decides to keep the risk, proper precautions are taken to decrease the occurrence and/or monetary losses associated with the risk.

Reduction. The fourth treatment, and arguably the most important, is the reduction of risks. Risk reduction is a proactive approach when managing risks. The objective of reduction is to reduce the chance for injury as well as the chance of litigation. The reduction section of the risk management plan establishes a variety of operational practices for reducing the likelihood of loss related to the identified risk. Every risk cannot be eliminated from an activity, but often the frequency and severity can be minimized by the proper maintenance of property and equipment, establishing emergency procedures, providing better staff training, and other risk reduction techniques. This should be the focus of any risk management program. For example, making an effort to reduce the frequency and severity of losses in a youth soccer league by utilizing appropriate reduction techniques makes it less likely that losses will occur. In this example, actions such as requiring shin guards, anchoring the soccer goals, and inspecting the soccer field for obstructions or holes are all specific risk reduction techniques.

The primary objective of reduction is for the responsible party to be aware of potential losses (after identifying the risks) and to do something to reduce the potential loss. There are **four major tools** that the recreation or sport manager can use to reduce risk.

The first is to *design a regular systematic inspection program*. A system of inspection must be established, a written record of that inspection must be kept, and a system of follow-up on hazards must be implemented. Inspection of facilities and equipment is a key to reducing loss. An organization is liable for the dangerous maintenance situations about which it knows and for those that it should have known if a proper professional job had been done on inspection (*Felipe v. Sluggers of Miami, Inc. and Sluggers, Inc.*, 2008).

Inspection of a fitness center would be an appropriate example. Examining the fitness center and its equipment would include items such as inspecting weight machine cables and the running deck on a treadmill; chlorine storage for a swimming pool would also be included in a regular inspection. Individuals knowledgeable about the items they are inspecting must complete these inspections. Also, this type of assessment helps locate newly created risks caused by vandalism, abuse or misuse, and theft.

If a hazard is found during the inspection, a system for addressing the hazard must be implemented. The system should include the following steps: (1) the hazard must be reported to maintenance personnel; (2) the individual overseeing the area where the hazard is located must be notified; (3) the equipment or area must be taken out of service until the repair is made; (4) once the identified hazard is eliminated, maintenance personnel must inform the manager; and (5) there should be established steps to follow in the event the repair has not been made in a reasonable period of time. (See also Chapter 2.31 *Premises Liability* and Chapter 4.22 *Audits in Risk Management*.)

The second major tool involves *establishing a maintenance program for facilities and equipment*. The maintenance program must be described in an organization's risk management plan and include both preventative and remedial maintenance that occurs on a regular basis. With the exception of slip and falls, the failure to provide proper maintenance is the leading cause of litigation against most sport/entertainment facilities (Ammon et al., 2016).

A third tool involves *training the facility's staff*. Staff should be trained to identify normal wear and tear and general deterioration of equipment, facilities, and other athletic areas that may lead to loss. Employees also need to understand how to conduct activities so that proper care is afforded to participants. The recreation or sport manager should verify that his or her staff knows how to ensure participants have the proper skill level and conditioning for activities, understands proper supervision, and understands how to enact the organization's emergency procedures (see also Chapter 2.34 *Supervision*). For most situations, it is important that the staff know certain information about the individual's ability to participate in the activity safely (van der Smissen, 1990). For example, in an age-group gymnastics program, the skill level and developmental stage of participants must be known in order to place them in the proper class. An organization must determine what skill and conditioning level is required for participation in the program for each activity or service.

Finally, the fourth tool recreation and sport managers must utilize is *a system under which documents related to program participation may be filed*. They also must be able to retrieve these documents when necessary. Technological advancements allow boxes of old forms to be digitized reducing storage space while allowing for easier access. Forms that should be retained include parental permission forms, agreements to participate, waivers, membership applications, contracts, inspection checklists, accident report forms, health records, records containing operations information, rules and regulations, copies of employee credentials, and any other program-related document.

With the growing threat of litigation, the need to document and to preserve documentation takes on added importance. In 2008, a 19-year-old plaintiff suffered a damaged testicle when a pitching machine delivered a 60 mph baseball when the machine's light indicated it was off. The plaintiff's attorney argued that the defendant did not have a maintenance log, checklist or manuals or any safety policies. The defendants also had prior knowledge that the machine was operable even when the light was off. The jury returned a $1.16 million award to the plaintiff (*Felipe v. Sluggers of Miami, Inc. and Sluggers, Inc.*, 2008).

When a risk manager develops a risk management plan, the most efficient and effective way to decrease the occurrence of various risks is to use reduction techniques such as those above. When a risk manager decides to retain or transfer the risks, he or she must be ready to also incorporate these reduction techniques to insure that each situation is handled in a manner that will reduce the chance of liability. *A crucial concept to remember is that risk reduction should be a risk management treatment any time an activity is offered—in conjunction with transfer or retention*. If the risks are not managed with the use of reduction techniques, more claims will occur and greater costs will be incurred. This will create a drain on funds allotted for retained risks and will eventually cause the insurer to raise the organization's premiums to cover the risks in question. By utilizing reduction techniques to reduce the occurrence of risks, the service provider should be able to keep insurance premiums and budgeted expenses at a minimum. In fact, by managing the risks, it is probable that the number of claims will decrease, which may cause the insurance rates to diminish as well (Ammon et al., 2016).

Implementing the Risk Management Plan (the "I" of the D.I.M. Process)

The second component in the D.I.M. process consists of implementing the risk management plan. Each individual in an organization must understand the overall risk management plan, risk reduction strategies and know what his or her role is in implementing the plan. Therefore, it can be said that the effectiveness of the overall plan is in direct proportion to the effectiveness of communicating the plan. If communication about the plan is nonexistent, incomplete, or inadequate, the program will become inoperable and the risks will not be reduced as they should be. Direct interpersonal communication is required to insure the plan functions properly.

A risk manager can supplement oral communication with printed guidelines outlining risk reduction techniques. These guidelines can be inserted in the employee manual during the first orientation. Examples of the items covered in the guidelines include: the organizational layout, personnel and organizational management, rules and regulations of the business, responsibilities of various employees, the correct methods of documenting records and reports, and emergency procedures. The manual is sometimes erroneously termed a "safety manual."

Some organizations make the mistake of placing the entire risk management plan into every employee manual. The sheer comprehensiveness of the plan will cause many new hires to avoid reading the manual. Only include the pertinent portions of the overall plan into the specific employee's manual. Employee dedication to the process is a key component for a successful risk management plan.

The utilization of a **sound training program** is another way to ensure effective communication and the implementation of the risk management plan. An in-service education program can be used to communicate staff responsibilities in relation to the plan and provide an opportunity for individuals to improve their ability to identify various types of risks. In-service educational opportunities allow the risk manager to explain the risk management plan to the organization's employees while stressing the importance of implementing the reduction strategies contained in the plan. For risk reduction to be effective, three in-service areas need to be addressed on a regular basis: (1) communication of responsibilities—what is each individual's role in implementing the plan; (2) development of professional judgment and decision making—what standard of care is required of each employee; and (3) credential education/training—the provision of expertise or an increased knowledge base that will lead to an increased ability to make sound judgments. The risk manager must verify that personnel are qualified for their positions and hold the necessary certifications.

Managing the Plan (the "M" of the D.I.M. Process)

The final component of the D.I.M. process is to **manage the plan**. The first step in managing the plan is to **designate a risk manager** and to select a risk management committee. Sport and recreation organizations may hire a risk manager or assign one individual the role of risk manager as part of his or her "other" duties. Effective risk managers and risk management committee members share many of the same traits. The risk manager must be a highly motivated individual, must be committed to risk management, and must be able to motivate others to believe in the risk management plan. Whichever system is chosen, the responsible party should monitor the risk management plan, implement changes, assist in fostering a genuine risk management attitude among other employees, conduct inspections, review accidents, and supervise in-service training (van der Smissen, 1990).

The second step in managing the plan is to provide the risk manager and committee with the **authority to lead**. This authority should be described in the policy statement of the organization because it provides a foundation for the plan. The policy statement should clearly delineate the responsibilities of the risk manager. The statement should outline and define the authority of the person responsible for administering the plan.

Upper management as well as the organization ownership must endorse and support the idea of risk management. They must be willing to assist the risk manager or risk management committee with verbal and financial support. Various costs are associated with any effective risk management plan—insurance comprising the greatest expense. Due to the society we live in and the potential for terrorism, the cost of some types of insurance has increased ten-fold. Therefore the organization's budget should include a line item devoted specifically for the implementation and continual assessment of the risk management plan. Without upper management's support a risk management plan will not succeed. The risk manager and the risk management committee must be given the freedom to act independently, but their actions must connect with the philosophy of the sport or recreation organization (Ammon et al., 2016).

The third step in managing the plan is to **provide employees with the opportunity for continuous input** into the risk management plan. Including some of the organization's employees, particularly those who have contact with clients, on the risk management committee is a possible source for this input. The continual success of a risk management plan mandates that employees, supervisors, and managers on all levels have the ability to interact with each other. Additionally, anyone whose expertise may improve the quality of the risk management plan should be included in the overall risk management process. The size of the committee depends on the overall goals and size of the organization.

As previously mentioned, risks are constantly changing and shifting due to the variety of activities and programs offered by an organization. The size of the organization, the type of activity being conducted, the age of the participants, the skill level of the participants and the age of any associated venue will cause the risks to vary. The risks will never remain the same so the assessment of these risks needs to be both flexible and constant. As soon as an organization ceases assessing the risks they open themselves up to potential litigation.

Risk management is a necessity for today's sport and recreation managers. Even though many risks can be identified, classified, and treated, some hazards will still exist and accidents will occur. It is impossible and unrealistic to expect a risk manager to eliminate all injuries and financial losses. However, by developing an extensive risk management plan, implementing the plan, and bestowing the authority to manage the plan upon a concerned risk manager, recreation and sport managers can diminish a number of dangerous risks as well as potential litigation.

SIGNIFICANT CASE

The case illustrates the concept of "inherent risks." A high school hockey player assumed the risk of having his foot cut by a skate blade because the player was aware that the risk of being injured by a skate blade was "inherent in the sport" of hockey. These types of accidents will occur no matter the type of risk management plan that is in effect. A reduction treatment of having a well-supplied first aid kit would help to mitigate these types of situations.

LITZ V CLINTON CENTRAL SCHOOL
126 AD3d 1306
March 20, 2015, Decided

I. Introduction

The Plaintiff filed suit against the Clinton Central School District, John Hughes, in his capacity as Head Hockey Coach of the Clinton High School Hockey Team, Rob Hameline, in his capacity as Assistant Hockey Coach of the Clinton High School Hockey Team and Michael Martini a teammate for negligence. Plaintiff commenced this action seeking damages for injuries he sustained in a locker room following hockey practice. Plaintiff was walking barefoot toward the shower area when defendant Michael Martini, one of plaintiff's teammates, stepped backwards onto plaintiff's right foot. Martini was still wearing his hockey skates at the time of the accident. The defendants moved separately for summary judgment dismissing the complaint on the ground that plaintiff had assumed the risks associated with the sport of hockey. The motions, were affirmed.

II. Background

On the date of the accident, plaintiff was practicing with his high school hockey team at the Clinton Arena, a municipal athletic and recreational facility. The accident took place immediately following practice in one of the arena's locker rooms, which was designated for the exclusive use of the high school hockey team. Contrary to the contention of plaintiff, the New York court concluded that the plaintiff was still "involved", or "participating" in the sport of hockey at the time of his injury." [T]he assumption [of risk] doctrine applies to any facet of the activity inherent in it". In this case the plaintiff and his teammates stored their hockey equipment, including their skates, in the arena locker room. During trial the Plaintiff described his routine as follows: "[G]et there before practice, get ready and get on the ice before you're supposed to be on the ice, get off, get undressed, shower and make sure your stuff is hanging up." Once practice had concluded on the night of the accident, the plaintiff and his teammates "all got off the ice as a team" and proceeded into the locker room to change out of their equipment. Martini and another teammate remained on the ice to pick up the nets and pucks, which took less than 10 minutes. The two players then headed into the locker room, put away the pucks, and began getting undressed. Martini was in the process of removing his equipment when the blade of his skate came into contact with the plaintiff's foot. At the time of the accident, plaintiff had been a member of his high school's varsity hockey team for three years and had been playing organized hockey for over a decade. Plaintiff acknowledged that the use of skates with very sharp edges is part of the sport of hockey, and he testified at his deposition that he was aware of the need to be careful around people wearing hockey skates.

The question posed to the court was whether plaintiff assumed the risk of the injury-causing acts at issue. "As a general rule, participants properly may be held to have consented, by their participation, to those injury-causing events which are known, apparent or reasonably foreseeable consequences of the participation". "Awareness of risk is not to be determined in a vacuum [but] . . . is, rather, to be assessed against the background of the skill and experience of the particular plaintiff. It is not necessary to the application of assumption of risk that the injured plaintiff have foreseen the exact manner in which his or her injury occurred, so long as he or she is aware of the potential for injury of the mechanism from which the injury results".

IV. Analysis

According to the New York State court "The assumption of risk doctrine applies where a consenting participant in sporting and amusement activities 'is aware of the risks; has an appreciation of the nature of the risks; and voluntarily assumes the risks." By engaging in such an activity, a participant "consents to those commonly appreciated risks which are inherent in and arise out of the nature of the sport generally and flow from such participation. The question of whether the consent was an informed one includes consideration of the participant's knowledge and experience in the activity generally."

The court agreed with the school district defendants and Martini that they met their burden of establishing that the risk of being injured by a skate blade is "inherent in the sport" of hockey and that the plaintiff was aware of, appreciated the nature of, and voluntarily assumed that risk. Notably, the plaintiff testified that he was "always worried" about the possibility of "being stepped on or something with a hockey skate, just getting cut by the skate", the precise mechanism of injury in this case, and he acknowledged that such a possibility was "part of the sport" of hockey. Although plaintiff was not aware of any similar incidents at the Clinton Arena, he testified that "there's been other injuries with skates in the [National Hockey League and] other leagues." Plaintiff further testified that he was aware that hockey players often wear their skates into the locker room: "I've always known since I was little, since I started—you know—after practice or a game, you walk in on skates" (emphasis added). Indeed, the floor of the arena locker room was rubberized for that very purpose. Plaintiff testified that he "always" walked around the locker room with bare feet when he did not have his skates on, and he acknowledged that he was "aware of the need to be careful walking with people still having skates on in the locker room." Defendants therefore established as a matter of law that being injured by a wayward blade in the locker room before, during, or immediately after a game or practice is "within the known, apparent and foreseeable dangers of the sport" of hockey.

The court concluded that it would be inconsistent with the purpose of the assumption of the risk doctrine to isolate the moment of injury and ignore the context of the accident. The policy underlying the assumption of the risk doctrine was to encourage free and vigorous participation in athletic and recreational pursuits by "shielding co-participants, activity sponsors or venue owners from 'potentially crushing liability'." Here, the school district defendants, "solely by reason of having sponsored or otherwise supported some risk-laden but socially valuable voluntary activity have been called to account in damages". The court concluded that there was a "suitably compelling policy justification . . . to permit an assertion of assumption of risk in the present circumstances".

The plaintiff failed to raise an issue of fact with respect to whether defendants "unreasonably increased the plaintiff's risk of injury." The Plaintiff contended that the risk of injury was unreasonably increased by the layout of the locker room. However, the court stated that while condition of the locker room was perhaps not ideal, any risks were readily appreciable. Thus, the school district defendants "fulfilled their duty of making the conditions as safe as they appeared to be." With respect to Martini, the plaintiff "failed to present evidence that [Martini]'s conduct was reckless or intentional." The plaintiff acknowledged that Martini was not engaged in horseplay or any other improper conduct at the time of the accident. Martini did not know that plaintiff was behind him when he stepped backwards, and plaintiff did nothing to alert Martini of his presence. As Martini testified at his deposition, he merely "took the wrong step at the wrong time."

V. Conclusion and Order

The court concluded that plaintiff's injuries were "simply the result of a 'luckless accident' "arising from his voluntary participation in a school-sponsored athletic activity and the trial court properly dismissed the complaint against the school district defendants and Martini based on assumption of the risk.

The appeal from an order of the Supreme Court, Oneida County granted the motions of defendants Clinton Central School District, John Hughes, in his capacity as Head Hockey Coach of the Clinton High School Hockey Team, Rob Hameline, in his capacity as Assistant Hockey Coach of the Clinton High School Hockey Team and Michael Martini for summary judgment and dismissed the complaint against those defendants.

CASES ON THE SUPPLEMENTAL WEBSITE

Clahassey v C Ami Inc. (2002 Mich. App. LEXIS 1352). The case illustrates the importance of a sound risk management plan. The reader needs to pay attention to how the location of the event and the failure to warn impacted the court's decision.

Maisonave v. Newark Bears (2005 N.J. LEXIS 1108). Examine what the NJ Supreme Court decided about the limited duty rule. When did it apply? What was the standard of care in the other sections of the ballpark?

John Hopkins v. Connecticut Sports Plex. LLC. (2006 Conn. Super. LEXIS 1710). The case illustrates the concept of foreseeability. While reading the case pay attention to the lack of a proper alcohol management plan, proper numbers of security staff and documentation of prior incidents.

Sciarrotta v. Global Spectrum, et al. (2008 N.J. LEXIS 314). The two aspects of the limited duty rule are discussed. Pay particular attention to the Supreme Court's conclusion pertaining to the pre-game warm-up.

Beglin v. Hartwick College, (2009 N.Y. LEXIS 7970). This case illustrates the importance of actual or constructive notice of a dangerous condition.

Chavez v. City of Santa Fe Springs (2011 Cal. App. LEXIS 9462). The trial court found the plaintiff's negligence claims which led to the death of her son were barred by the terms of a release signed by the mother and son, and granted the defendants' summary judgment motion. However, on appeal, the mother contended the trial court erred in granting summary judgment because the defendants' conduct constituted gross negligence that barred application of the release.

QUESTIONS YOU SHOULD BE ABLE TO ANSWER

1. Describe the significance of risk management.
2. Explain the DIM Process. What are the steps and how do they relate to each other?
3. Discuss the various types of transfer. Which of them do you believe is used most often?
4. Analyze as many reduction treatments as you can think of. If you were a sport or recreation venue manager which ones would be of the highest priority?
5. Identify two to three risks that a sport or recreation manager would encounter. Classify the risks and then select a treatment for each risk.

REFERENCES

Cases

Hatch v. V.P. Fair Foundation and Northstar Entertainment, 990 S.W.2d 126; 1999 Mo. App. LEXIS 315
Felipe v. Sluggers of Miami, Inc. and Sluggers, Inc., No. 07-18180 CA 22, Miami-Dade County Circuit Court, 11th, FL 2008
Noffke v. Bakke, 748 N.W.2d 195 (2008)

Publications

AAUW (2011). *Crossing the line: Sexual harassment at school*. Retrieved from http://www.aauw.org/learn/research/upload/CrossingTheLine.pdf
Ammon, R., Jr. (1993). Risk and game management practices in selected municipal football facilities. (Doctoral dissertation, University of Northern Colorado, 1993). *Dissertation Abstracts International, 54*, 3366A.
Ammon, R., Jr., Southall, R., & Nagel, M. (2016). *Sport facility management: Organizing events and mitigating risks* (3rd ed.) Morgantown, WV: Fitness Information Technology, Inc.
Corbett, R. (2002, August). *Risk management for sport organizations and sport facilities*. Presented at the Sports Management: Cutting Edge Strategies For Managing Sports as a Business Symposium, Toronto.
Cotten, D. (2013). Managing risk through insurance. In D. J. Cotten & J. Wolohan, (Eds.). Law for recreation and sport managers (6th Ed.) (pp. 340-350). Dubuque, IA: Kendall/Hunt Publishing Co.

Leopkey, B., & Parent, M. (2009). Risk management issues in large-scale sporting events: A stakeholder perspective. European Sport Management Quarterly 9(2), 187-208

Sharp, L. A., Moorman, A. M., & Claussen, C. L. (2007). *Sport law: A managerial approach*. Scottsdale, AZ: Holcomb Hathaway.

Spengler, J. O., Anderson, P. M., Connaughton, D. P., & Baker, T. A. (2009). *Introduction to sport law*. Champaign, IL: Human Kinetics.

van der Smissen, B. (1990). *Legal liability and risk management for public and private entities*. Cincinnati, OH: Anderson Publishing Co.

4.21 STANDARDS OF PRACTICE

Joann M. Eickhoff-Shemek | University of South Florida, Tampa

In a negligence lawsuit, a **standard of care** will be applied to measure the competence of a professional. If the professional's conduct falls below such a standard, he/she may be liable for injuries or damages resulting from such conduct (Black, 1991). The standard of care can be determined in various ways, but one way is from **standards of practice** developed and published by **professional** and **independent** organizations. This chapter will focus on the legal implications associated with these types of standards, not those dealing with accreditation, licensure, certification, statutes, or those developed by risk management authorities (*e.g.*, some states and municipalities) and insurance companies.

Standards of practice published by professional organizations are commonly referred to as standards, guidelines, recommendations, or position statements. Many professional organizations have published these documents to provide benchmarks of desirable practices for practitioners and managers. In addition to these types of standards, there are "technical physical specifications" (van der Smissen, 2000) published by independent organizations such as the American Society of Testing and Material (ASTM), the Consumer Product Safety Commission (CPSC), and equipment manufacturers. For example, ASTM has published standard specifications for safety signage for fitness equipment/facilities and standard specifications for playground equipment. CPSC has published standard specifications on equipment such as bicycle helmets and on facilities such as spas, hot tubs, and whirlpools. Equipment manufacturers also publish specifications regarding proper use, installation, maintenance, warnings, etc. with regard to the various types of equipment they sell.

Published standards of practice can be entered into evidence (via expert testimony) in a court of law to help determine the standard of care or **duty** that a defendant owes to a plaintiff. Therefore, it is critical for recreation and sport managers to incorporate these standards of practice into their risk management plans.

FUNDAMENTAL CONCEPTS

Potential Legal Impact of Published Standards of Practice

As demonstrated in Figure 4.21.1, published standards of practice can be introduced as evidence via expert testimony to help determine duty. If the defendant's conduct is inconsistent with these standards of practice, it can result in a breach of duty that can then lead to negligence. However, if the defendant's conduct is consistent with the standards of practice, it will be difficult for the plaintiff to prove there was a breach of duty.

Generally, the failure to adhere to published standards of practice can lead to claims of "ordinary" negligence against the defendant(s) as demonstrated in the Significant Case (*Elledge v. Richland/Lexington School District Five*) presented in this chapter. However, "gross" negligence claims also can be made against the defendant, *e.g.*, see *Xu v. Gay* (2003). (See this case on the Supplemental Web Site). In addition to ordinary and gross negligence claims, plaintiffs also might file a "breach of express warranty" claim against the defendant.

For example, the complaint filed in *Gloria Hicks v. Bally Total Fitness Corp.* not only included a wrongful death action for both ordinary and gross negligence, but also for breach of express warranty (Herbert, 2009). The wrongful death actions in this 2008 case involved the failure of Bally Total Fitness Corp. to provide appropriate emergency care to Malcolm Hicks when he suffered a sudden cardiac arrest while exercising at the fitness club. Mr. Hicks died several days later in the hospital. In the breach of express warranty claim, the plaintiff claimed that ". . . Bally pledged, agreed and warranted to its members that it would . . . conform to all relevant laws, regulations and published standards . . ." and ". . . would support and abide by guidelines and recommendations of the American College of Sports Medicine . . ." (Herbert, 2009, pp. 4-5).

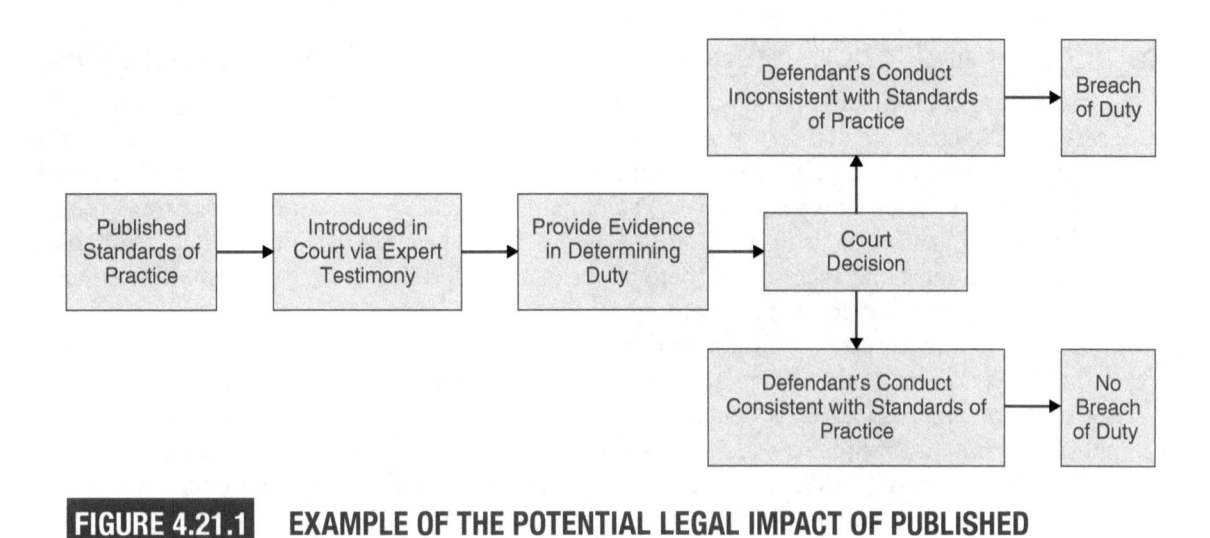

FIGURE 4.21.1 **EXAMPLE OF THE POTENTIAL LEGAL IMPACT OF PUBLISHED STANDARDS OF PRACTICE**

Standards of Practice Published by Professional Organizations

Following is a list of some of the professional organizations that have published standards of practice for various types of recreation and sport practitioners/managers. By no means is this a comprehensive list.

Exercise/Fitness Professionals
1. American College of Sports Medicine: *ACSM's Health/Fitness Facility Standards and Guidelines*
2. American College of Sports Medicine and American Heart Association Joint Position Statement: *Recommendations for Cardiovascular Screening, Staffing, and Emergency Policies at Health/Fitness Facilities* and *Automated External Defibrillators in Health/Fitness Facilities*
3. International Health, Racquet & Sportsclub Association: *IHRSA Club Membership Standards*

Strength and Conditioning Professionals
National Strength and Conditioning Association: *Strength and Conditioning Professional Standards and Guidelines*

Recreation Professionals
1. National Therapeutic Recreation Society and National Recreation and Park Association: *NTRS Code of Ethics and Interpretive Guidelines*
2. American Therapeutic Recreation Association: *ATRA Standards for the Practice of Therapeutic Recreation*
3. American Whitewater: *Safety Code of American Whitewater*

Physical Educators
Society of Health and Physical Educators (SHAPE) America—National Association for Sport and Physical Education: *National Standards & Grade-Level Outcomes for K-12 Physical Education*

Coaches
Society of Health and Physical Educators (SHAPE) America—National Association for Sport and Physical Education: *Quality Coaches, Quality Sports: National Standards for Sport Coaches*, 2nd Edition

Athletic Trainers
Board of Certification (BOC): *BOC Standards of Professional Practice* (affiliated with the National Athletic Trainers' Association)

Proliferation of and Inconsistency among Published Standards of Practice

One of the major purposes for developing and publishing standards of practice is to help standardize the delivery of services. Published standards of practice serve as "benchmarks" of practices that reflect the minimal acceptable level of service owed to participants and that should be universally applied by properly trained and educated professionals (Eickhoff-Shemek, Herbert, & Connaughton, 2009). Most often, these are developed by leaders within a given organization using a consensus and peer-review approach. However, a major challenge for some recreation and sport managers is that there has been a proliferation of such published statements, not to mention the many inconsistencies that exist among them.

This is especially true in the exercise/fitness field. In addition to the three published documents listed above under "exercise/fitness," several other organizations (*e.g.*, Medical Fitness Association, YMCA, Aerobics and Fitness Association of America) have also published standards of practice in recent years. The high number of these published standards of practice has led to many inconsistencies among them. For example, IHRSA's published standards of practice (IHRSA Club Membership Standards, 2005) do not require their clubs to have an Automated External Defibrillator (AED). However, ACSM does require health/fitness facilities to not only have an AED but to meet several other requirements related to AEDs such as having regular practice drills for staff members. (Tharrett & Peterson, 2012).

Not only do these inconsistencies make it difficult for exercise/fitness professionals to know which standards of practice they should follow, but these inconsistencies also allow expert witnesses to select—among the various standards of practice—those that best support their individual opinions. This can lead to differences in court rulings with regard to the establishment of the standard of care owed to participants in exercise and fitness programs. Therefore, given the inconsistencies that exist (discussed next), it is recommended that professionals **"follow those [published standards of practice] that are the most authoritative or safety oriented in their approach, regardless of how they are defined and/or stated . . ."** (Eickhoff-Shemek, Herbert, & Connaughton, 2009, p. 53).

Inconsistencies in Terminology

Certain professional organizations (*e.g.*, ACSM and NSCA) have distinguished, by definition, a standard from a guideline (Tharrett & Peterson, 2012; NSCA, 2009). Both ACSM and NSCA have defined **standards** as requirements and **guidelines** as recommendations. Standards are written as "shall" statements (ACSM) and "must" statements (NSCA) and guidelines are written as "should" statements. Other published standards of practice, e.g., *BOC Standards of Professional Practice* use the term "standards" in the title of their publication, but all the standards are written as "should" or "shall" statements, not "must" statements. Another inconsistency in the use of terminology is demonstrated in the ACSM and American Heart Association (AHA) joint position paper titled *Recommendations for Cardiovascular Screening, Staffing, and Emergency Policies at Health/Fitness Facilities* which includes requirements (must statements) and recommendations (should statements), though the title specifically states "recommendations."

Although differences clearly exist in how professional organizations define and use the terms standards and guidelines, does it make a difference to the courts when establishing the standard of care? It probably does not (see *Xu v. Gay* on the Supplemental Web Site). In *Xu*, Ning Yan died from a severe head injury resulting from a fall off a treadmill that had only 2½ feet clearance behind it at the defendant's fitness facility. The expert witness for the plaintiff, Dr. Marc Rabinoff, stated that the industry's standard of care for the safety distance behind treadmills should be a minimum of five feet. Though he did not specify the industry standards he was referring to, he did state that they were voluntary, not mandatory. Interestingly, the court made no distinction with regard to voluntary or mandatory stating that the "defendant's ignorance of and failure to implement these standards . . . establishes a case of ordinary negligence . . ." (p. 171). It appears from this case that even though the expert witness stated in his testimony that the industry standards were voluntary, the court still considered them as evidence of the standard of care that the defendant owed to Yan.

To add more concern with regard to how standards and guidelines are defined, a New York court ruled that the *ACSM's Health/Fitness Facility Standards and Guidelines* could not be applied to help determine the legal duties of the defendants because of a disclaimer included in the third edition of the publication (*Bloom v. ProMaxima Manufacturing Company*, 2009). The disclaimer (which was not included in the first and second editions) states that the standards are not to be used as evidence to determine the standard of care in the event of injuries and subsequent claims or lawsuits.

Two well-known expert witnesses, Harvey Voris and Marc Rabinoff, have often referred to these ACSM standards (as well as the NSCA and ASTM standards) in their expert testimony to communicate with courts as to what is appropriate with regard to facility operation and exercise equipment design and maintenance (Voris and Rabinoff, 2011). They state that, until the ruling in *Bloom*, these standards were never questioned with regard to their legal effect. They also state that "these statements need to be meaningful so they can be relied upon to establish . . . a standard of care especially when adherence to such a standard would prevent incidents from continuing to occur" (p. 21). In addition, they encourage ACSM and other professional organizations not to include damaging disclaimers in their publications because "how can a standard be a standard if the professional organization that writes them does not stand by them?" (p. 21). Despite this recommendation, the current (4th) edition of *ACSM's Health/Fitness Facility Standards and Guidelines* (Tharrett & Peterson, 2012) contains the same disclaimer as did the third edition.

The Law and Standards of Practice Continually Change

New issues arise which can potentially change the law as well as published standards of practice. It is important for recreation and sport managers to stay abreast of these changes. For example, in recent years several states have passed legislation that mandate fitness facilities to have an AED (Eickhoff-Shemek, Herbert, & Connaughton, 2009; Tharrett & Peterson, 2012). In addition, professional and independent organizations are continually updating/revising their published standards of practice. For example, the ASTM recently revised its standard dealing with motorized treadmills and the minimum clearance behind them (ASTM F2115, 2012). The ACSM has proposed significant changes in pre-activity screening procedures to be published in the next (10th) edition of *ACSM's Guidelines for Exercise Testing and Prescription* (Riebe, Franklin, & Thompson, et al., 2015). When developing a comprehensive risk management plan, it is essential for recreation and sport managers to carefully consider both "current" applicable laws and published standards of practice.

Standards of Practice as they Apply to Risk Management

It is essential for recreation and sport managers to incorporate applicable standards of practice into their risk management plan. Managers are ultimately responsible for the development and implementation of the risk management plan. However, all professionals responsible for the program must be involved in various aspects of the risk management process.

Head and Horn (1997) developed a five-step risk management decision-making process: (1) identifying and analyzing exposure to loss, (2) examining alternative risk management techniques, (3) selecting risk management techniques, (4) implementing techniques, and (5) monitoring results. This five-step approach can be adapted into the following four steps with regard to the application of standards of practice (see also Chapter 4.11 *Risk Management Process*)

Step 1. Identifying and Selecting Applicable Standards of Practice

Because there are so many published standards of practice from a variety of organizations, it is challenging for the recreation and sport manager to be aware of all applicable standards and to determine which ones should be selected and incorporated into the risk management plan. A risk management advisory committee (e.g., experts in the field, a knowledgeable lawyer, and an insurance expert) can provide excellent assistance in this step as well as the remaining steps. Because it is almost impossible to know which standards of practice will be introduced into a court of law, it is best to select those that are the most authoritative or safety oriented in their approach.

Step 2. Developing Risk Management Strategies That Reflect Standards of Practice

This step involves writing procedures that describe specific responsibilities or duties that staff members would carry out given a particular situation. For example, all programs should have written emergency procedures that not only reflect published standards of practice, but also describe specific tasks that staff members must perform when someone is hurt.

Once the written procedures are finalized, they should be included in the facility's policy and procedures manual. Policies and procedures from this manual can also be introduced as evidence in determining duty (see *Darling v. Charleston Community Hospital* (1964), where the defendant's own by-laws along with published standards were entered into evidence to determine duty). It is best for the procedures be written clearly and succinctly without too much detail. Too much detail in the written procedures will not allow for a certain amount of flexibility the staff members may need in a particular situation and may make it difficult for the staff to remember everything they are to do.

Step 3. Implementing the Risk Management Plan

Implementation of the risk management plan primarily involves staff training. Staff training will help ensure that staff members carry out the written policies and procedures properly. The policy and procedures manual should be used with initial training for new employees as well as with regular in-service training throughout the year for all employees. In regular in-service training, actual practice of a particular procedure (*e.g.*, emergency procedures) should take place. It is also important to explain to staff members why it is essential that they carry out their duties appropriately from a legal perspective.

Step 4. Evaluating the Risk Management Plan

Evaluation of the risk management plan should be done throughout the year. For example, the recreation and sport manager should regularly supervise staff to be sure they are carrying out their duties appropriately and if they are not, corrective action should take place, which may involve re-training. Evaluation should also occur after each injury to determine if the staff carried out the emergency procedures correctly and to determine if anything could be done to prevent a similar incident in the future. A formal evaluation of the entire risk management plan should be done at least annually. Like the law, standards of practice are not static and can change and evolve over time. Therefore, written procedures will need to be updated periodically to reflect these changes.

Recommendations for the New Business Owner

Recreation and sport managers who have been working in the field for a while often desire to start their own business. Before opening a business, the new owner must possess the necessary knowledge and skills to develop a comprehensive and effective risk management plan. Utilizing resources such as this text along with consulting with a competent lawyer will be necessary to help ensure applicable laws are built into the risk management plan. Regarding published standards of practice, the new business owner and his/her lawyer (or risk management advisory committee) need to follow the four steps described above.

Step 1 for the new business owner should be to make a concerted effort to identify and select applicable standards of practice. To get started with this step, seek out the standards of practice published by the professional organizations related to the business. For example, if opening a new sport performance facility, the business owner should research all the standards, guidelines, and position papers published by strength/conditioning and athletic professional organizations (e.g., NSCA and NATA) and then select those that are applicable to the daily operations of the facility and program. Related to exercise equipment, the standards and guidelines published by independent organizations (e.g., ASTM, CPSC) and the specifications published by equipment manufacturers must be thoroughly researched to identify and select those that are relevant.

Regarding **Step 2**, published standards of practice often do not describe "how" to implement them – only "what" to implement. This step requires the new business owner to possess the necessary knowledge/skills to prepare written risk management policies and procedures (to include in the facility's risk management manual) that reflect the "selected" applicable laws and standards of practice. Using resources such as this text along with obtaining assistance from legal/risk management experts and other competent, experienced professionals may be helpful with this step.

One of the most important tasks of the new business owner in **Step 3** (implementing the risk management plan) is to provide initial and on-going staff training. Given the legal principle, *respondeat superior*, business owners have a vested interest to help ensure their staff members are well-trained to properly carry out the policies and procedures in the facility's risk management manual. This legal principle basically states that employers can be held liable for the negligent acts of their employees. Numerous negligence lawsuits exist where the employer has been named as a defendant along with the employee who was negligent. In these cases, one of the most common claims is that the employer failed to train the employee. To minimize this liability exposure, the business owner needs to be an effective educator to carry out this important training task. If he/she does not possess these skills, there are many pedagogical resources that can help with the design and delivery of effective lesson plans for training purposes.

An essential task in **Step 4** requires the supervision of staff members to help ensure they are properly carrying out the risk management policies and procedures. The new business owner must take the time/effort to directly observe and evaluate "each" staff member while performing his/her job.

SIGNIFICANT CASE

The following case demonstrates that courts do allow expert witnesses to introduce published standards of practice as admissible evidence in determining duty in negligence cases. The trial court in this case excluded evidence provided by expert witnesses involving standards of practice published by ASTM and CPSC. The plaintiffs claimed that the trial court erred in excluding this evidence and appealed. The Court of Appeals of South Carolina (Elledge v. Richland/Lexington School District Five, 2000) found that the trial court did err in refusing to admit relevant evidence of the ASTM and CPCS industry standards. Citing a variety of cases to support its decision, the Court of Appeals stated: **"Safety standards promulgated by government or industry organizations in particular are relevant to the standard of care for negligence . . . Courts have become increasingly appreciative of the value of national safety codes and other guidelines issued by governmental and voluntary associations to assist in applying the standard of care in negligence cases . . . A safety code ordinarily represents a consensus of opinion carrying the approval of a significant segment of an industry, and it is not introduced as substantive law but most often as illustrative evidence of safety practices or rules generally prevailing in the industry that provides support for expert testimony concerning the proper standard of care"** *(pp. 477–478). (Emphasis added). The Court of Appeals reversed the trial court's decision and the Supreme Court of South Carolina affirmed the Court of Appeals decision. This is an excellent case to illustrate that not adhering to published standards of practice can lead to charges of negligence.*

ELLEDGE V. RICHLAND/LEXINGTON SCHOOL DISTRICT FIVE

Supreme Court of South Carolina
2002 S.C. LEXIS 235
November 25, 2002, Filed

Opinion: Justice Waller

We granted a petition for a writ of certiorari to review the Court of Appeals' decision in Elledge v. Richland/Lexington Sch. Dist. Five, 341 S.C. 473, 534 S.E.2d 289 (Ct. App. 2000). We affirm.

Facts

On December 9, 1994, nine-year-old Ginger Sierra (Ginger) slipped and fell on a piece of playground equipment at Irmo Elementary School where she attended fourth grade. The playground equipment was a metal monkey bar device which the children walked upon; it extended above the ground approximately two feet. As a result of the fall, Ginger broke her right leg. The growth plate in that leg was significantly damaged, and Ginger eventually underwent surgery in both legs to remove the growth plates. * * *

Ginger and her mother, Christine Elledge (collectively respondents), sued petitioner Richland/Lexington School District Five (the District) for negligence. A jury returned a verdict for the District. On appeal, the Court of Appeals reversed and remanded for a new trial. * * *

At trial, James Shirley, the principal at Irmo Elementary since 1990, testified that shortly after he arrived at the school, he had concerns about the school's playground. He was especially concerned by the lack of a fall surface and by the height of some of the playground equipment. As to the monkey bar which Ginger fell on, Shirley stated that children had been walking on it and this was also a concern. In 1991, Shirley contacted Jim Mosteller who redesigned the playground. As part of the playground renovations, the monkey bar which Ginger fell on was modified by Mosteller. Originally, the monkey bar was higher and had a bench underneath it. As part of the modifications performed in 1991, the height was lowered from about four feet to two feet, and the bench was removed. On the modified monkey bar, students would walk or crawl across it, although there were no handheld supports on the side. Shirley testified that he knew the children were walking across the apparatus after the modification.

Both of respondents' playground safety experts testified that the monkey bar was, in its original form, designed to develop children's upper body strength. Archibald Hardy stated that this piece of equipment was known as a "pull and slide" and the children were supposed to lie back on the bench underneath the bars and pull themselves along the apparatus. According to Hardy, the original design "definitely wasn't for walking" because the metal rungs were small enough for children's hands and were "fairly slick." The modification to the equipment encouraged children to "run up and jump on top of it;" however, Hardy stated that children "shouldn't have been playing on top of it at all." Hardy, who sold to and installed playground equipment for Irmo Elementary, had visited the playground on several occasions since 1992, and had recommended to Shirley that all the older equipment on the playground be "bulldozed."

Steven Bernheim, respondents' other expert, similarly testified about the equipment and stated that it "was not meant as a climber." According to Bernheim, the equipment was safe as originally designed, but in its modified form, it was unsafe because the narrow bars were originally designed for hands, not feet, and no grit had been placed on the metal bars to prevent slipping.

Bernheim stated generally that the playground at Irmo Elementary did not meet the proper safety standards in the industry. Respondents sought, however, to introduce specific evidence regarding the Consumer Product Safety Commission (CPSC) guidelines for playground safety and the American Society for Testing and Materials (ASTM) standards for playground equipment. The trial court granted the District's motion in limine to exclude this evidence. At trial, respondents argued that this evidence was relevant to establishing the District's common law duty of care. The trial court found the evidence inadmissible because the guidelines were not "binding" on the District and the District had not "adopted" them in any way.

Respondents proffered the following evidence. Bernheim would have testified that in 1994, when Ginger fell, the CPSC guidelines and ASTM standards were in effect and would have applied to "any group . . . utilizing the playground equipment for public use," including a school district. He stated that these guidelines are industry standards and are distributed to schools via superintendents' or principals' meetings. Significantly, Bernheim opined that the District should have had policies and procedures in place for retrofitting existing equipment so that it complied with the guidelines. Furthermore, Bernheim believed the modified monkey bar did not comply with the national guidelines because there were no handrails and no grit on the walking surface. According to Bernheim, because Ginger's injury involved getting caught in an entrapment between the ladder areas, it was the type of injury the guidelines are designed to prevent. While Bernheim acknowledged that the industry standards were guidelines only, he stated they are what the playground equipment industry "stands by."

Respondents also proffered testimony from the District's purchasing coordinator, Joe Tommie. According to Tommie, the District would specify in its bids for purchasing new playground equipment that the equipment must meet the CPSC guidelines and ASTM standards. He stated: "That's normally the standard we use to ensure that we purchase safe equipment."

* * *

On appeal, respondents argued the exclusion of this evidence was prejudicial error. The Court of Appeals agreed. Stating that "evidence of industry standards, customs, and practices is 'often highly probative when defining a standard of care,'" the Court of Appeals held the trial court erred by excluding evidence of the CPSC guidelines and ASTM standards. Elledge, 341 S.C. at 477, 534 S.E.2d at 290-91. * * * The Court of Appeals found the trial court was under "the mistaken belief that the District must have adopted these national protocols before such evidence was admissible. . . . While such proof might be necessary in attempting to establish negligence *per se*, it is not required when the evidence is offered to demonstrate an applicable standard of care." Id. at 478, 534 S.E.2d at 291. As to the District's argument there was no prejudice from any error, the Court of Appeals stated that the "exclusion of this testimony was clearly prejudicial since such evidence would tend to show the District's compliance with industry standards, which directly conflicts with the District's assertion that such standards were never recognized." Id. at 480, 534 S.E.2d at 292.

Issue

Did the Court of Appeals correctly decide that the trial court's exclusion of the CPSC guidelines and ASTM standards evidence was reversible error?

Discussion

The District argues that the trial court correctly excluded the CPSC guidelines and ASTM standards evidence. Specifically, the District maintains respondents failed to establish that these guidelines were accepted and used by school districts in South Carolina to determine the safety of existing playground equipment. In addition, the District contends that even if the trial court erred, the error was not prejudicial. We disagree.

To establish a cause of action in negligence, a plaintiff must prove the following three elements: (1) a duty of care owed by defendant to plaintiff; (2) breach of that duty by a negligent act or omission; and (3) damage proximately resulting from the breach of duty. * * * In our opinion, respondents' proffered evidence was relevant to, and admissible on, the first required element of negligence—the District's duty of care to respondents. * * * We agree with Chief Judge Hearn's observation that the trial court was under "the mistaken belief that the District must have adopted these national protocols before such evidence was admissible." Elledge, 341 S.C. at 478, 534 S.E.2d at 291.

As recognized by the Court of Appeals, the general rule is that evidence of industry safety standards is relevant to establishing the standard of care in a negligence case. See, e.g., McComish v. DeSoi, 42 N.J. 274, 200 A.2d 116, 120-21 (N.J. 1964) (holding that construction safety manuals and codes were properly admitted as objective standards of safe construction); Walheim v. Kirkpatrick, 305 Pa. Super. 590, 451 A.2d 1033, 1034-35 (Pa. Super. 1982) (holding that safety standards regarding the safe design and use of trampolines, including ASTM standards, were admissible on the issue of the defendants' negligence, even though the defendants were unaware of the standards); Stone v. United Eng'g, 197 W. Va. 347, 475 S.E.2d 439, 453-55 (W.Va. 1996) (no error to admit evidence of safety standards for the design and guarding of conveyors even though the standards had not been imposed by statute and did not have "the force of law"); see generally Daniel E. Feld, Annotation, *Admissibility in Evidence, on Issue of Negligence, of Codes or Standards of Safety Issued or Sponsored by Governmental Body or by Voluntary Association*, 58 A.L.R.3d 148, 154 (1974) (modern trend is to admit safety codes on the issue of negligence). This kind of evidence is admitted not because it has "the force of law," but rather as "illustrative evidence of safety practices or rules generally prevailing in the industry." McComish v. DeSoi, 200 A.2d at 121.

Indeed, the District even acknowledges this is the general rule. Respondents' expert, Bernheim, laid an adequate foundation for the admission of these safety standards when he stated they: (1) were in effect at the time of Ginger's accident, and * * * (2) would have applied to any group using playground equipment for public use, including a school district. Thus, the Court of Appeals correctly held that the trial court erred by excluding evidence of the CPSC guidelines and ASTM standards.

The District, however, argues this evidence was inadmissible because respondents did not show that school districts generally accepted or followed the guidelines with regard to existing playground equipment. * * * We find this argument completely unavailing. Since the evidence showed the District followed the CPSC guidelines when purchasing new playground equipment, and the guidelines are intended for general playground safety which logically includes the maintenance of existing playground equipment, the District's contention that the safety standards somehow did not apply to it on existing equipment is simply untenable. It is clear to us that a public school is exactly the type of entity to which the public playground safety guidelines should, and do, apply. Simply because the District did not utilize the guidelines in 1994 with regard to existing equipment does not mean that it should not have. * * *

We find this evidence is highly probative on the issue of defining the District's duty of care. Rules 401, 402, SCRE (evidence is relevant and admissible if it has any tendency to make the existence of any fact of consequence to the action more or less probable than it would be without the evidence); see also Elledge, 341 S.C. at 477, 534 S.E.2d at 290 ("Evidence of industry standards, customs, and practices is 'often highly probative when defining a standard of care.'") (quoting 57A Am.Jur.2d Negligence § 185 (1999)). Consequently, we hold the trial court abused its discretion by excluding this evidence. * * *

The District further argues that any error made by the trial court did not result in prejudice to respondents. The District contends that the evidence was cumulative to the admitted testimony of respondents' experts and the expert testimony was limited only by excluding specific references to the safety standards. We disagree.

Evidence of objective safety standards is generally offered "in connection with expert testimony which identifies it as illustrative evidence of safety practices or rules generally prevailing in the industry, and as such it provides support for the opinion of the expert concerning the proper standard of care." McComish v. DeSoi, 200 A.2d at 121 (emphasis added); see also Brown v. Clark Equip. Co., 62 Haw. 530, 618 P.2d 267, 276 (Haw. 1980) (evidence of safety codes is "admissible as an alternative to or utilized to buttress expert testimony") (emphasis added).

Respondents sought to introduce evidence of industry standards to identify and establish the duty of care owed by the District to respondents. According to respondents' expert, the modified monkey bar did not comply with the guidelines. According to the District's purchasing coordinator, the District utilized the guidelines to ensure the safety of new equipment purchases. The import of the expert's evidence is clear. Respondents sought to show that the same standards that were used to purchase safe new equipment, should have been used to safely modify and/or maintain the existing equipment.

Furthermore, this type of evidence constitutes an objective standard and as such would have greatly enhanced the opinions offered by respondents' experts. We therefore disagree with the District's argument that the evidence would have been cumulative to the experts' testimony. One of the main purposes of industry standard evidence is to provide support for an expert's opinion on what the applicable standard of care is, and thus, the evidence is not merely cumulative to the expert's testimony. * * *

In addition, we note that the bulk of the experts' testimony went to the element of breach of duty whereas the specific evidence of industry standards was intended to establish the applicable duty of care. In other words, while respondents' experts were allowed to offer their opinions that the equipment did not conform with the industry's guidelines and was not meant to be walked upon, this testimony primarily relates to breach of a duty, not to demonstrating precisely what the objective duty of care was. Since the evidence at issue went to a different element on the negligence cause of action—duty versus breach - clearly the evidence cannot be considered cumulative.

Accordingly, we hold the trial court's error in excluding this evidence prejudiced respondents' case.

CONCLUSION

The general rule is that evidence of industry safety standards is admissible to establish the standard of care in a negligence case. The evidence of CPSC guidelines and ASTM standards which respondents sought to have admitted in the instant case is exactly the type of evidence contemplated by this general rule. The Court of Appeals correctly held the trial court committed reversible error in excluding the evidence. Therefore, the Court of Appeals' opinion is **AFFIRMED.** * * *

CASES ON THE SUPPLEMENTAL WEBSITE

Bloom v. ProMaxima Manufacturing Company, 669 F.Supp. 2d 321 (2009 W.D.N.Y.). In this case, the court ruled that the *ACSM's Health/Fitness Facility Standards and Guidelines* could not be used as evidence to establish the standard of care because this publication contains a disclaimer that specifically states that the standards should not be used to give rise to a duty of care.

Corrigan v. Musclemakers, Inc. 686 N.Y.S2d 143 (1999 N.Y.App.Div. LEXIS 1954). This case involved a personal fitness trainer's failure to instruct his client on how to safely use the treadmill before using it. The court referred to the operator's manual that included a guideline that states the importance of understanding the treadmill's operation prior to use.

Jimenez v. 24 Hour Fitness USA, Inc., (237 Cal. App. 4th 546; 2015 Cal. App. LEXIS 494). In this case the health club failed to follow the distance specifications behind its treadmills (minimum of 6 feet) as stated in the manufacturer's assembly guide. Interestingly, the court also found the waiver signed by the plaintiff to be unenforceable. Consider why, from a safety and legal perspective, it is important to follow distance specifications (front, sides, and back) published by manufacturers of exercise equipment. Also, consider how the waiver in this case, if it had been written and administered properly, might have protected the defendant.

Xu v. Gay, 257 Mich. App. 263 (2003 Mich. App. LEXIS 1505). This case involved industry standards regarding the distance (clearance) behind treadmills. Explain why the court ruled that the failure to implement the standards did not establish a case of gross negligence.

L.A. Fitness International v. Mayer, 980 So. 2d 550 (2008 Fla. App. LEXIS 5893). This case involved IHRSA and ACSM standards regarding emergency procedures. Describe why most recreation and sport managers would not agree with the appellate court's ruling in this case.

QUESTIONS YOU SHOULD BE ABLE TO ANSWER

1. Describe the potential legal impact of published standards of practice.

2. Investigate and then develop a list of the standards of practice published by both professional and independent organizations that apply to your specific practice as a recreation and sport manager.

3. Explain what recreation and sport managers should do if they find inconsistencies among the published standards of practice.

4. Describe how published standards of practice can be applied to the four risk management steps. Include the specific actions that recreation and sport managers should take within each step.

5. Using the court's reasoning in the Significant Case (*Elledge*), explain how and why published standards of practice can be relevant to the standard of care.

REFERENCES

Cases
Bloom v. ProMaxima Manufacturing Company, 669 F.Supp. 2d 321 (W.D.N.Y. 2009).
Darling v. Charleston Community Hospital, 200 N.E.2d 149 (Ill. App. Ct. 1964.
Elledge v. Richland/Lexington School District Five, 341 S.C. 473 (S.C. Ct. App. 2000).
Elledge v. Richland/Lexington School District Five, LEXIS 235 (S.C. 2002).
Xu v. Gay, 668 N.W.2d 166 (Mich. App. 2003).

Publications
ASTM F2115 (2012). Standard Specification for Motorized Treadmills. West Conshohocken, PA: ASTM International.

Black, H. (1991). *Black's law dictionary* (6th ed.). St Paul, MN: West Publishing Company.

Head, G., & Head, S. (1997). *Essentials of risk management* (Vol. I, 3rd ed.). Malvern, PA: Insurance Institute of America.

Eickhoff-Shemek, J., Herbert, D. & Connaughton, P. (2009). *Risk management for health/fitness professionals: Legal issues and strategies*. Baltimore, MD: Lippincott Williams & Wilkins.

Herbert, D. (2009). New AED case filed. *The Exercise Standards and Malpractice Reporter, 23*(1), 1, 4–7.

IHRSA Club Membership Standards (2005). In *IHRSA's guide to club membership & conduct*. (3rd. ed.). Boston, MA: International Health, Racquet & Sportsclub Association (IHRSA).

National Strength and Conditioning Association (NSCA): Strength and Conditioning Professional Standards and Guidelines. (2009). *National Strength and Conditioning Journal, 31*(5), 14–38.

Reibe D, Franklin BA, Thompson PD, et al. (2015). Updating the American College of Sports Medicine's recommendations for the exercise pre-participation health screening process. *Medicine & Science in Sports & Exercise. 47*(11): 2473-2479.

Tharret, S. & Peterson, J. (Eds.) (2012). *ACSM's health/fitness facility standards and guidelines* (4th ed.). Champaign, IL: Human Kinetics.

van der Smissen, B. (2000). *Standards and how they relate to duty and liability*. Paper presented at the 13th Annual Sport, Physical Education, Recreation and Law Conference, Sponsored by the Society for the Study of the Legal Aspects of Sport and Physical Activity, Albuquerque, NM.

Voris, H.C. & Rabinoff, M. (2011). When is a standard of care not a standard of care? *The Exercise Standards and Malpractice Reporter, 25*(2), 20–21.

4.22 AUDITS IN RISK MANAGEMENT

Risk Management Plan

Legal Audit

Facility Audit

Todd L. Seidler | University of New Mexico

Jury Awards $15,000,000 to Paralyzed Teenager
Catastrophic Injury Leads to $8M Settlement
Pool Drain Cover Case Settled for $30.9 Million
Programs Eliminated: Title IX Lawsuit Follows
Two Students Shot in Gymnasium
Sandusky Scandal Costing PSU Millions
Teen Killed in Soccer Goal Post Accident
7 Die in Basketball Team Van Crash
$19.5M Settlement Reached in Weight Machine Suit
Overloaded Bleachers Collapse Killing One and Injuring Over 200

These are real headlines of actual incidents. Thousands of people are injured each year as a result of watching, volunteering, working, or participating in sport and recreational activities. As a result of those injuries, litigation against the sponsoring organization or recreation or sport business often occurs. Due in part to the expansion of programs, an increase in the number of participants, and the proliferation of personal injury lawsuits, risk management has become one of the most important concerns for today's sport or recreation manager. As covered throughout this text, managers of recreation and sport programs have a number of legal duties they are obligated to perform. Managers of sport and recreation organizations have a duty to use reasonable care for the safety of participants, spectators, and staff when providing programs, facilities, and equipment. As discussed in previous chapters, the establishment of a good, effective, formal risk management program has become the expected standard of practice for all sport and recreation programs.

In addition to litigation resulting from physical injury, sport and recreation managers are often faced with a wide variety of other legal actions such as contract disputes, employment issues, Title IX claims, compliance with Occupational Safety and Health Administration (OHSA) regulations, Americans with Disabilities Act (ADA) regulations, and allegations of Constitutional rights violations. As a result of the increase in litigation against recreation and sport organizations, managers of these agencies are increasingly called upon to defend themselves and their organizations from legal challenges. The purpose of this chapter is to present three risk management tools for recreation and sport managers—the **risk management plan**, the **legal audit**, and the **facility audit**. Each of these can be of immense value in protecting against harm to individuals and defending an organization from litigation. Other chapters throughout the text have focused on the risk management process and on many of the legal issues facing today's sport and recreation managers. Throughout this chapter, the reader will be directed to other sections of the text that will expand on the specific topic being discussed.

RISK MANAGEMENT PLAN

According to van der Smissen (1996), "There are two types of risks: the risk of financial loss and the risk of personal injury." She goes on to say, "A **risk management plan** is more than safety checklists! It is the systematic analysis of one's operations for potential risks or risk exposures and then setting forth a plan to reduce such exposures." A good risk management plan analyzes all potential risks that an organization faces and selects the optimal method to treat each.

As described in previous chapters, there are four methods of treating risks once they have been identified. They are (1) risk avoidance or elimination, (2) risk reduction, (3) risk retention, and (4) risk transfer (see also Chapter 4.11 *Risk Management Process*).

It is important to recognize that a risk management plan should be unique and be developed specifically for a particular organization. A youth baseball league will face different risks and have different requirements than a high school athletic department, a college recreation program, or a nonprofit organization sponsoring a large event. All components that are appropriate for a given situation should be included in the risk management plan.

In developing a risk management plan, it is important to understand the concept of developing **layers of protection**. This means that whenever an identified risk cannot be completely eliminated, several strategies should be used to treat the risk. For instance, instead of relying solely on a waiver to transfer the risk to the user, the waiver should be used in conjunction with other methods of treating the risk (e.g., an agreement to participate, special releases from a physician for a pre-existing condition, extra insurance, regular inspections, developing policies for transportation, or special training for personnel). In this way, if the waiver is successfully challenged in court, there are several other methods of protection still in place. The more layers of protection that are in place, the more likely the organization will be able to successfully defend itself in court—or avoid a lawsuit altogether.

The following are the major components of a risk management plan for a typical recreation or sport organization. This is only an outline as many of these concerns are discussed in depth in chapters throughout this text. References to the appropriate chapters will be provided when appropriate. It is also important to note that this is a generic outline and that each organization must develop a plan that is customized for its particular situation. Finally, the reader should realize there is no one best format or outline for a risk management plan. Most formats are acceptable as long as each of the sources of risk is addressed.

Organization Description

It is not always necessary but can be advantageous to begin with an overview and description of the organization along with its purpose and function. The following information may be useful:

- Organization mission statement, values and/or statement of philosophy
- A description of the services or programs provided
- An overview of the clientele served
- A description of the facilities and spaces that will be utilized
- The organizational structure of the organization—organizational chart
- Financial resources

Personnel

As part of an overall risk management plan, it may be desirable to review or develop policies and procedures for personnel such as might be found in the organization's personnel manual (see also Chapter 4.11 *Risk Management Process*). When discussing ways to avoid employment litigation, Schuler and Jackson (1996) state "One excellent avoidance technique is to undertake a comprehensive audit of all employment procedures, policies, and practices to ensure that all are in accord with the rapidly changing state and federal employment laws." A review of personnel-related policies and procedures should include the following:

- Develop thorough hiring procedures to ensure that employees are qualified to perform the job they are hired to do. This may include required initial and ongoing training for each position. Background checks, both in-state and out-of-state, should be required for all positions that work with children or other susceptible populations. This is a minimum requirement—it is advisable that they be conducted for all employees since responsibilities may change after one is employed.

- Develop complete and accurate job descriptions for all personnel, and describe the essential tasks necessary to do each job including individual responsibilities for safety and risk management. (This is also helpful in fully complying with the ADA.)
- Provide an evaluation and discipline process that allows for accurate and thoroughly written documentation of employee performance and discipline. This may include termination procedures. All procedures for discipline and termination should provide the employee with proper due process.
- Develop and implement a policy of nondiscrimination in the workplace. Comply with the requirements of federal and state laws that prohibit discrimination on the basis of race, religion, national origin, age, sex, pregnancy, and disability.
- Develop a procedure to field complaints of sexual harassment in the workplace. Be sure it effectively protects the rights of the accused and the accuser. Ensure compliance with government-mandated training requirements regarding the illegality of sexual harassment.
- Review all policies and procedures for possible due process considerations.
- Provide a location for conducting employment interviews that is fully accessible to those with disabilities, pursuant to the ADA.
- Ensure the hiring process is not subject to claims of discrimination because of a narrow applicant pool.
- Develop a policy manual or handbook for using volunteers. Ensure that all volunteers are properly trained and fully capable of performing the job they are being assigned to do. Just because someone is a volunteer does not relieve him/her from having to act reasonably.
- Update the employee handbook, manual, or policy to ensure compliance with recent changes to state and federal employment laws. Check your employment manual for any provisions that are contrary to state or federal law.
- Post all required notices in the workplace (e.g., "Sexual Harassment is Illegal," state and federal wage and hour laws, state and federal OSHA guidelines, state and federal fair employment laws, privacy laws and the Family and Medical Leave Act).
- Consider if a policy regarding violence in the workplace is appropriate for your situation.
- Ensure compliance with the Immigration and Naturalization Service requirement to complete work authorization (I-9) forms for all employees.

Conduct of Activities

This section of the risk management plan is a description of the programs being offered and the necessary standards for conduct (see also Chapter 2.34 *Supervision*). Issues to consider include:

- **Proper instruction.** Maintain policies ensuring adequate instruction and providing for proper methodology and progression.
- **Warnings and participation forms.** Review or develop all appropriate pre-participation forms: physical exam, waiver, warning, assumption of risk, parental consent, consent for emergency treatment, as well as any other appropriate forms necessary for the activities sponsored by the organization (see also Chapter 2.23 *Waivers and Releases* and Chapter 2.24 *Agreements Related to Inherent Risks*).
- **Mismatch situations.** Review or develop policies to avoid mismatches. (Should prevent mismatches between children and other participants as well as with staff/adults mismatches) (see also Chapter 2.34 *Supervision*).
- **Transportation policy.** If transportation is provided for participants, a thorough policy regarding vehicles, inspections, driver qualifications and training, insurance, maintenance and record keeping is necessary (see also Chapter 2.35 *Transportation*).
- **Hazing policy.** If applicable, a hazing policy should be developed, communicated, and enforced (see also Chapter 3.22 *Hazing*).
- **Rules.** Develop, communicate, and enforce rules that govern behavior of all participants, spectators, staff, and visitors.

General Supervisory Practices

Supervision is almost always an issue when injuries occur in recreation and sport programs and has to be an important aspect of the risk management plan (see also Chapter 2.34 *Supervision*). Some aspects of supervision that need to be addressed are:

- **A supervisory plan.** The plan should outline duties, responsibilities, qualifications, and schedules of supervisors.
- **Management of behavior of participants, spectators, staff, and visitors.** Crowd control can be considered an aspect of behavior management (see also Chapter 4.24 *Crowd Management*).
- **Rules and regulations for supervisors.** Supervisors must understand their duty and be well-trained in how to supervise properly. This may include a policy making it clear that an inappropriate relationship between a staff member and a participant is not allowed.
- **Security and access control.** A secure facility is a must.
- **Emergency care and accident reporting.** Preparedness for emergency care is a part of supervision (see also Chapter 2.33 *Emergency Care*).
- **Protection from foreseeable criminal acts.** The organization has an obligation to be prepared to protect participants, spectators, staff, and visitors from foreseeable criminal acts. There is generally no liability for unforeseeable criminal acts.
- **A plan for unplanned absence of supervisor.** Supervisors should be instructed as to the policy to follow in the event the supervisor unexpectedly has to leave persons in his or her charge without supervision for a period of time.

Facilities

The risk management plan should address the reduction or elimination of foreseeable hazards related to environmental conditions. A **facility audit** is a systematic method of identifying such hazards and risks related to a sport or recreation facility and determining the optimal method of treating each. The audit should cover all facilities, equipment, and all indoor and outdoor spaces. A detailed description of the facility risk audit is provided later in this chapter (see also Chapter 2.31 *Premises Liability*). The audit should address:

- Hazardous conditions
- Equipment
- Facility layout
- Maintenance
- OSHA
- Health hazards
- Security
- Access control
- ADA
- Signage

Crisis Management and Emergency Response Plans

The risk management plan should include a crisis management and/or emergency response plan. It is important to identify the crisis and emergency situations that are likely to occur and develop response plans and procedures for each. This should include all documentation and forms that are to be used. Once developed, regular training and testing of appropriate personnel is necessary to ensure that the plans are carried out as anticipated. The **emergency response plan** should include first-aid plans, reporting procedures (911) and medical services policies (see also Chapter 2.33 *Emergency Care* and Chapter 4.23 *Crisis Management*). Types of emergencies and crisis situations that may be planned for include:

- Serious personal injuries of participants, spectators, staff, visitors
- Weather related emergencies— tornado, hurricane, lightning, flood
- Dealing with participants, family members of victims, lawyers, and the media
- Active Shooter
- Civil disturbance
- Earthquake
- Fire
- Hazardous material spil
- Bomb or terrorism threat
- Medical emergencies

Insurance Coverage

Make certain the necessary insurance is in place and that it is adequate for foreseeable events (see also Chapter 4.25 *Managing Risk Through Insurance* and Chapter 4.26 *Workers' Compensation*). Every possible situation that can be envisioned should be considered to determine whether all staff, participants, volunteers, administrators and visitors will be adequately protected. Without such coverage, an injured party may feel it necessary to sue in order to pay medical bills and other costs. When evaluating insurance plan coverage, consider:

Organization or Business

- General liability
- Umbrella liability
- Employment practices liability

- Property
- Event
- Motor vehicle

Employee

- Workers' compensation
- Liability protecting employees

Participant

- Basic medical (often required of participant)
- Catastrophic injury

As mentioned previously, this is a generic risk management outline. The needs of each business or organization differ depending upon its goal, the activities offered, its size, whether it's public or private, and many other factors. In some organizations other areas should be included in the risk management plan. Some possible topics to add may be identified during a legal audit.

THE LEGAL AUDIT

A **legal audit** is a formal review of policies that attempts to address all pertinent legal aspects of the organization. A legal audit involves a complete legal checkup of the organization in which all aspects of the operation are examined in order to discover and minimize potential financial threats. Although the line between a risk management plan and a legal audit is often blurred, a legal audit typically includes more than what is thought of as a risk management plan. The legal audit helps ensure the *legal health* of a recreation or sport program and should be done in conjunction with the risk management plan of the organization. The legal audit is typically broken down into a four-step process.

Content of the Legal Audit

A list of the areas that are appropriate to address for each particular organization must be identified. Such a list can sometimes be obtained through legal counsel or from an insurer, but will most likely have to be developed within the organization. The structure of the legal audit covers a number of different categories and will vary somewhat from one organization to another. The legal requirements of a private sport organization may be very different from those of a nonprofit entity. Since some of the categories may not be applicable in certain situations and the number will vary somewhat, it is necessary for the sport or recreation manager to select those that are appropriate for a given situation. Such a comprehensive list of pertinent information helps to create a profile from which one can determine the current and potential *legal health* problems of the entity and to address these problems before they reach crisis proportions. If produced internally, it can be very helpful to develop the audit with the help of legal counsel, financial advisors, insurance specialists, and/or a risk management consultant.

According to Grange and Oliver (1985), some categories that may be included in a legal audit are:

- General information regarding the entity
- Governance/authority of the entity
- Function and purposes of the entity
- Policies related to contracts

- Employee and labor relations
- Personnel policies and records
- Operational licenses
- Records supporting tax-exempt status

- Financial information
- Books and records
- Regulatory requirements
- Copyright and/or patent records
- Information regarding property/facilities
- Compliance with gov't. reg. (e.g., Title IX, ADA)

Fried (1999) also provides a list of other issues that should be considered for inclusion:

- Partnership agreements
- Corporate formation procedures
- Tax issues
- Advertising liability
- Contract negotiations and compliance
- First aid and OSHA regulations
- Selling food and licensing/permits
- Government relations
- Zoning issues
- Nuisance from noise
- Alcohol-related concerns
- Copyright, trademark, and patent issues
- Spectator violence
- Insurance
- Facility rental agreements
- Sponsorship contracts
- Employment issues
- Employer liability
- Dangerous facilities
- Liability for the acts of volunteers
- Product liability
- Criminal law
- Real estate issues
- Crowd management
- Property rights
- Drug testing

Selecting the Manager and Committee

Once the list has been established, a qualified staff person must be selected and assigned to manage the legal audit process. It is crucial that a person be selected who is sensitive to detail, who has the ability and experience, and has the perceived authority to secure cooperation of other employees. The logical person may be the business manager if one exists in the organization. With smaller organizations, the athletic director or program administrator may be the best one to manage the process. Proper selection is key to a successful audit.

Once the manager has been chosen, a committee can then be selected to help carry out the audit. The members of the committee should represent the various major areas of the business operation. It is important to note that those selected for a legal audit committee are often different from those selected for a risk management committee.

It is also essential to obtain expert evaluation of the audit by legal, financial, and managerial counsel. For example, an attorney can examine the audit from a legal standpoint, a CPA can inspect it from a financial perspective, and a manager or someone from upper administration can study it from an operational point of view. Large organizations may have the necessary experts available to help, but others may have to hire outside consultants at this point. Specific examples include bringing in a specialist to study an athletic department's compliance with Title IX, hiring an insurance expert to evaluate the organization's current insurance package, or having an attorney review hiring policies and contracts.

Conducting the Audit

When an appropriate committee has been selected, it is time to conduct the audit. Each committee member is selected to study the policies and procedures specific to his or her area of expertise. Often, two or more will share interest areas and should collaborate on their evaluation. The committee should then come together and discuss each part individually with input from all members. As agreement on one area is achieved, the committee addresses the next item in the audit. Eventually, the committee should come to agreement on all aspects of the audit and prepare recommendations to the upper administration.

Implementing the Audit

For the final step, upper administration should receive copies of the completed legal audit. Typically, those overseeing the organization must then decide whether to act on each recommendation. A careful review of the document will help to sensitize them to areas that require immediate attention as well as those requiring long-range consideration. The more support garnered from these administrators, the stronger and more effective the entire process will be. It is important to note that this is an ongoing process. The audit should be reviewed on a regular basis and it should never be assumed that, because it was done before, it is still adequate.

The legal audit is becoming an essential task of sport and recreation managers and has a direct impact on the legal and financial health of their organizations. Sport and recreation managers must become familiar with the details of legal audits and be able to develop and refine them in order to improve the organization's protection from litigation.

THE FACILITY AUDIT

A **facility audit** is a systematic method of identifying the hazards and risks related to a sport or recreation facility and determining the optimal method of treating each. According to Sharp, Moorman and Claussen (2010), "Facility operations, maintenance and policies and procedures are often the foundation of a sport or recreation enterprise." A claim of unsafe facilities is one of the most common allegations made in lawsuits alleging negligence in recreation or sport programs. Addressing facility liability, Page (1988) called it one of the largest subcategories within the broad spectrum of tort law. When determining the conduct expected of a facility manager, courts have ruled that they be held to a standard of that of a reasonably prudent and careful facility manager. As specified in Chapter 2.31 *Premises Liability*, a facility operator has a general duty to exercise reasonable care for the safety of its patrons. That duty for ordinary care includes the obligation to:

- Keep the premises in safe repair
- Inspect the premises to discover obvious and hidden hazards
- Remove the hazards or warn others of their presence
- Anticipate foreseeable uses and take reasonable precautions to protect
- Conduct operations on the premises with reasonable care for the safety of all

A facility audit helps to ensure that the above obligations are carried out. If someone is injured in a facility and initiates a lawsuit claiming that the injury was caused by a situation the facility manager should not have allowed to exist, the court will partially base its findings of liability on the concept of foreseeability. Was it foreseeable that the situation in question was likely to cause an injury? If the court determines that a reasonable, prudent facility manager would have recognized a potential danger and acted to reduce or eliminate the hazard and the defendant did not, the chances of being found liable for the injury are greatly enhanced. However, if it is determined that a reasonable, prudent facility manager probably would not have identified the situation as likely to cause an injury, the potential for liability is greatly reduced.

It is the legal obligation of facility managers and program directors to address or treat all foreseeable risks in one way or another in order to reduce each unwanted risk as much as possible. According to Eickhoff-Shemek, Herbert, and Connaughton (2009), "In general, facilities should be properly designed, equipped, and maintained in all program areas if liability is to be controlled at manageable levels. All areas should be regularly checked and kept free of defects and nuisances to minimize the chances of participant injury, illness, or death." Additionally, Wolohan states, (2006) "Establishing a system of inspection, including documenting the dates of inspection, any potential problem areas and all necessary corrective measures, also can help dramatically cut down on a facility's potential liability." The best method of performing the above obligations and ensuring facility safety is through the development of a facility risk audit. This audit consists of a systematic inspection for potential hazards and developing a procedure for dealing with the hazards identified. The facility risk audit is broken down into two major parts: 1) the inspection (comprehensive, periodic, or daily), and 2) risk treatment.

Inspections

Comprehensive Inspections

The **comprehensive inspection** is conducted by one or more staff members who walk throughout the facility trying to identify as many potential risks or hazards as possible. Typically, the larger the organization or facility, the more people will make up an inspection team. It is often advantageous to include inspectors who have different backgrounds or specialties. A maintenance person will look at the facility from a different point of view than will a coach or a security officer. Each will look at the facility from his/her unique perspective and possibly identify different hazards.

It is also desirable and beneficial to have someone from outside the organization come in and inspect. It may be beneficial for two sport or recreation managers to trade off and inspect each other's facility. Often, those who work in a facility become used to the environmental conditions they see every day and may not notice a hazard, whereas someone looking at it from a fresh point of view may spot it easily. When more people are involved in inspections, fewer hazards will likely be overlooked.

An example of a hazardous condition that should have been identified and treated before someone was injured is illustrated in *Cohen v. Boys & Girls Club of Greater Salem Inc.* (2010) (see the Supplemental Web Site Website). Dillon Cohen was playing basketball when he struck an unpadded cement wall only 1½ feet from the end line. He suffered a skull fracture, a C-7 spinous process fracture, and a left clavicle fracture. An initial inspection by a qualified person should have identified the hazardous condition of the gym prior to play so it could be treated before someone was injured. It can also be beneficial to hire a professional risk management consultant to come in and assist in conducting the initial inspection and the development of checklists for daily, periodic, and comprehensive inspections.

In addition to identifying hazardous conditions, other facility issues must be addressed as part of the facility audit. Issues that may expose the organization to legal threats other than lawsuits from injury should be identified and dealt with. Among these are access control, security, compliance with ADA, Title IX and OSHA regulations, and proper signage regarding warnings and rules for facility usage.

The comprehensive inspection should include all interior areas (e.g., gyms, locker rooms, pools, hallways, lobbies, restrooms) as well as all exterior areas (e.g., playgrounds, fields, sidewalks, parking lots, fences). Each inspector should independently tour the entire facility and make a list of potential hazards. All of the individual lists should then be compiled into one comprehensive list of potential hazards. This comprehensive list must then be prioritized. The priority list will establish the order in which the hazards are treated. The more likely a hazard is to cause an injury and the more serious the potential injury, the higher the priority assigned to that hazard. Following completion of the priority list, each hazard must be considered and the best method of treating each determined (see Risk Treatment below). It is important to understand that a thorough, comprehensive inspection is not a one-time event and should occur on a regular basis (annually or more often if needed). In between these major inspections, periodic inspections should take place.

Periodic Inspections

After the comprehensive inspection is complete, an ongoing program of inspections should be implemented. In most facilities, it is appropriate to conduct **periodic inspections** on a daily, weekly, biweekly, and/or monthly basis, prior to each event, whatever is called for by the activities and usage of that particular facility. It is common practice to develop several different types of inspection checklists. It is often a good idea to develop checklists that can be used for **daily inspections**. Such an inspection may be done before opening the facility each day and should cover safety items that are likely to occur or change quickly such as checking for standing water or trash on a court, making sure doors are secure, or looking for holes on a softball field. An example of the need for frequent inspections is illustrated in *Zipusch v. LA Workout, Inc.*, 2007 Cal. App. LEXIS 1652 (see Significant Case). Zipusch filed suit for personal injuries sustained when she was injured on a treadmill. She claimed her foot became stuck to a sticky substance on the treadmill, causing her to fall. As part of her claim, she alleged the club's failure to inspect and maintain the exercise equipment resulted in the sticky substance remaining on the treadmill. The Court of Appeals felt that a reasonable argument could be made that inspecting the premises was especially important and the case was remanded to the trial court for further proceedings.

Inspections performed on a less frequent basis, such as weekly or monthly, might include looking for hazards that are less likely to occur or that take time to develop. Examples may include inspections of bleachers for loose bolts, bent or broken supports, damaged footboards or loose railings. Also, frayed cables or worn pulleys on weight machines, improper functioning of treadmills and other cardio equipment, and loose bolts and padding on basketball backboards and rims are examples of hazards that may occur over time. Inspections should occur as often as a reasonable and prudent professional would do in the same or similar circumstances. Facility managers should use their best professional judgment to determine the frequency of the periodic inspections. The more quickly a problem may occur or the greater the usage of the facility, the more often an inspection should be conducted.

In a spectator facility, however, it is often more appropriate to perform an inspection immediately **prior to each event**. The inspection in such a facility may focus on issues of spectator safety such as hazards that may cause a slip or trip and fall, the condition of seats and bleachers and emergency response equipment (e.g., fire extinguishers, alarms, and emergency lighting).

In addition to periodic inspections, it's important to ensure that there is a mechanism in place to quickly address hazards when actual notice occurs.

Developing the Checklists. Once the hazards identified through the comprehensive and periodic inspections have been identified, a checklist with which to perform periodic facility inspections on a regular, ongoing basis should be developed. This checklist should be designed for each facility and customized for that particular situation. It is all too common that sport and recreation managers will borrow a checklist from another facility, put their name and logo on it, and use it for their facility. This is not a safe or effective practice. Each facility and situation is unique. Therefore, every checklist should be customized for a given situation. It can be very helpful to study checklists from other facilities and borrow ideas from them, but it is essential that each item be applicable to the particular facility. It is also important to keep the checklist relatively straightforward and simple. If the checklist is so long and complex that it becomes a major operation to complete, the inspection probably won't be performed carefully, if at all. On the other hand, all items of importance must be included. All checklists should be kept up-to-date as facility conditions and equipment change. It is important to ensure that checklists are user-friendly, complete, and current.

When developing a facility checklist, the following items should be included in order for it to be as effective as possible:

- Name of the organization
- Inspector's name (printed)
- Inspector's signature
- Date of inspection
- Location of inspection (if needed)
- Problems discovered

Figure 4.22.1 is an example of a daily checklist while Figure 4.22.2 represents how a monthly checklist may appear. When writing the questions for the checklist, it can be very helpful to write them so that if each item is satisfactory, the *Yes* column will be checked (see Figures 4.22.1 and 4.22.2). This way it will be easy to look at each page of the list and see if any checks appear in the *No* column. If none exist, no problems were identified.

Risk Treatment

Once the potential hazards in the facility have been identified and prioritized, one or more **risk treatment** methods are utilized in order to eliminate each risk or at least make it as safe as possible. Chapter 4.11, *Risk Management Process*, provides a good description of treating risks after they have been identified. When treating physical hazards related to facilities or equipment, two methods are typically used:

1. **Risk elimination.** Fix it so that it is no longer a problem.
2. **Risk reduction.** If it cannot be eliminated, make it as safe as possible and identify other methods of treating the remaining hazard.

Daily Inspection Checklist

Inspector's Name _____Kevin Finn_____ Date __9/17/12__

Location of Inspection _____Main Gym_____

Inspector's Signature _____

Instructions for Inspector:

1. Inspect and complete all items.
2. Include comments on all "NO" responses.
3. Fill-out and report problems on completion of inspection.

# POTENTIAL HAZARD	YES	NO	COMMENTS
1. Floor clear of obstacles and debris	X		
2. Floor clear of standing water	X		
3. Floor swept, good traction	X		
4. All standards, mats & goals properly stored	X		
5. All other equipment properly stored	X		
6. Gym rules clearly posted	X		
7. Bleachers secure and in good repair	X		
8. Warning sign on bleachers clearly visible	X		
9. All lights undamaged and working		X	Light over center court is out
10. Emergency procedures clearly posted	X		
11. Emergency telephone accessible	X		
12. Emergency phone numbers and directions to facility are posted by the phone	X		
13. Rims unbroken, straight & in good shape	X		
14. Backboards unbroken & in proper position	X		
15. Wall pads in place	X		
16. Access—Ingress and egress points opened or locked as appropriate		X	N.E. outside door open
17. Supervisor present	X		
18. No unsupervised children present	X		
19. All of participants' equipment properly stored in hallway	X		
20. Other			

FIGURE 4.22.1 JOE DAILEY RECREATION CENTER DAILY INSPECTION CHECKLIST

Monthly Inspection Checklist

Inspector's Name _____Paul Edwards_____ Date __9/17/12__

Location of Inspection _____Weight Room_____

Inspector's Signature _____

Instructions for Inspector:

1. Inspect and complete all items.
2. Include comments on all "NO" responses.
3. Fill-out and report problems on completion of inspection.

# POTENTIAL HAZARD	YES	NO	COMMENTS
1. Weight machines clean & lubricated	X		
2. Cables, belts and pulleys undamaged		X	Belt on leg curl frayed
3. Benches, seats and back rests secure	X		
4. Proper storage available for weights, bars	X		
5. All other equipment properly stored	X		
6. Weight room rules clearly posted	X		
7. Instruction signs clearly visible		X	Missing on overhead press
8. Warning signs clearly visible	X		
9. Flooring flat and level	X		
10. Emergency procedures clearly posted	X		
11. Emergency telephone accessible	X		
12. Emergency phone numbers and directions to facility are posted by the phone	X		
13. Emergency exits clearly marked	X		
14. Electrical cords out of traffic flow	X		
15. Cardio machines in good working order	X		
16. Proper spacing between machines	X		
17. Other			

FIGURE 4.22.2 JOE DAILEY RECREATION CENTER MONTHLY INSPECTION CHECKLIST

Deciding on the optimal method(s) of risk treatment will rely on the best professional judgment of the facility and risk managers and staff involved. As each hazard is dealt with, the next one on the list can then be addressed. This does not mean that items with a lower priority on the list must wait until the ones before have been treated. If an item cannot be treated immediately (e.g., waiting on a part for repair), it is important to mark the equipment or area temporarily off limits, and deal with the next hazard on the list.

Many situations can be quickly and easily treated and removed from the priority list while others may take some time.

With some hazards it will be obvious how to best remedy the situation. For example, if there is a hole in a soccer field, repair it and determine its source. If it was a one-time incident, the hazard has been eliminated and no more concern is necessary. If, however, the problem is likely to recur, as when the holes are caused by gophers, the cause should be remedied as soon as possible. If it will take some time before it can be fixed permanently, it may be necessary to compensate for it by warning participants of the hazard, using cones to block off the area, posting warning signs, or closing the area until repair is completed.

Another example of risk reduction is illustrated when the sideline of a basketball court is two feet from a concrete block wall, an obvious hazard that must be dealt with. It is probably not possible to completely eliminate the hazard by moving the wall out several more feet. One method to reduce the hazardous situation might be to use floor tape and create a new sideline a few feet inside the current one. It may also be appropriate to warn the participants of the situation and to pad the wall. For a permanent fix, the boundary lines may be moved away from the wall, thereby increasing the buffer zone. The baskets may also have to be moved to match the new lines. Making the basketball court smaller may seem like an extreme measure but it is a totally appropriate way to reduce such a dangerous condition.

Again, for most facility hazards, completely eliminating the dangerous condition is the ideal method of risk treatment. However, when a hazard cannot be completely eliminated, sport and recreation managers must be creative and determine the optimal way to protect everyone involved. It's important to ensure that there is a mechanism in place to quickly address hazards when actual notice occurs (see the discussion on Actual vs. Constructive Notice in Chapter 2.31 *Premises Liability*). Once a hazardous condition has been identified, a reasonable facility manager will appropriately treat the hazard as soon as possible.

Documentation

Documenting and saving everything that relates to organizational legal issues, safety, and risk management is essential to protecting the assets of the organization and is good management practice. If litigation occurs, the court will want to see evidence of what the organization or business has done to protect others from harm. An organized, thorough, consistent method of documenting all efforts to make a program safe and legally sound is an integral part of any risk management program, legal audit, or facility audit. In each of these, documenting all efforts provides good protection for the organization. Keeping good records is essential if one has to demonstrate in court that everything that could be reasonably expected had been done. The old adage, "If it wasn't written down, it didn't happen" is a great one to apply to such programs. It is important to keep copies of all aspects of the risk management plan as well as the factors addressed in the legal audit. Finally, all records should be stored in such a way that they are safe, secure, and easily retrievable. Digitally saving documents on DVDs, external hard drives or using cloud backup is an excellent way to store large amounts of information. Multiple copies can then be stored in different locations to ensure availability in future years.

Conclusion

In order for a risk management program to be most effective, it must be valued by the organization. If the employees believe that the upper administration feels that the safety of all participants, spectators and staff is an important aspect of the culture of the organization, they are more likely to take their risk management responsibilities seriously. Administrators should communicate the need for and reward efforts toward making the facility as safe as it can be.

The need for recreation and sport managers to conduct risk management becomes increasingly clear every day. We have both a moral and legal obligation to do our best to both provide safe programs and to protect the assets of the organization. Along with the increased awareness of the necessity to provide risk management programs and legal audits has come a need for help in developing them. Sport and recreation managers often do not have the background and expertise required to develop a risk management plan that will keep injuries to a minimum and provide maximum protection against litigation. This has created an opportunity for those with such expertise to sell their services and help administrators devise appropriate plans, policies, and procedures. There are a number of risk management consultants that provide such a service in the recreation and sport fields and the number is increasing. Many risk management consultants have specialized knowledge in certain areas and have developed great expertise in their area. Examples of such areas include playgrounds, aquatics, strength and conditioning programs, crowd control, the use of waivers, and outdoor adventure programs. Along with specialized knowledge in managing risk for recreation and sport businesses, opportunities are appearing for positions as professional risk managers. More and more, large organizations are recognizing the need to have a person who is knowledgeable in risk management on the staff. Large arenas and stadiums, school districts, and city park and recreation departments are examples of entities that are now hiring professionals with these unique skills. Good risk management is now expected of all recreation and sport organizations.

SIGNIFICANT CASE

Yoko Zipusch joined a fitness club called LA Workout in 2004. A couple of months later, while walking on a treadmill, Zipusch claimed that her foot stuck to a sticky substance on the belt of the treadmill, causing her to fall and be injured. Zipusch filed a complaint against LA Workout for general negligence and premises liability alleging a failure to inspect and maintain the exercise equipment. This case provides an interesting discussion on the expectations for frequent inspections in a busy club.

ZIPUSCH V. LA WORKOUT, INC.
2007 Cal. App. LEXIS 1652
October 3, 2007, Filed

Procedural Posture

Plaintiff health club member brought an action for negligence and premises liability against defendant health club owner for personal injuries sustained when her foot became stuck to a sticky substance on a treadmill at the club. The owner purchased the club pursuant to bankruptcy proceedings. [LA Workout, Inc., is the predecessor-in-interest of Northridge GG, Inc. Northridge GG, Inc. purchased LA Workout on December 6, 2004, pursuant to bankruptcy proceedings. Northridge defended this action brought by Zipusch.] The Los Angeles County Superior Court, California, granted the owner's motion for summary judgment. The member appealed.

* * *

Facts and Proceedings

Zipusch signed a "Membership Agreement" in October 2004 and thereafter became a member of LA Workout. The double-sided membership agreement contained a readily identifiable assumption of risk provision located at the bottom of the front page which stated: "The use of the facility at LA Workout naturally involves the risk of injury to yourself or your guest, whether you or someone else cause [sic] it. As such you understand and voluntarily accept this risk and agree that LA Workout will not be liable for injury, including without limitation, personal, bodily or mental injury, economic loss or damage to you, your spouses [sic], guests, unborn child, or relatives resulting from the negligence or other acts of anyone else using LA Workout. If there is any claim by anyone based on injury loss or damage described here, which involves you or your guest, you agree to (1) defend LA Workout against such claims and pay LA Workout for all expenses relating to the claim and (2) indemnify LA Workout for all liabilities to you, your spouse, guests, relatives, or anyone else, resulting from such claims. The member or guest will defend and indemnify LA Workout for any negligence EXCEPT the sole negligence of the club. This agreement is not effective until you sign and date it. By signing below, you agree to the terms above."

On or about December 10, 2004, Zipusch allegedly sustained injuries when her foot became stuck to a sticky substance on a treadmill at the health club, causing her to lose her balance. Zipusch filed a complaint against LA Workout for general negligence and premises liability alleging its failure to inspect and maintain the exercise equipment resulted in the sticky substance remaining on the treadmill, causing her to lose her balance when her foot became stuck to it.

Northridge answered the complaint and later moved for summary judgment. In the motion, Northridge argued the release provision of the membership agreement exculpated the health club from claims arising during a member's use of the athletic facilities. Circumventing the exact wording of the release, Northridge argued in the health club context parties reasonably contemplate release provisions bar claims arising while exercising. Thus, Northridge appeared to argue, the unambiguous existence of a release exculpates a health club from claims arising while exercising without examining what the release's exact wording actually covers. Additionally, irrespective of the release provision, Northridge argued Zipusch could not raise a triable issue of material fact regarding any alleged negligence on the part of the health club, including its actual or constructive notice of the sticky substance on the treadmill.

Zipusch opposed the motion for summary judgment, arguing the release only barred claims against the health club caused by negligent third party conduct and, alternatively, the release contained an ambiguity which should be construed against the drafter, LA Workout. Either way, Zipusch argued the release did not bar claims against the health club for its own negligence. After addressing the threshold issue of the release, Zipusch presented evidence indicating the health club negligently inspected and maintained its equipment. First, Zipusch stated in her declaration, based on her own observations, 85 minutes had elapsed between the time of the accident and the last time a gym employee had inspected and cleaned the equipment. Zipusch argued a reasonable trier of fact could find the health club negligently inspected and maintained its exercise equipment by inferring the sticky substance was on the treadmill for this time period and concluding it was unreasonable and negligent to not remove the sticky substance during this time period. Additionally, at his deposition, an assistant manager of the health club testified the undersides of treadmill belts are not inspected in the normal course by gym employees monitoring the exercise area throughout the day. Zipusch argued a reasonable trier of fact could find this failure, in combination with the 85-minute gap between inspections, constituted negligence.

The trial court granted summary judgment in favor of Northridge based on the assumption of risk provision of the membership agreement, finding that while the release did not bar all claims arising during use of the health club, it did bar all claims involving third party conduct. The trial court found Zipusch had presented no evidence establishing the sticky substance materialized on the treadmill by non-third-party conduct.

* * *

Yoko Zipusch appealed from a summary judgment entered in favor of Northridge GG, Inc. (Northridge), in her negligence action for personal injuries sustained when her foot became stuck to a sticky substance on a treadmill at a health club owned by Northridge. Zipusch contends the trial court erroneously concluded there were no triable issues of material fact regarding two matters: first, whether the liability release contained in the signed membership agreement exculpated the health club from its own negligence; and second, whether the health club negligently failed to inspect and clean its exercise equipment. On de novo review, the court of appeal concluded (1) the release was too ambiguous to insulate the health club from liability to Zipusch for its own negligence, and (2) triable issues of material fact existed regarding whether the health club negligently failed to inspect and maintain its exercise equipment.

* * *

Discussion

LA Workout/Northridge's Alleged Negligent Inspection and Maintenance of Exercise Equipment is Not an Inherent Risk of Exercising at a Health Club

Absent a contractual release from liability, Northridge nonetheless can prevail on summary judgment if Zipusch's alleged injury was an inherent risk of exercising at a health club. As our Supreme Court has made clear, "resolution of the question of the defendant's liability in such cases turns on whether the defendant had a legal duty to avoid such conduct or to protect the plaintiff against a particular risk of harm." Rather than examining the "plaintiff's subjective knowledge or appreciation of the potential risk," the inquiry depends upon whether the defendant breached its general duty "to use due care not to increase the risks to a participant over and above those inherent in the sport." "Thus, although a ski resort has no duty to remove moguls from a ski run, it clearly does have a duty to use due care to maintain its towropes in a safe, working condition so as not to expose skiers to an increased risk of harm."

* * *

In determining whether the accident was an inherent risk of exercising at a health club we turn to the record and common sense. Generally, defective or unnecessarily dangerous equipment is not considered an inherent risk of a sport. This is entirely sensible. The main concern animating inherent risk analysis is the potential for chilling vigorous participation and altering the fundamental nature of a particular sport. However, these concerns are not present in lawsuits alleging defective or unnecessarily dangerous equipment where the issue is whether the defendant increased the risk above the inherent risk of the sport.

* * *

Here, Zipusch alleges the health club negligently inspected and maintained its exercise equipment, allowing a risk to remain for an unreasonable amount of time. Despite Northridge's misplaced reliance on *Leon v. Family Fitness Center (#107), Inc.*, we find nothing to support the contention the negligent inspection and maintenance of exercise equipment is an inherent risk of exercising at a health club. Unlike those who run outside on cracked sidewalks speckled with gum, Zipusch and other health club members pay dues in exchange for access to a safe and well-maintained exercise environment. Instead of chilling exercise at a health club, reasonably inspecting and maintaining exercise equipment should have the opposite effect. Further, Northridge acknowledges it already monitors and cleans the exercise facility. Accordingly, we find the negligent inspection and maintenance of exercise equipment is not an inherent risk of exercising at a health club.

* * *

Zipusch has Raised a Triable Issue of Material Fact Regarding Whether LA WorkOut/Northridge Negligently Inspected and Maintained its Exercise Equipment.

Given our interpretation of the release provision as set forth above, we find Northridge did not meet its burden on summary judgment of demonstrating Zipusch's causes of action have no merit. But even if Northridge had met its burden, we find Zipusch has raised a triable issue of material fact which precludes summary judgment.

Circumstantial evidence of a property owner's failure to inspect the premises before an accident is sufficient to infer the risk existed long enough for the property owner, in the exercise of due care, to have discovered and removed it. In other words, a property owner's failure to reasonably inspect can be used to infer constructive knowledge of the dangerous condition, providing a causal link between the accident and the time period between inspections. The determination of what constitutes a reasonable time period between inspections will necessarily vary according to the particular circumstances. For instance, " '[a] person operating a grocery and vegetable store in the exercise of ordinary care must exercise a more vigilant outlook than the operator of some other types of business where the danger of things falling to the floor is not so obvious.' " Thus, while a 15- to 30-minute interval between inspections at a busy commercial retail center may lead to an inference of negligence, the same inference might not be found elsewhere.

* * *

Zipusch has raised a triable issue of material fact regarding whether LA Workout negligently inspected and maintained its exercise equipment. In her declaration, Zipusch stated, based on her own observations, no staff member inspected or cleaned the exercise equipment in the 85-minute time period prior to the accident. In the health club context where numerous individuals are engaging in vigorous physical activity, a reasonable argument can be made that inspection of the premises is especially important, and an 85-minute time period between inspections is unreasonably long. Further, an LA Workout employee testified the undersides of the treadmill belts are not routinely inspected. From this evidence a reasonable trier of fact could find the health club negligently inspected and maintained its exercise equipment.

For the foregoing reasons, we conclude the trial court erred in granting Northridge's motion for summary judgment.

Disposition

The judgment is reversed and the case is remanded to the trial court for further proceedings. Appellant is entitled to recover her costs on appeal.

CASES ON THE SUPPLEMENTAL WEBSITE

Barnhard v. Cybex Intl. 2011 N.Y. App. Div. LEXIS 8264. Plaintiff claimed weight machine was defectively designed and tipped over and severely injured her.

Cohen v. Boys & Girls Club of Greater Salem Inc., 2010 N.H. Super. LEXIS 2. A dangerous condition existed in a gym where there was an inadequate buffer zone and no wall padding.

Flores v. 24 Hour Fitness, 2005 Cal. App. Unpub. LEXIS 207. Example of how a good inspection and maintenance program would have prevented an injury and lawsuit.

Guerra v. Howard Beach Fitness Center, 2011 N.Y. Misc. LEXIs 3346. A good inspection and maintenance program may have prevented a treadmill injury and lawsuit.

Range v. Abbott Sports Complex, 2005 Neb. LEXIS 36. Interesting discussion as to whether Range Sports Complex had constructive knowledge of a hole in a soccer field.

QUESTIONS YOU SHOULD BE ABLE TO ANSWER

1. When discussing a risk management plan, what is meant by "layers of protection?"
2. What is the difference between a legal audit and a facility audit?
3. What duty and obligations do facility managers owe to patrons using their facilities?
4. Why is it important to document the things that are done for safety and risk management?
5. How do you determine how often a facility inspection should be performed?

REFERENCES

Cases
Barnhard v. Cybex Intl. 2011 N.Y. App. Div. LEXIS 8264
Burkart v. Health & Tennis Corporation of America, Inc. 1987 Tex. App. LEXIS 7544.
Cohen v. Boys & Girls Club of Greater Salem Inc., 2010 N.H. Super. LEXIS 2
Flores v. 24 Hour Fitness, 2005 Cal. App. Unpub. LEXIS 207.
Guerra v. Howard Beach Fitness Center, 2011 N.Y. Misc. LEXIs 3346
Range v. Abbott Sports Complex, 2005 Neb. LEXIS 36
Zipusch v. LA Workout, Inc., 2007 Cal. App. LEXIS 1652.

Publications
Berg, R. (1994). Unsafe. *Athletic Business, 18*(4), 43–46.
Dougherty, N. J. (1993). *Principles of safety in physical education and sport.* Reston, VA: National Assn. for Sport and Physical Education.
Dougherty, N., & Seidler, T. (2007). Viewpoints: Injuries in the buffer zone: A serious risk management problem. *Journal of Physical Education Recreation and Dance, 78*(2), 4–7.
Eickhoff-Shemek, J., Herbert, D. & Connaughton, D. (2009). Risk Management for Health/Fitness Professionals. Philadelphia, PA: Lippincott, Williams & Wilkins.
Fried, G. B. (1999). *Safe at first.* Durham, NC: Carolina Academic Press.
Grange, G. R., & Oliver, N. S. (1985). Head off trouble with a legal audit. *Association Management.* Nov. 103 B 104.
Jewell, D. (1992). *Public assembly facilities* (2nd ed.). Malabar, FL: Krieger Publishing Co.
Kaiser, R., & Robinson, K. (1999). Risk management. In B. van der Smissen, M. Moiseichik, V. Hartenburg, and L. Twardgik (Eds.), *Management of park and recreation agencies* (pp. 713–741). Ashuba, VA: NRPA.
Maloy, B. P. (1993). Legal obligations related to facilities. *Journal of Physical Education, Recreation, and Dance, 64*(2), 28–30, 68.
Schuler, R.S. & Jackson, S.E. (1996). *Human resource management: Positioning for 21st century.* Minneaplois/St. Paul: West Publishing Co.

Sharp, L., Moorman, A., & Claussen, C. (2010). Premises liability and sport facility/event issues. In *Sport law: A managerial approach*. Scottsdale, AZ: Holcomb Hathaway.

Seidler, T. *(2006)*. Planning and designing safe facilities. *Journal of Physical Education Recreation and Dance, 77(5)*, 32–37, 44.

Seidler, T. (2009). Planning facilities for safety and risk management. in T.H. Sawyer, (Ed.), *Facility planning and design for health, physical activity, recreation and sport*. (12th ed.). Champaign, IL: Sagamore.

van der Smissen, B. (1990). *Liability and risk management for public and private enterprises*. Cincinnati, OH: Anderson Publishing Co.

van der Smissen, B. (1996). Tort liability and risk 5anagement. In Parkhouse, B.L. The Management of Sport (2nd Ed.) St. Louis: C.V.Mosby Company.

CRISIS MANAGEMENT

Daniel Connaughton | University of Florida
Thomas A. Baker, III | University of Georgia

4.23

> "If you prepare for everything you can think of,
> you will be prepared when the unthinkable happens."
>
> Rudy Giuliani, March 28, 2012
> Speaking about the 9-11 attack

How important is crisis management to the recreation or sport manager? Contrast two situations in which a crisis was reasonably foreseeable—the 1993 University of Wisconsin/Michigan football game, where it was announced in the school paper that the students would charge the field after a Wisconsin victory, and the June, 2000, Atlanta Braves/New York Mets baseball game that was John Rocker's first trip to New York after controversial remarks in a Sports Illustrated article. In each situation, there was the potential for a crisis and the likelihood of serious injury. In the University of Wisconsin situation, newspapers reported that University management increased uniformed security from about 55 to about 65 officers. The increase proved inadequate, resulting in more than 60 injuries. In contrast, the Mets and New York City increased the number of assigned officers from 60 to 560 (plus an unnamed number of plainclothes officers in the stands), the Mets placed a limit of two on the number of beers that could be purchased at one time, and the Mets constructed a chain-link fence to protect Rocker in the bullpen. As a result of the crisis management measures taken, there were no serious incidents, and consequently, the crisis was averted.

The potential for many crisis situations regularly confronts the recreation or sport manager. For example, an athletic director learns that one of his athletes just committed suicide. A fire breaks out in the gymnasium. A set of bleachers collapses injuring dozens of spectators. A coach is accused of sexual abuse (e.g., Jerry Sandusky, Penn State; Bernie Fine, Syracuse University) (Steinbach, 2012). An employee or athlete is arrested and charged with a crime. An active shooter or other act of terrorism (e.g., 2013 Boston Marathon bombings) occurs at a sport facility/event. Each of these situations constitutes a crisis situation. A common mistake that many sport or recreation managers make is thinking that they and their staff will automatically know what to do in the event of a crisis. However, in many crisis situations, there is no plan, and the staff does not know how to properly, quickly, and calmly react.

In recent years, crises have become a regular event for most organizations (Ashby & Diacon, 2000; Choi, Sung & Kim, 2010). According to a survey of intercollegiate athletic administrators, 93 percent of National Collegiate Athletic Association (NCAA) athletic departments experienced a crisis within the period studied (1999–2000), yet fewer than half of the respondents had written plans in place to deal with the crisis. Furthermore, only 22 percent of the athletic directors reported that they provided any crisis management training to their staffs (Syme, 2005). Approximately 40% of companies and organizations with either weak or non-existent crisis management plans that are impacted by a disaster will never reopen (Griffin, 2015). Having an established crisis philosophy and **Crisis Management Plan (CMP)** will prepare an organization in the event of an actual crisis. A comprehensive CMP will address major crisis risks ranging from fires, bleacher collapses, bomb threats, criminal activity, violent acts, litigation against the organization, and major power outages to environmental emergencies such as hurricanes and floods.

On a daily basis, numerous problems, incidents, and issues confront the recreation or sport manager. A medical emergency arises when a serious illness or injury occurs involving a participant, spectator, or staff member. Although such situations are important and may involve the utilization of an emergency medical plan, they typically do not constitute a crisis—unless they are improperly handled. Regular incidents require organizational resources to respond, but they are usually readily manageable, and normal business can still take place while the incident is dealt with. Nevertheless, these types of incidents can quickly escalate into crises if they are not brought under control, if there is significant media coverage, and/or if several resources are required from within, or from outside, the organization. Herman and Oliver (2001) defined a crisis as a sudden situation that threatens an organization's ability to survive: an emergency, a disaster, a catastrophe. A crisis may involve a death or injury, lost access to the use of facilities and/or equipment, disrupted or significantly diminished operations, unprecedented information demands, intense media scrutiny, and irreparable damage to an agency's reputation (p. 6).

Hermann (1972), whose definition is widely accepted in the literature, defined a **crisis** as a situation that incorporates three conditions: (1) a surprise to decision makers, (2) a threat to high-priority goals, and (3) a restricted amount of time available to respond. A crisis situation is generally an unforeseen situation that can be extensive in its scope of disruption and damages to the organization. Although a crisis may strike without warning, others may build over time. For example, the sudden accidental death of an athlete or employee may catch everyone in the organization by surprise. In other cases, the actions, or inactions, of key personnel may cause a crisis to come about slowly. In both examples, staff may claim they "never saw it coming." A crisis may result in extensive organizational damage that typically cannot be corrected very easily or quickly. Crises often threaten the organization's mission and reputation and can have an adverse effect on business, fund-raising, and overall public relations. Outside assistance is often necessary. The organization may even need to be closed for a period of time to reestablish services and repair damage.

In summary, crises have common characteristics. First, they are negative. Second, a crisis can create improper or distorted perceptions. Third, crises are almost always disruptive to the organization. Finally, a crisis typically takes the organization by surprise, placing the organization in a reactive mode. Therefore, having a crisis management plan is particularly important for smaller organizations because they often have fewer resources to draw from when a crisis erupts. The purpose of this chapter is to assist the recreation or sport manager in becoming more informed about crisis planning and management.

FUNDAMENTAL CONCEPTS

Crisis management, a subset of risk management, focuses on allowing the organization to achieve its mission under extraordinary circumstances. The primary goal in managing a crisis is public safety. Not addressing public safety can intensify the damage from a crisis (Coombs, 2007). Secondary goals are to prevent the crisis from damaging the organization's (1) ability to achieve its mission and goals, (2) reputation, and/or (3) finances. **Crisis management** is a process intended to prevent or reduce the damage a crisis can cause to an organization and its stakeholders (Coombs, 2007). Having a crisis management plan in place is critical because it facilitates the establishment of a unified organizational philosophy, thereby eliminating the need to decide how to respond and what to do during a crisis situation (Ajango, 2003). How an organization conducts itself during and after a crisis can mitigate the damage and its duration.

Crisis Management Plan

Every organization is at risk of facing a crisis. How and where a crisis occurs can seldom be controlled. What can be controlled is how an organization prepares, reacts, and responds. A key determinant of how well an organization will cope in the midst of a crisis is how well it addressed its crisis management plan (CMP) before the actual crisis occurs. The steps an organization takes months, or even years, prior to a crisis occurring may be as important as its immediate response to a crisis.

The primary goal of planning for crises is to develop comprehensive, written contingency plans based on currently existing resources and operational capabilities that will enable the organization to effectively deal with crises. CMPs cannot be copied from a book or from plans developed by other organizations, but rather must be specifically developed for each and every program. Every program has unique factors that must be considered. However, several basic components should form the foundation of CMPs.

A piece that is commonly missing or overlooked when developing CMPs lies in the relationship between the overall CMP and the organization's core values. Whether an organization wants to set, and present, a tone of open communication, care, and concern or one of quiet toughness, the long-term strategy will be a reflection of the organization's values. If employees at all levels do not agree with, or are not aware of, the philosophy behind the CMP, there is a high probability that the plan will not proceed smoothly once it is put into action. Perhaps one of the worst possible things that can happen to an organization undergoing a crisis is for an unexpected lack of agreement on core philosophies to surface. To avoid this pitfall, an organization should prioritize its intent and objectives regarding its CMP. There should be a stated purpose behind the plan, specifically as it relates to the organization's mission and philosophy. Well before a crisis occurs, CMP decision makers should freely discuss how a post-accident investigation would be conducted. Various opinions should be carefully considered. Several other questions should also be carefully considered prior to developing a CMP. Are the needs of victims a priority? Are employees' opinions secondary? Will legal ramifications drive the plan, or is public reputation more of a concern? It is important to discuss these issues and identify the organization's philosophy and goals prior to the onset of a crisis (Ajango, 2003).

Developing the Plan

The initial step in developing and writing a CMP is to **formulate a planning committee** who will begin the process. Awareness is the initial step to preparedness, and a crucial step in crisis planning is identification. Once the organization's philosophy and goals as they relate to managing a crisis are identified, the committee's primary task is to **identify the significant possible risks and crises** that may arise in their organization. The committee should scrutinize the core functions of the organization to identify and, in many cases, reduce or eliminate risks that could cast the organization into crisis mode. Examples of such crises may include an incident or event that would potentially result in serious injury or death, result in litigation, deter customers or otherwise impair income, impair the organization's ability to meet its core operating expenses, render the organization unable to deliver core services, or garner negative publicity and/or media attention resulting in the death of the organization.

Crisis risks can be categorized into avoidable (preventable) and unavoidable (unpreventable). Avoidable crisis risks may include actual or alleged client/participant maltreatment, service or product failure, severe injuries or death, transportation-related mishaps, and criminal conduct. Unavoidable crisis risks may include natural disasters (hurricanes, tornadoes, floods, wildfires, etc.), bomb threats, hazardous material incidents, terrorist attacks, and utility failures (Herman & Oliver, 2001). Although an organization may not be able to prevent these events from occurring, they can identify which ones are inherent to their area and are more likely to strike and then take steps to be as prepared as practically and reasonably possible to cope with the events if they occur.

Once crisis risks are identified, similar to a risk assessment, a **crisis assessment** is performed. However, instead of broadly focusing on any potential risk, a crisis assessment highlights the risks that would put the organization into crisis mode. Therefore, situations that could severely jeopardize the organization's credibility and/or resources should be the focus. Similar to classifying risks (see Chapter 4.11, *Risk Management Process*), potential crises should be individually assigned frequency and severity ratings. A frequency rating estimates how often this crisis may occur. A severity rating is based on how damaging to the organization the crisis would be if it does occur. Looking at the two ratings, an organization can determine its greatest risks (see Table 4.11.1, Risk Category Matrix, in Chapter 4.11, *Risk Management Process*).

The next step is to develop an **action plan for crisis response** for each major crisis risk that may confront the organization. An action plan is a document that details carefully considered courses of action. These alternatives can be selected when a crisis occurs. Herman and Oliver (2001) suggest keeping the format simple and easy to read, using short sentences and bulleted phrases, using flowcharts to indicate responsibilities and actions, including boxes that can be checked when the task is completed, and using tabs for quick access.

When developing such plans, identify all resources that may be needed in each crisis situation. Consider resources in the immediate area. Contact the local/state offices of the Federal Emergency Management Agency (FEMA), U.S. Department of Education, American Red Cross, local hospital, police and fire departments, and emergency medical services. Determine how they respond to crisis and how they may be able to assist your organization (Schirick, 2002).

Developing an action plan answers the crucial question: "What will we do if a crisis occurs?" In some cases, aspects of an organization's action plans may be identical, regardless of the cause, or source, of the crisis. For instance, a uniform step in an action plan may be contacting an insurance broker. In other cases, specific crises may require unique, specific responses. A beginning point for formulating action plans is to revisit the major crisis risks initially identified. The following sections present several components that should be considered as general guidelines when developing action plans.

Personnel Issues. There are two phases to personnel preparation. The first involves actions to be taken by the frontline leader (the person(s) in charge of the activity when the crisis occurs). Personnel should be educated on what immediate steps to follow (e.g., calling 911, activating the CMP). The second phase of personnel preparation involves subsequent actions to take in the crisis situation. The action plan should identify, by job title, those employees who will handle, or actively assist with, the crisis. Specific duties and responsibilities of each responder should be outlined in a simple and very clear format. The action plan should account for personnel trained to render emergency care, communication procedures, an incident reporting system, and a follow-up approach. In addition, personnel should know how to address the ongoing cause of the crisis (e.g., a gunman, terrorist, fire). They should know whom to contact for assistance (see Chapter 2.33, *Emergency Care*).

When developing the action plan and addressing the preceding components, input from various organizational levels and other affected agencies should be solicited. Both managerial and frontline staff should be consulted as well as athletes/participants and outside agencies, including groups such as local EMS, fire and police departments, legal counsel, crisis planning and management consultants, and the organization's insurance company.

Facility Issues. The location of emergency exits and shelters; gas, power, and water shutoff valves; alarm systems; backup power systems; main electrical panels; and fire hoses/extinguishers should be clearly identified. Location(s) for meeting EMS and other authorities (e.g., police, fire, and utility personnel) should be identified. Evacuation procedures should also be developed.

Emergency Equipment Issues. Identify the type of equipment available (e.g., public address and communication equipment, firefighting equipment, first aid kits, automated external defibrillators). Identify where each is stored and who will access it.

Communication Issues. Two major aspects of effective communication are necessary. The first involves the **immediate notification of the proper authorities** (e.g., police, medical personnel, mental health personnel). Designate who makes such calls and in what order. It is important to identify and get to know outside experts who will work side by side with your organization in a crisis. During a crisis is not the time to meet these key people. Train staff as to where and how to make emergency communications. The location of telephones and other communication devices should be specified, and emergency phone numbers should be identified. Finally, keeping communication channels open is vitally important during a crisis.

The second aspect of effective communications involves the need to **quickly communicate with constituencies**. For example, an athletic director may need to communicate with EMS, law enforcement, victims and their families, parents of athletes, school officials and other employees, professionals who can provide crisis counseling and other support, news media, and possibly others following a riot incident at a sporting event. Before the crisis occurs the following should be considered.

- Who will need to be contacted in the event of a crisis?
- What is the best method for communication during a crisis? Consider social media, email, Internet, telephone, broadcast fax, news conference, public address system, intercom, pagers, etc.
- What backup systems are available if the primary means of communication is compromised?
- Is the list of personnel who would need to be contacted readily available to more than one staff member?
- Who is responsible for communication during a crisis—one person or a group of people? (Herman & Oliver, 2001).

A crucial factor is **communication with the news media**. It is often the adverse publicity, rather than the actual damage from the crisis itself, that severely damages the organization. Therefore, a preassigned, trained spokesperson should contact the media at the earliest possible time. When speaking to these parties, the spokesperson should stick to the basic facts (e.g., type of crisis, which medical facility the victim was transported to, number of victims) and never assign or admit fault. The medical staff that provides care should only furnish medical or fatality information. Questions regarding insurance should be answered by the insurance agent/company. Finally, questions regarding liability should be addressed by the organization's risk management department or legal counsel. The staff should also be instructed not to speak to anyone regarding the incident unless approval has been obtained from the designated spokesperson. All requests for information should be immediately directed to the designated spokesperson. (For more on dealing with the media, see the following section.)

Documentation. Determine when and who completes what reports. Assigned personnel should know how to complete them and to whom they should be sent. Establish policies for filing and retaining reports.

Follow-up Procedures. There are several aspects to the follow-up procedures. First, it is necessary for the media spokesperson to follow up with the media. Depending on the crisis and its impact, there may need to be a follow-up with the victims, their families, classmates, colleagues, teammates, and/or friends, as well as with employees. Finally, it is important that the CMP be evaluated and modified where necessary.

Forming a Crisis Response Team

A small team should be formed to coordinate an organization's response to a crisis. This team needs to be formed and trained *before* a crisis occurs. Proper training will allow the team to react more calmly, effectively, and efficiently. The makeup of the crisis response team will vary depending on a number of factors, including the size of the organization, the nature of the services provided by the organization, the likely sources of crisis in the organization, and the organization's prior experience responding to a crisis. The makeup of the team may include the executive director, department heads, senior staff members, physical plant/building superintendent, board members, legal counsel, and outside advisors.

Practicing the Plan

Although responses to certain crises cannot be easily rehearsed, others can be simulated, practiced, or simply discussed to enhance readiness for an actual crisis and to identify any flaws in the action plans. When feasible, the plan should be tested in conditions as close to real life as possible. When flaws are noticed, the plans should be modified accordingly. Every time an organization conducts a CMP drill, key personnel involved should do a brief review of the exercise. Documentation of the review should be maintained by the organization. In between major drills, in-service training and tabletop exercises keep the strategies and process fresh in the minds of staff (Herman & Oliver, 2001; James, 2008).

Surviving a Crisis

The first step in addressing a crisis is to recognize and acknowledge it may be occurring. Oftentimes, individuals in organizations have different perceptions of when a crisis is at hand. It is important to recognize the signs of a crisis so the CMP has the best chance of working effectively.

Activating the Plan

Once a crisis has been recognized, the plan should be followed. According to Herman and Oliver (2001), the team leader should contact the crisis response team and attempt to answer the following questions.

- What has occurred?
- Who has been affected by the events thus far? Who are the known victims?
- What steps have been taken to control the crisis? Who has done what?
- Is the media aware of the crisis? Are we prepared to give a statement?

The crisis response team should discuss and carefully decide what steps need to be taken to:

- Provide and/or arrange care or support for the victims
- Notify key personnel
- Respond to media inquiries
- Brief the staff and key constituents of the organization
- Ensure continued service delivery or coordinate transfer to another provider

- Secure important documents, files, computer backups, etc.
- Ensure that the communication systems are up and operating

Proper Crisis Communication

One of the most important aspects of handling a crisis is communication. How an organization communicates with key constituents, responds to inquiries and criticisms, handles the media, and tells its story may very well determine its survival. A failed communications strategy can be disastrous for any organization. All communication during a crisis should be carefully considered and orchestrated. Whether it is directed to an internal or external audience and whether it is written, visual, or verbal, extra care should be taken when crafting messages. Seymour and Moore (2000) recommended applying the "Five Cs" to crisis communication.

1. **Care.** The public is often very reluctant to forgive a lack of compassion from an organization whose programs or services caused harm. An effective spokesperson is one who can express empathy and care with conviction and sincerity.
2. **Commitment.** The organization's message should clearly indicate that it is committed to investigating the incident and preventing future occurrences.
3. **Consistency.** A clear plan of how the organization will respond and what its spokesperson will say ensures a consistent message.
4. **Coherence.** It is important to be clear, be concise, and stick to the facts.
5. **Clarity.** Because the opportunity to convey a message may be slim and come without warning, it is vital to avoid jargon, technical terms, and other language that may confuse the listener.

Since communication is essential when managing a crisis, it has been recommended that schools with Sport Information Departments include such staff as part of crisis planning and response teams (McKindra, 2009). Sports information professionals are valuable campus assets who can help when communicating with the university community, staff, fans, and the media.

Use of Social Media in Crisis Management

For sport managers, social media can be a tool for managing a crisis or the instrument used to create a crisis that requires management. Social media communications in disaster situations have been shown to enhance situational awareness through the conveyance of social media broadcasts during a crisis situation (Vieweg, 2012). In order to make proper use of social media and control for problems caused by the medium, it is critical that sport managers stay current in communicative technologies, understand how social media is used, and stay current in communicative advances in technology. An important consideration in developing a CMP is the role social media will likely play. Recent sport-related crises (e.g., 2013 Boston Marathon), have demonstrated the importance of social media, not just in delivering timely information during a crisis but also strengthening relationships among stakeholders (e.g., EMS, media, customers, local community, general public).

An example of social media's potential use in managing crisis can be found in how it was used to locate earthquake victims in Haiti. On January 12, 2010, the worst earthquake in 200 years, a 7.0 in magnitude, occurred near the Haitian town of Port-au-Prince. The quake collapsed Haiti's communication infrastructure, impeding the rescue efforts of responders. Social media filled in for the traditional means of communication. Responders relied on social media. Twitter was used as a prime resource for communication and relief efforts were organized through both Google and Facebook (Palmer, 2010).

Social media may also be an effective mode of communication when satellite and cellular phones are not effectively working as was the case immediately following the 2013 Boston Marathon bombings. However, social media communications during crises have increased to the point that managers must now sift through hundreds of thousands, perhaps millions, of data points to find the most useful information during an event (Imran, Castillo, Diaz, & Vieweg, 2015). For this reason, sport managers need to consider developing policies and investing in proper technologies needed to maximize informational gains from data sourcing via social media during a crisis.

Sport managers have also made use of social media in responding to problems at their events. For example, both college and professional sports have made use of "**tattle texting**", a policy that provides patrons with a phone number that can be used to text complaints concerning unruly fans or other problems with the facility (e.g., being stuck in an elevator) (Reilly, n.d.). Patrons can use this service to text facility managers of problems that are occurring within the venue that require the attention from security officers or other facility personnel. This can help prevent a relatively minor problem from erupting into a major problem or crisis situation.

Social media can also be used by sport managers for crowdsourcing after a crisis (Stephens, 2011). **Crowdsourcing** is the term used to describe the process of distributing tasks to a crowd of people. During a crisis, social media serves as a valuable means for sport managers looking for immediate information from constituents concerning the crisis. After a crisis, sport managers could look to posts and pictures on Twitter, Facebook, and other social media forums to identify areas for improvement so as to better handle future crises. As communication technologies continue to advance and expand in use, so will the means for using these technologies to assist sport managers charged with the responsibility of managing crisis.

While social media has the potential to help in managing a crisis, it can also be the instrument used to create a crisis. Social media has been used by sport consumers to say things about the sport organization or sport facility that impact consumption and have the potential for instigating a crisis situation. For example, a person could post unflattering comments on a sports blog, on Yelp.com, or on Facebook about a sport organization that influences consumer opinion concerning the organization. It is important that sport managers understand that statements made on social media can be used to harm an organization's brand. Thus, sport managers should have a strategy for addressing a potential social media crisis. Henry (2010) advises managers to address rather than ignore the problem, utilize contacts in the media to counter the problem, be honest with consumers, and refrain from using "hot" language in any response. Also, managers should assign a point person to handle the matter until it subsides and continue to gauge consumer response by monitoring social media. Finally, when managing a crisis, it is critical to have experienced, dedicated staff monitoring all forms of electronic communication and social media (Roledo, Traylor, & Yu, 2013).

Dealing with the News Media

Organizations should educate designated spokespersons who will work with the news media during a crisis situation. This aspect of the CMP should address the following details.

- Who decides what information is released?
- Who speaks for the organization/releases materials to media? Typically one spokesperson should be designated. A central spokesperson provides a singular face for the media with whom the public becomes familiar. Centralized information also minimizes miscommunication. Backup spokespeople should be designated in the event that the central spokesperson is unavailable or is the subject of the crisis.
- Which members of the news media should be notified in a crisis?
- What are the phone numbers of key media people?
- What are the logistical details including locations where press conferences can be held; phone lines that media can use to call in; backup power supplies; parking area for the media; and what support staff is available to assist.

Preparations for a timely, accurate, and appropriate response must begin at the first sign of a potential crisis involving an organization, whether before or after exposure in the news media. News media will expect and demand an immediate response. In an effort to reduce panic and build trust, the sooner an organization is able to provide or relay accurate information, the better it is (Marinelli, 2015). If the organization does not provide an immediate response, others will. Others may provide inaccurate information, or may try to use the opportunity to attack the organization. Therefore, crisis managers must have a timely response (Coombs, 2007). An excellent example of providing the public with a timely response occurred after the 2013 Boston Marathon bombings. Within hours after the bombings, the public was kept informed via several press briefings provided by a collection of public officials. These collaborative presentations across several agencies presented a strong image of unified goals and coordinated actions. The briefings were factual, avoided speculation, and emphasized both what was known and what was not. They were direct, succinct, and calmly presented. During a time of great uncertainty and emotional turmoil, these presentations could not diminish all fears or provide all desired answers, but they were a calming and grounding influence that helped the public develop a more consistent and accurate set of shared facts (Leonard & Howitt, 2013).

A decision on whether a news conference and/or release would be an appropriate means of conveying information to the news media and public must be made. What means of internal communication will be used if the crisis affects employees and participants should also be determined. At the earliest possible stage, advise staff members of the situation. Give clear instructions regarding handling the media and telephone calls and alert them that they may be called to perform special duties related to the incident. Discuss alternative or additional means of conveying information. This might include such items as letters to parents, clients, or fans, letters to newspaper editors, or consultation with boards. Use of the Internet, websites, and social media can also help to provide a quick response.

Information files should be set up to contain all materials related to the incident. Internet, newspapers and television reports should be scanned daily for related stories. If necessary, arrange for videotaping of any TV coverage. Related material, including clippings, statements, memos, and any other documents should be filed in chronological order. Plan to frequently update employees and administrators on the status of the incident. Conduct a follow-up assessment to determine what did and did not work, and what changes might be made in the future for improved media relations during a crisis.

Guidelines for the Media Contact Person

Several strategies exist that will make dealing with the media as positive as possible. In any crisis, try to find out as much information as possible. That way, you avoid inadvertently saying the wrong thing or sending unintended messages.

The following are seventeen guidelines for dealing with the media.

1. Always return media calls, even if they call repeatedly and/or are hostile. Ignoring them will not make the problem disappear. The more cooperative you appear, the better.
2. Occasionally, a media representative will make a special request. If possible and if it does not violate the CMP, an effort should be made to accommodate reasonable requests.
3. Avoid antagonizing media representatives. A sharp tone at a press conference, during a telephone call, or elsewhere may affect your relationship with that individual and with others who may hear the conversation.
4. Try to remain levelheaded at all times when speaking to the media. Some of their questions may seem hostile or may seem like a personal attack. It must be remembered that they are trying to get as much information as possible on a crisis-oriented story that may have widespread impact to their audiences.
5. Refrain from getting mad or taking it personally when asked tough questions.
6. Always try to have an answer for reporters' questions and always tell the truth. However, never be afraid to say, "I don't know, but I'll find out."
7. Avoid using "no comment." Doing so often makes it appear that you have something to hide.
8. Additionally, stay "on the record" in all interviews. Any comment worth stating should be said "on the record." If you go "off the record," be prepared to hear or read it. Although it is unethical for reporters to report "off the record" comments, anything can, may, and will be done to advance a story.
9. Consider how information you release may affect others. If things you say will result in the media calling other organizations or individuals, call those individuals first to alert them to the information.
10. When speaking to the media, be sure to credit other agencies or individuals assisting with the crisis, including your staff. This enhances relationships and reflects well on you.
11. Try to be proactive with new information. If you acquire new information regarding the crisis advise the media.
12. When communicating with the media and/or the public, accurate information is important. People desire correct information about what occurred and how it may affect them. Due to the time pressure associated with a crisis response, there is a risk of providing inaccurate information. Incorrect statements can make an organization appear incompetent and/or inconsistent (Coombs, 2007). Admit when a

mistake has been made and correct it as soon as possible. This is often the first step to reestablishing confidence and credibility with the public and key constituencies.
13. Maintaining a sense of humor is important, but inappropriate humor will work against you.
14. Professional dignity is very important, particularly in unpleasant times.
15. As the crisis progresses, take notes. They can help you remember things and may be useful for later review.
16. If you are on camera, always dress professionally. Casual or mussed clothing may send a signal to viewers that things are out of control.
17. Try to give yourself some downtime and stress reduction. Overwork and little sleep can lead to misstatements and irritability.

Debrief Employees and Others Affected

When a crisis results in serious injuries or death(s), stress and trauma counseling for employees and other victims must be made available (Coombs, 2007). Even when victims survive, there may still be emotions to deal with, particularly for first responders. There may be feelings of guilt; others may recall their initial reaction, panic, or response. Some may wonder if they could have done more (James, 2008).

Critical Incident Stress Management (CISM) is a specific seven-stage group crisis intervention technique that has been adapted and used by rescue, disaster, and health-care groups in different settings, programs, and industries (Everly & Mitchell, 1999). This technique is designed to bring "psychological closure" to groups of victims or witnesses after a traumatic event and ideally is implemented 24 hours after the end of someone's involvement with the event. A professional needs to facilitate the process where each participant describes the event that occurred, their reaction to the event, and its psychological impact. The participant then learns how to manage the related stress (Herman & Oliver, 2001).

Have plans for dealing with emotional and mental health needs of staff, classmates, teammates, or friends and family of the victim(s) (Bacon & Anderson, 2003). Have procedures for communicating with the immediate families of all victims. Some organizations may have psychologists or mental health professionals available for the victims and/or their families, whereas others may refer affected individuals to available, trained professionals. Prior relationships with such trained professionals can be very helpful in these situations.

Evaluate the Response

Once the crisis is over, an evaluation should occur in a timely fashion.

- First, consider and review why the crisis occurred. What, if anything, could have been done to prevent or limit the crisis?
- Next, **how soon was the crisis noticed and how was it handled** should be evaluated. What was done appropriately or inappropriately should be addressed.
- Were others who were involved or affected timely informed?
- How effective was the crisis response team? Were certain skills or talents missing in the makeup of the team?
- How was the action plan followed? Was it effective and useful? What could have been done better?
- Also, **similar scenarios** should be examined. For example, what would you do in a similar situation in the future?
- Does the plan need to be changed? If so, how? Revising CMPs is an ongoing process.
- Finally, **send notes of appreciation** to those who have been of service, outside and inside the organization, including your own staff.

Terrorism and Crisis Management

The tragic events of September 11, 2011, signaled the emergence of terrorism as a foreseeable threat that warrants the attention and diligence of sport and recreation managers (Baker, Connaughton, Zhang, & Spengler, 2007). Terrorists tend to select acts designed to destroy critical infrastructure and key assets, cause mass fatalities, weaken the economy, and damage the nation's morale and confidence (Arquilla, Ronfeldt, & Zanini, 1999). Terrorists could accomplish these goals with an effective and impactful attack on a sport facility. In fact, the

U.S Department of Homeland Security (DHS) identified sport stadia and events as likely terrorist targets due to their potential for mass casualties, widespread media coverage, and social impact. Sports events occur at set times and set locations, attract large crowds, and involve activities that Americans hold dear; thus, they serve as effective targets for acts of terror. Accordingly, it is imperative that those charged with managing the threat of terrorism at sport events and facilities exercise reasonable care under the circumstances to protect participants and spectators from this foreseeable threat.

Specifically, it is critical that sport managers create, implement, and practice terrorism-specific crisis management plans. These plans should involve safety and security measures aimed at preventing and managing a crisis produced by acts of terror. Studies conducted on terrorism management have found that sport managers charged with managing the risk of terrorism at sport events should: conduct risk assessments; develop emergency response plans; properly train personnel in dealing with terrorism; and implement physical protection, access control, and crisis communication systems (Schwarz, Hall, & Shibli, 2010). Terrorism management strategies must also be coordinated with all first and second responder agencies and organizations on the local, state, and federal levels (Hall, Byon, & Baker, 2013). This includes law enforcement, fire and hazardous material management (hazmat), and emergency medical care (Hall, Fos, Marciani, & Zhang, 2011). The benefits of advance planning and training for a mass casualty incident during a large mass-gathering event were never more apparent than in the response to the 2013 Boston Marathon bombings that killed three and injured more than 260 people. Local, state and federal agencies, nongovernmental organizations, marathon organizers, and private-sector partners in Boston developed plans that defined roles and responsibilities during the Marathon. These agencies also regularly conducted drills to test these plans to facilitate coordination and communication during large-scale events. These plans and drills contributed to Boston's level of preparedness and multi-agency response that otherwise would not have been possible following the bombings. According to Richard Serino, FEMA Deputy Administrator, "the fact that the response was so well executed wasn't an accident – it was a result of years of planning and coordination." (FEMA, 2013, p. 3)

In an effort to examine emergency preparations and assess the city, state and federal government's response to the 2013 Boston Marathon bombings, the U.S. Senate's *Committee of Homeland Security and Governmental Affairs* conducted a hearing in July, 2013. The very informative and complete transcript, entitled "Lessons learned from the Boston Marathon bombings: Preparing for and responding to the attack", is available at http://www.fdsys.gov/

Useful Websites for Crisis Management Information and Materials

The *Nonprofit Risk Management Center* has a significant number of references (resources, articles, tutorials, tests, fact sheets, links, etc.) available regarding risk and crisis management. Their website is located at: http://www.nonprofitrisk.org/

The *U.S. Department of Education* provides many crisis management-related educational materials including but not limited to: Crisis Planning Guide, Practical Information on Crisis Planning, Action Guide for Emergency Management at Institutions of Higher Education, and Tips for Helping Students Recovering from Traumatic Events. Their website is located at: http://www.ed.gov/admins/lead/safety/emergencyplan/index.html

The *International Association of Venue Managers* (IAVM) provides information, training, and certification on several crisis management issues including but not limited to: crowd management and venue safety and security. Their website is located at: http://www.iavm.org/.

The *Center for Safe Schools* provides professional development and training, technical assistance, and acts as a resource clearinghouse for materials that address violence prevention and school safety. Their website provides links to a model school crisis management plan, crisis communication guides and toolkit, and other related references. Their website is located at: http://www.safeschools.info/about

The *Federal Emergency Management Agency* (FEMA) provides information and training on disasters, planning for emergencies, and risk management. Their website is located at: http://www.fema.gov/.

The *National Center for Spectator Sports Safety and Security* (NCS4) supports the advancement of sport safety and security through training, professional development, academic programs, and research. Their website is located at: https://www.ncs4.com/.

SIGNIFICANT CASE

In the Significant Case that follows, the defendants had a CMP that proved to be inadequate. Despite knowing in advance that the students planned to charge the field following a victory, insufficient precautions were taken to prevent the students from charging the field. More than 60 injuries resulted. Newspaper reports revealed that many University officials made potentially damaging statements to the press following the crisis. One official, in an attempt to make the necessary corrections to avoid a duplicate disaster, stated, "We can't ignore any possibility about what could be done to prevent this. We have to sit down and find some answers." Problems that were investigated included overcrowding in the student section, duplicate tickets, students moving from their seats in other sections of the stadium to the student section, use of alcohol inside the stadium, whether students should be assigned to seats instead of general admission, and whether the entire student section should be moved or dispersed (Schultz, 1993). Despite the failure of the crisis management plan to prevent the disaster, no defendant was found liable for his or her actions or inactions due to governmental immunity.

ENEMAN V. RICHTER
Court of Appeals of Wisconsin, District Four
217 Wis. 2d 288; 577 N.W.2d 386
February 5, 1998, Released

OPINION: ROGGENSACK, J. The appellants alleged they suffered personal injuries after a University of Wisconsin football game at Camp Randall Stadium, which injuries they claim resulted from the negligence of David Ward, Patrick Richter, Susan Riseling, Michael Green and David Williams, while the respondents were employed by the State on behalf of the University of Wisconsin. Respondents moved for summary judgment, based on the common law doctrine of public officer immunity. The circuit court concluded there were no material factual disputes and dismissed the appellants' claims. Because we agree that the material facts are not in dispute and that the respondents are entitled to immunity, we affirm.

* * *

Background

This is a consolidated appeal of summary judgments dismissing the claims of the appellants, all of whom are alleged to have suffered personal injuries when they were crushed by persons attempting to come onto the playing field at Camp Randall Stadium after the 1993 Wisconsin/Michigan football game. They assert their injuries would not have occurred if certain gates had not been closed by security personnel at the conclusion of the game and that the closing of the gates constituted negligence. David Ward, Chancellor for the University of Wisconsin Madison; Patrick Richter, Athletic Director for the University of Wisconsin-Madison; Susan Riseling, Chief of Police and Security for the University of Wisconsin-Madison; Michael Green, Camp Randall Facilities and Events Coordinator; and David Williams, a University police officer in Riseling's department, were state governmental employees on the date of the appellants' alleged injuries. They filed an answer denying negligence, and based on their status as state governmental employees, they asserted the affirmative defense of discretionary immunity, on which they moved for summary judgment.

Camp Randall Stadium is the site used for football games and other outdoor events at the University of Wisconsin-Madison. The football field is encircled by a chain link fence with a walkway between the fence and the bottom row of bleachers. Ingress and egress of the bleachers varies, depending on the section of the stadium. Sections O and P are at issue in this lawsuit. The lower rows of sections O and P exit to the walkway and then through the home team tunnel. It was also possible for those rows to exit to the field itself, even though security personnel directed spectators not to do so.

Prior to the 1993 football season, access to the field was limited by hand held ropes, which provided no real barrier to a spectator determined to enter the field. In anticipation of the 1993 football season, the University installed metal gates that could be positioned to close off the walkway at the bottom of the bleachers in order to permit the team to exit the field into the tunnel without interference from the spectators. When the walkway was closed off by the gates, sections O and P spectators' means of egress was restricted, until the team had made its way through the tunnel and the gates were opened again.

On October 30, 1993, after the University of Wisconsin's football team defeated the University of Michigan's team at Camp Randall, many of the students in sections O and P attempted to come onto the playing field. However, a few minutes before the game's end, the gates had been closed and latched by security personal. This provided a significant barrier to the spectators' egress onto the field, and it also created a dead end for tunnel egress from sections O and P, at a time when spectators were moving down the bleachers to exit the stadium or to push onto the field. The appellants were crushed against a metal railing and the gates when security personnel were unable to quickly unlatch the gates to open them.

Ward and Richter had no personal responsibility to manage the crowd at the Camp Randall games. On the other hand, Riseling's, Green's and Williams's activities at Camp Randall were arguably within the scope of the Standard Operating Procedures for Camp Randall relating to crowd control. Additionally, prior to the Michigan game, and subsequent to the installation of the gates, Riseling knew that it was possible that the students might try to rush onto the field at the game's end. In response to this potential for congestion in the student sections, she formulated and issued a directive entitled, "POST GAME CROWD TACTICS," whose goal was "to prevent injury to people—officers, band members and fans." The plan outlined a general strategy to follow which, in her judgment, would have prevented injury. Although her plan was implemented by security personnel, it was not successful.

Discussion

* * * It is well established that this court applies the same summary judgment methodology as the circuit court. Smith v. Dodgeville Mut. Ins. Co., 212 Wis. 2d 226, 232, 568 N.W.2d 31, 34 (Ct. App. 1997). We first examine the complaint to determine whether it states a claim, and then we review the answer to determine whether it presents a material issue of fact or law. Id. If we conclude that the complaint and the answer are sufficient to join issue, we examine the moving party's affidavits to determine whether they establish a prima facie case for summary judgment. Id. If they do, we look to the opposing party's affidavits to determine whether there are any material facts in dispute which entitle the opposing party to a trial. Id. at 233, 568 N.W.2d at 34.

Whether immunity lies because of the common law doctrine of public officer immunity is a question of law which we review de novo. Kimps v. Hill, 200 Wis. 2d 1, 8, 546 N.W.2d 151, 155 (1996) (citing K.L. v. Hinickle, 144 Wis. 2d 102, 109, 423 N.W.2d 528, 531 (1988)). A question of law is also presented when we decide whether the safe place statute applies to this case. Ruppa v. American States Ins. Co., 91 Wis. 2d 628, 639, 284 N.W.2d 318, 322 (1979).

Public Officer Immunity

* * *

Based on the information before us, we assume, without deciding, that there was a compelling and known danger of injury of sufficient magnitude to create a ministerial duty to act for Riseling, as Chief of Police and Security, due to her knowledge of the possibility of a crowd surge onto the field. However, Riseling did not ignore the potential danger. She, with the assistance of others, formulated a plan, the "POST GAME CROWD TACTICS," the goal of which was "to prevent injury to people—officers, band members and fans."

The plan established no specific tasks that were to be performed at a time certain; rather, it made general statements and set general guidelines such as,

We expect that if Wisconsin wins today, especially if it is a close game, there will be an attempt by fans to come onto the field.

> If there is a crowd surge, officers at that point will make the initial decision to move aside and begin pulling back to the goalpost assignment. Lt. Johnson will be observing from the press box and will make decisions on giving the command for all officers to pull back.

There may be times during and after the game when people crowd the fence and put pressure against it. Actively encourage them to move back. If it seems there is danger of the fence breaking (it has in the past) move back to a safe position. * * * Here, the formation of the post-game crowd control plan represented Riseling's judgment about how best to reduce the potential for injury to persons at the game. "A discretionary act is one that involves choice or judgment." Kimps, 200 Wis. 2d at 23, 546 N.W.2d at 161 (citation omitted). Additionally, the implementation of the plan required Riseling, Green and Williams to respond to their assessment of what the crowd's actions required. By its very nature, the way the plan was effected had to change from moment to moment because the plan was responsive to the crowd. Reacting to the crowd also constituted the exercise of discretion. Furthermore, neither the documents nor the testimony contained in any of the portions of the depositions submitted in opposition to respondents' motion for summary judgment established a factual dispute about whether any specific acts were required of any of the respondents. Therefore, we conclude that the decision about what type of a plan to formulate to safely manage the crowd, as well as the implementation of the chosen plan, were discretionary, not ministerial, acts.

4. Non-governmental acts.

* * *

Here, documents provided in support of, and in opposition to, the respondents' motion for summary judgment establish no inconsistency between the actions of those respondents whose job duties took them personally into crowd control management activities, and the University's policy of safe management of the crowd at football games. Rather, they acted in accord with the General Operating Procedures for Camp Randall Stadium. Neither the formulation of the plan nor the implementation of it required highly technical, professional skills, such as a physician's. Therefore, we conclude that the respondents' activities were governmental in nature and we decline to extend the exception to immunity found in Gordon in this context.

* * *

CONCLUSION

Because the appellants have submitted no evidentiary facts from which we could conclude that the respondents had ministerial duties which they failed to perform and because neither the safe place statute nor any other theory of liability put forth by the appellants applies to the respondents, we affirm the summary judgment dismissing appellants' claims against the respondents.

By the Court.—Judgment affirmed.

CASES ON THE SUPPLEMENTAL WEBSITE

Kleinknecht v. Gettysburg College (1993 U.S. App. LEXIS 6609). The reader should pay particular attention to the defendants' response to Kleinknecht's collapse on the field. How could they have been better prepared for such a crisis?

Mogabgab v. Orleans Parish School Board (1970 La. App. LEXIS 5219). Carefully review the coaches' response to this medical emergency. What should they have done differently?

Cater et al. v. City of Cleveland (1998 Ohio LEXIS 2212). Pay special attention to the defendant's lack of proper training and practice in how to call the emergency medical services. How did this affect the outcome of the crisis and lawsuit?

Dibartolomeo v. New Jersey Sports and Exposition Authority (2011, N.J. Super. LEXIS 345). While this case primarily deals with dangerous conditions and premises liability, note how the New Jersey Sports Authority handled crowd management after the manifestation of the dangerous condition. How can sport/recreation managers properly protect patrons from dangerous conditions when the primary means for ingress and egress are not functioning properly?

Maussner v. Atlantic City Country Club (1997 N.J. Super. LEXIS 155). Notice that Court noted the Country Club did not have a written "evacuation plan" for inclement weather nor was it posted anywhere at the Club. How could the Club have been better prepared for lightning? How can sport/recreation managers best plan for the dangers associated with inclement weather?

QUESTIONS YOU SHOULD BE ABLE TO ANSWER

1. Explain what is meant by the term "crisis."

2. Identify several possible crises that could affect a specific local recreation or sport business.

3. Identify and explain the main components of a Crisis Management Plan (CMP).

4. Search for examples of CMPs for recreation or sport management-related organizations/facilities on the Internet. Review them and identify their strengths and weaknesses.

5. Explain several ways you would practice different aspects of a CMP. How would you evaluate your response to a crisis?

REFERENCES

Case
Eneman v. Richter, 577 N.W.2d 386; 1998 Wisc. App.

Publications
Ajango, D. (2003). The ultimate goal in crisis response. In *Recreation & Adventure Program Law Conference Proceedings*. Vail, CO. p. C1–6.

Arquilla, J., Ronfeldt, D., & Zanini, M. (1999). Networks, netwar, and information-age terrorism. In Lesser, I.O., Hoffman, B., Arquilla, J., Ronfeldt, D., & Zanini, M. *Countering the new terrorism* (pp. 39–84). Santa Monica, CA: Rand Corporation.

Ashby, S., & Diacon, S. (2000). Strategic rivalry and crisis management. *Risk Management, 2*(2), 715.

Bacon, V. L. & Anderson, M. K. (2003). Crisis interventions for sport related incidents. *The Sport Journal, 6*(4). Retrieved December 15, 2005 from http://www.thesportjournal.org/2003Journal/Vol6-No4/crisis.asp

Baker, T.A., Connaughton, D.P., Zhang, J.J., & Spengler, J.O. (2007). Perceived risk of terrorism and related risk management practices of NCAA Division 1A football stadium managers. *Journal of Legal Aspects of Sport, 17*(1), 27-51.

Cheley, D. (1997, Spring). *Crisis at camp . . . What do we do now*? Paper presented at American Camping Association Mid-States Conference.

Choi, J. N., Sung, S. Y., & Kim, M. U. (2010). How do groups react to unexpected threats? Crisis management in organizational teams. *Social Behavior and Personality, 36*(6), 805–826.

CNN/Sports Illustrated. (2002, November 24). *That kind of Fiesta. . .. Postgame fires, car damage leads to 45 arrests of OSU fans*. Associated Press. Retrieved March 25, 2009 from http://sportsillustrated.cnn.com/football/college/news/2002/11/23/rowdy_fans_ap

Coombs, W.T. (2007). *Ongoing crisis communication: Planning, managing, and responding* (2nd ed.). Los Angeles: Sage.

Coombs, W.T. (2007, October 30). *Crisis management and communications*. Gainesville, FL: Institute for Public Relations. Retrieved March 20, 2009 from http://www.instituteforpr.org/essential_knowledge/detail/crisis_management_and_communications

Everly, G.S., & Mitchell, J.T. (1999). *Critical incident stress management: CISM, A new era and standard of care in crisis intervention* (2nd ed.). Elliot City, MD: Chevron Publishing.

Federal Emergency Management Agency (FEMA). (2013). Boston Marathon bombings: The positive effect of planning and preparation on response. *FEMA*. Retrieved January 4, 2016 from https://www.hsdl.org/

Griffin, J. (2015, April 13). Lessons learned from the Boston Marathon bombing. *Security InfoWatch*. Retrieved January 2, 2016 from http://www.securityinfowatch.com/article/12063830/lessons-learned-from-the-boston-marathon-bombing

Hall, S. A., Byon, K. K., & Baker, T. A. (2013). Managing the threat of terrorism in sport: Importance and performance analysis (IPA) of safety and security preparedness for NCAA sport facilities. *International Journal of Sport Management, 14*(4), 479-501.

Hall, S., Fos, P., Marciani, L., & Zhang, L. (2011). Multiple criteria decision making (MCDM) application in evaluating protective security measures for major sport events. *International Journal of Sport Management, 12*, 191–207.

Henry, L. (2010). Surviving a social networking crisis. *PR News*. Retrieved on January 1, 2012 from http://www.prnewsonline.com/prinsiders/Surviving-a-Social-Networking-Crisis_14077.html

Herman, M. L. & Oliver, B. B. (2001). *Vital signs: Anticipating, preventing and surviving a crisis in a nonprofit*. Washington, DC: Nonprofit Risk Management Center.

Hermann, C. F. (1972). *International crises: Insights from behavioral research*. New York: Free Press.

Imran, M., Castillo, C., Diaz, F., & Vieweg, S. (2015). Processing social media messages in mass emergency: A survey. *ACM Computing Surveys (CSUR), 47*(4), 67.

James, M. (2008, October). Sudden death at a fitness center. *Fitness Management*. Retrieved March 20, 2009 from http://fitnessmanagement.com/articles/article.aspx?articleid=2505&zoneid=28

Leonard, H.D. & Howitt, A.M. (2013, April 20). Preliminary thoughts and observations on the Boston Marathon bombings. Boston, MA: Harvard University. Retrieved December 2, 2015 from http://ksghauser.harvard.edu/index.php/content/download/67375/1242310/version/1/file/Leonard+and+Howitt_Boston+Marathon_Preliminary+Thoughts+HBL+AMH+2013+04+22+v3.pdf

Marinelli, V. (2015, December). Social media's role in crisis management. *Athletic Business*. Retrieved January 10, 2016 from http://www.athleticbusiness.com/web-social/social-media-s-role-in-crisis-management.html

McKindra, L. (2009, August 31). SIDs asked to be in the crisis-management loop. *The NCAA News*. Indianapolis: NCAA.

National Incident Management System. (2004). U.S. Department of Homeland Security. Washington D.C.

Palmer, J. (2010). Social networks and the web offer a lifeline in Haiti. *BBC mobile news*. Retrieved January 1, 2012 from http://news.bbc.co.uk/2/hi/8461240.stm

Reilly, R. (n.d.). Unruly fans, your days are done. Big Brother is watching. *ESPN The Magazine, Life of Reilly*. Retrieved December 28, 2012 from http://sports.espn.go.com/espnmag/story?id=4012452

Robledo, R., Traylor, N., & Yu, R. (2013, November/December). Surviving a crisis. *Aquatics International, 25*(10), 22-26, 50.

Seymour, M. & Moore, S. (2000). *Effective crisis management: Worldwide principles and practice*. New York: Cassell.

Schirick, E. (2002, March). Risk management and crisis response are you prepared? *Camping Magazine*. Retrieved March 20, 2009 from http://www.acacamps.org/campmag/rm023risk.php

Schwarz, E. C., Hall, S., & Shibli, S. (2010). *Sport Facility Operations Management: A Global Perspective*. Oxford, United Kingdom: Butterworth-Heinemann.

Schultz, R. (1993, November 1). Richter looks for solutions. *The Capital Times*, p. B1.

Steinbach, P. (2012, February). College coaches on the front lines of crisis management. *Athletic Business*. http://athleticbusiness.com/articles/article.aspx?articleid=3838&zoneid=38

Stephens, K. (2011). How can university emergency managers use social media? *Idisaster 2.0*. Retrieved on December 27, 2011 from http://idisaster.wordpress.com/2011/08/12/how-can-universities-use-social-media-for-emergency-management/

Stoldt, G. C., Miller, L. K., Ayres, T. D., & Comfort, P. G. (2000). Crisis management planning: A necessity for sport managers. *International Journal of Sport Management, 4*, 253–266.

Syme, C. (2005, January 17). Writing about crisis best way to avert one. *The NCAA News Online*. Retrieved March 20, 2009 from http://www.ncaa.org/wps/ncaa?ContentID=5760

USA Today. (2003, January 3). *Hello, Columbus*, p. C13. AP Wire.

U.S. Department of Education. (2009). *Emergency Planning*. Retrieved March 21, 2009 from http://www.ed.gov/admins/lead/safety/emergencyplan/index.html

Vieweg, S. (2012). Situational awareness in mass emergency: A behavioral and linguistic analysis of microblogged communications. Ph.D. Dissertation. University of Colorado at Boulder.

CROWD MANAGEMENT

Robin Ammon, Jr. | University of South Dakota
Nita Unruh | University of Nebraska/Kearney

4.24

Recreation, sport, and entertainment events share a number of common factors. First, each involves some type of activity. The activity may range from your state high school basketball tournament to the Bonnaroo Music and Arts Festival in Manchester, Tennessee. Second, all of these events are held in or at some type of venue. The venues take on numerous forms such as stadiums, arenas, swimming pools, golf courses, parks, and ski areas. Third, all of these events will entail numerous risks that could result in personal and/or financial loss. Examples of these risks include simple slip & falls, vandalism, fights among spectators, or an active shooter. The final similarity among these events is that, in most cases, they involve a crowd. A **crowd** is a group of individuals who gather to involve themselves in some specific event. A major element in providing a safe, entertaining, and valuable experience for the consumer is effective crowd management. This chapter will discuss the development of crowd management and modern techniques of effective crowd management.

FUNDAMENTAL CONCEPTS

A facility or event manager has a duty to provide as safe and secure an environment as possible. Crowd management was classified by van der Smissen (1990) as part of the duty facility managers owe to their patrons to protect them from unreasonable risk of harm from themselves or other individuals. Others have defined crowd management as a tool to assist facility or event managers in providing a safe and enjoyable environment for their guests by implementing the facility/event policies and procedures (Ammon, Southall & Nagel, 2016). A crowd manager's responsibilities include managing the movement and activities of the crowd/guests (*e.g.*, searching fans as they enter the facility), assisting with potentially dangerous situations (*e.g.*, preventing exuberant fans from storming the field of play or throwing objects on the field of play), and aiding guests with specific concerns related to their enjoyment and/or involvement with the event (*e.g.*, investigating a fan's text message pertaining to a potentially dangerous, intoxicated spectator).

Why is Crowd Management Important?

A facility manager has a legal duty to provide a reasonably safe environment (Seidler, 2005). Failure to meet this duty can result in legal liability for both the facility and the manager provided the incident was foreseeable. If the risk was not foreseeable, there can be no liability.

Foreseeability

As defined by Black (2011) foreseeability is the "The quality of being reasonably anticipatable." (p. 319). If the sport or recreation facility manager fails to foresee a crowd-related incident that would have been foreseen by a reasonable, prudent facility manager, injuries resulting from the incident leave the organization and manager vulnerable to a lawsuit. Therefore a prudent facility manager will need to anticipate rather than react (see also Chapter 2.11 *Negligence*).

Foreseeability, however, is not as clear as it once was. Due to the litigious nature of our society, individuals at various events *expect* to be kept safe no matter the risk. The plaintiff in *Cohen v Sterling Mets* (2007) was a vendor in the stands at Shea Stadium who was injured by a spectator scrambling for a t-shirt that had been launched into the stands during a between-the-innings promotional give-away. A public address announcement regarding the giveaway had been made prior to the promotion and security was present. Nevertheless, the vendor felt he should be compensated for his injuries. In 2010, another situation involving a promotion occurred when a plaintiff sued "Sluggerrr", the mascot of the KC Royals. The mascot had been shooting foiled wrapped hotdogs into the stands when one of them hit the plaintiff in the face. John Coomer, the plaintiff maintained that the Royals were negligent in failing to train the mascot on how to shoot the hotdogs. The Kansas State Supreme Court agreed with the plaintiff and found that the risk of being hit by a thrown hotdog was not an inherent risk to the game of baseball (*Coomer v Kansas City Baseball Corporation*, 2014). In both of these situations, the likelihood of injury should have been foreseeable by management.

The United States is not the only country with dangerous crowds. A variety of sporting events around the world have witnessed tragedy and death. In the United Kingdom the most famous incident took place in 1989 during a soccer match at Hillsborough stadium. Ninety-six spectators perished when too many spectators were allowed into an already full seating area at one end of the stadium. Two years later at Emirate Airlines Park in Johannesburg, South Africa, 43 fans were killed and 160 were injured during another soccer match. During a World Cup qualifying game between South Africa and Zimbabwe in 2000, bottles and other projectiles were thrown onto the field by incensed fans. As a result uniformed police officials, who had been hired to work the event, fired tear gas at the fans. Twelve spectators were killed as fans tried to evade the noxious fumes (Shaw, 2000). A similar situation occurred nine years later when 22 spectators were killed and over 130 were injured when agitated police officers fired tear gas into a crowd of unruly spectators during a World Cup qualifying match in Ivory Coast (Ammon & Surujlal, 2011). In February, 2012, more than 70 Egyptian soccer fans perished after hundreds of fans rushed the field following a match between two heated rivals. Reports surfaced after the tragedy that riot police had been told not to become involved as a result of previous sectarian violence (Fayed & Perry, 2012).

The results of an ineffective crowd management plan can also produce catastrophic results during non-sporting events. Therefore sport and recreation managers need to be aware of the distinct interaction between foreseeability and crowd management. For example, during a Black Friday event in 2008, a large crowd of frenzied New York shoppers at a Long Island Walmart trampled a security employee to death during the early morning hours of the biggest shopping day of the year. Walmart executives stated they could not have anticipated such a tragic incident. However, they expected a large number of early shoppers and employed additional outsourced crowd management staff, scheduled extra internal security and store associates, as well as used barricades to control the early morning shoppers. The Occupational Safety and Health Administration (OSHA) investigated the incident and fined Walmart $7000 for failing to adequately control the crowd (Jamieson, 2013). OSHA doesn't dictate that an organization must protect employees from customers but they have a policy that is termed the "general duty" clause. This clause dictates that an organization must implement specific safeguards that will ensure the health and safety of its employees under certain circumstances. The concept of *foreseeability* becomes prevalent; Walmart should have been able to foresee that uncontrolled crowds could result in a death (Jamieson, 2013). Whether shopping on Black Friday or attending a basketball game during March Madness, the potential for injury to patrons cannot be eliminated.

Injuries can arise from interactions among spectators outside of the venue as well; for example, the beating of Bryan Stow in the Los Angeles Dodgers parking lot after a game against the San Francisco Giants (Wilson, 2011). Another example occurred during a 49ers v. Raiders game, in the fall of 2011. A 26-year old man was severely beaten in a men's restroom and another was shot multiple times in the parking lot at Candlestick Park (Sherbert, 2011). In December, 2013, a man was beaten to death in a parking lot after falling asleep in the wrong vehicle during a Kansas City Chiefs' football game fight outside of Arrowhead Stadium (Associated Press, 2014). After losing to the New England Patriots in 2015, a number of Dallas Cowboy fans became embroiled in a physical confrontation. During the fracas, at urging of other bystanders, a fan shot another in the head (Hensley, 2015).

Physical problems with the facility caused by such things as fire and weather can also be a factor. For example, at least five people died at the Indiana State Fair during a Sugarland Concert when the stage blew apart during a summer storm (Usborne, 2011). In light of such incidents, event and facility managers should devise a crowd management plan to reduce the risk of injury resulting from common, foreseeable crowd activity.

Evolution of Crowd Management

An examination of the history of crowd management reveals some type of security measures have been used at major sport/entertainment events for over fifty years. During the late 1960s and early 1970s two of the early rock and roll band promoters, Bill Graham on the west coast and Barry Fey in the mid-west, are often credited with recognizing the need for adequately trained crowd management staff. They, along with a few other national concert promoters, realized that uniformed law officers were not the best individuals to protect bands and their fans. Graham and Fey introduced the concept of using "peer group" security personnel who were recruited from the same demographics as the concert fans. Not only were the early "peer group" security better able to relate to the crowds, but the **T-shirt security** (as they were called) also received specific training in how to deal with rock and roll fans.

Many sport and recreation managers contract with outside companies to provide the crowd management service for their venues. Contracting or outsourcing crowd management services eliminates the headaches associated with the hiring, firing, training, and scheduling of the crowd management staff and provides the requisite experience on how to deal with large crowds. This practice of contracting outside agencies is known as **outsourcing**. At most major sporting events, a shirt or jacket emblazed with a term such as "Event Staff" helps the spectator know that some measure of crowd management is being provided. Some events still use **uniformed** or **off-duty law enforcement** officers, but due to high salaries, improper training, and litigation concerns, using uniformed security extensively for crowd management duties is no longer the industry standard. However, uniformed security is still used to provide security services and to arrest intoxicated or unruly individuals at many events. In addition, because of the heightened concerns since September 11, 2001, many sport and recreation venues require the presence of armed law enforcement officers in addition to the outsourced crowd management staff.

Crowd Management since September 11, 2001

The horrific events that took place on September 11, 2001, have forever affected the way facilities and events are managed. Since that fateful day, a multitude of events have been classified as "National Special Security Events" (NSSE). This classification allows the federal government to take over the control of the security of the event. The Secret Service takes charge and, along with the Federal Emergency Management Agency (FEMA) and the FBI, devises a comprehensive security plan. There have been fewer than 50 of these occasions since President Clinton signed Presidential Decision Directive 62 creating this category of event in 1998. World governmental meetings, presidential inaugurations, presidential funerals, political conventions and various sporting events such as the Olympics have made up the bulk of these events.

Even for those events not classified as NSSE, operational costs have increased exponentially because insurers now view these types of events as attractive targets for terrorists. The availability of terrorist insurance will remain limited and the premiums astronomical for an indefinite period. Thus, it is paramount for sport/recreation/entertainment facility operators to recognize their venue's vulnerability and take corrective measures. Guidelines developed and security measures implemented to combat terrorism are effective crowd management techniques under any circumstances.

Physical Security Measures. A small vehicle loaded with explosives parked near a facility, such as the van used by Timothy McVeigh and Terry Nichols in Oklahoma City in 1995, can cause tremendous damage and multiple deaths. Therefore, the parking and delivery policies at sport and large scale recreation facilities should be examined. Security checks along with biometric verification can be utilized. Large concrete planters can be situated to keep trucks (or cars) from parking too close to the venue's walls. Filled with flowers and plants, these barriers need not appear ominous. Small steel posts known as bollards can be anchored in the ground or can be raised or lowered using a pneumatic process to monitor the flow of traffic into sensitive areas.

Technological communication networks, such as **closed circuit television** (CCTV) networks should be installed around venue access points (e.g., doors, gates, windows). In addition, sensors should also closely monitor access points for the air conditioning, ventilation and water systems. These sensors should be sensitive enough to quickly detect the release of chemical and biological agents. Smaller sport and recreation facilities may not have funding for extensive CCTV or chemical sensors, but they should insure that access points are secure.

No matter the level of preparedness, sport and recreation facility managers need to be able to adapt. For example, Hurricane Katrina taught facility managers that telephone service, water, heating/air conditioning, electricity and other essential services may be disrupted for extended periods of time. In addition, if the towers used by cell phones are damaged, a sport/recreation/entertainment facility (e.g., Louisiana Superdome) can have its communication system rendered totally inoperative. The purchase and use of satellite phones may need to be investigated.

Central Monitoring. A control room or command post should be established for crowd management and facility security, and should be located in a position that can survey the overall event. This is crucial for effective communication. Having the command post in a central location will allow crowd management and law enforcement personnel to view the entire venue, and enable them to utilize binoculars and video cameras to identify disruptive or intoxicated individuals. In the UK, the command post or control room, by law, must have a view of the stadium interior.

In larger sport and recreation venues (including commercial entities like Walmart), the trend has been to establish a centralized location that contains a variety of CCTV monitors. This control room is usually situated in a secure location inside the venue and is manned 24 hours a day, 365 days a year. In addition a game-day command post is located higher up in the facility that provides good lines of sight for representatives of the various command agencies such as law enforcement, emergency medical, facility maintenance, and crowd management. A specific number of staff members should be equipped with multi-channel radios, with each channel designated for specific groups (e.g., channel 1—peer group security; channel 2—housekeeping; channel 3—law enforcement; channel 4—medical services). Staff members from each group may then be contacted by the command post, via radio, to handle various situations quickly and safely.

Evacuation. Response time in an emergency requiring evacuation of the facility is critical. Each facility should have a specific evacuation plan in place for a variety of attack or other emergency scenarios. Electronic signs and emergency lighting are extremely important.

Panic can increase the number of deaths as well as spread any contamination resulting from an attack. Most facilities today have devised an evacuation plan but often leave out important components, such as the evacuation of their disabled guests. Sport venues such as PNC Park, AT & T Park and the Staples Center have all conducted mock evacuation drills to evaluate their current plans. One of the most successful evacuations in history took place in Madrid, Spain, at Santiago Bernabeu Stadium (home to Real Madrid, a professional soccer team). During a bomb scare on December 12, 2004, over 80,000 spectators were evacuated in an amazing eight minutes and 37 seconds. There were no fatalities and only a few minor injuries.

Fan Movement. Understanding crowd movement during an event becomes vital. The "storming" or "rushing" of a field (or basketball court for that matter) is an example of a *crush*. A "crush" is when fans or spectators rush towards something of perceived value (e.g., a goal post, a famous athlete/entertainer). The opposite would be a *stampede*. A "stampede" occurs when patrons rush away from something of perceived danger (i.e. someone with a weapon or an approaching storm).

There are a couple of philosophies pertaining to a crush. The first is to keep fans off the field, no matter what. The NFL has been quite specific about keeping fans off the field. However, some sport and recreation managers believe this tactic increases the chance for injury to the individual rushing the field as well as the peer group staff member attempting to prevent their access to the field. The second philosophy is to give the appearance of keeping fans off the fields, but to instruct crowd management to back off and only provide assistance to anyone who is in danger of becoming injured once the flow begins.

NFL Fan Behavior Policies

Although this section is specific to the National Football League (NFL), many of these concepts and procedures are adaptable to other organizations and venues.

Prior to the 2008 season, the NFL and its 32 teams agreed upon a Fan Code of Conduct. The Code states:

> When attending a game, you are required to refrain from the following behaviors: behavior that is unruly, disruptive, or illegal in nature, intoxication or other signs of alcohol impairment that results in

irresponsible behavior, foul or abusive language or obscene gestures, interference with the progress of the game (including throwing objects onto the field), failing to follow instructions of stadium personnel, and verbal or physical harassment of opposing team fans (McCarthy, 2008, ¶ 1-3).

Violators of the Code face various penalties that may include ejection and revocation of season tickets if the behavior is judged to be detrimental enough. The league has sent a firm message that they intend to hold season ticket owners responsible for the conduct of anyone using their tickets and occupying their seats (McCarthy, 2008).

The Code requires fans to abstain from behaviors that hamper the enjoyment of other fans or interfere with the product on the field of play ("NFL teams", 2008). With the increased scrutiny on potential alcohol problems inside the facility, some fans try to circumvent the policies by engaging in outlandish behavior outside the stadium while tailgating before the game begins. As a result many stadiums have increased the presence of uniformed police officers throughout their parking lots. In order to prevent problems with tailgaters during games, fans at Soldier Field and at Candlestick Park must either enter the game after kickoff or leave the parking lots.

The NFL has implemented additional strategies to reduce fan violence, and beginning in 2014, fans that were ejected from a stadium must complete a course on fan conduct and then reapply for entry to the team that ejected them. In 2015, the league took one additional step and began banning fans ejected from one stadium from attending games in other cities. Moving forward the challenge will be for technology to provide enough information to stadium security to catch fans that have been barred.

Additional initiatives have been put in place at numerous stadiums to stop intoxicated spectators from entering the stadium or from driving home drunk after the event. Several stadiums employ crowd management staff to walk among the spectators entering the stadium in the hopes of preventing intoxicated individuals from entering the stadium. Management at MetLife Stadium took another approach by utilizing an "anti-knucklehead" unit. Their task is to find intoxicated and disruptive fans and notify them they are being observed. If the behavior continues the offender may be ejected (Muret, 2011). Heinz Field management instituted the "Tattle text" program which allows fans to send a text message to the control room if they observe an obnoxious or intoxicated third party. Management also provides a 1-800 number for the same purpose. An alcohol management team is then dispatched to the location to assess the situation and eject the transgressors if deemed necessary. Other facilities offer "designated driver" programs where individuals sign a pledge card not to drink alcohol and oftentimes are rewarded by being provided with free soft drinks during the game. Elsewhere, venues such as Gillette Stadium and Lucas Oil Stadium have implemented "Fan Code of Conduct Awareness" courses. Fans that violate the venue's code of conduct must complete a course including topics such as alcohol abuse and the impact of obscene language (Muret, 2011). Each of these initiatives demonstrates the intent of the NFL and its teams to curtail alcohol transgressions and to enforce the Code of Conduct.

Criminal Trespass
Fans entering restricted areas may be subject to ejection or criminal charges. It should be noted that the charge for this type of offense varies from misdemeanor to felony, depending on the state. For example, during the summer of 2002, a father and son breached U. S. Cellular Field security, came onto the field, and proceeded to attack the Kansas City Royals' first base coach during a baseball game. This confrontation along with four incidents of field intrusion during the 2004 baseball season at The Great American Ball Park prompted state legislators in Ohio to pass state legislation pertaining to persons who enter any restricted area at a place of public amusement. Section 2911.23 of the Ohio Revised Code states "An owner or lessee of a place of public amusement, an agent of the owner or lessee, or a performer or participant at a place of public amusement may use reasonable force to restrain and remove a person from a restricted portion of the place of public amusement if the person enters or remains on the restricted portion of the place of public amusement and, as a result of that conduct, interrupts or causes the delay of the live performance, sporting event, or other activity taking place at the place of public amusement" (ORC 2911.23, 2006). Violators are charged with criminal trespass, punishable by jail term, fine, or other sentence including community service.

Searches and Resulting Litigation
Outsourced crowd management and security companies play a large role in managing and controlling the public in office buildings, schools, parks, recreation and sport facilities, and concert venues. However, the

courts have placed various limitations on the authority of private crowd management companies. Often, any violation of state law will cause a crowd manager to be held to the same civil and criminal liability as any private individual. In addition, the courts have ruled that a search of a person's belongings without their consent will generally be viewed as trespass. Many of the claims of illegal searches allege a violation of privacy rights and rely on the Fourth Amendment's guarantee of freedom from unreasonable searches. In determining if a search is legal, the courts look at three issues: 1) if the conduct was considered to be state action, 2) if the conduct could be considered a search, and finally 3) if the search was reasonable (see Chapter 6.15 *Search and Seizure/ Right to Privacy*).

With no further incidents since the terrorist attacks on September 11, 2001, many individuals have become less tolerant of increased security measures, especially those pertaining to searches. In addition, the legal question becomes: Have mass searches at athletic events crossed the line? Four cases illustrate the legal questions regarding pat-down searches and their impact on crowd management policies.

In 2005, the Supreme Court of North Dakota held that a mass pat-down search of spectators at college ice hockey games was unconstitutional (*State of North Dakota v. Seglen*, 2005). Seglen, a minor, was searched by a campus police officer upon entering the ice arena on the campus of the University of North Dakota. A can of beer was found in his possession for which he was cited. The court ruled that signage in the arena warning of the search did not mean Seglen consented to the search and that a physical "pat-down" search was more intrusive than a limited visual search. Even though the facility was privately owned, the officer conducting the search was found to be acting in an official capacity as a police officer for the University of North Dakota, so the Fourth Amendment applied. The North Dakota state Supreme Court ruled that the search was intrusive and violated Seglen's Fourth Amendment rights.

The next two incidents were a result of the NFL's "limited" pat-down search policy that was put into practice before the 2005 season. As per the new NFL directive, the San Francisco 49ers began searching all fans entering Candlestick Park during the 2005 football season. Mr. and Mrs. Sheehan purchased season tickets and were subjected to pat down searches during each home game during that season. In December, 2005, after the season was completed, the Sheehan's filed suit against the team claiming the 49ers violated their privacy rights. The trial court dismissed the action. The court stated the Sheehans did not have a reasonable expectation of privacy since they were subjected to the pat down searches at every game during the 2005 season. Therefore, they had full notice of the pat down policy, consented to the pat down prior to admittance to the game and never complained. The Sheehans appealed the decision and the state Court of Appeals dismissed the case (153 Cal. App. 4th 396, 2007 Cal.). In March, 2009, the state Supreme Court restored the case. The court stated they believed the case warranted further review and instructed the 49ers to justify the search policy. The Supreme Court reversed the Court of Appeals decision and remanded the case. It will be interesting to see how the decision of this case impacts the NFL's search policy (*Sheehan*, 2009).

Raymond James Stadium (home of the Tampa Bay Buccaneers) halted their searches after Gordon Johnston, a season ticket holder, sued the Tampa Bay Sports Authority (TSA), the government agency that manages Raymond James Stadium. Similar to the *Seglen* case, Johnston filed suit against the Tampa Bay Sports Authority (TSA) claiming that the pat-downs violated his Fourth Amendment rights. Johnston successfully challenged the NFL policy in two Florida state court decisions and one Federal court. However, in June, 2008, the 11th Circuit Court (U.S. Court of Appeals) ruled that Johnston gave up his right to challenge the searches when he consented to them. The court concluded that Johnston, as well as other fans, knew they were going to be subject to searches before they entered the stadium. In the judge's opinion, Johnston knew this information so he voluntarily submitted to the search. In January, 2009, the U.S. Supreme Court declined to hear the case (*Johnston v Tampa Sports Authority*, 2008).

Previous 11th Circuit decisions (*Bourgeois v Peters*, 2004) have used the unconstitutional conditions doctrine to nullify consent. In the *Bourgeois* case the 11th Circuit considered the constitutionality of suspicionless, warrantless searches of a group of protestors standing on public land. The court held the suspicionless search was unconstitutional and violated the plaintiff's rights under both the First and Fourth Amendments. In the *Bourgeois* case the government created the policy and performed the search. However, the appellate court recognized several differences between the *Bourgeois* and *Johnston*. First, the search utilized in *Bourgeois* prevented people from gathering on public land whereas the plaintiff in *Johnston* had no constitutional right to enter Raymond James Stadium for a Buccaneers football game and since the ticket was a revocable license Johnston could be barred from entering the stadium for any reason. Since the entrance policy was imposed by a private party, Johnston was not forced by the government to choose between his constitutional rights and a benefit to which he was entitled. Unlike the City's policy in *Bourgeois* the pat-down policy in *Johnston* was developed and mandated by the NFL Commissioner and applied exclusively to NFL events. The pat-down search was imposed by the NFL and the Buccaneers, who were both classified as private entities, and not a state actor.

While the *Seglen, Sheehan, Johnston* and *Bourgeois* decisions have had minimal effect on current searches, legal questions regarding pat-down searches and their impact on crowd management policies still exist. Claussen (2006) believes

> ....the threat of terrorism at large gathering events should not be considered sufficient justification to deviate from the value judgment embedded in the Constitution that freedom from the privacy invasion of unreasonable searches is worth protecting, despite the concomitant limits on governmental ability to provide greater security (pp.172).

Crowd Management Plan

A crowd management plan is an important component of the overall risk management plan of any organization whose activities or events are attended by large numbers of people. The facility manager is either directly or indirectly responsible for both risk management and crowd management. In order for the facility manager to effectively carry out these responsibilities, an effective crowd management plan addressing such issues as capacity of the venue, geographic location, demographics of guests, and type of event must be designed and implemented. In the event of litigation alleging failure to control crowds, courts will look to see if such a plan existed, if it was in writing, how it was implemented, and how it was disseminated to the involved employees. Each employee needs to be aware of his or her role in the plan, even if the role is only a small part of the plan (see also Chapter 4.11 *Risk Management Process*).

Trained and Competent Staff

The first component of a good plan is to have properly trained and competent staff to carry out the policies. Crowd managers must make their spectators feel safe while at the facility and adequate staff training becomes paramount. Crowd management staff, on the field or court, has to know what to do, or what not to do. At the end of some athletic events, the outsourced security company is asked to show a "presence" on the field. In most cases this is to deter spectators from trying to gain access to the field. Unfortunately a number of these staff have been redeployed from other locations in the facility where they have been performing other duties (e.g., pat downs at the entrance gates, preventing individuals trying to re-enter the facility after exiting, checking credentials in VIP areas, patrolling the concourses watching for overly intoxicated fans, helping close down the tailgating area). Sometimes due to timing these individuals don't receive a thorough briefing on their responsibility at their new position. This causes a lack of "game plan" and adds risk for those on the field or court.

Screeners/searchers may be employed as trained staff to identify prohibited items such as bottles, cans, coolers, cameras, weapons, fireworks, umbrellas, or alcoholic beverages. This "search," depending on local statutes, may be a visual screening or a physical "pat-down." In light of the terrorist threat emanating from the tragedies on September 11, 2001, this search has become a much more critical element of the crowd management plan. While a physical pat-down may prove effective at times, some fans still manage to smuggle in dangerous weapons. During the 2011 NFL season one fan managed to bring a "stun gun" into MetLife Stadium during a New York Jets-Dallas Cowboys game. During an altercation emanating from his refusal to stand during the national anthem, the individual used the weapon on several other fans. As a result, the NFL changed their search policy and began using handheld magnetometers (metal detectors or wands) at all 31 stadiums across the country. It remains to be seen if these types of searches would elevate to the "special needs" doctrine (Claussen, 2006).

The second group of crowd management personnel includes **ticket takers** who collect or scan the tickets of those entering the facility. The main role of the ticket taker is to ensure that everyone entering the event has a valid ticket for that day's event.

Ushers comprise the third wave of crowd management personnel. They should be well versed in the layout of the facility, including locations of first aid stations, pay phones, restrooms, concession stands, authorized smoking areas, and exits. Ushers should also assist the guests in finding their seats. The usher should observe the patrons and call for assistance when necessary to assist injured patrons, remove food and beverage spills, and defuse potential crowd altercations.

The last wave in crowd management is perhaps the most visible—**peer-group** or **T-shirt security**. Peer group security is trained to handle disturbances in the crowd such as unruly, disruptive, or intoxicated patrons. Peer group security will also assist in protecting the athletes or performers on the floor or field of the facility. Most recreation, sport, and entertainment facilities also require additional peer-group security personnel to fill various crowd management roles backstage and/or in the press box.

It is important to understand, peer-group or t-shirt security do not replace uniformed law enforcement officials. As previously mentioned using uniformed law enforcement extensively for crowd management duties is no longer the industry standard. Uniformed law enforcement officials, depending on the facility and local ordinances, often times do not go into the seating areas unless there is an enormous altercation. Undercover law enforcement officials may be present in a crowd, but they are usually looking for underage alcohol consumers or drug dealers. Depending on the type of venue and local ordinances, law enforcement officials will position themselves near the venue's entrances and exits or where VIPs are seated. In most cases peer group staff is responsible to bring intoxicated or unruly individuals out to where the law enforcement officials are located. At that time the officer will determine if the transgressor should be arrested or ejected. Due to the possibility of violent behavior, intoxicated fans, or potential terrorists, most sport and recreation venues require the presence of a number of armed law enforcement officers in addition to the outsourced crowd management staff.

To reduce the risk of a lawsuit due to personnel errors, whether outsourced personnel are used or the facility hires its own security personnel, it is paramount for all staff—ticket takers, screeners, ushers, or T-shirt security—to go through an **orientation program**. This orientation should include an understanding of the facility layout, location of first-aid stations, restrooms, telephones, lost and found, emergency exits, and perhaps most important, a clear understanding of their duties and authority (including the legal ramifications of their actions).

Unfortunately some venue managers (or outsourced agencies) have failed to properly screen potential employees. This failure has resulted in the hiring of individuals with a variety of criminal records. These negligent hiring practices have led to the necessity of criminal background checks for all potential employees. These investigations are costly but being proactive is far more important than the expense.

Crisis Management and Emergency Action Plan
The second major component in a crowd management plan is to prepare for crises or emergencies. Being prepared to handle these incidents includes the capacity to respond to two types of situations—a crisis or an individual injury or illness. **Crises** include events such as fire, bleacher collapses, bomb threats, power loss, tornados, and, in today's society, active shooters and terrorist activities. **Emergencies** generally take the form of individual medical problems (e.g., heart attacks, injuries from falls, heat-related illnesses). Crisis management plans and emergency action plans are necessary so minor problems don't become serious ones and serious ones don't become a disaster. Such plans must be designed and implemented by crowd managers, practiced, and documented (see also Chapter 2.33 *Emergency Care* and Chapter 4.23 *Crisis Management*).

Procedure for Handling Disruptive, Unruly, or Intoxicated Patrons
The third component of an effective crowd management plan pertains to dealing with **fan ejections**. Examples of behaviors that could result in an ejection include disruptive or unruly behavior, intoxication, possession of prohibited items, evasion of admission fees, or field intrusion. Plans also need to be in effect for enforcing the venue's policy when a fan behaves in a prohibited manner.

Another problem that may necessitate an ejection is third-party assaults. Third-party assaults occur for various reasons, some foreseeable and some not. Foreseeability does not depend on whether the exact incident was foreseeable. The question is whether an incident of that general nature was reasonably foreseeable. However, if there has been a history of violence or disruptive behavior, the courts have held that actions should be taken to prevent such occurrences (*Bishop v. Fair Lanes Georgia Bowling, Inc.*, 1986; *Cassanello v. Luddy*, 1997; *Leger v. Stockton*, 1988).

Well-written policies should be established that address ways to handle disruptive behavior. The language should be clear and concise, stating what actions will not be tolerated and what measures will result. Ejection policies should be printed on tickets and posted for patrons. Policies may differ among athletic event, recreational activity, or concert depending upon the request of the event manager. It is crucial for personnel with ejection authority to be well trained regarding the legal ramifications of their role (e.g., individual liability, understanding of human rights, protection of evidence, excessive force, rules of detention and arrest, and crimes against persons and property). It is also very important that ushers and other staff members who do not have ejection authority receive in-service training regarding their role.

Usually it is best to include a warning before an actual ejection takes place. If an ejection is necessary, it should be carried out swiftly. Handling patrons in this way sends a quick, but firm message to others in the crowd as to what will and will not be tolerated.

Every ejection must be properly documented. This is an extremely crucial step in the ejection process, as it serves to produce a valuable defense for the crowd management employee and facility administration if subsequent litigation ensues. In addition, photographs or video should be utilized as an additional step in the ejection process. This measure accurately portrays the ejected fan's condition and further protects the employees from unnecessary legal harassment. As previously mentioned, closed-circuit televisions (CCTV's) are prevalent in many sport and recreation venues and they can be used to document fights as well as ejections.

Effective Communication Network

An effective communication network is the fourth component of an effective crowd management plan. The network allows the crowd management staff to work efficiently and cooperatively to handle situations as they occur. Representatives from each group (facility management, medical, security, and law enforcement) should have input in the organization of the communication network. Familiarity with the communication network should be a part of the employee orientation and training for each event. Crowd management needs more than a *planning* emphasis; the timely implementation of communication policies is essential. The decisions made in the first two minutes *after* an incident will save lives.

Effective Signage

The fifth component of a crowd management plan is **signage**. Signage is an underutilized tool in risk and crowd management. Signage may be directional or informational in nature and each has its own specific function. **Directional signs** have a number of important uses. Directional signs provide patrons with directions to important locations such as interstate highway entrances and exits, main roadways, and parking areas. Other directional signs serve to indicate the correct entrance gate or portal, as well as directing the patrons to the ticket office.

Informational signs are signs that inform the public. Prohibited items (e.g., cans, bottles, backpacks, weapons, food, recording devices, and cameras) and rules (including ejection policies) are often communicated through such signs. In addition, informational signage helps to provide answers to spectator questions by identifying the location of concession stands, first-aid rooms, telephones, restrooms, smoking areas, and exits.

The United States is home to a number of nationalities and not everyone attending sport and recreation events speaks (or reads) English. Therefore, in some situations, facility managers must be aware of the need for bilingual signs. The number of Spanish-speaking fans is growing and so must the availability of signs in Spanish.

Implementation and Evaluation of the Plan

As with the risk management plan, the last step in a crowd management plan is the **implementation and evaluation** of the plan. A recreation or sport facility will not benefit from a well-written crowd management plan unless it is effectively implemented during an event. Implementation should start with a review of both the risk and crowd management policies before the event. Event-specific activities, such as half-time promotions, VIP guests on the sideline, or band members coming out into the crowd should be discussed. Each staff member should understand how the activity might affect his or her event responsibilities. After an event, all of the personnel should come together for a debriefing. They should also look into ways to improve the plan. As stated earlier, a crowd management plan should be flexible and allow for change as needed. Without implementation and evaluation, a well-organized crowd management plan becomes ineffective.

SIGNIFICANT CASE

This case involves the issues of negligence, contributory negligence, and assumption of risk. The plaintiff was a business invitee to a concert. During the concert an incident of crowd surfing occurred which caused the tortious act. The question is who was responsible for crowd management and did the plaintiff contribute to/or assume the risk of such injury.

MILLER V. LIVE NATION WORLDWIDE, INC., ET AL.
United States District Court For the District of Maryland, Southern Division
Civil Action No.: CBD-14-2697
2016 U.S. Dist. LEXIS 11369

FACTUAL BACKGROUND:

Kenneth K. Miller ("Plaintiff") alleges that on May 4, 2012, he was attending a rock concert at the Fillmore, a venue operated by Nation Worldwide, Inc. ("Live Nation"), in Silver Spring, Maryland. While observing the concert featuring the metal band Korn, Plaintiff was struck by a crowd surfer. Plaintiff, who was attending the concert with his teenage son, alleges that he was facing the stage, from the front row, when he was struck from behind. Plaintiff alleges that Noble (one of the promoters) was supposed to provide security and enforce the policy against crowd-surfing.

* * * *

Plaintiff alleges that there were several visible signs at the Fillmore prohibiting crowd-surfing. Plaintiff further alleges that there was little or no crowd-surfing at the beginning of the concert, but everything changed when Korn performed "Freak on a Leash," a song that is known to encourage crowd-surfing. Plaintiff alleges that the security personnel at the concert did not do anything to prohibit or discourage the crowd-surfing that ensued.

* * * *

As a result of the incident, Plaintiff suffered fractured vertebrae, and a severed right vertebral artery. Plaintiff underwent emergency surgery, and in the process, the surgeon had to manipulate Plaintiff's esophagus causing permanent injuries to his voice. Plaintiff alleges that as a result of the permanent injuries, he continues to experience pain in his esophagus, difficulty eating, a stabbing pain in his right bicep, decreased strength in his right bicep, and a numbness in his index finger and right thumb. As a result of the severed artery, Plaintiff has to take blood thinners for the rest of his life to prevent the possibility of a stroke.

On July 14, 2015, Noble filed its cross-claim against Live Nation ("Noble's Cross-Claim"). In the cross-claim, Noble alleges that on the day of the concert, Noble's only obligation was to provide consulting services. Noble claims its responsibility was not to provide **crowd control** services, as it was originally stipulated in the Services Agreement it signed with Live Nation.

The Services Agreement between Noble and Live Nation, executed on September 9, 2011 and set to terminate on August 1, 2013, provides that Noble was required to "provide crowd management services . . . including crowd management staff and security staff. Noble was required to provide "(i) **crowd control** . . ., (iv) direction and control of the audience to deter any crowd disturbances." More specifically, Noble was required to "use best efforts to monitor, keep secure and maintain reasonable control over those individuals . . . body-surfing in the general admission area located directly in front of the stage and/or in front of a staffed barricade." The Services Agreement provided that the agreement "may not be amended, revised or terminated orally but only by a written instrument executed by the Party against which enforcement of the amendment, revision or termination is asserted."

Noble asserts in its Cross-motion that it was Live Nation's responsibility to provide crowd management services, and that Live Nation owes Noble defense and indemnification for this incident. Noble's Count I, therefore, demands judgment against Live Nation for indemnification and/or contribution for any and all judgment that Plaintiff may receive against Noble. Noble's Count II for breach of contract alleges that under the Services Agreement, Live Nation owes Noble defense and indemnification.

* * * *

b. Live Nation had a duty to protect Plaintiff from crowd-surfing and Live Nation had actual or constructive notice that crowd-surfing was occurring at the concert.

As already stated, to establish a **negligence** claim, a plaintiff has to assert: (1) that the defendant was under a duty to protect the plaintiff from injury, (2) that the defendant breached that duty, (3) that the plaintiff suffered actual injury or loss, and (4) that the loss or injury proximately resulted from the defendant's breach of the duty. Whether there is enough evidence of the required elements in a **negligence** action is a question of fact to be determined by the fact finder, but the existence of a legal duty is a question of law that is decided by the court. ****

In this case, a reasonable jury or fact finder could infer from the evidence that Live Nation and Noble were aware that crowd-surfing was taking place at the concert. As the Plaintiff stated in his deposition, he saw a couple of crowd surfers at different times during the concert. Stephanie Steele, the corporate designee for Live Nation, acknowledged in her deposition that Live Nation was aware of crowd-surfing activities at a similar concert. This led Live Nation to determine it was necessary to place signs at the Fillmore prohibiting crowd-surfing. Edward Gilmore, Noble's Director of Security for the Fillmore, stated in his deposition that although Noble employees were aware of crowd-surfing, they were not told to stop it, and he did not observe any other security personnel trying to stop the crowd-surfing. Instead, according to Mr. Gilmore, the security personnel were assisting the crowd surfers over the barrier and did not tell them to leave the venue. Mr. Gilmore explained that crowd-surfing became an accepted practice, and there was no reason for Noble personnel to report it to Live Nation personnel

* * * *

Based on the evidence in this case, a fact finder could reasonably infer that Live Nation and Noble knew or should have known, based on past Korn concerts and what was happening the day of the concert, that crowd-surfing was either occurring or likely to occur. A fact finder could reasonably infer that Live Nation became aware with sufficient time to prevent more crowd-surfing or warn invitees such as Plaintiff. *** The Court rejects Live Nation's argument that it is not responsible for the tortious acts of a third person because the law on this issue is clear: if the business invitor could have anticipated the possible occurrence (crowd-surfing) and the probable results (injury to the business invitee), then liability may arise if the business invitor did not exercise reasonable care. **** (The court held that the defendants had a duty to protect their invitees from injuries associated with crowd-surfing, which the defendants were aware was occurring at the concert). In this case, there is evidence to suggest that Live Nation was aware of the crowd-surfing taking place at the concert and at previous Korn concerts. Whether Live Nation exercised reasonable care is a question for the jury.

c. The Court cannot conclude that Plaintiff was contributorily negligent as a matter of law.

Live Nation argues that Plaintiff was contributorily negligent as a matter of law when he failed to take reasonable care for his own safety. Live Nation states that Plaintiff "had a duty to exercise due care for his own safety by not placing himself in an area [the front of the stage] where crowd-surfing was occurring." ***

In response, Plaintiff cites **** and argues that contributory **negligence** is a fact-intensive defense for the jury to decide and it is only in the most rare of cases where the judge decides this issue. Further, Plaintiff argues that a reasonable jury could find that he was not contributorily negligent. In support thereof, Plaintiff advances five reasons: (1) Live Nation and Noble's finger-pointing at each other negates any suggestion that Plaintiff was contributorily negligent as a matter of law; (2) a reasonable jury could find that Plaintiff had no reason to believe that crowd-surfing would occur at the event because there were signs everywhere prohibiting crowd-surfing, no one crowd-surfed during most of the concert, and one of the two isolated people who crowd-surfed during a song stopped and the other was safely lowered at the barricade; (3) a jury could find that Plaintiff, knowing that crowd-surfing was prohibited, and not knowing that "Freak on Leash" would incite crowd-surfing, could not have reasonably anticipated that a crowd surfer would injure him; (4) a reasonable jury could find that Plaintiff did not negligently place himself at risk of injury by attending the concert; (5) even if the jury could find that Plaintiff negligently placed himself at risk of some injury, the kind of injury Plaintiff suffered, a broken neck, is not the kind of injury he could have imagined he was exposing himself to.

d. The Court cannot conclude that Plaintiff assumed the risk of his injuries as a matter of law.

**** Live Nation then suggests that, based on his deposition, Plaintiff understood and appreciated the danger of standing in a crowd when crowd-surfing was taking place; therefore, it is irrelevant that Plaintiff could not have predicted the exact injury he suffered. **** The defendant must prove three elements to establish the defense of assumption of the risk: (1) the plaintiff had knowledge of the risk of the danger; (2) the plaintiff appreciated that risk; and (3) the plaintiff voluntarily confronted the risk of danger. *** Live Nation then suggests that, based on his deposition, Plaintiff understood and appreciated the danger of standing in a crowd when crowd-surfing was taking place; therefore, it is irrelevant that Plaintiff could not have predicted the exact injury he suffered. ****

In this case, the Court cannot conclude that Plaintiff assumed the risk as a matter of law. There is no undisputed evidence that Plaintiff fully knew and understood the risk of the danger. Although Plaintiff had seen crowd surfers at the concert, he did not see anyone getting hurt by the crowd surfers. At most, Plaintiff saw crowd surfers that were stopped by the security guards or guards that were assisting the crowd-surfers. Plaintiff's Deposition, Live Nation points the Court to Plaintiff's deposition where he states that he "understood that it was possible" that a crowd surfer could fall in the process of crowd-surfing, and where Plaintiff acknowledges that he was aware that there was a "limited risk" of for example getting kicked in the shoulder or "smacked in the head." These acknowledgements from Plaintiff support a conclusion that he "would," "should" or "could" have known that there were risks associated with crowd-surfing. However, this evidence does not show that Plaintiff "must" have known that the risk of being injured by a crowd-surfer was actually present. Since there is no undisputed evidence that Plaintiff knew and understood the risk of the danger he was facing, and since there is a dispute as to whether Plaintiff assumed the risk, this issue is to be decided by the jury and not by the Court.

****

IV. Conclusion

For the foregoing reasons, the Court **GRANTS in part and DENIES in part** Live Nation's Motion. Live Nation's Motion is granted as to Noble's contract and indemnity claims and it is denied as to Plaintiff's claims. The Court also **DENIES** Noble's motion for summary judgment as to Plaintiff's claims, and **DENIES** Noble's Cross-motion against Live Nation.

CASES ON THE SUPPLEMENTAL WEBSITE

Bearman v University of Notre Dame (1983 Ind. App. LEXIS 3387). Analyze the court's reasoning about foreseeability. Even though the university may not know the particular danger posed by an intoxicated third party they should have foreseen that some people would become intoxicated and pose a general threat to the safety of other patrons.

Heenan v. Comcast Spectacor (2006 Phila. Ct. Com. Pl. LEXIS 138). This case is an excellent example of what can happen if a facility doesn't plan properly or utilize an effective crowd management plan. The operators were aware that the concert would likely be canceled, but they failed to make a timely announcement of the cancellation. In addition, they failed to formulate a plan to properly execute a safe and organized exit from the arena.

John Hopkins v Connecticut Sports Plex, L.L.C. (2006 Conn. Super. LEXIS 1710). The case illustrates the concept of foreseeability. Several key concepts such as the presence of a proper alcohol management plan, proper numbers of security staff and documentation of prior incidents are important to keep in mind while reading the case.

Cohen v Sterling Mets (2007 N.Y. Misc. LEXIS 5270). This case provides an excellent example of how the assumption of risk defense is viewed in comparison to the duty a sport venue has to protect employees and spectators. The concept of between-the-innings promotions and the risks they entail is also touched upon.

Schoneboom v B.B. King Blues Club (2009 N.Y. Misc. LEXIS 3914). This case involves a plaintiff injured during a "mosh pit" incident while watching a concert. The plaintiff claimed that additional security could have prevented the incident. The defendants maintained that the plaintiff assumed the risk of his injury and that additional security could not have prevented his injured knee.

Adrianne Armstrong v. Wal-Mart Stores East, L.P. (2014 Mass. App. LEXIS 36). This case demonstrates the obvious danger in dealing with crowd control and negligence.

QUESTIONS YOU SHOULD BE ABLE TO ANSWER

1. Describe three reasons why crowd management is a necessary component of an effective risk management plan.

2. Do an Internet search on Bill Graham and Barry Fey. What were some of the major concerns for the early promoters?

3. Research the NFL's Fan Code of Conduct. Do you believe it will be effective?

4. Analyze the *Seglen, Johnston, Sheehan* and *Bourgeois* cases. Name some of the similarities between the four cases.

5. Identify the components necessary for an effective crowd management plan. How would you implement a crowd management plan?

REFERENCES

Cases
Adrianne Armstrong v. Wal-Mart Stores East, L.P., 2014 Mass. App. Div. 109; 2014 Mass. App. Div. LEXIS 36
Bishop v. Fair Lanes Georgia Bowling, Inc., 803 F.2d 1548 (11th Cir. 1986).
Bourgeois v Peters 387 F.3rd 1303 (2004 U.S. App.)
Cassanello v. Luddy, 695 A.2d 325 (1997 N.J. Super.)
Cohen v Sterling Mets 840 N.Y.S.2d 527 (2007 N.Y. Misc.)
Leger v. Stockton, 249 Cal. Rptr. 688 (July 25, 1988).
John Hopkins v. Connecticut Sports Plex, LLC CV044002547S 2006 Conn. Super. LEXIS 1710
Johnston v Tampa Sports Authority, 530 F.3d 1320 (2008 U.S. App.)
Sheehan v. San Francisco 49ers, Ltd., 201 P.3d 472 (2009 Cal.)
Miller v. Live Nation Worldwide, Inc., 2016 U.S. Dist. LEXIS 11369
Stark v The Seattle Seahawks, et al., CASE NO. C06-1719JLR (2007 U.S. Dist.)
State of North Dakota v. Seglen, 700 N.W.2d 702 (2005 N.D.)

Publications
Ammon, R., Jr., Southall, R., & Nagel, M. (2016). *Sport facility management: Organizing events and mitigating risks* (3rd ed.) Morgantown, WV: Fitness Information Technology, Inc.
Associated Press. (2009, March 30). Ivory Coast soccer fans blame police for deadly stampede that killed 19. *FoxNews.com* Retrieved from http://www.foxnews.com/story/0,2933,511555,00.html
Associated Press. (February 21, 2014). Man charged in death of fan. Retrieved from http://espn.go.com/nfl/story/_/id/10496586/man-charged-death-fan-arrowhead-stadium
Black, H. C. (2011). *Black's Law Dictionary* (6th ed.). St. Paul: West Publishing Co.
Claussen, C. (2006). The constitutionality of mass searches of sports spectators. *Journal of Legal Aspects of Sport, 16*(2), 153-175.
Criminal Trespass on Place of Public Amusement, Ohio Revised Code § 2911.23 (2006)
Fayed, S. & Perry, T. (2012, February 2). Egyptians Incensed After 74 Die in Soccer Tragedy. *Reuters.com*. Retrieved http://www.reuters.com/article/2012/02/02/us-egypt-soccer-violence-idUSTRE81022D20120202
Hensley, N. (2015). Man shot in head during Dallas Cowboys tailgate fight outside AT&T Stadium after crowd goaded gunman. Retrieved from: http://www.nydailynews.com/news/national/man-shot-head-tailgate-fight-cowboys-game-article- 1.2393577.
Jamieson, D. (2013, November 21) Walmart Still Hasn't Paid Its $7,000 Fine For 2008 Black Friday Death. Retrieved from http://www.huffingtonpost.com/2013/11/21/walmart-black-friday-death_n_4312210.html
McCarthy, M. (2008, August 6). NFL unveils new code of conduct for its fans. *USA Today*. Retrieved from http://www.usatoday.com/sports/football/nfl/2008-08-05-fan-code-of-conduct_N.htm
Muret, D. (2011, November 21–27). Schooling fans on good behavior. *Street & Smith's SportsBusiness Journal 14* (14)25–26, 33.
NFL teams implement fan code of conduct. (2008). NFL.com. Retrieved from http://www.nfl.com/news/story?id=09000d5d809c28f9&template=without-video&confirm=true.
Seidler, T. (2005). Conducting a facility risk review. In H. Appenzeller, *Risk management in sport: Issues and strategies* (2nd ed.), 317-328. Durham, NC: Carolina Academic Press.
Shaw, A. (2000, July 10). Twelve dead in soccer stampede in Zimbabwe. *Chicago Sun Times*. Retrieved from http://www.highbeam.com/doc/1P2-4552349.html
Sherbert, E. (2011, April). Videos show abusive fans at 49ers and Raiders game, two people shot. *San Francisco Weekly*. http://blogs.sfweekly.com/thesnitch/2011/08/witnesses_sought_in_49ers_shoo.php
Usborne, D. (2011, August). Five killed as 'freak wind' blows down Indianapolis festival stage. *The Independent*. http://www.independent.co.uk/news/world/americas/five-killed-as-freak-wind-blows-down-indianapolis-festival-stage-2337797.html
van der Smissen, B. (1990). *Legal liability and risk management for public and private entities*. Cincinnati, OH: Anderson Publishing Co.
Wilson, S. (2011, May). Bryan Stow lawsuit: Family to sue Dodgers in L.A. Superior Court for slow security response to Stow's beating. *Los Angeles Weekly*. http://blogs.laweekly.com/informer/2011/08/stadium_violence_san_francisco.php
Wire reports. (2011, December 5). At least 12 injured as Oklahoma State fans celebrate. *USA Today*, 4C.

4.25 MANAGING RISK THROUGH INSURANCE

Doyice J. Cotten | Sport Risk Consulting

Insurance is a method by which an individual or business pays a defined expenditure (premium) to protect against the possibility of a large, undetermined future loss or expense. Conducting business without insurance is like rock climbing without a safety line—very risky. Insurance spreads the financial risks and costs of an individual or business among a large group of persons or businesses so that the losses of those few who experience them are shared with the many that do not. In so doing, insurance provides protection against financial catastrophe and is an indispensable risk management technique.

Many persons look at the purchase of insurance and risk management as one and the same. This, however, is not true. Risk management involves the identification of risks, determination of the extent of the risks, and the implementation of one or more control approaches. Control approaches include: (1) elimination of the activity; (2) reduction of risks through operational control; (3) retention (through such techniques as self-insurance, current expensing, and deductibles); (4) transfer by contract (through indemnity agreements, exculpatory clauses, and by requiring insurance by the other party); and (5) purchasing insurance from an insurance company.

Obviously, insurance is but one of many techniques available to help manage risks in a recreation or sport business. The recreation or sport manager should purchase insurance to protect against all risks that could have a significant impact upon the financial integrity of the business, but should not try to insure against every possible risk and potential loss. In addition to protection against property loss, loss of business income, and monetary judgments in lawsuits, insurance also protects the recreation or sport business from legal expenses resulting from litigation. It is usually less expensive to simply pay for minor losses when they occur. A major danger, however, is that failure to meet claim reporting requirements can jeopardize coverage when a seemingly minor injury (a strained knee) eventually reveals itself as a major injury (an ACL tear). It is obviously important that the recreation or sport manager be knowledgeable enough to determine which risks are of such a magnitude as to allow retention by the business, which can be transferred by contract, and which require protection through insurance coverage. The purpose of this chapter is to help the recreation or sport manager become more informed about this aspect of risk management and, subsequently, be able to better protect the business from financial risks.

FUNDAMENTAL CONCEPTS

The first thing to understand is that the insurance business is a very complex business and the average recreation or sport manager does not have the time or ability to become an expert in insurance. The recreation and sport manager should try to learn as much as he or she can about insurance, but must rely upon a trusted, knowledgeable insurance agent for real guidance.

The agent can work with the manager to identify the risks faced by your business, the types and amounts of coverage needed, and the appropriate insurance carrier for your needs. The agent should explain the terms of the policy, what is covered, what is not covered, and how they can fill in any holes in the coverage of the policy. While the entire policy is important, it is crucial that the recreation and sport manager clearly understands two sections of the policy: the exclusions section and the conditions section. The **exclusions section** of the policy describes what is NOT covered by the policy. Items that are often excluded from a standard commercial policy include landscaping, buildings under construction, and cash. Some perils that are usually excluded from the standard policy are earthquake; volcanic eruption; water damage from floods, sewers, or surface ground water;

power interruption; war; and nuclear hazard. When a needed coverage is not included in the policy, the agent can suggest riders or endorsements by which the coverage may be purchased. The **conditions section** sets forth the obligations of the insured in the event of a claim. Some conditions might include prompt reporting following a loss, giving sworn affirmation of loss, providing an inventory, or provision of receipts.

Types of Insurance Coverage

The type of coverage needed by your business depends upon the type and size of your business. Large businesses such as multi-activity recreation centers, summer camps, health clubs, country clubs, and ski resorts have definite insurance needs; however, those with small businesses such as personal trainers, dance instructors, tennis instructors, and martial arts instructors should not think they do not need insurance. Both need insurance, but their needs may differ.

Today, there are more sport and recreation businesses than ever before, but fortunately, there is more insurance available than in the past. Today, one can buy insurance for practically any sport activity (e.g., archery, basketball, cheerleading, racquetball, Frisbee golf) or any type of sport school or facility (e.g., baseball academy, dance studios, karate school, paintball facility, trampoline park). Likewise, insurance is available for all types of businesses and organizations (e.g., leagues, associations, hunting clubs, sports combines, special events, and day camps).

Sports Insurance Policies

Sports insurance policies are available that often include General Liability, Accident, Directors and Officers Liability, Equipment Insurance, and Crime Insurance. **General Liability** is one type of insurance that EVERY business should have. It protects you in the event of bodily injury or property damage lawsuits in which the injury or loss is caused by business or organization negligence. If the business is sued and the loss is covered, the policy will cover the legal costs and any award for damages up to the limit of the policy. The insurance company also has the option of paying a settlement to the plaintiff in order to avoid court expenses and risk of a larger award. **Accident Insurance** (also called Excess Accident Insurance, Participant Accident Insurance, or Medical Expense Insurance) covers the medical bills of injured participants. **Directors and Officers Liability** is a common coverage in larger organizations. It protects these officials in the event they are personally sued. Common allegations include discrimination, wrongful termination, and failure to follow organization bylaws. **Equipment Insurance** covers owned or leased equipment. Expensive equipment should be covered; policies generally protect against such risks as fire, wind, theft, and vandalism. Equipment can include items such as uniforms, scoreboards, bleachers, and maintenance equipment. **Crime Insurance** covers a multitude of areas including employee dishonesty (e.g., embezzlement), forgery/alteration (e.g., altering amount on a check), theft of money or securities, and computer fraud (e.g., hacking, transfer of funds). Crime claims are common in even small sport businesses.

Be careful to carefully examine policies for the exclusions. See that your policy also includes **coverage of athlete participants**, **punitive damages**, and **sex abuse/molestation claims**. If these are not included, add coverage by purchasing riders to cover them. In addition, some businesses will need **business auto insurance coverage**. **Pollution liability** is a coverage often purchased by some recreation or sport businesses (e.g., golf courses). This coverage protects the business if acts by the business result in pollution and damage to neighboring property. For instance, a chemical spill in a stream on a golf course could result in damage to the property of others and subsequent legal action against the business. **Employment practices liability** is sometimes available for protection from such claims as (1) wrongful termination, (2) sexual harassment, (3) equal pay violations, and (4) discrimination (racial, sex, age, and disability). Some policies cover any violation of certain state and federal statutes, including antidiscrimination laws, Americans with Disabilities Act (ADA), Age Discrimination in Employment Act (ADEA), and the Equal Pay Act. Other types of insurance include **cyber risk insurance**, **property insurance**, and **key person insurance**. Your agent can advise you regarding your need for these and possibly other types of coverage, riders, or endorsements available to you.

Other Coverage to Consider

Umbrella Liability. General Liability coverage is generally limited to $1,000,000 per covered incident. With the size of awards today, one million is not adequate for some types of activities. For activities like bowling and Frisbee golf, one million seems adequate; but when you consider activities like trampoline parks and cheerleading where catastrophic injuries are not unheard of, one million would be totally inadequate. For businesses that involve more risk, an **Umbrella Liability** policy would be advisable. The Umbrella Liability policy can raise your coverage to $5,000,000 at a reasonable cost. One can usually be purchased in increments per $1,000,000 dollars.

Liability Protecting Employees. Some recreation or sport businesses not only purchase liability insurance to protect the business, but also purchase insurance to protect employees in the event of legal action. The most common of these is **directors and officers liability** that usually provides general liability protection of $1 million or more for their "wrongful acts." Wrongful acts include error, misstatement, misleading statement, act, omission, and neglect of duty in the person's insured capacity. Coverage generally excludes: actions not within the scope of their duties; breach of contract; fines and penalties; dishonesty, infidelity, or criminal activities; human rights or sexual harassment violations; and failure to maintain adequate insurance.

Employee benefits liability is a type of coverage that is currently very popular, inexpensive, and easy to find. To illustrate the coverage, suppose a club pays for health insurance for its employees, but forgets to add a new employee to the policy. Sometime later the person is sick, has a claim, and finds no coverage. Employee benefits liability would cover this oversight. Coverage now is usually on a claims-made basis—meaning claims must be promptly and properly made within the term of the policy. Failure to do so may invalidate coverage.

Some recreation or sport businesses provide **professional** or **malpractice insurance** for some or all employees. The professional insurance is designed to protect the employee from liability for negligence in acts related to giving professional advice or counsel. Suits often name the employee personally because the practice today is to sue all who may be potentially at fault; because the act may be an *ultra vires* act leaving only the employee as vulnerable; and because with governmental entities, the entity may be immune, leaving only the employee. Malpractice insurance applies primarily to persons in legal or health-related areas. Malpractice insurance protects both the individual and the business.

Professional and malpractice insurance can also be purchased by the individual employee. Policies are often available through a professional organization at very reasonable rates. They may also be purchased from one's insurance company, but the charge will be significantly higher. One should be aware that many exclusions exist on the policies.

Motor Vehicle Insurance. The recreation or sport manager must be certain that all business vehicles are adequately covered. Maintain coverage for damage to the business vehicles (collision, comprehensive, and uninsured motorist); damage to other vehicles, property, or persons (liability); and medical coverage for injured parties. Business vehicles should be covered with a commercial automobile policy. One's personal automobile policy generally is inadequate for use with business vehicles.

In automobile insurance, as in property insurance, the amount of the deductible must be decided for both collision (damages to your automobile from the collision with another object) and comprehensive (damage to your automobile other than from collisions, e.g., vandalism to your auto, tree limb falling on your auto). Once again, the higher the deductible, the smaller the premium.

In some recreation or sport businesses, employees occasionally must drive personal automobiles for business purposes. A **non-owned automobile** endorsement may be purchased to insure the business in such cases. Coverage may also be extended to include volunteers who use their own vehicles. If the organization cannot insure the business use of personal vehicles for employees or volunteers, procedures should be instituted to ensure that the owners of all such vehicles have adequate coverage. (Both non-owned automobile and hired vehicle endorsements can be added to the CGL when there is no need for owned auto coverage.)

Many recreation or sport businesses have occasion to rent or lease vehicles for varying periods of time. The business may purchase a stand-alone policy or an endorsement on the firm's automobile policy that covers **hired vehicles**. This policy can provide both liability protection and coverage for the rental vehicle. Be aware, however, that neither the stand-alone policy nor the endorsement (nor for that matter, insurance purchased from the rental company) will cover the loss or theft of personal property or equipment stored in the vehicle.

In *Federal Insurance Company v. Executive Coach Luxury Travel, Inc.* (2010; see the Supplemental Website for Chapter 2.35 *Transportation*), Bluffton University contracted with Executive Coach to transport players to some baseball games. The bus, driven by an employee of Executive Coach, was involved in a serious accident. Federal Insurance, one of Bluffton's insurers, contended that the travel company was an independent contractor and that the driver was not using the bus with the university's permission. The University's insurance policy, however, stated that it covered "anyone else" driving the vehicle. The appellate court ruled that the driver was an "insured" and the case was remanded for further proceedings.

Other desirable endorsements are **uninsured/underinsured motorist coverage, bodily injury coverage**, and **property damage**. This coverage applies in the event that the other party has no insurance or the limits of that party's insurance have been reached.

Workers' Compensation. Workers' compensation is a no-fault, statutory-based insurance that provides for compensation to employees who suffer injury in the course of their employment. It is mandated in most states (see Chapter 4.26 *Workers' Compensation*). The worker receives compensation for lost income, both temporary and long term, and medical expenses incurred. The law in each state limits the amount of compensatory income allowed. In most states, all recreation or sport businesses with three or more full-time employees are required to carry workers' compensation insurance coverage.[1] The cost of this insurance varies with the amount of risk involved in that type of business and with the claims record of each individual sport business. The premium is based on a certain number of dollars per hundred of payroll for the business. Representative costs per $100 dollars of payroll might range from $15 for a riding club, $6 for a country club, $2 for a health spa, to less than $1 for a business involving all clerical or desk work.

Injured workers simply file a claim in order to receive compensation for work-related injuries. They neither have to file suit against the employer nor prove negligence or fault on the part of the employer. The employee, however, generally cannot receive compensation for pain and suffering through workers' compensation (see also Chapter 4.26 *Workers' Compensation*).

Event Insurance. Many recreation or sport businesses sponsor or conduct events either on an occasional or a regular basis. For any event, the business should purchase additional liability insurance if the event is not included in the CGL policy of the business. The amount of additional insurance coverage depends upon the event and how much investment is involved and/or whether the business is dependent upon a profit from the event. Also, many parties (e.g., venue, merchandisers, media, sponsors, concessionaires, and competing teams) may need to be named as additional insureds on your policy.

A common event liability policy would include bodily injury, personal injury, and property damage; an incident policy which would cover payment for medical expense for minor injuries (injured files a claim; no suit necessary); and settlement for uncontested claims in exchange for a release.

An important coverage for many events is that for **nonappearance/cancellation of event**. Bases for cancellation are specified and the policy generally includes costs, anticipated revenues, and anticipated profits. **Weather insurance** is an important coverage for some types of events in order to offset any loss of profit and expenses in the event of inclement weather. For some events, **life or accident coverage of participants** is purchased. Other typical endorsements include **automobiles, crime, prize indemnity**, **fire** (for damages that may not fall under the CGL), and **media coverage** (e.g., loss of signal, failure of transmission, breach of contract by media).

Summary. One might ask, "Do all sport and recreation businesses need insurance?" The answer is generally "yes." Whether a small, one-person business (e.g., a personal trainer, aerobics instructor, or a karate instructor); a moderate size business (e.g., a white-water rafting business, a country club, or a trampoline park); or a large sport business (e.g., the NCAA, the NBA, or a chain of health clubs), all need insurance protection. Their needs differ, depending upon the size of the business, the type of activity, and other variables.

Requiring Insurance of Other Parties

There are situations when it is important that a recreation or sport business require that other parties have insurance coverage. Some of these situations include (1) when another party or organization rents your facility for some type of event, (2) when a contractor or his workers are on the premises for remodeling, repair, or other work, and (3) when independent contractors make use of your facility.

---

[1] In California, the law requires that a business provide workers' compensation coverage even if there is only one employee.

Certificate of Insurance
It is good policy to require that such groups provide the recreation or sport business with a certificate of insurance. This proof of insurance is a form (called an ACORD form certificate) from the insurance company verifying that the party is covered by liability insurance. If the presence of the party covers a period of time, it may be necessary to require a certificate of insurance again at a later date to insure that coverage is still in force.

Endorsement
Many businesses require that the other party (e.g., building contractor doing renovations on the premises) name the recreation or sport business as an additional insured party on their insurance coverage. Additional insured status is intended to provide coverage when the additional insured (the sport or recreation business) has a claim made against it because of the activities of the named insured (e.g., the contractor, the other organization). The Additional Insured Endorsement is attached with the ACORD form. The form provides details about the coverage, including the insurance company name, the policy number, the dates and limits of coverage, and the name of the agent.

It is highly recommended that the sport or recreation business obtain the actual ISO additional insured form which evidences additional insured status, and not rely solely on a Certificate of Insurance which states that additional insured status applies. Often, agents and brokers will issue Certificates of Insurance which state that a party is listed as additional insured "if required by written contract;" as a result, in the absence of a written contractual obligation which demands the additional insured status, no additional insured status would be afforded despite this certificate's wording. An ISO additional insured endorsement provides additional insured status in the absence of a contractual requirement.

In some circumstances, parties are considered an additional insured without being named on an endorsement. In *Bedford Central School District v. Commercial Union Insurance Company* (2002; case is included on the Supplemental Website), Bedford allowed Iona Preparatory School to bring a class to use Bedford's obstacle course. The court found that the insurance policy was ambiguous and ruled against the relying insurance company. The court held that Iona and its students were additional insured and required Commercial Union to reimburse Bedford for its costs.

Event Policy
Recreation and sport businesses that make their facilities available to other groups generally require that the organization or group purchase and show proof of a specified amount of event insurance (see previous section). Health clubs, for instance, often make their club available to groups for a dance, party, or even sleepovers. These provide additional revenue and, at the same time, familiarize a number of potential clients with the club. The club generally requires that the group purchase a 24-hour event policy that can be obtained from a specialty insurance provider. Another example of when a user might be required to purchase event insurance would be when a rock group promoter rents a gymnasium for a rock concert.

Independent Contractors
Most recreation and sport businesses do not provide liability insurance coverage for independent contractors (e.g., physical therapists, massage therapists, and personal trainers in health clubs). While the event organizer's General Liability policy can extend coverage for the event organizer in the event an independent contractor's negligence causes injury or harm, this provides no protection for the independent contractor. It is good policy to require that the independent contractor carry liability insurance coverage.

Selecting the Agent and Carrier
Few administrators in recreation or sport management are insurance experts. This fact magnifies the importance of selecting both a good agent and a good carrier.

When selecting an agent, try to find one associated with a company that specializes in recreation or sport entity protection – one who is knowledgeable about and has experience dealing with sport and recreation businesses. The better the agent understands the recreation or sport business and its risks, the more helpful the agent can be 1) in recommending important coverages that might be critical to the business and 2) in eliminating, or reducing, unnecessary coverages. The agent should walk through your facility and discuss your exposures with you. Finally, do not select an agent who is inexperienced, will not take the time to explain coverages, or doesn't seem knowledgeable enough to help you evaluate your insurance needs.

There are many companies around the country that do this. Some offer policies applicable to many types of sports and recreational activities; others specialize in policies for only one or two types of sport. A few examples of companies **specializing in recreation and sport** are:

Sadler & Company, Inc. (www.sadlersports.com) Wide array of policies
The Monument Sports (http://www.monumentsports.com) Wide array of policies
Fairmont Insurance (www.fairmontins.com) Wide array of policies
Interwest Insurance Services, LLC (http://www.iwins.com/): Golf courses, concessionaires
Fitness Pak (www.fitnesspak.com): Western health club industry

The agent should have access to a number of companies who write policies. The agent should be able to help you find and select an appropriate carrier or MGA[2] who specializes in recreation and sport entities similar to yours. Such companies often offer enhancements and riders that non-specialists cannot provide. They know the unique types of problems faced by your type of business. Also, it is important to make certain the company has an A rating and has been in business for a number of years.

Some of the major sport and recreation **MGAs** include:

K & K Insurance Group, Inc. (www.kandkinsurance.com/)
RPS Bollinger Sports & Leisure (https://www.rpsbollinger.com/)
Markel Insurance (markelinsurance.com)

Some major **carriers** of sport and recreation insurance include:

American Specialty Insurance and Risk Services, Inc. (www.amerspec.com)
Nationwide Insurance (www.nationwide.com)
AIG (aig.com)
Philadelphia Insurance Companies (www.phly.com) or (https://www.phly.com/productsfw/default.aspx)

---

[2] *An MGA is an insurance organization that, for a fee, provides some of the services (e.g., underwriting, policy issuance, claims administration) normally provided by insurance carriers.*

SIGNIFICANT CASE

The York Insurance Company v. Houston Wellness Center, Inc. is a simple case that illustrates one of the most common mistakes made by the purchasers of insurance—failure to examine closely the exclusions in the coverage.

YORK INSURANCE COMPANY V. HOUSTON WELLNESS CENTER, INC.

Court of Appeals of Georgia, Third Division
261 Ga. App. 854; 583 S.E.2d 903; 2003 Ga. App. LEXIS 794
June 20, 2003, Decided

Opinion

BLACKBURN, Presiding Judge.

York Insurance Company ("York") appeals the trial court's denial of its motion for summary judgment, arguing that under the plain language of the policy it issued to Houston Wellness Center, Inc. ("Houston"), it had no duty to indemnify and defend Houston in a bodily injury suit filed against it. Finding that coverage was clearly and unambiguously excluded under the terms of the policy, we reverse the trial court's denial of York's motion.

The standard of review of the trial court's denial of [York's] motion for summary judgment is a de novo review of the evidence to determine whether there is any genuine issue of material fact as to the elements required to establish the causes of action stated in the complaint. To obtain summary judgment, [York] as the moving party must demonstrate that there is no genuine issue of material fact, and that the material evidence, viewed in the light most favorable to the nonmoving party, warrants judgment as a matter of law.

In a single enumeration of error, York contends that the trial court erred in denying its motion for summary judgment, arguing that under the unambiguous terms of the insurance policy which it issued to Houston, it was not required to defend and indemnify Houston in a bodily injury suit filed against it by Anne Vandalinda. Specifically, York argues that Vandalinda's allegations against Houston fit squarely within an exclusion in the policy.

An insurance policy is governed by the ordinary rules of contract construction. The hallmark of contract construction is to ascertain the intention of the parties. O.C.G.A. § 3-2-3. However, when the terms of a written contract are clear and unambiguous, the court is to look to the contract alone to find the parties' intent. Under Georgia law, an insurance company is free to fix the terms of its policies as it sees fit, so long as such terms are not contrary to law, and it is equally free to insure against certain risks while excluding others. An insurer's duty to defend is determined by comparing the allegations of the complaint with the provisions of the policy.(Citations and punctuation omitted.) *Capitol Indem. Corp. v. L. Carter Post 4472 Veterans of Foreign Wars.* n2 * * *

Vandalinda signed up for a three-month membership with Houston, a health and fitness club, in order to get physically fit. In her complaint, Vandalinda alleged that she was given instructions by one of Houston's employees on the use of various exercise machines. At the time of her injury, Vandalinda was using an exercise machine which develops the triceps. Vandalinda tried to release the machine using her arms as she had been instructed to do by Houston's employee. However, the complaint alleges the [*4] machine improperly released from Vandalinda's control "due to improper instructions" given by the employee, and, as a result, Vandalinda experienced pain in her left arm for which surgery was later required.

York issued to Houston a commercial general liability policy which contained the following exclusion: *This insurance does not apply to "bodily injury," "property damage" or "personal and advertising injury" arising out of the rendering of or failure to render any service, treatment, advice or instruction relating to physical fitness, including services or advice in connection with diet, cardio-vascular fitness, body building or physical training programs.* [Italics added]

It is apparent from the allegations of the complaint that Vandalinda's claim against Houston falls within the policy exclusion. Her "bodily injury arose out of the . . . failure" of Houston's employee "to render . . . advice or instruction relating to physical fitness, including . . . advice in connection with . . . body building or physical training programs." Accordingly, coverage for Vandalinda's bodily injury was excluded by the unambiguous language of the policy endorsement.

Where the language of the contract fixing the extent of coverage is unambiguous, as here, and but one reasonable construction is possible, this court must enforce the contract as written. A term in an insurance policy that unambiguously and lawfully limits the insurer's liability may not be extended beyond what is fairly within its plain terms. [York] was entitled to judgment as a matter of law because coverage was excluded for this loss. (Citation omitted.) *Bold Corp. v. Nat. Union Fire Ins. Co. & c.* n3

* * *

Judgment reversed. Ellington and Phipps, JJ., concur.

CASES ON THE SUPPLEMENTAL WEBSITE

Regan v. Mutual of Omaha Insurance Company, (2007 Ill. App. LEXIS 894). This case involves a swimming injury incurred by a baseball player on a team trip. Examine the wording of the policy restrictions and their interpretation by the court.

Maciasz v. Fireman's Fund Insurance Company and Chicago Insurance Company (988 So. 2d 991; 2008 Ala. LEXIS 11). In this case a client was injured in an automobile accident on the way to camp. The primary issue examined by the court is whether the insurance policy is ambiguous.

Ellison v. Kentucky Farm Bureau Mutual Insurance Company, 2010 Ky. App. Unpub. LEXIS 567. After one spectator assaulted a second spectator, the court ruled that the assaulting spectator's homeowner's insurance policy did not cover damages from the altercation.

Feszchak v. Pawtucket Mutual Insurance Company, 2008 U.S. Dist. LEXIS 29295. The insurance company failed to pay a claim due to an exclusion in the policy. The plaintiff filed suit and won.

Bedford Central School District v. Commercial Union Insurance Company (295 A.D.2d 295; 742 N.Y.S.2d 671; 2002 N.Y. App. Div. LEXIS 5737). A student lost an eye while participating on a challenge course owned by another school. The issue was whether the student was covered as an additional insured. Note the reasons given for the judgment.

QUESTIONS YOU SHOULD BE ABLE TO ANSWER

1. When a recreation or sport manager purchases insurance for a business or entity, what are the steps to take in determining the amount of coverage needed?
2. An independent contractor also needs insurance. Generally, what type of insurance is of most importance to the contractor? Explain why?
3. Explain what is meant by (1) exclusions and (2) conditions.
4. Distinguish between liability insurance and umbrella liability coverage.
5. What should be the major factors in selecting an agent and a carrier?

REFERENCES

Cases
York Insurance Company v. Houston Wellness Center, Inc., 2003 Ga. App. LEXIS 794.

Publications
Brooks, D. (1985). Property Insurance. *Risk management today*. Washington: ICMA.
Castle, G., Cushman, R., and Kensicki, P. (1981). *The business insurance handbook*. Homewood, Ill.: Dow Jones-Irwin.
Corbett, R. (1995). *Insurance in sport and recreation*. Edmonton, Alberta: Centre for Sport and Law.
Dahlgren, S. (2000, April). Covering your assets. *Athletic Business*. p. 59.
Kufahl, S. (2002, August). Business without a safety line? *Club Industry*, p. 18.
Mehr, R., Cammack, E., & Rose, T. (1985). *Principles of insurance*. Homewood, Ill.: Richard D. Irwin, Inc.
Novick, L. B. Murky waters: Insurance basics for nonprofits. Washington, D.C.: *Nonprofit Risk Management Institutes*.
Sundheim, F. (1983). *How to insure a business*. Santa Barbara, Calif: Venture Publications.
van der Smissen, B. (1990). *Legal liability and risk management for public and private entities*. Cincinnati: Anderson Publishing Co.
Wilkinson, D. G., (Ed.). (1988). *The event planning process*. Levine, M. A., Kirke, G., Zitterman, D. B., and Kert, E. Insurance. Willowdale, Ontario, Can.: The Event Management & Marketing Institute.

4.26 WORKERS' COMPENSATION

John T. Wolohan | Syracuse University

Under common law, when an employee was injured on the job, there was a good chance the injuries would go uncompensated due to the doctrines of assumption of risk, contributory negligence, and the fellow servant rule (Larson, 1992). Those injured workers who could overcome the preceding defenses usually faced a series of other problems before they received any compensation for their injuries. First, the injured workers, faced with little or no income, were under enormous financial pressure to settle their claims. The injured worker, therefore, usually received much less than the true value of his or her claim to support themselves and their families. Second, even if the injured employee was able to withstand the financial pressure and could afford to litigate the claim, the employer was often able to use the court system to his or her advantage and delay paying the employee any compensation. Finally, if the injured worker was lucky enough to recover his or her damages, the award was usually reduced by hefty attorney fees (Prosser & Keeton, 1984).

In an effort to protect injured workers and alleviate the injustice of the common law system, states began to enact workers' compensation legislation, modeled after the German and English systems. The first state to enact workers' compensation legislation was Maryland when it passed a cooperative accident fund for miners in 1902 (Larson, 1984). Subsequently, Congress passed legislation covering certain federal employees in 1908. By 1911, twenty-five states had enacted some form of law protecting employees; every state in the country having some form of workers' compensation law by 1949 (Larson, 1984). The **workers' compensation legislation**, which is different in every state, provides benefits, including lost wages, usually one-half to two-thirds of the employee's weekly wages, and medical care to an employee who is injured or killed in the course of employment, regardless of fault. The right of an employee to workers' compensation benefits is based on one simple test: Was the injury work-related? In exchange for this protection, the injured worker agrees to forego any tort claim he or she might have against the employer (Larson, 1992). The workers' compensation system, therefore, acts like a "bargain" between the employer and employee. The employer, in exchange for immunity from lawsuits, provides employees with swift, though limited, compensation for work-related injuries. In return, injured workers are guaranteed compensation for their injuries (Ashbrook, 2008).

Workers' compensation is, therefore, a form of strict liability. It makes no difference whether the injury was caused by the employee's negligence or pure accident; *all the employee has to show is that he or she was injured in the course of employment* (Larson, 1992). As a result, the injured worker receives quick financial assistance with minimal interruption in his or her life.

FUNDAMENTAL CONCEPTS

The basic policy behind the workers' compensation system is that the cost of the product should bear the blood of the worker (Prosser & Keeton, 1984). In other words, the employer is required by the state to compensate the employee through private insurance, state-funded insurance, or self-insurance for any damages suffered by the employee. The employer should treat the cost of workers' compensation insurance as part of the cost of production. These extra costs are then added to the cost of production and passed on to the consumer.

Eligibility Requirement

Although every state has its own workers' compensation laws, there are two basic eligibility requirements that an injured party must satisfy before he or she can recover workers' compensation benefits. The first requirement is that the person must show that he or she was an employee of the organization. An **employee** is defined as any person in the service of another under any contract of hire. In reviewing the relationship between an individual and a recreation or sport organization to determine if he or she was in fact an employee, the courts use an "economic reality test" (*Coleman v. Western Michigan University*, 1983). Under the **economic reality test**, the court examines the following factors to determine whether there existed an expressed or implied contract for hire.

1. Does the employer have the right to control or dictate the activities of the proposed employee?
2. Does the employer have the right to discipline or fire the proposed employee?
3. The payment of "wages" and, particularly, the extent to which the proposed employee is dependent upon the payment of wages or other benefits for his daily living expenses; and
4. Whether the task performed by the proposed employee was "an integral part" of the proposed employer's business (*Coleman v. Western Michigan University*, 1983 at 225).

In *Coleman v. Western Michigan University* (1983), the Michigan Court of Appeals, citing the *Rensing v. Indiana State University Board of Trustees* (1983) decision, concluded that scholarship athletes are not employees within the meaning of the workers' compensation statute. In particular, the court found that Coleman could only satisfy the third factor of the "economic reality test," that his scholarship did constitute wages. As far as the other factors, the court found that the university's right to control and discipline Coleman required by the first two factors was substantially limited. In considering the fourth factor, the court held "that the primary function of the defendant university was to provide academic education rather than conduct a football program." The term *integral*, the court held, suggests that the task performed by the employee is essential for the employer to conduct his business. The "integral part" of the university is not football, the court said, but education and research.

The second requirement every employee must meet before he or she can collect workers' compensation is that *the injury suffered by the employee must have occurred in the course of his or her employment.*

Workers' Compensation and Small Businesses

As mentioned earlier, workers' compensation is primarily regulated by the individual states, and therefore there is no single cohesive set of rules governing benefits, coverage, or premium computation. There are, however, some things that every business, no matter how big or small, must know.

First, in most states, it does not matter how small your business, if you have employees, you need workers' compensation insurance. As a result, workers' compensation insurance can be a significant expense for many small businesses.

Second, to satisfy the workers' compensation obligations, all an employer has to do is purchase an insurance policy. In most states, these policies can be purchased either through a state insurance fund or by private insurance from an insurance company. There are, however, some states that require employers to purchase coverage exclusively through state-operated funds.

Third, it is important to remember that if a business fails to carry workers' compensation insurance and an employee is injured, the employer can be required to not only pay the employee's medical expenses, death benefits, lost wages, and vocational rehabilitation out of pocket, but also be liable for any penalties levied by the state (Priz, 2005).

In addition, recreation and sport managers also need to be conscious of workers' compensation in the following areas: staff employees, independent contractors, and volunteers. With staff employees, it is clear that the recreation or sport manager should follow the local laws governing workers' compensation insurance. How independent contractors and volunteers are treated, however, will vary from state to state, so it is essential that employers inform their workers' compensation insurance agent if the organization uses independent contractors or volunteers.

Independent Contractors

Whether an individual is hired as an independent contractor or an employee may impact the obligation an employer has under each state's workers' compensation law. For example, some states require all workers to be covered under its workers' compensation programs, regardless of whether or not they are employees or independent contractors. Other states only require employees to be covered. As a result, it is important that employers know their state's laws to determine who must be covered and what is required of them to comply (Priz, 2005).

Volunteers

Although covering "volunteers" under your workers' compensation plan may seem like a less-attractive option considering the up-front expense for the organization of paying for workers' compensation insurance, there are a number of important benefits from this option. First, by covering "volunteers" under your workers' compensation plan, if a volunteer is injured, you can save your organization both time and money by avoiding a negligence lawsuit. Second, by covering "volunteers" under your workers' compensation plan, you save your organization from any bad publicity that a lawsuit would generate. Finally, you also protect your volunteers from financial hardship by providing them benefits under workers' compensation (Wong & Wolohan, 1996).

For example, in 1999, a girls' softball umpire in Montana was stepping away from the plate when a player accidentally hit him. When a workers' compensation claim was filed on behalf of the umpire, the investigation revealed that local recreation league umpires and referees had no workers' compensation insurance and possibly no medical coverage at all. Without workers' compensation, recreational league umpires have to rely on their own personal medical insurance. The cost for the league to cover the referees under workers' compensation would have been about $3.08 per referee (Hull, 2000).

Workers' Compensation and Professional Athletes

Satisfying the requirements for workers' compensation is usually not difficult for professional athletes. There is no question that professional athletes are employees of their teams and any injury suffered by an athlete is usually well documented and treated. The hard part, however, is to determine in which jurisdiction the athlete may file his or her claim. Historically, because of the state's liberal statute of limitations and the fact that it only required that an athlete had played at least one game within its jurisdiction to qualify for workers' compensation, California was often used "as the state of last resort" for the workers' compensation claims of professional athletes whose home states had more restrictive laws (Binning, 2014). Another reason that California was so attractive to professional athletes is because it was one of nine states to recognize workers' compensation claims for injuries resulting from "cumulative trauma" which result from repetitive traumatic activities extending over a period of time. Since professional athletes spend years performing the same tasks and perfecting repetitive movements, cumulative trauma injuries are a particular problem (Binning, 2014).

In the past few years, however, there have been two developments that have limited the rights of professional athletes under California's workers' compensation statutes. For example, in *Matthews v. National Football League Management Council*, Bruce Matthews a former offensive lineman with the Houston Oilers and the Tennessee Titans, who played in the NFL, filed for workers' compensation in California, claiming an array of disabilities that manifested from injuries sustained during his career. In rejecting "single-game rule," the Ninth Circuit Court found that although Matthews played thirteen games in California during his nineteen-year NFL career, "it is not clear that California would extend its workers' compensation regime to cover the cumulative injuries Matthews claims, given his limited contacts with the state" (*Matthews v. National Football League Management Council*, 2012).

In addition to the courts, the California State Legislature also acted to close the loophole in the system that was resulting in an average of 34 new claims each month and had paid nearly $42 million in claims to professional athletes since 2002 (Thompson and Olson, 2013). As a result, the state passed Assembly Bill AB1309, also known as Chapter 653 of the California Labor Code, limiting the state's workers' compensation exposure to professional athletes to those athletes who spent more than 20 percent of their professional time in California or worked for a California-based team for part of their professional or semi-professional career (Thompson and Olson, 2013).

Other than California, the majority of jurisdictions do not explicitly address the issue of workers' compensation benefits for professional athletes. In the absence of an explicit statutory provision protecting professional athletes, state courts are called to interpret the governing workers' compensation coverage of professional athletes. In most cases, the courts have held that athletes are considered "employees" within the controlling statutory system (McQueeney, 2014).

Some states, however, have amended their workers' compensation statutes to specifically exclude professional athletes. For example, in *Rudolph v. Miami Dolphins*, three professional football players, Council Rudolph, William Windauer, and Floyd Wells, sought workers' compensation benefits for injuries sustained during their employment with the Miami Dolphins. In upholding the Florida Workers' Compensation Statute which states that "'Employment' does not include services performed by or as . . . professional athletes, such as professional boxers, wrestlers, baseball, football, basketball, hockey, polo, tennis, jai alai, and similar players," the Florida Appellate Court held that the professional athlete exclusion was reasonable and not a wholly arbitrary one, since the players are frequently amenable to serious injuries, willfully hold themselves out to such injuries, and are generally well paid for their services.

Unlike the Florida's statutory system that applies a blanket exclusion to all professional athletes, Michigan's regime is organized such that professional athletes are statutorily included, but systematically or functionally excluded (McQueeney, 2014). Specifically, Section 360 of Michigan's Worker's Disability Compensation Act allows a professional athlete to claim benefits only insofar as the athlete earns less than 200% of the Michigan average weekly wage. The effect of this provision is to functionally exclude all professional athletes from the major professional leagues from claiming benefits (McQueeney, 2014).

In addition to Florida and Michigan, other states to exclude professional athletes from receiving workers' compensation under state statutes include Massachusetts, Wyoming, and Montana. Each of the three excludes professional athletes that are engaged in contact sports. Also, like Michigan, Pennsylvania's statute restricts eligibility for workers' compensation to only those professional athletes not making more than twice the state average weekly wage, which excludes all professional athletes from the major professional leagues from claiming benefits (Friede, 2015).

Chronic Traumatic Encephalopathy (CTE) and Long Term Injuries

One of the biggest issues facing professional athletes and workers' compensation coverage is the type of injuries professional athletes incur. For example, while concussions are generally acute traumas, they have recently been linked to degenerative brain diseases like chronic traumatic encephalopathy (CTE), Alzheimer's disease, and other dementia-type diseases. However, because they do not result from easily identifiable "accidents," professional athletes face a number of obstacles in trying to obtain benefits under state workers' compensation laws. For example, depending on the state, the statutes of limitation for long term workers' compensation disability claim will have usually tolled by the time athletes start to develop CTE or other long term cumulative trauma diseases.

For athletes in states in which the statute of limitations does not begin until after the disability is discovered the next obstacle to receiving compensation is the fact that their claims are based on cumulative trauma. Many states do not allow for cumulative trauma claims. Even if the courts allowed cumulative trauma claims, and even with all the current research showing a relationship between concussions and CTE, professional athletes would still need to show that their injury was caused by playing the sport (Friede, 2015).

Workers' Compensation and College Athletes

Early court cases involving college athletes generally ruled that the athletes were employees of the university and covered under the school's workers' compensation insurance (*University of Denver v. Nemeth*, 1953 and *Van Horn v. Industrial Accident Commission*, 1963). However, the courts began to change their position in the late 1950's when the Supreme Court of Colorado ruled that Ray Herbert Dennison, who was fatally injured while playing football for Fort Lewis A & M College, was not an employee of the university. In making its decision, the Supreme Court of Colorado held that "it was significant that the college did not receive a direct benefit from the activities, since the college was not in the football business and received no benefit from this field of recreation (*State Compensation Insurance Fund, et al. v. Industrial Commission of Colorado*, 1957). In the 65 years since the Supreme Court of Colorado's decision, courts in almost every jurisdiction have upheld the reasoning behind the decision and have ruled that students are not employees of their schools because the business of the university is education, not athletics.

State Legislation Regarding College Athletes

In affirming the decision of the California Workers' Compensation Appeals Board, the California Court of Appeals in *Graczyk v. Workers' Compensation Appeals Board* (1986), denied workers' compensation benefits to Ricky Graczyk after he sustained head, neck, and spine injuries while playing football for California

State University, Fullerton. The Court of Appeals ruled that it was the intent of the state legislature to exclude Graczyk, and all scholarship athletes, from receiving workers' compensation benefits for injuries received on the playing field. The court pointed out that the California State Legislature specifically amended the state's workers' compensation statute to define an "employee" to exclude "any person, other than a regular employee, participating in sports or athletics who receives no compensation for such participation other than the use of athletic equipment, uniforms, transportation, travel, meals, lodging, or other expenses incidental thereto."

The California State Legislature amended the statute further in 1981 when it specifically excluded from the definition of employee "[a]ny student participating as an athlete in amateur sporting events sponsored by any public agency, public or private nonprofit college, university or school, who receives no remuneration for such participation other than the use of athletic equipment, uniforms, transportation, travel, meals, lodging, scholarships, grants in aid, and other expenses" [*Graczyk v. Workers' Compensation Appeals Board*, 1986; West's Ann. Cal. Labor Code § 3353 (k)]. Hawaii, New York, and other states have followed California's example of expressly excluding scholarship athletes from workers' compensation benefits.

Consequences of Additional Coverage

As illustrated by *Rensing v. Indiana State University Board of Trustees* (1983), the issue of whether or not a scholarship athlete is an employee is a difficult one. For example, in most states, workers' compensation insurance rates are determined by actuarial tables that take into account the number of accidents and claims for that particular group of employees. If athletes were suddenly added into the group of school employees, the number of injuries and claims of the group would rise substantially. This would make it difficult, if not impossible, for colleges and universities to find an insurance company willing to insure them. Even if the school could find an insurance company, the increased exposure would require the insurance company to raise rates. Faced with higher insurance rates and/or the potential liability of self-insuring, many schools would be forced to evaluate whether the benefits of having an athletic program justify the increased cost and exposure.

Other Possible Consequences

Additional Workers' Compensation Claims. If scholarship athletes are considered employees of their school, there could be an increase in the number of workers' compensation claims filed and benefits paid (Wolohan, 1994).

Tax Effect on School. If scholarship athletes were considered employees of their school, there would be some interesting tax questions for both the colleges or universities and the scholarship athletes. For example, does the scholarship athlete now have to pay taxes on the value of the scholarship? Also, will schools now be required to pay FICA and Medicare tax on the student's income? If so, how are the taxes to be paid (Wolohan, 1994)?

Employee Benefits. If scholarship athletes are considered employees of the school, are scholarship athletes eligible for employee benefits? Besides tuition, room, board, and books, are scholarship athletes now going to be eligible for life, medical, and dental insurance? How about the school's employee retirement plan, would scholarship athletes be eligible (Wolohan, 1994)?

Nonscholarship Athletes. Even if scholarship athletes are considered employees of the school, what about athletes who do not receive athletic scholarships? Because these athletes receive no compensation, they have no contractual relationship with the university to compete in athletics. Therefore, the non-scholarship athlete could never be deemed an employee and would never be covered by workers' compensation (Wolohan, 1994).

NCAA Catastrophic Injury Insurance Program

One of the reasons scholarship athletes have sought workers' compensation benefits in the past is to recover out-of-pocket medical expenses. Although most schools will pay the medical expenses of injured athletes, there usually is a limit to their generosity. In fact, it is not uncommon for a school to stop paying an injured athlete's medical and other bills. This is especially true when the injury is permanently disabling, and the injured athlete requires prolonged medical care.

In an effort to alleviate such hardships, and perhaps to prevent future court challenges on the status of scholarship athletes, the NCAA, in August 1991, implemented a Catastrophic Injury Insurance Program. The NCAA's Catastrophic Injury Insurance Plan covers every student who participates in college athletics, student coaches, student managers, student trainers, and cheerleaders who have been catastrophically injured while participating in a covered intercollegiate athletic activity. The policy has a $75,000 deductible and provides benefits in excess of any other valid and collectible insurance up to $20,000,000.

The NCAA's Catastrophic Injury Insurance Program is similar to workers' compensation in that it provides medical, dental, and rehabilitation expenses plus lifetime disability payments to students who are catastrophically injured, regardless of fault. The plan also includes $25,000 if the individual dies within 12 months of the accident.

The NCAA plan is more attractive than workers' compensation in a number of ways. First, scholarship athletes can collect benefits without litigating the issue of whether or not the athlete is an employee of the college or university. Second, the NCAA's plan provides the athlete with benefits immediately, without time delays, litigation costs, and the uncertainties involved in litigation. Finally, another benefit of the NCAA's plan is that it guarantees that catastrophically injured athletes will receive up to $120,000 toward the cost of completing their undergraduate degree. (For more information on the NCAA's Catastrophic Injury Insurance Program go to the NCAA Website: http://www.ncaa.org/about/resources/insurance/student-athlete-insurance-programs

SIGNIFICANT CASE

Although maybe not the most recent case, the following case is significant in that it provides the reader with a thorough review of the issues surrounding scholarship athletes who suffer career-ending or life-threatening injuries. In particular, the case analyzes the definitions of "employee" for purposes of the workers' compensation laws.

RENSING V. INDIANA STATE UNIVERSITY BOARD OF TRUSTEES
Supreme Court of Indiana
444 N.E.2d 1170 (1983)
The facts established before the Industrial Board were summarized by the Court of Appeals:

"The undisputed testimony reveals that [Indiana State University Board of Trustees] the Trustees, through their agent Thomas Harp (the University's Head Football Coach), on February 4, 1974 offered Fred W. Rensing a scholarship or 'educational grant' to play football at the University. In essence, the financial aid agreement, which was renewable each year for a total of four years provided that in return for Rensing's active participation in football competition he would receive free tuition, room, board, laboratory fees, a book allowance, tutoring and a limited number of football tickets per game for family and friends. The 'agreement' provided, inter alia, the aid would continue even if Rensing suffered an injury during supervised play which would make it inadvisable, in the opinion of the doctor-director of the student health service, 'to continue to participate,' although in that event the University would require other assistance to the extent of his ability.

The trustees extended this scholarship to Rensing for the 1974–75 academic year in the form of a 'Tender of Financial Assistance.' Rensing accepted the Trustees' first tender and signed it (as did his parents) on April 29, 1974. At the end of Rensing's first academic year the Trustees extended a second 'Tender of Financial Assistance' for the 1975–76 academic year, which tender was substantially the same as the first and provided the same financial assistance to Rensing for his continued participation in the University's football program. Rensing and his father signed this second tender on June 24, 1975. It is not contested the monetary value of this assistance to Rensing for the 1975–76 academic year was $2,374, and that the 'scholarship' was in effect when Rensing's injuries occurred.

* * *

Rensing testified he suffered a knee injury during his first year (1974–75) of competition which prevented him from actively participating in the football program, during which time he continued to receive his scholarship as well as free treatment for his knee injury. The only requirement imposed by the Trustees (through Coach Harp) upon Rensing was attendance at his classes and reporting daily to the football stadium for free whirlpool and ultrasonic treatments for his injured knee.

* * *

As noted above, the financial aid agreement provided that in the event of an injury of such severity that it prevented continued athletic participation, 'Indiana State University will ask you to assist in the conduct of the athletic program within the limits of your physical capabilities' in order to continue receiving aid. The sole assistance actually asked of Rensing was to entertain prospective football recruits when they visited the University's Terre Haute campus.

During the 1975 football season, Rensing participated on the University's football team. In the spring of 1976 he partook in the team's annual three week spring practice when, on April 24, he was injured while he tackled a teammate during a punting drill.

* * *

The specific injury suffered by Rensing was a fractured dislocation of the cervical spine at the level of 4–5 vertebrae. Rensing's initial treatment consisted of traction and eventually a spinal fusion. During this period he developed pneumonia for which he had to have a tracheostomy. Eventually, Rensing was transferred to the Rehabilitation Department of the Barnes Hospital complex in St. Louis. According to Rensing's doctor at Barnes Hospital, one Franz Steinberg, Rensing's paralysis was caused by the April 24, 1976 football injury leaving him 95–100% disabled." *Rensing v. Indiana State University Board of Trustees*, supra, at pp. 80–82 (footnotes omitted).

Rensing's appeal to the Industrial Board was originally heard by a Hearing Member who found that Rensing had "failed to sustain his burden in establishing the necessary relationship of employer and employee within the meaning of the Indiana Workmen's Compensation Act," and rejected his claim. *Id.* at p. 83. The Full Industrial Board adopted the Hearing Member's findings and decision; then this decision was reversed by the Court of Appeals.

In this petition to transfer, the Trustees argue that there was no contract of hire in this case and that a student who accepts an athletic "grant-in-aid" from the University does not become an "employee" of the University within the definition of "employee" under the Workmen's Compensation Act, Ind. Code § 22-3-6-1(b), (Burns Supp., 1982). On the other hand, Rensing maintains that his agreement to play football in return for financial assistance did amount to a contract of employment.

Here, the facts concerning the injury are undisputed. The contested issue is whether the requisite employer-employee relationship existed between Rensing and the Trustees so as to bring him under the coverage of our Workmen's Compensation Act. Both the Industrial Board and the Court of Appeals correctly noted that the workmen's compensation laws are to be liberally construed. *Prater v. Indiana Briquetting Corp.*, (1969) 253 Ind. 83, 251 N.E. 2d 810. With this proposition as a starting point, the specific facts of this case must be analyzed to determine whether Rensing and the Trustees come within the definitions of "employee" and "employer" found in the statute, and specifically whether there did exist a contract of employment. Ind. Code § 22-3-6-1, supra, defines the terms "employee" and "employer" as follows:

"(a) 'Employer' includes the state and any political subdivision, any municipal corporation within the state, any individual, firm, association or corporation or the receiver or trustee of the same, or the legal representatives of a deceased person, using the services of another for pay."

"(b) The term 'employee' means every person, including a minor, in the service of another, under any contract of hire or apprenticeship, written or implied, except one whose employment is both casual and not in the usual course of the trade, business, occupation or profession of the employer."

The Court of Appeals found that there was enough evidence in the instant case to support a finding that a contract of employment did exist here. We disagree.

It is clear that while a determination of the existence of an employee-employer relationship is a complex matter involving many factors, the primary consideration is that there was an intent that a contract of employment, either express or implied, did exist. In other words, there must be a mutual belief that an employer-employee relationship did exist. *Fox v. Contract Beverage Packers, Inc.*, (1980) Ind. App., 398 N.E. 2d 709, *Gibbs v. Miller*, (1972) 152 Ind. App. 326, 283 N.E. 2d 592. It is evident from the documents which formed the agreement in this case that there was no intent to enter into an employee-employer relationship at the time the parties entered into the agreement.

In this case, the National Collegiate Athletic Association's (NCAA) constitution and bylaws were incorporated by reference into the agreements. A fundamental policy of the NCAA, which is stated in its constitution, is that intercollegiate sports are viewed as part of the educational system and are clearly distinguished from the professional sports business. The NCAA has strict rules against "taking pay" for sports or sporting activities. Any student who does accept pay is ineligible for further play at an NCAA member school in the sport for which he takes pay. Furthermore, an institution cannot, in any way, condition financial aid on a student's ability as an athlete. NCAA Constitution, Sec. 3-1-(a)-(1); Sec. 3-1-(g)-(2). The fundamental concerns behind the policies of the NCAA are that intercollegiate athletics must be maintained as a part of the educational program and student-athletes are integral parts of the institution's student body. An athlete receiving financial aid is still first and foremost a student.

All of these NCAA requirements designed to prohibit student-athletes from receiving pay for participation in their sport were incorporated into the financial aid agreements Rensing and his parents signed.

Furthermore, there is evidence that the financial aid which Rensing received was not considered by the parties involved to be pay or income. Rensing was given free tuition, room, board, laboratory fees, and a book allowance. These benefits were not considered to be "pay" by the University or by the NCAA since they did not affect Rensing's or the University's eligibility status under NCAA rules. Rensing did not consider the benefits as income as he did not report them for income tax purposes. The Internal Revenue Service has ruled that scholarship recipients are not taxed on their scholarship proceeds and there is no distinction made between athletic and academic scholarships. Rev. Rul. 77-263, 1977-31 I.R.B. 8.

As far as scholarships are concerned, we find that our Indiana General Assembly clearly has recognized a distinction between the power to award financial aid to students and the power to hire employees since the former power was specifically granted to the Boards of Trustees of state educational institutions with the specific limitation that the award be reasonably related to the educational purposes and objectives of the institution and in the best interests of the institution and the state. Ind. Code § 20-12-1-2(h) (Burns 1975).

Furthermore, we find that Ind. Code § 22-4-6-2 (Burns 1974) is not applicable to scholarship benefits. In that statute, which deals with contributions by employers to unemployment insurance, employers are directed to include "all individuals attending an established school . . . who, in lieu of remuneration for such services, receive either meals, lodging, books, tuition or other education facilities." Here, Rensing was not working at a regular job for the University. The scholarship benefits he received were not given him in lieu of pay for remuneration for his services in playing football any more than academic scholarship benefits were given to other students for their high scores on tests or class assignments. Rather, in both cases, the students received benefits based upon their past demonstrated ability in various areas to enable them to pursue opportunities for higher education as well as to further progress in their own fields of endeavor.

Scholarships are given to students in a wide range of artistic, academic and athletic areas. None of these recipients is covered under Ind. Code § 22-4-6-2, supra, unless the student holds a regular job for the institution in addition to the scholarship. The statute would apply to students who work for the University and perform services not integrally connected with the institution's educational program and for which, if the student were not available, the University would have to hire outsiders, e.g., workers in the laundry, bookstore, etc. Scholarship recipients are considered to be students seeking advanced educational opportunities and are not considered to be professional athletes, musicians or artists employed by the University for their skills in their respective areas.

In addition to finding that the University, the NCAA, the IRS and Rensing, himself, did not consider the scholarship benefits to be income, we also agree with Judge Young's conclusion that Rensing was not "in the service of" the University. As Judge Young stated:

> *"Furthermore, I do not believe that Rensing was 'in the service of' the Trustees. Rensing's participation in football may well have benefited the university in a very general way. That does not mean that Rensing was in the service of the Trustees. If a student wins a Rhodes scholarship or if the debate team wins a national award that undoubtedly benefits the school, but does not mean that the student and the team are in the service of the school. Rensing performed no duties that would place him in the service of the university." Rensing v. Indiana State University, at 90.*

Courts in other jurisdictions have generally found that such individuals as student athletes, student leaders in student government associations and student resident-hall assistants are not "employees" for purposes of workmen's compensation laws unless they are also employed in a university job in addition to receiving scholarship benefits.

All of the above facts show that in this case, Rensing did not receive "pay" for playing football at the University within the meaning of the Workmen's Compensation Act; therefore, an essential element of the employer-employee relationship was missing in addition to the lack of intent. Furthermore, under the applicable rules of the NCAA, Rensing's benefits could not be reduced or withdrawn because of his athletic ability or his contribution to the team's success. Thus, the ordinary employer's right to discharge on the basis of performance was also missing. While there was an agreement between Rensing and the Trustees which established certain obligations for both parties, the agreement was not a contract of employment. Since at least three important factors indicative of an employee-employer relationship are absent in this case, we find it is not necessary to consider other factors which may or may not be present.

We find that the evidence here shows that Rensing enrolled at Indiana State University as a full-time student seeking advanced educational opportunities. He was not considered to be a professional athlete who was being paid for his athletic ability. In fact, the benefits Rensing received were subject to strict regulations by the NCAA which were designed to protect his amateur status. Rensing held no other job with the University and therefore cannot be considered an "employee" of the University within the meaning of the Workmen's Compensation Act.

It is our conclusion of law, under the facts here, including all rules and regulations of the University and the NCAA governing student athletes, that the appellant shall be considered only as a student athlete and not as an employee within the meaning of the Workmen's Compensation Act. Accordingly, we find that there is substantial evidence to support the finding of the Industrial Board that there was no employee-employer relationship between Rensing and the Trustees, and their finding must be upheld.

For all of the foregoing reasons, transfer is granted; the opinion of the Court of Appeals is vacated and the Industrial Board is in all things affirmed.

CASES ON THE SUPPLEMENTAL WEBSITE

Coleman v. Western Michigan University, 125 Mich. App. 35; 336 N.W.2d 224; (1983). This case examines whether college sports are an integral part of business of a university.

Norfolk Admirals and Federal Insurance Company v. Ty A. Jones, 2005 Va. App. LEXIS 443. This case examines whether fighting, when following his coach's instructions, is part of a professional hockey player's job and therefore covered by workers' compensation.

Rudolph v. Miami Dolphins, 447 So. 2d 284 (Fla. App., 1983). This case examines the impact of the Florida Workers' Compensation Act on professional athletes.

Waldrep v. Texas Employers Insurance Association, 21 S.W.3d 692 (Tex. App, 2000). This case reexamines the issue of college athletes and whether they are employees of the schools.

QUESTIONS YOU SHOULD BE ABLE TO ANSWER

1. Are college athletes covered under workers' compensation?
2. How do you determine if an individual is an employee of an organization?
3. What are some of the benefits of the NCAA's Catastrophic Injury Insurance Program?
4. What are the benefits and disadvantages to workers of state enacted workers' compensation programs?
5. What are the benefits and disadvantages to employers of state enacted workers' compensation programs?

REFERENCES

Cases
Coleman v. Western Michigan Univ., 125 Mich. App. 35, 336 N.W.2d 224 (1983).
Graczyk v. Workers' Compensation Appeals Board, 184 Cal. App.3d 997, 229 Cal. Rptr. 494, 58 A.L.R. 4th 1245, 34 Ed. Law Rep. 523 (Cal. App. 2 Dist., Aug 8, 1986).
Matthews v. NFL Management Council, 688 F.3d 1107 (9th Cir. 2012).
Palmer v. Kansas City Chiefs, 621 S.W.2d 350 (Mo. Ct. App. 1981).
Rensing v. Indiana State University Board of Trustees, 437 N.E.2d 78 (1982).
Rensing v. Indiana State University Board of Trustees, 444 N.E.2d 1170 (1983).
Rudolph v. Miami Dolphins, 447 S.2d 284 (Fla. Dist. Ct. App. 1983).
State Compensation Fund v. Industrial Commission, 135 Colo. 570, 314 P.2d 288 (1957).
University of Denver v. Nemeth, 257 P.2d 423 (1953).
Van Horn v. Industrial Accident Commission, 219 Cal. App. 2d 457, 33 Cal. Rptr. 169 (1963).

Publications
Ashbrook, W. J. (Summer, 2008). Defining "Employee" Within Arizona's Workers' Compensation Statute: An Argument for Inclusion. *Arizona State Law Journal*, 40, 69–712.
Bacon, J. (1997, Oct. 21). Jury: Injured college athlete ineligible for workers' comp. *USA Today*.

Binning, R. (2014). Chapter 653: Tackling Players' End-Around the Laws of Their Home States: Restricting Professional Athlete Access to California's Workers' Compensation System. McGeorge Law Review, 45, 549 – 560

Friede, M. (2015). Professional Athletes are "Seeing Stars": How Athletes are "Knocked-Out" of States' Workers' Compensation Systems. Hamline Law Review, 38, 519 – 555.

Hull, R. (2000, April 26). Referees and umpires cry foul in workers' comp decision. *The Daily Inter Lake*.

Larson, A. (1984). *Workers' Compensation Law*. New York: Matthew Bender & Co.

Larson, A. (1992). *The law of workers' compensation*. New York: Matthew Bender & Co.

McQueeney, T. (2014). Fourth and Long: How the Well-Established System of Workers' Compensation Poses a Substantial Threat to the Financial Stability of the NFL. *University of Baltimore Law Review*, 43, 307 – 347.

NCAA Catastrophic Injury Insurance Policy. http://www.ncaa.org/insurance/catastrophic.html

Priz, E. (2005). *Ultimate guide to workers' compensation insurance*. Irvine, CA: Entrepreneur Press.

Prosser, W. L., & Keeton, W. P. (1984). *The law of torts* (5th ed.). St. Paul, MN: West Publishing Co.

Schwarz, A. (2010, April 7). Teams Dispute Workers' Comp Rights. *New York Times*, p. B10

Stumes, L. (2002a, Feb. 28). Rising premiums create unstable racing industry. *San Francisco Chronicle*, p. C7.

Stumes, L. (2002b, Dec. 22). Trainers, owners get some relief. *San Francisco Chronicle*, p. B15.

Thompson, D. and Olson, L. (2013). New California Law Limits Worker Comp for Pro Athletes. San Jose Mercury News. http://www.mercurynews.com/ci_24273989/new-california-law-limits-worker-comp-pro-athletes. Accessed April 21, 2016.

Wolohan, J. T. (1993, June). Ruling may have Texas-size impact. *Athletic Business*, 17, 22–23.

Wolohan, J. T. (1994). Scholarship athletes: Are they employees or students of the university? The debate continues. *Journal of Legal Aspects of Sport, 4*, 46–58.

Wong, G. M., & Wolohan, J. T. (1996, March). Pitching in. Schools have alternatives in determining volunteers' legal status. *Athletic Business*, 20, 10–14.

CONTRACT LAW 5.00

One of the most fundamental duties performed by sport and recreation administrators is contract negotiations. Therefore, it is important for everyone involved in the sport and recreation business to understand the basics of contract law and contract formation. Once a contract is drafted, the recreation or sport manager must also implement the terms of the contract and must understand the ramifications of failing to meet the contractual obligations. The following section examines the essentials of contract formation, the elements necessary for a legally valid contract and what are the legal implications of breaching a contract.

The *Contract Law* section is divided into three parts. The first part reviews the fundamental aspects of all contracts, presents some principles of interpretation used by the courts in deciding contract disputes, discusses the concept of breach of contract and the remedies for breach, refers to provisions that are typically found in all contracts, and familiarizes you with principles relating to signature authority. The first part is also meant as an introduction to subsequent sections that deal with sport-specific contract law topics in more detail. The second part applies the essential contract elements to employment contracts, and game, event, and sponsorship contracts. The third section looks at alternative dispute resolution methods and their growing role in sport and employment contracts.

# 5.10 CONTRACT ESSENTIALS

Bridget Niland | Daemen College

Contracts are the cornerstone of any business relationship. Since before medieval times, merchants have used contracts to formalize the promises that underlie business transactions (Simpson, 1986). Contract law has greatly evolved since then, but its principle function has remained the same: to provide a framework for the enforcement of promises (Davis, 1996; Hanson, 2006).

Contracts are pervasive throughout all sectors of the sport and recreation industry (Wong, 2010). Whether working in professional, amateur or recreational sport, administrators must consider existing agreements when making day to day decisions, and must know how to negotiate new contracts (Miller, Comfort & Stoldt, 2001). For example, on any given day a college athletics director will review or draft a sponsorship contract with a local company, an employment contract with a coach, a scholarship agreement with a student-athlete or a scheduling contract with another school. Other examples of contracts in the sport and recreation industry include: a professional sports team collective bargaining agreement; a standard player contract in professional sports; membership agreements at health and fitness facilities; liability waivers between participants and athletic event operators; vendor contracts between concessions and professional teams; facility lease agreements between club sport teams and school districts; purchase agreements between sports and memorabilia collectors.

Contract law is complex. As such, sport and recreation managers should consult a licensed attorney before entering into an agreement (Sharp, 2007). Not dismissing that advice, given the important role contracts play in the sport and recreation industry those wishing to work in it must understand the basic principles of contract law. Understanding the basics of contract law will allow sport and recreation managers to make informed decisions and limit the chance of costly lawsuits. The purpose of this chapter is to introduce the fundamental concepts of contract law and explore how those concepts apply within the sport and recreation industry.

FUNDAMENTAL CONCEPTS

Contract is a formal term used to describe a voluntary agreement that imposes duties and benefits upon the parties. It is a promise or a set of promises for which, if breached, the law will provide a remedy (Restatement (Second) Contracts $1). If properly formed, a contract creates a private law between the parties. If a dispute should arise between the parties, the contract is the first resource a court will consider in resolving the matter.

There are three sources of contract law in the United States: common law principles, the Uniform Commercial Code and the Restatement of Contracts. As mentioned in Chapter 1.10, common law is created by previous court decisions involving similar issues. The bulk of the common law of contracts evolved through state, rather than federal, court systems. The common law of contracts is the primary source of law for all contracts other than those for the sale of goods. Sale of goods contracts are governed by the Uniform Commercial Code (U.C.C.).

The U.C.C is a set of laws drafted by legal scholars and intended to create uniform commercial laws across the United States. If adopted by a state, the U.C.C. serves as a primary source of law. The U.C.C. includes nine articles. Article 2 of the U.C.C specifically applies to contracts for the sale of goods, and Article 2a applies to the lease of goods, either of which would cover the purchase of game tickets or lease of sporting equipment (Wong, 2010). Louisiana is the only state in the union that has not adopted Article 2 or 2a.

The third source of contract law is the Restatement of Contracts. It is a secondary source of law composed of a compilation of contract law principles drafted by judges and legal scholars from throughout the United States. Although it lacks the authority of common law or statutory laws like the U.C.C., courts often look to the Restatement for guidance in deciding contractual disputes.

Common law, the U.C.C. and the Restatement of Contracts all recognize that there are different classifications of contractual agreements. The most basic classification is between express contracts and implied contracts. In an **express contract**, the parties clearly state the terms of their agreement, verbally or in writing. The terms of an express contract, at minimum, include the identification of the parties, the subject matter of the contract, the length of time of the contract, and the cost of the contract for each party (Klass, 2010). The standard player contract common in professional sports is one example of an express contract.

Implied contracts occur when the conduct indicates that an agreement exists (this is also referred to as a *quasi contract*), yet there is no proof of a formal exchange of promises. Although implied contracts are rare in sport and recreation (Glover, 2009), there have been cases in which plaintiffs sue for breach of contracts that they claim existed based on the conduct of the two parties. For example, in *Mount Snow, Ltd., v. ALLI, the Alliance of Action Sports* (2013), the plaintiff, a Vermont ski resort, had an agreement with the defendant to host the Winter Dew Tour in both 2010 and 2011. The plaintiff signed a written agreement but the defendant did not. The two parties went on to work together to conduct Dew Tour in 2009 and 2010. In 2011, defendant moved the event to another site. The resort sued for breach of implied contract, among other claims. The district court denied the defendant's motion for summary judgement that argued no implied contract could be deduced from the conduct of the parties. The court disagreed stating that a trier of fact could find that an implied contract existed between the plaintiff and defendant due to their actions in both 2009 and 2010.

There is little legal consequence between an express or implied contract; however, it is easier to prove the existence of a contract that is expressed and in writing (Shubert, Smith & Trentadue, 1986). As such, it is best to formalize all agreements in a written document.

Contract law also classifies contracts by whether they are valid, void or voidable. If a court determines that a contract is **valid**, then it will enforce the contract or grant some other relief to the non-breaching party. A court will not enforce a contract that fails to meet the legal requirements or is contrary to some other rule of law. In such cases, the contract is rendered either **void**, meaning neither party is obligated to perform, or **voidable**, which provides one party the option of canceling the agreement.

Contract Formation

The goal of sport and recreation managers is to structure business agreements that are valid and enforceable should a dispute arise. To form a valid and enforceable contract the following elements must be present: agreement; consideration; capacity; and legality.

Agreement (Mutual Assent)

The first step in creating a valid and enforceable contract is to confirm that the parties mutually assent to the fundamental terms of the agreement. Mutual assent is simply evidence that the parties had a "meeting of the minds" as to the agreement. Courts will determine mutual assent by considering whether the parties had the same understanding as to the material terms of the agreement starting with the offer and acceptance (Miller, Comfort & Stoldt, 2001).

Offer

An **offer** is a conditional promise from the offeror (the party who makes the offer) to the offeree (the party to whom the offer was made). An offer occurs when one party demonstrates a willingness to enter into an agreement with **definite terms** that leaves another party in a position to respond (Restatement (Second) Contracts §24). Definite terms include: (1) the parties; (2) the subject matter; (3) the time and place for the subject matter to be performed; and (4) the consideration or price to be paid (Wong, 2010). For example, Sport Agent offers to represent Superstar in endorsement negotiations with a major sneaker company on January 28, 2010 in New York City, in exchange for Superstar agreeing to pay Sport Agent five percent of the endorsement earnings.

Offers are classified in two types of contracts: unilateral and bilateral. Most offers involve an exchange of promises that create a **bilateral contract**. An example of a bilateral contract within the sport and recreation industry is a scheduling agreement between college football teams, wherein the offeror, Private U, promises to pay the offeree, State U, $100,000 in exchange for State U's promise to play an away contest on Private U's campus. A **unilateral contract**, by contrast, involves the offeror making a promise to the offeree if the offeree takes some specified action. An example of a unilateral contract in recreational sports would be a 5 kilometer road race that offers prize money to the first finisher. The only method of accepting the offer is to win the race. Promising to win the race or even running in the race does not respond to the offer.

Acceptance

In addition to demonstrating a unilateral contract, the 5k road race also highlights the importance of **acceptance** in contract formation. The offeror is not bound and an agreement is not formed until the offeree accepts the offer. Only the offeree can accept the offer from the offeror. An offeree can accept an offer by signature, verbally, through performance (in the case of a unilateral contract) or any other mode permitted by the offeror (Restatement (Second) Contracts §30). Unless the parties agree otherwise, an offer is accepted when it is sent (i.e., mailed, faxed or by email), even if the acceptance is lost in delivery or transmission. This is known as the "mailbox rule."

In limited circumstances, silence by the offeree can be construed as acceptance of the offer. To avoid confusion as to acceptance, sport and recreation managers should formally respond to each offer (Wong, 2010). Failure to do so can lead to ambiguity between the parties and ultimately result in a lawsuit as to whether or not a contract existed. For example, in *Giuliani v. Duke University* (2009), the plaintiff, a recruited non-scholarship athlete, sued after he was removed from the team. The suit hinged on whether promises made during the recruitment process and statements contained in institutional manuals created a contract between the school and the student-athlete. In particular, the court was presented with the issue of what constitutes an offer on part of the institution and acceptance by the student-athlete. Similar issues existed in *LoPiccolo v. American University* (2012), where a recruited scholarship wrestling student-athlete attempted to enforce as a contract promises of a four-year athletic scholarship.

The acceptance also must mirror the offer (Restatement (Second) Contracts §58). A **counteroffer**, which alters the terms of the offer, is not acceptance. Rather, it terminates the offeror's offer and creates a new offer. Counteroffers are a critical part of any contract negotiation from small two-party employment contracts to large complex Collective Bargaining Agreements (CBA). A clear example of counteroffer can be found in the 2012 National Hockey League labor dispute that ultimately led to a lockout of players by the owners. The lockout occurred because players refused to accept the owner's CBA proposals as to the duration of the CBA, buyouts and annual salary. Rather than accepting the owner's initial proposals for these areas, the players association offered counteroffers thereby rejecting the owners' efforts to settle on the content of the CBA (Klein, 2012).

Consideration

In addition to offer and acceptance, an enforceable contract must include consideration. **Consideration** is the exchange of something of value between the parties. It involves each party giving-up something to gain the benefit of the contract. An agreement that lacks this exchange renders the contract unenforceable (Wong, 2010). Agreements that are based on **gifts** are typically dismissed for lack of consideration because there is no mutual exchange of detriment and benefit. One party is merely benefiting from another's generosity.

Because past actions occur prior to the making of a contract and were not intended to induce a promise in exchange, they are also insufficient consideration. In such instances, the offeror is making a promise because the event occurred; he is not making the promise in order to get the event to happen. For example, in *Blackmon v. Iverson* (2003), plaintiff sued basketball star Allen Iverson alleging that the plaintiff was the first to suggest that Iverson use "The Answer" as a nickname and for product merchandising. Iverson later decided to use the term for a line of apparel with Reebok. Iverson then promised to pay the plaintiff twenty-five percent of those earnings. Iverson recanted this promise and plaintiff sued to enforce what he argued was a valid oral contract. In dismissing the claim, the court held that the agreement lacked consideration for two reasons. First, plaintiff's suggestion of the nickname constituted a gift as there was no evidence he sought to be compensated at that time. Second, Iverson's after-the-fact offer to pay the plaintiff a portion of the earnings amounted to **past consideration** between the two parties.

Capacity

Contracts are voluntary agreements. As such, parties to a contract must possess the **capacity** to comprehend its terms and how those terms affect the party's legal interests. Courts will not enforce agreements in which one of the parties is shown to have lacked the capacity to represent his or her interests effectively (Wong, 2010). To void the contract, the party must show that they either lacked sufficient mental capacity, due to age or a medical condition, or were so intoxicated that the party could not understand the nature of the agreement. In either instance, contract law renders the agreement voidable by the impaired party.

For example, as a matter of public policy, courts protect "minors from the making of improvident contracts during their infancy by permitting them to rescind, or disaffirm, such contracts" (Burke & Grube, 2011). Accordingly, with the exception of the necessaries of life (e.g., food, clothes), contracts are unenforceable against the minor but enforceable against the other party (Sharp, 2007). The process of a minor rescinding a contract to which he or she is a party is known as **disaffirmance**. For example, in *Milicic v. Basketball Marketing Co., Inc.* (2004), the court upheld a professional basketball player's right to rescind an agency agreement he entered into as a minor.

A party can also **affirm** a contract entered into as a minor by simply continuing to perform his or her contractual duties as an adult. For example, the plaintiff in *Bagley v. Mt. Bachelor Ski and Summer Resort* (2014) was seventeen when he signed a season ski pass related at defendant ski area. Plaintiff's father signed a minor release and an indemnity agreement. The plaintiff continued to use the resort's services on 26 different occasions after he turned eighteen. Plaintiff was injured in defendant's terrain park. Plaintiff proceeded to file a negligence lawsuit against the defendant ski resort. In dismissing the suit, the court held that although a minor at the time he signed the release, it was nonetheless enforceable because plaintiff continued to use the services of the defendant ski resort after his eighteenth birthday.

Legality

Courts will not enforce a contract involving illegal action or a subject matter that violates public policy. For example, a court will not enforce an agreement between an athletic trainer and a professional athlete under which the athletic trainer agreed to inject the athlete with illegal performance enhancing drugs. Courts also will refuse to enforce employment contracts that include overly broad **covenants not to compete**. Also known as non-compete clauses or restrictive covenants, these provisions attempt to limit the ability of an employee to compete against the employer in the event that the employment is terminated or the employee resigns. Most coaching contracts include some type of non-compete clause, aimed at prohibiting a head coach from accepting another head coaching position within the same league, conference or state.

Sport managers, however, must take care in drafting non-compete clauses because courts will not enforce clauses that are geographically broad or extend for an unduly long period of time. Such agreements, courts have reasoned, constitute an unfair restraint of trade. If properly drafted, covenants not to compete can be an effective tool in limiting the coaching carousel described in *Northeastern University v. Brown*, (2004). An improperly drafted covenant not to compete may cost a company valued customer and also could result in a costly legal judgment.

For example, in *NASC v. Jervis (2008)*, defendants were a group of experienced soccer players and coaches that worked for the plaintiff, a company that ran soccer camps throughout the country. Each of the defendants signed an employment contract with plaintiff, which included a covenant not to compete with plaintiff after leaving the job. More specifically, the covenant agreed not to solicit NASC's customers and not to disclose NASC's confidential information. Over the course of several weeks, each defendant opted to work for a competitor helping it launch soccer camps in the New York City area. The plaintiffs sought to enforce the covenants preventing the defendants from conducting camps in the greater New York City region. The court struck down the covenants within the employment contracts finding the wording and application overly broad and unduly restrictive.

Special Doctrines of Contract Law

Promissory Estoppel

Promissory estoppel is a remedy courts will apply when an agreement lacks the requirements of a contract (i.e., agreement, consideration, capacity and legality), but nonetheless creates some form of detrimental reliance by one or more of the parties. Courts may apply promissory estoppel when plaintiff has shown that the agreement included (1) a promise that reasonably expected reliance, (2) there was reliance on the promise, and (3) an injustice to the party who relied on the promise.

Promissory estoppel is a common claim in breach of contract lawsuits filed by disgruntled student-athletes against college athletic programs (Epstein, 2005). For example, in *Fortay v. University of Miami* (1994), the plaintiff, a highly recruited football student-athlete, sued the university after he failed to secure the starting quarterback position. Fortay claimed that during the recruiting process and again while an enrolled student the university's football coaches promised him the position. After he was passed over for the spot, he filed the suit hoping to recover $10 million in damages (compensatory and punitive) for the broken promise. The case ultimately settled and the terms were not disclosed but it opened the door to similar lawsuits against college coaches who make unreasonable promises during the recruiting process.

Writing and Formality

The **Statue of Frauds** is a legal doctrine that dates back to common law in England. It is designed to prevent fraudulent claims and un-kept promises and encourage certain transactions to be reduced to writing (Wong, 2010). Under the doctrine, certain transactions must be in writing to be enforced. Transactions common to the sport and recreation industry and subject to the statute of fraud includes: (1) contracts that cannot be performed within a year; (2) agreements to guarantee another party's debt; (3) agreements for the sale or lease of land and; (4) contracts in which an executor or administrator promises to be personally liable for the debt of an estate. For example, courts have dismissed attempts by student-athletes to enforce a coach's verbal offer of a four- year athletic scholarship because such an agreement could not be performed within a year and thus must be in writing under the statute of frauds (*Shepard v. Loyola Marymount University*, 2002).

Parol Evidence Rule

Parol evidence consists of any oral or written terms outside the four corners of the final contract. It includes earlier versions of a contract or comments or statements made during contract negotiations.

The dilemma of how to handle parol evidence led courts to develop the parol evidence rule. According to the **Parol Evidence Rule**, if the contract is a complete final statement of the parties agreement (i.e., fully integrated), any prior or contemporaneous oral or written statements that alter, contradict or add new information regarding the agreement are inadmissible in any court proceeding concerning the contract (Restatement (Second) Contracts §213). The rule is intended to address breach of contract disputes in which one or more of the parties' referenced drafts of the contract or statements made in the negotiations process. The rule also covers contracts where it is unclear whether all relevant terms were included. *Vanderbilt University v. DiNardo* (1999), is a case in which the court had to consider whether to apply the parol evidence rule to bar comments made between a head football coach and an athletic director during contract negotiations. For another example of the parol evidence rule see *Haywood v. Univ. of Pittsburgh* (2013).

Yocca v. Pittsburgh Steelers, Inc. (2004), provides an another example of parol evidence and the conflict it creates for courts trying to resolve breach of contract disputes. The case focuses on the Pittsburgh Steelers sale stadium builder licenses (SBLs). Plaintiff completed the SBL application in accordance with a brochure issued by the Steelers purchasing Club I seats. Plaintiff went to a game and realized his seats had not been assigned Club I as noted in the brochure but rather Club II seats. Plaintiff filed suit for breach of contract. The trial court concluded that the parol evidence rule required dismissal of plaintiff's suit because the document entitled SBL Agreement contained an integration clause, which clarified that all the terms of the agreement were set forth in the application. On appeal, the court concluded that the agreement between plaintiff and the Steelers was formed when the plaintiff responded to the SBL Brochure prior to the deadline and sent in his first non-refundable deposit along with his application. The dismissal of the breach of contract claim was reversed.

Breach of Contract

A breach of contract occurs when a party to the contract fails to perform the duties imposed under the contract. The extent of the party's failure to perform determine the remedy sought by the non-breaching party. A minor breach exists when one party substantially performs most of its duties under the agreement. In such circumstances, the non-breaching party may negotiate with the breaching party as to the remaining duties owed under the contract or seek damages that resulted from the minor breach. A minor breach does not automatically relieve the non-breaching party from fulfilling its obligations under the contract. A material breach occurs when one party either fails to perform its duties under the contract or its performance was so inferior that it destroys the original intent of the agreement. If a material breach occurs, the non-breaching party may immediately rescind the contract and file a lawsuit to recover damages (Wong, 2010). To succeed on a breach of contract claim, the non-breaching party will have to show: (1) there was a valid contract; (2) plaintiff performed as specified by the contract; (3) defendant failed to perform as specified by the contract; and (4) plaintiff suffered an economic loss as a result of the defendant's breach of contract. Breach of Contract claims are common when colleges choose to not renew the athletics scholarships of student-athletes as in *Colli vs. Southern Methodist University* (2010).

Duty to Mitigate

Prior to awarding legal remedies for breach of contract, a court will consider whether the non-breaching party attempted to mitigate its damages. This duty to mitigate requires the non-breaching party to take actions that will reduce the loss incurred by the breach if possible. Basketball legend Michael Jordan's contract with now defunct communication company MCI provides an example of a plaintiff's duty to mitigate. In that case, Jordan attempted to collect compensation for an endorsement contract with MCI despite the company's bankruptcy. The company objected citing that upon learning of MCI's collapse Jordan made no attempts to mitigate his loss of the MCI compensation. The court agreed that Jordan did have an obligation to mitigate damages and required Jordan to submit additional evidence as to why his failure to mitigate should not bar recovery of his lost compensation (*In re Worldcom, Inc.*, 2007).

Defenses to a Breach of Contract Claim

To defeat a breach of contract claim, the breaching party often argues that the agreement lacked one or more elements of an enforceable contract. A defendant also may argue that one or more of the parties was mistaken as to the subject matter of the contract and thus there was no agreement. Mistake defenses are only successful if the breaching party can show that the mistake was a **mutual mistake** and involved the subject matter of the agreement. Generally, courts do not rescind contracts based on a **unilateral mistake** of the breaching party or contracts involving mutual mistakes over the value of the exchange.

Courts may rescind contracts involving **fraud** in either the inception of the contract or in the inducement to sign the contract. Prominent football coach Rich Rodriguez sought such relief in *West Virginia University v. Rodriguez* (2008). Rodriguez was under contract as the school's head football coach when he accepted the same position at the University of Michigan. WVU sued for breach of contract. In an attempt to defeat the institution's claim, Rodriguez argued that the employment contract was unenforceable because he had been fraudulently induced to sign the agreement by WVU's president. The case settled before the court could rule on the merits; however, WVU received its damage claim $4 million dollars with payments from Rodriguez and the University of Michigan.

A defendant also may contend that the contract is void because one or more of the parties lacked the authority to bind the organization or athlete to the contract. Employees act as agents of the employer or principal and subject to agency law have actual authority, apparent authority or no authority to bind the organization to a contract. Authority to contract was the focus, the company spent considerable resources on the dispute. For example, in *Kansas State Univ. v. Prince* (2009), the plaintiffs sought a declaratory judgment that an agreement signed by head football coach Ron Prince, and then KSU Athletics Director Robert Krause was not a valid or enforceable agreement following Prince's termination. A key issue in the dispute was whether Krause possessed authority to bind the institution to additional terms with the head football coach. To avoid such legal disputes and the associated costs, it is in the best interest of sport and recreation organizations to clearly communicate the authority and limits to authority of its employees in contractual settings (Sharp, 2007). Likewise, prior to entering into an agreement, companies working with a purported agent should confirm that agent's authority.

Remedies for a Breach of Contract

If a court finds that a party has breached a contract, it will grant relief that attempts to place the non-breaching party in the same position as if the contract had been performed (Restatement (Second) Contracts, 1981, §347). There are several types of remedies available to the non-breaching party: legal remedies; equitable remedies; and restitution.

Legal Remedies

Legal remedies are most prevalent and result in the court awarding the non-breaching party a monetary award for the damage incurred due to the breach. Monetary damages are divided into five categories: compensatory, consequential, nominal, punitive or liquidated.

Compensatory Damages

Compensatory damages are awarded to compensate the non-breaching party for the loss of the bargain. Compensatory damages are calculated according to one of three theories. Under an **expectation interest theory**, compensatory damages will reflect the benefit the non-breaching party expected to receive from the contract. An award based on reliance expectation reflects the losses suffered in the non-breaching party's belief that the breaching party would perform. A damage award under this theory could include expenses and investments made by the non-breaching party in anticipation that the breaching party would perform its duties under the contract. The restitution interest focuses on placing the non-breaching party in the condition it was in prior to the formation of the breached contract (Wong, 2010).

Consequential Damages

Consequential damages are awarded where there are foreseeable damages that result from circumstances out of the contract. To recover consequential damages, the non-breaching party must show that the breaching party knew or had reason to know that a breach will cause special damages to the other party. For example, a professional sports team buys computer software that will allow automated ticket purchases. The computer software fails and the team spends $15,000 on temporary employees who process orders over the phone. In this situation, the team may seek to recover the $15,000 paid to the temporary employees.

Nominal Damages

Courts will award nominal damages in situations when a breach of contract occurred but did not result in any significant economic loss. Cases resulting in nominal damages are usually motivated by principle, not money. Nominal damage awards amount to a few dollars. Nominal damages would be an appropriate remedy to a breach of contract claim involving a scheduling dispute in which the non-breaching party was able to secure another opponent and did not suffer any loss in revenue. A well-known nominal damages case is *United States Football League v. National Football League*, (1989). The USFL sued the NFL under federal antitrust law asserting a monopoly claim. Although the court found in favor of the USFL, it held that the league had not sufficiently established damages and thus only issued an award of $1.00.

Punitive Damages

Punitive damages are awarded to punish a defendant's reprehensible behavior and discourage others from doing the same in the future. Punitive damages are more common in tort lawsuits. Nonetheless, a small number of jurisdictions in the United States allow punitive damages in breach of contract claims involving malicious, bad faith or oppressive behavior.

Liquidated Damages

Liquidated damages are the only legal remedies not determined by a court or jury. These damages arise from a clause in the contract that specifies the damage award should either party fail to perform its duties under the agreement (Wong, 2010). In order for the clause to be enforced, it must be consistent with the actual harm suffered. Clauses that include a damage amount that far exceeds the actual harm constitute an unenforceable penalty.

Liquidated damage provisions are common in professional and college sport employment contracts, as well as contest scheduling agreements. An example of the prevalence and use of liquidated damages in sport and recreation law is the 2006 scheduling contract between the University of Buffalo and West Virginia University. The contract between the two schools contained a liquidated damages clause that required the breaching party to pay the non-breaching party $200,000. After the contract was signed, UB was contacted by Auburn University and offered $450,000 to play a game on their campus on the same day as the WVU game. UB accepted Auburn's offer and breached the contract with WVU. As a result, UB was obligated to pay WVU the $200,000 (Thamel, 2006).

Equitable Remedies

There are certain contractual disputes that cannot be adequately remedied by a monetary award. In such cases, courts will look to non-monetary judgments referred to as equitable remedies. The most common forms of equitable remedies are specific performance and injunctions.

Specific Performance

Specific performance requires the breaching party to perform its duties under the contract. Courts will award specific performance in cases that are unique, such as the purchase of an autographed jersey or tickets to a particular sporting event. Specific performance may be impossible depending on the terms of the contract. For example, courts rarely order specific performance for a breach of a personal service contracts such as a player's or coach's contract. In addition, plaintiffs seeking specific performance must show that there is no other appropriate legal remedy that will make them whole. A claim for specific performance will fail if requested to merely place a burden or penalty on the breaching party (*Brotherson v. the Professional Basketball Club, LLC*, 2008). In *Brotherson*, the plaintiffs were season ticket holders of the Seattle SuperSonics. They sought to punish the defendant for moving the team to Oklahoma City by requesting that the court enforce all the agreements with ticketholders residing in Seattle. Because the plaintiffs did not truly seek to retain the benefit of specific courts, the court rejected their claims for relief. For an additional example of season ticket holders seeking specific performance in a breach of contract case see *Yocca v. Pittsburgh Steelers, Inc.*, (2004).

Injunction

An injunction is the opposite of specific performance. It is sought when a party wishes to stop another party from acting. Courts will issue an injunction where there is evidence that a party will be irreparably harmed if relief is not granted (Wong, 2010). There have been numerous injunction cases against the NCAA in which a student-athlete seeks to enjoin the NCAA from applying a particular eligibility rule. In the context of a contract dispute involving a player or coach, this type of equitable relief is often referred to as a negative injunction because it is commonly used to block the player or coach from breaching a contract and going to play or work for another sport organization (Johnson, 1989).

Rescission and Restitution

Contracts that are unconscionable or involve illegal or fraudulent conduct, mistake or duress are often rescinded or voided by courts. The act of rescission undoes the contract. It is most often accomplished by ordering restitution, which requires all parties to return the consideration provided and any benefits reaped from the agreement (Sharp, 2007).

For example, rescission and restitution are often at issue in disputes involving health and fitness club memberships In *Robinson v. Lynmar Racquet Club, Inc.*, (1993), the plaintiff terminated her fitness club membership still owing two months of dues. The club filed a suit to collect the dues. Arguing that the contract violated the Colorado Consumer Protection Act, plaintiff also filed a lawsuit seeking rescission and restitution. In deciding the dispute, the court noted that the party seeking restitution must be capable of returning the opposite party to the position it occupied prior to entering into the contract. The court ultimately rejected plaintiff's claim noting that she was unable to do this. More specifically, plaintiff could not restore defendant with her use of its facilities and services that she had received over the course of the contract. As such, rescission was not a remedy available to resolve the dispute.

A court made the opposite ruling in *Taylor v. Wake Forest University* (1972). That case involved a scholarship student-athlete who became academically ineligible to play football for the institution. As a result, the institution cancelled his athletic scholarship. In response, the student-athlete filed a breach of contract suit. The court dismissed the student's case noting that he had failed to comply with his contractual obligation to the school and as such the school was entitled to rescind his athletic scholarship.

SIGNIFICANT CASE

The following case discusses whether a violation of the procedures outlined in the NCAA Division II Manual and the College Student Handbook amounts to a contractual agreement. The Student alleged breach of contract claims against the college and coach as her athletics scholarship was not renewed.

JENNIFER COLLI VS. SOUTHERN METHODIST UNIVERSITY AND RHONDA ROMPOLA
United States District Court for the Northern District Of Texas
2010 U.S. Dist. LEXIS 143582

Opinion

ORDER
Now before the Court is the Motion for Summary Judgment, filed by Defendants Southern Methodist University ("SMU") and Rhonda Leann Rompola ("Rompola") on February 1, 2010. A Response was filed by Plaintiff Jennifer Colli ("Colli") on February 24, 2010, and a Reply was filed on March 10, 2010. After careful consideration and for the reasons stated below, the Motion is GRANTED in PART and DENIED in PART.

I. Background
SMU is a private university located in Dallas, Texas and participates in a variety of National Collegiate Athletic Association ("NCAA") sports, including women's basketball. Rompola has been the head women's basketball coach for SMU for the past eighteen years. SMU and Rompola recruited Colli to play on the SMU women's basketball team, and Plaintiff signed a Letter of Intent to play basketball for SMU in November 2004.

Plaintiff received an athletic grant-in-aid to play basketball for SMU for the 2005-2006 season, which was memorialized in the initial Statement of Athletic Financial Aid signed on November 10, 2004. Under NCAA rules, "If a student's athletics ability is considered in any degree in awarding financial aid, such aid shall not be awarded in excess of one academic year." Accordingly, the Initial Statement makes it clear that Colli's award of financial aid was to cover the 2005-2006 academic year. The Initial Statement also references NCAA bylaws in its overview of the conditions of the financial aid, and in establishing the terms under which the financial aid may be reduced, cancelled or non-renewed.

Colli played basketball at SMU under Rompola's direction during the 2005-2006 season, and on April 27, 2006, Colli was presented with a renewal Statement of Athletic Financial Aid (the "Renewal Statement"), which provided Colli with a financial aid award that covered the 2006-2007 academic school year. On May 9, 2006, Colli signed the Renewal Statement which contained the same language regarding how financial aid may be reduced, cancelled or non-renewed as was found in the Initial Statement.

On June 23, 2006, Colli presented Steve Orsini ("Orsini"), SMU's Athletic Director, with a five page memorandum containing a list of complaints against Rompola and the SMU women's basketball program. Orsini then met with Rompola, and presented Colli's memorandum to her and asked Rompola "to go over each accusation and give him answers to it and check with the appropriate parties named in the in the accusations, the coaches, and what [she] knew about each accusation and answer it to the best of [her] knowledge." During her review of Colli's memorandum, Rompola chose not to interview any of the other members of the women's basketball team. Upon receiving Rompola's written response to Colli's memorandum, the determination was made "that the majority of Plaintiff's complaints were unsupported and that Plaintiff engaged in conduct that was detrimental to the women's basketball program." Accordingly, the decision was made to cancel Colli's scholarship.

On August 14, 2006, Orsini called Plaintiff's father and told him that he had decided not to renew Plaintiff's scholarship. On the following day, Orsini met with Plaintiff, and her mother and father, and informed them "that he was not renewing Plaintiff's scholarship because he found many of her allegations to be false and, because of the seriousness of some of her allegations, it would be detrimental to the team if she returned to play basketball for SMU." During this meeting, Orsini also informed Plaintiff and her parents that she had the right to appeal his decision.

On August 17, 2006 Marc Peterson ("Peterson"), the Director of Financial Aid at SMU, sent Plaintiff a letter notifying her that her "athletics grant-in-aid will not be renewed effective fall 2006." The letter also informed Plaintiff of her right to appeal, and the process for initiating the appeals process. On September 15, 2006, the Scholarship Appeals Board, after having Plaintiff present her case for reversing Orsini's decision and allowing Orsini and Rompola to present arguments to the contrary, denied Plaintiff's appeal. On September 15, 2008, Plaintiff filed the present action with this Court. On October 1, 2008, Plaintiff filed an Amended Complaint alleging 1) breach of contract; 2) intentional infliction of emotional distress; 3) promissory estoppel; 4) fraud; 5) breach of duty of good faith and fair dealing; 6) defamation; and 7) intentional interference with contractual and prospective advantage.

II. Summary Judgment Legal Standard

Summary judgment shall be rendered when the pleadings, depositions, answers to interrogatories, and admissions on file, together with affidavits, if any, show that there is no genuine issue of material fact and the moving party is entitled to judgment as a matter of law. Fed. R. Civ. P. 56(c). The moving party bears the burden of informing the district court of the basis for its belief that there is an absence of a genuine issue for trial and of identifying those portions of the record that demonstrate such absence. However, all evidence and reasonable inferences to be drawn therefrom must be viewed in the light most favorable to the party opposing the motion.

Once the moving party has made an initial showing, the party opposing the motion must come forward with competent summary judgment evidence of the existence of a genuine fact issue. Fed. R. Civ. P. 56(e). The party defending against the motion for summary judgment cannot defeat the motion unless he provides specific facts demonstrating a genuine issue of material fact, such that a reasonable jury might return a verdict in his favor. *Anderson v. Liberty Lobby, Inc.*, 477 U.S. 242, 247-48 (1986). Mere assertions of a factual dispute unsupported by probative evidence will not prevent a summary judgment. In other words, conclusory statements, speculation, and unsubstantiated assertions will not suffice to defeat a motion for summary judgment. Further, a court has no duty to search the record for evidence of genuine issues. *See Ragas v. Tenn. Gas Pipeline Co.*, 136 F.3d 455, 458 (5th Cir. 1998).

III. Analysis

As this Order concludes that some of Plaintiff's claims have merit and others fail as a matter of law, we will first address those claims that fail before turning our attention to claims in which a question of fact remains for a jury's determination.

* * *

Promissory Estoppel

The elements of a promissory estoppel claim are: (1) a promise; (2) reliance thereon that was foreseeable to the promisor; and (3) substantial reliance by the promisee to his detriment. *English v. Fischer*, 660 S.W.2d 521, 524 (Tex. 1983). Plaintiff alleges that SMU promised that she "would be entitled to a hearing before SMU's regular student disciplinary authority for allegations of misconduct." However, Plaintiff has provided no evidence as to how this promise was made to her or how she relied on this promise to her detriment. Accordingly, this claim fails as a matter of law.

* * *

Fraud

To establish her fraud claim, Plaintiff must prove (1) that a material representation was made; (2) that it was false; (3) that when the speaker made it he knew it was false or made it recklessly without any knowledge of the truth and as a positive assertion; (4) that he made it with the intention that it should be acted upon by the party; (5) that the party acted in reliance upon it; (6) that he thereby suffered injury. *Stone v. Lawyers Title Inc. Corp.*, 554 S.W.2d 183, 185 (Tex. 1977). However, as Defendants note, "Plaintiff's fraud claim is based on the same conduct that forms the basis for her breach of contract claim." Accordingly, Plaintiff's fraud claim fails as a matter of law.

Breach of Contract
1. Breach of the Athletic Scholarship

Under Texas law, "[t]he elements of a breach of contract cause of action are: (a) a valid contract; (b) the plaintiff performed or tendered performance; (c) the defendant breached the contract; and (d) the plaintiff was damaged as a result of that breach." *Case Corp. v. Hi-Class Bus. Sys. Of Am.*, 184 S.W.3d 760, 769 (Tex.App.--Dallas 2005). In their Motion for Summary Judgment and in their Reply, Defendants only challenge the third element, arguing that SMU's actions did not constitute a breach of the contract between the parties.

In presenting this defense, SMU argues that "[b]ecause the decision [to non renew Colli"s financial aid] was made outside the period of award, SMU had discretion whether or not to renew Plaintiff's athletic scholarship." Defendant adds that since "the NCAA guidelines are silent as to under what circumstances a university may cancel or not renew athletic grant-in-aid after the period of award, there is nothing which deprives a university from exercising this discretion." The Court finds this argument unpersuasive as it is clearly at odds with both NCAA bylaws and the SMU Student--Athlete Compliance Manual (the "Compliance Manual").

According to the Compliance Manual, "[a] final Athletic Department decision of nonrenewal or reduction of an athletic scholarship based upon documented policy violations . . . must be communicated to the student-athlete . . . [n]o later than May 15 for football, basketball, and soccer." If an incident warranting non renewal happens after this deadline, a nonrenewal notification "must be given as soon as is reasonably possible (but in no event later than the NCAA established deadline of July 1)." As the non renewal letter sent to Colli was dated August 17, 2006, it clearly fell outside of the deadline set by the NCAA and adopted by the Compliance Manual.

Defendant argues against this clear reading of both the NCAA Bylaws and the Compliance Manual, claiming that such an approach would create an "absurd result" in which student athletes could engage in misconduct after the July 1 "deadline" without threat of discipline or penalty as a university would be unable to cancel or not renew an athletic scholarship after the deadline had passed. However, recognition of a July 1 deadline for non renewals does not leave a university without disciplinary options. In fact, the NCAA Bylaws specifically anticipate and address the very situation that SMU claims it was faced with: the need to reduce a student athlete's financial aid after that student has signed her financial aid award letter.

Under NCAA Bylaw 15.3.4.3.2, "[a]n institution may not decrease . . . a student-athlete's financial aid from the time the . . . student athlete signs the financial aid award letter until the conclusion of the period set forth in the financial aid agreement, except under the conditions set forth in Bylaw 15.3.4.1." Accordingly, in addition to the July 1 deadline, once Plaintiff signed her Renewal Statement, SMU lost the right to non renew the scholarship. However, even though the July 1 deadline had passed and Colli had signed her Renewal Statement, SMU could still have sought cancellation of her scholarship under the guidelines set forth under 15.3.4.1. SMU's decision to non renew Colli's scholarship, however, was no longer an option under the Compliance Manual or NCAA Bylaws, and, accordingly, the non renewal violated SMU's contract with Colli. Therefore, the Court denies Defendant's motion for summary judgment on this claim.

2. Breach of the Student Handbook

The Southern Methodist University Student Handbook 2006-2007 (the "Handbook") states that every SMU student accused of violating institutional regulations retains the right to "a fair hearing before an impartial judiciary body of peers, or an administrative official, whichever is deemed appropriate by the judicial officer, after consultation with the student." At SMU, the regular student disciplinary authority is vested in the University Hearing Boards, as established under the University Judicial Code (the "Code") section of the Handbook.

In the present case, the cancellation of Colli's scholarship was supported, in part, by a finding that Colli had violated sections 3.05 and 3.14(a) of the Code. This alleged misconduct, however, was never established by either of proper disciplinary authorities as established in the Handbook and the Code. Additionally, it appears that Defendants did not maintain the rights of the accused as established under the Code, as Colli was allegedly not "informed of all alternatives and options by a counselor in the Counseling and Testing Center."

The Court finds that a reasonable jury could, on the evidence submitted, find that these allegations demonstrate a breach of SMU's responsibilities to Plaintiff under the terms of the Handbook, and therefore denies summary judgment on this claim.

* * *

CONCLUSION

For the foregoing reasons, Defendants' Motion for Summary Judgment is GRANTED IN PART and DENIED IN PART. .Summary judgment in Defendants' favor is GRANTED on Colli's claims . . . Promissory Estoppel and Fraud. Summary judgment is DENIED on Colli's claims for Breach of Contract. **IT IS SO ORDERED.**

CASES ON THE SUPPLEMENTAL CD

Blackmon v. Iverson, 324 F.Supp.2d 602 (E.D. Pa. 2003). This case looks at the issue of past consideration and whether an individual's promise created a valid contract.

Brotherson v. the Professional Basketball Club, LLC, 2009 U.S. Dist. LEXIS 13912 (W.D. Wash. 2009). This case discusses whether a brochure soliciting season tickets created a contract between the team and the buyers.

Haywood v. Univ. of Pittsburgh, 2013, U.S. Dist. LEXIS 140263 (W.D. Pa. Sept. 30, 2013). This case discusses basic contract interpretation and the ability to determine the parties' intent from the agreement as a whole, and the importance of word choice and meaning in drafting contracts.

HBCU Pro Football, LLC, v. New Vision Sports Properties, LLC, 2011 U.S. Dist. LEXIS 55976 (D. Md. 2011). This case provides an example of the contractual issues involved in the broadcasting of sport contests, including an agent's authority to contract on behalf of a third party, and the breach of contract claims that can result when such contracts are not fulfilled.

Giuliani v. Duke University, 2009 U.S. Dist. LEXIS 44412 (2009). This case discusses the various promises made by both prospective student-athletes and college athletic staff during the recruiting process and once on campus, and whether those promises can arise to a contractual relationship.

QUESTIONS YOU SHOULD BE ABLE TO ANSWER

1. What are some examples of contracts in the sport and recreation industry?
2. What are the three sources of contract law in the United States?
3. What are the four elements of an enforceable contract?
4. What will the non-breaching party have to show to succeed on a breach of contract claim?
5. What are the different remedies to a breach of contract claim?

REFERENCES

Cases

Bagley v. Mt. Bachelor, Inc, 2014 Ore. LEXIS 994 (2014)
Blackmon v. Iverson, 324 F.Supp.2d 602 (E.D. Pa. 2003).
Brotherson v. the Professional Basketball Club, LLC, 2009 U.S. Dist. LEXIS 13912 (W.D. Wash. 2009).
Chuy v. Philadelphia Eagles Football Club, 431 F.Supp. 254 (E.D. Pa. 1977).
Fortay v. University of Miami, 1994 U.S. Dist. LEXIS 1865 (D.N.J. 1994)
Giuliani v. Duke University, 2009 U.S. Dist. LEXIS 44412 (M.D.N.C. 2009)
Haywood v. Univ. of Pittsburgh, 2013, U.S. Dist. LEXIS 140263 (W.D. Pa. Sept. 30, 2013)
In re Worldcom, Inc., 2007 WL 446735 (Bkrtcy. S.D.N.Y. 2007)
LoPiccolo v. American University, 2012 U.S. Dist. LEXIS 1300 (D.D.C. 2012)
Milicic v. Basketball Marketing Co., Inc., 857 A.2d 689 (Pa. Super. Ct. 2004)
Mount Snow, Ltd., v. ALLI, 2013 U.S. Dist. LEXIS 118604 (D. Vt. 2013)
NASC Services v. Jervis, 2008 U.S. Dist. LEXIS 40502 (D.N.J. 2008)
Northeastern University v. Brown, 2004 Mass. Super LEXIS 64 (2004)
Robinson v. Lymar Racquet Club, 851 P.2d 274 (Colo. App. 1993)
Shepard v. Loyola Marymount Univ., 2002 Daily Journal DAR 11545 (Cal. App.2d Dist. 2002)
United States Football League v. National Football League, 842 F.2d 1335 (2nd Cir. 1988)
Vanderbilt University v. DiNardo, 174 F.3d 751 (6th Cir. 1999).
West Virginia University v. Rodriguez, 2008 WL 1739259 (Trial Pleading) (N.D.W.Va. Feb. 1, 2008)
Yocca v. Pittsburgh Steelers Sports, Inc., 854 A.2d 425 (Pa. 2004)

Publications

American Law Institute. (1981). *Restatement (second) of the law of contracts*. St. Paul, MN: American Law Institute.
Berry, R.C., & Wong, G.M. (1994). *The Law and Business of the Sports Industries* (3rd. ed.). Westport, CT: Prager Publishing.
Burke, D., & Grube, A. (2011). The NCAA Letter of Intent: A Voidable Agreement for Minors? 81 Miss. L.J. 265.
Davis, T. (1997). Balancing Freedom of Contract and Competing Values in Sports. *South Texas Law Review 38*, 1115.
Epstein, A. (2008). Sales and Sports Law. *Journal of Legal Aspects of Sport, 18*, 67.
Epstein, T. (2005). Splinters from the Bench: Feasibility of Lawsuits by Athletes Against Coaches and Schools for Lack of Playing Time4 Va. Sports & Ent. L.J. 174.
Glover, W. H. (2009*). Sports law handbook: (for coaches and administrators)*. Raleigh, NC: Lulu.com.
Hanson, S.M. (2006). Athletic Scholarships as Unconscionable Contracts of Adhesion: Has the NCAA Fouled Out? *Sports Law Journal 13*, 41–77.
Johnson, A.M. (1989). The Argument for Self-Help Specific Performance: Opportunistic Renegotiation of Player Contracts. *Connecticut Law Review 22*, 61.

Klein, J. (2012). *Union submits counteroffer and waits on NHL.* Retrieved from http://www.nytimes.com/2013/01/01/sports/hockey/players-union-submits-a-counteroffer-and-waits-on-nhl-response.html

Miller, L.K, Comfort, P.G., & Stoldt, G.C. (2001). Teaching Perspective: Contracts 101: Basics and Applications, *Journal of Legal Aspects of Sport 11*, 79.

Sharp, L. (2007). Contract essentials. In D.J. Cotton & J.T. Wolohan. *Law for recreation and sport managers* (4th ed.). pp. 364–374. Dubuque, IA: Kendall/Hunt Publishing

Shubert, G.W., Smith J.C., & Trentadue, R.K. (1986). *Sport law* (1st ed.). St. Paul, MN: West Publishing

Simpson, A.W.B., (1987). *A History of the Common Law of Contract: The Rise of the Action of Assumpsit* (2d ed.), Oxford: Oxford Publishing

Thamel, P. (2006, August 23). *In College Football, Big Paydays for Humiliation. New York Times*, p. A1.

Wong, G.M. (2010). *Essentials of Sports Law* (4th ed.), Santa Barbara, CA. ABC-CLIO, LLC.

EMPLOYMENT CONTRACTS

Rodney L. Caughron

5.21

Historically, employment contracts in sport and recreation were a matter of a handshake or a simple letter of agreement. With the increased level of compensation—both in salary and outside income—and the tenuous nature of a coach or administrator's position, employment contracts have evolved into complex legal documents. However, no matter how complicated the contracts have become, employment contracts are essentially the same as other contracts in the "real" world. The only difference is that they have the propensity to be broken on a much more frequent basis—often with the assent of both parties. That is why the more specific a contract can be crafted, specifically defining terms and reducing ambiguity, the more both parties will benefit (Yasser, McCurdy, Goplerud, & Weston, 2000).

FUNDAMENTAL CONCEPTS

Sport and recreation has become a big business in the United States. For example, in 2010–11, athletic programs at Division I colleges and universities generated over $6 billion in revenue (Berkowitz & Upton, 2011). With so much money involved in college and professional sports, there is an increased pressure on organizations to win in order to gain a bigger share of the potential revenue and ensure economic viability. As the pressure to win rises, it is only natural that the expectation on the coaches also increases. A perfect illustration of the tenuous nature of today's college coaching is the turnover in jobs that occurs at the end of each college basketball and football season. For example, in the end of the 2011 regular football season, out of the 66 schools that currently play in the big six football conferences (ACC, Big 10, Big 12, Big East, Pac 12 and the SEC), 12 coaches were fired or resigned to accept other jobs (Coaching Changes, 2011).

This continuous coaching carousel has required all parties, the organization, administrators and coaches, to develop specific contractual language to protect themselves and their interest if the contract is eventually breached. The more precise a contract can be crafted, reducing ambiguity and specifically defining the terms, the more both parties will benefit (Greenberg & Smith, 2007, and Yasser, McCurdy, Goplerud, & Weston, 2000). No matter how well the contract is drafted, however, when one party fails to meet its' obligation, or one side wishes to breach the contract, legal issues are sure to arise over what the proper damages should be.

Elements of a Common Contract

Although it is important to note that no two contracts will be alike, there are a number of elements that should be in every sports-related employment contract. These contracts often involve special perks and other common employment benefits as well as salary. For example, in John Calipari's $31.65 million deal with the University of Kentucky, his base pay was listed at just $400,000 per year. The contract, however, was packed with perks beyond his annual salary, including membership to the country club of his choice, two cars, 20 prime "lower-level" season tickets to UK home games, eight tickets for each UK home football game, and incentives for reaching the NCAA Sweet Sixteen and Final Four and a $375,000 bonus for winning the 2012 NCAA title. In Jim Harbaugh's contract with Michigan, Harbaugh gets $500,000 in base pay, with an additional $4.5 million in perquisites payed, a $2 million signing bonus, and other incentive bonuses added on (Biggers, 2015), and is almost fully guaranteed (Snyder, 2015).

While it is important to note that all contracts have most of the same elements, it is also important that each contract be tailored for the particular job. The following are some of the most common elements of a sport-related employment contract.

Duties and Responsibilities
- The contract should state that the employee agrees to devote his/her best effort to full-time performance as the position requires.
- There should be a specific list of responsibilities required to be performed by the employee.
- The contract should also include a general phrase that the employee agrees to perform other duties assigned to him or her, and mutually agreed upon.

Term of Employment
- The length of the contract should be explicit. For example in *Lindsey v. University of Arizona* (1987), the terms of employment were unclear. As a result, when the university breached an oral commitment to extend his contract for three additional years, Lindsey was forced to sue to recover the remainder of the contract. In another case, *Small v. Juniata College* (1997), the court found that Small's employment contract was for a one-year term and that the college personnel manual termination procedures did not affect the status of these one-year appointments.

Rollover Provisions
- Rollover provisions allow the organization to extend an employee's contract for an extra year, with the mutual agreement of the employee and organization. Rollover provisions tend to be one-sided in favor of the employee, exemplified in the statement by *Atlanta Journal-Constitution* reporter Jeff Schultz, "Now a coach can have an iron-clad, no escape contract signed in vampire blood . . . then weasel out of rollover contracts and jump across the street for a raise" (Schultz, 2006). This is especially true when the contract's rollover agreement requires specific terms of notice for terminating the employee, allowing the employee to collect more monetary damages if the contract is terminated by the organization. For example, in *Cherry v. A-P-A Sports, Inc.* (1983), Cherry's contract provided that if his contract was not renewed for an additional two years, he would automatically receive $35,000 in compensation.

Reassignment Clause
- A reassignment clause allows for the removal of the employee from the originally contracted position and reassigned to another position that is consistent with the employee's education and experience. For example, in *Monson v. State of Oregon* (1995), the University of Oregon had included a provision for reassignment, which they exercised, changing his assignment from men's basketball coach to golf coach. The court upheld the reassignment because it was part of the contractual language.
- The issue of reassignment and future loss of income due to the reassignment was addressed in *Smith v. Alanis & Zapata County Independent School District*, (2002). Smith was hired as the head high school football coach and athletic coordinator, but was reassigned midyear in accordance with his contract. Smith claimed that his removal as head coach, although not reducing his current salary per the contract, would have an effect on future income as a head coach. The court concluded that contract law in Texas did not allow compensation for future earning capacity, and therefore, the actions of the school district were within the scope of the employment contract.
- An interesting case dealing with reassignment was *Summey v. Monroe County Department of Education et al.* (2012), in which a high school football coach was reassigned, under the terms of his contract, to a middle school PE teaching position. Summey refused the position, and sued the school district for breach of contract. The court held Summey in breach due to his refusal to take the teaching assignment which was allowable under his contract.
- A reassignment clause should be coupled with the avoidance of any language in the contract that gives the employee the right to be in any specific titled position (e.g., head coach).

Compensation Clause
- A compensation clause should include the base salary, terms of pay increases over the time of the contract, fringe benefits, moving and relocation expenses, bonuses, additional retirement benefits, and all other compensation specifically delineated and agreed upon.

Fringe Benefits
- This area can include a myriad of benefits that organizations offer employees and administrators. Some of these fringe benefits may include: complementary cars, travel, loans, moving and housing expenses, and tickets. Many of the benefits are offered to the normal employee, but in many situations the benefits for the coach or administrator are inflated or outside the normal employees benefits. The type, amount, date the benefit is available, and penalties for termination of contract should be explicitly written out within the contract.

Bonuses and Incentives
- Bonuses and incentives are becoming more important to all employees. They may include signing bonuses, incentives based on team success, and in the case of college and university coaches and administrators, graduation rates of student–athletes. In *White v. National Football League* (2007), when Ashley Lelie did not report to training camp, he was fined by the Denver Broncos $220,000, the player's option bonus according to the team's interpretation of the NFL CBA. The court saw it differently and ruled that the option was earned as soon as it had been awarded and could not be recovered by the team (also see *Grillier* (2009) below).

Sovereign Immunity
- When dealing with various state organizations, depending on the state's sovereign immunity rules, an employee may not be able to sue the state organization, even for an alleged breach of the contract. In *Leach v. Texas Tech University* (2011), Mike Leach, the head football coach at Tech was fired prior to the conclusion of his contract. In dismissing Leach's claim that the university waived its immunity, the court held that the university was still protected under the state's sovereign immunity. In states that still have sovereign immunity, therefore, it is incumbent on employees to include an expressed waiver of that immunity in your employment contract.

Provisions for Outside and/or Supplemental Income
- These sources of income may include radio and television contracts; endorsements; shoe, apparel and equipment contracts; income from speeches and written materials, as well as camps and other sources of supplemental income.
- The organization should include in the contract that it is not legally liable for claims arising from these outside income sources, and that the organization retains all right of final approval for any outside income sources.
- Greenberg and Smith (2007) delineate the non-base income earned by Bruce Pearl, University of Tennessee Head Men's Basketball coach in the 2006–2007 season. Pearl's base salary was $300,000, but with his additional income sources, Pearl's reported income was approximately $1.5 million that season. Pearl was later fired in March 2011 after a series of university and NCAA violations.

Termination Clause
- A termination clause should state that termination may be caused by the death, disability, or criminal conduct. For example, in *Maddox v. University of Tennessee* (1995), the court upheld the dismissal of Maddox, an alcoholic, due to his arrest for drunk driving. Maddox contended that his dismissal was due to his alcoholism, which violated the Americans with Disabilities Act of 1990 (ADA) and the

Rehabilitation Act of 1973. The court did not agree, however, finding that the termination was for his criminal act and the subsequent negative publicity. In a similar case, ABC TV terminated an employee after he was arrested for selling cocaine. The plaintiff claimed he was covered under ADA, but the court ruled that his termination was based on the plaintiff's breach of the morals clause in his contract because he lied about the situation (*Nader v. ABC Television*, 2005).

- The contract should also contain a termination for "just cause" clause, so that if the employee violates either the organization's rules, its affiliation rules, civil or criminal laws, moral turpitude, refusal to perform duties, and so forth, the employee can be fired. These may be explicitly expressed or implied in the contract or in the "customs and mores" of the organization or society. For example, in *Deli v. University of Minnesota* (1994), the head women's gymnastics coach and her husband, the assistant coach, were terminated when the gymnasts viewed a videotape of the coach and her husband having sex. The court upheld the dismissal of both of the coaches, based on the indiscretions with the videotape and for other "just cause" reasons. Other examples are *McKenzie v. Wright State University* (1996), and *Farner v. Idaho Falls School District*, (2000). In *McKenzie v. Wright State University* (1996); the court upheld the dismissal of McKenzie for NCAA rules violations, which were specifically mentioned in her employment contract as cause for termination. The *Farner* case demonstrated how the master contract for high school teachers, when incorporating coaching and extra duties, requires the same "just cause" for termination as the teaching aspect of the contract. To terminate without just cause violates the individual's due process rights. In Nick Saban's (Head Football Coach at the University of Alabama) contract extension, the Termination for Cause section of the contract contained 15 specifically delineated reasons that the coach could be terminated.

- In *Haywood v. The University of Pittsburgh* (2013), Haywood – a football coach at the university – signed a contract that specifically stated that he could be terminated "with or without just cause." When Pittsburgh terminated his contract for just cause (domestic abuse charges), the court confirmed that he was not entitled to liquidated damages.

- The termination clause should also spell out the due process rights employees have to challenge their termination. This could include a formal hearing within the organization or the use of an arbitrator. For example, in *Stamps Public Schools v. Colvert* (1996), Colvert was able to prove that the school district had violated its own procedures and had not given him his contractually guaranteed due process. Another example involved Rick Neuheisel and the University of Washington. Neuheisel was fired as head football coach six months before the end of his original contract, based on his involvement in an NCAA men's basketball betting pool. In suing the university, Neuheisel claimed that Washington denied him his contractually guaranteed due process and the subsequent hearing. Neuheisel and Washington later settled for a cash payment of $2.5 million (from the NCAA for defamation) and $500,000 in cash and $1.5 million in a forgiven loan from the university (Greenberg & Thomas, 2005).

- Termination without cause allows the organization to fire the employee for any reason. This will usually come with a price, in that the organization will usually have to negotiate a settlement with the employee if a termination occurs. This was not the case in *Frazier v. University of the District of Columbia* (1990), however, where the court found that Frazier was an at-will employee and could be terminated at any time.

- In *O'Brien v. The Ohio State University*, (2007), James O'Brien, the Head Basketball Coach at The Ohio State University (OSU), was terminated by the athletic director for a "material breach" of his coaching contract. O'Brien gave a $6,000 loan to a recruited basketball player's mother in Yugoslavia in early 1999 (although the athlete was ruled a professional and was not able to play for OSU), based on humanitarian reasons and his belief that the athlete was not eligible anyway. O'Brien disclosed the loan to Ohio State, and OSU self-reported the loan as a NCAA violation. When OSU fired O'Brien on June 8, 2004, for a "material breach" of his contract, it referred to the loan as a "for cause" violation his contract. The court, however, concluded that OSU fired O'Brien for a major NCAA violation, prior to an NCAA determination. As a result, OSU was required to pay O'Brien the remainder of his contract, $2,494,972.83.

- In order to solve some of the problems involving in terminating an employee, employment contracts should contain an agreed upon liquidated damages amount, paid to the coach when he or she is fired (Greenberg, 2006). Along with *Vanderbilt University v. DiNardo* (1999), discussed later, a more recent case demonstrated the validity of liquidated damage clauses. Ford, men's basketball coach at Kent State University, resigned and signed a contract with Bradley University. As part of his contract, if he left prior to the completion of his contract he would owe Kent State the remainder of his contract salary to the university as damages. The court held the liquidated damages clause was a valid element to his contract and ordered him to pay Kent State $1.2 million (*Kent State University v. Ford*, 2015).

Buyout Provisions
- A buyout provision allows the employee or institution to terminate the contract on the payment of a specified amount of money. For example, in *Tolis v. Board of Supervisors of Louisiana State University* (1992), the court upheld an oral agreement to buy out Tolis's contract, which the defendants later violated. The court held that the Board of Supervisors must abide by their oral buyout agreement.
- A buyout provision may include a liquidated damages clause. For example, in January 2010, University of Connecticut coach Randy Edsall breached his contract with two years remaining to take the head coaching job at the University of Maryland (Clarke, Yanda, & Prisbell, 2011). In this type of situation, the schools generally allow the coach to breach his contract after paying an agreed on liquidated damage. In Edsall's instance, since he accepted the Maryland job on January 3, 2011, his contract required him to pay the University of Connecticut $400,000 (Football Bowl Subdivision coaches' salaries for 2010).
- Sometime, even when a written contract does not exist, a buyout may be warranted. For example, the University of Oregon gave Athletic Director, Mike Bellotti a $2.3 million buyout when after only nine months on the job he resigned. This type of situation demonstrates how both parties can come to an agreement for everyone to save face and avoid litigation (ESPN.com, 2010).

Arbitration Agreement
- An arbitration agreement is a clause in the contract that stipulates that if any dispute arises from the interpretation of the contract or other factors concerning the contract, the issues will be dealt with through arbitration (see *Miami Dolphins Ltd. v. Williams*, 2005).
- The areas to be arbitrated should be specifically delineated within the contract if arbitration is to be used. A dispute concerning this concept arose in *Grillier v. CSMG Sports, LTD.* (2009). Grillier was initially an independent contractor working as an agent. He and CSMG agreed upon a Consulting Agreement in which compensation and an arbitration clause were included. Subsequent to this agreement, Grillier was then hired as an employee, under an oral agreement. When a new employment contract was offered it did not include an extra compensation or an arbitration clause. Grillier later resigned and demanded payment for "extra compensation" (both during his Consulting Agreement and his employment contract), but disagreed that the dispute should be settled through arbitration, based on that oral employment agreement. The court allowed arbitration to go forward.
- An interesting case challenging the ability of NFL Commissioner Paul Tagliabue to serve as the arbitrator in contract disputes within the NFL involved coaches with the Minnesota Vikings, who after they were fired claimed they were entitled to incentive pay under their contract. The appellants filed suit to remove Tagliabue as the arbitrator in their dispute, but the court stated that nowhere in the Federal Arbitration Act is there an allowance to challenge an arbitrator—biased or not—prior to a decision by the arbitrator (*Alexander, et al. v. Minnesota Vikings Football Club LLC & National Football League*, 2002). In *State ex rel. Todd Hewitt v. Kerr* (2013), a Missouri Court of Appeals found that the maditory arbitration clause of the NFL player's contract was an unconscionable contract and not enforceable.

Covenant Not to Compete
- Covenants not to compete are also commonly used in coaching contracts. For example, in the new football coach's contract, the school could include a clause prohibiting the coach from accepting another head coaching position at any school in the same conference for five years after leaving his current school. The purpose of the clause is to protect the competitive advantage of the school, while at the same

time not overly restricting the coach's future earning possibilities. If the clause is too restrictive in scope or time (*MacGinnitie v. Hobbs Group*, 2005), courts will refuse to enforce it against the coach. If the non-compete provision of the contract is seen as a legitimate business requirement, the court, as it did in *Aim High Academy, Inc. v. Jessen* (2008), will uphold the provision as long as the provision is limited in scope
- An interesting case dealing with sports agencies and non-compete clauses in employment contracts was *Steinberg Moorad & Dunn, Inc. v. Dunn*, (2005). In reversing a lower court decision, the appeals court ruled that, under California law, non-compete clauses are invalid in contracts. Steinberg, Moorad & Dunn (SMD) had accused Dunn of breach of contract after he left the firm and started his own sports agency firm, taking several of SMD's professional athlete clients with him.

Discussion of Contract Issues

Typically in sports the employee has the advantage in any contractual situation in which the employee unilaterally decides to terminate the contract. If an employee unilaterally terminates his or her contract, thus breaching the conditions of the contract, the sport organization has essentially no remedy to "force" the employee to perform their duties. The reason the courts are unwilling to enforce such contracts is that to compel performance of a contractual duty would constitute a violation of the Thirteenth Amendment's prohibition against involuntary servitude. In addition, the court has stated that it would be unable to monitor the level of coaching performance and enforce proper coaching skills in a coaching contract (Cozzillio & Levinstein, 1997).

Although unable to compel the employee to perform his or her duties, the sport organization may acquire injunctive relief, which prohibits the employee from acquiring similar employment at another sport organization. This was evident in the case of Chuck Fairbanks and the New England Patriots. Fairbanks, who was head coach of the New England Patriots, breached his contract with New England to take the head coaching position with the University of Colorado. To prevent Fairbanks from leaving, the Patriots obtained injunctive relief, prohibiting the University of Colorado from entering into a coaching contract with Fairbanks (*New England Patriots Football Club Inc. v. University of Colorado*, 1979).

In some instances, problems arise between parties of an employment contract based on their personal relationships and friendship. One typical situation is when there is a verbal understanding that in the future a specific employment relationship will be consummated contractually by the two parties, and the agent of the organization does not have the authority to make such an agreement, or due to the fact that it is only an agreement and not yet a contract, the relationship does not transpire. This was the case in *Barnett v. Board of Trustees for State Colleges and Universities A/K/A University of Louisiana System*, (2001). Barnett was originally hired as basketball coach at Northwestern State University in 1994. A plan was formulated by Barnett and the then-university president, which would elevate Barnett to athletic director in 1996. A letter from the president was sent to Barnett confirming the agreement in 1995, pending approval by the university Board of Trustees (Louisiana state law required personnel appointments at the university to be approved by the Board of Trustees). Before Barnett could be appointed to the AD position, a new president took office at the institution, and someone else was hired as AD. Barnett filed suit against the University for breach of contract. The court ruled that no contract existed because all contracts had to be submitted to the Board, and Barnett was aware of this prerequisite from the beginning of the agreement. This case demonstrates the importance of employees knowing the exact procedural requirements for contracts with a particular institution or organization to become valid and actionable. *Meinders v. Dunkerton Community School District*, (2002) is an example of a similar situation at the high school level.

A similar situation involving knowing who can hire occurred in *Williams v. Smith* (2012), where Williams was offered an assistant men's basketball coaching position by the head coach, Tubby Smith. Smith did mention that the contract would have to be approved by the AD before it became effective. Due to Smith's NCAA violation history, the AD rejected the contract and Williams was not hired. Acting upon Smith's offer of employment, Williams resigned his previous position. The court rejected Williams' assertion of breach of contract. The lesson here is that you should not take any employment action until everyone that can reject the contract has signed on to the contract.

It is interesting to note that even when an employee breaches his or her contract and jumps from one organization to another, in most cases the parties involved eventually agree on a settlement, either financial or, in the case of professional teams, financial and possible trade of draft picks. For example, the New York Jets settled with the New England Patriots to obtain Bill Parcells for a reported $300,000 charitable donation and the Jets' third-and fourth-round draft picks in 1997, their second-round choice in 1998, and their first-round pick in 1999 (Rosenthal, 1997).

Another area where employers need to pay attention is the issue of perquisites that an employee may be entitled to. For example, in *Rodgers v. Georgia Tech Athletic Association*, (1983) (see the supplemental Web Site), Rodgers, the head football coach at Georgia Tech, asked the court to award him the value of the perquisites for the remainder of his terminated contract. In reaching its decision, the court eliminated those perquisites directly related to the function of Rodgers' job as head coach (i.e., a secretary), but awarded Rodgers the value of those items that were regularly provided to him either through the Association or from outside sources (i.e., television and radio revenues). The court also eliminated items that were gifts, and those items that the Association did not have knowledge of or contemplate as part of the contract. Therefore, the *Rodgers* case set a precedent that allows coaches or administrators to recover items that are specifically or tacitly provided for by the sport organization and those items that the coach or administrator and the organization would normally expect to be perquisites under the contract (*Rodgers v. Georgia Tech Athletic Association*, 1983).

Independent Contractors vs. Employee

A growing issue in the sport, fitness, and recreational industries is the hiring of independent contractors to perform duties that were typically performed by employees. Although the use of independent contractors is a good way to reduce costs and an organization's legal liability, not every individual will actually meet the standards of an "independent contractor." The classification of workers has significant implications for the employer in terms of taxes, tort liability, and other forms of employee compensation (Caughron & Fargher, 2004).

Darryll Halcomb Lewis brought to light the importance of this issue when dealing with sports officials. Halcomb Lewis states that if a sports official hurt on the job is considered an independent contractor, two consequences result: (1) the referee is barred from filing a worker's compensation claim, and (2) that absent legislated immunity, the organization hiring the official may be held liable for those injuries (Halcomb Lewis, 1998). This was echoed in *Wadler v. Eastern College Athletic Conference* (2003), in which a claim of Title VII discrimination based on race was dismissed against an athletic conference due to a lack of an employer–employee relationship—essentially recognizing a college baseball umpire as an independent contractor due to the employment relationship he had with the defendants in the case. A recent case, *Yonan v. United States Soccer Federation, Inc.* (2011), enforced the concept that most referees are considered independent contractors and not subject to employment discrimination statutes (in this case the Age Discrimination in Employment Act).

Although no specific test has been adopted universally by all jurisdictions, the Internal Revenue Service has developed a checklist that includes twenty criteria for determining whether someone is an independent contractor or an employee. The status of the individual is dependent on the following (the more reliant the individual is on the employer, the greater likelihood they are an employee):

1. **Instructions.** Level of instruction to accomplish the work, and the level of supervision;
2. **Training.** Initial and ongoing training;
3. **Integration.** Independence of individual within the workplace;
4. **Services rendered personally.** Ability of individual to subcontract;
5. **Hiring, supervising, and paying assistants.** Ability to hire and treat others as employees by the worker;
6. **Continuing relationship.** The relationship is based on a specific period of time or completion of a specific task;
7. **Set hours of work.** Role of the employer in setting the schedule of the individual;
8. **Full-time required.** Role of the employer in setting minimum or full-time work requirement;
9. **Doing work on employer's premises.** The level of on-site supervision and reliance on employer's facilities and equipment;
10. **Order or sequence set.** Level the employer sets the pattern of work by individual;
11. **Oral or written reports.** The amount of paperwork the individual must file with the employer;
12. **Payment by the hour, week, or month.** Method of payment and the inclusion of sick and vacation days;

13. **Payment of business and/or traveling expenses.** Level of compensation employer provides individual to perform work;
14. **Furnishing of tools and materials.** Level of use by individual of employer's equipment;
15. **Significant investment.** Records are kept to identify individual's contribution (e.g., purchase of equipment) to the employer's facilities;
16. **Realization of profit or loss.** The individual is responsible for their own business accounting and insurance;
17. **Working for more than one firm.** Do the customers pay the individual directly, and can the individual contract with other employers in the same business?
18. **Making services available to the public.** Level of independence the individual has in marketing, advertising, and working independent of employer;
19. **Right to discharge.** Level of ability of employer to discipline and fire individual;
20. **Right to terminate.** Can the individual end relationship with employer or are they bound contractually (Internal Revenue Service, pp. 298–299) (see Caughron & Fargher, 2004, for a full explanation of the classification process).

In 2015, the Obama administration issued a new interpretation of the Fair Labor Standards Act that an "econmonics realities" test should be used to determine a workers classification. The impact of this administrative move could have significant impact on the classification of current independent contractor in sport, such as officials and others (Bahmani, 2015; Smith, 2015).

SIGNIFICANT CASE

This case covers a multitude of contractual issues that are important to individuals involved in contract development and negotiations. The most important issue this case brings forward is that when developing a contract, each side must specifically state their expectations concerning elements of the agreement and write them out explicitly. This is illustrated in the reasons given in the contract for a lengthy contract, program stability, as well as the acceptance of liquidated damages, and the inclusion of the extension into the entire scope of the original contract. Lastly, this case shows that the court will recognize conditional acceptance of contracts, even verbal, which determine the enforcement of the contract.

VANDERBILT UNIVERSITY V. DINARDO
United States Court of Appeals for the Sixth Circuit

174 F.3d 751 (6th Cir. 1999)
On December 3, 1990, Vanderbilt University and Gerry DiNardo executed an employment contract hiring DiNardo to be Vanderbilt's head football coach. Section one of the contract provided:

> The University hereby agrees to hire Mr. DiNardo for a period of five (5) years from the date hereof with Mr. DiNardo's assurance that he will serve the entire term of this Contract, a long-term commitment by Mr. DiNardo being important to the University's desire for a stable intercollegiate football program. . . .

The contract also contained reciprocal liquidated damage provisions. Vanderbilt agreed to pay DiNardo his remaining salary should Vanderbilt replace him as football coach, and DiNardo agreed to reimburse Vanderbilt should he leave before his contract expired. Section eight of the contract stated:

> Mr. DiNardo recognizes that his promise to work for the University for the entire term of this 5-year Contract is of the essence of this Contract to the University. Mr. DiNardo also recognizes that the University is making a highly valuable investment in his continued employment by entering into this Contract and its investment would be lost were he to resign or otherwise terminate his employment. . . . Accordingly, Mr. DiNardo agrees that in the event he resigns or otherwise terminates his employment as Head Football Coach, prior to the expiration of this Contract, and is employed or performing services for a person or institution other than the University, he will pay to the University as liquidated damages an amount equal to his Base Salary (later negotiated as his net salary), . . . multiplied by the number of years (or portion(s) thereof) remaining on the Contract.

* * *

Vanderbilt initially set DiNardo's salary at $100,000 per year. DiNardo received salary increases in 1992, 1993, and 1994. On August 14, 1994, Paul Hoolahan, Vanderbilt's Athletic Director . . . talk(ed) to DiNardo about a contract extension. (DiNardo's original contract would expire on January 5, 1996). Hoolahan offered DiNardo a two-year contract extension. DiNardo told Hoolahan that he wanted to extend his contract, but that he also wanted to discuss the extension with Larry DiNardo, his brother and attorney.

Hoolahan telephoned John Callison, Deputy General Counsel for Vanderbilt, and asked him to prepare a contract extension. Callison drafted an addendum to the original employment contract which provided for a two-year extension of the original contract, specifying a termination date of January 5, 1998. Vanderbilt's Chancellor, Joe B. Wyatt, and Hoolahan signed the Addendum.

On August 17, Hoolahan returned to Bell Buckle with the Addendum. He took it to DiNardo at the practice field where they met in Hoolahan's car. DiNardo stated that Hoolahan did not present him with the complete two-page addendum, but only the second page, which was the signature page. DiNardo asked, "what am I signing?" Hoolahan explained to DiNardo, "it means that your contract as it presently exists will be extended for two years with everything else remaining exactly the same as it existed in the present contract." Before DiNardo signed the Addendum, he told Hoolahan, "Larry needs to see a copy before this thing is finalized." Hoolahan agreed, and DiNardo signed the document. . . .

On August 16, Larry DiNardo had a telephone conversation with Callison. They briefly talked about the contract extension, discussing a salary increase. Larry DiNardo testified that as of that date he did not know that Gerry DiNardo had signed the Addendum, or even that one yet existed.

On August 25, Callison faxed Larry DiNardo "a copy of the draft Addendum to Gerry's contract." Callison wrote on the fax: "let me know if you have any questions." The copy sent was unsigned. Callison and Larry DiNardo had several telephone conversations in late August and September, primarily discussing the television and radio contract. . . .

In November 1994, Louisiana State University contacted Vanderbilt in hopes of speaking with DiNardo about becoming the head football coach for L.S.U. Hoolahan gave DiNardo permission to speak to L.S.U. On December 12, 1994, DiNardo announced that he was accepting the L.S.U. position.

Vanderbilt sent a demand letter to DiNardo seeking payment of liquidated damages under section eight of the contract. Vanderbilt believed that DiNardo was liable for three years of his net salary: one year under the original contract and two years under the Addendum. DiNardo did not respond to Vanderbilt's demand for payment.

Vanderbilt brought this action against DiNardo for breach of contract. DiNardo removed the action to federal court, and both parties filed motions for summary judgement. The district court held that section eight was an enforceable liquidated damages provision, not an unlawful penalty, and that the damages provided under section eight were reasonable. *Vanderbilt University v. DiNardo*, 974 F. Supp. 638, 643 (M.D. Tenn. 1997). The court held that Vanderbilt did not waive its contractual rights under section eight when it granted DiNardo permission to talk to L.S.U. and that the Addendum was enforceable and extended the contract for two years. *Id*. at 643–45. The court entered judgement against DiNardo for $281,886.43. *Id*. at 645. DiNardo appeals.

I.

DiNardo first claims that section eight of the contract is an unenforceable penalty under Tennessee law. DiNardo argues that the provision is not a liquidated damage provision but a "thinly disguised, overly broad non-compete provision," unenforceable under Tennessee law.

* * *

Contracting parties may agree to the payment of liquidated damages in the event of a breach. *See Beasley v. Horrel*, 864 S.W.2d 45, 48 (Tenn. Ct. App. 1993). The term "liquidated damages" refers to an amount by the parties to be just compensation for damages should a breach occur. *See Id*. Court will not enforce such a provision, however, if the stipulated amount constitutes a penalty. *See Id*. A penalty is designed to coerce performance by punishing default. *See Id*. In Tennessee, a provision will be considered one for liquidated damages, rather than a penalty, if it is reasonable in relation to the anticipated damages for breach, measured prospectively at the time the contract was entered into, and not grossly disproportionate to the actual damages. *See Beasley*, 864 S.W.2d at 48; *Kimbrough & Co. v. Schmitt*, 939 S.W.2d 105, 108 (Tenn. Ct. App. 1996). When these conditions are met, particularly the first, the parties probably intended the provision to be for liquidated damages. However, any doubt as to the character of the contract provision will be resolved in favor of finding it a penalty.

* * *

DiNardo contends that there is no evidence that the parties contemplated that the potential damage from DiNardo's resignation would go beyond the cost of hiring a replacement coach. . . .

DiNardo's theory of the parties' intent, however, does not square with the record. The contract language establishes that Vanderbilt wanted the five-year contract because "a long-term commitment" by DiNardo was "important to the University's desire for a stable intercollegiate football program," and that this commitment was of "essence" to the contract. Vanderbilt offered the two-year contract extension to DiNardo well over a year before his original contract expired. Both parties understood that the extension was to provide stability to the program, which helped in recruiting players and retaining assistant coaches. Thus, undisputed evidence, and reasonable inferences there-from, establish that both parties understood and agreed that DiNardo's resignation would result in Vanderbilt suffering damage beyond the cost of hiring a replacement coach.

* * *

The stipulated damages clause is reasonable under the circumstances, and we affirm the district court's conclusion that the liquidated damages clause is enforceable under Tennessee law.

* * *

II.

DiNardo next argues that Vanderbilt waived its right to liquidated damages when it granted DiNardo permission to discuss the coaching position with L.S.U. Under Tennessee law, a party may not recover liquidated damages when it is responsible for or has contributed to the delay or nonperformance alleged as the breach. *See V.L. Nicholson Co. v. Transcom Inv. And Fin. Ltd., Inc.*, 595 S.W.2d 474, 484 (Tenn. 1980).

Vanderbilt did not waive its rights under section eight of the contract by giving DiNardo permission to pursue the L.S.U. position. *See Chattem, Inc. v. Provident Life & Accident Ins. Co.*, 676 S.W.2d 953, 955 (Tenn. 1984) (waiver is the intentional, voluntary relinquishment of a known right). First, Hoolahan's permission was quite circumscribed. Hoolahan gave DiNardo permission to talk to L.S.U. about their coaching position; he did not authorize DiNardo to terminate his contract with Vanderbilt. Second, the employment contract required DiNardo to ask Vanderbilt's athletic director for permission to speak with another school about a coaching position, and Hoolahan testified that granting a coach permission to talk to another school about a position was a "professional courtesy." Thus, the parties certainly contemplated that DiNardo could explore other coaching positions, and indeed even leave Vanderbilt, subject to the terms of the liquidated damages provision. *See Park Place Ctr. Enterprises, Inc. v. Park Place Mall Assoc.*, 836 S.W.2d 113, 116 (Tenn. Ct. App. 1992) ("all provisions of a contract should be construed as in harmony with each other, if such construction can be reasonably made . . ."). Allowing DiNardo to talk to another school did not relinquish Vanderbilt's right to liquidated damages.

* * *

III.

DiNardo claims that the Addendum did not become a binding contract, and therefore, he is only liable for the one year remaining on the original contract, not the three years held by the district court.

A.

DiNardo argues that the Addendum did not extend section eight, or that there is at least a question of fact as to whether the Addendum extended section eight.

. . . When the agreement is unambiguous, the meaning is a question of law, and we should enforce the agreement according to its plain terms. *Richland Country Club, Inc. v. CRC Equities, Inc.*, 832 S.W.2d 554, 557 (Tenn. Ct. App. 1991).

DiNardo argues that the original employment contract explicitly provides that section eight is limited to "the entire term of this five-year contract," and the plain, unambiguous language of the Addendum did not extend section eight. He points out that the Addendum did not change the effective date in section eight, unlike other sections in the contract.

The plain and unambiguous language of the Addendum read in its entirety, however, provides for the wholesale extension of the entire contract. Certain sections were expressly amended to change the original contract expiration date of January 5, 1996, to January 5, 1998, because those sections of the original contract contained the precise expiration date of January 5, 1996. The district court did not err in concluding that the contract language extended all terms of the original contract.

B.

DiNardo also claims that the Addendum never became a binding contract because Larry DiNardo never expressly approved its terms. DiNardo contends that, at the very least, a question of fact exists as to whether the two-year Addendum is an enforceable contract.

* * *

Under Tennessee law, parties may accept terms of a contract and make the contract conditional upon some other event or occurrence. *See Disney v. Henry*, 656 S.W.2d 859, 861 (Tenn. Ct. App. 1983). DiNardo argues that the Addendum is not enforceable because it was contingent on Larry DiNardo's approval.

There is evidence from which a jury could find that Larry DiNardo's failure to object did not amount to acceptance of the Addendum. The parties were primarily negotiating the radio and television contract during the fall of 1994. We cannot say that Larry DiNardo's failure to object by December 12, 1994, constituted an acceptance of the Addendum as a matter of law.

* * *

Accordingly, we affirm the district court's judgement that the contract contained an enforceable liquidated damage provision, and we affirm the portion of the judgement reflecting damages calculated under the original five-year contract. We reverse the district court's judgement concluding that the Addendum was enforceable as a matter of law. We remand for a resolution of the factual issues as to whether Larry DiNardo's approval was a condition precedent to the enforceability of the Addendum and, if so, whether the condition was satisfied by Larry DiNardo's failure to object.

We affirm in part, reverse in part, and remand the case to the district court for further proceedings consistent with this opinion.

CASES ON THE SUPPLEMENTAL WEB SITE

Grillier v. CSMG Sports, Ltd., 2009 U.S. Dist. LEXIS 50476. This case involves moving from one employment status to another and how contract language can affect the outcome of a case.

Leach v. Texas Tech University, 335 S.W.3d 386 (TX App. 7th, 2011). This case is interesting since it brings in the concept of sovereign immunity of a state against breach of contract charges.

Mullen v. Parchment School District, 2007 Mich. App. LEXIS 1704 (Mich. Ct. App. 2007). This case examines the impact of Collective Bargaining Agreement on extra duty coaching contracts.

Rodgers v. Georgia Tech Athletic Association, 303 S.E.2d 467 (Ga. Ct. App. 1983). This case examines the true value of college coaching contracts.

QUESTIONS YOU SHOULD BE ABLE TO ANSWER

1. Why is it important to distinguish between an employee and an independent contractor? And what process is used to make that distinction?
2. Why is it important to include language in a contract that defines the terms of termination of that contract?
3. Why is it important to be very specific in an employment contract when defining the terms of reassignment of the signee?
4. Are verbal employment contracts able to survive judicial scrutiny?
5. Despite the existence of a legally binding contract, why are employers unable to force the contracted employee or independent contractor to complete the agreed upon work required in the contract?

REFERENCES

Cases

Aim High Academy v. Jessen, 2008 R.I. Super. LEXIS 152.
Alexander, et al. v. Minnesota Vikings Football Club LLC & National Football League, 649 N.W.2d 464 (2002).
Barnett v. Board of Trustees for State Colleges and Universities A/K/A University of Louisiana System, 806 So. 2d 184; 2001 La. App. LEXIS 1676 (La. App. 1 Cir, 2001).
Cherry v. A-P-A Sports, Inc., 662 P.2d 200 (Colo. App. 1983).
Deli v. University of Minnesota, 511 N.W.2d 46 (Minn. Ct. App. 1994).
Farner v. Idaho Falls School District, 135 Idaho 337; 17 P.3d 281 (2000).
Frazier v. University of the District of Columbia, 742 F. Supp. 28 (D.D.C. 1990).
Grillier v. CSMG Sports, Ltd., 2009 U.S. Dist. LEXIS 50476.
Haywood v. The University of Pittsburgh, 976 F.Supp. 2d 606 (W.D. PA, 2013).
Kent State University v. Ford, 26 N.E.3d 868 (Ohio App. 2015).
Leach v. Texas Tech University, 335 S.W.3d 386 (TX App. 7th, 2011).
Lindsey v. University of Arizona, 157 Ariz. 48, 754 P.2d 1152 (Ariz. Ct. App. 1987).
MacGinnitie v. Hobbs Group, LLC, 2005 U.S. App. LEXIS 16853; 18 Fla. L. Weekly Fed. C 832 (11th Cir. 2005).
Maddox v. University of Tennessee, 62 F.3d 843 (6th Cir. 1995).
McKenzie v. Wright State University, 683 N.E.2d 381 (Ohio App. 1996).
Meinders v. Dunkerton Community School District, 645 N.W.2d 632 (IA Sup. 2002).
Miami Dolphins Ltd. v. Williams, 356 F. Supp. 2d 1301 (S.D. Fla. 2005).
Monson v. State of Oregon, 901 P.2d 904 (Or. App. 1995).
Nader v. ABC Television, 2005 U.S. App. LEXIS 19536 (2nd Cir. 2005).
New England Patriots Football Club Inc. v. University of Colorado, 592 F.2d 1196 (1st Cir. 1979).
O'Brien v. The Ohio State University, 2007 Ohio 4833 (Ohio App. 10th, 2007).
Rodgers v. Georgia Tech Athletic Association, 303 S.E.2d 467 (Ga. Ct. App. 1983).
Small v. Juniata College, 547 Pa. 731; 689 A.2d 235 (1997).
Smith v. Alanis & Zapata Independent School District, 2002 Tex. App. Lexis 5437 (TX App, 3rd 2002).
Stamps Public Schools v. Colvert, No. CA95–318 (Ark. Ct. App. 1996).
State ex rel. Hewitt v. Kerr, No. ED100479 (MO App E Dist, 2013).

Steinberg Moorad & Dunn, Inc. v. Dunn, 2005 U.S. App. LEXIS 5162 (9th Cir. 2005).
Summey v. Monroe County Department of Education et al. (No.E2011-01400-COA-R3-CV, 2012).
Tolis v. Board of Supervisors of Louisiana State University, 602 S.2d 99 (La. App. 1992).
Vanderbilt University v. DiNardo, 174 F.3d 751 (6th Cir. 1999).
Wadler v. Eastern College Athletic Conference, 2003 U.S. Dist. LEXIS 14212 (S. Dist, N.Y. 2003).
White v. National Football League, 183 L.R.R.M. (BNA) 2796 (D. Minn. 2007).
Williams v. Smith, 820 N.W.2d 807 (Sup Ct MN, 2012).
Yonan v. United States Soccer Federation, Inc., 2011 U.S. Dist. LEXIS 66383.

Publications

Bahmani, Shar. (2015, July 15). Employee or independent contractor? US Department of Labor provides new guidance. The National Law Review. Retrieved from http://www.natlawreview.com/article/employee-or-independent-contractor-us-department-labor-provides-new-guidance

Berkowitz, S. & Upton, J. (2011, June 15). Athletic departments see surge financially in down economy. *USA Today*. Retrieved from http://www.usatoday.com

Biggers, A. (2015, Jan. 25). Breaking down Jim Harbaugh's Michigan contract and how he could earn more. *Bleacher Report*. Retrieved from http://bleacherreport.com/articles/2342066-breaking-down-jim-harbaughs-michigan-contract-and-how-he-could-earn-more

Caughron, R., & Fargher, J. (2004). Independent contractor and employee status: What every employer in sport and recreation should know. *Journal of Legal Aspects of Sport, 14*(1), 47–61.

Clarke, L., Yanda, S. and Prisbell, E. (January 4, 2011). Terrapins welcome in Edsall. *The Washington Post*, D1.

Cozzillio, M., & Levinstein, M. (1997). *Sport law: Cases and materials*. Durham, NC: Carolina Academic Press.

ESPN.com (April 6, 2010). Lariviere: Bellotti getting $2.3M buyout. Retrieved from http://sports.espn.go.com/espn/print?id=5061452&type=story

Football Bowl Subdivision coaches' salaries for 2010 (2010, December 9). Retrieved from http://www.usatoday.com/sports/college/football/2010-coaches-contracts-table.htm

Greenberg, M. (2001, Fall). College coaching contracts revisited: A practical perspective. *Marq. Sports L.Rev., 12*, 153–226.

Greenberg, M. (2006, Fall). Symposium: National Sports Law Institute Board of Advisors: Termination of college coaching contracts: When does Adequate cause to terminate exist and who determines its existence? *Marquette Sports Law Review, 17*, 197–257.

Greenberg, M., & Smith, J. (2007, Fall). A study of Division I assistant football and men's basketball coaches' contracts. *Marquette Sport Law Review, 18*, 25–72.

Greenberg, M., & Thomas, R. (2005, April–June). The Rick Neuheisel case—lessons learned from the "washout" in Washington. *For the Record: The Official Newsletter of the National Sports Law Institute, 16*(2), 6–11.

Halcomb Lewis, D. (1998, Winter). After further review, are sports officials independent contractors? *American Business Law Journal, 35*, 249.

Hunt, M. (2003, June 3). Limbo tune doesn't get coaches dancing. *Milwaukee Journal Sentinel*, p. 01C.

Internal Revenue Service. (n.d.). *Internal Revenue Manual, 4600 Employment tax procedures*, Exhibit 4640–1. Washington, DC: Department of the Treasury, Internal Revenue Service.

NCAA president receives 2-year extension. (2005, August 5). *The Associated Press*, Sports News.

Rosenthal, J. (1997, March 7). Parcells case a journey through contract law precedent. *New York Law Journal*.

Schultz, J. (2006, January 13). AD exit strips Hewitt of ally. *The Atlanta Journal-Constitution*, p. 1H.

Smith, A. (2015, July 16). DOL narrows independent contractor classification. Society for Human Resource Management. Retrieved from http://www.shrm.org/legalissues/federalresources/pages/administrator-interpretation-independent-contractors.aspx

Snyder, M. (2015, Jan. 23). Jim Harbaugh's Michigan contract almost fully guaranteed. *USA Today Sport*. Retrieved from http://www.usatoday.com/story/sports/ncaaf/2015/01/23/jim-harbaugh-contract-details-michigan/22229001/

Yasser, R., McCurdy, J., Goplerud, C., & Weston, M. (2000). *Sports law: Cases and materials* (4th ed). Cincinnati, OH: Anderson Publishing Co.

GAME, EVENT, AND SPONSORSHIP CONTRACTS

5.22

Bridget Niland | Daemen College

The 2014 National Hockey League (NHL) Winter Classic game between the Detroit Red Wings and the Toronto Maple Leafs was record setting, but not for the reasons most sports fans would suspect. The event generated the largest attendance, broadcast viewership and profit posting in NHL history. Based on NHL calculations, the game held at the University of Michigan's football stadium, referred to as the "Big House," brought in nearly $30 million in revenue and posted expenses of only $20 million. The University of Michigan earned over $3 million through its rental agreement with the NHL. League executives attributed the record setting revenue to a variety of sources outside of the sale of game tickets, including the sale of licensed merchandise, sponsorships and proceeds from vendor contracts.

The 2014 Winter Classic provides recreation and sport managers with clear examples of the depth and breadth of **game, event and sponsorship contracts** as a number of each were involved in the hugely successful hockey game. These types of contracts often involve large sums of money and/or protect parties from the legal liabilities that accompany problems or accidents that can occur during a game or event. The purpose of this chapter is to clearly define the use of game, event and sponsorship contracts, and highlight for sport and recreation managers the various elements and issues involved in executing these contracts. The goal is to equip recreation and sport managers with the insights needed to facilitate the best possible outcome for their recreation and sport entities.

FUNDAMENTAL CONCEPTS

The United States recreation and sport industry is multifaceted and includes events that range from revenue producing juggernauts such as the National Football League's Super Bowl to high school athletics to small not for profit community recreation programs (Humphreys & Ruseski, 2009). Although the size and market power of sport and recreation events may vary, the use of **game, event and sponsorship contracts** is a common thread among each of these vastly different sectors of the industry (Greenwell, Danzey-Bussell, & Shonk, 2014). Whether the highly visible 2014 NHL Winter Classic or a small local road race, sport and recreation managers responsible for conducting events will rely on event and sponsorship contracts to ensure overall success (Masteralexis, Barr & Hums, 2015).

The common and statutory contract laws outlined in Chapter 5.10, *Contract Essentials*, apply to virtually all sport contracts including game, event and sponsorship contracts. Sport and recreation managers should also review the various applications of the **statute of frauds** to game, event and sponsorship contracts. Parties to game, event and sponsorship contracts frequently dictate additional terms unique to the event or sponsorship relationship. Game, event and sponsorship contracts may include a variety of parties including corporations serving as sponsors, vendors and concessionaires, insurance brokers and media outlets. Each party may demand bargained for exchange unique to the relationship and the event. As an example, the 2014 NHL Winter Classic required numerous contracts such as broadcast agreements with the NBC television network, sponsorship agreements with various corporate partners and a facility rental agreement with the University of Michigan. Similar to other larger sporting events, the core agreement to the Winter Classic was the game contract between the two hockey teams.

Game Contracts

The contracts discussed in this chapter are common throughout the sport and recreation industry, but **game contracts** often serve as the impetus for the other event contracts related to the event (e.g., sponsorship or endorsement contracts). The teams involved in a scheduled competition devote considerable time, effort and money to host or travel to a game. The scheduling of games and competitive contests is one of the most challenging and time consuming tasks in sport and recreation management. At the scholastic level, teams use online scheduling forms for their respective schools that ensure uniformity of terms among teams. At the collegiate level, conferences prepare game schedules for its member schools. The high cost of operating collegiate and professional teams make the use of game contracts necessary to avoid the monetary losses that can result from a cancelled contest.

OFFICIAL GAME CONTRACT   DATE REVISED

This Official Game Contract (the "Agreement"), is entered into on this _____ day of _____, _____, by and between _____ and _____, and stipulates the following:

1. Each party to the Agreement shall cause its _____ team to play _____ game(s) of _____ _____.

2. <u>Rules and regulations</u>. Said game(s) shall be governed by applicable National Collegiate Athletics Association (NCAA) legislation and playing rules, and by the rules of host institution's conference. The athletics eligibility of each team's student-athletes shall be governed by the rules and regulations of the represented institutions, of the institutions' athletics conferences and by the NCAA.

3. <u>Guarantee</u>. In consideration of the playing of said game(s), the home team's institution agrees to pay as a guarantee to the visiting team's institution the sum of _____ dollars (_____), or in lieu thereof, as an option, _____ percent of the _____ gate receipts of said game(s). Payment of these amount shall be made as soon as possible, but not later than thirty (30) days, after the close of said game(s).

4. <u>Game Proceeds</u>. The proceeds derived from programs, concessions, radio and television broadcasts and any other source shall belong to the home institution exclusively, or, shall be allocated according to Conference and/or League rules and regulation if applicable.

5. <u>Tickets</u>. Ticket prices shall be set by the home team's institution. The vising institution shall be allowed _____ complimentary tickets shall be made no later than _____ prior to the playing date of said game(s).

6. <u>Officials</u>. The officials for said game(s) shall be agreed upon by the represented institutions at least ten (10) days prior to the game(s), and the expenses for said officials shall be paid by the home institution. Officials shall be selected in the following manner.

7. <u>Change in NCAA Classification</u>. This Agreement may be voided by either party if either is reclassified to a different NCAA membership division after the contract has been executed.

8. <u>Other Terms</u>. Other provisions governing this Agreement are as follows:

9. <u>Violation of Terms</u>. In the event either party fails to produce its team and play said game(s) on said date(s) at the agreed upon site(s) or violates any clause of the Agreement without the express written permission of the other party, it shall pay to the party not at fault the sum of _____ dollars (_____), within one week of the date on which the breach of contract occurs. In addition, the violating party shall pay to the party not at fault all expenses incurred in pursuance of the Agreement by the party not at fault.

SIGNED IN QUADRUPLICATE

For: _____   For: _____
By: _____   By: _____
Its: _____   Its: _____
Date:_____   Date:_____

FIGURE 5.22-1

Imagine you are a college athletics director and it is the busiest weekend of the fall sports season. The college's men's and women's soccer teams are on a three-day bus trip that involves two away games and includes three hotel stays and food charges. The soccer trip is costing the college close to $10,000. During halftime of a home football game, you receive a panicked call from your women's soccer coach indicating that their opponent's coach just cancelled the soccer match. The coach provides very few details, but your first thoughts are regarding the costs of the cancellation. You immediately walk to your office and review the Game Contracts file to determine the actions you can take to either force the opposing team to play the game or to recover the costs associated with the now cancelled competition.

The example above illustrates the need for and use of Game Contracts in scholastic, college and professional sport. Sport and recreation managers use game contracts to clarify the terms of the agreement for a single competition or series of contests. Game contracts also provide a clear set of remedies should one of the parties attempt to cancel a contest (Greenwell, Danzey-Bussell, & Shonk, 2014). Game contracts include the date, time, location, and the rules and regulations that apply to the competition. If the contest is part of a game guarantee, the contract terms should include compensation for participating, any travel and meal reimbursement, and other items negotiated by the two the teams.

Guarantee Games are common among members of NCAA Division I and II levels in which the scheduling of profit rearing home games is critical to an athletic programs financial viability. The costs of **guarantee games** in Division I football and basketball is controversial as the games frequently involve a less resourced NCAA Division I team contracting with more successful and well-resourced Division I program (Lillig, 2009). The goal for the team paying the guarantee is to schedule a game that generates revenue and is likely result in a win. The benefit to the team receiving the guarantee is exposure of their student-athletes to top-ranked competition, as well as an additional source of revenue for their team or athletics program. The differing needs for guarantee games make it a necessity for sport and recreation managers to consult with an attorney before signing and returning the contract. An inadequately drafted game guarantee contract that lacks clear penalty for the party that breaches the agreement can result in a steep monetary loss. Figure 5-22.1 is a sample game contract and includes a clearly stated penalty in the event either party decides to breach the agreement.

Problems with scheduling guarantee games can exist even when a soundly drafted scheduling contract exists between the two teams. For example, *University of Louisville v. Duke University* (see significant case) provides an example of the problems that arise between schools that commit to multiple game guarantee contests over a period of years. Such contracts can be problematic should one of the parties see a significant increase or decrease in competitiveness.

Event Contracts

Event contracts, though similar in structure and content to game contracts, cover a wider range of activities. A game contract may cover a single game or series of games. Event contracts include the competition and/or the pre- or post- event activities associated with the competition (e.g., fan events, banquets). A **municipal sports commission** or convention and visitor's bureau in collaboration with specific team, college or youth sports program execute event contracts, but first the sanctioning body for the event conducts a formal bid process. The NCAA's championship bid process serves as an example. Cities or municipalities wishing to host an NCAA event must follow the association's formal bid process. The NCAA conducts a bid process for each sport in which it sponsors a national championship. The NCAA also accepts bids to host pre-championship qualifiers or playoff contests. The bid process requires NCAA members and cities wishing to host an event to submit a formal proposal that demonstrates the capability of hosting the event under parameters designated by the NCAA. Similar processes are in place for hosting professional sporting events such as the Super Bowl and the NHL, NFL and NBA draft events.

In addition to larger primary event contracts, there are smaller secondary event contracts. These contracts include facility rental agreements, leases, vendor contracts (e.g., concessions or apparel providers), personnel agreements and sponsorship agreements that expand the length of time or activity offerings of a multi-day event. Smaller secondary event contracts can be included in one large agreement or operate as separate agreements between the various parties.

Event contracts must include the provisions basic to any contract (see Chapter 5.10, *Contract Essentials*). Events contracts must also include provisions specific to the event such as venue designation, schedule for the event, competition regulations, delineation of responsibilities between the facility owner and the entity renting or leasing the facility (e.g., security), sponsorships related to the use of the facility, insurance and liability considerations, and risk of loss to the property (Lawrence & Wells, 2009).

Figure 5.22-2 is sample event contract for a sport related competition or event.

SAMPLE ELEMENTS OF EVENT CONTRACT

Title and Schedule
The official title of the EVENT shall be the "_____." The EVENT dates are: (Month Day, Year) - (Month, Day, Year).

Venue and Exclusivity
The EVENT held at (Location/Facility name, City) with the finals held at the (Location/Facility name, City) on (Dates). No other sports EVENT will be held at these sites while the EVENT is taking place.

Recognition of Sanctioning Body
The <sanctioning body> logo and/or the words "_____" and/or the word "_____" shall appear on all EVENT equipment, event merchandise, promotional material, administrative material and printed materials, including programs and web site.

Participants
The EVENT requires for a minimum of _____ teams or participants.

Rules of Play
The rules of play for the competition shall be the most recently approved _____, unless otherwise specified in writing.

Responsibility to Sanctioning Body
The <local organizing committee> is responsible to <sanctioning body> for all matters that concern the planning, organization, implementation and evaluation of (EVENT Name).

Event Coordination

A. <sanctioning body> Responsibilities

B. <local organizing committee> Responsibilities

Sponsorships
The procurement of corporate sponsors are used to offset event-related expenses and to enhance the participant/spectator experience.

Broadcasting, Videotaping, Photography and Website
<sanctioning body> has the right and responsibility in working with <local organizing committee> to award or limit broadcasting and videotaping rights and privileges at the EVENT.

FIGURE 5.22-2

Rental or Lease Agreements are perhaps the most widely used secondary event contracts. The location of the site for the primary event is the most critical detail to hosting any sporting event is (e.g., turf field complex, stadium, natatorium). Sport and recreation managers, especially those working in collegiate athletics or for municipalities, will use lease or rental agreements to secure practice or competition facilities for third parties conducting sporting events. The revenue earned through lease and rental agreements is an important source of income for the colleges and municipalities that own the facilities. **Rental agreements** pertain to short term (i.e., one-time or seasonal) use of a facility. For example, many small colleges or privately owned recreation facilities rent the use of their facility to youth sport organizations or adult recreation leagues. Sport and recreation managers working in those sectors must understand the importance of finalizing rental agreements and obtaining any required documentation (signed waivers, proof of insurance) prior to permitting use of the facility. For example, an event manager's failure to obtain signed waivers from facility renters could cause disqualification of insurance coverage as well as a liability judgement should injuries occur during use (see *Colony Insurance Co., v. Dover Indoor Climbing Gym*, 2009)

Sport and recreation managers use **lease agreements** to secure long-term and regular use of a stadium, gym, pool, ice rink or field. Most professional teams lease the use of their home stadiums or arenas from the city or town in which they are located. Such lease agreements are lengthy and complex in nature and require involvement of attorneys in the drafting and/or interpretation process.

Given the risk of either side breaching a lengthy facility lease, the agreements include liquidated damages provisions to provide some relief to the non-breaching party. For example, the lease agreement between the Buffalo Bills NFL team and the county that owns Ralph Wilson stadium, the Bills home competition and practice cite, includes a $400 hundred million penalty should the Bills leave the stadium prior to the end of the lease agreement. Even such a staggering amount of liquidated damage is often not a deterrent to a party breaching a lease and moving a team or event elsewhere. In *City of Seattle v. Prof's Basketball Club, LCC* (2009), the then owner of the NBA's Seattle Super Sonics agreed to pay the City of Seattle $75 million to terminate the team's lease with the city owned basketball arena, thus allowing the team to move to Oklahoma City. The City of Seattle had initially sued the team and the owner for breach of facility lease but relented during settlement talks (Helman, 2012).

Broadcasting Agreements. Another example of a secondary event contract, are the agreements between hosts and media outlets for the exclusive rights to media coverage of the event. Most commonly referred to **broadcasting agreements** or **media rights contracts**, these event contracts govern radio, television and internet live-stream of the athletic contest or event. The type and value of broadcasting or media rights contracts depends on the commercial draw of the event locally, or for highly visible sports, national interest in the event. Key components to broadcasting agreements are the quantity of coverage desired (i.e., single contest or entire season or series of events), the type of transmission for the broadcast (e.g., radio, television, internet live-stream), exclusivity of broadcast rights and advertisers and access to or set-up at the event.

Exclusivity clauses are a key component to effective sponsorship or media rights agreements because exclusivity assures the party purchasing the sponsorship or broadcast rights that it has exclusive right of access to the event over their competitors. Changes in ownership in the host team, facility or broadcasting company can affect the execution of the agreement (See *Fox Sports Net North, LLC v. Minnesota Twins Partnership*). Sport and recreation managers should be aware of any exclusivity clauses that apply to sponsorship or media outlet coverage of an event. Failure to recognize limitations that exist on business operations due to exclusivity provisions to a contract can result in costly attorney's fees. For example, an exclusivity term in a sponsorship contract was at the core of the dispute in *AT&T Mobility, LLC v. NASCAR*, (2009), which involved a dispute over logo exclusivity granted to Sprint Nextel, the official corporate sponsor of NASCAR and AT&T a corporate partner of NASCAR driver Jeff Burton.

Sponsorship Contracts

Walking through a college athletics or municipal recreation facility, you can help but notice the number of signs on the wall advertising various companies and their services. The logos of third party companies are also on athletics web sites, professional and youth team venues or at events held by local recreation clubs. All of these instances are examples of sport sponsorships, which are a major source of revenue within every sector of the sport and recreation industry. Companies in North America spend more than $13 billion annually on sponsorships of sport entities, events or activities (Ukman, 2010). Sponsorships exist between a company and an athlete (e.g., professional golfers), a sporting event (e.g., Buffalo Wild Wings Citrus Bowl), a college athletics department, a national governing body or a program conducted by a non-profit recreational sport club. Sponsorships also permeate professional sport events. For example, the official name of the 2014 NHL Winter Classic hockey game is the 2014 Bridgestone Winter Classic due to a sponsorship between the NHL and Bridgestone, the Official Tire of the NHL and the NHLPA (Botta, 2014).

Companies purchase sponsorships with the goal of building brand awareness and increasing sales with a targeted audience that follows the sport or entity selling the sponsorship (Branam, 2015). Sport and recreation managers secure sponsorships through a **sponsorship contract**, which is an agreement that confirms the legal obligations of two or more parties as to the sponsorship of an event, facility, team or other related sports entity. The complexity of a sport sponsorship contract is dependent on the overall value of the sponsorship as determined by the worth of the marketing elements included in the agreement. Smaller sponsorships offer simple marketing elements to a sponsor such covering signage, media advertising, and public address announcements. Sponsorships for larger events can include broadcasting of company logos during media broadcasts and advertising sports on web sites.

Sponsorships, especially in the educational or charitable setting, are at times confused with a corporate donation. Unlike a donation, a sponsorship contract is not a one-sided relationship. Sponsors, who are also known as corporate partners, purchase various marketing elements to align itself with the organization selling the sponsorship. A sponsorship contracts sets forth the terms or the partnership and details the beneficial marketing elements available to purchasing organization.

Sponsorship agreements of highly visible events are extensive and require substantial consideration of all parties. The content of sponsorship agreement can vary based on event size and the following or audience of the team or event. All sponsorship agreements should include: (1) the length of the agreement; (2) the rights granted to the sponsor; (3) the form of payment, (4) the right of the parties to use the marks or logos, and termination of the agreement (Lynde, 2007). Exclusive and proper use of logos and trademarks are especially important points to address so that all parties can avoid **ambush marketing**, a marketing tactic in which companies connect their product with a particular event without engaging in a sponsorship agreement with the event organizers. An example of ambush marketing is the use of a trademark or tagline of another company to indicate a corporate partnership, support or endorsement where there is none. Chapter 7.20 *Intellectual Property Law* also addresses the use of ambush marketing in the sport and recreation industry.

Athlete Sponsorships involve the sale of an athlete's name likeness or image to directly market the company and its products. **Endorsement contracts** secure athlete sponsorships and are very common among individual sport athletes in sports such as golf, tennis and distance running. Occasionally, the endorsement or sponsorship relationship requires an athlete or team to appear at a particular event pursuant to **appearance contract**, which guarantees the athlete or team is available to attend or participate in an event. Some national sport governing bodies and the NCAA prohibit endorsement for select products that does not align with the seller's reputation (e.g., tobacco, alcohol). Endorsement contracts also include strict cancellation clauses that allow the agreement to terminate immediately if the athlete places the company in bad light or brings harm to the company's reputation.

Circumstances that require the cancellation of an endorsement due to an athlete's or team's misdeed or egregious conduct are typically those that involve a crime or lack of character. In those cases, the athlete does not challenge the cancellation in part to avoid further discussion of their mistake. On occasion on athlete will step forward and challenge a canceled endorsement contract. For example, in *Mendenhall v. Hanesbrands, Inc.*, (2012), the plaintiff, a former NFL running back, challenged an athletic apparel company decision to cancel his endorsement contract after he posted controversial social media postings regarding terrorist attacks.

SIGNIFICANT CASE

This case centers on game contract under which the school's football programs agreed to play each other four times over ten years alternating the home team. This case illustrates the challenges with multiple year game commitments in college athletics and the affect that a team's success can have on the complete execution of those contracts.

UNIVERSITY OF LOUISVILLE V. DUKE UNIVERSITY

Commonwealth of Kentucky
Franklin Circuit Court
Case No. 07-CI-1765 (2008)

This matter is before the Court on Duke University's motion for judgment on the pleadings under CR 12.03. In this case, the University of Louisville has sued Duke University for breach of contract as a result of Duke's cancellation of football games scheduled for 2007, 2008 and 2009 under an Athletic Competition Agreement entered into by the parties in 1999. For the reasons stated below, Duke's motion is GRANTED as to the claims arising out of the 2007 and 2008 football seasons. The Court further holds that the claim arising out of the 2009 season is not ripe for adjudication, and must be DISMISSED without prejudice.

A motion for judgment on the pleadings is appropriate when a decision can be rendered in favor of the moving party as a matter of law, even though the Court must draw all factual inferences in favor of the party opposing the motion. City of Pioneer Village v. Bullitt County ex rel. Bullitt Fiscal Court, 104 S.W.3d 757 (2003). Here, the Court finds that none of the material facts are in dispute, and Duke is entitled to judgment as a matter of law regarding the claims arising out of the 2007 and 2008 football seasons.

The parties entered into an agreement on June 23, 1999, by which they agreed to play four games in 2002, 2007, 2008, and 2009. Following the 2002 game, Duke canceled the remaining games in the contract with Louisville. The contract signed by the parties contained a penalty of $150,000 per game for cancellation if the non-breaching party is unable to schedule a replacement game with a "team of similar stature."

The case at bar presents a question of contract interpretation. Absent an ambiguity, Kentucky courts are instructed to interpret contract terms according to their plain and ordinary meaning. Paragraph 13 of the contract between the parties states that the team which breaches the agreement is required to pay $150,000 per game to the non-beaching party. The breaching party is relieved of the obligation to pay liquidated damages, however, if the non-breaching team is able to schedule a replacement game "with a team of similar stature." The Court finds no ambiguity in this language, and thus this provision must be interpreted according to its plain and ordinary meaning.

To say that one thing is "of a similar stature" to another is to say that the two are on the same level. Nothing in the language of the agreement suggests that it is necessary or appropriate to conduct an in-depth analysis of the relative strengths and weaknesses of the breaching team and its potential replacements. Nor does the agreement specify that replacement teams must be from a particular major athletic conference or even a particular division of the National Collegiate Athletic Association (NCAA). The term "team of similar stature" simply means any team that competes at the same level of athletic performance as the Duke football team. At oral argument, Duke (with a candor perhaps more attributable to good legal strategy than to institutional modesty) persuasively asserted that this is a threshold that could not be any lower. Duke's argument on this point cannot be reasonably disputed by Louisville. Duke won only one football game, and lost eleven, during the 2007 football season.

Louisville concedes that it has filled its schedules for the 2007 and 2008 football seasons. Louisville does not even attempt to argue that any of the teams scheduled for 2007 or 2008 are inferior to Duke from the standpoint of athletic ability or success on the football field. Rather, Louisville argues that the term team "of a similar stature" is inherently ambiguous and the Court needs to allow further discovery and litigation over the meaning of that term, notwithstanding the enormous costs and lengthy delay to both parties that would result from such a ruling.

As explained above, the Court rejects this argument and finds that this term is unambiguous. Accordingly, it must be applied according to its plain meaning and common use. Louisville's alleged inability to schedule replacement games with teams from major athletic conferences or members of the Football Bowl Subdivision is irrelevant. Louisville does not, and cannot reasonably, contest the proposition that all of the teams it has scheduled for 2007 and 2008 are "of a similar stature" in terms of the one relevant criterion: the quality of those football teams compared to Duke's football team.

Duke is an NCAA Division I school that regularly competes with football teams in both the Football Bowl Subdivision and the Football Championship Subdivision, as does Louisville.[8] The Court therefore finds that it is reasonable as a matter of law to interpret the plain language of the contract in accordance with the established practice of both parties to this agreement, in which football games are regularly scheduled with Division I schools from both Subdivisions.

Accordingly, the Court finds there is a rebuttable presumption that any team designated by the NCAA as a Division I school, whether in the Football Bowl Subdivision or the Football Championship Subdivision, is a team of "similar stature" to Duke within the ordinary meaning of the language used in this Athletic Competition Agreement. While that presumption is not conclusive, Louisville should be required to produce at least some relevant, material and factual evidence that any of the teams on its schedule for 2007 or 2008 could be considered to be inferior to Duke's football team. Louisville has made no attempt to do this.

A breach qualifies as anticipatory when one repudiates an agreement using unequivocal words or conduct, and said repudiation substantially impairs the value of the contract. On March 24, 2003, Duke sent a letter to the University of Louisville stating that its team would not play the games scheduled for 2007, 2008, and 2009 under the Athletic Competition Agreement at issue in this case. This letter provides evidence of an unequivocal repudiation of the agreement, and refusing to play these games substantially impairs the value of the agreement. An anticipatory breach of a contract can, under some circumstances, give rise to an immediate action for damages. However, one may not collect on damages under the agreement until such damages become due. Damages under this contract for cancellation of the 2009 football game cannot be due until it is determined whether Louisville schedules a replacement game with a "team of similar stature" for the 2009 football season.

The Athletic Competition Agreement provides that the $150,000 penalty is waived when the non-breaching party schedules a contest with a "team of similar stature". Thus, under the terms of this contract, waiver of the penalty cannot be determined until the non-breaching team's schedule is final. If all the teams on this schedule are "teams of a similar stature", then the breaching party cannot be liable. The 2007 season has been completed, and it appears from the record that Louisville, on the weekend it had contracted to play Duke, instead played the University of Utah, an NCAA Division I Football Bowl Subdivision school. Louisville suggests, without offering any evidence, that Utah may not have been the replacement game for the canceled Duke game. Nevertheless, Louisville has not designated as Division I schools by the NCAA. Nor has Louisville offered any evidence that any of the Division I teams scheduled are not on a par with the Duke football team in terms of their "development or achievement."

Likewise, the 2008 schedule is now final. Louisville has failed to proffer any evidence that any of its scheduled opponents could be considered inferior to the Duke football team. Louisville has a full schedule of Division I opponents for 2008. Accordingly, Duke cannot be held liable for liquidated damages under the contract. Summary judgment must be granted in favor of Duke and against Louisville for all claims arising out of the 2008 season on the same grounds as for the 2007 season.

The issue of Duke's potential liability for the $150,000 penalty for the 2009 game cannot be determined until Louisville's schedule for 2009 becomes final. Duke argues that this claim is not ripe for adjudication. Although Louisville's 2009 schedule is not yet final, the Court notes that Louisville has gone on record as stating that "Louisville was able to fill the games in 2008 and 2009 with a home and home contract. It is 2007 that is the problem." Nevertheless, such a claim based on Louisville's 2009 schedule is certainly premature. While an anticipatory breach may have occurred, the contract itself.

Louisville argues that summary judgment is premature, and that it is entitled to take additional discovery. In light of the Court's ruling that the contract is not ambiguous and must be applied according to its plain meaning, the Court is at a loss to see how additional discovery could be warranted. Extensive written discovery has been completed. There are no additional disputed issues of material fact on which discovery could reasonably continue. Kentucky courts have long held that parties are only entitled to an adequate, not an unlimited, opportunity to complete discovery. Here, as in Rogers v. Professional Golfers Association, 28 S.W.3d 869, 874, the Court has found that the plaintiff's claims must fail as a matter of law and thus, "further discovery is unnecessary."

As the Court of Appeals has noted, in considering a motion for summary judgment "[t]he movant bears the initial burden of convincing the court by evidence of record that no genuine issue of fact is in dispute, and then the burden shifts to the party opposing summary judgment." Hallahan v. The Courier-Journal, 138 S.W.3d 699, 705 (2004). When a summary judgment has been made and properly supported, the party opposing the motion must produce "at least some affirmative evidence showing that there is a genuine issue of material fact for trial." Steelvest, Inc. v. Scansteel Service Center, Inc., 807 S.W.2d 476, 482 (1991). As the Supreme Court has explained, "[t]he party opposing summary judgment cannot rely on their own claims or arguments without significant evidence in order to prevent summary judgment." Wymer v. JH Properties, Inc., 50 S.W.3d 195, 199 (2001). Here, Duke has carried its burden to demonstrate that there are no material issues of disputed fact, and that it is entitled to judgment as a matter of law. Louisville has not produced any "significant evidence" that would support its claims or its argument that there are disputed material facts at issue. Accordingly, this Court must grant summary judgment on all claims arising out of the 2007 and 2008 football seasons. The claim arising out of the 2009 football season is not ripe, and must be dismissed without prejudice.

CONCLUSION

For the reasons stated above, the motion of defendant Duke University for judgment on the pleadings will be considered as a motion for summary judgment under CR 56. Hoke v. Cullinan, 914 S.W.2d 3335 (Ky. 1995). Duke's motion is GRANTED as to all claims arising out of the 2007 and 2008 football seasons, and those claims are DISMISSED with prejudice. Duke's motion to dismiss Louisville's claim regarding the 2009 season for lack of ripeness is GRANTED, and Louisville's claim arising out of the cancellation of the 2009 football game is DISMISSED without prejudice.

CASES ON THE SUPPLEMENTAL CD

AT&T Mobility, LLC v. NASCAR, Inc., 494 F.3d 1356 (2007 U.S. App. LEXIS 19182) (11th Cir. Ga., Aug. 13, 2007). This case outlines the use of sponsorship agreements and application of exclusivity clauses to sport and recreation events.

Fox Sports Net North, LLC v. Minnesota Twins Partnership, et al., 319 F.3d 329 (8th Cir. 2003). This case discusses a broadcast contract that was breached after third party network purchased initial network.

Mendenhall v. Hanesbrands, Inc., 856 F. Supp. 2d 717 (M.D.N.C. 2012). This case centers on the termination of an endorsement contract between Hanesbrands and former NFL running back Rashard Mendenhall due to statements plaintiff made through his personal Twitter account.

Race Tires America, Inc. v, Hoosier Racing Tire Corp (2010 U.S. App. LEXIS 15233). This case discusses the strength and purpose of exclusivity clauses.

TYR Sport, Inc., v. Warnaco Swimwear, Inc., et. al, 709 F. Supp. 2d 802 (2010). This case illustrates a problematic endorsement contract the need to employ a qualified attorney to review game and event related contracts.

SIGNIFICANT CASES FROM OTHER CHAPTERS:

Chapter 7.23 *Baltimore Orioles Inc. v. M.L.B. Players Assoc.* 805 F.2d. 663 (7th Cir. 1986). A case that discusses both intellectual property rights and the exclusive ownership of broadcast clips from former professional baseball players.

QUESTIONS YOU SHOULD BE ABLE TO ANSWER

1. What are the main distinctions between game, event and sponsorship contracts?
2. How do sponsorship contracts differ from endorsement contracts?
3. How do game, event and sponsorship contracts drive revenue for sport and recreation organizations?
4. What does effect does exclusivity have clauses have on event sponsorships and media rights to an event?
5. How does the statute of frauds apply to game, event and sponsorship contracts?

REFERENCES
Cases
AT&T Mobility, LLC v. NASCAR, Inc., 494 F.3d 1356, (2007 U.S. App. LEXIS 19182) (11th Cir. Ga., Aug. 13, 2007)
City of Seattle v. Prof's Basketball Clun, LCC, No. C07-1620RSM, (2007 WL 3217556) (W.D. Wash., Oct 29, 2007)
Colony Insurance Co., v. Dover Indoor Climbing Gym, No. 2008-759 (N.H. 2009). Retrieved at http://caselaw.findlaw.com/nh-supreme-court/1265598.html.
Fox Sports Net North, LLC v. Minnesota Twins Partnership, et al., 19 F.3d 329, (8th Cir. 2003).
Mendenhall v. Hanesbrands, Inc., 856 F. Supp. 2d 717 (M.D.N.C. 2012).
Race Tires America, Inc. v. Hoosier, (2008 Cal. App. LEXIS 222).
TYR Sport, Inc., v. Warnaco Swimwear, Inc., et. al, (2010 U.S. Dist. LEXIS 27566).
Univ. of Louisville v. Duke Univ., No. 07-CI-1765, at 1 (Franklin Cir. Ct. June 19, 2008). Retrieved at http://www.ncbusinesslitigationreport.com/Duke%20Opinion.pdf.

Publications
Ammon, R., Southall, R., & Nagel, M. (2010) *Sport Facility Management: Organization and Mitigating Risks*. (2d ed.) Morgantown, WV: Fitness Information Technology.
Branam, S. (2015). A modern approach to traditional sponsorship agreements. *Athletic Business*. Retrieved at http://www.athleticbusiness.com/marketing/a-modern-approach-to-traditional-sponsorship-agreements.html.
Botta, C. (2014). NHL Winter Classic Nets $20 Million. *Sports Business Journal*. Retrieved at http://www.sportsbusinessdaily.com/Journal/Issues/2014/01/13/Events-and-Attractions/Winter-Classic.aspx.
Conrad, M. (2011). *The business of sports: A primer for journalists* (2nd ed.). New York: Routledge.
County of Erie Non-Relocation Agreement. (n.d.). Retrieved at http://www2.erie.gov/exec/sites/www2.erie.gov.exec/files/uploads/Buffalo%20Bills%20Non-Relocation%20Agreement.pdf.
Greenwell, T. C., Danzey-Bussell, L. A., & Shonk, D. J. (2014). *Managing sport events*. Champaign, IL: Human Kinetics.
Helman, C. (2012). The sordid deal that created the Okla. City thunder. *Forbes*. Retrieved at http://www.forbes.com/sites/christopherhelman
Humphreys, B.R., & Ruseski, J.E. (2009). Estimates of the Dimensions of the Sports Market in the US. *International Journal of Sport Finance*, vol. 4, no. 2, pp. 94-113.
Lawrence, H., & Wells, M. (2009). *Event management blueprint: Creating and managing successful sports events*. Dubuque, IA: Kendall Hunt Publishing.
Lillig, J. (2009). "Magic" or Misery?: HBCUs, Guarantee Contracts and Public Policy. *DePaul Journal of Sports Law & Contemporary Problems*. Retrieved at http://via.library.depaul.edu/cgi/viewcontent.cgi?article=1049&context=jslcp.
Lynde, T. (2007). *Sponsorships 101*. Mableton, Georgia: Lynde and Associates.
Masteralexis, L. P., Barr, C. A., & Hums, M. A. (2015). Principles and practice of sport management. Sudbury, MA: Jones Bartlett.
Rosenthal, M., & Tamin, A. (2009). How to protect the exclusivity in your brand's sponsorship. *Athletic Business*. Retrieved at http://www.sportsbusinessdaily.com/Journal/Issues/2009/09/20090921/From-The-Field-Of/How-To-Protect-The-Exclusivity-In-Your-Brands-Sponsorship.aspx.
Steinbach, P. (2010) Non-Conference Scheduling Leads to Lopsided Scores, Balanced Books. *Athletic Business* Retrieved at http://www.athleticbusiness.com/College/non-conference-scheduling-leads-to-lopsided-scores-balanced-books.html.
Ukman, L. (2010). *IEG's Complete Guide to Sponsorship: Everything you need to know about sports, arts, event, entertainment and cause marketing*. Chicago: IEG, Incorporated.

5.30 ALTERNATIVE DISPUTE RESOLUTION

Arbitration, Negotiation, and Mediation

Rebecca J. Mowrey | Millersville University of Pennsylvania

Imagine; you are competing for a position on the USA Track & Field Olympic Team. This is your dream; your goal; your obsession. For over ten years you and your family and friends have made significant sacrifices and commitments enabling you to get to this elite level of athletic preparation and competition. Then, following a preliminary heat of your event you are notified that due to an eligibility rule violation you have been disqualified from further participation in the meet. With this one statement from a United States Olympic Committee (USOC) official, your dream, and all that you have worked so hard and so long to accomplish, has been crushed.

When you learn more about the alleged violation, you are absolutely certain that there has been a mistake. During the past twelve hours you and your coaches have already appealed the decision through all the USA Track & Field Association options available to you, and in each decision your appeal has been denied by Association officials. With your next preliminary heat scheduled to begin in fewer than six hours, you now turn your appeal efforts toward a group (**panel**) of neutral decision-makers (**arbitrators**) who are knowledgeable about track & field, as well as the USOC and USA Track & Field Association rules and procedures. This is the last level of appeal available to you. The panel has the full authority to listen to all parties, evaluate all evidence presented, and then make a final and in most cases **binding** (not open to further appeal or reversal) decision regarding your eligibility to continue to participate in the USA Olympic Team Trials in Track & Field. You may write the outcome of this imaginary story for yourself; however, it illustrates several of the unique elements of **arbitration**, and why the International Olympic Committee (IOC) and many International Sports Federations and National Governing Bodies representing a myriad of sport and recreation industries, support the use of arbitrators to address the complex disputes that arise during domestic and international events.

With the popularity of courtroom-themed dramas you might think of litigation as the only road to resolving legal disputes. In reality, litigation is just one, albeit the most popular, of several avenues that individuals or groups may pursue for legal remedy. However, litigation is not always an appropriate means for resolving a dispute. **Alternative dispute resolution** (ADR) is a blanket term that includes negotiation, mediation, and arbitration, among other options, as alternatives to adjudication of disputes, with mediation and arbitration being the most commonly used of the three (**www.law.cornell.edu/adr.html**). The use of ADR can be voluntarily pursued by the disputing parties or mandated by a contract or waiver (see also Chapter 2.23, *Waivers and Releases*). Recreation and sport managers with a working knowledge of ADR procedures, will not only be prepared when an ADR process is mandated, but also ready to recommend use of an ADR approach when appropriate. It is important to recognize issues and situations where ADR will be preferred over traditional litigation.

FUNDAMENTAL CONCEPTS

Court adjudication can be a costly and lengthy process. In recognition of this fact, the federal government established the **Administrative Dispute Resolution Act of 1990**, 5 U.S.C.A. 581, which requires all federal agencies to establish policies for the voluntary use of ADR as a "prompt, expert and inexpensive means of resolving disputes as an alternative to litigation in federal courts."

ADR Basics

Generally Assumed *ADR Benefits v. Litigation*

- Reduced costs (i.e., no attorney fees, limited discovery)
- Usually significantly faster/less time in dispute (i.e., limited pretrial discovery, overscheduled courts)
- "Expert's" decision can be rendered instead of a non-expert jury or judge. ADR panelists frequently specialize in the types of disputes they hear/decide.
- Greater flexibility and creative solutions instead of win/lose.
- Proceedings and outcome can be kept confidential
- ADR is considered to be the best option when there is a desire to maintain or reestablish the relationships in conflict. This could be critical to schools, offices, teams, or organizations.
- Increased satisfaction with the outcome and process

Generally Assumed *ADR Limitations v. Litigation*

- Legal precedent, if desired, is not established through ADR
- Absence of procedural safeguards if an arbitrator makes an error of law or fact
- Limited opportunity for appeal (in most cases appeals are only granted for arbitrator bias, fraud, or decisions rendered which exceed the arbitrator's authority)
- Enforcement of decisions is voluntary unless bound by contract (i.e., CBA)

Arbitration

Arbitration is the most formal of the ADR approaches discussed in this chapter, yet it is much less rigid than traditional litigation. Arbitration differs from negotiation and mediation significantly, as the arbitrator is not concerned with reaching a decision that is agreeable to the disputing parties. In this process a dispute is submitted to a neutral third party or arbitrator who listens to the disputants and considers the submitted evidence and then makes a decision or award.

The **Federal Arbitration Act of 1925**, 9 U.S.C. Section 1 (FAA) established federal law supporting arbitration as an alternative to litigation. The American Bar Association (ABA), the Uniform Law Commissioners (ULC), and the American Arbitration Association (AAA) approved the **Uniform Arbitration Act of 1955** (UAA) to establish procedure and policy standards for arbitration.

Since Congress's passage of the FAA and approval of the UAA, the number and complexity of arbitration cases has grown dramatically. In many of these cases, the FAA and the UAA failed to provide direction regarding substantive issues, and the need to update and modernize these Acts was evident. Specifically, consensus was reached by active arbitrators that revisions were needed to address the following points: (1) the need to modernize outdated provisions, clarify ambiguities under the Act, and codify important case-law developments; (2) the need to give primary consideration to the autonomy of contracting parties, provided their arbitration agreement conforms to basic notions of fundamental fairness because arbitration is a consensual process; (3) the need to maintain the essential character of arbitration as a means of dispute resolution distinct from litigation, particularly in regard to efficiency, timeliness and cost; and (4) because most parties intend arbitral decisions to be final and binding, the need to limit court involvement in the arbitration process unless unfairness or denial of justice produces clear need for such involvement." (www.nccusl.org). To address these concerns, the Revised Uniform Arbitration Act (RUAA) was approved in 2000 by the ULC, the ABA, and the AAA. The RUAA added significant procedural provisions absent from the UAA, including the use of electronic records and documents which was not a consideration in 1955 (www.aaa.org).

It might help you to think of the arbitration process as a simplified trial with limited discovery and relaxed rules regarding evidence (**www.adr.org**). Although organizations may attach unique elements to their **arbitration clause**, most proceedings contain the following five elements.

1. **Demand for arbitration.** A written demand for arbitration identifying the parties, the dispute, and the relief or remedy sought must be submitted to the opposing party. The arbitration request is less formal than writing a complaint in a civil action, but the issues to be arbitrated must be clear.
2. **Response.** The opposing party typically responds in writing, stating whether they agree that the issue is subject to arbitration under the existing contract or other relevant documents.

3. **Selection of arbitration panel.** A single arbitrator or panel with sufficient knowledge of the subject matter is selected. This process might be described in the arbitration clause of a contract or a permanent arbitrator might be designated.
4. **Arbitration hearing.** Although similar to a trial in some respects, namely, the presentation of witnesses, documents, briefs, memoranda, and closing arguments, the process differs from a trial in that written transcripts are only provided if the parties order them, the evidentiary rules are relaxed, and the extent of discovery and cross-examination are often limited (UAA of 1955).
5. **Decision.** After hearing from all parties (claimants, respondents, and affected parties) the arbitrator renders a decision (**www.adr.org**).

The decision of an arbitrator may be disputed and, under the RUAA, be vacated if: (1) the award was procured by corruption, fraud, or undue means; (2) there was evidence of partiality or corruption in the arbitrators; (3) the arbitrators were guilty of misconduct in refusing to postpone the hearing, on sufficient cause shown, or in refusing to hear evidence pertinent and material to the controversy; or of any other misbehavior by which the rights of any party have been prejudiced; or (4) the arbitrators exceeded their powers, or so imperfectly executed them that a mutual, final, and definite award on the subject matter submitted was not made (9 U.S.C. § 11).

The use of arbitration may be mandated in some contracts but be completely voluntary in others. In **voluntary arbitration** situations, the arbitration is mutually agreeable to both parties and may be **binding** or **nonbinding**, as determined in advance by the involved parties or the arbitration agreement. In **mandatory arbitration** situations, the disputing parties are often required to utilize arbitration as their sole method of addressing unresolved grievances according to the arbitration clause of their employment contracts (see Chapter 5.21, *Employment Contracts*), and in these cases the decision is typically binding (**www.adr.org**). Arbitration decisions are not typically subject to any further judicial review or appeal unless there is evidence that the arbitrator committed fraud or some other form of professional misconduct during the proceeding. If this is the case, the Federal Arbitration Act of 1925 provides for an appeal, and for review of the decision by a judge or court. There are two common approaches to determining the number of arbitrators; either the disputing parties agree on one arbitrator or they are each represented by their own arbitrators and a third impartial arbitrator joins them to form an **arbitration panel**. Disputing parties can seek assignment of an arbitrator from several nongovernment organizations, such as the **American Arbitration Association** (AAA), which maintains a registry of qualified arbitrators or "neutrals."

Arbitration agreements now commonly appear in waivers and service contracts, requiring signers to pursue arbitration, not litigation. For example, in *Cronin v. California Fitness* (2005), it was revealed that the two-page contract gym members sign includes an arbitration agreement capping damages for either party at an amount equal to the annual membership fee. Furthermore, the party making the claim must pay the arbitration cost, discovery is restricted, and the arbitration results must be kept confidential.

Negotiation

Negotiation refers to a consensual bargaining process used primarily to resolve disputes and complete transactions such as labor contracts. The intent of the negotiation process is to arrive at an agreement that is acceptable to all involved parties. The negotiators in these situations are attempting to obtain their client's goals and directives, so some concessions or compromises might be made to obtain the client's desired outcomes. You have likely engaged in hundreds of informal negotiations in your lifetime as you agree to trade resources with your friends, such as the use of your car, computer, phone, video games, or your proofreading skills, for something of theirs that you value. There are four basic steps to negotiation: (1) planning how you will approach the other parties, (2) exchanging information and requests, (3) offering and counter-offering concessions and compromises, and (4) reaching an agreement that is mutually acceptable to all parties (**www.adr.org**). Negotiations are typically confidential, so you will rarely have the opportunity to follow the progress of a negotiation unless you are one of the principal parties involved. However, information concerning many agreements in professional sports, including the standard player contracts for selected professional teams, can frequently be accessed electronically through websites.

Mediation

Mediation is a process in which a **neutral mediator** works collaboratively with the opposing parties to identify the areas of conflict and to assist them in reaching a settlement or agreement that is mutually satisfactory (**www.mediate.com**). Mediation is a consensual, nonbinding process, as the **mediators** have no power to impose or force a solution on the parties. The neutrality of the mediator is critical to ensure a sense of fairness while maintaining the integrity of the process. In some cases, the ability of the mediator to offer a different perspective will help resolve the conflict (**www.campus-adr.org**). You may have served unofficially as a mediator while keeping the peace between friends or classmates. If so, you have discovered one of the unique aspects of mediation versus negotiation or arbitration—the goal is to preserve the relationships and to reach an amicable resolution. As a result, mediation is a good choice for disputants who have strategic alliances or common interests that need to be maintained, such as teammates and coworkers (**www.mediate.com**). Another distinction of mediation is the potential to invoke the use of this process as a conflict intervention or conciliation as part of a larger conflict management program. In other words, as a conflict is developing and escalating, disputants might seek the involvement of a mediator before their conflict reaches a point of stalemate. The role of mediation in this manner is particularly effective when dealing with repetitive conflicts between individuals who need or wish to continue their working relationship (**www.adr.org**).

A less common approach for dispute management, but particularly useful when seeking to rebuild community or relationships i.e., team, staff, or inter-agency disputes; the **restorative justice (RJ)** process is focused on addressing the harm and restoring or rebuilding the prior relationship. Although RJ is actually a theory of criminal justice, often times the RJ results outperform the desired affect of traditional mediation approaches. The RJ process, among other restorative outcomes, provides the opportunity for victims and offenders to meet face to face in a mediated forum, and for each party to fully express the impact the event(s) or harm has had upon him/her. Offenders may reflect upon the impact of their decisions and be held accountable for their actions while victims may seek answers and meaningful restitution (www.restorativejustice.org). Restorative justice may be a good companion to criminal proceedings when crimes such as hazing, assault, or sexual harassment occur among those who must find a way to co-exist in the same school, organization, or community.

Collective Bargaining, Labor Disputes, and ADR

Many employee groups, including professional athletic players associations, have a **collective bargaining agreement** (CBA) with their employers. A CBA refers to an agreement between the employer and the labor union or organization that regulates the terms and conditions of employment for all the employees of a single employer. In some labor matters, the CBA may mandate that certain disputes (e.g., differences in interpretation of the CBA, grievances, salary issues) must be resolved through mandatory arbitration or that mediation may be sought by either party (**www.campus-adr.com**). The collective bargaining agreements of the professional sport leagues in the United States provide for grievances to be addressed through an arbitration process. However, every CBA contains specific clauses and procedures regarding how and when arbitration will be used that are unique to that CBA and the related parties. Since 1974, the CBA for Major League Baseball (MLB) has permitted eligible players to file for salary arbitration. From 1974–2009, a total of 487 MLB salary cases have been decided through arbitration (mlb.mlb.org).

When the parties of a CBA agree to enter into arbitration, the issues the arbitrator(s) is to address are clearly communicated. For example, in the *Matter of the Arbitration Between Terrell Owens and the National Football League (NFL) Players Association v. the Philadelphia Eagles and the NFL Management Council* (2005), an arbitrator was asked by the grievants, Terrell Owens and the NFL Players Association, to examine the decision of the Philadelphia Eagles' management to suspend Owens. Specifically, the arbitrator was asked to reach a decision on the following two issues: (1) Was the four-week disciplinary suspension for just cause; if not, what should be the remedy be? (2) Was it a violation of the CBA for the Club to exclude the Player from games and practices, following the four-week suspension? The arbitrator's conclusions and decision follow:

> In summary, there is ample room to find that the Club could respond to this Player's actions, suspending him without pay to the limits permitted by the collective bargaining agreement for his behavior

in this matter. Thereafter, the Coach properly exercised his inherent discretion to conclude that, on balance, the team would be better protected and better off by practicing and fielding a team that did not include Mr. Owens. The problem—a continuing one—was almost entirely off-field, and the response properly dealt with that reality. Both responses, the disciplinary and the discretionary, were specifically understood by these parties and fully countenanced as part of this collective bargaining relationship. The disciplinary side of the equation is expressly established in Article VIII. The non-disciplinary response is part of the core and character of a coaches discretion; significantly, but predictably, it is nowhere constrained by the CBA. The finding, therefore, is that the Club has shouldered its burden of providing clear and convincing evidence of the Player's misconduct and, moreover, that the four-week suspension was for just cause. Additionally, there was no violation of the labor agreement inherent in the Club's decision to pay Mr. Owens, but not to permit him to play or practice, due to the nature of his conduct and its destructive and continuing threat to the team.

AWARD, The grievance is denied. Richard I. Bloch, Esq. November 23, 2005

ADR Applications in Sport and Recreation

In professional sports almost all contract disputes between the players and / or coaches and teams are resolved through an arbitration process. For example, in 2008 an arbitrator ruled that former Dallas Mavericks coach Don Nelson was entitled to nearly 6.3 million dollars in deferred salary and compensation payments from his time as a coach at Dallas. Mavericks' owner Mark Cuban alleged that Nelson had violated a noncompete clause in his contract when he became head coach of the Golden State Warriors in 2006.

In the context of intercollegiate sports, the NCAA has utilized ADR approaches to resolve disputes in limited cases. In 1991, the NCAA enacted a legislative policy that capped or restricted the earnings or salaries of some coaching staff personnel at NCAA universities and colleges. These restricted-earnings coaches could not be compensated more than $12,000 during the traditional academic year and no more than $4,000 for summer employment (*Law v. NCAA*, 1998). The NCAA's restricted-earnings policy was found to be in violation of federal antitrust law (see Chapter 7.32, *Antitrust Law: Amateur Sport Applications*). The NCAA appealed the decision of the district court and also entered into mediation with the plaintiffs. As a result of the mediation process, a $54.5 million settlement was announced in 1999 (**www.ncaa.org**).

ADR and International Sport Disputes

Disputes in international sport settings raise several unique dilemmas, such as when to follow the legal system of the host country versus that of the athlete's country of residence. Also, most legal systems do not accommodate the need for nearly immediate decisions to remove athletes from further competition or to approve them for continued competition. The arbitration format is ideal for addressing international disputes that are bound by different judicial systems.

Members of the IOC realized the need for effective and efficient conflict resolution and established the Court of Arbitration for Sport (CAS) to address disputes submitted by international athletes, governing bodies, national Olympic committees, and sport federations (**www.tas-cas.org**). Since establishing the CAS, arbitration has been used to bridge the gap between differing legal systems and to reach a speedy decision that is imperative during multiday events such as the Olympics and world championships. The CAS consists of three divisions: the Appeals Arbitration Division, the Ad Hoc Division, and the Ordinary Arbitration Division. Athletes who disagree with the decisions of their sport federation or sport regulation body during non-Olympic times would seek arbitration through the CAS Appeals Arbitration Division. The Ad Hoc Division is charged with resolving disputes that occur during the Olympic Games, whereas the CAS Ordinary Arbitration Division addresses commercial contract disputes (i.e., official vendors and media). The CAS has courts in Lausanne, Switzerland; New York City, New York, USA; and Sydney, Australia. Unless all parties agree to follow another country's form of law, CAS will use Swiss law or the law of the country where the involved sport federation is located (**www.tas-cas.org**). The International Council of Arbitration for Sport (ICAS) was established in 1994 to administer the CAS and to provide a process for arbitration that is neutral and independent of the IOC. The primary responsibilities of the ICAS are to select neutral arbitrators and to protect the rights of all parties (Oschutz, 2002).

Since establishment, CAS has seen a dramatic increase in appeals filed for arbitration, with many cases tied to drug testing issues. In 2006, the Federation Internationale de Football Association (FIFA) requested that the CAS provide a legal opinion regarding the World Anti-Doping Agency's (WADA) World Anti-Doping Code (CODE). FIFA specifically wished to know if the CODE complied with Swiss law, and if FIFA's sanctions related to doping offences was in compliance with the CODE. The CAS determined that the FIFA policies were in compliance with the CODE. This complex case required arbitrators with knowledge of FIFA, Swiss law, and the WADA CODE.

In *United States Anti-Doping Agency v. Floyd Landis*, the CAS Panel upheld the 2007 American Arbitration Association Panel decision, resulting in Landis's disqualification from the 2006 Tour De France and suspending him from competition from January 30, 2007–January 30, 2009. Furthermore, the CAS Panel ordered Landis to pay $100,000 towards the United States Anti-Doping Agency's (USADA) CAS Arbitration costs. At the request of Landis, all court records were made public, and this was the first public anti-doping hearing ever conducted. The Supplemental Web Site includes the American Arbitration Association (AAA) Panel decision, the dissenting opinion of Christopher L. Campbell, a member of the AAA Arbitration Panel, and the CAS Panel decision.

Understandably, the number of CAS appeals usually increases during the years in which the Summer or Winter Olympic Games are held. In February, 2009, the CAS dismissed the appeal of Swedish wrestler Ara Abrahamian regarding the IOC decision to strip the bronze medal from him during the 2008 Summer Olympic Games. The IOC made their decision after Abrahamian dropped his medal on the floor in protest of a penalty call. In their ruling, the CAS stated that "the decision of the IOC Executive Board was not disproportionate in the circumstances."

In a perhaps more complicated Olympic medal dispute, the seven USA relay teammates of Marion Jones challenged the IOC decision to disqualify their 2000 medals due to the fact that Jones failed a drug test. These teammates included the 4x100m team that won the bronze medal, and the 4x400m team which won the gold medal. The teammates argued that at the time of these races there were no explicit rules in place explaining what should happen to the teammates if one or more members of the relay team tested positive for drug doping. The CAS panel agreed with the women and held that their relay results were not to be disqualified in the records nor were their medals or certificates to be forfeited (*Andrea Anderson, LaTasha Colander Clark, Jearl Miles-Clark, Torri Edwards, Chryste Gaines, Monique Hennagan, Passion Richardson v. International Olympic Committee* (2008) CAS, Aug. 30, 2010).

Although many CAS decisions involve an athlete as plaintiff, this Court has also been useful in disputes between governing bodies. In 2011 a dispute occurred between the Bulgarian Boxing Federation (BBF) and the European Boxing Confederation (EUBC). In January 2011 the BBF was selected to host the 2011 European Men Championships. However, at the time of this announcement the BBF was involved in a pending disciplinary investigation by the International Boxing Association (AIBA) that could result in suspension of the BBF. Due to uncertainty regarding the investigation outcomes, the EUBC revoked Bulgaria's hosting rights and awarded the 2011 European Men Championship to Turkey. The BBF appealed this decision to the CAS arguing that the EUBC had no legal grounds for their decision since the outcome of the AIBA investigation was unknown. Two months prior to the start of the 2011 European Men Championships, the Sole Arbitrator for the CAS decided in favor of the BBF; however, in an example of the unique ability of arbitration, the Arbitrator took the reality of the situation into account, including the cost and preparation to host that was already invested by Turkey, and the Arbitrator ruled that Turkey would still host the 2011 European Men Championship (*Bulgarian Boxing Federation v. European Boxing Confederation*, CAS, June 7, 2011). Additional CAS decisions can be found at their Website www.tas-cas.org.

Despite past acceptance of CAS decisions by Courts throughout the world, criticisms concerning the neutrality and transparency of the CAS and the ICAS have been raised, resulting in investigation by some nations and athletes. Mostly notably, five-time Olympic and German speed skater, Claudia Pechstein, sued for the right for her case to be tried through the German courts. The Higher Regional Court of Munich (*Claudia Pechstein v. German Speed Skating Association and International Skating Union*), ruled in her favor and Pechstein sued the International Skating Union (ISU) and Germany's speed skating association in civil court for loss of income (estimated in excess of 5 million dollars). Regardless of the final court decision in Germany, Pechstein has opened the door for other claimants to appeal CAS decisions through their home country's legal systems despite the fact that most sport governing bodies have adopted the CAS as their final appellate forum. It will be interesting to see if reforms are made by the ICAS to satisfy the discontent; if jurisdiction challenges are raised by the IOC and sport governing bodies; or if Pechstein has established a new direction in international sport litigation (conflictoflaws.net/2015/Pechstein).

Another growing area of international litigation is concerned with the protection of intellectual property, including Internet and electronic commerce. With the expansion of the Internet, an increasing number of **cybersquatters** have purchased domain names (.org, .com, .net) that potentially infringe on established trademarks (see Chapter 7.22, *Principles of Trademark Law*). This issue is especially important to professional and university athletic teams, sport merchandisers, and sport media, who stand to lose millions of dollars as a result of domestic and global trademark violations (**www.wipo.org**). As mentioned previously, international disputes are troublesome for those seeking traditional litigation as a remedy.

Established in 1994, the **World Intellectual Property Organization (WIPO)** resolves intellectual property disputes through arbitration and mediation (**www.wipo.org**). WIPO arbitration cases frequently resolve disputes regarding web domain name challenges. It is likely that the WIPO will be presented with a growing number of these cases as more companies compete in world-wide markets. For example, Spalding entered the Chinese market in 1995 at which time they completed Chinese trademark registration of the name Spalding. When the Chinese company Zhang Xue Ming registered the domain name spalding-cn.com, the Spalding company disputed the Chinese company's claim to this domain name. The WIPO Arbitration Panel agreed with Spalding and transferred the domain name to Spalding (2010, *SGC Lisco LLC v. Zhang Xue Ming*). Several additional examples of these cases are included on the Supplemental Web Site.

ADR, Sport Specialists, and Violence

The ICAS, AAA, and the professional player associations have already increased the demand for arbitration and negotiation specialists who are knowledgeable about sport. It is likely that the value of mediation will continue to be appreciated in these situations as well (Galton, 1998). Historically, it is common for the professional sport model to influence the intercollegiate, interscholastic, and club sport programs. Jeffrey Schalley (2001) argued that arbitration can be used to eliminate violence in sports. He proposed that language could be added to the CBA arbitration clauses to address "injury compensation resulting from reckless or intentional torts." Would this work as a deterrent? Without a CBA available in amateur sport settings, perhaps an arbitration clause regarding violence will begin to appear in athlete codes of conduct and/or in waivers (see Chapter 2.23, *Waivers and Releases*) and in participation agreements (see Chapter 2.24, *Informed Consents and Agreements to Participate*). As schools, universities, and communities address the growing concerns regarding "bullying," hazing, and conflict among their student athlete populations, the position of ADR sport specialist might become as commonplace as that of team physician.

The Globalization of Sport and the Role of Arbitration

The efforts to establish international and global sport leagues, coupled with the expansion of annual international competition, will result in increased disputes between participants, management, spectators, and other related constituents. U.S. professional sport programs continue to expand the number of contests that are scheduled outside the United States (NBA, NFL). As we have seen with Olympic situations, the arbitration model for addressing disputes between parties representing more than one country is preferable to litigation. The globalization of sport will continue to raise numerous challenges for the sport law community, and ADR procedures provide more flexibility and responsiveness than a common law system. We will likely see arbitration as the model for dispute resolution in the emerging international leagues, as sport federations have already seen the benefits of the Olympic Court of Arbitration.

CASES ON THE SUPPLEMENTAL WEB SITE

From reading chapter 5.30 you recognize that the parties selecting to utilize ADR may decide to make decisions directly available for review. Recent sport-related ADR decisions may be explored further through the following websites:

Court of Arbitration For Sport (http://www.tas-cas.org) Search in the Jurisprudence section

United States Olympic Committee (http://www.teamusa.org) Search in the Legal section under Governance

QUESTIONS YOU SHOULD BE ABLE TO ANSWER

1. Compare and contrast the common procedures of negotiation, mediation and arbitration.

2. Identify a recently tried sport or recreation case. Identify both the positive and negative arguments for using ADR vs. adjudication procedures to resolve this dispute.

3. Select Arbitration Decisions of interest from the Court of Arbitration For Sport or the United States Olympic Committee Web Sites. Determine if you agree with the decisions of the Arbitrators and indicate why. Review the five related Chapter 5.13 cases on the Supplemental Web Site. Determine if you agree with the Arbitrators and indicate why.

4. Research the current status of the Claudia Pechstein v. German Speed Skating Association and International Skating Union case (German Court Decision), and the impact this decision has had upon the relevance; jurisdiction; and authority of the CAS and the ICAS

5. Arbitration experts have stated that the MLB Salary Arbitration agreement has resulted in significantly higher salaries for players. Is this a direct result of the use of arbitration versus negotiation or other practices? Be prepared to debate the truth of these statements and support your position with facts

REFERENCES

Cases
Cronin v. California Fitness, 2005 Ohio App.LEXIS 3056.
Law v. NCAA, 134 F.3d 1010 (10th Cir. 1998).
Claudia Pechstein v. German Speed Skating Association and International Skating Union
Sprewell v. Golden State Warriors, 266 F.3d 979 (9th Cir. 2001).

Arbitration Proceedings
Administrative Panel Decision Adidas AG v. Zhifang Wu Case No. D2007–0032
Andrea Anderson, LaTasha Colander Clark, Jearl Miles-Clark, Torri Edwards, Chryste Gaines, Monique Hennegan Passion Richardson v. International Olympic Committee (IOC) CAS 2008 / A/ 1545 (July 16, 2010).
Bulgarian Boxing Federation v. European Boxing Confederation, CAS, June 7, 2011.
CAS 2007/A/1394 Floyd Landis v/United States Anti-Doping Agency
Mr. Ross Rebagliati and International Olympic Committee (IOC). (CAS, Ad Hoc Div., Ref: Arb., NAG 2, Final Award; www.tas-cas.org.
SGC Lisco LLC v. Zhang Xue Ming, 2010, WIPO Arbitration and Mediation Center, Case No. D2010–0748
United States—20 September 2007 Arbitration Case 30 190 00847 06 *United States Anti-Doping Agency v. Floyd Landis*, Majority Opinion

Publications
conflictoflaws.net/2015/Pechstein.
Cozzillio, M., & Levinstein, M. S. (1997). *Sports law cases and materials*. Durham, NC: Carolina Academic Press.
Donegan, F. (1994). Examining the role of arbitration in professional baseball. *Sports Lawyer Journal, 1*, 183.
Galton, E. (1998). Mediation programs for collegiate sports teams. *Dispute Resolution Journal, 53*, 37–39.
Haslip, S. (2001). A consideration of the need for a national dispute resolution system for national sports organizations in Canada. *Marquette Sports Law Review, 11*(2), 245–270.
Katsh, E., & Rifkin, J. (2001). *Online dispute resolution: Resolving conflicts in cyberspace*. San Francisco: Jossey-Bass.
McArdle, D. (2015). Dispute Resolution in Sport. New York, NY: Routledge.
Oschutz, F. (2002). Harmonization of anti-doping code through arbitration: The case law of the court of arbitration for sport. *Marquette Sports Law Review, 12*(2), 675–702.
Schalley, J. (2001). Eliminate violence from sports through arbitration, not the civil courts. *The Sports Lawyers Journal, 8*(1), 181–206.

Websites
www.aaa.org
www.adr.org
www4.law.cornell.edu/cgi-bi...re.law.cornell.edu/topics/adr.html
www.campus-adr.org
www.mediate.com
www.ncaa.org
www.sportslaw.org
www.restorativejustice.org
www.tas-cas.org
www.mediate.com
www.wipo.org

Legislation
Administrative Dispute Resolution Act of 1990, 5 U.S.C.A. 581.
Federal Arbitration Act of 1925, 9 U.S.C.
Revised Uniform Arbitration Act of 2000
Uniform Arbitration Act of 1955.

CONSTITUTIONAL LAW 6.00

The United States Constitution provides everyone certain rights and protections. Before the courts can apply those constitutional protections, however, certain threshold questions must be asked. The following section examines the constitutional safeguards of the First, Fourth, Fifth, and Fourteenth Amendments as they apply to freedom of the press, free speech, due process, equal protection, and the right to privacy and how they relate to the sport and recreation industries.

The *Constitutional Law* section is divided into two parts. The first part examines some of the fundamental principles of Constitutional law, including state action, due process, equal protection, and search and seizure. This part also serves as an introduction to the principles of Constitutional law. The second part examines how the issues of due process, equal protection, and search and seizure apply specifically to the sport, health and fitness, and recreation industries.

∗ ∗ ∗

6.11 JUDICIAL REVIEW, STANDING, AND INJUNCTIONS

Jim Masteralexis | Western New England University
Lisa Pike Masteralexis | University of Massachusetts

Sport and recreation managers make decisions regarding athletic rules and regulations on a daily basis. Although the courts generally take a "hands-off" approach to reviewing decisions by private athletic organizations, in a limited number of situations courts will review the actions of private athletic organizations to ensure that they have applied the rules and regulations properly. The following section examines when a court will review an athletic organization's action, when a plaintiff has standing to challenge a decision by private athletic organizations, and what types of injunctive relief the courts can order to bar the athletic organization from going forward with its decision.

FUNDAMENTAL CONCEPTS

Judicial Review

Scope of Review

As a general rule, the courts have declined to intervene in the internal affairs of private, voluntary organizations that govern professional and amateur sports. The reasoning behind this policy is that membership in the organizations is voluntary and the organizations are self-regulating. The court will, however, review the decisions where one of the following conditions is met:

1. The rule or regulation challenged by the plaintiff exceeds the scope of the athletic association's authority;
2. The rule or regulation challenged by the plaintiff violates an individual's constitutional rights;
3. The rule or regulation challenged by the plaintiff violates an existing law, such as the Sherman Antitrust Act or the Americans with Disabilities Act.;
4. The rule or regulation challenged by the plaintiff is applied in an arbitrary and/or capricious manner;
5. The rule or regulation challenged by the plaintiff violates public policy because it is considered fraudulent or unreasonable;
6. The athletic association breaks one of its own rules.

The harshness of a rule is not by itself grounds for judicial review. Relief is granted only where the plaintiff can prove to the court that one of the preceding conditions has been met. Even where a rule is subject to review, the court's role is limited. A court will not review the merits of the rule, but simply decide whether the application of the rule is invalid on the basis of meeting one of the six conditions listed.

Application. Despite the standards listed earlier, decisions to grant injunctions in cases that appear factually similar may vary. This is due to variations in precedent across jurisdictions or differences in regional standards, such as when a community is given the right to determine standards. An example would be in the distinction between free speech and obscenity. The U.S. Supreme Court has deferred to communities to define obscenity, so what may be considered obscene in Dallas might not be considered obscene in New York City. It may also be due to the application of state laws or state constitutional rights that grant greater protections than federal laws. One area in which this is common is where states have stronger privacy protections than the Fourth Amendment.

Married Students. One area where there has been some variation is when an amateur athletic association has imposed rules barring married students from participation in high school athletics. In one case, *Estay v. La Fourche Parish School Board* (1969), a married high school student challenged his exclusion from all extracurricular activities. The Louisiana Court of Appeals held that the school board had the authority to adopt the regulation. The regulation survived equal protection scrutiny because the court found there was a rational relationship between the rule and its stated objective of promoting completion of high school before marriage. Finally, the court held that the rule was not arbitrary and capricious, for it was applied uniformly and impartially against anyone who sought to participate in extracurricular activities, not simply athletics. Eight years later, and in another jurisdiction, the Colorado Court of Appeals ruled for the student-athlete, stating that he possessed a fundamental right to marry and the reasons proffered by the school board did not establish a compelling state interest to justify the violation of the plaintiff's equal protection rights (*Beeson v. Kiowa County School District*, 1977).

Alcohol and Drugs. Jurisdictions also vary when enforcing rules that prohibit the use of alcohol and drugs, often called good conduct rules. If the rules address a legitimate sport-related purpose, courts will often find that they are within the scope of the association's authority. But where the rule is intrusive and broadly attempts to regulate the conduct of a student-athlete during the off-season or conduct unrelated to athletic participation, a court will likely strike it down. In *Braesch v. De Pasquale* (1978), the Supreme Court of Nebraska ruled that a rule prohibiting drinking served a legitimate rational interest by directly affecting the discipline of a student-athlete. The court also ruled that the rule was not arbitrary nor an unreasonable means to attain the legitimate end of deterring alcohol use among student-athletes. On the other hand, in *Bunger v. Iowa High School Athletic Association* (1972), another court struck down a good conduct rule prohibiting the use of alcoholic beverages. During the summer, the plaintiff was riding in a car containing a case of beer. The car was pulled over by the police, and the four minors in the car were issued citations. The plaintiff reported the incident to his athletic program and was suspended in accordance with the state athletic association rule. The Iowa Supreme Court held the rule was invalid on the grounds that it exceeded the scope of the athletic association's authority. The Court based its decision on the fact that the incident was outside the football season, beyond the school year, and did not involve the illegal use of alcohol.

Athletic Associations. Cases involving athletic association rules that infringe on the constitutional right to freedom of expression have also exhibited variation. In *Williams v. Eaton* (1972), a group of fourteen African American football players for the University of Wyoming sought permission from their coach to wear black armbands in their game against Brigham Young University to protest the beliefs of the Mormon Church. The coach dismissed them from the team for violating team rules prohibiting protests. In a court action challenging the rule, the court held that the First Amendment rights of the players to freedom of speech could not be paramount to the rights of others to practice their religion free from a state-supported (University of Wyoming) protest. On the other hand, *Tinker v. Des Moines Independent School District* (1969), held that student-athletes wearing politically motivated black armbands protesting the Vietnam War in a public high school were found to have a constitutionally protected right to freedom of expression.

Standing

Standing is a plaintiff's right to bring a complaint in court. To establish standing, the plaintiff must meet three criteria:

1. The plaintiff bringing the action must have sustained an injury in fact;
2. The interest that the plaintiff seeks to be protected is one for which the court possesses the power to grant a remedy;
3. The plaintiff must have an interest in the outcome of the case.

The question of standing is generally raised by the defense seeking to dismiss a case and not one the court will raise on its own. In other words, as an initial matter, the plaintiff does not possess a burden of proof with regard to standing, but may be forced to show standing if the defendant raises the issue.

Application. The issue of standing was a determinative factor for the Federal Court when they ruled on a **motion to intervene** in the case of *ProBatter Sports, LLC v. Joyner Technologies*. A motion to intervene can be brought by anyone who is not involved in a court case if they have an interest in the case and it would be difficult for that person, or company, to protect their interest unless they were a party in the case. ProBatter was the owner of all the rights to a "unique" baseball video pitching simulator. In May 2005, ProBatter filed suit against

Joyner in the Federal District Court for the Northern District of Iowa alleging patent infringement of their "134 Patent" and "154 Patent". In December 2005, ProBatter filed another lawsuit in the Federal District Court for the District of Connecticut against another company, Sports Tutor, alleging patent infringement of two different patents, the "649 Patent" and the "924 Patent". Sports Tutor was the owner of the "Home Plate non-video pitching system". In February 2006, Sports Tutor filed a motion to intervene in the case in Iowa arguing that it had an interest in the subject matter of the case between ProBatter and Joyner and that their ability to protect their business interest would be impeded if they were not represented in the case. ProBatter opposed Sports Tutor's motion to intervene. The Federal Court for the Northern District of Iowa denied Sports Tutor's motion to intervene because the "649 Patent" and the "924 Patent" were not an issue in the Iowa case. In addition, Pro Batter did not make any claims in Iowa concerning Sports Tutor's Home Plate non-video pitching machine. The Iowa Federal Court held that Sports Tutor did not have standing to intervene because they did not sustain an injury in fact and they could adequately protect their interest in the Connecticut case.

On March 23, 2016, eleven (11) years after ProBatter filed suit against Sports Tutor in the Federal District Court in Connecticut, the Federal Court granted Summary Judgement for ProBatter for patent infringement and permanently enjoined Sports Tutor from making the "Home Plate" machines.

Injunctive Relief
Types of Injunctive Relief

There are four types of injunctive relief available: the temporary restraining order, the preliminary injunction, the permanent injunction, and specific performance.

The **temporary restraining order** is generally issued to a plaintiff in an emergency situation, without notice (appearance at hearing) to the defendant, and is usually effective for a maximum of ten days. Before a court will grant the temporary restraining order, a plaintiff must prove that he/she will face irreparable harm and that money damages would be an inadequate remedy.

The **preliminary injunction** is granted to a plaintiff prior to a trial on the merits of a legal action and lasts throughout the trial process of the case. The defendant is given notice to appear at the hearing for the injunction and may argue against the granting of the preliminary injunction. To be awarded a preliminary injunction, the plaintiff must prove:

1. The plaintiff will face a substantial threat of irreparable harm without the preliminary injunction. (Often where money damages would be an inadequate remedy, granting the injunction would provide the only remedy):
2. The balance of the hardships favors the plaintiff;
3. The plaintiff possesses a likelihood of success on the merits of the pending case;
4. Granting the injunction will serve the public interest.

Application. In the case of *Mancuso vs. Massachusetts Interscholastic Athletic Association*, (2009) the plaintiff was an accomplished swimmer. She has attended a private high school her freshmen year, was not a member of the swim team, but instead was a member of a private swim club. At the end of that year she transferred to her local high school and repeated her freshmen year because she had started school a year earlier than her peers. During this second freshman year she swam for her local high school and was considered one of the fastest swimmers in Massachusetts. She swam during her sophomore and junior years as well. Prior to the start of her senior year the MIAA determined that she was ineligible to compete because she has violated the "fifth year student rule" which states that "a student shall be eligible for interscholastic competition no more than 12 consecutive athletic seasons (i.e. four consecutive years) beyond the first completion of grade 8." Mancuso appealed to the MIAA for a waiver but it was denied. After exhausting the MIAA's internal review process, which included hearings before the Eligibility Review Board and the Massachusetts Interscholastic Athletic Council, the denial of the waiver was upheld.

Mancuso brought suit in Superior Court, a trial court, and claimed, in Count 1, that the MIAA's decision was an error and requested that the court vacate the denial of the waiver and allow her to compete. Count 2 and 3 claimed that the MIAA had violated her right to due process and her civil rights and requested an award of compensatory and punitive damages and an award of attorney's fees and costs. The Superior Court granted Mancuso a preliminary injunction and the plaintiff competed for her high school swim team during her senior year.

The case was scheduled for a trial, but prior to trial Mancuso filed a motion for partial judgment on the pleadings with regard to Count 1, which asserted that the MIAA was in error in denying her the waiver. The MIAA responded by filing a motion for summary judgment on all Counts. The Superior Court judge granted Mancuso's motion for partial summary judgment on Count 1 holding that the MIAA's decision to deny the waiver was "arbitrary and capricious" but denied the motion on the other counts.

At trial the Plaintiff was awarded $10,000 by the jury for the MIAA failing to provide Mancuso with due process, but the judge entered judgment notwithstanding the verdict (judgment n.o.v) which nullified the jury award. Mancuso appealed from this judgment and the MIAA cross-appealed from the entry of judgment on Count 1. The Massachusetts Supreme Judicial Court transferred the case on their own initiative from Appeals Court.

The Supreme Judicial Court found for the MIAA on the due process and civil rights claims and held that Mancuso has no property interest in participating in interscholastic athletics and no due process rights under the circumstances. The Court also held that Mancuso failed to establish an equal protection violation. However, the Court ruled that the MIAA's appeal on Count 1 was technically flawed and not properly before them and thus they did not review the decision of the trial judge, regarding Count 1, that the MIAA's denial of the waiver was arbitrary and capricious. In summary, Mancuso prevailed on Count 1, as it was not reversed on appeal, but she was not awarded any damages. This case, although complicated procedurally, illustrated that a preliminary injunction is a powerful tool which can be used to achieve a timely result, before a full trial, e.g. allowing Mancuso to compete for her local high school during her senior year.

A **permanent injunction** requires the plaintiff to prove the same four elements but is awarded as a remedy following a full hearing on the merits of the case. Finally, **specific performance** is a court order that may be available to the victim of a breach of contract. Specific performance requires that a defendant comply with (honor) the contract. Because money is generally an adequate remedy for a contract breach, specific performance is rarely used. The court will grant this remedy in situations where the subject matter is extremely rare. An example in sport where a court may be willing to grant specific performance is with a breach of a contract for the sale of sports memorabilia. There may be only one Honus Wagner baseball card in the world, and money may be an inadequate remedy to replace the card if the seller were to break the contract. In such a case the nonbreaching party might seek an injunction for specific performance because the card is priceless and rare.

Specific performance will not be granted to enforce a contract of a professional athlete. Although there may be only one LeBron James, if he were to break his contract with the Miami Heat, the court would not grant the Heat a specific performance injunction to force James to honor his contract with the club. The reason is that by granting such an injunction, the court would be forcing James to work and would find its order in conflict with the U.S. Constitutional prohibition against slavery. In such cases, however, there is a remedy for professional teams. Courts are willing to grant negative injunctions against athletes who breach their contracts. The effect of the negative injunction is to prohibit the player from playing his or her sport for any other team or event than the plaintiff's. In this way the court is not ordering the athlete to work, but simply prohibiting him/her from playing his/her sport anywhere except for the team possessing the valid and enforceable contract.

Scope. When a plaintiff seeks judicial review of a decision, the plaintiff will also request a temporary restraining order and/or a preliminary injunction to bar the rule from being applied. Injunctive relief is designed to prevent future wrongs, rather than to punish past actions. It is only used to prevent an irreparable injury that is suffered when monetary damages are inadequate to compensate the injured party. An injury is considered irreparable when it involves the risk of physical harm or death; the loss of a special opportunity; or the deprivation of unique, irreplaceable property. For example, a high school senior student-athlete may be granted an injunction to compete in a championship game because he/she may never again have that opportunity.

Application. In *Oliver v. National Collegiate Athletic Association* ("NCAA"), an Ohio state trial court applied both judicial review and injunctions in reversing a ruling of the NCAA. Andrew Oliver was a star high school pitcher in Ohio and in June 2006 the Minnesota Twins ("Twins") drafted him in the seventeenth (17th) round of the amateur baseball draft. Oliver retained the services of attorneys Robert Baratta, and Tim Baratta ("Baratta") to be his sports advisors and attorneys. Oliver had also been offered a full baseball scholarship at Oklahoma State University ("OSU"). At the end of the summer of 2006, Oliver, his father and Baratta met with representatives of the Twins at the Oliver home and the Twins offered Oliver $390,000 to sign with their team. Oliver rejected the offer and decided to attend OSU. In March of 2008 Oliver decided to terminate Baratta and hired the Boras Corporation to be his advisors and attorneys. Baratta sent an invoice for $113,750 to Oliver for legal services. Oliver brought the invoice to the OSU compliance office and to the Boras Corporation and refused to pay the bill.

In May 2008, Baratta mailed and faxed a letter to the NCAA alleging that Oliver violated NCAA rules by virtue of Baratta attending the meeting with the Twins in 2006. As a result of these complaints, OSU investigated Oliver's amateur status and indefinitely suspended him from playing baseball for violating NCAA Bylaw 12.3.1 by allowing Baratta to previously telephone the Twins on his behalf and attending the meeting at the Oliver home.

The relevant NCAA Bylaw, section 12.3.1, states:

> A lawyer may not be present during discussions of a contract offer with a professional organization or have any direct contact (in person, by telephone or by mail) with a professional sports organization on behalf of the individual. A lawyer's presence during such discussions is considered representation by an agent.

On August 18, 2008, Oliver was reinstated to play baseball at OSU when he was granted a temporary restraining Order by the Ohio Court of Common Pleas. However, in October 2008, OSU filed for reinstatement by the NCAA for Oliver, even though the Court had already granted him the reinstatement. The NCAA, in December 2008, suspended Oliver for one (1) year and charged him with a year of eligibility. The NCAA later reduced the penalty to a suspension from 70 percent of the baseball season and with no loss of eligibility. Oliver filed suit in Ohio court requesting that the court review the NCAA decision, declare that it was legally incorrect and requested injunctive relief to order the NCAA to allow him to play.

The Ohio court ruled that the NCAA's decision was arbitrary and capricious because it allows an athlete to retain an attorney but impermissibly limits what the attorney can do by prohibiting him from attending meetings with the professional organization. In addition, the court held that only the Ohio Supreme Court has the authority to regulate the conduct of Ohio attorneys, not the NCAA. The Court ruled that Oliver, a citizen of Ohio, had the right to have an attorney present when he met with the Twins to help him make an important decision. The Court granted Oliver a permanent injunction ordering the NCAA to reinstate his eligibility to play baseball.

After the Ohio Supreme Court's ruling, a trial was scheduled to determine the amount of damages that NCAA would pay Oliver. However, the case was settled prior to the trial and the NCAA paid Oliver $750,000. As part of the settlement, the trial judge vacated the order prohibiting the NCAA from enforcing Section 12.3.1. against Ohio citizens.

The case of *Starego v. The New Jersey Interscholastic Athletic Association* (NJIAA) is an appeal from a decision of an athletic association based upon the Americans with Disabilities Act (ADA). Anthony Starego was diagnosed with autism, attention deficit hyperactivity disorder and cognitive impairments, which qualified Anthony for an individualized education program ("IEP"). Because of his condition, Anthony was eligible to attend Brick Township High School ("Brick") until he turned twenty-one (21) years old. Anthony began playing football at Brick his freshman year in 2009 as a place kicker and played football for four (4) years, but he did not become the starting varsity place kicker until September 2012. Anthony turned nineteen (19) years old in June 2013 and in September 2013 Anthony began his fifth (5th) year at Brick. The eligibility rules of the NJIAA make a student ineligible to play sports, as in this case, if they turn nineteen (19) prior to September 1st and after the expiration of eight (8) consecutive semesters following his entrance into the 9th grade. Therefore, Anthony was ineligible to play football even though he had a legal right to attend Brick until he was twenty (21), which was an accommodation for his disabilities.

Anthony's parents applied for a waiver of the eligibility rules. After a hearing the NJIAA found that Anthony has already received the full benefit of participation in high school sports for four (4) years, he was a proven "difference-maker" who is a college-level kicker and his continued participation would provide his team with an actual advantage against other teams, and his participation would deny other students their opportunity to participate. Also, given his age and his size, Anthony was six foot two inches and 190 pounds, he may pose a safety risk to other players on the football field. The NJIAA denied his eligibility waiver but, because he "benefits tremendously from playing football from a developmental standpoint", the Association allowed Anthony to participate in team practices and scrimmage games.

Anthony's parents appealed this decision to the United States District Court for the District of New Jersey and requested an injunction ordering that Anthony be allowed to play football, based on the ADA. The appeal argued that the NJIAA's decision violated the ADA by refusing to provide Anthony, a disabled student, with a reasonable accommodation of continuing to play and participate in the sport of football for Brick.

The District Court, although sympathetic to Anthony, denied the parents appeal and request for an injunction. The Court disagreed with some important factual findings of the NJIAA. They stated that although Anthony was in a non-contact position of placekicker the safety concerns of the NJIAA were unwarranted as Anthony would most likely never cover kicks or tackle anyone. The Court also held that the NJIAA overstated Anthony's athletic ability as he would not be able to play Division I football.

The court held that the NJIAA must conduct an individualized review of each disabled student's situation to ensure the protections intended and contemplated by the ADA are followed. The Court concluded that granting Anthony a waiver would be a reasonable accommodation under the ADA. However, the court denied injunctive relief to Anthony because it held that Anthony was not denied the waiver to play football because of his disabilities but because he was not eligible to play football at Brick because of his age. The court reasoned "the ADA does not provide Anthony additional opportunities because of his disabilities, but rather, the statute puts him on an equal footing with every other student player." The court recognized that Anthony had played football for four (4) year, just as any other high school student would be allowed to do, and he had aged out of eligibility to play and was thus not "otherwise qualified" to play football because of the age eligibility rules. The court discussed that "enforcing age limit rules is not discriminatory because the limits are based only on the neutral factor of age, and as such, they apply equally to disabled and non-disabled students."

SIGNIFICANT CASE

The case that follows provides an excellent example of an appellate court's review of the grounds for granting a preliminary injunction against conduct that is arbitrary and capricious and conduct that violates an organization's own rules. The case also discusses in detail the concept of public interest in the granting of injunctive relief. The case involves an appeal by Indiana High School Athletic Association (IHSAA) of the trial court's issuance of a permanent injunction against the IHSAA's denial of full eligibility and a hardship exception for a student–athlete. The trial court found that the IHSAA's decision was arbitrary and capricious. Upon appeal, the IHSAA asserts that the trial court's findings are clearly erroneous, given the broad discretion afforded to its eligibility decisions.

INDIANA HIGH SCHOOL ATHLETIC ASSOCIATION V. DURHAM
Court of Appeals of Indiana, Fifth District
748 N.E.2d 404 (2001)

In the summer of 1999, Bernard Durham (B.J.) transferred from Park Tudor High School (Park) to North Central High School (North Central). B.J. participated in varsity cross-country and track during his freshman and sophomore years at Park. B.J. had attended private school, either at Park or at St. Richard's School since second grade. B.J. has three brothers who also attended private schools.

During 1998, B.J.'s mother, Joan Durham, and her husband, Tim Durham, separated and initiated divorce proceedings. Tim is not B.J.'s biological father.

B.J.'s biological father lives in France and does not contribute to B.J.'s support. * * * [T]he time came to sign 1999–2000 re-enrollment contracts for B.J. and his three brothers in their private schools. At that time, Joan and Tim's divorce was not yet final. Joan decided not to sign the contracts because she could no longer afford the tuition to send her children to private schools. She instead enrolled her sons in the public school system where they resided. B.J. enrolled in North Central. In the fall of 1999, an IHSAA transfer form was completed on behalf of B.J. so that he could continue participating in sports at North Central. Joan indicated on the form that the recent divorce created such a financial burden on her that she could not afford to keep B.J. enrolled at a private school. Joan also provided the IHSAA with financial information and court filings to support the listed reason for B.J.'s transfer.

* * *

Park, as the sending school, also had to offer the reason for B.J.'s transfer. Initially, Park had included in the transfer form that B.J. told coaches, administrators, and other students that "he wanted to go to a better track/c.c. [crosscountry] program and that is why he is leaving." B.J. denied making such statements. However, Park changed its position after speaking with its athletic director who had subsequently learned that B.J.'s family situation prompted the transfer. Park recommended that B.J. be awarded full eligibility to compete in sports at North Central. On August 25, 1999, IHSAA Assistant Commissioner Sandy Searcy granted B.J. only limited eligibility, which prohibited B.J. from competing at the varsity level, and denied B.J. a hardship exception.

The Durhams, through North Central's athletic director, appealed that decision to the IHSAA Executive Committee. The Durhams were led to believe that the question of whether B.J. transferred for athletically motivated reasons would not be an issue discussed at the hearing scheduled before the Executive Committee. A hearing was held, at which B.J., Joan, and the athletic directors from both schools testified. Evidence was presented that B.J. had been running with the junior varsity cross-country team at North Central, and that if he enjoyed full eligibility, B.J. would be one of the school's top runners. Joan testified that B.J. had suffered a great deal as a result of the IHSAA's decision. She relayed that he had problems with anxiety in the past, and that his running had helped him through this difficult time for his family. B.J. testified that he did not want to leave Park, and that he refused to explain why he was leaving when asked about the move at Park. Assistant Commissioner Searcy also testified that she was convinced that the change in the Durham's financial circumstances was permanent and substantial although not beyond their control. Park's athletic director, referring to Park's initial comment on B.J.'s transfer form, stated that the reference was the result of bantering between athletes and coaches due to the rivalry with North Central.

The Executive Committee agreed with Assistant Commissioner Searcy's decision, denying B.J. full eligibility and issuing findings. The Executive Committee concluded that B.J. transferred schools without a change in residence and failed to fit within any of the criteria of the Transfer Rule to gain full eligibility. Further, the Committee determined that B.J. did not meet the necessary conditions to gain full eligibility through the hardship exception to the Transfer Rule. Even though Searcy had testified that there had been a permanent and substantial change in financial circumstances, the IHSAA Executive Committee reasoned that B.J. failed to produce sufficient proof that the reason for transfer was beyond the control of him and his family. The IHSAA also noted that some evidence existed that the transfer may have been motivated by athletic reasons, even though the Durhams did not know that this was an issue before the Executive Committee.

District Court's Order

The Durhams sought a temporary restraining order in court. On September 17, 1999, the trial court granted the temporary restraining order. On September 20, 1999, B.J. filed the complaint asking that the IHSAA's decision be overturned and that a permanent injunction be issued. * * * On October 22, 1999, the court granted the permanent injunction and found that the IHSAA's findings were arbitrary and capricious. * * * The IHSAA appealed.

Discussion

Upon appeal, the IHSAA asserts that the trial court applied the standard of review over its decisions improperly. The IHSAA contends that its rulings are entitled to great deference and should be reversed only if they are willful and unreasonable without consideration of the facts and circumstances in the case. In this case, the IHSAA argues that the trial court merely reweighed the evidence and substituted its own decision. The Durhams insist that this case is moot because the time for the injunction has expired * * *. Alternatively, the Durhams counter that the IHSAA's conduct is not free from judicial review, and the IHSAA violated its own rules in denying B.J. a hardship exception.

I. IHSAA—Background and Rules

The IHSAA is a voluntary association designed to regulate interschool athletic competition. It establishes standards for eligibility, competition, and sportsmanship. For each school year, the IHSAA publishes a manual containing * * * specific rules regarding eligibility. The rule in question in this case is Rule 19, known as the Transfer Rule. The Transfer Rule guides athletic eligibility when a student moves to a new school district. Rule 19-4 provides that a student will be ineligible for 365 days if he or she transfers schools for "primarily athletic reasons." Further, Rule 19-6.2 gives the IHSAA the authority to grant limited eligibility to a student who transfers to another school without a corresponding change of residence by his or her parent(s)/guardian(s). However, if one or more of the criteria under Rule 19-6.1 are met, then a student may enjoy full and immediate eligibility, even without a change of residence by his or her parent(s)/guardian(s).

If none of the criteria in Rule 19-6.1 are met, then a student must fall within the hardship exception to the Transfer Rule to gain full and immediate eligibility. Rule 17.8, entitled "Hardship" grants the authority to set aside any rule, including the Transfer Rule, if certain conditions are met. In particular, Rule 17-8.1 lists these three conditions:

a. Strict enforcement of the Rule in the particular case will not serve to accomplish the purpose of the Rule;
b. The spirit of the Rule has not been violated; and
c. There exists in the particular case circumstances showing an undue hardship that would result from enforcement of the Rule.

Further, among those situations to receive general consideration for a hardship exception is: "a change in financial condition of the student's family may be considered a hardship, however, such conditions or changes in conditions must be permanent, substantial and significantly beyond the control of the student or the student's family." IHSAA Manual, Rule 17-8.4.

When a student moves to a new school district, an investigation and a transfer report must be completed if athletic eligibility at the new school is desired. Included in this report are forms filled out by the sending school, the receiving school, and the student and/or the student's parent(s)/ guardian(s). The report must include the relevant circumstances and documents and recommendations regarding immediate eligibility from both schools.

II. Mootness

Initially, the Durhams assert that the IHSAA's appeal should be denied because the case is moot. The Durhams contend that there are no outstanding issues between the parties because the injunction has been lifted, the issue of attorney fees has been decided, and North Central did not win any State titles with B.J.'s participation. However, the IHSAA replies that the problem with the majority of litigation surrounding eligibility decisions is that the injunction granted by the trial court expires before the matter has been fully litigated and appealed. The IHSAA also contends that the case is not moot because its Restitution Rule, below, allows the IHSAA to make the school forfeit victories, team awards, and funds received from a tournament if it has been determined that an ineligible student athlete has competed for that school.

The Restitution Rule, Rule 17-6 of the IHSAA Bylaws, reads:

If a student is ineligible according to Association Rules but is permitted to participate in interschool competition contrary to Association Rules but in accordance with the terms of a court restraining order or injunction against the student's school and/or the Association and the injunction is subsequently voluntarily vacated, stayed, or reversed or it is finally determined by the court *that injunctive relief is not or was not justified, any one or more of the following action(s) against such school in the interest of restitution and fairness to competing schools shall be taken:*

a. Require individual or team records and performances achieved during participation by such ineligible student be vacated or stricken;
b. Require team victories be forfeited to opponents;
c. Require team or individual awards earned be returned to the Association; and/or
d. If the school has received or would receive any funds from an Association tournament series in which the ineligible individual has participated, require that the school forfeit its share of net receipts from such competition, and if said receipts have not been distributed, authorize the withholding of such receipts by the Association.

Alternatively, the IHSAA argues that even if the issues have been decided in this case, this court should hear the case because it involves questions of public interest.

An issue becomes moot when it is no longer live and the parties lack a legally cognizable interest in the outcome or when no effective relief can be rendered to the parties. * * * When the principal questions in issue have ceased to be matters of real controversy between the parties, the errors assigned become moot questions and the court will not retain jurisdiction to decide them. * * * An actual controversy must exist at all stages of the appellate review, and if a case becomes moot at any stage, then the case is remanded with instructions to dismiss. The Durhams insist that the IHSAA failed to assert evidence that there is a live controversy. The evidence about how the Restitution Rule may create a live controversy was introduced only through the Appendix to the IHSAA's Reply Brief.

* * *

Regardless of whether we consider the affidavit, an exception to the mootness doctrine applies. The IHSAA relies upon the exception that an otherwise moot case may be decided on the merits if the case involves a question of great public interest. Indiana courts recognize that a moot case can be reviewed under a public interest exception when it involves questions of great public importance. * * * The IHSAA argues that this exception applies to the instant case because the issue involves children and education, matters that are considered of great public concern, and our court has previously held that a challenge to an IHSAA eligibility rule is an issue of substantial public interest. * * * We agree.

While at first glance high school athletics may not seem to be of great public importance, according to the IHSAA, over 160,000 students statewide participate in sports under the IHSAA eligibility rules. Thus, this issue touches many in our state. Further, the issue of eligibility when a student transfers schools has arisen several times and has been the subject of much litigation * * * Also, the specific issue of a student transferring schools after his or her parents' divorce is likely to recur. * * * The public interest exception to the mootness doctrine applies to this case, allowing us to decide the merits.

III. Were the Trial Court's Findings Clearly Erroneous?

A. Our Standard of Review

The IHSAA asserts that the trial court's findings were clearly erroneous. In this case, the trial court issued an injunction to prevent the IHSAA from enforcing its ruling against B.J. When we review an injunction, we apply a deferential standard of review. * * * The grant or denial of an injunction is discretionary, and we will not reverse unless the trial court's action was arbitrary or constituted a clear abuse of discretion.* * *An abuse of discretion occurs when the trial court's decision is clearly against the logic and effect of the facts and circumstances or if the trial court misinterprets the law. *Id.*

* * *

B. Did the Trial Court Fail to Apply the Correct Standard of Review Governing IHSAA Decisions?

The IHSAA argues that the trial court failed to apply the deferential standard of review afforded to its administrative rulings in granting the Durham's request for a permanent injunction. In *Carlberg*, 694 N.E.2d 222, our supreme court delineated how a trial court should review an administrative ruling made by the IHSAA. Although the IHSAA is a voluntary association, the court held that student challenges to IHSAA decisions are subject to judicial review. *Id.* at 230. The court reasoned that student athletes in public schools do not voluntarily subject themselves to IHSAA rules, and students have no voice in rules and leadership of the IHSAA. *Id.* The court then determined that IHSAA decisions are analogous to government agency decisions and, hence, adopted the "arbitrary and capricious" standard of review used when courts review government agency action. *Id.* at 231. The arbitrary and capricious standard of review is narrow, and a court may not substitute its judgment for the judgment of the IHSAA. *Carlberg*, 694 N.E.2d at 233. "The rule or decision will be found to be arbitrary and capricious 'only where it is willful and unreasonable, without consideration and in disregard of the facts or circumstances in the case, or without some basis which would lead a reasonable and honest person to the same conclusion.'" *Id.* (quoting *Dep't of Natural Res. v. Ind. Coal Council, Inc.*, 542 N.E.2d 1000, 1007 (Ind. 1989), *cert. denied*, 493 U.S. 1078 (1990)).

In particular, the IHSAA takes issue with the trial court's holding that because B.J. met all of the criteria for the hardship exception, the IHSAA erred in denying him one. The IHSAA contends that even if B.J. would have met all of the criteria listed in the Hardship Rule, Rule 17–8.1, he is not entitled to mandatory relief. Rather, the IHSAA maintains that relief under the Hardship Rule is a matter of grace. In other words, the IHSAA has the discretion of whether to grant a hardship exception even if the Durhams proved that (1) strict enforcement of the Transfer Rule will not serve to accomplish the purpose of the Rule, (2) the spirit of the Transfer Rule has not been violated, and (3) an undue hardship would result if the Transfer Rule was enforced

* * *

However, the IHSAA's position leaves its administrative decisions denying a hardship exception free from judicial review of any sort. While the text of the Hardship Rule states that the IHSAA "shall have the authority to set aside the effect of any Rule," the IHSAA's stance that it can deny a hardship exception even when the student meets the listed criteria implies both that it may have no ascertainable standards for granting or denying a hardship and that its hardship determinations are free from judicial review. IHSAA Manual, Rule 17–8.1. If the IHSAA is truly analogous to a governmental agency, then it must also establish standards on which to base its decisions.

Our supreme court in *Carlberg*, established the appropriate standard of review for IHSAA decisions in no uncertain terms. To reiterate, the *Carlberg* court stated that an IHSAA decision is arbitrary and capricious if it is "willful and unreasonable, without consideration and in disregard of the facts or circumstances in the case, or without some basis which would lead a reasonable and honest person to the same conclusion." 694 N.E.2d at 233 (citation omitted). The IHSAA's suggestion that the Hardship Rule is entitled to an increasingly narrow standard of judicial review flies in the face of the *Carlberg* decision. In *Carlberg*, the supreme court upheld the IHSAA's Transfer Rule in part because there are provisions in place to lessen the severity of the rule. *Carlberg*, 694 N.E.2d at 233. The court reasoned that granting immediate and full eligibility either under the listed exceptions to the Transfer Rule or under the Hardship Rule and granting limited eligibility at the junior varsity or freshman level serves to balance the possible harsh effects of the Transfer Rule. *Id.* If we accepted the IHSAA's assertion that its decisions to deny a hardship exception fall under a more stringent standard of review than the arbitrary and capricious standard enunciated in *Carlberg*, then we would be taking away one of the underpinnings of that case.

Thus, we hold that trial courts may determine whether the denial of a hardship exception in a particular case was the result of arbitrary and capricious action by the IHSAA. In this case, the trial court did not fail to give weight to the IHSAA's broad discretion, as the IHSAA alleges. Rather, in rendering its decision that the IHSAA acted arbitrarily and capriciously, the trial court looked at the IHSAA's particular decision with respect to B.J., applied the appropriate standard, and concluded that the IHSAA's conduct rose to the level of willful and unreasonable decision making that was in disregard of the facts and circumstances before it. For this, the trial court was well within its discretion.

C. Were the IHSAA's Findings Clearly Erroneous?

Finally, the IHSAA asserts that even if the trial court used the appropriate standard of review governing its decisions, the trial court's findings were clearly erroneous. The IHSAA asserts that the evidence, as adduced in its written findings, supports its denial of full eligibility and a hardship exception. In particular, the IHSAA asserts that some evidence existed that B.J. transferred for athletically motivated reasons. It points to the bantering about North Central having a better cross-country and track program. The trial court concluded that this was "hearsay within hearsay" and was not substantial evidence. The IHSAA counters that hearsay is admissible during administrative proceedings, and can be found to be substantial evidence of probative value. * * * The IHSAA also contends that the Durhams failed to establish that the purpose of the Transfer Rule would not be served by denying B.J. a hardship exception due to this evidence of "school jumping."

Here, the trial court did not abuse its discretion in holding that the IHSAA's conclusion that there was some evidence supporting that B.J. transferred for athletic reasons was arbitrary and capricious. Although hearsay may be admissible in administrative proceedings, this evidence of bantering was based upon Park Tudor's mistaken assumption that B.J. was transferring for athletic reasons. As soon as Park Tudor officials learned of the Durhams' circumstances, the transfer report was corrected to reflect that they recommended that B.J. be given full eligibility under a hardship exception. Thus, any evidence of athletic motivation was recanted by Park Tudor. Further, Park Tudor's retraction is against their own interest, as it would seem that Park Tudor would be interested in not having B.J. compete against it due to its rivalry with North Central. Despite this, Park Tudor supported B.J.'s pursuit of a hardship exception.

Additionally, the Durhams were led to believe that athletic motivation would not be an issue in B.J.'s case. It is unfortunate that the IHSAA listed athletic motivation as a reason for transfer even though little or no evidence supports it. This practice was denounced in *Martin*, 731 N.E.2d at 11, which noted that the IHSAA uses the possibility of an athletically-motivated transfer, although admittedly not primarily athletically motivated, as a "poison pill" to keep students from receiving a hardship exception even if there is no substantial evidence to that effect. In the instant case, the trial court recognized this practice and found no evidence in the record to support the IHSAA's conclusion that athletic motivation played a role in B.J.'s transfer. Thus, the trial court's findings with respect to athletic motivation were not clearly erroneous.

Further, the IHSAA argues that B.J. did not establish undue hardship because he failed to show that his family's circumstances were beyond his or his family's control and that he could not afford to attend private school. The IHSAA contends that the trial court merely reweighed the evidence of the family's finances, and that the Durhams still enjoyed a high standard of living. The IHSAA concluded that the decision to send B.J. to North Central was a choice.

Rule 17–8.1, the general section of the Hardship Rule, states that the IHSAA may grant a hardship exception if (1) strict enforcement of the rule in the particular case will not serve to accomplish the purpose of the rule; (2) the spirit of the rule has not been violated; and (3) there exists in the particular case circumstances showing an undue hardship that would result from enforcement of the rule. Thereafter, specific circumstances are listed as candidates for hardship exceptions. One such circumstance that may be considered a hardship is a change in financial condition of the student or a student's family if the change is permanent, substantial, and significantly beyond the control of the athlete or the athlete's family.

The Seventh Circuit Court of Appeals considered this issue in *Crane*, 975 F.2d 1315, and held that the IHSAA's denial of full eligibility was arbitrary and capricious where a student whose parents were divorced had transferred schools after a change in custody. *Crane*, 975 F.2d at 1322. The IHSAA has concluded that the student failed to prove that the move was beyond his control, as the change in custody occurred after Crane had some discipline problems and trouble with his grades in school. The Seventh Circuit, finding that this decision was arbitrary and capricious, reasoned that the IHSAA had ignored the plain language of its rules and instead used "rambling rationalizations" to come to a "pre-ordained result." *Id.* at 1323, 1325. The court noted that the IHSAA changes its interpretation of its rules depending upon the situation before it. *Id.* At 1325. We also addressed this issue in *Avant*, 650 N.E.2d 1164 (Ind. Ct. App. 1995). In *Avant*, we held that the IHSAA's denial of a hardship exception was supported by the evidence. *Id.* at 1169. Avant transferred from a private to a public school, and Avant's enrollment at a private school created a financial hardship on the family. However, the family's financial situation had not changed, and there was also evidence that Avant had disagreements with his basketball coach. Further, the family's financial situation was never listed on the transfer report. Thus, we concluded that the IHSAA's decision to deny Avant a hardship exception was not arbitrary and capricious. *Id.*

Unlike *Avant*, in this case there was a change in the Durhams' family finances due to the divorce, and this change was documented in the transfer report submitted to the IHSAA. This change was caused by something beyond their control, Joan's recent divorce. Included in the specific list of situations receiving consideration for a hardship exception is a substantial and permanent change in financial condition of the student or the student's family significantly beyond the control of the student or the student's family.

With the evidence submitted by Joan in the IHSAA administrative proceedings regarding her recent divorce and family's change in finances, no reasonable and honest person could conclude that the Durhams have not met this specific consideration listed within the Hardship Rule.

The trial court in the case before us found that the IHSAA ignored its own rules and instead interjected a condition of undue hardship not found in its rules that the Durhams prove their poverty before B.J. be given a hardship exception. We agree.

Contrary to IHSAA's assertion, the Hardship Rule does not read that an athlete's family must prove that it is a hardship case. In fact, financial hardship or poverty is not contained within the change in financial condition provision or the Hardship Rule generally. Instead, the "hardship" referred to in the Hardship Rule focuses on the hardship faced by the student athlete if the rule is strictly enforced. In this case, B.J. would face a hardship if he had to run at the junior varsity level because through no fault of his own and without any athletic motivation, B.J. was forced to transfer schools because of a substantial and permanent change in his family's financial condition. Just as in *Crane*, the IHSAA is attempting to adjust its interpretation of the Hardship Rule to meet the particulars of this case.

Even if we were to read a financial hardship requirement into the Hardship Rule, the Durhams would meet such a condition. The evidence in the record is undisputed that Joan had a significant amount of debt and her income had decreased by sixty-seven percent as a result of the divorce. At first glance, Joan's taxable income of $134,620 may not appear to suggest a family in financial hardship. However, a closer look reveals that Joan's monthly expenses are about equal to her monthly income. Joan's mortgage and utilities total $ 96,000 yearly, and she has many other regular expenses including health care, insurance, and various household expenses. Joan also has no assets that she could access to alleviate her financial burdens. Although Joan may be able to sell her house, she would net very little in proceeds after her mortgage debt was satisfied. Further, Joan would like to keep her children in the family home to avoid more disruption in their lives, in light of the divorce. The IHSAA should not be in the business of second-guessing personal financial decisions, but should accept the circumstances as they are.

Given the evidence in this case, the trial court did not abuse its discretion in overturning the IHSAA's denial of full eligibility and refusal to grant a hardship exception. While it may be true that in other cases, see *IHSAA v. Vasario*, 726 N.E.2d 325, 333 (Ind. Ct. App. 2000) and *Avant*, 650 N.E.2d at 1169, we have recognized the IHSAA's broad discretion in refusing to grant a student a hardship exception, this discretion is not unreviewable and is subject to the arbitrary and capricious standard upon review. The evidence in this case overwhelmingly leads to the conclusion that the reasons the IHSAA created the Transfer Rule, deterrence of athletic recruiting and equality in competition, would not be served by denying B.J. a hardship exception. The trial court did not simply reweigh the evidence and substitute its opinion, but instead found that the IHSAA ignored the facts and circumstances before it in rendering its decision. No reasonable and honest person would have concluded that B.J. should be denied a hardship exception in this case. This case embodies the reason the Hardship Rule was created. Although the IHSAA contends that its decisions are virtually unreviewable, a court does have the discretion to identify arbitrary and capricious conduct. The trial court in this case properly identified arbitrary and capricious action by the IHSAA.

Judgment affirmed.

CASES ON THE SUPPLEMENTAL CD

ProBatter Sports, LLC. v. Joyner Technologies, 2006 WL 625874 (N.D. Iowa 2006). The courts description of the lack of standing because the cases in Iowa and Connecticut concerned different patents illustrates problems in standing.

Oliver v. National Collegiate Athletic Association, Court of Common Pleas, Erie County Ohio, Docket 2008-CV-0762 (February 9, 2009). The courts description and analysis of the rule prohibiting lawyers from being present to negotiate professional contracts for amateur athletes and the unfairness that is creates is instructive.

NFL v. Coors Brewing and NFL Players Incorporated, 1999 U.S. Lexis 32547. The court gives a clear review of the preliminary injunction elements concerning a trademark infringement case concerning the phrase "the official beer of the NFL players".

Starego v. New Jersey Interscholastic Athletic Association, 970 F. Supp 203 (2013). The court considers an appeal from a decision of an athletic association prohibiting a disabled student from playing a 5th year of high school football based on an application of a federal law, the Americans with Disabilities Act (ADA), and concludes that the athletic associations decision did not violate the act.

QUESTIONS YOU SHOULD BE ABLE TO ANSWER

1. What standard will a court use to review a decision of a private voluntary organization such as the NCAA?
2. What standards will the court use to determine if a person has standing to bring an action in court?
3. What are the four types of injunctive relief?
4. When and under what circumstances will a court issue a permanent injunction?
5. What is specific performance?

REFERENCES
Cases
Beeson v. Kiowa County School District, 567 P.2d 801 (Colo. Ct. App. 1977).
Braesch v. De Pasquale, 265 N.W.2d 842 (Neb. Sup. Ct. 1978).
Bunger v. Iowa High School Athletic Association, 197 N.W.2d 555 (Sup. Ct. 1972).
Estay v. La Fourche Parish School Board, 230 So.2d 443 (La. Ct. App. 1969).
Indiana High School Athletic Association, Inc. v. Durham, 748 N.E.2d 404 (2001).
Mancuso vs. Massachusetts Interscholastic Athletic Association, 453 Mass. 116, 900 N.E.2d 518, 2009 Mass. Lexis 15 (2009)
Oliver v. National Collegiate Athletic Association, Court of Common Pleas, Erie County Ohio, Docket 2008-CV-0762 (February 9, 2009).
ProBatter Sports, LLC. v. Joyner Technologies, 2006 WL 625874 (N.D. Iowa 2006).
ProBatter Sports, LLC. v. Sports Tutor, 2016 WL 1178050 (D Conn 2016).
Starego v. New Jersey Interscholastic Athletic Association, 970 F. Supp 203 (2013).
Tinker v. Des Moines Independent School District, 383 F.2d 988, rev'd 393 U.S. 503 (1969).
Williams v. Eaton, 468 F.2d 1079 (10th Cir. 1972).

6.12 STATE ACTION

John Wolohan | Syracuse University

In writing the United States Constitution, the authors were concerned with protecting the individual rights and liberties of the citizens from the government. As a result, the protections guaranteed in the Constitution and its amendments apply only to the actions of governmental entities. The only exception to this rule is the Thirteenth Amendment's prohibition on slavery, which is designed to control the actions of private individuals. While at first, the Constitution only applied to the activities of the Federal Government, the protections were eventually expanded to protect individuals from state, city, town or other governmental subdivision (Rotunda and Nowak, 1999). Therefore, the first question we must ask in any case involving actions that limit or interfere with an individual's constitutionally protected rights is whether the defendant's actions constitute state action (Rotunda and Nowak, 1999).

In cases where the complained of action is performed by a governmental entity, such as the police or a public university, college or high school, state action is a given. Where, however, the complained of action is performed by an otherwise private organization, such as a golf course, college conference or professional sports league, the court must consider whether the conduct is fairly attributable to the state, and thus subject to constitutional claims (*Lugar v. Edmondson Oil Co.*,1982).

FUNDAMENTAL CONCEPTS

Determining when private conduct is state action and thus subject to the constitutional limitations has long been one of the most difficult issues in constitutional law. To assist courts in determining whether the alleged wrongdoer has sufficient connection to the states to subject their actions to the constitutional limitations, the United States Supreme Court has developed three basic tests: 1) the **public function test;** (2) the **nexus or entanglement test**; and 3) the **state compulsion test**.

The Public Function Theory

When using the public function theory, courts consider whether a private actor is performing functions that have been traditionally reserved to government or that is governmental in nature (Rotunda & Nowak, 1999). If private organizations or people are engaged in an activity that has been traditionally reserved to the government, their actions will be subject to the same constitutional limitations as if the state were performing the action. Since the state could engage in any activity, the fact that a private organization or person engages in an activity which could be performed by the state, however, will not in itself subject them to the constitutional scrutiny. It is only those activities or duties that are traditionally associated with sovereign governments, and are operated almost exclusively by government entities that are deemed public functions (Rotunda & Nowak, 1999).

In *Jackson v. Metropolitan Edison Co.* (1974) and *Flagg Brothers v. Brooks* (1978), the Supreme Court held that private activities would only constitute state action under the public function theory if: 1) the activity involved a function that is traditionally been performed exclusively by the state; and 2) the private entity assumption of the function replaces the government's performance of the function. In at least one case the National Collegiate Athletic Association (NCAA) had been found subject to the Constitution under the pubic function theory (*Buckton v. NCAA*, 1973).

The Nexus or Entanglement Theory

The nexus/entanglement theory examines whether the state's involvement or relationship with the private actor is so entangled that it transforms the private conduct into state action and therefore subject to constitutional review. For example, in *Burton v. Wilmington Parking Authority* (1961), the Supreme Court found that the action of a private restaurant that leased space in a public parking facility was subject to the equal protect clause when it refused service to minorities. In reaching this decision, the Supreme Court hed that even though the restaurant did not receive any direct governmental aid, the Court held that they were in a "symbiotic relationship" because restaurant benefited from the location and the facility benefited from the rent it received.

The scope of the nexus/entanglement theory was limited by three 1982 Supreme Court decisions: *Blum v. Yaresky*, *Rendell-Baker v. Kohn* and *Lugar v. Edmondson Oil Co.* In *Blum*, the Court refused to find such a symbiotic relationship between government and a privately owned nursing home despite the fact that the state heavily subsidized the operation of nursing home and paid for 90 percent of the patient's medical expenses. The mere receipt of state funds, the court held, did not transform otherwise private acts into state action unless the state exercises coercive power or provides significant encouragement. In *Rendell-Baker v. Kohn*, the court refused to find state action when a private school, funded primarily from public funds and regulated by public authorities, because its action in dismissing an employee was neither compelled or influenced by the state. In *Lugar v. Edmondson Oil Co.*, the court found states action when a private party, with the assistance of the country sheriff seized another person of his property without due process.

As a result of the Supreme Court cases, the nexus/entanglement theory has been limit, such that neither state funding nor state regulation, without more, is enough to trigger state action. Now, in order for the court to find state action, there must also be significant joint participation between the state and private party.

The State Compulsion Theory

Before the state compulsion test can be satisfied, the Supreme Court held that there must be proof that the state significantly encouraged or somehow coerced the private party, either overtly or covertly, to take a particular action so that the choice is really that of the state (*Adickes v. S. H. Kress & Co.*, 1970)

Application to Sport and Recreation Organizations

As mentioned above, the courts have traditionally held that the activities of public schools, universities and their officials is state action and subject to constitutional review. What is not so clear is how to view the actions of private sports and recreational organizations that govern high school, college Olympic and professional sports.

Recreational Clubs and Facilities

While public lands are constitutionally protected, the question of whether a park and amusement area controlled by a private organization is also constitutionally protected depending on the facts of the case. For example, in *Evans v. Newton* (1966), the Supreme Court held that a park owned by private trustees constituted state action when it allowed only white people to use the park. In the decision, the court implied that the operation of the park was an essential municipal function, which could not be delegated to private persons so as to avoid constitutional review (Evans, 1966).

However, the court has narrowed the public function theory since *Evans v. Newton*. As a result, the operation of other recreational facilities, such as country clubs or amusement parks, have not been construed as state action (*UAW* and *City of N.Y. Dep't of Parks & Rec*). A notable exception is the interesting case of *Pitt v. Pine Valley Golf Club* (1988), where the plaintiff claimed that a membership rule, that restricted homeownership in the Borough of Pine Valley to members of the Pine Valley Golf Club, violated the 5th and 14th Amendments of the Constitution. When making the requisite state action inquiry, the court noted that the club was in essence issuing a zoning ordinance. Because the power to make zoning ordinances is traditionally reserved to the state, the court found state action to be involved.

In *Perkins v. Londonderry Basketball Club* (1999), the court held that a voluntary, non-profit organization that enjoyed tax-exempt status was not a state actor even though it availed itself of public facilities free of charge and its board members were also members of the town's Recreation Commission. In *Hippopress v. SMG* (2003), the plaintiff was unable to demonstrate that there was a sufficiently close relationship between SMG, a facility management group and the City of Manchester which had contracted with SMG to manage its multipurpose sports and entertainment venue to establish SMG's conduct as state action. Without meeting this threshold, Hippopress was unable to proceed with its state and federal constitutional claims.

Cases where state action was found to exist in circumstances similar to those describe above include: *Fortin v. Darlington Little League* (1975), where the extent of public facility use has been important and *Stevens v. New York Racing Association* (1987), where the plaintiff was able to show the existence of state action under the "symbiotic relationship" theory. The court noted that state action existed because of the extent state funding. (See also Section 6.26, *Private Clubs in Sport and Recreation*).

High School Athletic Associations

As illustrated by *Brentwood v. Tennessee Secondary School Athletic Association*, the significant case below, a number of courts have held statewide athletic associations to be state actors under either the entanglement or public function theory. (See, e.g.,; *Griffin High School v. Illinois High School Assn.*, (1987); *Clark v. Arizona Interscholastic Assn.*, (1982), cert. denied, (1983); *In re United States ex rel. Missouri State High School Activities Assn.*, (1982); *Louisiana High School Athletic Assn. v. St. Augustine High School*, (1968); *Oklahoma High School Athletic Assn. v. Bray*, (1963); *Indiana High School Athletic Assn. v. Carlberg*, (Ind. 1997); *Mississippi High Sch. Activities Ass'n v. Coleman*, (Miss. 1994); *Kleczek v. Rhode Island Interscholastic League, Inc.*, (1992); *Cmtys. for Equity v. Mich. High School Athletic Ass'n*, (2006); *Jones v. W. Va. State Bd. of Educ.*, (2005); *Christian Heritage Academy v. Oklahoma Secondary School Activities Ass'n*, (2007); and *Mancuso v. Massachusetts Interscholastic Athletic Ass'n*, 2009); see also *Moreland v. Western Penn. Interscholastic Athletic League*, (1978).

National Organizations Governing College Athletics

The National Collegiate Athletic Association (NCAA) is a privately funded, unincorporated association made up of four-year colleges and universities. Two other organizations that govern college athletics are: the National Junior College Athletic Association (NJCAA), which is made up of junior and community colleges, and the National Association of Intercollegiate Athletics (NAIA), which is made up of those schools that have chosen not to join the NCAA. All of these associations are private organizations composed of both public and private schools and membership is voluntary.

Despite the NCAA's status as a private association, courts up until the mid-1980 historically had found that the NCAA's actions constituted state action and constitutional review. For example, in *Buckton v. NCAA* (1973), the court held that in supervising and policing most intercollegiate athletics nationally, the NCAA performed a public function, sovereign in nature, which subjected it to constitutional scrutiny. In *Howard University v. NCAA* (1975), the D.C. Circuit Court in ruling that the NCAA's enforcement of its five-year competition rule constituted state action found that the influence of state-supported universities in the NCAA required a finding of state action.

Following the Supreme Court's 1982 trilogy of state action cases, the courts began to move away from this position. The first case to find the NCAA not to be a state actor and its activities not subject to constitutional review was *Arlosoroff v. NCAA*, (1984). In *Arlosoroff v. NCAA*, the Fourth Circuit Court held that the NCAA's regulation of intercollegiate athletics was not a function traditionally reserved to the state. Mere indirect involvement of state government, the court held could no longer convert private actions into state action.

In *NCAA v. Tarkanian* (1988), the United States Supreme Court held that the NCAA's conduct, resulting in Tarkanian's two-year suspension as basketball coach by the University of Nevada, Las Vegas (UNLV) did not constitute state action. In rejecting Tarkanian's argument that the NCAA acted jointly with UNLV, a state university, to deprive him of his due process right, the court held that the NCAA did not have the power to directly discipline a university employee or to mandate UNLV to take any action against Tarkanian. The university, the court held, retained the power not to comply with or reject any of the NCAA rules. UNLV, the court ruled voluntarily chose to abide by the NCAA's rules rather than face future penalties. As a result of the court's decision in Tarkanian, the NCAA rules and activities have no longer been found to constitute state action. However, in a case distinguishable from Tarkanian, the Second Circuit Court in *Cohane v. NCAA* (2007) found that that a coach who was dismissed by his school in the hope of placating the NCAA could show that the NCAA was a "willful participant in joint activity with the state" if all the facts alleged in the case was true.

College Conferences
In determining whether intercollegiate athletic conferences are state actors, the courts have generally examined whether the members of the college athletic conference were public or private, if the conference received direct or indirect or tax breaks or concessions from the state, and if the conference members use public facilities. For example, in *Stanley v. Big Eight Conference* (1978), in finding the actions of the conference constituted state action, the court found important the fact that the conference was composed solely of state supported public universities that delegated supervision over intercollegiate athletics to the Big Eight.

As a result of the Supreme Court's decision in *NCAA v. Tarkanian* (1988) the question of whether a college conference is a state action is a little more difficult, especially when the conference is not made up entirely of public institutions. For example, in *Hairston v. Pac-10 Conference* (1994), the court held that "on the issue of whether state action is involved, *NCAA v. Tarkanian* is dispositive."

The United States Olympic Committee (USOC)
Even though created by federal statute and the recipient of federal funding, the courts have held that the USOC's actions do not constitute state action. Two cases that illustrate this conclusion are: *DeFrantz v. USOC*, (1980) and *San Francisco Arts & Athletics, Inc. v. USOC* (1987). In ruling that the USOC's decision to boycott the 1980 Moscow Olympics did not constitute state action the court held that "the USOC is an independent body, and nothing in its chartering statute gives the federal government the right to control that body or its officers. Furthermore, the facts here do not indicate that the federal government was able to exercise any type of 'de facto' control over the USOC" *DeFrantz v. USOC*, (1980).

Similarly, in *San Francisco Arts & Athletics, Inc. v. USOC*, the Supreme Court held that the USOC's refusal to grant SFAA the right to use the word "Olympic" and certain other Olympic symbols did not constitute state action even though the organization was created by federal statute, received federal funds, and was granted the exclusive right to control the word and symbols by the Amateur Sports Act of 1978 because there was no involvement by the government in withholding the permission.

Other Legislatively Created Sport Organizations
In *Johnston v. Tampa Sports Authority* (2006), the court noted that the TSA was a public entity created by the Florida Legislature and that it could not simply "contract away" its public status. Rather, TSA, the court held, has an obligation to maintain the stadium it manages in a manner that protects the constitutional rights of its patrons. In subsequent litigation, the TSA continued to be deemed a state actor (*Johntson v. TSA*, 2008). (See Supplemental CD.) In *Sheehan v. San Francisco 49er* (2009), the court analyzed a similar pat-down policy and came to the conclusion that only private action was involved in the searches at issue there.

Professional Sports Leagues
Since professional sports teams and leagues do not perform a function that has been traditionally reserved to the state, nor are they so entwinement with the government that the state is involved in their decisions, their actions have historically been found not to constitute state action. That being said, has been limited. For example, in *Long v. NFL* (1994), the court ruled that the mere fact that a city collected an amusement tax on tickets and that it constructed the stadium for a team was not enough to establish state action in a constitutional challenge to the NFL's drug testing policy.

As professional sport franchises seek new facilities, however, largely funded and maintained by tax payer dollars, they should be careful that they do not get so entwined with the city or state government that their actions constitute state action. For example, in *Ludtke v. Kuhn* (1978), the court ruled that the New York Yankees were sufficiently entwined with government to consider the team's enforcement of the MLB Commissioner's policy of excluding female reporters from the clubhouse state action. The Yankees, the court noted leased the stadium from the city, public funds were used to improve the stadium, the city provide the Yankees with additional police on game days and the city had exercised its power of eminent domain to acquire Yankee Stadium.

SIGNIFICANT CASE

In Brentwood Academy v. Tennessee Secondary School Athletic Association, the United States Supreme Court is asked to consider whether a private state high school athletic association should be considered a state actor. In making its' decision, the court examines the relationship between the private association and its' public members.

BRENTWOOD ACADEMY V. TENNESSEE SECONDARY SCHOOL
Athletic Association Supreme Court of the United States
531 U.S. 288 (2001)

JUSTICE SOUTER delivered the opinion of the Court.

The issue is whether a statewide association incorporated to regulate interscholastic athletic competition among public and private secondary schools may be regarded as engaging in state action when it enforces a rule against a member school. The association in question here includes most public schools located within the State, acts through their representatives, draws its officers from them, is largely funded by their dues and income received in their stead, and has historically been seen to regulate in lieu of the State Board of Education's exercise of its own authority. We hold that the association's regulatory activity may and should be treated as state action owing to the pervasive entwinement of state school officials in the structure of the association, there being no offsetting reason to see the association's acts in any other way.

I

Respondent Tennessee Secondary School Athletic Association (Association) is a not-for-profit membership corporation organized to regulate interscholastic sport among the public and private high schools in Tennessee that belong to it. No school is forced to join, but without any other authority actually regulating interscholastic athletics, it enjoys the memberships of almost all the State's public high schools (some 290 of them or 84% of the Association's voting membership), far outnumbering the 55 private schools that belong. A member school's team may play or scrimmage only against the team of another member, absent a dispensation.

The Association's rulemaking arm is its legislative council, while its board of control tends to administration. The voting membership of each of these nine-person committees is limited under the Association's bylaws to high school principals, assistant principals, and superintendents elected by the member schools, and the public school administrators who so serve typically attend meetings during regular school hours. Although the Association's staff members are not paid by the State, they are eligible to join the State's public retirement system for its employees. Member schools pay dues to the Association, though the bulk of its revenue is gate receipts at member teams' football and basketball tournaments, many of them held in public arenas rented by the Association.

The constitution, bylaws, and rules of the Association set standards of school membership and the eligibility of students to play in interscholastic games. Each school, for example, is regulated in awarding financial aid, most coaches must have a Tennessee state teaching license, and players must meet minimum academic standards and hew to limits on student employment. Under the bylaws, "in all matters pertaining to the athletic relations of his school," App. 138, the principal is responsible to the Association, which has the power "to suspend, to fine, or otherwise penalize any member school for the violation of any of the rules of the Association or for other just cause," id. at 100.

Ever since the Association was incorporated in 1925, Tennessee's State Board of Education (State Board) has (to use its own words) acknowledged the corporation's functions "in providing standards, rules and regulations for interscholastic competition in the public schools of Tennessee," id. at 211. More recently, the State Board cited its statutory authority, Tenn. Code Ann. § 49-1-302 (App. 220), when it adopted language expressing the relationship between the Association and the Board. Specifically, in 1972, it went so far as to adopt a rule expressly "designating" the Association as "the organization to supervise and regulate the athletic activities in which the public junior and senior high schools in Tennessee participate on an interscholastic basis." Tennessee State Board of Education, Administrative Rules and Regulations, Rule 0520-1-2-.26 (1972) (later moved to Rule 0520-1-2-.08). The Rule provided that "the authority granted herein shall remain in effect until revoked" and instructed the State Board's chairman to "designate a person or persons to serve in an ex-officio capacity on the [Association's governing bodies]." App. 211. That same year, the State Board specifically approved the Association's rules and regulations, while reserving the right to review future changes. Thus, on several occasions over the next 20 years, the State Board reviewed, approved, or reaffirmed its approval of the recruiting

Rule at issue in this case. In 1996, however, the State Board dropped the original Rule 0520-1-2-.08 expressly designating the Association as regulator; it substituted a statement "recognizing the value of participation in interscholastic athletics and the role of [the Association] in coordinating interscholastic athletic competition," while "authorizing the public schools of the state to voluntarily maintain membership in [the Association]." Id. at 220.

The action before us responds to a 1997 regulatory enforcement proceeding brought against petitioner, Brentwood Academy, a private parochial high school member of the Association. The Association's board of control found that Brentwood violated a rule prohibiting "undue influence" in recruiting athletes, when it wrote to incoming students and their parents about spring football practice. The Association accordingly placed Brentwood's athletic program on probation for four years, declared its football and boys' basketball teams ineligible to compete in playoffs for two years, and imposed a $3,000 fine. When these penalties were imposed, all the voting members of the board of control and legislative council were public school administrators.

Brentwood sued the Association and its executive director in federal court under Rev. Stat. § 1979, 42 U.S.C. § 1983, claiming that enforcement of the Rule was state action and a violation of the First and Fourteenth Amendments. The District Court entered summary judgment for Brentwood and enjoined the Association from enforcing the Rule. 13 F. Supp. 2d 670 (MD Tenn. 1998). In holding the Association to be a state actor under § 1983 and the Fourteenth Amendment, the District Court found that the State had delegated authority over high school athletics to the Association, characterized the relationship between the Association and its public school members as symbiotic, and emphasized the predominantly public character of the Association's membership and leadership. The court relied on language in *National Collegiate Athletic Ass'n* v. *Tarkanian*, 488 U.S. 179, 193, n. 13, 102 L. Ed. 2d 469, 109 S. Ct. 454 (1988), suggesting that statewide interscholastic athletic associations are state actors, and on other federal cases in which such organizations had uniformly been held to be acting under color of state law.

The United States Court of Appeals for the Sixth Circuit reversed. 180 F.3d 758 (1999). It recognized that there is no single test to identify state actions and state actors but applied three criteria derived from *Blum* v. *Yaretsky*, 457 U.S. 991, 73 L. Ed. 2d 534, 102 S. Ct. 2777 (1982), *Lugar* v. *Edmondson Oil Co.*, 457 U.S. 922, 73 L. Ed. 2d 482, 102 S. Ct. 2744 (1982), and *Rendell-Baker* v. *Kohn*, 457 U.S. 830, 73 L. Ed. 2d 418, 102 S. Ct. 2764 (1982), and found no state action under any of them. It said the District Court was mistaken in seeing a symbiotic relationship between the State and the Association, it emphasized that the Association was neither engaging in a traditional and exclusive public function nor responding to state compulsion, and it gave short shrift to the language from *Tarkanian* on which the District Court relied.

* * *

II

A

Our cases try to plot a line between state action subject to Fourteenth Amendment scrutiny and private conduct (however exceptionable) that is not. *Tarkanian*, *supra*, 488 U.S. at 191; *Jackson* v. *Metropolitan Edison Co.*, 419 U.S. 345, 349, 42 L. Ed. 2d 477, 95 S. Ct. 449 (1974). The judicial obligation is not only to "'preserve an area of individual freedom by limiting the reach of federal law' and avoid the imposition of responsibility on a State for conduct it could not control," *Tarkanian*, *supra*, 488 U.S. at 191 (quoting *Lugar*, *supra*, at 936-937), but also to assure that constitutional standards are invoked "when it can be said that the State is *responsible* for the specific conduct of which the plaintiff complains," *Blum*, *supra*, at 1004 (emphasis in original). If the Fourteenth Amendment is not to be displaced, therefore, its ambit cannot be a simple line between States and people operating outside formally governmental organizations, and the deed of an ostensibly private organization or individual is to be treated sometimes as if a State had caused it to be performed. Thus, we say that state action may be found if, though only if, there is such a "close nexus between the State and the challenged action" that seemingly private behavior "may be fairly treated as that of the State itself." *Jackson*, *supra*, at 351.

What is fairly attributable is a matter of normative judgment, and the criteria lack rigid simplicity. From the range of circumstances that could point toward the State behind an individual face, no one fact can function as a necessary condition across the board for finding state action; nor is any set of circumstances absolutely sufficient, for there may be some countervailing reason against attributing activity to the government. See *Tarkanian*, 488 U.S. at 193, 196; *Polk County* v. *Dodson*, 454 U.S. 312, 70 L. Ed. 2d 509, 102 S. Ct. 445 (1981).

Our cases have identified a host of facts that can bear on the fairness of such an attribution. We have, for example, held that a challenged activity may be state action when it results from the State's exercise of "coercive power," *Blum*, 457 U.S. at 1004, when the State provides "significant encouragement, either overt or covert," *ibid*. or when a private actor operates as a "willful participant in joint activity with the State or its agents," *Lugar*, *supra*, at 941 (internal quotation marks omitted). We have treated a nominally private entity as a state actor when it is controlled by an "agency of the State," *Pennsylvania* v. *Board of Directors of City Trusts of Philadelphia*, 353 U.S. 230, 231, 1 L. Ed. 2d 792, 77 S. Ct. 806 (1957) (per curiam), when it has been delegated a public function by the State, cf., *e.g.*, *West* v. *Atkins*, *supra*, at 56; *Edmonson* v. *Leesville Concrete Co.*, 500

U.S. 614, 627-628, 114 L. Ed. 2d 660, 111 S. Ct. 2077 (1991), when it is "entwined with governmental policies" or when government is "entwined in [its] management or control," *Evans* v. *Newton*, 382 U.S. 296, 299, 301, 15 L. Ed. 2d 373, 86 S. Ct. 486 (1966).

Amidst such variety, examples may be the best teachers, and examples from our cases are unequivocal in showing that the character of a legal entity is determined neither by its expressly private characterization in statutory law, nor by the failure of the law to acknowledge the entity's inseparability from recognized government officials or agencies. *Lebron* v. *National Railroad Passenger Corporation*, 513 U.S. 374, 130 L. Ed. 2d 902, 115 S. Ct. 961 (1995), held that Amtrak was the Government for constitutional purposes, regardless of its congressional designation as private; it was organized under federal law to attain governmental objectives and was directed and controlled by federal appointees. *Pennsylvania* v. *Board of Directors of City Trusts of Philadelphia*, *supra*, held the privately endowed Gerard College to be a state actor and enforcement of its private founder's limitation of admission to whites attributable to the State, because, consistent with the terms of the settlor's gift, the college's board of directors was a state agency established by state law. Ostensibly the converse situation occurred in *Evans* v. *Newton*, *supra*, which held that private trustees to whom a city had transferred a park were nonetheless state actors barred from enforcing racial segregation, since the park served the public purpose of providing community recreation, and "the municipality remained entwined in [its] management [and] control,' id. at 301.

These examples of public entwinement in the management and control of ostensibly separate trusts or corporations foreshadow this case, as this Court itself anticipated in *Tarkanian*, *supra*. *Tarkanian* arose when an undoubtedly state actor, the University of Nevada, suspended its basketball coach, Tarkanian, in order to comply with rules and recommendations of the National Collegiate Athletic Association (NCAA). The coach charged the NCAA with state action, arguing that the state university had delegated its own functions to the NCAA, clothing the latter with authority to make and apply the university's rules, the result being joint action making the NCAA a state actor.

To be sure, it is not the strict holding in *Tarkanian* that points to our view of this case, for we found no state action on the part of the NCAA. We could see, on the one hand, that the university had some part in setting the NCAA's rules, and the Supreme Court of Nevada had gone so far as to hold that the NCAA had been delegated the university's traditionally exclusive public authority over personnel. Id. at 190. But on the other side, the NCAA's policies were shaped not by the University of Nevada alone, but by several hundred member institutions, most of them having no connection with Nevada, and exhibiting no color of Nevada law. Id. at 193. Since it was difficult to see the NCAA, not as a collective membership, but as surrogate for the one State, we held the organization's connection with Nevada too insubstantial to ground a state action claim. Id. at 193, 196.

But dictum in *Tarkanian* pointed to a contrary result on facts like ours, with an organization whose member public schools are all within a single State. "The situation would, of course, be different if the [Association's] membership consisted entirely of institutions located within the same State, many of them public institutions created by the same sovereign." Id. at 193, n. 13. To support our surmise, we approvingly cited two cases: *Clark* v. *Arizona Interscholastic Assn.*, 695 F.2d 1126 (CA9 1982), cert. denied, 464 U.S. 818, 78 L. Ed. 2d 90, 104 S. Ct. 79 (1983), a challenge to a state high school athletic association that kept boys from playing on girls' interscholastic volleyball teams in Arizona; and *Louisiana High School Athletic Assn.* v. *St. Augustine High School*, 396 F.2d 224 (CA5 1968), a parochial school's attack on the racially segregated system of interscholastic high school athletics maintained by the athletic association. In each instance, the Court of Appeals treated the athletic association as a state actor.

B

Just as we foresaw in *Tarkanian*, the "necessarily fact-bound inquiry," *Lugar*, 457 U.S. at 939, leads to the conclusion of state action here. The nominally private character of the Association is overborne by the pervasive entwinement of public institutions and public officials in its composition and workings, and there is no substantial reason to claim unfairness in applying constitutional standards to it.

The Association is not an organization of natural persons acting on their own, but of schools, and of public schools to the extent of 84% of the total. Under the Association's bylaws.

Although the findings and prior opinions in this case include no express conclusion of law that public school officials act within the scope of their duties when they represent their institutions, no other view would be rational, the official nature of their involvement being shown in any number of ways. Interscholastic athletics obviously play an integral part in the public education of Tennessee, where nearly every public high school spends money on competitions among schools. Since a pickup system of interscholastic games would not do, these public teams need some mechanism to produce rules and regulate competition. The mechanism is an organization overwhelmingly composed of public school officials who select representatives (all of them public officials at the time in question here), who in turn adopt and enforce the rules that make the system work. Thus, by giving these jobs to the Association, the 290 public schools of Tennessee belonging to it can sensibly be seen as exercising their own authority to meet their own responsibilities. Unsurprisingly, then, the record indicates that half the council or board meetings documented here were held during official school hours, and that public schools have largely provided for the Association's financial support. A small portion of the Association's revenue comes from membership dues paid by the schools, and the principal part from gate receipts at tournaments among the member schools. Unlike mere public buyers of contract services, whose payments for services rendered do not convert the service providers into public actors, see *Rendell-Baker*, 457 U.S. at 839-843, the schools here obtain membership in the service organization and give up sources of their own income to their collective association. The Association thus exercises the authority of the predominantly public schools to charge for admission to their games; the Association does not receive this money from the schools, but enjoys the schools' moneymaking capacity as its own.

In sum, to the extent of 84% of its membership, the Association is an organization of public schools represented by their officials acting in their official capacity to provide an integral element of secondary public schooling. There would be no recognizable Association, legal or tangible, without the public school officials, who do not merely control but overwhelmingly perform all but the purely ministerial acts by which the Association exists and functions in practical terms. Only the 16% minority of private school memberships prevents this entwinement of the Association and the public school system from being total and their identities totally indistinguishable.

To complement the entwinement of public school officials with the Association from the bottom up, the State of Tennessee has provided for entwinement from top down. State Board members are assigned ex officio to serve as members of the board of control and legislative council, and the Association's ministerial employees are treated as state employees to the extent of being eligible for membership in the state retirement system.

It is, of course, true that the time is long past when the close relationship between the surrogate association and its public members and public officials acting as such was attested frankly. As mentioned, the terms of the State Board's Rule expressly designating the Association as regulator of interscholastic athletics in public schools was deleted in 1996, the year after a Federal District Court held that the Association was a state actor because its rules were "caused, directed and controlled by the Tennessee Board of Education," *Graham* v. *TSSAA*, 1995 U.S. Dist. LEXIS 3211, No. 1:95- CV-044, 1995 WL 115890, *5 (ED Tenn., Feb. 20, 1995).

But the removal of the designation language from Rule 0520-1-2-.08 affected nothing but words. Today the State Board's member-designees continue to sit on the Association's committees as nonvoting members, and the State continues to welcome Association employees in its retirement scheme. The close relationship is confirmed by the Association's enforcement of the same preamendment rules and regulations reviewed and approved by the State Board (including the recruiting Rule challenged by Brentwood), and by the State Board's continued willingness to allow students to satisfy its physical education requirement by taking part in interscholastic athletics sponsored by the Association. The most one can say on the evidence is that the State Board once freely acknowledged the Association's official character but now does it by winks and nods. The amendment to the Rule in 1996 affected candor but not the "momentum" of the Association's prior involvement with the State Board. *Evans* v. *Newton*, 382 U.S. at 301. The District Court spoke to this point in finding that because of "custom and practice," "the conduct of the parties has not materially changed" since 1996, "the connections between TSSAA and the State [being] still pervasive and entwined." 13 F. Supp. 2d at 681.

The entwinement down from the State Board is therefore unmistakable, just as the entwinement up from the member public schools is overwhelming. Entwinement will support a conclusion that an ostensibly private organization ought to be charged with a public character and judged by constitutional standards; entwinement to the degree shown here requires it.

C

Entwinement is also the answer to the Association's several arguments offered to persuade us that the facts would not support a finding of state action under various criteria applied in other cases. These arguments are beside the point, simply because the facts justify a conclusion of state action under the criterion of entwinement, a conclusion in no sense unsettled merely because other criteria of state action may not be satisfied by the same facts.

The Association places great stress, for example, on the application of a public function test, as exemplified in *Rendell-Baker* v. *Kohn*, 457 U.S. 830, 73 L. Ed. 2d 418, 102 S. Ct. 2764 (1982). There, an apparently private school provided education for students whose special needs made it difficult for them to finish high school. The record, however, failed to show any tradition of providing public special education to students unable to cope with a regular school, who had historically been cared for (or ignored) according to private choice. It was true that various public school districts had adopted the practice of referring students to the school and paying their tuition, and no one disputed that providing the instruction aimed at a proper public objective and conferred a public benefit. But we held that the performance of such a public function did not permit a finding of state action on the part of the school unless the function performed was exclusively and traditionally public, as it was not in that case. The Association argues that application of the public function criterion would produce the same result here, and we will assume, *arguendo*, that it would. But this case does not turn on a public function test, any more than *Rendell-Baker* had anything to do with entwinement of public officials in the special school.

For the same reason, it avails the Association nothing to stress that the State neither coerced nor encouraged the actions complained of. "Coercion" and "encouragement" are like "entwinement" in referring to kinds of facts that can justify characterizing an ostensibly private action as public instead. Facts that address any of these criteria are significant, but no one criterion must necessarily be applied. When, therefore, the relevant facts show pervasive entwinement to the point of largely overlapping identity, the implication of state action is not affected by pointing out that the facts might not loom large under a different test.

D

This is not to say that all of the Association's arguments are rendered beside the point by the public officials' involvement in the Association, for after application of the entwinement criterion, or any other, there is a further potential issue, and the Association raises it. Even facts that suffice to show public action (or, standing alone, would require such a finding) may be outweighed in the name of some value at odds with finding public accountability in the circumstances. In *Polk County*, 454 U.S. at 322, a defense lawyer's actions were deemed private even though she was employed by the county and was acting within the scope of her duty as a public defender. Full-time public employment would be conclusive of state action for some purposes, see *West* v. *Atkins*, 487 U.S. at 50, accord, *Lugar*, 457 U.S. at 935, n. 18, but not when the employee is doing a defense lawyer's primary job; then, the public defender does "not act on behalf of the State; he is the State's adversary." *Polk County*, supra, at 323, n.13. The state-action doctrine does not convert opponents into virtual agents.

The assertion of such a countervailing value is the nub of each of the Association's two remaining arguments, neither of which, however, persuades us. The Association suggests, first, that reversing the judgment here will somehow trigger an epidemic of unprecedented federal litigation. Brief for Respondents 35. Even if that might be counted as a good reason for a *Polk County* decision to call the Association's action private, the record raises no reason for alarm here. Save for the Sixth Circuit, every Court of Appeals to consider a statewide athletic association like the one here has found it a state actor. This majority view began taking shape even before *Tarkanian*, which cited two such decisions approvingly, see *supra*, at 9, (and this was six years after *Blum*, *Rendell-Baker*, and *Lugar*, on which the Sixth Circuit relied here). No one, however, has pointed to any explosion of § 1983 cases against interscholastic athletic associations in the affected jurisdictions. Not to put too fine a point on it, two District Courts in Tennessee have previously held the Association itself to be a state actor, see *Graham*, 1995 U.S. Dist. LEXIS 3211, 1995 WL 115890, at *5; *Crocker* v. *Tennessee Secondary School Athletic Assn.*, 735 F. Supp. 753 (MD Tenn. 1990), affirmance order, 908 F.2d 972, 973 (CA6 1990), but there is no evident wave of litigation working its way across the State. A reversal of the judgment here portends nothing more than the harmony of an outlying Circuit with precedent otherwise uniform.

The judgment of the Court of Appeals for the Sixth Circuit is reversed, and the case is remanded for further proceedings consistent with this opinion.

It is so ordered.

CASES ON THE SUPPLEMENTAL CD

Johnston v. Tampa Sports Authority, 442 F. Supp. 2d 1257 (M.D. Fla., 2006). After reading this case and the Section 7.12 Significant Case, try to determine what teams have relationships with their stadium/host city that might subject their practices to constitutional analysis.

NCAA v. Tarkarnian, 488 U.S. 179 (1988). Most courts and commentators maintain that this case removed any question of whether the NCAA could be considered a state actor. Can you find any support in the opinion or elsewhere for an alternate view?

Stark v. the Seattle Seahawks, 2007 U.S. Dist. LEXIS 45510. The case examines the "pat-down policies" at a professional sport venue and the relationship between teams, leagues, and stadium managers.

Fricano v. Chicago White Sox, 2012 Ill. App. Unpub. LEXIS 278. The case examines the legal status of off-duty police when they are employed as security guards for private organizations.

QUESTIONS YOU SHOULD BE ABLE TO ANSWER

1. Why is it important to understand what organizations could be deemed state actors?
2. Summarize the state action analysis in a paragraph or less.

3. Has there ever been a case in which a sport or recreation organization has been considered to be performing a "public function"?

4. What makes in the outcome in *Johnston* different than the outcome in *Sheehan*?

5. Draft a fact pattern that you think would present a challenging state action analysis.

REFERENCES
Cases
Adickes v. S. H. Kress & Co., 398 U.S. 144 (1970)
Arlosoroff v. NCAA, 746 F.2d 1019 (4th Cir. 1984).
Blum v. Yaresky, 457 U.S. 991 (1982).
Brentwood v. Tennessee Secondary Sch. Ath. Ass'n, 531 U.S. 288 (2001).
Buckton v. NCAA, 366 F.Supp. 1152 (D. Mass. 1973).
Burton v. Wilmington Parking Authority, 365 U.S. 715 (1961).
Cohane v. NCAA, 215 Fed. Appx. 13 (2nd.Cir. 2007).
Cmtys. for Equity v. Mich. High Sch. Ath. Ass'n, (6th Cir. 2004).
DeFrantz v. USOC, 492 F.Supp. 1181 (D.D.C. 1980).
Edmondson v. Leesville Concrete, 500 U.S. 614 (1991).
Evans v. Newton, 382 U.S. 296 (1966).
Fortin v. Darlington Little League, 514 F.2d 344 (1st Cir. 1975).
Griffin High Sch. v. Illinois High Sch. Ass'n (7th Cir. 1987).
Hairston v. PAC-10 Conference, 893 F.Supp 1485 (W.D. Wash. 1994) aff 'd, 101 F.3d 1315 (9th Cir. 1996).
Hippopress, LLC v. SMG, 837 A.2d 347 (N.H. 2003).
Howard Univ. v. NCAA, 510 F.2d 21 (D.C. Cir. 1975).
Jackson v. Metropolitan Edison, Co., 419 U.S. 345 (1974).
Jones v. West Virginia State Bd. Of Educ., 622 S.E.2d 289 (W.Va. 2005).
Johnston v. Tampa Sports Authority, 442 F.Supp. 2d 1257 (M.D. Fla 2006).
Johnston v. Tampa Sports Authoirty, 490 F.3d 820 (11th Cir. 2007).
Long v. NFL, 870 F.Supp 101 (N.D. Pa. 1994).
Louisiana High Sch. Ath. Ass'n v. St. Augustine High School, 396 F.2d 224 (5th Cir. 1968).
Ludtke v. Kuhn, 461 F.Supp. 86 (S.D. N.Y. 1978).
Lugar v. Edmondson Oil Co., 457 U.S. 922 (1982).
Mancuso v. Massachusetts Interscholastic Ath. Ass'n. Inc., 900 N.E.2d 518 (Mass. 2009).
Moreland v. West Pennsylvania Interscholastic Ath. League, 572 F.2d 121 (3rd Cir. 1978).
NCAA v. Tarkanian, 488 U.S. 179 (1988).
Oklahoma High Sch. Ass'n v. Bray, 321 F.2d 269 (10th Cir. 1963).
Perkins v. Londonderry Basketball Club, 196 F.3d 13 (1st Cir. 1999).
Pitt v. Pine Valley Golf Club, 695 F.Supp.778 (D. NJ, 1988).
Rendell-Baker v. Kohn, 457 U.S. 830 (1982).
San Francisco Arts & Athletics, Inc. v. USOC, 483 U.S. 522 (1987).
Sheehan v. San Francisco 49ers, Ltd., 2009 Cal. LEXIS 1638 (Ca. 2009).
Stanley v. Big Eight Conference, 463 F.Supp. 920 (W.D. Mo. 1978).
Stark v. The Seattle Seahawks, 2007 U.S. Dist. LEXIS 45510 (W.D.Wash 2007).
Stevens v. New York Racing Ass'n, 665 F.Supp 164 (E.D.N.Y. 1987).

Publications
Rotunda, R and Nowak, J. (1999). *Treatise on Constitutional Law: Substance and Procedure (3rd ed.)*. St. Paul, MN: West Group

6.13 DUE PROCESS

John T. Wolohan | Syracuse University

The Due Process Clause found in the Fifth Amendment of the United States Constitution states that: "No person shall . . . be deprived of life, liberty, or property without due process of law." There is a second Due Process Clause found in the Fourteenth Amendment, passed in 1868, which applies the Due Process requirement to the states. Based on the clauses' language, it would seem that the due process only referred to the procedures required before any person is deprived of life, liberty or property (Sullivan and Gunther, 2007). However, as we will learn, there are two basic types of due process protected by the courts: Procedural Due Process and Substantive Due Process. **Procedural Due Process** requires that before a governmental entity (State Actor) deprives an individual of his or her "life, liberty or property" interests, that he or she be provided with the proper procedural due process or procedural fairness (Rotunda and Nowak, 1999). The amount of "due process" required, generally depends on the rights being deprived. The more important the right, the more procedural due process that the state is required to provide. **Substantive Due Process** provides individuals with a level of protection against state interference with certain fundamental rights and liberty interests not specifically protected under the constitution, and ensures that these rights cannot be taken without appropriate governmental justification, regardless of the procedures used to do the taking (Rotunda and Nowak, 1999).

FUNDAMENTAL CONCEPTS

Due process has been defined as "a course of legal proceedings which have been established in our system of jurisdiction for the protection and enforcement of private rights" (Pennoyer v. Neff, 1877). In order to determine whether there has been a violation of the Due Process Clause, a court must ask three questions: 1) is there governmental or state action; 2) does the government's action deprive an individual of "life, liberty or property;" and 3) how much due process was due? (Pierce, 2002)

State Actor

Before a court can conclude that someone's due process rights have been violated, the court must first find that the defendant is a **state actor.** For an extended discussion of state action, see Section 6.12, *State Action*. In general, however, public schools and universities, as well as state high school athletic associations are all considered state actors. Once the court has determined that there is state action, it can then determine whether a person's due process has been violated.

Life, Liberty, Or Property Interest

Since the Constitution states that "No person shall . . . be deprived of life, liberty, or property without due process of law," it is essential that sport and recreation managers understand what the words life, liberty and property actually mean. It should be noted, however, that since sport and recreation associations are not involved in depriving individuals of their lives, the two interests examined in this chapter are liberty and property.

Liberty Interest

While usually associated with taking away someone's liberty or freedom by sending them to jail, the Supreme Court has always recognized that "liberty" encompasses far more than freedom from jail (Pierce, 2002). The Supreme Court has defined liberty interest to include "the right of the individual to contract, to engage in any of the common occupations of life, to acquire useful knowledge, to merry, establish a home and bring up children, enjoy those privileges long recognized . . . as essential to the orderly pursuit of happiness by free men" (*Meyer v. Nebraska*, 1923). These "unenumerated" rights, those rights not explicitly mentioned in the Constitution, are protected under the "liberty" interests under Substantive Due Process (Hawkins, 2006). Substantive Due Process, therefore, is simply the recognition that no procedure can be just if it is being used to unjustly deprive a person of his basic human liberties. For example, in *Gross v. Lopez* (1975), the Supreme Court held that a public school student who was suspended from school for alleged misconduct without being provided the opportunity to challenge the charge, was deprived of his liberty interest. The liberty interest identified by the court in Gross was the student's interest in his good name and reputation. Charges of misconduct, the court held, "could seriously damage the student's standing with their fellow pupils and their teachers as well as interfere with later opportunities for higher education and employment" (Gross v. Lopez, 1975)

Since the Supreme Court's decision in *Gross v. Lopez* (1975), the court has begun to limit its interpretation of liberty interests. For example, in 1976, only a year after its decision in *Gross v. Lopez*, the Supreme Court in *Paul v. Davis* (1976) held that a state agency's actions deprive: "that reputation alone, apart from some more tangible interests such as employment," is insufficient "to invoke the ... protections of the Due Process Clause" (*Paul v. Davis*, 1976). In *Siegert v. Gilley* (1991), the court held that even when the stigmatizing act was undertaken with malice and has the effect of significantly impairing an individual's future employment opportunities, a person still does not have a protectable liberty interest in his or her reputation. This "more tangible interests" requirement has become known as the "**stigma plus**" test (Schoonmaker, 2010). An example of the "stigma plus" test in the sport industry is *Stanley v. Big Eight Conference* (1978). When Jim Stanley was relieved of his duties as head football coach and reassigned to other duties in accordance with his contract at Oklahoma State University, based on the Big Eight Conference's investigation of NCAA rules violations, Stanley sued the Big Eight Conference. In particular, Stanley claimed that he had a liberty interest under the Fourteenth Amendment due process clause "in his good name and reputation for integrity as they bear directly upon his ability to obtain employment as a collegiate football coach in the future" (*Stanley v. Big Eight Conference*, 1978). In ruling that "Stanley passes the stigma plus test required by *Paul v. Davis*," the court held that "Stanley's interest are more accurately termed 'liberty interest' for Stanley has no contractual or statutory entitlement to continued employment ... not that his contract has been terminated" (*Stanley v. Big Eight Conference*, 1978).

Arbitrary and Capricious. While the courts do not want to get judicially involved in the internal decision making of voluntary state athletic associations, substantive due process also allow the courts to review the internal decision making of a voluntary state athletic associations if they find the rules were applied arbitrary and capricious (Pierce, 2002). Generally, it is not the responsibility of the courts to inquire into the expediency, practicability, or wisdom of the bylaws and regulations of voluntary associations, no matter how seemingly silly, such as hair length (Long v. Zopp, 1973). However, if the rule is applied in an arbitrary and capricious, or the case involving mistake, fraud, or collusion, the courts will review the internal decisions regarding rules and regulations of voluntary state athletic associations (Schoonmaker, 2010).

In addition to Due Process, the Administrative Procedure Act (APA) also instructs the courts to set aside any agency action that is "arbitrary, capricious, or an abuse of discretion" (Administrative Procedure Act).

Property Interest

Up until 1970, the Supreme Court used the traditional common law definition of property. For example, if an individual owned something of value he or she had a property right protected from arbitrary government deprivation without due process (Pierce, 2002). Benefits an individual received from the government, such as a job, or unemployment / welfare benefits, were only privileges that the government could take away at any time for any reason (Pierce, 2002). The courts began to move away from this position in 1961 when it adopted the doctrine of unconstitutional conditions in *Cafeteria & Restaurant Workers Union v. McElroy* (1961).

In *Goldberg v. Kelly* (1970), the Supreme Court held that governmental "benefits are a matter of statutory entitlement for persons qualified to receive them and procedural due process is applicable to their termination" (*Goldberg v. Kelly*, 1970). In 1972, the Supreme Court expanded on its' decision in *Goldberg v. Kelly* (1970), when it held that "to have a property interest in a benefit, a person clearly must have more than an abstract need or desire for it. He must have more than a unilateral expectation of it. He must instead, have a legitimate claim of entitlement" (*Board of Regents v. Roth*, 1972).

High School Sports. Once a State extends the right to an education, students have a constitutionally protected property right in their education, and the State may not withdraw that right absent fundamental fair process (*Goss v. Lopez*, 1975). Since the courts have determined that students, in most cases, have a protected right in a public education, students have argued that they are also "entitled" to the same property interest in participating in sports. However, even if a student has a constitutionally protected right to an education based on mandatory attendance or mandatory physical education requirement, as a general rule, the courts have ruled "that participation in interscholastic sports a privilege, not a right" (*Reid v. Renowa Hills Public Schools*, 2004).

For example, in *Indiana High School Athletic Association v. Carlberg* (1998), Jason Carlberg and his parents sued the Indiana High School Athletic Association (IHSAA) over its' Transfer Rule. The Transfer Rule stated that a student who transfers schools for nonathletic reasons without a change of permanent residence by the student's parents or guardians has only limited athletic eligibility following enrollment. After spending his freshman year at Brebeuf Preparatory School where he swam on the varsity swim team, Carlberg transferred to Carmel High School for academic reasons.

While the trial court ruled that enforcement of the Transfer Rule violated Carlberg's constitutional right to substantive due process, the Supreme Court of Indiana ruled that participation in interscholastic sports was not one of the rights or interests protected by substantive due process. While recognizing that the importance of participation in interscholastic sports, the Supreme Court of Indiana held that the right to participate in interscholastic athletics did not rise "to the level of the kinds of fundamental rights and liberties" protected by substantive due process (Indiana High School Athletic Association v. Carlberg, 1998). As a result, the court citing its' decision in *Hass v. South Bend Community School Corportation*, (1972) held that "[A] student has no constitutional right to participate in interscholastic athletics" (Indiana High School Athletic Association v. Carlberg, 1998).

In addition to Indiana, the majority of courts have also found that participation in interscholastic sports falls outside due process: *Bruce v. S.C. High School League*, (1972) (participation in high school extracurricular activities is a privilege); *Albach v. Odle*, (1976) (interscholastic athletic participation not a constitutionally protected right); *Hamilton v. Tenn. Secondary School Athletic Association*, (1976) (privilege of participation in interscholastic sports is outside due process protections); *Menke v. Ohio High School Athletic Association*, (1981) (holding that student has no fundamental right to participate in high school athletics); *Whipple v. Oregon School Activities Association*, (1981) ("While we think that participation in interscholastic sports is an important part of the educational process, we are not persuaded by plaintiff's argument that it is a liberty or property interest of constitutional proportions"); *Niles v. Univ. Interscholastic League*, (1983) (student's interest in interscholastic activities falls outside of due process rights); *Davenport v. Randolph Co. Board of Education*, (1984) (privilege of participation in sports falls outside due process); *Simkins v. S.D. High School Activities Association*, (1989) (interscholastic participation is mere expectancy); *Zehner v. Central Berkshire Regional School District*, (1995) (taking part in interscholastic athletics was not constitutionally protected claim of entitlement). It should be noted, however, that some jurisdictions have found that participation in interscholastic athletics was a protected right and not a privilege: *Moran v. School District #7, Yellowstone County*, (1972) and *Duffley v. New Hampshire Interscholastic Athletic Association*, (1982).

While there are no cases addressing the issue, it is interesting to note that as more and more school districts charge athletes a fee to participate in high school sports, the question of whether participation in interscholastic sports is going to be elevated to due process protection.

College Sports. Because college students pay for college, the courts have ruled that "a student's interest in attending a university is a property right protected by due process" (Abbariao v. Hamline University School of Law, 1977). With college athletes, students have asserted that they either have a property right because he or she has a property interest in their scholarship or a property right in a future professional career. For example, in *Hall v. University of Minnesota* (1982), Mark Hall asserted that he has been denied his due process right after the university denied him admission into an academic program after three years at the university, thereby causing him to lose his basketball scholarship. In ruling that Hall had a protected property right based on his future opportunity to play professional basketball, the court found that "the interest at stake here, although ostensibly academic, is Hall's ability to obtain a "no cut" contract with the National Basketball Association" (Hall v. University of Minnesota, 1982). In support of its' decision, the court noted that Hall had used his college career as a means of entry into professional sports as do many college athletes. The court found that Hall had "put all of his "eggs" into the "basket" of professional basketball . . . and that he would suffer a substantial loss if his career objectives were impaired" (Hall v. University of Minnesota, 1982). It should be noted that most courts do not like to assign a property right to future events, such as professional athletic careers, because they are too speculative to be protected. In addition, the courts generally have not recognized a right of non-scholarship athletes to participate in intercollegiate athletics (*Colorado Seminary v. NCAA*, 1978).

While students have also been successful in arguing that they had a property right in the present economic value in a college athletic scholarship, *Gulf South Conference v. Boyd* (1979), depending on the length of athletic scholarships, students may not have the same property interests in their scholarships as Boyd and Hall. Up until 2015, when the NCAA started to move back to four-year scholarships for some athletes, as long as schools followed proper NCAA procedures, scholarships athletes only had a property interest for a single year. For example, in Conrad v. The University of Washington, (1992), the court upheld the school's dismissal of a football player when it ruled that he did not have a protected interest in his athletic scholarship.

Another case, dealing with due process property right, is *National Collegiate Athletic Association v. Tarkanian*, (1988). Jerry Tarkanian was the head basketball coach and a tenured teacher at UNLV when the NCAA, after conducting an investigation into improper recruiting practices and other rule violations proposed a series of sanctions against the university. Included in the sections was a 2-year probation, and a request that the university show cause why additional penalties should not to be imposed, if the university failed to remove the coach completely from the university's intercollegiate athletic program during the probation period (National Collegiate Athletic Association v. Tarkanian, 1988).

When the president of the university ordered that Tarkanian be suspended for the probation period, Tarkanian brought suit in a Nevada state court against the university alleging that he had been deprived of his due process right under the Fourteenth Amendment. While the Supreme Court of Nevada agreed with Tarkanian and held that the NCAA's regulatory activity constituted state action and that the procedures used by the NCAA had violated the due process clause, the case was eventually overturned by the United States Supreme Court on the grounds that the NCAA was no a state actor, and therefore not subject to the due process clause (National Collegiate Athletic Association v. Tarkanian, 1988).

Due Process Analysis

Having established that the government's action deprive an individual of "life, liberty or property," an individual must now show how much **Procedural Due Process** was required. Up until the Supreme Court's decision in *Goldberg v. Kelly* (1970), the court generally held that due process required a hearing, resembling a judicial trial (Pierce, 2002). By 1973, however, the Court had moved from this position and held that a "hearing" is an ambiguous term that could refer to a wide range of decision making procedures (*U.S. v. Florida East Coast Ry*, 1973). While there is no established requirements, generally the amount of due process required will depend on the right being deprived an individual. For example, if the state was attempting to put you in jail for 10 year, the due process required would be high, including the right to an unbiased trial, the right to present evidence, to view all the evidence, the right to cross examine witnesses, and the right to counsel. If, however, it was a $10 parking ticket, the due process required would be much lower and you would not have many of the same procedural protection.

In 1976, the Court developed a four part balancing test to be used to determine the extent to procedural due process. The first part of the test, looks at "the private interest that will be affected by the official action; second, the risk of an erroneous deprivation of such interest through the procedures used; third the probable value, if any, of additional or substitute procedural safeguards; and finally, the Government's interest, including the function involved and the fiscal and administrative burdens that the additional or substitute procedural requirement would entail" (*Mathews v. Eldridge*, 1976, p. 335). For example, in *Gross v. Lopez* (1975), a number of students were suspended for ten days for disruptive behavior. The students sued claiming their due process rights had been violated. In agreeing with the students, the Supreme Court held that a public school student was entitled to a hearing of some kind before he was suspended for 10 days. Absent the hearing, which the court held could be as simple as an informal meeting between a school official and the student in which the student had a chance to tell his side of the story; the Court held that there was too great a chance that the student would be erroneously deprived an important liberty and property interest (*Goss v. Lopez*, 1975). The Court further outlined the procedures that needed to be followed to meet the standard they had established. Specifically, the student must be given oral and written notice of the charges against him and, if he or she denies them, an explanation of the evidence the authorities have and an opportunity to present his side of the story. The court also held that there need be no delay between the time of the notice and the time of the hearing (*Goss v. Lopez*, 1975).

As a result of *Goss v. Lopez*, if a high school or state high school athletic association would like to suspend a student from athletic competition due process requirements require that the student receive published standards; notice of the specific charges; advance written notice of the time and place of the hearing notice; a hearing (*Kelley v. Metropolitan County Board of Education of Nashville*, 1968); the right to an impartial decision maker (*Butler v. Oak Creek-Franklin School District*, 2001); a written report of the findings of fact and the basis for punishment; and an appeals procedure (*Behagen v. Intercollegiate Conference of Faculty Representatives*, 1972).

SIGNIFICANT CASE

In seeking due process protection, Joscelin Yeo urged the court to protect her reputation as an athlete. In addressing this question, the court examined the plaintiff's potential financial opportunities and the due process she might be owed.

NATIONAL COLLEGIATE ATHLETIC ASSOCIATION V. JOSCELIN YEO
Supreme Court of Texas
171 S.W.3d 863 (2005)

OPINION

Construing the Texas Constitution's guarantee of due course of law,[1] we held twenty years ago in *Spring Branch I.S.D. v. Stamos*, 695 S.W.2d 556, 560-61, 28 Tex. Sup. Ct. J. 554 (Tex. 1985) like "the overwhelming majority of jurisdictions" construing other constitutional guarantees of due process, that "students do not possess a constitutionally protected interest in their participation in extracurricular activities." We have endorsed the rule in *Stamos* twice since. Respondent nevertheless contends that because of her unique situation as "the most decorated athlete in the history of the Republic of Singapore", to disqualify her from participating in an intercollegiate swimming competition would deprive her of protected property and liberty interests in her reputation and existing and future financial opportunities in violation of the Texas Constitution. The lower courts agreed, distinguishing this case from *Stamos*. We conclude that the rule in *Stamos* applies and therefore reverse the judgment of the court of appeals and render judgment that respondent take nothing.

[1] TEX. CONST. art. I, § 19 ("No citizen of this State shall be deprived of life, liberty, property, privileges or immunities, or in any manner disfranchised, except by the due course of the law of the land.").

When Coach Michael Walker recruited Joscelin Yeo, a high school student in the Republic of Singapore, to enroll at the University of California at Berkeley, she had already achieved fame in her country as a swimmer. At Berkeley, she won numerous All-American awards and was a member of a world-record-setting relay team in 1999.

Before the 2000-2001 school year, Walker left Berkeley for the University of Texas at Austin ("UT-Austin"). He was helping coach the Singapore Olympic team, of which Yeo was a member, and she went with him to UT-Austin. Berkeley and UT-Austin are both members of the National Collegiate Athletic Association ("NCAA"), which prescribes rules for determining the eligibility of student athletes to engage in competition. A member that violates these rules is subject to sanctions. NCAA rules generally prohibit a student who transfers from one four-year member institution to another from participating in intercollegiate athletic competitions for one full academic year, but this restriction may be waived under certain circumstances if the former institution does not object. Berkeley refused to waive the restriction, and thus Yeo was ineligible to compete at UT-Austin for an academic year.

As permitted by NCAA rules, Yeo did not enroll in classes for the fall semester of 2000 in order to compete in the Olympics. In compliance with the one-year restriction, she did not participate in intercollegiate events during that semester or the spring semester, when she was enrolled in classes. UT-Austin mistakenly believed that

Yeo's first semester had counted toward satisfying the restriction and that she was free to engage in competition beginning the fall semester of 2001. After Yeo competed in four events, Berkeley complained to the NCAA. UT-Austin confessed its error and agreed that Yeo would sit out the remainder of the semester, but the NCAA required that she not participate in the first four events the following spring, to match the four events in which she had been disqualified. Yeo did not know of UT-Austin's discussions with the NCAA and simply did as UT-Austin told her.

UT-Austin then added three swimming events at the beginning of its spring semester schedule. After Yeo had sat out those events and a fourth one, UT-Austin allowed her to rejoin the swim team, but Berkeley again complained, arguing that the added events could not be used to satisfy the one-year restriction. NCAA staff agreed and on March 6 issued a decision that Yeo not participate in the next three regularly scheduled events, including the 2002 NCAA women's swimming and diving championship on March 22. UT-Austin immediately appealed the staff decision to the NCAA Student-Athlete Reinstatement Committee ("the SARC"), and a telephonic hearing was scheduled for the next day. For the first time, UT-Austin told Yeo of the problem and advised her simply to plea for sympathy. She did, but at the conclusion of the hearing, the SARC upheld the staff decision.

At UT-Austin's suggestion, Yeo then obtained legal counsel, who persuaded Berkeley on March 15 to waive Yeo's one-year restriction, something it had refused to do before. Counsel moved the SARC to reconsider, especially in light of this development, but it refused.

On March 20, Yeo sued UT-Austin and its vice president for institutional relations and legal affairs, Patricia Ohlendorf, to enjoin them from disqualifying her from competing in the championship meet two days later and for a declaration that UT-Austin had denied her procedural due process as guaranteed by the Texas Constitution. That same day, the trial court issued a temporary restraining order granting Yeo the injunctive relief requested. On March 21, the NCAA intervened in the action, but Yeo moved to strike the intervention, and after a hearing later that day, the trial court granted Yeo's motion. The next morning, the NCAA sought mandamus relief from the court of appeals, and UT-Austin appealed from the temporary restraining order. That afternoon, the court of appeals denied the petition for mandamus and dismissed the interlocutory appeal for want of jurisdiction. Yeo competed in the championship meet.

In November 2002, after a trial to the bench, the trial court rendered judgment for Yeo, declaring that UT-Austin had denied Yeo procedural due process guaranteed by the Texas Constitution, thereby depriving her of protected liberty and property interests. The court permanently enjoined UT-Austin from declaring Yeo ineligible in the future without affording her due process and from punishing her for participating in past competitions, including the 2002 women's championship. The trial court also awarded Yeo $ 164,755.50 in attorney fees through an appeal to this Court.

The NCAA appealed from the order striking its intervention, and UT-Austin appealed from the judgment. The court of appeals affirmed. We granted the NCAA's and UT-Austin's petitions for review.

Since the championship meet in March 2002, Yeo has, of course, moved on. When briefs were filed in this case, we were told that Yeo had graduated from UT-Austin, received a Rhodes Scholarship, and ended her college swimming career. But none of the parties argues that the case has become moot, because the injunction prevents the NCAA from imposing retroactive sanctions under its "Restitution Rule". We agree that the case is not moot.

We first consider whether Yeo has an interest protected by due course of law under article I, section 19 of the Texas Constitution. In so doing, we look as usual to cases construing the federal constitutional guarantee of due process as persuasive authority. The parties have not identified any difference between the state and federal guarantees material to the issues in this case.

Yeo does not challenge our holding in *Stamos* that a student has no interest in participating in extracurricular activities that is protected by the Texas Constitution's guarantee of due course of law. Nor does she dispute that under NCAA rules, she was ineligible to participate in the 2002 NCAA women's swimming and diving championship. Yeo argues that she was entitled to notice and a meaningful hearing before NCAA rules were applied to her because of her unique reputation and earning potential. Had she been disqualified from competing in the championship meet, she contends, people would have suspected that it was for her own misconduct and not for UT-Austin's mistakes in attempting to comply with NCAA rules. Yeo acknowledges that the United States Supreme Court has held that reputation alone is not a protected liberty or property interest. But it is the degree of her interests, Yeo contends, and not merely their character, that bring them within constitutional protection. A student-athlete with a lesser reputation or less certain of her earning potential, she concedes, would not have the same rights. The court of appeals agreed:

> In connection with the permanent injunction, the trial court made several material findings of fact that are essentially unchallenged: (1) Yeo had already established a world-class reputation and her "good name, outstanding reputation, high standing in her community, her unblemished integrity and honor are particularly important in the Republic of Singapore and in light of her cultural background"; (2) if NCAA rules did not prohibit athletes from accepting professional compensation while competing in NCAA sanctioned events, Yeo "would be immediately eligible to capitalize on her public persona by entering into lucrative endorsement and marketing opportunities

as well as being eligible for prize winnings due to her performance as a member of Singapore's national team"; and (3) "UT-Austin represented to [Yeo] at the time she transferred from [Cal-Berkeley] to become a student-athlete at UT-Austin that UT-Austin would not jeopardize or compromise [Yeo's] eligibility to compete on behalf of UT-Austin in NCAA athletic competition."

These findings of fact support Yeo's theory that her athletic reputation, which was established *even before* she began attending Cal-Berkeley and competing under NCAA regulations, constitutes a protected interest for purposes of due course of law. Yeo had competed in two Olympic games before attending college and had been named sportswoman of the year and Olympic flag-bearer for her native country, Singapore. At both the temporary restraining order and permanent injunction hearings, Yeo represented that it was this continuing interest in her athletic and professional reputation that UT-Austin had damaged by its actions.

* * *

Here, Yeo presented testimony from multiple witnesses indicating that she had established a reputation as a world-class athlete in her home country of Singapore *separate and apart from her intercollegiate swimming career.* As a result, much of her reputation had been built outside of the United States and the structure of NCAA intercollegiate athletics. We cannot say that the trial court erred in holding that Yeo had a protected interest under these facts.

UT-Austin, joined by various *amici curiae*, contends that an affirmance in this case will create a protected interest in every intercollegiate student-athlete to participate in athletic events. We reject this argument and note that we reach this decision because of the unique fact pattern with which we are presented. Based upon the largely undisputed findings of fact, Yeo had already established a protected interest in her reputation as an athlete long before she came to this country to swim competitively as a student-athlete under NCAA rules. Our holding that Yeo, under these facts, has a protected interest should not be read as extending that same protection to every other intercollegiate athlete. The determination of whether a student-athlete has a protected interest is necessarily fact-specific, depending on that athlete's specific situation and reputation. Each such case must be decided on its own merits, in light of the financial realities of contemporary athletic competition. We hold that Yeo's established liberty interest in her reputation as an athlete is entitled to due course of law protection and we affirm the trial court's decision in that regard.

We reject Yeo's argument and the court of appeals' holding. The United States Supreme Court has stated, and we agree, that whether an interest is protected by due process depends not on its *weight* but on its *nature.* Yeo does not take issue with this principle but argues in effect that the weight of an interest can determine its nature. A stellar reputation like hers, Yeo contends and the court of appeals concluded, is categorically different from a more modest reputation. We disagree. The loss of either may be, to its owner, substantial. The court of appeals held that whether a reputation is constitutionally protected must be decided case by case, but it did not suggest a measure for distinguishing one case from another, and neither does Yeo. We see none, which convinces us that the *nature* of one's interest in a good reputation is the same no matter how good the reputation is.

Yeo's claimed interest in future financial opportunities is too speculative for due process protection. There must be an actual legal entitlement. While student-athletes remain amateurs, their future financial opportunities remain expectations.

Yeo argues that her reputation and future financial interests are entitled to constitutional protection under our decision in *University of Texas Medical School v. Than.* There we held that a medical student charged with academic dishonesty had a protected liberty interest in a graduate education. But since *Than* we have refused to accord a student's interest in athletics the same protection. We decline to equate an interest in intercollegiate athletics with an interest in graduate education.

Accordingly, we hold that Yeo has asserted no interests protected by article I, section 19 of the Texas Constitution. The case must therefore be dismissed. While we need not reach the NCAA's arguments that it should have been permitted to intervene, we expressly disapprove the court of appeals' conclusions that the NCAA's interests were not sufficiently implicated to warrant intervention, and that intervention would have unduly complicated the case.

We have twice reminded the lower courts that "judicial intervention in [student athletic disputes] often does more harm than good." As the Fifth Circuit has said, judges are not "super referees". Along the same vein, the United States Supreme Court has observed: "Courts do not and cannot intervene in the resolution of conflicts which arise in the daily operation of school systems and which do not directly and sharply implicate basic constitutional values." We reiterate this counsel to the trial courts and courts of appeals.

The judgment of the court of appeals is reversed, and judgment is rendered that Yeo take nothing.

CASES ON THE SUPPLEMENTAL CD

Stanley v. Big Eight Conference, 463 F. Supp. 920 (W.D. MO. 1978). The case examines what due process an athletic conference that is investigating a coach must supply to satisfy the coach's due process rights.

Stone v. Kansas State High School Activities Association, 761 P.2d 1255 (Kan. App. 1988. In this case the court holds that high school students do have a constitutionally protected interest in participating in extracurricular activities.

Palmer v. Merluzzi, 868 F.2d 90 (3rd Cir. 1989). This case examines whether a student was adequately notified of the accusation against him and was provided a meaningful opportunity to argue against his scholastic and athletic suspensions.

Mancuso vs. Massachusetts Interscholastic Athletic Association, 453 Mass. 116; 900 N.E.2d 518 (2009). This case examines whether students have a "legitimate claim of entitlement," to her participation in interscholastic athletics under State law, if the law recognizes a right to an education, which includes physical education.

QUESTIONS YOU SHOULD BE ABLE TO ANSWER

1. Due process protections are found in what Amendments?
2. The three rights protected by the Due Process clause are?
3. In determining whether your substantive due process has been violated, the courts will review whether the regulation or rule is . . . ?
4. In determining whether your procedural due process has been violated, the courts will review what?
5. Is participation in high school sports a privilege or a protected right?

REFERENCES
Cases
Abbariao v. Hamline University School of Law, 258 N.W.2d 108 (Minn.1977)
Albach v. Odle, 531 F.2d 983 (10th Cir. 1976)
Behagen v. Intercollegiate Conference of Faculty Representatives, 346 F. Supp. 602 (D. Minn. 1972).
Board of Regents v. Roth, 408 U.S. 564 (1972).
Bruce v. South Carolina High School League, 189 S.E.2d 817 (S.C. 1972)
Butler v. Oak Creek-Franklin School District, 172 F. Supp. 2d 1102 (E.D. Wis. 2001).
Cafeteria & Restaurant Workers Union v. McElroy 367 U.S. 885 (1961)
Colorado Seminary v. NCAA, 417 F. Supp. 885 (D. Colo. 1976), aff 'd, 570 F.2d 320 (10th Cir. 1978).
Conrad v. The University of Washington, 834 P.2d 17 (Wash, 1992)
Davenport v. Randolph Co. Board of Education, 730 F.2d 1395 (11th Cir. 1984)
Duffley v. New Hampshire Interscholastic Athletic Association, 446 A.2d 462 (Sup. Ct. N.H. 1982).
Goldberg v. Kelly, 397 U.S. 254 (1970).
Goss v. Lopez, 419 U.S. 565 (1975).
Gulf South Conference v. Boyd, 369 So. 553 (Sup. Ct. Ala. 1979).
Hall v. University of Minnesota, 530 F. Supp. 104 (D. Minn. 1982).
Hamilton v. Tenn. Secondary School Athletic Association, 552 F.2d 681 (6th Cir. 1976)
Hass v. South Bend Community School Corporation, 289 N.E.2d 495 (Ind. 1972)
Indiana High School Athletic Association v. Carlberg, 694 N.E.2d 222 (Ind. 1998),
Kelley v. Metropolitan County Board of Education of Nashville, 293 F. Supp. 485 (M.D. Tenn. 1968).
Long v. Zopp, 476 F.2d 180 4th Cir. 1973).
Mathews v. Eldridge, 424 U.S. 319 (1976).
Menke v. Ohio High School Athletic Association, 441 N.E.2d 620 (Ohio Ct. App. 1981)
Meyer v. Nebraska, 262 U.S. 390 (1923).
Moran v. School District #7, Yellowstone County, 350 F. Supp. 1180 (D. Mont. 1972).
National Collegiate Athletic Association v. Tarkanian, 488 U.S. 179 (1988)

National Collegiate Athletic Association v. Yeo, 114 S.W. 3d 584, rev'd 171 S.W. 3d 863 (Tex. 2003).
Niles v. University Interscholastic League, 715 F.2d 1027 (5th Cir. 1983).
Palmer v. Merluzzi, 868 F.2d 90 (3rd Cir. 1989).
Paul v. Davis, 424 U.S. 693 (1976).
Pennoyer v. Neff, 95 U.S. 714 (1877).
Reid v. Renowa Hills Public Schools, 680 N.W.2d 62 (Mich. App. 2004),
Siegert v. Gilley, 500 U.S. 226 (1991)
Simkins v. South Dakota High School Activities Association, 434 N.W.2d 367 (S.D. 1989)
Spring Branch Independent School District, et al. v. Stamos, 695 S.W.2d 556 (Tex. 1985).
Stanley v. Big Eight Conference, 463 F. Supp. 920 (W.D. MO. 1978).
Stone v. Kansas State High School Activities Association, 761 P.2d 1255 (Kan. App. 1988).
U.S. v. Florida East Coast Ry, 410 U.S. 224 (1973).
Whipple v. Oregon School Activities Association, 629 P.2d 384 (Or. Ct. App. 1981)
Zehner v. Central Berkshire Regional School District, 921 F. Supp. 850 (D. Mass. 1996).

Publications

Hawkins, B. (2006). The Glucksberg Renaissance: Substantive Due Process since Lawrence v. Texas. *Michigan Law Review* 105, 409.

Pierce, R. (2002). Administrative Law Treatise (4th. Ed.). New York, NY: Aspen Press

Schoonmaker, L. (2010). State action. In D. J. Cotton & J. T. Wolohan (Eds.), Law for recreation and sport managers (5th Ed.) pp. 428–439. Dubuque, IA: Kendall/Hunt Publishing Co.

Sullivan, K. and Gunther, G. (2007). *Constitutional Law* (17th ed.). New York, NY: Foundation Press

Rotunda, R and Nowak,, J. (1999). *Treatise on Constitutional Law: Substance and Procedure (3rd ed.)*. St. Paul, MN: West Group

Legislation

Administrative Procedure Act, 5 U.S.C. §§ 551 et seq.

EQUAL PROTECTION

Sarah K. Fields | University of Colorado Denver

6.14

In 1868, just after the Civil War, Congress enacted the Fourteenth Amendment to the United States Constitution. The Equal Protection Clause of the Fourteenth Amendment decreed that "no state shall . . . deny to any person within its jurisdiction the equal protection of the laws." According to contemporary debates on the floor of the House of Representatives and the Senate, the Equal Protection Clause was not intended to be applied literally to all people: it was meant to provide some rights to African-American men; those rights were not intended to include the right to vote, to serve on a jury, or to marry white women. The framers of the Fourteenth Amendment never intended that the clause be applied to women of any race. Thus from the first day, the Equal Protection Clause's literal universal inclusion has been limited, and the challenge for the courts over the past century and a half has been to determine what those limitations are and how to apply the Equal Protection Clause both practically and fairly.

Society and the laws constantly distinguish or discriminate between different groups of individuals. Not everyone is treated equally; for example, eight year olds are not allowed legally to drink alcohol, to join the military, or to drive cars. The Equal Protection Clause simply requires that similarly situated people be treated similarly and that the states be able to articulate and justify why they treat one group differently than another group. Over time, the courts have concluded that to determine if the government's classification is legal under the Equal Protection Clause, the test, or standard of review, will vary according to what category of people the classification describes. Today, courts usually use one of three different standards of review: (1) the easiest test to survive is **mere rationality** and most classifications are tested under this standard; (2) a more difficult middle tier, sometimes called **intermediate scrutiny**, applies to gender classifications; and (3) a very difficult to pass test of **strict scrutiny** applies to deprivations of fundamental rights and to classifications which are suspect—race, **alienage** (status of a foreigner legally within the country) and national origin.

The legal reach of equal protection derives from several sources. Although originally the Fourteenth Amendment only applied to the actions of the states, subsequent Supreme Court interpretation has concluded that the federal government must also comply with equal protection, both because it would be irrational to assume that the state governments must provide equal protection but the federal government would not and because the Fifth Amendment includes a "due process" clause. The Supreme Court ruled in *Bolling v. Sharpe* (1954), that the Fifth Amendment's due process clause inferred an equal protection component for the federal government. Equal protection also derives from the Civil Rights Act of 1871 (42 USC § 1983) which prohibits persons acting under color of law from depriving people of "rights, privileges, or immunities secured by the Constitution." This law protects individuals from having a governmental actor infringe upon their constitutional rights, including their right of equal protection. Additionally, every state constitution has some parallel language to the Equal Protection Clause of the Fourteenth Amendment to the U.S. Constitution, and individuals may file suit in state courts under their state Equal Protection Clause.

FUNDAMENTAL CONCEPTS

State Actor

Before a court can conclude that one's equal protection rights have been violated, the court must find that the defendant is a **state actor.** For an extended discussion of state action, what this means, and how to determine who a state actor is, see Section 6.12, *State Action*. In general, however, public schools and universities are considered state actors, as are community parks and recreation organizations. This means that they must comply with equal protection. Although in general, purely private organizations have greater freedom to discriminate between groups and are not usually limited by equal protection, occasionally courts have concluded that some private organizations have been so intertwined with governmental powers (such as using public facilities or acting in lieu of a governmental agency) that they too can be deemed state actors.

Standing

In order for a plaintiff to file a constitutional claim, the plaintiff must have a direct stake in the outcome of the case in order to have *standing*, see Section 6.11, *Judicial Review, Standing, and Injunctions*. Simply having an interest in the outcome of a case or the topic in general does not satisfy the standing requirement.

Purposeful Discrimination

Courts have determined that the Equal Protection Clause only protects individuals from intentional or **purposeful discrimination.** Unintentional discrimination or a **disparate impact**—when one group is more greatly burdened by a classification than another—on one group does not necessarily mean that equal protection has been violated. For example, on average men are taller than women, so if a fire department has a height minimum taller than the average height of women, more women may be excluded than men. This would be a disparate impact, but by itself, it would not be purposeful discrimination; to prove the regulation violated the Equal Protection Clause, a plaintiff would need evidence to indicate the height minimum was intended to exclude women.

Standards Of Review

Lowest Tier Rational Basis Review

The rational basis review or "**mere rationality**" test is the easiest standard of review and many classifications have survived legal challenges because the state actor has been able to establish that *the classification is rationally related to a legitimate governmental interest.* As mentioned in the example in the introduction to this section, eight year old children cannot legally drink alcohol, join the military, or drive because the vast majority of eight year olds are too young to make safe, informed decisions about their choices and drinking, joining the military, or driving could be dangerous to them and to others. The government has a legitimate interest in the safety of its children and its citizens, and the legal limitations placed on children are rationally related to that legitimate interest. This test applies when the classification the state uses is not subject to one of the more difficult standards of review as described later in this section.

Residency Classifications. Sport and recreation have provided a variety of examples of classifications that have been challenged on equal protection grounds. For example, in *Baldwin v. Fish & Game Commission of Montana* (1978), the Supreme Court concluded that the different classification of residents and non-residents of a state, and charging them different fees for hunting licenses, was rationally related to the legitimate state purpose of preserving a finite resource. The Tenth Circuit Court of Appeals cited *Baldwin* when it concluded that even though non-resident hunting fees were ten to twenty times more than residents fees and awarded significantly fewer licenses to non-residents, the differences were not violations of the Equal Protection Clause because the state had acted rationally to protect its legitimate interest in protecting state resources (*Schutz v. Thorne*, 2005).

Classifications of Students Involved in Extracurricular Activities Compared to Other Students. In *Hageman v. Goshen County School* District (2011), a Wyoming school district adopted a policy of random, suspicionless drug and alcohol testing of all students who participated in extracurricular activities. When challenged on equal protection grounds, the courts upheld the policy because the district had a legitimate interest in deterring the use of drugs and alcohol and that the policy was rationally related to that interest (for more information on this topic see Section 6.23, *Drug Testing*). Similarly when a state high school athletic association required that no more than 50% of an independent or club team be made up of starting players for that sport from any single school or the school would be disqualified from play, athletes filed an Equal Protection claim arguing that the rule made two categories: athletes who can play on club and school teams and athletes who can play only club or school. The court concluded that the rule was rationally related to the states' legitimate interest in promoting fair competition by not allowing a team to play year round and encouraging many students to play rather than an elite few. (*B.A. v. Mississippi High School Activities Association*, 2013). (This case is available on the accompanying computer disc).

Eligibility Rules. A number of eligibility rules have survived equal protection challenges in which mere rationality was the test. A few examples include, a federal district court in New York upholding a school district rule that athletes have tetanus shots prior to participation in outdoor sports. A young man whose family's religious beliefs precluded vaccinations had argued that the rule violated his equal protection rights. The court concluded that the classification was rationally related to the state's legitimate interest in the safety of its students (*Hadley v. Rush Henrietta Center School District*, 2007). In Virginia, a boy's parents chose to have him repeat the third grade because of a learning disability. As a senior in high school, the student turned 19 on August 31, one day before the state's age eligibility rule's September 1 deadline. In upholding the Virginia High School League rules holding him ineligible, the court found that the rule was reasonably related to a legitimate state interest, and that he had no fundamental right to compete (*Sisson v. Virginia High School League*, 2010).

Not all eligibility rules survive equal protection challenges, however. For example, in Indiana, an appellate court concluded that the state high school athletic association had violated the equal protection rights of a student who had received poor grades and ultimately withdrawn from the eleventh grade because of illness. The school allowed him to repeat the grade, but the athletic association deemed him ineligible. The court concluded that excluding the student, who had not withdrawn from school to gain any kind of athletic competitive advantage, was arbitrary and capricious (*Indiana High School Athletic Ass'n v. Schafer*, 1992).

Courts have been divided about the constitutionality of banning home-schooled children from school based athletic participation. The West Virginia Supreme Court found that the state had a legitimate interest in promoting academics rather than athletics and that excluding home-schooled children from its interscholastic program was rationally related to that interest (*Jones v. West Virginia State Board of Education*, 2005). On the contrary, however, a Massachusetts state court concluded that excluding home-schooled students from sport was not rationally related to a legitimate state interest (*Davis v. Massachusetts Interscholastic Athletic Association*, 1995).

Workers' Compensation. A Missouri court concluded that workers' compensation to professional athletes can be limited because the state has a legitimate interest in controlling costs, and professional athletes choose to work in a high risk venue, thus distinguishing between a professional athlete and another worker is rationally related to that interest (*Dubinsky v. St. Louis Blues Hockey Club*, 2007).

Fantasy Sport. Two daily fantasy sport websites which allowed individual to purchase players' statistics and create their own sports team and then win money based on the success of that team challenged a New York assertion that their sites violated New York laws against gambling. FanDuel and Draftkings claimed that their equal protection rights had been violated, but a New York state court rejected that argument because the two could not produce evidence that other similarly situated gaming sites had been treated differently (*New York v. FanDuel*, 2015). In 2016, the two sides reached an agreement allowing the sites to continue operating.

Intermediate Scrutiny

Quasi-suspect classifications are subject to intermediate scrutiny. Thus far the Supreme Court has consistently found *gender and illegitimacy to be quasi-suspect categories*, but gender is the most relevant quasi-suspect classification for the sport and recreation manager. The Supreme Court created this middle tier of testing in a series of gender discrimination lawsuits in the 1970s. Prior to the 1970s, gender discrimination had been traditionally examined under the mere rationality test and government discrimination against women frequently survived this test. For example, in *State v. Hunter* (1956), a woman convicted of wrestling without a state license appealed her conviction on the grounds that the state law violated her equal protection rights: the state at that time only issued wrestling licenses to men. She lost her case because the Oregon Supreme Court concluded that the classification was rationally related to the state's legitimate interest in protecting public health, morals, and participants' safety.

As the Women's Rights movement of the twentieth century progressed, however, the Supreme Court made it more difficult for local, state and Federal governments to utilize gender classifications. In *Craig v. Boren* (1976), the majority of the Court held that to survive equal protection scrutiny, *a gender classification must be substantially related to an important governmental objective.*

Gender Classifications and Contact Sport. Female athletes have used the Equal Protection Clause to gain the right to try out for contact sports teams such as football in *Force by Force v. Pierce City R-VI School District*, (1983), and wrestling in *Beattie v. Line Mountain School District*, (2014). (The *Beattie* case is available on the accompanying computer disc.) In each case the courts recognized that other gender discrimination legislation like Title IX would not help the athlete. The enforcement regulations for Title IX, for example, exempt contact sport from the law, and the Equal Protection Clause can be used to close that exemption. For more information see Section 7.11, *Gender Equity: Opportunities to Participate*. In *Force* and *Beattie*, the defendant school districts had argued primarily that the state had an important interest in protecting the female athletes from the dangers of co-educational contact sport, in protecting the psyche of the boys' they would compete against, and in maintaining a smoothly run sports program.

The courts rejected the arguments that the state had an important interest in the psyche of only the male athletes and in logistical ease (like needing a separate changing space for the female athlete). Although the courts agreed that the safety of all students was an important state interest, they did not agree that a gender classification was substantially related to that important interest because that classification erroneously presumed that all boys were bigger and stronger than all girls and thus a gender classification failed to have a substantial relationship with the important governmental interest in children's safety. The Equal Protection Clause does not, however, require that a school create a separate female team in a contact sport, only that the school allow females to try out for sports on the contact sport team (*Mansourian v. Board of Regents*, 2011).

In the converse, schoolboys who have filed equal protection lawsuits to gain access to traditionally female sports like field hockey have been much less successful. For example in 1991 in Rhode Island, the federal district court concluded that the state athletic association could prohibit a boy from playing on the girls' field hockey team because the state had an important governmental interest in redressing past discrimination against girls in sport. The court noted that excluding boys from playing on girls' teams was substantially related to that interest. (*Kleczek v. Rhode Island Interscholastic League*).

Gender Discrimination and Scheduling Seasons. In 2006, the Sixth Circuit Court of Appeals ended a battle between the Communities for Equity and the Michigan High School Athletic Association. MHSAA had, for years, scheduled many girls' sports in non-traditional seasons. For example, although the game of basketball is usually a winter sport, in Michigan, high school girls played in the fall season. Communities for Equity believed this distinction to be a violation of equal protection. MHSAA argued that scheduling girls' sport in nontraditional seasons allowed more girls and boys to play sports and also allowed both boys and girls access to the best facilities and practice and competition times without having internal fights for court or game times. The Sixth Court of Appeals affirmed the decision that the distinction was a violation of the Equal Protection Clause because the state failed to establish that the gender classification was substantially related to that important interest. The court particularly condemned the MHSAA for only scheduling girls' teams in the off-seasons, noting that if scheduling was really so challenging and if non-traditional scheduling was really so helpful, the burden could have been borne equally by boys' and girls' teams (2006). Similarly in 2012, the Seventh Circuit Court of Appeals overturned a district court's dismissal of an equal protection lawsuit against an Indiana school district. The plaintiffs complained that about 95% of boys' high school basketball games were scheduled for primetime nights whereas only 53% of the girls' games were, and they argued that this was a violation of the girls' equal protection rights. The Appellate Court agreed (*Parker v. Franklin County Community School Corp.*, 2012). (This case is available on the accompanying computer disc).

Transgender athletes. To date, no published decision regarding transgender athletes' attempts to play on the gendered team of their choice has been decided on equal protection grounds. However, given the increased visibility of these athletes, such a decision seems inevitable. When it occurs, the likely test will be intermediate scrutiny because at least one court has concluded that discrimination against transgendered people is sex discrimination (*Glenn v. Brumby*, 2011).

Strict Scrutiny

Fundamental Rights Deprivation. Strict scrutiny is triggered when a state deprives a person of his or her fundamental rights. These fundamental rights include those articulated in the Constitution—freedom of speech and the right to assemble peaceably for example—and also some rights not articulated. The right to vote, to travel, and to privacy have all been established as fundamental rights. Education has been deemed a non-fundamental right and participating in sport has simply been deemed a privilege; therefore, for sport and recreation managers, fundamental rights deprivations are relatively uncommon.

Fundamental rights deprivations, however, can occur. For example, a Texas school district had a rule prohibiting married students from participating in extracurricular activities including sport. The district argued that the rule was intended to help a married student succeed in his or her education and marriage as well as to discourage early marriage between students. The court concluded that because the right to marry is fundamental, the district needed to prove that the *classification was necessary to achieve a compelling governmental interest.* The court found the district failed to do this because the district had no evidence that banning married students from extracurricular activities helped married students in any aspect of their lives (*Bell v. Lone Oak Independent School District*, 1974).

Suspect Classifications. Suspect classifications can also trigger strict scrutiny. The Supreme Court has concluded that race, national origin, and alienage are suspect classifications. To survive an equal protection challenge, the state must prove that *the suspect classification is necessary to achieve a compelling governmental interest, and the classification must be the least restrictive means of achieving that interest.* This test is very stringent and very few laws involving suspect classifications have survived the test and been deemed constitutional. For example, in 1999 a Washington state court concluded that the transfer rules were discriminatory because they had a disparate impact on foreign students and the rules could not survive strict scrutiny (*Fusato v. Washington Interscholastic Activities Association*). (This case is included on the accompanying computer disc.)

Racial discrimination in sport and recreation, however, has long been an issue, and allegations of racial discrimination are still made. In 2011 in *Boyd v. Feather River Community College District*, African-American members of the football team claimed that they had been cut from the team because of their race after a season of suffering verbal and physical abuse that was racially motivated. A federal district court rejected the defendants' request to dismiss the case, concluding that sufficient evidence of racial discrimination existed. In 2013, a white female collegiate basketball player who had lost her scholarship claimed that she had been victim of racial discrimination, but the court found no evidence supporting her claim (*Heike v. Guevara*).

Shifting Tests

The three-tier level of testing as described above evolved from the traditional two-tier level of testing (mere rationality and strict scrutiny). As a practical matter, courts, including the U.S. Supreme Court, have tinkered with the levels of tests in their analyses. For example, in 1996 in *U.S. v. Virginia*, the Virginia Military Institute (VMI) attempted to justify its male-only admission policy against the federal government's claims that the policy violated the Equal Protection Clause. Writing for a six-person majority, Justice Ruth Bader Ginsberg seemed to rely on the intermediate level of scrutiny, but added that a state actor must have an "exceedingly persuasive" justification for gender segregation, adding that gender classifications would trigger "skeptical scrutiny." The majority found that the state had failed to provide that exceedingly persuasive justification. In his concurrence Chief Justice William Rehnquist supported in the decision of the majority but did so while clearly articulating the traditional intermediate scrutiny test. Justice Anton Scalia, in his dissent, argued adamantly against Justice Ginsberg's ratcheted-up test for gender classifications.

Relying on the "exceedingly persuasive" language, a federal court allowed an equal protection challenge to a community golf tournament which was limited to men only to go to trial. A woman had been excluded based on her gender, and the community club justified this because they offered the occasional tournament for women only. The court suggested that tradition was not an exceedingly persuasive justification for gender discrimination (*Joyce v. Town of Dennis*, 2010). As a result, the sport and recreation manager should be aware that the tests surrounding equal protection have evolved over time and are likely to continue to do so.

Over and Under-Inclusive

Perhaps the most common reason that courts reject classifications as violating equal protection is because the classification includes more people than it should or, both alternatively and sometimes simultaneously, the classification does not include all the people it should in order to meet the objective of the law. For example in *Sullivan v. University Interscholastic League* (1981), the state athletic association argued that their rule making transfer students ineligible to compete in varsity basketball and football was rationally related to their legitimate interest in discouraging the recruiting of athletes, a practice which undermined the educational experience of a student. The Texas Supreme Court agreed that the state did have a legitimate interest in emphasizing education over athletics and in discouraging the recruitment of athletes. The court, however, thought the rule was not rationally related to the interest because it was over-inclusive; the rule applied to all transfer students, even those who transferred for reasons completely unrelated to sport. (This case is included on the accompanying computer disc.)

Another example was that of a student-athlete who challenged a rule preventing married students from participating in high school sports. The state argued that the rule existed to promote a wholesome high school atmosphere, to discourage married students from discussing sex in the locker room, to reduce drop-out rates, and to encourage married students to focus on their education and marriage. In ruling for the student, the court concluded that the rule was over-inclusive: some married students of good character would not detract from a wholesome atmosphere. This student had played while the case was pending, and his grades improved, he held a part-time job, and he remained married. The court concluded the rule was also under-inclusive because it did not bar the participation of students who engaged in pre-marital sex nor those students who were of poor character (*Indiana High School Athletics Ass'n v. Raike*, 1975).

SIGNIFICANT CASE

Hayden v. Greensburg Community School Corporation is an example of an unusual gender discrimination case but the arguments follow the traditional intermediate scrutiny test.

HAYDEN V. GREENSBURG COMMUNITY SCHOOL CORPORATION
United States Court of Appeals for the Seventh Circuit
743 F.3rd 569 (7th Cir., 2014)

JUDGES: Before EASTERBROOK, MANION, and ROVNER, Circuit Judges. MANION, Circuit Judge, concurring in part and dissenting in part.

Rovner, *Circuit Judge*. On behalf of their son, A.H., Patrick and Melissa Hayden challenge a policy which requires boys playing interscholastic basketball at the public high school in Greensburg, Indiana, to keep their hair cut short. The Haydens make two principal arguments: (1) the hair-length policy arbitrarily intrudes upon their son's liberty interest in choosing his own hair length, and thus violates his right to substantive due process, and (2) because the policy applies only to boys and not girls wishing to play basketball, the policy constitutes sex discrimination. The district court rejected both claims and granted judgment to the defendants. *Hayden ex rel. A.H. v. Greensburg Cmty. Sch. Corp.*, 2013 U.S. Dist. LEXIS 34494, 2013 WL 1001947 (S.D. Ind. Mar. 13, 2013). We reverse in part. Because the hair-length policy on its face treats boys and girls differently, and because the record tells us nothing about any comparable grooming standards applied to girls playing basketball, the evidence entitles the Haydens to judgment on their sex discrimination claims.

A.H.'s home is in Greensburg, Indiana, a city of approximately 11,500 people in the south-central region of the state. The Greensburg Community School Corporation comprises an elementary school, a junior high school, and a senior high school, which combined have an enrollment of 2,290 students.

The board of trustees that establishes policy for the school district has adopted a provision—Policy 5511, entitled "Dress and Grooming"—which in relevant part directs the district superintendent to "establish such grooming guidelines as are necessary to promote discipline, maintain order, secure the safety of students, and provide a healthy environment conducive to academic purposes"; these guidelines are to include dress standards for members of school athletic teams. The district guidelines implementing this directive leave it to the individual principal of each school, in consultation with staff, parents, and/or students, to develop and enforce appropriate dress and grooming policies.

* * *

Stacy Meyer, the head varsity basketball coach at Greensburg High School, has established an unwritten hair-length policy which applies to the boys basketball teams. That policy provides that each player's hair must be cut above the ears, eyebrows, and collar. Coach Meyer has explained the policy as one that promotes team unity and projects a "clean cut" image. The boys baseball teams have a similar hair-length policy, whereas the boys track and football teams do not. No girls athletic team is subject to a hair-length policy. * * *

A.H. is seventeen years old and currently is a junior in high school. He wishes to play basketball, but he also wishes to wear his hair longer than the hair-length policy permits.

* * *

After A.H. refused to cut his hair and was removed from the boys junior high school basketball team in the Fall of 2010, his parents sued the Greensburg Community School Corporation, its governing school board, and various district and school officials, alleging that the hair-length policy violated multiple state and federal constitutional and statutory provisions.

* * *

Equal Protection

A more meritorious contention is that the hair-length policy deprives A.H. of equal protection because it discriminates against him on the basis of his sex. Because A.H. is a boy, he must cut his hair in order to play interscholastic basketball at Greensburg; were he a girl, he would not be subject to that requirement, as the girls team has no hair-length policy. (All school athletes apparently are subject to the ban on hair styles that pose health, sanitation, or vision problems, display initials, numbers, or insignia, incorporate hair coloring, or are otherwise extreme in some way, but the hair-length policy is distinct from these restrictions.) The equal protection clause of the Fourteenth Amendment protects individuals against intentional, arbitrary discrimination by government officials. *Village of Willowbrook v. Olech*, 528 U.S. 562, 564, 120 S. Ct. 1073, 1074-75, 145 L. Ed. 2d 1060 (2000) (per curiam); *see also, e.g., Nabozny v. Podlesny*, 92 F.3d 446, 453-56 (7th Cir. 1996) (applying equal protection clause in school context). Gender is a quasi-suspect class that triggers intermediate scrutiny in the equal protection context; the justification for a gender-based classification thus must be exceedingly persuasive. *United States v. Virginia*, 518 U.S. 515, 533, 116 S. Ct. 2264, 2275, 135 L. Ed. 2d 735 (1996).

* * *

The parties have litigated the hair-length policy in isolation rather than as an aspect of any broader grooming standards applied to boys and girls basketball teams. We were told, when we raised the subject at oral argument, that male and female athletes alike are subject to grooming standards; and indeed the parties jointly stipulated below for purposes of the preliminary injunction hearing that whereas only the boys basketball and baseball teams have hair-length policies, the other school athletic teams do have grooming policies. But the content of those grooming policies has never been established, and the fact that there are grooming standards for both girls and boys teams was not even mentioned in the stipulated facts submitted to the district court for purposes of resolving the case. The stipulated facts reveal only that there is a hair-length policy for the boys basketball team but for not for the girls basketball team (or, for that matter, any other girls team). As such, the stipulated facts indicate that a boy wishing to play basketball at Greensburg is subject to a requirement, impinging upon a recognized liberty interest, that a girl is not.

The defendants argue that this is not sex-based discrimination because the hair-length policy applies to only two of the boys athletic teams. Boys wishing to compete on the football or track teams, for example, would be free to do so without having to keep their hair cut short. As the defendants apparently see it, the fact that the policy does not apply to all boys teams demonstrates that the policy does not categorically discriminate against boys. The district court agreed.

The argument is untenable. That the policy is not universally applied to boys does not negate the fact that it is based on sex: Again, boys wishing to play basketball (or baseball) are subject to a requirement that girls are not. The fact that other boys playing other sports are not burdened by that requirement is neither here nor there. The equal protection clause protects the individual rather than the group, and the individual plaintiff in this case wishes to play basketball. (citations omitted) He is subject to a burden that a girl in the same position is not.

Equally problematic is the school district's alternative contention that the sex discrimination claim fails for lack of proof that any such discrimination is intentional. *See, e.g., Nabozny*, 92 F.3d at 454. This is a case of disparate treatment rather than disparate impact; the hair-length policy, being applicable only to boys teams, draws an explicit gender line. The intent to treat boys differently from girls is therefore evident from the one-sided nature of the policy. (citations omitted)

* * *

The Haydens plainly have made out a prima facie case of discrimination. The hair-length policy applies only to male athletes, and there is no facially apparent reason why that should be so. Girls playing interscholastic basketball have the same need as boys do to keep their hair out of their eyes, to subordinate individuality to team unity, and to project a positive image. Why, then, must only members of the boys team wear their hair short? Given the obvious disparity, the policy itself gives rise to an inference of discrimination. To defeat that inference, it was up to the school district to show that the hair-length policy is just one component of a comprehensive grooming code that imposes comparable although not identical demands on both male and female athletes. In the face of such evidence, the parties might cross swords on such questions as whether community norms dictate separate grooming standards, whether the burdens imposed by those standards on boys and girls are indeed comparable, whether the respective grooming standards are enforced equally, and, irrespective of comparability and even-handedness, whether a sex-specific grooming standard like the hair-length policy is compatible with *Price Waterhouse.* But absent any evidence as to the content of the grooming standards that are applicable to female athletes, we are not prepared to simply assume that an otherwise facially-discriminatory rule is justified.

The dissent looks to the parties' stipulation that there are grooming standards for all teams, coupled with the hair-style provision of the athletic code of conduct as proof that male and female athletes are in fact subject to comparable grooming standards. Yet, the mere stipulation that there *are* grooming standards applicable to girls as well as boys teams does not establish the content of those standards. Nor does the hair-style provision fill that void. That provision proscribes hair styles "which create problems of health and sanitation, obstruct vision, or call undue attention to the athlete"; and it goes on to cite a variety of specific methods of wearing or styling one's hair that are forbidden to all athletes, including hair coloring, Mohawks, and cuts that display insignia, numbers, initials, or the like. If this is the sum total of the broader grooming code applicable to both male and female athletes referenced by the parties' stipulation, the parties themselves have not identified it as such in their supplemental submissions to the court. Nor is it obvious to us that it is, as this provision merely declares certain extreme hairstyles to be off-limits (and no one is suggesting that A.H.'s preferred hairstyle would run afoul of these prohibitions). Beyond that, the policy delegates to each varsity head coach the responsibility to determine "acceptable" hair lengths for his or her respective sport, which does not explain why short hair may be thought necessary for boys who play basketball but not girls.

The fact is, beyond the outer limits articulated in the hairstyle provision, we know virtually nothing about the grooming standards to which female athletes at Greensburg are subject. May they wear earrings or other types of jewelry, for example, and if so, what if any restrictions are imposed on these items? If the goal for all interscholastic athletes is a neat, clean-cut appearance, which is one of the reasons that Coach Meyer gave for the hair-length policy, are girls required to maintain their hair to particular standards? Beyond the limits on mohawks and other extreme hairdos set forth in the hair-style provision, are there any limits on the manner in which girls may style their hair? Although girls can evidently wear their hair as *long* as they wish, could a female basketball player wear her hair in an extremely short "buzz-cut," which might literally qualify as "clean cut" but perhaps not in the sense that Coach Meyer means it and perhaps not in synch with local norms? Surely girls with longer hair must do something to keep their hair out of their eyes while playing basketball, as the dissent points out. But, at the risk of stating the obvious, boys with longer hair could do the same. In fact, male athletes use head and hair bands to do this very thing, as anyone who has watched professional basketball or football games recently can confirm.

* * *

What we have before us is a policy that draws an explicit distinction between male and female athletes and imposes a burden on male athletes alone, and a limited record that does not supply a legally sufficient justification for the sex-based classification. We know that there is a rule prohibiting both male and female athletes at the junior high school from wearing hairstyles that might in some way interfere with their vision or pose some other type of problem; we have assumed that the same rule applies to high school athletes of both sexes. But there is no suggestion that A.H. wishes to wear his hair in an extreme fashion, let alone that hair worn over a boy's ears or collar or eyebrows is invariably problematic. The record also tells us that Coach Meyer offered two reasons for the policy: promoting team unity, by having team members wear their hair in a uniform length, and projecting a "clean-cut" image. We may assume that the hair-length rule is consistent with these reasons and that both reasons are legitimate grounds for grooming standards that apply to interscholastic athletes. What is noteworthy, for purposes of the Haydens' equal protection claim, is that the interests in team unity and projecting a favorable image are not unique to male interscholastic teams, and yet, so far as the record reveals, those interests are articulated and pursued solely with respect to members of the boys basketball team (and baseball team, assuming that the hair-length rule is applied to that team for the same reasons). If there is an argument that the goals of team unity and a "clean-cut" image are served through comparable, albeit different, grooming standards for female athletes, it has neither been advanced nor supported in this case. And the fact that other boys teams are not subject to a hair-length policy casts doubt on whether such an argument could be made.

The parties consented to the entry of final judgment on the record as it stands, and that record entitles the Haydens to judgment on the equal protection claim. The policy imposes a burden on only male athletes. There has been no showing that it does so pursuant to grooming standards for both male and female athletes that, although not identical, are comparable. Finally, no rational, let alone exceedingly persuasive, justification has been articulated for restricting the hair length of male athletes alone.

* * *

On the record presented to us, the Haydens have established that the hair-length policy applicable to boys wishing to play basketball impermissibly discriminates based on sex.

Manion, *Circuit Judge*, concurring in part and dissenting in part.

Having ruled against A.H.'s primary argument, the court decides this case on equal protection arguments that A.H. did not make, rooted in authority he did not cite. However, the court does not actually tell us why the policies here are not comparable under the correct standard. Rather, the court decides that the school loses by default because the record is missing *some* of the grooming provisions that are applicable to female athletes. But there is enough in the record to compare the grooming policies applicable to male and female athletes, and if anything that is missing were included, it would only make the burden of the grooming policy applicable to male athletes even more clearly balanced out by the burden on female athletes. Although I agree with the court's general summary of the law of equal protection, I write separately because the record does not establish any violation of the Equal Protection clause or Title IX.

Imitating a policy established by the celebrated Hoosier and legendary basketball coach John Wooden, Coach Meyer insists that the boys on the Greensburg basketball team cut their hair shorter than A.H. prefers cut his hair. Meyer hopes that this policy will promote team unity and at the same time project a clean-cut image, but A.H. doesn't "feel like himself" with a shorter haircut. The policy of the Greensburg school board allows the coach of each team to determine any limitation on his players' hair length, and according to the parties' stipulation, Meyer and the baseball coach are the only coaches at Greensburg who impose haircut requirements. A.H. refuses to be compared to the male athletes in other sports who do not have to cut their hair. Rather, because the members of the Greensburg girls basketball team do not have to cut their hair, A.H. claims he is being discriminated against because of his sex.

As the court recognizes, sex-based equal protection analysis is much more nuanced than a simple "but for" test. Discrimination based on sex violates the Equal Protection clause unless the state has an exceedingly persuasive justification. *United States v. Virginia*, 518 U.S. 515, 533, 116 S. Ct. 2264, 135 L. Ed. 2d 735 (1996). However, maintaining different grooming standards for men and women is not usually discrimination.

* * *

Even the sports that overlap have differences: a girls' basketball is smaller than a boys' basketball and a softball is bigger than a baseball—and despite the similarities of the sports, girls softball teams often wear shorts while boys baseball teams must always wear baseball pants.

With this context, the grooming decisions reveal a common thread: as long as a grooming or appearance policy applies to both men and women, the fact that it has different provisions based on different social norms or community standards for men and women (or based on different athletic traditions) is acceptable. Distinction is not discrimination. The court and I agree that the rule permits a policy that is different for men and women so long as it is comparable.

* * *

On the record we have, the grooming policies for boys and girls, as a whole, are comparable. Requiring men, but not women, to keep their hair at a certain length has never been held to be unequally burdensome. Further, there is no evidence (or argument) that the policies fail for other reasons; for example, there is no evidence that the distinctions are ungrounded in social norms or community standards or are arbitrary, nor is there evidence that the policies are not evenhandedly applied. Absent such proof, the otherwise comparable policies do not amount to sex discrimination.

* * *

The stipulations in this case indicate that there is an athletic "hair style" policy that applies to both male and female athletes, with a "cut" requirement that applies only to (some) male athletes (and there may be other provisions applicable to female athletes, but we assume there are not to A.H.'s favor). Even with *no* additional grooming provisions applicable to female athletes, and therefore *no* additional burdens on females athletes (besides the athletic code's hairstyle provision), the policies are comparably burdensome. *Knott*, 527 F.2d at 1250 (holding that a policy was not discrimination where "[n]o similar regulation restricts the hair length or hair style of female employees, but both male and female employees must conform to certain standards of dress"—exactly the scenario stipulated to here). * * * The policies here are not sex-based discrimination.

met.

* * *

Accordingly, I would affirm the district court. I concur in part but respectfully dissent in part and in the judgment.

CASES ON THE SUPPLEMENTAL CD

B.A. v. Mississippi High School Activities Association, 983 F. Supp. 2d 857 (N.D. Miss., 2013). Consider the case from the players' perspective. How does this rule harm them?

Beattie v. Line Mountain School District, 992 F.Supp.2d 384 (M.D. Pa., 2014). The reader should note the state's justifications for gender discrimination and how the court characterized them.

Fusato v. Washington Interscholastic Activities Association, 970 P.2d 774 (Washington Ct. of App., 1999). Explore why the court rejects the state's argument that the test should rationally related and not strict scrutiny.

Parker v. Franklin County Community School Corp., 2012 U.S. App. LEXIS 1783 (7th Cir. Jan. 31, 2012). Examine the court's discussion of the substantive experiences of game times in light of the equal protection claims.

Sullivan v. University Interscholastic League, 616 S.W.2d 170 (Tex. 1981). Texas recognized the dangers of high schools recruiting strong athletes, but the state's answer is an example of how a statute can be overbroad.

QUESTIONS YOU SHOULD BE ABLE TO ANSWER

1. Imagine you wanted to start a youth league based on the religious identification of the athletes. What would you need to do to make sure that your league was not in violation of the Equal Protection Clause?

2. What are the three different standards of review for classifications under the Equal Protection Clause? Explain which standard should be used for which classification.

3. What does it mean for a statute to be void for being over- or under-inclusive? How can a statue be both over and under-inclusive simultaneously?

4. In *Hayden v. Greensburg Community School Corporation*, why did the dissent disagree with the majority opinion? Who do you think had a more compelling argument?

5. Some scholars argue that the middle level of scrutiny for gender classifications should be collapsed into the strict scrutiny category. Explain why you think this is a logical or illogical argument.

REFERENCES

Cases

Adams v. Baker, 919 F. Supp. 1496 (D. Kan. 1996).
B.A. v. Mississippi High School Activities Association, 983 F. Supp. 2d 857 (N.D. Miss., 2013).
Baldwin v. Fish & Game Commission of Montana, 436 U.S. 371 (1978).
Bell v. Lone Oak Independent School District, 507 S.W.2d 636 (Tex. Civ. App. 1974).
B.C. v. Cumberland Regional School District, 531 A.2d 1059 (N.J. Super. 1987).
Bolling v. Sharpe 347 U.S. 497 (1954).
Boyd v. Feather River Community College District, No. 2:11-CV-0231 JAM-EFB, 2011 U.S. Dist. LEXIS 12168 (E.D. Cal. Oct. 20, 2011).
Communities for Equity v. Michigan High School Athletic Ass'n, 178 F. Supp. 2d 805 (W.D. Mich. 2001), *aff'd*, 459 F. 3d 676 (6th Cir. 2006).
Craig v. Boren, 429 U.S. 190 (1976).
Davis v. Massachusetts Interscholastic Athletic Association No., 94-2887, 1995 Mass. Super. LEXIS 791, (Super., Jan. 18, 1995).
Dubinsky v. St. Louis Blues Hockey Club, 229 S.W.3d 126 (Mo. Ct. App. 2007).
Force by Force v. Pierce City R-VI School District, 570 F. Supp. 2010 (S.W. Mo. 1983).
Hadley v. Rush Henrietta Center School District, No. 05-CV-6331T, 2007 U.S. Dist LEXIS 30586 (W.D. N.Y., April 25, 2007).
Heike v. Guevara, No. 10-1728, 2013 U.S. App. LEXIS 5420 (6th Cir. March 18, 2013).
Glenn v. Brumby, 663 F.3d. 1312 (11th Cir., 2011).
Indiana High School Athletics Ass'n v. Raike, 329 N.E.2d 66 (Ind. Ct. App. 1975).

Indiana High School Athletic Ass'n v. Schafer, 598 N.E.2d 540 (Ind. App. 1992).
Jones v. West Virginia State Board of Education, 622 S.E.2nd 289 (W.Va., 2005).
Joyce v. Town of Dennis, 705 F. Supp. 2d 74 (D. Mass. 2010).
Kleczek v. Rhode Island Interscholastic League, 768 F.Supp. 951 (D. R.I., 1991)
Mansourian v. Board of Regents, NO. 2:03-cv-2591 FCD EFB, 2011 U.S. Dist. LEXIS 85396 (E.D. Cal. Aug. 3, 2011).
McGee v. Virginia High School League, 801 F. Supp. 2d 526 (W.D. Va. 2011).
New York v. FanDuel, 453056/15, 2015 N.Y. Misc. LEXIS 4521 (N.Y. App. Div. December 11, 2015).
Palmer v. Thompson, 403 U.S. 217 (1971).
Parker v. Franklin County Community School Corp., No. 10-3595, 2012 U.S. App. LEXIS 1783 (7th Cir. Jan. 31, 2012).
Hageman v. Goshen County School District, 256 P.3d 487 (Wyo. 2011).
Schutz v. Thorne, 415 F.3rd 1128 (10th Cir., 2005).
Sisson v. Virginia High School League, No.7:10CV00530, 2010 U.S. Dist. LEXIS 132264 (W.D. Va. Dec. 14, 2010).
State v. Hunter, 300 P.2d 455 (Ore. 1956).
St. Augustine High School v. Louisiana High School Athletic Ass'n., 270 F. Supp. 767 (E.D. La. 1967), *aff 'd.*, 396 F.2d 224 (5th Cir. 1968).
Sullivan v. University Interscholastic League, 616 S.W.2d 170 (Tex. 1981).
United States v. Virginia, 518 U.S. 515 (1996).

Publications

Buzuvis, Erin E. (2011). Transgender Student-Athletes and Sex-Segregated Sport: Developing Policies of Inclusion for Intercollegiate and Interscholastic Athletes. *Seton Hall Journal of Sports and Entertainment Law 21*, 1-59.

Engdahl, Sylvia. (2009). *Amendment XIV: Equal Protection.* Farmington Hills, MI: Greenhaven Press/Gale Cengage Learning.

Fields, Sarah K. (2005). *Female Gladiators: Gender, Law, and Contact Sport in America.* Champaign, IL: University of Illinois Press.

Karst, Kenneth (1977). Equal Citizenship under the Fourteenth Amendment. *Harvard Law Review 91*, 1–69.

Legislation

U.S. Constitution, Amend. 5.
U.S. Constitution, Amend. 14 § 1.
42 U.S.C. § 1983.

6.15 SEARCH AND SEIZURE/RIGHT TO PRIVACY

Margaret E. Ciccolella | University of the Pacific

The right of privacy is fundamental to American heritage and to rights guaranteed by the United States Constitution. While the word "privacy" is not found in the United States Constitution, privacy interests are found in the "penumbra" of rights guaranteed throughout the Constitution, e.g., the First, Fourth, Fifth, and Fourteenth Amendments safeguard privacy interests relevant to freedom of expression, substantive due process, equal protection, and search and seizure of one's person and/or personal effects.

The interpretation of the nature and extent of privacy protections have been contested within the context of education and its athletic programs. First Amendment protections dealing with personal conduct and expression have been challenged by considering the authority of the schools to regulate hair length (*Menora v. Illinois High School Assn.*, 1982; *Tinker v. Des Moines Indep. Comm. School District*, 1969), dress (*Dunham v. Pulsifer*, 1970; *Zeller v. Donegal School District*, 1975), on- and off-court/field behavior (*Bunger v. Iowa H.S. Athletic Assn.*, 1972) and marriage/parenthood of student-athletes (*Davis v. Meek*, 1972; *Estay v. LaFourche Parish School Board*, 1969; *Indiana High School Athletic Assn. v. Raike*, 1975; *Perry v. Granada Municipal School District*, 1969). Confidentiality of educational records protected by the Family Educational Rights and Privacy Act, also known as the "Buckley Amendment," has been challenged (*Marmo v. NYC Board of Education*, 1968). The Freedom of Information Act, often used as a basis on which to challenge confidentiality, has been challenged itself (*Arkansas Gazette Co. v. Southern State College*, 1981). Clearly, privacy exceeds Fourth Amendment protections and is addressed throughout the Constitution and in federal statutory law.

However, it is the Fourth Amendment of the United States Constitution that is considered the "heart" of privacy protection and is therefore central to any discussion of the issue. It is the primary purpose of this chapter to focus upon privacy interests of student-athletes as they relate specifically to the Fourth Amendment of the United States Constitution. Perhaps no issue illustrates this better than case law on urinalysis-drug-testing of high school and intercollegiate athletes.

FUNDAMENTAL CONCEPTS

In addition to protecting individuals from illegal search and seizure, the United States Constitution, e.g., the First, Fourth, Fifth, and Fourteenth Amendments also safeguards privacy interests relevant to freedom of expression.

The Fourth Amendment

The Fourth Amendment to the United States Constitution states:

> The right of the people to be secure in their persons, houses, papers, and effects against unreasonable searches and seizures, shall not be violated, and no Warrant shall issue, but upon probable cause, supported by Oath or affirmation, and particularly describing the place to be searched, and the persons or things to be seized. (United States Constitution, Amendment IV)

The Fourth Amendment, made applicable to the states by virtue of the Fourteenth Amendment, guarantees that individuals are protected against "***arbitrary invasions by governmental officials***" (*O'Connor v. Ortega*, 1987). Note that only unreasonable searches and seizures are prohibited. Also, in the context of conduct by law enforcement, warrants based upon probable cause are required.

Once a search or seizure is characterized as "unreasonable," it is unconstitutional and therefore is prohibited. In the context of athletics, searches of lockers, personal items, or a person become potentially serious invasions of privacy by the language of the Fourth Amendment. Valid warrants based upon probable cause are rarely the situation in athletics because school searches are not typically under the authority of law enforcement. More commonly, in the context of public school-aged and college-aged athletes, searches and seizures occur under the authority of school officials.

It is important to distinguish constitutionally permissible from constitutionally prohibited conduct as determined by the Fourth Amendment. Fourth Amendment analysis of search and seizure privacy interests must consider three basic issues. First, does the conduct represent state (governmental) action? Second, is the conduct a search? Third, is the search reasonable?

Is There State Action?

The Fourth Amendment protects individuals from invasions of privacy by the government. It does not protect against the conduct of private individuals or organizations. The NCAA is not subject to Fourth Amendment scrutiny because the regulatory functions of the NCAA are considered to represent private and not state action (*Arlosoroff v. NCAA*, 1984). Action or conduct by state, local, or federal officials is state or governmental action for purposes of the Fourth Amendment. For example, public but not private schools are subject to Fourth Amendment standards of review.

Is the Conduct a Search?

Under Fourth Amendment analysis, a search occurs when an expectation of privacy which society is prepared to consider reasonable is infringed (*Schaill v. Tippecanoe County School Corp.*, 1989). The United States Supreme Court has held that the collection and testing of urine constitute a search under the Fourth Amendment (*Skinner v. Railway Labor Executives' Assn.*, 1989). This is especially relevant to athletes subject to mandatory urine testing. In *Skinner*, the Court stated:

> It is not disputed, however, that chemical analysis of urine, like that of blood, can reveal a host of private medical facts about an employee, including whether he or she is epileptic, pregnant, or diabetic. Nor can it be disputed that the process of collecting the sample to be tested, which may in some cases involve visual or aural monitoring of the act of urination, itself implicates privacy interests (*Skinner v. Railway Labor Executives' Assn.*, 1989).

There remains a legitimate expectation of privacy for both the college and public school student that a student's urine is not subject to public scrutiny. The courts continue to hold that the mandatory urine testing of student-athletes constitutes a search and seizure (*University of Colorado v. Derdeyn*, 1993; *O'Halloran v. University of Washington*, 1988; *Vernonia v. Acton*, 1995). This does not mean that mandatory urine testing of students will result in a violation of the Fourth Amendment. In *O'Halloran v. University of Washington* (1988), the constitutionality of drug testing college athletes was upheld even though it was concluded that, "the NCAA's urine testing program is a search for Fourth Amendment analysis." In 1995, the Supreme Court held that mandatory, random urinalysis testing of public school athletes represented a reasonable search under a Fourth Amendment analysis (*Vernonia v. Acton*, 1995). Most recently, the Supreme Court extended this holding to public school students who participate in competitive extramural activities (*Board of Education v. Earls*, 2002).

It is clear that urine testing of student-athletes represents a search. The more crucial question is whether the search is reasonable. Reasonableness, by considering all of the events or the "totality of the circumstances" surrounding a search, will ultimately determine whether a Fourth Amendment violation has occurred.

Is the Conduct a Reasonable Search?

The Fourth Amendment prohibits only unreasonable searches. However, the test of reasonableness under the Fourth Amendment is not capable of precise definition or mechanical application. The Supreme Court consistently asserts what is "reasonable" depends on the context within which a search takes place (*National Treasury Employees Union v. Von Raab*, 1989; *O'Connor v. Ortega*, 1987; *Skinner v. Railway Labor Executives' Assn.*,

1989). In *New Jersey v. T.L.O.* (1985), the proper standard for assessing the legality of a school search by school officials was determined. In this case, school officials searched a student's purse for drugs. *The Supreme Court held that reasonableness of a search involved a two-fold inquiry.* First, *was the search justified at its inception*, e.g., was there reasonable suspicion for the search? Second, *was the search reasonable in its scope*, e.g., were the measures adopted reasonably related to the objectives of the search and not excessively intrusive in light of the age and sex of the student and the nature of the infraction?

In light of the *T.L.O.* holding and in the context of warrantless school searches, it is common for a court to determine reasonableness by a) considering the existence of reasonable suspicion for the search, and b) balancing the degree of intrusion on individual privacy interests against governmental interests in conducting the search.

Reasonable Suspicion. Reasonable suspicion has been defined as "the existence of reasonable circumstances, reports, information, or reasonable direct observation" leading to the belief that illegal drugs have been used (*Horsemen's Benevolent & Protective Assn. v. State Racing Commission*, 1989). The University of Colorado (CU) amended its suspicionless urine testing program by including a rapid eye examination (REE). REE became the basis for a subsequent mandatory urinalysis on the basis that a positive REE test provided reasonable suspicion of drug use. Other physical and behavioral characteristics were also used as a basis for reasonable suspicion including excessive aggressiveness and poor health habits (*University of Colorado v. Derdeyn*, 1993).

New Jersey v. T.L.O. (1985) required individualized suspicion, but because of the facts of that case, the Court was not required to consider whether circumstances could ever exist that could negate the need for individualized suspicion. *Vernonia v. Acton* (1995) may well have provided the circumstances missing in *New Jersey*. See *Significant Case*, below.

Balancing Test. In addition to considering the existence of reasonable suspicion, the courts typically balance the degree of the intrusion on an individual's privacy interests against the government's interests in testing.

Privacy Interests of the Student-Athlete

Privacy interests of athletes have included the following arguments (*Hill v. NCAA*, 1994):

1. There are few activities in our society more personal or private than the passing of urine. Therefore, the visual or aural monitoring of urination implicates privacy interests.
2. Monitored urine collection is embarrassing and degrading thereby violating privacy and dignitary interests protected by the Fourth Amendment.
3. Chemical analysis of urine violates medical confidentiality because it can reveal a host of private medical facts, e.g., epilepsy, pregnancy, diabetes.
4. Urinalysis testing interferes with privacy rights associated with the right to control one's own medical treatment, including the right to choose among legal medications.
5. Urinalysis testing attempts to regulate "off-the-field" personal conduct thereby violating the right to engage in constitutional protections for enormously diverse personal action and belief.

Alternatively, it has been argued that athletes subject to drug testing have diminished expectations of privacy rendering a Fourth Amendment analysis an insufficient basis on which to declare a Constitutional violation. For example, "communal undress" inherent in athletic participation suggests a reduced expectation of privacy. Also, health examinations are fairly routine to participants in vigorous activities. In the context of such examinations, viewing and touching is tolerated among relative strangers that would be firmly rejected in other contexts (*O'Halloran v. University of Washington*, 1988). More recently the Supreme Court of the United States in *Vernonia v. Acton* (1995) has stated:

> Legitimate privacy expectations are even less with regard to student-athletes. School sports are not for the bashful. They require "suiting up" before each practice or event, and showering and changing afterwards. Public school locker rooms, the usual sites for these activities, are not notable for the privacy they afford (*Vernonia v. Acton*, 1995).

Governmental Interests Served by Urine Testing

The other side of the balancing test considers the governmental interests served by urine testing. In the context of urine testing of student-athletes, the government must show a special need because the testing exceeds the normal need for law enforcement and occurs in the absence of a warrant or probable cause. A search unsupported by probable cause can be constitutional, we have said, "when special needs, beyond the normal need for law enforcement, make the warrant and probable-cause requirement impracticable" (*Vernonia v. Acton*, 1995).

Examples of special needs that have been successfully asserted to justify warrantless, mandatory urine testing of the intercollegiate athlete include: 1) providing fair and equitable competition, 2) guarding the health and safety of student-athletes, and 3) deterring drug use by testing (*Hill v. NCAA*, 1994; *O'Halloran v. University of Washington*, 1988). With regard to public school athletes, these needs as well as the role of the school standing *in loco parentis* to the children entrusted to it has recently and successfully been argued to support mandatory, random urinalysis testing of public school athletes (*Vernonia v. Acton*, 1995). The doctrine of *in loco parentis* has no role in higher education. The role of guardian may help distinguish disparate holdings of cases dealing with random, suspicionless drug testing of college as opposed to public school athletes:

"[A] proper educational environment requires close supervision of schoolchildren, as well as the enforcement of rules against conduct that would be perfectly permissible if undertaken by an adult" (*New Jersey v. T.L.O.*, 1985).

"Fourth Amendment rights ... are different in public schools than elsewhere; the "reasonableness" inquiry cannot disregard the schools' custodial and tutelary responsibility for children ... So also when the government acts as guardian and tutor the relevant question is whether the search is one that a reasonable guardian and tutor might undertake" (*Vernonia v. Acton*, 1995).

"We therefore find of only marginal relevance holdings by other courts that high school student-athletes have a diminished expectation of privacy under the Fourth Amendment" (*University of Colorado v. Derdeyn*, 1993) [in reference to drug testing of college athletes by the University of Colorado]).

SIGNIFICANT CASE

This case offers a thorough Fourth Amendment analysis of a school district policy mandating suspicionless urinalysis drug testing of high school athletes. Privacy expectations of students and governmental interests served in the policy were examined. The Supreme Court concluded that the district drug testing policy was reasonable by Constitutional standards and did not violate the Fourth Amendment.

VERNONIA SCHOOL DISTRICT V. ACTON
United States Supreme Court
115 S. Ct. 2386 (1995)

In the fall of 1991, respondent James Acton, then a seventh grader, signed up to play football at one of the District's grade schools. He was denied participation, however, because he and his parents refused to sign the testing consent forms. The Actons filed suit, seeking declaratory and injunctive relief from enforcement of the Policy on the grounds that it violated the Fourth and Fourteenth Amendments to the United States Constitution ...

* * *

II.

The Fourth Amendment to the United States Constitution provides that the Federal Government shall not violate "the right of the people to be secure in their persons, houses, papers, and effects, against unreasonable searches and seizures. . . ." We have held that the Fourteenth Amendment extends this constitutional guarantee to searches and seizures by state officers.

* * *

As the text of the Fourth Amendment indicates, the ultimate measure of the constitutionality of a governmental search is "reasonableness." [Whether] a particular search meets the reasonableness standard "'is judged by balancing its intrusion on the individual's Fourth Amendment interests against its promotion of legitimate governmental interests." Where a search is undertaken by law enforcement officials to discover evidence of criminal wrongdoing, this Court has said that reasonableness generally requires the obtaining of a judicial warrant. Warrants cannot be issued, of course, without the showing of probable cause required by the Warrant Clause. But a warrant is not required to establish the reasonableness of all government searches; and when a warrant is not required (and the Warrant Clause therefore not applicable), probable cause is not invariably required either. A search unsupported by probable cause can be constitutional, we have said, "when special needs, beyond the normal need for law enforcement, make the warrant and probable-cause requirement impracticable." *Griffin v. Wisconsin*, 107 S. Ct. 3164 (1987).

We have found such "special needs" to exist in the public school context. There, the warrant requirement "would unduly interfere with the maintenance of the swift and informal disciplinary procedures [that are] needed," and "strict adherence to the requirement that searches be based on probable cause" would undercut "the substantial need of teachers and administrators for freedom to maintain order in the schools." T. L. O., 469 U.S. at 340, 341. The school search we approved in T. L. O., while not based on probable cause, was based on individualized suspicion of wrongdoing. As we explicitly acknowledged, however, "'the Fourth Amendment imposes no irreducible requirement of such suspicion.'" Id., at 342, n. 8. We have upheld suspicionless searches and seizures to conduct drug testing of railroad personnel involved in train accidents . . . to conduct random drug testing of federal customs officers who carry arms or are involved in drug interdiction . . . and to maintain automobile checkpoints looking for illegal immigrants and contraband . . . and drunk drivers.

III.

The first factor to be considered is the nature of the privacy interest upon which the search here at issue intrudes. The Fourth Amendment does not protect all subjective expectations of privacy, but only those that society recognizes as "legitimate." What expectations are legitimate varies, of course, with context, depending, for example, upon whether the individual asserting the privacy interest is at home, at work, in a car, or in a public park. In addition, the legitimacy of certain privacy expectations vis-a-vis the State may depend upon the individual's legal relationship with the State. For example, in Griffin, we held that, although a "probationer's home, like anyone else's, is protected by the Fourth Amendment," the supervisory relationship between probationer and State justifies "a degree of impingement upon [a probationer's] privacy that would not be constitutional if applied to the public at large." 483 U.S. at 873, 875. Central, in our view, to the present case is the fact that the subjects of the Policy are (1) children, who (2) have been committed to the temporary custody of the State as schoolmaster.

Traditionally at common law, and still today, unemancipated minors lack some of the most fundamental rights of self-determination—including even the right of liberty in its narrow sense, i. e., the right to come and go at will. They are subject, even as to their physical freedom, to the control of their parents or guardians . . . When parents place minor children in private schools for their education, the teachers and administrators of those schools stand in loco parentis over the children entrusted to them. In fact, the tutor or schoolmaster is the very prototype of that status . . .

In T. L. O. we rejected the notion that public schools, like private schools, exercise only parental power over their students, which of course is not subject to constitutional constraints. Such a view of things, we said, "is not entirely 'consonant with compulsory education laws,'" and is inconsistent with our prior decisions treating school officials as state actors for purposes of the Due Process and Free Speech Clauses, T. L. O., at 336. But while denying that the State's power over schoolchildren is formally no more than the delegated power of their parents, T. L. O. did not deny, but indeed emphasized, that the nature of that power is custodial and tutelary, permitting a degree of supervision and control that could not be exercised over free adults. "[A] proper educational environment requires close supervision of schoolchildren, as well as the enforcement of rules against conduct that would be perfectly permissible if undertaken by an adult." 469 U.S. at 339. While we do not, of course, suggest that public schools as a general matter have such a degree of control over children as to give rise to a constitutional "duty to protect" . . . we have acknowledged that for many purposes "school authorities act in loco parentis" . . . with the power and indeed the duty to "inculcate the habits and manners of civility. "Id., at 681. Thus, while children assuredly do not "shed their constitutional rights . . . at the schoolhouse gate," *Tinker v. Des Moines Independent Community School Dist.*, 89 S. Ct. 733 (1969), the nature of those rights is what is appropriate for children in school . . .

Fourth Amendment rights, no less than First and Fourteenth Amendment rights, are different in public schools than elsewhere; the "reasonableness" inquiry cannot disregard the schools' custodial and tutelary responsibility for children. For their own good and that of their classmates, public school children are routinely required to submit to various physical examinations, and to be vaccinated against various diseases. Particularly with regard to medical examinations and procedures, therefore, "students within the school environment have a lesser expectation of privacy than members of the population generally."

Legitimate privacy expectations are even less with regard to student athletes. School sports are not for the bashful. They require "suiting up" before each practice or event, and showering and changing afterwards. Public school locker rooms, the usual sites for these activities, are not notable for the privacy they afford. The locker rooms in Vernonia are typical: No individual dressing rooms are provided; shower heads are lined up along a wall, unseparated by any sort of partition or curtain; not even all the toilet stalls have doors. As the United States Court of Appeals for the Seventh Circuit has noted, there is "an element of 'communal undress' inherent in athletic participation," Schaill by Kross v. *Tippecanoe County School Corp.*, 864 F.2d 1309, 1318 (1988).

There is an additional respect in which school athletes have a reduced expectation of privacy. By choosing to "go out for the team," they voluntarily subject themselves to a degree of regulation even higher than that imposed on students generally. In Vernonia's public schools, they must submit to a preseason physical exam (James testified that his included the giving of a urine sample, App. 17), they must acquire adequate insurance coverage or sign an insurance waiver, maintain a minimum grade point average, and comply with any "rules of conduct, dress, training hours and related matters as may be established for each sport by the head coach and athletic director with the principal's approval." Record, Exh. 2, p. 30, P 8. Somewhat like adults who choose to participate in a "closely regulated industry," students who voluntarily participate in school athletics have reason to expect intrusions upon normal rights and privileges, including privacy. See Skinner, 489 U.S. at 627.

IV.

Having considered the scope of the legitimate expectation of privacy at issue here, we turn next to the character of the intrusion that is complained of. We recognized in Skinner that collecting the samples for urinalysis intrudes upon "an excretory function traditionally shielded by great privacy." 489 U.S. at 626. We noted, however, that the degree of intrusion depends upon the manner in which production of the urine sample is monitored. Under the District's Policy, male students produce samples at a urinal along a wall. They remain fully clothed and are only observed from behind, if at all. Female students produce samples in an enclosed stall, with a female monitor standing outside listening only for sounds of tampering. These conditions are nearly identical to those typically encountered in public restrooms, which men, women, and especially school children use daily. Under such conditions, the privacy interests compromised by the process of obtaining the urine sample are in our view negligible.

The other privacy-invasive aspect of urinalysis is, of course, the information it discloses concerning the state of the subject's body, and the materials he has ingested. In this regard it is significant that the tests at issue here look only for drugs, and not for whether the student is, for example, epileptic, pregnant, or diabetic. See id., at 617. Moreover, the drugs for which the samples are screened are standard, and do not vary according to the identity of the student. And finally, the results of the tests are disclosed only to a limited class of school personnel who have a need to know; and they are not turned over to law enforcement authorities or used for any internal disciplinary function.

Respondents argue, however, that the District's Policy is in fact more intrusive than this suggests, because it requires the students, if they are to avoid sanctions for a falsely positive test, to identify in advance prescription medications they are taking. We agree that this raises some cause for concern. In Von Raab, we flagged as one of the salutary features of the Customs Service drug-testing program the fact that employees were not required to disclose medical information unless they tested positive, and, even then, the information was supplied to a licensed physician rather than to the Government employer. See Von Raab, 489 U.S. at 672–673, n. 2. On the other hand, we have never indicated that requiring advance disclosure of medications is per se unreasonable. Indeed, in Skinner we held that it was not "a significant invasion of privacy." 489 U.S. at 626, n. 7. It can be argued that, in Skinner, the disclosure went only to the medical personnel taking the sample, and the Government personnel analyzing it, . . . and that disclosure to teachers and coaches—to persons who personally know the student—is a greater invasion of privacy. Assuming for the sake of argument that both those propositions are true, we do not believe they establish a difference that respondents are entitled to rely on here.

The General Authorization Form that respondents refused to sign, which refusal was the basis for James's exclusion from the sports program, said only (in relevant part): "I . . . authorize the Vernonia School District to conduct a test on a urine specimen which I provide to test for drugs and/or alcohol use. I also authorize the release of information concerning the results of such a test to the Vernonia School District and to the parents and/or guardians of the student." App. 10–11. While the practice of the District seems to have been to have a school official take medication information from the student at the time of the test, see id., at 29, 42, that practice is not set forth in, or required by, the Policy, which says simply: "Student athletes who . . . are or have been taking prescription medication must provide verification (either by a copy of the prescription or by doctor's authorization) prior to being tested." Id., at 8. It may well be that, if and when James was selected for random testing at a time that he was taking medication, the School District would have permitted him to provide the requested information in a confidential manner—for example, in a sealed envelope delivered to the testing lab. Nothing in the Policy contradicts that, and when respondents choose, in effect, to challenge the Policy on its face, we will not assume the worst. Accordingly, we reach the same conclusion as in Skinner: that the invasion of privacy was not significant.

V.

Finally, we turn to consider the nature and immediacy of the governmental concern at issue here, and the efficacy of this means for meeting it. In both Skinner and Von Raab, we characterized the government interest motivating the search as "compelling." Skinner, supra, at 628 (interest in preventing railway accidents); Von Raab, supra, 489 U.S. at 670 (interest in ensuring fitness of customs officials to interdict drugs and handle firearms). Relying on these cases, the District Court held that because the District's program also called for drug testing in the absence of individualized suspicion, the District "must demonstrate a 'compelling need' for the program." 796 F. Supp. at 1363. The Court of Appeals appears to have agreed with this view. See 23 F.3d at 1526. It is a mistake, however, to think that the phrase "compelling state interest," in the Fourth Amendment context, describes a fixed, minimum quantum of governmental concern, so that one can dispose of a case by answering in isolation the question: Is there a compelling state interest here? Rather, the phrase describes an interest that appears important enough to justify the particular search at hand, in light of other factors that show the search to be relatively intrusive upon a genuine expectation of privacy. Whether that relatively high degree of government concern is necessary in this case or not, we think it is met. That the nature of the concern is important—indeed, perhaps compelling—can hardly be doubted. Deterring drug use by our Nation's schoolchildren is at least as important as enhancing efficient enforcement of the Nation's laws against the importation of drugs, which was the governmental concern in Von Raab, supra, at 668, or deterring drug use by engineers and trainmen, which was the governmental concern in Skinner, supra, at 628. School years are the time when the physical, psychological, and addictive effects of drugs are most severe. "Maturing nervous systems are more critically impaired by intoxicants than mature ones are; childhood losses in learning are lifelong and profound"; "children grow chemically dependent more quickly than adults, and their record of recovery is depressingly poor." . . . And of course the effects of a drug-infested school are visited not just upon the users, but upon the entire student body and faculty, as the educational process is disrupted. In the present case, moreover, the necessity for the State to act is magnified by the fact that this evil is being visited not just upon individuals at large, but upon children for whom it has undertaken a special responsibility of care and direction. Finally, it must not be lost sight of that this program is directed more narrowly to drug use by school athletes, where the risk of immediate physical harm to the drug user or those with whom he is playing his sport is particularly high. Apart from psychological effects, which include impairment of judgment, slow reaction time, and a lessening of the perception of pain, the particular drugs screened by the District's Policy have been demonstrated to pose substantial physical risks to athletes . . .

As for the immediacy of the District's concerns: We are not inclined to question—indeed, we could not possibly find clearly erroneous—the District Court's conclusion that "a large segment of the student body, particularly those involved in interscholastic athletics, was in a state of rebellion," that "disciplinary actions had reached 'epidemic proportions,'" and that "the rebellion was being fueled by alcohol and drug abuse as well as by the student's misperceptions about the drug culture." 796 F. Supp. at 1357. That is an immediate crisis of greater proportions than existed in Skinner, where we upheld the Government's drug-testing program based on findings of drug use by railroad employees nationwide, without proof that a problem existed on the particular railroads whose employees were subject to the test . . .

As to the efficacy of this means for addressing the problem: It seems to us self-evident that a drug problem largely fueled by the "role model" effect of athletes' drug use, and of particular danger to athletes, is effectively addressed by making sure that athletes do not use drugs. Respondents argue that a "less intrusive means to the same end" was available, namely, "drug testing on suspicion of drug use." Brief for Respondents 45–46. We have repeatedly refused to declare that only the "least intrusive" search practicable can be reasonable under the Fourth Amendment. Skinner, supra, at 629, n. 9 (collecting cases). Respondents' alternative entails substantial difficulties—if it is indeed practicable at all. It may be impracticable, for one thing, simply because the parents who are willing to accept random drug testing for athletes are not willing to accept accusatory drug testing for all students, which transforms the process into a badge of shame.

Respondents' proposal brings the risk that teachers will impose testing arbitrarily upon troublesome but not drug-likely students. It generates the expense of defending lawsuits that charge such arbitrary imposition, or that simply demand greater process before accusatory drug testing is imposed. And not least of all, it adds to the ever-expanding diversionary duties of schoolteachers the new function of spotting and bringing to account drug abuse, a task for which they are ill prepared, and which is not readily compatible with their vocation . . .

VI.

Taking into account all the factors we have considered above—the decreased expectation of privacy, the relative unobtrusiveness of the search, and the severity of the need met by the search—we conclude Vernonia's Policy is reasonable and hence constitutional.

We caution against the assumption that suspicionless drug testing will readily pass constitutional muster in other contexts. The most significant element in this case is the first we discussed: that the Policy was undertaken in furtherance of the government's responsibilities, under a public school system, as guardian and tutor of children entrusted to its care. n4 Just as when the government conducts a search in its capacity as employer (a warrantless search of an absent employee's desk to obtain an urgently needed file, for example), the relevant question is whether that intrusion upon privacy is one that a reasonable employer might engage in, see *O'Connor v. Ortega*, 107 S. Ct. 1492 (1987); so also when the government acts as guardian and tutor the relevant question is whether the search is one that a reasonable guardian and tutor might undertake. Given the findings of need made by the District Court, we conclude that in the present case it is.

We may note that the primary guardians of Vernonia's schoolchildren appear to agree. The record shows no objection to this district wide program by any parents other than the couple before us here—even though, as we have described, a public meeting was held to obtain parents' views. We find insufficient basis to contradict the judgment of Vernonia's parents, its school board, and the District Court, as to what was reasonably in the interest of these children under the circumstances.

The Ninth Circuit held that Vernonia's Policy not only violated the Fourth Amendment, but also, by reason of that violation, contravened Article I, § 9, of the Oregon Constitution. Our conclusion that the former holding was in error means that the latter holding rested on a flawed premise. We therefore vacate the judgment, and remand the case to the Court of Appeals for further proceedings consistent with this opinion.

It is so ordered.

CASES ON THE SUPPLEMENTAL CD

Brannum v. Overton County School Board, 956 F.3d. 498 (2007). Middle-school students successfully sued alleging violations of their privacy rights under the Fourth Amendment when video-surveillance cameras were installed in locker rooms.

University of Colorado v. Derdeyn, 863 P.2d 929 (1993). A random suspicionless urinalysis drug testing program on college athletes was held to violate the Fourth Amendment. The court held that the program was not constitutionally reasonable and that voluntary consent was not obtained from the student-athletes.

Herrera v. Santa Fe Public Schools, 956 Fed Supp 2d.1191 (2013). The Fourth Amendment was violated when a school principal requested New Mexico guards to perform pat-down searches at a prom that included lifting the female students' skirts.

Hill v. NCAA, 7 Cal.4th 1 (1994). Stanford University student-athletes sued contending that the NCAA's drug testing program violated the right of privacy as explicitly guaranteed under the California Constitution. The Fourth Amendment was not used since a private actor's conduct was at issue. This case meticulously analyzes privacy rights, examines the competing arguments of the NCAA and students, and details the requirements for a privacy cause of action.

Wooten v. Pleasant Hope R-VI School District, 139 F.Supp.2d 835 (2000). High school student sued alleging common law violations of privacy when her coach publicly disclosed her dismissal from the softball team. Public disclosure of private facts and the distinction of false light and defamation are specifically addressed in this case.

QUESTIONS YOU SHOULD BE ABLE TO ANSWER

1. What language in the Fourth Amendment protects against privacy intrusions by government?

2. The Fourth Amendment protects against "unreasonable" searches. Define and give an example of a "search". Describe/explain the analysis used to determine a "reasonable search".

3. On what basis has it been concluded that student-athletes have "diminished expectations of privacy" with regard to a Fourth Amendment analysis?

4. In *Vernonia*, what governmental interests were served by the drug testing program of the school district?

5. In addition to drug testing, give examples in sport and recreation of searches that could be violations of the Fourth Amendment.

REFERENCES

Cases
Arlosoroff v. NCAA, 746 F.2d 1019 (1984).
Arkansas Gazette Co. v. Southern State College, 620 S.W.2d 258 (1981).
Board of Education v. Earls, 122 S.Ct. 2559.
Bunger v. Iowa H. S. Athletic Assn., 197 N.W.2d 555 (1972).
Davis v. Meek, 344 F. Supp. 298 (1972).
Dunham v. Pulsifer, 312 F. Supp. 41 (1970).
Estay v. LaFourche Parish School Board, 230 So.2d 443 (1969).
Horsemen's Benevolent & Protective Assn. v. State Racing Commission, 532 N.E.2d 644 (1989).
Indiana High School Athletic Assn. v. Raike, 329 N.E.2d 66 (1975).
Marmo v. NYC Board of Education, 289 N.Y.S.2d 51 (1968).
Menora v. Illinois High School Assn., 683 F.2d 1030 (1982).
National Treasury Employees Union v. Von Raab, 109 S.Ct. 1384 (1989).
New Jersey v. T.L.O., 105 S.Ct. 733 (1985).
O'Connor v. Ortega, 107 S.Ct. 1492 (1987).
O'Halloran v. University of Washington, 679 F. Supp. 997 (1988).
Perry v. Granada Municipal School District, 300 F. Supp. 748 (1969).
Schaill v. Tippecanoe County School Corporation, 864 F.2d. 1309 (1989).
Skinner v. Railway Labor Executives' Assn., 109 S.Ct. 1402 (1989).
Tinker v. Des Moines Indep. Comm. School District, 89 S.Ct. 733 (1969).
University of Colorado v. Derdeyn, 863 P.2d 929 (1993).
Vernonia School District 47J v. Action, 115 S.Ct. 2386 (1995).
Zeller v. Donegal School District, 517 F.2d 600 (1975).

Legislation
United States Constitution, First, Fourth and Fourteenth Amendments.

FIRST AMENDMENT

John T. Wolohan | Syracuse University

The First Amendment, which establishes the freedom of speech, freedom of the press and freedom of religion, has been called "the indispensable condition of nearly every other form of freedom" (*Palko v. Connecticut*, 1937). As we will discover below, however, even though the First Amendment is one of most litigated Amendments to the United States Constitution it is still considered to be "a work in progress" (Weaver and Lively, 2003). The reasons the First Amendment has kept the Supreme Court so busy is not only because of the continued development of new means of expression, but also the inherent conflicts in the Amendment's language protecting the freedoms of speech, press and religion.

FUNDAMENTAL CONCEPTS

"Congress shall make no law respecting an establishment of religion, or prohibiting the free exercise thereof; or abridging the freedom of speech, or of the press; or the right of the people peaceably to assemble, and to petition the Government for a redress of grievances."

(United States Constitution, Amendment I)

While the language of the First Amendment is clear and would seem to leave little room for misinterpretation, the judicial history of the First Amendment illustrate that the freedoms provided under the law are not set in stone. For example, even though the First Amendment provides for freedom of speech, the government has a legitimate reason to restrict our speech in some instances. Therefore, in evaluation our rights under the First Amendment, the Court must determine whether the enumerated guarantee must give way to some higher governmental priority (Weaver and Lively, 2003).

Freedom of Speech

As the Supreme Court found in *United States v. Schwimmer*, (1937), the First Amendment is not designed to protect the "free thought for those who agree with us, but freedom for the thoughts that we hate." Not all speech is entitled First Amendment protection, however. For example, in *Schenck v. United States*, (1919) a case in which the Supreme Court upheld the conviction of anti-war protesters who urged draft eligible men to resist the draft, the court held that words that create a "clear and present danger" would not be protected. To illustrate the point that not all speech is protected under the First Amendment, the court held that even "the most stringent protection of free speech would not protect a man in falsely shouting fire in a theatre and causing a panic" (*Schenck v. United States*, 1919). As a general rule, the Supreme Court has deemed the following categories of speech: defamation, obscenity, fighting words, and words that create a clear and present danger as unprotected expression. If the court determines that the challenged speech or expression falls into one of these unprotected categories, it receives less than full First Amendment protection and the courts will review it using the rational basis test. (See Chapter 6.14 Equal Protection for a discussion of the rational basis test).

If, however, the Court classifies the speech as protected, it is reviewed using a strict scrutiny. For example, political speech and speech critical of governmental policies, is regarded as high value and protected speech and consistent with this classification, the government would have to show that restricting such speech was necessary to achieve a compelling state interest or that the speech presented a clear and present danger. In addition, the Supreme Court has viewed some speech, such as advertising and other commercial speech and sexually explicit, but non-obscene speech, as protected, but not enjoying the full protections of the First Amendment. In these cases of speech, the court uses an intermediate level of scrutiny (Weaver and Lively, 2003). (See Chapter 6.14 *Equal Protection* for a discussion of the strict and intermediate scrutiny tests).

Therefore, before the Court can determine whether someone's free speech rights have been deprived, the court must first determine what category the speech falls into: protected or non-protected. Once it determines the category, it can then apply the standard of review, essentially balancing the competing constitutional right of the individual and the state's interest. In weighting these factors the Court also considers the medium that was used, if any, to disseminate expression, since some media, like newspapers, are afforded more First Amendment protection than others (Weaver and Lively, 2003).

Standard of Review

In reviewing freedom of speech cases involving students, the leading case is *Tinker v. Des Moines Independent Community School District*, (1969). In *Tinker*, three students were suspended from public school for wearing black armbands to protest the war in Vietnam. In finding that "students and teachers do not shed their constitutional rights to freedom of speech or expression at the schoolhouse gate" the United States Supreme Court held that the wearing of armbands was entirely divorced from actually or potentially disruptive conduct and as such was closely akin to "pure speech" which is entitled to comprehensive protection under the First Amendment (*Tinker v. Des Moines Independent Community School District*, 1969).

In order for the State, in this case school officials, to justify prohibiting speech or a particular expression of opinion, the court ruled that the action must be based on "something more than a mere desire to avoid the discomfort and unpleasantness that always accompany an unpopular viewpoint" (*Tinker v. Des Moines Independent Community School District*, 1969). If the state cannot show that engaging in the forbidden conduct would "materially and substantially interfere with the requirements of appropriate discipline in the operation of the school," the Supreme Court held that the state cannot prohibit the speech or expression. In *Tinker*, the Court found that the school officials failed to show that they had any reason to anticipate that the students wearing of the armbands would substantially interfere with the work of the school or impinge upon the rights of other students. In fact, the Court found that the action of the school authorities was based on an urgent wish to avoid any controversy which might result from the silent symbol of armbands. Such a prohibition, the Court held was not constitutionally permissible.

While the *Tinker* test is the standard of review most frequently applied to student speech cases, the Supreme Courts has expanded the exemptions provided school officials in free speech cases (Hayes, 2010). For example, in *Frederick v. Morse*, (2007) a student was suspended from school after he refused the principal's direction to take down a banner that he unfurled while watching the Olympic Torch Relay pass through town. The viewing of the relay was a school-sanctioned and school-supervised event. The fourteen-foot banner, which the principal regarded as promoting illegal drug use, read "BONG HiTS 4 JESUS" (*Frederick v. Morse*, 2007).

In overturning the Ninth Circuit Court's decision, the Supreme Court held that consistent with the First Amendment a school official may restrict student speech at a school event, when that speech is reasonably viewed as promoting illegal drug use or other illegal activity. In support of this conclusion, the Supreme Court ruled that the "substantial disruption" rule of *Tinker* was not the only basis for restricting student speech. Considering the special characteristics of the school environment and the governmental interest in stopping student drug abuse, the Court held that schools were entitled to take steps to safeguard those entrusted to their care from speech that could reasonably be regarded as encouraging illegal drug use.

Besides the "substantial disruption" and the "encouraging illegal activity" exemptions, the Supreme Court in *Bethel School District No. 403 v. Fraser*, (1986) found another exemption to a student's free speech. In *Fraser*, a high school student delivered a speech, nominating a fellow student for student government office, at an assembly attended by about 600 students. The entire speech referred to the candidate in terms of sexual metaphor, employing such phrases as "he's firm in his pants . . . his character is firm," "a man who takes his point and pounds it in," and "a man who will go to the very end—even the climax, for each and every one of you." During the speech, some students were observed to react by hooting and yelling, others by making sexually suggestive gestures, and still others appeared to be bewildered and embarrassed. The morning after the assembly, the student was notified that the school considered his speech to have been a violation of the disciplinary rule, that he would be suspended for 3 days, and that his name would be removed from a list of potential graduation speakers (*Bethel School District No. 403 v. Fraser*, 1986). The District Court, holding that the suspension violated the student's First Amendment right, awarded him damages and enjoined the school district from preventing him from speaking at graduation. The Ninth Circuit Court of Appeals affirmed the judgment of the District Court, rejecting the argument that the speech had a disruptive effect on the education process and that the school district had an interest in protecting students from lewd and indecent language in a school-sponsored setting.

In overturning the decision of the lower courts, the United States Supreme Court held that the First Amendment did not prevent the school district from suspending the student for giving the offensively lewd and indecent speech at the assembly. While the Court found that under the First Amendment, the use of an offensive form of expression would be allowable to adults making what the speaker considers a political point, the Supreme Court held that it does not follow that the same latitude must be permitted to children in a public school. In addition, the Supreme Court held that the First Amendment recognizes a state interest in protecting minors from exposure to vulgar and offensive spoken language, as well as limitations on the otherwise absolute interest of the speaker in reaching an unlimited audience where the speech is sexually explicit and the audience may include children.

Freedom of Speech in Athletics. Students' freedom of speech "rights do not embrace merely the classroom hours. When he is in the cafeteria, or on the playing field, or on the campus during the authorized hours, he may express his opinions, even on controversial subjects . . . if he does so without materially and substantially interfere with the requirements of appropriate discipline in the operation of the school and without colliding with the rights of others" (*Tinker v. Des Moines Independent Community School District*, 1969). Although the Court has recognized that students have freedom of speech rights on the "playing field," since most actions taken by an athlete or a group of athletes are generally going to "materially and substantially interfere" with or disrupt the team, and thus, school activities, student athletes tend to have less freedom to speak out or complain about their coaches. For example, in *Pinard v. Clatskanie School District 6J*, (2006), several members of the boys' basketball team alleged that the school violated their First Amendment rights by suspending them in retaliation for speaking out against their coach. The students had signed a petition requesting the removal of the team's head coach.

Using the *Tinker* standard, the Ninth Circuit ruled that the students' petition and complaints against the coach were protected speech because they could not reasonably have led school officials to forecast substantial disruption of or material interference with a school activity. However, even though the students' actions in signing the petition may have been constitutionally protected, the Ninth Circuit held that the students' protect in refusing to board the bus was properly punishable by school officials as unprotected speech; the game boycott substantially disrupted and materially interfered with the operation of the basketball program (*Pinard v. Clatskanie School District 6J*, 2006).

This standard was reaffirmed by the Sixth Circuit Court of Appeals in *Lowery v. Euverard*, (2007). In Lowery, like in Pinard, a group of high school athletes signed a petition that stated "I hate Coach (coach's name) and I don't want to play for him." Although the petition was to be held until after the football season and then given to the principal of school, in order to have the coach replaced, the coach found out about the petition during the season. When he did, the coach interviewed all the players individually to discover who signed the petition. Players who signed the petition but apologized to the coach were allowed to remain on the team; any player who did not apologize to the coach was removed from the team.

In trying to find the proper balance between a student athlete's First Amendment rights and a coach's need to maintain order and discipline, the Sixth Circuit Court of Appeals rejected the students' argument that the petition did not substantially disrupted the team. In ruling that this argument misapplies the *Tinker* standard, the Sixth Circuit held that school officials "were not obligated to wait until the petition substantially disrupted the team before acting, nor are they now required to demonstrate that it was certain that the petition would substantially disrupt the team. Rather, [the Court held,] school officials must show that it was reasonable for them to forecast that the petition would disrupt the team" (*Lowery v. Euverard*, 2008). Based on the circumstances, the Court held that it was reasonable for school officials to believe that the petition would disrupt the team, by eroding the coach's authority and dividing players into opposing camps. As a result, the Sixth Circuit held that the petition was not protected by *Tinker*, and coach did not violate the students' First Amendment rights by removing them from the football team. *Tinker* did not require teachers to surrender control of the classroom to students, and the standard does not require coaches to surrender control of the team to players.

If the protest is not likely to substantially disrupt the team or erode or interfere with the coach's authority, the courts will allow the speech. For example in *Hysaw v. Washburn University of Topeka*, (1987), several black football players on the Washburn team expressed discontent with their scholarships; that promises had not been carried out and that white players on the team were being favored by the coaching staff. To protest, the players boycotted team practices. The Athletic Director responded to the players' boycott by outlining the administration's position. In particular, he pointed out that "missing practice without an excuse from the coaching staff is a violation of disciplinary rules affecting all players and will be treated in the same manner as any player's unexcused absence" (*Hysaw v. Washburn University of Topeka*, 1987). The players were given a chance to apologize and rejoin the team, those players that did not apologize, were removed from the team.

At trail, the school claimed that even if the players were dismissed for protesting racial mistreatment, the dismissal was justified under *Tinker*, because the activity by students "materially and substantially interfered with the requirements of appropriate discipline in the operation of the school" (*Hysaw v. Washburn University of Topeka*, 1987). In particular, the school argued that the boycott severely disrupted the football team and infringed upon the rights of others participating in the football program. In rejecting this argument, the District Court held that since the coach testified that any absence caused by protesting racial mistreatment would be excused, there was no way the protest could be considered disruptive. To do so, the court held, would be to hold that the coaching staff followed a policy—excusing the players to protest—which caused disruption to the team. In addition, the court also rejected the schools argument that the players' actions infringed upon the rights of others participating in the football program. The *Tinker* exception, the court held, is a narrow one. As such, the court was not prepared to hold that players' actions infringed upon the "rights" of the other players. The boycott may have made practice more difficult, the team's morale may have been dampened by the players' actions, and the season's play may have suffered. But the team's "rights" were not infringed upon, at least not under the narrow definition of "rights" spelled out in *Tinker*. The court will not place the interests of participants in a university extracurricular activity above the rights of any citizen to speak out against alleged racial injustice without fear of government retribution.

Freedom of Speech in Recreational Sports. One of the most troubling areas involving freedom of speech is the use of email to criticize coaches and administrators. For example in *Robinson v. Hicks; King; City of Harrisburg*, (2011) the parents of a minor child, sent numerous emails to league officials expressing their disapproval over comments made by the coach and demanded a new coach. As a result of the Robinson's actions, the Harrisburg Youth Soccer Club (HYSC) Board of Directors unanimously voted to suspend the three Robinsons from HYSC for one year because of their alleged inappropriate behavior, such as using profanity and threats with the staff and players. The Robinsons argued that the city's conduct violated their First Amendment right by retaliating against them for speaking out against Hicks and the soccer program.

In ruling against the Robinsons' the Third Circuit Court ruled that to "state a claim for actionable retaliation under the First Amendment, the Robinsons must allege (1) constitutionally protected conduct, (2) retaliatory action sufficient to deter a person of ordinary firmness from exercising his constitutional rights, and (3) a causal link between the constitutionally protected conduct and the retaliatory action" (*Robinson v. Hicks; King; City of Harrisburg*, 2011). In reviewing the facts, the Third Circuit Court ruled that even if the Robinsons' comments to the city youth soccer president were considered constitutionally protected speech and that they were suspended from the soccer team in retaliation, there was insufficient evidence that the league and its president participated in the retaliatory conduct to subject them to liability. Given the history of the parents' aggressive and disruptive behavior, the Third Circuit Court ruled the decision to suspend them from the soccer team would have been the same even without the exercise of their First Amendment rights.

Freedom of the Press

In examining the question of "Freedom of the Press," the courts have generally interpreted the clause as having no significance independent of the speech clause. Therefore, when presented with a First Amendment Freedom of the Press claim, the court will first examine whether the content is protected under the First Amendment. The constitutional inquiry, however is usually more layered when freedom of press rights are involved. The first consideration is the nature of the speech. Is it protected, is it commercial, or is it unprotected. The higher the value of the speech, the more protection it receives and the higher the level of scrutiny applied. Once the court determines the nature of the speech, it must next look at the nature of the medium used. For each medium of expression, newspaper, radio or television broadcast, cablecast or internet, the standard of First Amendment review varies. The print medium has the highest level of First Amendment protection, and broadcasting, because of the scarcity of broadcast frequencies and it's invasive and accessibility to children has the least. The consequence of this analytical framework is that the same expression published without constitutional constraints in print may be the basis for liability in broadcasting" (Weaver and Lively, 2003).

An example of the different standards of review used by the courts, strict scrutiny applied to content in print media and an intermediate standard of review applied to broadcast media is *Zacchini v. Scripps-Howard Broadcasting* (1977). In Zacchini, a television station secretly taped Hugo Zacchini's performance as the "human cannonball" and broadcast the performance on the 11 o'clock newscast. Since each performance occupies some 15 seconds; the entire act was shown on the news program that night, together with favorable commentary. While holding that a "TV station has a privilege to report in its newscasts matters of legitimate public interest which would otherwise be protected by an individual's right of publicity," the Supreme Court found that the free speech privilege afforded respondent under United States Constitution did not extend to broadcasting Zacchini's entire performance (*Zacchini v. Scripps-Howard Broadcasting*, 1977). The Court emphasized that the broadcast of an entire act was categorically different from reporting on an event, in that it posed a substantial threat to the economic value of the performance, and to Zacchini's livelihood. Zacchini's interest, the Supreme Court held that was more like a patent or copyright, interests which were not subject to claims of constitutional privilege (*Zacchini v. Scripps-Howard Broadcasting*, 1977).

The development of the Internet, and its widespread adoption inside the home poses significant challenges to the traditional model of medium specific analysis (Weaver and Lively, 2003). For example in *Layshock v. Hermitage School District*, (2007), the court was asked to determine whether the school district violated a student's First Amendment right when it suspended him for creating and posting a parody profile of the principal on an Internet website at home outside of school hours. The school district claimed the punishment was justified under either the *Tinker* or *Fraser* tests.

In balancing the freedom of expression of a student with the right and responsibility of a public school to maintain an environment conducive to learning, the court found that the mere fact that the internet may be accessed at school does not authorize school officials to become censors of the world-wide web. Public schools are vital institutions, but their reach is not unlimited. Schools have an undoubted right to control conduct within the scope of their activities, but they must share the supervision of children with other, equally vital, institutions such as families, churches, community organizations and the judicial system (*Layshock v. Hermitage School District*, 2007). In the current case, the court found that the school district failed to demonstrate a sufficient causal nexus between the student's conduct and any substantial disruption of school operations. In particular, the court noted that the school district was unable to show that the "buzz" or discussions in school were caused by this particular student's profile as opposed to the reaction of administrators. Accordingly, the School's right to maintain an environment conducive to learning does not trump the student's First Amendment right to freedom of expression.

The Future of the Press. Before leaving this section, it is important to think about "who is the press"? In 1791 when the First Amendment was adopted, there was only print media. In the past 100 years, we added radio, television and Internet. So when you think about who is the press: is it only the traditional print media? Print and broadcast media? What about an ESPN reporter who also blogs for ESPN's website? What about if he blogs on his own site? What if he creates a website criticizing the play calling of his child's youth basketball coach?

Freedom of Religion

As the Supreme Court stated in *Walz v. Tax Commission*, (1970) "we will not tolerate either governmentally established religion or governmental interference with religion. Short of those expressly proscribed governmental acts there is room for play in the joints productive of a benevolent neutrality which will permit religious exercise to exist without sponsorship and without interference." With so much room for play, it is easy to see why the courts have continuously struggled with First Amendment Freedom of Religion cases and the inherent conflict that exist between the **Establishment Clause**, which prohibits Congress or the states from making any law establishing or promoting a religion, and **Free Exercise Clause**, which prohibits Congress or the states from making any law interfering with the free exercise of religion (Brown-Foster, 2010).

The Establishment Clause

"In the words of [Thomas] Jefferson, the clause against establishment of religion by law was intended to erect a wall of separation between Church and State" (*Everson v. Board of Education*, 1947). Since 1971, the Court's primary test for analyzing Establishment Clause cases is the **Lemon Test**, first developed in *Lemon v. Kurtzman*, (1971). Under the Lemon Test, the Court uses a three prong analysis in which: "[First], the statute must have a secular legislative purpose; second, its principal or primary effect must be one that neither advances nor inhibits religion; finally, the statute must not foster an excessive government entanglement with religion" (*Lemon v. Kurtzman*, 1971).

The Lemon Test, however, has been criticized as "simply not providing adequate standards for deciding Establishment Clause cases" (*Wallace v. Jaffree*, 1985). As a result, the Court has begun to focus on whether a law or policy accommodates (constitutionally acceptable), endorses (constitutionally unacceptable) or coerces others conform to (constitutionally unacceptable) religion. For example in *Lee v. Weisman* (1992), the Court developed the **Coercion Test**, which analyzes whether school-sponsored religious activity has a coercive effect on students. The third test developed by the court is the Endorsement Test. The **Endorsement Test** asks whether government policies or practices are religiously neutral (constitutionally acceptable) or convey or communicate a message of endorsement or disapproval of religion (constitutionally unacceptable) (Brown-Foster, 2010).

In reviewing cases involving prayer in public schools, the courts tend to examine whether students felt coerced into participation in religion. For example in *Santa Fe High Independent School District v. Doe* (2000), a student elected as Santa Fe High School's student council chaplain delivered a prayer over the public address system before each home varsity football game. A group of students challenged this practice under the Establishment Clause of the First Amendment. The United States Supreme Court in striking down the policy held that for purposes of analysis under the Federal Constitution's First Amendment, there is a crucial difference between government speech endorsing religion, which the First Amendment's establishment of religion clause forbids; and private speech endorsing religion, which the First Amendment's free speech and free exercise of religion clauses protect. In ruling that the school district's policy endorses religion, the Supreme Court citing *Lee v. Weisman*, (1992) held that "at a minimum, the Constitution guarantees that government may not coerce anyone to support or participate in religion or its exercise, or otherwise act in a way which 'establishes a [state] religion or religious faith, or tends to do so" (*Lee v. Weisman*, 1992). By delivering a prayer over the public address system before each home varsity football game, the court found that the school district's conduct amounted to an endorsement of religion. In cases involving state participation in a religious activity, the relevant question is whether an objective observer would perceive the school's practice as a state endorsement of prayer in public schools. Regardless of the listener's support for, or objection to, the message, the Court held that an objective Santa Fe High School student would unquestionably perceive the school's pregame prayer as state approved.

Free Exercise Clause

The "Free Exercise [clause] embraces two concepts—freedom to believe and freedom to act. The first is absolute but, in the nature of things, the second cannot be. The freedom to act must have appropriate definition to preserve the enforcement of that protection [although] the power to regulate must be so exercised as not, in attaining a permissible end, unduly to infringe the protected freedom" of others (*Cantwell v. Connecticut*, 1940). In other words, the state cannot enact any laws that interfere with, by making it illegal or otherwise burdens, an individual's right to exercise his or her religious beliefs unless the general application of the law has a nonreligious purpose. In addition, the state cannot require, or otherwise encourages, a specific religious practice or conduct that may be forbidden by some religious belief (Shiffrin and Choper, 2006). For example, in ruling that the use of controlled substances during religious ceremonies could be prohibited by the state laws, the Supreme Court found that the purpose of the law was nonreligious and of general applicability (*Employment Division, Department of Human Resources of Oregon v. Smith*, (1990)). Laws of general applicability thus can be analogized to content neutral regulation in the freedom of speech context. When such enactments are challenged, and even if they impose a substantial burden upon free exercise interest, the court will review the law under the rational basis test not strict scrutiny (See Chapter 6.14 Equal Protection for a discussion of the tests). The courts will use the strict scrutiny only in those cases where a law is found aimed directly at religion.

For example, in *Borden v. School District of the Township of East Brunswick* (2008), the head football coach at East Brunswick High School had established a tradition where he would lead the team in prayer. Borden decided to change the tradition where he said prayer for the first pre-game dinner of each season. For every game thereafter, he asked everyone to stand and chose a senior to say a prayer. Additionally, Borden asked the players to take a knee in the locker room to discuss game strategy after which he again led the team in prayer. After a complaint was filed against the coach for his practices, the school district directed Borden to stop what he was doing and provided him with guidelines that coincided with previous court rulings that any prayer had to be truly student-initiated. These guidelines also stipulated that any representative of the school district could not participate.

Upset he could no longer engage in the silent act of bowing his head during his team's pre-meal grace and taking a knee with his team during a locker-room prayer, Borden brought suit seeking a declaratory judgment that the East Brunswick School District's policy prohibiting his participation in student-initiated prayer was unconstitutionally overbroad and vague, and violated his First Amendment rights. In upholding the school district's policy, the Third Circuit Court of Appeals held that even Borden's silent acts could be construed as an endorsement of religion (*Borden v. School District of the Township of East Brunswick*, 2008). In support of this conclusion, the Third Circuit Court held that Borden's silent acts violate the Establishment Clause because, when viewing the acts in light of Borden's twenty-three years of prior prayer activities with the East Brunswick High School football team during which he organized, participated in, and even led prayer activities with his team, a reasonable observer would conclude that Borden was endorsing religion in violation of the Establishment Clause (*Borden v. School District of the Township of East Brunswick*, 2008).

SIGNIFICANT CASE

In this case, the court examines whether the students First Amendment Right of Free Speech was violated when the students were punished for non-disruptive speech made outside of the school setting.

T.V. v. SMITH-GREEN COMMUNITY SCHOOL CORPORATION
United States District Court for the Northern District of Indiana
807 F. Supp. 2d 767 (2011)

Here's what the record reveals: during the summer of 2009, T.V. and M.K. were both entering the 10th grade at Churubusco High School, a public high school of approximately 400 students. Both T.V. and M.K. were members of the high school's volleyball team, an extracurricular activity, and M.K. was also a member of the cheerleading squad, also an extracurricular activity, as well as the show choir, which is a cocurricular activity. Cocurricular activities provide for academic credit but also involve activities that take place outside the normal school day.

Try-outs for the volleyball team for the coming year would occur in July. A couple of weeks prior to the tryouts, T.V., M.K. and a number of their friends had sleepovers at M.K.'s house. Prior to the first sleepover, the girls bought phallic-shaped rainbow colored lollipops. During the first sleepover, the girls took a number of photographs of themselves sucking on the lollipops. In one, three girls are pictured and M.K. added the caption "Wanna suck on my cock." In another photograph, a fully-clothed M.K. is sucking on one lollipop while another lollipop is positioned between her legs and a fully-clothed T.V. is pretending to suck on it.

* * *

T.V. posted most of the pictures on her MySpace or Facebook accounts, where they were accessible to persons she had granted "Friend" status. Some of the photos involving the lollipops were also posted on Photo Bucket, where a password is necessary for viewing. None of the images identify the girls as students at Churubusco High School. Neither T.V. nor M.K. ever brought the images to school either in digital or any other format. In their depositions, both T.V. and M.K. characterized what they did as "just joking around" and disclaimed that the images conveyed any scientific, literary or artistic value or message, but testified that the photos were taken and were shared on the internet because the girls thought what they had done was funny and "wanted to share with [their] friends how funny it was."

Around August 4, a parent brought printouts of the photographs to Steve Darnell, the Superintendent of Smith-Green Community School Corporation. The parent reported that the images were posted on Facebook and Photo Bucket and that the photographs were causing "divisiveness" among the girls on the volleyball teams, because "two camps" had formed—girls that were "in favor . . . of what was going on with the pictures" and "girls that just wanted to have no part in it." Evidently, this woman's daughter did not play volleyball in the fall of 2009. Superintendent Darnell immediately took the pictures to Principal Couch, reported that the photos were "causing a disruption in extracurricular teams," and told him to "follow code with this." . . .

The Churubusco High School Student Handbook for 2008-2009 contains an "EXTRA-CURRICULAR/CO-CURRICULAR CODE OF CONDUCT AND ATHLETIC CODE OF CONDUCT." On page 25, this code provides: The purpose of the "Extra-Curricular Code of Conduct" is to demonstrate to students at Churubusco High School who participate in organized extra-curricular activities that they not only represent themselves, but also represent Churubusco High School, as well. Therefore, those students who choose to participate in extra-curricular activities are expected to demonstrate good conduct at school and outside of school. . . . This code will be in force for the entire year including out of season and during the summer.

Separately, under the heading "EXTRA-CURRICULAR/CO-CURRICULAR ACTIVITIES" on page 24, the Student Handbook states: "If you act in a manner in school or out of school that brings discredit or dishonor upon yourself or your school, you may be removed from extra-curricular activities for all or part of the year."

After confirming the identities of the girls in the images, and discussing the matter with the Athletic Director and the Assistant Principal, within a day of Principal Couch's receipt of the photographs, he informed M.K. and T.V. that they had violated the athletic code and faced suspension from extracurricular and cocurricular activities. At the time, T.V. and M.K. were both participating in volleyball practices and M.K. was attending rehearsals for the show choir. Principal Couch did not discuss the situation with any member of the volleyball coaching staff, other than approaching the volleyball coach to confirm that the girls were playing volleyball and to inform the coach that he needed to speak with the girls because of an extracurricular violation. Principal Couch did not speak with the director of the show choir until after M.K. was suspended, and then simply to advise the teacher of the suspension.

Defendants explain the basis for Principal Couch's decision as his "determination that the photographs were inappropriate, and that by posing for them, and posting them on the internet, the students were reflecting discredit upon the school." In addition, Principal Couch determined that the photographs had the potential for causing disruption of school activities. . . . Against this background, Principal Couch wanted the new 2009-2010 school year "to get off on the right foot," and "needed to do something before this blew up." The conclusion that the photographs represented a violation of the Student Handbook coupled with the anticipation of potential school disruption from the situation served as the basis for the discipline imposed.

Principal Couch informed T.V. and M.K. that they were being suspended from extracurricular and cocurricular activities for a calendar year pursuant to the school's 2008-2009 policy, for bringing discredit on themselves and the school. The portion of the policy cited provided that "If you act in a manner in school or out of school that brings discredit or dishonor upon yourself or your school, you may be removed from extracurricular activities for all or part of the year." It was explained to the girls that, under the policy, they could obtain a reduction of their punishment by making three visits to a counselor and then meeting with the school's Athletic Board to apologize for their actions. When he was contacted by T.V.'s parents, Superintendent Darnell indicated that he supported Couch's decision.

Both T.V. and M.K. opted to visit the counselor, and completed those requirements by August 13, 2009. Subsequently, the girls each appeared separately before the Athletic Board, a panel consisting of Principal Couch, the Athletic Director, the Assistant Principal and the coaches. As a result, the punishment was modified and the girls were excluded from only 25% of their fall extracurricular activities, which meant that T.V. missed six volleyball games and M.K. missed five games and a show choir performance.

Analysis
Is the speech involved nonetheless unprotected?

The parties dispute whether the case involves speech protected by the First Amendment. Defendants contend that, under distinct standards, the photographs constitute both obscenity and child pornography, neither of which is protected by the First Amendment. *United States v. Stevens*, 130 S.Ct. 1577, 1584, 176 L. Ed. 2d 435 (2010). At the May 27th hearing, after being pressed on the point, counsel for defendants conceded that the law on obscenity and child pornography are not applicable here, and with good reason.

Obscene material is not protected by the First Amendment. Smith-Green and Couch initially invoked the three-part test for obscenity set out by the Supreme Court in *Miller*. The second part of that test asks whether "the work depicts or describes, in a patently offensive way, sexual conduct specifically defined by the applicable state law." *Id*. at 24. The state law defendants cite to is Indiana's definition of "sexual conduct" in its statutes on child exploitation and possession of child pornography:

"Sexual conduct" means sexual intercourse, deviate sexual conduct, exhibition of the uncovered genitals intended to satisfy or arouse the sexual desires of any person, sadomasochistic abuse, sexual or deviate sexual conduct with an animal, or any fondling or touching of a child by another person or of another person by a child intended to arouse or satisfy the sexual desires of either the child or the other person.

I.C. §35-42-4-4(a). Tacitly acknowledging that the only item in this list that might apply to the photographs here is "deviate sexual conduct," defendants then turn to the definition of that term in I.C. §35-41-1-9: "'Deviate sexual conduct' means an act involving: (1) a sex organ of one person and the mouth or anus of another person; or (2) the penetration of the sex organ or anus of a person by an object."

Although Smith-Green and Couch once blithely asserted that the photographs depict "deviate sexual conduct" within this definition, as necessary to meet the second element of the *Miller* obscenity test, I cannot reach the same conclusion. Not even a single photograph meets the definition of "deviate sexual conduct" because none of them depicts the sex organ, mouth or anus of two people, and none of the images depicts actual penetration. From the plain meaning of the words of the statutory definition, I conclude—consistent with the defendants' concession on the point—that the photographs do not depict "deviate sexual conduct" as defined in Indiana law, and that as a result the photographs do not constitute obscenity under the Supreme Court's criteria in *Miller*.

Neither do the photographs constitute child pornography under either state or federal statutes. Indiana's statutes addressing child pornography refer to images that include, depict or describe "sexual conduct by a child," using the same definition of "sexual conduct" as has been considered and rejected previously with respect to the obscenity analysis. I.C. §35-42-4-4(b) & (c). Defendants, while glossing over the inapplicable Indiana statutory definition of "sexual conduct" as discussed above, also initially argued that M.K. and T.V. have "admitted" that the photographs depicted oral and anal sexual acts. But this is a complete stretch of the girls' deposition testimony. The testimony referred to does not address the statutory definition of the term, and in any event could not do so, as these lay witnesses cannot offer such legal analysis and conclusions.

The federal definition, found at 18 U.S.C. §2256(8), requires a "visual depiction involv[ing] the use of a minor engaging in sexually explicit conduct." The phrase "sexually explicit conduct" has a multi-part definition, from which defendants invoke this portion: "actual or simulated . . . sexual intercourse, including genital-genital, oral-genital, anal-genital, or oral-anal, whether between persons of the same or opposite sex." §2256(2)(A)(i). With only candy phalluses and toy tridents, the photographs cannot be said to depict simulated oral-genital sexual intercourse or anal-genital sexual intercourse within the meaning of this statute. Instead, the conduct depicted "must have created the realistic impression of an actual sex act to constitute simulated sexual intercourse." *Tilton v. Playboy Entertainment Group, Inc.*, 554 F.3d 1371, 1376 (11th Cir. 2009). An act "only constitutes simulated sexual intercourse . . . if it creates the realistic impression of an *actual* sexual act." *Giovani Carandola, Ltd. v. Fox*, 470 F.3d 1074, 1080 (4th Cir. 2006) (emphasis in original). Given this analysis, and defendants' later concession, the students' First Amendment claim is not defeated by a contention that their speech is unprotected obscenity or child pornography.

What free speech standards apply?

Having rejected Smith-Green and Couch's arguments that the photographs are not protected by the First Amendment, I must next determine what constitutional free speech standards apply. Relying upon *Bethel School District No. 403 v. Fraser*, 478 U.S. 675, 106 S. Ct. 3159, 92 L. Ed. 2d 549 (1986), Smith-Green and Couch first argue that the photographs are not entitled to First Amendment protection because they are lewd, vulgar and/or plainly offensive. In *Fraser*, the Supreme Court held that the First Amendment does not prevent school officials from punishing "a vulgar and lewd speech . . . [that] would undermine the school's basic educational mission." *Id*. at 685. The speech being made by the student in *Fraser* was at a school assembly. M.K. and T.V.'s photographs were taken inside the privacy of their own homes and were published to the internet from outside of school. Defendants contend that "it is undisputed that the photographs did in fact make it into the school." While this may be true, it's beside the point. Neither M.K. nor T.V. brought the material into the school environment. Others did.

Fraser cannot be interpreted as broadly as Smith-Green and Couch want. Context matters, as *Fraser* itself notes: "A high school assembly or classroom is no place for a sexually explicit monologue directed towards an unsuspecting audience of teenage students." *Id*. But as Justice Brennan noted in his concurrence, the Court's holding was limited: "If respondent had given the same speech outside of the school environment, he could not have been penalized simply because government officials considered his language to be inappropriate." *Id*. at 688.

Indeed, the Supreme Court itself has noted *Fraser*'s limited scope: . . . in *Morse v. Frederick*, 551 U.S. 393 (2007), the Supreme Court plainly stated that "[h]ad Fraser delivered the same speech in a public forum outside the school context, it would have been protected," echoing the observation of Justice Brennan in his *Fraser* concurrence. So here Smith-Green and Couch cannot prevail on a characterization of the photographs as lewd and vulgar in reliance on *Fraser* because, simply put, "[t]he School District's argument fails at the outset because *Fraser* does not apply to off-campus speech."

The Tinker standard and its limits

All of which brings us to *Tinker v. Des Moines Indep. Cmty. Sch. Dist.*, 393 U.S. 503 (1969), where the Supreme Court considered a schools' punishment of students who wore black armbands to school to represent their objections to the Vietnam War and their support for a truce. The case presented a conflict between the rights of the students to free expression and the interest of the school officials in maintaining order in the educational environment. The Court balanced those competing interests by announcing the following standard: school officials can restrict student expression only if the officials can show "that the students' activities would materially and substantially disrupt the work and discipline of the school." *Id.* at 513. The Supreme Court found that there was "no evidence whatever of petitioners' interference, actual or nascent, with the schools' work or of collision with the rights of other students to be secure and to be let alone." *Id.* at 508. Therefore, the suspension of the students for their expression by wearing the armbands was found to violate their First Amendment rights. *Id.* at 514.

Smith-Green and Couch first argue that students have no constitutional right to participate in extracurricular activities, and therefore the discipline imposed upon M.K. and T.V. requires no showing of "substantial disruption."

But *Tinker* itself defeats this argument: The principle of these cases [on student free speech] is not confined to the supervised and ordained discussion which takes place in the classroom . . . A student's rights, therefore, do not embrace merely the classroom hours. When he is in the cafeteria, or on the playing field, or on the campus during the authorized hours, he may express his opinions, even on controversial subjects like the conflict in Vietnam, if he does so without 'materially and substantially interfer(ing) with the requirements of appropriate discipline in the operation of the school' and without colliding with the rights of others. *Tinker*, 393 U.S. at 512–13.

The constitutional right at issue is freedom of expression, not that of participation in extracurricular activities. That there is no constitutional right to participate in athletics or other extracurricular activities may be pertinent to an analysis of other sorts of constitutional claims, such as a Due Process claim, a Privileges and Immunities claim, or an Equal Protection claim, but as *Tinker* itself notes, not to a freedom of expression claim.

What this means is that a student cannot be punished with a ban from extracurricular activities for non-disruptive speech. For example, in a case involving suspension from a high school football team, the Ninth Circuit observed: "In holding that a student's First Amendment rights are 'not confined to the supervised and ordained discussion which takes place in the classroom,' the Court extended *Tinker's* principles to school activities broadly defined, including extracurricular activities." *Pinard v. Clatskanie School District 6J*, 467 F.3d 755, 769 (9th Cir. 2006).

* * *

In the present context, I will also assume without deciding that *Tinker* applies, because even under its contextual narrowing of the right of free speech, I conclude that the school officials violated the First Amendment rights of plaintiffs T.V. and M.K.

Substantial disruption

Finally then, I arrive at the First Amendment standard to be applied, namely whether in the circumstances present here, Principal Couch reasonably found that the pictures posted on the internet had disrupted, or would materially and substantially disrupt, the work and discipline of the school. I agree with Principal Couch and Smith-Green that a showing of actual disruption is not required for the punishment to pass constitutional muster. School officials are not required to wait and allow a disruption of their school environment to occur before taking action. However, "*Tinker* requires a specific and significant fear of disruption, not just some remote apprehension of disturbance" *Saxe v. State College Area School District*, 240 F.3d 200, 211 (3rd Cir. 2001).

M.K. and T.V. are under the impression that the defendants concede the actual disruption argument, and that the disciplinary decision was made entirely on the basis of potential future disruption. But this isn't the case. The school defendants rely on the assertion that Principal Couch acted in part on the report of the complaining parent that the photographs *had already caused* divisiveness on school teams. The mother who brought the photos to Darnell reported that they were "causing issues" with her daughter and the extracurricular teams. The trouble was further described as "divisiveness" with the girls on the volleyball teams, that is, the girls' division into "two camps"—those "in favor, you know, of what—was going on in the pictures" and those who "just wanted to have no part of it."

* * *

Comparison of this testimony reflects a discrepancy in the record as to whether actual disruption of school-sponsored student activity was in fact a basis for the imposition of the discipline meted out to M.K. and T.V. But even assuming it was, the actual disruption in this case does not come close to meeting the *Tinker* standard. Here's what *Tinker* says on that point:

> [I]n our system, undifferentiated fear or apprehension of disturbance is not enough to overcome the right to freedom of expression. Any departure from absolute regimentation may cause trouble. Any variation from the majority's opinion may inspire fear. Any word spoken, in class, in the lunchroom, or on the campus, that

deviates from the views of another person may start an argument or cause a disturbance. But our Constitution says we must take this risk.... In order for the State in the person of school officials to justify prohibition of a particular expression of opinion, it must be able to show that its action was caused by something more than a mere desire to avoid the discomfort and unpleasantness that always accompanies an unpopular viewpoint. Certainly where there is no finding and no showing that engaging in the forbidden conduct would 'materially and substantially interfere with the requirements of appropriate discipline in the operation of the school,' the prohibition cannot be sustained. Tinker, 393 U.S. at 508–09, quoting Burnside, 363 F.2d at 749.

Defendants' showing of actual disruption is extremely weak. Petty disagreements among players on a team—or participants in clubs for that matter—is utterly routine. This type of unremarkable dissension does not establish disruption with the work or discipline of the team or the school, much less disruption that is "substantial" or "material."

* * *

Here, school officials cannot point to any *students* creating or experiencing actual disruption *during any school activity*. Instead, the officials merely responded to the complaints of parents (two in all), and the complaints do not appear to have been confirmed with any students or coaches. As was true of the armbands in *Tinker*, the photos in this case could be said, at best, to have "caused discussion outside of the classrooms, but no interference with work and no disorder." Tinker, 393 U.S. at 514. Certainly no evidence has been presented of the kind of serious issues enumerated recently by the Seventh Circuit as indicative of substantial disruption: "[s]uch facts might include a decline in students' test scores, an upsurge in truancy, or other symptoms of a sick school." *Zamecnik v. Indian Prairie School District*, 636 F.3d 874, 876 (7th Cir. 2011).

In sum, at most, this case involved two complaints from parents and some petty sniping among a group of 15 and 16 year olds. This can't be what the Supreme Court had in mind when it enunciated the "substantial disruption" standard in *Tinker*. To find otherwise would be to read the word "substantial" out of "substantial disruption."

* * *

To sum up: no reasonable jury could conclude that the photos of T.V. and M.K. posted on the internet caused a substantial disruption to school activities, or that there was a reasonably foreseeable chance of future substantial disruption. And while the crass foolishness that is the subject of the protected speech in this case makes one long for important substantive expressions like the black armbands of *Tinker*, such a distinction between the worthwhile and the unworthy is exactly what the First Amendment does not permit. With all respect to the important and valuable function of public school authorities, and the considerable deference to their judgment that is so often due, it would be an unseemly and dangerous precedent to allow the state, in the guise of school authorities, to reach into a child's home and control his/her actions there to the same extent that it can control that child when he/she participates in school sponsored activities. Plaintiffs' motion for partial summary judgment will therefore be granted, and defendants' summary judgment motion denied, on the issue whether T.V. and M.K. were punished in violation of their First Amendment rights.

* * *

Conclusion

Today I determine as a matter of law that the punishment imposed on T.V. and M.K. for their out of school expression violated their First Amendment rights.... Finally, I conclude that a Student Handbook provision that authorizes discipline for out of school conduct that brings "dishonor" or "discredit" upon the school or the student is so vague and overbroad as to violate the Constitution. I wish the case involved more important and worthwhile speech on the part of the students, but then of course a school's well-intentioned but unconstitutional punishment of that speech would be all the more regrettable.

CASES ON THE SUPPLEMENTAL CD

Besig, Cook, and Garda v. The Dolphin Boating and Swimming Club, 683 F.2d 1271 (9th Cir. 1982). In this case the court examines the right to associate, or right not to associate of private clubs.

Borden v. School District of the Township of East Brunswick, 533 F. 3d. 153 (3rd Cir. 2008). This case closely examines personal rights of an employee serving as a state actor with the rights of a school district to enforce religious freedoms found in the First Amendment to the United States Constitution.

Jordan v. Jewel Food Stores, Inc., 83 F. Supp. 3d 761 (2015). This case examines the free speech clause after a Chicago grocery store took out a page in Sports Illustrated congratulating Michael Jordan on his 2009 induction into the Hall of Fame, Jordan sued for using his identity without permission.

Tinker v. Des Moines Independent Community School District, 393 U.S. 503 (1969). This case examines the free speech rights of high school students in school and when school officials have the right to prevent student speech.

Zacchini v. Scripps-Howard Broadcasting, 433 U.S. 562 (1977). This case compares the First Amendment protections granted television stations in broadcasting news, to an individual's right of publicity and economic value of his performance.

QUESTIONS YOU SHOULD BE ABLE TO ANSWER

1. What standard of review did the Court develop in *Tinker v. Des Moines Independent Community School District*?
2. In addition to the *Tinker* standard, when else can public school officials restrict student speech?
3. Discuss when a public school coach can and cannot be involved in prayer before a game.
4. Explain why there is a conflict between the Establishment Clause and Free Exercise Clause.
5. Discuss why the Courts protect print media differently than broadcast media?

REFERENCES

Cases

Bethel School District No. 403 v. Fraser, 478 U.S. 675 (1986).
Borden v. School District of the Township of East Brunswick, 523 F. 3d 153 (3rd Cir. 2008).
Cantwell v. Connecticut, 310 U.S. 296 (1940).
Doe v. Duncanville Independent School Dist., 70 F.3d 405 (1995).
Employment Division, Department of Human Resources of Oregon v. Smith, 494 U.S. 872 (1990).
Everson v. Board of Education, 330 U.S. 1 (1947).
Frederick v. Morse, 551 U.S. 393 (2007).
Gitlow v. New York, 268 U.S. 652 (1925).
Hysaw v. Washburn University of Topeka, 690 F. Supp. 940 (1987).
Layshock v. Hermitage School District, 496 F. Supp. 2d 587 (2007).
Lee v. Weisman, 505 U.S. 577 (1992).
Lemon v. Kurtzman, 403 U.S. 602 (1971).
Lowery v. Euverard, 497 F.3d 584 (6th Cir. 2007).
Palko v. Connecticut, 302 U.S. 319 (1937).
Pinard v. Clatskanie School District 6J, 446 F.3d 964 (9th Cir. 2006).
Robinson v. Hicks, King and City of Harrisburg, 450 Fed. Appx. 168 (3rd Cir. 2011).
Santa Fe High Independent School District v. Doe, 530 U.S. 290 (2000).
Schenck v. United States, 249 U.S. 47 (1919).
Tinker v. Des Moines Independent Community School District, 393 U.S. 503 (1969).
United States v. Schwimmer, 279 U.S. 644 (1937).
Wallace v. Jaffree, 472 U.S. 38 (1985).
Walz v. Tax Commission of City of New York, 397 U.S. 664 (1970).
Zacchini v. Scripps-Howard Broadcasting, 433 U.S. 562 (1977).

Publications

Brown-Foster, S. (2010). Religious Issues. In D. J. Cotton & J. T. Wolohan (Eds.), Law for Recreation and Sport Managers (5th Ed.) pp. 517–527. Dubuque, IA: Kendall/Hunt Publishing Co.
Hayes, A. (2010). From Armbands to Douchebags: How *Doninger v. Niehoff* Shows the Supreme Court Needs to Address Student Speech in the Cyber Age. *Akron Law Review*, 43, 247–289.
Sullivan, K., and Gunther, G. (2007). *Constitutional Law* (17th ed.). New York, NY: Foundation Press.
Shiffrin, S. and Choper, J. (2006). *The First Amendment: Cases—Comments—Questions* (4th ed.) St. Paul, MN: West Publishing.
Weaver, R. and Lively, D. (2003). *Understanding the First Amendment*. Newark, NJ: LexisNexis

Legislation

United States Constitution, Amendment I.

VOLUNTARY ASSOCIATIONS AND ELIGIBILITY ISSUES

Colleen Colles | Metropolitan State University of Denver

By definition, a **voluntary association** is "a group of individuals joined together on the basis of mutual interest or common objectives, especially a business group that is not organized or constituted as a legal entity" (*Random House Inc.*, 2016). This fundamental right to associate is protected by the **First and Fourteenth Amendments.** State high school athletic associations, the National Federation of High Schools (NFHS), the National Collegiate Athletic Association (NCAA), the National Parks and Recreation Association (NPRA) are all examples of voluntary sport and recreation associations.

In reviewing the rules voluntary associations establish for eligibility or the right to participate in the organization, the courts have historically been reluctant to overturn the bylaws, rules, regulations, or decisions of these associations unless they violate constitutional law, public policy or were enforced in an **arbitrary or capricious** manner (see *Indiana High School Athletic Association, Inc. v. Watson, 2010* on Supplemental CD). By joining voluntary associations, the courts have held that participants agree to follow the rules and regulations of such organizations and essentially form reciprocal restraints that function as contracts (Andrzejewski, 2013).

The following section examines the jurisdiction of courts with regard to voluntary associations and some of the specific eligibility requirements enacted by such organizations. In particular, the section will examine the eligibility requirements of both state high school athletic associations and the NCAA.

FUNDAMENTAL CONCEPTS

Voluntary associations get their authority to govern through a combination of federal, state, and local legislation, and in some cases, litigation. States often grant school boards the authority to join governing associations, thereby relieving themselves of the oversight, decision-making, and enforcement. Local schools have significant independence in determining the rules and regulations regarding their participation in interscholastic sports; however, state athletic associations play a significant role by providing state-wide governance for interscholastic athletics (Van Ann, 2011).

On occasion, an athletic association's governing authority has been challenged.

In *Louisiana High School Athletic Association v. State of Louisiana* (2013), state legislative action was found to restrict the association's ability to govern. The Louisiana High School Athletic Association (LHSAA) effectively argued that the Legislature passed statutes which interfered with the LHSAA's internal operations by attempting to make rules and regulations *for* the association instead of allowing LHSAA to do so on its own. The Louisiana constitution prohibits the legislature from passing any law that amends, changes, or explains the charters of any private corporation. The state laws, which amended association bylaws regarding residency, transfer rules and eligibility for home school students, were declared unconstitutional. The court held that the LHSAA is a private entity and the legislature's actions violated the association's constitutional rights to equal protection and due process of the law.

Judicial Review

As discussed in Section 6.11, generally the courts will not interfere with the internal affairs of a voluntary association. For example in *Rottmann v. Penn Interscholastic Athletics Association (2004)*, the court held that:

> In the absence of mistake, fraud, collusion or arbitrariness, the decisions of such associations will be accepted by the courts as conclusive. Such associations may adopt reasonable rules which will be

deemed valid and binding upon the members of the association unless the rule violates some law or public policy. It is not the responsibility of the federal courts to inquire into the expediency, practicability, or wisdom of those regulations (*Rottmann v. Penn Interscholastic Athletics Association*, 2004).

As noted in *NCAA v. Yeo (2005)*, "judicial intervention in [student athletic disputes] often does more harm than good . . . " and "judges are not 'super referees.'" This notion of judicial deference to the associations was highlighted by the court in *NCAA v. Lasege (2001)*, when it stated that members of voluntary associations should be free from unwarranted interference from the courts and members should be allowed to "paddle their own canoe."

However, there are exceptions to this non-interference tenet. For example, in *Florida High School Athletic Association v. Marazzito (2005)*, the court affirmed that intervention in the internal affairs of a voluntary association may be appropriate under *exceptional circumstances*. Specifically, a court should only intervene under the following two conditions: (1) a substantial property, contract or economic rights will be adversely affected by the association's action and the internal procedures of the association were unfair or inadequate or (2) the association acted maliciously or in bad faith.

The courts have also consistently ruled that the regulations and/or decisions of associations cannot be unreasonable, arbitrary, or capricious. In a case involving a student's request to transfer schools under a hardship exception, the Indiana High School Athletic Association's (IHAA) decision to deny the student-athlete eligibility was deemed arbitrary and capricious because the IHSAA did not take into account that a substantial change to the family's financial condition had occurred and that the change was out of the student's control. Thus, the court determined that the student should have met the requirements for a hardship waiver (*IHAA v. Durham, 2001*). When allegations of "unreasonableness" arise, courts will decide if the rule has a rational relationship to a reasonable goal of the association.

It is important to recognize that the member *schools* are considered "voluntary" members of the governing associations, so judicial review is very limited; however, *students* are not deemed "voluntary" members and are therefore afforded the stricter arbitrary and capricious standard of review. The focus of many lawsuits involving voluntary sport and recreation associations is on the arbitrary and capricious standard and violations of constitutional rights.

Arbitrary and Capricious Standard

In *Indiana High School Athletic Association v. Carlberg (1997)*, the Supreme Court of Indiana found that the transfer rule advanced a legitimate goal of the IHSAA, and as enforced against Carlberg was not arbitrary and capricious and therefore did not violate the student's federal right of equal protection. In reaching this decision, two important points were noted by the court. First, the arbitrary and capricious standard of review is narrow and the court cannot substitute its judgment for the judgment of the IHSAA. Second, the court stated "the rule or decision will be found to be arbitrary and capricious only where it is willful and unreasonable, without consideration and in disregard of the facts or circumstances in the case, or without some basis which would lead a reasonable and honest person to the same conclusion" (*Indiana High School Athletic Association v. Carlberg*, 1997).

State or Federal Constitutional Rights

Since high school athletic associations are widely accepted as **state actors**, the decisions of these associations are subject to constitutional review. *(see Section 6.12 State Action)*. As state actors, these voluntary associations cannot deny citizens equal protection and/or due process guaranteed by the Federal Constitution. (*See sections 6.13 Due Process and 6.14 Equal Protection*). The **Equal Protection Clause of the Fourteenth Amendment** provides a constitutional method for checking the fairness of the application of the law. If an association cannot demonstrate a connection between the rule and its purpose, then an equal protection violation may have occurred. Thus, voluntary associations must practice due diligence by providing procedural due process whenever disciplinary action is taken.

In Kentucky, the parents of non-public school students alleged violations of their rights under the First and Fourteenth Amendments through the application of Bylaw 13, which places limits on the amount and type of merit-based scholarship assistance a student can receive and remain eligible to participate in athletics (*Seger v. Kentucky High School Athletic Association*, 2011). The appellate court affirmed the decision of the district court to dismiss the federal claims stating that the Bylaw applied to all non-public schools equally. Of interest in this case are the plaintiffs' allegations that the restrictions in Bylaw 13 are discriminatory on the basis of religion and that a strict scrutiny standard should be applied. The court disagreed and ruled that the bylaw does not discriminate based on a "suspect" or "quasi-suspect" classification and thus is subject to review under the rational basis standard.

In *Sisson v. Virginia High School League* (2010), the plaintiff was one day too old under the league's participation rules and was prohibited from participating in varsity athletics. After a failed appeal to the state athletic association, the plaintiff filed action alleging violations of his right to due process and equal protection and requested that a temporary restraining order be granted. The court, which denied the request, based its ruling on the plaintiff's inability to establish the necessary elements for a preliminary injunction: (1) irreparable harm and (2) a likelihood of success based on the merits. A key consideration by the court was the fact that the plaintiff's parents elected to hold him back a year on the recommendation of the school, he was not held back by the school for academic reasons.

It should be noted that while high school athletic associations have been deemed state actors for constitutional purposes, thereby limiting their regulatory authority, the NCAA has not. Therefore, while the actions of state high school associations are subject to Constitutional review, the courts will not review those of the NCAA (see *NCAA v. Tarkanian*, 1988).

High School Privilege
High school eligibility rules are essentially the products of state high school activities/athletics associations. These associations are created to deal with the management of **extracurricular activities**, which by definition are all those activities for students that are sponsored or sanctioned by an educational institution that supplement or complement, but are not a part of, the institution's required academic program or regular curriculum.

It is well-established that students do not have a general constitutional right to participate in athletics. Participation is voluntary and, more important, a **privilege.** A school board may decide, usually through its participation in the state high school athletics association, the terms under which students may exercise the privilege. When eligibility standards are challenged in the courts, they must in most circumstances withstand only rational basis scrutiny. This means that if the requirements are rationally related to a legitimate purpose of association and not arbitrary, capricious, or unjustly discriminatory, they will be upheld by the courts (*IHSAA v. Watson, 2010*).

High School Regulations
High school athletic association eligibility by-laws often address, but are not limited to, issues regarding residency, attendance, transfers, age limits, recruiting, amateurism, and behavior. The areas currently attracting the most attention and legal scrutiny are transfer rules and allegations of illegal recruiting. In fact, high school basketball in New Jersey has been described as having a "transferring epidemic" (Stanmyre, 2014), and the Dallas Morning News recently published a 4-part series on high school transfer issues in the state of Texas (Smith, C., Wixon, M., & Riddle, G., 2015).

Transfer Rules
High school athletic associations create transfer rules to preclude student-athletes from **"jumping"** (enrolling at a different school) for reasons pertaining to athletics. There are many legitimate reasons for students to transfer such as family relocations, changes in employment, divorce, academic offerings, etc., thus establishing a basis for exceptions to the rules.

Recently, a group of private schools sued the New York State Public High School Athletic Association alleging that new rules governing transfers limit school choice. In this case, which is currently in the Albany County Supreme Court, the nine plaintiff schools contend that three new amendments to the transfer rule are arbitrary and violate state education law. The defendant states that the changes were necessary to curb illegal recruiting and keep students from gaining an "athletic advantage" (Kennedy, 2015).

In an unpublished decision by the Superior Court of New Jersey (*Board of Education of the Township of North Bergen Hudson County v. New Jersey State Interscholastic Athletic Association (2015)*, a state appellate panel denied North Bergen High School's bid to reinstate the 2011 state football championship. The school had been stripped of the championship for illegally recruiting two players. In its decision the panel stated, "players were cheated of the opportunity to learn the most valuable lesson of competitive sports." These widespread allegations of illegal recruiting have prompted athletic associations across the country to continually investigate ways to create and enforce transfer policies that are equitable for both students and schools.

Although transfer rules will likely remain popular targets for legal challenges based upon claims of violations of equal protection, freedom of religion, a right to travel, and due process, the courts have generally upheld transfer rules under rational judicial scrutiny.

Home-Schooled Student Eligibility

Many states currently require public schools to allow homeschoolers access to sports (See current list at: http://www.hslda.org/docs/nche/Issues/E/Equal_Access.pdf). Specific eligibility requirements vary from state to state, but generally include 1) being in compliance with the state homeschool law, 2) meeting the same eligibility requirements (residence, age, etc.) as public school students, and 3) submitting verification that the student is passing his or her core subjects (additional details available at: http://www.hslda.org/docs/nche/issues/s/state_sports.asp).

Even though some state legislatures have supported home-schoolers in providing access to the privilege of public school activities, the courts in many states have taken a different position (Batista & Hatfield, 2005). For example, in *Jones v. West Virginia State Board of Education (2005)*, the state Supreme Court overturned a trial court ruling that the West Virginia Secondary School Activities Commission (WVSSAC) violated a home-schooled student's rights to equal protection and breached its duty to promulgate reasonable rules and regulations. In reversing the decision, the Supreme Court stated that the WVSSAC did not violate the student's rights because the challenged statute pertained to providing educational resources, not athletic resources, to home-schooled students. Athletic competitions and leagues for "homeschoolers" have become more commonplace at the local, regional and national levels.

The Pennsylvania Interscholastic Athletic Association (PIAA) Attendance Rule was recently challenged by Shonda Chapman, mother of a home-schooled child who was ruled ineligible. The child was not enrolled full-time at a private school, but wanted to participate on the private school's sports teams. The PIAA Attendance Rule stated that a home-schooled student that is not enrolled full-time at a private school cannot play sports for the private school but must instead play sports in the public school district in which he resides. Chapman filed a civil action claiming the rule violated her Fourteenth Amendment rights of freedom of religion. The claims were dismissed as the court held that the Attendance Rule was facially neutral as it applies to all children, regardless of their religious belief and the burden on the plaintiff's free exercise of religion was minimal *(Chapman v. Pennsylvania Interscholastic Athletic Association, 2014)*.

Redshirting

The practice of delaying or postponing an athlete's competition in order to extend the athlete's career is known as **"redshirting."** For purposes of maximizing athletic success, redshirting is an effective strategy to take advantage of an extra year's growth and maturity and, of course, skill development. High school athletics association rules do not permit the practice of redshirting because it is contrary to the educational mission. Furthermore, redshirting creates unfair competition advantages, possible dangerous mismatches, and unwarranted exclusion of peer student-athletes.

On the other hand, high school athletics associations recognize illness or injury and purely academic determinations of grade level as legitimate reasons for exceptions to rules precluding redshirting and make appropriate allowances. To address potential problems related to redshirting, **rules of longevity** must be invoked. Longevity rules determine the limits for participation in terms of (1) semesters/years allowed to complete competition, and (2) a maximum age beyond which interscholastic competition may not continue. For example, most high school association rules limit a student-athlete to eight consecutive semesters in which to complete interscholastic competition. Similarly, most associations do not permit competition among student-athletes who have reached their nineteenth birthday before beginning his/her senior year. In general, courts have agreed with the rational argument that longevity and redshirting regulations preserve the privilege of interscholastic sports competition, consistent with their educational mission.

Intercollegiate Regulations

Individual eligibility rules for intercollegiate competition begin at the specific institution where the student is enrolled. Depending upon the institution's characteristics and mission, specific eligibility standards for representing that institution in intercollegiate athletic competition may be imposed. Such standards must reflect at a minimum the requirements of the conference in which it competes and, further, the association of conferences and institutions in which it holds membership. The largest such association of four-year institutions is the National Collegiate Athletic Association (NCAA). Therefore, this discussion will focus on the eligibility rules and bylaws of the NCAA and various legal challenges to those rules (see www.NCAA.org).

Article 1.3.1 of the *NCAA Manual* (2015–16) declares its basic purpose:

> The competitive athletics programs of member institutions are designed to be a vital part of the educational system. A basic purpose of this Association is to maintain intercollegiate athletics as an integral part of the educational program and the athlete as an integral part of the student body and, by so doing, retain a clear line of demarcation between intercollegiate athletics and professional sports.

Thus, the NCAA is a private, voluntary association of four-year institutions that share a common interest in preserving amateur intercollegiate athletics as part of the educational mission.

Academic Regulations

To maintain the educational mission, the NCAA has legislated explicit rules for qualifying individuals academically for competition on two dimensions: initial and continuing. To meet *initial* qualifications for competing at an NCAA Division I institution, the student-athlete must currently demonstrate the following (Bylaw 14.3.1.1):

a. Graduation from high school
b. Successful completion of a required core curriculum of 16 approved academic courses in specified subjects
c. Specified minimum GPA in the core curriculum, and
d. Specified minimum SAT or ACT score.
e. Effective August 2016, the minimum GPA for initial eligibility will increase from 2.0 to 2.3 and the specified minimum SAT/ACT score will be determined according to a sliding scale (see http://fs.ncaa.org/Docs/eligibility_center/Quick_Reference_Sheet.pdf for an example of the index). Also effective in August 2016 is a new designation of an *academic redshirt*. This term applies to student-athletes who have a GPA lower than 2.3, but higher than 2.0. They may receive athletically related funding, but cannot compete during the first year of residence.

Determination of initial eligibility is conducted by the Eligibility Center and includes a review of academic and amateurism standards. If the student satisfactorily meets the standards, the student is deemed a "qualifier" and is academically eligible to participate and receive athletically related financial aid. If the standards are not met, the applicant is restricted from competing (but may practice), may not receive athletically related financial aid, and surrenders one of his or her four years of competition eligibility.

To satisfy **continuing eligibility** requirements, the student-athlete must demonstrate a consistent record of progress toward a degree. To register "satisfactory progress" the student-athlete's academic record at the beginning of the fall semester or quarter of each year in residence must indicate completion of a requisite percent of course requirements in the student-athlete's particular academic program at a requisite percent of the GPA required for graduation at the particular institution. In addition, the student-athlete must be enrolled full-time (minimum 12 semester credit hours) in order to maintain current athletic eligibility. Dropping below full-time enrollment immediately disqualifies the student for athletic competition.

Amateurism
As stated previously, the NCAA's basic purpose highlights a focus on the amateur status of student athletes and the NCAA Manual (2015–16) consistently refers to the maintenance of a "clear line of demarcation between college athletics and professional sports" (NCAA Manual, 2011–12). Bylaws applied to amateurism contain restrictions on activities that occur prior to and after enrollment. Initial amateur certification is managed by the Eligibility Center and must be retained throughout the student-athlete's enrollment. A significant case challenging the NCAA's authority to regulate eligibility is *Bloom v. NCAA*, (2004). In the case, which highlighted Bloom's amateur status, the court held that the NCAA had not been arbitrary and capricious in enforcing its rules and denying a waiver for Bloom.

Transfer Rules
NCAA rules governing eligibility following transfer from one institution to another are rather complex. The purposes of transfer rules are to preclude recruitment of athletes from one institution to another and to discourage interruptions of academic progress due to transfers because of reasons pertaining to athletics. The general principle stated in Bylaw 14.5.1 requires a student who transfers to a member institution from any other collegiate institution to complete one full academic year of residence at the certifying institution before being eligible to compete. There are multiple exceptions to this requirement; the most notable being those involving transfers from two-year colleges.

In January 2009, the NCAA adopted more stringent rules (bylaw 14.5.4) for athletes transferring from two-year institutions that required increased requirements with regard to math and English credit hours. Another area of note is Bylaw 14.1.9.1 which applies to graduate students. The bylaw allows student athletes that had graduated with remaining eligibility to transfer and play at another institution where they were enrolled in a graduate degree. Critics of this rule suggested that it created "free agency" in college sports (Martin, 2008).

In November 2015, Devin Pugh, a collegiate football player, filed a class action lawsuit alleging the National Collegiate Athletic Association's (NCAA) rule restricting its collegiate athletes to sit out for a year when transferring between top-level schools and capping the number of scholarships a school can offer are anti-competitive. Although this case is primarily focused on unfair business practices and anti-trust issues, the transfer rules of the NCAA and their impact on player eligibility have come under increased scrutiny. *Pugh v. NCAA* is currently in the U.S. District Court for the Southern District of Indiana.

Longevity
The NCAA also is concerned with the problems presented by interminable eligibility and older-than-expected participants. With regard to the former, the NCAA decided four years of intercollegiate competition is the maximum allowed, regardless of where or at how many institutions the competition takes place. Further, the individual student-athlete is permitted five consecutive calendar years from original matriculation to complete four years of eligibility. Thus, an accommodation is possible following a transfer, or even a redshirt year for maturation or injury, etc. In addition, student-athletes may also seek waivers if they undertake military service, serve with religious organizations, or become pregnant.

With regard to age, the membership became alarmed at the infusion of older athletes, particularly foreign athletes with the advantage of seasoning and experience, supplanting the scholarships of younger athletes. So, in 1980 the membership passed "the age rule," Bylaw 14.2.4.5, which credits any organized sports competition in a particular sport in each 12-month period following the athlete's twentieth birthday as a year of NCAA competition eligibility.

The Restitution Rule
Bylaw 19.7 or the Restitution Rule has undergone a series of modifications since it was introduced in 1975. The current bylaw approved in 2010 applies to a "student-athlete who is ineligible under the terms of the constitution, bylaws or other legislation of the Association" and "is permitted to participate in intercollegiate competition contrary to such NCAA legislation but in accordance with the terms of a court restraining order

or injunction operative against the institution attended by such student-athlete or against the Association, or both". Subsequently, if the "injunction is voluntarily vacated, stayed or reversed or it is finally determined by the courts that injunctive relief is not or was not justified", the institution must pay restitution to the NCAA. Restitution can range from individual and team records being stricken to loss of television coverage and ineligibility for future championship play.

SIGNIFICANT CASE

In a case examining the impact of NCAA rules on high school athletes and lawyers, readers should pay particular attention to the court's reasoning regarding the arbitrary nature of the challenged bylaw and the violation of good faith and fair dealing.

ANDREW A. OLIVER V. NATIONAL COLLEGIATE ATHLETIC ASSOCIATION
Court of Common Pleas, Erie County
2009 Ohio 6587; 920 N.E.2d 203 (2009)

Facts

The plaintiff, Andrew Oliver, is a resident of Vermilion, Erie County, Ohio. In 2006, the plaintiff graduated from Vermilion High School, where he was the primary pitcher for its baseball team. The plaintiff is currently in his junior year of college at Oklahoma State University ("OSU"). Since August 2006, the plaintiff has pitched for the baseball team at OSU.

The defendant, the National Collegiate Athletic Association ("NCAA"), is an unincorporated business association having its principal place of business in Marion County, Indiana; it has member institutions not only in Oklahoma but also in Ohio. OSU is a member institution of the defendant; the NCAA association regulates the student-athlete activities at OSU.

The plaintiff, in February 2006, retained the services of Robert M. Baratta, Tim Baratta, and Icon Sports Group, d.b.a. Icon Law Group, as his sports advisors and attorneys. In June of the same year, the Minnesota Twins of Major League Baseball drafted the plaintiff in the 17th round of the draft. At the end of the summer, the Minnesota Twins met with the plaintiff and his father at the Oliver family home in Vermilion before the plaintiff left for his freshman year of college. Tim Baratta also attended the meeting, at his own request, at the Oliver home. During the meeting the Minnesota Twins offered the plaintiff $ 390,000 to join their organization. After heeding the advice of his father, the plaintiff rejected the offer and chose to attend OSU in the fall on a full scholarship for which he had already signed a letter of intent in the fall of 2005.

As a result of deciding to go to OSU and accepting amateur status, the plaintiff would not be eligible for the draft again until his junior year of college in June 2009. The plaintiff played his freshman and sophomore years for OSU, and during that period he never received any invoices requesting payment for any services rendered by his advisors. In fact, the plaintiff avers that the advisors provided nothing of value to him.

In March 2008, plaintiff decided to terminate the Barattas and Icon Sports and retain the Boras Corporation. The plaintiff communicated his intentions of termination to Robert Baratta. At that time, Robert Baratta attempted to reconnect with the plaintiff and his father, but to no avail. In April 2008, the plaintiff received a letter and an invoice from the Barattas for $ 113,750 for legal services. The invoice did not contain any detail of services rendered or time entries. The plaintiff took the invoice to the OSU baseball team coach, the OSU Athletic Compliance Office, and the Boras Corporation. Subsequently, the plaintiff retained attorney Michael Quiat to assist him with the matter. Quiat requested the time records supporting Baratta's invoice. In May, in response to the request, the Barattas sent a letter dated February 8, 2006, and a contract dated February 8, 2006, to Quiat. The letter listed six items of assistance rendered by them on behalf of the plaintiff. The plaintiff has argued that the contract is fictitious and the assistance stated in it was in fact never performed.

On May 19, 2008, the previous attorneys mailed, faxed, and e-mailed a letter to the defendant complaining about the plaintiff and reporting alleged violations by the plaintiff, i.e. the meeting at the Olivers' home that Tim Baratta had attended. As a result of the allegations, OSU and the defendant investigated the alleged violations in relationship to the plaintiff's amateur status. In May

2008, the plaintiff was indefinitely suspended from playing baseball and was informed by OSU staff that he had violated NCAA Bylaw 12.3.1 by (1) allowing his previous attorneys to contact the Minnesota Twins by telephone and (2) by allowing Tim Baratta to be present in his home when a representative from the Minnesota Twins tendered an offer to him.

On August 18, 2008, the plaintiff was reinstated as a result of a temporary restraining order issued by this court. However, in October 2008, OSU filed for reinstatement of the plaintiff with the NCAA even though the temporary restraining order had reinstated the plaintiff. Subsequently, in December 2008, the plaintiff was suspended for one year and charged a year of eligibility by the defendant. The penalty was subsequently reduced to 70 percent of the original suspension and no loss of eligibility for the plaintiff.

Arguments

The plaintiff requests that this court enter a declaratory judgment and injunctive relief enjoining the NCAA Bylaw 12.3.2.1 as unenforceable because the plaintiff retained legal counsel (the Barattas) to represent him and that legal counsel is subject to the exclusive regulation of the Ohio Supreme Court. Therefore, the defendant has no authority to promulgate a rule that would prevent a lawyer from competently representing his client. As such, the plaintiff maintains that, NCAA Bylaw 12.3.2.1 is void because it is against the public policy of the state of Ohio.

Furthermore, the plaintiff argues that NCAA Bylaw 12.3.2.1 is arbitrary and capricious because, it does not impact a player's amateur status but instead limits the player's ability to effectively negotiate a contract that the player or a player's parent could negotiate. In that regard, the plaintiff contends that he was the victim of unethical attorneys who, under the laws of the state of Ohio, had a duty to protect him, but instead the defendant punished him even though he bore no fault. Thus, according to the plaintiff, the defendant should vacate the findings that were the foundation of the plaintiff's suspension and reinstate him immediately with no further punishment.

Finally, the plaintiff requests that this court also enter a declaratory judgment and permanent injunction enjoining the defendant from enforcing NCAA Bylaw 19.7. The plaintiff argues that the bylaw interferes with the Ohio Constitution's delegation of all judicial power to the courts of this state and, consistent with that premise, exists solely to coerce or direct its agents and members to ignore court orders that are binding upon member institutions of the defendant.

Contrarily, the defendant argues that the plaintiff did not overcome the presumption that its bylaws and decisions as a voluntary association are valid. As such, the defendant contends that it has the right to manage its affairs and apply its bylaws, within legal limits, without interference from the judiciary and since the plaintiff has failed to prove that its bylaws are illegal, arbitrary or fraudulent, the defendant's internal affairs are presumptively correct.

The defendant argues that the plaintiff must prove by clear and convincing evidence that any decision made by the defendant was arbitrary or capricious. The defendant also argues that the plaintiff has failed to sustain such proof. The decision made to reinstate the plaintiff's eligibility, even though a penalty was imposed, was based on admitted and objective evidence obtained by the defendant and this court should not substitute its judgment for that of the defendant's.

Furthermore, the defendant argues that it is not in contract with the plaintiff and that such a relationship must be proven in order to support an entry of a permanent injunction. Likewise, the defendant maintains that since there is no underlying contract claim, there can be no independent basis for granting declaratory relief. The defendant argues that it did not owe a contractual duty of good faith and fair dealing since there can be no implied duty where there is no underlying contract. The defendant supports its contention by stating that Oklahoma's law does not allow this court to imply terms in a contract that the parties did not bargain for, nor does it allow the court to disregard the plaintiff's violation.

The defendant also argues that the plaintiff waived any contractual benefits by his prior breaches, namely, violation of NCAA bylaws and concealing his agent relationship. In accordance with this argument, the defendant declares that these prior breaches bar recovery of any equitable relief since the plaintiff has failed to come to court with clean hands. Similarly, the defendant professes that even if the plaintiff had proven liability on a contract claim, the remedy, according to the defendant, is not immediate reinstatement or revisions to the "agent rule." The defendant states that what the plaintiff is seeking is overreaching and the remedy sought is dramatic and improper.

* * *

The defendant also proclaims that the balance of harm militates against the entry of injunctive relief. The defendant contends that its bylaws are rationally related to the NCAA constitution and preserving the amateur model of collegiate athletics and the bylaws, in particular Bylaw 12.3.2.1, help to retain a clear line of demarcation between collegiate and professional sports, which is a goal of its members. Consequently, the defendant argues that striking Bylaw 19.7 leaves the members without a remedy, and it admonishes the court that it should not strike a bylaw simply because the court believes the members of the institution should govern themselves in a different way.

* * *

II. Breach of Contract

* * *

To the extent that the plaintiff's claim of arbitrary and capricious action asserts a violation of the duty of good faith and fair dealing that is implied in the contractual relationship between the NCAA and its members, his position as a third-party beneficiary of that contractual relationship affords him standing to pursue his claims. . . . Previously, Ohio law held that not every contract implicates an implied obligation to use good faith and fair dealing. . . . There had to be a distinction between written terms and implied promises within a contract. Without explaining the history of the distinctions, the Sixth Appellate District of Ohio, in whose jurisdiction this court lies, holds that the parties to a contract "are bound toward one another by standards of good faith and fair-dealing." *Bolling v. Clevepak Corp.* (1984), 20 Ohio App.3d 113, 121, 20 Ohio B. 146, 484 N.E.2d 1367. Ohio law now supports that good faith is part of a contract claim. . . . Furthermore, the court in *Brown v. Otto C. Epp Mem. Hosp.* determined that "good faith is required of every contract," and this court is in agreement with that premise. *Brown* (1987), 41 Ohio App.3d 198, 199, 535 N.E.2d 325. Thus, this court holds that a party can be found to have breached its contract if it fails to act in good faith.

III. Good Faith and Fair Dealing

Even though the obligation of good faith exists in a contractual relationship, this is not an invitation for this court to rewrite the benefit bestowed on the parties. The court agrees with the defendant that this is not a case about whether the court agrees or disagrees with the bylaws in question. Neither is it a case about how the defendant voted at either the 1975 or 2002 membership conventions. However, since this court has determined that the agreement between the defendants has an implied covenant of good faith and fair dealing as it relates to the plaintiff, there must be in fact honesty and reasonableness in the enforcement of the contract. Therefore, the defendant, and for that matter OSU, was required to deal honestly and reasonably with the plaintiff as a third-party beneficiary regarding their contractual relationship. Surely each party is entitled to the benefit of its bargain. With that stated, if this court determines that Bylaw 12.3.2.1 is void because it is against the public policy of Ohio or because it is arbitrary and capricious, and Bylaw 19.7 interferes with the delegation of judicial power to the courts of this state, then the defendant has not dealt with the plaintiff honestly or reasonably and the defendant has breached the contract.

* * *

NCAA Bylaw 12.3.2.1.

However, the crux of this case falls under Bylaw 12.3.2, which carves out an exception to the no agent rule by allowing a student-athlete to retain a lawyer (not even the defendant can circumvent an individual's right to counsel). Yet, the exception to the rule, i.e., NCAA Bylaw 12.3.2 which allows legal counsel for student-athletes attempts to limit an attorney's role as to that representation and, in effect, such as in the case here, puts the onus on the student-athlete. See NCAA Bylaw 12.3.2.1.

The status of the no-agent rule, as firmly pointed out in the direct testimony of Kevin Lennon, vice president of membership services, is a prohibition against agents, not lawyers. Therein lies the problem.

It is impossible to allow student-athletes to hire lawyers and attempt to control what that lawyer does for his client by Bylaws 12.3.2 or 12.3.2.1. These rules attempt to say to the student-athlete that he or she can consult with an attorney but that the attorney cannot negotiate a contract with a professional sport's team. This surely does not retain a clear line of demarcation between amateurism and professionalism. The student-athlete will never know what his attorney is doing for him or her, and quite frankly neither will the defendant. The evidence is very clear that this rule is impossible to enforce and as a result is being enforced selectively. Further, as in this case, it allows for exploitation of the student-athlete "by professional and commercial enterprises," in contravention of the positive intentions of the defendant.

Was Barratta's presence in that room a clear indication that the plaintiff, a teenager who had admitted at trial that he was in no position to negotiate a professional contract and whose father testified to the same, was a professional? According to Bylaw 12.3.2.1, the no-agent rule, he was. As such the following issues must be resolved: Is the no-agent rule against the public policy of Ohio? Is it arbitrary? Is it capricious?

* * *

For a student-athlete to be permitted to have an attorney and then to tell that student-athlete that his attorney cannot be present during the discussion of an offer from a professional organization is akin to a patient hiring a doctor, but the doctor is told by the hospital board and the insurance company that he cannot be present when the patient meets with a surgeon because the conference may improve his patient's decision-making power. Bylaw 12.3.2.1 is unreliable (capricious) and illogical (arbitrary) and indeed stifles what attorneys are trained and retained to do.

* * *

This court appreciates that a fundamental goal of the member institutions and the defendant is to preserve the clear line of demarcation between amateurism and professionalism. However, to suggest that Bylaw 12.3.2.1 accomplishes that purpose by instructing a student-athlete that his attorney cannot do what he or she was hired to do is simply illogical. An example of a clear line of demarcation between amateurism and professionalism is indeed drawn within the bylaws and is done so in Bylaw 12.02.3: A professional athlete is one who receives any kind of payment, directly or indirectly, for athletics participation except as permitted by the governing legislation of the Association.

If the membership and the NCAA decide that Bylaw 12.02.3 does not accomplish that purpose, so be it. But no entity, other than that one designated by the state, can dictate to an attorney where, what, how, or when he should represent his client. With all due respect, surely that decision should not be determined by the NCAA and its member institutions, no matter what the defendant claims is the purpose of the rule. If the defendant intends to deal with this athlete or any athlete in good faith, the student-athlete should have the opportunity to have the tools present (in this case an attorney) that would allow him to make a wise decision without automatically being deemed a professional, especially when such contractual negotiations can be overwhelming even to those who are skilled in their implementation.

IV. Arbitrary and Capricious

With that stated, the court now addresses the issue of whether Bylaw 19.7 is arbitrary and capricious. Bylaw 19.7 states:

If a student athlete who is ineligible under the terms of the constitution, bylaws or other legislation of the Association is permitted to participate in intercollegiate competition contrary to such NCAA legislation but in accordance with the terms of a court restraining order or injunction operative against the institution attended by such student-athlete or against the Association, or both, and said injunction is voluntarily vacated, stayed or reversed or it is finally determined by the courts that injunctive relief is not or was not justified, the Board of Directors may take any one or more of the following actions against such institution in the interest of restitution and fairness to competing institutions: (a) through (e).

Following the above-mentioned paragraph, subsections (a) through (e) list penalties that impinge on institutions, student-athletes, or team records for following the dictates of a court order that may later be overturned by a higher court. The plaintiff would ask: "How could any entity punish an individual for accessing their right to Court?" The defendant argues that the member institutions agreed that it was improper to allow an institution to reap the benefits of playing a student-athlete who was finally adjudicated to be ineligible. Just because member institutions agree to a rule or bylaw does not mean that the bylaw is sacrosanct or that it is not arbitrary or capricious.

Throughout the history of this country many institutions and entities have agreed to bylaws that were against the notion of a fair judicial process. The regulations must be fair to the people to whom they were meant to serve, especially when it comes to the right of an individual to petition the court system. Courts of appeal have never been without remedies for cases that they overturn as it relates to the parties that are involved. Student-athletes must have their opportunity to access the court system without fear of punitive actions against themselves or the institutions and teams of which they belong. The old adage that you can put lipstick on a pig, but it is still a pig, is quite relevant here. The defendant may entitle Bylaw 19.7 "Restitution" but it is still punitive in its achievement, and it fosters a direct attack on the constitutional right of access to courts.

Bylaw 19.7 takes the rule of law as governed by the courts of this nation and gives it to an unincorporated business association. The bylaw is overreaching. For example, if a court grants a restraining order that permits a student-athlete the right to play, the institution will find itself in a real dilemma. Does the institution allow the student-athlete to play as directed by the court's ruling and in so doing face great harm should the decision be reversed on appeal? Alternatively, does the institution, in fear of Bylaw 19.7, decide that it is safer to disregard the court order and not allow the student-athlete to play, thereby finding itself in contempt of court? Such a bylaw is governed by no fixed standard except that which is self-serving for the defendant. To that extent, it is arbitrary and indeed a violation of the covenant of good faith and fair dealing implicit in its contract with the plaintiff, as the third-party beneficiary.

* * *

After this court has engaged in a balancing process that was designed to weigh the equities between the parties, the court determines by clear and convincing evidence that the plaintiff would suffer immediate and irreparable injury, loss, or damage if injunctive relief is not granted. If an injunction is not granted, the plaintiff would suffer loss of his college baseball experience, impairment or loss of his future baseball professional career, loss in being available for the upcoming draft because he is less likely to be seen, and ongoing damage to the plaintiff's reputation and baseball career.

In comparison, the defendant's witnesses stated that if relief were granted, it would be confusing as to which institutions would have to follow this court's ruling. Would it be Ohio members, Oklahoma members, all institutions? However, since this court has personam jurisdiction, this argument is not as persuasive as the plaintiff's and the scales of justice have tilted in the plaintiff's favor.

Judgment accordingly.

CASES ON THE SUPPLEMENTAL CD

Indiana High School Athletic Association v. Watson, (2010 Ind. LEXIS 800). Examine the court's acceptance of hearsay testimony and the conclusion that the transfer was primarily for athletic reasons.

Jones v. West Virginia State Board of Education, (2005 W. Va. LEXIS 96). Readers should review the Supreme Court's discussion of the challenged statute's application to educational and athletic resources.

Louisiana High School Athletic Association v. State of Louisiana, (2013 La. LEXIS 247). Examine the court's determination of a "public body" and what is considered a legitimate state interest.

Rottmann v. Pennsylvania Interscholastic Athletic Association, (2004 U.S. Dist. LEXIS 27506). Readers should pay particular attention to the court's discussion of vague and overbroad regulations.

Seger v. Kentucky High School Athletic Association, (2011 U.S. App. LEXIS 25799 (6th Cir. 2011). Pay particular attention to the discussion regarding religious discrimination and the appropriate standard of review.

Significant Cases from Other Chapters
Chapter 6.12 State Action - *Brentwood Academy v. Tennessee Secondary School Athletic Association*, 531 U.S. 288 (2001). Note the court's analysis of the Tennessee Secondary School Athletic Association as a state actor and compare it to the Supreme Court's analysis of the NCAA as a state actor in *National Collegiate Athletic Association v. Tarkanian*, (1988 U.S. LEXIS 5613).

QUESTIONS YOU SHOULD BE ABLE TO ANSWER

1. What does it mean to enforce a rule or policy in an arbitrary and capricious manner? Give a specific sport or recreation related example.

2. High school athletic associations generally accepted as state actors. Why?

3. In general, how have the courts ruled with regard to challenges brought against high school transfer rules?

4. In order to be *initially* qualified as eligible to compete in NCAA athletics, what academic achievements must a student-athlete demonstrate?

5. Explain the Restitution Rule and how it applies to NCAA eligibility.

REFERENCES

Cases
Board of Education of the Township of North Bergen, Hudson County v. New Jersey State Interscholastic Athletic Association, (2015 N.J. Super. Unpub. LEXIS 811).
Bloom v. National Collegiate Athletics Association, (2004 Colo. App. LEXIS 781).
Brentwood Academy v. Tennessee Secondary School Athletic Association, 531 U.S. 288 (2001).
Chapman v. Pennsylvania Interscholastic Athletic Association, (2014 U.S. Dist. LEXIS 17702).
Communities for Equity v. Michigan High School Athletic Association, 80 F. Supp. 2d. 729 (W.D. Mich. 2000).
Florida High School Athletic Association v. Marazzito, 891 So. 2d 653 (Fl. App. 2005).
Indiana High School Athletic Association v. Carlberg, 694 N.E.2d 222 (Supr. Ct. Ind. 1997).
Indiana High School Athletic Association v. Durham, 748 N.E.2d 404 (Ind. App. 2001).
Indiana High School Athletic Association v. Watson, (2010 Ind. LEXIS 800).
Jones v. West Virginia State Board of Education, (2005 W. Va. LEXIS 96).
Louisiana High School Athletic Association v. State of Louisiana, (2013 La. LEXIS 247).
National Collegiate Athletic Association v. Lasege, 53 S.W. 3d (Supr. Ct. KY, 2001).
National Collegiate Athletic Association v. Tarkanian, 488 U.S. 179 (1988).
National Collegiate Athletic Association v. Yeo, 171 S.W. 3d 863 (Supr. Ct. Texas 2005).
Rottmann v. Pennsylvania Interscholastic Athletic Association, (2004 U.S. Dist. LEXIS 27506).
Seger v. Kentucky High School Athletic Association, (2011 U.S. App. LEXIS 25799 (6th Cir. 2011).
Sisson v. Virginia High School League, (2010 U.S. Dist. LEXIS 132264).
Topp v. Big Rock Foundation, Inc, (2013 N.C. LEXIS 54).

Publications
Andrzejewski, L. C. (2013). Reeling in the Supreme Court of North Carolina: Judicial Intervention in the Internal Dispute Resolution of Voluntary Associations under Topp v. Big Rock Foundation, Inc. NCL Rev., 92, 2119.
Bastista, P.J., & Hatfield, L.C. (2005). Learn at home, play at school: A state-by-state examination of legislation, litigation and athletic association rules governing public school athletic participation by homeschool students, *Journal of Legal Aspects of Sport*, 15(2), p. 213–265.

Martin, W. C. (2008). Comment: The Graduate Transfer Rule: Is the NCAA Unnecessarily Hindering Student-athletes from Traversing the Educational Paths they Desire?, *Villanova Sports and Entertainment Law Journal, 15*, p. 103, 106–107.

NCAA Manual (2015–16). Indianapolis: NCAA.

Sander, L. (2011). Junior-College athletes sue NCAA over transfer rules. Retrieved on March 5, 2012 from https://chronicle.com/blogs/players/junior-college-athletes-sue-ncaa-over-transfer-rules/28270

Smith, C., Wixon, M., & Riddle, G. (July 23, 2015). On the Move, Dallas Morning News. Retrieved on January 8th fromhttp://interactives.dallasnews.com/2015/on-the-move/

Stanmyre, M. (2014). Transferring 'epidemic' sweeping across New Jersey high school basketball landscape. Retrieved on January 18, 2016 from http://highschoolsports.nj.com/news/article/transferring-epidemic-sweeping-across-new-jersey-high-school-basketball-landscape/

Van Ann, B. (2011). Varsity blues: A call to reconfigure the judicial standard for high school athletic association transfer rules. *Columbia Journal of law & the arts, 34*(2), 231–260.

Voluntary association. (n.d.). Dictionary.com *Unabridged (v 1.1)*. Retrieved January 8, 2016, from Dictionary.com. Website: http://dictionary.reference.com/browse/voluntary association

Legislation

United States Constitution, Amendment I
United States Constitution, Amendment XIV

CONDUCT ISSUES

W.S. Bill Miller | University of Wisconsin-Parkside

As most parents, student-athletes and school administrators would likely acknowledge, it is possible that today's student-athlete faces more conduct-related regulations than any student-athletes ever. While players have always faced rules and basic codes of conduct implemented by coaches and schools, today's student-athletes and athletic administrators have to deal with those rules along with a seemingly ever-increasing amount of regulations implemented by state governments, state high school athletic associations, leagues, and conferences. Basic team rules authored by coaches are now often accompanied by rules created by the aforementioned governing bodies that cover uniform characteristics, off-campus conduct, grade point averages, grooming, appearance, and student expression which can include regulating what players can or cannot do on their social networking pages.

This growing body of regulation creates three issues. First, there is more opportunity than ever for student-athletes (and their parents in some cases) to commit conduct-related violations which could have a negative impact on their participation in sports. Second, administrators need to be aware of all of these various rules and the potential legal issues that can be created when they attempt to enforce these rules. Third, administrators also need to be aware of new changes in technology and social media platforms that often require monitoring by school officials and could necessitate additional rules or changes in existing rules to ensure that they can achieve the conduct-regulating objectives that they originally implemented.

FUNDAMENTAL CONCEPTS

An important item for athletic administrators to understand is that the individual pieces of this growing body of conduct-related regulation are not always viewed the same in the eyes of the law. This means that understanding the different types of conduct and the legal implications of addressing these potential violations is essential to protect the interests of both the school and the individual administrator. Potential conduct violations which do not have a connection to a student-athlete's constitutional rights are typically much easier to address from an administrative perspective. Schools have consistently been given wide latitude by the courts to articulate policies and create various forms of discipline in an attempt to regulate conduct that does not affect a student's constitutional rights. As discussed later in this chapter, schools and athletic administrators that articulate and follow basic rules regarding the regulation of non-constitutionally implicated conduct by student-athletes have traditionally been given great deference by the legal system.

In contrast, attempts to regulate conduct that have constitutional implications such as restricting a student's freedom of speech or freedom of expression usually create more substantial challenges for athletic administrators in terms of prohibiting or restricting the conduct. As one might suspect, the courts have generally been very reluctant to allow school administrators to restrict the constitutional rights of students. However, over the past three decades, the United States Supreme Court has articulated several situations in which administrators can restrict the rights of students through a variety of means including the use of student codes and impose discipline for violations of those codes.

As you will see in the next two sections of this chapter, the biggest challenge for athletic administrators can be in trying to identify what types of student conduct create constitutional implications. Most would understand that student codes of conduct or other rules which attempt to restrict one's freedom of speech or expression could create potential constitutional implications. For example, rules that attempted to eliminate or restrict a student's ability to speak about political or controversial issues in either school or non-school settings would obviously fall into that category. However, seemingly harmless attempts by administrators to create a better learning environment for students by creating regulations which prohibit a student from wearing a shirt or piece of apparel to school that features a flag or support for a cancer-related charity can also create constitutional implications. And as noted above, most students, parents and especially their attorneys understand that being able to link conduct-related regulation and discipline with constitutional protections enhances the chances of success for the student-athlete in getting the potential discipline overturned.

Constitutionally Implicated Conduct

The types of cases that feature student conduct issues with constitutional implications have typically fallen into one of two categories: freedom of religion and freedom of expression.

Freedom of Expression

Over the past four decades, the United States Supreme Court has issued four key rulings which address student-related freedom of expression issues in school settings. These cases have established a framework through which athletic administrators are encouraged to view their attempts to regulate student conduct.

The Tinker Cases

In *Tinker v. Des Moines Independent Community School District* (1969), two public high school students were planning to show their objection to the Vietnam War by wearing black armbands to school along with engaging in several other activities. School administrators found out about the plan and adopted a policy stating that students would be asked to remove all armbands and would be suspended if they refused to do so. The students followed through on their protest and wore the black armbands to school. The administration also followed through on its threat and suspended the students for wearing the armbands.

In its ruling, the Supreme Court offered arguably one of its more famous lines and a key principle that administrators need to keep in mind when considering constitutionally-implicated conduct issues. "First Amendment rights applied in light of the special characteristics of the school environment, are available to teachers and students" (*Tinker v. Des Moines Independent Community School District*, 1969). "It can hardly be argued" the court held "that either students or teachers shed their constitutional rights to freedom of speech or expression at the schoolhouse gate" (*Tinker v. Des Moines Independent Community School District*, 1969). The Court went on to note that discomfort, unpleasantness or unsubstantiated fear of a disturbance caused by the student's freedom of expression was not enough for schools to restrict the constitutional rights of students. The court then added that "in the absence of constitutionally valid reasons to regulate their speech, students are entitled to freedom of expression of their views" (*Tinker v. Des Moines Independent Community School District*, 1969). The Court went on to state, however, that student conduct that had the potential to materially and substantially interfere with the operations of the school or the rights of others was not constitutionally protected. One more additional important item for sports administrators to note is that the *Tinker* ruling specifically stated that the playing field was among the places where students could utilize their constitutionally-protected rights of freedom of expression.

In *Bethel School District No. 403 v. Fraser* (1986), the Supreme Court offered more guidance as to how schools can regulate student conduct with regard to freedom of expression issues. Fraser was a high school student invited to deliver a nominating speech for a fellow student running for office to an assembly of approximately 600 high school students. The speech featured large amounts of sexual innuendo that led some members of the audience to become confused in the words of the Court while others began to make gestures which simulated the acts described in the speech. Fraser was suspended by the school for three days and removed from the potential commencement speaker list because of violations of the school's student code of conduct which prohibited the use of obscene language. The Court upheld the suspension stating that it is appropriate for public school officials to regulate the use of vulgar and offensive terms by students as part of the educational process. It then added that the speech in this situation had no political viewpoint unlike the student conduct in *Tinker*.

Two years after *Fraser*, the Court added further *Tinker* clarification in *Hazelwood School District v. Kuhlmeier* (1988). Hazelwood East High School had a student newspaper which was written by a journalism class at the school and overseen by a teacher and school administrators. In an edition scheduled for publication late in the 1982–83 academic year, school officials removed two pages of content from the proposed six-page newspaper because of content that discussed divorce and teen pregnancy issues. A group of students sued the school district claiming their First Amendment rights were violated. The Court upheld the rights of the school district to remove the pages from the newspaper. While acknowledging *Tinker*, the Court stated that the type of speech in this case was different than *Tinker* because of the fact that it was school-sponsored speech. The Court specifically stated in its ruling that, "We hold that educators do not offend the First Amendment by exercising editorial control over the style and content of student speech in school-sponsored expressive activities so long as their actions are reasonable related to legitimate pedagogical concerns." (*Hazelwood School District v. Kuhlmeier*, 1988)

After nearly two decades of silence on student freedom of expression issues, the final case of the Supreme Court's four major rulings in this area is *Morse v. Frederick* (2007). The Olympic torch relay was passing in front of the high school and school administrators decided to allow students to watch the event as part of a school-sponsored activity. At the relay, Frederick unveiled a 14-foot banner stating "Bong Hits 4 Jesus" in full view of the crowd. The school's principal demanded that he remove the banner stating that it encouraged illegal activity. Frederick was eventually suspended for eight days as allowed for by school board policy. The Court upheld the suspension and included a long discussion on the problems of illegal drug use both in society and schools as part of its reasoning. It went on to discuss the apparent lack of political value in Frederick's banner. It also acknowledged *Tinker's* concern about restricting speech that features unpopular viewpoints. But it added, "the particular concern to prevent student drug abuse at issue here, embodied in established school policy, extends well beyond an abstract desire to avoid controversy" (*Morse v. Frederick*, 2007).

Applying the Tinker Cases

In reviewing the four major student freedom of expression cases, a few guidelines for sports administrators dealing with such issues in conduct-related cases become evident. *Tinker* offers substantial protection for student freedom of expression absent any constitutionally-valid reasons for restricting or prohibiting student expression. *Frasor* begins to allow administrators to restrict those rights when the speech is in-school, vulgar and appears to offer no political value. *Hazelwood* gives administrators greater control over school-sponsored forms of speech. Finally, *Morse* allows the restriction of student speech when advocating illegal drug use. Two major challenges confront sport administrators when attempting to regulate student conduct in light of the *Tinker* quartet of decisions. First, while the *Tinker* decisions offer guidelines they do not articulate a firm list of rules for officials to follow when evaluating student conduct. Second, as will be shown throughout this section, there are a larger number of student conduct issues that have constitutional implications under the *Tinker* cases than many school administrators would typically suspect.

Student Expression About Coaches

Use of the guidelines created by the *Tinker* cases regarding schools regulating freedom of expression can be seen in a series of cases involving actions taken by schools against student-athletes who expressed their discontent with their coaches. In *Pinard v. Clatskanie School District 6J* (2006), several members of the boys basketball team signed a petition requesting the removal of the team's head coach. According to the players, administrators gave the team two options upon learning of the petition. The players could play in the game that evening and participate in mediation or they could maintain their call for the coach's removal and skip the bus trip to that evening's game. Most of the players skipped the trip to the game and were subsequently suspended. Citing *Tinker*, the Ninth Circuit Court of Appeals concluded that the players' petition and subsequent complaints to school administrators about the coach were protected speech. However, the Court of Appeals also found that the players' refusal to board the bus for the team's game was a substantial disruption of school activity as discussed in *Tinker*. As a result, those actions were not constitutionally protected and the suspensions were upheld.

In *Lowery v. Euverard* (2008) a group of high school football players signed a petition stating that they hated the team's head coach and no longer wished to play for him. The coach found out about the petition and later removed any player from the team who did not apologize to the coach. The Sixth Circuit Court of Appeals upheld the player dismissals using many of the *Tinker* quartet precedents stating that the defendants could reasonably believe that the petition would divide the team and erode the authority of the coach. The Court of Appeals went on to add, "Plaintiffs' regular education has not been impeded, and, significantly, they are free to continue their campaign to have the coach fired. What they are not free to do is continue to play football for him while actively working to undermine his authority" (*Lowery v. Euverard*, 2008).

Student Expression through Social Networking

The effects of the *Tinker* quartet can also be seen in how courts view freedom of expression issues in which the student makes the expression through social networking sites outside of the school. Students often erroneously think that off-campus social networking activities cannot be addressed by school administrators. However, these issues can be addressed under some circumstances by administrators and the courts under the *Tinker* quartet. The following three cases feature recent court rulings on social networking issues. In light of technological advancements and the ever-growing use of such social sites, it is highly likely that there will be a growing amount of litigation in this area going forward.

In *J.C. v. Beverly Hills Unified School District* (2010), the plaintiff and a group of students made a four-minute video that contained disparaging remarks about a classmate. The video was posted on YouTube and the plaintiff contacted a group of students encouraging them to watch the video, including the student who was the focus of the video. After school officials were made aware of the video, the plaintiffs were eventually suspended for four days in accordance with school policy. In ruling that the suspensions violated the students' First Amendment right of expression, the court stated that while the school had the ability to suspend the student under the principles advanced in the *Tinker* quartet if the facts warranted it, in this case, the facts did not warrant such an action because no reasonable jury could find that the plaintiffs' video would create a reasonably foreseeable risk of substantial disruption. The court went on to state that the school could not point to the discipline itself as a substantial disruption, since that the biggest effects of the video appeared to be that the two students were sent home from school.

In *T.V. v. Smith-Green Community School Corporation* (2011) a group of high school volleyball players took a series of provocative photos during a summer group sleepover. Racy comments were later added to the photos which were subsequently posted on MySpace and Facebook. The photos, while never brought to school, were brought to the attention of school officials by a parent who said that the photos were causing a division within the team. The student-athletes were suspended from the team for one year due to a violation of the school's student-athlete code of conduct. The suspension were later reduced to smaller portions of the team's schedule once the student-athletes underwent counseling and apologized to the school's Athletic Board for their actions. In ruling that the school violated the student's First Amendment rights, the court found that the photos were taken in a non-school setting and published to the internet outside of school eliminating the *Fraser* argument. The court then used the *Tinker* reasoning to determine while students may not have a constitution right to participate in athletics that does not mean that they cannot pursue their constitutionally-guaranteed rights of freedom of expression. The ruling specifically stated, "What this means is that a student cannot be punished with a ban from extracurricular activities for non-disruptive speech." In reviewing the facts of the case, the court found the issue to be minor disagreements among team members and complaints from two parents, both of which did not rise to the level of substantial disruption as called for in *Tinker*.

Finally, in *Bell v. Itawamba County School Board* (2015), a student posted a rap recording on his Facebook page and YouTube in which he alleged misconduct by two teachers/coaches against female students. The recording, which was later described by the court as 'incredibly profane and vulgar,' contained multiple examples of intimidating language and physical threats against the two coaches in the eyes of school administrators. The student was suspended, prohibited from attending school functions and placed in an alternative school for the remainder of the grading period. The Fifth Circuit Court of Appeals upheld the punishment using the substantial disruption reasoning from *Tinker* stating, "It goes without saying that a teacher, which includes a coach, is the cornerstone of education . . . It equally goes without saying that threatening, harassing, and intimidating a teacher impedes, if not destroys, the ability to educate. It disrupts, if not destroys, the discipline necessary for an environment in which education can take place." (*Bell v. Itawamba County School Board*, 2015).

Student Expression through Apparel

One of the ways that students often express themselves is through the apparel that they choose to wear. While not usually likely thought of as a constitutional issue, the apparel issue is one that has been addressed by a variety of courts through the years. A series of recent cases using the *Tinker* reasoning illustrate how courts have looked at the apparel issue. While these cases do not involve student-athletes, they are indicative of the types of issues that sport administrators can face on a daily basis. In *Defoe v. Spiva* (2010) the school developed a code of student conduct that prohibited students from wearing apparel which drew attention to them as opposed to the learning environment and articulated a variety of example of items that were prohibited. The plaintiff wore a t-shirt and a belt buckle featuring the Confederate flag on two separate occasions. He refused to comply with school officials, requests to comply with the dress code and was subsequently suspended. The Sixth Circuit Court of Appeals using the *Tinker* cases upheld the dress code and the suspension stating that it was reasonable for school officials to foresee a substantial disruption at the school which could be caused by the display of the Confederate flag. The Court of Appeals added that it was not a political viewpoint issue as all apparel that could cause a disruption was banned under the code.

The challenge school administrators face in addressing expression issues can be seen in a series of cases revolving around students all wearing "I (heart) Boobies. (Keep a Breast)" bracelets. In B.*H. v. Easton Area School District* (2013), a Pennsylvania middle school enacted a policy banning students from wearing bracelets that supported breast cancer awareness which featured the word "boobies." Several students refused to remove the bracelets and were subsequently suspended in-school for a day and a half and prohibited from attending an upcoming school dance. In ruling for the students, the Third Circuit Court of Appeals held that the word boobies is not lewd or vulgar as defined by *Fraser*. As such, the court ruled that no substantial disruption could be caused or foreseen at the school by the students wearing the bracelets. However, two different district courts subsequently acknowledged and explicitly rejected the *Easton* reasoning and sided with school administrators banning the bracelets. In *J.A. v. Fort Wayne Community Schools* (2013), the court noted the bracelet slogan could reasonably be interpreted as vulgar and went on to state, "School officials, who know the age, maturity, and other characteristics of their students better than federal judges, are in a better position to decide whether to allow these products into their schools." (*J.A. v. Fort Wayne Community Schools*, 2013).

Student Expression through Grooming
Another way students can choose to express themselves is through their personal grooming habits. As such, any attempted restrictions on student-athletes such as hair length or whether they can wear a beard or a mustache can also unwittingly create constitutional implications for sport administrators. In *Dunham v. Pulsifer* (1970), the high school had recently enacted a student-athlete code of conduct which included a variety of apparel and grooming requirements. For example, males had to be clean shaven and their hair was to be tapered in the back and on the sides of the head with no hair over the collar. The plaintiffs were three male tennis players who were ranked as the top three players on the team. All three players were prevented from playing in a match by school officials because of violations of the code. In fact six of the top eight players on the team were eventually dismissed from the team because they violated the aforementioned code provisions. While *Tinker* was discussed in the case, the court utilized an Equal Protection Clause analysis to determine that the school singled out these student-athletes. The court then looked at the reasonableness of the regulation in comparison to its intended purpose and stated that it would allow the regulation if it was not arbitrary and had some reasonable connection with a legislative or administrative purpose. Upon analyzing the facts of the case, the court found no evidence that the grooming rule enhanced team performance, reduced team dissension or created discipline. In addition, while the court acknowledged the important role of the coach, stating that "during the actual competition, the coach's instructions must be accepted without question" (*Dunham v. Pulsifer*, 1970). The court went on to state that the "coach's right to regulate the lives of his team members does have limits" (*Dunham v. Pulsifer*, 1970) and overturned the suspensions and reinstated the players to the team.

Freedom of Religion
In terms of regulating student-athlete conduct, there has been very little litigation with regard to religious freedom issues. However, the litigation that has occurred has an obvious constitutional impact. In *Moody v. Cronin* (1980), the plaintiff was suspended from high school for three days for refusing to attend physical education classes. The dispute arose due to a state law that required students to attend physical education classes on a daily basis and the then-relatively recent passage of Title IX which introduced co-ed physical education classes at the school. The student was a member of the United Pentecostal Church whose tenets include a requirement that members wear modest apparel. Moody believed that the attire required for the physical education class did not satisfy that requirement. The court ruled that the plaintiff had deep religious convictions about the attire issue and the State of Illinois could not deny the plaintiff's free exercise of their religious beliefs absent sufficient state interest. In finding that the state failed to show such an interest, the court noted that the state had a variety of

alternative educational methods it could have used to achieve its objectives without restricting the religious rights of the plaintiff.

Non-Constitutionally-implicated Conduct

As shown in the previous section, student-athlete conduct that implicates one's constitutional rights such as Freedom of Expression or Freedom of Religion has often been afforded great protection by the courts. In contrast, schools and administrators are given great latitude in regulating, prohibiting and implementing various forms of discipline when non-constitutionally implicated conduct is at the center of the dispute. In litigation surrounding non-constitutional conduct situation, the main issue courts often examine is whether the student-athlete received proper due process from the school and administrators. (see, Section 6.13 Due Process.) The basic concept you should be aware of is that student-athletes need to be given proper notice of the charges against them and be given a proper ability to respond. As discussed in chapter 6.13, *Goss v. Lopez* (1975) is the key case in this area, especially for academic suspensions.

When dealing with athletic suspensions on top of the academic suspension, the case of *Palmer v. Merluzzi* (1989) illustrates how courts often handle these situations. Palmer was a high school football player who was suspended for ten days academically and later given a 60-day athletic suspension after being caught smoking marijuana and drinking at the school's radio station. The plaintiff challenged the fact that he was not given a second notice and hearing for the athletic suspension. The Third Circuit Court of Appeals upheld the suspension stating that the school handbook and Interscholastic Athletic Program warned that students who did not demonstrate good citizenship were subject to suspension. The Court of Appeals then stated that based on the code provisions, the nature of the offense and common sense, Palmer should have known his athletic status was at risk as well. The ruling went on to add, "[W]e believe it would be unduly disruptive of a school's educational process to require one disciplinary process for football players and similarly situated athletes and another disciplinary process for other students" (*Palmer v. Merluzzi*, 1989).

The limited extent to which student-athletes can challenge conduct-related discipline without Constitutional implications can be seen in a series of decisions authored by the courts over the past few decades. In *Wooten v. Pleasant Hope R-VI School District* (2000), the plaintiff was dismissed from the team in accordance with the school's student-parent handbook after failing to show up for a game. The plaintiff met with the coach and school officials the following week and was allegedly told at the meeting by the coach that her teammates did not wish to see her reinstated. Wooten later claimed that she found out this statement was not true and requested a hearing from school officials about her dismissal from the team. School officials did not honor her request and a lawsuit was filed on procedural due process grounds. Despite the alleged misstatements of the coach, the court rejected Wooten's claims stating that the meeting gave the plaintiff notice of the charges against her and an opportunity to present her case.

In *Sala v. Warwick Valley Central School District* (2009), the student-athlete was arrested after marijuana was found in his home. He was initially suspended for the remainder of the season but this penalty would be reduced to four games if the school's code of conduct was followed. While under suspension, Sala was caught driving too fast in a school parking lot. The school's athletic director asked him to slow down and Sala reportedly responded with obscenities. Following the incident, he was dismissed from the team. Sala appealed to the superintendent claiming the athletic director had "antipathy" toward his family. Following the meeting, the superintendent upheld the suspension and a lawsuit was filed. In ruling for the school district, the court stated that Sala met with the coach on multiple occasions and received written notice of the reason for his dismissal. In addition, the court noted that Sala met with the superintendent where he could present his story and then received a letter explaining the basis for the decision and notice of his right to appeal to the school board.

In *Dennis v. Board of Education of Talbot County* (2014), two lacrosse players were suspended from school after a pocket knife and butane lighter were discovered in their equipment bags during an administrator search of the team bus for alcohol. As part of the appeal process, the student-athletes argued they used the prohibited items to work on their sticks and they were not dangerous weapons as claimed by school officials. The court rejected the players' arguments that they did not have notice about the prohibition of the items because school policy stated 'dangerous items' instead of providing a specific list. It also rejected the players' use of the items as tools argument stating, "School policies are not open to due process challenges simply because a student wishes to use a dangerous weapon for a non-deadly purpose." (*Dennis v. Board of Education of Talbot County*, (2014).

SIGNIFICANT CASE

The following case illustrates how courts often use the principles first articulated in the Tinker case to decide Freedom of Expression lawsuits involving students in a dispute with their coach. As a result, the reader should consider the issues that administrators need to examine when faced with these types of issues.

PINARD V. CLATSKANIE SCHOOL DISTRICT 6J
United States Court of Appeals (Ninth Circuit)
467 F.3d 755 (9th Cir. 2006).

I. Factual and Procedural Background

Plaintiffs are eight former members of the 2000–01 Clatskanie High School varsity boys basketball team in Clatskanie, Oregon. The defendants include the Clatskanie School District, Jeff Baughman (the varsity boys basketball coach), Michael Corley (the high school principal), Lester Wallace (the high school athletic director), and Earl Fisher (the superintendent). Baughman, a teacher at the high school before taking on coaching responsibilities, became the team's head coach for the 2000–01 school year.

Considering the evidence in the light most favorable to the plaintiffs, as we must at this stage of the litigation, see *Bingham v. City of Manhattan Beach*, 341 F.3d 939, 945–46 (9th Cir.2003), Baughman was verbally abusive and highly intimidating. * * * Linn explained that the players did not report Baughman's behavior because Baughman made it clear that "anything that happened in the locker room stays in the locker room."

After one particular home game, Baughman told the players that if they wanted him to quit, they should say so, and he would resign. The players apparently took Baughman at his word. On February 12, 2001, several weeks after Baughman's statement, co-captains Jacob Pinard and Christopher Somes called a team meeting at a local restaurant to discuss Baughman's behavior. Before the meeting, one of the plaintiffs typed up a petition requesting that Baughman resign. The petition stated:

> As of February 12, 2001, the Clatskanie Tigers Boys Varsity Basketball Team would like to formally request the immediate resignation of Coach Jeff Baughman. As a team we no longer feel comfortable playing for him as a coach. He has made derogative [sic] remarks, made players uncomfortable playing for him, and is not leading the team in the right direction. We feel that as a team and as individuals we would be better off if we were to finish the season with a replacement coach. We, the undersign [sic], believe this is in the best interest of the team, school, town, and for the players and fans. We would appreciate the full cooperation of all the parties involved.

With the exception of a foreign exchange student, every varsity player attended the meeting, including Baughman's son. No coaches, teachers or parents attended. After discussing the petition, all but one of the players (Baughman's son) signed it. The players also added a type-written note beneath the signatures stating: "[W]e will not be approached individually on this. This was a team decision and we will be addressed as a team."

The following morning, co-captain Somes delivered the petition to Baughman. The coach immediately took it to the high school principal, defendant Corley, who was in a meeting with the superintendent, defendant Fisher. The three defendants met for 10 to 15 minutes, during which time Baughman expressed that he was "confused," "very upset" and "hurt." Although none of these defendants could recall exactly what was discussed during this meeting, Corley remembers recommending that Baughman not resign, and Superintendent Fisher suggested that they meet with the players to "find out the detail" of the petition. Baughman was also concerned because the team was scheduled to play an important away game that evening. Upset by the events of the morning, Baughman asked Corley for permission to take off the remainder of the day, which Corley granted. Corley did not ask Baughman whether he would coach the game that night.

Once home, Baughman called the junior varsity coach, Gary Points, "to inform him of the situation." According to Points, Baughman stated that he "wanted to know who his back-stabbers were" and wanted "to corner the little sons-of-bitches and not give them an out." When Points asked what Baughman meant, Baughman responded that Corley had given him two options: he could either resign, or decide not to resign and tell the players to either get on the bus and play or if they chose not to board the bus to turn in their uniforms. According to Points, Baughman claimed that Corley and Wallace were advising him to choose the second option.

After Baughman left the school, Corley called a meeting with athletic director Wallace and all of the players who had signed the petition. The players told Corley and Wallace about Baughman's derogatory remarks, stated he was unfair and expressed their discomfort in playing for him. When the players indicated that they would not play on the team if Baughman was going to coach them, Corley and Wallace explained they could not have Baughman immediately removed without an investigation. According to the plaintiffs, Corley and Wallace presented the players with two options: the players could participate in a mediation process with the two of them serving as mediators and board the team bus for the game that evening, or they could adhere to their position and forfeit their privilege to play in the game. The plaintiffs contend that neither Corley nor Wallace advised them that they would be disciplined further for choosing the second option. The meeting ended without the players expressing whether they intended to board the bus.

Later in the day, Baughman informed Corley and Wallace that he was not going to coach the game that evening. Wallace then made arrangements for a substitute coach to replace Baughman. Corley and Wallace did not inform the players of Baughman's decision.

With the exception of Somes, each of the players who had signed the petition chose not to board the bus and did not play in the game. The junior varsity team played in place of the eight missing players along with Somes, Baughman's son and the foreign exchange student, losing the game by more than 50 points. Baughman did not coach the team, and most of the plaintiffs attended the game as spectators. The plaintiffs contend they decided not to board the bus to demonstrate their resolve and sincerity concerning the petition and complaints against Baughman. They also maintain they would not have refused to travel with the team had they known Baughman was not coaching.

The next day, Corley and Wallace met with the plaintiffs, Somes and several of the players' parents. According to two of the parents in attendance, Corley announced that "all of the players *who signed the petition* were permanently suspended from the team" (emphasis added). Corley stated in the district court that he alone decided to suspend the players from the team, but that he did *not* suspend Somes (who had signed the petition but boarded the bus and played in the game). Rather, the suspension applied only to those members of the team "who had refused to board [the] team bus . . . and play basketball that evening." Although the defendants now argue that Corley had authority to suspend the plaintiffs under the school's "Code of Conduct and Appearance for Athletes," it is not clear from the record that the Code played any role in Corley's decision. Indeed, Corley conceded in a deposition that he was unfamiliar with the Code's contents.

* * *

III. Discussion

The plaintiffs argue that their petition, complaints to Corley and Wallace and decision to take the option of not playing in the away game constitute speech protected by the First Amendment. The defendants agree that the petition standing alone is "pure speech." See *Bartnicki v. Vopper*, 532 U.S. 514, 526–27, 121 S.Ct. 1753, 149 L.Ed.2d 787 (2001) (suggesting that the "delivery of a tape recording," "handbill" or "pamphlet" are forms of "pure speech"). The defendants also agree that the plaintiffs' refusal to board the bus-while itself not "pure speech"-was "inseparable" from the petition. However, the defendants argue that the plaintiffs' entire course of conduct-the petition, complaints against Baughman and the boycott of the game-was not constitutionally protected because it had no political dimension, was not a matter of public concern and materially interfered with the school's basketball program. The defendants further contend that the plaintiffs were suspended not for their petition or complaints against Baughman, but *only* for their refusal to board the bus.

We have long held that students in public schools do not "shed their constitutional rights to freedom of speech or expression at the schoolhouse gate." See *Chandler v. McMinnville Sch. Dist.*, 978 F.2d 524, 527 (9th Cir.1992) (quoting Tinker, 393 U.S. at 506, 89 S.Ct. 733). However, our precedents make equally clear that the First Amendment rights of public school students "'are not automatically coextensive with the rights of adults in other settings' and must be 'applied in light of the special characteristics of the school environment.'" *LaVine v. Blaine Sch. Dist.*, 257 F.3d 981, 988 (9th Cir.2001) (quoting *Hazelwood Sch. Dist. v. Kuhlmeier*, 484 U.S. 260, 266, 108 S.Ct. 562, 98 L.Ed.2d 592 (1988)). Thus, in the school context, "we have granted educators substantial deference as to what speech is appropriate." *Id*. But "deference does not mean abdication; there are situations where school officials overstep their bounds and violate the Constitution." *Id*. Our task is to determine whether the district court erred in concluding that this case does not present such a situation.

A. Plaintiffs' Speech

This case involves both a petition-a form of "pure speech"-as well as potentially expressive conduct in the form of the plaintiffs' refusal to board the bus. See, e.g., Tinker, 393 U.S. at 505–06, 89 S.Ct. 733 (describing the wearing of armbands as akin to "pure speech"); see also *Baldwin v. Redwood City*, 540 F.2d 1360, 1366 (9th Cir.1976) (suggesting that the "element of conduct" in pure speech is "minimal"). Although the defendants concede that the petition "standing alone" is pure speech, they characterize the plaintiffs' petition, complaints against Baughman and refusal to board the bus as both "concerted action" and one "course of conduct," the entirety of which is constitutionally punishable under *Tinker*. We disagree with that view. As we discuss in Section III.C, because the plaintiffs' petition and grievances against Baughman are a form of pure speech, the defendants may not constitutionally punish the plaintiffs just for filing their petition or complaining about Baughman unless they show "facts which might reasonably have led [them] to forecast substantial disruption of or material interference with school activities" *as a result of the petition or complaints. Tinker, 393 U.S. at 514, 89 S.Ct. 733*.

As for the plaintiffs' refusal to board the bus and play in the game, the plaintiffs assume that this conduct falls within the ambit of the First Amendment's protections because it is expressive in nature. *See, e.g., Rumsfeld v. Forum for Academic & Institutional Rights, Inc., 547 U.S. 47, 126 S.Ct. 1297, 1310, 164 L.Ed.2d 156 (2006)* ("*FAIR*") (explaining that the Supreme Court has "extended First Amendment protection only to conduct that is inherently expressive"); *Roulette v. City of Seattle*, 97 F.3d 300, 302-03 (9th Cir.1996) ("The First Amendment protects not only the expression of ideas through printed or spoken words, but also symbolic speech-nonverbal 'activity . . . sufficiently imbued with elements of communication.'" (quoting *Spence v. Washington, 418 U.S. 405, 409, 94 S.Ct. 2727, 41 L.Ed.2d 842 (1974)*)). As we explain below, however, we ultimately need not decide whether the plaintiffs' boycott of the game constitutes "inherently expressive" conduct encompassed by the First Amendment, because even if it does the boycott was properly punishable under *Tinker*.

* * *

C. Applying Tinker

Because the plaintiffs' speech falls within *Chandler's* third category of "all other speech," the defendants must justify their decision to suspend the players permanently by showing "facts which might reasonably have led[them] to forecast substantial disruption of or material interference with school activities." *Tinker*, 393 U.S. at 514, 89 S.Ct. 733. The *Tinker* rule is a "flexible one," *Karp*, 477 F.2d at 174, and in applying it, "we look to the totality of the relevant facts," including not only the plaintiffs' actions, but "all of the circumstances confronting the school officials" at the time. *LaVine*, 257 F.3d at 989. "[U]ndifferentiated fear or apprehension of disturbance is not enough to overcome the right to freedom of expression," and the "mere desire to avoid the discomfort and unpleasantness that always accompany an unpopular viewpoint" cannot justify a school official's decision to punish or prohibit student speech. *Tinker*, 393 U.S. at 508–09, 89 S.Ct. 733.

Applying these guiding principles here, we conclude that the First Amendment protects the players' petition and their complaints to Corley and Wallace during the ensuing meeting. The defendants do not dispute that the petition and meeting neither disrupted school activities nor impinged on the rights of other students, and the record contains no evidence that Corley suspended the plaintiffs out of any such concern. The players handed their petition to Baughman directly at the start of a school day, and after Baughman left the school, they explained their complaint only to Corley and Wallace in a private meeting. These facts closely resemble those reviewed by the Tenth Circuit in *Seamons v. Snow*, 84 F.3d 1226 (10th Cir.1996). *Seamons* held that the First Amendment protected a student athlete's report to school authorities of a physical assault, because the student's speech "was responsibly tailored to the audience of school administrators, coaches, family and participants who needed to know about the incident." *Id*. at 1237–38.

It is also relevant that neither Corley nor Wallace informed the players of Baughman's decision not to coach the team that evening, even though the players had clearly stated that Baughman was the reason they did not want to play. Thus, to the extent that the petition and meeting might have given the school officials a "reason to anticipate" disruption of the game, the totality of the relevant facts reveals that any such expectation would have been unreasonable given Corley's and Wallace's knowledge of Baughman's decision. Had Corley and Wallace told the players that Baughman was not coaching that night-and the record reveals no reason why they could not have-it appears that the players would have boarded the bus.

Finally, assuming without deciding that the plaintiffs' refusal to board the bus constituted expressive conduct encompassed by the First Amendment, we agree with the district court that the plaintiffs' boycott of the game substantially disrupted and materially interfered with a school activity. Comparing the conduct at issue here with the wearing of armbands in *Tinker* demonstrates why the district court's decision was correct.

In holding that the First Amendment protected the students' right to wear a black armband to school to protest the Vietnam War, *Tinker* noted that "the wearing of armbands . . . was entirely divorced from actually or potentially disruptive conduct by those participating in it." 393 U.S. at 505, 89 S.Ct. 733. The Court emphasized that the "school officials banned and sought to punish petitioners for a silent, passive expression of opinion, unaccompanied by any disorder or disturbance on the part of petitioners." *Id*. at 508, 89 S.Ct. 733. It also noted that the district court made "no finding and no showing that engaging in the forbidden conduct would materially and substantially interfere with the requirements of *appropriate discipline in the operation of the school*," *id*. at 509, 89 S.Ct. 733 (internal quotation marks omitted) (emphasis added), and that there was "no evidence whatever of [the protestors'] interference, actual or nascent, with the *schools' work*," *id*. at 508, 89 S.Ct. 733 (emphasis added). In holding that a student's First Amendment rights are "not confined to the supervised and ordained discussion which takes place in the classroom," the Court extended *Tinker's* principles to school activities broadly defined, including extracurricular activities:

> When [a student] is in the cafeteria, *or on the playing field*, or on the campus during the authorized hours, he may express his opinions . . . if he does so without materially and substantially interfer(ing) with the requirements of appropriate discipline in the operation of the school. . . . But conduct by the student, *in class or out of it*, which for *any reason*-whether it stems from time, place, or type of behavior-materially disrupts classwork or involves *substantial disorder* or invasion of the rights of others is, of course, not immunized by the constitutional guarantee of freedom of speech. *Id*. at 512–13, 89 S.Ct. 733.

In this case, unlike in *Tinker*, there is undisputed evidence to support the district court's explicit finding that the plaintiffs' refusal to board the bus for the away game "material[ly] disrupt[ed] . . . the operation of the boys' varsity basketball team." As a general matter, school districts spend much time and money scheduling and hosting their extracurricular events-part of the school's educational program-which involve the coordination of multiple school officials, students, parents and often times volunteers, referees and bus drivers. Here, there is no dispute that the plaintiffs constituted all but three members of the varsity team. Similarly, it is undisputed that the boycotted event was a regularly scheduled out of town game against a rival school, part of the school's varsity basketball program, that the varsity team was scheduled to travel to the game on a school bus and that the plaintiffs refused to board the bus only a few hours before the game was scheduled to begin. The last minute boycott of a regularly scheduled game by nearly every member of the team forced the district either to play the game with replacement players or cancel the event. That the school succeeded in obtaining substitute players-albeit of lesser experience and ability-may have mitigated the disruptive effects of the plaintiffs' actions, but it did not eliminate them or render them less than substantial. Either option materially interfered with the school district's operation of a bona fide school activity.

Under these circumstances, the plaintiffs' conduct plainly "interrupted school activities" and "intrude[d] in the school['s] affairs." *Tinker*, 393 U.S. at 514, 89 S.Ct. 733. Thus, even if we viewed the plaintiffs' boycott as symbolic speech within the First Amendment, school officials could permissibly discipline the players for this disruptive conduct. Like Justice Brennan, we recognize that "[t]he vigilant protection of constitutional freedoms is nowhere more vital than in the community of American schools." *Keyishian v. Board of Regents*, 385 U.S. 589, 603, 87 S.Ct. 675, 17 L.Ed.2d 629 (1967) (quoting *Shelton v. Tucker*, 364 U.S. 479, 487, 81 S.Ct. 247, 5 L.Ed.2d 231 (1960). At the same time, we cannot ignore *Tinker's* admonition that the First Amendment is properly read to permit a school district's "reasonable regulation of speech-connected activities in *carefully restricted* circumstances." *Tinker*, 393 U.S. at 513, 89 S.Ct. 733 (emphasis added). Those circumstances were met here.

* * *

CASES ON THE SUPPLEMENTAL CD

Bell v. Itawamba County School Board, 799 F.3d 379 (2015). Note how the court used the *Tinker* analysis to examine and resolve an issue surrounding a student's posts on social networking sites from an off-campus location.

Bethel School District No. 403 v. Fraser, 478 U.S. 675 (1986). Study how the Supreme Court distinguished Fraser's situation from that seen in the *Tinker* case and the effect this had on the court's analysis in this and future cases.

Lowery v. Euverard, 497 F.3d 584 (6th Cir. 2008). Examine how the court used a *Tinker* analysis to uphold the dismissals of the players from the football team.

Palmer v. Merluzzi, 868 F.2d 90 (3rd Cir. 1989). Study how the court uses a different analysis when examining non-constitutionally-implicated student-athlete conduct versus constitutionally-implicated conduct.

T.V. v. Smith-Green Community School Corporation, 807 F.Supp.2d 767 (N.D. Ind. 2011). The reader should look at how the court used the *Tinker* analysis to examine and resolve a social networking dispute involving student-athletes and an athletic code of conduct.

QUESTIONS YOU SHOULD BE ABLE TO ANSWER

1. Why do students try to make constitutional claims when filing lawsuits against schools and school administrators for conduct-related issues?

2. How did the *Fraser*, *Hazelwood* and *Morse* rulings impact how school administrators view Freedom of Expression conduct cases through the *Tinker* analysis?

3. Do you agree with the *Easton* or the *Fort Wayne* decision regarding the "I (heart) Boobies. (Keep a Breast)" bracelet issue? Why did you reach this conclusion?

4. In your opinion, should cases revolving around issues like grooming and apparel be considered Freedom of Expression issues with constitutional implications?

5. Should school athletic departments be able to discipline student-athletes for any pictures, videos or written content that are posted on social networking sites from off-campus?

REFERENCES
Cases

Bell v. Itawamba County School Board, 799 F.3d 379 (5th Cir. 2015).
Bethel School District No. 403 v. Fraser, 478 U.S. 675 (1986).
B.H. v. Easton Area School District, 725 F.3d 293 (3rd Cir. 2013).
Defoe v. Spiva, 625 F.3d 324 (6th Cir. 2010).
Dennis v. Board of Education of Talbot County, 21 F.Supp.3d 497 (D. Md. 2014).
Dunham v. Pulsifer, 312 F. Supp. 411 (D. Vermont 1970).
Goss v. Lopez, 419 U.S. 565 (1975).
Hazelwood School District v. Kuhlmeier, 484 U.S. 260 (1988).
J.A. v. Fort Wayne Community Schools, 2013 U.S. Dist. LEXIS 117667 (N. Ind. 2013).
J.C. v. Beverly Hills Unified School District, 711 F. Supp.2d 1094 (D. Calif. 2010).
Lowery v. Euverard, 497 F.3d 584 (6th Cir. 2008).
Moody v. Cronin, 484 F. Supp. 270 (C.D. Ill. 1979).
Morse v. Frederick, 551 U.S. 393 (2007).
Palmer v. Merluzzi, 868 F.2d 90 (3rd Cir. 1989).
Pinard v. Clatskanie School District 6J, 467 F.3d 755 (9th Cir. 2006).
Sala v. Warwick Valley Central School District, 2009 WL 225493 (S.D.N.Y.)
Tinker v. Des Moines Independent Community School District, 393 U.S. 503 (1969).
T.V. v. Smith-Green Community School Corporation, 807 F.Supp.2d 767 (N.D. Ind. 2011).
Wooten v. Pleasant Hope School District, 139 F.Supp.2d 835 (W.D. Missouri 2000).

Legislation
United States Constitution, Amendment I.
United States Constitution, Amendment XIV.

6.23 DRUG TESTING

John T. Wolohan | Syracuse University

Since the beginning of time, there have always been athletes who have sought to gain an advantage in competition. For example, since the beginning of the ancient Olympic Games, many of the athletes tried to improve their performance by experimenting with their diet and or the use of stimulants (Yesalis & Bahrke, 2001). Today, whether through elite training, sleeping in oxygen tents, specialized diet, vitamin supplements, or less ethical methods such as anabolic steroids and other Performance Enhancing Drugs (PEDs), athletes are still seeking ways to get bigger, faster, and stronger (Sigman, 2008).

Perhaps no athlete illustrates that point more than Lance Armstrong. In 2012, the United States Anti-Doping Agency (USADA) sent a notice letter to Armstrong, informing him it was opening formal action against him and five others for their alleged roles in a doping conspiracy beginning in January 1998 and running through 2010. Specifically, USADA claimed that not only did Armstrong "use prohibited substances and/or methods including EPO, blood transfusions, testosterone, corticosteroids and masking agents but that he also encouraged his teammates to use and/or assisted them in using doping products and/or methods, including EPO, blood transfusions, testosterone and cortisone" (Armstrong v. Tygart, 2012). When Armstrong refused to arbitrate the case against USADA, the organization stripped him of all victories and prizes and barred him from international athletic competition for life. Armstrong would later confess to all the allegations against him, setting off various court battles that are still going on today.

Worried about the impact PEDs were having on the integrity of sports, as well as the health and safety of athletes, athletic administrators and organizations from the interscholastic, intercollegiate, Olympic, and professional levels have implemented a series of drug-testing programs. However, in their haste to rid sports of performance-enhancing drugs, some people have voiced concern that sports and recreational organizations may be violating the rights of the very athletes they are trying to protect. This section examines the various legal principles raised when an institution or organization implements a drug-testing program for athletes.

FUNDAMENTAL CONCEPTS

The main legal areas governing drug testing of athletes are constitutional law and labor law. The law that will govern a particular complaint depends on the individual. For example, drug testing high school or college athletes raises a number of constitutional issues concerning the athlete's right to due process and privacy, as well as protection against illegal search and seizure and self-incrimination. The drug testing of professional athletes will usually be resolved through internal grievance and arbitration systems set up within the league's collective bargaining agreement (CBA). As for international and Olympic athletes drug testing programs are regulated by the World Anti-Doping Agency (WADA); national anti-doping agencies such as the United States Anti-Doping Agency (USADA) and the Court of Arbitration for Sport (CAS).

Constitutional Law

The first question to ask whenever a constitutional law issue arises: "is there **state action**?" The safeguards of the U.S. Constitution apply only when state action is present. State action is defined as any action taken directly or indirectly by a state, municipal, or federal government. Therefore, before an athlete can claim that a drug-testing program violated his or her constitutional rights, the entity being challenged must be shown to be part of the federal, state, or municipal government. (For more information on state action, see Chapter 6.12, *State Action*).

Since public high schools and colleges are state actors, the students attending these institutions benefit from the protections afforded under the constitution. Private entities, such as the NCAA and professional sports teams, on the other hand, are not subject to constitutional challenges. For example, in *Long v. National Football League* (1994), a NFL player sued the league after he tested positive for anabolic steroids and was suspended pursuant to the league's drug-testing policy. In dismissing his claim, the court held that Long failed to show a sufficiently close nexus between the actions of the city and city officials and the decision of the NFL to establish state action.

Even when the state is involved in the drug testing of professional athletes, the courts have afforded wide latitude to such programs. For example, in *Shoemaker v. Handell* (1986), five jockeys challenged the New Jersey Racing Commission's regulations requiring drug testing of jockeys. The jockeys claimed that the test constituted an illegal search and seizure and was a violation of their Fourth Amendment rights. The Court of Appeals, in upholding the regulations, held that the commission's concern for racing integrity warranted the tests and that as long as the commission kept the results confidential, there was no violation of the jockeys' rights.

The Fourth Amendment

Once state action has been established, an organization must meet the safeguards of the Fourth Amendment to the United States Constitution before it can implement a drug-testing program. The Fourth Amendment provides that:

> [T]he right of the people to be secure in their persons, houses, papers and effects, against unreasonable searches and seizures, shall not be violated, and no Warrants shall issue, but upon probable cause, supported by Oath or affirmation, and particularly describing the place to be searched and the persons or things to be seized.

Therefore, before any drug test program can be ruled constitutional under the Fourth Amendment, the "search" or test must be reasonable. To determine whether a drug test satisfies the reasonableness requirement, the court must balance the intrusion of the test on an individual's Fourth Amendment interests against its promotion of legitimate governmental interests. This is even more important when considering high school students, who are generally minors. In conducting this balancing test, the court examines the following three factors: legitimate privacy expectation; character of the intrusion and the nature and immediacy of the governmental concern.

The first factor the courts consider is whether the individual has a **legitimate privacy expectation** on which the search intrudes. What expectations are legitimate varies depending on where the individual asserting the privacy interest is: e.g., at home, at work, in a car, or in a public park. In addition, the legitimacy of certain privacy expectations may depend on the individual's legal relationship with the state. For example, the expectation of privacy by high school students in school is less than college students, members of the general population or even high school students outside the school grounds. Also affecting the privacy expectations of athletes is the fact that athletes shower and change together before and after each practice or game; therefore, their expectation of privacy is small. As the Supreme Court noted in *Vernonia School District v. Acton* (1995), "high school sports are not for the bashful."

The second factor to be considered is the **character of the intrusion.** In determining the character of the intrusion, the court examines the manner in which the samples are collected and monitored. For example, is the individual required to give a blood test, which courts would find highly invasive, or a urine sample, which is far less invasive? In *Vernonia School District v. Acton* (1995), the Supreme Court noted that under the school district's testing program, male students produce samples at a urinal along a wall. They remain fully clothed and are only observed from behind, if at all. Female students produce samples in an enclosed stall, with a female monitor standing outside listening only for sounds of tampering. These conditions are nearly identical to those typically encountered in public restrooms, which men, women, and especially schoolchildren use daily. Under such conditions, the Supreme Court held that the privacy interests compromised by the process of obtaining the urine sample are negligible (*Vernonia School District v. Acton*, 1995).

In addition, to the manner in which the samples are collected, the court also considers the type of information being collected by the test, illegal drug and performance-enhancing drugs, and who receives the test results and how the information is used. The test information should only be disclosed to those limited individuals who have a need to know. For example, in *Vernonia School District v. Acton* (1995), the Supreme Court held that it was "significant that the tests at issue here look only for drugs, and not for whether the student is, for example, epileptic, pregnant, or diabetic." Moreover, the Court found that the drugs for which the samples are screened are standard, and do not vary according to the identity of the student. Finally, the Supreme Court noted that the results of the tests are disclosed only to a limited class of school personnel who have a need to know; and they are not turned over to law enforcement authorities or used for any internal disciplinary function (*Vernonia School District v. Acton*, 1995).

The final factor to be considered is the **nature and immediacy of the governmental concern** and the efficacy of the drug test in meeting those concerns. In other words, the court must determine whether the state's interest in conducting the drug test is important enough to justify intruding on an individual's expectation of privacy. For example, in *Vernonia School District v. Acton* (1995), the Supreme Court found that the schools had a compelling state interest in "deterring drug use by our Nation's schoolchildren." Moreover, the court found that the necessity for the State to act is magnified by the fact that this evil is being visited not just upon individuals at large, but upon children for whom it has undertaken a special responsibility of care and direction. Finally, it must not be lost sight of that this program is directed more narrowly to drug use by school athletes, where the risk of immediate physical harm to the drug user or those with whom he is playing his sport is particularly high (*Vernonia School District v. Acton*, 1995).

Not all high school drug tests meet this standard, however, for example is *Gruenke v. Seip*, (2000), a high school swimming coach who suspected that a member on the team was pregnant, required the athlete to take a pregnancy test. In ruling that the coach's actions constituted an unreasonable search under the Fourth Amendment, the Third Circuit Court ruled that even though student athletes have a very limited expectation of privacy, in order to compel a student to take a pregnancy test the school must show a legitimate health concern.

Finally, while the Fourth Amendment also requires that before any search can be conducted there must be **probable cause**, the Supreme Court has recognized that a search unsupported by probable cause can be constitutional when the state has special needs. As the Supreme Court noted in *Vernonia School District v. Acton* (1995), because of the student's age, the state has "special needs" in the public school context.

Post–Vernonia Expansions

Since the United States Supreme Court's decision in *Vernonia*, high schools have sought to extend drug testing to more and more students. In 2002, the United States Supreme Court, in *Board of Education v. Earls* (2002), extended the scope of *Vernonia* to include all extracurricular activities. In Earls, the school district instituted a policy that required all students who participated in any competitive extracurricular activities, including band members, choir members, academic team members, and athletic team members, to submit to drug testing. In upholding the policy, the Supreme Court held that the drug-testing policy reasonably served the school district's important interest in detecting and preventing drug use, and the policy did not violate the Fourth Amendment's prohibition against unreasonable searches and seizures.

In *Safford Unified Sch. Dist. # 1 v. Redding* (2009), the United States Supreme Court was asked to determine whether 13-year-old's Fourth Amendment right was violated when she was subjected to a strip search by school officials acting on reasonable suspicion that she had brought forbidden prescription and over-the-counter drugs to school. In holding that the strip search of the student was unreasonable and a violation of the Fourth Amendment, the Supreme Court ruled that in order for a school search to be permissible in its scope, the measures adopted must be reasonably related to the objectives of the search and not excessively intrusive in light of the age and sex of the student and the nature of the infraction. In the Redding case, the court found that the content of the suspicion failed to match the degree of intrusion. In particular, the Supreme Court noted that the school official knew before the search that the pills were only prescription-strength ibuprofen and over-the-counter naproxen, common pain reliever equivalent to two Advil, or one Aleve. In addition, there was no reason to suspect that the drugs were concealed in her bra and underwear.

State High School Athletic Associations. In addition to individual high schools, state high school athletic associations have also started mandatory testing of athletes. In December 2005, New Jersey became the first state to require random steroid testing for athletes on high school teams that qualify for postseason play. The program, which costs $100,000.00 per year, only tests for performance-enhancing drugs in championship tournaments and requires that 60% of the tests come from football, wrestling, track and field, swimming, lacrosse, and baseball. Following New Jersey's example, Illinois, Texas and Florida also started steroid testing programs. After two years and having spent close to $100,000, Florida discontinued its program in 2009. In justifying the decision, Florida officials pointed to the fact that out of the 600 tests it conducted only one athlete tested positive (Popke, 2009). In 2013, however, after learning that high school athletes were linked to the Biogenesis clinic that supplied PEDs to a number of athletes, including high school students, the Florida High School Athletic Association announced it will push individual member schools to conduct their own steroid testing programs (Navarro, 2013). In 2015, after having spent 10 million dollars on its program, and only finding 11 athletes that tested positive for steroids, Texas Governor Greg Abbott signed a law killing the state-mandated program (Cook, 2015).

College Athletics. As mentioned above the NCAA is not a state actor under the constitution, therefore it is free to test athletes attending member institutions without fear of violating the constitution protections provided under the Fourth Amendment. As a result, the NCAA, at the January 1986 Convention enacted legislation implementing a uniform drug-testing program for all college athletes. The program allows for year-round testing of anabolic steroids, diuretics and masking agents, peptide hormones, beta-2 agonists and beta blockers. Athletes competing NCAA championship events may be tested for all banned drug classes, and include tests for street drugs. For more information on the NCAA program, as well as a list of banned substances, see: http://www.ncaa.org/sites/default/files/Drug%20Testing%20Program%20for%202015%20FINAL.pd. Although the NCAA might be free to test athletes without fear of violating the constitution protections of the Fourth Amendment, the same is not true of those individual colleges and universities who conduct their own drug testing programs.

Consent Forms

An individual can voluntarily waive his or her Fourth Amendment rights and submit to a drug-testing program. However, even when there is consent to a drug test, the court has ruled that not all consent is voluntary. For example, in *University of Colorado v. Derdeyn* (1993), a group of student-athletes who had signed consent forms challenged the university's mandatory drug testing program. In upholding the students' challenge, the Colorado Supreme Court held that the university failed to show that the students' consent to such testing was voluntary. Absent such voluntary consent, the court concluded that the university's random, suspicionless urinalysis drug-testing program violated the students' constitutional rights.

State Constitutions

It is also important to note that individual state constitutions may afford more liberal protections to citizens with respect to search and seizure when compared to the U.S. Constitution. For example, in *Hill v. NCAA* (1994), after the NCAA implemented its' drug testing program Jennifer Hill, a member of the swimming team at Stanford University, challenged the NCAA's drug testing program by arguing that it violated her privacy rights under the California State Constitution. In particular, Hill pointed to the NCAA's procedure for collecting urine samples and the consent form, which asked students to disclose medical and sexual information. In ruling against Hill, the California Supreme Court held that the NCAA's drug-testing policy did not violate the students' constitutional right to privacy. In holding that the program was consistent with the privacy provisions of the state constitution, the California Supreme Court held that the NCAA's interest in protecting both the health and safety of the athletes and the integrity of the programs outweighed Hill's privacy interests *Hill v. NCAA*, (1994).

Another case involving a state constitutional challenge is *York v. Wahkiakum School District No. 200*, (2008), in which the Supreme Court of Washington ruled that the random and suspicionless drug testing of student athletes violates article I, section 7 of the Washington State Constitution. (See Significant Case)

Due Process

Another theory used by athletes to challenge the constitutionality of drug-testing programs is due process. As discussed in Chapter 6.13, *Due Process*, to establish a violation of due process, an individual must establish that he or she has some type of property or liberty interest that has been adversely affected. Unfortunately, for the student–athletes, it is clear from past court decisions that participation in athletics is not a property right, but is a privilege not protected by Constitutional due process safeguards. For example, in *Brennan v. Board of Trustees* (1997), John Brennan, a student-athlete at the University of Southwestern Louisiana, challenged a positive drug test for anabolic steroids on due process grounds. In the case, Brennan requested and received two administrative appeals in which he contended that the positive test results were "false" due to a combination of factors, including heavy drinking and sexual activity the night before the test and his use of nutritional supplements. Following the unsuccessful appeals, USL complied with the NCAA regulations and suspended Brennan from intercollegiate athletic competition for one year. In rejecting his claim, the court held that Brennan had no liberty or property interest in participating in intercollegiate athletics.

Labor Law

Another legal area governing drug testing is labor law. In professional sports, the conduct of the players is governed by a contract that is negotiated between the league, representing the owners, and the players' association, representing the players. This contract or Collective Bargaining Agreement (CBA) addresses the conditions of the athletes' employment. Because drug-testing programs affect an athlete's condition of employment (if they test positive, they cannot play), it is a mandatory subject of bargaining and must be part of the CBA. (For more information on Labor Relations in Professional Sports, see Chapter 7.33). The first professional sports league to subject its players to drug tests was the National Basketball Players. The program, which only covered street drugs, was adopted in 1983. The NBA added steroids to the list of banned substances in 1999. The first league to test players for steroid use was the NFL in 1987.

One problem with drug testing in professional sports, as demonstrated by the fight over drug testing in Major League Baseball, is the conflict of interest both the union and management have in having a strong testing program. Because the job of the MLB Players Association is to protect the players from anything that might impact their work, which the current drug testing program clearly does, it is in the union's best interest to fight to keep testing out of baseball. As a result of this conflict, it is not surprising that the union only agreed to allow drug testing of players under the threat of Congressional intervention and if baseball could demonstrate that there was a problem. As a result, MLB conducted survey tests in 2003 to gauge the use of steroids among players. If more than 5 percent of the major league players tested had tested positive, the threshold established by the union, MLB could implement a full drug testing program in 2004. At the end of the 2003 season a total of 103 players tested positive, and MLB has had a drug testing program ever since. The penalties under the current Major League Baseball Drug Testing Policy, which was updated in 2014, are: an 80-game suspension for the first offense; 162-game/183-days of pay suspension for a second offense; and a permanent suspension from the major or minor leagues for a third. (mlb.mlb.com).

World Anti-Doping Agency

In 1998, the sport world was rocked by a series of high profile doping scandals. For example, before the 1998 Tour de France a masseur for one of the teams was stopped at the boarder when his car is found to contain more than 400 doping products, including EPO, a drug that increases oxygen in red blood cells. During the race, the police raided a number of the hotel rooms of team members, forcing five teams drop out of the race along with some individuals, including former world champion Luc Leblanc. In addition to the Tour, 1998 also saw members of the Chinese national swim team test positive before the 1998 world championships and vials of human growth hormone were found in the team's luggage while traveling to the event. On top of that, in 1998, three-time gold medal winner, Michelle Smith de Bruin was banned from competition for four years by the International Swimming Federation (FINA) after finding that she had manipulated a drug test by spiking her urine sample with alcohol. Finally, Canadian snowboarder Ross Rebagliati won the Olympic gold medal in Nagano Olympics Olympic Winter Games tested positive for marijuana, and was automatically disqualified. Rebagliati was able to keep the gold, however, since the International Ski Federation (FIS) never banned marijuana (Sigman, 2008).

Worried about the impact the drug scandals might have on the future of the Olympic Games, the International Olympic Committee held the First World Conference on Doping in Sport in February 1999 in Lausanne,

Switzerland. As a result of the conference, the International Olympic Committee (IOC) and the international sport governing bodies created the Lausanne Declaration on Doping in Sport, which called for the creation of a global anti-doping agency. In November 1999, the World Anti-Doping Agency (WADA) was established to fill this role.

In March 2003, WADA announced a consolidated drug-control program for all international sports. The World Anti-Doping Code (the Code) was signed by sixty-five sports federations and over fifty nations, including the United States, United Kingdom, Russia, France, Germany, and Australia, and covers all Olympic sports, the federations that govern them, and all their athletes. In developing the Code, WADA sought to create a single list of banned drugs, a uniform system for testing for them, and penalties for violators. Up until the Code was developed, each Olympic sport operated under its own drug program. Since it entered into force on January 1 2004, the Code has led to several significant advances in the global fight against doping in sport, and has brought about harmonization to a system where previously rules had varied, and in some cases did not exist.

Under the WADA Code each athlete is responsible for all positive findings, no matter how the drug got into their bodies. For a first violation under the 2015 Code, an athlete received an automatic 4-year ban from competition; a second violation and the athlete is banned for life. In an effort to provide some flexibility, the 2003 Code was revised in 2009 and 2015 to allow for WADA to reduce the mandatory penalties if "an athlete or other Person can establish how a Specified Substance entered his or her body or came into his or her Possession and that such Specified Substance was not intended to enhance the Athlete's sport performance or mask the Use of a performance-enhancing substance" (WADA Code). As of January 1, 2009, however, the Code also requires athletes to submit to no-notice, out-of-competition tests anytime, anywhere. To do this, every athlete on the national testing register, and any elite athlete in an Olympic or major team sport, must report his or her whereabouts to their national anti-doping organizations for at least one hour a day between the hours of 6 am and 11 pm, seven days a week, three months in advance. Failure of the athlete to be where he or she said they would be counts as a strike. (For more information on the 2015 WADA Code, see: http://www.wada-ama.org/).

An example of the impact the WADA Code has on international sports is *Landis v. USADA* (2007). During the 2006 Tour de France, Floyd Landis, who would eventually win the race, tested positive for the presence of exogenous testosterone. The Court of Arbitration for Sport (CAS), in *Landis v. USADA* (2007), upheld USADA's penalty stripping Landis of his 2006 Tour de France win and declaring him ineligible to compete for two years and requiring Landis to pay the $100,000 in legal expenses USADA incurred in the arbitration.

SIGNIFICANT CASE

The following case examines whether the drug testing of student–athletes violates the students state constitutional rights of privacy.

HANS YORK ET AL., V. WAHKIAKUM SCHOOL DISTRICT NO. 200
Supreme Court of Washington
178 P.3d 995 (Wash. 2008)

The question before us is whether random and suspicionless drug testing of student athletes violates article I, section 7 of the Washington State Constitution.

1 Article I, section 7 of the Washington Constitution provides:

No person shall be disturbed in his private affairs, or his home invaded, without authority of law.

Facts

The Wahkiakum School District (school district) requires its student athletes to refrain from using or possessing alcohol or illegal drugs. Beginning in 1994, the school district implemented myriad ways to combat drug and alcohol use among the student population. Nevertheless, drug and alcohol problems persisted. Acting independently of the school district, the Wahkiakum Community Network (community network) began surveying district students. From these surveys, the community network ranked teen substance abuse as the number one problem in Wahkiakum County. As reiterated by the trial court, the community network's surveys showed that in 1998, 40 percent of sophomores reported previously using illegal drugs and 19 percent of sophomores reported illegal drug use within the previous 30 days, while 42 percent of seniors reported previously using illegal drugs and 12.5 percent reported illegal drug use within the previous 30 days. Clerk's Papers (CP) at 484-85 (Undisputed Facts 10(c), (d)). In 2000, 50 percent of student athletes self-identified as drug and/or alcohol users. *Id.*

As a result, the school district decided to implement random drug testing where all student athletes may be tested initially and then subjected to random drug testing during the remainder of the season. The school district formed the Drug and Alcohol Advisory Committee (now the Safe and Drug Free Schools Advisory Committee) to help deal with the student substance abuse problems. CP at 485. The committee evaluated the effectiveness of its previous programs, such as D.A.R.E. (Drug Abuse Resistance Education) and support groups, and contemplated adopting policy 3515, which would require random drug testing of student athletes. The trial court found:

Based upon the evidence of substantial alcohol and drug use among students and pursuant to the School District's statutory authority and responsibility to maintain order and discipline in its schools, to protect the health and safety of its students, and to control, supervise and regulate interschool athletics, the Board of Directors adopted the policy. CP at 486.

As part of the policy, all student athletes must agree to be randomly drug tested as a condition of playing extracurricular sports. The drug testing is done by urinalysis, with the student in an enclosed bathroom stall and a health department employee outside. The sample is then mailed to Comprehensive Toxicology Services in Tacoma, Washington. If the results indicate illegal drug use, then the student is suspended from extracurricular athletic activities; the length of suspension depends on the number of infractions and whether the student tested positive for illegal drugs or alcohol. Also, the school district provides students with drug and alcohol counseling resources. The results are not sent to local law enforcement or included in the student's academic record. And the student is not suspended from school, only from extracurricular sports.

During the 1999-2000 school year, Aaron York and Abraham York played sports and were tested under the policy. And Tristan Schneider was tested under the policy during the 2000-2001 year. The York and Schneider parents brought suit arguing the school district's policy violated the Washington State Constitution. Their motion for a preliminary injunction was denied by superior court Judge Penoyar, and the Court of Appeals dismissed the petition as moot. *See York v. Wahkiakum Sch. Dist. No. 200*, 110 Wn. App. 383, 40 P.3d 1198 (2002). The trial court then held that while the school district's policy "approached the tolerance limit" of our constitution, the policy was nevertheless constitutional and narrowly tailored to reach a compelling government end. CP at 497.

The York and Schneider parents sought and obtained direct review in our court of a summary judgment order and ask us to determine whether the school district's policy 3515 is constitutional.

* * *

Analysis

We are aware there are strong arguments, policies, and opinions marshaled on both sides of this debate, but we are concerned only with the policy's constitutionality. And while we are loath to disturb the decisions of a local school board, we will not hesitate to intervene when constitutional protections are implicated. . . . No matter the drawbacks or merits of the school district's random drug testing, we cannot let the policy stand if it offends our constitution. Students "do not 'shed their constitutional rights' at the schoolhouse door." *Goss v. Lopez*, 419 U.S. 565, 574, 95 S. Ct. 729, 42 L. Ed. 2d 725 (1975).

The question before us is narrow: Whether Wahkiakum School District's blanket policy requiring student athletes to submit to random drug testing is constitutional. The United States Supreme Court has held such activity does not violate the Fourth Amendment to the federal constitution. *Vernonia Sch. Dist. 47J v. Acton*, 515 U.S. 646, 115 S. Ct. 2386, 132 L. Ed. 2d 564 (1995). But we have never decided whether a suspicionless, random drug search of student athletes violates article I, section 7 of our state constitution. Therefore, we must decide whether our state constitution follows the federal standard or provides more protection to students in the state of Washington.

I. May Wahkiakum School District Perform Suspicionless, Random Drug Tests of Student Athletes?

a. Federal cases concerning public school searches

The school district argues we should follow federal cases and allow suspicionless, random drug testing of its student athletes. Two federal cases are apposite to our consideration. These cases, while helpful, do not control how we interpret our state constitution. *City of*

Seattle v. Mighty Movers, 152 Wn.2d 343, 356, 96 P.3d 979 (2004). There are stark differences in the language of the two constitutional protections; unlike the Fourth Amendment, article I, section 7 is not based on a reasonableness standard.

The United States Supreme Court has held public school searches presented a "special need," which allowed a departure from the warrant and probable cause requirements. New Jersey v. T.L.O., 469 U.S. 325, 105 S. Ct. 733, 83 L. Ed. 2d 720 (1985). The T.L.O. Court held school teachers and administrators could search students without a warrant if (1) there existed reasonable grounds for suspecting that the search will turn up evidence that the student has violated or is violating either the law or the rules of the school" and (2) the search is "not excessively intrusive in light of the age and sex of the student and the nature of the infraction." Id. at 341–42.

Next, in Acton, a public school district implemented a random drug testing of school athletes, similar to the one at issue here. Acton, 515 U.S. 646. Each student athlete was tested at the beginning of the season, and then each week 10 percent were randomly selected for testing. Most critics of Acton are not persuaded the majority's analysis justifies a suspicionless search of the student athletes. But the Acton majority claimed individualized suspicion would unduly interfere with the government's goals and might actually make the situation worse. Its reasoning was based primarily on three rationales: (1) individualized suspicion would "transform [ ] the process into a badge of shame," id. at 663, where teachers could claim any troublesome student was abusing drugs; (2) teachers and student officials are neither trained nor equipped to spot drug use; and (3) individualized suspicion creates an unnecessary loss of resources in defending claims and lawsuits against arbitrary imposition, when students and parents will inevitably challenge whether reasonable suspicion did indeed exist. Id. at 664 ("In many respects, we think, testing based on 'suspicion' of drug use would not be better, but worse.").

But these arguments were unpersuasive several years earlier when the Court applied an individualized suspicion standard to public schools in T.L.O. The Acton majority never adequately explained why individual suspicion was needed in T.L.O. but not in Acton. Justice O'Connor spent much of her dissent taking issue with this standard:

[N]owhere is it less clear that an individualized suspicion requirement would be ineffectual than in the school context. In most schools, the entire pool of potential search targets—students—is under constant supervision by teachers and administrators and coaches, be it in classrooms, hallways, or locker rooms. . . .

. . . The great irony of this case is that most (though not all) of the evidence the District introduced to justify its suspicionless drug testing program consisted of first- or second-hand stories of particular, identifiable students acting in ways that plainly gave rise to reasonable suspicion of in-school drug use—and thus that would have justified a drug-related search under our T.L.O. decision. Acton, 515 U.S. at 678–79 (O'Connor, J., dissenting).

The Wahkiakum School District modeled its policy after the one used by the Vernonia School District. But simply passing muster under the federal constitution does not ensure the survival of the school district's policy under our state constitution. The Fourth Amendment provides for "[t]he right of the people to be secure in their persons, houses, papers, and effects, against unreasonable searches and seizures." U.S. CONST. amend. IV. Therefore, a Fourth Amendment analysis hinges on whether a warrantless search is reasonable, and it is possible in some circumstances for a search to be reasonable without a warrant. See Acton, 515 U.S. at 652 ("As the text of the Fourth Amendment indicates, the ultimate measure of the constitutionality of a governmental search is 'reasonableness.'"). But our state constitutional analysis hinges on whether a search has "authority of law"—in other words, a warrant. WASH. CONST. art. I, § 7.

b. Search and seizure analysis under article I, section 7

Our state constitution provides: "No person shall be disturbed in his private affairs, or his home invaded, without authority of law." WASH. CONST. art. I, § 7. It is well established that in some areas, article I, section 7 provides greater protection than its federal counterpart—the Fourth Amendment. State v. McKinney, 148 Wn.2d 20, 29, 60 P.3d 46 (2002); State v. Myrick, 102 Wn.2d 506, 510, 688 P.2d 151 (1984) ("[T]he unique language of Const. art. 1, § 7 provides greater protection to persons under the Washington Constitution than U.S. Const. amend. 4 provides to persons generally."). When determining whether article I, section 7 provides greater protection in a particular context, we focus on whether the unique characteristics of the constitutional provision and its prior interpretations compel a particular result. State v. Walker, 157 Wn.2d 307, 317, 138 P.3d 113 (2006). We look to the constitutional text, historical treatment of the interest at stake, relevant case law and statutes, and the current implications of recognizing or not recognizing an interest. Id.

This requires a two-part analysis. First, we must determine whether the state action constitutes a disturbance of one's private affairs. Here that means asking whether requiring a student athlete to provide a urine sample intrudes upon the student's private affairs. Second, if a privacy interest has been disturbed, the second step in our analysis asks whether authority of law justifies the intrusion. The "authority of law" required by article I, section 7 is satisfied by a valid warrant, limited to a few jealously guarded exceptions. Because the Wahkiakum School District had no warrant, if we reach the second prong of the analysis, we must decide whether the school district's activity fits within an exception to the warrant requirement. Relying on federal law, the school district claims there is a "special needs" exception to the warrant requirement that we should adopt. The York and Schneider parents point out we have not adopted such an exception and urge us not to do so here.

II. Suspicionless, Random Drug Testing Disturbs a Student Athlete's Private Affairs

When inquiring about private affairs, we look to "'those privacy interests which citizens of this state have held, and should be entitled to hold, safe from governmental trespass absent a warrant'." *State v. Young*, 123 Wn.2d 173, 181, 867 P.2d 593 (1994) (quoting *Myrick*, 102 Wn.2d at 511). This is an objective analysis.

The private affair we are concerned with today is the State's interference in a student athlete's bodily functions. Specifically, does it intrude upon a privacy interest to require a student athlete to go into a bathroom stall and provide a urine sample, even against that student's protest? Federal courts and our court both agree the answer is an unqualified yes, such action intrudes into one's reasonable expectation of privacy. Indeed, we offer heightened protection for bodily functions compared to the federal courts.

But the school district claims student athletes have a lower expectation of privacy. Certainly, students who choose to play sports are subjected to more regulation. For example, RCW 28A.600.200 provides, "Each school district board of directors is hereby granted and shall exercise the authority to control, supervise and regulate the conduct of interschool athletic activities." And certainly there is generally less privacy in locker rooms than in other parts of a school. But the district does not link regulations and the communal atmosphere of locker rooms with a student's lowered expectation of privacy in terms of being subjected to suspicionless, random drug testing. We do not see how what happens in the locker room or on the field affects a student's privacy in the context of compelling him or her to provide a urine sample. A student athlete has a genuine and fundamental privacy interest in controlling his or her own bodily functions. The urinalysis test is by itself relatively unobtrusive. Nevertheless, a student is still required to provide his or her bodily fluids. Even if done in an enclosed stall, this is a significant intrusion on a student's fundamental right of privacy. *See Robinson*, 102 Wn. App. at 822.

This analysis should in no way contradict what we have previously said about students' privacy interests. Generally, we have recognized students have a lower expectation of privacy because of the nature of the school environment. Courts have held a school official needs some "reasonable" or "individualized" suspicion in order to protect students from arbitrary searches, yet still give officials sufficient leeway to conduct their duties. *T.L.O.*, 469 U.S. at 341; *State v. McKinnon*, 88 Wn.2d 75, 558 P.2d 781 (1977). Our court discussed student searches and student rights under the Fourth Amendment prior to the United States Supreme Court's holding in *T.L.O.*

In *McKinnon*, we said: Although a student's right to be free from intrusion is not to be lightly disregarded, for us to hold school officials to the standard of probable cause required of law enforcement officials would create an unreasonable burden upon these school officials. Maintaining discipline in schools oftentimes requires immediate action and cannot await the procurement of a search warrant based on probable cause. We hold that the search of a student's person is reasonable and does not violate his Fourth Amendment rights, if the school official has reasonable grounds to believe the search is necessary in the aid of maintaining school discipline and order. *McKinnon*, 88 Wn.2d at 81. And in *Kuehn*, we also opined in dicta that although a warrant or probable cause might be unnecessary to search a student's backpack, the school nevertheless needed to articulate some reasonable suspicion to justify a search of a student under both the Fourth Amendment and article I, section 7. . . .

We decided these cases before the United States Supreme Court decided *T.L.O.*, which cited *McKinnon* when it also held reasonable suspicion was necessary to search a student. *T.L.O.*, 469 U.S. at 333 n.2. Nevertheless, in *State v. Brooks*, 43 Wn. App. 560, 568, 718 P.2d 837 (1986), the Court of Appeals analyzed *McKinnon* and *Kuehn* and said, "Accordingly, since the holding in *T.L.O.* is consistent with our Supreme Court's holding in *McKinnon*, we conclude that article 1, section 7 affords students no greater protections from searches by school officials than is guaranteed by the Fourth Amendment." The school district points to this one sentence to say we should adopt whole cloth the federal analysis with regards to both student searches and student drug testing. But *Brooks* did not involve drug testing and was decided before *Acton*. Nor are we bound to the Court of Appeals' broad language.

Because we determine that interfering with a student athlete's bodily functions disturbs one's private affairs, we must address the second prong of the article I, section 7 analysis: does the school district have the necessary authority of law to randomly drug test student athletes?

III. Under Article I, Section 7 There Is No Authority of Law that Allows a School District to Conduct Random Drug Tests

We have long held a warrantless search is per se unreasonable, unless it fits within one of the "'jealously and carefully drawn exceptions.'" *State v. Hendrickson*, 129 Wn.2d 61, 70, 917 P.2d 563 (1996). These exceptions include "exigent circumstances, consent, searches incident to a valid arrest, inventory searches, the plain view doctrine, and *Terry* investigative stops." *Robinson*, 102 Wn. App. at 813. Any exceptions to the warrant requirement must be rooted in the common law. *State v. Ladson*, 138 Wn.2d 343, 979 P.2d 833 (1999); *Robinson*, 102 Wn. App. at 813. And it is always the government's burden to show its random drug testing fits within one of these narrow exceptions. *City of Seattle v. Mesiani*, 110 Wn.2d 454, 457, 755 P.2d 775 (1988). Today the school district asks us to accept an analog to the federal special needs doctrine to justify its drug testing policy. The York and Schneider parents point out we have never formally adopted a special needs exception and therefore claim no exception to the warrant requirement exists here.

* * *

c. Washington State cases concerning suspicionless searches

Though we have not considered drug testing in public schools, we have a long history of striking down exploratory searches not based on at least reasonable suspicion. *State v. Jorden*, 160 Wn.2d 121, 127, 156 P.3d 893 (2007) ("[T]his court has consistently expressed displeasure with random and suspicionless searches, reasoning that they amount to nothing more than an impermissible fishing expedition."); *Robinson*, 102 Wn. App. at 815 ("Our Supreme Court has thus not been easily persuaded that a search without individualized suspicion can pass constitutional muster."). In *Mesiani*, this court held a random roadblock sobriety checkpoint program initiated by Seattle police was a "highly intrusive" search and violated "the right to not be disturbed in one's private affairs guaranteed by article I, section 7." *Mesiani*, 110 Wn.2d at 458–60. In *Kuehn*, this court held a search of student luggage required by school officials as a condition of participation in a school-sponsored trip to Canada violated both the Fourth Amendment and article I, section 7. 103 Wn.2d at 595. We opined, "[i]n the absence of individualized suspicion of wrongdoing, the search is a general search. '[W]e never authorize general, exploratory searches,'" (alteration in original) and such searches are "anathema to the Fourth Amendment and Const. art. 1, § 7 protections." *Id*.

The few times we have allowed suspicionless searches, we did so either relying entirely on federal law or in the context of criminal investigations or dealing with prisoners. In *Meacham*, 93 Wn.2d at 738–39, we upheld mandatory blood tests of putative fathers. In *Juveniles A, B, C, D, E*, 121 Wn.2d at 90, we upheld mandatory HIV tests of convicted sexual offenders. In *Olivas*, 122 Wn.2d at 83, we upheld blood tests of convicted felons without individualized suspicion. And recently in *State v. Surge*, 160 Wn.2d 65, 156 P.3d 208 (2007), we held a DNA (deoxyribonucleic acid) sampling of convicted felons did not violate article I, section 7. That case allowed for warrantless testing without individualized suspicion because we asserted such testing did not disturb a reasonable right to privacy. But these cases present far different factual situations from drug testing student athletes. A felon has either already pleaded guilty or been found guilty beyond a reasonable doubt of a serious crime; a student athlete has merely attended school and chosen to play extracurricular sports. Most troubling, however, is that we can conceive of no way to draw a principled line permitting drug testing of only student athletes. If we were to allow random drug testing here, what prevents school districts from either later drug testing students participating in any extracurricular activities, as federal courts now allow, or testing the entire student population?

We cannot countenance random searches of public school student athletes with our article I, section 7 jurisprudence. As stated earlier, we require a warrant except for rare occasions, which we jealously and narrowly guard. We decline to adopt a doctrine similar to the federal special needs exception in the context of randomly drug testing student athletes. In sum, no argument has been presented that would bring the random drug testing within any reasonable interpretation of the constitutionally required "authority of law." See *Mesiani*, 110 Wn.2d at 458.

Accordingly, we hold the school district's policy 3515 is unconstitutional and violates student athletes' rights secured by article I, section 7. Therefore, we reverse the superior court. The York and Schneider parents shall recover their costs.

CASES ON THE SUPPLEMENTAL CD

Board of Education of Independent School District No. 92 of Pottawatomie County v. Earls, 536 U.S. 822 (2002). This case examines whether the state can expand drug testing programs to include all middle and high school students who participate in any extracurricular activity, not just sport.

Doe v. Little Rock School District, 380 F.3d 349 (8th Cir. 2004). This cases examines whether the district's practice of conducting random, suspicionless searches of students and their belongings of randomly selected classrooms by school officials violated the students Fourth Amendment rights.

Hill v. National Collegiate Athletic Association, 865 P.2d 633 (1994). This case examines whether the NCAA drug testing program violates state constitutional protections.

Shoemaker v. Handell, 795 F.2d 1136 (1986). This case examines the state's interest in drug testing jockeys in the horse-racing industry.

Williams v. National Football League, 582 F.3d 863 (8th Cir. 2009). This case examines the rights of professional athletes to challenge positive drug test under state law, instead of the collective bargaining agreement (CBA).

York v. Wahkiakum School District No. 200, 178 P.3d 995 (2008). This case examines whether a school district's policy of random and suspicionless drug test was unconstitutional under Washington State's Constitution.

QUESTIONS YOU SHOULD BE ABLE TO ANSWER

1. What are some of the constitutional protections available to fight an unwanted drug test?
2. Why are NCAA athletes unable to challenge the NCAA drug testing program under the fourth Amendment of the United States Constitution?
3. How does the court determine if a drug test is reasonable under the Fourth Amendment of the United States Constitution?
4. Drug testing of professional team athletes in the Unites States are governed by what?
5. What is WADA? What role does it play in sports?

REFERENCES

Cases
Armstrong v. Tygart, 886 F. Supp. 2d 572, 2012).
Board of Education of Independent School District No. 92 of Pottawatomie County v. Earls, 536 U.S. 822 (2002).
Brennan v. Board of Trustees, 691 So.2d 324 (1997).
Gruenke v. Seip, 225 F.3d 290 (3rd Cir. 2000).
Hill v. National Collegiate Athletic Association, 865 P.2d 633, 26 Cal. Rptr.2d 834 (1994).
Landis v. USADA, CAS 2007/A/1394
Long v. National Football League, 870 F. Supp. 101 (1994).
Safford Unified Sch. Dist. # 1 v. Redding, 2009 U.S. LEXIS 4735.
Shoemaker v. Handell, 795 F.2d 1136 (1986).
University of Colorado v. Derdeyn, 863 P.2d 929 (Colo. 1993).
USOC v. IOC, CAS 2011/0/2422
Vernonia School District 47J v. Acton, 515 U.S. 646 (1995).

Publications
Popke, M. (2009, April). Drug Wars. *Athletic Business*, p.12.
Sigman, S. (2008). Doping in Sports: Legal and Ethical Issues: Are We All Dopes? *Marquette Sports Law Review* 19, 125 - 208.
Yesalis, C & Bahrke, M. (2001). History of Doping in Sport. *International Sports Studies, 24, 42-76*

Legislation
United States Constitution, Amendment IV.

Websites
Cook, Bob. 2015. "Why Testing High School Athletes for PEDs is a Big, Fat Failure." June 7, Forbes.com. http://www.forbes.com/sites/bobcook/2015/06/07/why-testing-high-school-athletes-for-peds-is-a-big-fat-failure/#239ec44994f4. Accessed June 15, 2016.
Major League Baseball's Joint Drug Prevention and Treatment Program. http://mlb.mlb.com/pa/pdf/jda.pdf Accessed June 15, 2016.
Navarro, Manny. 2013. "Steroid tests urged for Florida high school athletes." August 7, Miami Herald.com. http://www.miamiherald.com/sports/high-school/prep-miami-dade/article1953875.html. Accessed June 15, 2016.
New Jersey State Interscholastic Athletic Association Steroid Testing Program, http://www.njsiaa.org/NJSIAA/09steroidmemo.pdf. World Anti-Doping Agency, http://www.wada-ama.org/

PARTICIPANTS WITH DISABILITIES

John T. Wolohan | Syracuse University

In the sport and recreation field, the line between lawful refusal to extend eligibility requirements and illegal discrimination against individuals with disabilities is getting clearer all the time. This has especially true since 1990, when the Americans with Disabilities Act (ADA) was originally signed into law and particularly true when the Americans with Disabilities Act Amendment Act (ADAAA) was passed in 2008. Even with the enactment of the ADAAA, individuals with disabilities continue to face a number of obstacles in their effort to participate in and attend sport and recreation events. This chapter examines some of the obstacles individuals with disabilities face in their fight to participate in sport and recreation activities.

FUNDAMENTAL CONCEPTS

As recently as 1970, children with learning disabilities were denied access to a number of state public school systems because it was thought that their presence would interfere with the learning environment of students without disabilities (Clement, 1988). To remedy this situation, in 1973, Congress passed federal legislation designed to increase the opportunities available to individuals with disabilities. The first law passed by Congress was the Rehabilitation Act of 1973.

The Rehabilitation Act of 1973

Section 504 of the Rehabilitation Act states that:

> "No otherwise qualified handicapped individual in the United States, . . . shall solely by reason of his handicap, be excluded from participation in, be denied the benefits of, or be subjected to discrimination under any program or activity receiving Federal financial assistance . . . " (29 U.S.C. § 794).

One of the stated intents of the Rehabilitation Act is to provide individuals with disabilities the opportunity to participate in physical education and athletic programs or activities without being discriminated against due to their disability. For an individual to successfully pursue a claim under § 504, he or she must establish four elements:

1. that he or she is an *individual with a disability* (Section 504 defines a person with a disability as one who has, one who has a record of having, or one who has been regarded as having a physical or mental impairment that *substantially limits* a major life activity);
2. that he or she is *otherwise qualified* for the athletic activity (the individual with a disability must show that, with reasonable accommodation, he or she can participate);
3. that he or she is being excluded from athletic participation *solely by reason of* their disabilities (the person with a disability must demonstrate that he or she is being discriminated against due to his/her disability); and
4. that the *school, or institution is receiving federal financial assistance* (29 U.S.C. 794) (all public schools in the United States would fall in this category.)

Because most challenges under § 504 hinge on the determination of the "otherwise qualified" element or the "solely by reason of" element, an examination of the meaning of those two elements is important. The U.S. Supreme Court, in *Southeastern Community College v. Davis* (1979), interpreted the phrase "otherwise qualified" to mean someone who is able to meet all of a program's requirements in spite of his or her disability (*Southeastern Community College v. Davis*, 422 U.S. 397, at 406, 1979). Davis, who has a hearing disability, sought entry into Southeastern Community College's School of Nursing. The Supreme Court, in finding that Davis's hearing disability made it impossible for her to safely complete the nursing program, stated that § 504 of the Rehabilitation Act does not compel an institution to disregard an individual's ability or to make substantial modifications in their programs to accommodate individuals with disabilities. However, the institution must demonstrate that its rules, policies and procedures represent essential elements to the program.

In *Alexander v. Choate* (1985), the Supreme Court addressed what types of modifications would be required under § 504 when it held that although an organization need not be required to make fundamental or substantial modifications to accommodate an individual's disability, ***it may be required to make reasonable ones.*** Reasonable accommodation may include (1) making facilities used by employees readily accessible to and usable by individuals with disabilities, and (2) job restructuring, part-time or modified work schedules, acquisition or modification of equipment or devices, the provision of readers or interpreters, and similar actions (34 C.F.R. § 104.12. (b)). For example, in *S.S. v. Whitesboro Central School District*, (2012), a student who suffered severe anxiety attacks that would trigger thoughts of drowning. Due to this fear, S.S. requested the accommodation of permitting S.S. to exit the pool for indeterminate periods of time—on unannounced occasions during practices and swim competitions—to calm her nerves, without being kicked off of the team. In rejecting the students § 504 claim the court held that there was nothing the school could do to reasonably accommodate S.S.'s disability. There is no reasonable accommodation that a swim team coach could make for an athlete who is suddenly and sporadically afraid of the water and thus has to exit the pool during practices and competitions. As stated above, one of the essential requirements of swim team members is the ability to enter, and remain in, the pool when required by the coach during practices and competitions. To require otherwise would fundamentally change the nature of the swim team and thus be unreasonable.

Another area of growing concern for sports administrators is whether para-athlete on high school track teams should be able to earn team points when competing in meets. In *K. L. v. Missouri State High School Activities Association*, (2016), the court "concluded that such scoring would fundamentally alter the nature of track and field events in the able-bodied divisions, and that . . . if a requested accommodation violates the fundamental alteration principle, it is by definition 'not reasonable'" (*K. L. v. Missouri State High School Activities Association*, 2016). In support of the decision, the court noted that since only four schools currently had para-athletes competing in track, out of the 506 high schools in Missouri, those four schools would "be afforded unequal and preferential treatment against teams without para-athletes who would have their accomplishments altered by an unfair and inequitable distribution of points they have no chance to earn without para-athletes" (*K. L. v. Missouri State High School Activities Association*, 2016).

Beside Missouri, this issue has also been heard by courts in Alabama, *Badgett v. Alabama High School Athletic Association* (2007), and Maryland, *McFadden v. Grasmick* (2007), where courts have also held that the para-athletes requested modifications in scoring of track and field events would fundamentally alter the nature of the track and field program.

The requirement that an individual be excluded ***solely by reason of*** the disability is met if an individual is being excluded due to their disability. For example, school districts may have policies that require participants to have both of any type of paired organ (e.g., kidneys) for safety reasons. In *Poole v. South Plainfield Board of Education* (1980), the South Plainfield Board of Education denied Richard Poole the right to participate in South Plainfield's interscholastic wrestling program due to the fact that he was born with one kidney. The court concluded that Poole was being excluded from participation in athletics "solely by reason of" the fact he had one kidney.

The issue of whether someone is being excluded "solely by reason of" their disability is more difficult when an individual, due to an illness or learning disability, is over the athletic association's maximum age requirement. *University Interscholastic League (UIL) and Bailey Marshall v. Buchanan* (1993) is a good illustration of the challenge presented in these cases. In *UIL v. Buchanan* two nineteen-year-old students with diagnosed learning disabilities sought a permanent injunction against the enforcement of UIL's rule requiring all athletes to be under 19 years old. In support of the age requirement, the UIL argued that the age requirement was necessary to ensure the safety of the participating student–athletes and to reduce the competitive advantage of having older participants. The UIL also argued that the age rule did not discriminate against the plaintiffs because of their disability, but was applied equally to all students. Therefore, the plaintiffs were ineligible due to their ages, not their disability.

The Court of Appeals in affirming the trial court's injunction, enjoined UIL from enforcing the age rule against the plaintiffs, held that except for their disability, the students would have turned nineteen after September 1 of their senior year and would have been age-eligible to participate in interscholastic athletics. In determining whether UIL had made reasonable accommodations for the plaintiffs' disabilities, the Court of Appeals examined the waiver mechanism UIL had in place for other eligibility rules. The waiver of the age rule, the Court of Appeals found, would be a reasonable accommodation by UIL to ensure that individuals with disabilities achieve meaningful access. The UIL's "no exception" policy to the age requirement, therefore, had to yield to the reasonable accommodation requirement of § 504 of the Rehabilitation Act.

For other cases challenging high school athletic association eligibility rules, see: *Dennin v. Connecticut Interscholastic Athletic Conference* (1996); *J.M. v. Montana High School Association* (1994); *Johnson v. Florida High School Activities Association* (1995); *Pottgen v. Missouri State High School Athletic Association* (1994); and *Sandison v. Michigan High School Athletic Association* (1995).

Individuals with Disabilities Education Act (Idea)

In 1975, Congress enacted the *Education for All Handicapped Children Act of 1975*. The purpose of this Education law was to increase the educational opportunity available to school-aged students with disabilities by providing a free appropriate public education in the least restrictive environment emphasizing special education and related services designed to meet their unique needs (20 U.S.C. 1400 (c)). In 1990, the *Education for All Handicapped Children Act* was amended and renamed the **Individuals with Disabilities Education Act (IDEA)** and applies to students with diagnosed disabilities from birth to graduation, or a maximum age of 21. In 2004, the IDEA was reauthorized as the **Individuals with Disabilities Education Improvement Act (IDEIA).** The major changes emphasize key requirements in the special education process, increased monitoring of student progress and the use of accommodations outlined in the Individual Education Plan (IEP). Although there was a title change at the time of reauthorization, the current law is still referred to as IDEA.

To satisfy the goal of IDEA, local educational agencies, together with the student's teachers and parents or guardians, are required to develop a written plan or IEP, outlining achievable educational goals and objectives, reasonable accommodations and related services. Although less specific with regard to athletics than those pursuant to § 504 of the Rehabilitation Act, the regulations adopted under IDEA do require each public agency to ensure that a variety of educational programs and services, including physical education, available to students without disabilities are available to those covered under the act. Besides providing educational programs and services, each public agency is also required to provide nonacademic and extracurricular activities and services in such manner as is necessary to afford children with disabilities an equal opportunity for participation in those services and activities (34 C.F.R. § 300.306(a)). For example, in *Lambert v. West Virginia State Board of Education* (1994), a high school basketball player, who has been deaf since birth, won the right to require her school to provide her with a sign language interpreter so that she could compete on the girls' basketball team. In holding that the Board of Education was required to provide a sign language interpreter for the plaintiff, the court found that the assistance of an interpreter was a reasonable accommodation that provided the plaintiff with equal access to extracurricular activities.

Another example of a student–athlete successfully using IDEA to gain participation is *Crocker v. Tennessee Secondary School Athletic Association* (1992). In *Crocker* the plaintiff transferred from a private school into his local public high school so that he could receive the special education he needed, which was not available in the private school. When the plaintiff attempted to participate in interscholastic athletics at his new school, the TSSAA ruled that he was ineligible. According to TSSAA rules, any student who transfers from one TSSAA member school to another is ineligible to participate in interscholastic sports for 12 months. The plaintiff argued that the TSSAA, by enforcing its transfer rule, was depriving him of his rights guaranteed under IDEA. In ruling for Crocker, the Court held that because the plaintiff's transfer was motivated by his disability and not athletics, TSSAA's refusal to waive its transfer rule violated IDEA.

Another important issue under IDEA is whether the student's participation in interscholastic athletics is a related service that should have been incorporated into his or her IEP. The importance of including participation in interscholastic athletics in a student's IEP can be seen in *T.H. v. Montana High School Association* (1992). In *T.H. v. MHSA*, the plaintiff, after being diagnosed as having a learning disability, was provided with an IEP in accordance with IDEA. One component of the student's plan was for the student to participate in interscholastic athletics as a motivational tool. Before his senior year, the Montana High School Association ruled T.H. ineligible to compete in interscholastic athletics due to his age. The court, in finding for the plaintiff, held that when participation in interscholastic sports is included as a component of the IEP, the privilege of competing in interscholastic sports is transformed into a federally protected right. Conversely, when a student's IEP does not include interscholastic athletic participation, the student has no protect right under the IDEA (*J.M. v. Montana High School Association*, 1996).

Ted Stevens Olympic And Amateur Sports Act

Another piece of legislation impacting the rights of individuals with disabilities is the **Ted Stevens Olympic and Amateur Sports Act.** Originally passed in 1978 and called the Amateur Sports Act (36 U.S.C. §371), the law grants the United States Olympic Committee (USOC) exclusive jurisdiction over amateur athletics in the United States, including all matters pertaining to United States participation in the Olympic Games, the Paralympic Games, and the Pan-American Games.

In particular, the Amateur Sports Act required the USOC to "encourage and provide assistance to amateur athletic programs and competition for handicapped individuals, including, where feasible, the expansion of opportunities for meaningful participation by handicapped individuals in programs of athletic competition for able-bodied individuals" (36 U.S.C. § 374 (13)). The USOC attempted to accomplish this goal by establishing the Committee on Sport for the Disabled and by financially supporting various other sports organizations, such as Disabled Sports USA and the Wheelchair Sports USA.

In 1998, the Amateur Sports Act was amended and renamed Ted Stevens Olympic and Amateur Sports Act, after the law's sponsor, Senator Ted Stevens of Alaska. The Ted Stevens Olympic and Amateur Sports Act places a greater responsibility on the USOC and its constituent organizations to serve elite athletes with a disability, in particular Paralympic athletes. As a result of the 1998 amendments, the USOC has sought to expand the opportunities available to athletes with disabilities by establishing a Paralympic Division within the USOC, providing increased funding and logistical support for athletes and sporting bodies, recognizing Paralympic athletes as members of the USOC Athletes Advisory Committee and providing other avenues for input from Paralympic athletes.

Not everyone, however, has been satisfied with the funding and support the USOC provides to Paralympic athletes. For example, in *Hollonbeck v. USOC*, (2008) the Tenth Circuit Court of Appeals rejected a lawsuit filed by Scot Hollonbeck, a wheelchair racer who had won multiple medals at three Paralympics, who challenged the USOC's policy of providing Athlete Support Programs only to Olympic team members, to the exclusion of Paralympic team members. In finding that the USOC's policy of excluding Paralympic athletes from Athlete Support Programs was not discriminatory, the court noted that the eligibility requirements that the USOC used to distribute the benefits under the policy was that the athlete must be "eligible to represent the United States and . . . intended to compete, if selected, in the next Olympic or Pan American Games." On its face, the court held that such a policy does not contain an explicit requirement of not being disabled. Thus, the court held, the requirement to be an Olympic athlete to be eligible for the Athlete Support Programs is not discriminatory to Paralympic athletes.

The Americans With Disabilities Act (ADA)

The **Americans with Disabilities Act (ADA)** was signed into law July 26, 1990, extending many of the provisions of Section 504 of Rehabilitation Act to the private sector. The purpose of this civil rights statute is "to provide a clear and comprehensive national mandate for the elimination of discrimination against individuals with disabilities" (42 U.S.C. 12101 (b)(1). The ADA focuses on eradicating barriers by requiring entities to consider whether reasonable accommodations could be made to remove any barrier created by a person's disability (Wolohan, 1997a). The ADA defines a "qualified individual with a disability" as any individual with a disability, either physically or mentally, "who, with or without reasonable modifications to rules, policies, or practices, the removal of architectural, communication . . . barriers, or the provision or auxiliary aids and services, meets the essential eligibility requirements for the receipt of services or the participation in programs or activities provided by a public entity" (42 U.S.C. 12115). The ADA is divided into five sections covering the areas of: employment, public services, public services operated by private entities, transportation, and telecommunications. The three sections of which sport and recreational professionals should be aware of are *Title I*, which covers employment; *Title II*, which covers public services; and *Title III*, which covers public accommodations and services operated by private entities.

Title I—Employment
Title I provides that "no covered entity shall discriminate against a qualified individual with a disability because of the disability of such individual in regard to job application procedures, the hiring, advancement, or discharge of employees, employee compensation, job training, and other terms, conditions, and privileges of employment" (42 U.S.C. § 12112). For more information on Title I of the ADA, see Chapter 7.16, *Title I of the Americans with Disabilities Act*.

Title II—Public Services
Title II, which is based on Section 504 of the Rehabilitation Act, provides that "no qualified individual with a disability shall, by reason of such disability, be excluded from participation in or be denied the benefits of the services, programs, or activities of a public entity, or be subjected to discrimination by any such entity" (42 U.S.C. § 12132). In the case of public schools and state athletic associations, the courts have generally determined that athletic associations are given oversight authority by public schools of their athletic programs, participation rules, and competition rules, thus giving them a major role in the public service provided. Given this authority, the athletic association often falls within the provision of both Title II of the ADA and Section 504 of the Rehabilitation Act.

In interpreting the meaning of Title II, the Courts apply the same four standards established under Section 504 of the Rehabilitation Act. Therefore, to establish a violation of Title II of the ADA an individual must demonstrate:

1. that he or she is a "qualified individual with a disability;"
2. that he or she is "otherwise qualified" for the activity;
3. that he or she is being excluded from athletic participation "solely by reason of" their disabilities; and
4. that he or she is being discriminated against by a public entity.

Title III—Public Accommodations and Services Operated by Private Entities
The provisions of Title III provide that "no individual shall be discriminated against on the basis of disability in the full and equal enjoyment of the goods, services, facilities, privileges, advantages, or accommodations of any place of public accommodation by any person who owns, leases, or operates a place of public accommodation" (42 U.S.C. § 12182). Places of public accommodation include stadiums, golf courses, gymnasiums, recreational facilities and other places of public gathering. In addition, policies, practices, and procedures of these facilities must ensure equal opportunity for people with disabilities. For example, if a commercial sport facility uses a turnstile for spectators to gain entry, they must be an accessible option to the turnstile for a wheelchair user. As a result, "the ADA has been instrumental in opening access in sports facilities for people with disabilities" (Hums et al., 2016).

One case that illustrates this point is *Miller v. California Speedway Corp.*, (2008). Robert Miller, a quadriplegic who uses an electric wheelchair, was unable to see races at the California Speedway when the fans immediately in front of him stood up during the most exciting parts of the race. In ruling that the Speedway has violated Title III of the ADA, the court held that the regulation requiring that wheelchair areas "provide people with physical disabilities . . . lines of sight comparable to those for members of the general public" included lines of sight over standing spectators (*Miller v. California Speedway Corp.*, 2008).

Overall, the ADA and Section 504 are civil rights laws that provide protection from discrimination based on disability. For example, in a consent decree issued in 1998, it was determined that Title III of the ADA applies to the National Collegiate Athletic Association (NCAA), as an organization with some public colleges and universities as members. Consequently, the NCAA has a duty to accommodate student athletes with disabilities and must have a process in place to consider modifications to its policies and procedures on a case-by-case basis.

Even if an individual is able to meet all the requirements under Title II or Title III of the ADA, the law still does not require an organization to accommodate a person "**when that individual poses a direct threat to the health or safety of others**" (28 C.F.R. § 36.208). For example, in *Anderson v. Little League Baseball, Inc.* (1992), a youth baseball coach, who was a wheelchair user and had coached Little League Baseball for the previous three years as an on-field coach, sued the league after it adopted a policy prohibiting coaches in wheelchairs from on-field coaching. In support of the policy, the league claimed that the coach posed a direct threat to the health or safety of the athletes and that the policy was intended to protect the players from collisions with the wheelchair. In ruling for the coach, the Court said that the league's policy fell markedly short of the requirements of the ADA. The court found no evidence indicating that the plaintiff posed a direct threat to the health or safety of others.

Another area of concern for sport and recreation administrators around the country, especially after the United States Supreme Court's ruling in *PGA v. Martin* (2001), was what rules are essential to the nature of sport. For example, in *Kuketz v. Petronelli*, (2005), Stephen Kuketz, a nationally ranked wheelchair racquetball player, wanted to join the Brockton Athletic Club men's "A" league so that he could compete against the best able-bodied players available to help prepare for upcoming international wheelchair competitions. Because of his physical limitations, however, Kuketz requested that the club allow him the wheelchair-racquetball-standard two bounces during "A" league play, instead of the one bounce allowable under standard racquetball rules.

Citing safety reasons, the club rejected Kuketz's request (Wolohan, 2005). Disappointed with the decision, Kuketz sued the club claiming the decision violated both federal and state antidiscrimination laws. In evaluating whether the club unlawfully discriminated against Kuketz when it refused to modify its policies and practices, the Supreme Judicial Court of Massachusetts held that the allowance for more than one bounce in racquetball was inconsistent with the fundamental character of the game. As expressly articulated in the rules of racquetball, the court found that the essence of the game of racquetball is the hitting of a moving ball with a racquet before the second bounce. Giving a player in a wheelchair two bounces and a player on foot one bounce in head-to-head competition would alter such an essential aspect of the game that it would be unacceptable, even if it affected all competitors equally. In addition, the court found that unlike golf, the speed at which racquetball is played is important and is one of the factors distinguishing players in different levels. Therefore, if one player were allowed to play the game with two bounces, it would require a change in the strategy, positioning, and movement of the players during the game and would essentially create a new game, with new strategies and new rules.

In 2008, the ADA was reauthorized as the ADA Amendments Act (ADAAA). The major purpose of the ADAAA was to legislatively overturn a series of court decisions that interpreted the ADA in a way that made it difficult to prove that an impairment is a disability. For example, in the original law, a person with a disability was one who had an impairment that "substantially limits" his/her participation in a major life activity. The ADAAA revises the language to describe a person with a disability as one who has an impairment that "significantly restricts" participation, thus broadening the scope of coverage under **both** the ADA and Section 503 of the Rehabilitation Act and opening the door to a wider range of people with disabling conditions.

SIGNIFICANT CASE

The following case raises two interesting questions concerning the application of the Americans with Disabilities Act: first, whether the Act protects access to professional golf tournaments by a qualified entrant with a disability; and second, whether a disabled contestant may be denied the use of a golf cart because it would "fundamentally alter the nature" of the tournaments to allow him to ride when all other contestants must walk.

PGA TOUR V. CASEY MARTIN
United States Supreme Court
532 U.S. 661 (2001)

This case raises two questions concerning the application of the Americans with Disabilities Act . . . to a gifted athlete: first, whether the Act protects access to professional golf tournaments by a qualified entrant with a disability; and second, whether a disabled contestant may be denied the use of a golf cart because it would "fundamentally alter the nature" of the tournament, to allow him to ride when all other contestants must walk.

I.

Petitioner PGA TOUR, Inc., a nonprofit entity formed in 1968, sponsors and cosponsors professional golf tournaments conducted on three annual tours. About 200 golfers participate in the PGA TOUR; about 170 in the NIKE TOUR; and about 100 in the SENIOR PGA TOUR. PGA TOUR and NIKE TOUR tournaments typically are 4-day events, played on courses leased and operated by petitioner. The entire field usually competes in two 18-hole rounds played on Thursday and Friday; those who survive the "cut" play on Saturday and Sunday and receive prize money in amounts determined by their aggregate scores for all four rounds. The revenues generated by television, admissions, concessions, and contributions from cosponsors amount to about $ 300 million a year, much of which is distributed in prize money.

There are various ways of gaining entry into particular tours. For example, a player who wins three NIKE TOUR events in the same year, or is among the top-15 money winners on that tour, earns the right to play in the PGA TOUR. Additionally, a golfer may obtain a spot in an official tournament through successfully competing in "open" qualifying rounds, which are conducted the week before each tournament. Most participants, however, earn playing privileges in the PGA TOUR or NIKE TOUR by way of a three-stage qualifying tournament known as the "Q-School."

Any member of the public may enter the Q-School by paying a $ 3,000 entry fee and submitting two letters of reference from, among others, PGA TOUR or NIKE TOUR members. The $ 3,000 entry fee covers the players' greens fees and the cost of golf carts, which are permitted during the first two stages, but which have been prohibited during the third stage since 1997. Each year, over a thousand contestants compete in the first stage, which consists of four 18-hole rounds at different locations. Approximately half of them make it to the second stage, which also includes 72 holes. Around 168 players survive the second stage and advance to the final one, where they compete over 108 holes. Of those finalists, about a fourth qualify for membership in the PGA TOUR, and the rest gain membership in the NIKE TOUR.

Three sets of rules govern competition in tour events. First, the "Rules of Golf," jointly written by the United States Golf Association (USGA) and the Royal and Ancient Golf Club of Scotland, apply to the game as it is played, not only by millions of amateurs on public courses and in private country clubs throughout the United States and worldwide, but also by the professionals in the tournaments conducted by petitioner, the USGA, the Ladies' Professional Golf Association, and the Senior Women's Golf Association. Those rules do not prohibit the use of golf carts at any time.

Second, the "Conditions of Competition and Local Rules," often described as the "hard card," apply specifically to petitioner's professional tours. The hard cards for the PGA TOUR and NIKE TOUR require players to walk the golf course during tournaments, but not during open qualifying rounds. On the SENIOR PGA TOUR, which is limited to golfers age 50 and older, the contestants may use golf carts. Most seniors, however, prefer to walk.

Third, "Notices to Competitors" are issued for particular tournaments and cover conditions for that specific event. Such a notice may, for example, explain how the Rules of Golf should be applied to a particular water hazard or man-made obstruction. It might also authorize the use of carts to speed up play when there is an unusual distance between one green and the next tee.

The basic Rules of Golf, the hard cards, and the weekly notices apply equally to all players in tour competitions. As one of petitioner's witnesses explained with reference to "the Masters Tournament, which is golf at its very highest level . . . the key is to have everyone tee off on the first hole under exactly the same conditions and all of them be tested over that 72-hole event under the conditions that exist during those four days of the event."

II.

Casey Martin is a talented golfer. As an amateur, he won 17 Oregon Golf Association junior events before he was 15, and won the state championship as a high school senior. He played on the Stanford University golf team that won the 1994 National Collegiate Athletic Association (NCAA) championship. As a professional, Martin qualified for the NIKE TOUR in 1998 and 1999, and based on his 1999 performance, qualified for the PGA TOUR in 2000. In the 1999 season, he entered 24 events, made the cut 13 times, and had 6 top-10 finishes, coming in second twice and third once.

Martin is also an individual with a disability as defined in the Americans with Disabilities Act. Since birth he has been afflicted with Klippel-Trenaunay-Weber Syndrome, a degenerative circulatory disorder that obstructs the flow of blood from his right leg back to his heart. The disease is progressive; it causes severe pain and has atrophied his right leg. During the latter part of his college career, because of the progress of the disease, Martin could no longer walk an 18-hole golf course. Walking not only caused him pain, fatigue, and anxiety, but also created a significant risk of hemorrhaging, developing blood clots, and fracturing his tibia so badly that an amputation might be required. For these reasons, Stanford made written requests to the Pacific 10 Conference and the NCAA to waive for Martin their rules requiring players to walk and carry their own clubs. The requests were granted.

When Martin turned pro and entered petitioner's Q-School, the hard card permitted him to use a cart during his successful progress through the first two stages. He made a request, supported by detailed medical records, for permission to use a golf cart during the third stage. Petitioner refused to review those records or to waive its walking rule for the third stage. Martin therefore filed this action. A preliminary injunction entered by the District Court made it possible for him to use a cart in the final stage of the Q-School and as a competitor in the NIKE TOUR and PGA TOUR. Although not bound by the injunction, and despite its support for petitioner's position in this litigation, the USGA voluntarily granted Martin a similar waiver in events that it sponsors, including the U.S. Open.

Congress enacted the ADA in 1990 to remedy widespread discrimination against disabled individuals. In studying the need for such legislation, Congress found that "historically, society has tended to isolate and segregate individuals with disabilities, and, despite some improvements, such forms of discrimination against individuals with disabilities continue to be a serious and pervasive social problem." . . .

To effectuate its sweeping purpose, the ADA forbids discrimination against disabled individuals in major areas of public life, among them employment (Title I of the Act), public services (Title II), and public accommodations (Title III). At issue now, as a threshold matter, is the applicability of Title III to petitioner's golf tours and qualifying rounds, in particular to petitioner's treatment of a qualified disabled golfer wishing to compete in those events.

Title III of the ADA prescribes, as a "general rule": "No individual shall be discriminated against on the basis of disability in the full and equal enjoyment of the goods, services, facilities, privileges, advantages, or accommodations of any place of public accommodation by any person who owns, leases (or leases to), or operates a place of public accommodation." 42 U.S.C. § 12182(a).

The phrase "public accommodation" is defined in terms of 12 extensive categories, which the legislative history indicates "should be construed liberally" to afford people with disabilities "equal access" to the wide variety of establishments available to the nondisabled.

It seems apparent, from both the general rule and the comprehensive definition of "public accommodation," that petitioner's golf tours and their qualifying rounds fit comfortably within the coverage of Title III, and Martin within its protection. The events occur on "golf courses," a type of place specifically identified by the Act as a public accommodation. § 12181(7)(L). In addition, at all relevant times, petitioner "leases" and "operates" golf courses to conduct its Q-School and tours. § 12182(a). As a lessor and operator of golf courses, then, petitioner must not discriminate against any "individual" in the "full and equal enjoyment of the goods, services, facilities, privileges, advantages, or accommodations" of those courses. *Ibid.* Certainly, among the "privileges" offered by petitioner on the courses are those of competing in the Q-School and playing in the tours; indeed, the former is a privilege for which thousands of individuals from the general public pay, and the latter is one for which they vie. Martin, of course, is one of those individuals. It would therefore appear that Title III of the ADA, by its plain terms, prohibits petitioner from denying Martin equal access to its tours on the basis of his disability. . . .

Petitioner argues otherwise. To be clear about its position, it does not assert (as it did in the District Court) that it is a private club altogether exempt from Title III's coverage. In fact, petitioner admits that its tournaments are conducted at places of public accommodation. Nor does petitioner contend (as it did in both the District Court and the Court of Appeals) that the competitors' area "behind the ropes" is not a public accommodation, notwithstanding the status of the rest of the golf course. Rather, petitioner reframes the coverage issue by arguing that the competing golfers are not members of the class protected by Title III of the ADA.

According to petitioner, Title III is concerned with discrimination against "clients and customers" seeking to obtain "goods and services" at places of public accommodation, whereas it is Title I that protects persons who work at such places. As the argument goes, petitioner operates not a "golf course" during its tournaments but a "place of exhibition or entertainment," . . . and a professional golfer such as Martin, like an actor in a theater production, is a provider rather than a consumer of the entertainment that petitioner sells to the public. Martin therefore cannot bring a claim under Title III because he is not one of the "'*clients or customers* of the covered public accommodation.'" Rather, Martin's claim of discrimination is "job-related" and could only be brought under Title I—but that Title does not apply because he is an independent contractor (as the District Court found) rather than an employee.

* * *

We need not decide whether petitioner's construction of the statute is correct, because petitioner's argument falters even on its own terms. If Title III's protected class were limited to "clients or customers," it would be entirely appropriate to classify the golfers who pay petitioner $3,000 for the chance to compete in the Q-School and, if successful, in the subsequent tour events, as petitioner's clients or customers. In our view, petitioner's tournaments (whether situated at a "golf course" or at a "place of exhibition or entertainment") simultaneously offer at least two "privileges" to the public—that of watching the golf competition and that of competing in it. Although the latter is more difficult and more expensive to obtain than the former, it is nonetheless a privilege that petitioner makes available to members of the general public. In consideration of the entry fee, any golfer with the requisite letters of recommendation acquires the opportunity to qualify for and compete in petitioner's tours. Additionally, any golfer who succeeds in the open qualifying rounds for a tournament may play in the event. That petitioner identifies one set of clients or customers that it serves (spectators at tournaments) does not preclude it from having another set (players in tournaments) against whom it may not discriminate. It would be inconsistent with the literal text of the statute as well as its expansive purpose to read Title III's coverage, even given petitioner's suggested limitation, any less broadly.

* * *

As we have noted, 42 U.S.C. § 12182(a) sets forth Title III's general rule prohibiting public accommodations from discriminating against individuals because of their disabilities. The question whether petitioner has violated that rule depends on a proper construction of the term "discrimination," which is defined by Title III to include: "a failure to make reasonable modifications in policies, practices, or procedures, when such modifications are necessary to afford such goods, services, facilities, privileges, advantages, or accommodations to individuals with disabilities, *unless the entity can demonstrate that making such modifications would fundamentally alter the nature* of such goods, services, facilities, privileges, advantages, or accommodations." § 12182(b)(2)(A)(ii) (emphasis added).

Petitioner does not contest that a golf cart is a reasonable modification that is necessary if Martin is to play in its tournaments. Martin's claim thus differs from one that might be asserted by players with less serious afflictions that make walking the course uncomfortable or difficult, but not beyond their capacity. In such cases, an accommodation might be reasonable but not necessary. In this case, however, the narrow dispute is whether allowing Martin to use a golf cart, despite the walking requirement that applies to the PGA TOUR, the NIKE TOUR, and the third stage of the Q-School, is a modification that would "fundamentally alter the nature" of those events.

In theory, a modification of petitioner's golf tournaments might constitute a fundamental alteration in two different ways. It might alter such an essential aspect of the game of golf that it would be unacceptable even if it affected all competitors equally; changing the diameter of the hole from three to six inches might be such a modification. Alternatively, a less significant change that has only a peripheral impact on the game itself might nevertheless give a disabled player, in addition to access to the competition as required by Title III, an advantage over others and, for that reason, fundamentally alter the character of the competition. We are not persuaded that a waiver of the walking rule for Martin would work a fundamental alteration in either sense.

As an initial matter, we observe that the use of carts is not itself inconsistent with the fundamental character of the game of golf. From early on, the essence of the game has been shot-making—using clubs to cause a ball to progress from the teeing ground to a hole some distance away with as few strokes as possible. That essential aspect of the game is still reflected in the very first of the Rules of Golf, which declares: "The Game of Golf consists in playing a ball from the *teeing ground* into the hole by a *stroke* or successive strokes in accordance with the rules." . . . Over the years, there have been many changes in the players' equipment, in golf course design, in the Rules of Golf, and in the method of transporting clubs from hole to hole. Originally, so few clubs were used that each player could carry them without a bag. Then came golf bags, caddies, carts that were pulled by hand, and eventually motorized carts that carried players as well as clubs. "Golf carts started appearing with increasing regularity on American golf courses in the 1950's. Today they are everywhere. And they are encouraged. For one thing, they often speed up play, and for another, they are great revenue producers." There is nothing in the Rules of Golf that either forbids the use of carts, or penalizes a player for using a cart. That set of rules, as we have observed, is widely accepted in both the amateur and professional golf world as the rules of the game. The walking rule that is contained in petitioner's hard cards, based on an optional condition buried in an appendix to the Rules of Golf, is not an essential attribute of the game itself.

Indeed, the walking rule is not an indispensable feature of tournament golf either. As already mentioned, petitioner permits golf carts to be used in the SENIOR PGA TOUR, the open qualifying events for petitioner's tournaments, the first two stages of the Q-School, and, until 1997, the third stage of the Q-School as well. Moreover, petitioner allows the use of carts during certain tournament rounds in both the PGA TOUR and the NIKE TOUR. . . .

Petitioner, however, distinguishes the game of golf as it is generally played from the game that it sponsors in the PGA TOUR, NIKE TOUR, and (at least recently) the last stage of the Q-School—golf at the "highest level." According to petitioner, "the goal of the highest-level competitive athletics is to assess and compare the performance of different competitors, a task that is meaningful only if the competitors are subject to identical substantive rules." The waiver of any possibly "outcome-affecting" rule for a contestant would violate this principle and therefore, in petitioner's view, fundamentally alter the nature of the highest level athletic event. The walking rule is one such rule, petitioner submits, because its purpose is "to inject the element of fatigue into the skill of shot-making," and thus its effect may be the critical loss of a stroke. As a consequence, the reasonable modification Martin seeks would fundamentally alter the nature of petitioner's highest level tournaments even if he were the only person in the world who has both the talent to compete in those elite events and a disability sufficiently serious that he cannot do so without using a cart.

The force of petitioner's argument is, first of all, mitigated by the fact that golf is a game in which it is impossible to guarantee that all competitors will play under exactly the same conditions or that an individual's ability will be the sole determinant of the outcome. For example, changes in the weather may produce harder greens and more head winds for the tournament leader than for his closest pursuers. . . . Whether such happenstance events are more or less probable than the likelihood that a golfer afflicted with Klippel-Trenaunay-Weber Syndrome would one day qualify for the NIKE TOUR and PGA TOUR, they at least demonstrate that pure chance may have a greater impact on the outcome of elite golf tournaments than the fatigue resulting from the enforcement of the walking rule.

Further, the factual basis of petitioner's argument is undermined by the District Court's finding that the fatigue from walking during one of petitioner's 4-day tournaments cannot be deemed significant. The District Court credited the testimony of a professor in physiology and expert on fatigue, who calculated the calories expended in walking a golf course (about five miles) to be approximately 500 calories—"nutritionally . . . less than a Big Mac." 994 F. Supp. at 1250. What is more, that energy is expended over a 5-hour period, during which golfers have numerous intervals for rest and refreshment. In fact, the expert concluded, because golf is a low intensity activity, fatigue from the game is primarily a psychological phenomenon in which stress and motivation are the key ingredients. . . .

Moreover, when given the option of using a cart, the majority of golfers in petitioner's tournaments have chosen to walk, often to relieve stress or for other strategic reasons. . . .

Even if we accept the factual predicate for petitioner's argument—that the walking rule is "outcome affecting" because fatigue may adversely affect performance—its legal position is fatally flawed. Petitioner's refusal to consider Martin's personal circumstances in deciding whether to accommodate his disability runs counter to the clear language and purpose of the ADA. As previously stated, the ADA was enacted to eliminate discrimination against "individuals" with disabilities, and to that end Title III of the Act requires without exception that any "policies, practices, or procedures" of a public accommodation be reasonably modified for disabled "individuals" as necessary to afford access unless doing so would fundamentally alter what is offered, § 12182(b)(2)(A)(ii). To comply with this command, an individualized inquiry must be made to determine whether a specific modification for a particular person's disability would be reasonable under the circumstances as well as necessary for that person, and yet at the same time not work a fundamental alteration. . . .

To be sure, the waiver of an essential rule of competition for anyone would fundamentally alter the nature of petitioner's tournaments. As we have demonstrated, however, the walking rule is at best peripheral to the nature of petitioner's athletic events, and thus it might be waived in individual cases without working a fundamental alteration. Therefore, petitioner's claim that all the substantive rules for its "highest-level" competitions are sacrosanct and cannot be modified under any circumstances is effectively a contention that it is exempt from Title III's reasonable modification requirement. But that provision carves out no exemption for elite athletics, and given Title III's coverage not only of places of "exhibition or entertainment" but also of "golf courses," . . . its application to petitioner's tournaments cannot be said to be unintended or unexpected. . . .

Under the ADA's basic requirement that the need of a disabled person be evaluated on an individual basis, we have no doubt that allowing Martin to use a golf cart would not fundamentally alter the nature of petitioner's tournaments. As we have discussed, the purpose of the walking rule is to subject players to fatigue, which in turn may influence the outcome of tournaments. Even if the rule does serve that purpose, it is an uncontested finding of the District Court that Martin "easily endures greater fatigue even with a cart than his able-bodied competitors do by walking." The purpose of the walking rule is therefore not compromised in the slightest by allowing Martin to use a cart. . . . As a result, Martin's request for a waiver of the walking rule should have been granted.

* * *

The judgment of the Court of Appeals is affirmed.

CASES ON THE SUPPLEMENTAL CD

Poole v. South Plainfield Board of Education, 490 F. Supp. 948 (D. N.J. 1980). The case examines whether school officials have the right to prevent a student from participating in athletics due to a medical condition.

Sandison v. Michigan High School Athletic Association, 64 F.3d 1026 (6th Cir. 1995). In this case, the court ruled that waiving an eligibility requirement was not a reasonable accommodation required under the ADA for high school athletic associations.

Dennin v. Connecticut Interscholastic Athletic Conference, 913 F. Supp. 663 (1996). In this case, the court ruled that waiving an eligibility requirement was a reasonable accommodation required under the ADA for high school athletic associations.

K. L. v. Missouri State High School Activities Association, 2016 U.S. Dist. LEXIS 47621. In this case, the court examined whether awarding points for para-athletes on the track team was a reasonable accommodation.

Miller v. Cal. Speedway Corp. 536 F. 3d 1020 (2008). In this case, the plaintiff, an individual with a physical disability, sued the speedway citing violations of Title III of the ADA, related to violation of lines of site for people with disabilities during NASCAR events.

QUESTIONS YOU SHOULD BE ABLE TO ANSWER

1. Under Section 504 of the Rehabilitation Act, what four elements must be established in order to pursue a claim?
2. What has been an acceptable process for a scholastic athlete with a disability to gain access to athletic participation under the IDEA?
3. What are the three sections of the ADA that have greatest applicability to sport and how does the ADA define an individual with a disability who is "other qualified"?
4. Under which titles of the ADA would interscholastic sports cases related to athletic associations, age participation, academic eligibility policies, and paired-organ decisions apply?
5. What are the major obstacles faced by participants with disabilities in gaining access to intercollegiate and professional sport?

REFERENCES

Cases
Alexander v. Choate, 469 U.S. 287 (1985).
Anderson v. Little League Baseball, 794 F. Supp. 342 (1992).
Badgett v. Alabama High School Athletic Association, 2007 U.S. Dist. Lexis 36014
Crocker v. Tennessee Secondary School Athletic Association, 980 F.2d 382 (6th Cir. 1992).
Dennin v. Connecticut Interscholastic Athletic Conference, 913 F. Supp. 663 (1996).
Hollonbeck v. USOC, 513 F.3d 1191 (10th Cir. 2008)
J.M. v. Montana High School Association. 875 P. 2d. 1026 (D. Mont. 1994)
Johnson v. Florida High School Activities Association Inc., 899 F. Supp. 579 (M.D. Fla. 1995).
K. L. v. Missouri State High School Activities Association, 2016 U.S. Dist. LEXIS 47621.
Kuketz v. Petronelli, 821 N.E.2d 473 (MA. 2005).
Lambert v. West Virginia State Board of Education, 447 S.E.2d 901 (W.Va. 1994).
McFadden v. Grasmick, 485 F.Supp. 2d 642 (D.Md. 2007).
Miller v. California Speedway Corp. 536 F. 3d 1020 (2008).
PGA Tour v. Casey Martin, 532 U.S. 661 (2001).
Poole v. South Plainfield Board of Education, 490 F. Supp. 948 (D. N.J. 1980).
Pottgen v. Missouri State High School Athletic Association, 40 F.3d 926 (8th Cir. 1994).
Sandison v. Michigan High School Athletic Association, 64 F.3d 1026 (6th Cir. 1995).
Southeastern Community College v. Davis, 422 U.S. 397 (1979).
S.S. v. Whitesboro Central School District, 2012 U.S. Dist. LEXIS 11727
T.H. v. Montana High School Association, CV 92-150-BLG-JFB (1992).
University Interscholastic League and Bailey Marshall v. Buchanan, 848 S.W. 2d. 298 (1993).

Publications
Clement, A. (1988). *Law in sport and physical activity*. Dubuque, IA: Brown & Benchmark.
Hums, M., Schmidt, S., Novak, A. & Wolff, E. (2016). Universal Design: Moving the Americans With Disabilities Act From Access to Inclusion. Journal of Legal Aspects of Sport, 26, 36-51.
Wolohan, J. (1997a). An ethical and legal dilemma: Participation in sports by HIV infected athletes. *Marquette. Sports Law Journal, 7*, 345.
Wolohan, J. (1997b). Are age restrictions a necessary requirement for participating in interscholastic athletic programs? *UMKC. Law Review, 66*, 345.
Wolohan, J. (2003, March). The big dance: Administrators must tread carefully when deciding whether to accommodate individuals with disabilities. *Athletic Business*, pp. 20–24.

Wolohan, J. (2005, June). Bounce check: A club is not required to change its racquetball league rules for a wheelchair athlete. *Athletic Business*, pp. 18–22.

Legislation

The Rehabilitation Act of 1973, 29 U.S.C. § 701 *et seq*.
The Individuals with Disabilities Education Act, 20 U.S.C. § 1400 *et seq*.
The Individuals with Disabilities Education Improvement Act, 20 U.S.C. § 1400 *et seq*.
The Amateur Sports Act, 36 U.S.C. § 371–396.
Ted Stevens Olympic and Amateur Sports Act, 36 U.S.C. § 220501–220529.
The Americans with Disabilities Act, 42 U.S.C. § 12101 *et seq*.
The Americans with Disabilities Amendments Act, 42 U.S.C. §12101–12102.

PRIVATE CLUBS IN SPORT AND RECREATION

Anne DeMartini | Flagler College
Mark Dodds | SUNY Cortland

Historically, many groups and organizations, including sport and recreation organizations, have discriminated in their membership criteria against various groups of people based on race, national origin, religion, gender or sexual orientation. For example, in the early 1990's, the PGA Tour and LPGA were forced to create a policy that required a Tour's host country club to have an open membership policy (Lieber, 2003). The policy was necessary due to the media attention and pressure from sponsors when Shoal Creek (Alabama) Country Club, which was hosting the 1990 PGA Championship, did not allow African Americans as members. The club eventually changed its' policy just prior to hosting the event because of media and social pressure. Media and social pressure, however, are not always enough to force organizations to open up their membership policies. For example, in 2003 Martha Burk from the National Council of Women's Organizations protested Augusta National Country Club's male-only membership policy (Lieber, 2003). Even though the protest generated substantial media attention and calls for change, because The Masters golf tournament is a non-PGA co-sponsored event, Augusta National did not have to comply with the PGA rule and the club retained its' male members only policy.

FUNDAMENTAL CONCEPTS

While the discriminatory membership practices of country clubs like Augusta National have been well documented, they are not the only clubs that have discriminatory policies. The purpose of this section, therefore, is to examine the statutory protections as they relate to private sport and recreation clubs, as well as identify the multi factor test used by the courts to identify if a club is truly private. Some of the areas explored include: Freedom of Association; the Civil Rights Act of 1964; the Americans with Disabilities Act; and state anti-discrimination laws.

Freedom of Association

Private clubs, including country clubs or other exclusive sport clubs, are selective by nature. These clubs decide who may join and who to exclude. In most cases, this discrimination is legal, since citizens of the United States enjoy the freedom to associate with persons of their choice, without government intervention or interference (*Roberts v. United States Jaycees*, 1984). Freedom of association also includes the right *not* to associate with certain people. While "Freedom of Association" is not an enumerated right in the Constitution, it has been judicially recognized as one of the rights represented by the concept of liberty (Osborne, 2006). The United States Constitution protects the Freedom of Association under the First and Fourteenth Amendments in two distinct ways: expressive association and intimate association (Jolly-Ryan, 2006).

Expressive Association

The First Amendment states that, "Congress shall make no law respecting an establishment of religion, or prohibiting the free exercise thereof; or abridging the freedom of speech, or of the press; or the right of the people peaceably to assemble, and to petition the Government for a redress of grievances" (United States Constitution, Amendment I). Although the Constitution does not directly state that individuals have the right to freely form their own associations, the Supreme Court has interpreted the First Amendment to allow for this based on the right to freedom of expression (Dees, 2010). As a result, citizens of the United States have the protected right to freely form their own associations "in pursuit of a wide variety of political, social, economic, educational, religious, and cultural ends" (*Roberts v. United States Jaycees*, 1984).

The freedom of expressive association is characterized by the size of the group, its purpose, its policies, its selectivity, and congeniality (*Roberts v. United States Jaycees*, 1984). The right of freedom of expressive association is fundamental to our Constitution and receives the highest degree of protection. However, this most fundamental freedom is seldom relevant for private golf or country clubs, since generally the purpose of joining these organizations is for recreation, sport, or social opportunities, rather than for engaging in free speech or expression (Jolly-Ryan, 2006).

Intimate Association

Citizens of the United States also have the freedom of intimate association; the constitutional right to enter into and maintain certain intimate human relationships (*Roberts v. United States Jaycees*, 1984). Intimate association originates from the right to privacy implied in the Due Process Clause of the Fourteenth Amendment and is characterized by its relative smallness, high degree of selectivity and seclusion of others. Intimate association cases have generally been used to describe intimate family matters such as marriage, contraception, abortion, family housing, raising children, and homosexuality (Osborne, 2006). The United States Supreme Court, however, has made it clear that some relationships outside of the family may qualify as intimate associations. According to *Roberts v. United States Jaycee* (1984) any relationship between a small group of people that carries "deep attachments and commitments" and forms because individuals share "distinctly personal aspects of one's life" is protected by intimate association (*Roberts v. United States Jaycees*, 1984).

Balancing Freedom of Association with Anti-Discrimination

Though citizens hold the constitutional rights of expressive and intimate association, the right to associate for expressive purposes is not absolute (*Roberts v. United States Jaycees*, 1984). *The government may interfere with expressive association when there is a compelling state interest.* For example, the government has a compelling interest in eradicating discrimination, so preventing discrimination is usually enough of a compelling social objective that it may warrant governmental interference in private affairs. Therefore, in determining whether a club's membership policy is discriminatory the state must balance a club member's fundamental rights of association with another person's fundamental right to be free from unlawful discrimination (Osborne, 2006). The legislatively created private club exemptions within many federal anti-discrimination laws display evidence of the attempt to establish this balance.

Anti-Discrimination Legislation

If an organization is truly private, it will generally be exempt from most federal and state anti-discrimination laws. To determine if a club is private for employment issues, the Equal Employment Opportunity Commission (EEOC), which is charged with enforcing Title VII of the Civil Rights Act of 1964, has established a set of factors for the courts to use. In addition to the EEOC guidelines for Civil Rights cases, the courts can also use the Americans with Disabilities Act and state anti-discrimination laws to determine if a club fits within the legal designation of a private club.

Civil Rights Act of 1964

Congress enacted the Civil Rights Act of 1964 (Civil Rights Act) to protect citizens' constitutional rights and prohibit various forms of discrimination in the areas of public accommodations (Title II) and in employment (Title VII) (Dees, 2010).

Title II

Title II of the Civil Rights Act of 1964 prohibits discrimination in places of public accommodation (42 U.S.C. § 2000a). While the law makes it clear that a **place of public accommodation** includes a "sports arena, stadium or other place of exhibition or entertainment" (42 U.S.C. § 201b(3)), due to the freedom of association guarantees found in the United States Constitution, Title II creates an exemption for private clubs (42 U.S.C. 2000a(e)). When addressing whether a club is truly private under Title II, rather than examining one particular issue, the courts use a "factor analysis" approach (Dees, 2010). Courts examine the following relevant factors:

1. The genuine selectivity of the group in the admission of its members;
2. The membership's control over the operations of the establishment;
3. The history of the organization;
4. The use of the facilities by nonmembers;
5. The purpose of the club's existence;
6. Whether the club advertises for members;
7. Whether the club is profit or nonprofit;
8. The formalities observed by the club such as bylaws, meetings, etc. (U.S. v. Lansdowne Swim Club, 1989).

Out of the eight factors, no one factor controls the determination of public or private status. The courts however have given particular attention to two factors: (1) the club's selectivity with respect to membership, and (2) the use of the club's facilities by nonmembers (Dees, 2010). To determine selectivity, courts examine the number of members of a club, the cost of joining the club, and if the club advertises for members (Osborne, 2006; Jolly-Ryan, 1997). The more exclusive the club, those with fewer members, higher membership fees, stricter standards, and more member control over the selection procedure, the more likely it is to be considered to be private. For example, in *Thornton v. Shaker Ridge Country Club*, (2007) the court found that a country club that advertised for members and had its facilities available to the public was a place of public accommodation under Title II. In another case, *Anderson v. Pass Christian Isles Golf Club, Inc.*, (1974), the court ruled that a golf course that had an arrangement with local hotels to allow hotel guests use of the course was not a private club, but a place of public accommodation.

A genuinely private club, the courts have held, must demonstrate strict exclusivity in its selection processes (Dees, 2010). For example, *Durham v. Red Lake Fishing & Hunting Club, Inc.*, (1987), the court ruled that a private fishing and hunting club that did not have a selective membership application process and allowed public access to its roads was not a private club under the Title II exemption. Historically, the courts have ruled against finding a club private if the club offers too many services to nonmembers or open areas of the club to the public for commercial purposes. For example, *New York v. Ocean Club*, (1984) the court found that the club was a public accommodation and not a private club because membership was extended to a large indefinite segment of the public without any standards of eligibility and without any requirements that might have indicated exclusivity. Additionally, the court noted that club's tennis courts were offered for use by the general public. Finally, any organization or club that receives public benefits will generally be considered a place of public accommodation. For example, in *United States v. Slidell Youth Football Association*, (1974) a non-profit youth football program was not considered a private club because it received public benefits such as rent-free use of the fields, and operating revenue.

Title VII

Title VII of the Civil Rights Act of 1964 deals with discrimination in an employment setting for governmental agencies, labor unions and employers with 15 or more employees (42 U.S.C. § 2000e-2(a)). This law, therefore, applies to all sport and recreation organizations that employee 15 or more people. However, like Title II of the Civil Rights Act, Title VII makes an exception for "**bona fide private membership club.**" To qualify for the exemption, an organization must show both that it is tax-exempt and that it is a "bona fide private membership club." The EEOC's Compliance Manual (2000), defines a "bona fide private membership club" as an organization that:

1. Is a club in the ordinary sense of the word;
2. Is private; and
3. Has meaningful conditions of limited membership.

A "**club**" is an association of persons for social and recreational purposes or for the promotion of some common purpose who meet periodically. These clubs usually vote in new members who then earn the privilege of using the club property. In determining whether a club is private, the EEOC considers the extent to which the club limits its facilities and services to club members and their guests, the extent to which and/or the manner in which the facilities are controlled or owned by its membership. The EEOC also considers to what extent and in what manner the club publicly advertises to solicit its members and to promote the use of its facilities or services by the general public. Courts address the question as to whether an organization is private on a case-by-case basis, the presence or absence of any one of these factors while important, is not determinative. Finally, to determine whether a club meets the requirement of meaningful conditions of limited membership, the EEOC considers both the size of the membership, including the existence of any limitations on its size, and membership eligibility requirements (EEOC, 2000).

It is important to note, however, that since under Title VII the clubs are discriminating in the employment practices, unlike Title II where the clubs discriminate in membership issues, the courts are going to analyze Title VII claims differently than a Title II claim. For example, in *EEOC v. Chicago Club*, (1996) the court held that a private club's employment decisions are not constitutionally relevant to the individual members' abilities to define their own identities by choosing with whom they wish to associate. For a more in-depth review of the law, see chapter 7.13 Title VII of the Civil Rights Act of 1964.

Americans with Disabilities Act (ADA)

In 1990, Congress passed the **Americans with Disabilities Act (ADA)** (42 U.S.C. § 12101) and in 2008, the **Americans with Disabilities Act Amendment Act (ADAAA)** (42 U.S.C. §12101), to provide a clear and comprehensive national mandate for the elimination of discrimination against individuals with disabilities (42 U.S.C. § 12101 *et seq.*). For a more in-depth review of the law, see chapters 6.24 Participants with Disabilities and 7.16 Title I of the Americans with Disabilities Act.

Under Title III of the ADA, the owners and operators of places of public accommodation must make reasonable accommodations to individuals with disabilities to participate equally in the goods, services, and accommodations provided by the establishment (Thornton, 2011). For a successful claim, a plaintiff must prove: 1. He or she is an individual with a disability, 2. the defendant owned, leased, or operated a place of public accommodation, and 3. the defendant discriminated against the plaintiff on the basis of his/her disability. Title III of the ADA, however, has an exemption for private clubs and religious organizations which states that:

> The provisions . . . shall not apply to private clubs or establishments exempted from coverage under Title II of the Civil Rights Act of 1964 (42 U.S.C. 2000-a(e)) or to religious organizations or entities controlled by religious organizations, including places of worship (42 U.S.C. § 12187).

Therefore, if an entity is exempt under Title II of the 1964 Civil Rights Act, it is also exempt under Title III of the ADA. Likewise, an entity that would fail the test of a private club under Title II would also fail the test under Title III of the ADA (Dees, 2010).

An example of the factor analysis used by the courts to determine if a private organization qualifies for an exemption under Title III of the ADA is *Bommarito v. Grosse Pointe Yacht Club* (2007). In Bommarito, the court was asked to consider whether a yacht club was private and therefore qualified for the exemption under the ADA. In ruling that the club was private, the court examined the extent that the club's facilities or services were limited to club members and their guests; the extent to which the management of the club controlled the club and its access; and how the club advertised publicly for new membership or for its services (*Bommarito v. Grosse Pointe Yacht Club*, 2007). In another case, *Staley v. Nat'l Capital Area Council* (2011) the court ruled that the Boy Scouts, despite the large size of the organization and how it acquired new members, were also a private club for the purposes of the ADA and not required to provide sign language interpreters for deaf members. The court reached this conclusion based on the organizations' selectivity, history and purpose.

The court considered those same factors in *Nicholls v. Holiday Panay Marina* (2009), when the court held that even though a marina restricted access to tenants-only, it still did not qualify as a public accommodation under Title III of the ADA. In ruling that the marina had to comply with the ADA and modify the facility to become wheelchair accessible, the court declared that just because the marina "restricted access does not make an accommodation nonpublic" (*Nicholls v. Holiday Panay Marina*, 2009).

In contrast, the court found a five-thousand acre recreational ranch owned by approximately 1700 individual owners was a private entity exempt from the ADA in *Pappion v. R-Ranch Prop. Owners Ass'n*, (2013). The court considered the use of facilities by nonmembers, the purpose of the facility's existence, advertisement to the public, and its profit or non-profit status (*Pappion v. R-Ranch Prop. Owners Ass'n*, 2013). R-Ranch and

Ranch Headquarters limited use to owners and owners' guests, owners were required to supervise guests at all times, and the number of guest stays were limited (*Pappion v. R-Ranch Prop. Owners Ass'n*, 2013). The R-Ranch's Covenants, Conditions and Restrictions expressly stated that the facility's purpose was purely recreation, and "[n]o business or commercial activities of any kind whatsoever shall be conducted within the R-Ranch Properties" (*Pappion v. R-Ranch Prop. Owners Ass'n*, 2013). The Ranch selectively attempted to increase membership and was a non-profit corporation; therefore, supporting its characterization as a private entity and not a public accommodation (*Pappion v. R-Ranch Prop. Owners Ass'n*, 2013).

State Anti-Discrimination Statutes

In addition to federal law, a number of states have passed anti-discrimination laws that prohibit discrimination based on gender, sexual orientation, race, color, religion and national origin (Kamp, 1998). Since they are state laws, there is no interstate commerce requirement, thus narrowing the private club exemption. Many plaintiffs, particularly women, have a better chance of succeeding on a state anti-discrimination lawsuit than bringing a federal civil rights action (Kamp, 1998). Some state anti-discrimination statutes are broader in scope than the federal anti-discrimination laws. As of 2015, twenty-one states and the District of Columbia's public accommodation statutes explicitly prohibit sexual orientation discrimination in commerce (Courtney, 2015).

For example, in *Apilado v. The North American Gay Amateur Athletic Alliance* (2011), The North American Gay Amateur Athletic Alliance (NAGAAA) disqualified plaintiffs' softball team from the Gay Softball World Series for violating a rule requiring team rosters to hold a maximum of two heterosexual players. The plaintiffs claimed that the NAGAAA was a public accommodation and unlawfully discriminated against them because of their real or perceived sexual orientation. After determining that the NAGAAA met the definition of public accommodation, the court moved on to evaluate if the First Amendment freedom of association protected NAGAAA's ability to exclude someone from membership.

In ruling in favor of the NAGAAA, the court found NAGAAA to be an expressive association since its mission included helping the community and transmitting the value of sportsmanship. In addition, the court concluded the forced inclusion of heterosexual members would diminish NAGAAA's ability to express its message, the "promotion of an athletic, competitive, sportsmanlike gay identity, with a unique set of values, in response to a particular need" (*Apilado v. NAGAAA*, 2011). Based on these factors, the court determined the plaintiffs did not prove that the state interest in eliminating NAGAAA's exclusionary policies outweighed NAGAAA's associational rights, reasoning "if state public-accommodation statutes truly prohibited discrimination against all groups and in any form, then freedom of association would be toothless" (*Apilado v. NAGAAA*, 2011).

SIGNIFICANT CASE

A truly private club does not have to comply with discrimination laws including Title II and Title VII of the Civil Rights Act of 1964 and Title III of the Americans with Disabilities Act. In order to be considered truly private, courts use a multi-factor test. The following case illustrates how a court evaluates a private club using this test.

UNITED STATES OF AMERICA V. LANSDOWNE SWIM CLUB
United States Court of Appeals for the Third Circuit
894 F. 2d 83 (1990)

This appeal is taken from the judgment of the district court, after a non-jury trial, that the Lansdowne Swim Club (LSC) discriminated against blacks on the basis of race or color in violation of Title II of the Civil Rights Act of 1964,

42 U.S.C. §§ 2000a-2000a-6 (1982). LSC challenges the findings of the district court on three grounds: that it is an exempted private club, that it is not a place of public accommodation, and that the United States failed to prove a pattern or practice of racial discrimination. We will affirm the judgment of the district court.

I. Because the district court opinion thoroughly sets forth the facts, *United States v. Lansdowne Swim Club*, 713 F. Supp. 785 (E.D. Pa. 1989), we shall only summarize them here. LSC, a nonprofit corporation organized under the laws of Pennsylvania, is the only group swimming facility in the Borough of the Lansdowne, Pennsylvania. Since its founding in 1957, LSC has granted 1400 full family memberships. Every white applicant has been admitted, although two as limited members only. In that time, however, LSC has had only one non-white member.

The uncontroverted experiences of the following Lansdowne residents are significant. In 1976, the Allisons wrote to LSC requesting an application but LSC did not respond. Dr. Allison is black; his three children are part-black. In 1977, the Allisons twice again wrote for an application but LSC did not respond. The following year, the Allisons repeated the procedure with similar results. In 1983, the Allisons filed a timely application and otherwise qualified for membership. Nonetheless, they were rejected. Two of the Ryans' adopted children are black. The Ryans then complained to the media and picketed LSC, joined by the Allisons. In 1986, the Iverys, who are black, filed a timely application and otherwise qualified for membership. Nonetheless, they were rejected (as were the Ryans and Allisons who had again applied).

* * *

II. LSC's first argument is that it is a private club. Under Title II, "a private club or other establishment not in fact open to the public" is exempt from the statute. 42 USC. § 2000a(e). LSC has the burden of proving it is a private club. *See Anderson v. Pass Christian Isles Golf Club, Inc.*, 488 F.2d 855, 857 (5th Cir. 1974). Although the statute does not define "private club", cases construing the provision do offer some guidance. The district court distilled eight factors from the case law as relevant to this determination. Three of which it found dispositive of LSC's public nature: the genuine selectivity of its membership process, e.g., *Tillman v. Wheaton-Haven Recreation Ass'n.*, 410 U.S. 431 (1973), its history, e.g., *Cornelius v. BPOE*, 382 F. Supp. 1182 (D. Conn. 1974), and use of its facilities by nonmembers, *Id*. Appellant disputes these findings.

First, the court concluded that LSC's membership process was not genuinely selective. Essential to this conclusion was the court's finding that "LSC possesses no objective criteria or standards for admission." The court identified four "criteria" for admission to LSC: being interviewed, completing an application, submitting two letters of recommendation and tendering payment of fees. We agree, and LSC apparently concedes, that these criteria were not genuinely selective. Nonetheless, LSC challenges the court's failure to consider membership approval a criterion for admission. We agree with the district court, however, that a formal procedure requiring nothing more than membership approval is insufficient to show genuine electivity. See Tillman, 410 U.S. at 438–39. In addition, LSC stipulated that the only information given to the members prior to the membership vote is the applicants' names, addresses their children's names and ages, and the recommenders' identities. In such a situation, the court was correct to conclude that LSC "provides no information to voting members that is useful in making an informed decision as to whether the applicant and his or her family would be compatible with existing members." Therefore, even if membership approval were considered a fifth criterion, it would not make the process any more genuinely selective in this case.

The district court also found the yields of the membership process indicative of lack of selectivity. Since 1958, LSC has granted full memberships to at least 1400 families while denying them to only two non–black families. LSC contends that emphasizing the few instances of nonblack applicant rejection "misconstrues the significance of selectivity. The crucial question should be whether the members exercised their right to be selective rather than the statistical results of the exercise of that right." As the Court of Appeals for the Fourth Circuit noted a decade ago, formal membership requirements "have little meaning when in fact the club does not follow a selective membership policy." *Wright v. Salisbury Club, Ltd.*, 632 F.2d 309, 312 (4th Cir. 1980) (citing Tillman, 410 U.S. at 438–39). We find the evidence of lack of selectivity convincing.

Second, the court concluded that "the origins of LSC suggest that it was intended to serve as a 'community pool' for families in the area and not as a private club." We believe there was ample evidence to support this finding. A founder of LSC testified that LSC was created as a community pool for the neighborhood children. LSC's stipulations confirm the public nature of the facility: organizers solicited Lansdowne-area residents, conducted public recruitment meetings an accepted every family that applied for membership before opening.

Third, the court concluded that use of the facility by nonmembers "undercut LSC's claim that it is a private club." Among other reasons, the court cited the following factors. LSC hosts several swim meets and diving meets each year but does not prohibit the general public form attending. LSC also sponsors two to four pool parties each year, for which members and association may sell an unlimited number of tickets to persons who are not members. In addition, LSC's basketball and volleyball courts, located on its parking lot, are open to the public. Finally, LSC permits the local Boys' Club to use its parking lot for an annual Christmas tree sale that is open to the public. Although LSD contends such use is de minimus, we are persuaded otherwise.

III. LSC also contends that it is not a "place of public accommodation" as defined in Title II. Under the statute, a place of public accommodation has two elements: first, it must be one of the statutorily enumerated categories of establishments that serve the public, 42 U.S.C. § 2000a(b); second, its operations must affect commerce, Id.

A. The district court concluded that the whole complex, both the recreational areas and the snack bar, was an establishment which served the public. The court began by identifying LSC as a "place of . . . entertainment", one of the categories of covered establishments. "LSC concedes that its swimming and other recreational areas make it an 'establishment'", but maintains that the snack bar is not a covered establishment. The district court held that "bifurcation has no support in the plain language of the Act of the case law interpreting it." Under the facts in the case, we agree. Nonetheless, the court also found the snack bat to be a "facility principally engaged in selling food for consumption on the premises", another category of covered establishments. LSC stipulated that "food for consumption on the premises of the Club is sold" at the snack bar. We believe these findings were sufficient to render the entire facility a covered establishment which serves the public.

B. The district court also concluded that the "affecting commerce" requirement was met. Initially, the court discussed the recreational areas, which it correctly deemed a place of entertainment under § 2000a(b)(3). Under Title II, the operations of a place of entertainment affect commerce if "it customarily presents . . . sources of entertainment which move in commerce". Id. § 2000a(c)(3). The court found the slicing board, manufactured in Tesac, and guests from out of state to be sources of entertainment which moved in commerce. See *Scott v. Young*, 421 F.2d 143, 144–45 (4th Cir.) (both recreational apparatus originating out of state and patrons from out of state who entertain other patrons by their activity constitute "sources of entertainment which move in commerce") (relying on *Daniel v. Paul*, 395 U.S. 298, 307–08, 23 L. Ed. 2d 318, 89 S. Ct. 1697 (1969)), cert. Denied, 398 U.S. 929, 90 S. Ct. 1820, 26 L. Ed. 2d 91 (1970). Implicitly conceding this, LSC argues that they do not satisfy "the requisite degree of interstate involvement." Nonetheless, the court found both to be "customarily presented" the sliding board because it is permanently installed, and the out of state guests because the attend regularly and constitute a significant percentage of the guests (13% in 1986, 8% in 1987). We believe these findings, and the court's consequent finding that operation of the recreational areas affects commerce, are supported by the evidence.

The court then considered the snack bar, which it correctly deemed a facility principally engaged in selling food for consumption on the premises under § 2000a(b)(2). Under Title II, the operations of this category covered establishments affect commerce if "it serves or offers to serves interstate travelers or a substantial portion of the food which it serves . . . has moved in commerce". Id. § 2000a(c)(2). The court found the "affecting commerce" requirement satisfied in three ways. First, it was stipulated that the snack bar serves interstate travelers. Although LSC contends that the statute is meant to cover tourists lured from other states by advertising, the plain language of the statute provides no support for this view. Second, the court found that the snack bar offers to serve all users of the facility, including guests. Third, the court found that a substantial portion of the food served by the snack bar has moved in interstate commerce. The parties stipulated that the syrup in the "Coca-Cola" beverages was produced in Maryland. The court found that many of the purchases at the snack bar were for cold drinks, of which "Coca-Cola" beverages were the most popular. Nonetheless, appellant claims the substantiality test has not been met, citing *Daniel v. Paul*, 395 U.S. 298, 23 L. Ed. 2d 318, 89 S. Ct. 1697 (1969), in which the Supreme Court found the test met when three of the four foods sold had moved in interstate commerce. Id. at 305. In light of the broad remedial purpose of Title II, we refuse to read the requirement or Daniel so narrowly. These findings are not clearly erroneous.

* * *

CASES ON THE SUPPLEMENTAL CD

Apilado v. North American Gay Amateur Athletic Alliance, 792 F. Supp. 2d 1151 (W.D. Wash. 2011). This case examines the application of state law to sexual orientation discrimination.

Thornton v. Shaker Ridge Country Club, Inc., 2007 U.S. Dist. LEXIS 94082 (N.D.N.Y. 2007). This case specifically evaluates if a country club is a private club.

EEOC v. Chicago Club, 86 F.3d 1423 (7th Cir. 1996). This case considers a private club and Title VII implications.

Staley v. Nat'l Capital Area Council, Case No. RWT 10cv2768, 2011 U.S. Dist. LEXIS 61986 (D. Md. 2011). This case analyzes the Boy Scouts' selectivity, history and purpose to establish if they are a private club.

United States. v. Slidell Youth Football Ass'n, 387 F. Supp. 474 (E. D. La. 1974). A non-profit football organization was deemed a place of public accommodation and had to face a racial discrimination claim.

QUESTIONS YOU SHOULD BE ABLE TO ANSWER

1. Explain the factors courts examine to determine if a sport and recreational club is truly "private."
2. Research a local club and analyze it to see if it could be considered truly "private."
3. How can public pressure change a discriminatory club's membership policy?
4. Identify the most effective way to eliminate discrimination in private sport and recreation clubs. Justify your answer.
5. If you were to establish your own sport club, would you establish it as a public or private organization? Justify your answer.

REFERENCES

Cases

Anderson v. Pass Christian Isles Golf Club, Inc., 488 F.2d 855, 857 (5th Cir. 1974).
Apilado v. The North American Gay Amateur Athletic Alliance, 792 F. Supp. 2d 1151 (W.D. Wash, May 27, 2011).
Bommarito v. Grosse Pointe Yacht Club, 2007 U.S. Dist. LEXIS 21064 (E.D. Mich. 2007).
Cornelius v. BPOE, 382 F. Supp. 1182 (D. Conn. 1974).
Daniel v. Paul, 395 U.S. 298 (1969).
Durham v. Red Lake Fishing & Hunting Club, Inc., 666 F. Supp. 954 (W.D. Tex. 1987).
EEOC v. Chicago Club, 86 F.3d 1423 (7th Cir. 1996).
New York v. Ocean Club, 602 F. Supp. 489 (E.D. N.Y. 1984).
Nicholls v. Holiday Panay Marina, 173 Cal. App. 4th 966, 93 Cal. Rptr. 3d 309 (Cal. App. 2d Dist. 2009).
Roberts v. United States Jaycees, 468 U.S. 609 (1984).
Pappion v. R-Ranch Prop. Owners Ass'n, 2015 U.S. Dist. LEXIS 66808 (E.D. Cal. 2013)
Staley v. Nat'l Capital Area Council, Case No. RWT 10cv2768, 2011 U.S. Dist. LEXIS 61986 (D. Md. 2011).
Thornton v. Shaker Ridge Country Club, Inc. 2007 U.S. Dist. LEXIS 94082 (N.D.N.Y. 2007).
United States v. Lansdowne Swim Club, 894 F.2d 83, 1990 U.S. App. LEXIS 790 (3d Cir. Pa. 1990).
United States. v. Slidell Youth Football Ass'n, 387 F. Supp. 474 (E. D. La. 1974)
Wright v. The Cork Club, 315 F. Supp. 1143 (S.D. Tex. 1970).

Publications

Courtney, P. (2015). Prohibiting sexual orientation discrimination in public accommodations: A common law approach, *University of Pennsylvania Law Review, 163*, 1497–1537.
Dees, W. (2010). *Private Clubs in Sport and Recreation.* In D. J. Cotton & J. T. Wolohan (Eds.), Law for Recreation and Sport Managers (5th Ed.) pp. 528–536. Dubuque, IA: Kendall/Hunt Publishing Co.
Jolly-Ryan, J. (1997). Chipping away at discrimination at the country club, *Pepperdine Law Review*, 25, 495–527.
Jolly-Ryan, J. (2006). Teed off about private club discrimination on the taxpayer's dine: Tax exemptions and other government privileges to discriminatory private clubs, *William and Mary Journal of Women and the Law*, 13, 235–272.
Kamp, N. (1998). Gender Discrimination at Private Golf Clubs, *Sports Lawyers Journal*, 5, 94.
Lieber, J. (2003). *Golf's host clubs have open-and-shut policies on discrimination*, Retrieved from http://www.usatoday.com/sports/golf/2003-04-09-club-policies_x.htm
Osborne, B. (2006). Gender, employment, and sexual harassment issues in the golf industry. *Journal of Legal Aspects of Sport, 16*, 25–84.
Thornton, P. (2011), Sports Law, Jones and Bartlett, Sudbury, MA p. 405.
U.S. Equal Employment Opportunity Commission. (2000) *EEOC Compliance Manual Section 2: Threshold Issues #2IIIB4aii.* Retrieved from http://www.eeoc.gov/policy/docs/threshold.html#2-III-B-4-a-ii

Legislation

United States Constitution Amendment I.
United States Constitution Amendment XIV.
Civil Rights Act of 1964, 42 U.S.C. § 2000a (2000).
Civil Rights Act of 1964, 42 U.S.C. § 2000e (2000).
Civil Rights Act of 1964, 42 USC § 12101
ADA Amendments Act of 2008 (P.L. 110-325), 42 U.S.C. §12101–12102.
The Americans with Disabilities Act, 42 U.S.C. § 12101 *et seq*.

SPORT AND LEGISLATION

7.00

In addition to the federal Constitution, Congress has also enacted a number of laws that affect the sport and recreation industry. The *Sport and Legislation* section examines those laws and the impact they have on the industry. The section is divided into four parts. The first part reviews federal laws as they apply to discrimination in the sport and recreation industry. The section examines such areas as gender equity and race, age, sex, and disability discrimination. The second part examines intellectual property law. In particular, the sections review how important rights of publicity, rights of privacy, copyright, trademark, and patent law are to the sport and recreation industries. The third part examines federal antitrust and labor laws and how they are applied to professional and amateur sports. The final part of the *Sport and Legislation* section examines sport agent legislation. In particular, the section reviews sport agent legislation and the impact of the Uniform Athlete Agent Act of sport agents.

7.11 GENDER EQUITY: OPPORTUNITIES TO PARTICIPATE

Linda Jean Carpenter | Professor Emerita, Brooklyn College

Sport is the laboratory experience through which students may gain skills such as decision-making, risk evaluation, teamwork, leadership, self-appraisal, and personal esteem. These skills are the same skills that allow graduates to successfully use their other academic skills in their adult lives and employment circumstances. As a result, sport's place on campus in the form of intramurals, recreation, athletics, and physical education is defensible, not because of any possible revenue generation or because of fan support, but because of the valuable skills it provides, which are not easily obtained elsewhere in the educational setting. The skills obtained through sport have value to both female and male participants. The legal imperatives for equity found in the Fourteenth Amendment of the United States Constitution and Title IX of the Education Amendments of 1972 (and a variety of similarly worded state legislation) are the two most frequently used tools to judicially increase gender equitable participation in sport. Between the Fourteenth Amendment and Title IX, most circumstances within education are covered. The Fourteenth Amendment requires a state actor; Title IX does not. Title IX requires the presence of federal financial assistance; the Fourteenth Amendment does not. Both cover gender discrimination. Both cover employees and students.

FUNDAMENTAL CONCEPTS

Constitutional Issues

The Equal Protection Clause of the Fourteenth Amendment is the generic protector of equal rights. It guarantees that no **state actor** such as a federal, state, or local governmental agency, or, for example, public school or recreation program, can gratuitously classify people and treat them differently based on those classifications without having a defensible reason.

Levels of Scrutiny

Strict/High: Necessary to Accomplish a Compelling State Interest. The defensible reason required for a state actor to constitutionally treat people differently varies depending on the classification scheme employed. If, for example, a public school (*state actor*) classified its students by race and then treated its African-American students differently, the reason used to defend the constitutionality of such an action would have to withstand the Court's highest level of scrutiny. The school would need to show that its racially based discrimination was *necessary to accomplish a compelling state interest*. It is difficult to imagine a reason for racial discrimination that would meet such a test.

Mild/Low: Rationally Related to a Legitimate State Interest. As an alternative example, consider the scenario where a public school's (*state actor*) physical education program classified its students by skill level and, as a result, restricted its beginning-level students to a beginning-level course while allowing the more highly skilled students to have access to a variety of advanced electives. The Court would use a lower level of scrutiny to determine if discrimination based on skill level was constitutional. The school would only have to show that its discrimination was *rationally related to a legitimate state interest*. Protecting beginners from the injuries likely to occur if they participated with highly skilled athletes or performed advanced movements for which they were either untrained or unconditioned would appear to be rationally related to the legitimate state interest of protecting the health and safety of the community's schoolchildren.

Intermediate/Midlevel: An Evolving Middle Ground. Most classification schemes are reviewed by the courts using either the strict/high or mild/low levels of scrutiny. Typically, only those classifications based on race, alienage, or national origin (R.A.N.) face strict/high scrutiny. Almost all other classification schemes face only the mild/low level. In the last few decades, however, we have seen the judicial review of classification schemes based on age, gender, and disability elevated from the mild/low level of scrutiny to a reasonably amorphous midlevel of scrutiny.

In its June 1996 decision involving coeducation at Virginia Military Institute (116 S.Ct. 2264) the Supreme Court elevated the scrutiny applied to *gender* discrimination even higher within this middle ground to a level requiring an exceedingly persuasive justification. Thus if a state actor discriminates on the basis of gender, it will need to show that doing so was considerably more than rationally related to a legitimate state interest, but it will not need to show that it was necessary to accomplish a compelling state interest.

Cases involving gender discrimination in sport and recreation have used the Fourteenth Amendment, but the more prevalently used tool is Title IX. For this reason, and because of the presence of a fuller discussion of constitutional issues elsewhere in this text, the remaining portion of this section dealing with participation issues will focus on Title IX. However, before proceeding to a deeper discussion of Title IX, a brief mention of an issue involving the interrelationship of the Constitution's Fourteenth Amendment and Title IX is appropriate. May the victim of discrimination (in this particular case, discrimination was in the form of sexual harassment) sue using both Title IX and the Fourteenth Amendment? The Supreme Court answered that question in *Fitzgerald v. Barnstable School Community* in the affirmative, when it held that the plaintiff does not have to lose constitutional rights at the school-house door or playground gate. Neither did Congress intend for Title IX to be the solitary mechanism for combating gender-based discrimination in school settings.

Title IX

A Brief History

Title IX was enacted by Congress on June 23, 1972, to prohibit gender discrimination in the nation's education programs. Three basic elements must all exist for Title IX's jurisdiction to be triggered. The elements are:

1. **Gender Discrimination.** Title IX does not protect against discrimination based on race or age; it protects solely against discrimination based on gender;
2. **Federal Funding.** The receipt of federal funding is required so that the enforcement of Title IX has administrative teeth. If an institution is found to be violating Title IX, its federal funding may be terminated. However, it should be noted, no federal money has ever been removed from a campus due to a Title IX violation;
3. **Education Program.** The definition of this element brought early controversy to the implementation of Title IX. The U.S. Supreme Court's 1984 *Grove City v. Bell* decision resulted in the word *program* being defined as a "subunit" of an institution. As a result of *Grove City*, any subunit that did not receive federal funding would not be obligated to refrain from gender discrimination. Thus college-level athletics and physical education programs, which typically receive no federal funding, were no longer obligated by Title IX to refrain from gender discrimination. In 1988, however, Congress passed the Civil Rights Restoration Act of 1987 over presidential veto saying, in effect, that the Court had misunderstood Congress' intent to have Title IX apply on an institution-wide basis. So, as of 1988, Title IX once again applies to college-level athletics and physical education programs, as well as to all education programs in institutions that receive federal funding.

Title IX Enforcement

There are three main pathways to enforce Title IX. The complainant or plaintiff may select any of the three and need not exhaust, nor even initiate, in-house remedies first.

The first method is internal. Each institution under the jurisdiction of Title IX must have a designated Title IX officer. The Title IX officer's job is to educate the faculty, staff, and students about the rights and responsibilities imposed by Title IX and to deal with any Title IX complaints filed in-house.

The second method of enforcement is through the Office for Civil Rights (OCR) of the U.S. Department of Education. Once an administrative complaint is filed with the OCR (legal standing is NOT required in order to file), the OCR investigates and, if violations are found, negotiates a "letter of resolution" with the institution in which the institution agrees to a time frame and a list of changes to be made.

The third method involves the filing of a federal lawsuit by someone with legal standing. This method has found increasing favor among plaintiffs since the Supreme Court's unanimous 1992 *Franklin v. Gwinnett County Public Schools* (see the Supplemental CD) decision, which made it clear that compensatory and perhaps even punitive damages are available to victims of intentional gender discrimination under Title IX.

Title IX Requirements

When Title IX was enacted in 1972, there was only the one-sentence law saying:

> *"No person in the United States shall, on the basis of sex, be excluded from participation in, be denied the benefits of, or be subjected to discrimination under any education program or activity receiving Federal financial assistance."*

In addition to the one-sentence law, formal regulations were promulgated and ultimately gained the force of law. Even though most Title IX cases and controversies have related to its application to sport, Title IX applies to all of education. However, because of continuing controversy about the details of Title IX's implementation in the area of sport, policy interpretations were adopted in 1979. Policy interpretations do not have the force of law but courts are required to give them significant deference. Policy interpretations are not intended to alter the meaning of the regulations but merely provide a fuller explanation of what compliance with the regulations would look like or how compliance would be evaluated. Another, yet much weaker, source of information about the requirements of Title IX is found in the 1990 *OCR Investigator's Manual*, which provides insight into how the OCR views its own requirements. OCR also has the ability and, some would argue the obligation, to clarify areas of the law that are found to be confusing. Letters of clarification have been issued over the years to explain specific issues that have been the center of controversy such as the applicability of a three pronged test relating to the measurement of the adequacy of opportunities to participate. Letters of clarification do not have the force of law but theoretically simply restate the law. However, some OCR letters of clarification, such as the "Additional Clarification" issued in 2005 concerning the use of surveys to determine interest in participation, exceeded a simple restatement and attempted to alter the law. The 2005 Additional Clarification was rescinded in April, 2010.

Recreation Program Application

Recreation programs are also often under the jurisdiction of Title IX. As long as all three elements (federal money, allegations of sex discrimination, and education program) are met, recreation programs are included in the jurisdiction of Title IX. It would be difficult to conceive of a campus-based recreation program that would not be under Title IX jurisdiction. Nonscholastic, community-based recreation programs need not be operated by the state or federal government to be under the jurisdiction of Title IX. State action is not required to trigger Title IX jurisdiction. The recreation program's primary activity need not be conducting educational programs; it only needs to include an educational component in its programs to be under the jurisdiction of Title IX. If a recreation program is found to be under the jurisdiction of Title IX, offering more activities or more participation opportunities for its male clients, offering those activities in better facilities, or providing a higher quality officiating staff for its male clients, would be examples of potential Title IX violations.

Athletics Application

There are many specific requirements of Title IX relating to coaching, facilities, equipment, travel, and so on. However, if you are not on the team, you don't need a uniform, coaching and the other items, so this section will focus on the legal requirements for participation rather than on the treatment of athletes once they are participating. Title IX's regulations require that "the selection of sports and levels of competition effectively accommodate the interests and abilities of members of both sexes." According to the policy interpretations (U.S. Department of Education Athletic Guidelines, 1979), an institution has effectively accommodated the interests of its students if it satisfies any ONE of the following three benchmarks:

1. Participation opportunities for male and female students are provided in numbers substantially proportionate to their respective enrollments;
2. The institution can show a history and continuing practice of program expansion demonstrably responsive to the developing interest and abilities of the members of the underrepresented sex;
3. The institution can show that it is fully and effectively meeting the interests and abilities of the underrepresented sex.

Institutions that have maintained their commitment to the legal requirements of gender equity over the years have had no difficulty in meeting either Benchmark 2 or 3 and thus don't even need to address the issue of proportionality found in Benchmark 1. However, institutions that have ignored the requirements of Title IX or that have failed to implement plans to provide equitable athletic participation opportunities for their female students, more than four decades after the passage of Title IX, are now facing a quandary. They have not satisfied Benchmark 2 because they have not expanded their program for their female students. Similarly, if a group of female athletes demonstrates interest and ability sufficient to support the creation of a team in a particular sport in which it would be reasonable to find suitable competition in the school's traditional competitive region, the institution cannot claim that it has satisfied Benchmark 3. That leaves Benchmark 1: proportionality.

For many reasons, including past discrimination, social influences, and the changing enrollment gender balance, very few schools meet Benchmark 1. Typically, the courts have also found such institutions to be in violation of Title IX's requirement to effectively accommodate the interests and abilities of its female (historically underrepresented sex) student-athletes because it is unlikely that Benchmarks 2 or 3 have been met either. Such institutions are therefore at risk of losing their federal funding in addition to being liable for possible compensatory and punitive damages. Consternation and controversy surrounding the measurement of equitable participation has been unabated by the fact that the status of the law and the application of the three-prong test (as found in the 1979 Policy Interpretations and as reiterated unchanged in the form of a 1996 clarification letter from the Office for Civil Rights) has been very straightforward.

One of the three tests of participation, the proportionality prong (Benchmark 1) was created to provide a "safe harbor." In this context "safe harbor" means that a school that can show it has met the proportionality prong will be exempt from creating additional participation opportunities for females, even if there remain significant numbers of females who are denied participation. The school would be granted the "safe harbor" exemption because it is assumed that if its ratio of female athletes mirrors the ratio of females in the student body, gender equity in participation has been met. Reality has demonstrated that schools that have not gradually moved toward compliance over the years or that have left favored teams' budgets and inflated participation numbers unrestrained find that they can meet none of the three prongs in any reasonable way. They cannot rewrite history to meet prong 2, and they cannot claim that they have met the interests and abilities of the underrepresented sex (prong 3) as long as there are sufficient able and interested females wanting to participate. Therefore, the only prong over which an institution that has not moved toward compliance over the years has retained any degree of control is the proportionality prong.

Some institutions have manipulated compliance within the proportionality prong in ways that, in effect, reduce participation for males and sometimes even the historically underrepresented females. By canceling men's minor sport teams, the absolute number of male participants is reduced, and the male/female athlete ratio moves closer to the ratio in the student body without having to increase participation opportunities for women. This manipulation is contrary to the spirit of Title IX. Even so, administrators have often defended their decision to cut men's minor sport teams, rather than restrain favored teams, by disingenuously placing the blame on Title IX. The popularity of various sports waxes and wanes even in the absence of Title IX, but those whose sports are cut are understandably frustrated.

Data on both the high school and college levels make it clear that the absolute number of males and females participating as varsity athletes is continuing to expand. The massive increase in women's participation from 16,000 female intercollegiate athletes in 1971 to over 200,000 in 2016 has not come at the cost of men's participation opportunities which are among the highest ever. The same is true for the high school levels where there were 4,519,312 boys and 3,287,735 girls participating in interscholastic athletics as of 2014-15. The number of participation opportunities continues to increase although specific teams at specific schools are sometimes cut.

Manipulation of the proportionality prong by capping men's participation slots or cutting a men's team in order to alter the proportion of female to male athletes without having to increase participation opportunities for females is not an appropriate Title IX compliance technique within the spirit of the law. Although roster manipulation is contrary to the spirit of the law, it is sometimes permissible under the law and sometimes not. Frustration born of the manipulation of the proportionality prong most typically arises when a men's team is cut. The frustration is sometimes heightened when the athletic administration blames Title IX for the loss.

However, sometimes the manipulation involves replacing one or more smaller roster women's teams with a single larger roster women's team. Such was the case at Quinnipiac University according to the allegations found in *Biediger v Quinnipiac University* (See Significant Case). Quinnipiac's women's volleyball team was slated for replacement by a competitive cheer team. Competitive cheer teams carry much larger rosters than volleyball teams thus helping an institution to meet the proportionality prong. The Quinnipiac case involved accusations of dishonest, not merely strategic, manipulation of rosters. In addition, the case involved a determination of whether the competitive cheer group met the standards to be considered a 'sport' for Title IX purposes.

Not every activity that involves motion or athleticism fulfills the subjective requirements promulgated by the OCR for the designation, 'sport'. There is a rebuttable presumption that an activity labeled a 'sport' by an intercollegiate athletic association, such as the NCAA, also meets the Title IX 'sport' requirements of OCR if the offering institution is an association member and fulfills the association's requirements for offering the activity as a 'sport'. When the presumption fails to apply or has been rebutted, the OCR may evaluate the particular activity on a case-by-case basis. Among the issues reviewed by the OCR (simplified and condensed for this discussion) are:

1. Are the budget, support services, and coaching staffs provided in a manner consistent with other established sports in the institution's athletics program?
2. Are the participants eligible to receive financial aid and recruited in a manner consistent with established sports at the institution?
3. Are practice opportunities, competitive opportunities (number and length predetermined by a governing athletics organization or group of institutions, defined season) and pre/post season competition available in a manner consistent with established sports at the institution?
4. Is the primary purpose of the activity that of supporting/promoting other athletic activities or to provide intercollegiate or interscholastic competition at varsity levels?
5. Is the selection of participants based on factors related primarily to athletic ability?

The *Biediger* decision determined that Quinnipiac's competitive cheer group was not a 'sport' for the purposes of Title IX and thus the group's members could not be counted for the purposes of meeting the proportionality prong. The NCAA continues to debate whether competitive cheer should be designated as an emerging sport but whatever the NCAA's decision, the NCAA's characterization is not binding on the OCR but simply helps to establish a rebuttable presumption. There are likely to be more institutions desiring to count participants in competitive cheer; large roster women's sports assist an institution in meeting the proportionality prong. Whatever the final determination at a particular institution, it will be interesting to watch the process of determining whether competitive cheer is or is not a sport for the purposes of Title IX.

Opportunities to Participate Free from Harassment

Having the opportunity to participate but facing sexual harassment while participating is not much of an opportunity at all. Sexual harassment invades many areas of human interaction, and the Fourteenth Amendment to a small degree and Titles VII and IX to a larger degree are useful tools with which to combat sexual harassment. Title IX is specifically applicable to sexual harassment of students by both their teachers and coaches. Title VII, on the other hand, applies only in the workplace, and thus does not protect students. See Section 7.14, *Sexual Harassment* for a full discussion of harassment.

SIGNIFICANT CASE

The replacement of a smaller roster women's team by a new, larger roster women's team in an attempt to alter the ratio needed to satisfy Prong/Benchmark 1(proportionality) brings into question the validity of the replacement activity as a 'sport' as well as the accuracy of the method of counting participation slots. The Biediger settlement plan is included on the Supplemental Web Site and provides very interesting reading about the potential results of failing to comply with Title IX's requirement to provide equitable access to participation opportunities.

BIEDIGER, ET AL V. QUINNIPIAC UNIVERSITY
United States District Court
District of Connecticut
728 F. Supp. 2d 62 (2010)

In March 2009, the defendant, Quinnipiac University ("Quinnipiac" or the "University"), announced plans to cut three of its sports teams: the women's volleyball team, the men's golf team, and the men's outdoor track team. Contemporaneously, the University pledged to create a new varsity sport, competitive cheerleading, for the 2009-10 season. Those decisions form the basis of this lawsuit. Plaintiffs *** are five current Quinnipiac women's varsity volleyball players, and *** their coach. Together, they allege that Quinnipiac's decision to eliminate its volleyball team violates Title IX of the Education Amendments of 1972 (20 U.S.C. § 162, et seq.) and the regulations adopted pursuant thereto (34 C.F.R. Part 106) ("Title IX").

On May 22, 2009, I granted the plaintiffs' motion for a preliminary injunction, holding that the manner in which Quinnipiac managed its varsity rosters – essentially, by setting artificial ceilings for men's varsity teams and floors for women's varsity teams – deprived female athletes of equal athletic participation opportunities. ***

Although the plaintiffs allege several theories for relief under Title IX, the parties agreed to sever and try independently the plaintiffs' first claim: that Quinnipiac discriminates on the basis of sex in its allocation of athletic participation opportunities. The parties tried that claim in a bench trial held from June 21 to June 25, 2010. My findings of fact and conclusions of law are set forth herein.

I conclude, as a matter of law, that Quinnipiac discriminated on the basis of sex during the 2009-10 academic year by failing to provide equal athletic participation opportunities for women. Specifically, I hold that the University's competitive cheerleading team does not qualify as a varsity sport for the purposes of Title IX and, therefore, its members may not be counted as athletic participants under the statute. Competitive cheer may, sometime in the future, qualify as a sport under Title IX; today, however, the activity is still too underdeveloped and disorganized to be treated as offering genuine varsity athletic participation opportunities for students.

Second, I hold that, although cross-country, indoor track, and outdoor track are usually considered different sports, Quinnipiac may not count some runners who participate in each sport three times. Quinnipiac's practice of requiring women cross-country runners to participate on the indoor and outdoor track teams, and its treatment of the indoor and outdoor track teams as, in essence, an adjunct of the cross-country team, are sufficient to show that some cross-country runners who participate on the indoor and outdoor track teams should not be counted under Title IX. Specifically, cross-country runners who were injured or red-shirted during the 2009-10 indoor and outdoor track seasons cannot be counted because their activity does not amount to genuine athletic participation opportunities.

Finally, although I find, as a matter of fact, that Quinnipiac is no longer engaged in the same roster manipulation that was the basis for my preliminary injunction order, the University is still continuing to deflate the size of its men's rosters and inflate the size of its women's rosters. Although that roster management is insufficient to conclude that Quinnipiac violated Title IX as a matter of law, it supports the ultimate conclusion that the University is not offering equal participation opportunities for its female students.

1. Findings of Fact

***

Historically, men's and women's basketball and ice hockey have been the school's premier sports. Quinnipiac, however, sponsors seven varsity men's athletic teams and 12 varsity women's athletic teams, including, inter alia, women's volleyball, women's cross-country, women's indoor track and field, women's outdoor track and field, and women's competitive cheer.

During the 2009-10 academic year, 5,686 students were enrolled in the University's undergraduate program. That year, 2,168 students, or 38.13 percent of the student body, were male, and 3,518 students, or 61.87 percent of the student body, were female. Based on the varsity rosters for the first day of teams' competitions, 166 male athletes and 274 female athletes participated during the academic year. Using those first day of competition figures, in 2009-10 male athletes made up 37.73 percent, and female athletes 62.27 percent, of the University's varsity athletes. If Quinnipiac's numbers were accepted, the University would not be liable under Title IX because the school would be offering athletic opportunities for women in numbers proportional to the percentage of women in the school's undergraduate population.

To succeed, the plaintiffs must undermine the way Quinnipiac counts its varsity athletes. Plaintiffs seek to do so by raising three areas of factual disagreement. First, the plaintiffs claim that Quinnipiac's roster numbers are inaccurate and the University's policy of setting varsity roster targets leads to artificially undersized men's teams and oversized women's teams. Second, the plaintiffs claim that Quinnipiac's female cross-country runners should not be counted multiple times for their participation on the indoor and outdoor track teams because the indoor and outdoor track teams are not true independent sports teams but serve, instead, as a more structured nontraditional season for the University's female cross-country runners. Third and finally, the plaintiffs claim that the Quinnipiac competitive cheerleaders should not be counted because competitive cheer is not yet a legitimate intercollegiate varsity sport.

* * *

A. Roster management

Following the 2008-09 academic year, Quinnipiac changed its practice with respect to setting roster targets for its teams – the practice that formed the basis of my preliminary injunction order. Rather than establish ceilings for men's teams and floors for women's teams, and implicitly encourage coaches to manipulate their rosters before and after the first dates of competition – the dates on which the University collected its roster data to prove its Title IX compliance – Quinnipiac established a new policy of setting roster targets. That policy required coaches to meet roster numbers prescribed by the University after consultation with its coaches.

* * *

The plaintiffs allege two potential ways in which Quinnipiac's practice of setting roster targets could result in a Title IX violation. First, the University may have manipulated its roster sizes by misidentifying student athletes, specifically, by erroneously discounting individual athletes from men's teams and adding individual athletes to women's teams. In other words, the plaintiffs claim that Quinnipiac's varsity teams were not actually complying with the roster targets the University assigned, and the actual number of athletes was not captured by the roster target totals. And, second, the University may have set artificially low roster numbers for its men's teams and high numbers for its women's teams, thus creating de facto ceilings and floors for squads on the basis of sex, which had the effect of denying genuine athletic participation opportunities to some women athletes.

* * *

B. Competitive cheer

Following the 2008-09 academic year, Quinnipiac decided to create a new women's varsity sport: competitive cheer. Competitive cheer is an outgrowth of traditional sideline cheerleading. Competitive cheer teams use many of the moves and techniques that sideline cheer squads have developed over the decades, and their routines look like more athletic and aerobatic sideline cheer orchestrations. But whereas sideline cheerleaders primarily work to entertain audiences or solicit crowd reaction at other teams' games or school functions, competitive cheer teams strictly engage in sport. Participants do not perform for a crowd's approval or involvement – they compete to win. In order to distinguish their activity from their sideline roots, cheer teams do not attempt to elicit crowd response; generally do not use pom-poms, megaphones, signs, or other props associated with traditional cheerleading teams; do not wear skirts and sleeveless or cropped tops, but wear uniforms consisting of shorts and jerseys, much like what women's volleyball players don; and emphasize the more gymnastic elements of sideline cheerleading, such as aerial maneuvers, floor tumbling, and balancing exercises, to the exclusion of those activities intended to rally the watching audience. As I noted in my preliminary injunction ruling, competitive cheer is an athletic endeavor that "could be easily described as 'group floor gymnastics. *** Despite its athletic elements, however, competitive cheer is not recognized as a sport by the NCAA. Nor does the NCAA recognize competitive cheer as an "emerging sport," a provisional designation that allows a university to count the activity toward NCAA revenue distribution and minimum sports sponsorship requirements.

* * *

Furthermore, the Department of Education has not recognized competitive cheerleading to be a sport. Indeed, schools reporting their athletic participation data to the Department of Education under the Equity in Athletics Disclosure Act ("EADA") are instructed to report their cheerleading team rosters only if they have received a letter from OCR determining that their cheerleading squads are legitimately engaged in sport.18 U.S. Dep't of Educ., *** The EADA is a law separate from Title IX that requires an educational institution receiving federal funding and participating in intercollegiate athletics to report its athletic participation data for men and women to the Department of Education.

* * *

Although the schools held some basic common beliefs about the sport – for example, the members were unanimous that competitive cheer teams should only engage in competition, and not support other varsity teams in a sideline capacity – there was no consensus on finer questions, such as how many players should compete, how the sport should be scored, and how the regular and post-seasons should be structured. Indeed, even the organization of the NCSTA still had to be determined; at the time of the meeting, and to this day, the NCSTA is a loosely defined, unincorporated association with no board of directors, subcommittees, voting or petition systems for its members, or other hallmarks of a governing national athletics organization.

* * *

The University plans to cancel the women's volleyball program, thus eliminating the team's 12 roster spots. Those positions will be made up for – and, in fact, exceeded, should the new indoor and outdoor track positions count under Title IX – by the new roster spots on the women's cross-country and competitive cheer teams. If, however, the University does not cut the women's volleyball program, it has set a roster target of 14 players for the team. Besides the changes to the women's cross-country, indoor track, outdoor track, and volleyball teams, the University also plans on increasing the men's basketball team by two spots, decreasing the women's soccer team by two spots, increasing the women's lacrosse team by one spot, and decreasing the women's softball team by one spot.

* * *

The first factor, and the one relevant to the decision of this case, is "[w]hether the selection of sports and levels of competition effectively accommodate the interests and abilities of members of both sexes." ***In 1979, HEW published a policy interpretation in the Federal Register defining the phrase "effectively accommodate the interests and abilities of members of both sexes"*** That policy interpretation states that whether a university meets its obligation to "effectively accommodate the interests and abilities of members of both sexes" will be determined in one of the following three ways: (1) Whether intercollegiate level participation opportunities for male and female students are provided in numbers substantially proportionate to their respective enrollments; or (2) Where the members of one sex have been and are underrepresented among intercollegiate athletes, whether the institution can show a history and continuing practice of program expansion which is demonstrably responsive to the developing interest[s] and abilities of the members of that sex; or (3) Where the members of one sex are underrepresented among intercollegiate athletes, and the institution cannot show a continuing practice of program expansion such as that cited above, whether it can be demonstrated that the interests and abilities of the members of that sex have been fully and effectively accommodated by the present program.

* * *

In this case, Quinnipiac defends against the plaintiffs' allegations of sex discrimination by relying on the first prong, contending that, because it provides athletic participation opportunities for women in numbers substantially proportionate to its undergraduate female enrollment, the University is in compliance with Title IX. The University does not argue that it meets Title IX's mandate by satisfying the second or third prongs of the 1979 Policy Interpretation. On December 16, 1996, OCR, the body responsible for enforcing Title IX, published a letter that clarified, inter alia, the meaning of the first prong: "[w]hether intercollegiate level participation opportunities for male and female students are provided in numbers substantially proportionate to their respective enrollments." OCR stated that, in determining whether a university provides substantially proportionate participation opportunities for its male and female students, its "analysis begins with a determination of the number of participation opportunities afforded to male and female athletes in the intercollegiate athletic program." ***

The 1979 Policy Interpretation defines "athletes" as students: a. Who are receiving the institutionally-sponsored support normally provided to athletes competing at the institution involved, e.g., coaching, equipment, medical and training room services, on a regular basis during a sport's season; and b. Who are participating in organized practice sessions and other team meetings and activities on a regular basis during a sport's season; and c. Who are listed on the eligibility or squad lists maintained for each sport; and d. Who, because of injury, cannot meet a, b, or c above but continue to receive financial aid on the basis of athletic ability.

* * *

OCR stated that "[a]s a general rule, all athletes who are listed on a team's squad or eligibility list and are on the team as of the team's first competitive event are counted as participants" and "an athlete who participates in more than one sport will be counted as a participant in each sport in which he or she participates."

Finally, OCR clarified that a participant on a team need not meet minimum criteria of playing time or athletic ability to count for Title IX purposes. OCR includes, among others, those athletes who do not receive scholarships (e.g., walk-ons), those athletes who compete on teams sponsored by the institution even though the team may be required to raise some or all of its operating funds, and those athletes who practice but may not compete.

OCR's investigations reveal that these athletes receive numerous benefits and services, such as training and practice time, coaching, tutoring services, locker room facilities, and equipment, as well as important non-tangible benefits derived from being a member of an intercollegiate athletic team. Because these are significant benefits, and because receipt of these benefits does not depend on their cost to the institution or whether the athlete competes, it is necessary to count all athletes who receive such benefits when determining the number of athletic opportunities provided to men and women. Id. Although the scope of who counts as an athlete is broader than scholarship athletes who receive playing time, OCR was careful to emphasize, in a letter accompanying the 1996 Clarification, that for an athlete to be counted, he or she must be afforded a participation opportunity that is "real, not illusory," and offers the same benefits as would be provided to other bona fide athletes.

* * *

Once all athletes – or, stated differently, all genuine participation opportunities – are counted, the second and final part of analyzing a university's compliance under the first prong is deciding whether the numbers of genuine participation opportunities are substantially proportionate for men and women.

* * *

OCR was clear that substantial proportionality does not require exact proportionality. Rather, whether a school meets the first prong is determined on a case-by-case basis, and involves assessing the percentage of female athletes relative to female enrollment and taking into account "the institution's specific circumstances and the size of its athletic program.". To provide a baseline, OCR said that a university would fail to satisfy the substantial proportionality test if, assuming the school lacked perfect proportionality, the number of additional women to achieve such proportionality would be insufficient to constitute a varsity team. So, for example, if a school has five fewer female athletes than needed to reach exact proportionality, OCR would find the athletic program to be substantially proportional because no varsity team can be sustained with so few participants.

Finally, in the letter that accompanied the 1996 Clarification, OCR stated that, although universities will be subject to the agency's counting methodology, schools retained "flexibility and choice regarding how they will provide nondiscriminatory participation opportunities." That flexibility includes eliminating teams or placing caps on their rosters in order to achieve substantial proportionality. Nonetheless, regardless of the means it chooses -to comply with the 1979 Policy Interpretation's first prong, a university will not meet the substantial proportionality threshold if the participation opportunities it provides to women are not genuine.

* * *

Thus, the facts introduced about what Quinnipiac will do in the future do not change my ruling that Quinnipiac violated Title IX and, currently, is not in compliance with the law and its regulations. IV. Remedy The plaintiffs have proved that Quinnipiac failed to provide equal athletic participation opportunities to its female students. I now turn to the remedy to which they are entitled. Both parties are in agreement that if I conclude that Quinnipiac violated Title IX then injunctive relief is appropriate. The parties disagree, however, what kind of injunctive relief should be entered. The plaintiffs have requested an injunction that the women's volleyball team continue during the 2010-11 season. But Quinnipiac has requested the right to develop its own compliance plan to be submitted to the court for approval. Both parties can and should be accommodated. Quinnipiac shall submit a compliance plan describing how it will bring itself into Title IX compliance for 2010-11 and thereafter. *** The University is entitled to determine its own method for achieving statutory compliance; the OCR regulations are clear that, although educational institutions must offer equal athletic participation opportunities to both sexes, Title IX gives schools flexibility in deciding for themselves how to best meet that legal obligation.

* * *

Conclusion

I find in favor of the plaintiffs on their first claim for relief in their first amended complaint***A declaratory judgment shall issue that the defendant, Quinnipiac University, has violated Title IX and the regulations promulgated pursuant thereto by failing to provide equal athletic participation opportunities to its female students. Furthermore, Quinnipiac is hereby enjoined from continuing to discriminate against its female students on the basis of sex by failing to provide equal athletic participation opportunities.

Therefore: IT IS HEREBY ORDERED that, within 60 days, Quinnipiac University shall submit to the court a compliance plan detailing how it will achieve compliance with Title IX and its regulations. That compliance plan shall provide for the continuation of the women's volleyball team during the 2010-11 season.

CASES ON THE SUPPLEMENTAL CD

Biediger, et al v Quinnipiac University, Case 3:09 –cv621-SRU (2010) This case from the US District Court, District of Connecticut, examines the method of counting participation slots for the purposes of complying with Title IX and also considers whether competitive cheer should or should not be considered a sport for the purposes of Title IX and *Biediger v Quinnipiac University* Settlement, filed April 26, 2013.

Fitzgerald v. Barnstable School Committee, 129 S.Ct. 788 (2009). This case examines whether Title IX was the exclusive mechanism for addressing gender discrimination in schools or a substitute for § 1983 suits as a means of enforcing constitutional rights.

Franklin v. Gwinnett County Public Schools, 503 U.S. 60 (1992). This case examines whether Title IX provides a damages for individual students.

Roberts v Colorado State University, 998 F 2d 824 (10th Cir. 1993). This case relates to a suit brought by current and former members of the Colorado State University's fast pitch softball team regarding the discontinuation of the softball program. The students, suing as individuals claimed Title IX violations. A permanent injunction was issued reinstating the softball team.

United States v. Virginia, 518 U.S. 515 (1996). This case examines Virginia's policy of denying women admission to the Virginia Military Institute, a publicly funded university.

QUESTIONS YOU SHOULD BE ABLE TO ANSWER

1. Does Title IX protect members of discontinued men's teams and is the lack of money a defense to Title IX? Provide reasons to support your determination.

2. Should failure of Benchmark 1 (proportionality) solely create an irrefutable presumption of either compliance with or violation of Title IX's accommodation/opportunity requirement? If yes, why? If no, why?

3. May a student who has been discriminated against sue using both Title IX and the 14th Amendment as legal theories or must the student select only one theory? Why do you think this determination is supportable and fair?

4. Evaluate the recreational sport program at your school or in your community and determine if you think the program is complying with the requirements of Title IX.

5. Review the settlement for the Biediger v Quinnipiac case found in the Supplement Case website. Select 3 specific settlement requirements and discuss how effectively their implementation might impact gender equity in the future.

REFERENCES
Cases
Biediger, et al v. Quinnipiac University, 728 F. Supp. 2d 62 (2010).
Cohen v. Brown University, 991 F.2d 888 (1st Cir. 1993), 8879 F. Supp. 185 (D. R.I. 1995), cert. denied.
Fitzgerald v. Barnstable School Committee, 555 U.S. 246 (2009).
Franklin v. Gwinnett County Public Schools, 503 U.S. 60 (1992).
Grove City v. Bell, 465 U.S. 555 (1984).
Roberts v. Colorado State University, 814 F. Supp. 1507 (D. Colo.) aff 'd in relevant part sub nom. *Roberts v. Colorado State Bd. of Agric.*, 998 F.2d 824 (10th Cir.), cert. denied, 114 S. Ct. 580 (1993).
United States v. Virginia Military Institute, 116 S.Ct. 2264 (1996).

Publications
U.S. Department of Education.(1979). Athletic Guidelines.
Dear Colleague Letter, September 17, 2008, Office for Civil Rights, US Department of Education. http://www2.ed.gov/about/offices/list/ocr/letters/colleague-20080917.html

Legislation
Title VII: 42 USC sections 2000e –17, plus additions made by the Civil Rights Act of 1991, Pub.L. No. 102–166, 105 Stat 1071 (1991).
Title IX: Education Amendments of 1972, §§ 901–909 as amended, 20 U.S.C.A. §§ 11681-11688. 40 Fed. Reg. 24, 128 (1975) currently appearing at 34 C.F.R. §§ 106 (1992).
U.S. Department of Education Athletic Guidelines; Title IX of the Education Amendments of 1972; A Policy Interpretation; Title IX and Intercollegiate Athletics, 44 Fed. Reg. 71, 413, 71, 423 (1979).

GENDER EQUITY: COACHING AND ADMINISTRATION

Barbara Osborne | University of North Carolina at Chapel Hill

Although opportunities to participate for girls and women in sport in the United States have increased dramatically over the past 40 years leadership and employment opportunities for women have not. In some cases, women's opportunities in sport management have actually decreased. The Institute for Diversity and Ethics in Sport conducts research on discrimination in the sport industry and publishes a "Report Card" annually. The 2015-16 Racial and Gender Report Cards assigned letter grades from A through F for intercollegiate athletics and professional sports leagues. The WNBA earned the highest grade of A+, followed by the NBA (A), MLS, NFL, NCAA and MLB (B), for gender policies and employment. The Associated Press received a D.

Vivian Acosta and Linda Jean Carpenter have conducted a longitudinal study, "Women in Intercollegiate Sport" since 1977. Although there are more women employed in administrative and coaching positions in intercollegiate athletics than ever before, the number of women as a percentage of total administrators and coaches is not close to the 90% representation in the 1970's when most colleges and universities had separate men's and women's athletics departments. As of 2015, only 22.3% of athletics directors at all NCAA institutions were women, with Division III having the highest percentage of female athletics directors at 34%. However, 11.3% of schools have no women employed in athletics administration. Less than half (43.4%) of women's athletics teams have a female head coach, but less than 3% of men's teams are coached by women. There are more paid assistant coaches in women's college athletics than ever before, and 56.8% of those positions are held by women. Sports medicine and sports information lag woefully behind, with only 32.4% of women employed as head athletics trainers. Athletics communications appears to mirror the professional sports media, as only 12.1% of sports information directors are women (Acosta & Carpenter, 2015). In addition to barriers in employing women in college athletics programs, a gender gap also exists in salaries, with female coaches earning on average only 62% of what male coaches make (Osborne & Yarbrough, 2001).

There are many possible explanations for the decline in women's employment as athletics administrators and coaches. Combining men's and women's athletics programs in the 1970's and 1980's was less of a merger of two departments and more of take-over by the men's athletics department resulting in elimination of female athletics administrators. This transition also resulted in paid positions and improved pay for coaches of women's teams, making positions coaching women more attractive to men. Research indicates the sex of the person making the employment decision matters, and male athletics directors are more likely to hire men (Acosta & Carpenter, 2015). Fewer female coaches and administrators results in fewer role models for female athletes. Lack of interaction with female coaches may have also influenced preference for male coaches by female athletes (Women's Sports Foundation, n.d.). Cultural stereotypes also persist that female coaches are not as qualified, and are softer than male coaches.

A high school coaching case illustrates the sports cultural bias against hiring female coaches. Geraldine Fuhr was the girls' varsity basketball coach at Hazel Park for 10 years, and had also served as the assistant boys varsity basketball coach for 8 years. When the boys' varsity coach announced his retirement, Fuhr and John Barnett, who had been coaching the boys' freshman basketball team for the past two years, were the only two applicants for the position. Both candidates were interviewed by the search committee, and at the end of the process, the Superintendent of Schools informed the search committee that several members of the school board did not want Fuhr as the boys coach and that they had to honor their wishes. The president of the school board announced that he "was very concerned about a female being the head boys' basketball coach in Hazel Park" (*Fuhr v. School District of Hazel Park*, 2004, p. 757). Barnett was hired, and Fuhr was told by the school principal that she did not get the job because of her gender. She sued the school district for sex discrimination under Title VII and the Elliot-Larsen Act, a Michigan civil rights act that prohibits discrimination. A jury held in Fuhr's favor, awarding her $245,000 in present damages and $210,000 in future damages. Subsequently, the district court ordered Hazel Park to hire Fuhr as the boys' varsity basketball coach, and struck the jury's award of future damages, but granted Fuhr attorney's fees. Hazel Park appealed, but the Sixth Circuit affirmed, finding that Hazel Park had intentionally discriminated against Fuhr on the basis of sex by not hiring her as the head boys' basketball coach.

FUNDAMENTAL CONCEPTS

Employment discrimination laws prevent employers, including sport and recreation organizations, from discriminating on the basis of race, sex, religion, country of national origin, disability, and age. These laws seek to prevent bias in all aspects of employment including hiring, work assignment, compensation, promotion, and termination. The United States Equal Employment Opportunity Commission (EEOC) is the federal agency responsible for these laws. This chapter will examine constitutional and statutory protection against employment discrimination based on gender, including the issues of pay equity, pregnancy, and retaliation.

Constitutional Law and Civil Rights Acts

Constitutional law claims for discrimination based on gender may be made under the equal protection clause of the Fourteenth Amendment. Because the proposed Equal Rights Amendment to the United States Constitution was never ratified, sex is not a protected category under the Constitution so the federal courts apply an intermediate scrutiny standard, meaning that the government action must be substantially related to an important government interest. Additionally, 42 U.S.C. §1983 of the Civil Rights Act of 1871 provides for damages when federal constitutional rights are violated. §1983 claims may also be used to redress deprivation of a right guaranteed by a federal statute.

State Constitutions may also provide heightened protection from discrimination based on sex. For example, the State Constitution of Illinois states in its Bill of Rights that all persons have the right to be free from discrimination on the basis of race, color, creed, national ancestry, and sex. States that include sex as a protected category in the state constitution heighten protection by providing strict scrutiny review by the courts. State civil rights legislation also provides additional protection from gender discrimination. In Michigan, the Elliott-Larsen Civil Rights Act prohibits discriminatory practices on the basis of religion, race, color, national origin, sex, age, height, weight, familial status and marital status in the exercise of civil rights. As protection against discrimination varies from state to state, and federal Constitutional protection is only at an intermediate level, additional federal legislation has been needed to address gender inequity in the workforce.

Equal Pay Act of 1963

An amendment to the Fair Labor Standards Act of 1938 (29 U.S.C.A. §201–219), the Equal Pay Act (EPA) prohibits employers from discriminating on the basis of sex between employees at the same establishment who perform equal work in equivalent positions under similar working conditions. An employee may have a claim for relief under the EPA if the employee proves that the employer pays a higher wage to an employee of the opposite sex for equal work on a job that requires equal skill, effort and responsibility when the job is performed under similar working conditions. Skill is measured as equal based on experience, training, education and ability required in performing the job, effort is the amount or degree of physical or mental exertion required to perform the job successfully, and responsibility is measured by the degree of accountability required with emphasis on the importance of the job obligation. Once the employee has proved differential pay for equal work, the burden then shifts to the employer to justify the wage difference through one of the defenses enumerated in the Act: seniority, merit, quantity or quality of production, and any factor other than the sex of the employee. If the employer offers a justification, the employee has one final opportunity to provide evidence that the employer's defense is pretext and that the real reason for the pay inequity is gender discrimination. The burden of proof standard in an Equal Pay Act claim is very high, making it difficult for an employee to win a claim.

The *Stanley v. University of Southern California* case illustrates this difficulty. In 1993, Marianne Stanley was the successful coach of the USC women's basketball program. As her four-year contract was nearing completion, she began negotiating a new contract with Michael Garrett, Athletics Director at USC. Stanley asked for a contract equal to that of the men's basketball coach at USC. The athletics director agreed that Stanley was worth more, but explained that the athletics department could not afford to pay that type of an increase. Stanley then retained an attorney to negotiate the terms of a new contract and the athletics director responded by withdrawing a multi-year offer, and instead offered a one-year contract. Stanley asked for additional time to consider the offer, and in the meantime, her current contract expired. Garrett, however, sent a memo to Stanley withdrawing his offer and informing her that he would be seeking other candidates to fill her position.

Stanley filed a lawsuit claiming that the athletics director and USC had engaged in sex discrimination and retaliation. She argued that she was entitled to be paid a salary that was equal to the salary of the men's basketball coach as the positions required equal skill, effort and responsibility, and are performed under similar working conditions. USC refuted the claim, offering evidence that the men's basketball coach had substantially different qualifications and experience. The men's coach had substantial public relations and revenue generating skills including nine years of marketing experience, Additionally, he had authored two best-selling novels, performed as an actor in a movie, and had appeared on television. USC also refuted that the men's and women's basketball coaching positions are not equivalent positions, as the men's coaching position required promotional activities related to generating revenue. The university argued that the men's basketball team generated greater attendance, attracted more media interest, inspired larger donations, and produced substantially more revenue than the women's basketball team, which placed greater pressure on the men's basketball coach. The court agreed with the university and found that factors other than gender caused the difference in salary; the appellate court affirmed the decision of the lower court.

It is very difficult for a plaintiff to make a successful Equal Pay Act claim in sports settings. The first hurdle is to establish an equal comparator position. Female athletics administrators, however, are often in a unique position within the athletics department and have no male counterpart in a job that is substantially equal to her own. Coaches may have less difficulty when there are both male and female versions of the same team, but as in the *Stanley* case, courts do not always find that the coach of the men's team and the coach of the women's team in the same sport have substantially equal positions. A coach may choose to compare her position with that of a male coach of another sport, but differences in the number of athletes coached, number of assistant coaches necessary, variety of player positions to train, number of games in a season and other sport-related factors make it easy for the court to conclude that working conditions are not similar.

If the coach or administrator is able to establish an equal comparator, it is still extremely difficult to refute the employer's affirmative defense. Employers are quite successful at establishing that their pay decisions stem from any factor other than sex. Athletics programs have successfully asserted the following justifications for paying male coaches more than comparable female coaches: the men's team produces more revenue than the women's team; the coaching marketplace demands higher salaries for the best coaches; current salary was based on past salary; and the male coach has additional duties. Sex of the athletes coached should not be an acceptable defense, as the sex of the student-athlete is a factor based on sex and not a gender neutral factor (EEOC Guidelines, 1997).

Title VII of Civil Rights Act of 1964

Title VII protects broadly against discrimination on the basis of race, color, religion, country of national origin and sex. Like the Equal Pay Act, Title VII protects against discrimination in compensation. However, the Equal Pay Act is limited to equal pay for equal work, while Title VII offers a victim significantly broader protection. Victims may make claims for failure to hire or promote, or for improper firing on the basis of sex. Additionally, employers may not discriminate on the basis of sex with respect to the terms, conditions, and privileges of employment beyond pay (See Chapter 7.13 for a thorough examination and analysis of Title VII).

An example of the broader protection provided by Title VII is the case of Kathryn Tomlinson who filed a complaint with the EEOC against the Phoenix Suns. Tomlinson was employed as a member of the "Zoo Crew", an entertainment troupe that shoots T-shirts into the stands, assists with half-time promotions, performs with the team mascot, and participates in community events to promote the Suns. Although Tomlinson and two other female employees performed well as members of the Zoo Crew, the Suns adopted a new hiring policy for the following season, limiting the positions to talented males with athletic ability. Unable to reapply for their former jobs, the women filed a complaint against the Suns and the stadium management team. To resolve the case, the Suns paid over $100,000 to the plaintiffs, and were required to provide training to employees, supervisors, and management prohibiting sex discrimination as well as establishing policies to ensure that sex-restrictive job announcements would not be created in the future.

Title IX of Education Amendments of 1972

Although Title IX of the Education Amendments of 1972 is best known for providing opportunities for girls to participate in athletics, the statute was enacted to address sex discrimination in educational institutions. Inequities also existed for women who were working at educational institutions. In 1972, the majority of women working in education were teaching in elementary and secondary schools. Although there have been increasing opportunities for women employed in education, compared to their male peers, women on average are still paid less, hold a lower ranking title, and are not tenured. Title IX is enforced by the Office for Civil Rights (OCR) in the United States Department of Education. Title IX Regulations Subpart E addresses employment discrimination in educational institutions.

The Title IX Regulations prohibit any educational institution that is a recipient of federal funding from discriminating against an applicant or employee on the basis of sex. It further prohibits discrimination on the basis of sex in hiring, promoting, awarding tenure, demoting, transferring, laying off or terminating an employee. Job classifications, assignments, and training may not be made on the basis of sex either. Rate of pay, or any other form of compensation or benefits may not be related to sex, and the language of the compensation section (§106.54) mirrors the requirements of the Equal Pay Act.

Although Title IX provides a cause of action for coaches who complain of employment discrimination on the basis of sex at federally funded schools, coaches still have difficulty winning these cases in court. Anderson & Osborne (2008) report that only half of Title IX claims of employment discrimination litigated and appealed were favorable to the plaintiff coach or administrator. It is also important to note that a Title IX claim of discrimination based on the gender of the athlete coached will be dismissed; the statute only provides protection against discrimination because of the gender of the coach.

Retaliation

One of the most recent developments in the law involves claims for retaliation when coaches have been wrongfully terminated for speaking out against inequities in the men's and women's athletics programs in violation of Title IX. Retaliation occurs when an employee suffers an adverse employment action in response to an action that the employer perceives negatively, such as complaining about unfair treatment to athletes, lack of comparable facilities for practice and/or competition, or other inequitable situations. Neither the plain language of the statute nor the Regulations specifically allows for a claim of retaliation, and the Federal Court of Appeals were split, with some allowing the claim to proceed, and others dismissing the claim for failure to state a recognizable claim. The issue was decided by the Supreme Court in *Jackson v. Birmingham Board of Education* (2005) when it concluded that teachers, coaches, and administrators who complain of sex discrimination on behalf of themselves or others have a right to sue if they are victims of retaliation. Since that decision, there have been a myriad of lawsuits against colleges and universities across the country, including several in California that have attracted attention because of the large jury awards and settlements.

For example, Fresno State University has been battling complaints about gender discrimination within the athletics program for several years. First, Diane Milutinovich, an athletics administrator, was dismissed from her position for "budget reasons" after she complained about inequities in the men's and women's athletics programs. Then the women's volleyball coach, Lindy Vivas, and women's basketball coach, Stacy Johnson-Klein were fired after questioning administrators and complaining about inequities in facilities, staffing, and employment demands between the men's and women's athletics programs. Fresno State agreed to pay Milutinovich $3.5 million in settlement. Juries in separate trials found that the university intentionally discriminated against the coaches and awarded $5.85 million to Vivas and $19.1 million to Johnson-Klein.

Pregnancy Discrimination Act of 1978
The fundamental physical difference between men and women is the ability to bear children, and childbearing as well as child rearing responsibilities have contributed to bias against women in hiring, promotion, and salaries. This physiological difference has historically been used to justify differential treatment between the sexes in a variety of situations. For example, in *Muller v. Oregon*, the Supreme Court upheld an Oregon law that prohibited women from working for more than 10 hours per day because "woman's physical structure and the performance of maternal functions place her at a disadvantage in the struggle for subsistence" (*Muller v. Oregon*, 1908). Although medicine and science have refuted those old-fashioned opinions regarding the proper role of women in society, many people still believe that working mothers are less productive employees who should be paid less because they will have childcare responsibilities that may conflict with work priorities. The Pregnancy Discrimination Act combats that discriminatory reasoning by prohibiting employers from negatively impacting employment or benefits on the basis of pregnancy and childbirth.

Lilly Ledbetter Fair Pay Act of 2009
The gender wage gap in the United States in 2016 is about 21 percent, which translates to women earning about 79 cents for each dollar that a man would earn in the same circumstances. The limitations of the Equal Pay Act, reluctance of women to file lawsuits against their employers, and contrary legal decisions have all contributed to the persistent gender wage gap in the United States. For example, Lilly Ledbetter worked as a supervisor at the Goodyear plant in Gadsden, Alabama for almost twenty years. Just as Ledbetter prepared to retire, she was informed through an anonymous note that she had been paid significantly less than her male peers who were doing the same job. Ledbetter filed suit under Title VII and the trial jury awarded Ledbetter back pay and damages worth more than $3 million. The case was appealed all the way to the United States Supreme Court which overturned the decision, holding that employees must file wage discrimination complaints within 180 days of the original pay decision, no matter when they became aware of the disparity, so Ledbetter was left with nothing (*Ledbetter v. Goodyear Tire & Rubber Co.*, 2007). This decision significantly restricted the time period in which victims may file claims, severely weakening the statutory protections provided under Title VII.

Unhappy with the precedent that the Supreme Court established in the Ledbetter case, Congress passed the Lilly Ledbetter Fair Pay Act of 2009 which allows victims of pay discrimination to assert their rights under the Equal Pay Act and Title VII for full compensatory and punitive damages. The legislation establishes that an unlawful employment practice occurs each time an individual is paid if that compensation is affected by application of a discriminatory compensation practice or decision. The Act also requires the EEOC to issue regulations and survey pay data that will allow it to improve enforcement of the law. To correct for legal decisions that may have relied on the Supreme Court precedent established in the *Ledbetter v. Goodyear Tire & Rubber Co.* case, the legislation is retroactive to all claims pending on or after May 28, 2007. Unfortunately, the gender wage gap has not budged since this legislation was enacted.

SIGNIFICANT CASE

This recent Supreme Court decision has expanded the scope of Title IX protection for coaches and administrators who suffer retaliation for speaking out against gender inequity in their athletics programs.

RODERICK JACKSON V. BIRMINGHAM BOARD OF EDUCATION

Supreme Court of the United States
544 U.S. 167 (2005)

Roderick Jackson, a teacher in the Birmingham, Alabama, public schools, brought suit against the Birmingham Board of Education (Board) alleging that the Board retaliated against him because he had complained about sex discrimination in the high school's athletic program. Jackson claimed that the Board's retaliation violated Title IX of the Education Amendments of 1972, Pub L 92–318, 86 Stat 373, as amended, *20 U.S.C. § 1681 et seq.* The District Court dismissed Jackson's complaint on the ground that Title IX does not prohibit retaliation, and the Court of Appeals for the Eleventh Circuit affirmed. *309 F.3d 1333 (2002).* We consider here whether the private right of action implied by Title IX encompasses claims of retaliation. We hold that it does where the funding recipient retaliates against an individual because he has complained about sex discrimination. I

Because Jackson's Title IX claim was dismissed under *Federal Rule of Civil Procedure 12(b)(6)* for failure to state a claim upon which relief can be granted, "we must assume the truth of the material facts as alleged in the complaint." *Summit Health, Ltd. V. Pinhas, 500 U.S. 322, 325, 114 L. Ed. 2d 366, 111 S. Ct. 1842 (1991).*

According to the complaint, Jackson has been an employee of the Birmingham school district for over 10 years. In 1993, the Board hired Jackson to serve as a physical education teacher and girls' basketball coach. Jackson was transferred to Ensley High School in August 1999. At Ensley, he discovered that the girls' team was not receiving equal funding and equal access to athletic equipment and facilities. The lack of adequate funding, equipment, and facilities made it difficult for Jackson to do his job as the team's coach.

In December 2000, Jackson began complaining to his supervisors about the unequal treatment of the girls' basketball team, but to no avail. Jackson's complaints went unanswered, and the school failed to remedy the situation. Instead, Jackson began to receive negative work evaluations and ultimately was removed as the girls' coach in May 2001. Jackson is still employed by the Board as a teacher, but he no longer receives supplemental pay for coaching.

After the Board terminated Jackson's coaching duties, he filed suit in the United States District Court for the Northern District of Alabama. He alleged, among other things, that the Board violated Title IX by retaliating against him for protesting the discrimination against the girls' basketball team. Amended Complaint 2–3, App. 10–11. The Board moved to dismiss on the ground that Title IX's private cause of action does not include claims of retaliation. The District Court granted the motion to dismiss.

The Court of Appeals for the Eleventh Circuit affirmed. *309 F.3d 1333 (2002).* It assumed, for purposes of the appeal, that the Board retaliated against Jackson for complaining about Title IX violations. It then held that Jackson's suit failed to state a claim because Title IX does not provide a private right of action for retaliation, reasoning that "[n]othing in the text indicates any congressional concern with retaliation that might be visited on those who complain of Title IX violations." *Id., at 1344.* Relying on our decision in *Alexander v. Sandoval, 532 U.S. 275, 149 L. Ed. 2d 517, 121 S. Ct. 1511 (2001),* the Court of Appeals also concluded that a Department of Education regulation expressly prohibiting retaliation does not create a private cause of action for retaliation: "Because Congress has not created a right through Title IX to redress harms resulting from retaliation, [the regulation] may not be read to create one either." *309 F.3d, at 1346.* Finally, the court held that, even if Title IX prohibits retaliation, Jackson would not be entitled to relief because he is not within the class of persons protected by the statute.

We granted certiorari, *542 U.S. 903, 159 L. Ed. 2d 266, 124 S. Ct. 2834 (2004),* to resolve a conflict in the Circuits over whether Title IX's private right of action encompasses claims of retaliation for complaints about sex discrimination. Compare *Lowrey v. Texas A & M Univ. System, 117 F.3d 242, 252 (CA5 1997)* ("[T]itle IX affords an implied cause of action for retaliation"); *Preston v. Virginia ex rel. New River Community College, 31 F.3d 203, 206 (CA4 1994)* (same), with the case below, *supra.*

II. A. Title IX prohibits sex discrimination by recipients of federal education funding. The statute provides that "[n]o person in the United States shall, on the basis of sex, be excluded from participation in, be denied the benefits of, or be subjected to discrimination under any education program or activity receiving Federal financial assistance."*20 U.S.C. § 1681(a).* More than 25 years ago, in *Cannon v. University of Chicago*, 441 U.S. 677, 690–693, 60 L. Ed. 2d 560, 99 S. Ct. 1946 (1979), we held that Title IX implies a private right of action to enforce its prohibition on intentional sex discrimination. In subsequent cases, we have defined the contours of that right of action. In *Franklin v. Gwinnett County Public Schools*, 503 U.S. 60, 117 L. Ed. 2d 208, 112 S. Ct. 1028 (1992), we held that it authorizes private parties to seek monetary damages for intentional violations of Title IX. We have also held that the private right of action encompasses intentional sex discrimination in the form of a recipient's deliberate indifference to a teacher's sexual harassment of a student, *Gebser v. Lago Vista Independent School Dist.*, 524 U.S. 274, 290–291, 141 L. Ed. 2d 277, 118 S. Ct. 1989 (1998), or to sexual harassment of a student by another student, *Davis v. Monroe County Bd. of Ed.*, 526 U.S. 629, 642, 143 L. Ed. 2d 839, 119 S. Ct. 1661 (1999).

In all of these cases, we relied on the text of Title IX, which, subject to a list of narrow exceptions not at issue here, broadly prohibits a funding recipient from subjecting any person to "discrimination on the basis of sex."*20 U.S.C. § 1681*. Retaliation against a person because that person has complained of sex discrimination is another form of intentional sex discrimination encompassed by Title IX's private cause of action. Retaliation is, by definition, an intentional act. It is a form of "discrimination" because the complainant is being subjected to differential treatment. See generally *Olmstead v. L. C.*, 527 U.S. 581, 614, 144 L. Ed. 2d 540, 119 S. Ct. 2176 (1999) (Kennedy, J., concurring in judgment) (the "normal definition of discrimination" is "differential treatment"); see also *Newport News Shipbuilding & Dry Dock Co. v. EEOC*, 462 U.S. 669, 682, n. 22, 77 L. Ed. 2d 89, 103 S. Ct. 2622 (1983) (discrimination means "less favorable" treatment). Moreover, retaliation is discrimination "on the basis of sex" because it is an intentional response to the nature of the complaint: an allegation of sex discrimination. We conclude that when a funding recipient retaliates against a person *because* he complains of sex discrimination, this constitutes intentional "discriminationon the basis of sex," in violation of Title IX.

The Court of Appeals' conclusion that Title IX does not prohibit retaliation because the "statute makes no mention of retaliation," *309 F.3d, at 1344*, ignores the import of our repeated holdings construing "discrimination" under Title IX broadly. Though the statute does not mention sexual harassment, we have held that sexual harassment is intentional discrimination encompassed by Title IX's private right of action. *Franklin, 503 U.S., at 74–7* . . . Thus, a recipient's deliberate indifference to a teacher's sexual harassment of a student also "violate[s] Title IX's plain terms." *Davis, supra, at 64* . . . Likewise, a recipient's deliberate indifference to sexual harassment of a student by another student also squarely constitutes "discrimination on the basis of sex." *Davis, 526 U.S., at 64* . . . "Discrimination" is a term that covers a wide range of intentional unequal treatment; by using such a broad term, Congress gave the statute a broad reach. See *North Haven Bd. of Ed. V. Bell*, 456 U.S. 512, 521. . . . . .

Congress certainly could have mentioned retaliation in Title IX expressly, as it did in § 704 of Title VII of the Civil Rights Act of 1964, 78 Stat 257, as amended, 86 Stat 109, *42 U.S.C. § 2000e–3(a)* (providing that it is an "unlawful employment practice" for an employer to retaliate against an employee because he has "opposed any practice made an unlawful employment practice by [Title VII], or because he has made a charge, testified, assisted, or participated in any manner in an investigation, proceeding, or hearing under [Title VII]"). Title VII, however, is a vastly different statute from Title IX, see *Gebser, 524 U.S., at 283–284, 286–28* . . . and the comparison the Board urges us to draw is therefore of limited use. Title IX's cause of action is implied, while Title VII's is express. See *id., at 283–284*. . . . Title IX is a broadly written general prohibition on discrimination, followed by specific, narrow exceptions to that broad prohibition. See *20 U.S.C. § 1681*. By contrast, Title VII spells out in greater detail the conduct that constitutes discrimination in violation of that statute. See *42 U.S.C. §§ 2000e–2* (giving examples of unlawful employment practices), 2000e–3 (prohibiting "[o]ther unlawful employment practices," including (a) "[d]iscrimination" in the form of retaliation; and (b) the discriminatory practice of "[p]rinting or publication of notices or advertisements indicating prohibited preference . . ."). Because Congress did not list *any* specific discriminatory practices when it wrote Title IX, its failure to mention one such practice does not tell us anything about whether it intended that practice to be covered.

Title IX was enacted in 1972, three years after our decision in *Sullivan v. Little Hunting Park, Inc.*, 396 U.S. 229 (1969). In *Sullivan*, we held that Rev Stat § 1978, *42 U.S.C. § 1982*, which provides that "[a]ll citizens of the United States shall have the same right . . . as is enjoyed by white citizens . . . to inherit, purchase, lease, sell, hold, and convey real and personal property," protected a white man who spoke out against discrimination toward one of his tenants and who suffered retaliation as a result. Sullivan had rented a house to a black man and assigned him a membership share and use rights in a private park. The corporation that owned the park would not approve the assignment to the black lessee. Sullivan protested, and the corporation retaliated against him by expelling him and taking his shares. Sullivan sued the corporation, and we upheld Sullivan's cause of action under *42 U.S.C. § 1982* for "[retaliation] for the advocacy of [the black person's] cause." *396 U.S., at 237*. Thus, in *Sullivan* we interpreted a general prohibition on racial discrimination to cover retaliation against those who advocate the rights of groups protected by that prohibition.

Congress enacted Title IX just three years after *Sullivan* was decided, and accordingly that decision provides a valuable context for understanding the statute. As we recognized in *Cannon*, "it is not only appropriate but also realistic to presume that Congress was thoroughly familiar with [*Sullivan*] and that it expected its enactment [of Title IX] to be interpreted in conformity with [it]." *441 U.S., at 699.* . . .. Retaliation for Jackson's advocacy of the rights of the girls' basketball team in this case is "discrimination on the basis of sex," just as retaliation for advocacy on behalf of a black lessee in *Sullivan* was discrimination on the basis of race.

B. The Board contends that our decision in *Alexander v. Sandoval, 532 U.S. 275 (2001)*, compels a holding that Title IX's private right of action does not encompass retaliation. *Sandoval* involved an interpretation of Title VI of the Civil Rights Act of 1964, 78 Stat 252, as amended, *42 U.S.C. § 2000d et seq.*, which provides in *§ 601* that no person shall, "on the ground of race, color, or national origin, be excluded from participation in, be denied the benefits of, or be subjected to discrimination under any program or activity" covered by Title VI. *42 U.S.C. § 2000d. Section 602 of Title VI* authorizes federal agencies to effectuate the provisions in *§ 601* by enacting regulations. Pursuant to that authority, the Department of Justice promulgated regulations prohibiting funding recipients from adopting policies that had "the effect of subjecting individuals to discrimination because of their race, color, or national origin."*28 C.F.R. § 42.104(b)(2) (1999)*. The *Sandoval* petitioners brought suit to enjoin an English-only policy of the Alabama Department of Public Safety on grounds that it disparately impacted non-English speakers in violation of the regulations. Though we assumed that the regulations themselves were valid, see *532 U.S., at 281*, we rejected the contention that the private right of action to enforce intentional violations of Title VI encompassed suits to enforce the disparate-impact regulations. We did so because "[i]t is clear . . . that the disparate-impact regulations do not simply apply *§ 601*—since they indeed forbid conduct that *§ 601* permits—and therefore clear that the private right of action to enforce *§ 601* does not include a private right to enforce these regulations. "*Id., at 285* . . . . Thus, *Sandoval* held that private parties may not invoke Title VI regulations to obtain redress for disparate-impact discrimination because Title VI itself prohibits only intentional discrimination.

The Board cites a Department of Education regulation prohibiting retaliation "against any individual for the purpose of interfering with any right or privilege secured by [Title IX],"*34 C.F.R. § 100.7(e) (2004)* (incorporated by reference by *§ 106.71*), and contends that Jackson, like the petitioners in *Sandoval*, seeks an "impermissible extension of the statute" when he argues that Title IX's private right of action encompasses retaliation. Brief for Respondent 45. This argument, however, entirely misses the point. We do not rely on regulations extending Title IX's protection beyond its statutory limits; indeed, we do not rely on the Department of Education's regulation at all, because the statute *itself* contains the necessary prohibition. As we explain above . . . the text of Title IX prohibits a funding recipient from retaliating against a person who speaks out against sex discrimination, because such retaliation is intentional "discrimination on the basis of sex." We reach this result based on the statute's text. In step with *Sandoval*, we hold that Title IX's private right of action encompasses suits for retaliation, because retaliation falls within the statute's prohibition of intentional discrimination on the basis of sex.

C. Nor are we convinced by the Board's argument that, even if Title IX's private right of action encompasses discrimination, Jackson is not entitled to invoke it because he is an "indirect dvers[m]" of sex discrimination. Brief for Respondent 33. The statute is broadly worded; it does not require that the victim of the retaliation must also be the victim of the discrimination that is the subject of the original complaint. If the statute provided instead that "no person shall be subjected to discrimination on the basis of *such individual's* sex," then we would agree with the Board. Cf. *42 U.S.C. § 2000e–2(a)(1)* ("It shall be an unlawful employment practice for an employer . . . to discriminate against any individual . . . because of *such individual's* race, color, religion, sex, or national origin" (emphasis added)). However, Title IX contains no such limitation. Where the retaliation occurs because the complainant speaks out about sex discrimination, the "on the basis of sex" requirement is satisfied. The complainant is himself a victim of discriminatory retaliation, regardless of whether he was the subject of the original complaint. As we explain above . . . this is consistent with *Sullivan*, which formed an important part of the backdrop against which Congress enacted Title IX. *Sullivan* made clear that retaliation claims extend to those who oppose discrimination against others. See *396 U.S., at 237*, (holding that a person may bring suit under *42 U.S.C. § 1982* if he can show that he was "punished for trying to vindicate the rights of minorities").

Congress enacted Title IX not only to prevent the use of federal dollars to support discriminatory practices, but also "to provide individual citizens effective protection against those practices." *Cannon, 441 U.S., at 704* . . . We agree with the United States that this objective "would be difficult, if not impossible, to achieve if persons who complain about sex discrimination did not have effective protection against retaliation." Brief for United States as *Amicus Curiae* 13. If recipients were permitted to retaliate freely, individuals who witness discrimination would be loathe to report it, and all manner of Title IX violations might go unremedied as a result. See *Sullivan, supra, at 237*.

Reporting incidents of discrimination is integral to Title IX enforcement and would be discouraged if retaliation against those who report went unpunished. Indeed, if retaliation were not prohibited, Title IX's enforcement scheme would unravel. Recall that Congress intended Title IX's private right of action to encompass claims of a recipient's deliberate indifference to sexual harassment. See generally *Davis, 526 U.S. 629*. Accordingly, if a principal sexually harasses a student, and a teacher complains to the school board but the school board is indifferent, the board would likely be liable for a Title IX violation.

See generally *Gebser, 524 U.S. 274*. But if Title IX's private right of action does not encompass retaliation claims, the teacher would have no recourse if he were subsequently fired for speaking out. Without protection from retaliation, individuals who witness discrimination would likely not report it, indifference claims would be short circuited, and the underlying discrimination would go unremedied.

Title IX's enforcement scheme also depends on individual reporting because individuals and agencies may not bring suit under the statute unless the recipient has received "actual notice" of the discrimination. *Id., at 288, 289–290* . . . If recipients were able to avoid such notice by retaliating against all those who dare complain, the statute's enforcement scheme would be subverted. We should not assume that Congress left such a gap in its scheme.

Moreover, teachers and coaches such as Jackson are often in the best position to vindicate the rights of their students because they are better able to identify discrimination and bring it to the attention of administrators. Indeed, sometimes adult employees are "'the only effective dversary[ies]'" of discrimination in schools. See *Sullivan, supra, at 237* . . .

D. The Board is correct in pointing out that, because Title IX was enacted as an exercise of Congress' powers under the Spending Clause, see, *e.g., Davis, supra, at 640*, . . ., "private damages actions are available only where recipients of federal funding had adequate notice that they could be liable for the conduct at issue," *Davis, supra, at 640*. When Congress enacts legislation under its spending power, that legislation is "in the nature of a contract: in return for federal funds, the States agree to comply with federally imposed conditions."*Pennhurst StateSchool and Hospital v. Halderman, 451 U.S. 1, 17 (1981)*. As we have recognized, "[t]here can . . . be no knowing acceptance [of the terms of the contract] if a State is unaware of the conditions [imposed by the legislation on its receipt of funds]."*Ibid.*

The Board insists that we should not interpret Title IX to prohibit retaliation because it was not on notice that it could be held liable for retaliating against those who complain of Title IX violations. We disagree. Funding recipients have been on notice that they could be subjected to private suits for intentional sex discrimination under Title IX since 1979, when we decided *Cannon*. *Pennhurst* does not preclude private suits for intentional acts that clearly violate Title IX. *Davis, supra, at 642*.

Indeed, in *Davis*, we held that *Pennhurst* did not pose an obstacle to private suits for damages in cases of a recipient's deliberate indifference to one student's sexual harassment of another, because the deliberate indifference constituted intentional discrimination on the basis of sex. *Davis, supra, at 650* . . . Similarly, we held in *Gebser* that a recipient of federal funding could be held liable for damages under Title IX for deliberate indifference to a teacher's harassment of a student. *524 U.S., at 287–28.* In *Gebser*, as in *Davis*, we acknowledged that federal funding recipients must have notice that they will be held liable for damages. See *Davis, supra, at 642* . . . But we emphasized that "this limitation on private damages actions is not a bar to liability where a funding recipient intentionally violates the statute." *Davis, supra, at 642* . . . Simply put, "*Pennhurst* does not bar a private damages action under Title IX where the funding recipient engages in intentional conduct that violates the clear terms of the statute." *Davis, supra, at 642* . . .

Thus, the Board should have been put on notice by the fact that our cases since *Cannon*, such as *Gebser* and *Davis*, have consistently interpreted Title IX's private cause of action broadly to encompass diverse forms of intentional sex discrimination. Indeed, retaliation presents an even easier case than deliberate indifference. It is easily attributable to the funding recipient, and it is always—by definition—intentional. We therefore conclude that retaliation against individuals because they complain of sex discrimination is "intentional conduct that violates the clear terms of the statute," *Davis, 526 U.S., at 642*, and that Title IX itself therefore supplied sufficient notice to the Board that it could not retaliate against Jackson after he complained of discrimination against the girls' basketball team.

The regulations implementing Title IX clearly prohibit retaliation and have been on the books for nearly 30 years. Cf., *e.g., id., at 643* (holding that Title IX's regulatory scheme "has long provided funding recipients with notice that they may be liable for their failure to respond to the discriminatory acts of certain nonagents"). More importantly, the Courts of Appeals that had considered the question at the time of the conduct at issue in this case all had already interpreted Title IX to cover retaliation. See, *e.g., Lowrey, 117 F.3d, at 252; Preston, 31 F.3d, at 206*. The Board could not have realistically supposed that, given this context, it remained free to retaliate against those who reported sex discrimination. Cf. *Davis, supra, at 644* (stating that the common law of torts "has put schools on notice that they may be held responsible under state law for their failure to protect students from the tortious acts of third parties"). A reasonable school board would realize that institutions covered by Title IX cannot cover up violations of that law by means of discriminatory retaliation.

To prevail on the merits, Jackson will have to prove that the Board retaliated against him *because* he complained of sex discrimination. The amended complaint alleges that the Board retaliated against Jackson for complaining to his supervisor, Ms. Evelyn Baugh, about sex discrimination at EnsleyHigh School. At this stage of the proceedings, "[t]he issue is not whether a plaintiff will ultimately prevail but whether the claimant is entitled to offer evidence to support the claims."*Scheuer v. Rhodes, 416 U.S. 232, 236 (1974)*. Accordingly, the judgment of the Court of Appeals for the Eleventh Circuit is reversed, and the case is remanded for further proceedings consistent with this opinion.

It is so ordered. * * *

CASES ON THE SUPPLEMENTAL CD

Deli v. University of Minnesota, 863 F. Supp. 958 (D. Minn. 1994) (female coach of women's gymnastics team failed to prove comparator positions of coaches of men's team in Equal Pay Act claim; court also indicated that Title VII and the Equal Pay Act to not prohibit salary discrimination based on the gender of the athletes on the team).

Fuhr v. Sch. Dist. of Hazel Park, 364 F.3d 753 (6th Cir. 2004) (successful employment discrimination case for high school basketball coach).

Medcalf v. Trustees of the Univ. of Pa., 2001 U.S. Dist. LEXIS 10155 E.D. Pa., June 19, 2001 (male coach claimed he was best qualified candidate but did not receive interview because of his sex).

Stanley v. University of Southern California, 13 F.3d 1313 (1994) (unsuccessful pay discrimination claims under Equal Pay Act, Title VII and Title IX for women's basketball coach).

Weaver v. The Ohio State University, 71 F. Supp.2d 789 (S.D. Ohio 1998).

QUESTIONS YOU SHOULD BE ABLE TO ANSWER

1. What are the limitations of Constitutional protections against discrimination based on sex?
2. Explain the elements of an Equal Pay Act claim and how the burden of proof shifts from plaintiff to defendant and back to plaintiff as a case proceeds.
3. Explain the protection against employment discrimination under Title IX. What are the limitations of this legislation?
4. How does Title IX protect employees from employer retaliation for complaining about gender inequities within athletics programs?
5. How does the Lilly Ledbetter Fair Pay Act improve protection against pay discrimination compared to the Equal Pay Act?

REFERENCES

Cases
Cannon v. University of Chicago, 441 U.S. 677 (1979).
Deli v. University of Minnesota, 863 F. Supp. 958 (D. Minn. 1994).
Fuhr v. Sch. Dist. of Hazel Park, 364 F.3d 753 (6th Cir. 2004).
Grove City College v. Bell, 464 U.S. 555 (1984).
Jackson v. Birmingham Board of Education, 544 U.S. 167 (2005)
Ledbetter v. Goodyear Tire & Rubber Co., 550 U.S. 618 (2007)
Lowrey v. Texas A & M University, 11 F. Supp.2d 895 (S.D. Tex. 1998).
Medcalf v. Trustees of the Univ. of Pa., 2001 U.S. Dist. LEXIS 10155 E.D. Pa., June 19, 2001.
Muller v. Oregon, 208 U.S. 412 (1908)
Stanley v. University of Southern California, 13 F.3d 1313 (9th Cir. 1994).
Stanley v. University of Southern California, 178 F.3d 1069 (9th Cir. 1999).
Weaver v. The Ohio State University, 71 F. Supp.2d 789 (S.D. Ohio 1998).

Publications
Acosta, V., & Carpenter, L. (2016). Women in intercollegiate sport—A longitudinal, National study—Thirty-seven year update,. at http://acostacarpenter.org

Anderson, P. & Osborne, B. (2008). A Historical Review of Title IX Litigation. *Journal of Legal Aspects of Sport*, 18(1), 127–168.

Lapchick, R. (2015/16). Racial and Gender Report Card at http://www.tidesport.org/reports.html

Osborne, B. & Yarbrough, M.V. (2001). Pay Equity for Coaches and Athletic Administrators: An Element of Title IX? *University of Michigan Journal of Law Reform*, 34(1&2), 231–251.

Press Release (2003 October 9). EEOC Resolves Sex Discrimination Lawsuit Against NBA's Phoenix Suns and Sports Magic for $104,500. Retrieved from the U.S. Equal Employment Opportunity Commission website on April 7, 2009, at http://www.eeoc.gov/oress/10-9-03b.html

Women's Sports Foundation (n.d.). Coaching-Do Female Athletes Prefer Male Coaches?: The Foundation Position. Retrieved May 4, 2009, from http://www.womenssportsfoundation.org/Content/Articles/Issues/Coaching/C/Coaching—Do-Female-Athletes-Prefer-Male-Coaches-The-Foundation-Position.aspx

Legislation

Civil Rights Act of 1987 (Pub. L. No. 100–259, 102 Stat. 28).
EEOC Notice Number 915.002, *Enforcement Guidance on Sex Discrimination in the Compensation of Sports Coaches in Educational Institutions* (Oct. 29, 1997). Retrieved on May 1, 2009, from http://www.eeoc.gov/policy/docs/coaches.html
Elliott-Larsen Civil Rights Act, Mich. C. L. § 37.2101 (2009).
Equal Pay Act of 1963, 29 U.S.C. § 206(d).
Fair Labor Standards Act of 1938, 52 Stat. 1060.
Ill. Const. Art. 1, Sec. 17 (2009).
Lilly Ledbetter Fair Pay Act, 111 P.L. 2 (2009).
Pregnancy Discrimination Act of 1978 (42 U.S.C.A. §2000e(k)).
Title VII of Civil Rights Act of 1964, 42 U.S.C. § 2000 2(a)(1)(2).
Title IX of the Educational Amendments of 1972, 20 U.S.C. § 1681–1688.

TITLE VII OF THE CIVIL RIGHTS ACT OF 1964

Stephanie A. Tryce | Saint Joseph's University
Lisa Pike Masteralexis | University of Massachusetts - Amherst

The Civil Rights Act of 1964 is a comprehensive federal law prohibiting discrimination in many settings, including elections, housing, federally funded programs, education, employment, and public facilities and accommodations. Title VII of the Civil Rights Act addresses employment discrimination and is the focal point of the act. It became the first comprehensive federal law prohibiting employment discrimination. Generally, a distinction that is made on the basis of an employee's characteristics (race, gender, religion, national origin) is discriminatory under Title VII.

FUNDAMENTAL CONCEPTS

Scope

Title VII broadly prohibits discrimination in employment. Section 703 (a) states:

> *It shall be an unlawful employment practice for an employer—(1) to fail or refuse to hire or to discharge any individual, or otherwise discriminate against any individual with respect to his compensation, terms, conditions, or privileges of employment, because of such individual's race, color, religion, sex, or national origin; or (2) to limit, segregate, or classify his employees or applicants for employment in any way which would deprive or tend to deprive any individual of employment opportunities or otherwise adversely affect his status as an employee, because of such individual's race, color, religion, sex, or national origin [42 U.S.C. §§ 2000e-2(a)].*

Title VII applies to employers with fifteen or more employees working at least twenty calendar weeks whose organizations affect interstate commerce. Employers can be individuals, partnerships, joint ventures, corporations, unincorporated associations, and government entities. The definition also includes employment agencies and labor organizations (unions or players associations). Title VII, however, excludes from its definition of employer the U.S. government and some departments of the District of Columbia, Native American tribes, and bona fide membership clubs, such as country clubs.

Graves v. Women's Professional Rodeo Association, Inc. ("WPRA") (1990), provides a clear example that professional associations, which sanction events, will not be considered employers unless they clearly fit the definition of employer. In *Graves*, a male rodeo barrel racer charged that the defendant nonprofit association, which organized female rodeo contestants and sanctioned events, had discriminated against him on the basis of gender when it denied him membership. WPRA was not an "employer" under Title VII because its members were not employees. WPRA did not pay wages, withhold taxes, or pay insurance for members. Furthermore, rules only permitted an opportunity for members to compete for prize money raised by rodeo sponsors, not by the WPRA. Similarly, in *Day v. Jeannette Baseball Association et al* (2013), the court concluded the male plaintiff was a volunteer baseball coach for the Jeannette Baseball Association, for which he received no compensation or benefits. The court in granting the defendant's motion for summary judgment concluded Jeannette Baseball Association was not a business, but a community voluntary organization and its volunteer coaches were not employees and therefore it is not an "employer" under Title VII.

Administration of Title VII
A five-member, presidential-appointed administrative agency, the Equal Employment Opportunity Commission ("EEOC") is charged with the administration of Title VII. The EEOC carries out a number of functions, including investigating charges of employment discrimination. It attempts to conciliate alleged violations. Where the EEOC does not find reasonable cause to go forward with conciliation or where conciliation is not fruitful, the complaining party may proceed with a private Title VII lawsuit. The EEOC may also file suit in federal district court to enforce Title VII, or it may intervene in any private employment discrimination lawsuit. For example, in *EEOC v. National Broadcasting Co., Inc.*, the EEOC sued on behalf of a female applicant for the position of television sports director alleging sex discrimination in violation of Title VII. Further, the EEOC creates guidelines and regulations for the interpretation of Title VII. Although the guidelines and regulations do not possess the full force and effect of law, they are subject to great judicial deference. For example, in *Meritor Savings Bank, FSB v. Vinson* (1986), the U.S. Supreme Court relied on EEOC guidelines to define hostile environment sexual harassment.

Civil Rights Act of 1991
The Civil Rights Act of 1991 established a Glass Ceiling Commission and a Glass Ceiling Initiative through the Department of Labor to examine whether a glass ceiling existed to keep women and minorities underrepresented in management and decision-making positions. Additionally, this Act amended the Civil Rights Act of 1964 to permit jury trials and compensatory and punitive damages in addition to back pay for *all* claims of intentional discrimination under Title VII, not just racial and ethnic discrimination.

Furthermore, the Civil Rights Act of 1991 prohibits "race norming," a practice whereby test scores are adjusted on the basis of race or other Title VII classification. It also adopted the defenses of "business necessity" and "job-related" practices as bases for which an employer can justify an employment practice challenged as discriminatory. Finally, the 1991 Act eliminated challenges to affirmative action consent decrees from individuals who had notice and an opportunity to object when the decree was entered or whose interests were adequately represented by another individual or organization.

Classes Protected under Title VII
Title VII prohibits employment discrimination on the basis of race, color, religion, gender, or national origin in hiring, firing, training, compensating, designating work assignments, promoting, demoting, or any other employment activity. Thus, any employment decision, practice, or policy that segregates individuals and treats them differently on the basis of the preceding classifications violates Title VII.

Race
Although much of the U.S. Civil Rights Movement focused on the treatment of African Americans, Title VII's definition of race is much broader. It is not limited to ethnological races, but protects all classes of people from dissimilar treatment, including, but not limited to Hispanics/Latinos, Native Americans, and Asian Americans.

Racial discrimination cases involving coaches and athletic directors arose from decisions made in the course of public school desegregation. For example, in *Cross v. Board of Education of Dollarway, Arkansas School District* (1975), the plaintiff, a black high school football coach at a black high school in a segregated school district, was demoted to assistant coach when his school integrated with a white high school. Cross was passed over for the position twice, and white coaches with fewer qualifications were hired. On the second instance, the school superintendent suggested the school board deviate from its policy to promote within to search outside the district for a white coach. The superintendent was of the opinion that the white players would not play for a black coach and the community was not ready for a black head coach and athletic director. The court found the school board's refusal to even consider Cross's application was clear evidence of individual disparate treatment on the basis of his race. As a result Cross was entitled to back pay equal to the difference in the amount he would have received as head coach and that which he did receive as assistant coach. Additionally, the defendant was ordered to promote Cross to the position of head football coach and athletic director or to compensate him at a salary comparable to the position.

In April 2005, a California jury awarded Mike Terpstra, former California State University Stanislaus men's basketball coach, $540,000 in damages in a reverse race discrimination case. Terpstra, a white male, claimed his race was a factor in the university's decision to allow his contract to expire after the 2002–2003 season, because they were interested in replacing him with a black coach. Although Terpstra was ultimately replaced with another white male coach, the jury found that race was a factor in allowing his contract to expire.

Racial discrimination has expanded to include cases where plaintiff and defendant are from the same-race. In *Ross v. Douglas County* (2001), the Eighth Circuit Court of Appeals held that an African-American employee could assert a claim of racial harassment directed toward him by his African-American supervisor's use of racial epithets. The court found that the African-American supervisor's behavior was discriminatory "whatever the motive" and that the supervisor's race "did not alter this." The case, however, does not serve to clarify the distinction between the content of the improper behavior at issue and the motivation for the behavior in the first instance. Juries are likely to have difficulty separating the racially obvert nature of the conduct from whether racial bias was the reason for the harassment in the first instance.

Color
An employer's distinction on the basis of skin pigment or the physical characteristics of an applicant or employee's race are discriminatory. For instance, if an employer favors light-skinned African Americans over dark-skinned African Americans, it is treating African Americans differently on the basis of color. Color discrimination often intersects with racial discrimination.

National Origin
In national origin discrimination cases, the focus is on one's ancestry (excluding U.S. territories such as Puerto Rico or the Virgin Islands). Title VII does not prohibit employment discrimination solely on the basis of citizenship. For example, in *Dowling v. United States* (1979), the plaintiff argued that the National Hockey League and the World Hockey Association only hired Canadian referees, and thus, discriminated against him on the basis of his national origin. The court dismissed the claim, stating that Title VII did not bar employment discrimination on the basis of alienage or citizenship. However, the lack of U.S. citizenship may not be used as a method of disguising discrimination that is actually based on race or national origin. An employer may follow a policy of employing only U.S. citizens, but may not give unequal treatment to different noncitizens based on their country of origin.

Sex
Title VII's sex discrimination cases have involved female plaintiffs primarily; however, it also applies to men. For example, in *Medcalf v. University of Pennsylvania* (1998), an EEOC investigation found that University of Pennsylvania ("Penn") had discriminated against male applicants when hiring the new women's crew coach. The EEOC found that Penn took extraordinary measures to recruit only female candidates, and that the university failed to interview Andrew Medcalf, its assistant men's rowing coach, even though he was highly recommended. An example is the case of *Mollaghan et al v. Varnell (2013)*, where three male coaches of the University of Southern Mississippi's (USM) woman's soccer team brought a claim of gender discrimination, sexual harassment and retaliation against Sonya Varnell, the senior women's administrator for women's sports at USM, averring that she wanted to replace the male coaches of women's teams with female coaches. Although the jury in the trial rendered a verdict for the male plaintiffs, the trial court granted a judgment notwithstanding the verdict in favor defendants Varnell and USM, with the exception of the sexual harassment claim. Upon appeal, the Supreme Court of Mississippi ruled that there was insufficient evidence to support any of the jury's verdicts, as the coaches' contracts expired and neither coach was replaced with a female.

It is the gender of the employee discriminated against, not the gender of the athletes an employee coaches, which form the basis for Title VII discrimination. The plaintiffs in *Jackson v. Armstrong School District* (1977) lost their Title VII claim because they alleged they were paid less money because they were coaching girls' basketball, rather than alleging that they were discriminated against because they were women. The defendant avoided liability by establishing that men coaching girls' basketball were paid the same amount as the women.

The theory of sexual harassment comes from this section of the Act. Liability for sexual harassment was introduced as a legal theory in the late 1970s and continues to evolve, with the most recent decisions focusing on same-sex harassment and employer liability (both are discussed in Section 7.14, *Sexual Harassment*).

Historically, Title VII's protection against sex-based discrimination did not include discrimination on the basis of sexual orientation. In 1978 Congress amended Title VII's language "on the basis of sex" to include protection against discrimination on the basis of pregnancy, childbirth, or other related medical conditions (including abortion). Although Title VII does not protect against sexual orientation discrimination in the workplace, twenty-two states have added protection against discrimination on the basis of sexual orientation in their employment discrimination laws. At the same time, and possibly in response to this movement, a number of jurisdictions have sought to prohibit homosexuality in their state and/or local governments. In *Price Waterhouse v. Hopkins* (1989), the U.S. Supreme Court stated that where the employer bases employment decisions on gender stereotyping, a Title VII claim might be sustained. The key in the determination is whether the harassment occurred because of the victim's sex. In *Bibby v. Philadelphia Coca Cola Bottling Co.*, (2001), the Third Circuit of Appeals rejected a plaintiff's claim of unlawful harassment and enumerated three ways to prove where same-sex harassment occurred on account of the victim's sex: "(1) proof that the harasser sexually desires the victim; (2) proof that the harasser displays hostility to the presence of a particular sex in the workplace; and (3) proof that the harasser's conduct was motivated by a belief that the victim failed to conform to the stereotypes of his or her gender" (*Bibby v. Philadelphia Coca Cola Bottling Co.*, 2001),

The scope of Title VII sex discrimination claims now also includes transsexual. In *Smith v. City of Salem* (2004), the Sixth Circuit Court of Appeals held that a transsexual has a viable cause of action under Title VII if he is discriminated against because of his failure to conform to sex stereotypes by exhibiting less masculine and more feminine mannerisms and appearance or vice versa. The Sixth Circuit, relying on *Price Waterhouse*, found that "sex" encompasses both the biological differences between men and women, and gender discrimination, which are based on the failure to conform to stereotypical gender norms. Although Title VII does not expressly protect against sexual orientation discrimination,, it is possible that the decision in *Salem* could be used by the Lesbian, Gay, Bisexual, Transgender, Questioning/Queer Intersex and Asexual ("LBGTQIA") community to bring claims under Title VII by asserting that they have been discriminated against for failure to conform to stereotypical gender norms. Further supporting LGBTQIA protection under Title VII, in a July 2015 historic decision in *Complainant v. Anthony Foxx*, (2015) regarding same-sex employment discrimination the EEOC concluded "that sexual orientation is inherently a "sex-based consideration" and allegation of discrimination based on sexual orientation is necessarily an allegation of sex discrimination under Title VI."

Religion
All well recognized faiths and even those considered unorthodox (provided the court is convinced that the purported belief is sincere and genuinely held, and not simply adopted for an ulterior motive) are protected under Title VII. An employer must make *a reasonable accommodation* to an employee's religious practices and observances, unless it would place an **undue hardship** on the employer. An employer's obligation is simply to make a reasonable accommodation to an employee.

Theories of Liability
Courts applying Title VII have established four theories of liability: individual disparate treatment, systemic disparate treatment, disparate impact, and retaliation.

Individual Disparate Treatment
There are two ways to prove intentional discrimination. The first is through **direct evidence** of intent from the defendant's statements. In *Morris v. Bianchini, et al.* (1987), the plaintiff and another woman were passed over for promotion to athletic director of the health and fitness club in favor of less qualified males. The reason they were given was that the club sought "a macho, male image" for its athletic director. This statement was used as evidence of intent by the club's management to discriminate against two qualified women in favor of a less qualified candidate on the basis of gender. Another example is *Biver v. Saginaw Township Community Schools, et al.* (1986), in which the plaintiff alleged discrimination in failing to hire her for a boys' or girls' basketball

team coaching position. Accepted as evidence of the superintendent's discriminatory intent, the court cited his statement that "hell would freeze over before he would hire a woman for a boys' coaching position" (*Biver v. Saginaw Township Community Schools*, et al., 1986). The superintendent claimed it was not discriminatory, as his policy was to hire men to coach boys and women to coach girls. The plaintiff challenged his credibility by showing many instances in which he had hired men to coach girls.

A second method by which one can prove discrimination is through the use of an ***inference***. A plaintiff can establish an inference for the court by comparing how an employer treats similarly situated employees of different protected classes. The model for using an inference to prove discriminatory intent was established in *McDonnell Douglas Corp. v. Green*, (1973). The McDonnell Douglas model is as follows:

> "[f]irst, the plaintiff has the burden of proving by the preponderance of the evidence a prima facie case of discrimination. Second, if the plaintiff succeeds in proving the prima facie case the burden shifts to the defendant 'to articulate some legitimate nondiscriminatory reason for the employee's rejection.' Third, should the defendant carry this burden, the plaintiff must then have an opportunity to prove by a preponderance of the evidence that the legitimate reasons offered by the defendant were not its true reasons, but were a pretext for discrimination" (*McDonnell Douglas Corp. v. Green*, 1973).

Under this widely relied upon standard, a ***prima facie case*** is established by the plaintiff showing:
(If applicant)

1. Applicant is a member of a protected class,
2. Applicant applied for a job for which the employer was seeking applicants
3. Applicant was qualified to perform the job,
4. Applicant was not hired, and
5. Employer continues to seek applicants after rejection.

(If employee)

1. Employee is within the protected class,
2. Employee was performing the task satisfactorily,
3. Employee was discharged or adversely affected by change in working conditions, and
4. Employee's work was assigned to one in a nonminority category.

The burden then shifts to the defendant to rebut the plaintiff's presumption by producing evidence that the plaintiff was rejected and someone else preferred for a ***legitimate, nondiscriminatory reason*** (*Texas Department of Community Affairs v. Burdine*, 1981). The defendant's burden is one of production, not persuasion. For the reason to be legitimate, it must be lawful, clear, and reasonably specific. In other words, when comparing the chosen applicant or employee with the plaintiff, the defendant should elaborate on the criteria necessary for hiring or promotion, the basis for the comparison of the candidates, and that the person hired or promoted, rather than the plaintiff, possessed the qualities the defendant was seeking (*Herman v. National Broadcasting Co., Inc.*, 1984). The defendant need not prove that the chosen employee was a superior candidate, but simply that there were legitimate, nondiscriminatory reasons to justify the employer's decision. It is difficult for a defendant to raise this defense without clear qualification criteria for hiring. For instance, in *Jackson v. World League of American Football* (1994), the court refused to grant summary judgment in a racial discrimination case where the World League of American Football had not set clear qualifications for the position of head football coach. Once the employer provides a legitimate, nondiscriminatory reason for the alleged discrimination, the burden then shifts back to the employee to prove that the legitimate reason is in fact a ***pretext*** for intentional discrimination. A plaintiff may establish evidence of pretext by:

1. providing direct evidence of prejudice toward the plaintiff or members of the protected class,
2. presenting statistical evidence, and
3. presenting comparative evidence that members of a protected class were treated less favorably or members of the majority were treated favorably.

An example of the last point occurred in *Davis v. McCormick* (1995), where a female coach was subject to a more stringent disciplinary policy and her discipline was arguably more severe than any male coach's discipline.

The court found that this raised a reasonable inference that the plaintiff's discipline was a pretext for intentional discrimination. In *Riley v. Birmingham Board of Education* (2005), the plaintiff, a white male, alleged that board decided not to renew his head coaching position, nor appoint his as a head coach for another school, but instead designate him as an assistant coach was discrimination on the basis of race. As evidence, the plaintiff offered that the school's principal, a black female, made a statement about "taking care of our own." The court concluded that this statement was not direct evidence of discrimination because it was not made during the decision making process. The court explained that under the McDonnell Douglas framework, an inferential step was required before concluding that the statement was race-based and that the reasons offered for the nonrenewal of his contract were a pretext.

A plaintiff may also present the fact that the legitimate, nondiscriminatory reason was not given to the plaintiff at the time the employment decision was made as evidence that it was an afterthought and, thus, a pretext. For example, in *Baylor v. Jefferson County Board of Education* (1984), a black teacher-coach proved the defendant school board's transfer of him to a teaching-only position was racially motivated. Baylor successfully proved that the defendant's legitimate, nondiscriminatory reason for the job transfer was developed after his hearing and decision to transfer him out of coaching were made.

Finally, failing to comply with the usual hiring procedures may indicate discriminatory actions. For instance, as noted earlier in *Cross* (1975), the school superintendent suggested that the school board deviate from its policy of promoting from within to search outside the district for a white coach. In *Peirick, v. Indiana University-Purdue* (2005), the Court refused to grant summary judgment in a sex discrimination case where the plaintiff offered sufficient evidence that demonstrated "either that a discriminatory reason more likely motivated the employer or that the employer's proffered explanation is unworthy of credence" (*Peirick, v. Indiana University-Purdue*, 2005).

Harassment. The Supreme Court in *Meritor Savings Bank, FSB v. Vinson* (1986), stated the EEOC "has held and continues to hold that an employer has a duty to maintain a working environment free of harassment based on race, color, religion, sex, [or] national origin . . . and that the duty requires positive action where necessary to eliminate such practices or remedy their effects" (*Meritor Savings Bank, FSB v. Vinson*, 1986). Courts have applied this theory to harassment on the basis of race (*Johnson v. NFL*), religion (*Compston v. Borden, Inc.*, 1976), national origin (*Cariddi v. Kansas City Chiefs Football Club*, 1977), and gender (*Meritor Savings Bank, FSB v. Vinson*, 1986). By far, the application of the harassment theory is most developed for discrimination on the basis of sex. A thorough discussion of sexual harassment is found in Section 7.14, *Sexual Harassment*.

Systemic Disparate Treatment

Under the theory of systemic disparate treatment, plaintiffs challenge broad sweeping employment policies that are discriminatory, such as an employer's policy not to hire women or to segregate employees by race. A plaintiff's initial burden is to "establish by preponderance of the evidence that discrimination is an employer's standard operating procedure—the regular, rather than the unusual practice" (*Lowery v. Circuit City*, 1998, quoting *Teamsters v. United States*, 1977). This creates an inference that hiring or promotion practices were made in furtherance of this discriminatory policy.

When challenging system wide patterns or practices, plaintiffs often rely on statistical evidence bolstered with evidence of individual discriminatory treatment. The statistics will compare the racial, ethnic, or gender balance of the qualified labor population with the population of a workforce that draws employees from that population. In *Teamsters v. United States* (1977), the court stated that statistics showing an imbalance are probative because such imbalance is often a telltale sign of purposeful discrimination. Absent discrimination, it is assumed that over time nondiscriminatory workplace practices will result in a workforce that is representative of a region's general population.

Once a plaintiff establishes a presumption of a discriminatory pattern or practice, the burden then shifts to the employer to demonstrate why an inference of discrimination could not be drawn from the plaintiff's evidence. Here the defendant has two options. First, the defendant can attack the plaintiff's statistical evidence as inaccurate or insignificant. Second, the employer may seek to provide a nondiscriminatory explanation for the apparently discriminatory result. As with individual disparate treatment, once a defendant produces this explanation, the burden will shift to the plaintiff to persuade the court that the defendant's stated explanation is in fact a pretext for discrimination.

Disparate Impact

Disparate impact discrimination exists where a plaintiff is challenging a neutral employment practice, regardless of intent, that has a discriminatory effect on a protected group. This model only applies where the employer has instituted a specific procedure, usually a criterion for employment, which the plaintiff can show has a causal connection with a protected class's imbalance in the workforce (*Pouncy v. Prudential Insurance Co. of America*, 1982).

The prima facie case requires proof that the employment practice or policy has an adverse impact on the protected group to which the employee belongs. This is usually established through statistical evidence documenting the impact of the practice on the protected class. The use of statistical evidence is difficult and the plaintiff's methodology may be attacked as flawed. For instance, in *Wynn v. Columbus Municipal Separate School District* (1988), a female coach used the disparate impact model to challenge her employer's practice of having the head football coach also serve as the athletic director. She argued that the practice had a disparate impact on females, because it was extremely rare that a female would be qualified to be a head football coach. The plaintiff presented statistical evidence from her state of Mississippi. Of the 192 high school athletic directors in the state only 62 were not head football coaches, no women were head football coaches, and just two athletic directors were women. The court found her theory flawed on two grounds. First, the fact that few women in Mississippi were selected to serve as athletic director had little relationship to the issue of whether the defendant, Columbus School District, discriminates against women as athletic director. Second, the plaintiff's statistical evidence is drawn from a pool that includes not only females from the protected class, but a number of nonmembers of that class, namely males who are not qualified as football coach and thus, are denied the athletic director position. The court stated the better approach would be to consider the discriminatory treatment of qualified female coaches in the Columbus schools who had been denied the position of athletic director. Thus, the plaintiff lost on her disparate impact claim, but was successful under her disparate treatment theory.

In addition to attacking statistical evidence, an employer may also rebut the plaintiff's argument by producing evidence that the practice is "job-related." This requires proof that the challenged employment practice is necessary to achieve some legitimate business objective, the practice actually achieves that objective, and there is no reasonable alternative for accomplishing the objective without discriminating. Once the employer establishes the barrier is "job-related," the burden shifts back to the plaintiff to prove that the barrier is a pretext for discrimination, by showing there are other adequate devices that do not discriminate against a protected class.

Retaliation

Title VII provides a cause of action for retaliation in response to a plaintiff's filing of a claim of employment discrimination. Section 704 (a) of Title VII states:

> *it shall be an unlawful employment practice for an employer to discriminate against any of his employees . . . because [that employee] has opposed any practice made an unlawful employment practice by this title or because he has made charge, testified, assisted or participated in any manner in an investigation proceeding, or hearing under this title [42 U.S.C. § 2000e-3(a)].*

The plaintiff's burden of proof in retaliation claims mirrors that in other Title VII suits. The plaintiff bears the initial burden of establishing a prima facie case of retaliation. To establish the prima facie retaliation case, the plaintiff must show by a preponderance of the evidence that (1) the plaintiff engaged in a statutorily protected activity, (2) adverse action was taken against the plaintiff by the employer subsequent to and contemporaneously with such activity, and (3) a causal link exists between the protected activity and the adverse action (*Jalil v. Advel Corp.*, 1989). Once the plaintiff has established a prima facie case, the defendant may introduce evidence providing legitimate, non-retaliatory reasons for its conduct. If the defendant properly introduces such evidence, the burden shifts back to the plaintiff to show that the defendant's justification is merely pretext for unlawful retaliation. See *Lowery v. Texas A&M University d/b/a Tarleton State University* (1998), where a Lowery, former women's basketball coach, alleged that defendants were liable under Title VII, Title IX, 42 U.S.C. §1983 and the Constitution's First and Fourteenth Amendments for retaliating against her by removing her as Women's Athletics Coordinator in response to comments she made criticizing the university and its officials on gender equity issues.

Additional Defenses

Bona Fide Occupational Qualification

It is not illegal to discriminate on the basis of religion, gender, or national origin if an employer can show the classification is a bona fide occupational qualification (BFOQ). Race and color are never BFOQs. The BFOQ defense requires the employer to prove that members of the excluded class could not safely and effectively perform essential job duties and the employer must have a factual basis for believing that persons in the excluded class could not perform the job. The BFOQ must also be reasonably necessary to the normal operation of the business. An example might be a situation where a boys' overnight recreational program hires only male floor counselors. If the counselors will live in dorms with the boys, the recreation program may prefer males for the comfort of the boy campers and for role modeling. Finally, customer preference cannot be the basis for a BFOQ.

Business Necessity

Business necessity serves as a defense to a disparate impact discrimination claim, where a particular practice causes a protected class to face discrimination. The employer may prove that a particular practice is "job related" and thus a business necessity despite the discriminatory impact of the practice (*Griggs v. Duke Power Co.*, 1971).

Affirmative Action

Affirmative action involves creating policies for giving preference to those underrepresented in the workplace. The policies often possess goals/timetables for increasing percentages of underrepresented workers to rectify past discrimination. The affirmative-action policy may be voluntary or court ordered as a result of a lawsuit. Affirmative action policies often result in discrimination against the overrepresented classes, termed reverse discrimination. It is legal provided:

- The discrimination results from a formal, systematic program,
- The program is temporary, operating only until its goals are reached,
- The program does not completely bar the hiring/promotion of non-minorities,
- The program does not result in the firing of non-minority workers,
- The program does not force the employer to hire/promote unqualified workers.

Where the program is court-ordered, it must be based on actual evidence of discrimination. Where the program is voluntary, it must be based actual evidence of discrimination or evidence that those in underrepresented groups had been underutilized in the past.

Remedies

Section 706(g) provides the following power to remedy employment discrimination under Title VII:

> *If the court finds that the respondent has intentionally engaged in or is intentionally engaging in an unlawful employment practice . . . the court may enjoin the respondent from engaging in such unlawful employment practice, and order such affirmative action as may be appropriate, which may include, but is not limited to, reinstatement or hiring of employees with or without back pay . . . or any other equitable relief as the court deems appropriate. . .*

A successful plaintiff most often is awarded back pay. A back pay order requires the defendant to pay all lost wages and benefits that would have been earned were it not for the illegal discrimination. The trial court may grant interest on these wages.

SIGNIFICANT CASE

The following case is an example of a Title VII lawsuit involving a retaliation claim. The employees argued that they were dismissed due to their opposition to the NFL's discriminatory employment practices.

THOMAS V. NATIONAL FOOTBALL LEAGUE PLAYERS ASSOCIATION
U.S. Court of Appeals for the District of Columbia Circuit
131 F.3d 198 (1997)

A principal claim in this case is that the defendant, acting pursuant to "mixed motives," unlawfully retaliated against the plaintiffs in violation of Title VII, 42 U.S.C. § 2000e et seq. (1994). The issues on appeal require us to delimit the requirements of *McDonnell Douglas Corp. v. Green*, 411 U.S. 792, (1973), *Texas Dep't of Community Affairs v. Burdine*, 450 U.S. 248 (1981), and *Price Waterhouse v. Hopkins*, 490 U.S. 228 (1989), with respect to a plaintiff's *prima facie* case, a defendant's burden of production, and the ultimate burdens of persuasion, in a retaliation/mixed-motives case.

The actions giving rise to this lawsuit occurred when Eugene Upshaw, Executive Director of the National Football League Players Association ("NFLPA"), first laid off, then terminated employees Valerie Thomas and Rita Raymond on the stated grounds that they had been disloyal in criticizing NFLPA staff and policies in an anonymously distributed document and in several legally taped telephone calls. Julie Taylor-Bland (Bland at the time of the events) resigned in the aftermath of the firing of the other two. Before leaving the employ of the NFLPA, Thomas and Bland had suggested to management that NFLPA promotion policy discriminated against African-American women. The three women subsequently sued the NFLPA, charging that the lay-off and discharge of Thomas and Raymond, and the alleged constructive discharge of Bland, came in retaliation to their opposition to discriminatory employment practices, and hence violated Title VII.

After trial, the District Court granted judgment as a matter of law to the NFLPA on the plaintiffs' claim that there existed a pattern and practice of discrimination at the NFLPA. * * * It then found that Thomas had been unlawfully fired, that Raymond had not made out a *prima facie* case of retaliation, and that Bland had not been fired at all. The trial court granted Thomas back pay and prejudgment interest, but declined to reinstate her. *Thomas, et al., v. National Football League Players Ass'n*, 941 F. Supp. 156 (D.D.C. 1996), *reprinted in* J.A. 279. * * *Thomas, et al., v. National Football League Players Ass'n*, No. 91-3332 (D.D.C. Nov. 26, 1996). The NFLPA now appeals the decision adverse to it; Thomas, Raymond, and Bland cross appeal the decisions adverse to them.

We affirm the District Court's judgment on the merits as to Thomas, Raymond, and Bland's claims.

* * *

I. BACKGROUND

In 1988, Thomas, Raymond, and Bland worked for the NFLPA and belonged to Office and Professional Employees International Union, Local 2 ("Local 2"). After the NFLPA's unsuccessful strike against the owners during the 1987 season, the NFLPA's finances suffered, and Executive Director Upshaw devised a new budget for the NFLPA, which sought to reduce personnel costs through attrition. The board of directors of the NFLPA met during the first week of March 1988, and elected George Martin president and Mike Davis vice president. The board declined to adopt Upshaw's proposed budget, instead demanding a ten percent reduction in personnel costs by layoff.

Thomas, Bland and others complained about promotional opportunities for African-Americans and women in the Local 2 bargaining unit to Martin in an informal meeting. Sometime after March 10, 1988, Martin organized a second meeting, which Thomas and Bland also attended. Similar concerns were raised, and someone present accused Upshaw of racism.

In the weeks that followed, Martin and Davis conducted personal and telephone interviews with staff on a range of employment-related subjects. Interviewees were assured of confidentiality. In their interviews, Thomas and Bland expressed views on race and sex discrimination at the NFLPA. Davis also interviewed Raymond. Around the same time, Upshaw implemented the NFLPA board's directive to lay off some employees to cut costs. Prior to the lay-offs, Upshaw heard from Davis that Thomas and Raymond had criticized various employees in telephone conversations with Davis, and were suspected of producing and circulating a document harshly critical of the NFLPA. The document was headed and referred to as "What every player should know about the NFLPA." It included, among other allegations, a variety of claims about unfair promotion practices at the NFLPA. It did not include allegations of racial discrimination.

On March 18, 1988, Upshaw laid off six employees, including Thomas and Raymond. At a time proximate to the lay-offs, Martin undertook to investigate the employees' allegations of misconduct at the NFLPA, and asked Upshaw about minority issues at the NFLPA. Martin told Upshaw that Thomas had called him a racist and had complained about promotion of African-Americans and women. Martin and Davis each gave copies of the "What every player should know" memorandum to Upshaw. Davis told Upshaw about his telephone conversations with Thomas and Raymond and that Raymond had mailed him a copy of the memorandum.

On March 23, 1988, Davis gave Upshaw tapes of his telephone conversations with Thomas and Raymond. According to Upshaw's un-contradicted testimony, the conversations included ad hominem attacks on various NFLPA employees, including Upshaw. On the tapes, Raymond promised to send a copy of the "What every player should know" memorandum to Davis. Upshaw concluded that Thomas and Raymond had written the memo.

On April 12, 1988, five of the six employees laid off on March 18 were fired for cause. Upshaw sent each employee an identical letter explaining the firing on the grounds that the employees had libeled and slandered NFLPA personnel, had violated confidentiality, and had shown disloyalty towards and intentionally embarrassed the NFLPA. Upshaw later testified that he fired Thomas and Raymond for what he believed they had said and written about the NFLPA employees. Some weeks later, Bland asked Upshaw about a newly open paralegal/secretary position, and Upshaw told her that he "did not see her in the job"; on May 20, 1988, Bland resigned.

Local 2 pursued grievances against the NFLPA on behalf of Thomas and Raymond. The grievances were appealed to arbitration and an arbitrator ruled that the two had been dismissed without just cause. The arbitrator's award ordered reinstatement, but the NFLPA failed to comply. Thomas, Raymond, and Bland also filed timely charges with the Equal Employment Opportunity Commission ("EEOC"), which issued "no cause" determinations on all their claims. At trial, the District Court dismissed as a matter of law plaintiffs' claim of a pattern and practice of discrimination. It found for Thomas and awarded her back pay, without reinstatement, with prejudgment interest for twenty-one months after her firing, based on expert testimony that estimated the time it should have taken Thomas to find new employment. The District Court found against Raymond, who did not appear at trial. Finally, the District Court found that Bland had not been constructively discharged.

II. ANALYSIS

Burdens of Pleading, Production, and Persuasion Under Title VII.

Title VII makes it unlawful to retaliate against an employee who "has opposed any practice made an unlawful practice" by the statute. 42 U.S.C. § 2000e–3(a).

As in all Title VII cases, the plaintiff must first make out a *prima facie* case of unlawful employment action. *McDonnell Douglas Corp. v. Green*, 411 U.S. 792 (1973). Where retaliation is alleged, a *prima facie* case requires a showing that (1) plaintiff engaged in protected activity, (2) plaintiff was subjected to adverse action by the employer, and (3) there existed a causal link between the adverse action and the protected activity. *Mitchell v. Baldrige*, 759 F.2d 80, 86 (D.C. Cir. 1985). A rebuttable presumption of unlawful discrimination arises when a plaintiff makes out a *prima facie* case. *Texas Dep't of Community Affairs v. Burdine*, 450 U.S. 248, 254 (1981). The defendant may rebut the presumption by asserting a legitimate, nondiscriminatory reason for its actions. The defendant's responsibility at this stage has been characterized as a "burden of production," because the ultimate burden of persuasion remains with the plaintiff.

When a defendant satisfies the burden of production, the presumption of discrimination dissolves; however, the plaintiff still has the opportunity to persuade the trier of fact that the defendant's proffered reason was not the actual or sole basis for the disputed action. The plaintiff may aim to prove that a discriminatory motive was the only basis for the employer's action, or the plaintiff may seek to show that the employer was motivated by both permissible and impermissible motives. The plaintiff often will—quite reasonably—argue both alternatives. *See Price Waterhouse v. Hopkins*, 490 U.S. 228, 247 n.12 (Brennan, J.) * * * Where a plaintiff argues that discriminatory motivation constituted the only basis for the employer's action, the plaintiff may persuade the trier of fact of the pre-textual nature of the defendant's asserted reason "either directly by persuading the court that a discriminatory reason more likely motivated the employer or indirectly by showing that the employer's proffered explanation is unworthy of credence." *Burdine*, 450 U.S. at 256.

On the other hand the plaintiff argues that the action resulted from mixed motives, a slightly different model operates. A plaintiff asserting mixed motives must persuade the trier of fact by a preponderance of the evidence that unlawful retaliation constituted a substantial factor in the defendant's action. *Price Waterhouse*, 490 U.S. at 276 (O'Connor, J., concurring); *Id.* at 259 (White, J., concurring). When the plaintiff successfully shows that an unlawful motive was a substantial factor in the employer's action, the defendant may seek to prove in response that it would have taken the contested action even absent the discriminatory motive. If the defendant fails to persuade the trier of fact by a preponderance of the evidence that it would have taken the action even absent the discriminatory motive, the plaintiff will prevail.

This burden on a defendant in a mixed-motives case has been characterized both as an affirmative defense, and as a shifting burden of persuasion. Under *Price Waterhouse* a defendant who is guilty of acting pursuant to an unlawful motive may escape liability by proving that it would have made the same decision in the absence of the unlawful motivation. In short, the ultimate burden of persuasion as to the facts constituting the defense properly falls on the defendant in a mixed-motives case, because the plaintiff has proven that unlawful motivation constituted a substantial factor in the defendant's action.

APPELLANT'S CLAIMS
Meaning and Requirement of Direct Evidence
Appellant NFLPA, the defendant below, argues that, under *Price Waterhouse*, the burden of persuasion shifts to the defendant only where the plaintiff has provided "direct" rather than "inferential" evidence of discriminatory animus. We reject this contention. Under *Price Waterhouse*, the burden of persuasion shifts to the defendant when the plaintiff has shown by a preponderance of "any sufficiently probative direct or indirect evidence" that unlawful discrimination was a substantial factor in the employment decision. *White v. Federal Express Corp.*, 939 F.2d 157, 160 (4th Cir. 1991).

* * *

As this court recently noted, "the distinction between direct and circumstantial evidence has no direct correlation with the strength of [a] plaintiff's case." *Crawford-El v. Britton*, 93 F.3d 813, 818 (D.C. Cir. 1996) (*en banc*), *cert. granted*, 117 S. Ct. 2451 (U.S. 1997). The purported distinction between "circumstantial" or "inferential" and "direct" evidence urged here does not make logical sense, because the decision to shift the burden of persuasion properly rests upon the strength of the plaintiff's evidence of discrimination, not the contingent methods by which that evidence is adduced.

* * *

District Court Decision on the Merits
The District Court * * * found that Thomas engaged in protected activity by participating in two conversations with Martin in which she raised the issue of discrimination against women and African-Americans in promotion at the NFLPA, and by distributing the memo to Martin. The District Court found that the NFLPA fired Thomas "immediately following" the protected activity, and permissibly concluded that Thomas had made out a prima facie case. Because it did not find evidence that Raymond engaged in protected conduct, the District Court correctly found that Raymond had not made out a *prima facie* case. The District Court further found that Bland was not constructively discharged, because she had not presented evidence of aggravating factors making her work intolerable. Neither of these conclusions was clearly erroneous; the legal framework for both was correct.

The District Court then assessed the evidence that served to refute the NFLPA's claim that it had non-discriminatory reasons sufficient to fire Thomas. It found that the way in which the firing followed Upshaw's learning of Thomas's taped comments; the unusual security measures surrounding the firing; and Upshaw's possession of the memorandum which he believed Thomas had co-authored sufficed to prove that Thomas's firing was motivated "in substantial measure" by her protected activity. This constituted an acceptable finding of mixed motives, and was not clearly erroneous. Although the District Court did not cite *Price Waterhouse*, it correctly concluded that the burden of persuasion had shifted, and that as a result "it was NFLPA's burden to demonstrate that Thomas would have been discharged regardless of her protected activity." In the District Court's view, "the NFLPA failed to sustain that burden" in that it did not successfully separate permissible from impermissible motives in its decision. This conclusion was not clearly erroneous, either, but reflected the fact finder's assessment of the evidence surrounding the firing.

Rejection of Statistical Evidence
The District Court correctly ruled as a matter of law that plaintiffs did not make out a prima facie statistical case of a pattern and practice of discrimination on the part of the NFLPA. The crucial basis for this ruling was that plaintiffs' expert did not consider the relevant qualifications of those passed over or approved for promotion. A *prima facie* case of statistical disparity must include the minimum objective qualifications of the applicants. Here, the expert did not account for minimum qualifications. Indeed, he could not have done so, because Appellees never specifically requested qualification standards from Appellant in discovery. We need not reach the District Court's other reasons for dismissal, because even if the trial court had found adequate sample size and statistical significance (which it did not), a non-discriminatory, qualifications-based reason for the disparate impact could have existed. * * *

The Relief
The District Court awarded Thomas back pay from the date of her firing to December 1989, by which time, it found, she should have secured employment. The District Court did not abuse its discretion in weighing expert testimony regarding job availability to arrive at this time period.

* * *

The District Court did not abuse its discretion in declining to reinstate Thomas. Although the acrimony of litigation alone probably would not suffice to rule out reinstatement, *see Dickerson v. Deluxe Check Printers, Inc.*, 703 F.2d 276, 281 (8th Cir. 1983), the District Court's denial of reinstatement reflected its own observation that some of Thomas's actions "might well have warranted discharge [as it] reasonably concluded that reinstatement would not serve the interests of justice where the employee engaged in behavior that could conceivably have given rise to a legitimate discharge under other circumstances.

The District Court awarded Thomas prejudgment interest on the back pay. The presumption strongly favors prejudgment interest, but the trial court may disallow interest where attributable to substantial, unexplained delay by the plaintiff. Although Thomas reasonably awaited the EEOC's disposition of her request for a right to sue letter, which was delayed through no fault of her own, the same cannot be said of the three-year period during which Thomas and her co-plaintiffs repeatedly amended their complaint. The District Court must reconsider this issue on remand.

* * *

III. CONCLUSION

For the foregoing reasons, the judgment of the District Court is affirmed regarding Thomas, Raymond, and Bland.

So ordered.

CASES ON THE SUPPLEMENTAL CD

Lowery v. Texas A&M University System, 11 F. Supp. 2d 895 (1998). This case examines whether the university and its' officials discriminated against the coach on the basis of her sex and retaliated against her for complaining about the alleged discrimination.

Peirick v. Indiana University-Purdue University Indianapolis, 2005 U.S. Dist. LEXIS 32479. This case examines whether the university had a legitimate reason for firing an employee.

Medcalf v. University of Pennsylvania, 71 Fed. Appx. 924 2003; U.S. Appl LEXIS 16110. This reverse gender discrimination case examines whether the evidence supported the rejection of the Defendant University's proffered reason for hiring a woman over a man.

McClure v. Sports & Health Club, 370 N.W. 2d 844 (1985). The issues in this case are at the intersection of religious rights and gay rights. The Minnesota Supreme court ruled against for profit owners of a gym chain who claimed that employing individuals who lived in ways that were "antagonistic to the Bible" violated their religious beliefs.

Minnis v. Bd. Of Sup'rs of La. State Univ. and Agric. And Mech. Coll., 972 F.Supp.2d 878 (2013). The plaintiff was an African American head woman's tennis coach who was fired after twenty-one years at Louisiana State University (LSU). The plaintiff brought an employment discrimination suit; however, the court held that her claims of disparate treatment as is related to performance evaluations and a reprimand did not constitute adverse employment action, and LSU's proffered reasons for his termination were legitimate, nondiscriminatory and not pre-textual in nature.

QUESTIONS YOU SHOULD BE ABLE TO ANSWER

1. What classes are protected under Title VII?

2. How does a plaintiff establish a prima facie case of discrimination under Title VII, if the plaintiff is an applicant for a job? What if the plaintiff is an employee?

3. What are the differences between cases based on disparate impact and disparate treatment discrimination under Title VII?

4. What defenses are available to a defendant accused of violating Title VII?

5. What are the remedies available for engaging in intentional unlawful employment practices in violation of Title VII?

REFERENCES

Cases

Baylor v. Jefferson County Board of Education, 733 F.2d 1527 (11th Cir. 1984).
Bianchi v. City of Philadelphia, No. 99-CV-2409, 2002 WL 23942 (E.D. Pa. Jan 2, 2002).
Bibby v. Philadelphia Coca Cola Bottling Co., No. 00-1261 (3d Cir. August 1, 2001).
Biver v. Saginaw Township Community Schools, et al., 805 F.2d 1033 (6th Cir. 1986).

Cariddi v. Kansas City Chiefs Football Club, 568 F. Supp. 87 (8th Cir. 1977).
Complainant v. Anthony Foxx, Secretary, Department of Transportation (FAA), Appeal No. 0120133080
Compston v. Borden, Inc., 424 F. Supp. 157 (S.D. Ohio 1976).
Cross v. Board of Education of Dollarway, Arkansas School District, 395 F. Supp. 531 (E.D. Ark. 1975).
Davis v. McCormick, 898 F. Supp. 1275 (C.D. Ill. 1995).
Day v. Jeannette Baseball Association et al., 2013 U.S. Dist. LEXIS 154399
Dowling v. United States, 476 F. Supp. 1018 (D. Mass. 1979).
EEOC v. National Broadcasting Co., Inc., 753 F. Supp. 452 (S.D. N.Y. 1990).
Graves v. Women's Professional Rodeo Association, Inc., 907 F.2d 71 (8th Cir. 1990).
Griggs v. Duke Power Co., 401 U.S. 424 (1971).
Herman v. National Broadcasting Co., Inc., 774 F.2d 604 (7th Cir. 1984).
Jackson v. Armstrong School District, 430 F. Supp. 1050 (W.D. Penn. 1977).
Jackson v. World League of American Football, 65 Fair Emp. Prac. Cas. 358 (S.D. N.Y. 1994).
Johnson v. NFL, 1999 U.S. Dist. LEXIS 15983 (S.D.N.Y. October 18, 1999).
Jalil v. Advel Corp., 873 F. 2d 701 (3rd Cir. 1989).
Lowery v. Circuit City, 158 F.3d 742 (1998).
Lowery v. Texas A&M University d/b/a Tarleton State University, 11 F. Supp.2d 895 (1998).
McDonnell Douglas Corp. v. Green, 411 U.S. 792 (1973).
McClure v. Sports & Health Club, 370 N.W. 2d 844 (1985).
Medcalf v. University of Pennsylvania, 2001 U.S. Dist. Lexis 10155.
Meritor Savings Bank, FSB v. Vinson, 477 U.S. 57 (1986).
Minnis v. Bd. Of Sup'rs of La. State Univ. and Agric. And Mech. Coll., 972 F.Supp.2d 878 (2013).
Mollaghan v. Varnell, 134 S. Ct. 63 (U.S. 2013).
Morris v. Bianchini, et al., 43 Fair Emp. Prac. Cases 647 (E.D. Va. 1987).
Peirick v. Indiana University-Purdue, 2005 U.S. Dist. LEXIS 32479.
Pouncy v. Prudential Insurance Co. of America, 668 F.2d 795 (5th Cir. 1982).
Price Waterhouse v. Hopkins, 490 U.S. 228, 250-51 (1989).
Riley v. Birmingham Board of Education, 154 Fed. Appx. 114; 2005 U.S. App. LEXIS 21317
Ross v. Douglas County, 244 F.3d 620 (2001).
Smith v. City of Salem, 378 R.3d 566 (6th Cir. 2004).
Teamsters v. United States, 431 U.S. 324 (1977).
Texas Department of Community Affairs v. Burdine, 450 U.S. 248 (1981).
Wynn v. Columbus Municipal Separate School District, 692 F. Supp. 672 (N.D. Miss. 1988).

Publications
Player, M. A. (1988). *Employment discrimination law*. St. Paul, MN: West Publishing Co.
Zimmer, M. J., Sullivan, C. A., & Richards, R. F. (1988). *Cases and materials on employment discrimination.* Boston: Little, Brown, and Co.

Legislation
Title VII of the Civil Rights Act of 1964, 42 U.S.C. § 2000e et seq. (1990).

7.14 SEXUAL HARASSMENT

Barbara Osborne | University of North Carolina at Chapel Hill

With increasing numbers of girls and women participating and working in sports and recreation settings, managers today need to be aware of and prevent sexual harassment. Whether it is a health club owner promising to promote an aerobics instructor in exchange for sexual favors, a coach initiating inappropriate conversations, touching, or engaging in sexual relationships with an athlete at the club, middle school, high school, or collegiate levels, a journalist who is propositioned by a team owner, or an athlete sexually teasing or taunting a peer, sexual harassment is a major problem not only in the sports and recreation industry but in society as a whole.

FUNDAMENTAL CONCEPTS

Sexual Harassment in the Workplace

Although the Civil Rights Act of 1964 was enacted to prevent discrimination on the basis of race, color, religion, sex, or national origin, the Court did not recognize sexual harassment as sex discrimination until *Williams v. Saxbe* in 1976. In that case, the Supreme Court ruled that sexual harassment is a form of sex discrimination actionable under Title VII if the harassment places an artificial barrier on employment. Other cases, *Barnes v. Costle* (1977) and *Miller v. Bank of America* (1979) narrowly recognized sexual harassment only in situations when the subordinate's employment opportunities were conditioned on entering into a sexual relationship with a superior, commonly described as quid pro quo sexual harassment.

The Equal Employment Opportunity Commission (EEOC) is the administrative agency charged with enforcing Title VII. It was not until 1980 that the EEOC Guidelines first acknowledged sexual harassment as "discrimination because of sex". The Guidelines took a broader approach than the courts and defined sexual harassment as:

Unwelcome sexual advances, requests for sexual favors, and other verbal or physical conduct of a sexual nature constitute sexual harassment when:

1. submission to such conduct is made either explicitly or implicitly a term or condition of an individual's employment;
2. submission to or rejection of such conduct by an individual is used as the basis for employment decisions affecting such individual; or
3. such conduct has the purpose or effect of unreasonably interfering with an individual's work performance or creating an intimidating, hostile or offensive working environment.

It is important to note "unwelcome" as a key to the definition of sexual harassment. Conduct is unwelcome if the employee did not solicit or incite it and when the employee regards the conducts as undesirable or offensive. A charging party's claim will fail if the allegedly offensive conduct was "welcome." Table 1 provides a list of behaviors or actions that may be considered harassment given the circumstances.

The first condition listed in the EEOC definition refers to **quid pro quo** sexual harassment—when an employer conditions an employment benefit on some form of sexual favor. The second condition expands beyond quid pro quo behavior to all **tangible employment actions**, defined as any significant change in employment status, such as hiring, firing, failing to promote, or reassignment. Submitting to sexual advances in order to retain employment is also a tangible employment action, although there is no advancement or demotion in the employee's work status (*Jin v. Metropolitan Life Ins. Co*, 2002). The critical factor is the link between the sexual conduct and the benefit, even if the person demanding the sexual benefit is not the employer. In these cases, the courts uniformly apply strict liability in the same manner that they apply it in racial or religiously motivated cases under Title VII (see Chapter 7.13).

TABLE 1	SEXUALLY HARASSING BEHAVIORS
Behavioral	
Ogling, leering, staring, gestures, mooning, flashing	
Verbal	
Request for dates, asking personal questions, lewd comments, dirty or sexual jokes, whistling, catcalling, obscene calls, sexual comments or rumors	
Written/Visual	
Love letters, poems, obscene letters, cards, notes, posters, pictures, cartoons, graphics, sexual graffiti	
Touching	
Violation of personal space, patting, rubbing, pinching, bra-snapping, caressing, blocking movement, kissing, groping, grabbing, tackling, hazing	
Power	
Retaliation, using position to request dates or suggest sexual favors, gender-directed favoritism, disparate treatment, hazing rituals, bullying, intimidation, condescending or patronizing behavior	
Threats	
Quid pro quo demands, conditioning evaluations or references on sexual favors, retaliation for refusal to comply with requests	
Force	
Attempted rape or assault, rape, assault, pantsing, stripping, extreme forms of hazing, stalking, sexual abuse, physical abuse, vandalism	

The third condition listed in the EEOC definition of sexual harassment is commonly known as **hostile environment.** The first case recognizing hostile environment sexual harassment was *Meritor Savings Bank, FSB v. Vinson* (1986). The Supreme Court referred to the EEOC guidelines in recognizing that the repeated actions of a supervisor could so contaminate the work environment that it altered the conditions of employment. The Court also expanded the scope of Title VII to include situations that did not result in direct or tangible economic loss. However, the Supreme Court did not define what behavior would constitute a hostile environment, only stating that the harassment must be so severe that it creates an abusive working environment.

Determining whether there is a hostile environment is a three-step approach examining:

1. The totality of the circumstances;
2. Whether a reasonable person in the same or similar circumstance would find the conduct sufficiently severe or pervasive to create an intimidating, hostile or abusive work environment (objective test); and
3. Whether the plaintiff perceived the environment to be hostile or abusive (subjective test).

Totality of the Circumstances. Because sexual attraction may play a role in the day-to-day social exchange between employees, the distinction between invited, uninvited-but-welcome, offensive-but-tolerated, and flatly rejected sexual advances may be difficult to discern. An examination of the totality of the circumstances—the nature of the conduct, the context in which the incidents occurred, the frequency of the conduct, its severity and pervasiveness, whether it was physically threatening or humiliating, whether it was unwelcome, and whether it unreasonably interfered with an employee's work performance—is necessary. Whether there is a repeated pattern of relatively benign behavior or a single incident of gross behavior is not conclusive. The most important analysis is whether the conduct negatively altered the work environment.

Reviewing all the circumstances in determining whether an environment is hostile or abusive also requires both a subjective and an objective test. The **reasonable person (objective test)** requires the plaintiff to prove that the conduct is severe or pervasive enough that a reasonable person would objectively find it hostile or abusive. The **employee's perception (subjective test)** requires that the plaintiff subjectively perceive the environment to be so hostile and abusive that it altered the employment climate. However, in *Harris v. Forklift Systems*, (1993), the Supreme Court established that the plaintiff does not have to prove psychological injury to prove that she was sexually harassed.

Under the EEOC guidelines issued in 1999, an employer is always liable for the actions of a supervisor that result in a tangible effect of employment status of the victim. The employer is liable for harassment by coworkers if the employer knew or should have known of the misconduct, unless it can show that it took immediate and appropriate corrective action. Harassment by non-employees—for example customers, vendors, or club members—are the employer's responsibility under a similar negligence standard, which also takes into account the extent of the employer's control over the harasser.

The Supreme Court and the 1999 Guidance allow for an employer to avoid liability with a two-part **affirmative defense**. The employer bears the burden of proving by a preponderance of the evidence both of these elements:

1. The employer exercised reasonable care to prevent and promptly correct harassment.
2. The employee unreasonably failed to take advantage of any preventive or corrective opportunities provided by the employer or to avoid harm otherwise.

To show reasonable care to prevent and correct harassment, the employer must have established, publicized, and enforced anti-harassment policies and grievance procedures prior to the complaint of harassment. This includes handing out a copy of the policy and complaint procedure to every employee, posting them in central locations, and including them in employee handbooks. The policy and procedures should include a clear explanation of prohibited conduct, an assurance of protection from retaliation for the complainant, a clearly described complaint process, and a promise of confidentiality. The complaint procedure should also provide accessible contact people to receive complaints (although some courts have ruled that reporting to any employee in a supervisory role is sufficient). A prompt, thorough, and impartial investigation should be conducted as soon as the employer learns of a complaint. The employee should be assured that immediate and appropriate corrective measures will be taken, and the employer should initiate intermediate protective measures against further harassment. If it is determined that harassment has occurred, the employer must take immediate corrective/disciplinary action to effectively end the harassment.

The Guidance also established that the employer must show that the employee did not exercise reasonable care by taking advantage of preventive opportunities, complaint procedures, or other ways to avoid harm. A failure to complain in a timely manner about persistent harassment could eliminate the employer's liability. If some, but not all, of the harm could have been avoided by an earlier compliant, damages awarded would likely be reduced.

Once the employer has established both parts of the affirmative defense, the employee has the opportunity to rebut the employer's assertion that the employee unreasonably failed to complain or otherwise avoid harm. The 1999 Guidance lists three explanations that may be reasonable: (1) risk of retaliation, (2) employer-created obstacles in the complaint process or procedures, and (3) belief that the complaint mechanism is not effective.

Although it is illegal to retaliate against an individual for opposing employment practices that discriminate based on sex or for filing a discrimination charge, testifying, or participating in any way in an investigation, proceeding, or litigation under Title VII, research indicates that most employees who fail to report harassment fear retaliation. It is the employer's burden to prove that this fear is unwarranted. One of the easiest ways to satisfy this burden is to have and promote a complaint process that maintains confidentiality and does not punish employees who complain.

State Legislative Protection. State legislation can greatly enhance protection against sexual harassment in the workplace. In *Morehouse v. Berkshire Gas Co.*(1997), obscenely defaced photos of Morehouse were posted at the Berkshire Gas Company Fall Classic Golf Tournament (one was hung at the first tee, another was affixed to a garbage barrel at the fifth tee and was urinated on, another was attached to the flag at the ninth hole, and at least five more defaced photos were recovered from various other spots). Under *Mass. Gen. Lawsch. 151B, s 4(5)* individuals may be held liable for aiding or abetting discriminatory conduct that is prohibited under state law. Under Title VII, only the employer is liable for the acts of employees under the guidelines previously outlined in Table 1. Massachusetts legislation broadens the application of sexual harassment protection by holding individuals liable for their behavior, as well as others as aiders or abettors. This state legislation also extends the scope of responsibility of the employer, even when the supervisory employees are not acting within the scope of their employment (such as socially golfing at an outing).

Sexual Harassment in the Schools

The other major act of legislation related to sexual harassment is Title IX of the Education Act of 1972. Although it is most often referenced in relation to girls' participation in sport (see Chapter 7.11), Title IX prohibits discrimination on the basis of sex by any educational institution receiving federal funds. Sexual harassment is discrimination based on sex that is prohibited by Title IX because it disrupts and deprives students of equal access to education.

The Office of Civil Rights (OCR) in the U.S. Department of Education is responsible for enforcing Title IX. In the 2001 OCR guidance, sexual harassment is defined as it applies to educational institutions as unwelcome conduct of a sexual nature that rises to a level that denies or limits a student's ability to participate in or benefit from the school's programs.

Because the employment case law under Title VII is more developed, the courts have often referred to Title VII to guide them in Title IX cases. However, the Supreme Court takes a very different approach to institutional liability under Title IX compared to employer liability under Title VII. *Gebser v. Lago Vista Independent School District* (1998) indicates that damages under Title IX are only available when the institution has actual knowledge of the offensive behavior. The Court explicitly rejected the application of agency principles that it applies in Title VII sexual harassment cases. Relying on the "contractual nature" of Title IX, the Court reasoned that Title IX as a Spending Clause statute requires that the institution have actual notice and be deliberately indifferent to the reported behavior before it would be held liable.

For example, in *Davis v. Monroe County Board of Education* (1999), a fifth grader suffered sexual harassment by one of her classmates over several months. Although the victim and her mother repeatedly informed her teachers of the harassment, no one at the school made any effort to separate the two students (who sat next to each other in class) or to discipline the harasser. The Supreme Court concluded that student–student sexual harassment claims under Title IX should be analyzed in the same way as teacher–student sexual harassment. The Court found that schools are responsible for both preventing peer sexual harassment and for handling claims of peer sexual harassment in a prompt and effective manner once an appropriate administrator has actual notice.

The OCR Revised Sexual Harassment Guidance explains the liability of the educational institution under Title IX. If the employee engages in sexual harassment while carrying out responsibilities to provide benefits and services to students, the institution is responsible for the discriminatory conduct, remedying its effects, and preventing future occurrences whether or not it has notice of the harassment. If the employee is acting outside the scope of his or her assigned duties (and sexually harassing behavior is almost always considered outside the scope of the employee's duties), the institution must take prompt and effective action to stop the harassment and prevent its recurrence on notice of the harassment. The institution is considered to have engaged in its own discrimination if it fails to act and allows the student to be subjected to a hostile environment that denies or limits the student's ability to participate in or benefit from the school's program. The institution is responsible for peer or third-party harassment if the institution knew or reasonably should have known of the harassment and failed to take prompt and effective action. This liability is based on the contractual nature of Title IX, which promises an educational environment free from discrimination.

Whether the harasser is an employee or a peer, the victim of sexual harassment bears the burden of proving the following elements:

1. That she is a member of a protected group based on her sex
2. That she was subjected to unwelcome conduct of a sexual nature
3. That the conduct was so severe, pervasive, and objectively offensive that it denied equal access to the school's educational opportunities or benefits
4. That a school official with authority to take corrective action had actual knowledge or notice of the behavior
5. That the school official was deliberately indifferent to the conduct and failed to reasonably respond.

The Supreme Court in *Gebser v. Lago Vista Independent School District* (1998) and *Davis v. Monroe County Board of Education* (1999) did not address the issue of whether a school could raise an affirmative defense by having an effective sexual harassment policy. Schools are required by Title IX regulations to adopt and publish grievance procedures to address sexual discrimination. The procedures do not have to be specific to harassment, but should provide an effective manner for preventing and addressing sexual harassment. The OCR in 2000 reissued the following criteria for evaluating a school's grievance procedure:

1. Notice of policies and procedures must be sent to students, parents (for elementary and secondary students), and employees, including where complaints may be filed.
2. The procedure must actually be applied to complaints alleging harassment.
3. An adequate, reliable, and impartial investigation of the complaints must be conducted, including the opportunities to present witnesses and other evidence.
4. A designated, prompt time frame should be established for the complaint and investigative process.
5. Notice of the outcome of the complaint must be given to the parties involved.
6. An assurance must be made that the school will take corrective measures to eliminate current harassment and similar instances of harassment in the future.

If an educational institution implements these guidelines when developing its sexual harassment policies and procedures, it should function to reduce instances of harassment and provide protection for its students. It may also mitigate liability if a complaint is made to the OCR or a civil suit is filed.

Coach/Athlete Sexual Harassment

Although the liability of the institution is the same when the harasser is a coach and the victim is an athlete as that for teacher/student harassment, there are unique circumstances in the athletics context that merit closer attention. Although the number of female athletes has increased dramatically over the past 40 years, the percentage of female coaches has decreased. This increases the number of men coaching female athletes and also increases the opportunity and possibility of sexual harassment. Male coach/female athlete is not the only context in which sexual harassment occurs, but it is significantly greater than any other combination.

Touching, keeping track of the athlete's life outside athletics, and nicknames are routinely accepted as part of a coach–athlete relationship and could be harmless. However, this conduct should be measured by the unwelcomeness standard: conduct is unwelcome if the athlete did not request or invite it and it is offensive to the victim. The power dynamic in coach–athlete relationships (factors such as power, trust, and control) may affect the ability of a female athlete to freely consent or decline sexual contact, so administrators and coaches must measure whether the conduct is harassing by its impact on the athlete, and not just by the intent of the coach.

Peer Sexual Harassment in Athletics

Complaints of peer harassment are increasing dramatically. A female swimmer from the University of Pittsburgh filed a civil suit seeking reinstatement to the university swim team claiming she was released as a result of her complaints of harassment against a swimmer on the men's team. A former placekicker on the University of Colorado football team publicly alleged that she was sexually harassed by her teammates, which led to her transfer to the University of New Mexico. She stated that she was "treated like a piece of meat" and constantly called "names that are unrepeatable." The student–athlete indicated she reported the incidents to the coach several times during the season, but the harassment persisted. An educational institution is liable for peer harassment when the harassing conduct is reported and the administration fails to reasonably respond.

Athletics departments may also be held liable under Title IX when a student-athlete (or even a recruit) sexually assaults a student, whether the assault occurred on or off campus. The first case to find that a school may be liable was *Williams v. Board of Regents of the University System of Georgia* (2007). In this case, a female student was allegedly gang raped by three male athletes. The plaintiff claimed that the university was liable under Title IX because the coach, athletics director and university president were aware that the student–athlete who attacked the plaintiff had a history of sexual assaults before he was recruited and admitted to the university. The Eleventh Circuit Court held that given the past history of the recruited student–athlete, the institution had "before the fact notice" and should have made efforts to prevent future harassment from occurring. The Tenth Circuit Court made a similar ruling regarding the alleged rape of female students by football players and recruits at the University of Colorado (see *Simpson v. University of Colorado* in the Supplemental Web Site).

These cases, and a series of high profile situations at Yale, Notre Dame, Eastern Michigan, Wake Forest, and several other schools prompted the US Department of Education, Office for Civil Rights to distribute a Dear Colleague Letter addressing Sexual Violence in April 2011. This letter is intended to be a significant guidance document that supplements the 2001 Revised Sexual Harassment Guidance and will be provided deference by the courts.

The 2011 Dear Colleague defines sexual violence as "... physical sexual acts perpetrated against a person's will or where a person is incapable of giving consent..." (p. 1). OCR requires that a school take "immediate action to eliminate the harassment, prevent its recurrence, and address its effects" when the school knows or reasonably should know about peer harassment that creates a hostile environment (p. 4). This standard is to be applied for victims filing administrative complaints with OCR or for plaintiffs that are requesting injunctive relief. It differs from the precedent established by the Supreme Court in *Davis v. Monroe County Board of Education* (1999) which requires the plaintiff to prove that the school had actual knowledge and was deliberately indifferent in order to be compensated with monetary damages. The Office for Civil Rights is currently investigating hundreds of colleges and universities for failing to properly manage sexual assaults.

SIGNIFICANT CASE

This is the leading case of sexual harassment in the recreation industry. The Supreme Court addressed the conflict of opinions issued by the lower courts and thoroughly explains the new standards for establishing employer liability under Title VII.

BETH ANN FARAGHER V. CITY OF BOCA RATON
United States Supreme Court
524 U.S. 775 (1998)

Between 1985 and 1990, Beth Ann Faragher worked part time and during the summers as an ocean lifeguard for the Marine Safety Section of the Parks and Recreation Department of respondent, the City of Boca Raton, Florida (City). During this period, Faragher's immediate supervisors were Bill Terry, David Silverman, and Robert Gordon. In June 1990, Faragher resigned.

In 1992, Faragher brought an action against Terry, Silverman, and the City, asserting claims under Title VII, *42 U.S.C. § 1983*, and Florida law. So far as it concerns the Title VII claim, the complaint alleged that Terry and Silverman created a "sexually hostile atmosphere" at the beach by repeatedly subjecting Faragher and other female lifeguards to "uninvited and offensive touching," by making lewd remarks, and by speaking of women in offensive terms. The complaint contained specific allegations that Terry once said that he would never promote a woman to the rank of lieutenant, and that Silverman had said to Faragher, "Date me or clean the toilets for a year." Asserting that Terry and Silverman were agents of the City, and that their conduct amounted to discrimination in the "terms, conditions, and privileges" of her employment, Faragher sought a judgment against the City for nominal damages, costs, and attorney's fees.

Following a bench trial, the United States District Court for the Southern District of Florida found that throughout Faragher's employment with the City, Terry served as Chief of the Marine Safety Division, with authority to hire new lifeguards, to supervise all aspects of the lifeguards' work assignments, to engage in counseling, to deliver oral reprimands, and to make a record of any such discipline. Silverman was a Marine Safety lieutenant from 1985 until June 1989, when he became a captain. Gordon began the employment period as a lieutenant and at some point was promoted to the position of training captain. In these positions, Silverman and Gordon were responsible for making the lifeguards' daily assignments, and for supervising their work and fitness training.

The lifeguards and supervisors were stationed at the city beach and worked out of the Marine Safety Headquarters, a small one-story building containing an office, a meeting room, and a single, unisex locker room with a shower. Their work routine was structured in a "paramilitary configuration," with a clear chain of command. Lifeguards reported to lieutenants and captains, who reported to Terry. He was supervised by the Recreation Superintendent, who in turn reported to a Director of Parks and Recreation, answerable to the City Manager. The lifeguards had no significant contact with higher city officials like the Recreation Superintendent.

In February 1986, the City adopted a sexual harassment policy, which it stated in a memorandum from the City Manager addressed to all employees. In May 1990, the City revised the policy and reissued a statement of it. Although the City may actually have circulated the memos and statements to some employees, it completely failed to disseminate its policy among employees of the Marine Safety Section, with the result that Terry, Silverman, Gordon, and many lifeguards were unaware of it.

From time to time over the course of Faragher's tenure at the Marine Safety Section, between 4 and 6 of the 40 to 50 lifeguards were women. During that 5-year period, Terry repeatedly touched the bodies of female employees without invitation, would put his arm around Faragher, with his hand on her buttocks, and once made contact with another female lifeguard in a motion of sexual simulation. He made crudely demeaning references to women generally, and once commented disparagingly on Faragher's shape. During a job interview with a woman he hired as a lifeguard, Terry said that the female lifeguards had sex with their male counterparts and asked whether she would do the same.

Silverman behaved in similar ways. He once tackled Faragher and remarked that, but for a physical characteristic he found unattractive, he would readily have had sexual relations with her. Another time, he pantomimed an act of oral sex. Within earshot of the female lifeguards, Silverman made frequent, vulgar references to women and sexual matters, commented on the bodies of female lifeguards and beachgoers, and at least twice told female lifeguards that he would like to engage in sex with them. Faragher did not complain to higher management about Terry or Silverman. Although she spoke of their behavior to Gordon, she did not regard these discussions as formal complaints to a supervisor but as conversations with a person she held in high esteem. Other female lifeguards had similarly informal talks with Gordon, but because Gordon did not feel that it was his place to do so, he did not report these complaints to Terry, his own supervisor, or to any other city official. Gordon responded to the complaints of one lifeguard by saying that "the City just [doesn't] care."

In April 1990, however, two months before Faragher's resignation, Nancy Ewanchew, a former lifeguard, wrote to Richard Bender, the City's Personnel Director, complaining that Terry and Silverman had harassed her and other female lifeguards. Following investigation of this complaint, the City found that Terry and Silverman had behaved improperly, reprimanded them, and required them to choose between a suspension without pay or the forfeiture of annual leave.

On the basis of these findings, the District Court concluded that the conduct of Terry and Silverman was discriminatory harassment sufficiently serious to alter the conditions of Faragher's employment and constitute an abusive working environment. The District Court then ruled that there were three justifications for holding the City liable for the harassment of its supervisory employees. First, the court noted that the harassment was pervasive enough to support an inference that the City had "knowledge, or constructive knowledge" of it. Next, it ruled that the City was liable under traditional agency principles because Terry and Silverman were acting as its agents when they committed the harassing acts. Finally, the court observed that Gordon's knowledge of the harassment, combined with his inaction, "provides a further basis for imputing liability on [sic] the City." The District Court then awarded Faragher one dollar in nominal damages on her *Title VII claim*.

A panel of the Court of Appeals for the Eleventh Circuit reversed the judgment against the City. Although the panel had "no trouble concluding that Terry's and Silverman's conduct . . . was severe and pervasive enough to create an objectively abusive work environment," it overturned the District Court's conclusion that the City was liable. The panel ruled that Terry and Silverman were not acting within the scope of their employment when they engaged in the harassment, that they were not aided in their actions by the agency relationship, and that the City had no constructive knowledge of the harassment by virtue of its pervasiveness or Gordon's actual knowledge. * * *

Since our decision in *Meritor*, Courts of Appeals have struggled to derive manageable standards to govern employer liability for hostile environment harassment perpetrated by supervisory employees. While following our admonition to find guidance in the common law of agency, as embodied in the Restatement, the Courts of Appeals have adopted different approaches. We granted certiorari to address the divergence, and now reverse the judgment of the Eleventh Circuit and remand for entry of judgment in Faragher's favor.

II

A

Under Title VII of the Civil Rights Act of 1964, "it shall be an unlawful employment practice for an employer to fail or refuse to hire or to discharge any individual, or otherwise to discriminate against any individual with respect to his compensation, terms, conditions, or privileges of employment, because of such individual's race, color, religion, sex, or national origin." *42 U.S.C. § 2000e–2*(a)(1). We have repeatedly made clear that although the statute mentions specific employment decisions with immediate consequences, the scope of the prohibition " 'is not limited to "economic" or "tangible" discrimination,'" and that it covers more than " 'terms' and 'conditions' in the narrow contractual sense." Thus, in *Meritor* we held that sexual harassment so "severe or pervasive" as to " 'alter the conditions of [the victim's] employment and create an abusive working environment' " violates *Title VII*.

So, in *Harris*, we explained that in order to be actionable under the statute, a sexually objectionable environment must be both objectively and subjectively offensive, one that a reasonable person would find hostile or abusive, and one that the victim in fact did perceive to be so. We directed courts to determine whether an environment is sufficiently hostile or abusive by "looking at all the circumstances," including the "frequency of the discriminatory conduct; its severity; whether it is physically threatening or humiliating, or a mere offensive utterance; and whether it unreasonably interferes with an employee's work performance." Most recently, we explained that Title VII does not prohibit "genuine but innocuous differences in the ways men and women routinely interact with members of the same sex and of the opposite sex." A recurring point in these opinions is that "simple teasing," offhand comments, and isolated incidents (unless extremely serious) will not amount to discriminatory changes in the "terms and conditions of employment."

These standards for judging hostility are sufficiently demanding to ensure that Title VII does not become a "general civility code." Properly applied, they will filter out complaints attacking "the ordinary tribulations of the workplace, such as the sporadic use of abusive language, gender-related jokes, and occasional teasing." We have made it clear that conduct must be extreme to amount to a change in the terms and conditions of employment, and the Courts of Appeals have heeded this view.

While indicating the substantive contours of the hostile environments forbidden by Title VII, our cases have established few definite rules for determining when an employer will be liable for a discriminatory environment that is otherwise actionably abusive. Given the circumstances of many of the litigated cases, including some that have come to us, it is not surprising that in many of them, the issue has been joined over the sufficiency of the abusive conditions, not the standards for determining an employer's liability for them. There have, for example, been myriad cases in which District Courts and Courts of Appeals have held employers liable on account of actual knowledge by the employer, or high-echelon officials of an employer organization, of sufficiently harassing action by subordinates, which the employer or its informed officers have done nothing to stop. In such instances, the combined knowledge and inaction may be seen as demonstrable negligence, or as the employer's adoption of the offending conduct and its results, quite as if they had been authorized affirmatively as the employer's policy. * * *

Finally, there is nothing remarkable in the fact that claims against employers for discriminatory employment actions with tangible results, like hiring, firing, promotion, compensation, and work assignment, have resulted in employer liability once the discrimination was shown.

A variety of reasons have been invoked for this apparently unanimous rule. Some courts explain . . . that when a supervisor makes such decisions, he "merges" with the employer, and his act becomes that of the employer. Other courts have suggested that vicarious liability is proper because the supervisor acts within the scope of his authority when he makes discriminatory decisions in hiring, firing, promotion, and the like. Others have suggested that vicarious liability is appropriate because the supervisor who discriminates in this manner is aided by the agency relation. Finally, still other courts have endorsed both of the latter two theories.

The soundness of the results in these cases (and their continuing vitality), in light of basic agency principles, was confirmed by this Court's only discussion to date of standards of employer liability, in *Meritor*, which involved a claim of discrimination by a supervisor's sexual harassment of a subordinate over an extended period. In affirming the Court of Appeals' holding that a hostile atmosphere resulting from sex discrimination is actionable under Title VII, we also anticipated proceedings on remand by holding agency principles relevant in assigning employer liability and by rejecting three *per se* rules of liability or immunity. We observed that the very definition of employer in Title VII, as including an "agent," expressed Congress's intent that courts look to traditional principles of the law of agency in devising standards of employer liability in those instances where liability for the actions of a supervisory employee was not otherwise obvious, and although we cautioned that "common-law principles may not be transferable in all their particulars to Title VII," we cited the Restatement § 219–237, with general approval.

We then proceeded to reject two limitations on employer liability, while establishing the rule that some limitation was intended. We held that neither the existence of a company grievance procedure nor the absence of actual notice of the harassment on the part of upper management would be dispositive of such a claim; while either might be relevant to the liability neither would result automatically in employer immunity. Conversely, we held that Title VII placed some limit on employer responsibility for the creation of a discriminatory environment by a supervisor, and we held that Title VII does not make employers "always automatically liable for sexual harassment by their supervisors," contrary to the view of the Court of Appeals, which had held that "an employer is strictly liable for a hostile environment created by a supervisor's sexual advances, even though the employer neither knew nor reasonably could have known of the alleged misconduct," *477 U.S. at 69–70.*

Meritor's statement of the law is the foundation on which we build today. * * *

B

The Court of Appeals identified, and rejected, three possible grounds drawn from agency law for holding the City vicariously liable for the hostile environment created by the supervisors. It considered whether the two supervisors were acting within the scope of their employment when they engaged in the harassing conduct. The court then enquired whether they were significantly aided by the agency relationship in committing the harassment, and also considered the possibility of imputing Gordon's knowledge of the harassment to the City. Finally, the Court of Appeals ruled out liability for negligence in failing to prevent the harassment. Faragher relies principally on the latter three theories of liability.

I

A "master is subject to liability for the torts of his servants committed while acting in the scope of their employment." Restatement § 219(1). This doctrine has traditionally defined the "scope of employment" as including conduct "of the kind [a servant] is employed to perform," occurring "substantially within the authorized time and space limits," and "actuated, at least in part, by a purpose to serve the master," but as excluding an intentional use of force "unexpectable by the master."

Courts of Appeals have typically held, or assumed, that conduct similar to the subject of this complaint falls outside the scope of employment. In so doing, the courts have emphasized that harassment consisting of unwelcome remarks and touching is motivated solely by individual desires and serves no purpose of the employer. For this reason, courts have likened hostile environment sexual harassment to the classic "frolic and detour" for which an employer has no vicarious liability.

These cases ostensibly stand in some tension with others arising outside Title VII, where the scope of employment has been defined broadly enough to hold employers vicariously liable for intentional torts that were in no sense inspired by any purpose to serve the employer . . .

The proper analysis here, then, calls not for a mechanical application of indefinite and malleable factors set forth in the Restatement, but rather an enquiry into the reasons that would support a conclusion that harassing behavior ought to be held within the scope of a supervisor's employment, and the reasons for the opposite view. The Restatement itself points to such an approach, as in the commentary that the "ultimate question" in determining the scope of employment is "whether or not it is just that the loss resulting from the servant's acts should be considered as one of the normal risks to be borne by the business in which the servant is employed."

In the case before us, a justification for holding the offensive behavior within the scope of Terry's and Silverman's employment was well put in Judge Barkett's dissent: "[A] pervasively hostile work environment of sexual harassment is never (one would hope) authorized, but the supervisor is clearly charged with maintaining a productive, safe work environment. The supervisor directs and controls the conduct of the employees, and the manner of doing so may inure to the employer's benefit or detriment, including subjecting the employer to Title VII liability." It is by now well recognized that hostile environment sexual harassment by supervisors (and, for that matter, co-employees) is a persistent problem in the workplace. An employer can, in a general sense, reasonably anticipate the possibility of such conduct occurring in its workplace, and one might justify the assignment of the burden of the untoward behavior to the employer as one of the costs of doing business, to be charged to the enterprise rather than the victim.

Two things counsel us to draw the contrary conclusion. First, there is no reason to suppose that Congress wished courts to ignore the traditional distinction between acts falling within the scope and acts amounting to what the older law called frolics or detours from the course of employment. Such a distinction can readily be applied to the spectrum of possible harassing conduct by supervisors, as the following examples show. First, a supervisor might discriminate racially in job assignments in order to placate the prejudice pervasive in the labor force. Instances of this variety of the heckler's veto would be consciously intended to further the employer's interests by preserving peace in the workplace. Next, supervisors might reprimand male employees for workplace failings with banter, but respond to women's shortcomings in harsh or vulgar terms. A third example might be the supervisor who, as here, expresses his sexual interests in ways having no apparent object whatever of serving an interest of the employer. If a line is to be drawn between scope and frolic, it would lie between the first two examples and the third, and it thus makes sense in terms of traditional agency law to analyze the scope issue, in cases like the third example, just as most federal courts addressing that issue have done, classifying the harassment as beyond the scope of employment.

The second reason goes to an even broader unanimity of views among the holdings of District Courts and Courts of Appeals thus far. Those courts have held not only that the sort of harassment at issue here was outside the scope of supervisors' authority, but, by uniformly judging employer liability for co-worker harassment under a negligence standard, they have also implicitly treated such harassment as outside the scope of common employees' duties as well. If, indeed, the cases did not rest, at least implicitly, on the notion that such harassment falls outside the scope of employment, their liability issues would have turned simply on the application of the scope-of-employment rule.

It is quite unlikely that these cases would escape efforts to render them obsolete if we were to hold that supervisors who engage in discriminatory harassment are necessarily acting within the scope of their employment. The rationale for placing harassment within the scope of supervisory authority would be the fairness of requiring the employer to bear the burden of foreseeable social behavior, and the same rationale would apply when the behavior was that of co-employees. The employer generally benefits just as obviously from the work of common employees as from the work of supervisors; they simply have different jobs to do, all aimed at the success of the enterprise. As between an innocent employer and an innocent employee, if we use scope of employment reasoning to require the employer to bear the cost of an actionably hostile workplace created by one class of employees (*i.e.*, supervisors), it could appear just as appropriate to do the same when the environment was created by another class (*i.e.*, co-workers).

The answer to this argument might well be to point out that the scope of supervisory employment may be treated separately by recognizing that supervisors have special authority enhancing their capacity to harass, and that the employer can guard against their misbehavior more easily because their numbers are by definition fewer than the numbers of regular employees. But this answer happens to implicate an entirely separate category of agency law (to be considered in the next section), which imposes vicarious liability on employers for tortious acts committed by use of particular authority conferred as an element of an employee's agency relationship with the employer. Since the virtue of categorical clarity is obvious, it is better to reject reliance on misuse of supervisory authority (without more) as irrelevant to scope-of-employment analysis.

2

The Court of Appeals also rejected vicarious liability on the part of the City insofar as it might rest on the concluding principle set forth in § 219(2)(d) of the Restatement, that an employer "is not subject to liability for the torts of his servants acting outside the scope of their employment unless . . . the servant purported to act or speak on behalf of the principal and there was reliance on apparent authority, or he was aided in accomplishing the tort by the existence of the agency relation." Faragher points to several ways in which the agency relationship aided Terry and Silverman in carrying out their harassment. She argues that in general offending supervisors can abuse their authority to keep subordinates in their presence while they make offensive statements, and that they implicitly threaten to misuse their supervisory powers to deter any resistance or complaint. Thus, she maintains that power conferred on Terry and Silverman by the City enabled them to act for so long without provoking defiance or complaint.

The City, however, contends that § 219(2)(d) has no application here. It argues that the second qualification of the subsection, referring to a servant "aided in accomplishing the tort by the existence of the agency relation," merely "refines" the one preceding it, which holds the employer vicariously liable for its servant's abuse of apparent authority. But this narrow reading is untenable; it would render the second qualification of § 219(2)(d) almost entirely superfluous (and would seem to ask us to shut our eyes to the potential effects of supervisory authority, even when not explicitly invoked). The illustrations accompanying this subsection make clear that it covers not only cases involving the abuse of apparent authority, but also to cases in which tortious conduct is made possible or facilitated by the existence of the actual agency relationship.

We therefore agree with Faragher that in implementing Title VII it makes sense to hold an employer vicariously liable for some tortious conduct of a supervisor made possible by abuse of his supervisory authority, and that the aided-by-agency-relation principle embodied in § 219(2)(d) of the Restatement provides an appropriate starting point for determining liability for the kind of harassment presented here. Several courts, indeed, have noted what Faragher has argued, that there is a sense in which a harassing supervisor is always assisted in his misconduct by the supervisory relationship. The agency relationship affords contact with an employee subjected to a supervisor's sexual harassment, and the victim may well be reluctant to accept the risks of blowing the whistle on a superior. When a person with supervisory authority discriminates in the terms and conditions of subordinates' employment, his actions necessarily draw upon his superior position over the people who report to him, or those under them, whereas an employee generally cannot check a supervisor's abusive conduct the same way that she might deal with abuse from a co-worker. When a fellow employee harasses, the victim can walk away or tell the offender where to go, but it may be difficult to offer such responses to a supervisor, whose "power to supervise—[which may be] to hire and fire, and to set work schedules and pay rates—does not disappear . . . when he chooses to harass through insults and offensive gestures rather than directly with threats of firing or promises of promotion." Recognition of employer liability when discriminatory misuse of supervisory authority alters the terms and conditions of a victim's employment is underscored by the fact that the employer has a greater opportunity to guard against misconduct by supervisors than by common workers; employers have greater opportunity and incentive to screen them, train them, and monitor their performance.

In sum, there are good reasons for vicarious liability for misuse of supervisory authority. That rationale must, however, satisfy one more condition. We are not entitled to recognize this theory under Title VII unless we can square it with *Meritor's* holding that an employer is not "automatically" liable for harassment by a supervisor who creates the requisite degree of discrimination, and there is obviously some tension between that holding and the position that a supervisor's misconduct aided by supervisory authority subjects the employer to liability vicariously; if the "aid" may be the unspoken suggestion of retaliation by misuse of supervisory authority, the risk of automatic liability is high. To counter it, we think there are two basic alternatives, one being to require proof of some affirmative invocation of that authority by the harassing supervisor, the other to recognize an affirmative defense to liability in some circumstances, even when a supervisor has created the actionable environment.

There is certainly some authority for requiring active or affirmative, as distinct from passive or implicit, misuse of supervisory authority before liability may be imputed. That is the way some courts have viewed the familiar cases holding the employer liable for discriminatory employment action with tangible consequences, like firing and demotion. And we have already noted some examples of liability provided by the Restatement itself, which suggests that an affirmative misuse of power might be required.

But neat examples illustrating the line between the affirmative and merely implicit uses of power are not easy to come by in considering management behavior. Supervisors do not make speeches threatening sanctions whenever they make requests in the legitimate exercise of managerial authority, and yet every subordinate employee knows the sanctions exist; this is the reason that courts have consistently held that acts of supervisors have greater power to alter the environment than acts of co-employees generally. How far from the course of ostensible supervisory behavior would a company officer have to step before his orders would not reasonably be seen as actively using authority? Judgment calls would often be close, the results would often seem disparate even if not demonstrably contradictory, and the temptation to litigate would be hard to resist. We think plaintiffs and defendants alike would be poorly served by an active-use rule.

The other basic alternative to automatic liability would avoid this particular temptation to litigate, but allow an employer to show as an affirmative defense to liability that the employer had exercised reasonable care to avoid harassment and to eliminate it when it might occur, and that the complaining employee had failed to act with like reasonable care to take advantage of the employer's safeguards and otherwise to prevent harm that could have been avoided. This composite defense would, we think, implement the statute sensibly, for reasons that are not hard to fathom.

Although Title VII seeks "to make persons whole for injuries suffered on account of unlawful employment discrimination," its "primary objective," like that of any statute meant to influence primary conduct, is not to provide redress but to avoid harm. As long ago as 1980, the Equal Employment Opportunity Commission (EEOC), charged with the enforcement of Title VII, *42 U.S.C. § 2000e–4*, adopted regulations advising employers to "take all steps necessary to prevent sexual harassment from occurring, such as . . . informing employees of their right to raise and how to raise the issue of harassment." and in 1990 the Commission issued a policy statement enjoining employers to establish a complaint procedure "designed to encourage victims of harassment to come forward [without requiring] a victim to complain first to the offending supervisor." It would therefore implement clear statutory policy and complement the Government's Title VII enforcement efforts to recognize the employer's affirmative obligation to prevent violations and give credit here to employers who make reasonable efforts to discharge their duty. Indeed, a theory of vicarious liability for misuse of supervisory power would be at odds with the statutory policy if it failed to provide employers with some such incentive.

The requirement to show that the employee has failed in a coordinate duty to avoid or mitigate harm reflects an equally obvious policy imported from the general theory of damages, that a victim has a duty "to use such means as are reasonable under the circumstances to avoid or minimize the damages" that result from violations of the statute. An employer may, for example, have provided a proven, effective mechanism for reporting and resolving complaints of sexual harassment, available to the employee without undue risk or expense. If the plaintiff unreasonably failed to avail herself of the employer's preventive or remedial apparatus, she should not recover damages that could have been avoided if she had done so. If the victim could have avoided harm, no liability should be found against the employer who had taken reasonable care, and if damages could reasonably have been mitigated no award against a liable employer should reward a plaintiff for what her own efforts could have avoided.

In order to accommodate the principle of vicarious liability for harm caused by misuse of supervisory authority, as well as Title VII's equally basic policies of encouraging forethought by employers and saving action by objecting employees, we adopt the following holding in this case and in *Burlington Industries, Inc.* v. *Ellerth*, also decided today. An employer is subject to vicarious liability to a victimized employee for an actionable hostile environment created by a supervisor with immediate (or successively higher) authority over the employee. When no tangible employment action is taken, a defending employer may raise an affirmative defense to liability or damages, subject to proof by a preponderance of the evidence, see *Fed. Rule. Civ. Proc. 8(c)*. The defense comprises two necessary elements: (a) that the employer exercised reasonable care to prevent and correct promptly any sexually harassing behavior, and (b) that the plaintiff employee unreasonably failed to take advantage of any preventive or corrective opportunities provided by the employer or to avoid harm otherwise. While proof that an employer had promulgated an antiharassment policy with complaint procedure is not necessary in every instance as a matter of law, the need for a stated policy suitable to the employment circumstances may appropriately be addressed in any case when litigating the first element of the defense. And while proof that an employee failed to fulfill the corresponding obligation of reasonable care to avoid harm is not limited to showing an unreasonable failure to use any complaint procedure provided by the employer, a demonstration of such failure will normally suffice to satisfy the employer's burden under the second element of the defense. No affirmative defense is available, however, when the supervisor's harassment culminates in a tangible employment action, such as discharge, demotion, or undesirable reassignment.

Applying these rules here, we believe that the judgment of the Court of Appeals must be reversed. The District Court found that the degree of hostility in the work environment rose to the actionable level and was attributable to Silverman and Terry. It is undisputed that these supervisors "were granted virtually unchecked authority" over their subordinates, "directly controlling and supervising all aspects of [Faragher's] day-to-day activities." It is also clear that Faragher and her colleagues were "completely isolated from the City's higher management." The City did not seek review of these findings.

While the City would have an opportunity to raise an affirmative defense if there were any serious prospect of its presenting one, it appears from the record that any such avenue is closed. The District Court found that the City had entirely failed to disseminate its policy against sexual harassment among the beach employees and that its officials made no attempt to keep track of the conduct of supervisors like Terry and Silverman. The record also makes clear that the City's policy did not include any assurance that the harassing supervisors could be bypassed in registering complaints. Under such circumstances, we hold as a matter of law that the City could not be found to have exercised reasonable care to prevent the supervisors' harassing conduct. Unlike the employer of a small workforce, who might expect that sufficient care to prevent tortious behavior could be exercised informally, those responsible for city operations could not reasonably have thought that precautions against hostile environments in any one of many departments in far-flung locations could be effective without communicating some formal policy against harassment, with a sensible complaint procedure. . . .

III

The judgment of the Court of Appeals for the Eleventh Circuit is reversed, and the case is remanded for reinstatement of the judgment of the District Court.

It is so ordered.

CASES ON SUPPLEMENTAL CD

Davis v. Monroe County Board of Education, 526 U.S. 629 (1999). This case establishes the standards for institutional liability for peer sexual harassment.

Fitzgerald v. Barnstable School Committee, 129 S. Ct. 788 (2009). The examines whether a complaint of sexual harassment under Title IX preclude a second constitutional claim under § 1983.

Morehouse v. Berkshire Gas Co. 989 F. Supp. 54, 61 (D. Mass. 1997). This case examines a Title VII sexual harassment claim involving harassment of a female employee at a company sponsored golf outing.

Simpson v. Univ. of Colorado, 500 F.3d 1170 (10th Cir. 2007). This case examines the liability of an educational institution for the sexual assault of students at off campus party by recruits and student-athletes.

Williams v. Board of Regents of University System of Georgia, 477 F.3d 1282 (11th Cir. 2007). This case examines the liability of an educational institution for the sexual assault of a student in a dormitory by student-athletes.

QUESTIONS YOU SHOULD BE ABLE TO ANSWER

1. Define sexual harassment under Title VII.

2. Define sexual harassment under Title IX.

3. Explain the similarities and differences between the elements of a plaintiff's complaint and employer or institutional liability under Title VII and Title IX.

4. Explain what an employer must do in order to avoid liability with an affirmative defense.

5. Explain the school's liability for sexual violence under Title IX and why this is different than criminal liability.

REFERENCES

Cases
Barnes v. Costle, 561 F.2d 983 (D.C. 1977).
Burlington Industries, Inc. v. Ellerth, 524 U.S. 742 (1998).
Davis v. Monroe County Board of Education, 119 S.Ct. 1161 (1999).
Faragher v. City of Boca Raton, 524 U.S. 775 (1998).
Gebser v. Lago Vista Independent School District, 524 U.S. 274 (1998).
Harris v. Forklift Systems, Inc., 510 U.S. 17 (1993).
Jin v. Metropolitan Life Ins. Co., 295 F.3d 335 (2nd Cir. 2002).
Meritor Savings Bank, FSB v. Vinson, 477 U.S. 57 (1986).
Miller v. Bank of America, 600 F.2d 211 (9th Cir. 1979).
Morehouse v. Berkshire Gas Co. 989 F. Supp. 54, 61 (D. Mass. 1997).
Simpson v. University of Colorado, 500 F.3d 1170 (10th Cir. 2007).
Williams v. Board of Regents of University System of Georgia, 477 F.3d 1282 (11th Cir. 2007).
Williams v. Saxbe, 1976 413 F.Supp. 654 (DDC 1976).

Legislation
Title VII of the Civil Rights Act, 42 U.S.C. 2000e et seq. (2008).
Title VII Guidelines on Discrimination Because of Sex, 29 C.F.R. 1604.11
EEOC Notice 915.002 (6/18/1999) Enforcement Guidance: Vicarious Employer Liability for Unlawful Harassment by Supervisors.
Title IX of the Education Act of 1974, 20 U.S.C. 1681 (2008).
OCR Notice: Revised Sexual Harassment Guidance: Harassment of Students by School Employees, Other Students, or Third Parties (11/02/2000) 65 Fed. Reg. 213. pp. 66091–66114.
Dear Colleague Letter: Sexual Violence (4/04/2011). Available at http://www2.ed.gov/about/offices/list/ocr/letters/colleague-201104.html

AGE DISCRIMINATION IN EMPLOYMENT

Anne DeMartini | Flagler College

The White House Conference on Aging (2015) announced in 2013 there were 44.7 million Americans aged 65 and older and over the next 50 years that number is expected to more than double. Individuals live and work longer than ever before, and workers over the age of 40 represent an increasingly large percentage of the U.S. workforce (Glenn & Little, 2014). Between 1990 and 2013, the labor force participation rate of people 65 and over increased from 12% to 19% ("A statistical profile," 2015).

As Americans get older, there is a fear that employers and colleagues may unfairly stereotype older workers as close-minded, less productive, less adaptable to new technology and ideas, slower, less physically active, and more prone to sickness (Glenn & Little, 2014). Relying on these stereotypes can lead to ageism, the discrimination against persons of a certain age group and the tendency to regard older persons as debilitated, unworthy of attention, or unsuitable for employment (ageism, 2016). Additionally, employers may hold biases against older workers based on financial concerns, including reluctance to pay the higher salaries that older workers can command, or fear that older workers will cost them more in health and retirement benefits. Employers may be unwilling to invest resources in training an older worker when they perceive that younger employees will provide a higher return on that investment (Stack, 2013).

When employers take adverse actions against employees because of these unfounded fears, the result is age discrimination. Employment age discrimination is not a new phenomenon. Throughout much of the twentieth century, employers made such discrimination explicit through the establishment of workplace policies requiring retirement of older workers by a certain age and the use of job postings that specified the desired age of prospective applicants (Stack, 2013).

Rather than decreasing over time, the problem of age discrimination in the workplace has grown (Stack, 2013). According to an AARP study (2013), older workers' observations of age discrimination have risen since 2007. Almost two-thirds of the 1502 respondents in the nationally representative sample of 45-74 year-old workers reported seeing or experiencing age discrimination ("Staying ahead," 2013). Sixteen percent of workers cited age discrimination as the reason they were not confident that they could quickly find a new job if their current one was eliminated. In the last decade, claims of age discrimination increased fifteen percent, with the Equal Employment Opportunity Commission (EEOC) reporting receipt of 20, 588 charges in 2014 ("Enforcement" 2015).

FUNDAMENTAL CONCEPTS

Congress enacted the **Age Discrimination in Employment Act** (ADEA) in 1967 after a Secretary of Labor study found employers often discriminated against older workers based on unsubstantiated assumptions about the effect of age on their ability to do a job (Van Ostrand, 2009). The purposes of the ADEA are: promoting the employment of older persons based on their ability rather than age, prohibiting arbitrary age discrimination in employment, and helping employers and workers mediate problems arising from the impact of age on employment (Van Ostrand, 2009). Emphasizing the individual and social costs of age discrimination, Congress' original intent was to give age the same protected status that extended to race and sex under Title VII (Stack, 2013).

Age Discrimination in Employment Act of 1967

Who is subject to the ADEA?

Employers with 20 or more employees, including state, local, and the federal government, must comply with the ADEA (Age discrimination, 2015). The ADEA defines an employer as "a person engaged in an industry affecting commerce who has twenty or more employees for each working day in each of twenty or more calendar weeks in the current or preceding calendar year" (29 U.S.C. 630 (b)). A "person" includes individuals, partnerships, associations, labor organizations, corporations, business trusts, legal representatives, or any organized groups of persons (29 U.S.C. 630 (a)). The ADEA defines employee as "any individual employed by an employer" (29 U.S.C. 631(f)). The term employee must be distinguished from an independent contractor or volunteer, neither of which are considered employment relationships under the law (Epstein, 2006).

In *Yonan v. United States Soccer Federation*, (2011), the 50 year-old plaintiff, who worked as a soccer official for over twenty-five years was not considered an employee for the purposes of the ADEA. The court concluded all five factors of the "economic realities test" indicated that Yonan was an independent contractor for the United States Soccer Federation (USSF), not an employee. The court noted the USSF did not supervise him, Yonan was free to officiate soccer games not governed by the USSF without penalty, the USSF did not reimburse Yonan's clothing, equipment or registration fee, only covered his travel expenses for USSF sponsored games and did not pay Yonan, except for individual games sponsored by the USSF. Yonan's own tax returns stated he was "self-employed" operating as a "sole proprietor," and never listed the USSF as his employer.

Who is protected by the ADEA?

The ADEA protects individuals who are 40 years of age or older from employment discrimination based on age ("Age discrimination," 2015). The law initially protected employees who were between the ages of forty and sixty-five, but the upper age limit was extended to seventy in 1978, and removed completely in 1986 (Van Ostrand, 2009). The ADEA's protections apply to both employees and job applicants ("Age discrimination," 2015). *In Blasi v. Pen Argyl Area School District* (2013), the court dismissed the 58 year old plaintiff's ADEA claim finding that Blasi had not actually applied for the baseball coaching job, so he was not a job applicant protected by the ADEA. Blasi expressed an interest in being the middle school boys' basketball coach to Pen Argyl's Athletic Director during a phone conversation six months prior to the hiring of the new coach, who was under 30. Blasi did not again express an interest in the basketball position and did not indicate that he applied for or even expressed an interest in the assistant boys' baseball coaching position to anyone. The court concluded Blasi did not make "every reasonable attempt to convey his interest in the coaching positions as required" . . . by the ADEA.

The ADEA prohibits employers from discriminating against a person *because of his/her age* with respect to any term, condition, or privilege of employment, including hiring, firing, promotion, layoff, compensation, benefits, job assignments, and training ("Age discrimination," 2015). The ADEA makes it "unlawful for an employer . . . to fail or refuse to hire or to discharge any individual or otherwise discriminate against any individual with respect to his compensation, terms, conditions, or privileges of employment, because of such individual's age" (29 U.S.C. 623(a)(1)). The ADEA does not prevent an employer from asking a job applicant's age or date of birth although this could be evidence in a trial that might demonstrate that one was treated differently because of his or her age (Epstein, 2006).

In *Peterson v. National Football League*, the NFL terminated the 66 year old plaintiff, a former Regional Security Representative, in 1996. Peterson claimed that the NFL failed to consider him for four newly created security positions because of his age in violation of the ADEA and New York Executive Law 296. The court held that the NFL stated legitimate, non-discriminatory reasons for restructuring the security department and redistributing the regional security representative's responsibilities among the local representatives and new specialist positions in order to enhance department efficiency in the handling of background investigations. Of the individuals hired for new specialist positions, two were 58 years old and one was 30 years old. The only evidence suggesting a discriminatory motive behind the decision to restructure the department was testimony concerning a stray remark that the court concluded alone did not negate the legitimate reasons for the restructuring. The court found Peterson did not show a triable issue of fact as to whether age played a motivating role, or contributed to, the filling of the positions, and granted the NFL summary judgment.

Enforcement and Remedies

Congress charged the **Equal Employment Opportunity Commission** (EEOC) with responsibility for enforcing employment laws including the ADEA (29 U.S.C. 628). Congress incorporated two primary mechanisms to enforce the ADEA: the EEOC may file a suit on behalf of the alleged victim of age discrimination for injunctive and monetary relief, or a private civil action can be brought by the individual (Van Ostrand, 2009). However, before bringing a lawsuit under the ADEA, a plaintiff must exhaust his or her administrative remedies by filing a charge of discrimination with the EEOC within 180 days of the alleged discriminatory incident (42 U.S.C. 2000e-5(e)(1)).

Dreith v. The National Football League (1991) illustrates the relationship between these two enforcement mechanisms. Dreith worked as a referee for the NFL and had officiated many post-season playoff games. In 1998, the NFL informed Dreith that he would not be able to officiate any of that year's playoff games and demoted him to line judge. Dreith filed a complaint that was transferred to the EEOC alleging that he had been demoted because of his age. Thereafter, the NFL informed Dreith that it was not renewing his contract. The EEOC determined that the NFL's policy to scrutinize its officials' on-field performance after they reached age 60 violated the ADEA. After the EEOC made this determination, Dreith commenced with his private ADEA claim and the EEOC later filed its own action against the NFL. The NFL moved to dismiss Dreith's claim, arguing that EEOC's filing of a claim superseded the private one. The court held that a commencement of an ADEA action by the EEOC does not preclude or require dismissal of an earlier-filed private ADEA action and denied the NFL's motion.

An ADEA claimant may recover unpaid wages, liquidated damages, and attorney's fees. In addition to these remedies, the ADEA authorizes federal district courts to afford relief such as reinstatement, back pay, injunctive relief, declaratory judgment, and attorney's fees (29 U.S.C. 216(b)). However, most age discrimination claims were and are handled administratively or resolved out of court ("Enforcement," 2015).

Moore v. The Univ. of Notre Dame (1998) explains several types of remedies. Notre Dame fired assistant football coach Joe Moore, then sixty-five. Moore brought an action against Notre Dame under the ADEA alleging that head football coach Bob Davie told him he was fired because he was "too old" and would not be able to continue to coach for another full five-year period and a fan magazine reported that Davie said that Moore could only coach a few more years due to his age. The official reason Notre Dame later gave for firing Moore was because he did not measure up to the standards of Notre Dame, claiming Moore had intimidated, abused and made offensive remarks to players. In 1998, a jury found for Moore and awarded him back pay of $ 42,935.28 and liquidated damages of the same amount because the jury felt Notre Dame's conduct was willful. Post-trial, Moore filed motions requesting reinstatement, front pay, attorney's fees and costs. The court held that reinstatement was not the preferred remedy in this case because reinstatement would cause significant friction as well as disruption of the current football program, and someone else currently occupied Moore's former position. The court did award Moore $75,577.68 in front pay, which was based upon his new job salary minus what he would have made at Notre Dame, finding that since the coach was near retirement age and was unlikely to obtain a coaching position that provided similar prestige and compensation, he was entitled to an award of front pay for that relatively short time period. The court also awarded reasonable attorney's fees and expenses and costs of over $400,000.

Theories of liability and Elements of a Claim

The anti-discrimination language of the ADEA mirrors Title VII; both statutes prohibit discrimination "because of" an individual's membership in a protected class. Traditionally, courts have interpreted the ADEA by analogy to Title VII (Stack, 2013). However, not all theories of discrimination available under Title VII are wholly obtainable under the ADEA.

Disparate impact claims hold that employment discrimination occurs when a facially neutral employment practice impacts a particular group more adversely than another and cannot otherwise be justified by a legitimate business necessity (*Int'l Bhd. of Teamsters v. United States*, 1977). Under a disparate impact theory of liability, the plaintiff does not have to show intentional discrimination; the fact that the practice has a disparate effect on the protected class is sufficient (Van Ostrand, 2009). Under the ADEA these types of claims are much narrower in scope than under Title VII (Stack, 2013). Unlike Title VII, the ADEA creates an exception under which an employer will not be liable for disparate impact if the neutral employment action is based on "'reasonable factors other than age'" (*Smith v. City of Jackson*, 2005).

In *Wards Cove Packing Co. v. Atonio*, the Supreme Court set out the elements a plaintiff must prove for a successful disparate impact claim. Plaintiffs must:

1. identify "the specific or particular employment practice" that resulted in the disparate impact;
2. rather than demonstrating its policy was job-related and consistent with business necessity, the defendant's policy justification is only subject to a "reasoned review;" and
3. the burden of proof would "remain with the plaintiff at all times."

In 1991, less than two years later, Congress enacted The Civil Rights Act of 1991, amending Title VII to more or less overturn *Wards Cove* and to return the law to the standards applied prior to the decision. Interestingly, in *Smith v. City of Jackson* (2005) the Supreme Court declined to impute that congressional intent to ADEA claims, leaving the stricter *Wards Cove* standards in place that require the plaintiff to "isolate . . . and identify. . .the specific employment practices that are allegedly responsible for any observed statistical disparities."

Disparate Treatment. Most ADEA plaintiffs bring their cases under disparate treatment theory (Day, 2014). Disparate treatment claims allege that the employer treated the plaintiff less favorably than other employees because of the plaintiff's age, which requires that the plaintiff prove the employer had a discriminatory motive. ADEA plaintiffs making a disparate treatment claim must prove intentional discrimination by demonstrating that age "actually played a role" and "had a determinative influence on the outcome" of an adverse employment decision (*Reeves v. Sanderson Plumbing Products*, 2000). Plaintiffs can prove their employer intentionally discriminated against them by either direct or circumstantial evidence *(Desert Palace, Inc. v. Costa*, 2003).

Since direct evidence of discrimination based on the protected class is very rare, proving intentional discrimination is not an easy task for plaintiffs. Previously, courts applied the same analysis to ADEA disparate treatment claims as disparate treatment claims under Title VII (Van Ostrand, 2009). However, a Supreme Court case, *Gross v. FBL Financial Services*, (2009), disrupted any uniformity in analysis.

The leading Title VII disparate treatment case established the evidentiary and analytical framework for claims where no direct evidence is available (*McDonnell Douglas Corp. v. Green*, 1973). Though the Supreme Court has not directly addressed whether the analytical framework of *McDonnell Douglas* applies to ADEA claims, lower courts continue to apply variations of the *McDonnell Douglas* framework to ADEA cases. The typical prima facie case in ADEA cases requires the plaintiff to show that he or she:

1. is in the protected age group;
2. suffered an adverse employment action;
3. was qualified; and
4. the employer selected a person younger than plaintiff.

If the plaintiff can establish a prima facie case, the defendant has the burden of production to present evidence of a legitimate nondiscriminatory reason for the adverse employment action. Once the employer-defendant does so, the burdens of production and persuasion return to the plaintiff to prove that the employer intentionally discriminated against the plaintiff based on age (Day, 2014).

Sport and Recreation Cases. In *Beery v. University of Oklahoma Bd. of Regents* (2000), the court held that the plaintiff Beery could not prove the last element of her prima facie case that similarly situated younger employees were treated more favorably, because she could not show she was replaced by a younger individual. Beery worked as an administrative assistant to the Athletic Director, performing administrative and secretarial functions, for almost 30 years. In 1997, when Beery was 48, the Athletic Director terminated her as part of a reorganization of the Athletic Department. Beery alleged a violation of the ADEA arguing that Bob King, a recently hired, 40 year old, Special Assistant to the Athletic Director took over some of Beery's high-level duties. However, the court found that Beery's duties were redistributed among King, the accounting department, and a new Administrative Coordinator. Since King's duties were more related to his budgetary and supervisory roles, his salary was much higher, and the fact that he performed his job for four months before Beery was discharged, the court concluded he had not replaced Beery.

Rickert v. Midland Lutheran College, (2009) demonstrates an employer's successful use of a legitimate nondiscriminatory reason to avoid ADEA liability. Rickert served as part-time head volleyball coach and part-time

Student Activities Director, resulting in the equivalent of a full time job with benefits. When the school created a full time Student Activities Director position, Rickert did not apply since she would not have been able to continue coaching volleyball if hired. When the athletic program changed from NAIA to NCAA, the volleyball coaching position changed to full time. A search committee interviewed candidates, including Rickert, and offered the position to a qualified 25 year old. The defendant conceded Rickert offered a sufficient prima facie case for both positions, but argued the plaintiff's failure to apply for the full-time Student Activities Director position was a clear nondiscriminatory reason for not hiring the plaintiff to perform that job and that there was no evidence Rickert was more qualified than the 30 year old who was hired. Additionally, the defendant argued the search committee for the volleyball coaching position considered both objective and subjective factors and traits in comparing the candidates and recommending its choices, and chose the strongest candidate in light of the changes to the athletic department and the increased emphasis on recruiting.

The court concluded that stray references to youth made by one search committee member was not sufficient evidence to prove intent to discriminate based on age. The court granted the defendant's motion for summary judgment, noting the plaintiff may disagree with Midland's decision, but the courts do not "sit as super-personnel departments reviewing wisdom or fairness of employer's judgments unless they were intentionally discriminatory."

Similarly, in *Yost v. Chicago Park District* (2015) the court refused to rule on the accuracy or wisdom of an employer's decision, limiting its concern to only if the reason provided by the Park District for hiring someone other than Yost was a lie. Yost, 47, worked as a Music Instructor for the Chicago Park District and applied for an open position as a playground supervisor. The Park District followed its typical, highly structured employment procedure, which includes a two-stage evaluation process. The Human Resources department identified 34 people to interview who met the minimum qualifications identified in the bid application. Then, two interviewers asked the candidates the same list of questions, independently completed their Interview Rating Forms, averaged their numeric scores and then ranked the candidates accordingly. Yost earned an average score of 2.5 (out of a possible 4.0). The district offered the position to a 29-year old female working as a Park Kids and Recreation Leader who received an average score of 3.17.

The defendant conceded that Yost proved his prima facie case, but argued the legitimate non-discriminatory reason for not promoting Yost was that the other candidate was more qualified for the position. Yost claimed that he "possessed superior qualifications . . . based upon [his] comparative experience, well-roundedness, and educational background," and that the reason given by the Park District was pretext for intentional age discrimination. The Court found that it could not infer that the Park District's decision was pretextual based on the difference in credentials between Yost and the other candidate. While Yost had a college degree, the other candidate provided a more detailed application, including more ideas relevant to the position, and her education supported work in the field. Both evaluators found the other candidate more qualified for the position than Yost. In granting the defendant's motion for summary judgment, the court concluded that several of the evaluation criteria may have been subjective, but there is no evidence that these criteria were a "mask for discrimination."

In contrast, in *Ryther v. KARE 11* (1997), Thomas Ryther, a 53 year old sportscaster successfully proved intentional age discrimination under the traditional McDonnell Douglas framework. The broadcast network did not contend that Ryther failed to establish a prima facie case of age discrimination. Ryther was within the protected age group, his contract renewals and KARE 11's own evaluations demonstrated he had been performing his job satisfactorily for over twelve years, his contract in 1991 was not renewed, and KARE 11 replaced him with 33 year old who had a lower performance rating than Ryther. The network argued they had a legitimate non-discriminatory reason for not renewing Ryther's contract – market research from Gallup that showed he had a lower viewer recognition percentage than a sportscaster at a competitor station.

Ryther argued this reason was pretext for age discrimination because of evidence that his ratings were due to KARE 11's failure to emphasize sports and not his performance, the survey itself was poorly designed, and an overall corporate atmosphere unfavorable toward older employees. Testimony showed several older employees were suddenly given poor performance ratings and forced to choose between early retirement and demotions and that others in the sports department made cutting remarks about Ryther's age, calling him an "old fart," an "old man," and saying he was "too old to be on the air," and "had no business being in the industry any more for his age" *Ryther v. KARE 11* (1997).

The court concluded even though much of the evidence was circumstantial, a reasonable jury could infer that KARE 11's asserted reason for discharging Ryther was false, and that the evidence was sufficient to allow a jury to find that KARE 11 engaged in age discrimination. The court of appeals affirmed the judgment of the district court and affirmed the jury's verdict to award Ryther $1,254,535 in back pay, front pay, liquidated damages, and attorneys' fees.

Mixed Motives. Significantly different than Title VII is the lack of a recognized **mixed-motives discrimination claim** under the ADEA since the Supreme Court's decision in *Gross v. FBL Financial Services*, (2009). Congress ensured that a mixed-motive discrimination claim would allow a plaintiff to recover for an employer's discriminatory actions if the plaintiff's membership in the protected class was a 'motivating factor' in the decision, even if other factors also motivated the practice (42 U.S.C. § 2000e-2(m), e-5(g)(2)(B). *Gross* clarified that a plaintiff must prove that age was the "but-for" cause of the adverse employment action in order to prevail on a disparate treatment claim under the ADEA, eliminating mixed-motives age discrimination claims. Therefore, after *Gross*, the burden of persuasion never shifts to the defendant in an ADEA case, even where a plaintiff demonstrates age partly motivated the defendant (Van Ostrand, 2009). Employers need only to show that factors other than age led to the adverse employment action to avoid ADEA liability (Jay, 2014).

In *Shreve v. Cornell University* (1988), the court concluded that the Shreve's age was not the determining factor in the university's employment decisions. Shreve, 56, worked as an assistant football coach. When the head football coach, Blackman, retired, Shreve applied for that open position. When the head coaching position was offered to the defensive coordinator for the Detroit Lions of the National Football League, Baughan, Shreve then applied to retain his assistant coaching position under the Baughan.

Shreve alleged the Athletic Director Silve maintained age-based bias that impacted both the decision not to hire him for the head coaching position and Baughan's subsequent decision not to retain him as an assistant. Shreve testified that after Slive informed him that he would not be named head coach at Cornell following Blackman's retirement, Slive again asked Shreve his age and told him that Slive's father had changed professions "late in life" and had great success. Finally, Shreve testified that an Associate Athletic Director frequently referred to him as the "old fart" and the "old chestnut." The court was unwilling to conclude that these incidents were sufficient to infer age-based animus.

Though noting Shreve was qualified, the court concluded that Baughan's superior coaching credentials and engaging personality would have won him the top coaching position irrespective of plaintiff's age. The court found Baughan's decision not to offer Shreve a position as an assistant coach at Cornell was based on Baughan's impression, based on conversations with others, that Shreve was a poor football coach and that he was not aware of Shreve's age at the time. The court concluded even if Baughan's assessment of plaintiff's abilities was drawn from conversations he conducted with Slive and Blackman, age-based animus could not be fairly attributed to them.

Defenses

The text of the ADEA itself provides employers' first defense when it states that "it shall not be unlawful for an employer . . . to take any action otherwise prohibited . . . where the differentiation is based on reasonable factors other than age . . . ." (29 U.S.C.623(f)(1)). This "reasonable factors other than age" (RFOA) provision affords employers an independent "safe harbor" from liability insuring that employers may use neutral criteria other than age even if the employment action has a disparate adverse impact on older workers (Epstein, 2006). However, if an employer relies on an unreasonable non-age factor, a plaintiff may use that as evidence that the employer's explanation is a pretext for intentional discrimination (Epstein, 2006).

Bona Fide Occupational Qualification. Similar to Title VII, the ADEA provides an affirmative defense to liability where age is a **bona fide occupational qualification** (BFOQ) reasonably necessary to the normal operation of the particular business. The Supreme Court outlined the extremely narrow test for what constitutes a BFOQ (*Western Air Lines v. Criswell*, (1985)).

Reduction in Force. An employer will likely have a legitimate defense to a claim under the ADEA if the employer discharges an employee in connection with a reduction in work force (RIF), and does not replace the plaintiff with another employee (Epstein, 2006). A plaintiff-employee discharged as part of a RIF must present additional direct, circumstantial, or statistical evidence indicating that the employer singled out the plaintiff for discharge for discriminatory reasons (*Barnes v. GenCorp.*, (1990)).

In *King v. True Temper Sports* (2011), a manufacturer of steel golf club shafts implemented a workforce reduction that included the decision to eliminate three production supervisor positions. The plaintiff, King, 59, was a supervisor in the golf shaft department and filed an ADEA claim alleging True Temper illegally discriminated against him based on age when he was terminated as part of a company-wide reduction in force (RIF). Generally, a RIF reduction is itself a legitimate nondiscriminatory reason for a discharge and the defendant argued that the decision to lay off King and two others was because they were the three weakest supervisors in the facility. King did not persuade the court that he was clearly more qualified than the younger supervisor who was retained. The court noted that a mere showing that two of the three terminated supervisors were the oldest supervisors was too small a statistical sample to allow for an inference of age discrimination. The court granted True Temper's motion for summary judgment since King could not prove that the legitimate nondiscriminatory reason was pretext.

Seniority Systems. A bona fide seniority system provides a valid defense to ADEA claims, as long as the system is not a subterfuge (29 U.S.C. 623(i)(2)). The system must be based primarily on length of service; although the system may be qualified by merit factors as well (Epstein, 2006).

Business Necessity Defense and Business Judgment Rule. Luce (2004) noted the business necessity defense allows employers to defend any action by proving they considered neutral criteria, unrelated to age, which are job-related and consistent with business necessity. The business judgment rule protects directors so that they may take some risk without fear of being held liable for every decision, if the decisions were on an informed basis, in good faith and in the best interests of the company (*Aronson v. Lewis*, (1984)). An employer could use this rule as a legitimate defense related to reduction in work force, layoffs, termination of employment and other practices that affect those over age forty (Epstein, 2006).

Older Workers Benefit Protection Act (OWBPA)

The Older Workers Benefit Protection Act of 1990 (OWBPA) amended the ADEA to specifically prohibit employers from denying benefits to older employees. Congress recognized that the cost of providing certain benefits to older workers is greater than the cost of providing those same benefits to younger workers, and that those greater costs might create a disincentive to hire older workers. Therefore, in limited circumstances, an employer may be permitted to reduce benefits based on age, as long as the cost of providing the reduced benefits to older workers is no less than the cost of providing benefits to younger workers ("Age discrimination," 2015). Although Congress created the OWBPA to protect the benefits of older workers, the law provides flexibility to employers, permitting them to observe the terms of "bona fide employee benefit plans," such as retirement, pension, or insurance plans that do contain age-based distinctions, as long as those distinctions are cost-justified (Glenn & Little, 2014).

State Laws

The ADEA does not preempt state age discrimination laws and states may expand the coverage of the ADEA. Similarly, states cannot usurp this federal law (29 U.S.C. 633(a)). Many states offer stronger protections against age discrimination than the federal ADEA (Neumark & Button, 2013). As of 2011, forty-four states and the District of Columbia have age discrimination laws with lower minimum firm sizes, therefore covering more workers than the ADEA which only applies to firms with 20 or more workers (Neumark & Button, 2013). Twenty-nine states and the District of Columbia go beyond the ADEA, offering compensatory or punitive damages whether or not they require proof of intent (Neumark & Button, 2013). This results in larger potential damages awarded to successful plaintiffs.

Additionally, some state laws take the position that age discrimination should not be limited just to those over forty (Epstein, 2006.) According to the National Conference of State Legislatures (2015) twenty-five states and the District of Columbia either expand the protected age range, or eliminate a particular age requirement entirely. For example, the District of Columbia's age discrimination statute protects ages 18–65 with some exceptions and the Connecticut statute does not specify an age ("State employment," 2015).

SIGNIFICANT CASE

This recent case in the fitness industry clearly outlines the burden shifting framework of an ADEA claim and further elucidates how "qualified" a plaintiff must be to sustain a prima facie case. The case addresses which arguments the court will consider when a plaintiff establishes a prima facie case versus which arguments the court will reserve to consider in its analysis of pretext. The case also highlights the requirements for a plaintiff to prove that the employer's legitimate non-discriminatory reason was pretext.

D'AGOSTINO V. LA FITNESS INTERNATIONAL
United States District Court for the Eastern District of New York
901 F. Supp. 2d 413 (2012)

Maria D'Agostino ("Plaintiff") brings this action against LA Fitness International, LLC. and Michael Sharp, (together "Defendants") alleging age and gender discrimination in violation of the New York State Human Rights Law ("NYSHRL"), N.Y. Exec. Law § 290 et seq., Title VII of the Civil Rights Act of 1964 ("Title VII") and the Age Discrimination in Employment Act ("ADEA"). Defendants have moved for summary judgment, alleging that they acted appropriately in demoting Plaintiff. For the reasons that follow, the court grants Defendants' motion in its entirety.

***

II. Background

On January 3, 2007, Maria D'Agostino, forty-seven years old at the time, began her employment as a Training Assistant Manager ("TAM") at the Lake Success, New York facility for LA Fitness — a nationwide network of sports clubs. TAMs are responsible for selling personal training sessions and are promoted in large part based on their ability to achieve sales goals. Michael Sharp, as District Vice President, was responsible for monitoring personal training sales. On or about August 9, 2007, Sharp promoted Plaintiff to Weekend General Manager ("WGM"), which was approved by Dorian Gallagher, Regional Vice President. *** Plaintiff was promoted in light of her sales figures and received a transfer to LA Fitness' Staten Island facility because she had requested to be closer to her home. As WGM of the Staten Island facility, Plaintiff was responsible for running the weekend sales team, supervising trainers, setting schedules, and participating in the interview process for new hires. In February of 2008, after approximately six months as the WGM at the Staten Island facility, Gallagher again promoted Plaintiff to Training General Manager ("TGM") on a probationary basis. As TGM, Plaintiff was responsible for overall sales at the club, sales training, supervising the sales staff, hiring and firing, training of physical trainers, and training TAMs to be promoted to WGMs *** Plaintiff reported directly to Michael Sharp.

Over the course of her tenure as TGM, Plaintiff alleges that Sharp made several comments disparaging her in particular and women in general. In addition to these remarks, Plaintiff alleges that her younger male counterparts received preferential treatment. On November 11, 2008, Plaintiff sent an email to Linda Bessant, Employee Relations Manager in LA Fitness' Human Resources department *** complain[ing] about a recent conference call that she had been on with Sharp and other TGMs. Plaintiff referred to Sharp's tone as "loud," and characterized his statements as "demoralizing, insulting, degrading, and threatening." *** Plaintiff filed a formal complaint against Sharp with Human Resources complaining about his abusive conduct.

On Tuesday, November 18, 2008, Plaintiff received an email from Sharp seeking to discuss "the direction we are currently heading in Staten Island, and what gameplan [Plaintiff] had in mind to implement to turn it around." Sharp included in the email sales data comparing LA Fitness' Staten Island facility to the national average for all its clubs. Sharp admonished Plaintiff that he "need[ed] to see improvement . . . Not only improvement in numbers, but improvement in manpower and staff quality." In this regard, Sharp noted that he was currently interviewing TAMs to fill the WGM position to help alleviate some of Plaintiff's staffing concerns, but asked Plaintiff to send him "an email of your gameplan for turning [the facility's sale numbers] around and let [him] know what interviews [Plaintiff had] scheduled for the near future." Plaintiff responded to Sharp's email, advising him that she was aware of her responsibilities and was "performing at 100% of [her] potential Plaintiff also indicated that she was "well aware of where [the Staten Island facility's] numbers are and where they need to be." She did not send him a game plan. Following her response to Sharp's email, Plaintiff forwarded the conversation to Bessant for her "file with H[uman] R[esources]."

***

On November 24, 2008, Plaintiff again emailed Bessant "just for [her] records," complaining that Sharp had commented to two other employees that she was "probably on [her] way out." * * * Plaintiff also testified that she called Bessant and had a call with her, Michu Welch, and a third party whose name Plaintiff could not recall. *** In that call, Plaintiff avowed that she felt she was being discriminated against because of her age. * * * Plaintiff acknowledged that, other than during this call and in an email sent to Welch following her resignation, she had never stated that she felt she was being discriminated against.

* * *

On November 28, 2008, Gallagher drove to the Staten Island facility to meet with Plaintiff to discuss her failure to meet her responsibilities, but he discovered that she was not at work. *** When Plaintiff arrived at the facility some time later that day, Gallagher approached her with two options for moving forward; Plaintiff could either accept a demotion to WGM at Lake Success or resign. According to Plaintiff, Gallagher stated that he was giving her the option to transfer because it was clear that she did not enjoy working under Sharp's jurisdiction, but Plaintiff also acknowledged that they had a discussion about her sales and the fact that they "ha[dn't] been spectacular." At the time, Plaintiff believed that Gallagher's stated reasons for demoting her were true, and in a November 30, 2008 email to Welch, even accepted that she must "of course take accountability, somewhat" for the facility's low sales numbers. Nonetheless, Plaintiff declined the demotion and opted to resign.

* * *

III. DISCUSSION

Under Title VII, the ADEA and the NYSHRL, a plaintiff establishes a prima facie case of intentional discrimination by showing that (1) she is a member of a protected class; (2) she was qualified for the position she held; (3) she suffered an adverse employment action; and (4) the adverse action took place under circumstances giving rise to [an] inference of discrimination. See Gorzynski v. JetBlue Airways Corp., 596 F.3d 93, 107, 110 (2d Cir. 2010) (ADEA). Although the evidence necessary to establish plaintiff's initial burden has been characterized by the Second Circuit as "minimal" and "de minimis," see Zimmermann v. Associates First Capital Corp., 251 F.3d 376, 381 (2d Cir. 2001).

* * *

1. Plaintiff has established a prima facie case of discrimination under Title VII, the ADEA, and the NYSHRL

Defendants do not appear to contest that Plaintiff is a member of a protected class, has suffered an adverse employment action, or that the adverse action took place under circumstances that give rise to an inference of discrimination. Rather, they argue only that Plaintiff has not established a prima facie because she did not possess the basic skills necessary to perform as a TGM and has therefore failed to demonstrate that she was qualified for the position. In support, Defendants point to sales statistics from Plaintiff's tenure as TGM, indicating that she had among the lowest, or in some cases the lowest, sales out of all of the facilities in her district. However, as the Second Circuit has "long emphasized," "the qualification prong must not be interpreted in such a way as to shift into the plaintiff's prima facie case an obligation to anticipate and disprove the employer's proffer of a legitimate nondiscriminatory basis for its decision." Gregory v. Daly, 243 F.3d 687, 696 (2d Cir. 2001). Thus, a plaintiff "need not show perfect performance or even average performance." Id. Instead, a plaintiff "need only make the 'minimal showing' that 'she possesses the basic skills necessary for performance of [the] job.'" Id. The court finds that Plaintiff has met her burden.

Plaintiff worked at LA Fitness for nearly two years, had always held positions in which sales constituted a large part of her job function, and was twice promoted into successively higher positions, at least once based, "in large part," on her ability to achieve sales goals. On this record, the court has little difficulty in concluding that Plaintiff has demonstrated the "minimal qualifications" required for her prima facie case.

* * *

2. Plaintiff has failed to demonstrate that Defendants' Legitimate Non-Discriminatory Reason for Demoting her was a Mere Pretext

Assuming then, that Plaintiff has established her prima facie case, the burden shifts to Defendants to articulate a legitimate non-discriminatory reason for their actions. Meeting that challenge, Defendants have asserted, based on sales data from Plaintiff's tenure as TGM, that Plaintiff was demoted for not achieving sales goals, and because the facility she managed was often ranked at or near the bottom in sales when compared to other facilities in her district. Under Plaintiff's management, the Staten Island facility was only meeting 25 percent of its sales goals while the national average was 50 percent). In addition, Defendants assert that Plaintiff was demoted for failing to maintain staffing levels and not properly handling her day-to-day responsibilities. Plaintiff does not dispute the accuracy of this information, noting at her deposition that she only met her daily sales goals approximately "65 percent" of the time, and acknowledging to Gallagher that her sales numbers "were not spectacular" when she was notified of her demotion. Given Defendants' facially non-discriminatory justifications for Plaintiff's termination, the burden again falls to Plaintiff to demonstrate the existence of a material fact as to whether the reasons proffered by Defendants are mere pretexts for a discriminatory motive.

* * *

a. Plaintiff Has Not Establish Pretext Based on Sharp's Discriminatory Remarks

To establish discriminatory intent, Plaintiff relies on a series of comments allegedly made by Sharp. Specifically, Plaintiff testified that over the two years she worked at LA Fitness, Sharp commented that "females," and Plaintiff in particular, "can't take credit cards," that women "didn't know how to do the job" and were not "tough enough," and that he visited the Staten Island facility because "there are a lot of pretty things to look at." Sharp also allegedly passed by Plaintiff while she was training and commented that "the old lady can't work out."

Notwithstanding Sharp's inappropriate comments, Plaintiff does not appear to dispute that he played no role in the decision to demote her and points to no evidence that would indicate otherwise. To the contrary, both Plaintiff and Gallagher's testimonies suggest that the decision to demote Plaintiff was made by Gallagher alone. *** Nor does Plaintiff allege that Gallagher in any way discriminated against her. Finally, Plaintiff acknowledged that the justifications Gallagher provided to her for her demotion and transfer were both correct; she had, in fact, not been meeting sales expectations and did not enjoy working with Sharp. Under these circumstances, Plaintiff cannot establish, via Sharp's comments, that Gallagher's justifications for Plaintiff's demotion masked a discriminatory purpose.

* * *

b. Plaintiff Has Not Established Pretext Based on the Alleged Preferential Treatment Received By Younger Male Employees

Plaintiff also claims that the justifications for her demotion are mere pretext as demonstrated by the preferential treatment provided to younger male managers. More to the point, Plaintiff asserts that these managers — who Plaintiff named at her deposition — were promoted when asked, moved to different clubs at their request, came in late, disappeared for days, and took drugs and were arrested in the club, all without reprimand or repercussion. *** As a preliminary issue, Defendants argue that Plaintiff has not demonstrated that these individuals are similarly situated to her. Plaintiff was allegedly demoted for poor sales, but she has not demonstrated that any of these individuals had similar sales numbers and yet were treated differently. In fact, Plaintiff has provided no evidence as to what these younger male managers' sales numbers actually were or for how long their sales numbers suffered, and even admitted at her deposition that she "didn't watch the [sales] numbers [of other clubs]. Given the lack of any sales data regarding these younger male managers, the court agrees with Defendants that, on the record before it, Plaintiff has failed to establish that these younger male managers were in the same position as she — someone who was demoted based on poor sales performance.

* * *

Even assuming, however, that these managers were similarly situated to Plaintiff, Plaintiff's allegations fall far short of meeting her burden. First, despite Plaintiff's allegation that these managers' were abusing drugs in the clubs and had prison records, Plaintiff did not testify whether any of her superiors were aware of such conduct, did not say whether any of these individuals were ever disciplined, and admitted that she never reported any of this information to her superiors, either because she believed it to be "open knowledge" or because she "didn't want to get involved." Second, as to Plaintiff's claims that other managers were allowed to take vacation without prior notice or to come in late, Plaintiff testified that in the one instance where she personally observed a male co-worker coming in late and brought it to Sharp's attention, that Sharp eventually addressed the issue. Third, although Plaintiff testified that she believed a former supervisor — not Sharp — excluded her from certain meetings, Plaintiff later admitted that the supervisor never directed her not to attend meetings. In fact, Plaintiff did attend the meetings, and testified that any meeting she missed was due to the fact that she "wasn't in the building when those [meetings] occurred." Fourth, although Plaintiff argues that her younger male counterparts were allowed to transfer to other facilities at their request, she offers no specifics regarding how often these individuals requested transfers, how often such requests were granted, or what other circumstances, if any, surrounded these requests. And, in any event, although Plaintiff was denied a second transfer in the less than two years she had worked for LA Fitness, she was granted her request to transfer to the Staten Island facility to be closer to her home.

In sum, in the court's view, Plaintiff has offered little more than speculation and vague allegations of similarly-situated employees receiving more favorable treatment, many of which are controverted by Plaintiff's own testimony. Under such circumstances, Plaintiff's allegations are simply insufficient to satisfy her burden and demonstrate that the reasons proffered by Defendants for her demotion were mere pretext. The court finds that Plaintiff has not proffered sufficient evidence to raise a genuine issue of material fact as to whether her demotion was motivated by discriminatory animus, it grants Defendants' motion for summary judgment.

* * *

IV. CONCLUSION

For the reasons set forth above, Defendants' motion for summary judgment is GRANTED.***

CASES ON THE SUPPLEMENTAL CD

Gross v. FBL Financial Services, 557 U.S. 167 (2009). The U.S. Supreme Court held that a claim for disparate treatment under the ADEA could not shift the burden of persuasion to the defendant, even after the plaintiff had established that age was a motivating factor in the defendant's adverse employment decision.

Smith v. City of Jackson, 544 U.S. 228 (2005). The Supreme Court articulated the standard for analyzing disparate-impact claims under the ADEA.

Ryther v. KARE 11, 108 F.3d 832 (8th Cir. Minn. 1997). This case illustrates a rare instance where the plaintiff in an ADEA case prevails, illustrating each of the steps of a traditional McDonnell Douglas framework.

Shreve v. Cornell University, 1988 U.S. Dist. LEXIS 3109 (N.D.N.Y, 1988). A classic sport case, it demonstrates a court's analysis of how much employment decisions must be predicated on the basis of age to trigger ADEA liability.

QUESTIONS YOU SHOULD BE ABLE TO ANSWER

1. Explain the history and purpose of the Age Discrimination in Employment Act.
2. Identify who is subject to the ADEA and who is protected by it.
3. List the theories of liability available under the ADEA and the elements a plaintiff must prove under each to sustain a valid claim.
4. Explain how ADEA claims have changed since *Smith v City of Jackson* and *Gross v FBL Financial Services*.
5. Create a hypothetical situation in the sport or recreation industry where there is a risk of age discrimination. Apply what you've learned about the ADEA to determine if a plaintiff would have a valid claim under the ADEA.

REFERENCES

Cases

Beery v. University of Oklahoma Bd. of Regents, 203 F.3d 834 (10th Cir. Okla., 2000)
Blasi v. Pen Argyl Area School District, 2013 U.S. Dist. LEXIS 172173; 120 Fair Empl. Prac. Cas. (BNA) 1850 (2013)
Dreith v. The National Football League, 777 F. Supp. 832 (D. Colo., 1991)
Gross v. FBL Financial Services, 557 U.S. 167 (2009)
Int'l Bhd. of Teamsters v. United States, 431 U.S. 324 (1977)
King v. True Temper Sports, 2011 U.S. Dist. LEXIS 60631 (N.D. Miss., 2011)
McDonnell Douglas Corp. v. Green, 411 U.S. 792 (1973)
Moore v. The Univ. of Notre Dame, 22 F. Supp. 2d 896 (N.D. Ind. 1998)
Peterson v. National Football League, 1999 U.S. Dist. LEXIS 13403; 80 Fair Empl. Prac. Cas. (BNA) 1714 (1999)
Rickert v. Midland Lutheran College, 009 U.S. Dist. LEXIS 78886; 22 Am. Disabilities Cas. (BNA) 590 (2009).
Ryther v. KARE 11, 108 F.3d 832 (8th Cir. Minn. 1997)
Shreve v. Cornell University, 1988 U.S. Dist. LEXIS 3109 (N.D.N.Y, 1988)
Smith v. City of Jackson, 544 U.S. 228 (2005)
Wards Cove Packing Co. v. Atonio, 490 U.S. 642 (1989)
Yonan v. United States Soccer Fed'n, Inc., 833 F. Supp. 2d 882 (N.D. Ill., 2011)
Yost v. Chicago Park Dist., 2015 U.S. Dist. LEXIS 122339 (N.D. Ill., 2015)

Publications

Ageism. 2016. In *Random House Dictionary*. Retrieved January 6, 2016 from http://dictionary.reference.com/browse/ageism
AARP Research (2014). Staying ahead of the curve 2013: The AARP work and career study – Older workers in an uneasy job market. Washington, DC.
Day, J. (2014). Closing the loophole—Why intersectional claims are needed to address discrimination against older women. *Ohio State Law Journal*, 75, 447–476.
Doyle, K. (2013, October 2). One in three older adults reports age discrimination. *Reuters Health*. Retrieved from http://uk.reuters.com/article/us-older-adults-idUKBRE9970ZS20131008
Epstein, A. (2006). The ADED and sports law. *Journal of Legal Aspects of Sport*, 16, 177–196.

Neumark, D. & Button, P. (2013). Did age discrimination protections help older workers weather the great recession? (Working paper No: WP 2013-287) University of Michigan Retirement Research Center. http://www.mrrc.isr.umich.edu/publications/papers/pdf/wp287.pdf

Neumark, D., Burn, I. & Button, P. (2015). Is it harder for older workers to find jobs? New and improved evidence from a field experiment (Working paper No. 21669). National Bureau of Economic Research.

Glenn, J.J. & Little, K.E. (2014). A study of the Age Discrimination in Employment Act of 1967. GP Solo, a publication of the American Bar Association, 31 (6). Retrieved from http://www.americanbar.org/publications/gp_solo/2014/november_december/a_study_the_age_discrimination_employment_act_1967.html

Stack, E.M. (2013). Note: A new split on old age: Preclusion of §1983 claims and the ADEA. *Fordham Law Review, 82*, 331–371.

National Conference of State Legislatures (2015). State employment-related discrimination statutes. Washington, D.C. Retrieved from http://www.ncsl.org/documents/employ/Discrimination-Chart -2015.pdf

U.S. Equal Employment Opportunity Commission (2015). Age discrimination. Washington, DC. Retrieved from http://www.eeoc.gov/eeoc/publications/age.cfm

U.S. Equal Employment Opportunity Commission (2015). Enforcement and litigation statistics: Age Discrimination in Employment Act. Washington, DC. Retrieved from http://www.eeoc.gov/eeoc/statistics/enforcement/adea.cfm

Van Ostrand, L.A. (2009). Note: A close look at ADEA mixed-motives claims and Gross v. FBL Financial Services, Inc. *Fordham Law Review, 78*, 399–451.

White House Conference on Aging. (2015). A statistical profile of older Americans. Washington, DC. Retrieved from http://www.whitehouseconferenceonaging.gov/about/statistics.html

Legislation
The Age Discrimination in Employment Act, 29 U.S.C. § 621-34
Civil Rights Act of 1991

TITLE I OF THE AMERICANS WITH DISABILITIES ACT

Mary A. Hums | University of Louisville

It is becoming more common to see people with disabilities participating in sport. Events geared specifically for athletes with disabilities such as the Paralympic Games, the Para-PanAmerican Games, and the Warrior Games draw thousands of participants and spectators. Athletes with disabilities are now being included in events such as the Boston Marathon and the Commonwealth Games. The recent Dear Colleague Letter provides guidance for students with disabilities to participate in interscholastic and intercollegiate sport.

Events such as the ones listed above and the athletes with disabilities who compete in them are becoming more visible every day. But what about other people with disabilities who wish to work as sport and recreation managers in some segment of the sport and recreation industry? What barriers do they face and what kind of legal protections do they have against employment discrimination? In addition to addressing facility issues, the Americans with Disabilities Act (ADA) provides guidelines for employers when dealing with employees with disabilities. These guidelines help ensure equal opportunity for people with disabilities by opening up the definition of who is a "qualified individual" to include people of all abilities.

FUNDAMENTAL CONCEPTS

The Americans with Disabilities Act of 1990 (ADA) is not limited to facility accessibility and stadium sightline issues, as the legislation also addresses employment issues as well. It is important to remember that the ADA covers the entire scope of the employment process. Title I of the ADA states "[N]o covered entity shall discriminate against a qualified individual with a disability because of the disability of such individual in regard to job application procedures, the hiring, advancement or discharge of employees, employee compensation, job training, and other terms, conditions, and privileges of employment" [42 U.S.C. 12112(a)]. According to Masteralexis and Wong (2015, p. 115), "The sport industry is people intensive, so sport managers must have a working knowledge of how the law affects human resource management, particularly a basic knowledge of labor and employment laws," and this includes The Americans With Disabilities Act. This section focuses primarily on the question of reasonable accommodation. Before examining the ADA's application to sport organizations, some basic definitions must be established.

Employer

According to Title I, § 12111 [sec. 101] (5)(a) of the ADA, the term *employer* means "a person engaged in an industry affecting commerce who has 15 or more employees for each working day in each of 20 or more calendar weeks in the current or preceding calendar year, and any agent of such person." In *Jones v. Southeast Alabama Baseball Umpires Association* (1994), an umpire who wore a prosthetic leg had his request to work an increased number of varsity high school baseball games denied and chose to file an ADA claim. The Umpires' Association filed for summary judgment, claiming it did not fall under ADA coverage because it did not employ umpires for more than twenty weeks. Jones was able to show that because the Association assigned umpires during both the school year and for summer youth games, it actually employed umpires for approximately six months, and therefore the Association's request for summary judgment was denied.

Disability

Under the ADA, the term *disability* means (1) a physical or mental impairment that substantially limits one or more of the major life activities of such individual; (2) a record of such impairment; or (3) being regarded as having such an impairment [§ 12103 (Sec. 3)] (2). Although the ADA does not specifically define "major life activities," the Department of Health and Human Services defines those as "functions such as caring for one's self, performing manual tasks, walking, seeing, hearing, speaking, breathing, learning, and working" [45 C.F.R. 84.3(j)(2)(i)(1985)].

Qualified Individual with a Disability

According to Title I, § 12111 [Sec. 101] (8) of the ADA, a "qualified individual with a disability" means: "an individual who, with or without reasonable accommodation, can perform the essential functions of the employment position that such an individual holds or desires." In order to be qualified, a person must still meet certain prerequisites for the position. For example, a teacher who could not pass the required national teachers' examination could be considered not qualified for a teaching position (*Pandazides v. Virginia Board of Education*, 1992). In *Sawhill v. Medical College of Pennsylvania* (1996), the plaintiff, a licensed clinical pathologist, was told his termination was because he did not fit into his department's future plans, but later discovered his termination was related to his disability (clinical depression). The plaintiff alleged termination based on his disability violated the ADA. The defendant's motion to dismiss was denied. The term "qualified individual with a disability" does "not include any employee or applicant who is currently engaging in illegal use of drugs, when the covered entity acts on the basis of such use" (42 U.S.C. 12112(a)). In *Collings v. Longview Fibre Company* (1995), Collings and seven other employees alleged Longview Fibre wrongfully terminated them for their drug addiction disability in violation of the Americans with Disabilities Act. The employees were discharged because of their drug-related misconduct at work and not because of their alleged substance abuse disability. The regulations accompanying the ADA indicate that employers may discharge or deny employment to people illegally using drugs, and the courts have recognized a distinction between termination of employment because of misconduct and termination because of a disability.

Reasonable Accommodation/Undue Hardship

According to the Job Accommodation Network (n.d., p. 1): "In relation to the ADA, reasonable accommodation is any modification or adjustment to a job or the work environment that will enable a qualified applicant or employee with a disability to participate in the application process or to perform essential job functions. Reasonable accommodation also includes adjustments to assure that a qualified individual with a disability has rights and privileges in employment equal to those of employees without disabilities."

A reasonable accommodation means making some modifications in the work environment that allows a person with a disability an equal employment opportunity. These accommodations take place in three aspects of employment (Colker & Milani, 2005):

- To ensure equal opportunity in the employment process;
- To enable a qualified individual with a disability to perform the essential functions of a job;
- To enable an employee with a disability to enjoy equal benefits and privileges of employment (p. 20).

It is good to ask the following questions when considering reasonable accommodations:

1. What limitations is the employee experiencing?
2. How do these limitations affect the employee and the employee's job performance?
3. What specific job tasks are problematic as a result of these limitations?
4. What accommodations are available to reduce or eliminate these problems? Are all possible resources being used to determine possible accommodations?
5. Has the employee with a disability been consulted regarding possible accommodations?
6. Once accommodations are in place, would it be useful to meet with the employee with a disability to evaluate the effectiveness of the accommodations and to determine whether additional accommodations are needed?

7. Do supervisory personnel and employees need training regarding disabilities? (Job Accommodation Network, 2013, Accommodating Employees Who Use Wheelchairs section).

To comply with the ADA, employers must make reasonable accommodations for their workers with disabilities. However, employers only need to do so if providing the reasonable accommodation does not result in undue hardship. According to Title I, § 12111 [sec. 101] (9) of the ADA, a "***reasonable accommodation***" may include:

> Making existing facilities used by employees reasonably accessible to and usable by individuals with disabilities; and Job restructuring, part-time or modified work schedules, reassignment to a vacant position, acquisition or modification of equipment or devices, appropriate adjustment or modifications of examinations, training materials or policies, the provision of qualified readers or interpreters, and other similar accommodations for individuals with disabilities.

When making reasonable accommodations, employers should consider using the following steps for accommodation (U.S. Department of Labor, 2009):

1. Notify employees
2. Facilitate requests
3. Analyze jobs
4. Identify functional limitations
5. Determine potential accommodations
6. Determine reasonable solutions
7. Make the accommodation
8. Monitor effectiveness

According to Title I, § 12111 [sec. 101] (10)(a) of the ADA, an ***undue hardship*** is "an action requiring significant difficulty or expense, when considered in light of the factors set forth in subparagraph (b)":

(b) In determining whether an accommodation would impose an undue hardship on a covered entity, factors to be considered include:

i. the nature and cost of the accommodation needed under this Act;
ii. the overall financial resources of the facility or facilities involved in the provision of reasonable accommodation; the number of persons employed at such a facility; the effect on expenses and resources, or the impact otherwise of such accommodation upon the operation of the facility;
iii. the overall financial resources of the covered entity; the overall size of the business of the covered entity with respect to the number of its employees; the number, type and location of its facilities; and
iv. the type of operation or operations of the covered entity, including the composition, structure, and functions of the workforce of such entity; the geographic separateness, administrative, or fiscal relationship of the facility or facilities in question to the covered entity.

The courts have interpreted the meaning of reasonable accommodation and undue hardship differently in different cases (Churchill, 1995). Some reasonable accommodations include working at home for an employee who experiences pain while commuting (*Sargent v. Litton Systems*, 1994); taking a leave of absence for alcoholism treatment (*Schmidt v. Safeway*, 1994); eliminating heavy lifting and strenuous work (*Henchey v. Town of North Greenbush*, 1993); allowing a police officer to carry food, glucose, and an insulin injection kit (*Bombrys v. City of Toledo*, 1993); and transferring an employee to a city where better medical care was available (*Buckingham v. United States*, 1993).

There are instances, however, when the courts have indicated that the requested accommodations were unreasonable or would have resulted in undue hardship. Reasonable accommodation did not require allowing an employee who has unpredictable violent outbursts to remain in the workplace (*Mazzarella v. U.S. Postal Service*, 1993), accommodating frequent or unpredictable absences (*Jackson v. Veteran's Administration*, 1994), or assigning limited tasks that substantially reduce an employee's contribution to the company (*Russell v. Southeastern Pennsylvania Transportation Authority*, 1993).

Accommodations do not have to be expensive according to the Job Accommodation Network (2015, Finding #2):

> Of the employers who gave cost information related to accommodations they had provided, 389 out of 673 (58%) said the accommodations needed by employees cost absolutely nothing. Another 251 (37%) experienced a one-time cost. Only 24 (4%) said the accommodation resulted in an ongoing, annual cost to the company and 9 (1%) said the accommodation required a combination of one-time and annual costs; however, too few of these employers provided cost data to report with accuracy. Of those accommodations that did have a cost, the typical one-time expenditure by employers was $500. When asked how much they paid for an accommodation beyond what they would have paid for an employee without a disability who was in the same position, employers typically answered around $400.
>
> Here are some examples of specific costs of accommodations:
>
> - A cancer patient who dealt with fatigue and low concentration had his desk moved to a quieter location to avoid distraction. Cost = $0
> - A scientist with carpel tunnel syndrome experienced pain when working on regular reports received an ergonomic keyboard. Cost = $70

A janitor with a back impairment had trouble lifting and carrying items. The company purchased ergonomic and lightweight cleaning equipment (Job Accommodation Network, 2015, para. 11).

Providing reasonable accommodations for employees need not be excessively expensive or complicated. Working off EEOC guidance, here are examples of reasonable accommodations:

- Making existing facilities accessible
- Job restructuring
- Reassignment to a vacant position
- Part-time or modified schedules
- Acquiring or modifying equipment
- Changing the physical layout of the work area
- Removing requirements to stand when a job is performed
- Changing tests, training materials, or policies
- Providing readers or interpreters

On the other hand, these are examples of what the EEOC says it may view as an unreasonable accommodation:

- Eliminating an essential job function
- Lowering production standards (after reasonable accommodations have been instituted)
- Having to provide personal-use items for daily activities (prosthetics, wheelchairs, hearing aids, etc.)
- Arrangements that conflict with the company's seniority system, regardless of whether it is a product of collective bargaining or simply of management decision (Schleifer, 2007, p. 1).

The following are examples of what reasonable accommodations might look like in sport industry settings. An Associate Athletic Director with low vision could have a larger screen desktop computer. A Marketing Manager with Seasonal Affective Disorder could have full-spectrum light bulbs installed in his office light fixtures. Flexible scheduling could help YMCA staffers who have fibromyalgia or other disabilities where fatigue is an issue of their condition. A Stadium Facility Manager who uses a wheelchair could take his service dog to any meetings in appropriate areas of the facility. A Community Service Department employee with cerebral palsy who uses a motorized chair would have access to key-restricted elevators. All of these accommodations are easily done and cost very little for the investment made in helping good employees do their jobs even better.

Americans with Disabilities Act Amendments Act of 2008

In September of 2008, President George W. Bush signed the Americans with Disabilities Act Amendments of 2008. These Amendments went into law on 1 January 2009. According to the Equal Employment Opportunity

Commission (2009, ¶3), the Act retains the ADA's basic definition of "disability" as an impairment that substantially limits one or more major life activities, a record of such an impairment, or being regarded as having such an impairment. However, it changes the way that these statutory terms should be interpreted in several ways. Most significantly, the Act:

- Directs EEOC to revise that portion of its regulations defining the term "substantially limits";
- Expands the definition of "major life activities" by including two non-exhaustive lists:
  1. The first list includes many activities that the EEOC has recognized (e.g., walking) as well as activities that EEOC has not specifically recognized (e.g., reading, bending, and communicating);
  2. The second list includes major bodily functions (e.g., "functions of the immune system, normal cell growth, digestive, bowel, bladder, neurological, brain, respiratory, circulatory, endocrine, and reproductive functions");
- States that mitigating measures other than "ordinary eyeglasses or contact lenses" shall not be considered in assessing whether an individual has a disability;
- Clarifies that an impairment that is episodic or in remission is a disability if it would substantially limit a major life activity when active;
- Changes the definition of "regarded as" so that it no longer requires a showing that the employer perceived the individual to be substantially limited in a major life activity, and instead says that an applicant or employee is "regarded as" disabled if he or she is subject to an action prohibited by the ADA (e.g., failure to hire or termination) based on an impairment that is not transitory and minor;
- Provides that individuals covered only under the "regarded as" prong are not entitled to reasonable accommodation.

"Under the new amendments, effective January 1, 2009, the determination of whether a person has an impairment that substantially limits a major life activity, a "*disability*" in the legal sense under the ADA, must be made, with a few exceptions, *without regard* to the beneficial effects of a mitigating action, such as taking medication" (Prosser, n.d., p. 1). This legislation can help both employees and employers. Employees can more readily establish they have a disability, and employers can more clearly determine if one of their employees is disabled.

There have been some additional interesting sport related developments in this area as well. In 2006, the United Nations rarified the Convention on the Rights of Persons with Disabilities. The United States is now a signatory to that convention. While it remains to be seen exactly how the Convention will be codified into law in the United States, discussions have now begun regarding its implementation in countries around the world. The Convention deals with access to sport and physical activity for people with disabilities, but also contains language about sport managers (United Nations, 2006, p. 22):

> (b) To ensure that persons with disabilities have an opportunity to *organize, develop* and participate in disability-specific sporting and recreational activities and, to this end, encourage the provision, on an equal basis with others, of appropriate instruction, training and resources.

A high-profile sport related occurrence was the firing of Steve Sarkisian, the head football coach at the University of Southern California (USC) after his apparent alcohol-related behavior at university events. "It comes as no surprise, then, that the focus of Sarkisian's litigation is the claim that at the time he worked for USC he was a "person with a disability" in that he suffered from alcoholism, and that alcoholism limited one or more of his major life activities" (Sampson, 2015 para. 2). The events surrounding Sarkisian should remind employers to "tread carefully with respect to issues related to alcohol dependency and understand that while inappropriate behavior or failure to perform the essential job functions isn't excused by an employee's alcoholism, the employer still must evaluate whether a reasonable accommodation is appropriate and can be provided" (Kim, 2015, para. 7). In addition, Royce White a first-round draft pick of the Houston Rockets in 2012, who has an anxiety disorder that manifests itself as fear of flying, was reassigned to the NBA developmental league, and consequently suspended for failure to provide services. "If litigated, the White case will present an interesting application of the ADA to the sports world and the NBA in particular. Among the issues will be the extent of the reasonable accommodations that the Rockets would need to provide in order to allow White to perform the essential functions of his job as a professional athlete. Given the nature of the NBA life, specifically its schedule and the air travel required as part of the job, it would be interesting to see what a court would determine to be reasonable accommodations under these facts." (Rhoads & Sinon, 2016, para. 4).

SIGNIFICANT CASE

This case offers a good example of the ADA in action. It also involves an illness we do not always think of as being a disability, alcoholism. We usually think of disability in terms of a mobility disability or perhaps a hearing or visual impairment.

MADDOX V. UNIVERSITY OF TENNESSEE
United States Court of Appeals for the Sixth Circuit
62 F.3d 843 (1995)

Opinion: Bailey Brown, Circuit Judge.

The plaintiff-appellant, Robert Maddox, a former assistant football coach at the University of Tennessee, brought suit against the school, its Board of Trustees, and its athletic director, Doug Dickey (collectively "UT"), under § 504 of the Rehabilitation Act of 1973, as amended, 29 U.S.C. § 701, et seq., and the Americans with Disabilities Act of 1990 ("ADA"), 42 U.S.C. § 12101, et seq., alleging discriminatory discharge on the basis of his disability, alcoholism. The district court granted UT's motion for summary judgment, concluding that Maddox was not terminated solely by reason of, or because of, his handicap, but rather, because of a well-publicized incident in which Maddox was arrested for driving under the influence of alcohol. Maddox appealed. We AFFIRM.

I. FACTS

On February 17, 1992, Doug Dickey, acting as UT's athletic director, extended to Maddox an offer of employment as an assistant football coach. The position did not carry tenure and was terminable at will in accordance with the policies of the Personnel Manual. As part of the hiring process, Maddox completed an application. On the line after "Describe any health problems or physical limitations, which . . . would limit your ability to perform the duties of the position for which you are applying," Maddox wrote "None." In response to the question "have you ever been arrested for a criminal offense of any kind?" Maddox replied "No." These responses were not accurate. According to what Maddox alleges in this lawsuit, he suffers from the disability of alcoholism. Also, Maddox was arrested three times before 1992, once for possession of a controlled substance, and twice for driving a motor vehicle under the influence of alcohol. As to the first answer, Maddox claims that it is in fact correct because "it has never affected my coaching ability . . . I never drank on the job." As to the second question, Maddox claims that another university employee, Bill Higdon, advised him not to include the information concerning his prior arrests on the application.

On May 26, 1992, after Maddox began working at UT, a Knoxville police officer arrested Maddox and charged him with driving under the influence of alcohol and public intoxication. According to newspaper reports, the accuracy of which is not contested, Maddox backed his car across a major public road at a high rate of speed, almost striking another vehicle. When stopped by the officer, Maddox was combative, his pants were unzipped, and he refused to take a breathalyzer. He also lied to the arresting officer, stating that he was unemployed. This incident was highly publicized, and UT was obviously embarrassed by the public exposure surrounding the event.

Maddox entered an alcohol rehabilitation program at a UT hospital after his arrest. UT first placed Maddox on paid administrative leave. In June 1992, however, Dickey and then Head Coach Johnny Majors determined that the allegations were accurate and jointly issued a letter notifying Maddox that his employment was being terminated. They testified that termination was necessary because of: (1) the criminal acts and misconduct of Maddox; (2) the bad publicity surrounding the arrest; and (3) the fact that Maddox was no longer qualified, in their minds, for the responsibilities associated with being an assistant coach. Both Dickey and Majors deny that they were aware that Maddox was an alcoholic or that Maddox's alcoholism played any part in the decision to discharge him. Nevertheless, Maddox brought this action alleging that the termination was discriminatory on the basis of his alcoholism in violation of his rights under the Rehabilitation Act and the ADA. UT responded by filing a motion for summary judgment which the district court granted. The court recognized that, under both statutes, a plaintiff must show that he was fired by reason of his disability. In the court's view, summary judgment was appropriate because Maddox could not establish the existence of a genuine issue of material fact with respect to whether he had been fired by reason of his status as an alcoholic rather than by reason of his criminal misconduct. Maddox now appeals.

II. Analysis

1. Standard of Review

Review of a grant of summary judgment is de novo, utilizing the same test used by the district court to determine whether summary judgment is appropriate. A court shall render summary judgment when there is no genuine issue as to any material fact, the moving party is entitled to judgment as a matter of law, and reasonable minds could come to but one conclusion, and that conclusion is adverse to the party against whom the motion is made.

2. Maddox Was Not Terminated Because of His Disability

Maddox raises a number of issues on appeal which he contends show that the district court erred in granting summary judgment to the defendants. Maddox first alleges that the district court erred in analyzing his claim under the Rehabilitation Act. Section 504 of the Act provides, "no otherwise qualified individual with a disability . . . shall, solely by reason of her or his disability, be excluded from the participation in, be denied the benefits of, or be subject to discrimination under any program or activity receiving Federal financial assistance." 29 U.S.C. § 794(a). Thus, in order to establish a violation of the Rehabilitation Act, a plaintiff must show:

(1) The plaintiff is a "handicapped person" under the Act; (2) The plaintiff is "otherwise qualified" for participation in the program; (3) The plaintiff is being excluded from participation in, being denied the benefits of, or being subjected to discrimination under the program solely by reason of his handicap; and (4) The relevant program or activity is receiving Federal financial assistance.

It is not disputed in this case that UT constitutes a program receiving Federal financial assistance under the Act. Likewise, we assume, without deciding, that alcoholics may be "individuals with a disability" for purposes of the Act. . ... Thus, our analysis focuses on whether Maddox is "otherwise qualified" under the Act and whether he was discharged "solely by reason of" his disability. The burden of making these showings rests with Maddox.

In support of its motion for summary judgment, UT contended that both factors weighed in its favor. First, Dickey and Majors contended that they did not even know that Maddox was considered an alcoholic in making both the decision to hire and fire him. Moreover, they contended that Maddox was discharged, not because he was an alcoholic, but because of his criminal conduct and behavior and the significant amount of bad publicity surrounding him and the school. UT alternatively contended that Maddox is nevertheless not "otherwise qualified" to continue in the position of assistant football coach.

The district court granted UT's motion for summary judgment, specifically holding that UT did not discharge Maddox solely by reason of his disability. The court found it beyond dispute that Maddox's discharge resulted from his misconduct rather than his disability of alcoholism. The court noted,

It cannot be denied in this case, Mr. Maddox was charged with . . . [driving while under the influence and public intoxication] which would not be considered socially acceptable by any objective standard. The affidavit testimony of Mr. Dickey and Mr. Majors is clear on the point that it was this specific conduct, not any condition to which it might be related, which provoked the termination of Mr. Maddox's employment.

As a result, the court found it unnecessary to decide the alternative ground of whether Maddox was "otherwise qualified."

Maddox contends that the district court erred in distinguishing between discharge for misconduct and discharge solely by reason of his disability of alcoholism. Maddox claims that he has difficulty operating a motor vehicle while under the influence of alcohol and therefore he characterizes drunk driving as a causally connected manifestation of the disability of alcoholism. Thus, Maddox contends that because alcoholism caused the incident upon which UT claims to have based its decision to discharge him, UT in essence discharged him because of his disability of alcoholism. In support, Maddox relies on *Teahan v. Metro-North Commuter R.R. Co.*, 951 F.2d 511, 516–17 (2d Cir. 1991), cert. denied, 121 L. Ed. 2d 24, 113 S. Ct. 54 (1992), in which the Second Circuit held that a Rehabilitation Act plaintiff can show that he was fired "solely by reason of" his disability, or at least create a genuine issue of material fact, if he can show that he was fired for conduct that is "causally related" to his disability. In *Teahan*, the defendant company discharged the plaintiff because of his excessive absenteeism. The plaintiff responded by claiming that his absenteeism was caused by his alcoholism and therefore protected under the Rehabilitation Act. The district court disagreed and granted summary judgment for the employer because, the court found, Teahan was fired for his absenteeism and not because of his alcoholism. The Second Circuit reversed the district court's grant of summary judgment on appeal, however, rejecting the court's distinction between misconduct (absenteeism), and the disabling condition of alcoholism. The court presumed that Teahan's absenteeism resulted from his alcoholism and held that one's disability should not be distinguished from its consequences in determining whether he was fired "solely by reason" of his disability. *Id.* Thus, Maddox argues that, in the instant case, when UT acted on the basis of the conduct allegedly caused by the alcoholism, it was the same as if UT acted on the basis of alcoholism itself.

We disagree and hold that the district court correctly focused on the distinction between discharging someone for unacceptable misconduct and discharging someone because of the disability. As the district court noted, to hold otherwise, an employer would be forced to accommodate all behavior of an alcoholic which could in any way be related to the alcoholic's use of intoxicating beverages; behavior that would be intolerable if engaged in by a sober employee or, for that matter, an intoxicated but nonalcoholic employee.

Despite Teahan, a number of cases have considered the issue of misconduct as distinct from the status of the disability. In *Taub v. Frank*, 957 F.2d 8 (1st Cir. 1992), the plaintiff Taub, a heroin addict, brought suit against his former employer, the United States Postal Service, alleging discriminatory discharge under the Rehabilitation Act. The Post Office discharged Taub after he was arrested for possession of heroin for distribution. The district court granted the Post Office's motion for summary judgment and Taub appealed. The First Circuit affirmed and held that Taub could not prevail on his Rehabilitation Act claim because his discharge resulted from his misconduct, possession of heroin for distribution, rather than his disability of heroin addiction. The court reasoned that addictionrelated criminal conduct is simply too attenuated to extend the Act's protection to Taub.

The conduct/disability distinction was also recognized by the Fourth Circuit in *Little v. F.B.I.*, 1 F.3d 255 (4th Cir. 1993). In *Little*, the F.B.I. discharged the plaintiff, known by his supervisors to be an alcoholic, after an incident in which he was intoxicated on duty. The district court granted summary judgment in favor of the F.B.I. on the basis that the plaintiff was no longer "otherwise qualified" to serve as an F.B.I. agent. The Fourth Circuit affirmed, noting as an additional basis that the plaintiff's employment was not terminated because of his handicap. The court noted, "based on no less authority than common sense, it is clear that an employer subject to the . . . [Rehabilitation] Act must be permitted to terminate its employees on account of egregious misconduct, irrespective of whether the employee is handicapped." *Id.*; see also *Landefeld v. Marion Gen. Hosp., Inc.*, 994 F.2d 1178, 1183 (6th Cir. 1993) (Nelson, J., concurring) ("The plaintiff was clearly suspended because of his intolerable conduct, and not solely because of his mental condition.")

Moreover, language within the respective statutes makes clear that such a distinction is warranted. Section 706(8)(c) of the Rehabilitation Act states:

"Individuals with a disability" does not include any individual who is an alcoholic whose current use of alcohol prevents such individual from performing the duties of the job in question or whose employment, by reason of such current alcohol abuse, would constitute a direct threat to property or the safety of others.

Likewise, the ADA specifically provides that an employer may hold an alcoholic employee to the same performance and behavior standards to which the employer holds other employees "even if any unsatisfactory performance is related to the alcoholism of such employee." 42 U.S.C. § 12114(c)(4). These provisions clearly contemplate distinguishing the issue of misconduct from one's status as an alcoholic.

At bottom, we conclude that the analysis of the district court is more in keeping with the purposes and limitations of the respective Acts, and therefore, we decline to adopt the Second Circuit's reasoning in Teahan. Employers subject to the Rehabilitation Act and ADA must be permitted to take appropriate action with respect to an employee on account of egregious or criminal conduct, regardless of whether the employee is disabled. In the instant case, for example, while alcoholism might compel Maddox to drink, it did not compel him to operate a motor vehicle or engage in the other inappropriate conduct reported. Likewise, suppose an alcoholic becomes intoxicated and sexually assaults a coworker? We believe that it strains logic to conclude that such action could be protected under the Rehabilitation Act or the ADA merely because the actor has been diagnosed as an alcoholic and claims that such action was caused by his disability.

3. Pretext

Maddox alternatively contends that even if UT has successfully disclaimed reliance on his disability in making the employment decision, the district court nevertheless erred in determining that Maddox had produced no evidence that the reasons articulated by UT were a pretext for discrimination. A Rehabilitation Act plaintiff may demonstrate pretext by showing that the asserted reasons had no basis in fact, the reasons did not in fact motivate the discharge, or, if they were factors in the decision, they were jointly insufficient to motivate the discharge.

Maddox first alleges that Dickey and Majors knew that Maddox was an alcoholic. Setting aside for a moment the legal significance of this statement, it is not supported factually in the record.

Maddox also claims that he knew of other coaches in the football program who drank alcohol in public and who were arrested for DUI but who were not discharged. This point is also irrelevant. Whether Maddox had such knowledge is immaterial. There is no evidence in the record establishing that Majors or Dickey had knowledge of the public intoxication of any other coach, or failed to reprimand or terminate any coach who they knew to have engaged in such behavior.

Maddox finally contends that UT's conclusion that he is no longer qualified to be an assistant coach at UT is without merit. Maddox claims that his misconduct did not affect his "coaching" responsibilities because an assistant coach's duties are limited to the practice and playing fields, and do not comprise of serving as a counselor or mentor to the players or serving as a representative of the school. Maddox relies on the fact that none of these functions were explained to him in his formal job description.

We first note that this allegation seems more appropriate for determining whether he was "otherwise qualified" rather than whether he was discharged because of his disability. Nevertheless, Maddox's position is simply unrealistic. It is obvious that as a member of the football coaching staff, Maddox would be representing not only the team but also the university. As in the instant case, UT received full media coverage because of this "embarrassing" incident. The school falls out of favor with the public, and the reputation of the football program suffers. Likewise, to argue that football coaches today, with all the emphasis on the misuse of drugs and alcohol by athletes, are not "role models" and "mentors" simply ignores reality.

The district court's grant of summary judgment in favor of the defendants is AFFIRMED.

CASES ON THE SUPPLEMENTAL CD

McFadden v. Grasmick, 485 F. Supp. 2d 642 (2007). This case examines whether a wheelchair athlete should be allowed to compete with able-bodied runners.

PGA Tour v. Martin, 532 U.S. 661 (2001). This case examines whether walking is an essential element in the game of golf.

Bowers v. The National Collegiate Athletic Association, 475 F.3d 524 (3rd Cir. 2007). This case examines the rights of college athletes under the Americans with Disabilities Act of 1990 (ADA) and the Rehabilitation Act of 1973.

QUESTIONS YOU SHOULD BE ABLE TO ANSWER

1. Define reasonable accommodation.

2. Give two examples of how you could make a reasonable accommodation for:

    a. An Assistant Athletic Director with a hearing impairment
    b. A Director of Marketing who uses a wheelchair
    c. A Ticket Account Executive with a visual impairment

3. What is meant by a qualified person with a disability?

4. What criteria must a person meet to be a person with a disability? How has the Americans with Disabilities Act Amendments changed this?

5. Which of the following would be classified as an employer? Why or why not?

    a. A National Football League team
    b. A two-week summer soccer camp
    c. A major metropolitan downtown YMCA

REFERENCES

Cases
Bombrys v. City of Toledo, 849 F. Supp. 1210 (N.D. Ohio 1993).
Buckingham v. United States, 998 F.2d 735 (9th Cir. 1993).
Collings v. Longview Fibre Company, 63 F.3d 828 (1995).

Henchey v. Town of North Greenbush, 831 F. Supp. 960 (N.D. N.Y. 1993).
Jackson v. Veterans' Administration, 22 F.3d 277 (11th Cir. 1994).
Jones v. Southeast Alabama Baseball Umpires Association, 864 F. Supp. 1135 (M.D. Ala. 1994).
Mazzarella v. U.S. Postal Service, 849 F. Supp. 89 (D. Mass. 1993).
Pandazides v. Virginia Board of Education, 804 F. Supp. 794 (1992).
Russell v. Southeastern Pennsylvania Transportation Authority, 2 A.D. Cas. [BNA] 1419 (E.D. Pa. 1993).
Sargent v. Litton Systems, 841 F. Supp. 956 (N.D. Cal. 1994).
Sawhill v. Medical College of Pennsylvania, 1996 U.S. Dist. LEXIS 4097.
Schmidt v. Safeway, 864 F. Supp. 991 (D. Ore. 1994).

Publications

Churchill, S. S. (1995, June). Reasonable accommodations in the workplace: A shared responsibility. *Massachusetts Law Review*, 73–83.

Colker, R., & Milani, A. A. (2005). *The law of disability discrimination handbook*. Newark, NJ: Lexis Nexis.

Equal Employment Opportunity Commission. (n.d.). Notice concerning the Americans with Disabilities Act Amendments of 2008. Retrieved from http://www.eeoc.gov/ada/amendments_notice.html

Hums, M. A. (1994). AIDS in the sport arena: After Magic Johnson, where do we go from here? *Journal of Legal Aspects of Sport, 4*(1), 59–65.

Hums, M. A., & Wolff, E. A. (2006, January). *Inclusion of athletes with disabilities: Connections and collaborations*. Presented at the Annual NAKPEHE Conference, San Diego, CA.

Job Accommodation Network. (n.d.). Frequently asked questions. Retrieved from http://askjan.org/links/faqs.htm#1

Job Accommodation Network. (2006). Technical assistance manual: Title I of the ADA. Retrieved from http://www.jan.wvu.edu/links/ADAtam1.html#III

Job Accommodation Network. (2013). Accommodation and compliance series: Employees who use wheelchairs. Retrieved from http://askjan.org/media/wheelchair.html

Job Accommodation Network. (2015). Accommodation and compliance series: Workplace accommodations: Low cost, high impact. Retrieved from http://askjan.org/media/lowcosthighimpact.html

Kim, D.L. (2015). Alcoholism and how USC may have violated ADA by firing Steve Sarkisian. Retrieved from http://blogs.hrhero.com/entertainhr/2015/10/19/alcoholism-and-how-usc-may-have-violated-the-ada-by-firing-steve-sarkisian/

Masteralexis, L. P., & Wong, G. (2015). Legal principles applied to sport management. In L.P. Masteralexis, C. A. Barr, & M. A. Hums, *Principles and practice of sport management* (5th ed.) (pp. 97-130). Burlington, MA: Jones & Bartlett Publishing.

Prosser, A. (n.d.). Americans with Disabilities Act: Big changes in 2009. Retrieved from http://fchr.state.fl.us/fchr/resources/commissioners_speak_out/americans_with_disabilities_act_big_changes_in_2009

Rhoads and Sinon. (2016). Employment laws apply to professional sports, too. Retrieved from http://blog.rhoadssinon.com/employment-laws-apply-to-professional-sports-too/

Samson, R.L. (2015). A fired football coach's lawsuit provides a cautionary tale for employers. Retrieved from http://www.dickinsonlaw.com/2015/12/fired-football-coachs-lawsuit-cautionary-tale-employers/

Schleifer, J. (2009). Finally . . .. a reasonable explanation of ADA reasonable accommodation. Retrieved from http://hrdailyadvisor.blr.com/archive/2007/07/05/ADA_Americans_with_Disabilities_Act_reasonable_accommodation_undue_hardship_definitions.aspx

United Nations. (2006). *Convention on the Rights of Persons with Disabilities*. New York: Author.

U.S. Department of Labor. (2009). The job accommodation process: Steps to collaborative solutions. Retrieved from http://www.dol.gov/odep/pubs/misc/job.htm

INTELLECTUAL PROPERTY LAW

7.20

Whether it is athletes seeking to gain more control over the use of their images and publicity rights, or teams and organizations trying to protect the values of their trademarks or copyrights, one area of the law that is seemingly growing in importance is Intellectual Property Law. The following section examines the four main areas of intellectual property: copyright and patent law; trademark law and image rights.

COPYRIGHT AND PATENT LAW

Merry Moiseichik | University of Arkansas

Copyright and patent are both forms of intellectual property. The United States Constitution gives Congress the power to enact laws governing patents and copyrights. Article 1, Section 8 of the Constitution states: "Congress shall have the power . . . to promote the Progress of Science and useful Arts, by securing for limited Times to Authors and Inventors the exclusive Right to their respective Writings and Discoveries." The use and protection of intellectual property is becoming more important to the sport and recreation industry. For example, copyright law becomes an issue in designs of logos and stadiums, ownership of television and video game rights, and use of music in recreational settings.

FUNDAMENTAL CONCEPTS

Copyright Law

Congress enacted the United States Copyright Act of 1909 to *protect the work of authors and other creative persons from the unauthorized use of their copyrighted materials and to provide a financial incentive* for artists to produce, thereby increasing the number of creative works available in society. This legislation was completely revised in 1976 to take into account changing technology, and to become more inclusive of the types of medium technology produced. In 1989 the United States became a member of the Berne Convention, where an international copyright treaty was created. This brought new revisions of the Copyright Act in 1990. The act was revised again in 1994, 1999 and 2002 to reflect changing technology and the Internet.

Copyright Protection

The purpose of the copyright law is to protect those who have put time and energy into some creative project. The law is economically motivated, designed to protect the rights of those who produce the many creative endeavors we hear and see daily. A copyright gives the owner of the work the exclusive right to copy, reproduce, distribute, publish, perform, or display the work. There are two fundamental criteria for copyright protection: 1) the work must be original, and 2) it must be in some tangible form that can be reproduced (17 U.S.C. § 102). Registration of a copyright is not required for protection, although no action for infringement can be instituted until the copyright has been registered (17 U.S.C. § 401). The protection exists as soon as the work is fixed in some tangible form, such as on paper, CD, DVD, canvas, and so forth. Copyright protection lasts 70 years beyond the death of the author or for 95 years for anonymous works or works made for hire (17 U.S.C. § 301). The federal government grants registration of a copyright, which provides procedural advantages in enforcing rights under law.

There are eight broad categories of copyright protection, including:

1. literary works;
2. musical works;
3. dramatic works;
4. pantomime and choreographic works;
5. pictorial, graphic, and sculptural works;
6. motion pictures and other audiovisual works;
7. sound recordings; and
8. architectural works (17 U.S.C. § 102).

To appreciate what can be copyrighted, it is instructive to consider what cannot be. "In no case does copyright protection for an original work of authorship extend to any idea, procedure, process, system, method of operation, concept, principle, or discovery, regardless of the form in which it is described, explained, illustrated, or embodied in such work" (17 U.S.C. § 102). Government documents and works in the public domain do not have copyright protection either. Works in the public domain include those with expired copyrights and works where copyright has not been requested (17 U.S.C. § 105).

Works that are not original cannot be considered for copyright (17 U.S.C. § 104). This would include standard works such as calendars, height and weight charts, tape measures, and lists of tables (U.S. Copyright Office, 2012). This allows freedom to make use of these articles. The outline of a calendar cannot be copyrighted, but the format and the pictures that go with the calendar can be. This allows recreation or sport programs, for example, to use a common calendar and add their own dimensions including pictures, special events, and any additional information specific to their programs. Similarly, no copyright can be held for blank forms that are used to obtain information (U.S. Copyright Office, 2015). Therefore, agencies can use anyone's accident report form or registration form as long as the forms do not include creative authorship but rather, just request information.

Athletic competitions/games are not copyrightable as they do not fall within "original works of authorship" (*National Basketball Association v. Motorola, Inc.*, 1997). You can, however, copyright the broadcasts, just not the underlying games. To illustrate this point, the Second Circuit Court in *National Basketball Association v. Motorola* (1997) stated that "if the inventor of the T-formation in football had been able to copyright it, the sport might have come to an end instead of prospering. Even where athletic preparation most resembles authorship—figure skating, gymnastics, and, some would uncharitably say, professional wrestling—a performer who conceives and executes a particularly graceful and difficult—or, in the case of wrestling, seemingly painful—acrobatic feat cannot copyright it without impairing the underlying competition in the future" (*National Basketball Association v. Motorola, Inc.*, 1997, p. 846).

Copyright protection also only extends to works that are the fruits of intellectual labor or those that are significantly creative. Therefore, works where authorship is small, also cannot hold a copyright (17 U.S.C. § 102). This includes slogans, titles, names, variations, typographic ornamentation, lettering, or coloring. If slogans, titles, names, etc., were copyrighted, there would be a loss of freedom to speak. For example, in *Syrus v. Bennett* (2011) the Tenth Circuit Court held Charles Syrus did not have a protected copyright in the phrases "Go Thunder" "Let's Go Thunder" and "Thunder Up" as used by the NBA's Oklahoma City Thunder because adding the team name to a common cheer required "no intellectual labor" (*Syrus v. Bennett*, 2011). These short sayings are protected by the trademark laws (see Chapter 7.22 *Principles of Trademark Law*).

Facts are also not copyrightable. Research data are facts. Any raw data collected can be used by anyone. In *Feist Publications v. Rural Telephone Service Co.* (1991), Feist Publications published a telephone book. Rural Telephone Service used all the information from Feist book, reorganized it, and published their own book using addresses as the listing. In ruling that Rural Telephone had not infringed the copyright law, the court held that Feist had only published non-copyrightable facts. Rural Telephone used the facts, just in a different way. This issue has come up in the area of fantasy sports, where players' game statistics are used. Since the statistics used in fantasy sports are merely facts, they are not copyrightable.

Rights of the Copyright Owner
A copyright gives its owner certain rights to the works, including:

1. the right to reproduction;
2. the right to preparation of derivative works including translation from language to language and from one form to another (i.e., from book to movie, from movie to play);
3. the right to public distribution;
4. the public performing rights, which include live renditions that are face to face, on recordings, broadcasts, and retransmissions by cable;
5. the right to the public display, specifically written or art work; and
6. to perform the copyrighted work publicly by means of a digital audio transmission (17 U.S.C. § 106).

This section was strengthened with the passage of the Visual Artists Rights Act of 1990 (VARA, 17 U.S.C. § 106A). Among the rights afforded artists by this law is the right to prevent any intentional distortion, mutilation, or other modification of that work. This allows the artist to control the visual art work until his or her death. In

Phillips v. Pembroke Real Estate (2003), the city of Boston had granted permission to a developer to build an office building and a convention center in a public sculpture park on Boston Harbor. Phillips, the sculptor, sought an injunction against the manager of the park and sought to prevent the park from moving the sculpture to a different location, from modifying the park and from altering sculptures that he created specifically for the park. Phillips stated that his design was created with the environment in mind and that it would negatively affect the art if it were moved. In rejecting Phillips' argument, the court found that VARA does not protect site specific art and that art can be moved to a different location (*Phillips v. Pembroke Real Estate*, 2006).

Copyright Ownership

Copyright ownership vests initially in the author or creator of the work. However, in the case of a "work made for hire," the owner of the copyright is the employer or person for whom the work was prepared. The Copyright Act provides that "the employer or other person for whom the work was prepared is considered the author for the purpose of this title, and, unless the parties have expressly agreed otherwise in a written instrument signed by them, owns all of the rights comprised in the copyright" (17 U.S.C. § 201(b)). For example, in *Baltimore Orioles v. Major League Baseball Players* (1986), the players claimed ownership in the copyright of televised games. In rejecting the players' claim, the Seventh Circuit Court found that since the players were working for the club, the Orioles owned the copyright, not the players.

Fair Use

An important section of the Copyright Law for users of copyrighted works is the fair use section (17 U.S.C. §107). This section was passed to strike a balance between the copyright monopoly and the greater interest of society including criticism, comment, news reporting, teaching, scholarship, or research. There are four factors to ascertain fair use: 1) the purpose and the character of use, whether it is for commercial or for nonprofit educational purposes; 2) the nature of the copyrighted work; 3) the amount and substantiality of the material used in comparison with the whole; and 4) the effect of the use on the potential market or value of the work (17 U.S.C. § 107).

Ted Giannoulas, the creator of the sports mascot, "the Chicken," was sued by the owners of Barney, a purple dinosaur in a children's TV show. The Chicken, as part of a pregame show, beat up on Barney. The owners of Barney said they did not approve of their character being used in that manner and that it negatively affected the small children who loved Barney. In upholding Giannoulas' right to use Barney, the court ruled it was a parody and thus fair use (*Lyons Partnership, L.P. v. Giannoulas*, 1999).

A primary motivator for the passage of the fair use section was the use of copyrighted works for educational purposes. The educational fair use test is based on three rules: 1) brevity (using small parts of the whole); 2) spontaneity (if there is time to request permission, it should be requested); and, 3) cumulative effect (how will it affect the creator). The copying is not allowed when it replaces a book that would be purchased. Consumables are not allowed to be copied under any circumstances. Therefore coloring books, consumable material, cannot be copied for use in after school or day care programs (House Report No. 94-1478, 1977).

Music and Performance

Musical scores that are performed by bands and choruses should be purchased. However, there are guidelines in §110 of the Copyright Act that allow for music and dramatic performances by nonprofit agencies, religious institutions, or for educational purposes. Performance of music is legal without paying royalties if it is not for profit and all money goes to charity. Music and dramatic works can be performed in classrooms, for religious assembly, and for transmission to the public, without any purpose of direct or indirect commercial advantage and without payment of any fee or other compensation for the performance to its performers, promoters, or organizers. There can be no direct or indirect admission charged unless the proceeds, after deducting the reasonable costs of producing the performance, are used exclusively for educational, religious, or charitable purposes and not for private financial gain (17 U.S.C. § 110). The 2002 amendments specifically discuss the transmission of these performances. It is not legal to make digital displays of these works unless they are specifically and only for registered students. They also cannot be transmitted or stored where public has access to them for any length of time other than what is absolutely necessary. Section 110 does not include colleges and universities playing their pep music at games or for fraternities and sororities using music at parties, unless the function is to raise money for charity. Licenses must be secured from performance rights agencies.

Public Performance Restrictions

According to the Copyright Act a performance or display is public if it is open to the public or at any place where a substantial number of persons outside a normal circle of a family and its social acquaintances are gathered (17 U.S.C. § 101). For public performances, a license must be obtained. This even includes dormitory public areas. Music is also affected by public performance restrictions. Playing CDs, for example, in a public place is prohibited without a license. If a manager of a fitness center, for example, wants to play background music in the center and people paid to be members, the manager must obtain a license. If that same center has an aerobics instructor who plays CD's during exercises, the center must have a license, especially if there is profit. It is not the responsibility of the aerobics instructor to get the license. It is the responsibility of the center in which the class is being given to get the license, which are not particularly expensive and depends on the size of the facility, the amount of use, and the number of participants in the program. Cases involving copyright infringement for public performances of music include: *Tallyrand Music, Inc. v. Frank Stenko* (1990), involving background music played in a skating rink; *Broadcast Music, Inc. v. Melody Fair Enterprises, Inc.* (1990), involving a club where musical compositions were performed by live artists; *Lorimar Music v. Black Iron Grill Co.* (2010), where a restaurant tried to play karaoke music without a license; and *Broadcast Music Inc. v. Blueberry Hill Family Restaurants, Inc.* (1995), where a restaurant chain operated jukeboxes that patrons played for free. Each of these defendants was found guilty of playing copyrighted music without a license and fined.

Television and Radio Broadcasting

The Copyright Act protects any original works of authorship fixed in any tangible medium, including motion pictures and other audiovisual works. The broadcast, by radio or television, of a live sporting event is eligible for protection. The Act has become a significant source of protection for the major professional sport leagues to combat the unauthorized interception of commercial-free feeds of broadcast signals. For live transmissions "the first fixation is made simultaneously with its transmission, the copyright owner may, either before or after such fixation takes place, institute an action for infringement . . . if . . . the copyright owner (1) serves notice upon the infringer not less than 48 hours before such fixation . . . and (2) makes registration for the work . . . within three months after its first transmission" (17 U.S.C. § 411(c)). For example, in *Live Nation Motor Sports, Inc. v. Davis*, (2007) Live Nation Motor Sports sued Davis for copyright infringement after he transmitted through his website live audio feeds of motor cross events that were being produced live by Live Nation Motor Sports, Inc. for TV. In ruling for Live Nation Motor Sports, the court found that even though the transmission were live and therefore not yet fixed, the broadcast was copyrighted at the time of transmission.

Another issue involving copyright law and television focuses on sports bars that broadcast games that can only be seen through the use of satellite dish antenna systems. The professional sport leagues contend that this piracy of network satellite signals both devalues advertising revenues when patrons at sport bars watch contests commercial free, and affects local ticket sales when a blacked-out game is broadcast in a local sports bar. Under the "home-use" exemption, which is intended to limit the exclusive rights granted copyright owners when the transmission is received by equipment similar to the type "commonly used in private homes" (17 U.S.C. § 110(5)), the sport bars claim that satellite dish equipment is commonly used in private homes and therefore legal. Such arguments, however, have been unsuccessful to date and any sports bar or other public establishments desiring to transmit cable or pay-per-view broadcasts must have a license (*Cablevision Systems Corp. v. 45 Midland Enterprises, Inc.*, (1994); *National Football League v. McBee & Bruno's, Inc.*, (1986); *National Football League v. Rondor*, (1993)).

This "home-use" exemption clause does not include rebroadcasting. It is a copyright infringement, therefore, to tape a copyrighted program and exhibit it at another time in a public setting without explicit permission from the producers. For example, if a sport bar recorded a game for later viewing in their establishment, such a viewing would be a violation of copyright law. The broadcasting rights of time and place are reserved for the broadcasters. On the other hand, it is legal to tape a show for later viewing if it is done in the confines of a home with friends and family. This is considered time shifting and has been held legal in nonpublic settings (*Sony Corp. v. Universal Studios*, 1984).

Internet

The internet is a major issue in copyright infringement as it has made pirating copyrighted material, such as music and movies, easily available to the general public. For example, in *A & M Records, Inc. v. Napster, Inc.*, 2002, Napster created a website that allowed free downloading of music. Although the court eventually shut down Napster, finding the website vicariously libel for copyright infringement since it provided the method for file sharing and should have known copyright infringement was occurring; there continues to be a battle over copyright protection on the internet as more sophisticated software is developed.

In 1998 The Digital Millenium Copyright Act (17 USCS § 512) was passed to take the responsibility off the provider of the websites that make infringing easy and pass it on to the actual infringer, the person who copies or passes on copyrighted material through the service provider's website. The service provider, for example You Tube, provides the site, which could allow for legal uploading and downloading of material, but through that process could be used to infringe as well. The service provider should not receive financial benefit from the infringing material and must respond expeditiously to remove it when notified of its presence.

In an effort to stop online piracy and protect the TV, music and movie industry, Congress attempted to pass two bills: Stop Online Piracy Act (SOPA) and Protect IP Act (PIPA). When the public however protested that the bills would limit the freedom of the internet, Congress pulled the bills back for further review (Pepitone, 2012). Whether it is the music industry fighting to remove music from the Fair Use section of the Copyright law and prevent the use of music in YouTube videos, short sections in films, or backgrounds in political ads (Henslee, 2009), or internet reporters struggling to blog games, it is clear that the internet will continue to be in the forefront of copyright issues.

SIGNIFICANT CASE

The following case examines the issues surrounding who owns the rights to copyright, the players who provide the entertainment or the owners and producers. The case explains how a game can be a copyrighted work and what constitutes copyright.

BALTIMORE ORIOLES INC. V. M.L.B. PLAYERS ASSOCIATION
United States Court of Appeals for the Seventh Circuit
805 F.2d 663 (1986)

The primary issue involved in this appeal is whether major league baseball clubs own exclusive rights to the televised performances of major league baseball players during major league baseball games.

This appeal arises out of a long-standing dispute between the Major League Baseball Clubs ("Clubs") and the Major League Baseball Players Association ("Players") regarding the ownership of the broadcast rights to the Players' performances during major league baseball games. After decades of negotiation concerning the allocation of revenues from telecasts of the games, the Players in May of 1982 sent letters to the Clubs, and to television and cable companies with which the Clubs had contracted, asserting that the telecasts were being made without the Players' consent and that they misappropriated the Players' property rights in their performances.

The mailing of these letters led the parties to move their dispute from the bargaining table to the courtroom.

On June 14, 1982, the Clubs filed an action (entitled *Baltimore Orioles, Inc. v. Major League Baseball Players Association*, No. 82 C 3710) in the United States District Court for the Northern District of Illinois, in which they sought a declaratory judgment "that the telecasts of Major League Baseball games constitute copyrighted 'works made for hire' in which defendant and Major League Baseball players have no rights whatsoever." Baltimore Orioles Complaint. The district court found that the Clubs, not the Players, owned a copyright in the telecasts as works made for hire and that the Clubs' copyright in the telecasts preempted the Players' rights of publicity in their performances.

* * *

Our analysis begins by ascertaining whether the Clubs own a copyright in the telecasts of major league baseball games. In general, copyright in a work "vests initially in the author or authors of the work," 17 U.S.C. § 201(a); however, "in the case of a work made for hire, the employer or other person for whom the work was prepared is considered the author . . . and, unless the parties have expressly agreed otherwise in a written instrument signed by them, owns all of the rights comprised in the copyright." 17 U.S.C. § 201(b). A work made for hire is defined in pertinent part as "a work prepared by an employee within the scope of his or her employment." 17 U.S.C. § 101. Thus, an employer owns a copyright in a work if (1) the work satisfies the generally applicable requirements for copyrightability set forth in 17 U.S.C. § 102(a), (2) the work was prepared by an employee, (3) the work was prepared within the scope of the employee's employment, and (4) the parties have not expressly agreed otherwise in a signed, written instrument.

* * *

The district court concluded that the telecasts were copyrightable works. We agree. Section 102 sets forth three conditions for copyrightability: first, a work must be fixed in tangible form; second, the work must be an original work of authorship; and third, it must come within the subject matter of copyright. See 17 U.S.C. § 102(a). Although there may have been some question at one time as to whether simultaneously recorded live broadcasts were copyrightable, this is no longer the case. Section 101 expressly provides that "[a] work consisting of sounds, images, or both, that are being transmitted, is 'fixed' . . . if a fixation of the work is being made simultaneously with its transmission." Since the telecasts of the games are videotaped at the same time they are broadcast, the telecasts are fixed in tangible form.

* * *

Moreover, the telecasts are original works of authorship. The requirement of originality actually subsumes two separate conditions, i.e., the work must possess an independent origin and a minimal amount of creativity. * * * It is obvious that the telecasts are independent creations, rather than reproductions of earlier works.

It is important to distinguish among three separate concepts—originality, creativity, and novelty. A work is original if it is the independent creation of its author. A work is creative if it embodies some modest amount of intellectual labor. A work is novel if it differs from existing works in some relevant respect. For a work to be copyrightable, it must be original and creative, but need not be novel. (Thus, in contrast to patent law, a work that is independently produced by two separate authors may be copyrighted by both.)

* * *

As for the telecasts' creativity, courts long have recognized that photographing a person or filming an event involves creative labor. * * * For example, one court held that the Zapruder film of the Kennedy assassination was copyrightable because it embodied many elements of creativity. Among other things, Zapruder selected the kind of camera (movies, not snapshots), the kind of film (color), the kind of lens (telephoto), the area in which the pictures were to be taken, the time they were to be taken, and (after testing several sites) the spot on which the camera would be operated.

The many decisions that must be made during the broadcast of a baseball game concerning camera angles, types of shots, the use of instant replays and split screens, and shot selection similarly supply the creativity required for the copyrightability of the telecasts. * * * ("When a football game is being covered by four television cameras, with a director guiding the activities of the four cameramen and choosing which of their electronic images are sent to the public and in which order, there is little doubt that what the cameramen and the director are doing constitutes 'authorship.'").

The Players argue that their performances are not copyrightable works because they lack sufficient artistic merit. We disagree. Only a modicum of creativity is required for a work to be copyrightable. Contrary to the Players' contentions, aesthetic merit is not necessary for copyrightability. * * * A recording of a performance generally includes creative contributions by both the director and other individuals responsible for recording the performance and by the performers whose performance is captured. * * * Judged by the above standard, the Players' performances possess the modest creativity required for copyrightability. As Justice Holmes once declared, "if . . . [certain works] command the interest of any public, they have a commercial value—it would be bold to say that they have not an aesthetic and educational value—and the taste of any public is not to be treated with contempt." *Bleistein v. Donaldson Lithographing Co.*, 188 U.S. 239, 252, 47 L. Ed. 460, 23 S. Ct. 298 (1903) (holding circus poster copyrightable). Courts thus should not gainsay the copyrightability of a work possessing great commercial value simply because the work's aesthetic or educational value is not readily apparent to a person trained in the law. That the Players' performances possess great commercial value indicates that the works embody the modicum of creativity required for copyrightability.

Moreover, even if the Players' performances were not sufficiently creative, the Players agree that the cameramen and director contribute creative labor to the telecasts. The work that is the subject of copyright is not merely the Players' performances, but rather the telecast of the Players' performances. The creative contribution of the cameramen and director alone suffices for the telecasts to be copyrightable.

Furthermore, the telecasts are audiovisual works, which under § 102 come within the subject matter of copyright. See 17 U.S.C. § 101 (definition of "audiovisual works"); * * * the telecasts are, therefore, copyrightable works.

Section 102(a) provides: Copyright protection subsists . . . in original works of authorship fixed in any tangible medium of expression, now known or later developed, from which they can be perceived, reproduced, or otherwise communicated, either directly or with the aid of a machine or device. Works of authorship include the following categories:

1. literary works;
2. musical works, including any accompanying words;
3. dramatic works, including any accompanying music;
4. pantomimes and choreographic works;
5. pictorial, graphic, and sculptural works;
6. motion pictures and other audiovisual works; and
7. sound recordings. 17 U.S.C. § 102(a). "Audiovisual works" are works that consist of a series of related images which are intrinsically intended to be shown by the use of machines or devices such as projectors, viewers, or electronic equipment, together with accompanying sounds, if any, regardless of the nature of the material objects, such as films or tapes, in which the works are embodied. 17 U.S.C. § 101.

b. Employer-employee relationship

With regard to the relationship between the Clubs and the Players, the district court found, and the Players do not dispute, that the Players are employees of their respective Clubs. We add only that this finding is consistent with the broad construction given to the term "employee" by courts applying the "work made for hire" doctrine. * * * (a person acting under another's direction and supervision is an employee for the purpose of the work made for hire doctrine) * * *.

c. Scope of employment

The district court further found that the scope of the Players' employment encompassed the performance of major league baseball before "live and remote audiences." See Baltimore Orioles, 1985 Copyright L. Dec. at 19,731. On appeal the Players argue that there exist genuine issues of material fact as to whether the performance of baseball for televised audiences is within the scope of the Players' employment. * * * * However, they never claimed that the performance of baseball before televised audiences was not within the scope of their employment. Indeed, the only issue as to which Players argued that there was a genuine issue of material fact concerned the parties' written agreements respecting ownership of the telecasts' copyright. * * * The Players, therefore, failed to preserve this argument.

Moreover, even on appeal, the Players do not identify any evidence that would create a genuine issue of material fact as to the scope of the Players' employment. In contrast to the Players' perfunctory claim that playing baseball for television audiences is not within the scope of their employment, see Appellant's Brief 29, the Clubs brought forth detailed evidence in support of their motion for summary judgment that the scope of the Players' employment encompassed performances before broadcast audiences. Because of the Players' failure to point to any evidence to the contrary, we would not reverse the district court's finding that the performance of baseball before remote audiences is within the Players' scope of employment even if the Players had preserved their contention. * * *

For example, the Clubs adduced evidence that the Players are acutely aware of the fact that major league baseball games are televised, and that the Players understand that television revenues have a bearing on the level of the salaries that they receive.

d. Written agreements

Because the Players are employees and their performances before broadcast audiences are within the scope of their employment, the telecasts of major league baseball games, which consist of the Players' performances, are works made for hire within the meaning of § 201(b). (The parties can change the statutory presumption concerning the ownership of a copyright in a work made for hire, but cannot vary the work's status as a work made for hire). Thus, in the absence of an agreement to the contrary, the Clubs are presumed to own all of the rights encompassed in the telecasts of the games. The district court found that there was no written agreement that the Clubs would not own the copyright to the telecasts, and, therefore, that the copyright was owned by the Clubs.

* * *

The provisions of the three written agreements on which the Players rely to establish a genuine issue of material fact are paragraph 3(c) of the Uniform Player's Contract, paragraph 7 of the Benefit Plan, and article X of the Basic Agreement. First, the Uniform Player's Contract is the standard form contract between individual players and their respective clubs. In 1947, the first year that the Clubs sold network television rights to major league baseball games, the following language was added to the contract:

The Player agrees that his picture may be taken for still photographs, motion pictures or television at such times as the Club may designate and that all rights in such pictures shall belong to the Club and may be used by the Club for publicity purposes in any manner it desires. Uniform Player's Contract 3(c). The language of paragraph 3(c) has remained materially unchanged over the years.

Second, the Benefit Plan sets forth the particulars of the Players' pension fund. First entered into in 1967, the Benefit Plan arose in large part out of the parties' long-standing dispute as to the allocation of national television revenues to the pension fund. In negotiations over the 1969 Benefit Plan, the Players asserted their long-held claim that broadcasts of baseball games without their consent violated their rights of publicity in their performances. The Clubs, however, maintained that the Players had no rights whatsoever in the telecasts. The parties accordingly agreed to the following compromise provision:

The execution of this Agreement shall not be deemed to change any rights or obligations of the Clubs or the Players with respect to the funding of the Plan (except to the extent set forth in other Paragraphs of this Agreement) or with respect to radio and television, as such rights and obligations existed immediately after the execution of the Agreement Re Major League Baseball Players Benefit Plan of January 1, 1967.

Third, the Basic Agreement represents the collective bargaining agreement between the Players and the Clubs. The original Basic Agreement entered into in 1968 provided that grievances would be arbitrated by the Commissioner of Baseball. When the parties entered into the 1970 Basic Agreement, they agreed to arbitration of grievances by a tripartite panel, rather than by the Commissioner; however, the Clubs did not agree to submit to impartial arbitration those disputes concerning the right to broadcast major league baseball games. The parties thus agreed that:

Anything in the Grievance Procedure provided for in the Basic Agreement to the contrary notwithstanding, complaints or disputes as to any rights of the Players or the Clubs with respect to the sale or proceeds of sale of radio or television broadcasting rights in any baseball games by any kind or method of transmission, dissemination or reception shall not be subject to said Grievance Procedure. However, nothing herein or in the Grievance Procedure shall alter or abridge the rights of the parties, or any of them, to resort to a court of law for the resolution of such complaint or dispute. 1970 Basic Agreement art. X. This language has been included verbatim in each Basic Agreement entered into since 1970.

The Players contend that these three provisions create a genuine issue of material fact with respect to the parties' agreements concerning the ownership of the copyright to the telecasts. We disagree. Section 201(b) states that the employer owns the copyright in a work made for hire "unless the parties have expressly agreed otherwise in a written instrument signed by them." The requirement that an agreement altering the presumption that an employer owns the copyright in a work made for hire represents a substantial change in the "work made for hire" doctrine. Under prior law, "such an agreement could be either oral or implied." However, § 201(b) requires that an agreement altering the statutory presumption be both written and express.

* * *

In this case, the parties have not expressly agreed to rebut the statutory presumption that the Clubs own the copyright in the telecasts. Paragraph 3(c) of the Uniform Player's Contract does not declare that the copyright in the telecasts is owned by the Players, rather than by the Clubs. Instead, it merely grants the Clubs the rights to take the Players' pictures for still photographs, motion pictures, and television and to use the pictures for publicity purposes. A limitation on the Clubs' rights to televise the Players' performances perhaps might be implied by the grant of these particular rights; however, even if such an implied limitation were plausible, paragraph 3(c) nowhere contains an express statement that the Clubs do not own the copyright in the telecasts of the Players' performances.

* * *

Paragraph 7 of the Benefit Plan and Article X of the Basic Agreement similarly do not declare that the Players, rather than the Clubs, own the copyright in the telecasts. The two provisions simply preserved whatever rights in the telecasts that the parties might possess and reserved each party's right to have disputes concerning television rights be resolved in court, rather than by arbitration. They nowhere state that either the Clubs or the Players own the copyright in the telecasts. These provisions thus do not represent an express agreement that the Players own the copyright in the telecasts. If anything, they reflect the parties' express disagreement as to the copyright's ownership.

The Players point to the absence of a provision expressly granting the Clubs the right to televise the games as support for their assertion that they have "reserved" their rights of publicity in their performances. Nonetheless, there is no need for such an express declaration because under § 201(b) the Clubs are presumed to own the copyright in the works produced by their employees unless the parties expressly agree otherwise in a signed, written instrument.

The Players also argue that these three provisions must be read in light of the agreements' collective bargaining history, and that the circumstances surrounding the agreements cannot be determined without a trial. We disagree. Under § 201(b), an agreement altering the statutory presumption that the employer owns the copyright in a work made for hire must be express. This is to say, the parties' agreement must appear on the face of the signed written instrument. Section 201(b) thus bars the use of parol evidence to imply a provision not found within the four corners of the parties' agreement. * * * Moreover, even if extrinsic evidence were admissible to explain an ambiguity in the parties' agreement, the provisions relied upon by the Players are unambiguous with respect to the ownership of the copyright in the telecasts. Since the contractual terms regarding television rights are clear, it is unnecessary to examine the parties' collective bargaining history to ascertain the meaning of the agreements.

The Players rely on labor law cases concerning the construction of collective bargaining agreements. Such cases, however, have no bearing on the consideration in a copyright case of the parties' agreements concerning the ownership of the copyright in a work made for hire. Congress considered incorporating in § 201(b) the "shop right" doctrine of patent law under which the employer would acquire the right to use the employee's work to the extent needed for the purposes of the employer's regular business, but the employee would retain all other rights so long as he or she refrained from authorizing competing uses. Congress rejected this change because it would create uncertainty as to the ownership of the copyright in a work made for hire. * * * In any event, the collective bargaining history behind the parties' agreements similarly reflects a sharp dispute as to the ownership of the television rights to the games. A fortiori, it cannot establish that the parties agreed that the Players would own the copyright in the televised broadcasts.

The Players further assert that the parties' traditional practice of devoting approximately one-third of the revenues derived from nationally televised broadcasts to the Players' pension fund establishes a genuine issue of material fact as to the ownership of the copyright in these telecasts. We disagree. The allocation of revenues from nationally televised broadcasts is determined by the parties' relative bargaining strength and ability. Depending on the Players' bargaining power, they can negotiate a greater or a lesser share of the national telecast revenues. Nevertheless, there is no relationship between the division of revenues from nationally televised broadcasts and the ownership of rights in those telecasts. For example, a motion picture star might negotiate to receive a certain number of "points" from a film's profits; however, that she shares in the film's profits does not mean that she owns some share of the copyright in the film. (Indeed, the producer most likely holds the copyright in the work.) Just as the ownership of points in a film's profits does not represent a proportionate ownership of the copyright in the film, the Players' receipt in the form of pension contributions of a certain fraction of the revenues from nationally televised broadcasts in no way suggests that they own any part of the copyright in the telecasts.

The Players do not claim that they traditionally have received some share of the revenues from locally televised broadcasts. Therefore, even under the Players' analysis, the division of revenues from national broadcasts does not create a genuine issue of material fact as to the ownership of the copyright in local telecasts. Moreover, the Clubs contest the assertion that they traditionally have devoted to the Players' pension fund approximately one-third of the revenues from nationally televised broadcasts. They argue that since it was first entered into in 1967, the Benefit Plan simply has provided for the Clubs to contribute to the pension plan a flat dollar amount from whatever source of revenue they choose, and never has required the Clubs to contribute any amount, let alone one-third, of the national telecast revenues. Nonetheless, as our subsequent discussion indicates, we need not resolve this dispute because it is not material to the ownership of the copyright in the national telecasts.

* * *

We thus conclude that there are no genuine issues of material fact as to the ownership of the copyright in the telecasts, and that the parties did not expressly agree to rebut the statutory presumption that the employer owns the copyright in a work made for hire. We, therefore, hold that the Clubs own the copyright in telecasts of major league baseball games.

* * *

CASES ON THE SUPPLEMENTAL CD

Baltimore Orioles, Inc. v. M.L.B. Players Assoc, 805 F.2d 663 (1986). This is the continuation of the case as it relates to copyright and pre-emption, right to publicity and master servant.

Incredible Technologies Inc. v. Virtual Technologies Inc, 400 F.3d 1007 (2005). This case examines what one has to prove to succeed in a copyright infringement case.

Lorimar Music A Corp v. Black Iron Grill, 2010 U.S. Dist. LEXIS 76484 (W.D. MO. 2010). This case shows how an infringement case is handled (Note the amount the infringement cost).

Kelley v. Chicago Park District, 635 F.3d 290 (7th Cir. 2011). Note how the elements of copyright are evaluated. Do you agree with the outcome? Explain.

Brigams Yoga College of India v. Evolation Yoga LLC 803 F.3d 1032 (9th Cir. 2015) This case discusses what can obtain a copyright and what cannot.

QUESTIONS YOU SHOULD BE ABLE TO ANSWER

1. For what can you get a copyright and what cannot carry a copyright?

2. Explain the difference between public and private and contrast how they are treated differently when playing music or watching videos.

3. What is meant by "fair use" and what rights and privileges does it confer?

4. Many musicians claim that the internet may be the demise of music as a career as musician can no longer make a living through music. Discuss this statement in relation to the copyright law.

5. Look through social media and determine how much of it may be breaking copyright law. Suggest some methods that might be used to curb such infringement.

REFERENCES
Cases
A & M Records, Inc. v. Napster, Inc., 284 F.3d. 1091 (9th Cir. 2002).
Baltimore Orioles v. Major League Baseball Players, 805 F.2d 663 (7th Cir. 1986).
Broadcast Music, Inc. v. Blueberry Hill Family Restaurants, Inc., 899 F. Supp. 474 (N.D. Nev, 1995).
Broadcast Music, Inc. v. Melody Fair Enterprises, Inc., 1990 WL 284743 (W.D. N.Y. 1990).
Cablevision Systems Corp. v. 45 Midland Enterprises, Inc., 858 F. Supp. 42 (S.D. N.Y. 1994).
Feist Publications v. Rural Telephone Service Co., 111 S.Ct. 1282 (1991).
Live Nation Motor Sports, Inc. v. Davis, 81 U.S.P.Q.2d (BNA) 1826 (2007)
Lorimar Music A Corp v. Black Iron Grill, 2010 U.S. Dist. LEXIS 76484 (W.D. MO. 2010)
Lyons Partnership, L.P. v. Giannoulas, 179 F.3d 384 (5th Cir. 1999).
National Basketball Association and NBA Properties, Inc. v. Motorola, Inc., 105 F.3d 841 (2nd Cir., 1997).
National Football League v. McBee & Bruno's, Inc., 792 F.2d 726 (8th Cir. 1986).
National Football League v. Rondor, 840 F. Supp. 1160 (N.D. Oh. 1993).
Phillips v. Pembroke Real Estate, Inc., 459 F.3d 128 (1st Cir. 2006).
SONY Corp. v. Universal Studios, 104 S. Ct. 774 (1984).
Syrus v. Bennett, 455 Fed. Appx. 806 (10th Cir. 2011).
Tallyrand Music Inc. v. Frank Stenko, 1990 WL 169163 (M.D. Pa. 1990).

Publications
H. Rep. No. 94-1478, at 51 (1977)
Kukkonen, C. A. (1998). Be a good sport and refrain from using my patented putt: Intellectual property protection for sports related movements. *Journal of the Patent and Trademark Office Society*, 80, 808.
Patent Office Reform. Hearing before the Courts, The Internet, and Intellectual Property of the Committee of the Judiciary, House of Representatives, 109th Cong., 1 (2005).
Pepitone, J. (2012, Jan 20) SOPA and PIPA postponed indefinitely after protests. *CNN Money*. Retrieved from http://money.cnn.com/2012/01/20/technology/SOPA_PIPA_postponed/index.htm
Smith, J. A. (1999). It's your move—No it's not! The application of patent law to sports moves. *University of Colorado Law Review*, 70, 1051.
U.S. Copyright Office (2015) Blank forms and other works not protected by copyright. Retrieved from: http://copyright.gov/circs/circ32.pdf
U.S. Copyright Office (2012) Copyright basics. Retrieved from: http://www.copyright.gov/circs/circ01.pdf3
Weber, L. (2000) Something in the way she moves: The case for applying copyright protection to sports moves. *Columbia–VLA Journal of Law and the Arts*, 23, 317.
Wilson, D. C. (1997). The legal ramifications of saving face: An integrated analysis of intellectual property and sport. *Villanova Sports and Entertainment Law Journal*, 4, 227.

Legislation
Copyright Remedy Clarification Act, 104 U.S.C. 2749 (1990).
The 1976 Copyright Act 17 U.S.C. § 101 et seq. (2008).
Patents 35 U.S.C. § 101 et seq. (2008).
Visual Artists Rights Act of 1990, 104 U.S.C. 5128 (1990).

7.22 PRINCIPLES OF TRADEMARK LAW

Paul M. Anderson | National Sports Law Institute of Marquette University Law School

One of the most valuable assets for a recreation or sport organization is its name, logo, or some other defining characteristic that the public will recognize when viewing its products or services. These characteristics help promote the organization and help to sell these products and services. Because such identifying marks are so valuable, competitors will often engage in counterfeiting and other illegal behavior that harms the original organization. A recent study by the Organization for Economic Cooperation and Development (OECD) estimate that the total global economic value of counterfeit and pirated products is as much as $650 billion a year—a value expected to increase to as much as $1.7 trillion (Frontier Economics, 2011). In the United States alone the current estimate is between approximately $215 million annually (Global Intellectual Property Center, 2013). One of the strongest ways for an organization to protect itself is by seeking trademark protection for its name, logo, or other defining symbols.

FUNDAMENTAL CONCEPTS

The two main purposes of trademark law are to protect the owner of a mark and to prevent others from using the mark in a way that will cause consumer confusion. The Federal Trademark Act of 1946, known as the Lanham Act, governs trademarks, registration, and provides measures to protect from infringement.

Federal Trademark Act of 1946/the Lanham Act

According to the Lanham Act, a **trademark** is any word, name, symbol, or device, or any combination thereof, adopted or used by some entity to identify their goods and distinguish them from those manufactured or sold by others (15 U.S.C §1127). A trademark (1) identifies a seller's goods and distinguishes them from those sold by others, (2) signifies that goods come from one particular source, (3) indicates that products are of a certain quality, and (4) advertises, promotes and assists in selling the particular goods (McCarthy, Schechter, & Franklyn 2004).

Trademarks can also be categorized by strength. The strongest marks are **arbitrary** or **fanciful marks** that bear no direct relationship to the product itself, such as "Adidas" for sports apparel, and "Ping" for golf clubs. These marks are inherently distinctive because they serve as an indicator of the source of the goods rather than describing the goods themselves.

Next are **suggestive marks** that hint at the characteristics of the goods or services, but require some consumer imagination to be understood as descriptive. For instance, although some consumers would understand a "Hot Pocket" to be a warm food item, it takes a bit of imagination to understand that the name stands for a meal wrapped in a flaky crust.

Descriptive marks identify a characteristic or quality of a good or service. For example, "SwingAway" is the name of a hitting net with a ball attached on a rope so that the hitter can swing away at the ball and it will come back to the same spot. These marks only receive trademark protection after they obtain "**secondary meaning**." Secondary meaning is obtained through widespread use and public recognition so that the mark primarily indicates the source of the good or service instead of the good or service itself. For example, in *Board of Supervisors v. Smack Apparel Co.* (2008) several universities sued a company that made apparel using identifiable color schemes from these universities, such as purple and gold for LSU, crimson and cream for the University of Oklahoma, scarlet and gray for the Ohio State University, and cardinal and gold for the University of Southern California. In ruling that such color schemes could receive trademark protection because they had obtained secondary meaning the court found that the defendants had infringed upon the schools' trademarks.

Generic marks receive no trademark protection because they refer to the name or class of the good or service and are so common or descriptive that they are not indicative of the source or sponsorship of the good or service. Some companies who originally adopt distinctive names or logos eventually lose their trademark rights in these same names or logos because they become so well known, such as *Kleenex* for facial tissue and *Jell-O* for gelatin.

The Lanham Act also protects service marks and collective marks. A **service mark** is a mark used in the sale of advertising or services to identify and distinguish the services of one entity from the services of others. Whereas a trademark identifies the source and quality of a product, a service mark identifies the source and quality of an intangible service. The mark "NCAA," as it stands for events and services related to the National Collegiate Athletic Association, is a service mark. A **collective mark** is a trademark or service mark used by the members of a cooperative, association, or other collective organization to indicate membership in that organization. Examples of collective marks in sports include "NBA," "NFL" and "Big East."

Use and Registration

To create ownership rights in a trademark, the trademark owner must be the first to use the mark in trade and make continuous, uninterrupted use from then on. Once the trademark is used, consumers can rely on it to identify and distinguish the owner's particular goods or services from those of others. Federal registration is not required to establish common law trademark rights nor is it required to begin using a trademark. However, with registration, trademark rights extend to the use of the mark across the United States. Federal registration also provides constructive notice to others that the registrant owns the trademark and the right to exclusively use the mark. Every ten years the trademark can be reregistered to provide continuous protection.

Any sport or recreation organization that wants to ensure that its logo, design, or other insignia is not already registered as a trademark can search all federally registered trademarks online at http://tmsearch.uspto.gov/bin/gate.exe?f=tess&state=4809:r4y599.1.1. The following is information for the trademark *National Sports Law Institute of Marquette University Law School*.

Word Mark	NATIONAL SPORTS LAW INSTITUTE MARQUETTE UNIVERSITY LAW SCHOOL
Goods and Services	IC 041. US 100 101 107. G & S: Educational services; namely, conducting educational and international classes, workshops, meetings and seminars in the field of sports law. FIRST USE: 20000531. FIRST USE IN COMMERCE: 20000531
Mark Drawing Code	(3) DESIGN PLUS WORDS, LETTERS, AND/OR NUMBERS
Design Search Code	05.15.02 - Laurel leaves or branches (borders or frames); Wreaths 13.01.02 - Blow torch; Propane torches; Torches; Welding torch 26.01.08 - Circles having letters or numerals as a border; Circles having punctuation as a border; Letters, numerals or punctuation forming or bordering the perimeter of a circle
Serial Number	76133371
Filing Date	September 22, 2000
Published for Opposition	November 6, 2001
Registration Number	2533880
Registration Date	January 29, 2002
Owner	(REGISTRANT) Marquette University CORPORATION WISCONSIN 615 N. 11th Street Room 015 Milwaukee WISCONSIN 53233
Disclaimer	NO CLAIM IS MADE TO THE EXCLUSIVE RIGHT TO USE "SPORTS LAW INSTITUTE" APART FROM THE MARK AS SHOWN
Type of Mark Distinctiveness	SERVICE MARK
Limitation Statement	as to "NATIONAL SPORTS LAW INSTITUTE"

Infringement

Even if a recreation or sport organization registers its trademarks, legal disputes may still occur when another organization develops a product that seems to include similar marks. The first organization can then sue the offending organization for trademark infringement.

In order to demonstrate trademark infringement under Section 1114(a) of the Lanham Act, the owner of the trademark must show that she has a protectable property right in the trademark. Use and registration can establish a valid protectable right in a particular trademark. The trademark owner must also show that the other party's use of a similar mark is likely to cause confusion, mistake, or deceive consumers as to who is the true source of the mark. When analyzing potential consumer confusion, the courts focus on the following factors:

1. Strength of the mark,
2. Similarity between the marks,
3. Similarity between the products and marketing channels used to sell them,
4. Likelihood that the trademark owner will expand their use of the mark on future products,
5. Evidence of actual confusion,
6. Defendant's "good faith" intent in adopting the mark,
7. Quality of the defendant's product, and
8. Sophistication of the consumers.

Ohio State University v. Thomas (2010), involved a challenge by the Ohio State University to the use of various federally registered trademarks such as "Buckeyes," "Ohio State," and "OSU," for two electronic magazines, "Buckeye Gameday" and "Ohio State Buckeyes E-Book," as well as a print publication and website, www.buckeyeillustrated.com. In analyzing whether the defendants' use of the word Buckeyes created a likelihood of confusion, the court looked to a combination of the factors listed above, including; strength of the plaintiff's mark, relatedness of the goods or services, similarity of the marks, evidence of actual confusion, marketing channels used, likely degree of purchaser care, intent of the defendant in selecting the mark, and likelihood of expansion of the product lines. Finding that these factors weighed in favor of a likelihood of consumer confusion, the court granted Ohio State's motion for a temporary restraining order and preliminary injunction stopping the plaintiff and his marketing company from infringing upon the university's marks.

Counterfeiting

Another form of trademark infringement is counterfeiting, often known as piracy. The Lanham Act defines a **counterfeit mark** as "a spurious mark that is identical with, or substantially indistinguishable from, a registered mark" (15 U.S.C. § 1127). Counterfeiting is an intentional effort to produce products that reproduce a genuine trademark without a license or permission. The problem is extensive within the sports and recreation industry. For example, a recent joint nationwide law enforcement effort between the federal government and the NFL, called Operation Team Player, seized more than $21.6 million in counterfeit sports merchandise (U.S. Immigration and Customs Enforcement, 2014). Organizations that attempt to counterfeit the trademarks of a recreation or sport management organization are subject to severe criminal and civil penalties.

Dilution

Dilution law protects the distinctive quality and selling power of a trademark, even if consumers are not actually confused by a non-trademark owner's use of the mark. The Federal Trademark Dilution Act of 1995 defines **dilution** as the lessening of the capacity of a famous mark to identify and distinguish goods or services, regardless of either the presence or absence of competition between the parties, or a likelihood of confusion, mistake, or deception. The Trademark Dilution Revision Act of 2006 helped further define the standard for dilution claims emphasizing that in a claim for dilution a trademark owner only needs to show a likelihood of dilution rather than actual dilution.

The University of Kansas sued an online retailer that was incorporating the school's trademarks on t-shirts that used offensive language and referred to sex and alcohol. Kansas fans complained that these t-shirts reflected negatively on the school's reputation. The court confirmed that a reasonable jury could find that this use of the widely recognized Kansas athletic marks could cause dilution, especially when considered in combination with the fan complaints regarding the negative effect of the t-shirts on the school's reputation (*University of Kansas v. Sinks*, 2008).

Unfair Competition and False Advertising

Unfair competition refers to a broader area of law than trademark infringement. It can involve any activity wherein one party attempts to deceive or mislead consumers by using the trademarks of another party to give the consumer the mistaken belief that the products of the infringer are actually the products of the true trademark owner. Unfair competition claims can be brought under Section 1125(1)(a) of the Lanham Act, which provides a cause of action for false designation of origin alleging that an infringer has used the trademark rights of another to deceive consumers as to the affiliation, connection, or association of the infringer with the legitimate trademark owner, and Section 1125(1)(b), which provides a cause of action for false advertising alleging that another party has used commercial advertising or promotions to misrepresent the nature, characteristics, quality, or origin of their products.

An example of an unfair competition and false advertising case that involved two well-known football helmet producers is *Riddell, Inc. v. Schutt Sports, Inc.* (2010). Riddell relied heavily on a certain concussion study in its advertisements, citing various results of the study that concerned concussion rates for players wearing Riddell helmets. Schutt asserted that these advertisements amounted to false advertising and deceptive trade practices. However, the court noted that Schutt did not have any evidence of actual consumer confusion based on the advertisements. Therefore, it could prevail only if it could show that Riddell's statements were literally false, which they failed to do.

Defenses

Often a recreation and sport organization will fight an infringement claim by arguing that the plaintiff does not have any protectable rights in the trademark, or the defendant's use will not cause consumer confusion. In addition, the organization may claim the trademark has been abandoned, that the doctrine of laches applies, that it is disparaging, that the use was a fair use or parody, or that there has been no infringement due to the presence of certain disclaimers.

Abandonment

Although trademark rights can be renewed continuously through registration, a trademark owner must still actively use the mark for it to remain valid. Section 1127 of the Lanham Act defines **abandonment** as discontinued use of a trademark with the intent not to resume such use, or when any act or omission of the owner of a mark causes it to become the generic name for the goods in connection with which it is used. When a defendant asserts abandonment as a defense, the claim is that the mark has fallen into the public domain because of the plaintiff's lack of use and intent not to resume use. An abandoned mark may be claimed and used by the public at large.

Action Ink registered the phrase "Ultimate Fan" as a service mark to use in promotional contests at sporting events. The company did not use the mark from 1995-2012. From 2006–2012 the New York Jets and Anheuser-Busch used the mark for various "Ultimate Fan" promotions. In 2012, Action Ink sued both Anheuser-Busch and the Jets for trademark infringement for the use of the mark. The court noted that typically nonuse of a mark for three consecutive years is evidence of abandonment. Although Action Ink claimed that it had used the mark, the lower courts found that its use consisted almost entirely of challenges to allegedly infringing uses of the mark. As a result, because Action Ink did not use the mark in any contests for seventeen years, it had abandoned its "Ultimate Fan" service mark (*Action Ink, Inc. v. N.Y. Jets, 2014*).

Laches

In certain circumstances if trademark owners have neglected to assert their trademark rights in a timely manner, the **doctrine of laches** may limit them from recovery, if such recovery would be prejudicial to the potential infringer. After finding out that NFL Films used video footage of them playing football without their permission, several former NFL players brought a false endorsement claim against the NFL. Noting that other courts have found that a delay of more than six years is unreasonable before bringing such a claim, and that the players had no excuse for their decades long delay here, the court found that the doctrine of laches barred their claim against the NFL (*Dryer v. NFL, 2014*).

Fair Use or Parody

Section 1115(b)(4) of the Lanham Act provides that where a trademark is used fairly and in good faith only to describe the goods or services involved, there is no trademark infringement. For example, an artist's renderings of famous University of Alabama football plays containing depictions of players dressed in University uniforms with the University's marks was deemed to be fair use of the marks. The court found that the defendants used their own marks to identify the source of the paintings, which was evidence of good faith and made it clear that the source was the artist and not the University of Alabama (*University of Alabama Board of Trustees. v. New Life Art Inc.*, 2009).

Courts have also held that parody of a trademark is not infringement. In *World Wrestling Federation Entertainment, Inc. v. Big Dog Holdings, Inc.* (2003), the court found that the defendant's use of dog caricatures of WWE wrestlers on novelty items, when used in conjunction with its own registered trademark, dog design logo, and a disclaimer indicating the parody nature, made it clear that the items were spoofs of the WWE and its characters such that there was no likelihood of confusion.

Disparaging Marks

Trademark protection can also be denied if a mark is shown to be immoral, deceptive, scandalous, or disparaging under Section 1052(a) of the Lanham Act. In *Harjo, et al. v. Pro-Football, Inc.* (1999), Native Americans petitioned to cancel the trademark registrations for the marks "Washington Redskins" and "Redskins," both owned by Pro-Football, Inc., the owners of the NFL's Washington Redskins franchise. The Patent and Trademark Office initially granted the petition to cancel the marks. The team then sued for summary judgment to avoid the cancellation of the marks. The district court reversed, finding that the plaintiff presented insufficient evidence that the marks were disparaging to Native Americans and that the claim was barred by the doctrine of laches because there was a twenty-five-year delay in bringing the suit (2003). After further litigation the district court's decision was affirmed 2009, however, this was not the end of the dispute. Finding that the Redskins marks were disparaging to Native Americans at the time they were registered, the United States Patent and Trademark Office canceled the mark in 2014 (*Blackhorse, et. al.*, 2014). The team has appealed and the dispute was still in court when this book went to press.

Disclaimers

A potential trademark infringer may also argue that a conspicuously placed **disclaimer** alerting consumers that the product or service does not contain certain attributes or features, and that it is not from a certain source organization, absolves it from liability for infringement. In *Heisman Trophy Trust v. Smack Apparel Co.* (2009), the plaintiff alleged trademark infringement regarding various t-shirts produced by Smack Apparel that promoted the candidacy of potential Heisman winners. Smack Apparel claimed that disclaimers it included on each of the t-shirts helped to dispel any consumer confusion that may have existed. The court rejected this argument and held that where a substantial likelihood of confusion otherwise exists, and the disclaimers are not prominently featured on the products, such disclaimers are of limited value.

Licensing

Merchandisers, manufacturers and sponsors often wish to associate themselves with a recreation or sport organization. One way to do this is through the grant of a license. A **license** is a written document in which the trademark owner grants another entity the right to associate their business and/or product with the name, goodwill, logos, symbols, emblems, and designs of the trademark owner. By paying some form of compensation, the company that receives the license (the licensee) can then use the trademark of the licensor to sell its own products. Problems occur when entities other than the licensee attempt to use the licensor's marks or when the licensor becomes unhappy with the licensee's use of the license.

Professional Sports. Most professional sports leagues have developed profitable licensing programs to capitalize on public demand for sports-related items with team and league affiliations. Each of the four major sports leagues (NFL, NBA, NHL, and MLB) have created separate properties divisions (i.e., NBA Properties) that deal with licensing of league and club trademarks to vendors who manufacture and sell products to consumers. The revenue realized from the sale of such licensed products is then divided among the teams within the league, normally on an equal basis.

The players' associations also have formed separate entities that handle licensing issues for athletes (i.e., Players, Inc. for the NFL Players Association, and the Players Choice Group Licensing Program for the MLB Players Association). These entities provide marketing and licensing services to companies interested in using the names and likenesses of current and past players. Revenues are normally distributed among the players that make up the association on a pro rata basis.

Some players have even gone so far as to seek trademark protection for their own name and likeness. Michael Jordan owns a trademark for his name for use in the promotion and endorsement of goods and services, clinics, and camps. Major sportswear companies have also recognized the potential value of trademarking a famous athlete's name, as Nike actually owns the name, "LEBRON," for shoes, sports bags, and other sporting goods.

The NCAA. The National Collegiate Athletic Association (NCAA) protects the intellectual property of the approximately 65 trademarks and service marks associated with the NCAA and its 90 annual championships through the development of various licensing and marketing programs (www.ncaa.org). However, the NCAA does not monitor individual university marks. Rather, universities are responsible for monitoring their own respective marks.

For example, in 1988, the University of Wisconsin created its Office for Trademark Licensing to promote and protect its trademarks. Through this office the university has licensing agreements with close to 400 companies and has generated more than $39 million in revenues (http://licensing.wisc.edu/).In addition, many schools utilize the Collegiate Licensing Company (CLC). Through a complex licensing application process, the CLC aids colleges in protecting their marks and developing their brands and is currently utilized by approximately 200 colleges, universities, bowl games, conferences, the Heisman Trophy, and the NCAA (http://www.clc.com/).

The licensing and monitoring of college and university marks has become a thorny issue since many high schools use logos and marks either substantially similar, or sometimes even identical, to collegiate marks. As high school athletics have become more high-profile through enhanced media coverage, colleges have been forced to take an increased interest in the logos and trademarks these high schools use for their athletic programs. Recognizing the value of their trademarks, universities are increasingly demanding that high schools stop using these similar or identical logos that have the potential to cause confusion or dilution. In the past, colleges became aware of these high schools often by accident; now however, universities actively protect their marks and search for potential infringers at the high school level. For example, in 2011 Notre Dame forced an El Paso Catholic School to stop referring to themselves as the "fighting Irish" and made them remove their fighting leprechaun logo (Hunt, 2012).

The Olympics. The International Olympic Committee (IOC) owns the familiar "Olympic Rings" logo and the right to use the mark all over the world. The United States Olympic Committee (USOC) owns the exclusive right to use and license the Olympic marks in the United States and vigorously protects the use of its protected marks and terminology. Unauthorized use of the Olympic name or marks may also be held to violate the Ted Stevens Olympic and Amateur Sports Act.

For example, the USOC sued an operator of a children's summer camp operating under the name, "Camp Olympik" where various Olympic-style athletic events were part of the camp activities. The USOC had previously contacted the defendant, which originally operated under the name "Camp Olympic" and made various uses of the Olympic rings and Olympic torch, to request that they stop using the Olympic words and symbols as they were violating the Amateur Sports Act. In response, the camp changed the name to "Camp Olympik" and slightly altered the logo with the Olympic ring. In agreeing with the USOC, the court found that the changes the camp made were not enough and that a likelihood of confusion still existed (*USOC v. Tobyhanna Camp Corporation, 2010*).

The Internet

In the mid-1990s, as recreation and sport organizations began to promote their products and services on the Internet, many found that someone else had already registered their preferred domain name. These "cybersquatters" attempt to register famous trademarks as domain names in the hopes of selling them to the famous entity for substantial profit.

In the fall of 1999, two measures were established to combat the widespread problem of cybersquatting. The Anti-cybersquatting Consumer Protection Act (ACPA) amended the Lanham Act by creating a specific claim against cybersquatters. The Act outlawed the act of registering, with the bad-faith intent to profit, a domain name that is confusingly similar to a registered or unregistered mark or dilutes a famous mark. The Act allows a court to resolve domain name disputes even when the disputed owner of the name cannot be found or cannot be served in the United States.

A case dealing with a claim under the ACPA involved the NCAA, the Illinois High School Association (IHSA), and the domain name "marchmadness.com." The IHSA began using the phrase "March Madness" to refer to its boys' basketball tournaments in the 1940s. The NCAA's first use was in 1982, when CBS broadcaster Brent Musberger used the phrase to describe the NCAA men's basketball tournament. In the early 1990s both the IHSA and the NCAA claimed exclusive trademark rights to the phrase. After going through some initial litigation, the NCAA and IHSA agreed to work together to protect their rights. In 2000, they formed the March Madness Athletic Association (MMAA), and each retained a license to use the phrase in association with their tournaments. After falsely claiming association with the NCAA, Netfire acquired the domain name "marchmadness.com" in 1996. MMAA sued claiming that Netfire was engaging in cybersquatting in violation of the ACPA. Finding that Netfire acted with bad faith to profit from use of the trademarked phrase, and that the domain name was identical or confusingly similar to the actual trademark, the court upheld the district court determination that Netfire had violated the ACPA (*March Madness Athletic Association, LLC v. Netfire Inc.*, 2005).

In addition to the ACPA, trademark owners can submit their dispute to a form of alternative dispute resolution. The Uniform Dispute Resolution Process (UDRP) is administered by the Internet Corporation for Assigned Names and Numbers (ICANN). By using the UDRP, a trademark owner must allege that its mark is "identical or confusingly similar" to the mark used by the cybersquatter who has no legitimate rights or interests in the domain name, and that the cybersquatter registered and used the domain name in bad faith. In addition, a UDRP proceeding does not preclude a lawsuit under the ACPA.

In 2011, the PAC-10 Conference filed a complaint with the World Intellectual Property Organization (WIPO) Arbitration and Mediation Center against defendant Lee, challenging registration of the domain names, "pac-12network.com," "pac12network.com," and "pac-12network.org"—names registered following the Pac-10 commissioner's announcement that the conference was looking to expand its membership (*Pac-10 Conference v. Lee*, 2011). The Pac-10 Conference alleged that these domain names were confusingly similar to its trademarks, that Lee had no legitimate interest in the domain names, and that the domain name were registered in bad faith. The arbitration panel agreed and ordered Lee to transfer the domain names to the Pac-10.

Ambush Marketing

With rights fees for events such as the Super Bowl and Olympic Games costing several millions of dollars, official sponsors of these events want to ensure they are the only company given the exposure associated with the particular event. **Ambush marketing** refers to the efforts of companies to weaken or attack a competitor's official association with a sports organization or event by using advertising and promotional campaigns designed to confuse consumers and to misrepresent the official sponsorship of the event. Unfortunately for the official sponsor, these corporations have been able to successfully defend their ambush marketing campaigns with claims of commercial free speech. In addition, most ambush campaigns are short-lived, and courts support the use of disclaimers allowing ambush companies to make limited use of a registered trademark as long as they avoid creating consumer confusion.

Following AT&T's purchase of Cingular Wireless, AT&T wished to replace the Cingular logo on Jeff Burton's NASCAR race car with an AT&T logo. The Cingular logo on the car had been grandfathered in, but NASCAR would not allow a change to the AT&T logo, as it would interfere with Nextel's exclusive sponsorship agreement with NASCAR. Following a U.S. District Court ruling that would have allowed the AT&T logo, NASCAR filed a countersuit against AT&T, alleging among other things, ambush marketing, as the logo on the vehicle would provide an avenue for circumventing Nextel's exclusive sponsorship rights in the NASCAR series.

Regardless of the limited success of ambush marketing claims, sport organizations can minimize the negative effects associated with these tactics by developing a comprehensive anti-ambush marketing plan. As part of this plan, official sponsors should monitor nonsponsor signage and advertisements to ensure that official event names, marks, and logos are not being used.

SIGNIFICANT CASE

The following case illustrates how a court will examine likelihood of consumer confusion in a trademark infringement case. Of special note is the court's examination of the similarity of the marks and products and overlap in the geographical markets. The court discussed survey evidence used to demonstrate consumer confusion. The court also noted that even though the Colts did not use the contested mark, they did not abandon it over the intervening period of time.

INDIANAPOLIS COLTS V. METROPOLITAN BALTIMORE FOOTBALL CLUB
United States Court of Appeals for the Seventh Circuit
34 F.3d 410 (7th Cir. 1994)

POSNER, *Chief Judge.* The Indianapolis Colts and the National Football League, to which the Colts belong, brought suit for trademark infringement *(15 U.S.C. §§ 1051 et seq.)* against the Canadian Football League's new team in Baltimore, which wants to call itself the "Baltimore CFL Colts." (Four of the Canadian Football League's teams are American.) The plaintiffs obtained a preliminary injunction against the new team's using the name "Colts," or "Baltimore Colts," or "Baltimore CFL Colts," in connection with the playing of professional football, the broadcast of football games, or the sale of merchandise to football fans and other buyers. The ground for the injunction was that consumers of "Baltimore CFL Colts" merchandise are likely to think, mistakenly, that the new Baltimore team is an NFL team related in some fashion to the Indianapolis Colts, formerly the Baltimore Colts. From the order granting the injunction the new team and its owners appeal to us under *28 U.S.C. § 1292*(a)(1). Since the injunction was granted, the new team has played its first two games—without a name.

A bit of history is necessary to frame the dispute. In 1952, the National Football League permitted one of its teams, the Dallas Texans, which was bankrupt, to move to Baltimore, where it was renamed the "Baltimore Colts." Under that name it became one of the most illustrious teams in the history of professional football. In 1984, the team's owner, with the permission of the NFL, moved the team to Indianapolis, and it was renamed the "Indianapolis Colts." The move, sudden and secretive, outraged the citizens of Baltimore. The city instituted litigation in a futile effort to get the team back—even tried, unsuccessfully, to get the team back by condemnation under the city's power of eminent domain—and the Colts brought a countersuit that also failed. *Indianapolis Colts v. Mayor & City Council of Baltimore, 733 F.2d 484, 741 F.2d 954 (1984), 775 F.2d 177 (7th Cir. 1985).*

Nine years later, the Canadian Football League granted a franchise for a Baltimore team. Baltimoreans clamored for naming the new team the "Baltimore Colts." And so it was named—until the NFL got wind of the name and threatened legal action. The name was then changed to "Baltimore CFL Colts" and publicity launched, merchandise licensed, and other steps taken in preparation for the commencement of play this summer.

* * *

The Baltimore team wanted to call itself the "Baltimore Colts." To improve its litigating posture (we assume), it has consented to insert "CFL" between "Baltimore" and "Colts." A glance at the merchandise in the record explains why this concession to an outraged NFL has been made so readily. On several of the items "CFL" appears in small or blurred letters. And since the Canadian Football League is not well known in the United States—and "CFL" has none of the instant recognition value of "NFL"—the inclusion of the acronym in the team's name might have little impact on potential buyers even if prominently displayed. Those who know football well know that the new "Baltimore Colts" are a new CFL team wholly unrelated to the old Baltimore Colts; know also that the rules of Canadian football are different from those of American football and that teams don't move from the NFL to the CFL as they might from one conference within the NFL to the other. But those who do *not* know these things—and we shall come shortly to the question whether there are many of these football illiterate—will not be warned off by the letters "CFL." The acronym is a red herring, and the real issue is whether the new Baltimore team can appropriate the name "Baltimore Colts." The entire thrust of the defendants' argument is that it can.

They make a tremendous to-do over the fact that the district judge found that the Indianapolis Colts abandoned the trademark "Baltimore Colts" when they moved to Indianapolis. Well, of course; they were no longer playing football under the name "Baltimore Colts," so could not have used the name as the team's trademark; they could have used it on merchandise but chose not to, until 1991 (another story—and not one we need tell). When a mark is abandoned, it returns to the public domain, and is appropriable anew—in principle. In practice, because "subsequent use of [an] abandoned mark may well evoke a continuing association with the prior use, those who make subsequent use may be required to take reasonable precautions to prevent confusion." 2 McCarthy, *supra*, § 17.01[2], at p. 17–3. This precept is especially important where, as in this case, the former owner of the abandoned mark continues to market the same product or service under a similar name, though we cannot find any previous cases of this kind. No one questions the validity of "Indianapolis Colts" as the trademark of the NFL team that plays out of Indianapolis and was formerly known as the Baltimore Colts. If "Baltimore CFL Colts" is confusingly similar to "Indianapolis Colts" by virtue of the history of the Indianapolis team and the overlapping product and geographical markets served by it and by the new Baltimore team, the latter's use of the abandoned mark would infringe the Indianapolis Colts' new mark. The Colts' abandonment of a mark confusingly similar to their new mark neither broke the continuity of the team in its different locations—it was the same team, merely having a different home base and therefore a different geographical component in its name—nor entitled a third party to pick it up and use it to confuse Colts fans, and other actual or potential consumers of products and services marketed by the Colts or by other National Football League teams, with regard to the identity, sponsorship, or league affiliation of the third party, that is, the new Baltimore team.

* * *

Against this the defendants cite to us with great insistence *Major League Baseball Properties Inc. v. Sed Non Olet Denarius, Ltd., 817 F. Supp. 1103, 1128 (S.D.N.Y. 1993)*, which, over the objection of the Los Angeles Dodgers, allowed a restaurant in Brooklyn to use the name "Brooklyn Dodger" on the ground that "the 'Brooklyn Dodgers' was a non transportable cultural institution separate from the 'Los Angeles Dodgers.' " The defendants in our case argue that the sudden and greatly resented departure of the Baltimore Colts for Indianapolis made the name "Baltimore Colts" available to anyone who would continue the "nontransportable cultural institution" constituted by a football team located in the City of Baltimore. We think this argument very weak, and need not even try to distinguish *Sed Non Olet Denarius* since district court decisions are not authoritative in this or any court of appeals. *Colby v. J.C. Penney Co., 811 F.2d 1119, 1124 (7th Cir. 1987)*. If it were a Supreme Court decision it still would not help the defendants. The "Brooklyn Dodger" was not a baseball team, and there was no risk of confusion. The case might be relevant if the Indianapolis Colts were arguing not confusion but misappropriation: that they own the goodwill associated with the name "Baltimore Colts" and the new Baltimore team is trying to take it from them. Cf. *Quaker Oats Co. v. Mills Co., 134 F.2d 429, 432 (7th Cir. 1943)*. They did make a claim of misappropriation in the district court, but that court rejected the claim and it has not been renewed on appeal. The only claim in our court is that a significant number of consumers will think the new Baltimore team the successor to, or alter ego of, or even the same team as the Baltimore Colts and therefore the Indianapolis Colts, which is the real successor. No one would think the Brooklyn Dodgers baseball team reincarnated in a restaurant.

* * *

. . . for if everyone *knows* there is no contractual or institutional continuity, no pedigree or line of descent, linking the Baltimore-Indianapolis Colts and the new CFL team that wants to call itself the "Baltimore Colts" (or, grudgingly, the "Baltimore CFL Colts"), then there is no harm, at least no harm for which the Lanham Act provides a remedy, in the new Baltimore team's appropriating the name "Baltimore Colts" to play under and sell merchandise under. If not everyone knows, there is harm. Some people who might otherwise watch the Indianapolis Colts (or some other NFL team, for remember that the NFL, representing all the teams, is a coplaintiff) on television may watch the Baltimore CFL Colts instead, thinking they are the "real" Baltimore Colts, and the NFL will lose revenue. A few (doubtless very few) people who might otherwise buy tickets to an NFL game may buy tickets to a Baltimore CFL Colts game instead. Some people who might otherwise buy merchandise stamped with the name "Indianapolis Colts" or the name of some other NFL team may buy merchandise stamped "Baltimore CFL Colts," thinking it a kin of the NFL's Baltimore Colts in the glory days of Johnny Unitas rather than a newly formed team that plays Canadian football in a Canadian football league. It would be naive to suppose that no consideration of such possibilities occurred to the owners of the new Baltimore team when they were choosing a name, though there is no evidence that it was the dominant or even a major consideration.

Confusion thus is possible, and may even have been desired; but is it likely? There is great variance in consumer competence, and it would be undesirable to impoverish the lexicon of trade names merely to protect the most gullible fringe of the consuming public. The Lanham Act does not cast the net of protection so wide. * * * The legal standard under the Act has been formulated variously, but the various formulations come down to whether it is likely that the challenged mark if permitted to be used by the defendant would cause the plaintiff to lose a substantial number of consumers. Pertinent to this determination is the similarity of the marks and of the parties' products, the knowledge of the average consumer of the product, the overlap in the parties' geographical markets, and the other factors that the cases consider. The aim is to strike a balance between, on the one hand, the interest of the seller of the new product, and of the consuming public, in an arresting, attractive, and informative name that will enable the new product to compete effectively against existing ones, and, on the other hand, the interest of existing sellers, and again of the consuming public, in consumers' being able to know exactly what they are buying without having to incur substantial costs of investigation or inquiry.

To help judges strike the balance, the parties to trademark disputes frequently as here hire professionals in marketing or applied statistics to conduct surveys of consumers. * * *

Both parties presented studies. The defendants' was prepared by Michael Rappeport and is summarized in a perfunctory affidavit by Dr. Rappeport to which the district judge gave little weight. That was a kindness. The heart of Rappeport's study was a survey that consisted of three loaded questions asked in one Baltimore mall.

* * *

The plaintiffs' study, conducted by Jacob Jacoby, was far more substantial and the district judge found it on the whole credible. The 28-page report with its numerous appendices has all the trappings of social scientific rigor. Interviewers showed several hundred consumers in 24 malls scattered around the country shirts and hats licensed by the defendants for sale to consumers. The shirts and hats have "Baltimore CFL Colts" stamped on them. The consumers were asked whether they were football fans, whether they watched football games on television, and whether they ever bought merchandise with a team name on it. Then they were asked, with reference to the "Baltimore CFL Colts" merchandise that they were shown, such questions as whether they knew what sport the team played, what teams it played against, what league the team was in, and whether the team or league needed someone's permission to use this name, and if so whose. If, for example, the respondent answered that the team had to get permission from the Canadian Football League, the interviewer was directed to ask the respondent whether the Canadian Football League had in turn to get permission from someone. There were other questions, none however obviously loaded, and a whole other survey, the purpose of which was to control for "noise," in which another group of mallgoers was asked the identical questions about a hypothetical team unappetizingly named the "Baltimore Horses." The idea was by comparing the answers of the two groups to see whether the source of confusion was the name "Baltimore Colts" or just the name "Baltimore," in which event the injunction would do no good since no one suggests that the new Baltimore team should be forbidden to use "Baltimore" in its name, provided the following word is not "Colts."

* * *

Jacoby's survey of consumers reactions to the "Baltimore CFL Colts" merchandise found rather astonishing levels of confusion not plausibly attributable to the presence of the name "Baltimore" alone, since "Baltimore Horses" engendered much less. * * * Among self-identified football fans, 64 percent thought that the "Baltimore CFL Colts" was either the old (NFL) Baltimore Colts or the Indianapolis Colts. But perhaps this result is not so astonishing. Although most American football fans have heard of Canadian football, many probably are unfamiliar with the acronym "CFL," and as we remarked earlier it is not a very conspicuous part of the team logo stamped on the merchandise. Among fans who watch football on television, 59 percent displayed the same confusion; and even among those who watch football on cable television, which attracts a more educated audience on average and actually carries CFL games, 58 percent were confused when shown the merchandise. Among the minority not confused about who the "Baltimore CFL Colts" are, a substantial minority, ranging from 21 to 34 percent depending on the precise sub-sample, thought the team somehow sponsored or authorized by the Indianapolis Colts or the National Football League.

* * *

But with all this granted, we cannot say that the district judge committed a clear error (the standard, *Scandia Down Corp. v. Euroquilt, Inc.*, supra, 772 F.2d at 1427–28) in crediting the major findings of the Jacoby study and inferring from it and the other evidence in the record that the defendants' use of the name "Baltimore CFL Colts" whether for the team or on merchandise was likely to confuse a substantial number of consumers. This mean[s]—given the defendants' failure to raise any issue concerning the respective irreparable harms from granting or denying the preliminary injunction—that the judge's finding concerning likelihood of confusion required that the injunction issue.

* * *

The defendants make some other arguments but they do not have sufficient merit to warrant discussion. The judgment of the district court granting the preliminary injunction is AFFIRMED.

CASES ON THE SUPPLEMENTAL CD

Dallas Cowboys Football Club, Ltd. v. America's Team Properties, Inc., 616 F. Supp. 2d 622 (N.D. Tex. 2009). Focuses on how a court examines various factors in order to determine if there is a likelihood of confusion.

National Football League Properties, Inc. v. New York Football Giants, Inc., 637 F. Supp. 507 (D.N.J. 1986). Examines the league's efforts to control its collective trademark rights.

Pro Football, Inc. v. Harjo, 565 F.3d 880 (D.C. Cir. 2009). Examines the application of laches regarding allegedly disparaging team marks.

Abdul-Jabbar v. GMC, 85 F.3d 407 (9th Cir. 1996). Discusses abandonment and fair use defenses to trademark infringement claims.

Board of Supervisors v. Smack Apparel Co., 550 F.3d 465 (5th Cir. 2008). Focuses on the application of trademark principles to nontraditional marks as well as defenses such as fair use and laches.

QUESTIONS YOU SHOULD BE ABLE TO ANSWER

1. Explain the functions of a trademark for a recreation and sport management organization.
2. What is the benefit of federally registering your organization's trademarks?
3. What must a trademark owner establish in order to show infringement by another organization?
4. If your recreation or sport management organization is accused of infringing another organization's trademarks, what defenses can you use to show that no infringement took place?
5. As a recreation or sport management organization, why would you want to provide other organization's with a license to use your trademark on their goods or services?

REFERENCES

Cases

Action Ink, Inc. v. N.Y. Jets, 576 Fed. Appx. 321 (5th Cir. 2014).
Blackhorse et. al. v. Pro Football, Inc., Cancellation No. 92046185 (June 18, 2014).
Dryer v. NFL, 55 F.Supp.3d 1181 (D. Minn. 2014)
Harjo, et al. v. Pro-Football, Inc., 50 U.S.P.Q. 1705 (1999), rev'd, summary judgment granted in part, summary judgment denied in part, 68 U.S.P.Q.2d 1225 (2003).
Heisman Trophy Trust v. Smack Apparel Co., 637 F. Supp. 2d 146 (S.D.NY 2009)
March Madness Athletic Association, LLC v. Netfire Inc., 120 Fed. Appx.540 (5th Cir. 2005).
Ohio State University v. Thomas, 738 F. Supp. 2d 743 (S.D. Ohio 2010).
Pac-10 Conference v. Lee, WIPO Case No.D2011-0200 (2011) (Sorkin, David, Arb.).
Riddell, Inc. v. Schutt Sports, Inc., 724 F. Supp. 2d 963, 975 (W.D. Wis. 2010).
University of Alabama Board of Trustees. v. New Life Art Inc., 677 F. Supp. 2d 1238 (D. Ala. 2009).
University of Kansas v. Sinks, 565 F. Supp. 2d 1216 (D. Kan. 2008).
USOC v. Tobyhanna Camp Corp., 2010 U.S. Dist. LEXIS 117650 (D. Pa. 2010).
World Wrestling Federation Entertainment, Inc. v. Big Dog Holdings, Inc., 280 F. Supp. 2d 413, 440 (D. Pa. 2003).

Publications

Frontier Economics Ltd., London (2011, February). Estimating the global economic and social impacts of counterfeiting and piracy: A report commissioned by business action to stop counterfeiting and piracy (BASCAP). Retrieved April 28, 2011, from http://www.iccwbo.org/uploadedFiles/BASCAP/Pages/Global%20Impacts%20-%20Final.pdf.Global Intellectual Property Center, U.S. Chamber of Commerce. (2013, January 8). Domestic counterfeiting and piracy cost U.S. $215B. Retrieved January 28, 2016, from http://www.theglobalipcenter.com/counterfeit-piracy-facts/.
Hunt, Darren. (2012, July 15). Notre Dame forcing Cathedral High to drop 'Fighting,' change mascot. Retrieved January 26, 2016, from http://www.kvia.com/news/Notre-Dame-Forcing-Cathedral-High-To-Drop-Fighting-Change-Mascot/541108.
McCarthy, J. Thomas, Schechter, Roger E., & Franklyn, David J. (2004, 3rd Edition). *McCarthy's desk encyclopedia of intellectual property*. Washington, DC: Bureau of National Affairs.
U.S. Immigration and Customs Enforcement (2014, January 30). Federal agencies seize more than $21.6 million in fake NFL merchandise during 'Operation Team Player.' Retrieved January 26, 2016, from https://www.ice.gov/news/releases/federal-agencies-seize-more-216-million-fake-nfl-merchandise-during-operation-team.

Legislation

The Anti-cybersquatting Consumer Protection Act, 15 U.S.C. § 1125(d) (2016).
The Federal Trademark Act, 15 U.S.C. §§ 1051–1127 (2016).
The Federal Trademark Dilution Act, 15 U.S.C. § 1125(c) (2016).
The Federal Trademark Dilution Revision Act, 15 U.S.C. § 1051 (2016).
Ted Stevens Olympic and Amateur Sports Act, 36 U.S.C. §§ 220501–220529 (2016).

IMAGE RIGHTS

John T. Wolohan | Syracuse University

7.23

The image rights of athletes and other celebrities, if properly managed, can be worth hundreds of millions of dollars over an athlete's career. In fact, for most high profile athletes, endorsing products or lending their name to them has become more lucrative then their professional playing contracts. A good example of the value of an athlete's image is Tiger Woods. In 2009, Tiger Woods earned roughly $100 million more annually in endorsement income, then he did on the golf course. That all changed, however, on November 27, 2009, when Woods crashed his car crash outside his home. Following the crash, a series of news reports linking Woods to numerous extra material affairs came to light. Woods wife eventually divorced him and his public image as a family man was damaged forever. As a result, according to the 2016 list of Forbes Highest Paid Athletes Woods only earned $50 million from his various endorsements in 2015. The $50 million was still significant considering that Woods only made $600,000 on the golf course(Forbes.com, 2016).

With so much money at stake, it is not surprising that athletes would carefully protect the value of their image. The only way to truly protect the value of their image or name, however, is by controlling the use of the image. In the United States there are numerous legal foundations that are available to help athletes and other people control their image rights. However, as we will also see below, the ability to control their image is not absolute.

FUNDAMENTAL CONCEPTS

The term "image rights" has become closely associated with the right of privacy and the right of publicity. Generally, a person's image right relates to his or her name or likeness, such as photograph or other visual representation of the person. Recently, however, the courts have expanded the "traditional meaning of 'name and likeness' to include such things as nicknames, drawings, celebrity look-alikes or by including characteristics such as vocal idiosyncrasies within a more general formulation of identity" (Clay, 1994). As a way of introducing "image rights" this chapter examines the legal theories and protections behind the rights.

Right of Privacy

"Instantaneous photographs and newspaper enterprise have invaded the sacred precincts of private and domestic life; and numerous mechanical devices threaten to make good the prediction that what is whispered in the closet shall be proclaimed from the roof-tops. For years there has been a feeling that the law must afford some remedy for the unauthorized circulation of portraits of private persons; and the evil of the invasion of privacy by newspapers" (Warren and Brandeis, 1890).

These words are as true today as they were in 1890 when they were first published by Samuel Warren and Louis Brandeis in their article entitled "The Right of Privacy." In the article, Warren and Brandeis argued that the courts should recognize a new legal theory "the right to privacy" as a way to protect private individuals against the outrageous and unjustifiable infliction of mental distress caused by the press and advertisers (Warren and Brandeis, 1890).

The court, however, were reluctant to accept Warren and Brandeis' the new theory however. For example, the Court of Appeals of New York in *Roberson v. Rochester Folding Box Company* (1902) held that a young woman, whose picture had been used on flour advertisement without her consent could not recover damages based on a violation of her right to privacy. In finding that there was no such right recognized at common law, the court concluded that the injury was of a purely mental character, not physical, and that recognizing such a right would potentially flood the courts in lawsuits. Perhaps most importantly, the court feared that due to the difficulty of determining a private from public figure, recognizing a right of privacy would restrict the First Amendment guarantees of freedom of the press.

As a result of the public storm that followed the court's decision in Roberson, the New York State Legislature responded by amending the New York State Civil Rights Law to establish a statutory right to privacy. For the first time, the new law made it illegal for a person or corporation to use for advertising purposes, or for the purposes of trade, the name, portrait or picture of any living person without having first obtained the written consent of such person (N.Y. Civ. Rights Law, § 50). In addition to making such use illegal, the law also allowed individuals to recover civil damages under tort law, including injunctive relief, compensatory damages, and, if the defendant acted knowingly, exemplary damages (N.Y. Civ. Rights Law, § 51). After New York codified the right of privacy, a majority of states followed suit and now provide private citizens a legally protected right of privacy either under common law or state statutes. The issue, however, was not so clear for people in the sports and entertainment industry. Even after finding a right of privacy, the courts refused to recognize a celebrity's right of privacy. In support of this position, the court found that since college and professional athletes and celebrities had dedicated their life to the public, they had thereby waived their right of privacy. For example, in *O'Brien v. Pabst Sales Co.* (1941), David O'Brien, a famous college football player, tried to invoke a right of privacy against a brewery after it used his photograph in uniform on calendars. In rejecting O'Brien's right of privacy argument, the court held that because O'Brien was famous and had completely publicized his name and image he had waived his right of privacy.

The courts started extending the right of privacy to include a "Right of Publicity" in order to protect athletes and other celebrities against commercial misappropriation, and prevent the unjust enrichment of others off a celebrity's reputation in *Haelan Laboratories v. Topps Chewing Gum, (1953)*. Topps, knowing of Haelan's contracts with various professional baseball players, deliberately entered into contracts with the players to use their photograph in connection with the sales of Topps' gum. Haelan's contract with the players provided the company the exclusive right to use the player's photograph in connection with the sales of its' chewing-gum.

In rejecting Topps claim that their contracts were valid since the contract between Haelan and the player was no more than a release by the player, which give Haelan the right to use the photographs, the Second Circuit Court of Appeals held that "in addition to and independent of the right of privacy, a man has a right in the publicity value of his photograph, i.e., the right to grant the exclusive privilege of publishing his picture," and that the licensees and assignees of that right could enforce the right against infringing third parties (*Haelan Laboratories v. Topps Chewing Gum, 1953*). It is common knowledge, the court held "that many prominent persons (especially actors and ball-players), far from having their feelings bruised through public exposure of their likenesses, would feel sorely deprived if they no longer received money for authorizing advertisements" (*Haelan Laboratories v. Topps Chewing Gum, 1953*).

Right of Publicity

Since the Second Circuit Court's decision in *Haelan Laboratories v. Topps*, (1953) the right of publicity has been acknowledged in most states either by common law or statute. Although the right of publicity is not uniformly applied by all the states, most states agree with the three goals behind the right's general purpose. "First, the right to publicity recognizes the economic value of an individual's identity. Second, the publicity right is an incentive for creativity, encouraging the production of entertaining and intellectual works. Finally, the right prevents unjust enrichment of those who usurp the identity of another" (*Cardtoons v. MLBPA*, 1993).

Some States have even begun broaden the right of publicity by expanding the "traditional meaning of "name and likeness" to include such things as nicknames, drawings, celebrity look-alikes or by including characteristics such as vocal idiosyncrasies within a more general formulation of identity" (Clay, 1994). For example, in *Palmer v. Schonhorn Enterprises*, (1967) Arnold Palmer, and other well-known professional golfers, sought an injunction to prevent the use of their names and biographical information in conjunction with a game. Palmer and the other golfers claimed that the use of their names was an invasion of their privacy and an unfair exploitation and commercialization of their names and reputations. Schonhorn claimed that since the information contained in the profiles was readily obtainable public data and available to all, it should not be denied the privilege of reproducing that which is set forth in newspapers, magazine articles and other periodicals.

After acknowledging that Palmer was a celebrity who derived a substantial portion of his earnings from professional golf and the marketability of his name for endorsement purposes, the Superior Court of New Jersey held that there was little doubt that a person was entitled to relief when his name is used without his consent, either to advertise the defendant's product or to enhance the sale of an article. In particular, the court held that "the basic and underlying theory is that a person has the right to enjoy the fruits of his own industry free from unjustified interference" (*Palmer v. Schonhorn Enterprises*, 1967). Therefore, even though "the publication of biographical data of a well-known figure does not per se constitute an invasion of privacy, the use of that data for the purpose of capitalizing upon the name by using it in connection with a commercial project other than the dissemination of news or articles or biographies does" (*Palmer v. Schonhorn Enterprises*, 1967).

Common Law Misappropriation

In addition to the right of privacy and publicity, a majority of states recognize a common law cause of action for the misappropriation of a person's name, photograph, and likeness for commercial purposes. In order to establish a cause of action for common law misappropriation in these situations, the courts have generally held that an individual must demonstrate four elements:

1. the defendant used the plaintiff's identity;
2. the appropriation of plaintiff's name or likeness provided the defendant some advantage, commercially or otherwise;
3. lack of consent; and
4. resulting injury (*Eastwood v. Superior Court*, 1983).

In determining whether there is a cause of action for common law misappropriation, one of the hardest questions for the court to answer is whether an individual's identity or likeness was even used. For example, in *Newcombe v. Adolf Coors*, (1998) the Ninth Circuit Court of Appeal was asked to determine whether a beer ad featuring an old time baseball game, showing a pitcher in a windup position misappropriated Newcombe's likeness. Newcombe was a former All Star and the only player in Major League Baseball history to ever win the Most Valuable Player Award, the Cy Young Award, and the Rookie of the Year Award. Even though the player's uniforms did not depict an actual team, and the background did not depict an actual stadium, the Ninth Circuit Court ruled that the player's windup was so distinctive that it made the identity of the player readily identifiable as Newcombe.

Another example is *Motschenbacher v. R.J. Reynolds Tobacco Co.* (1974). In the case, R.J. Reynolds produced some television ads utilizing a stock color photograph depicting several racing cars on a race track and even though the drivers in the cars were not visible in the photo, and the cars had been altered, the numbers were changed, and a spoiler was added on which the company placed their product's name, the Ninth Circuit Court of Appeals still found that the ads violated Motschenbacher's right of publicity. The Ninth Circuit Court reasoned that even though the driver's personal likeness was unrecognizable, his identity could still be inferred by the distinctive decorations on his car (*Motschenbacher v. R.J. Reynolds Tobacco Co.*, 1974).

Statutory Protections

In addition to the common law, "twenty-two states recognize the Right of Publicity in some capacity via statute: Alabama, Arizona, California, Florida, Hawaii, Illinois, Indiana, Kentucky, Massachusetts, Nebraska, Nevada, New York, Ohio, Oklahoma, Pennsylvania, Rhode Island, Tennessee, Texas, Utah, Virginia, Washington and Wisconsin (rightofpublicity.com). The two states that have been most active in protecting the right of publicity are New York and California.

An example of the rights available under statutory law is *Ali v. Playgirl*, (1978). In their February 1978 issue, *Playgirl* printed a portrait of a nude black man in the corner of a boxing ring. The man is unmistakably recognizable as Muhammad Ali, former heavyweight boxing champion, and is accompanied by the phrase "the Greatest." In defense of their use, *Playgirl* argued that because Ali was a public figure, he waived his right of privacy and therefore no consent was needed. In examining Ali's rights under section 51 of the New York

Civil Rights Law, the federal District Court held that it was clear that *Playgirl* used Ali's portrait or picture for the purpose of trade within the meaning of § 51 without his consent. Such use, the court held, amounted to a wrongful appropriation of the market value of Ali's likeness. As for *Playgirl*'s argument that the use was privileged, the court ruled that "the privilege of using a public figure's picture in connection with an item of news does not extend to commercialization of his personality" (*Ali v. Playgirl, Inc.*, 1978).

Another example is *John Doe, a/k/a Tony Twist, v. TCI Cablevision*. Tony Twist, a former NHL player who had a reputation as an enforcer on the ice sued the creator of the comic book, *Spawn*, for including a villainous character in the book sharing his name. In trying to determine whether the use of a person's name and identity violated Twist's right to publicity, the Supreme Court of Missouri held that the issue was whether the use of a Twist's name and identity is "expressive," in which case it is fully protected, or "commercial," in which case it is generally not protected (*Doe, a/k/a Tony Twist, v. TCI Cablevision*, 2003). For instance, the court went on, "the use of a person's identity in news, entertainment, and creative works for the purpose of communicating information or expressive ideas about that person is protected "expressive" speech. On the other hand, the use of a person's identity for purely commercial purposes, like advertising goods or services or the use of a person's name or likeness on merchandise, is rarely protected (*Doe, a/k/a Tony Twist, v. TCI Cablevision*, 2003).

Intellectual Property Provisions

In addition to state law, federal law can also be an effective tool in defending a person's right of publicity. Federal law is especially important because the right of privacy is only available to individuals, and corporations and partnerships must rely on theories such as trademark law and copyright law to prevent the unauthorized commercial use of their identity.

Federal Trademark Law (The Lanham Act)

The Federal Trademark Act of 1946, also known as the Lanham Act, defines a trademark as "any word, name, symbol, or device, or any combination thereof, adopted or used by a manufacturer or merchant to identify their goods and distinguish them from those manufactured or sold by others" (15 U.S.C. §§ 1051 *et seq*). Although mainly thought of as a means for manufacturers to identify their goods and distinguish them from those manufactured or sold by others, the Lanham Act also protects consumers and competitors from a wide variety of misrepresentations of products and services in commerce, including the unauthorized use of an individual's image rights. Therefore, although narrower in scope than the right of publicity or misappropriation, the federal Trademark Act can be a powerful tool in protecting an athlete's image rights. (See also Chapter 7.22, Principles of Trademark Law).

False Endorsement Claims. Commonly referred to as "false endorsement claims," the Lanham Act bars the unauthorized commercial use of a celebrity's identity to help sell a defendant's goods or services, which is likely to cause confusion among consumers, as to the association, sponsorship, or approval of goods or services by another person (15 U.S.C. § 1125(a)). In deciding whether the unauthorized use of a celebrity's identity is going to cause confusion in the mind of consumers, the courts consider the following factors:

1. the strength of plaintiff's marks and name;
2. relatedness of the goods;
3. similarity of plaintiff's and defendant's marks;
4. evidence of actual confusion;
5. marketing channels used;
6. likely degree of purchaser care (sophistication of the defendant's audience); and
7. defendant's intent in selecting the mark (*Abdul-Jabbar v. General Motors*, 1996).

Personal names can only receive trademark protection after they obtain secondary meaning. The rationale behind the requirement that names obtain secondary meaning is that a personal name is not distinctive enough to pinpoint a single source of goods or services (McCarthy, 2004). In order to obtain secondary meaning, the name or mark, must have widespread use and public recognition so that the mark primarily indicates the source of the good or service instead of the good or service itself. For example, in

Hirsch v. S.C. Johnson & Son (1979) a case involving the use of Hirsch's nickname "Crazylegs" on a shaving gel, the Supreme Court of Wisconsin found that under Trademark law there need be no evidence of prior marketing of a product or service under the nickname Crazylegs. All that was necessary, the court ruled was that Hirsch "show that Crazylegs designated the plaintiff's vocation or occupation as a sports figure and that the use of the name on a shaving gel for women created a likelihood of confusion as a sponsorship" (*Hirsch v. S.C. Johnson & Son*, 1979).

Another example of an athlete using trademark law to prohibit the use of his name is *Abdul-Jabbar v. General Motors Corp* (1996). Kareem Abdul-Jabbar sued General Motors after they used the name Lew Alcindor in a television commercial without his consent. Born Frederick Lewis Alcindor, Abdul-Jabbar used the name Lew Alcindor throughout his college and early professional career, but began using the name Kareem Abdul-Jabbar in 1971, after he converted to Islam.

In overturning the lower court, the Ninth Circuit Court of Appeals held that there was a genuine issue as to whether the use of Abdul-Jabbar old name implied his endorsement or sponsorship. In rejecting General Motors claim that Abdul-Jabbar had abandoned the name Lew Alcindor, the Ninth Circuit refused to extend the abandonment theory to cover a person's name. One's birth name, the court held, "is integral part of one's identity; it is not bestowed for commercial purposes, nor is it 'kept alive' through commercial use" (*Abdul-Jabbar v. General Motors Corp*, 1996). As for General Motors claim that its' use of the name Lew Alcindor was protected under the "fair use" doctrine, which protects the unauthorized use of a trademark when "the mark is used only to describe the goods or services of a party or their geographic origin" (*Abdul-Jabbar v. General Motors Corp*, 1996). The Ninth Circuit ruled that a commercial user is entitled to the nominative fair use defense if it meets three requirements:

1. that the product or service in question must be one not readily identifiable without use of the trademark;
2. that only so much of the mark may be used as is reasonably necessary to identify the product or service; and
3. the user must do nothing that would, in conjunction with the mark, suggest sponsorship or endorsement by the trademark holder. (*New Kids on the Block v. New America Pub., Inc.*, 1992)

In ruling that there was a genuine issue of fact as to the third requirement, implied endorsement or sponsorship, the Ninth Circuit held that the use of celebrity endorsements in television commercials was so well established by commercial custom that many people may assume that when a celebrity's name is used in a television commercial, the celebrity endorses the product advertised. Likelihood of confusion as to endorsement is therefore a question for the jury. Had GMC limited itself to the "trivia" portion of its ad, the court held that GMC could likely defend the reference to Lew Alcindor as a nominative fair use. "But by using Alcindor's record to make a claim for its car—like the basketball star, the Olds 88 won an "award" three years in a row, and like the star, the car is a "champ" and a "first round pick"—GMC has arguably attempted to "appropriate the cachet of one product for another," if not also to "capitalize on consumer confusion" (*Abdul-Jabbar v. General Motors Corp*, 1996).

Federal Copyright Act

In addition to the Lanham Act, another piece of federal legislation that can be used to protect an individual's image right is the 1976 Federal Copyright Act (17 U.S.C. § 101 et seq.). The Copyright Act was enacted to protect the creators of all "original works of authorship fixed in any tangible medium of expression" (17 U.S.C. § 102). Included in the list of works that can receive copyright protection are "pictorial, graphic and ... motion pictures and other audiovisual works" (17 U.S.C. § 102). Once created, the Act gives the owner of the copyrighted work control over how the work is reproduced and distributed. (See also Chapter 7.21, Copyright & Patent Law).

It is important to note, however, that while the Act may give the owner of the copyright exclusive control over the work, (17 U.S.C. § 110) there are some areas where copyright law and image rights clash. For example, in *Downing v. Abercrombie & Fitch*, (2001) Abercrombie & Fitch purchased three surfing photos from a photographer to include in an upcoming catalog. One of the photos, taken at the 1965 Makaha International Surfing Championships, was of George Downing. After seeing the catalog, Downing sued Abercrombie & Fitch claiming that the use of the photo violated his publicity rights. Abercrombie & Fitch, however, argued that as the copyright owner, it had the exclusive right to control the reproduction and distribution of the photos. In addition, Abercrombie & Fitch argued that Downing's state law right of privacy claim was preempted by federal copyright law.

In analyzing whether federal copyright law preempts an individual's state law right of privacy claim, the court held that Downing's state law right of privacy was not preempted by the Federal Copyright Act. In support of this position, the Ninth Circuit Court held that while the photograph, as a pictorial work of authorship, was protected under the Copyright Act, Downing's name and his image, which were also used in the photo, were not. "A person's name or likeness is not a work of authorship within the meaning of 17 U.S.C. § 102. This is true notwithstanding the fact that Downing 's name and likeness is embodied in a copyrightable photograph" (*Downing v. Abercrombie & Fitch*, 2001).

Game Data & Statistics. Another issue of concern for the leagues is who owns the player statistics and game data. Under copyright law, facts and statistics are not copyrightable. However, with an estimated 58 million people in the U.S. and Canada playing fantasy sports (Fantasy Sports Trade Association, 2016) generating billions of dollars, it is not surprising that the professional leagues and players' associations would want to control the right of others to use the players' profiles and statistics. In *C.B.C. Distribution v. Major League Baseball Advanced Media*, (2007) C.B.C. sought a declaratory judgment against Major League Baseball Advanced Media to establish its right to use, without license, the names of and information about major league baseball players in connection with its fantasy baseball products. Advanced Media counter-claimed, maintaining that CBC's fantasy baseball products violated the players' rights of publicity, and that the players, through their association, had licensed those rights to Advanced Media, the interactive media and Internet company of major league baseball.

In ruling against Major League Baseball Advanced Media, the Eighth Circuit Court found that "the information used in CBC's fantasy baseball games is all readily available in the public domain, and that it would be a strange law that a person would not have a first amendment right to use information that is available to everyone" (*C.B.C. Distribution v. Major League Baseball Advanced Media*, 2007). When balanced against CBC's first amendment rights in offering its fantasy baseball products, the Eighth Circuit ruled the players' rights of publicity was not enforceable.

First Amendment Defenses

Because the intent of the First Amendment is to protect the dual freedoms of speech and the press, the courts will allow the "unauthorized use of an individual's name or likeness" when it is used for the "dissemination of ideas and information" or for other cultural purposes (McCarthy, 2004). However, if an individual's name or likeness is used for commercial purposes, the courts will not protect it. The following are some of the First Amendment defenses involving image rights.

Newsworthiness Doctrine. The newsworthiness doctrine permits the media to use the unauthorized likeness of celebrities or anyone of interest in connection with a news item about the person. The definition of "news" has been given a broad reading and includes matters of public concern and interest. One example of how the doctrine relates to athletes and their image rights is *Montana v. San Jose Mercury News*, (1995). Joe Montana sued the San Jose Mercury News newspaper for reproducing his name, photograph, and likeness in poster form and selling it to the general public without his consent. In ruling that the newspaper had the right to use Montana's image, the California Court of Appeal held that the newspaper accounts of Montana's performance in two Super Bowls and four championships constituted publication of matters in the public interest and was entitled to protection by the First Amendment of the United States Constitution. In particular, the Court of Appeal held that Montana's name and likeness appeared in the posters for the same reason they appeared on the original newspaper pages: because he was a major player in contemporaneous newsworthy sports events and therefore may be republished in another medium, without the person's written consent.

The Incidental Use Exception. The courts have recognized an incidental use exception in cases where a newspaper or magazine has used, for advertising purposes, the image or photo of an athlete or other celebrity previously printed in a story. The advertisements, the courts have held, are simply "incidental" to the original, newsworthy publication. A good example is *Joe Namath v. Sports Illustrated*, (1975). Joe Namath sued Sports Illustrated after the magazine used his photograph in advertisements promoting subscriptions without his consent. The photograph used was originally used in the magazine in conjunction with an article published by Sports Illustrated concerning the 1969 Super Bowl game. In holding that the publication and use of Namath's photo in the advertisements did not violate the law, the court held that the use of the photograph was merely incidental advertising of the magazine. In particular, the court noted that the reproduction was used to illustrate the quality and content of the magazine in which Namath had earlier been properly and fairly depicted and in no way indicated Namath's endorsement of the magazine.

Parody Defense. The First Amendment also allows for the use of parodies under certain circumstances. For example, parodies that use another person's image, when used in a traditionally noncommercial medium such as a newspaper, magazine, television program, book, or movie will likely be granted First Amendment protection. Parodies used in a commercial context, however, will generally not receive First Amendment protection. An example of the parody defense is *Cardtoons, L.C. v. Major League Baseball Players Association*, (1993). Cardtoons, a trading card company, designed "parody" trading cards of active major league baseball players. Cardtoons did not obtain either a license or consent from Major League Baseball Players Association (MLBPA). In ruling for MLBPA, the court stated that the primary purpose behind Cardtoons' parody was commercial. Commercial speech, the Court held, does not receive the same type of Constitutional protection. First Amendment rights end, the court held when Cardtoons preys on the MLBPA's names and likenesses for purely commercial purpose

Transformative Use Defense. If the challenged work contains significant transformative elements or if the value of the work does not derive primarily from the celebrity's fame, the courts will allow the use under the transformative use defense. The defense "poses what is essentially a balancing test between the First Amendment and the right of publicity" (*Keller v. Electronic Arts*, 2010). To determine whether a work is transformative, the court must first inquire into whether the athlete's likeness is one of the "raw materials" from which an original work is synthesized, or whether the depiction or imitation of the athlete is the very sum and substance of the work in question (*Keller v. Electronic Arts*, 2010). If the court believes that distinctions exist, the First Amendment would bar a right of publicity claims based on appropriation of the plaintiff's identity or likeness; if not, the claims are not barred.

An example of the transformative use defense is *Keller v. Electronic Art*, (2010). Sam Keller a former starting quarterback for the Arizona State University and University of Nebraska football teams sued Electronic Arts, Inc. (EA), the NCAA and the Collegiate Licensing Company (CLC) over the use of his image in EA's video game "NCAA Football" (*Keller v. Electronic Arts*, 2010). Keller alleged that, to make the games realistic, EA designs the virtual football players to resemble their real-life counterparts: they share the same jersey numbers, have similar physical characteristics and come from the same home state. Although EA omits the real-life athletes' names from "NCAA Football," Keller filed suit against EA claiming that its use of his likeness without his consent was in violation of California's statutory and common law rights of publicity.

EA asserted that Keller's right of publicity claim was barred by the First Amendment Transformative Use Defense. In rejecting EA's defense, the court held that EA's depiction of Keller in "NCAA Football" was not sufficiently transformative to bar his California right of publicity claims as a matter of law (*Keller v. Electronic Arts*, 2010). In support of this conclusion, the court noted that in the game, the quarterback for Arizona State University shares many of Keller's characteristics. Further, the game's setting is identical to where the public found Keller during his collegiate career: on the football field. As for EA's assertion that the video game, taken as a whole, contains transformative elements. The court held that such a broad view was not supported by precedent.

The Keller case would eventually be consolidated with a number of other lawsuits involving current and past college athletes In RE: Student-Athlete Name & Likeness Litigation, 763 F. Supp. 2d 1379 (2011). In 2014, the NCAA settled the case by agreeing to pay $20 million to current and former college athletes whose likenesses were used in the video games. The video game maker EA Sports and the Collegiate Licensing Company, which handles licensing rights for many of the universities, also settled for $20 million each, which brought the total settlement paid to the athletes to $60 million (Strauss & Eder, 2014).

SIGNIFICANT CASE

In this case, the Seventh Circuit Court is asked to determine a magazine advertisement linking a grocery store's logo and marketing slogan to an image relating to Michael Jordan was properly classified as noncommercial speech that was protected by the First Amendment.

MICHAEL JORDAN V. JEWEL FOOD STORES, INC.
United States Court of Appeals for the Seventh Circuit
743 F.3d 509 (7th Cir. 2014)

This trademark and right-of-publicity dispute pits basketball legend Michael Jordan against Jewel Food Stores, Inc., the operator of 175 Jewel-Osco supermarkets in and around Chicago. On the occasion of Jordan's induction into the Naismith Memorial Basketball Hall of Fame in September 2009, Time, Inc., the publisher of *Sports Illustrated*, produced a special commemorative issue of *Sports Illustrated Presents* devoted exclusively to Jordan's remarkable career. Jewel was offered free advertising space in the issue in exchange for agreeing to stock the magazine in its stores. Jewel accepted the offer and submitted a full-page ad congratulating Jordan on his induction into the Hall of Fame. The ad ran on the inside back cover of the commemorative issue, which was available on newsstands for a three-month period following the induction ceremony.

To Jordan the ad was not a welcome celebratory gesture but a misappropriation of his identity for the supermarket chain's commercial benefit. He responded with this $5 million lawsuit alleging violations of the federal Lanham Act, the Illinois Right of Publicity Act, the Illinois deceptive-practices statute, and the common law of unfair competition. Jewel denied liability under these laws and also claimed a blanket immunity from suit under the First Amendment. The district court sided with Jewel on the constitutional defense, prompting this appeal.

Jewel maintains that its ad is "noncommercial" speech and thus has full First Amendment protection. Jordan insists that the ad is garden-variety commercial speech, which gets reduced constitutional protection and may give rise to liability for the private wrongs he alleges in this case. As the case comes to us, the commercial/noncommercial distinction is potentially dispositive. If the ad is properly classified as commercial speech, then it may be regulated, normal liability rules apply (statutory and common law), and the battle moves to the merits of Jordan's claims. If, on the other hand, the ad is fully protected expression, then Jordan agrees with Jewel that the First Amendment provides a complete defense and his claims cannot proceed. The district court held that the ad was fully protected noncommercial speech and entered judgment for Jewel.

We reverse. Jewel's ad, reproduced below, prominently features the "Jewel-Osco" logo and marketing slogan, which are creatively and conspicuously linked to Jordan in the text of the ad's congratulatory message. Based on its content and context, the ad is properly classified as a form of image advertising aimed at promoting the Jewel-Osco brand. The ad is commercial speech and thus is subject to the laws Jordan invokes here. The substance of Jordan's case remains untested, however; the district court's First Amendment ruling halted further consideration of the merits. We remand for further proceedings.

A copy of Jewel's ad at the end of this opinion.

* * *

II. Discussion

A. Some Context for the Commercial-Speech Classification

Jordan's appeal requires us to decide whether Jewel's ad is properly classified as commercial speech or noncommercial speech under the Supreme Court's First Amendment jurisprudence. Before addressing the substance of that question, we take a moment to place it in the context of the claims raised in this litigation, which arise from different sources of law but all center on Jordan's allegation that Jewel misappropriated his identity for its commercial benefit.

Jordan is a sports icon whose name and image are deeply embedded in the popular culture and easily recognized around the globe. His singular achievements on the basketball court have made him highly sought after as a celebrity endorser; as a retired player who continues to reap the economic value of his reputation in the history of the game, he understandably guards the use of his identity very closely. The Lanham Act and the other laws he invokes here enable him to do that.

Jewel argues that Jordan's claims can't succeed because its ad is fully protected noncommercial speech under the First Amendment. We understand this to be an argument that the First Amendment prevents the court from applying these laws to any speech that is considered "noncommercial" in the constitutional sense, thus providing a complete constitutional defense to all claims. Jordan accepts this legal premise, so we take the point as conceded. But the law in this area is considerably more complex than the parties' agreement implies.

The Supreme Court has generally worked out its commercial-speech doctrine in public-law cases. . . . In the public-law context, the commercial/noncommercial classification determines the proper standard of scrutiny to apply to the law or regulation under review in the case.

This is not a public-law case; it's a clash of private rights. Even if Jewel's ad qualifies as noncommercial speech, it's far from clear that Jordan's trademark and right-of-publicity claims fail without further ado. According to a leading treatise on trademark and unfair-competition law, there is no judicial consensus on how to resolve conflicts between intellectual-property rights and free-speech rights; instead, the courts have offered "a buffet of various legal approaches to [choose] from."

* * *

Jordan's litigating position allows us to sidestep this complexity. The parties have agreed that if Jewel's ad is "noncommercial speech" in the constitutional sense, then the First Amendment provides a complete defense to all claims in this suit. We're not sure that's right, but for now we simply note the issue and leave it for another day. With that large unsettled question reserved, we move to the task of classifying Jewel's ad as commercial or noncommercial speech for constitutional purposes.

B. Commercial or Noncommercial Speech?

1. *The commercial-speech doctrine*

The First Amendment prohibits the government from "abridging the freedom of speech." U.S. CONST. amend. I. Because "'not all speech is of equal First Amendment importance,'" *Snyder v. Phelps*, 131 S. Ct. 1207, 1215, 179 L. Ed. 2d 172 (2011) (quoting *Hustler Magazine, Inc. v. Falwell*, 485 U.S. 46, 56, 108 S. Ct. 876, 99 L. Ed. 2d 41 (1988)), certain categories of speech receive a lesser degree of constitutional protection. Commercial speech was initially viewed as being outside the ambit of the First Amendment altogether. See *Valentine v. Chrestensen*, 316 U.S. 52, 54, 62 S. Ct. 920, 86 L. Ed. 1262 (1942). That understanding has long since been displaced. Current doctrine holds that commercial speech is constitutionally protected but governmental burdens on this category of speech are scrutinized more leniently than burdens on fully protected noncommercial speech. See *Fox*, 492 U.S. at 477 ("Our jurisprudence has emphasized that commercial speech [enjoys] a limited measure of protection, commensurate with its subordinate position in the scale of First Amendment values, and is subject to modes of regulation that might be impermissible in the realm of noncommercial expression." (internal quotation marks omitted)); *Zauderer v. Office of Disciplinary Counsel of the Sup. Ct. of Ohio*, 471 U.S. 626, 637, 105 S. Ct. 2265, 85 L. Ed. 2d 652, 17 Ohio B. 315 (1985) ("There is no longer any room to doubt that what has come to be known as 'commercial speech' is entitled to the protection of the First Amendment, albeit to protection somewhat less extensive than that afforded 'noncommercial speech.'").

The Court's rationale for treating commercial speech differently rests on the idea that commercial speech is "more easily verifiable by its disseminator" and "more durable"—that is, less likely to be chilled by regulations—than fully protected noncommercial speech. *Va. Pharmacy Bd.*, 425 U.S. at 771 n.24. Other cases explain that the more deferential degree of judicial scrutiny is justified because commercial speech "'occurs in an area traditionally subject to government regulation.'" *Lorillard Tobacco Co. v. Reilly*, 533 U.S. 525, 554, 121 S. Ct. 2404, 150 L. Ed. 2d 532 (2001) (quoting *Cent. Hudson*, 447 U.S. at 562). Whatever the justification, the Court has not strayed from its commercial-speech jurisprudence despite calls for it to do so. See *id*. at 554-55 (acknowledging disagreement among members of the Court as to what level of scrutiny applies to regulations on commercial speech but nonetheless refusing to "break new ground").

To determine whether speech falls on the commercial or noncommercial side of the constitutional line, the Court has provided this basic definition: Commercial speech is "speech that proposes a commercial transaction."

It's important to recognize, however, that this definition is just a starting point. Speech that does *no more than* propose a commercial transaction "fall[s] within the core notion of commercial speech," *Bolger*, 463 U.S. at 66, but other communications also may "'constitute commercial speech notwithstanding the fact that they contain discussions of important public issues,'" *Fox*, 492 U.S. at 475 (quoting *Bolger*, 463 U.S. at 67-68).

Indeed, the Supreme Court has "'made clear that advertising which links a product to a current public debate is not thereby entitled to the constitutional protection afforded noncommercial speech.'" . . . Although commercial-speech cases generally rely on the distinction between speech that proposes a commercial transaction and other varieties of speech, it's a mistake to assume that the boundaries of the commercial-speech category are marked exclusively by this "core" definition. . . . To the contrary, there is a "commonsense distinction" between commercial speech and other varieties of speech, and we are to give effect to that distinction.

The Supreme Court's decision in *Bolger* is instructive on this point. *Bolger* dealt with the question of how to classify speech with both noncommercial and commercial elements. There, a prophylactics manufacturer published informational pamphlets providing general factual information about prophylactics but also containing information about the manufacturer's products in particular. *Bolger*, 463 U.S. at 62. The manufacturer brought a pre-enforcement challenge to a federal statute that prohibited the unsolicited mailing of advertisements about contraceptives. The Supreme Court held that although the pamphlets did not expressly propose a commercial transaction, they were nonetheless properly classified as commercial speech based on the following attributes: the pamphlets were a form of advertising, they referred to specific commercial products, and they were distributed by the manufacturer for economic purposes. *Id.* at 66-67.

We have read *Bolger* as suggesting certain guideposts for classifying speech that contains both commercial and noncommercial elements; relevant considerations include "whether: (1) the speech is an advertisement; (2) the speech refers to a specific product; and (3) the speaker has an economic motivation for the speech." *See United States v. Benson*, 561 F.3d 718, 725 (7th Cir. 2009) (citing *Bolger*, 463 U.S. at 66-67). This is just a general framework, however; no one factor is sufficient, and *Bolger* strongly implied that all are not necessary.

2. *Applying the doctrine*

Jewel argues that its ad doesn't propose a commercial transaction and therefore flunks the leading test for commercial speech. As we have explained, the commercial-speech category is not limited to speech that directly or indirectly proposes a commercial transaction. Jewel nonetheless places substantial weight on this test, and the district judge did as well. Although neither relies exclusively on it, the district court's opinion and Jewel's defense of it on appeal both press heavily on the argument that the ad doesn't propose a commercial transaction, so we will start there.

It's clear that the textual focus of Jewel's ad is a congratulatory salute to Jordan on his induction into the Hall of Fame. If the literal import of the words were all that mattered, this celebratory tribute would be noncommercial. But evaluating the text requires consideration of its context, and this truism has special force when applying the commercial-speech doctrine. Modern commercial advertising is enormously varied in form and style.

We know from common experience that commercial advertising occupies diverse media, draws on a limitless array of imaginative techniques, and is often supported by sophisticated marketing research. It is highly creative, sometimes abstract, and frequently relies on subtle cues. The notion that an advertisement counts as "commercial" only if it makes an appeal to purchase a particular product makes no sense today, and we doubt that it ever did. An advertisement is no less "commercial" because it promotes brand awareness or loyalty rather than explicitly proposing a transaction in a specific product or service. Applying the "core" definition of commercial speech too rigidly ignores this reality. Very often the commercial message is general and implicit rather than specific and explicit.

Jewel's ad served two functions: congratulating Jordan on his induction into the Hall of Fame and promoting Jewel's supermarkets. The first is explicit and readily apparent. The ad contains a congratulatory message remarking on Jordan's record-breaking career and celebrating his rightful place in the Basketball Hall of Fame. Jewel points to its longstanding corporate practice of commending local community groups on notable achievements, giving as examples two public-service ads celebrating the work of Chicago's Hispanocare and South Side Community Services. The suggestion seems to be that the Jordan ad belongs in this "civic booster" category: A praiseworthy "fellow Chicagoan" was receiving an important honor, and Jewel took the opportunity to join in the applause.

But considered in context, and without the rose-colored glasses, Jewel's ad has an unmistakable commercial function: enhancing the Jewel-Osco brand in the minds of consumers. This commercial message is implicit but easily inferred, and is the dominant one.

We begin by making a point that should be obvious but seems lost on Jewel: There is a world of difference between an ad congratulating a local community group and an ad congratulating a famous athlete. Both ads will generate goodwill for the advertiser. But an ad congratulating a famous athlete can only be understood as a promotional device for the advertiser. Unlike a community group, the athlete needs no gratuitous promotion and his identity has commercial value. Jewel's ad cannot be construed as a benevolent act of good corporate citizenship.

As for the other elements of the ad, Jewel-Osco's graphic logo and slogan appear just below the textual salute to Jordan. The bold red logo is prominently featured in the center of the ad and in a font size larger than any other on the page. Both the logo and the slogan are styled in their trademarked ways. Their style, size, and color set them off from the congratulatory text, drawing attention to Jewel-Osco's sponsorship of the tribute. Apart from the basketball shoes, the Jewel-Osco brand-name is the center of visual attention on the page. And the congratulatory message specifically incorporates Jewel's slogan: "as we honor a fellow Chicagoan who was 'just around the corner' for so many years." The ad is plainly aimed at fostering goodwill for the Jewel brand among the targeted consumer group—"fellow Chicagoans" and fans of Michael Jordan—for the purpose of increasing patronage at Jewel-Osco stores.

The district judge nonetheless concluded that the ad was not commercial speech based in part on his view that "readers would be at a loss to explain what they have been invited to buy," a reference to the fact that the ad features only the tribute to Jordan, the Jewel-Osco logo and slogan, and a pair of basketball shoes. Granted, Jewel does not sell basketball shoes; it's a chain of grocery stores, and this ad contains not a single word about the specific products that Jewel-Osco sells, nor any product-specific art or photography. The Supreme Court has said that the failure to reference a specific product is a relevant consideration in the commercial-speech determination. *See Bolger*, 463 U.S. at 66-67. But it is far from dispositive, especially where "image" or brand advertising rather than product advertising is concerned.

Image advertising is ubiquitous in all media. Jewel's ad is an example of a neighborly form of general brand promotion by a large urban supermarket chain. What does it invite readers to buy? Whatever they need from a grocery store—a loaf of bread, a gallon of milk, perhaps the next edition of *Sports Illustrated*—from *Jewel-Osco*, where "good things are just around the corner." The ad implicitly encourages readers to patronize their local Jewel-Osco store. That it doesn't mention a specific product means only that this is a different genre of advertising. It promotes brand loyalty rather than a specific product, but that doesn't mean it's "noncommercial."

The district judge was not inclined to put much stock in the ad's use of Jewel-Osco's slogan and graphic logo. Specifically, he considered the logo as little more than a convenient method of identifying the speaker and characterized the slogan as simply a means of ensuring "that the congratulatory message *sounded* like it was coming from Jewel." Dismissing the logo and slogan as mere nametags overlooks their value as advertising tools. The slogan is attached to the Jewel-Osco graphic logo and is repeated in the congratulatory message itself, which describes Jordan as "a fellow Chicagoan who was 'just around the corner' for so many years." This linkage only makes sense if the aim is to promote shopping at Jewel-Osco stores. Indeed, Jewel's copywriter viewed the repetition of the slogan the same way we do; she thought it was "too selly" and "hitting too over the head."

In short, the ad's commercial nature is readily apparent. It may be generic and implicit, but it is nonetheless clear. The ad is a form of image advertising aimed at promoting goodwill for the Jewel-Osco brand by exploiting public affection for Jordan at an auspicious moment in his career.

Our conclusion is confirmed by application of the *Bolger* framework, which applies to speech that contains both commercial and noncommercial elements. Again, the *Bolger* inquiry asks whether the speech in question is in the form of an advertisement, refers to a specific product, and has an economic motive. *See Benson*, 561 F.3d at 725 (explaining the three *Bolger* factors).

Jewel's ad certainly qualifies as an advertisement in form. Although the text is congratulatory, the page nonetheless promotes something to potential buyers: Jewel-Osco supermarkets. Jewel's ad is easily distinguishable from the magazine's editorial content. Although the district court properly characterized it as "embrac[ing] the issue's theme," the ad obviously isn't part of the editorial coverage of Jordan's career. It isn't an article, a column, or a news photograph or illustration. It looks like, and is, an advertisement.

We can make quick work of the second and third *Bolger* factors. As we have explained, although no *specific* product or service is offered, the ad promotes patronage at Jewel-Osco stores more generally. And there is no question that the ad serves an economic purpose: to burnish the Jewel-Osco brand name and enhance consumer goodwill. The record reflects that Jewel received Time's offer of free advertising space enthusiastically; its marketing representatives said it was a "great offer" and it "would be good for us to have our logo in *Sports Illustrated*" because "having your logo in any location where people see it is going to help your company." Indeed, Jewel gave Time valuable consideration—floor space in Jewel-Osco grocery stores—in exchange for the full-page ad in the magazine, suggesting that it expected valuable brand-enhancement benefit from it. We don't doubt that Jewel's tribute was in a certain sense public-spirited. We only recognize the obvious: that Jewel had something to gain by conspicuously joining the chorus of congratulations on the much-anticipated occasion of Jordan's induction into the Basketball Hall of Fame. Jewel's ad is commercial speech.

A contrary holding would have sweeping and troublesome implications for athletes, actors, celebrities, and other trademark holders seeking to protect the use of their identities or marks. Image advertising (also known as "institutional advertising") is commonplace in our society. Rather than expressly peddling particular products, this form of advertising features appealing images and subtle messages alongside the advertiser's brand name or logo with the aim of linking the advertiser to a particular person, value, or idea in order to build goodwill for the brand.

To pick a current example for illustrative purposes, think of the television spots by the corporate sponsors of the Olympics. Many of these ads consist entirely of images of the American athletes coupled with the advertiser's logo or brand name and an expression of support for the U.S. Olympic team; nothing is explicitly offered for sale. Jewel's ad in the commemorative issue belongs in this genre. It portrays Jewel-Osco in a positive light without mentioning a specific product or service—in this case, by invoking a superstar athlete and a celebratory message with particular salience to Jewel's customer base. To say that the ad is noncommercial because it lacks an outright sales pitch is to artificially distinguish between product advertising and image advertising. Classifying this kind of advertising as constitutionally immune noncommercial speech would permit advertisers to misappropriate the identity of athletes and other celebrities with impunity.

Nothing we say here is meant to suggest that a company cannot use its graphic logo or slogan in an otherwise noncommercial way without thereby transforming the communication into commercial speech. Our holding is tied to the particular content and context of Jewel's ad as it appeared in the commemorative issue of *Sport Illustrated Presents*.

* * *

To wrap up, we hold that Jewel's ad in the commemorative issue qualifies as commercial speech. This defeats Jewel's constitutional defense, permitting Jordan's case to go forward. We note that the lone federal claim in the suit—a false-endorsement claim under § 43(a) of the Lanham Act, 15 U.S.C. § 1125(a)—requires proof that Jewel's congratulatory ad caused a likelihood of confusion that Jordan was a Jewel-Osco sponsor or endorsed its products and services. Because the merits have not been briefed, we express no opinion on the substance of Jordan's claims under the Lanham Act or any of the state-law theories. We remand to permit the parties to address whether the Lanham Act claim warrants a trial, and if not, whether the district court should retain or relinquish supplemental jurisdiction over the state-law claims.

REVERSED AND REMANDED.

CASES ON THE SUPPLEMENTAL CD

Abdul-Jabbar v. General Motors Corp., 85 F.3d 407 (9th Cir 1996). The case examines whether a person retains an interest in their birth name, when he or she adopts another name.

Cardtoons v. Major League Baseball Players Association, 95 F.3d 959 (10th Cir 1996). This case examines the parody defense under the First Amendment and whether it applies to commercial activity.

John Doe, a/k/a Tony Twist v. TCI Cablevision, 110 S.W.3d 363 (2003). The case examines whether the use of a fictional character named "Anthony 'Tony Twist' Twistelli" in the Spawn comic book violated Tony Twist's image rights, even though the characters bear no physical resemblance to each other and, aside from the common nickname, are similar only in that each can be characterized as having an "enforcer" or tough-guy persona.

Hirsch v. S. C. Johnson & Son, Inc., 280 N.W.2d 129 (1979). This case examines the unauthorized use of the plaintiff's nickname "Crazy Legs" on a shaving gel for women and whether common law trade name infringement applies.

Newcombe v. Adolf Coors Co., 157 F.3d 686 (9th Cir. 1998). The case examines whether an image in a magazine was the plaintiff and, it so, whether it violated the plaintiff's image rights.

QUESTIONS YOU SHOULD BE ABLE TO ANSWER

1. What are some of the laws available to protect the unauthorized use of your image?
2. Historically, the right of publicity only covered the use of a person's "name or likeness"; however, the courts have now expanded the right to include what else?
3. What are some of the specific uses of a person's image that are protected?
4. What are some of the First Amendment defenses available?
5. What are some of the specific uses of a person's image that are prohibited?

REFERENCES

Cases

Abdul-Jabbar v. General Motors Corp., 85 F.3d 407 (9th Cir. 1996).
Ali v. Playgirl, Inc., 447 F.Supp. 723 (1978).
Cardtoons, L.C. v. Major League Baseball Players Association, 838 F. Supp 1501 (N.D. Okla. 1993).
C.B.C. Distribution v. Major League Baseball Advanced Media, 505 F.3d 818 (8th Cir. 2007).
Downing v. Abercrombie & Fitch, 265 F.3d 994 (2001).
Eastwood v. Superior Court, 149 Cal. App. 3d 409, 198 Cal. Rptr. 342 (1983).
Haelan Laboratories, Inc. v. Topps Chewing Gum, Inc., 202 F.2d 866 (2nd. Cir. 1953).
Hirsch v. S.C. Johnson & Son, 280 N.W. 129 (Wis. 1979).
Joe Namath v. Sports Illustrated, 48 A.D.2d 487; 371 N.Y.S.2d 10 (1975).
John Doe, a/k/a Tony Twist, v. TCI Cablevision, 110 S.W.3d 363 (2003).
Keller v. Electronic Arts, 2010 U.S. Dist. LEXIS 10709 (N.D. Cal., Feb. 8, 2010).
Montana v. San Jose Mercury News, 40 Cal. Rptr. 2d 639 (1995).
Motschenbacher v. R.J. Reynolds Tobacco Co., 498 F.2d 821 (1974).
Newcombe v. Adolf Coors Co., 157 F.3d 686 (9th Cir. 1998).
New Kids on the Block v. New America Pub., Inc., 971 F.2d 302, (9th Cir. 1992).
O'Brien v. Pabst Sales Co., 124 F.2d 167 (1941).
Palmer v. Schonhorn Enterprises, 232 A.2d 458 (1967).
RE: Student-Athlete Name & Likeness Litigation, 763 F. Supp. 2d 1379 (2011).
Roberson v Rochester Folding Box Co., 171 N.Y. 538, 64 N.E. 442 (1902).

Publications

Clay, S. (1994). Starstruck: The overextension of celebrity publicity rights in state and federal courts. *Minnesota Law Review, 79*, 485–517.

Das, Souray. 2016. "*Forbes Highest Paid Athletes 2016.*" Forbes.com. http://sporteology.com/forbes-highest-paid-athletes-2015/. Accessed June 16, 2016.

Fantasy Sports Trade Association. 2016. http://fsta.org/fantasy-sports-grows-to-57-4-million/. Accessed June 16, 2016.

McCarthy, J. T. (2004). *The rights of publicity and privacy* (3rd ed.). Deerfield IL: Clark Boardman Callaghan.

Prosser, W. (1960). Privacy. *California Law Review, 48*, 383–423.

Spencer, B. (April 4, 2011). *Bill for Pounds 82 Million Tiger's Sex Romps; Loss of Sponsors hit Earnings*. Daily Record, p. 11

Strauss, B & Eder, S. (2014, June 10). NCAA Settles One Video Game Suit for $20 Million as a Second Begins. *The New York Times*, sec. B, p. 11.

Right of Publicity. A Brief History of Right of Publicity. http://rightofpublicity.com/brief-history-of-rop. Accessed June 16, 2016.

Warren, S., & Brandeis, L. (1890). The right of privacy. *Harvard Law Review, 4*, 193–220.

Legislation

California Civil Code § 990.

Federal Copyright Act, 17 U.S.C. § 101 *et seq.*

The Lanham Act, 15 U.S.C. § 1051 *et seq.*

N.Y. Sess. Laws 1903, ch.132 § 1. Amended in 1921, now cited as N.Y. Civ. Rights Law, § 50.

N.Y. Sess. Laws 1903, ch.132 § 2. Amended in 1921, now cited as N.Y. Civ. Rights Law, § 51.

7.31 ANTITRUST LAW: PROFESSIONAL SPORT APPLICATIONS

Lisa Pike Masteralexis | University of Massachusetts-Amherst

Antitrust cases have left an indelible mark on professional sport leagues' structure and labor management relations. No other industry employs such restrictive rules and policies. Restraints on free agency and salary spending and restrictions on franchise ownership have exposed leagues to antitrust challenges by players, owners, prospective owners, competitor leagues, cities possessing franchises, cities seeking franchises, and media entities.

FUNDAMENTAL CONCEPTS

Antitrust Law

In 1890, Congress passed the Sherman Antitrust Act to break up business trusts and monopolies. Section 1 of the Act prohibits "every contract, combination . . . or conspiracy in restraint of trade or commerce among the several states [interstate commerce]" (15 U.S.C. §1). Under the statute violators pay three times the damage suffered. Section 2 of the Act makes it a felony, "to monopolize, attempt to monopolize, or combine or conspire . . . to monopolize" (15 U.S.C. § 2).

The Sherman Act's language is vague and thus, dependent on judicial interpretation as to the Act's intent and meaning (Roberts, 1990). To that end, the Supreme Court has adopted three approaches to determine violations of Section 1 of the Act. The first is a "**rule of reason**" defense that recognizes some restraints are necessary business practices. To evaluate the rule of reason defense, the Court weighs the pro-competitive effects of the rule or practice against the anti-competitive effects. The defense requires an inquiry as to the necessary business practices of the industry, and the defendant must overcome the plaintiff's allegation that the defendant's conduct is unreasonable. The rule of reason is applied frequently in sport due to the numerous, and arguably, necessary rules and restrictions adopted for competitive balance among teams in a league. Such restrictions include player drafts; free agency restrictions; restraints on salary, franchise sale, ownership, territories, and movement; and revenue sharing, among others, all of which can be argued as necessary for the proper operation of the leagues. Courts will, however, judge such restrictions on their reasonableness, balancing the business necessity against the degree of anticompetitive behavior of the practice.

The second approach is adopted when anticompetitive conduct is deemed **illegal per se**. *Illegal per se* activities are presumed to have no benefit to competition. Use of the *illegal per se* approach is limited and applied in two situations: when the Court is examining agreements between traditional business competitors and when the Court is seeking to avoid a lengthy inquiry into an industry's business operations. Application of *illegal per se* to professional sport is rare because there is likely a business justification for anti-competitive behavior.

A third approach occurs when the Court focuses on the effect a challenged practice has on consumer welfare (Roberts, 1990). This approach has yet to be applied in professional sport cases. Roberts (1990) has argued the consumer welfare standard may be very important for sport-related antitrust cases and, if applied, would likely limit a plaintiff's success as the plaintiff would be forced to demonstrate that league conduct injures consumer welfare. The success of this approach may vary, for instance, with restrictions in the player market harder to prove under this application than other aspects of the business of professional sport, such as restrictions on franchise relocation. Recently, consumers of MLB, NHL and NFL game broadcasts have brought antitrust lawsuits alleging that leagues used anti-competitive practices to control the broadcasting market, enabling them to charge higher prices for their game telecasts. The leagues accomplish this by granting territorial protections to teams to protect their home markets and those of their competitors. As a result, fans are not able to watch their favorite teams without purchasing an all-league subscription, thereby forcing consumers to pay more for the product than a market free from monopolization would cost. The MLB and NHL suits have settled, but the NFL suit continues at the time of publication (Stempel, 2015; Emert, 2016). If the NFL suit does not settle, it may provide an opportunity for this third effect to be tried in court.

Antitrust Law Applied to Baseball

Baseball possesses a unique status in professional sport, as well as in American business, by virtue of its antitrust **exemption**. In *Federal Baseball Club of Baltimore, Inc. v. National League of Professional Baseball Clubs, et al.* (1922), the Supreme Court concluded that baseball was neither interstate nor commerce—two elements necessary for federal antitrust laws to apply. The Supreme Court considered the baseball business to be a local exhibition consisting of personal service contracts with players, rather than commerce. Further, it found the travel of players across state lines was not essential to the baseball business, but purely incidental to the game. Over time the exemption has faced attack and been amended, but, *Federal Baseball* is still controlling. In *Toolson v. New York Yankees* (1953) and *Flood v. Kuhn* (1972), cases challenging the *Federal Baseball* verdict, baseball players contended that the player reserve system violated federal antitrust laws. Under the reserve system, teams perpetually renewed player contracts, and without a free market in which to sell their services, the players were forced to play with their teams or retire from baseball. In both cases the Supreme Court reaffirmed baseball's exemption by shifting the burden to Congress to create legislation abolishing the exemption. *Flood* also noted that baseball players could use labor relations rather than antitrust law to resolve disputes over the reserve clause. Incidentally, the Major League Baseball Players Association used labor arbitration to successfully challenge the player reserve system, ultimately limiting the reserve clause to a one-year renewal favoring the club, ushering in free agency in baseball (*In Re Twelve Clubs Comprising the National League and Twelve Clubs Comprising the American League and Major League Baseball Players Association*, 1975).

In 1998, Congress codified baseball's exemption through the Curt Flood Act (15 U.S.C. § 27). This Act clarified baseball's trilogy of cases by exempting the business of baseball, but not the labor of major baseball players. The Act defines the business of baseball as: the minor leagues and minor league player reserve clause; the amateur draft; franchise expansion, location, or relocation; franchise ownership; marketing and sales of the entertainment product of baseball; and licensed properties. In 2015, the City of San Jose challenged MLB's antitrust exemption over a failed bid to bring the Oakland A's to San Jose. The trial court dismissed on the precedent of baseball's antitrust exemption because it found franchise relocation to fit squarely within the business of baseball. The Ninth Circuit affirmed explaining that excluding franchise relocation from those aspects for which were subject to antitrust laws meant that Congress was "aware of the possibility that the baseball exemption could apply to franchise relocation and did not overturn it as it had with labor issues. (*City of San Jose v. Office of the Com'r of Baseball*, 2015).

Antitrust Law Applied to Other Sports

Numerous antitrust suits have been filed by players, owners and prospective owners, and competitors in other sports. *United States v. International Boxing Club* (1955) was the first case to successfully apply antitrust law to professional sport. Soon after, football became subject to antitrust law. In *Radovich v. National Football League* (1957), a professional football player challenged a rule that restricted his ability to sign a contract with a team other than the one that held his rights and that blacklisted him from signing as a player-coach with a team affiliated with the NFL. Radovich contended that the blacklist was a group boycott in restraint of trade. The trial and appellate courts dismissed Radovich's claims on the ground that football, like baseball, was exempt from antitrust law. The Supreme Court, however, reversed and held that due to the NFL's radio and television contracts, the NFL was engaged in interstate commerce and subject to the Sherman Act. Shortly thereafter, golf, too, was subject to antitrust (*Deesen v. PGA of America*, 1966) and the argument that baseball's exemption should apply to other sports fell by the wayside.

Single-Entity Status

In an attempt to gain Section 1 immunity, a number of leagues structured themselves as single entities with owners investing in the league rather than in teams. The leagues adopt centralized operations for business and personnel decisions. Centrally administered leagues operated by owner–investors, argue they are a single entities. The single entity defense is based on a defendant's inability to contract, combine, or conspire in restraint of trade as is required of Section 1. Single-entity status for traditionally organized sports leagues has been rejected by the U.S. Supreme Court (*American Needle v. NFL*, 2010). In *American Needle v. NFL*, the Supreme Court ruled that the NFL was not a single entity because it consisted of distinct businesses with independent centers of decision making that competed and cooperated with one another. This ruling mirrored that in numerous lower court rulings when the NFL had raised the single entity defense (*Sullivan v. NFL*, 1994; *Los Angeles Mem'l Coliseum Comm'n v. NFL*, 1984; *NASL v. NFL*, 1982; *Smith v. Pro Football, Inc.*, 1978; and *Mackey v. NFL*, 1976).

In *Fraser v. Major League Soccer* (2000), the First Circuit Court of Appeals determined that Major League Soccer (MLS) was a hybrid single entity organized as a limited liability company made up of operator-investors who sacrificed local autonomy for centralized operations. MLS owns all the teams in the league, including their intellectual property rights, tickets, and broadcast rights. It sets team schedules, negotiates stadium leases and assumes related liabilities, pays the salaries of league personnel including referees, and supplies certain equipment. *Fraser* makes clear that a sports league can be organized uniquely and avoid antitrust liability provided it is a single entity from its inception, not as a result of restructuring itself to avoid antitrust liability.

Antitrust Challenges by Competitor Leagues

A few Section 2 cases challenge competitor leagues over the practices of established leagues as monopolistic. Only one case, *Philadelphia World Hockey, Inc. v. Philadelphia Hockey Club, Inc.* (1972), was substantially successful for the plaintiff. The World Hockey Association successfully argued that the NHL monopolized the labor pool of talented players through the use of the reserve system. The NHL's reserve system perpetually bound players to a team. The World Hockey Association successfully argued that the system restrained their ability to acquire marquee NHL players.

Two other cases brought by upstart competitors were not as successful. In *American Football League v. National Football League* (1963), the AFL was unable to prove that the NFL, by expanding into Dallas and Minneapolis, two cities the AFL was also considering for expansion, was monopolizing the market for professional football. In *United States Football League v. National Football League* (S.D.N.Y., 1986), a jury found that the NFL had monopolized the market for football in the United States, but only awarded nominal damages.

Antitrust Challenges by Prospective Team Owners and Team Owners

Individual franchise owners have challenged league rules, on the theory that rules diminish competition. Many league rules restrict individual opportunities in favor of the good of the league. Prospective team owners have challenged league ownership restrictions that have kept them from becoming owners. The courts in *Levin v. National Basketball Association* (1974), and *Mid-South Grizzlies v. National Football League* (1983), upheld rules requiring three-fourths approval of league owners for transfer of ownership (*Levin*), and admission to the league (*Mid-South Grizzlies*). The most recent of these challenges, *Piazza v. Major League Baseball* (1993), involved potential owners prevented from purchasing and relocating the San Francisco Giants. The case settled out of court after the *Piazza* court entered a declaratory judgment that the claim should not be dismissed on the basis of baseball's antitrust exemption.

The *Los Angeles Memorial Coliseum and the Los Angeles Raiders v. National Football League*, (1984) is the most celebrated ownership challenge to a restrictive franchise policy. The Raiders' owner Al Davis successfully argued that a three-fourths vote needed to relocate into the Los Angeles market was an unreasonable restraint of trade. At the time, it was highly unusual for an owner to sue co-owners. However, a new breed of owners who have made large investments to purchase teams appear more willing to challenge league policies on antitrust grounds. This represents a major shift away from the "league-think" philosophy championed by former NFL Commissioner Pete Rozelle.

Other lawsuits filed by franchise owners involve challenges to the number of games telecast nationally on a superstation (*Chicago Professional Sports Limited Partnership v. National Basketball Association*, 1996); ownership policies, such as restrictions against public ownership and relocation (*Sullivan v. National Football*

League, 1994, *VKK v. National Football League*, 1999); and marketing and revenue sharing (*Dallas Cowboys v. NFL Trust*, 1995).

Antitrust Challenges by Individual Athletes
Suspended athletes have used antitrust to challenge league actions. In *Molinas v. National Basketball Association* (1961), a NBA player suspended for wagering on games in which he was participating, sued the league when his application for reinstatement was rejected. Molinas argued that expulsion from the league was a group boycott and constituted a restraint of trade because he had no economic alternative to playing in the NBA. In upholding the suspension, the court held that the restraint was reasonable, as the NBA had a legitimate interest in banning gambling.

On the other hand, in *Blalock v. LPGA* (1973), professional golfer Jane Blalock successfully argued that a board composed of five of her competitors who suspended her for one year after initially recommending probation was an unreasonable restraint of trade by an organization engaged in interstate commerce. Blalock was distinguished from *Molinas* and *Deeson v. PGA of America* (1966), where both athletes were suspended by their sports' commissioners rather than their competitors. Additionally, in *Deeson*, the plaintiff was not excluded from all tournaments and thus, could still earn winnings playing golf.

Antitrust Exemption for Sport Broadcasting Contracts
In 1961, Congress exempted sports leagues' national television deals from antitrust liability (15 U.S.C. §§ 1291–1294). The statute grants professional leagues an exemption to pool their television rights when negotiating league-wide television packages.

Convergence of Labor and Antitrust Laws
In the early 1900s, employers used the Sherman Act against labor movements, claiming workers organizing boycotts or work stoppages were committing conspiracies in restraint of trade. Employers used injunctions to thwart labor activities and the threat of treble damages to chill the labor movement. In 1914, Congress enacted the Clayton Act to exempt organized labor acting in its own self-interest from antitrust liability. However, the federal courts continued to grant injunctions against labor activity. In response, Congress passed the Norris-La Guardia Act in 1932, often called the Anti-Injunction Act, because it restricted the federal judiciary's power to grant injunctions against labor unions in labor disputes (see Section 7.33, *Labor Law: Professional Sports Applications*). In *Brady v. NFL* (2011), NFL players sought an injunction preventing the league from locking the players out. In rejecting the players' request, the court held that the Norris-LaGuardia and the Clayton Acts barred the federal courts from issuing injunctions in disputes between employers and employees.

During the Term of the Collective Bargaining Agreement
Together, the Clayton and Norris-La Guardia Acts created an antitrust exemption for unions acting in their own self-interest, but did not protect union-management actions, such as entering into collective bargaining agreements (CBAs). CBAs are contracts that contain restrictive provisions and as such could be deemed "contracts in restraint of trade." The U.S. Supreme Court addressed this issue in a number of non-sport cases and established the non-statutory labor exemption to antitrust law. In balancing the interests of antitrust law against labor law, the court held that the goal of federal labor policy is to bring labor and management together to negotiate a CBA that best suits their needs. Congress, the court held, did not intend for antitrust laws to subvert the goal of achieving labor peace through labor-management relations. The objective of the labor exemption is to protect those mandatory subjects agreed to through good faith bargaining from antitrust scrutiny by a party to the collective agreement. It would not be fair to agree to a restrictive practice, receive concessions in exchange for the agreement, and then turn around and sue a counterpart under antitrust law over the practice (*Brown v. Pro-Football*, 1996). The Supreme Court has established that terms negotiated between labor and management in their collective agreement, which outside a collective agreement

would be subject to antitrust law, are in fact exempt from antitrust scrutiny, provided the defendant meets this test:

1. The injured party is a party to the collective bargaining agreement.
2. The subject contested on antitrust grounds is a mandatory subject for bargaining (hours, wages, and other terms and conditions of employment).
3. The collective bargaining agreement was reached through bona fide arms' length bargaining.

Scope of the Labor Exemption

A number of cases address the scope of the labor exemption in the professional sport industry. The league and union are protected from antitrust suits by the labor exemption for suits brought by players not in the league when a collective bargaining agreement with restrictive policies is negotiated (*Wood v. National Basketball Association*, 1987; *Clarett v. National Football League*, 2003). At the time restrictive provisions limit a players' earning capacity, a player is then in the league and must take the burdens of collective bargaining to receive the benefits. The same holds true for suits by former players who may disagree with a union's negotiating decisions and challenge restrictive practices agreed to in negotiation (*Reynolds v. National Football League*, 1978).

Courts have examined practices such as restrictions on free agency, the draft, and salary caps as mandatory subjects. As long as the restriction affects hours, wages, or terms and conditions of employment, courts have found the provisions to be mandatory subjects of collective bargaining. For example, in *Mackey v. National Football League* (1976), the court found that although the Rozelle Rule, a restriction on free agency that required teams signing free agents to pay compensation to the player's former team, did not directly deal with hours, wages, and terms and conditions of employment, its effect was to depress player salaries (wages), and thus it was deemed a mandatory subject.

Mackey v. National Football League (1976), and *McCourt v. California Sports, Inc.* (1979) highlight the concept of arm's length bargaining. In *Mackey*, a number of former and current football players challenged the Rozelle Rule, while owners argued that the labor exemption applied. The court disagreed, finding that there was no bona fide arm's length bargaining because the Rozelle Rule remained unchanged from the time it was unilaterally implemented in 1963. Further, there was no evidence that players agreed to the Rozelle Rule as a *quid pro quo* for better pension benefits and the right to individually negotiate their salaries (as was argued by the NFL's defense). In fact, the *Mackey* Court found that there was no direct bargaining on the Rozelle Rule. Contrast *Mackey* with *McCourt*, where the NHL's By-Law 9A, a similar free agent compensation structure, was subject to antitrust attack by Dale McCourt, a player named as compensation. The court found that the labor exemption protected the NHL because the players' association had bargained vigorously against By-Law 9A. The court stated that player benefits were bargained for in connection with the reserve system remaining unchanged, and the inclusion of the free agent compensation clause was not the result of collusion, but of good-faith bargaining.

Duration of the Labor Exemption

The labor exemption continues to protect parties from antitrust scrutiny even after a collective bargaining agreement (CBA) has expired. Collective bargaining agreement provisions survive its expiration because labor law requires parties to maintain the status quo and continue bargaining for a new agreement until impasse. Impasse occurs when there is a total breakdown in negotiations between union and management and often leads to a strike or a lockout. Like the subjects of the CBA, the labor exemption survives the agreement's expiration provided the parties maintain the status quo. If this were not the case, the players' association may have no incentive to bargain and may opt to drag its feet in negotiations until the expiration of the agreement to seek treble damages through an antitrust suit, thereby increasing its leverage in labor negotiations. The duty to maintain the status quo only extends to impasse, and once an employer has bargained in good faith to impasse, they may unilaterally impose changes to the mandatory bargaining subjects without incurring antitrust liability, provided those changes are consistent with the latest proposals made to the union prior to impasse. In *Powell v. NFL* (1989), the court ruled that the labor exemption does not end with impasse and the players association cannot challenge the league on antitrust grounds provided a collective bargaining relationship exists. That result led the players to decertify so they could sue on antitrust grounds. Similarly the NFLPA and NBPA voted to disclaim or decertify their unions in 2011.

SIGNIFICANT CASE

In this case, a corporation that designed, manufactured and sold headwear carrying trademarked names and logos of NFL teams brought an antitrust suit against the NFL, its teams, and the competitor, Reebok that had received exclusive licensing agreement for trademarked headwear and apparel. The case examines whether the NFL's actions are exempt from antitrust scrutiny under the single entity defense.

AMERICAN NEEDLE INC. V. NATIONAL FOOTBALL LEAGUE
United States Supreme Court
130 S.Ct. 2201(2010)
Justice STEVENS delivered the opinion of the Court.

"Every contract, combination in the form of a trust or otherwise, or, conspiracy, in restraint of trade" is made illegal by § 1 of the Sherman Act, as amended, 15 U.S.C. § 1. The question whether an arrangement is a contract, combination, or conspiracy is different from and antecedent to the question whether it unreasonably restrains trade. This case raises that antecedent question about the business of the 32 teams in the National Football League (NFL) and a corporate entity that they formed to manage their intellectual property. We conclude that the NFL's licensing activities constitute concerted action that is not categorically beyond the coverage of § 1. The legality of that concerted action must be judged under the Rule of Reason.

I

Originally organized in 1920, the NFL is an unincorporated association that now includes 32 separately owned professional football teams. Each team has its own name, colors, and logo, and owns related intellectual property. Like each of the other teams in the league, the New Orleans Saints and the Indianapolis Colts, for example, have their own distinctive names, colors, and marks that are well known to millions of sports fans.

Prior to 1963, the teams made their own arrangements for licensing their intellectual property and marketing trademarked items such as caps and jerseys. In 1963, the teams formed National Football League Properties (NFLP) to develop, license, and market their intellectual property. Most, but not all, of the substantial revenues generated by NFLP have either been given to charity or shared equally among the teams. However, the teams are able to and have at times sought to withdraw from this arrangement.

Between 1963 and 2000, NFLP granted nonexclusive licenses to a number of vendors, permitting them to manufacture and sell apparel bearing team insignias. American Needle, Inc., was one of those licensees.

In December 2000, the teams voted to authorize NFLP to grant exclusive licenses, and NFLP granted Reebok International Ltd. an exclusive 10-year license to manufacture and sell trademarked headwear for all 32 teams. It thereafter declined to renew American Needle's nonexclusive license.

American Needle filed this action in the Northern District of Illinois, alleging that the agreements between the NFL, its teams, NFLP, and Reebok violated §§ 1 and 2 of the Sherman Act. In their answer to the complaint, the defendants averred that the teams, NFL, and NFLP were incapable of conspiring within the meaning of § 1 "because they are a single economic enterprise, at least with respect to the conduct challenged." App. 99. After limited discovery, the District Court granted summary judgment on the question "whether, with regard to the facet of their operations respecting exploitation of intellectual property rights, the NFL and its 32 teams are, in the jargon of antitrust law, acting as a single entity." *American Needle, Inc. v. New Orleans La. Saints*, 496 F.Supp.2d 941, 943 (2007). The court concluded "that in that facet of their operations they have so integrated their operations that they should be deemed a single entity rather than joint ventures cooperating for a common purpose." *Ibid.*

The Court of Appeals for the Seventh Circuit affirmed. The panel observed that "in some contexts, a league seems more aptly described as a single entity immune from antitrust scrutiny, while in others a league appears to be a joint venture between independently owned teams that is subject to review under § 1." 538 F.3d, 736, 741 (2008). Relying on Circuit precedent, the court limited its inquiry to the particular conduct at issue, licensing of teams' intellectual property. The panel agreed with petitioner that "when making a single-entity determination, courts must examine whether the conduct in question deprives the marketplace of the independent sources of economic control that competition assumes." *Id.*, at 742. The court, however, discounted the significance of potential competition among the teams regarding the use of their intellectual property because the teams "can function only as one source of economic power when collectively producing NFL football." *Id.*, at 743. The court noted that football itself can only be carried out jointly. See *ibid.* Moreover, "NFL teams share a vital economic interest in collectively promoting NFL football . . . [to] compet[e] with other forms of entertainment." *Ibid.* "It thus follows," the court found, "that only one source of economic power controls the promotion of NFL football," and "it makes little sense to assert that each individual team has the authority, if not the responsibility, to promote the jointly produced NFL football." *Ibid.* Recognizing that NFL teams have "license[d] their intellectual property collectively" since 1963, the court held that § 1 did not apply. Id., at 744.

We granted certiorari.

II

As the case comes to us, we have only a narrow issue to decide: whether the NFL respondents are capable of engaging in a "contract, combination . . ., or conspiracy" as defined by § 1 of the Sherman Act, 15 U.S.C. § 1, or, as we have sometimes phrased it, whether the alleged activity by the NFL respondents "must be viewed as that of a single enterprise for purposes of § 1." *Copperweld Corp. v. Independence Tube Corp.*, 467 U.S. 752, 771 (1984).

Taken literally, the applicability of § 1 to "every contract, combination . . . or conspiracy" could be understood to cover every conceivable agreement, whether it be a group of competing firms fixing prices or a single firm's chief executive telling her subordinate how to price their company's product.

The meaning of the term "contract, combination . . . or conspiracy" is informed by the " 'basic distinction' " in the Sherman Act " 'between concerted and independent action' " that distinguishes § 1 of the Sherman Act from § 2 *Copperweld*, 467 U.S., at 767. Section 1 applies only to concerted action that restrains trade. Section 2, by contrast, covers both concerted and independent action, but only if that action "monopolize[s]," 15 U.S.C. § 2, or "threatens actual monopolization," *Copperweld*, 467 U.S., at 767 a category that is narrower than restraint of trade. Monopoly power may be equally harmful whether it is the product of joint action or individual action.

Congress used this distinction between concerted and independent action to deter anticompetitive conduct and compensate its victims, without chilling vigorous competition through ordinary business operations. The distinction also avoids judicial scrutiny of routine, internal business decisions.

* * *

III

We have long held that concerted action under § 1 does not turn simply on whether the parties involved are legally distinct entities. Instead, we have eschewed such formalistic distinctions in favor of a functional consideration of how the parties involved in the alleged anticompetitive conduct actually operate.

As a result, we have repeatedly found instances in which members of a legally single entity violated § 1 when the entity was controlled by a group of competitors and served, in essence, as a vehicle for ongoing concerted activity. . . . We have similarly looked past the form of a legally "single entity" when competitors were part of professional organizations or trade groups. [footnotes and citations omitted].

Conversely, there is not necessarily concerted action simply because more than one legally distinct entity is involved. . . .

The roots of this functional analysis can be found in the very decision that established the intraenterprise conspiracy doctrine. In *United States v. Yellow Cab Co.*, 332 U.S. 218 (1947), we observed that "corporate interrelationships . . . are not determinitive of the applicability of the Sherman Act" because the Act "is aimed at substance rather than form." *Id.*, at 227. We nonetheless held that cooperation between legally separate entities was necessarily covered by § 1 because an unreasonable restraint of trade "may result as readily from a conspiracy among those who are affiliated or integrated under common ownership as from a conspiracy among those who are otherwise independent."*Ibid.*

* * *

We finally reexamined the intraenterprise conspiracy doctrine in *Copperweld Corp. v. Independence Tube Corp.*, 467 U.S. 752 (1984), and concluded that it was inconsistent with the " 'basic distinction between concerted and independent action.' " *Id.*, at 767. Considering it "perfectly plain that an internal agreement to implement a single, unitary firm's policies does not raise the antitrust dangers that § 1 was designed to police," *id.*, at 769, we held that a parent corporation and its wholly owned subsidiary "are incapable of conspiring with each other for purposes of § 1 of the Sherman Act," *id.*, at 777. We explained that although a parent corporation and its wholly owned subsidiary are "separate" for the purposes of incorporation or formal title, they are controlled by a single center of decisionmaking and they control a single aggregation of economic power. Joint conduct by two such entities does not "depriv[e] the marketplace of independent centers of decisionmaking," *id.*, at 769, and as a result, an agreement between them does not constitute a "contract, combination . . . or conspiracy" for the purposes of § 1. . . . [footnotes and citations omitted].

IV

As *Copperweld* exemplifies, "substance, not form, should determine whether a[n] . . . entity is capable of conspiring under § 1." 467 U.S., at 773, n. 21. This inquiry is sometimes described as asking whether the alleged conspirators are a single entity. That is perhaps a misdescription, however, because the question is not whether the defendant is a legally single entity or has a single name; nor is the question whether the parties involved "seem" like one firm or multiple firms in any metaphysical sense. The key is whether the alleged "contract, combination . . ., or conspiracy" is concerted action—that is, whether it joins together separate decisionmakers. The relevant inquiry, therefore, is whether there is a "contract, combination . . . or conspiracy" amongst "separate economic actors pursuing separate economic interests," id., at 769, such that the agreement "deprives the marketplace of independent centers of decision making," ibid., and therefore of "diversity of entrepreneurial interests," *Fraser v. Major League Soccer, L.L. C.*, 284 F.3d 47, 57 (C.A.1 2002), and thus of actual or potential competition . . .

Thus, while the president and a vice president of a firm could (and regularly do) act in combination, their joint action generally is not the sort of "combination" that § 1 is intended to cover. Such agreements might be described as "really unilateral behavior flowing from decisions of a single enterprise."*Copperweld*, 467 U.S., at 767. Nor, for this reason, does § 1 cover "internally coordinated conduct of a corporation and one of its unincorporated divisions," id., at 770, because "[a] division within a corporate structure pursues the common interests of the whole," ibid., and therefore "coordination between a corporation and its division does not represent a sudden joining of two independent sources of economic power previously pursuing separate interests," id., at 770–771. Nor, for the same reasons, is "the coordinated activity of a parent and its wholly owned subsidiary" covered. See id.,at 771. They "have a complete unity of interest" and thus "[w]ith or without a formal 'agreement,' the subsidiary acts for the benefit of the parent, its sole shareholder." Ibid.

Because the inquiry is one of competitive reality, it is not determinative that two parties to an alleged § 1 violation are legally distinct entities. Nor, however, is it determinative that two legally distinct entities have organized themselves under a single umbrella or into a structured joint venture. The question is whether the agreement joins together "independent centers of decisionmaking." Id., at 769. If it does, the entities are capable of conspiring under § 1, and the court must decide whether the restraint of trade is an unreasonable and therefore illegal one.

V

The NFL teams do not possess either the unitary decision making quality or the single aggregation of economic power characteristic of independent action. Each of the teams is a substantial, independently owned, and independently managed business. "[T]heir general corporate actions are guided or determined" by "separate corporate consciousnesses," and "[t]heir objectives are" not "common" *Copperweld*, 467 U.S., at 771; see also *North American Soccer League v. NFL*, 670 F.2d 1249, 1252 (C.A.2 1982)(discussing ways that "the financial performance of each team, while related to that of the others, does not . . . necessarily rise and fall with that of the others"). The teams compete with one another, not only on the playing field, but to attract fans, for gate receipts and for contracts with managerial and playing personnel.

Directly relevant to this case, the teams compete in the market for intellectual property. To a firm making hats, the Saints and the Colts are two potentially competing suppliers of valuable trademarks. When each NFL team licenses its intellectual property, it is not pursuing the "common interests of the whole" league but is instead pursuing interests of each "corporation itself," *Copperweld*, 467 U.S., at 770; teams are acting as "separate economic actors pursuing separate economic interests," and each team therefore is a potential "independent cente[r] of decision making," id., at 769. Decisions by NFL teams to license their separately owned trademarks collectively and to only one vendor are decisions that "depriv[e] the marketplace of independent centers of decision making," ibid., and therefore of actual or potential competition. See *NCAA*, 468 U.S., at 109, n. 39 (observing a possible § 1 violation if two separately owned companies sold their separate products through a "single selling agent").

In defense, respondents argue that by forming NFLP, they have formed a single entity, akin to a merger, and market their NFL brands through a single outlet. But it is not dispositive that the teams have organized and own a legally separate entity that centralizes the management of their intellectual property. An ongoing§ 1 violation cannot evade § 1 scrutiny simply by giving the ongoing violation a name and label. . . .

The NFL respondents may be similar in some sense to a single enterprise that owns several pieces of intellectual property and licenses them jointly, but they are not similar in the relevant functional sense. Although NFL teams have common interests such as promoting the NFL brand, they are still separate, profit-maximizing entities, and their interests in licensing team trademarks are not necessarily aligned. . . . Common interests in the NFL brand "*partially* unit[e] the economic interests of the parent firms," Broadley, Joint Ventures and Antitrust Policy, 95 Harv. L.Rev. 1521, 1526 (1982) (emphasis added), but the teams still have distinct, potentially competing interests.

It may be, as respondents argue, that NFLP "has served as the 'single driver" of the teams' "promotional vehicle," " 'pursu[ing] the common interests of the whole.' " Brief for NFL Respondents 28 (quoting *Copperweld*, 467 U.S., at 770–771; brackets in original). But illegal restraints often are in the common interests of the parties to the restraint, at the expense of those who are not parties. It is true, as respondents describe, that they have for some time marketed their trademarks jointly. But a history of concerted activity does not immunize conduct from § 1 scrutiny. "Absence of actual competition may simply be a manifestation of the anticompetitive agreement itself." *Freeman*, 322 F.3d, at 1149.

Respondents argue that nonetheless, as the Court of Appeals held, they constitute a single entity because without their cooperation, there would be no NFL football. It is true that "the clubs that make up a professional sports league are not completely independent economic competitors, as they depend upon a degree of cooperation for economic survival." *Brown*, 518 U.S., at 248. But the Court of Appeals' reasoning is unpersuasive.

The justification for cooperation is not relevant to whether that cooperation is concerted or independent action. A "contract, combination . . . or conspiracy," § 1, that is necessary or useful to a joint venture is still a "contract, combination . . . or conspiracy" if it "deprives the marketplace of independent centers of decision making," *Copperweld*, 467 U.S., at 769 See *NCAA*, 468 U.S., at 113 ("[J]oint ventures have no immunity from antitrust laws"). Any joint venture involves multiple sources of economic power cooperating to produce a product. And for many such ventures, the participation of others is necessary. But that does not mean that necessity of cooperation transforms concerted action into independent action; a nut and a bolt can only operate together, but an agreement between nut and bolt manufacturers is still subject to § 1 analysis. Nor does it mean that once a group of firms agree to produce a joint product, cooperation amongst those firms must be treated as independent conduct. The mere fact that the teams operate jointly in some sense does not mean that they are immune.

In any event, it simply is not apparent that the alleged conduct was necessary at all. Although two teams are needed to play a football game, not all aspects of elaborate inter league cooperation are necessary to produce a game. Moreover, even if league wide agreements are necessary to produce football, it does not follow that concerted activity in marketing intellectual property is necessary to produce football.

The Court of Appeals carved out a zone of antitrust immunity for conduct arguably related to league operations by reasoning that coordinated team trademark sales are necessary to produce "NFL football," a single NFL brand that competes against other forms of entertainment. But defining the product as "NFL football" puts the cart before the horse: Of course the NFL produces NFL football; but that does not mean that cooperation amongst NFL teams is immune from § 1 scrutiny. Members of any cartel could insist that their cooperation is necessary to produce the "cartel product" and compete with other products.

The question whether NFLP decisions can constitute concerted activity covered by § 1 is closer than whether decisions made directly by the 32 teams are covered by § 1. This is so both because NFLP is a separate corporation with its own management and because the record indicates that most of the revenues generated by NFLP are shared by the teams on an equal basis. Nevertheless we think it clear that for the same reasons the 32 teams' conduct is covered by § 1, NFLP's actions also are subject to § 1, at least with regards to its marketing of property owned by the separate teams. NFLP's licensing decisions are made by the 32 potential competitors, and each of them actually owns its share of the jointly managed assets. Apart from their agreement to cooperate in exploiting those assets, including their decisions as the NFLP, there would be nothing to prevent each of the teams from making its own market decisions relating to purchases of apparel and headwear, to the sale of such items, and to the granting of licenses to use its trademarks.

We generally treat agreements within a single firm as independent action on the presumption that the components of the firm will act to maximize the firm's profits. But in rare cases, that presumption does not hold. Agreements made within a firm can constitute concerted action covered by § 1 when the parties to the agreement act on interests separate from those of the firm itself, and the intrafirm agreements may simply be a formalistic shell for ongoing concerted action [citations and footnotes omitted].

For that reason, decisions by the NFLP regarding the teams' separately owned intellectual property constitute concerted action. Thirty-two teams operating independently through the vehicle of the NFLP are not like the components of a single firm that act to maximize the firm's profits. The teams remain separately controlled, potential competitors with economic interests that are distinct from NFLP's financial well-being. . . . Unlike typical decisions by corporate shareholders, NFLP licensing decisions effectively require the assent of more than a mere majority of shareholders. And each team's decision reflects not only an interest in NFLP's profits but also an interest in the team's individual profits. . . . The 32 teams capture individual economic benefits separate and apart from NFLP profits as a result of the decisions they make for the NFLP. NFLP's decisions thus affect each team's profits from licensing its own intellectual property. "Although the business interests of" the teams "will *often* coincide with those of the" NFLP "as an entity in itself, that commonality of interest exists in every cartel." *Los Angeles Memorial Coliseum Comm'n v. NFL*, 726 F.2d 1381, 1389 (C.A.9 1984) (emphasis added). In making the relevant licensing decisions, NFLP is therefore "an instrumentality" of the teams. . . .

If the fact that potential competitors shared in profits or losses from a venture meant that the venture was immune from § 1, then any cartel "could evade the antitrust law simply by creating a 'joint venture' to serve as the exclusive seller of their competing products." *Major League Baseball Properties, Inc. v. Salvino, Inc.*, 542 F.3d 290, 335 (C.A.2 2008) (Sotomayor, J., concurring in judgment). "So long as no agreement," other than one made by the cartelists sitting on the board of the joint venture, "explicitly listed the prices to be charged, the companies could act as monopolies through the 'joint venture.'" *Ibid*. (Indeed, a joint venture with a single management structure is generally a better way to operate a cartel because it decreases the risks of a party to an illegal agreement defecting from that agreement). However, competitors "cannot simply get around" antitrust liability by acting "through a third-party intermediary or 'joint venture'." *Id*., at 336.

VI

Football teams that need to cooperate are not trapped by antitrust law. "[T]he special characteristics of this industry may provide a justification" for many kinds of agreements. *Brown*, 518 U.S., at 252 (STEVENS, J., dissenting). The fact that NFL teams share an interest in making the entire league successful and profitable, and that they must cooperate in the production and scheduling of games, provides a perfectly sensible justification for making a host of collective decisions. But the conduct at issue in this case is still concerted activity under the Sherman Act that is subject to § 1 analysis.

When "restraints on competition are essential if the product is to be available at all,"*per se* rules of illegality are inapplicable, and instead the restraint must be judged according to the flexible Rule of Reason. *NCAA*, 468 U.S., at 101; see *id.*, at 117 ("Our decision not to apply a *per se* rule to this case rests in large part on our recognition that a certain degree of cooperation is necessary if the type of competition that petitioner and its member institutions seek to market is to be preserved"); . . . In such instances, the agreement is likely to survive the Rule of Reason. See *Broadcast Music, Inc. v. Columbia Broadcasting System, Inc.*, 441 U.S. 1, 23 (1979) ("Joint ventures and other cooperative arrangements are also not usually unlawful . . . where the agreement . . . is necessary to market the product at all"). And depending upon the concerted activity in question, the Rule of Reason may not require a detailed analysis; it "can sometimes be applied in the twinkling of an eye." *NCAA*, 468 U.S., at 109, n. 39.

Other features of the NFL may also save agreements amongst the teams. We have recognized, for example, "that the interest in maintaining a competitive balance" among "athletic teams is legitimate and important," *NCAA*, 468 U.S., at 117. While that same interest applies to the teams in the NFL, it does not justify treating them as a single entity for § 1 purposes when it comes to the marketing of the teams' individually owned intellectual property. It is, however, unquestionably an interest that may well justify a variety of collective decisions made by the teams. What role it properly plays in applying the Rule of Reason to the allegations in this case is a matter to be considered on remand.

* * *

Accordingly, the judgment of the Court of Appeals is reversed, and the case is remanded for further proceedings consistent with this opinion.

CASES ON THE SUPPLEMENTAL CD

Brown, v. Pro Football, Inc., d/b/a Washington Redskins, 518 U.S. 231 (1996). This case examines whether the NFL violated the Sherman Act, when they implemented unilateral changes after the parties had bargained to an impasse.

City of San Jose v. Office of the Commissioner of Baseball, 776 F.3d 686 (9th Cir. 2015), cert. denied sub nom 136 S. Ct. 36 (2015). This case examines whether baseball is still exempt from antitrust law when engaged in business decisions, specifically to stall a bid for relocation of a team from Oakland to San Jose.

Flood v. Kuhn, 407 U.S. 258 (1972). This case examines whether the reserve clause in baseball was exempt Federal Antitrust law.

Fraser v. Major League Soccer, L.L.C., 284 F.3d 47 (2002). This case examines whether Major League Soccer was a single entity for antitrust purposes.

National Basketball Ass'n v. SDC Basketball Club, Inc., 815 F.2d 562 (Cal. 1987). This case considers a franchise's relocation and whether a league can sanction franchise for failing to seek league approval prior to relocation without violating antitrust laws.

QUESTIONS YOU SHOULD BE ABLE TO ANSWER

1. Why is baseball exempt from antitrust law? Why does it continue to be exempt over 90 years after the original decision granting the exemption by the U.S. Supreme Court? What are the limitations on the exemption?

2. What is the single entity defense and why do leagues and tours seek to be declared single entities?

3. Why would professional sports leagues want unions to protect themselves from antitrust challenges?

4. What arguments must a league raise in order to exert the labor exemption defense?

5. Why are sports leagues "magnets" for antitrust litigation?

REFERENCES

Cases

Abrahamian, et al. v. National Football League Inc., et al., Case No. 2:15-cv-04606 (C.D. Calif. 2015).
American Football League v. National Football League, 323 F.2d 124 (4th Cir. 1963).
American Needle v. National Football League, 130 S.Ct. 2201 (2010).
Brady v. National Football League, 644 F. 3d 661 (8th Cir. 2011).
Brown v. Pro-Football, Inc., 518 U.S. 231 (1996).
City of San Jose v. Office of the Commissioner of Baseball, 776 F.3d 686 (9th Cir. 2015), cert. denied sub nom 136 S. Ct. 36 (2015)
Chicago Professional Sports Limited Partnership v. National Basketball Association, 95 F.3d 593 (7th Cir. 1996).
Clarett v. National Football League, 306 F.Supp.2d 379 (S.D.N.Y. 2004).
Dallas Cowboys v. NFL Trust, 94-C-9426 (N.D. Cal. 1995).
Deesen v. PGA of America, 358 F. 2d 165 (9th Cir. 1966), *cert denied* 385 U.S. 846 (1966).
Federal Baseball Club of Baltimore, Inc. v. National League of Professional Baseball Clubs, et al., 259 U.S. 200 (1922).
Flood v. Kuhn, 407 U.S. 258 (1972).
Fraser v. Major League Soccer, 97 F. Supp. 2d 130 (D. Mass. 2000).
Garber, et al. v. Office of the Commissioner of Baseball, et al., Case No. 1:12-CV-03704 (S.D. N.Y. 2014).
Laumann, et al. v. National Hockey League, et al., Case No. 12-cv-01817 (S.D. N.Y. 2014).*Levin v. National Basketball League*, 385 F. Supp. 149 (S.D. N.Y. 1974).
Los Angeles Memorial Coliseum and the Los Angeles Raiders v. National Football League, 726 F.2d 1381 (9th Cir. 1984).
Mackey v. National Football League, 543 F.2d 606 (8th Cir. 1976).
McCourt v. California Sports, Inc., 600 F.2d 1193 (6th Cir. 1979).
Mid-South Grizzlies v. National Football League, 550 F. Supp. 558 (E.D. Pa. 1982), *aff'd* 720 F.2d 772 (3rd Cir. 1983), *cert. denied*, 467 U.S. 1215 (1984).
Molinas v. National Basketball Association, 190 F. Supp. 241 (S.D. N.Y. 1961).
Philadelphia World Hockey, Inc. v. Philadelphia Hockey Club, Inc., 351 F. Supp. 462 (E.D. Pa. 1972).
Piazza v. Major League Baseball, 831 F. Supp 420 (E.D. Pa. 1993).
Powell v. National Football League, 930 F.2d 1293 (8th Cir. 1989).
Radovich v. National Football League, 352 U.S. 445 (1957).
Reynolds v. National Football League, 584 F.2d 280 (8th Cir. 1978).
Sullivan v. National Football League, 34 F.3d 1091 (1st Cir. 1994).
Toolson v. New York Yankees, 346 U.S. 356 (1953).
United States v. International Boxing Club, 348 U.S. 236 (1955).
United States Football League v. National Football League, 644 F. Supp. 1040 (S.D. N.Y. 1986).
VKK v. National Football League, 55 F. Supp. 196 (S.D.N.Y. 1999).
Wood v. National Basketball Association, 809 F.2d 954 (2nd Cir. 1987).

Publications

Emert, J. (2016, January 19). "MLB tv settlement is "big win" for fans, *Washington Post*. Retrieved May 12, 2016 from https://www.washingtonpost.com/news/early-lead/wp/2016/01/19/mlb-tv-settlement-is-big-win-for-baseball-fans/
Roberts, G. (1990). Antitrust issues in professional sports. In G. Uberstine (Ed.), *Law of professional and amateur sports* (pp. 19-1–19-54. Deerfield, IL: Clark Boardman Callaghan.
Stempel, J.(2015, June 11). "NHL, broadcasters settle lawsuit over TV blackouts," *Reuters*. Retrieved May 12, 2016 from http://www.reuters.com/article/nhl-broadcasters-antitrust-settlement-idUSL1N0YX2O620150611

Legislation

The Clayton Act of 1914, 15 U.S.C. §§ 12–27 (1989).
The Curt Flood Act of 1998, 15 U.S.C. § 27 (1998).
National Labor Relations Act, 29 U.S.C. § 151-69 (1988).
The Sherman Antitrust Act of 1890, 15 U.S.C. § 1, et seq. (1989).

ANTITRUST LAW: AMATEUR SPORT APPLICATIONS

John T. Wolohan | Syracuse University

Unlike professional sports organizations, the courts have traditionally have been reluctant to apply the antitrust laws against the NCAA and its member schools. The basic rational behind this theory is that the NCAA is the guardian of amateur sports in America and that they should be free to control eligibility requirements and other rules regulating the relationship between member schools as they seem fit. That reluctance, however, seems to fading away. Since the 2015 NCAA Convention, when the five biggest and wealthiest college-sports conferences (the Power Five): Atlantic Coast (ACC), Big Ten, Big 12, Pacific-12 (Pac 12), and Southeastern (SEC) were granted autonomy to create new legislation granting athletes' financial benefits in addition the ones they already receive. As the 65 major colleges become more and more like professional sports, the courts seem more willing to hold the NCAA and other amateur athletic organizations under the antitrust law. These lawsuits, which range from the unlawful restraint of trade in the college athlete market, the television market and the college basketball coaches' market to the unlawful use of their monopoly power to destroy another amateur athletic organization, will all be explored in the following section.

FUNDAMENTAL CONCEPTS

In reviewing Federal Antitrust challenges against the NCAA, the first question the courts must determine is which of the two major sections of the Sherman Act apply. The two sections of the Sherman Act are: Section 1 (15 U.S.C. § 1) which prohibits restraints of trade or commerce; and Section 2 (15 U.S.C. § 2) which prohibits monopolies or attempted monopolies. Once the court determines what section of the Sherman Act applies, it must then determine whether the NCAA's rule or policy has a pro-competitive benefit to the consumer (athletes and sports fans) or an anti-competitive effect.

Sherman Antitrust Act
Section 1 of the Sherman Act

Section 1 of the Sherman Act states that "[E]very contract, combination in the form of trust or otherwise, or conspiracy, in restraint of trade or commerce among the several States, or with foreign nations, is hereby declared to be illegal" (15 U.S.C. § 1).

As we will see below, it is important to note, that not every restraint of trade violates the antitrust law. Because nearly every contract that binds the parties to an agreed course of conduct "is a restraint of trade" of some sort, the Supreme Court has limited the restrictions contained in Section 1 to bar only **unreasonable restraints of trade**" (*NCAA v. Board of Regents of University of Oklahoma*, 1984). Therefore, in order to prevail on a Section 1 claim under the Sherman Act, the plaintiff must show that the defendant (1) participated in an agreement that restrained interstate trade or commerce; and (2) that the agreement unreasonably restrained trade in the relevant market.

Establishing a Section 1 Violation

In determining whether a defendant's conduct is an unreasonable restraint of trade, the courts have developed three categories of antitrust analysis: the *per se* rule; the rule of reason analysis; and an abbreviated or "quick look" rule of reason analysis.

***Per Se* Rule.** The reasoning behind the *per se* rule is that certain types restraints or agreements, such as price fixing among competitors, resale price maintenance, and market allocations, are almost always antitrust violations, regardless of the intent of the participants or the justifications offered. Once the courts identify something as a *per se* violation, they will refuse to engage in a detailed (and costly) market and effects analysis of conduct. There are only a handful of categories that will trigger the *per se* rule, as such, the courts tend to limit the application of the *per se* rule (Hovenkamp, 2005).

Rule of Reason. Unlike the per se rule, when conducting a rule of reason analysis, the court will take a careful look at the type of restraint or agreement and whether it has positive or negative impact on competition in the relevant product market (Hovenkamp, 2005). The focus of the rule of reason inquiry, therefore, is not so much the legal category in which the conduct falls, but rather the actual purpose and effects of the restraint and how it affects competition. Under the rule of reason analysis, the court must perform an economic and legal analysis, not only evaluating the restraint, but also the actual history and purpose behind the restraint and whether it "unreasonably" affects competition.

Since Section 1 only bars "unreasonable restraints of trade," an agreement to restrain trade may still survive scrutiny under Section 1 if the pro-competitive benefits of the restraint reasonably justify the anticompetitive effects. Justifications offered under the rule of reason may be considered only to the extent that they tend to show that, on balance, "the challenged restraint enhances competition" (*NCAA v. Board of Regents of University of Oklahoma*, 1984).

"Quick Look" Rule of Reason. When a practice has obvious anticompetitive effects, almost to the point of deserving per se condemnation, the courts will apply a "quick look" rule of reason analysis which allows the courts to proceed directly to the question of whether the pro-competitive justifications advanced for the restraint outweigh the anticompetitive effects (Hovenkamp, 2005). For example, in *Law v. National Collegiate Athletic Association* (1998), the court, using a quick look rule of reason analysis, found that an "anticompetitive effect is established, even without a determination of the relevant market, where the plaintiff shows that a horizontal agreement to fix prices exists, that the agreement is effective, and that the price set by such agreement is more favorable to the defendant than otherwise would have resulted from operation of market forces"(*Law v. National Collegiate Athletic Association*, 1998).

Section 2 of the Sherman Act

Section 2 of the Sherman Act states that "[E]very person who shall monopolize, attempt to monopolize, or combine or conspire with any other person or persons, to monopolize any part of the trade or commerce among the several States, or with foreign nations, shall be deemed guilty of a felony..." (15 U.S.C. 2).

Establishing a Section 2 Violation

Unlike Section 1, which requires that at least two parties combine or conspire in restraint of trade, it is important to note that Section 2 of the Sherman Act can be triggered by a single party acting alone. In order to establish a violation under Section 2, the Supreme Court has identified two elements that must be present: "(1) the possession of monopoly power in the relevant market and (2) the willful acquisition or maintenance of that power as distinguished from growth or development as a consequence of a superior product, business acumen or historical accident" (*United States v. Grinnell Corp.*, 1966) "and has exercised that power" (*Verizon Communications v. Law Office of Curtis v. Trinko*, 2004).

Monopoly power has traditionally been defined as "the power to control market prices or exclude competition" (*United States v. E.I.duPont Nemours & Co.*, 1956). However, in addition to having the ability to control market prices or exclude competition, it is essential that the courts identify the relevant markets adversely affected by the anticompetitive actions. For example, while the NCAA may have a monopoly over college sports, it has very little control over professional sports.

The NCAA and Antitrust Law

The following section looks at just some of the antitrust lawsuits filed against the NCAA. In particular, the cases examine the difficulty the courts have in distinguishing between rules and regulations that are designed to protect the amateur nature of intercollegiate athletes and those that are commercial in nature.

Student-Athletes

In *Banks v. NCAA* (1992), Braxston Banks, while still a college football player, entered his name into the NFL draft. When he was not drafted, Banks sued the NCAA seeking to have his final year of eligibility to play intercollegiate football restored. Banks alleged that the NCAA rule revoking an athlete's eligibility once he or she chooses to enter a professional draft or engages an agent to help him secure a position with a professional team is an illegal restraint in violation of the Sherman Antitrust Act. In rejecting Bank's argument, the Seventh Circuit Court of Appeals held that Bank's failed to allege an anticompetitive effect on a relevant market; at best, the court held, Banks had merely attempted to frame his complaint in antitrust language. Although Banks alleged a restraint on the market of college football players, the complaint failed to explain how the alleged restraint diminished competition in or among the markets.

In *Smith v. NCAA* (1998), Renee Smith sued the NCAA, alleging that the NCAA's enforcement of a bylaw prohibiting her from participating in athletics while enrolled in a graduate program at an institution other than her undergraduate institution violated the Sherman Antitrust Act. The Court of Appeals held that as matter of first impression, the Sherman Act's restraint of trade provision did not apply to NCAA eligibility rules. Even if the Sherman Act was applicable, the court held that the challenged rule was not an unlawful restraint of trade.

In *Agnew v. NCAA* (2012), two former NCAA Division I football players, who had suffered career-ending football injuries and lost their scholarships, sued the NCAA claiming that the NCAA's regulations on the number of scholarships given per team and the prohibition of multi-year scholarships prevented them from obtaining scholarships that covered the entire cost of their college education. These regulations, according Agnew, have an anticompetitive effect on the market for student-athletes, and therefore violate § 1 of the Sherman Act. Although the Seventh Circuit Court of Appeals disagreed with the district court that the former players could not have alleged a relevant cognizable market, the court ultimately concluded that the former players did not sufficiently identify a commercial market, an obvious necessity for Sherman Act violations, and therefore held that the district court's dismissal was justified.

In O'Bannon v. NCAA, (2015), a group of former student-athletes who played Division I basketball and football players filed an Antitrust claim against the NCAA claiming that the NCAA conspired to restrain trade in violation of Section 1 of the Sherman Act by agreeing to fix at zero the amount of compensation the athletes were allowed to receive under NCAA rules for the use of their names, images, and likenesses in products or media. In overturning the district court's decision, allowing students to be paid cash compensation of up to $5,000 per year, the Ninth Circuit Court held that the NCAA is not above the antitrust laws, and courts cannot and must not shy away from requiring the NCAA to play by the Sherman Act's rules. In this case, the court held the NCAA's rules have been more restrictive than necessary to maintain its tradition of amateurism in support of the college sports market. The Rule of Reason, therefore, requires that the NCAA permit its schools to provide up to the cost of attendance to their student athletes. It does not require NCAA member schools to pay student-athletes up to $5,000 per year in deferred compensation (O'Bannon v. NCAA, 2015).

Television

In *NCAA v. Board of Regents of the University of Oklahoma* (1984), the U.S. Supreme Court ruled that the NCAA's plan for televising college football games of member institutions violated the Sherman Antitrust Act. The Supreme Court held that the plan on its face constituted a restraint on the operation of a free market; that the relevant market was college football; and that the restraint was not justified on the basis of procompetitive effect, protecting live attendance, or maintaining competitive balance among amateur athletic teams (See Significant Case).

Women's Athletics

When it was first created, the NCAA only sponsored men's intercollegiate athletic programs. Women's intercollegiate athletic programs were governed by the Association for Intercollegiate Athletics for Women (AIAW), which had 961 member colleges and universities by 1980–81. In 1981, the NCAA began to sponsor women's championships for the first time. Forced to pick between the AIAW and the NCAA, the AIAW suffered a significant drop in membership and participation in its events. As a result of the membership loses, the National Broadcasting Company (NBC) decided not to exercise its exclusive television rights to telecast AIAW championships. In addition, the Eastman Kodak Company and the Broderick Company also sought to withdraw sponsorship of AIAW achievement awards. Because the AIAW's leadership expected these financial hardships only to worsen, it decided to close for business on June 30, 1982.

Claiming that the NCAA unlawfully used its monopoly power in men's college sports to facilitate its entry into women's college sports and to force the AIAW out of existence, the AIAW sued the NCAA. In *Association for Intercollegiate Athletics for Women v. NCAA* (1984), the Court held that the AIAW failed to prove an illegal agreement between the NCAA and NBC to "tie" television rights to the NCAA's newly instituted women's basketball championship to NBC's contract with the NCAA and their men's basketball tournament. The court also held that even if the conduct of the NCAA was avowedly anticompetitive in purpose, the record did not support a finding that its effect on the AIAW was the result of anything but direct competition.

College Coaches

In *Law v. National Collegiate Athletic Association* (1998), the NCAA attempted to reduce the costs of intercollegiate athletics "without disturbing the competitive balance" among member institutions, by limiting the number of coaches on a Division I basketball staff to four members, one head coach, two assistant coaches, and one entry-level coach called a "restricted-earnings" coach. The compensation for the Restricted Earnings Coach (REC) was restricted to a total of $12,000 for the academic year and $4,000 for the summer months or $16,000 per year. Since the NCAA did not dispute that the cost reduction had effectively reduced restricted-earnings coaches' salaries, thereby artificially lowering the price of coaching services, the Tenth Circuit Court of Appeals using a "quick look" rule of reason analysis found that the restricted-earnings coaches' rule was anticompetitive and had no procompetitive rationales and therefore was an unlawful restraint of trade. As a result, the court found the NCAA liable for nearly $22.3 million damages, which when trebled, made the NCAA potentially liable for approximately $67 million. The NCAA eventually settled the case for $54.5 million (Dauner, 2000).

In *Bassett v. NCAA*, (2008), Claude Bassett an assistant football coach for the University of Kentucky filed suit against NCAA, the Southeastern Conference and the University of Kentucky, after he resigned due to allegations of NCAA rules infractions. In rejecting Bassett claim that the actions of the defendants' amounted to a group boycott that prevented him from coaching at any NCAA member school in violation of the Sherman Act, the Sixth Circuit Court found that Bassett's complaint lacked the critical commercial activity component required to permit application of the Sherman Act. The court found that NCAA's rules on recruiting student athletes, specifically those rules prohibiting improper inducements and academic fraud were explicitly non-commercial. Because the rules and the corresponding sanctions were not commercial, the enforcement of the rules could not be commercial. The Sixth Circuit also held that Bassett's complaint failed to allege any antitrust injury because it was devoid of any allegation of the anticompetitive effect of NCAA's enforcement of its non-commercial rules on the coaching market.

SIGNIFICANT CASE

The following antitrust case establishes the precedent that even though the NCAA plays a vital role in protecting and preserving the nature of amateur athletics, when its regulations are purely commercial in nature, it will be held to same antitrust standards as other commercial businesses.

NCAA V. BOARD OF REGENTS OF THE UNIVERSITY OF OKLAHOMA
United States Supreme Court
468 U.S. 85 (1984)

The University of Oklahoma and the University of Georgia contend that the National Collegiate Athletic Association has unreasonably restrained trade in the televising of college football games. After an extended trial, the District Court found that the NCAA had violated section 1 of the Sherman Act and granted injunctive relief. The Court of Appeals agreed that the statute had been violated but modified the remedy in some respects. We granted certiorari, and now affirm.

I.

The NCAA

Since its inception in 1905, the NCAA has played an important role in the regulation of amateur collegiate sports. It has adopted and promulgated playing rules, standards of amateurism, standards for academic eligibility, regulations concerning recruitment of athletes, and rules governing the size of athletic squads and coaching staffs. In some sports, such as baseball, swimming, basketball, wrestling, and track, it has sponsored and conducted national tournaments. It has not done so in the sport of football, however. With the exception of football, the NCAA has not undertaken any regulation of the televising of athletic events.

The NCAA has approximately 850 voting members. The regular members are classified into separate divisions to reflect differences in size and scope of their athletic programs. Division I includes 276 colleges with major athletic programs; in this group only 187 play intercollegiate football. Divisions II and III include approximately 500 colleges with less extensive athletic programs. Division I has been subdivided into Divisions I-A and I-AA for football.

Some years ago, five major conferences together with major football-playing independent institutions organized the College Football Association (CFA). The original purpose of the CFA was to promote the interests of major football-playing schools within the NCAA structure. The Universities of Oklahoma and Georgia, respondents in this Court, are members of the CFA.

* * *

The Current Plan

The plan adopted in 1981 for the 1982–1985 seasons is at issue in this case. This plan, like each of its predecessors, recites that it is intended to reduce, insofar as possible, the adverse effects of live television upon football game attendance. It provides that "all forms of television of the football games of NCAA member institutions during the Plan control periods shall be in accordance with this Plan." The plan recites that the television committee has awarded rights to negotiate and contract for the telecasting of college football games of members of the NCAA to two "carrying networks."

* * *

In separate agreements with each of the carrying networks, ABC and the Columbia Broadcasting System (CBS), the NCAA granted each the right to telecast the 14 live "exposures" described in the plan, in accordance with the "ground rules" set forth therein. Each of the networks agreed to pay a specified "minimum aggregate compensation to the participating NCAA member institutions" during the 4-year period in an amount that totaled $131,750,000. In essence the agreement authorized each network to negotiate directly with member schools for the right to televise their games. The agreement itself does not describe the method of computing the compensation for each game, but the practice that has developed over the years and that the District Court found would be followed under the current agreement involved the setting of a recommended fee by a representative of the NCAA for different types of telecasts, with national telecasts being the most valuable, regional telecasts being less valuable, and Division II or Division III games commanding a still lower price. The aggregate of all these payments presumably equals the total minimum aggregate compensation set forth in the basic agreement. Except for differences in payment between national and regional telecasts, and with respect to Division II and Division III games, the amount that any team receives does not change with the size of the viewing audience, the number of markets in which the game is telecast, or the particular characteristic of the game or the participating teams. Instead, the "ground rules" provide that the carrying networks make alternate selections of those games they wish to televise, and thereby obtain the exclusive right to submit a bid at an essentially fixed price to the institutions involved. See 546 F.Supp., at 1289-1293.

The plan also contains "appearance requirements" and "appearance limitations" which pertain to each of the 2year periods that the plan is in effect. The basic requirement imposed on each of the two networks is that it must schedule appearances for at least 82 different member institutions during each 2-year period. Under the appearance limitations no member institution is eligible to appear on television more than a total of six times and more than four times nationally, with the appearances to be divided equally between the two carrying networks. See *Id.*, at 1293. The number of exposures specified in the contracts also sets an absolute maximum on the number of games that can be broadcast.

Thus, although the current plan is more elaborate than any of its predecessors, it retains the essential features of each of them. It limits the total amount of televised intercollegiate football and the number of games that any one team may televise. No member is permitted to make any sale of television rights except in accordance with the basic plan.

Background of this Controversy

Beginning in 1979 CFA members began to advocate that colleges with major football programs should have a greater voice in the formulation of football television policy than they had in the NCAA. CFA therefore investigated the possibility of negotiating a television agreement of its own, developed an independent plan, and obtained a contract offer from the National Broadcasting Co. (NBC). This contract, which it signed in August 1981, would have allowed a more liberal number of appearances for each institution, and would have increased the overall revenues realized by CFA members.

In response the NCAA publicly announced that it would take disciplinary action against any CFA member that complied with the CFA-NBC contract. The NCAA made it clear that sanctions would not be limited to the football programs of CFA members, but would apply to other sports as well. On September 8, 1981, respondents commenced this action in the United States District Court for the Western District of Oklahoma and obtained a preliminary injunction preventing the NCAA from initiating disciplinary proceedings or otherwise interfering with CFA's efforts to perform its agreement with NBC. Notwithstanding the entry of the injunction, most CFA members were unwilling to commit themselves to the new contractual arrangement with NBC in the face of the threatened sanctions and therefore the agreement was never consummated. See *Id.*, at 1286-1287.

* * *

II.

There can be no doubt that the challenged practices of the NCAA constitute a "restraint of trade" in the sense that they limit members' freedom to negotiate and enter into their own television contracts. In that sense, however, every contract is a restraint of trade, and as we have repeatedly recognized, the Sherman Act was intended to prohibit only unreasonable restraints of trade.

It is also undeniable that these practices share characteristics of restraints we have previously held unreasonable. The NCAA is an association of schools which compete against each other to attract television revenues, not to mention fans an athletes. As the District Court found, the policies of the NCAA with respect to television rights are ultimately controlled by the vote of member institutions. By participating in an association which prevents member institutions from competing against each other on the basis of price or kind of television rights that can be offered to broadcasters, the NCAA member institutions have created a horizontal restraint—an agreement among competitors on the way in which they will compete with one another. A restraint of this type has often been held to be unreasonable as a matter of law. Because it places a ceiling on the number of games member institutions may televise, the horizontal agreement places an artificial limit on the quantity of televised football that is available to broadcasters and consumers. By restraining the quantity of television rights available for sale, the challenged practices create a limitation on output; our cases have held that such limitations are unreasonable restraints of trade. Moreover, the District Court found that the minimum aggregate price in fact operates to preclude any price negotiation between broadcasters and institutions, thereby constituting horizontal price fixing, perhaps the paradigm of an unreasonable restraint of trade.

Horizontal price fixing and output limitation are ordinarily condemned as a matter of law under an "illegal per se" approach because the probability that these practices are anticompetitive is so high; a per se rule is applied when "the practice facially appears to be one that would always or almost always tend to restrict competition and decrease output." *Broadcast Music, Inc. v. Columbia Broadcasting System, Inc.*, 441 U.S. 1, 19-20 (1979). In such circumstances a restraint is presumed unreasonable without inquiry into the particular market context in which it is found. Nevertheless, we have decided that it would be inappropriate to apply a per se rule to this case. This decision is not based on a lack of judicial experience with this type of arrangement, on the fact that the NCAA is organized as a nonprofit entity, or on our respect for the NCAA's historic role in the preservation and encouragement of intercollegiate amateur athletics. Rather, what is critical is that this case involves an industry in which horizontal restraints on competition are essential if the product is to be available at all.

As Judge Bork has noted: "[Some] activities can only be carried out jointly. Perhaps the leading example is league sports. When a league of professional lacrosse teams is formed, it would be pointless to declare their cooperation illegal on the ground that there are no other professional lacrosse teams." R. Bork, The Antitrust Paradox 278 (1978). What the NCAA and its member institutions market in this case is competition itself—contests between competing institutions. Of course, this would be completely ineffective if there were no rules on which the competitors agreed to create and define the competition to be marketed. A myriad of rules affecting such matters as the size of the field, the number of players on a team, and the extent to which physical violence is to be encouraged or proscribed, all must be agreed upon, and all restrain the manner in which institutions compete. Moreover, the NCAA seeks to market a particular brand of football—college football. The identification of this "product" with an academic tradition differentiates college football from and makes it more popular than professional sports to which it might otherwise be comparable, such as, for example, minor league baseball. In order to preserve the character and quality of the "product," athletes must not be paid, must be required to attend class, and the like. And the integrity of the "product" cannot be preserved except by mutual agreement; if an institution adopted such restrictions unilaterally, its effectiveness as a competitor on the playing field might soon be destroyed. Thus, the NCAA plays a vital role in enabling college football to preserve its character, and as a result enables a product to be marketed which might otherwise be unavailable. In performing this role, its actions widen consumer choice—not only the choices available to sports fans but also those available to athletes—and hence can be viewed as procompetitive.

* * *

Respondents concede that the great majority of the NCAA's regulations enhance competition among member institutions. Thus, despite the fact that this case involves restraints on the ability of member institutions to compete in terms of price and output, a fair evaluation of their competitive character requires consideration of the NCAA's justifications for the restraints.

Our analysis of this case under the Rule of Reason, of course, does not change the ultimate focus of our inquiry. Both per se rules and the Rule of Reason are employed "to form a judgment about the competitive significance of the restraint." *National Society of Professional Engineers v. United States*, 435 U.S. 679, 692 (1978). A conclusion that a restraint of trade is unreasonable may be "based either (1) on the nature or character of the contracts, or (2) on surrounding circumstances giving rise to the inference or presumption that they were intended to restrain trade and enhance prices. Under either branch of the test, the inquiry is confined to a consideration of impact on competitive conditions." Per se rules are invoked when surrounding circumstances make the likelihood of anticompetitive conduct so great as to render unjustified further examination of the challenged conduct. But whether the ultimate finding is the product of a presumption or actual market analysis, the essential inquiry remains the same—whether or not the challenged restraint enhances competition. Under the Sherman Act the criterion to be used in judging the validity of a restraint on trade is its impact on competition.

III.

Because it restrains price and output, the NCAA's television plan has a significant potential for anticompetitive effects. The findings of the District Court indicate that this potential has been realized. The District Court found that if member institutions were free to sell television rights, many more games would be shown on television, and that the NCAA's output restriction has the effect of raising the price the networks pay for television rights. Moreover, the court found that by fixing a price for television rights to all games, the NCAA creates a price structure that is unresponsive to viewer demand and unrelated to the prices that would prevail in a competitive market. And, of course, since as a practical matter all member institutions need NCAA approval, members have no real choice but to adhere to the NCAA's television controls.

The anticompetitive consequences of this arrangement are apparent. Individual competitors lose their freedom to compete. Price is higher and output lower than they would otherwise be, and both are unresponsive to consumer preference. This latter point is perhaps the most significant, since "Congress designed the Sherman Act as a 'consumer welfare prescription.' " *Reiter v. Sonotone Corp.*, 442 U.S. 330, 343 (1979). A restraint that has the effect of reducing the importance of consumer preference in setting price and output is not consistent with this fundamental goal of anti-trust law. Restrictions on price and output are the paradigmatic examples of restraints of trade that the Sherman Act was intended to prohibit. See *Standard Oil Co. v. United States*, 221 U.S. 1, 52-60 (1911). At the same time, the television plan eliminates competitors from the market, since only those broadcasters able to bid on television rights covering the entire NCAA can compete. Thus, as the District Court found, many telecasts that would occur in a competitive market are foreclosed by the NCAA's plan.

Petitioner argues, however, that its television plan can have no significant anticompetitive effect since the record indicates that it has no market power—no ability to alter the interaction of supply and demand in the market. We must reject this argument for two reasons, one legal, one factual.

As a matter of law, the absence of proof of market power does not justify a naked restriction on price or output. To the contrary, when there is an agreement not to compete in terms of price or output, "no elaborate industry analysis is required to demonstrate the anticompetitive character of such an agreement." *Professional Engineers*, 435 U.S., at 692. Petitioner does not quarrel with the District Court's finding that price and output are not responsive to demand. Thus the plan is inconsistent with the Sherman Act's command that price and supply be responsive to consumer preference. We have never required proof of market power in such a case. This naked restraint on price and output requires some competitive justification even in the absence of a detailed market analysis.

As a factual matter, it is evident that petitioner does possess market power. The District Court employed the correct test for determining whether college football broadcasts constitute a separate market—whether there are other products that are reasonably substitutable for televised NCAA football games. Petitioner's argument that it cannot obtain competitive prices from broadcasters since advertisers, and hence broadcasters, can switch from college football to other types of programming simply ignores the findings of the District Court. It found that intercollegiate football telecasts generate an audience uniquely attractive to advertisers and that competitors are unable to offer programming that can attract a similar audience. These findings amply support its conclusion that the NCAA possesses market power. Indeed, the District Court's subsidiary finding that advertisers will pay a premium price per viewer to reach audiences watching college football because of their demographic characteristics is vivid evidence of the uniqueness of this product. Moreover, the District Court's market analysis is firmly supported by our decision in *International Boxing Club of New York, Inc. v. United States*, 358 U.S. 242 (1959), that championship boxing events are uniquely attractive to fans and hence constitute a market separate from that for nonchampionship events. See *Id.*, at 249-252. Thus, respondents have demonstrated that there is a separate market for telecasts of college football which "[rests] on generic qualities differentiating" viewers. *Times-Picayune Publishing Co. v. United States*, 345 U.S. 594, 613 (1953). It inexorably follows that if college football broadcasts be defined as a separate market—and we are convinced they are—then the NCAA's complete control over those broadcasts provides a solid basis for the District Court's conclusion that the NCAA possesses market power with respect to those broadcasts. "When a product is controlled by one interest, without substitutes available in the market, there is monopoly power."

Thus, the NCAA television plan on its face constitutes a restraint upon the operation of a free market, and the findings of the District Court establish that it has operated to raise prices and reduce output. Under the Rule of Reason, these hallmarks of anticompetitive behavior place upon petitioner a heavy burden of establishing an affirmative defense which competitively justifies this apparent deviation from the operations of a free market. See Professional Engineers, 435 U.S., at 692–696. We turn now to the NCAA's proffered justifications.

IV.

Relying on Broadcast Music, petitioner argues that its television plan constitutes a cooperative "joint venture" which assists in the marketing of broadcast rights and hence is procompetitive. . . . The essential contribution made by the NCAA's arrangement is to define the number of games that may be televised, to establish the price for each exposure, and to define the basic terms of each contract between the network and a home team. The NCAA does not, however, act as a selling agent for any school or for any conference of schools. The selection of individual games, and the negotiation of particular agreements, are matters left to the networks and the individual schools. Thus, the effect of the network plan is not to eliminate individual sales of broadcasts, since these still occur, albeit subject to fixed prices and output limitations. Unlike Broadcast Music's blanket license covering broadcast rights to a large number of individual compositions, here the same rights are still sold on an individual basis, only in a noncompetitive market.

The District Court did not find that the NCAA's television plan produced any procompetitive efficiencies which enhanced the competitiveness of college football television rights; to the contrary it concluded that NCAA football could be marketed just as effectively without the television plan. There is therefore no predicate in the findings for petitioner's efficiency justification. Indeed, petitioner's argument is refuted by the District Court's finding concerning price and output. If the NCAA's television plan produced procompetitive efficiencies, the plan would increase output and reduce the price of televised games. The District Court's contrary findings accordingly undermine petitioner's position. In light of these findings, it cannot be said that "the agreement on price is necessary to market the product at all." Broadcast Music, 441 U.S., at 23. In Broadcast Music, the availability of a package product that no individual could offer enhanced the total volume of music that was sold. Unlike this case, there was no limit of any kind placed on the volume that might be sold in the entire market and each individual remained free to sell his own music without restraint. Here production has been limited, not enhanced. No individual school is free to televise its own games without restraint. The NCAA's efficiency justification is not supported by the record.

Neither is the NCAA's television plan necessary to enable the NCAA to penetrate the market through an attractive package sale. Since broadcasting rights to college football constitute a unique product for which there is no ready substitute, there is no need for collective action in order to enable the product to compete against its nonexistent competitors. This is borne out by the District Court's finding that the NCAA's television plan reduces the volume of television rights sold.

V.

Throughout the history of its regulation of intercollegiate football telecasts, the NCAA has indicated its concern with protecting live attendance. This concern, it should be noted, is not with protecting live attendance at games which are shown on television; that type of interest is not at issue in this case. Rather, the concern is that fan interest in a televised game may adversely affect ticket sales for games that will not appear on television.

Although the NORC studies in the 1950's provided some support for the thesis that live attendance would suffer if unlimited television were permitted, the District Court found that there was no evidence to support that theory in today's market. Moreover, as the District Court found, the television plan has evolved in a manner inconsistent with its original design to protect gate attendance. Under the current plan, games are shown on television during all hours that college football games are played. The plan simply does not protect live attendance by ensuring that games will not be shown on television at the same time as live events.

There is, however, a more fundamental reason for rejecting this defense. The NCAA's argument that its television plan is necessary to protect live attendance is not based on a desire to maintain the integrity of college football as a distinct and attractive product, but rather on a fear that the product will not prove sufficiently attractive to draw live attendance when faced with competition from televised games. At bottom the NCAA's position is that ticket sales for most college games are unable to compete in a free market. The television plan protects ticket sales by limiting output—just as any monopolist increases revenues by reducing output. By seeking to insulate live ticket sales from the full spectrum of competition because of its assumption that the product itself is insufficiently attractive to consumers, petitioner forwards a justification that is inconsistent with the basic policy of the Sherman Act. "[The] Rule of Reason does not support a defense based on the assumption that competition itself is unreasonable."

VI.

Petitioner argues that the interest in maintaining a competitive balance among amateur athletic teams is legitimate and important and that it justifies the regulations challenged in this case. We agree with the first part of the argument but not the second.

Our decision not to apply a per se rule to this case rests in large part on our recognition that a certain degree of cooperation is necessary if the type of competition that petitioner and its member institutions seek to market is to be preserved. It is reasonable to assume that most of the regulatory controls of the NCAA are justifiable means of fostering competition among amateur athletic teams and therefore procompetitive because they enhance public interest in intercollegiate athletics. The specific restraints on football telecasts that are challenged in this case do not, however, fit into the same mold as do rules defining the conditions of the contest, the eligibility of participants, or the manner in which members of a joint enterprise shall share the responsibilities and the benefits of the total venture.

The NCAA does not claim that its television plan has equalized or is intended to equalize competition within any one league. The plan is nationwide in scope and there is no single league or tournament in which all college football teams compete. There is no evidence of any intent to equalize the strength of teams in Division I-A with those in Division II or Division III, and not even a colorable basis for giving colleges that have no football program at all a voice in the management of the revenues generated by the football programs at other schools. The interest in maintaining a competitive balance that is asserted by the NCAA as a justification for regulating all television of intercollegiate football is not related to any neutral standard or to any readily identifiable group of competitors.

The television plan is not even arguably tailored to serve such an interest. It does not regulate the amount of money that any college may spend on its football program, nor the way in which the colleges may use the revenues that are generated by their football programs, whether derived from the sale of television rights, the sale of tickets, or the sale of concessions or program advertising. The plan simply imposes a restriction on one source of revenue that is more important to some colleges than to others. There is no evidence that this restriction produces any greater measure of equality throughout the NCAA than would a restriction on alumni donations, tuition rates, or any other revenue-producing activity. At the same time, as the District Court found, the NCAA imposes a variety of other restrictions designed to preserve amateurism which are much better tailored to the goal of competitive balance than is the television plan, and which are "clearly sufficient" to preserve competitive balance to the extent it is within the NCAA's power to do so. And much more than speculation supported the District Court's findings on this score. No other NCAA sport employs a similar plan, and in particular the court found that in the most closely analogous sport, college basketball, competitive balance has been maintained without resort to a restrictive television plan. Perhaps the most important reason for rejecting the argument that the interest in competitive balance is served by the television plan is the District Court's unambiguous and well-supported finding that many more games would be televised in a free market than under the NCAA plan. The hypothesis that legitimates the maintenance of competitive balance as a procompetitive justification under the Rule of Reason is that equal competition will maximize consumer demand for the product. The finding that consumption will materially increase if the controls are removed is a compelling demonstration that they do not in fact serve any such legitimate purpose.

VII.

The NCAA plays a critical role in the maintenance of a revered tradition of amateurism in college sports. There can be no question but that it needs ample latitude to play that role, or that the preservation of the student-athlete in higher education adds richness and diversity to intercollegiate athletics and is entirely consistent with the goals of the Sherman Act. But consistent with the Sherman Act, the role of the NCAA must be to preserve a tradition that might otherwise die; rules that restrict output are hardly consistent with this role. Today we hold only that the record supports the District Court's conclusion that by curtailing output and blunting the ability of member institutions to respond to consumer preference, the NCAA has restricted rather than enhanced the place of intercollegiate athletics in the Nation's life. Accordingly, the judgment of the Court of Appeals is Affirmed.

CASES ON THE SUPPLEMENTAL CD

Agnew v. NCAA, 683 F.3d 328 (7th Cir. 2012). This case examines whether the NCAA's cap on the number of scholarships given per team and the prohibition of multi-year scholarships violate antitrust law.

Association for Intercollegiate Athletics for Women v. NCAA, 735 F.2d 577 (1984). The case examines whether the NCAA's move into women's athletics violated antitrust law.

Banks v. NCAA, 977 F.2d 1081 (7th Cir. 1992). The case examines the NCAA's rules on player eligibility and whether they restrain the trade of college athletes.

Law v. NCAA, 134 F.3d 1010 (10th Cir. 1998). This case examines the NCAA's rule on the salaries colleges could pay certain coaches and whether the rule violates antitrust law.

NCAA v. Board of Regents of the University of Oklahoma, 468 U.S. 85 (1984). This case examines the NCAA's rule in broadcasting college football games.

McCormack v. National Collegiate Athletic Association, 845 F.2d 1338 (5th Cir. 1988). This case examines whether the NCAA's rules restricting benefits awarded to student athletes violates antitrust law.

Worldwide Basketball & Sport Tours v. NCAA, 388 F.3d 955 (6th Cir. 2004). Compare the district court's use of "quick-look" approach compared to the traditional rule of reason analysis.

QUESTIONS YOU SHOULD BE ABLE TO ANSWER

1. How do courts determine a restraint of trade under a Rule of Reason analysis?
2. What is the significant case concerning women college athletics and antitrust, and what was its impact?
3. How do you define monopoly power?
4. Considering the cases mentioned in the chapter, why do student-athlete eligibility issues often give rise to potential antitrust violations?
5. In evaluating NCAA rules and bylaws, what are some of the things the court look for when considering the reasonableness of the rule?

REFERENCES

Cases
Agnew v. NCAA, 683 F.3d 328 (7th Cir. 2012).
Association for Intercollegiate Athletics for Women v. NCAA, 735 F.2d 577 (1984).
Banks v. NCAA, 977 F.2d 1081 (7th Cir. 1992).
Hairston v. Pacific 10 Conference, 101 F.3d 1315 (9th Cir. 1996).
Law v. NCAA, 134 F.3d 1010 (10th Cir. 1998).
McCormack, v. National Collegiate Athletic Association, 845 F.2d 1338 (1988).
NCAA v. Board of Regents of the University of Oklahoma, 468 U.S. 85 (1984).
O'Bannon v. NCAA, 802 F.3d 1049 (9th Cir. 2015).
Smith v. NCAA, 139 F.3d 180 (3rd Cir. 1998).
United States v. E.I. DuPont Nemours & Co., 351 U.S. 377 (1956).
United States v. Grinnell Corp., 384 U.S. 563 (1966).
Verizon Communications v. Law Office of Curtis v. Trinko, 540 U.S. 398 (2004).
Worldwide Basketball and Sports Tours, Inc. v. NCAA, 388 F.3d 955 (6th Cir. 2004).

Publications
Dauner, J. T. (2000, June 14). Court hears payout arguments from restricted earnings coaches. *The Kansas City Star*, p. D4.
Hovenkamp, H. (2005). Federal Antitrust Policy: The law of Competition and its practice (3rd ed.) St. Paul, MN: West Publishing Group.

Legislation
The Sherman Antitrust Act of 1890, 15 U.S.C.A. § 1 *et seq.*
The Clayton Act of 1914, 15 U.S.C.A. § 12–27.

LABOR LAW: PROFESSIONAL SPORT APPLICATIONS

Lisa Pike Masteralexis | University Of Massachusetts Amherst

Labor law has been critical to the U.S. workforce as it created structures for employees to bargain for safe and productive work environments. Labor laws, along with employment laws, delineate what conduct is acceptable in the workplace. Labor laws exist on both state and federal levels. State labor laws apply to public entities, such as a city or state's sports authority or a state university athletic or recreation department. Federal labor laws apply to private employers engaged in a business involving interstate commerce, such as a professional sports league or an arena operated by a facility management company.

The National Labor Relations Act in particular sets forth the parameters of conduct by employers and employees in private-sector unionized workplaces through a process of collective bargaining that allows employees and employers to determine what issues must be resolved in their particular workplace and negotiate a contract for their workplace. As a manager in the sport industry, it is critical that management decisions are made with an eye toward the collective bargaining agreement and its rules, policies, and procedures, lest you find yourself facing a grievance and arbitration process.

FUNDAMENTAL CONCEPTS

Fair Labor Standards Act

The Fair Labor Standards Act of 1938 (FLSA) guarantees minimum hourly wages, overtime pay of not less than one and a half times the employees regular rate for work exceeding 40 hours, and child labor protections.. There are numerous exemptions from the overtime pay and/or the minimum wage provisions and some from the child labor provisions. FLSA section 13(a)(1) exempts from these minimum wage and overtime pay protections "white collar" employees classified as executive, administrative, or professional, where no more than 20% of their time is spent engaged in non-exempt work. The Code of Federal Regulations defines exempt white color employees as:

- An exempt executive is in management and regularly directs the work of at least two employees and holds authority or involvement in hiring or firing.
- An exempt administrative employee's primary duty involves the exercise of discretion and independent judgment with respect to matters of significance
- An exempt professional is one whose work requires advanced knowledge, work that is original and creative in a recognized field of artistic endeavor, work teaching in a school system or educational institution, or work in the computer field. An exempt professional employee must exercise discretion and judgment, or require invention, imagination, or talent in a recognized field of artistic endeavor. Examples of these professionals would be musicians, dancers, artists, doctors, lawyers, engineers, pharmacists, and the like. (FLSA, 29 CFR 541.300; 541.300(a)(2); 541.303; 541.400)
- An exempt highly compensated executive is one whose annual compensation is at least $100,000. This exemption applies only to those whose primary duty is office work, not manual labor. Thus, those involving work with hands, physical skill and energy are not exempt no matter how highly paid.

Other exemptions likely to apply in the sport industry are for those engaged in commissioned sales for the retail or service industry, of which sports and recreation are a part. An exempt outside salesperson must be customarily and regularly engaged away from the employer's place of business and have a primary duty of making sales, or obtaining orders or contracts for services or for the use of facilities.

In addition, an amusement or recreational establishment, "if (1) it does not operate for more than seven months in any calendar year, or (2) during the preceding calendar year, its average receipts for any six months of such year were not more than 33-1/3 per centum of its average receipts for the other six months of such year" [FLSA, 29 USC § 213 (a)(3) (2005)] are also exempt from FLSA wage and overtime provisions.

In 2014, President Obama directed the Department of Labor to update "the salary level and total annual compensation requirements to more effectively distinguish between overtime-eligible white collar employees and those who may be exempt, thereby making the exemption easier for employers and employees to understand, but also to update the salaries with the times. (Department of Labor, 2016). The new rules take effect December 1, 2016 and raises the salary threshold of those exempt from overtime pay from $455 per week ($23,660 annual) to $913 per week ($47,476 annual).. This rule will likely impact the professional sports industry and convert some formerly exempt employees to non-exempt leaving the employer with the choices of elevating exempt workers' salaries, providing overtime of comp time, or re-evaluating workloads; all of which were original goals of FLSA. The rule will also require salary and compensation levels to be updated every 3 years beginning January 1, 2020.

The FLSA requires employers keep records on exemptions and overtime pay. Exemptions are narrowly construed against the employer. Consequently, employers and employees should always closely check the exact terms and conditions of an exemption in light of the employee's actual duties before assuming that the exemption might apply to an employee. The burden of proving the exemption rests with the employer.

There has recently been a rash of FLSA cases brought in the professional sports industry, among the plaintiffs are minor league baseball players, NFL cheerleaders, and student interns. In ongoing litigation former minor leaguers have sued Major League Baseball (MLB), its franchises, and former Commissioner Bud Selig on the grounds that requiring them to attend practice sessions and participate in off-season activities without compensation and paying them a fixed salary without overtime during the season while requiring them to exceed the 40-hour work week. (Senne v. Kansas City Royals Baseball Corp., 2015). The group of players has been certified as a class, but is awaiting trial. The players are suing MLB rather than Minor League Baseball (MiLB) because the major league franchises hire and pay the players whom they supply to the MiLB affiliates. Among MLB's defenses is that minor league baseball is seasonal and falls within the amusement or recreational establishment exemption or that minor leaguers are exempt professionals (performers with special skills). Historically, professional athletes, including baseball players have turned to antitrust law to wage these labor battles, but with the Curt Flood Act, the minor leagues are specifically exempted from antitrust laws.

In the past few years NFL cheerleaders have sued the Oakland Raiders, Buffalo Bills, Cincinnati Bengals, New York Jets, and Tampa Bay Buccaneers for violations of wage and hour laws. The cases are in various stages of litigation. For instance, the Raiders settled with their cheerleaders in September 2014 for $1.25 million and a promise to pay minimum wage going forward. The suit has resulted in legislation that defines pro cheerleaders in all professional sports in California to be employees and not independent contractors, thus affording them a wealth of protections under state labor and employment laws (BNA, 2015). The Buccaneers settled for $825,000 (Waldron, 2015) and the Bills cheerleaders have just been certified as a class in January 2016 so the case is still in the discovery phase (Fight Wage Theft, 2016). The Bills suspended their cheerleading team, as have a handful of others while the issues are resolved.

Another group of recent FLSA cases of interest to the sport and recreation industry are those challenging unpaid internships. Unpaid internships are a staple in sport and recreation business. In recent years unpaid interns in the sport and entertainment industries have challenged the unpaid internships on the grounds that they serve as a free labor pool, arguing that interns are in jobs that should be done by paid employees. The Department of Labor has set forth criteria for unpaid internships. The rules state that the work must be similar to vocational training given in an educational environment, that the experience be for the benefit of the interns rather than the advantage of the employer, and that the interns work must not displace that a regular employees. Some employers feel that as long as interns are receiving college credit, the academic requirements should dictate that the interns need not be paid. In *Glatt v. Fox Searchlight Pictures* (2016), the Second Circuit

Court of Appeals adopted a primary beneficiary test and set forth the following list of considerations for unpaid internships:

1. The extent to which the intern and the employer clearly understand that *537 there is no expectation of compensation. Any promise of compensation, express or implied, suggests that the intern is an employee—and vice versa.
2. The extent to which the internship provides training that would be similar to that which would be given in an educational environment, including the clinical and other hands-on training provided by educational institutions.
3. The extent to which the internship is tied to the intern's formal education program by integrated coursework or the receipt of academic credit.
4. The extent to which the internship accommodates the intern's academic commitments by corresponding to the academic calendar.
5. The extent to which the internship's duration is limited to the period in which the internship provides the intern with beneficial learning.
6. The extent to which the intern's work complements, rather than displaces, the work of paid employees while providing significant educational benefits to the intern.
7. The extent to which the intern and the employer understand that the internship is conducted without entitlement to a paid job at the conclusion of the internship.

Under the primary beneficiary test, the employer should ask whether the intern or the employer is the primary beneficiary of the relationship. That question plus the above criteria are important considerations for businesses when considering whether to create an unpaid internship program.

National Labor Relations Act

The National Labor Relations Act of 1935 (NLRA) applies to private employers. It was enacted to "eliminate . . . or mitigate the causes of certain substantial obstructions to the free flow of commerce . . . by encouraging collective bargaining and by protecting the exercise by workers of full freedom of association, self-organization, and designation of representatives of their own choosing, for the purpose of negotiating the terms and conditions of their employment or other mutual aid or protection" (NLRA, § 151, 2005). The NLRA set forth employee rights to join or assist unions, engage in concerted activity for economic benefits and work protections, and to engage in collective bargaining. It applies to employees and employers in the private sector, drawing distinctions between employees for assignment to bargaining units, such that employees who are in the same bargaining unit need not do the exact same job, but must have common bargaining interests.

Through the NLRA, Congress created the National Labor Relations Board (NLRB) because it believed a specialized agency charged with regulating labor relations was necessary. The two primary activities of the NLRB are to conduct secret ballot union elections for certification and decertification and to prevent and remedy unfair labor practices.

Employee Rights

The NLRA § 7 established three significant employee rights:

1. The right to join or assist unions and the right not to join or assist unions;
2. The right to engage in collective bargaining through representative of own choosing; and
3. The right to engage in concerted activity for one's own mutual aid and protection (29 USCS § 157, 2005).

When employees want to join a union, they must petition the NLRB to conduct a secret ballot election under § 9 of the act to determine whether at least one-third of all employees are interested in conducting an election and whether the group is an appropriate unit to collectively bargain with the employer. The NLRB examines the community of interests of the group to determine if there is enough in common to make bargaining successful. **Community of interests** include: commonality of supervision, work rules, and personnel policies; shared work areas, similarity of job duties and working conditions; similarity of methods for evaluation; similarity in pay and benefits; integration and interdependence of operations; and history, if any, of collective bargaining between the parties (Feldacker, 2000; Gold, 1998).

In *North American Soccer League (NASL) v. NLRB*, (1980), the league challenged the NLRB's certification of all players into a national bargaining unit for purposes of collective bargaining. The NASL argued that employee units at the local team level were the appropriate bargaining unit. The NLRB disagreed, finding that where an employer has assumed sufficient control over the working conditions of employees of its franchisees, the NLRB may require employers to bargain jointly. The court agreed that labor relations were in fact conducted at a league wide level and not delegated to individual teams, and thus, the NLRB's designation was appropriate. If the NASL had successfully limited bargaining to the local level, employers could easily undermine solidarity by trading union supporters. Local units could also undermine the union's strike threat, such that if a team in Boston went on strike, the league could continue to play and give any team playing Boston a bye. By continuing without a franchise, the strike's force would be severely limited. With the shared revenue structures in place in most leagues, the Boston franchise could also still receive a cut of revenues from the league, severely disabling the leverage of the union.

Once a union is designated as an appropriate bargaining unit, elections are held, and a union is certified as the exclusive bargaining representative for employees, granting two important changes for employees. First, management then has a duty to bargain in good faith with the union and second, the union has a duty of fair representation for its employee members.

Duty to Engage in Collective Bargaining. Once a union is in existence, management *must* engage in collective bargaining over mandatory subjects of bargaining or risk being charged with an unfair labor practice under § 8 (a)(5) of the NLRA for failing to bargain in good faith (*NLRB v. Katz*, 1962). Mandatory subjects are hours, wages, and terms and conditions of employment. They are those things "plainly germane to the 'working environment' and not those 'managerial decisions which lie at the core of entrepreneurial control'" (*Ford Motor Co. v. NLRB* at 498, 1979). The result of good faith negotiations is to create a collective bargaining agreement (CBA). Wages are basically anything else that has monetary value including salaries, per diem, bonuses, severance and termination pay, and fringe benefits, such as health care, life or disability insurance. Hours provisions cover anything related to time spent at work. Terms and conditions of employment cover the majority of remaining provisions in one's work life, including job security, seniority, grievance and arbitration provisions, drug-testing provisions, safety concerns, and the like.

There are also permissive subjects for bargaining, over which management is not obligated to negotiate and the union cannot bargain to impasse. An example of a permissive subject is if the National Basketball Players Association wanted its logo to appear in all NBA advertisements. If the NBA refused, the players could not require the NBA to negotiate to an impasse over the issue. An impasse is a stalemate in negotiations that often leads to a strike or a lockout.

Duty of Fair Representation. After certification by the NLRB, a union becomes the exclusive bargaining representative for *all* employees. The duty of fair representation requires that a union represent *all* employees fairly, even those employees who are not union members (*Steele v. Louisville & Nashville Railroad*, 1944). If the union does not represent employees fairly, it commits an unfair labor practice under § 8(b) (1) (A). Fair representation requires that unions must not discriminate or act in an arbitrary or bad faith manner (*Vaca v. Sipes*, 1967). Most duty of fair representation cases challenge decisions to pursue grievances on behalf of employees. In *Peterson v. Kennedy and the NFLPA*, a NFL player sued his union for failing to fairly represent him when it erred in not filing his grievance in a timely manner (1985). The court held that because the union's conduct amounted to no more than negligence, it did not meet the standard required for a duty of fair representation case. The court emphasized that unions are not liable for good faith, nondiscriminatory errors of judgment made in interpreting CBAs, in processing grievances or representing them in the process.

Unfair Labor Practices

Section 8 of the NLRA is the mechanism used to protect § 7 rights as it establishes employer and union unfair labor practices.

Employer Discrimination or Retaliation for Union Activity. It is an unfair labor practice for the employer to interfere with, restrain or coerce employees who are engaged in union activity [NLRA, § 8(a)(1)]. It is also an unfair labor practice to discriminate against employees for engaging in union activities and for support of the union [NLRA, § 8(a)(3)]. Often workplace discipline, demotion, or termination decisions arise from mixed motives—union animus by the employer combined with an employee's poor work performance or misconduct. As a result these cases are often difficult to decide.

Duty to Bargain in Good Faith. Once a union is certified by the NLRB, management and union have a duty to bargain in good faith over hours, wages, and terms and conditions of employment. Either party can negotiate to impasse and decide whether to use their economic weapons of imposing a strike or a lockout. In practice, management may unilaterally implement its last best offer and still fulfill the duty to bargain in good faith (*Brown v. Pro Football*, 1996). Because there is no duty to bargain over permissive subjects, employers can unilaterally impose permissive and "management rights" subjects. Management rights subjects generally encompass managerial decisions that "lie at the core of entrepreneurial control" (*Ford Motor Co. v. NLRB* at 498, 1979). Management need not negotiate management rights, but it may have to negotiate their effect when they impact mandatory subjects for bargaining. For example, management need not negotiate with the union to relocate a sports franchise to a new city, but will have to negotiate with the players' association over the effects of the decision –for instance, how players will cover relocation costs.

Duty to bargain in good faith cases may arise in professional sports when the commissioner attempts to make a new rule that impacts mandatory subjects. For instance, in *National Football League Players Association v. National Labor Relations Board*, the NFLPA argued that the NFL Commissioner's imposition of a rule and corresponding fines for players leaving the bench during fights without negotiating with the union was a refusal to bargain in good faith (1974). Often a conflict arises between the Commissioner's best interest powers and the players' right to negotiate over mandatory subjects. Keep in mind that *NFLPA v. NLRB* does not limit the NFL's ability to impose rules or fines for bench clearing fights, it simply requires that such rules be negotiated with the union.

Taft-Hartley Act of 1947

There is no doubt that the NLRA was pro-labor. A dozen years later the Taft-Hartley Act amended the NLRA to give balance to labor relations by focusing on rights of employers and non-union members.

Collective Bargaining Relationship

The collective bargaining agreement (CBA) is a contract that expresses the final negotiations between management and union over the mandatory subjects of their business. The collective bargaining relationship is an ongoing one; there may be a need for additional negotiations after the CBA is formed that require union and management to continue to discuss or negotiate other issues that affect mandatory subjects. Either side has the right to convince the other side to come back to the bargaining table to discuss or negotiate over a new or current term of employment.

Over the term of the collective bargaining relationship, there is considerable time spent by union and management in the administration of the CBA. As issues evolve that require union and management to communicate with one another. Sometimes those communications result in memoranda of understanding that are incorporated into the contract and ongoing relationship.

An important component of the administration is arbitration; arbitration clauses are common in all labor agreements and create a mechanism for employees and employers to resolve disputes. Arbitration is a less costly, more efficient alternative to the court system, to union striking or to management locking employees out as a means of resolving disagreements. There are two forms of arbitration: rights and interest. Rights arbitration is for disputes over the interpretation or application of the contract. Interest arbitration deals with disputes over the actual terms of contract, such as salary arbitration (*Silverman v. MLBPRC*, 1995). In salary arbitration for example, the contract provision delegates to the arbitrator(s) the power to determine the compensation term for a given player based on a salary dispute between the player and the team.

Despite the quality of negotiating or the clarity of expression in the CBA, disputes are bound to arise during the course of the agreement. Disputes can be lodged through a grievance process negotiated into the CBA. The road to an arbitration case starts with union or management filing a grievance against the other. The contract will set forth a process for resolving the disputes that leads up to a final, binding arbitration hearing. The Steelworkers Trilogy cases (*U.S. Steelworkers v. American Mfg. Co.*, 1960; *U.S. Steelworkers v. Warrior Gulf Co.*, 1960; *U.S. Steelworkers v. Enterprise Corp.*, 1960) established federal policy that an arbitrator's decision should not be the subject of judicial intervention provided that the arbitrator's award is based on the essence of the collective bargaining agreement. Thus, a court cannot substitute its decision for an arbitrator's if it does not agree with the arbitrator's decision. A court can only overturn a decision if the plaintiffs prove the arbitrator has exceeded the scope of the authority granted in the CBA or by the parties or that the arbitrator has decided the grievance in an arbitrary or capricious manner (*MLBPA v. Garvey*, 2001).

A recent issue being addressed through collective bargaining is testing for drugs and/or human growth hormones. Despite Congress' threats to impose uniform policies for these items on professional leagues, policies achieved through collective bargaining will be effective in protecting the rights and obligations of employees and employers. Through a bargaining process an employee's privacy rights, confidentiality of tests, medical concerns, the determination of what to test for and what amounts of those drugs or hormones must be in one's system to be subject to suspension, concerns over "what else" the organization might discover in testing, the role of results and international competition, and the like will be negotiated to develop fair provisions. The bargaining table also provides a forum for the two sides to add educational and rehabilitative components. Further, union and management may negotiate testing policies and procedures in the context of other aspects of their employment relationship, such as disciplinary actions and arbitration provisions.

Professional Sport Labor Relations

The labor movement in professional sports occurred 30–40 years later than other industries. Despite the NLRA's enactment in 1935, the first decision to enforce union certification in professional sports involved baseball umpires in 1969. In the *American League of Professional Baseball Clubs and the Association of National Baseball League Umpires* (1969), Major League Baseball challenged the NLRB's jurisdiction. MLB argued that because it was exempt from antitrust laws under the 1922 U.S. Supreme Court decision in *Federal Baseball*, then it should likewise be exempt from labor laws. Next, MLB argued that it had an internal system of self-regulation, eliminating the need for NLRB involvement. The NLRB disagreed, arguing that MLB's internal system would put the umpire before the Commissioner for a final resolution of disputes. The NLRB recognized that the system was designed by the employers, who also hire and manage the Commissioner. Without evidence of a neutral third party as the final arbiter, the NLRB noted that this case had the potential to be the beginning of a whole host of employees who might seek NLRB assistance in the future including professional athletes, clubhouse attendants, front office staff, scouts, groundskeepers, and maintenance staff.

Today, virtually all major league teams are unionized workplaces for professional athletes, but not for the other employees envisioned by that umpires case in 1969. The reasons for this are varied, and among them might be (1) there are fewer white-collar workers in unions, (2) there is high turnover in front office and coaching positions, (3) the competition for jobs might deter people from working together in a union organizing movement, and (4) organizing front office staff or coaches on a national, multiemployer level like the professional athletes is challenging.

Unionized workplaces for professional athlete are unique because the dynamics of the collective bargaining relationship make every negotiation a battle. Short careers lead to a high employee turnover rate for professional athletes. A majority of athletes lack job security, causing players to want to achieve the best deal possible in collective bargaining negotiations. With an average career length hovering around three years and most collective bargaining agreements covering three to six-year terms, unions are motivated to negotiate for the best contract possible. Players might conceivably work their entire career under one CBA, whereas in other industries, an employee's career lasts through multiple CBA negotiations, creating more patience in the process. There is a great disparity between players' talent and thus, their need for the union. A superstar will have far different bargaining goals than a bench player. When negotiating for their collective interests, unions struggle to keep the superstars and average players equally satisfied. Without the solidarity of all players, a players' association loses its strength.

Players' associations are transnational employee bargaining units that negotiate with a transnational multiemployer bargaining unit. Players associations must constantly spread their message to new members. In spreading the message, the associations face logistical challenges of a large, diverse, geographically expansive bargaining unit. In the high-pressure world of professional team sports, the multiemployer bargaining team also faces challenges by having disparate bargaining priorities, such as large versus small market clubs; corporate versus family ownership; ownership stake in one club versus ownership stakes in a more diverse set of sport/entertainment business venture, such as those ownership groups that have cross-ownership in teams, media ventures, and/or facilities. Despite the very contentious labor struggles between owners and players, leagues favor unionized workforces in professional sport for the labor exemption protection from antitrust liability that unions provide.

College Athletes and Labor Relations

In March 2014 the NLRB Regional Director in Chicago, in response to a petition for an election, ruled that Northwestern University grant-in-aid scholarship football players were employees for purposes of the N.L.R.A. and directed an election to determine whether they had the votes to unionize. The director's decision focused on the fact that he viewed the college athletes as employees in an employer relationship with the University. He distinguished this from a typical student's relationship with their school. The elements of the relationship that he focused on were the revenues generated from that relationship, the control that the university and coaches exerted over the football players, and the scholarship ($61,000 per academic year and $76,000 with summer school) serving as payment for their employment. The decision only applied to those athletes under scholarship. The working conditions he detailed were the hours logged in during practice, games, study hall, and travel as well as the control coaches exerted over players' lives in terms of rules and codes of conduct, such as the use of social media, dress codes, automobile registrations and the like.

The ruling was short-lived as Northwestern appealed to the NLRB which in August 2015 overturned the ruling. The decision was "primarily premised on a finding that, because of the nature of sports leagues (namely the control exercised by the leagues over the individual teams) and the composition and structure of FBS football (in which the overwhelming majority of competitors are public colleges and universities over which the Board cannot assert jurisdiction), it would not promote stability in labor relations to assert jurisdiction." (Northwestern University and CAPA, 2015 at 3). The Football Bowl Subdivision is made up of 125 teams of which, just 17 are private universities. The NLRA would, thus, only apply to those 17 institutions and the other 108 public institutions would be subject to jurisdiction under state labor law. Conceivably, having various labor situations across those states, from non-union to collective bargaining agreements with differing hours, wages, and working conditions. Further, while not making a determination as to whether college athletes were employees, this narrow ruling did leave open the possibility for a future case.

While the Northwestern football players did not win the right to unionize, the conditions under which NCAA Division I athletes changed as a result of this case, along with antitrust cases challenging NCAA restrictions. These cases have pushed the NCAA and the five power conferences to loosen their restrictions and create better "working conditions" for athletes in terms of more scholarship guarantees including some up to the full cost of attendance, better medical care and insurance, limits on practice times, liberalization of transfer rules, better access to assistance from agents, and the like. The challenge for college athletes is that these rules are not guaranteed by a collective bargaining process with athletes across the table, but are limited to the whims of those in charge of the conferences (Staples, 2015).

SIGNIFICANT CASE

Silverman v. Major League Baseball Player Relations Committee reviews when the National Labor Relations Board (NLRB) can seek a section 10 (j) injunction under National Labor Relations Act as part of unfair labor practice charges filed against baseball owners before NLRB. It also examines whether free agency, reserve issues, and salary arbitration are mandatory subjects of collective bargaining.

SILVERMAN V. MAJOR LEAGUE BASEBALL PLAYER RELATIONS COMMITTEE
United States Court of Appeals for the Second Circuit
67 F. 3d 1054 (1995)

WINTER, CIRCUIT JUDGE:
This is an appeal by the Major League Baseball Player Relations Committee, Inc. ("PRC") and the constituent member clubs of Major League Baseball ("Clubs") from a temporary injunction issued by Judge Sotomayor pursuant to section 10(j) of the National Labor Relations Act ("NLRA"), 29 U.S. C. §160(j). The PRC is the collective bargaining representative for the twenty-eight Clubs.

The Major League Baseball Players Association is a union that is the exclusive bargaining representative for the forty-man rosters of each major league club. The injunction is based on the district court's conclusion that appellants violated NLRA §§ 8(a)(1) and (5), 29 U.S.C. §§ 158(a) (1) and (5) by unilaterally implementing terms and conditions of employment that differed from those in the last collective agreement. It orders the PRC and the Clubs to: (i) abide by the terms of an expired collective agreement, (ii) rescind any actions taken that are inconsistent with that agreement and (iii) bargain in good faith with the Players Association. *See Silverman v. Major League Baseball Player Relations Comm., Inc.*, 880 F. Supp. 246, 261 (S. D. N.Y. 1995). The injunction is to remain in effect until either (i) the expired agreement is replaced by a new collective bargaining agreement, (ii) the National Labor Relations Board ("NLRB") renders a final disposition of the matters pending before it in the related administrative case, or (iii) the district court finds, upon petition of either of the parties, that an impasse has occurred. We affirm.

BACKGROUND

On January 1, 1990, the most recent collective agreement ("CBA") between appellants and the Players Association became effective. It contained provisions implementing a combination of free agency and a reserve system—that is, a compromise between free competitive bidding for a player's services and an individual club's exclusive rights to those services.

Free agency, in its purest form, is a status in which the rights to a player's athletic services are not owned by a club and may be shopped around by the player in a quest for the most attractive bid. However, for more than a century, Major League Baseball has had a reserve system that to one degree or another affords individual clubs exclusive property rights to the athletic services of certain players. Before the players were organized and a collective bargaining relationship was established, the standard player's contract with a club reserved to the club exclusive rights to a player's services and provided for an annual right of renewal of the contract by the club in question. The Clubs interpreted the contract as allowing the club in question to renew all of an individual player's contract, including the right of renewal provision. So interpreted, this provision—known generally as the "reserve clause"—bound a player to one club in perpetuity until traded or released. After the Clubs recognized the Players Association and entered into a collective agreement with it, an arbitrator held in a grievance proceeding that the reserve clause allowed a renewal for only one year rather than a succession of years. *See National & American League Professional Baseball Clubs v. Major League Baseball Players Assn.*, 66 Lab.Arb. (BNA) 101 (1976) (Seitz, Arb.). Since then, appellants and the Players Association have struggled to accommodate their conflicting interests in the free agency and reserve issues, and a variety of compromises have from time to time been reached. However, relations have been acrimonious, and several strikes and lockouts have occurred. This appeal itself arises out of a strike that terminated the 1994 season before the playoffs and World Series.

Article XX of the CBA that became effective in 1990 contains a series of provisions that govern free agency and reserve rights. Players with six or more years of major league service are free agents and may seek competing bids in an effort to obtain the best contract, which may of course give exclusive rights to the club for a stipulated number of years. Free agency is guaranteed by an anti-collusion provision, Article XX(F), which prohibits the Clubs from acting in concert with each other with respect to the exercise of rights under Article XX. Article XX(F) thus prevents the Clubs from agreeing either to refuse to bid for the services of free agents or to offer only low bids to them. Article XX(F) also prohibits players from acting in concert with regard to Article XX rights. (citations omitted).

Players with less than six years of service remain under reserve to their individual clubs, although a club may reserve a player only once. Although a minimum annual salary is provided, players with less than three years of major league service must negotiate with their clubs to determine their salary for the coming season. Article XX allows certain reserved players—generally those with more than three but less than six years of service—to demand salary arbitration. Salary arbitration is a mechanism for determining the individual salaries for that group of reserved players if they cannot arrive at an agreement with their clubs. The player and the club each present the arbitrator with a suggested salary figure for a new one-year contract. The arbitrator then inserts either the player's or the club's figure into a blank uniform contract that the parties have already signed. Article VI(F)(12) provides the following with regard to the criteria to be used, and the evidence to be heard, by the arbitrator:

(12) *Criteria.* (a) The Criteria will be the quality of the Player's contribution to his Club during the past season (including but not limited to his overall performance, special qualities of leadership and public appeal), the length and consistency of his career contribution, the record of the Player's past compensation, comparative baseball salaries . . ., the existence of any physical or mental defects on the part of the Player, and the recent performance record of the Club including but not limited to its League standing and attendance as an indication of public acceptance (subject to the exclusion stated in subparagraph (b)(i) below). Any evidence may be submitted which is relevant to the above criteria, and the arbitrator shall assign such weight to the evidence as shall to him appear appropriate under the circumstances. The arbitrator shall, except for a Player with five or more years of Major League service, give particular attention, for comparative salary purposes, to the contracts of Players with Major League service not exceeding one annual service group above the Player's annual service group. This shall not limit the ability of a Player or his representative, because of special accomplishment, to argue the equal

relevance of salaries of Players without regard to service, and the arbitrator shall give whatever weight to such argument as he deems appropriate.

   (b) Evidence of the following shall not be admissible:

    (i) The financial position of the Player and the Club;

    (ii) Press comments, testimonials or similar material bearing on the performance of either the Player or the Club, except that recognized annual Player awards for playing excellence shall not be excluded;

    (iii) Offers made by either Player or Club prior to arbitration;

    (iv) The cost to the parties of their representatives, attorneys, etc.;

    (v) Salaries in other sports or occupations.

The CBA expired on December 31, 1993, pursuant to the PRC's notice of termination. Although negotiations for a successor agreement did not get underway until March 1994, the PRC and the Players Association continued to observe the terms of the expired CBA. Prior to the commencement of negotiations, the Clubs and the Players Association had completed individual salary arbitration hearings and had entered into individual player contracts for the 1994 baseball season, which began in April 1994. (citations omitted).

Negotiations for a new collective bargaining agreement continued unsuccessfully. The PRC offered its first formal economic proposal to the Players Association at a meeting on June 14, 1994. It included a "salary cap," a mechanism that establishes a ceiling on the total player salaries paid by each club. The ceiling may allow some flexibility, depending on the details. Generally, the aggregate salaries of each team are determined by an agreed upon formula and must remain above a minimum percentage of industry revenues, also determined by an agreed upon formula, but below a maximum percentage of those revenues. *See Wood v. National Basketball Assn*, 809 F. 2d 954, 957 (2d Cir. 1987). The PRC proposal also eliminated the salary arbitration system and substituted restricted free agency rights for those reserved players previously eligible for salary arbitration. As an alternative to the PRC's proposed salary cap, the Players Association suggested a revenue sharing and luxury "tax" plan that would impose a tax on high-paying clubs. Subsequent proposals reflected disagreement over appropriate tax rates and payroll thresholds above which clubs would be subject to the tax. (citations omitted).

The players struck on August 12, and the 1994 baseball season never resumed. On December 22, 1994, the PRC declared an impasse in negotiations and stated that it intended unilaterally to impose a salary cap and to implement other changes in the terms and conditions of employment, including the elimination of salary arbitration. The Players Association responded with a unilateral ban on players signing individual contracts with the Clubs. (citations omitted).

Thereafter, cross-charges of unfair labor practices were filed with the NLRB by the Players Association and the Clubs. The Players Association alleged that the Clubs had engaged in unfair labor practices by unilaterally implementing the salary cap and other terms because the parties were not at an impasse.

On February 3, 1995, counsel for the PRC notified the NLRB General Counsel that the PRC would revoke the implementation of unilateral changes and restore the status quo ante. The General Counsel indicated that the Players Association charges would be dismissed as a result. Counsel for the PRC informed the General Counsel, however, that the PRC did not believe itself obligated to maintain provisions of the CBA that involved non-mandatory subjects of bargaining. He mentioned salary arbitration in that regard and also suggested that the Clubs might decide to bargain exclusively through the PRC. The NLRB General Counsel declined to offer an advisory opinion on these matters.

Three days later, by memorandum dated February 6, counsel for the PRC notified the Clubs that, until a new collective bargaining agreement was ratified or until further notice, individual clubs had no authority to negotiate contracts with individual players because the PRC was now the Clubs' exclusive bargaining representative. This amounted to an agreement among the Clubs not to hire free agents and thus was a departure from the anti-collusion provision, Article XX(F) of the CBA. It also amounted to an elimination of salary arbitration, because salary arbitration is a method of arriving at a wage for an individual player contract with a club.

The Players Association thereupon filed a new unfair labor practice charge, and the General Counsel issued a complaint alleging, *inter alia*, that the Clubs and the PRC had violated Sections 8(a)(1) and (5) of the NLRA by unilaterally eliminating, before an impasse had been reached, competitive bidding for the services of free agents, the anti-collusion provision, and salary arbitration for certain reserved players. The NLRB found that these matters were related to wages, hours, and other terms and conditions of employment and were therefore mandatory subjects for collective bargaining. It then authorized its General Counsel to seek an injunction under NLRA § 10(j). On March 27, the NLRB Regional Director filed a petition seeking a temporary injunction restraining the alleged unfair labor practices.

The district court agreed that the NLRB had reasonable cause to conclude that free agency and salary arbitration were mandatory subjects of bargaining and that the Clubs' unilateral actions constituted an unfair labor practice. The district court also concluded that injunctive relief was warranted. This appeal followed.

DISCUSSION

The NLRB is authorized under Section 10(j) of the NLRA to petition for temporary injunctive relief from a district court to enjoin ongoing unfair labor practices. If the court has reasonable cause to believe that an unfair labor practice has occurred and that injunctive relief would be just and proper, it should grant appropriate relief. . . .

We turn now to the merits of the regional director's petition. The petition invokes basic principles of labor law. Section 8(d) of the NLRA mandates that employers and unions bargain in good faith over "wages, hours, and other terms and conditions of employment." These are so-called mandatory subjects of bargaining. Under case law, the parties may propose and bargain over, but may not insist upon, permissive subjects of bargaining. *NLRB v. Wooster Div. of Borg-Warner Corp.*, 356 U.S. 342, 349 (1958). When a collective agreement expires, an employer may not alter terms and conditions of employment involving mandatory subjects until it has bargained to an impasse over new terms. *NLRB v. Katz*, 369 U.S. 736, 741–43 (1962 Thereafter, it may implement the new terms. Generally, when an agreement expires, an employer need not bargain to an impasse over terms and conditions involving permissive subjects but may alter them upon expiration. *Allied Chem. & Alkali Workers v. Pittsburgh Plate Glass Co.*, 404 U.S. 157, 187–88 (1971).

Many of the usual issues that arise in impasse cases are not disputed in the instant matter. The parties agree that the PRC, in directing the Clubs to decline to bargain individually with free agents, unilaterally departed from much of Article XX, which provides for a limited form of free agency and forbids collusive behavior by the Clubs in negotiating with free agents. It is also undisputed that the PRC unilaterally departed from the CBA's provisions with regard to salary arbitration. The PRC does not claim that it had bargained to an impasse over the free agency, the anti-collusion, or the salary arbitration provisions. Finally, it is also agreed that, if those provisions involved mandatory subjects of bargaining, their unilateral abrogation before impasse was a refusal to bargain in good faith.

The PRC and the Clubs argue that the anti-collusion and free agency provisions of the CBA do not involve mandatory subjects of bargaining and are therefore not subject to the *Katz* rule that unilateral implementation of new terms is an unfair labor practice unless the employer has bargained to an impasse over these new terms. The PRC and the Clubs contend that an injunction compelling them to maintain the free agency and anti-collusion provisions undermines their right as a multi-employer group to bargain collectively through an exclusive representative. If so, they would be permissive subjects of bargaining. With regard to salary arbitration, the PRC and the Clubs argue that it is the equivalent of interest arbitration—arbitration of the terms of a new collective agreement—and thus not a mandatory subject of bargaining. (citations omitted).

We are unpersuaded that an injunction compelling the PRC and the Clubs to observe the anti-collusion and free agency provisions of the CBA infringes on their right as a multiemployer group to bargain through an exclusive representative. Free agency and the ban on collusion are one part of a complex method—agreed upon in collective bargaining—by which each major league player's salary is determined under the CBA. They are analogous to the use of seniority, hours of work, merit increases, or piece work to determine salaries in an industrial context. The PRC and the Clubs describe free agency and the ban on collusion as provisions undermining their right to select a joint bargaining representative because those provisions entail individual contracts with clubs. However, the argument ignores the fact that free agency is simply a collectively bargained method of determining individual salaries for one group of players. The anti-collusion provision is not designed to prevent the PRC from representing the Clubs. Rather, that provision guarantees that free agency will be a reality when permitted by the CBA. . .

The question, therefore, is whether the free agency, anti-collusion, and reserve issues are—or there is reasonable cause to believe they are—otherwise mandatory subjects of bargaining. Section 8(d) of the NLRA defines the duty to bargain as "the obligation . . . to meet . . . and confer in good faith with respect to wages, hours, and other terms and conditions of employment. . . ." In *Wood v. National Basketball Assn.*, we noted that free agency and reserve issues are "at the center of collective bargaining in much of the professional sports industry," and that "it is precisely because of [free agency's] direct relationship to wages and conditions of employment that [it is] so controversial and so much the focus of bargaining in professional sports." 809 F. 2d 954, 961–62 (2d Cir. 1987).

Wood noted that collective bargaining between professional athletes and leagues raises "numerous problems with little or no precedent in standard industrial relations."*Id*. Such is the case with a free agency and reserve system. For the most part, unionized employees in the industrial sector may leave one employer for another without restriction. The employee may have no bargaining rights with regard to the terms of hire by the new employer, which may be set by a collective agreement, but is nevertheless generally free to go from one unionized job to another.

The professional sports industry has a very different history and very different economic imperatives. Most professional sports leagues have always had some form of what has become known as the reserve system. (citations omitted). . . . Until the arbitration decision in 1976, the reserve system prevented players from offering their services to competing teams. A player's services were thus the property of a single team until he was traded or released. In enforcing a complete reserve system, Major League Baseball was exercising monopsony power—a buyer's monopoly.

However, there are many reasons, apart from maximizing the transfer of revenues from players to clubs, why reserve systems exist within professional sports.

Fans might not be interested in games between teams that had entirely new lineups for every contest. Moreover, high quality play may require that individuals practice and play with the same teammates for at least some period of time. Teams may also want to recoup what they regard as training costs invested in players while they gained experience. In antitrust litigation, the leagues perennially argue that some form of reserve system is necessary for competitive balance (citation omitted). Indeed, even in a system of complete free agency, one would expect to see many long-term agreements binding individual players to particular clubs.

There are also reasons, apart from maximizing the transfer of revenues to players, why a union of professional athletes would seek free agency. It is very difficult to set individual salaries in professional sports through collective bargaining. Although unions of professional athletes may bargain for uniform benefits and minimum salaries, they do not usually follow their industrial counterparts and seek relatively fixed salaries by job description, seniority, or other formulae. Players often play positions requiring very different skills. Moreover, the level of performance and value to a team in attracting fans differs radically among players, with star athletes or popular players being far more valuable than sub-par or nondescript players. Usually, therefore, players unions seek some form of free agency as a relatively simple method of setting individual salaries.

Most importantly, however, both the leagues and the players unions view free agency and reserve issues as questions of what share of revenues go to the clubs or to the players. The more restrictive the reserve system is, the greater the clubs' share. The greater the role of free agency, the greater the players' share.

To hold that there is no reasonable cause for the NLRB to conclude that free agency and reserve issues are mandatory subjects of bargaining would be virtually to ignore the history and economic imperatives of collective bargaining in professional sports. A mix of free agency and reserve clauses combined with other provisions is the universal method by which leagues and players unions set individual salaries in professional sports. Free agency for veteran players may thus be combined with a reserve system, as in baseball, or a rookie draft, as in basketball, for newer players. A salary cap may or may not be included. (citations omitted). To hold that any of these items, or others that make up the mix in a particular sport, is merely a permissive subject of bargaining would ignore the reality of collective bargaining in sports.

Indeed, free agency is in many ways nothing but the flip side of the reserve system. A full reserve system does not eliminate individual bargaining between teams and players. It simply limits that bargaining to one team. If free agency were a permissive subject of collective bargaining, then so would be the reserve system.

With regard to salary arbitration, we will assume, but not decide, that if it is a form of interest arbitration, it may be unilaterally eliminated. *See George Koch & Sons, Inc.*, 306 N.L.R.B. 834, 839 (1992)(interest arbitration permissive subject of bargaining). Interest arbitration is a method by which an employer and union reach new agreements by sending disputed issues to an arbitrator rather than settling them through collective bargaining and economic force. (citation omitted). The salary arbitration provisions of the CBA are a method by which salaries for some players who are not eligible for free agency—those with three to six years of major league service—are set. The CBA sets forth criteria by which the arbitrator is to reach a decision. These criteria include the player's performance in the prior year, the length and consistency of career contribution, physical or mental defects, recent performance of the team on the field and at the gate, and salaries of certain comparable players. The CBA also forbids the arbitrator from considering certain facts that might otherwise be relevant. Finally, the CBA requires that the arbitrator pick either the club's suggested salary or the player's.

We decline to analogize Article VI(F) of the CBA to interest arbitration. Salary arbitration provides limited discretion to the arbitrator to set salaries for designated players who are not eligible for free agency. The discretion afforded the arbitrator is arguably less than the discretion afforded arbitrators in grievance arbitration involving disputes arising under an existing collective agreement, which is beyond question a mandatory subject of bargaining. In grievance arbitration, an arbitrator may permissibly imply a term even though the term has no explicit support in the text of the collective agreement. Similarly, a term may be implied from past practices even though somewhat inconsistent with the agreement. (citations omitted). We thus decline to analogize salary arbitration to interest arbitration, and, therefore, we hold that there is reasonable cause to believe that it is a mandatory subject of bargaining.

With regard to whether the granting of relief was "just and proper," we review the district court's determination only for abuse of discretion. We see no such abuse in the present matter. Given the short careers of professional athletes and the deterioration of physical abilities through aging, the irreparable harm requirement has been met. The unilateral elimination of free agency and salary arbitration followed by just three days a promise to restore the status quo. The PRC decided to settle the original unfair labor practice charges while embarking on a course of action based on a fallacious view of the duty to bargain. We see no reason to relieve it of the consequences of that course.

We therefore affirm.

CASES ON THE SUPPLEMENTAL CD

National Football League Players Association v. National Labor Relations Board, 503 F.2d 12 (1974). This case explores the duty to bargain in good faith over mandatory subjects for bargaining.

North American Soccer League v. National Labor Relations Board, 613 F. 2d. 1379 (5th Cir. 1980). This case explores the appropriate bargaining units in professional sports unions and when management has a duty to bargain with players versus its ability to change terms of conditions of employment unilaterally.

Morio v. North American Soccer League, 501 F. Supp. 633 (S.D. N.Y. 1980.) This case explores the parameters duty to bargain collectively with an exclusive bargaining representative in a setting where individual contract negotiations are also present. To avoid undermining a union's authority, management must not bargain with individual employees until an agreement or impasse in bargaining is reached.

Silverman v. Major League Baseball Player Relations Committee, 880 F. Supp. 246 (1995). This case examines the parameters of an employer's ability to impose unilateral changes after impasse and after players have gone on strike.

Palace Sports & Entertainment, Inc. D/B/A/ St. Pete Forum v. National Labor Relations Board, 411 F. 3d 212 (2005). This case explores the concept of an employee's right to organize a union in the workplace. It also examines when an employer may terminate a union leader's employment in the workplace when the firing is allegedly made through mixed motives—alleged anti-union animus toward the employee and alleged employee misconduct.

Northwestern University and College Athletes Players Association (CAPA), Petitioner. Case 13–RC–121359 (August 17, 2015). This case determines that the National Labor Relations Board does not have proper jurisdiction over athletes and teams in the Football Bowl Subdivision.

QUESTIONS YOU SHOULD BE ABLE TO ANSWER

1. Examine the definitions of employees who are exempt under the Fair Labor Standards Act and apply them to positions you know are held in the sport industry. Determine what workers would fit in each category.

2. What are the mandatory subjects for bargaining? Give an example of each. Examine how college athletes might argue that they are employees and identify what their mandatory subjects for bargaining might be.

3. Why are provisions, such as drug testing, better addressed through collective bargaining than through an Act of Congress?

4. What are the unique aspects of professional sports labor relations?

5. What is the difference between rights and interest arbitration?

REFERENCES

Cases

Brown v. Pro Football, Inc., 518 U.S. 231 (1996).
Ford Motor Co. v. NLRB, 441 U.S. 488, 498 (1979).
Glatt v. Fox Searchlight Pictures, Inc. 811 F. 2d 528 (2d Cir. 2016).
MLBPA v. Garvey, 532 U.S. 504 (2001).
National Football League Players Association v. National Labor Relations Board, 503 F.2d 12 (1974).
NLRB v. Katz, 369 U.S. 736 (1962).
North American Soccer League v. NLRB, 613 F. 2d. 1379 (5th Cir. 1980).
Northwestern University and CAPA, NLRB Case 13–RC– 121359 (August 17, 2015).
Peterson v. Kennedy and the NFLPA, 771 F.2d 1244 (1985).
Silverman v. Major League Baseball Player Relations Committee, 880 F. Supp. 246 (1995).
Steele v. Louisville & Nashville Railroad Co., 323 U.S. 192 (1944).

The American League of Professional Baseball Clubs and the Association of National Baseball League Umpires, 180 N.L.R.B. 190 (1969).
U.S. Steelworkers v. American Mfg. Co., 363 U.S. 564 (1960).
U.S. Steelworkers v. Warrior Gulf Co., 363 U.S. 574 (1960).
U.S. Steelworkers v. Enterprise Corp., 363 U.S. 593 (1960).
Vaca v. Sipes, 386 U.S. 171 (1967).

Publications

Department of Labor (2016)." Final Rule: Overtime." Retrieved on May 28, 2016 from https://www.dol.gov/WHD/overtime/final2016/

Feldacker, B. (2000). *Labor guide to labor law* (4th ed.). Upper Saddle River, NJ: Prentice Hall.

Fight Wage Theft (2016, Jan. 3). "Court certifies class in Buffalo Bills cheerleaders wage theft lawsuit." Retrieved May 2, 2016 from http://www.fightwagetheft.com/news/buffalo-jills-class-certified

Gold, M. E. (1998). *An introduction to labor law* (2nd ed.). Ithaca, NY: ILR Press/Cornell University Press.

Staples, A. (2015, Aug. 17). "Despite NLRB setback, Northwestern unionization effort still a success." Retrieved Jun 1, 2016 from http://www.si.com/college-football/2015/08/17/northwestern-football-players-union-nlrb-ruling

Waldron, T. (2015, Mar. 9). "NFL teams who underpaid cheerleaders lose millions in settlements." Retrieved May 3, 2016 from http://thinkprogress.org/sports/2015/03/09/3631369/tampa-bay-buccaneers-settle-minimum-wage-lawsuit-cheerleaders-825000/

Legislation

Fair Labor Standards Act, 29 USCS § 201, et seq. (2005).
Fair Labor Standards Act, 29 CFR § 541, et seq. (2016).
Labor Management Relations Act, 29 USCS § 141, et. seq. (2005).
National Labor Relations Act, 29 USCS § 151, et. seq. (2005).

7.40 SPORT AGENT LEGISLATION

John T. Wolohan | Syracuse University

Although the creation of the modern sports agent is usually credited to Boston attorney Bob Woolf in the mid-1960s, individuals have been representing athletes as far back as the 1920s. One of the first sports agents was Charles "Cash & Carry" Pyle, who in 1925 negotiated a $3,000-per-game contract between Red Grange and the Chicago Bears (Shropshire & Davis, 2008). In truth, however, it was only the rare and special athlete that needed an agent before the 1970s. Before free agency, most professional athletes were bound to their team through a reserve system and were left with few alternatives and little negotiating power. As a result, the only real contract negotiation in these circumstances was a matter of taking what was offered or refusing to play.

Beginning in the mid-1970s, due to court decisions, arbitration, collective bargaining, and in some instances, the emergence of competing professional leagues, players gained greater freedom and bargaining leverage to market their skills to the highest bidder. At this same time, large sums of money were coming into the leagues via increased television and radio rights. These events expanded media coverage, escalating rights fees paid by networks to leagues, and made professional sports more popular and profitable. As a result, team owners had more money to spend, albeit grudgingly, on attracted high quality and high priced players to their teams. With all the millions of dollars coming into professional sports, it became more and more essential for many athletes to seek the help of professional "sports agents" to maximize their salary and other compensation.

FUNDAMENTAL CONCEPTS

Although few would argue that the services of a competent agent can be extremely valuable for a professional athlete, the emergence of the sport agent in professional sports has not been without problems. For example, there is only a limited supply of quality athletes. In the four major sports in America, there are only a total of 4,374 professional athletes playing at the very top level.

League	Number of Teams	Game Day Roster	Practice Players	Total
NBA	30	12	0	360
NFL	32	53	10	2,016
NHL	30*	20	2	660
MLB	30	25	0	750
MLS	21*	18	10	588
Totals		128	22	4,374

* League were voting on expansion in 2016.

At the same time, there are over 2,000 Certified agents in those same sports (sports-agent-directory, 2016). While this numbers might not seem so bad to those considering entering the business, two players for every agent for every agent, when you consider that the top two Scott Boras alone represents 69 MLB players and Tom Condon represents 41 NFL players, the odds of landing a client go down significantly (Forbes.com, 2015). As a result, there is a lot of competition to secure and sign a client. It should not be all that surprising therefore that agents, and or their employees, are providing college athletes all types of illegal inducements to get the athlete to sign with them. The following section outlines some of the attempts by the state and federal governments and other various organizations to protect college and professional athletes, as well as colleges and universities, from actions of unscrupulous agents.

Sport Agent Legislation

There have been numerous attempts to regulate sport agents, unfortunately, due to a variety of reasons these attempts have mostly failed to stop the unethical, unscrupulous, and illegal conduct of sport agents.

State Legislative Efforts

In 1981, California became the first state to pass legislation regulating sport agents when it enacted the California Athlete Agents Act. Thirty-Five (35) years later, the number of states regulating the activities of sport agents has grown to Forty-Three (43). However, instead of protecting the athletes from unethical and unscrupulous agents, the focus of current state sport agent statutes has shifted to addressing the economic damage an unscrupulous agent could cause for a college or university. This current legislative trend is characterized by provisions requiring notice to school and state before and/or after the signing of a representation contract, waiting periods for valid contracts, the creation of causes of action in favor of colleges and universities for agent misconduct resulting in damages, and an abandonment or modification of the onerous registration requirements common in earlier legislative schemes.

Uniform Athlete Agent Act

The most recent attempt by states to regulate the sport agent profession began in 1997, when the National Conference of Commissioners on Uniform State Laws (NCCUSL), at the request of several major universities and the NCAA, appointed a drafting committee to develop a uniform statute for regulating sport agents. The NCCUSL is a national association, which endeavors to promote the uniformity of state laws. As a result of their work, the NCCUSL developed the **Uniform Athlete Agents Act (UAAA)** in the fall of 2000. The stated goal of the UAAA is the protection of student-athletes from unscrupulous agents (Viltz, *et. al.* 2014). To achieve this goal, the UAAA contains a number of important provisions regulating the conduct between athletes and agents. For example, the UAAA requires an agent to provide important information, both professional and criminal in nature. This information enables student-athletes, their parents and family, and university personnel to better evaluate the prospective agent. The UAAA also requires that written notice be provided to institutions when a student-athlete signs an agency contract before their eligibility expires. In addition, the UAAA gives authority to the secretary of state to issue subpoenas that would enable the state to obtain relevant material that ensures compliance with the act. Finally, the UAAA provides for criminal, civil, and administrative penalties with enforcement at the state level (Viltz, *et. al.* 2014).

In addition, the UAAA also covers such key areas as agent registration requirement; liability insurance; notice to educational institution; a student-athletes' right to cancel, and penalties. Perhaps the most important part of the UAAA is the section allowing an agent's valid certificate of registration from one state to be honored in all other states that have adopted the act. The success of the reciprocal registration process is contingent on states establishing a reasonable fee schedule, including lower registration fees for reciprocal applications and renewals. Thus, more agents are likely to register due to the efficiency of this process, its practical cost-saving implications for the agent, and the benefits of complying with a single set of regulations.

As of 2016, the UAAA had been passed in forty (40) states. In addition, three states have laws dealing with agent behavior on the books that do not conform to the UAAA (see Table 7.40.1). However, some critics argued that the UAAA is more interested in protecting NCAA member institutions, than athletes. For example, the UAAA requires agents and student-athletes to notify the institution within seventy-two hours of the signing of a contract, or before the student-athlete's next scheduled athletics event, whichever occurs first. If a prospective student-athlete has signed a contract, the agent must notify the institution where the agent has reasonable grounds to believe the prospect will enroll. Finally, the act provides institutions with a right of action against the agent or former student–athlete for any damages caused by a violation of this act.

The UAAA has not been the panacea many anticipated, however. Since not every state has passed the Act, there is still a lack of uniformity, which in turn, has had an impact on the number of agents registering with the states. Therefore, it is not surprising that agents prone to abuse have ignored these statutory provisions and continued to conduct business as usual. In addition, differing state requirements have created an administrative nightmare for many honest agents doing business in several states. This, coupled with a perceived lack of enforcement, often encourages the breach of these provisions. For example, in *Howard v. Mississippi Secretary of State* (2015), sports agent Fred Howard was fined $15,000 by the Mississippi Secretary of State for violating the Mississippi Athlete Agents Act after he signed two college football plyers at Jackson State University without first registering as an athlete agent with the Secretary of State as required. Although Howard claimed that he was unaware of his obligation to register with the Secretary of State's Office before signing the players, the court found that by representing himself as an agent and signing clients in Mississippi, Howard had violated Mississippi Code Annotated section 73-42-33 (Rev. 2012) by failing to register as an athlete agent prior to entering into an agency contract with a student-athlete (Howard v. Mississippi Secretary of State, 2015).

This has led some states to be more active in attempting to control the corruption of sports agents. For example, in 2011, Texas passed a bill that would lead to a felony conviction and up to 10 years in prison for any sports agents or runners who bait college athletes into signing contracts that cause them to lose their eligibility. Under the new bill, prospective agents would have to post a $50,000 bond with the state before signing a student-athlete to a contract. Before a student-athlete's last intercollegiate game, agents would be restricted from directly contacting or providing anything of value from anyone related to the student-athlete, among other limitations. In addition to Texas, Arkansas and Oklahoma also stiffened the penalties for agents who violate state laws governing agent conduct. Under the new Arkansas law, the maximum fine for agents would go up to $250,000 and make violations punishable by up to six years in jail (Arkansas Statute Chapter 16, subchapter 1). In Oklahoma, the fine for a first offense can be up to $250,000 and up to $500,000 for a second offense. In addition to civil damages and penalties the law also imposes criminal penalties ranging up to three years in jail (Oklahoma Statute 70 O.S. § 821). In 2014 Oregon amended the UAAA in include marketing agents, and financial advisors, as well as player agents. Besides broadening the definition of who is an agent, the new law also requires agents to not only register with the state, but also with each individual school (Mullen, 2013).

TABLE 7.40.1 STATES THAT HAVE PASSED THE UAAA, AS OF JULY 2016

Alabama	Illinois	Nebraska	Rhode Island
Arizona	Indiana	Nevada	South Carolina
Arkansas	Iowa	New Hampshire	South Dakota
Colorado	Kansas	New Mexico	Tennessee
Connecticut	Kentucky	New York	Texas
Delaware	Louisiana	North Carolina	Utah
Florida	Maryland	North Dakota	Washington
Georgia	Minnesota	Oklahoma	West Virginia
Hawaii	Mississippi	Oregon	Wisconsin
Idaho	Missouri	Pennsylvania	Wyoming
States That Have Passed the Non-UAAA Designed to Regulate Athlete Agents			
California	Ohio	Michigan	
States That Have No Existing Laws Regulating Athlete Agents			
Alaska	Massachusetts	New Jersey*	Virginia
Maine	Montana	Vermont	
Source: www.ncaa.org, 2016.			

National Legislative Efforts

To correct some of the shortcomings of the states' laws, the Unites States Congress passed the **Sports Agent Responsibility and Trust Act (SPARTA)** (15 U.S.C. § 7801 - 7807). Sponsored by Tom Osborne, a Republican from Nebraska and the former football coach at the University of Nebraska, SPARTA was signed into law in 2004. Under SPARTA "it is unlawful for an athlete agent to:

1. directly or indirectly recruit or solicit a student athlete to enter into an agency contract, by
   a. giving any false or misleading information or making a false promises or representation; or
   b. providing anything of value to a student athlete or anyone associated with the student athlete before the student athletes enters into an agency contract, including any consideration in the form of a loan, or acting in the capacity of a guarantor or co-guarantor for any debt;

2. enter into an agency contract with a student athlete without providing the student athlete with a disclosure document described in subsection (b); or
3. predate or postdate an agency contract (15 U.S.C. § 7802a).

As part of the disclosure document that agents are required to give student athletes, the law states that:

> "the disclosure document must contain, in close proximity to the signature of the student athlete, or, if the student athlete is under the age of 18, the signature of such student athlete's parent or legal guardian, a conspicuous notice in boldface type stating: 'Warning to student athlete: If you agree orally or in writing to be represented by an agent now or in the future you may lose your eligibility to compete as a student athlete in your sport. Within 72 hours after entering into this contract or before the next athletic event in which you are eligible to participate, whichever occurs first, both you and the agent by whom you are agreeing to be represented must notify the athletic director of the educational institution at which you are enrolled, or other individual responsible for athletic programs at such educational institution, that you have entered into an agency contract.'"
>
> (15 U.S.C. § 7802b3)

SPARTA is enforced by the Federal Trade Commission (FTC). The law, however, also allows the attorney general of any state to bring a civil action against any agent it believes is in violation of the law (15 U.S.C. § 7804). Under the law, the state may recover any actual losses and expenses an educational institution may incur as a result of the conduct of the agent (15 U.S.C. § 7805b2).

SPARTA, however, has been criticized. First, some people argue that the limits it places on who can take action if a sport agent does not live up to his or her duties leaves the student athlete with no recourse if the attorney general or the FTC do not want to act on an agents wrongdoing. This point is illustrated by the fact that the FTC has not imposed a single penalty against an agent since the law was passed. As for the individual states, less than half the states that have enacted the UAAA have ever withdrawn a agents license or impose any penalty against an agent (Viltz, et. al. 2014). Second, like the UAAA, which SPARTA encourages every state to enact, the main goal of SPARTA is to protect colleges and universities by ensuring that student athletes keep their NCAA eligibility. The law, therefore, does nothing to protect professional athletes who no longer have any college eligibility left.

Other Regulatory Efforts

Agent-specific legislation is not the only legal means used to regulate the conduct of athlete agents. Other common law or statutory remedies, although not specifically directed at agents, have been used to attempt to control their abusive conduct. For example, the common law civil remedies of breach of contract, misrepresentation, fraud, deceit, and negligence have been applied in cases of agent misconduct (Shropshire & Davis, 2008). In addition, such organizations as the NCAA, professional sport players' associations, and the American Bar Association can also be used in regulating this relationship between athletes and agents.

The National Collegiate Athletic Association (NCAA)

In the mid-1980s, the NCAA was rocked by one of the largest sports agent abuse cases ever. Norby Walters, a successful agent in the music industry, and his partner Lloyd Bloom signed 58 college football and basketball athletes to postdated contracts. The contracts were dated for after the athlete's eligibility expired. On entering into the contracts, under which the athletes agreed to use Walters as their agent in negotiating professional contracts, Walters provided the students with cash and other perks while they were still in college. When all but two of the students tried signed with new agents and tried to back out of their contracts with Walters, Walters sued the athletes for breach of contract. The federal government eventually got involved in the case and Walters and Bloom were charged with various federal conspiracies and racketeering crimes (*United States v. Norby Walters*, 1993). As a result of the Walters scandal, and other reports of agent abuse, the NCAA has worked with individual states encouraging them to adopt the UAAA as a means of limiting the damage resulting from the impermissible and oftentimes illegal practices of some athlete agents.

Even though the NCAA and its member schools suffer media embarrassment and financial loss every time a new scandal comes to light, as an organization, the NCAA has very little control over agents. The NCAA can only directly punish its members, the colleges and universities, and indirectly the student athletes. For example, under NCAA Bylaw 12.3.1

> "An individual shall be ineligible for participation in an intercollegiate sport if he or she ever has agreed (orally or in writing) to be represented by an agent for the purpose of marketing his or her athletics ability or reputation in that sport. Further, an agency contract not specifically limited in writing to a sport or particular sports shall be deemed applicable to all sports, and the individual shall be ineligible to participate in any sport" (NCAA Manual, 2015–16).

In addition to sports agents, the NCAA Bylaws also prohibits athletes from accepting gift from runner (individuals who befriend student-athletes and frequently distribute impermissible benefits on behalf of sports agents) and financial advisors.

At the 2016 NCAA Convention, the Power Five schools approved Proposal No. 2015-18 allowing high school baseball players drafted by a professional baseball team to be represented by an agent or attorney during contract negotiations, prior to full-time collegiate enrollment, without losing their college eligibility. However, in order to retain their eligibility to play in college, the athlete must not sign with the professional team and pay the agent his standard fee for the negotiating services.

In 2012, the NCAA broadened the of agent to include any individual, agency or organization that represents a prospective student-athlete for compensation in placing the prospective student-athlete in a collegiate institution as a recipient of institutional financial aid shall be considered an agent or organization marketing the individual's athletics ability or reputation (NCAA Bylaw 12.3.3). The goal of the new language is to close a loophole in the NCAA's rules that did not cover the actions of parents, relatives, and friends of student athletes. The "Cam Newton" loophole, which was brought to light in the controversy surrounding former Auburn University star quarterback Cam Newton and the allegations that his father attempted to broker a "pay for play" arrangement with several SEC schools, is designed to prevent parents, relatives, and friends from shopping the athlete around to the highest bidder. The problem with NCAA regulations, however, is that they do not directly apply to sport agents. NCAA rules and regulations are only applicable to the academic institutions in which the athletes are enrolled. The NCAA lacks the authority to penalize agents or athletes once they turn professional. Therefore, an agent can violate NCAA regulations without fear of NCAA sanctions. While the NCAA can revoke the remaining eligibility of student athlete with whom the agent dealt, the real loser in any NCAA sanctions is the academic institution.

Professional Team Sports Players' Associations

The power of the players' associations of the four major sports leagues to regulate sport agents derives from the National Labor Relations Act and other federal labor law. Essentially, the players' associations regulate agents by "requiring their members to hire regulated agents only, and by obtaining the agreement of teams to negotiate with regulated agents only" (Fluhr, 1999). The first professional team sport players' union to initiate a player-agent certification program was the National Football League Players' Association (NFLPA) in 1983. The 1982 collective bargaining agreement between the NFL and NFLPA had reserved the exclusive right for the NFLPA or "its agent" to negotiate individual NFL player contracts. The 1983 program was established to certify agents as "NFLPA Contract Advisors," who, under the program, are required to use a standard representation agreement, comply with certain limits on compensation for contractual negotiations, and attend periodic training seminars. Fines, suspensions, and/or revocations of licenses are among the penalties imposed for noncompliance.

Despite the program's intent to protect athletes from agent incompetence and corruption, several problems still persisted. First, the program, in its original form, did not address the corruption occurring in intercollegiate athletics. Only agents representing current NFL players were covered. Alerted to the potential for agent abuse of athletes who had yet to sign their first NFL contract, the program was amended to prohibit agents from communicating with a college football player who is ineligible to be drafted, including a player who has applied for early eligibility, until his name appears on the NFL's official list of draft-eligible players. Second, the plan was limited in scope. The plan regulated only "contract advisors" of NFL players, and its rules prohibited the charging of excessive fees for only contract negotiation and money-handling services. Agents providing other services could charge excessive fees and effectively evade the plan's restrictions (Dunn, 1988). Third, the plan was devoid of any specific criteria for granting or denying agent certification.

Since 1998, however, the NFLPA, by trying to enforce higher standards, has taken a more active role in policing agents. The union has rolled back the maximum percentage that agents can charge players to negotiate a contract from 4 percent to 3 percent (Freeman, 1998). In 1999, concerned about the quality of the agents representing its players, the NFLPA started testing anyone who registers to become a NFL player's agent. The test covered such areas as the collective bargaining agreement, salary cap issues, and free agency. Any agent who fails the test will not be certified (Freeman, 1998). The NFLPA also requires current agents to pass a test yearly. If the agent fails the exam, his or her certification is suspended until he or she passes the test. Under the CBA, NFL teams are prohibited from engaging in individual contract negotiations with any agent who has not been certified by the NFLPA. If a team does negotiate a contract with a non-certified agent, the Commissioner is obligated to reject the contract and impose a fine of $30,000 upon the Club.

The requirements to be an NFL player agent, however, are still low. According to the NFLPA website, all a person has to do to become an NFL player agent is:

- Non-refundable Application fee of $2,500.00
- Undergraduate AND Post Graduate degree (Masters or Law) from an accredited college/university.
- Authorization to perform a background investigation
- Mandatory attendance at a 2016 two (2) day seminar in a location TBD
- Successful completion of written proctored examination
- Valid Email address (NFLPA, 2016).

In 1985, the Major League Baseball Players' Association (MLBPA) became the next union to adopt an agent certification plan. The National Basketball Players' Association (NBPA) followed the MLBPA in 1986, when it adopted its agent certification plan. The National Hockey League (NHL), which was the last union to start regulating agents, joined the other major sports leagues in 1996 when it drafted its agent certification program (Couch, 2000). In November 2004, Major League Soccer (MLS) and the MLS Players Union included language in their collective bargaining agreement that allows the union to develop and implement an agent certification program. However, at the present time, no such program exists.

The general scheme in professional sports leagues is that only those agents registered with the unions can negotiate on behalf of the players. The unions also require annual registration and fees, annual attendance at seminars, a disciplinary system including an arbitration provision, and the ban on specific conflict of interest situations. Generally, a sports agent earns between 4 and 10 percent of an athlete's playing contract, though some leagues place limits on what percentage an agent can charge in commission. For example, the National Football League states that an agent cannot receive more than 3 percent of player salaries. The National Basketball Association places the limit at 3 percent too. Major League Baseball and the National Hockey League do not have any limits on agent commissions (Viltz, et. al. 2014).

Even with all the safeguards the unions have tried to build into their program, agents are still taking advantage of unsuspecting athletes. For example, in *Hillard and Taylor v. Black*, (2000) two NFL players, Issac Hilliard and Fred Taylor, sued their agent William "Tank" Black to recover over a million dollars. Hilliard and Taylor claimed that Black, who was licensed by the NFLPA as a Contract Advisor, perpetrated two major financial scams. First, Black obtained free stock in a company, which he then sold to Hilliard and some of his other clients for more than $ 1,000,000 dollars and deposited into his personal bank account. Second, Black persuaded Hilliard and Taylor, and other clients to invest approximately $ 8.4 million in a promissory notePonzi schemeby saying that the notes were safe and extremely lucrative. Taylor alone invested $3.4 million in the scheme. Black assured the players that he had no financial interest in the promissory notes; however, he retained 40 percent of the investment returns (*Hillard and Taylor v. Black*, 2000).

The American Bar Association (ABA)
While the ABA's Model Code of Professional Responsibility establishes standards of integrity and conduct for all attorneys, unfortunately, even though many sport agents are attorneys, the code has no effect on agents who are not lawyers. As a result, some commentators have argued that the best way to regulate sport agents would be to require that all agents are licensed attorneys (Evanoff, 2011 and Amoona, 2008). The benefit of

such a requirement, they argue would be that athletes who believed they were cheated by an attorney agent would have more of a recourse than simply attempting to have an agent suspended from the league's union. Athletes cannot only sue his or her agent for malpractice, they can also report attorney agents to the state bar, and they could be disbarred for unethical behavior if necessary. The requirement that all agents be licensed to practice law would also protect athletes, by preventing agents who are not licensed to practice law from engaging in the unauthorized practice of law. In addition, requiring a law degree would establish a minimum educational requirement. Currently, there is no educational degree requirement. Finally, rather than taking two to four percentage of a player's contract, attorney agents treat athletes like all other clients and charge them an hourly-fee basis (Amoona, 2008). Tim Duncan, *Shane Battier*, Ray Allen, *Tamika Catchings* and Grant Hill all employed the Williams & Connolly Law Firm to negotiate their contracts. By charging the athletes on an hourly-fee basis rather than a percentage-of-income basis, the firm claims that it can save its athletes hundreds of thousands, if not millions, of dollars over the course of a professional career. For example, when Grant Hill signed his first contract, a six-year, $45 million deal with the Detroit Pistons, Hill paid a reported $100,000 fee. If Hill would have been represented by an agent, the deal would have cost Hill approximately $1.8 million (Amoona, 2008).

Requiring all sports agents to be attorneys does pose a couple of problems however. First, such a requirement would surely be challenged under antitrust law as a restraint of trade. Second, such a requirement would require agents to pass multiple bar exams.

Financial Advisors

In addition to negotiating contracts, a number of agents and their firms act as financial advisor to their clients. In 2002, the National Football League Players Association (NFLPA) became the first sports union to establish regulations governing financial advisor to players. The voluntary program attempts to pre-select and qualify financial advisors for services to NFL players (Yasser, McCurdy, Goplerud & Weston, 2011). To be eligible for the NFLPA's Financial Advisors Program, which is a voluntary program financial advisors must apply to the NFLPA and submit to annual background checks, developed in conjunction with the Securities and Exchange Commission.

In *Atwater v. The National Football League Players Association*, (2010) several current and former NFL players who had invested with Kirk Wright, a financial advisor approved by the NFLPA sued the NFL and the NFLPA after Wright defrauded the players of around $20 million. The players argued that they would not have invested money with Wright had the NFL and the NFLPA given them accurate information about Wright. More specifically, the players argued that the NFLPA listed Wright with the NFLPA's Financial Advisors Program without first conducting a proper investigation. As for the NFL, Plaintiffs asserted that several Plaintiffs requested, and the NFL provided an inadequate background check on Wright.

In rejecting the players' argument, the Eleventh Circuit Court of Appeals pointed to the disclaimer in the Financial Advisors Program that stated:

> "The parties will use best efforts to establish an in-depth, comprehensive Career Planning Program. The purpose of the program will be to help players enhance their career in the NFL and make a smooth transition to a second career. The program will also provide information to players on handling their personal finances, it being understood that players shall be solely responsible for their personal finances" (*Atwater v. The National Football League Players Association*, 2010).

The only recourse for the players therefore was to try and recover their money from Wright. Wright was eventually convicted on 47 counts of mail fraud, securities fraud, and money laundering and faced up to 710 years and $16 million in fines. However, before he could be sentenced, Wright killed himself in prison (Tierney, 2008).

SIGNIFICANT CASE

The following case examines the fiduciary duty between an agent to his or her client, and when he or she breaches that duty by failing to disclose material facts that may influence the athlete's contract negotiation.

DETROIT LIONS AND BILLY SIMMS V. JERRY ARGOVITZ
United States Court of Appeals for the Sixth Circuit
767 F.2d 919 (6th Cir. 1985)

This is a cross-appeal from a judgment by which the district court rescinded a contract to play football executed between Billy Sims and the Houston Gamblers, a United States Football League (USFL) franchise. The district court found that the contract resulted from an unconscionable breach of a fiduciary duty by Sim's [Simm's] agent Jerry Argovitz, who was also partial owner of the Houston Gamblers. On this appeal, Argovitz assigns numerous errors in the district court's finding of fact. The Detroit Lions and Sims primarily appeal the district court's denial of two motions to amend their complaints. Upon review of the issues before us, we affirm the district court's rescission of the contract and remand the case for consideration by the district court of two motions to amend the Detroit Lions' and Billy Sims' [Simms'] complaints.

In 1980 the Detroit Lions, a National Football League franchise, drafted Sims and signed him to a four year contract that expired on February 1, 1984. Argovitz entered into an agency agreement with Sims early in 1980 and counseled him on numerous matters. Sims and Argovitz developed a confidential relationship in which, Argovitz testified, Sims looked up to him like a father. Sims sought Argovitz's advice on significant professional, financial, and personal matters.

From April 1982 through June 1983, Argovitz negotiated with the Lions for a renewed contract with Sims. On May 5, 1983, Argovitz announced at a press conference that his application for what became the Gambler's franchise had been approved. Sims was present at the press conference. The district court found that Argovitz manipulated Sims' contract negotiations with the Lions during the spring of 1983 in light of Argovitz's own interest in the Gamblers. The court also found that Argovitz misrepresented the negotiations with the Lions as not progressing when in fact they were progressing well. Sims received information on the Lions' negotiations only from Argovitz, the court found. During May or June, 1983, Argovitz decided to seek a contract for Sims with the Gamblers. On June 29, 1983, Sims arrived in Houston, believing that the Lions were not negotiating in good faith and were not really interested in his services. On June 30, 1983 the Gamblers offered Sims a $3.5 million, five year contract that included nonmonetary fringe benefits Sims valued greatly. Argovitz told Sims that he thought the Lions would match the Gamblers' financial package and offered to telephone them. Although Sims told Argovitz not to call the Lions, the district court found that to have two teams bidding for a single athlete is "the dream of every agent," and that Argovitz breached his fiduciary duty to Sims by not following the common practice described by both expert witnesses of informing the Lions of the Gamblers' offer. On the afternoon of June 30, while negotiations were proceeding, the Lions' attorney called Argovitz. Argovitz was present at his office, but declined to accept the call. Argovitz attempted to return the call only after 5:00 p.m., when the Lions' attorney had left for the July 4th weekend. The district court found these actions to further breach Argovitz's fiduciary duty towards Sims. Argovitz then left for the holiday weekend. The next day, July 1, 1983, Sims signed an exclusive contract with the Gamblers.

In July 1983, uninformed by anyone of these events, the Lions sent Sims a further offer through Argovitz. On November 12, 1983, at Argovitz's instigation, Sims met with him and reexecuted the Gamblers' contract. Sims also signed a waiver of any claim he might have against Argovitz. Although at this time Argovitz had sold his agency business and no longer represented Sims, Argovitz did not inform Sims' new agent of his intention to have Sims sign a waiver. Nor did Argovitz, despite his fiduciary relationship with Sims, advise Sims to seek independent advice before signing the waiver. On December 16, 1983, Sims executed a second exclusive contract with the Lions for $1 million more than his Gamblers' contract.

On December 18, 1983, the Lions and Sims brought this suit in Michigan state court against Argovitz and the Gamblers seeking rescission of the Gamblers' contract with Sims. After an evidentiary hearing, the district court found that it had subject matter jurisdiction on the basis of complete diversity of citizenship. Argovitz and the Gamblers challenge this finding on the ground that Sims' domicile was Texas, and complete diversity is lacking. A person's domicile determines his citizenship for diversity purposes. *Kaiser v. Loomis*, 391 F.2d 1007,

1009 (6th Cir. 1968). The location of a person's domicile at any given time is a question of intent: what is the fixed location to which he intends to return when he is elsewhere? *Mas v. Perry*, 489 F.2d 1396, 1399 (5th Cir.), cert. denied, 419 U.S. 842 (1974). As such, determination of domicile is primarily a question of fact, that will not be reversed unless clearly erroneous. *Holmes v. Sopuch*, 639 F.2d 431, 434 (8th Cir. 1981) (Per Curiam). See also *Hawes v. Chub Ecuestre El Comandante*, 598 F.2d 698, 702 (1st Cir. 1979). The relevant time at which to determine citizenship and one's intent to remain domiciled in a given state is the time suit is filed. *Napletana v. Hillsdale College*, 385 F.2d 871, 872 (6th Cir. 1967). During the four years preceding this controversy Sims was employed in Michigan, owned and resided in a home there. He also owned a ranch in Hooks, Texas. No evidence emphasized by the appellants establishes a definite and firm conviction in our minds that the district court erred when it found that Sims' domicile was Michigan at the time of this suit. Argovitz and the Gamblers simply ask this court to reweigh the evidence on a cold record.

The district court found that it had personal jurisdiction over Argovitz individually and over the numerous partnerships and corporations that he represented as an agent. Michigan's long arm statutes provide for personal jurisdiction over individuals, partnerships, and corporations that transact business in the state. See M.C.L.A. §§ 600.701, 600.721, 600.725, 600.715. The goal of Michigan's jurisdictional statutes is to reach "the outer limits of personal jurisdiction consistent with due process." *Speckine v. Stanwick International, Inc.*, 503 F. Supp. 1055, 1057 (W.D. Mich. 1980). Due Process requires "certain minimum contacts with [the state] such that the maintenance of the suit does not offend 'traditional notions of fair play and substantial justice.'" *International Shoe Co. v. Washington*, 326 U.S. 310, 316 (1945) (quoting *Milliken v. Meyer*, 311 U.S. 457, 463 (1940)). Under *Hanson v. Denckla*, 357 U.S. 235 (1958), the defendants must have availed themselves of the privilege of conducting business in the forum state. Most recently the Supreme Court has emphasized foreseeability as critical: "the defendant's conduct and connection with the forum State are such that he should reasonably anticipate being hauled into court there." *World-Wide Volkswagen Corp. v. Woodson*, 444 U.S. 286, 297 (1980). Argovitz had conducted business in Michigan for over three years as the agent of Sims, a Michigan citizen. He was acting on behalf of his player representative organizations in doing so. The Houston Gamblers defendants contracted with Billy Sims as an attraction for their football team, which planned to use his contracted services in football games conducted in Michigan under USFL auspices and contracts. The contract between Billy Sims and the Gamblers was negotiated and signed in Texas, but it certainly was to be performed in part in Michigan. The district court was not in error.

The district court granted rescission of the contract between the Gamblers and Sims because it found that Argovitz had breached his fiduciary duty as Sims' agent and confidant. It is uncontested that Argovitz had a personal interest in Sims contracting with the Gamblers, who as a new team in a new football league would greatly benefit from the star attraction of a player of Sims' caliber. Argovitz's self-dealing arose from this conflict with his fiduciary duty to advance Sims' best interests.

As the district court found, under Texas law, where an agent has an interest adverse to that of his principal in a transaction in which he purports to act on behalf of his principal, the transaction is voidable by the principal unless the agent disclosed all material facts within his knowledge that might affect the principal's judgment. *Burleson v. Earnest*, 153 S.W.2d 869, 874–75 (Tex. Civ. App. 1941). This remains true even if the contract is fair. Id. The district court found as a matter of fact that "[a]t no time prior to December 1, 1983, was Sims aware" of all material facts regarding Argovitz's involvement with the Gamblers and Argovitz's failure to pursue Sims' interests in negotiations with the Lions. Argovitz accepts the legal standard as defined by the district court. He maintains that he satisfied his duty of disclosure simply by telling Sims that he was partial owner of the Gamblers and by telling Sims that the Lions would match the financial elements of the Gamblers' offer. A review of the facts as found by the district court reveals that these are but a few of the material disclosures that Argovitz should have made. The district court was not clearly erroneous.

Argovitz maintains that rescission of the contract, an equitable remedy, is improper for a number of reasons having to do with Sims' behavior during 1983. The key to these issues is that the district court found as a matter of fact that Sims was not aware of all material imformation [information] concerning his contract with the Gamblers until at least December 1983. Argovitz and the Gamblers do not point to evidence of behavior by Sims that would render the district court's factual findings clearly erroneous.

The district court denied the Lions' and Sims' motions to amend their complaints without explanation, and in one case without making an explicit ruling. Such action represents an abuse of discretion under *Foman v. Davis*, 371 U.S. 178, 182 (1962). See also *Gootee v. Colt Industries, Inc.*, 712 F.2d 1057, 1065 n.7 (6th Cir. 1983). The district court should reconsider the motions to amend in light of the standards of Foman, which looks to considerations such as undue delay, bad faith, and futility of the amendment. Id. If, on remand, the district court denies leave to amend, it should state its reasons for doing so.

Therefore, the district court's rescission of the contract between Billy Sims and the Houston Gamblers is AFFIRMED. The matter is REMANDED for consideration of the motions to amend the Lions' and Sims' complaints.

CASES ON THE SUPPLEMENTAL CD

Brown v. Woolf, 554 F.Supp. 1206 (1983). The case looks at the fiduciary relationship between players and their agents.

Hillard and Taylor v. Black, 125 F. Supp. 2d 1071 (2000). The case looks at the fiduciary relationship between players and their agents and the agents' obligation to disclose certain facts.

Smith v. IMG Worldwide, Inc., 2006 U.S. Dist. LEXIS 82566. This case examines the recruitment of athletes, and when what agents can say about another firm or agent.

Steinberg Moorad & Dunn, Inc. v. Dunn, 2002 U.S. Dist. LEXIS 26752. This case examines the fiduciary duty between agents and their firm.

United States of America v. Piggie, 303 F.3d 923 (8th Cir. 2002). The case looks at whether secretly paying high school athletes in violation of NCAA rules and then falsely certifying that they had not previously received payments, was a violation of criminal law.

QUESTIONS YOU SHOULD BE ABLE TO ANSWER

1. What were some of the events that brought about the need for professional sports agent?
2. What was the first state to pass legislation regulating sport agents?
3. What are some of the benefits of the Uniform Athlete Agents Act (UAAA)?
4. What are some of the negatives of the Uniform Athlete Agents Act (UAAA)?
5. What role should the professional sports leagues and their unions play in regulating an agent's relationship with college athletes?

REFERENCES

Cases
Atwater v. The National Football League Players Association, 626 F.3d 1170 (11th Cir., 2010)
Detroit Lions, Inc. v. Argovitz, 580 F.Supp. 542 (1984).
Hillard and Taylor v. Black, 125 F. Supp. 2d 1071 (2000).
Howard v. Mississippi Secretary of State, 184 So. 3d 295 (2015).
United States v. Norby Walters, 997 F.2d 1219 (7th Cir. 1993).

Publications
Amoona, J. (2008). Top Pick: Why A Licensed Attorney Acting as a Sports Agent Is a "Can't Miss" Prospect. Georgetown Journal of Legal Ethics Georgetown Journal of Legal Ethics, 21, 599–613.
Couch, B. (2000). How agent competition and corruption affects sports and the athlete-agent relationship and what can be done to control it. *Seton Hall Journal of Sport Law, 10*, 111–137.
Dunn, D. (1988). Regulation of sports agents: Since at first it hasn't succeeded, try federal legislation. *TheHastings Law Journal, 39*, 1031–1078.
Evanoff, C. (2011). Show me the Money: How the Model *Rules of Professional Conduct* Can Deter NCAA Rules Violations Involving Sports Agents & College Athletes. *DePaul Journal of Sports Law & Contemporary Problems*, 8, 63 - 93.
Fluhr, P. (1999). The regulation of sports agents and the quest for uniformity. *Sports Lawyers Journal*, 6,1–25.
Freeman, M. (1998, July 26). Protecting players from their agents: Misconduct leaves N.F.L. Union fearful of incompetence and greed. *The New York Times*, sec. 8, p. 1, col. 1.
NCAA Constitution, Bylaw 12.3 NCAA Manual (2015–16).
Mullen, L. (2013, December 16-22). Oregon agent law to cover marketing agents, financial advisers. *SportsBusiness Journal*. P. 16.
Mullen, L. (2016, January 7). Angent Ben Dogra Decertified by NFLPA, Bus can Rep Players During Appeal. *SportsBusiness Journal*. http://www.sportsbusinessdaily.com/Daily/Issues/2016/01/07/Labor-and-Agents/Dogra.aspx?ana=SBD%20Email. Accessed June 22, 2016.
Shropshire, K., & Davis, T. (2008). *The business of sport agents* (2nd ed.). Philadelphia, Pa: University of Pennsylvania Press.
Tierney, M. (2008, June 2). *After Financier's Death, Suit against Union Lives On*. The New York Times, p. D 3.

Viltz, R, Seifried, C. & Foreman, J. (2014). An Analysis of Sport Agent Regulation: A Call fot Cooperation. *Journal of Legal Aspects of Sport*, 24, 62–77.

Yasser, R., McCurdy, J., Goplerud P., & Weston, M. (2011). Sports Law: Cases and Materials (7th. Ed.). New Providence, NJ: LexisNexis

Legislation

Sports Agent Responsibility and Trust Act, 15 U.S.C. 7801 *et seq*.
Arkansas Statute Chapter 16, subchapter 1
Oklahoma Statute 70 O.S. 821
Texas Statute Chapter 2051, subchapter A

Websites

Forbes.com 2015 Sports Agents. http://www.forbes.com/sports-agents/list/#tab:overall. Retrieved June 22, 2016
NCAA.org. http://fs.ncaa.org/Docs/ENF/UAAA/map/index.html. Retrieved June 22, 2016
NFLPA.com. https://www.nflpa.com/agents/how-to-become-an-agent. Retrieved June 22, 2016
Sports Agent Directory. https://sports-agent-directory.com/. Retrieved June 22, 2016

CASE INDEX

A

Abdul-Jabbar v. General Motors Corp., 612, 616, 617, 624
Action Ink, Inc. v. N.Y. Jets, 605
Adickes v. S. H. Kress & Co., 417
Adrianne Armstrong v. Wal-Mart Stores East, L.P., 338
Agnew v. NCAA, 639, 645
A.H. v. Greensburg Cmty. Sch. Corp., 440
Aim High Academy, Inc. v. Jessen, 378
Akins v. Glens Falls City Sch. Dist., 133
Albach v. Odle, 428
Albertson v. Fremont County, 143
Alexander, et al. v. Minnesota Vikings Football Club LLC & National Football League, 377
Alexander v. Choate, 502
Alexander v. Sandoval, 537, 539
Alexson v. White Memorial Foundation, Inc., 145–147
Ali v. Playgirl, Inc., 615, 616
Allen v. Donath, 65, 66
Allied Chem. & Alkali Workers v. Pittsburgh Plate Glass Co., 656
American Football League v. National Football League, 628
American Needle Inc. v. National Football League, 628, 631–635
A & M Records, Inc. v. Napster, Inc., 596
Anderson v. Liberty Lobby, Inc., 369
Anderson v. Little League Baseball, Inc., 506
Anderson v. Pass Christian Isles Golf Club, Inc., 515, 518
Andrew A. Oliver v. National Collegiate Athletic Association, 473–476
Angland v. Mountain Creek Resort, Inc., 65
Apilado v. North American Gay Amateur Athletic Alliance, 517, 519
Appellants, v. Kirkwood Resort Company, 12
Aramony. v. District of Chapman Beach, 140
Archibald v. Kemble, 223
Arguello v. Sunset Station, Inc., 202, 211
Arkansas Gazette Co. v. Southern State College, 446
Arlosoroff v. NCAA, 418, 447
Armstrong v. Best Buy Co., 25
Armstrong v. Tygart, 490
Armstrong v. United States, 144
Aronson v. Lewis, 575

Arvada v. Nissen, 222
Ashburn v. Bowling Green, 151
Ash v. Royal Caribbean Cruises LTD, 208
Association for Intercollegiate Athletics for Women v. NCAA, 640, 645
Atcovitz v. Gulph Mills Tennis Club, Inc., 153
AT&T Mobility, LLC v. NASCAR, Inc., 389, 392
Atwater v. The National Football League Players Association, 666
Auburn School District No. 408 v. King County, 81
Auckenthaler v. Grundmeyer, 66, 73
Avenoso v. Mangan, 61, 97
Avila v. Citrus Community College District, 63, 154, 250
Azzano v. Catholic Bishops of Chicago, 65
Azzarello v. Black Bros. Co., 196

B

Badgett v. Alabama High School Athletic Association, 502
Bagley v. Mt. Bachelor Ski and Summer Resort, 363
Bailey v. Palladino, 114
Baldwin v. Fish & Game Commission of Montana, 436
Baldwin v. Redwood City, 486
Balthazor v. Little League Baseball, Inc., 68
Baltimore Orioles v. Major League Baseball Players, 393, 594, 600
Banks v. NCAA, 639, 645
Banovitch v. Commonwealth, 222
Barakat v. Pordash, 169
Barnes v. Costle, 556
Barnes v. GenCorp, 575
Barnett v. Board of Trustees for State Colleges and Universities A/K/A University of Louisiana System, 378
Barnhard v. Cybex Intl., 311
Barnhart v. Cabrillo Community College, 182
Barretto v. City of New York, 171
Barry v. Time, Inc., 234
Bartell v. Mesa Soccer Club, Inc., 87
Bartnicki v. Vopper, 486
Bassett v. NCAA, 640
Baumeister v. Plunkett, 220
B.A. v. Mississippi High School Activities Association, 437, 444
Baylor v. Jefferson County Board of Education, 548
Bearman v. Notre Dame, 137
Beasley v. Horrel, 381

Beattie v. Line Mountain School District, 438, 444
Beaver v. Foamcraft, Inc., 82
Beckett v. Clinton Prairie School Corp., 171
Becksfort v. Jackson, 66
Bedford Central School District v. Commercial Union Insurance Company, 344, 347
Beery v. University of Oklahoma Bd. of Regents, 572
Beeson v. Kiowa County School District, 405
Beggerly v. Walker, 187
Beglin v. Hartwick College, 284
Behagen v. Intercollegiate Conference of Faculty Representatives, 430
Belik v. Carlson Travel Group, Inc., 207, 211
Belliconish v. Fun Slides Carpet Skate Park and Party Center, LLC, 114
Bell v. Itawamba County School Board, 482, 488
Bell v. Lone Oak Independent School District, 439
Bell v. the Associated Press, 228
Bengals v. William Bergey, 240
Benitez v. New York City Board of Education, 69, 170
Bennett v. Hidden Valley Golf and Ski, Inc., 79
Bennett v. Stanley, 145
Bennison v. Stillpass Transit Co., 25
Bergman v. Anderson, 222
Berrier v. Simplicity Manufacturing, Inc., 195
Beth Ann Faragher v. City of Boca Raton, 561–567
Bethel School District No. 403 v. Fraser, 456–457, 463, 480, 488
Beydoun v. Wataniya Restaurants Holding, 210
B.H. v. Easton Area School District, 483
Bibby v. Philadelphia Coca Cola Bottling Co., 546
Biediger, et al. v. Quinnipiac University, 527–530
Bilney v. Evening Star Newspaper Co., 237, 238
Bingham v. City of Manhattan Beach, 485
Bishop v. Fair Lanes Georgia Bowling, Inc., 334
Biver v. Saginaw Township Community Schools, et al., 546, 547
BJ'S Wholesale Club, Inc. v. Rosen, 114
Blackmon v. Iverson, 362, 370
Blalock v. LPGA, 629
Blashka v. South Shore Skating, Inc., 166
Blasi v. Pen Argyl Area School District, 570
Bleistein v. Donaldson Lithographing Co., 597
Bloom v. NCAA, 472
Bloom v. ProMaxima Manufacturing Company, 288, 294
Blum v. Yaretsky, 417, 421
Board of Education of Independent School District No. 92 of Pottawatomie County v. Earls, 499
Board of Education of the Township of North Bergen Hudson County v. New Jersey State Interscholastic Athletic Association, 470

Board of Education v. Earls, 447, 492
Board of Supervisors v. Smack Apparel Co., 602, 612
Board v. Ruiz, 169
Bojko v. Lima, 241, 242, 244
Bold Corp. v. Nat. Union Fire Ins. Co., 346
Bolling v. Clevepak Corp., 475
Bolling v. Sharpe, 435
Bolton v. Tulane University, 183
Bombrys v. City of Toledo, 583
Bommarito v. Grosse Pointe Yacht Club, 516
Borden v. School District of the Township of East Brunswick, 461, 465
Borne v. Haverhill Golf, 48
Bouillon v. Harry Gill Company, 198
Bowers v. The National Collegiate Athletic Association, 589
Boyd v. Feather River Community College District, 439
Boyd v. Lufthansa, 206
Brady v. NFL, 629
Braesch v. De Pasquale, 405
Brahatcek v. Millard School Dist., 169, 171, 176
Brannum v. Overton County School Board, 453
Bray v. Marriott International, 201
Brennan v. Board of Trustees, 494
Brentwood v. Tennessee Secondary School Athletic Association, 418, 420–424, 477
Brett v. Hillerich & Bradsby Co., 191
Brewer v. Rogers, 234
Bridgewater v. Carnival Corp., 207
Brigams Yoga College of India v. Evolution Yoga LLC, 600
Broadcast Music Inc. v. Blueberry Hill Family Restaurants, Inc., 595
Broadcast Music, Inc. v. Columbia Broadcasting System, Inc., 635, 642
Broadcast Music, Inc. v. Melody Fair Enterprises, Inc., 595
Brokaw v. Winfield-Mt. Union Community School District, 218–219
Brotherson v. the Professional Basketball Club, LLC, 367, 370
Brown v. Atlas-Kona Kai, 156
Brown v. Bally Total Fitness Corporation, 156
Brown v. Clark Equip. Co., 293
Brown v. Day, 55
Brown v. Otto C. Epp. Mem. Hosp., 475
Brown v. Pro Football, Inc., 629, 635, 651
Brown v. Woolf, 669
Bruce v. S.C. High School League, 428
B.R. v. Little League Baseball, Inc., 61
Bubis v. Kassin, 141
Buckingham v. United States, 583

Buckton v. NCAA, 416, 418
Buell Industries, Inc. v. Greater New York Mutual Ins. Co., 136
Bulgarian Boxing Federation v. European Boxing Confederation, 399
Bull v. Ball State University, 234
Bunger v. Iowa High School Athletic Association, 405, 446
Burleson v. Earnest, 668
Burlington Industries, Inc. v. Ellerth, 566
Burton v. State of Rhode Island, 145
Burton v. Wilmington Parking Authority, 417
Bushnell v. Japanese-American Religious and Cultural Center, 68
Butler v. Newark Country Club, 145
Butler v. Oak Creek-Franklin School District, 430

C

Cablevision Systems Corp. v. 45 Midland Enterprises, Inc., 595
Cafeteria & Restaurant Workers Union v. McElroy, 427
Calandri v. Ione Unified School Dist., 171
Caldwell v. Griffin Spalding County Board of Education, 261
Calhanas v. South Amboy Roller Rink, 65
Cannon v. University of Chicago, 538
Cantwell v. Connecticut, 460
Capitol Indem. Corp. v. L. Carter Post 4472 Veterans of Foreign Wars, 346
Carabba v. Anacortes School District No. 103, 69, 171
Cardtoons, L.C. v. Major League Baseball Players Association, 614, 619, 624
Cariddi v. Kansas City Chiefs Football Club, 548
Carnival Cruise Lines, Inc. v. Shute, 205
Carter v. Baldwin, 157
Carter v. City of Cleveland, 154
Case Corp. v. Hi-Class Bus. Sys. Of Am., 369
Cash v. Six Continents Hotels, 59
Cassanello v. Luddy, 334
Cassie v. Walled Lake Consolidated Schools, 244
Cater et al. v. City of Cleveland, 325
Cavoto v. Chicago National Baseball Club, 252
C.B.C. Distribution v. Major League Baseball Advanced Media, 618
Cerny v. Cedar Bluffs Junior/Senior Public School, 46, 70
Cervantes v. Ramparts, Inc., 204
Chai v. Sport and Fitness Clubs of America, 156
Chandler v. McMinnville Sch. Dist., 486
Chapman v. Nichols, 270

Chapman v. Pennsylvania Interscholastic Athletic Association, 470
Charnis v. Watersport Pro LLC, 107
Chattem, Inc. v. Provident Life & Accident Ins. Co., 382
Chauvlier v. Booth Creek Ski Holdings, Inc., 112
Chavez v. City of Santa Fe Springs, 284
Cherry v. A-P-A Sports, Inc, 374
Chicago Professional Sports Limited Partnership v. National Basketball Association, 628
Chrisman v. Brown, 90
Chuy v. Philadelphia Eagles Football Club, 228, 242
Cicconi v. Bedford Central School District, 87
Cioffi v. Averill Park Central School District Board of Education et al., 262, 270
Cirillo v. City of Milwaukee, 47
City of Bainbridge Island v. Brennan, 140
City of Dallas v. Hughes, 143
City of Los Angeles v. Patel, 203
City of Mangum v. Powell, 130
City of Pioneer Village v. Bullitt County exrel, 391
City of San Jose v. Office of the Commissioner of Baseball, 627, 635
City of Santa Barbara v. Superior Court, 44, 45
City of Seattle v. Mesiani, 499
City of Seattle v. Mighty Movers, 496–497
City of Seattle v. Prof's Basketball Club, LCC, 389
C.J.R. v. G.A., 65
Clahassey v. C Ami Inc., 284
Clarett v. National Football League, 630
Clark v. Arizona Interscholastic Assn., 422
Claudia Pechstein v. German Speed Skating Association and International Skating Union, 399, 401
Clayton v. New Dreamland Roller Skating Rink, 218
Clemens v. McNamee, 234
Clement v. Griffin, 188
Cobb v. Time Inc., 230
Cohane v. NCAA, 418
Cohen v. Boys & Girls Club of Greater Salem Inc., 303, 311
Cohen v. Cowles Publishing Co., 231
Cohen v. Five Brooks Stable, 87, 111, 114
Colby v. J.C. Penney Co., 610
Coleman v. Oregon Parks & Recreation Dept., 143
Coleman v. Western Michigan University, 349, 356
Collings v. Longview Fibre Company, 582
Colon v. Chelsea Piers Mgmt., 157
Colony Insurance Co., v. Dover Indoor Climbing Gym, 388
Colorado Seminary v. NCAA, 429
Complainant v. Anthony Foxx, 546

Compston v. Borden, Inc., 548
Conant v. Stroup, 131
Conkwright v. Globe News Publishing Company, 231
Conley v. MLT, Inc., 204
Connell v. Payne, 65
Conradt v. Four Star Promotions, 113
Cookson v. Brewer School Department, 262
Coomer v. Kansas City Royals Baseball Corporation, 134, 137
Cooperman v. David, 68
Cooper v. The Aspen Skiing Company, 82
Copperweld Corp. v. Independence Tube Corp., 35
Copperweld Corp. v. Independence Tube Corp., 632
Cornelius v. BPOE, 518
Corrigan v. Musclemakers, Inc., 169, 294
Covell v. Bell Sports, Inc., 191, 195–198
Craig v. Amateur Softball Association of America, 50
Craig v. Boren, 437
Crase v. Kent State University, 127
Crawford-El v. Britton, 553
Creely v. Corpus Christi Football Team, Inc., 129
Crespin v. Albuquerque Baseball Club, 18
Criminal Law v. Civil Law, 247
Crocker v. Tennessee Secondary School Athletic Association, 424, 503
Cronin v. California Fitness, 396, 401
Cronk v. Suffern Senior High School, 242
Cross v. Board of Education of Dollarway, 544
Cruz v. City of New York, 170
Cruz v. Drezek, 136
Cruz v. Gloss, 67
Culli v. Marathon Petroleum Co., 132
Cunico v. Miller, 218
Curtis Publishing Co. v. Butts, 227, 228

D

D'agostino v. La Fitness International, 576–578
Dailey v. Los Angeles Unified School Dist., 166, 169
Dallas Cowboys Football Club, Ltd. v. America's Team Properties, Inc., 611
Dallas Cowboys v. NFL Trust, 629
Daniel v. Paul, 519
Darling v. Charleston Community Hospital, 290
Daubenmire v. Sommers, 228, 229
Davenport v. Randolph Co. Board of Education, 428
David v. County of Suffolk, 165
Davis v. Berwind Corp., 196
Davis v. LeCuyer, 67
Davis v. Massachusetts Interscholastic Athletic Association, 437
Davis v. McCormick, 547
Davis v. Meek, 446

Davis v. Monroe County Board of Education, 263, 538, 559, 561, 567
Day v. Jeannette Baseball Association et al., 543
Deesen v. PGA of America, 627
Defoe v. Spiva, 482–483
DeFrantz v. USOC, 419
DeGooyer v. Harkness, 169
Deguilio v. Gran, Inc., 98
Deli v. University of Minnesota, 376, 541
Delta Tau Delta v. Johnson, 135
Dendrite International v. Doe, 231
Dennin v. Connecticut Interscholastic Athletic Conference, 503, 510
Dennis v. Board of Education of Talbot County, 484
Dep't of Natural Res. v. Ind. Coal Council, Inc., 412
Desert Palace, Inc. v. Costa, 572
Detroit Lions and Billy Simms v. Jerry Argovitz, 240, 667–668
Dibartolomeo v. New Jersey Sports and Exposition Authority, 325
Dickerson v. Deluxe Check Printers, Inc., 553
Diebella v. Hopkins, 229, 234
Dilallo v. Riding Safely Inc., 107–108
Dilger v. Moyles, 65
Disney v. Henry, 382
Diversified Products Corp. v. Faxon, 191
Dixon v. Whitfield, 188
Doe, a/k/a Tony Twist, v. TCI Cablevision, 616
Doe v. Cahill, 231
Doe v. Little Rock School District, 499
Doe v. TCI Cablevision, 238, 244
Dominion Sports Services, Inc. v. Bredehoft, 240
Domino v. Mercurio, 166
Don King Productions v. James "Buster" Douglas, 240
Dotzler v. Tuttle, 65
Dougherty v. Montclair High School, 151
Dowling v. United States, 545
Downing v. Abercrombie & Fitch, 617, 618
Doyle v. Volkswagenwerk Aktiengesellschaft, 197
Dreith v. The National Football League, 571
Drury v. Blackston, 142
Dryer v. NFL, 605
Dubinsky v. St. Louis Blues Hockey Club, 437
Dudley Sports Co. v. Schmitt, 191
Duffley v. New Hampshire Interscholastic Athletic Association, 428
Dugan v. Thayer Academy, 69, 151
Duitch v. Canton City Schools, 260, 270
Dunagan v. Coleman, 65
Duncan v. Kelly, 67
Dunham v. Pulsifer, 446, 483
Durham v. Red Lake Fishing & Hunting Club, Inc., 515

E

Eastman v. Yutzy, 61, 82
Eastwood v. Superior Court, 615
Edmonson v. Leesville Concrete Co., 421
Edward C. v. City of Albuquerque, 133
Edwards v. National Audubon Society, 231
EEOC v. Chicago Club, 516, 519
EEOC v. National Broadcasting Co., Inc., 544
Elbaz v. Beverly Hills Unified School District, 261
Elledge v. Richland/Lexington School District Five, 286, 291–294
Ellison v. Kentucky Farm Bureau Mutual Insurance Company, 347
Ellis v. Marriott International, 204
Emerick v. Fox Raceway, 108
Employment Division, Department of Human Resources of Oregon v. Smith, 460
Eneman v. Richter, 323–325
English v. Fischer, 369
Erie Railroad Co. v. Tompkins, 196
Escola v. Coca-Cola Bottling Co. of Fresno, 192
Esshaki v. Millman, 218
Estate of Deshaun Newton, et al. v. Wes Grandstaff, et. al, 155
Estate of Newton v. Grandstaff, 161
Estay v. La Fourche Parish School Board, 405, 446
Estes v. Tripson, 66
Evans v. Newton, 417, 422, 423
Everett v. Bucky Warren, 67, 190
Everson v. Board of Education, 460

F

Fabend v. Rosewood Hotels and Resorts, 203
Fact v. Expressions, 229
Fagan v. Summers, 167
Fairchild v. Amundson, 124, 125–127
Fallhowe v. Hilton Worldwide, Inc., 204, 211
Farner v. Idaho Falls School District, 376
Fazzinga v. Westchester Track Club, 57
Feagins v. Waddy, 89
Federal Baseball Club of Baltimore, Inc. v. National League of Professional Baseball Clubs, et al., 627
Federal Insurance Company v. Executive Coach Luxury Travel, Inc., 188, 342
Federation v. European Boxing Confederation, 399
Feist Publications v. Rural Telephone Service Co., 593
Feld v. Borkowski, 65
Felipe v. Sluggers of Miami, Inc. and Sluggers, Inc., 279, 280
Ferguson v. DeSoto Parish School Board, 166, 170
Feszchak v. Pawtucket Mutual Insurance Company, 347
Figure World v. Farley, 47
Filler v. Rayex Corp., 194
Fischer v. Olde Towne Tours, LLC, 190
Fitzgerald v. Barnstable School Community, 523, 531, 567
Flagg Brothers v. Brooks, 416
Fleuhr v. City of Cape May, 165
Flood v. Kuhn, 627, 635
Flores v. 24 Hour Fitness, 311
Florida High School Athletic Association v. Marazzito, 468
Focke v. United States, 187
Foman v. Davis, 668
Force v. Pierce City R-VI School District, 438
Ford Motor Co. v. NLRB, 650–651
Forster v. Town of Henniker, 142
Fortay v. University of Miami, 364
Fortier v. Los Rios Community College Dist., 68
Fortin v. Darlington Little League, 418
Foster v. Board of Trustees of Butler County Community College, et al., 180, 182, 185–187
Foster v. Houston General Insurance Co, 171
Fowler v. Harper, 222
Fowler v. Tyler Independent School District, 103
Fox Sports Net North, LLC v. Minnesota Twins Partnership, et al., 389, 392
Fox v. Contract Beverage Packers, Inc., 354
Franklin v. Gwinnett County Public Schools, 524, 531
Fraser v. Major League Soccer, L.L.C., 33–38, 628, 633, 635
Frazier v. University of the District of Columbia, 376
Frederick v. Morse, 456
Fricano v. Chicago White Sox, 424
Frith v. Lafayette County School District, 151
FSB v. Vinson, 544
Fuhr v. Sch. Dist. of Hazel Park, 532, 541
Fusato v. Washington Interscholastic Activities Association, 439, 444

G

Galloway v. Walker, 65
Gamble v. Bost., 67
Garda v. The Dolphin Boating and Swimming Club, 465
Garrett v. Nissen, 191
Gault v. Sequin School District, 151
Gebser v. Lago Vista Independent School Dist., 538, 559
Gehling v. St. George's University School of Medicine, 157

Geiersbach v. Frieje, 69
Generally Assumed ADR Limitations v. Litigation, 394, 395
Gertz v. Robert Welch, Inc., 225, 228, 229
Giampietro v. Viator, Inc., 207
Gibbs v. Miller, 354
Gilbert v. McLeod Infirmary, 33
Gilbert v. Seton Hall University, 90
Gill v. Tamalpais Union High School District, 44
Giovani Carandola, Ltd. v. Fox, 463
Giuffra v. Vantage Travel Service, Inc., 207
Giuliani v. Duke University, 362, 371
Gladon v. Greater Cleveland Regional Transit Auth., 25
Glankler v. Rapides Parish School Board, 168
Glatt v. Fox Searchlight Pictures, 648
Glenn v. Brumby, 438
Gloria Hicks v. Bally Total Fitness Corp., 286
Glucksman v. Walters, 55
Godfrey v. Iverson, 220
Goff v. Clarke, 218
Goldberg v. Kelly, 427, 429
Golden Gate Water Ski Club v. County of Contra Costa, 141
Golden v. Milford Exempted Village School District Board of Education, 260
Goldstein v. Hard Rock Café International, Inc., 204
Goldstein v. Pataki, 140, 147
Gonzalez-Martinez v. Royal Caribbean Cruises LTD., 205
Gootee v. Colt Industries, Inc., 668
Gorthy v. Clovis Unified Sch. Dist., 241
Gorzynski v. JetBlue Airways Corp., 577
Goss v. Lopez, 484, 496
Grace v. Kumalaa, 83
Graczyk v. Workers' Compensation Appeals Board, 351, 352
Graham v. TSSAA, 423
Graves v. Women's Professional Rodeo Association, Inc., 543
Green v. Orleans Parish School Board, 169, 171, 176
Gregory v. Daly, 577
Griffin v. Wisconsin, 450
Griggs v. Duke Power Co., 550
Grillier v. CSMG Sports, LTD., 377, 383
Gross v. FBL Financial Services, 572, 574, 579
Gross v. Lopez, 427, 429–430
Grove City v. Bell, 523
Gruenke v. Seip., 492
Guerra v. Howard Beach Fitness Center, 311
Gulf South Conference v. Boyd, 429
Gutman v. Allegro Resorts Marketing Corp., 203, 209–210
Gyuriak v. Millice, 65

H

Hackbart v. Cincinnati Bengals, Inc., 220, 223
Hacking v. Town of Belmont, 69
Hadley v. Rush Henrietta Center School District, 437
Haelan Laboratories v. Topps Chewing Gum, 614
Hageman v. Goshen County School District, 436
Hairston v. Pac-10 Conference, 419
Hallahan v. The Courier-Journal, 392
Hallman v. Unique Vacations, 207
Hall v. University of Minnesota, 428
Halper v. Vayo, 154
Hames v. State, 157
Hamill v. Town of Southampton, 171
Hamilton v. Tenn. Secondary School Athletic Association, 428
Hammond v. Allegretti, 132
Hanson v. Kynast, 55, 160
Hans York et al., v. Wahkiakum School District No. 200, 495–499
Hanus v. Loon Mountain Recreation Corp., 59–61, 103
Harjo, et al. v. Pro-Football, Inc., 606
Harris v. Forklift Systems, 557
Harting v. Dayton Dragons Professional Baseball Club, LLC, 43
Harvey v. Ouachita Parish School Board, 170
Hass v. South Bend Community School Corportation, 428
Hatch v. V.P. Fair Foundation and Northstar Entertainment, 56, 279
Hauter v. Zogarts, 194
Hawes v. Chub Ecuestre El Comandante, 668
Hawkins v. Peart, 82
Hayden v. Greensburg Community School Corporation, 440–443
Hayden v. University of Notre Dame, 135
Hayes v. City of Plummer, 142
Haywood v. Univ. of Pittsburgh, 364, 370, 376
Hazelwood School District v. Kuhlmeier, 480–481, 486
HBCU Pro Football, LLC, v. New Vision Sports Properties, 371
Heard v. City of Villa Rica, 9
Hearon v. May, 70, 171
Heenan v. Comcast Spectacor, 338
Heike v. Guevara, 439
Heisman Trophy Trust v. Smack Apparel Co., 606
Henchey v. Town of North Greenbush, 583
Hennessey v. Pyne, 217

Case Index 677

Henson v. Seabourn Cruise Line Limited, Inc, 206
Herman v. National Broadcasting Co., Inc., 547
Herrera v. Santa Fe Public Schools, 453
Herring v. Bossier Parish School Board, 167
Hewitt v. Miller, 113
Hillard and Taylor v. Black, 665, 669
Hillsmere Shores Improvement Association v. Singleton, 140
Hill v. National Collegiate Athletic Association, 448, 449, 453, 493, 499
Hippopress v. SMG, 418
Hirsch v. S. C. Johnson & Son, Inc., 617, 624
Hofer v. Gap, Inc., 207
Hohe v. San Diego Unified Sch. Dist., 109
Hoke v. Cullinan, 65, 392
Hollinger v. Jane C. Stormont Hospital and Training School for Nurses, 187
Hollonbeck v. USOC, 504
Holmes v. Sopuch, 668
Hoopla Sports and Entertainment, Inc. v. Nike, Inc., 17
Horsemen's Benevolent & Protective Assn. v. State Racing Commission, 448
Horvath v. Ish., 65
Hospital v. Halderman, 539
Hot Rod Hill Motor Park v. Triolo, 144
Howard University v. NCAA, 418
Howard v. Mississippi Secretary of State, 661–662
Howard v. Missouri Bone and Joint Center, Inc., 50
Howard v. United States of America, 144
Hughes v. Jones, 186
Hunt v. Radwanski et al., 270
Hustler Magazine, Inc. v. Falwell, 621
Hysaw v. Washburn University of Topeka, 458

I

Iacco v. Bohannon, 230
IHSAA v. Vasario, 414
Image Rights. Vanna White v. Samsung Electronics America, 244
Incredible Technologies Inc. v. Virtual Technologies Inc., 600
Indiana High School Athletic Ass'n v. Raike, 440, 446
Indiana High School Athletic Ass'n v. Schafer, 437
Indiana High School Athletic Association v. Carlberg, 428, 468
Indiana High School Athletic Association v. Durham, 409–414, 468
Indiana High School Athletic Association v. Watson, 476, 469

Indianapolis Colts v. Mayor & City Council of Baltimore, 609
Indianapolis Colts v. Metropolitan Baltimore Football Club, 609–611
Indus. v. Whirlpool Corp., 38
Institute of Athletic Motivation v. Univ. of Ill., 230
International Boxing Club of New York, Inc. v. United States, 643
International Shoe Co. v. Washington, 668

J

Jackson v. Armstrong School District, 545
Jackson v. Birmingham Board of Education, 535
Jackson v. Livingston Country Club, Inc., 67
Jackson v. Metropolitan Edison Co., 416, 421
Jackson v. Veteran's Administration, 583
Jackson v. World League of American Football, 547
Jaeger v. Western Rivers Fly Fisher, 56, 58
Jalil v. Advel Corp., 549
Jane Doe II v. St. Joseph University, 259
Jane Doe v. St. Joseph's University, 259
J.A. v. Fort Wayne Community Schools, 483
Jaworski v. Kiernan, 65, 71
J.C. v. Beverly Hills Unified School District, 482
Jiminez v. 24 Hour Fitness USA, Inc., 114, 294
Jin v. Metropolitan Life Ins. Co, 556
J.M. v. Montana High School Association, 503, 504
Joe Namath v. Sports Illustrated, 619
John Doe, a/k/a Tony Twist, v. TCI Cablevision, 616, 624
John Hopkins v. Connecticut Sports Plex. LLC., 284
Johnson v. Florida High School Activities Association, 503
Johnson v. Gibson and Stillson, 131
Johnson v. NFL, 548
Johnson v. Ubar, LLC, 114
Johnston v. Tampa Sports Authority, 419, 424
Jones v. Southeast Alabama Baseball Umpires Association, 581
Jones v. West Virginia State Board of Education, 437, 470, 476
Jordan v. Jewel Food Stores, Inc., 465
Joyce v. Town of Dennis, 439

K

Kabella v. Bouschelle, 65, 222
Kaczmarcsyk v. City & County of Honolulu, 168
Kahler v. Town of Middleboro, 142
Kahn v. East Side Union High School District, 45, 68, 72, 165, 170–175

Kaiser v. Loomis, 667
Kane v. National Ski Patrol System, Inc., 68
Kansas State Univ. v. Prince, 365
Karas v. Strevell, 73
Kavanaugh v. Trustees of Boston University, 69, 71
Keesee v. Board of Education of the City of New York, 169
Keller v. Electronic Arts, 619
Kelley v. Chicago Park District, 600
Kelley v. Metropolitan County Board of Education of Nashville, 430
Kelly v. Crown Equip. Co, 197
Kelly v. McCarrick, 68, 170
Kelly v. N. Highlands Recreation & Park Dist., 241
Kelly v. Priceline.com, Inc., 207
Kennedy v. Syracuse University, 154
Kent State University v. Ford, 377
Keyishian v. Board of Regents, 488
Kiley v. Patterson, 65
Kimbrough & Co. v. Schmitt, 381
Kimps v. Hill, 324
King v. CJM Country Stables, 127
King v. True Temper Sports, 575
King v. University of Indianapolis, 124, 127
Kinsman v. Winston, 219
Kleczek v. Rhode Island Interscholastic League, 438
Kleinknecht v. Gettysburg College, 149, 154, 158–161, 325
Kline v. OID Assocs., Inc., 68, 72
K.L. v. Hinickle, 324
K. L. v. Missouri State High School Activities Association, 502, 511
Knight v. Jewett, 44, 65, 86, 174
Knoll v. Board of Regents of the University of Nebraska, 261
Koch v. Billings School Dist. No. 2, 172
Koffman v. Garnett, 221
Konneker v. Romano, 139
Kopczynski v. Barger, 145
Kross v. Tippecanoe County School Corp., 451
Krueger v. La Quinta Inn, 203
Kuketz v. Petronelli, 506
Kuykendall v. Young Life, 90
Kyriazis v. University of West Virginia, 156

L

L.A. Fitness International v. Mayer, 156, 161, 294
LaFlamme v. Dallessio, 136
Lambert v. West Virginia State Board of Education, 503
Lamp v. Reynolds, 2002, 44

Landefeld v. Marion Gen. Hosp., Inc., 588
Landers v. School District No. 203, 169
Landis v. USADA, 495
Lang v. Silva, 65
Lash v. Cutts, 83
Lasseigne v. American Legion, Nicholson Post #38, 155
Lautieri v. Bai v. USA Triathlon, Inc., 58, 67
LaVine v. Blaine Sch. Dist., 486
LaVine v. Clear Creek Skiing Corp, 67
Law v. National Collegiate Athletic Association, 398, 401, 638, 640, 645
Layden v. Plante, 76, 84–86
Layshock v. Hermitage School District, 459
Leach v. Texas Tech University, 375, 383
Leakas v. Columbia Country Club, 79
Lebron v. National Railroad Passenger Corporation, 422
Ledbetter v. Goodyear Tire & Rubber Co., 536
Lee v. Weisman, 460
Leger v. Stockton, 334
Lemoine v. Cornell University, 156
Lemon v. Kurtzman, 460
Leonard v. Behrens, 65
Leon v. Family Fitness Center (#107), Inc., 310
Levin v. National Basketball Association, 628
Lewin v. Fitworks of Cincinnati, LLC, 156
Lewis v. Coffing Hoist Division, 197
Lewis v. Elsin, 208
Liberman v. Gelstein, 231
Liberty Mutual v. Zurich Insurance, 202
Lilley v. Elk Grove Unified School Dist., 166
Limones v. School District of Lee County, 153, 161
Lindsey v. University of Arizona, 374
Little v. F.B.I, 588
Little v. State of Arizona, 84
Live Nation Motor Sports, Inc. v. Davis, 595
LLC v. NBC Universal Media LLC, 231
LLC v. Team AK, Inc., 244
Longfellow v. Corey, 165, 171
Longin v. Kelly, 54
Long v. National Football League, 419, 491
LoPiccolo v. American University, 362
Lorillard Tobacco Co. v. Reilly, 621
Lorimar Music A Corp. v. Black Iron Gril, 600
Lorimar Music v. Black Iron Grill Co., 595
Los Angeles Mem'l Coliseum Comm'n v. NFL, 628, 634
Los Angeles Raiders v. National Football League, 628
Louisiana High School Athletic Assn. v. St. Augustine High School, 422
Louisiana High School Athletic Association v. State of Louisiana, 467, 477

Case Index 679

Lovett v. Omni Hotels Management Corp, 203
Lowery v. Circuit City, 548
Lowery v. Euverard, 457, 481, 488
Lowery v. Texas A&M University d/b/a Tarleton State University, 537, 549, 554
Lowe v. Texas Tech University, 170
Ludtke v. Kuhn, 419
Lugar v. Edmondson Oil Co., 416, 417, 421
Lyons Partnership, L.P. v. Giannoulas, 594
Lystedt v. Tahoma School District, 151

M

MacGinnitie v. Hobbs Group, 378
Maciasz v. Fireman's Fund Insurance Company and Chicago Insurance Company, 347
Mackey v. NFL, 628, 630
Maddox v. University of Tennessee, 375, 586–589
Madsen v. Wyoming River Trips, Inc., 82
Maheshwari v. City of New York, 137
Maisonave v. Newark Bears Professional Baseball Club, 18, 284
Major League Baseball Properties, Inc. v. Salvino, Inc., 634
Major League Baseball Properties Inc. v. Sed Non Olet Denarius, Ltd., 610
Mangone v. Pickering, 65
Manning v. Grimsley, 220, 223
Mann v. Shusteric Enterprises, 133
Mansourian v. Board of Regents, 438
Marcantonio v. Dudzinski et al., 270
Marchetti v. Kalish, 68
March Madness Athletic Association, LLC v. Netfire Inc., 608
Mark v. Moser, 64
Marmo v. NYC Board of Education, 446
Martino-Valdes v. Renaissance Hotel, 204
Mason v. Bristol, 144
Mason v. Cohn, 217
Mas v. Perry, 668
Matheny v. United States, 142
Matherson v. Marchello, 226, 231
Mathews v. Eldridge, 429
Matter of the Arbitration Between Terrell Owens and the National Football League (NFL) Players Association v. the Philadelphia Eagles and the NFL Management Council, 397
Matthews v. National Football League Management Council, 350
Maurer v. Cerkvenik-Anderson Travel, 208
Maussner v. Atlantic City Country Club, 135, 157, 325
Mazzarella v. U.S. Postal Service, 583

McAfee MX v. Foster, 147
McArthur v. Kerzner International Limited, 205
McCarthy v. New York State Canal Corp., 144
McClure v. Sports & Health Club, 554
McComish v. DeSoi, 293
McCormack v. National Collegiate Athletic Association, 646
McCourt v. California Sports, Inc., 630
McCrann v. Riu Hotels, 203
McDermott v. Carie, 127
McDonnell Douglas Corp. v. Green, 547, 551, 552, 572
McElroy & Canestero v. Bellmore-Merrick School District, 263
McFadden v. Grasmick, 502, 589
McGue v. Kingdom Sports Center, Inc., 25, 26–27, 132
McKenzie v. Wright State University, 376
McPherson v. Tennessee Football Incorporated, 131
Medcalf v. University of Pennsylvania, 541, 545, 554
Meeker v. Edmunson, 262
Meek v. Wal-Mart Stores, Inc., 136
Meinders v. Dunkerton Community School District, 378
Mendenhall v. Hanesbrands, Inc., 390, 392
Menke v. Ohio High School Athletic Association, 428
Menora v. Illinois High School Assn., 446
Menough v. Woodfield Gardens, 133
Meritor Savings Bank, FSB v. Vinson, 548, 557
Merten v. Nathan, 105
Meyer v. Nebraska, 426
Miami Dolphins Ltd. v. Williams, 377
Michael Jordan v. Jewel Food Stores, Inc., 620–623
Mid-South Grizzlies v. National Football League, 628
Miglino v. Bally Total Fitness of Greater New York, Inc., 99, 153
Milicic v. Basketball Marketing Co., Inc., 363
Milkovich v. Lorain Journal Co., 229
Miller v. Bank of America, 556
Miller v. California Speedway Corp., 505, 511
Miller v. Live Nation Worldwide, Inc. et al., 336–338
Milliken v. Meyer, 668
Minass v. HHC TRS Portsmouth, LLC, 200
Minnis v. Bd. Of Sup'rs of La., 554
Mirand v. City of New York, 176
Mitchell v. Baldrige, 552
Mitchell v. WSG Bay Hills IV, LLC, 145, 147
MLBPA v. Garvey, 652
Mogabgab v. Orleans Parish School Board, 154, 161, 325
Molinas and Deeson v. PGA of America, 629
Molinas v. National Basketball Association, 629

Mollaghan et al v. Varnell, 545
Monson v. State of Oregon, 374
Montana v. San Jose Mercury News, Inc., 237, 244, 618
Moody v. Cronin, 483
Moore v. Fargo Public School District 1, 142
Moore v. Phi Delta Theta Co., 65
Moore v. Stills, 140
Moore v. The Univ. of Notre Dame, 571
Moore v. Waller, 114
Moose v. Massachusetts Institute of Technology, 67
Morehouse v. Berkshire Gas Co., 558, 567
Morio v. North American Soccer League, 658
Morris v. Bianchini, et al., 546
Morse v. Frederick, 463, 481
Motschenbacher v. R.J. Reynolds Tobacco Co., 615
Mount Snow, Ltd., v. ALLI, 361
Mounts v. Van Beeste, 103
Mullen v. Parchment School District, 383
Muller v. Jackson Hole Mt. Resort, 198
Muller v. Oregon, 536
Muraco v. Sandals Resort International, 204
Murray v. Zarger, 181
Myers v. Friends of Shenendehow Crew, Inc., 155
Myricks v. Lynwood Unified School District, 54, 180, 188

N

Nabozny v. Barnhill, 64
Nabozny v. Podlesny, 441
Nader v. ABC Television, 376
Namath v. Sports Illustrated, 237
Napletana v. Hillsdale College, 668
NASC v. Jervis, 363
NASL v. NFL, 628
National Basketball Ass'n v. SDC Basketball Club, 635
National Basketball Association v. Motorola, Inc., 17, 593
National Collegiate Athletic Association v. Joscelin Yeo, 430–432, 468
National Collegiate Athletic Association v. Tarkanian, 421, 429, 477, 418, 419, 424, 469
National Football League Management Council v. NFLPA, 15
National Football League Players Association v. National Labor Relations Board, 658
National Football League Properties, Inc. v. New York Football Giants, Inc., 611
National Football League v. McBee & Bruno's, Inc., 595
National Football League v. Rondor, 595
National Society of Professional Engineers v. United States, 643
National Treasury Employees Union v. Von Raab, 447
NCAA v. Board of Regents of the University of Oklahoma, 637, 639, 640–645, 646
Newcombe v. Adolf Coors Co., 615, 624
New England Patriots Football Club Inc. v. University of Colorado, 378
New England Patriots, L.P. v. Stubhub, Inc., 252
New Jersey v. T.L.O., 448, 449, 497
New Kids on the Block v. New America Pub., Inc., 617
Newport News Shipbuilding & Dry Dock Co. v. EEOC, 538
New York Times Co. v. Sullivan, 227
New York v. FanDuel, 437
New York v. Ocean Club, 515
NFLPA v. NLRB, 651
NFL v. Coors Brewing and NFL Players Incorporated, 414
Nice v. Centennial Area School District, 262
Nicholls v. Holiday Panay Marina, 516
Niles v. Univ. Interscholastic League, 428
NLRB v. Katz, 650, 656
NLRB v. Wooster Div. of Borg-Warner Corp., 656
Norfolk Admirals and Federal Insurance Company v. Ty A. Jones, 356
North American Soccer League v. National Labor Relations Board, 650, 658
North American Soccer League v. NF, 633
Northeastern University v. Brown, 363
North Haven Bd. of Ed. V. Bell, 538
Northwestern Nat.Cas. Co. v. McNulty, 219
Novak v. Virene, 64, 67
NPS, LLC. v. StubHub, Inc., 256

O

O'Bannon v. NCAA, 639
O'Brien v. Pabst Sales Co., 614
O'Brien v. The Ohio State University, 376
O'Connor v. Ortega, 446, 447, 453
Official Brands, Inc. v. Roc Nation Sports, 240, 241, 243
O'Halloran v. University of Washington, 447, 448, 449
Ohio State University v. Thomas, 604
Oliver v. National Collegiate Athletic Association, 407, 414
Olmstead v. L. C., 538
Onyx Acceptance Corp. v. Trump Hotel & Casino Resorts, Inc., 201
Ortega v. Kmart Corp., 134
Orth v. Novelli, 67
Oswald v. Township High School District No. 214, 64

Ouellette v. Blanchard, 131
Overall v. Kadella, 65, 218, 223

P

Pac-10 Conference v. Lee, 608
Palace Sports & Entertainment, Inc. D/B/A/ St. Pete Forum v. National Labor Relations Board, 658
Palko v. Connecticut, 455
Palmer v. Merluzzi, 433, 484, 488
Palmer v. Mount Vernon Township High School District 201, 170
Palmer v. Schonhorn Enterprises, Inc., 238
Pandazides v. Virginia Board of Education, 582
Pappion v. R-Ranch Prop. Owners Ass'n, 516–517
Parisi v. Harpursville Central School District, 67
Parker v. Franklin County Community School Corp., 438, 444
Park Place Ctr. Enterprises, Inc. v. Park Place Mall Assoc., 382
Partin v. Vernon Parish School Board, 167
Partnership v. NBA, 37
Passantino v. Board of Educ., 166
Passion Richardson v. International Olympic Committee, 399
Patrick v. Miller, 270
Paul v. Davis, 427
Pavlides v. Galveston Yacht Basin, 191
Pechstein v. German, 401
Peirick v. Indiana University-Purdue University Indianapolis, 548, 554
Pelletier v. Bilbiles, 55
Pennsylvania v. Board of Directors of City Trusts of Philadelphia, 421, 422
People of the State of Colorado v. Hall, 256
People of the State of New York v. Shacker, 256
People v. Freer, 249, 255
People v. Greer, 250
People v. Shacker, 251
People v. Solak, 217
Perkins, et al. v. Alamo Heights Independent School District, 262
Perkins & Phillips v. Alamo Heights Independent School District et al., 270
Perkins v. Commonwealth, 222
Perkins v. Londonderry Basketball Club, 418
Perry v. Granada Municipal School District, 446
Peterson v. Kennedy and the NFLPA, 650
Peterson v. National Football League, 570
Pfenning v. Lineman, 135
Pfister v. Shusta, 45, 65
PGA Tour, Inc. v. Martin, 7, 17, 506–510, 589

Phelps v. Firebird Raceway, Inc., 157
Philadelphia World Hockey, Inc. v. Philadelphia Hockey Club, Inc., 628
Phillips v. Cricket Lighters, 196
Phillips v. Pembroke Real Estate, 594
Piazza v. Major League Baseball, 628
Picou v. Hartford Ins. Co., 65
Pinard v. Clatskanie School District 6J, 457, 464, 481, 485–488
Pinero v. the city of new york, 48–50
Pinson v. State of Tennessee, 151, 154
Pitt v. Pine Valley Golf Club, 417
Plains Resources, Inc. v. Gable, 186
Plevretes v. La Salle University, 151
Polk County v. Dodson, 421
Poole v. South Plainfield Board of Education, 502, 510
Pottgen v. Missouri State High School Athletic Association, 503
Pouncy v. Prudential Insurance Co. of America, 549
Powell v. NFL, 630
PPA v. The Pop Warner Football Team of Shelton, Inc., 242, 244
Prater v. Indiana Briquetting Corp., 354
Prejean v. East Baton Rouge Sch. Brd., 171
Preston v. Virginia ex rel. New River Community College, 537
Price Waterhouse v. Hopkins, 546, 551, 552
Pride Park Atlanta v. City of Atlanta, 82
Private v. Public Facts, 238–239
ProBatter Sports, LLC v. Joyner Technologies, 405, 414
Pro Football, Inc. v. Harjo, 612
Pugh v. NCAA, 472

Q

Quaker Oats Co. v. Mills Co., 610

R

Radovich v. National Football League, 627
Ragas v. Tenn., 369
Range v. Abbott Sports Complex, 311
Rantapaa v. Black Hills Chair Lift Co., 66
Reddell v. Johnson, 65
Reed v. City of Portsmouth, 143–144
Reeves v. Sanderson Plumbing Products, 572
Regan v. Mutual of Omaha Insurance Company, 347
Regina v. Cey, 223
Regina v. Green, 255
Regina v. Maki, 255
Rendell-Baker v. Kohn, 417, 421, 423

682 Case Index

Rensing v. Indiana State University Board of Trustees, 349, 352, 353–356, 355
Reynolds v. National Football League, 630
Ribaudo v. La Salle Institute, 86
Ricci v. Schoultz, 67
Richland Country Club, Inc. v. CRC Equities, Inc, 382
Rickert v. Midland Lutheran College, 572
Riddell, Inc. v. Schutt Sports, Inc., 605
Ridder v. Tennis Enterprises, Ltd et al., 136–137
Riddle v. Universal Sport Camp, 79
Riker v. Boy Scouts of America, 57
Riley v. Birmingham Board of Education, 548
Ritchie-Gamester v. City of Berkley, 65, 218
Roberson v. Rochester Folding Box Company, 613
Robertson v. Travis, 83
Roberts v. Kling, 269
Roberts v. United States Jaycees, 513–514
Robinson v. Chicago Park District, 156
Robinson v. Hicks; King; City of Harrisburg, 458
Robinson v. Lynmar Racquet Club, Inc., 367
Roderick Jackson v. Birmingham Board of Education, 537–540
Rodgers v. Georgia Tech Athletic Association, 379, 383
Rodrigo v. Koryo Martial Arts, 68
Rogers v. Fred R. Hiller Company of GA., Inc., 55
Rogers v. Professional Golfers Association, 392
Rollins v. Concordia Parish School Board, 168
Romaine v. Kallinger, 226
Rosania v. Carmona, 65
Rosenblatt v. Baer, 226, 227
Rosenbloom v. Metromedia, Inc., 229, 236
Ross v. Clouser, 65
Ross v. Douglas County, 545
Rostai v. Neste Enterprises, 61
Rotolo v. San Jose Sport and Entertainment, LLC, 153, 156
Rottmann v. Pennsylvania Interscholastic Athletic Association, 467–468, 477
Roulette v. City of Seattle, 487
Rowe v. Pinellas Sports Auth., 18
Rubbo v. Guilford Board of Education, 65
Rudolph v. Miami Dolphins, 350, 356
Rumsfeld v. Forum for Academic & Institutional Rights, Inc., 487
Ruppa v. American States Ins. Co., 324
Russell v. South eastern Pennsylvania Transportation Authority, 583
Rutecki v. CSX Hotels, 46
Rutnik v. Colonie Center Club, Inc., 153
Ryther v. KARE 11, 573, 579

S

Safford Unified Sch. Dist. # 1 v. Redding, 492
Sala v. Warwick Valley Central School District, 484
Salte v. YMCA, 153
Sanders v. Laurel Highlands River Tours, Inc, 198
Sandison v. Michigan High School Athletic Association, 503, 510
San Francisco Arts & Athletics, Inc. v. USOC, 419
Santa Fe High Independent School District v. Doe, 460
Santiago v. Clark, 66
Santoro v. Unique Vacations Inc., 59
Sargent v. Litton Systems, 583
Savino v. Robertson, 64
Sawhill v. Medical College of Pennsylvania, 582
Saxe v. State College Area School District, 464
Scandia Down Corp. v. Euroquilt, Inc., 611
Schafer v. United States of America, 143
Schaill v. Tippecanoe County School Corp., 447
Schenck v. United States, 455
Scheuer v. Rhodes, 540
Schick v. Ferolito, 65
Schmidt v. Boardman Co., 196
Schmidt v. Safeway, 583
Schneider v. American Hockey and Ice Skating Center, Inc., 129
Schutz v. Thorne, 436
Sciarrotta v. Global Spectrum, 284
Scott v. News-Herald, 230
Scott v. Pacific West Mountain Resort, 112
Scott v. Rapides Parish School Board, 165, 169
Scott v. United States, 143
Scott v. Young, 519
Seamons v. Snow, 262, 267, 487
Searles v. Trustees of St. Joseph College, 46
Seger v. Kentucky High School Athletic Association, 469, 477
Sellers v. Rudert, et al., 151
Senne v. Kansas City Royals Baseball Corp., 648
SGC Lisco LLC v. Zhang Xue Ming, 400
Sheehan v. San Francisco 49er, 419
Sheehan v. St. Peter's Catholic School, 166
Shelton v. Tucker, 488
Shepard v. Loyola Marymount University, 364
Sherwood v. Danbury Hospital, 136
Shoemaker v. Handell, 491, 499
Shreve v. Cornell University, 574, 579
Shridhar v. Vantage Travel Service, Inc., 208
Siegert v. Gilley, 427
Siesto v. Bethpage Union Free School District, 261
Silverman v. Major League Baseball Player Relations Committee, 651, 653–657, 658

Case Index **683**

Simkins v. S.D. High School Activities Association, 428
Simpson v. Univ. of Colorado, 560, 567
Sisino v. Island Motocross of N.Y., Inc., 44
Sisson v. Virginia High School League, 437, 469
Skinner v. Railway Labor Executives' Assn., 447
Small v. Juniata College, 374
Smith v. Alanis & Zapata County Independent School District, 374
Smith v. City of Jackson, 571, 572, 579
Smith v. City of Salem, 546
Smith v. Dodgeville Mut. Ins. Co., 324
Smith v. Gardner, 180
Smith v. IMG Worldwide, Inc., 669
Smith v. NCAA, 639
Smith v. Pro Football, Inc, 628
Smith v. Royal Caribbean Cruises LTD., 206
Smith v. YMCA of Benton Harbor/St. Joseph, 108
Snelling & Snelling v. Fall Mountain Regional School District, et al., 263
Snyder v. Phelps, 621
Sony Corp. v. Universal Studios, 595
Southeastern Community College v. Davis, 501
Southwest Key Program, Inc. v. Gil-Perez, 46, 50
Southwick v. City of Rutland, 57, 61
Spahn v. Messner, Inc., 239
Spahr v. Ferber Resorts, 201
Spear v. Marriott Hotel Services, Inc., 203
Speckine v. Stanwick International, Inc., 668
Spence v. Washington, 487
Spiegelhalter v. Town of Hamden, 144
Spiegler v. State of Arizona, 155
Spotlite Skating Rink, Inc. v. Barnes, 50, 157, 160
Spring Branch I.S.D. v. Stamos, 430
S.S. v. Whitesboro Central School District, 502
Stadt v. United Center Joint Venture, 132
Staley v. Nat'l Capital Area Council, 516, 519
Stamps Public Schools v. Colvert, 376
Standard Oil Co. v. United States, 643
Stanley v. Big Eight Conference, 419, 427, 433
Stanley v. University of Southern California, 534, 541
Starego v. The New Jersey Interscholastic Athletic Association, 408, 414
Starkey v. G Adventures, Inc., 205, 211
Stark v. the Seattle Seahawks, 424
State Compensation Insurance Fund, et al. v. Industrial Commission of Colorado, 351
State ex rel. Todd Hewitt v. Kerr, 377
Staten v. Superior Court, 65
State of Minnesota v. Yang, 202
State of North Dakota v. Seglen, 332
State of Ohio v. Wright, 202
State of Washington v. Shelley, 249, 250, 256

State v. Brooks, 498
State v. Dunham, 255
State v. Floyd, 249, 250, 255
State v. Forbes, 249
State v. Guidugli, 249, 250, 253
State v. Hendrickson, 498
State v. Hunter, 437
State v. Jorden, 499
State v. Ladson, 498
State v. Limon, 249
State v. McKinnon, 498
State v. Murphy, 216
State v. Myrick, 497
State v. Shelley, 255
State v. Surge, 499
State v. Walker, 497
State v. Young, 498
Steele v. Louisville & Nashville Railroad, 650
Steele v. State, 217
Steelvest, Inc. v. Scansteel Service Center, Inc., 392
Steinberg Moorad & Dunn, Inc. v. Dunn, 378, 669
Steinfield v. EmPG Int'l, LLC, 208
Stephenson v. Redd, 65
Stepien v. Franklin, 229
Stevens v. Chesteen, 167
Stevens v. New York Racing Association, 418
Stevens v. Payne, 58
Stimson v. Carlson, 65
St. Margaret Mercy Healthcare Centers, Inc. v. Poland, 166, 170, 176
Stobaugh v. Norwegian Cruise Line, 205
Stokes v. Bally's Pacwest, 115
Stone v. Continental Airlines, 205
Stone v. Kansas State High School Activities Association, 433
Stone v. Lawyers Title Inc. Corp, 369
Stone v. United Eng'g, 293
Stowers v. Clinton Central School Corporation, 124
Stringer v. Minnesota Vikings Football Club, L.L.C., 157
Strout v. Packard, 258
Suarez v. City of Texas City, 143
Suchomajcz v. Hummel Chem. Co., 161
Sullivan-Coughlin v. Palos Country Club, Inc., 157
Sullivan v. Little Hunting Park, Inc., 538
Sullivan v. National Football League, 37, 628–629
Sullivan v. Nissen Trampoline Company, 191
Sullivan v. University Interscholastic League, 439, 444
Summit Health, Ltd. v. Pinhas, 537
Sweeney v. City of Bettendorf, 121, 127
Symonds v. City of Pawtucket, 142
Syrus v. Bennett, 593

T

Tally Bissell Neighbors, Inc. v. Eyrie Shotgun Ranch, LLC, 144, 147
Tallyrand Music, Inc. v. Frank Stenko, 595
Taub v. Frank, 588
Taylor v. Hesser, 65
Taylor v. Wake Forest University, 368
Teahan v. Metro-North Commuter R.R. Co., 587
Teamsters v. United States, 548, 548
Tepper v. City of New Rochelle School District, 171
Texas Dep't of Community Affairs v. Burdine, 547, 551, 552
Thomas, et al., v. National Football League Players Ass'n., 551
Thomas v. national football league players association, 551–554
Thomas v. Sport City, Inc., 169
Thompson v. McNeill, 65, 72, 222
Thompson v. Rochester Community Schools, 103
Thornton v. Shaker Ridge Country Club, Inc., 515, 519
Thurston Metals & Supply Co. v. Taylor, 67
T.H. v. Montana High School Association, 503
Ticketmaster, L.L.C. v. RMG Technologies, Inc., 252
Tillman v. Wheaton-Haven Recreation Ass'n., 518
Tilton v. Playboy Entertainment Group, Inc., 463
Time, Inc. v. Hill, 239
Times-Picayune Publishing Co. v. United States, 643
Tinker v. Des Moines Independent Community School District, 405, 446, 450, 456, 457, 464, 465, 480
Tolis v. Board of Supervisors of Louisiana State University, 377
Toller v. Plainfield School District, 202, 165
Toolson v. New York Yankees, 627
Toone v. Adams, 220, 230
Townsend v. The State of California, 55
Traub v. Cornell University, 198
Tremblay v. West Experience Inc., 79
Trotter v. School District, 156
Trujillo v. Yeager, 69, 70–72
Turner v. Mandalay Sports Entm't, LLC, 242
T.V. v. Smith-Green Community School Corporation, 461–465, 482, 488
Twardy v. Northwest Airlines, Inc., 205
TYR Sport, Inc., v. Warnaco Swimwear, Inc., et. al., 392

U

Uddin v. Embassy Suites Hotel, 25
UnderHanson v. Denckla, 668
United States Anti-Doping Agency v. Floyd Landis, 399
United States Football League v. National Football League, 366, 628
United States of America v. Landsdowne Swim Club, 517–519
United States of America v. Piggie, 669
United States v. Benson, 622
United States v. E.I.duPont Nemours & Co., 638
United States v. International Boxing Club, 627
United States v. Norby Walters, 663
United States v. Schwimmer, 455
United States v. Slidell Youth Football Association, 515, 519
United States v. Stevens, 462
United States v. Virginia, 441, 443, 531
United States v. Yellow Cab Co., 632
Universal Gym Equipment, Inc. v. Vic Tanny International, Inc., 55
University Interscholastic League (UIL) and Bailey Marshall v. Buchanan, 502
University of Alabama Board of Trustees. v. New Life Art Inc, 606
University of Colorado v. Derdeyn, 447, 448, 449, 453, 493
University of Denver v. Nemeth, 351
University of Kansas v. Sinks, 604
University of Louisville v. Duke University, 387, 390–392
University of Texas at Arlington v. Williams, 144
University of Texas Medical School v. Than, 432
USOC v. Tobyhanna Camp Corporation, 607
U.S. Steelworkers v. American Mfg. Co., 651
U.S. Steelworkers v. Enterprise Corp., 651
U.S. Steelworkers v. Warrior Gulf Co., 651
U.S. v. Burke, 251
U.S. v. Florida East Coast Ry, 429
U.S. v. Lansdowne Swim Club, 515
U.S. v. Virginia, 439

V

Vaca v. Sipes, 650
Valentine v. Chrestensen, 621
Vanderbilt University v. DiNardo, 364, 376, 380–382
Van Dusen v. Barrack, 196
Van Horn v. Industrial Accident Commission, 351
Van Horn v. Watson, 98
Vaughan v. Nielson, 127
Vaughn v. Barton, 103
Vendrell v. School District No. 26C, 222
Verizon Communications v. Law Office of Curtis v. Trinko, 638
Vernonia School District v. Acton, 447, 448, 449–453, 491–492, 492, 496

Village of Willowbrook v. Olech, 441
VKK v. National Football League, 629
V.L. Nicholson Co. v. Transcom Inv. And Fin. Ltd., Inc., 382
Vumbaca v. Terminal One Group Assn., 205

W

Wadler v. Eastern College Athletic Conference, 379
Wager v. Pro, 216
Waldbaum v. Fairchild Publications, Inc., 228
Waldrep v. Texas Employers Insurance Association, 356
Walheim v. Kirkpatrick, 293
Walker v. Daniels, 156
Wallace v. Jaffree, 460
Walsh v. Luedtke, 82
Walt Disney World Co. v. Wood, 55
Walz v. Tax Commission, 459
Wards Cove Packing Co. v. Atonio, 572
Ward v. Mount Calvary Lutheran Church, 166
Warford v. Lexington Herald, 227
Warren v. United States Specialty Sports Ass'n, 242
Washburn v. Klara, 222
Waters v. Michael Drake et al., 263
Weaver v. The Ohio State University, 541
Webb v. City of Richland, 142, 147
Webb v. Zern, 196
Western Air Lines v. Criswell, 574
West Virginia University v. Rodriguez, 365
Whipple v. Oregon School Activities Association, 428
Whitacre v. Halo Optical Products, Inc., 191
White v. Federal Express Corp., 553
White v. National Football League, 375
Whittemore v. Country Inn & Suites, 201
Willey v. Carpenter, 222
Williams v. Board of Regents of the University System of Georgia, 560, 567
Williams v. Butler, 54
Williams v. City of Albany, 58
Williams v. Community Drive-in Theater, Inc., 187
Williams v. Eaton, 405
Williams v. National Football League, 500
Williams v. Saxbe, 556
Williams v. Smith, 378
Williams v. Wood, 67
Wilson v. Daily Gazette Co., 239
Wilson v. O'Gorman High School, 69
Wilson v. United States of America, 57
Wissell v. Ohio High School Athletic Association, 198
Wolf v. Celebrity Cruises, Inc., 208
Wolf v. Rawlings Sporting Goods Co., 192, 195
Wolf v. Tico Travel, 208
Woodbury v. Courtney, 222
Woodman v. Kera, 108
Wood v. National Basketball Assn., 655, 656
Wooten v. Pleasant Hope R-VI School District, 453, 484
Worldwide Basketball & Sport Tours v. NCAA, 646
World-Wide Volkswagen Corp. v. Woodson, 668
World Wrestling Federation Entertainment, Inc. v. Big Dog Holdings, Inc., 606
Wright v. Salisbury Club, Ltd., 518
Wykidal v. Bain, 141
Wynn v. Columbus Municipal Separate School District, 549

X

Xu v. Gay, 286, 288, 294

Y

Yagle v. United States, 142
Yang v. Voyagaire Houseboats, Inc., 82
Yatsko v. Berezwick, 154
Yi v. Pleasant Travel Service, Inc., 203, 211
Yocca v. Pittsburgh Steelers, Inc., 364, 367
Yonan v. United States Soccer Federation, Inc., 379, 570
Yoneda v. Tom, 157
York Insurance Company v. Houston Wellness Center, Inc., 346
York v. Wahkiakum School District No. 200, 493, 496, 500
Yost v. Chicago Park District, 573
Young v. New Southgate Lanes, et al., 137
Yount v. Johnson, 67

Z

Zacchini v. Scripps-Howard Broadcasting, 459, 466
Zamecnik v. Indian Prairie School District, 465
Zauderer v. Office of Disciplinary Counsel of the Sup. Ct. of Ohio, 621
Zavras v. Capeway Rovers Motorcycle Club, 50
Zehner v. Central Berkshire Regional School District, 428
Zeller v. Donegal School District, 446
Zimmermann v. Associates First Capital Corp., 577
Zipusch v. LA Workout, Inc., 124, 132, 134, 176, 303, 308–310
Zivich v. Mentor Soccer Club, 109
Zurla v. Hydel, 67

SUBJECT INDEX

A

AAA. *See* American Arbitration Association
Abandonment of trademarks, 605
Abrahamian, Ara, 399
Absolute privilege, 230
Academic Legal Journals, 19
Academic standards, eligibility and, 471–472
Acceptance of contracts, 362
Access control, 299
Accident coverage of participants, 341, 343
Accommodations
 Americans with Disabilities Act, 504–506
 public, places of, 505–506, 514–515
 reasonable, 503, 504, 546, 582–584
Acosta, Vivien, 532
ACPA. *See* Anti-cybersquatting Consumer Protection Act
ACSM's Health/Fitness Facility Standards and Guidelines, 289
Action plans for crisis response, 315
Activity-related injuries, 81
Acts of commission, 40
Acts of omission, 40
Actual contact, 117
Actual damages, 219
Actual malice, 225, 227
Actual notice, 132
Actus reus, 247
ADA. *See* Americans with Disabilities Act
ADAAA. *See* Americans with Disabilities Act Amendment Act
Additional Insured Endorsement, 344
ADEA. *See* Age Discrimination in Employment Act
Ad Hoc Division, 398
Administration, gender equity in, 532–541
Administrative court system, 5–6
Administrative Dispute Resolution Act of 1990, 394
Administrative Procedure Act (APA), 427
Admiralty law, 106–107, 109
ADR. *See* Alternative dispute resolution
Adverse possession, 140
AED. *See* Automated External Defibrillator
Affirm, 363
Affirmative action, 550
Affirmative defense, 558
Affirmative easements, 141

Affirmed decisions, 12
Affirmed in part, 12
Age Discrimination in Employment Act (ADEA), 569–578
 defenses against claims, 574–575
 enforcement and remedies, 571
 Older Workers Benefit Protection Act and, 575
 protection by, 570
 sport and recreation cases, 572–574
 state laws, 575
 United States Soccer Federation, 570
Agency, free, 630
Agency law, 206–208
Agents, 206
 breach of fiduciary duty and, 240
 insurance, 344–345
 principal–agent relationships, 181, 206–207
 sport, legislation on, 660–668
Age rule, 472
Aggravated negligence, 44
Agreements, in contract law, 361
Agreements to participate, 80, 120–124
Air travel, 205
Alcohol use, 405, 484
 crowd management and, 334
 hazing and, 258–259
Alienage, 435
A.L.R. *See* Annotated Law Reports
Alternative dispute resolution (ADR), 11, 394–400
 arbitration, 395–396
 collective bargaining and labor disputes, 397–398
 definition of, 394
 fundamental concepts of, 394–400
 globalization of sport and, 400
 in international sport disputes, 398–400
 mediation, 11, 109–110, 394, 397
 negotiation, 394, 396
 sponsorships and, 394–395
 in sport and recreation, 398
 sport specialists in, 400
 trademarks and, 608
Amateur athletes, antitrust law and, 637–645
Amateur Sports Act, 504
Amateur status, 472
Ambush marketing, 390, 608
American Arbitration Association (AAA), 396

687

American Bar Association (ABA), 665–666
American College of Sports Medicine, 116–117, 167, 286, 287
American Heart Association, 168, 287
American Jurisprudence, 19
American Law Source On-Line, 21
American Society of Testing and Material (ASTM), 286
Americans with Disabilities Act (ADA), 501, 504–506, 516–517
  Amendments Act of 2008, 584–586
  disability definition in, 582
  employer definition in, 581
  fundamental concepts in, 581
  qualified individual with a disability in, 582
  on reasonable accommodation/undue hardship, 582–584
  Title I, 581–589
Americans with Disabilities Act Amendment Act (ADAAA), 501, 506, 516
Amusement rides, 102
Anderson County High School, 261
Andover High School, 266
Annotated Law Reports (A.L.R.), 19
Annotations, 16, 19
Answer, filing, 9
Anticipate foreseeable uses, 135
Anti-cybersquatting Consumer Protection Act (ACPA), 607–608
Anti-discrimination legislation, 514–517
  Age Discrimination in Employment Act, 569–578
  Americans with Disabilities Act, 504–506, 516–517, 581–589
  disabled participants and, 501–510
  freedom of association and, 514
  gender, 522–542
  National Labor Relations Act, 649–651
  Title VII, 543–554
Anti-Injunction Act, 629
Antitrust law, 31, 398, 626–645
  amateur sport applications, 637–645
  baseball and, 627
  challenges by individual athletes, 629
  challenges by team owners, 628–629
  coaches and, 640
  competitor leagues challenges in, 628
  fundamental concepts in, 626
  labor law and, 629–630
  professional sport applications, 626–635
  Sherman Antitrust Act, 637–639
  student-athletes and, 639
  television and, 639
  women's athletics and, 639–640
APA. *See* Administrative Procedure Act
Apparel, freedom of expression and, 482–483
Apparent agents, 207
Apparent authority, 58–59
Appeal
  definition of, 4
  notice of, 11
Appearance contracts, 390
Appellate courts, 11–12, 16–18
  federal, 4, 5
  state, 5
Appellate Divisions of Supreme Court, 5
Appellate phase, 11–13
Appreciation
  notes of, 321
  of risk, 79
Appropriation, 236–238
Aquatics, 156, 203
Arbitrary and capricious, 427, 468
Arbitrary/fanciful marks, 602
Arbitration, 11, 395–396
  clauses, 395–396
  collective bargaining and, 397–398, 651–652
  employee termination and, 376
  employment contracts and, 376
  panels, 396
  parental arbitration agreements, 109–110
  salary, 651
Arbitrators, 394
Armstrong, Lance, 490
Assault and battery, 213
  crowd management and, 334
  defenses to, 218–219
  definition of, 216, 248
  elements of, 216, 217
  simple *vs.* aggravated, 248
  sport-related, 248
  tort remedies, 219–220
  vicarious liability, 220
Association for Intercollegiate Athletics for Women, 639
Association, freedom of, 513–514
Assumption of risk agreements, 80, 124–125
ASTM. *See* American Society of Testing and Material
Athens Convention, 206
Athlete sponsorships, 390
Athlete Support Programs, 504
Athletic trainers, 287

Atlanta Journal-Constitution, 374
Attractive nuisance, 145
At-will employees, 376
Audits, risk management, 296–310
    facility, 299, 302–308
    legal, 300–302
Authority to lead, 281
Automated External Defibrillator (AED), 288
    statutes, 84, 98–99, 152
Automobile insurance, 342, 343
Avoidance of risk, 277, 278

B

Bailee, 202
Bailment, 202
Bailor, 202
Balancing test, 448
Baseball, 102, 494, 627
Battery, 116, 217. *See also* Assault and battery
BBF. *See* Bulgarian Boxing Federation
Bedbugs, 200–201
Behavior management, 299
Bellotti, Mike, 377
Beyond a reasonable doubt, 215n3
Bicycling, 102
Bilateral contracts, 361
Binding arbitration, 394, 396
Binding precedent, 3
Black's Law Dictionary, 19, 40, 168, 225
Blogs, 20–21
Board members, 54
Board of Certification (BOC), 287
BOC. *See* Board of Certification
BOC Standards of Professional Practice, 287, 288
Bodily injury coverage, 343
Bona fide occupational qualification (BFOQ), 550, 574
Bona fide private membership clubs, 515
Bonuses, 375
Brandeis, Louis, 613
Breach of contract, 365–368
    defenses to, 365–366
    duty to mitigate, 365
    employment contracts, 376
    parol evidence rule in, 364
    promissory estoppel in, 364
    remedies for, 366
    sport agents and, 663
Breach of duty, 40, 43–46
Breach of fiduciary duty, 213, 239–240
Breach of warranty, 192–195

Brewer School Department, 262
Broadcasting Agreements, 388
Bryant, Dez, 241
Buckley Amendment, 446
Bulgarian Boxing Federation (BBF), 399
Bullying laws, 266
Bungee jumping, 2
Burk, Martha, 513
Bush, George W., 584
Business/academic journals, 19–20
Business auto insurance coverage, 341
Business income insurance, 340
Business invitees, 129
Business necessity defense, 550
Business operations, 276
Business structure, 29–33
    corporations, 31–33
    limited liability company, 31
    limited partnerships, 30
    partnerships, 30–31
    sole proprietorship, 29
Buyout provisions, 377

C

California Athlete Agents Act, 661
Calipari, John, 373
Call person, 151
"Cam Newton" loophole, 664
Campus recreation centers, 155–156
Campus Security Act (CSA), 266
Cancellation clauses, 390
Cancellation insurance, 343
Capacity to contract, 363
Cardiac Arrest Survival Act (CASA), 99
Cardio-pulmonary resuscitation (CPR), 156. *See also* Emergency care
Carpenter, Linda Jean, 532
CAS. *See* Court of Arbitration for Sport
CASA. *See* Cardiac Arrest Survival Act
Case law, 3, 252
Catastrophic Injury Insurance Program, 353
Cause-in-fact, 46–47
CBA. *See* Collective bargaining agreements
C corporations, 32
CCTV networks. *See* Closed circuit television networks
Center for Safe Schools, 322
Centers for Disease Control Injury Center, 149
Central monitoring, 330
Certificates of insurance, 179, 344
Certifications, emergency care, 152–154

Certified class, 8
Certiorari, 4, 17
C.F.R. *See* Code of Federal Regulations
Character of the intrusion, 491
Charge person, 151
Charitable immunity, 84, 89–90
Checklists
   facility audit, 304–306
   IRS independent contractor *vs.* employee, 379–380
Child abuse, 276
Chronic traumatic encephalopathy (CTE), 351
Circuit Courts, 4–7
CISM. *See* Critical Incident Stress Management
Citizen's Media Project, 237
Civil litigation, 260–263
Civil Rights Act of 1871, 435, 533
Civil Rights Act of 1964, 514–516
   gender equity and, 534–535
   sexual harassment and, 556
   Title II, 514–515
   Title VII, 515–516, 534–535, 543–550
Civil Rights Act of 1991, 544, 572
Class action lawsuits, 8
Classification of risk, 276
Clayton Act, 629
CLC. *See* Collegiate Licensing Company
Closed circuit television (CCTV) networks, 329, 330
Clothing, freedom of expression and, 482–483
Coaches, 249
   age discrimination and, 570
   antitrust law and, 640
   gender equity and, 532–541
   hazing and, 259, 261–264
   sexual harassment and, 560
   standards of practice, 287
   student expression about, 481
   turnover among, 373
Code of Federal Regulations (C.F.R.), 16
Codes of conduct, 479
Coercion, 171–172
Coercion Test, 460
Collective bargaining, 397–398, 647
   antitrust law and, 629–630
   duty to engage in, 650
   professional athletes and, 652
   Taft-Hartley Act on, 651–653
Collective bargaining agreements (CBA), 397–398, 490, 494, 651–652
Collective marks, 603

College athletes and athletics, 493
   due process and, 428–429
   gender equity in, 532
   state action and, 418–419
   workers' compensation and, 351–353
College conferences, 419
Collegiate Licensing Company (CLC), 607
Colorado Ski Safety Act, 67
Columbine High School shooting, 266
Common carriers, 179, 205
Common law, 3, 76–80
   misappropriation, 615
Communication
   in crisis management, 316
   in crowd management, 335
   issues, 316
Community of interests, 649
Comparative fault, 80, 83
Comparative negligence, 80, 261
Compensation clauses, 375
Compensatory damages, 47–48, 219, 366
Complaint, 9, 10
Comprehensive inspections, 303
Compulsory participation standards, 170
Concurrent jurisdiction, 7
Condemnation of property, 140
Conditions section, insurance, 341
Conduct issues, 479–488
   freedom of expression and, 480–483
   freedom of religion and, 483–484
   fundamental concepts on, 479–480
   non-constitutionally implicated, 484
Conduct of activities, 298
Confidentiality, 396, 446
Conflict management, 397
Conflicts of interest, 240
Consent, 116. *See also* Informed consent
   in assault and battery, 217–218
   for drug testing, 493
   express or implied, 218
   hazing and, 266
Consequential damages, 366
Consideration, 106, 362
   past, 362
Constitutional issues, gender equity and, 522–523
Constitutional law, 16, 403–519
   conduct issues and, 479–488
   defamation and, 227–230
   drug testing and, 490–493
   due process, 426–434
   on eminent domain, 140

equal protection in, 435–445
  Fifth Amendment and, 215
  First Amendment and, 226–229, 236–238, 455–465, 467, 468, 513, 517
  Fourteenth Amendment and, 236, 262–263, 435, 446–448, 467, 468
  Fourth Amendment and, 491–492
  fundamental concepts in, 404–415
  gender equity and, 533–535
  hazing and, 262–263
  on involuntary servitude, 378
  jurisdiction and, 6–7
  on participants with disabilities, 501–510
  on privacy, 236
  private clubs and, 513–519
  researching, 24
  school officials, 262–263
  search and seizure in, 446–453
  standing and, 405–406
  state action and, 416–419
  students, 262
  Thirteenth Amendment and, 378
  voluntary associations and eligibility in, 467–476
Constitutions, 2, 15, 16
  state, 493
Constructive contact, 117
Constructive notice, 132
Consumer Product Safety Commission (CPSC), 286
Consumer welfare standard, 626
Contact sports
  and competitive sports, 66–67
  exception, 64
  gender classifications and, 438
Continuing eligibility, 471
Continuous input, in risk management, 281
Contract law, 359–400
  alternative dispute resolution and, 394–400
  breach of contract, 365–368
  corporate liability and, 55–57
  employment contracts, 373–382
  essentials of, 360–370
  on formation, 361–363
  fundamental concepts in, 360–370
  game, event, and sponsorship contracts, 385–392
  negligence defenses based on, 80–82
  overbooking and, 201
  privity of contract and, 193
  risk transfer and, 278
  special doctrines of, 364
  tortious interference and, 213, 240–241
  waivers and, 106
Contracts
  definition of, 360
  express, 361
  formation of, 361–363
  implied, 361
  Restatement of, 19
  validity of, 361
Contributory fault, 79–80
Contributory negligence, 79–80
Control of activities, 141
Control person, 151
Convention on the Rights of Persons with Disabilities, 585
Co-participants, negligence and, 45
Copyright law, 592–600
  on fair use, 594
  image rights and, 617–618
  Internet and, 596
  on music and performance, 594–595
  owner rights under, 593–594
  on ownership, 594
  protection under, 592–593
  public performance restrictions in, 595
  television and radio and, 595
Corporate entities, 52, 54–55
Corporations, 31–33
  C, 32
  liability and, 52, 55–59
  nonprofit, 32–33
  public, 33
  publicly traded, 32
  S, 32
Corpus Juris Secundum, 19
Counseling, crisis management and, 321
Counterfeit marks, 604
Counteroffers, 362
Course and scope of employment, 180
Court Decisions, 15
Court decisions, as source of law, 16–17
Court of Appeals, 5
Court of Arbitration for Sport (CAS), 398, 399, 490, 495
Court system, 4–7
Covenants not to compete, 363, 377–378
Covenants not to sue, 105, 111
Coverage of athlete participants, 341
Coverages section, insurance, 341–343
CPR. *See* Cardio-pulmonary resuscitation
CPSC. *See* Consumer Product Safety Commission

Crime insurance, 341, 343
Crimes against government, 251–252
Crimes against persons, 248–251
Crimes against public health, safety, and welfare, 251
Crimes, classifications of, 248–252
Criminal hazing, 264–266
Criminal law
   definition of, 213
   hazing and, 258–272
   origins of, 247–248
   sport-related crimes, 247–257
Criminal negligence, 248–249
Criminal trespass, 331
Crisis management, 313–324
   communication in, 316
   debriefing after, 321
   definition of, 314
   media contact person in, 320–321
   news media in, 316, 319–320
   plan activation for, 317–318
   planning for, 314–317
   practicing, 317
   response evaluation, 321
   social media in, 318–319
   terrorism and, 321–322
   websites on, 322
Crisis management plans (CMP), 299, 313–317, 333–335
Crisis response teams, 317
Critical Incident Stress Management (CISM), 321
Crowd management, 299, 327–338
   companies for, 329
   criminal trespass and, 331
   evolution of, 329
   implementation and evaluation, 335
   importance of, 327–328
   NFL fan behavior policies and, 330–331
   operational procedures and, 329
   plans for, 333–335
   searches and, 331–333
   signage and, 335
Crowdsourcing, 319
Cruise line exception, 107
Cruises, 206
CSA. *See* Campus Security Act
CTE. *See* Chronic traumatic encephalopathy
Cuban, Mark, 398
Curt Flood Act, 627
Cyber risk insurance, 341
Cybersquatters, 400, 607, 608

D

Daily inspections, 303
Damage(s), 11, 40, 47
   for assault and battery, 215, 219
   for breach of contract, 366–367
   compensatory, 366
   consequential, 366
   for defamation, 231
   definition of, 40
   liquidated, 366–367, 377
   nominal, 366
   punitive, 45, 48, 219, 366
   sponsorship contracts and, 389
Dangerous activities, participants in, 171
Dedication of land, 140
Defamation, 213, 225–235
   damages for, 231
   defenses to, 230–231
   false light intrusion and, 239
   First Amendment and, 226–229
   and internet, 231
   private figures and, 229
   public figures and, 227–228
   public officials and, 227
   statements of fact *vs.* expressions of opinion, 229–230
   types of, 226
Defects, product, 191–192
Defendants, 8, 216
Defenses against negligence, 75–87
   agreements related to inherent risks, 116–128
   based on common law, 76–80
   based on statutory law, 83–84
   fundamental concepts in, 75–76
   immunity, 88–104
   waivers and releases, 105–115
Definite terms, 361
Descriptive marks, 602
Design defects, 191
Digests, 15, 23
Digital Millennium Copyright Act, 252
Dilution of trademarks, 604
D.I.M. process of risk management, 275–282
   developing risk management plan in, 275–280
   implementing the plan in, 280–281
   managing the plan in, 281–282
Directional signs, 335
Directors and officers liability insurance, 341, 342

Disability, definition of, 582, 585
Disabled participants, 171
    Americans with Disabilities Act and, 501, 516–517, 581–589
    anti-discrimination legislation and, 516
    definition of, 501
    Individuals with Disabilities Education Act and, 503–504
    Rehabilitation Act of 1973 and, 501–503
    Ted Stevens Olympic and Amateur Sports Act and, 504
Disaffirmance, 363
Disclaimers, 106, 110, 606
Disclosure, duty of, 207
Disclosure, in informed consent, 116
Discovery, 9
Discretionary acts, 89
Discretionary/ministerial doctrine, 89
Discrimination, purposeful, 436
Disparaging marks, 606
Disparate impact, 436, 549, 571–572
Disparate treatment, 546–549, 572
Dispute management, 398–400
Disruptive patrons, 334
Distraction exception, 133
District Courts, 4, 17
Diversity of citizenship jurisdiction, 6
Doctrine of laches, 605
Documentation, in risk management, 280
    crisis management, 317
    of ejections, 334
    facility audits, 307
Domain names, Internet, 400, 607, 608
Doping, 399. *See also* Drug testing
    World Anti-Doping Code on, 399, 495
Double jeopardy, 215
Draft, 630
Dreith, Ben, 571
Drivers, negligence and, 180. *See also* Transportation
Drug testing, 490–499
    collective bargaining and, 652
    consent forms for, 493
    constitutional law on, 490–493
    due process and, 493–494
    Fourth Amendment and, 491–492
    governmental interests and, 449
    labor law and, 494
    search and seizure and, 447
    World Anti-Doping Agency and, 490, 494–495

Drug use, 405
    alcohol, 258–259, 334, 405, 484
    college sports, 428–429
    high school sports, 427–428
Due process, 376, 426–434
    drug testing and, 493–494
    eligibility and, 468–469
    liberty interests and, 426–427
    procedural, 426
    property interests, 427–429
    substantive, 426
Duty, 40–42
    to bargain in good faith, 651
    breach of, 40, 43–46
    of care, 129, 178–179, 261
    to disclose, 207
    emergency care and, 149–150
    to engage in collective bargaining, 650
    of fair representation, 650
    to mitigate, 365
    not to increase inherent risks, 76
    for ordinary care, 302
    to provide transportation, 178–182
    shared responsibility statutes and, 99
    sources of, 41–42
    standards of practice and, 286
    to supervise, 165–167
    to warn, 169–170

E

Easements, 141
East Brunswick High School, 461
Economic loss, 47
Economic reality test, 348–349
Edsall, Randy, 377
Education Act of 1972, 559
Educational fair use test, 594
Education Amendments of 1972, 535–536
Education for All Handicapped Children Act of 1975, 503
EEOC. *See* Equal Employment Opportunity Commission
Effective communication network, 335
Ejection of fans, 334
Electronic research, 20
Eleemosynary corporations, 33
Elevated risk, 169
Eligibility
    academic regulations and, 471–472
    amateur status and, 472
    arbitrary and capricious standard in, 468

Eligibility *(Continued)*
  continuing, 471
  equal protection and, 437
  high school privilege and, 469
  home-schooled students, 470
  longevity of, 472
  married students, 404–405
  redshirting, 470–471
  Restitution Rule and, 472–473
  transfer rules, 469–470
Elimination of risk, 277, 278, 304
Emergency action plans, 334
Emergency care, 98–99, 149–164
  AED statutes, 84, 98–99, 152
  certifications/equipment for, 152–154
  crowd management and, 334
  definition of, 149
  duty of, 149–150
  elements of, 150–154
  implementation of procedures, 154
  injury assessment in, 151–152
  personnel for, 151–152
  planning for, 150–151
  for recreation/fitness participants, 155–157
  risk management plans and, 299
  for spectators, 157
  sport and recreation applications, 154–157
  supervision and, 172
  waivers and, 111
Emergency equipment issues, 316
Emergency response plans (ERPs), 150, 299
Eminent domain, 140
Emotional distress, 47
  intentional infliction of, 213, 237, 241–242
  negligent infliction of, 242
Employee benefits, 352, 515–516
Employee benefits liability insurance, 342
Employee's perception test, 557
Employees/service personnel, 53. *See also* Gender discrimination; Labor law
  age discrimination and, 569–578
  Americans with Disabilities Act on, 504–506, 581–589
  at-will, 376
  categories of, liability and, 52–54
  in crisis management, 315
  in crowd management, 333–334
  discrimination laws, 533
  game and event contract, 396
  gender equity and, 533–541
  independent contractors, 56
  orientation for, 334
  rights of, 649–650
  in risk management, 275, 276, 281
  screening, 333
  Title VII on, 543–544
  workers' compensation eligibility and, 348–349
Employee vehicles, 181–182
Employment contracts, 373–382
  arbitration agreements, 395–396
  bonuses and incentives, 375
  buyout provisions, 377
  compensation clauses, 375
  covenants not to compete, 377–378
  discussion of issues in, 378–379
  duties and responsibilities, 374
  elements of, 373–380
  fringe benefits in, 375
  fundamental concepts in, 373–382
  game and event, 396
  independent contractors *vs.* employees, 379–380
  provisions for outside/supplemental income, 375
  reassignment clauses, 374
  sovereign immunity, 375
  termination clauses, 375–377
  term of employment in, 374
Employment practices liability insurance, 341
Endorsement contracts, 390, 613
Endorsements, 341
Endorsement Test, 460
Entanglement theory, 417
Equal Employment Opportunity Commission (EEOC), 514, 533, 544, 556
  age discrimination and, 569, 571
  Americans with Disabilities and, 584, 585
Equal Pay Act of 1963, 533–534
Equal protection, 435–445
  eligibility and, 468–469
  freedom of expression and, 483
  gender equity and, 522–523
  purposeful discrimination and, 436
  standards of review for, 436–440
  state actors and, 435–436
Equine liability statutes, 100
Equipment insurance, 341
Equipment rental agreements, 81
Equipment, safe environment and, 170
Equitable relief, 220
Equitable remedies, 367–368
ERPs. *See* Emergency Response Plans
Establishment Clause, 460
EUBC. *See* European Boxing Confederation

European Boxing Confederation (EUBC), 399
Evacuation, 330
Event insurance policies, 343
Exclusions section, insurance, 340–341
Exclusive rights, 389
Exclusivity clauses, 389
Exculpatory agreements, 105
Executive branch, 3, 5
Exemplary damages, 45, 48, 219
Exemption, antitrust, 627, 630
Expectation interest theory, 366
Express assumption of risk, 76
Express contracts, 361
Express/implied consent, 218–219, 266
Expressions
   freedom of, 405, 480–483
   of opinion, 229–230
Expressive association, 513–514
Express warranties, 194, 286
Extracurricular activities, 436–437, 469

F

Facilities, leasing, 56, 81, 388
Facility audit, 296, 299, 302–308
   checklists for, 304–306
   documentation of, 307
   inspections in, 303–306
   risk treatment in, 304, 306–307
Factor analysis approach, 515, 516
Facts, copyright of, 593
Failure to supervise, 47
Fairbanks, Chuck, 378
Fair comment, 230
Fair Labor Standards Act of 1938 (FLSA), 533, 647–649
Fair representation, duty of, 650
Fair use, 594, 605–606, 617
False advertising, 604–605
False endorsement claims, 616–617
False light invasion of privacy, 239
Falwell's declaration further states, 10
Family Educational Rights and Privacy Act, 446
Fan Code of Conduct, 330–331
Fan ejections, 334
Fan movement, 330
Fantasy sport, 437
Federal Arbitration Act, 395, 396
Federal Copyright Act, 617–618
Federal court system, 4, 5, 7, 17
Federal Educational Rights and Privacy Act (FERPA), 266

Federal Emergency Management Agency (FEMA), 322, 329
Federal funding, 523, 535
Federal Motor Carrier Safety Administration, 179
Federal question jurisdiction, 6
Federal Reporter, 17
Federal Supplement, 17
Federal Supplement Second Series, 17
Federal Tort Claims Acts, 84, 88–89
Federal Trademark Act of 1946, 602–605, 616–617
Federal Trademark Dilution Act, 604
Federation Internationale de Football Association (FIFA), 399
Fees
   recreational user statutes and, 143
   simple absolute, 139
   sponsorship, 389
FEMA. *See* Federal Emergency Management Agency
FERPA. *See* Federal Educational Rights and Privacy Act
Fey, Barry, 329
Fiduciaries, definition of, 239
Fiduciary duty, breach of, 213, 239–240
FIFA. *See* Federation Internationale de Football Association
Financial advisors, 666
Financial sponsorship, 57–58
FindLaw, 20, 21, 23
Fine, Bernie, 249
Fire insurance, 343
First Aid Statutes, 97–98
First Amendment, 455–465
   defamation and, 226–229
   freedom of association and, 513–514
   freedom of expression and, 482
   freedom of religion and, 459–461
   freedom of speech and, 226–229, 236–239, 455–458
   freedom of the press, 226–229, 236–239, 458–459
   Free Exercise clause, 460–461
   hazing and, 262
   image rights defenses and, 618–619
   private clubs and, 513, 517
Fishing, 102
Fitness challenges, 157
Florida state law, 261
Florida State University, 219
FLSA. *See* Fair Labor Standards Act of 1938
Follow-up procedures, 317

Foreseeability, 42, 46, 131–132
   crowd management and, 327–328
   reasonably foreseeable test, 250
   supervision and, 166–167
Foreseeable uses, anticipating, 135
Forum non conveniens, 204
Forum selection clauses, 204–205
Fourteenth Amendment, 236, 262–263
   eligibility and, 467, 468
   equal protection and, 435, 468
   gender discrimination and, 523
   search and seizure and, 446–448
Fourth Amendment, drug testing and, 491–492
Fraud, 663
   breach of contract and, 365
   statute of, 364
Free agency, 630
Freedom of association, 513–514
Freedom of expression, 405, 480–483
Freedom of Information Act, 446
Freedom of religion, 459–461, 483–484
Freedom of speech, 455–458
   defamation and, 226–229
   freedom of expression and, 480–481
   standard of review for, 456–458
Freedom of the press, 458–459
   defamation and, 226–229
   invasion of privacy and, 236–239
Free Exercise clause, 460–461
Fresno State University, 536
Fringe benefits, 375
Fundamental rights deprivation, 438–439

G

Gambling, 252, 629
Game data, ownership of, 618
Game, event, and sponsorship contracts, 385–392
   game and event, 386–389
   sponsorship, 388–390
Gender discrimination, 438, 517
   benchmarks for, 525
   in coaching and administration, 532–541
   federal legislation against, 522–531
   levels of scrutiny in, 522–523
   sexual harassment and, 526
   Title IX and, 23, 24, 438, 523–526
Gender equity, 532–541
   constitutional law on, 533–535
   Equal Pay Act on, 533–534
   Lilly Ledbetter Fair Pay Act and, 536
   Pregnancy Discrimination Act and, 536
   retaliation and, 535–540
   Title IX on, 535–536
   Title VII on, 534–535
General damages, 231
General liability insurance, 341
General recreation and sport immunity statutes, 102
General supervision, 167
Gifts
   contracts and, 362
   of property, 140
Gilpin, Max, 250
Giveaways, 328
Glass Ceiling Commission, 544
Glass Ceiling Initiative, 544
Globalization of sport, 400
Golf, 157, 513–515
Golfing Gizmo, 194
Good faith, 96, 97
   duty to bargain in, 651
Good Samaritan statutes, 45, 84, 97–98, 150
Google, 20, 21
Governing organizations, 58
Governmental functions, 89
Governmental immunity, 53, 80, 88
Governmental interest, 449
Governmental/proprietary doctrine, 89
Government, crimes against, 251–252
Government research sources, 21–22
GPA. *See* Grade point average
Grade point average (GPA), 471
Graham, Bill, 329
Grooming, freedom of expression and, 483
Gross negligence, 44
Group waivers, 110
Guarantee games, 387
Guidelines, 288

H

Halcomb Lewis, Darryll, 379
Hang gliding, 102
Harassment
   racial, 545, 556–567
   sexual, 526, 545, 546, 548
Hazardous recreational activity immunity statutes, 102
Hazards
   obvious and hidden, 134
   removing/warning of, 134–135
Hazing, 213, 258–272
   anti-hazing laws and, 264–265
   bullying laws and, 266

definition of, 249, 260
penalties for, 267
policies on, 298
rights and, 262-263
sex crimes and, 263-264
Head injuries, 150-151, 191-192
Health clubs, emergency care in, 156-157
Highly offensive facts, 238, 239
High school athletic associations, 418, 532-541
High school privilege, 469
Hired vehicles, 342
Hiring procedures, discriminatory, 548
Hockey, 102
Hockey North America, 240
Hold harmless agreements, 57, 278
Holyfield, Evander, 216
Home-schooled students, eligibility of, 470
Home-use exemption, 595
Homicide, 248-249
Hospitality and tourism law, 200-212
  agency law, 206-208
  fundamentals of, 200-201
  guest privacy and, 202-203
  jurisdiction in, 203-205
  overbooking and, 201
  protection of guest property, 201-202
  recreational facilities and, 203
  transportation and, 205-206
Hostile environment, 557
Human growth hormones, 652
Human resources law, 54
Human subject research, 116-117

I

IAVM. *See* International Association of Venue Managers
ICANN. *See* Internet Corporation for Assigned Names and Numbers
ICAS. *See* International Council of Arbitration for Sport
IDEA. *See* Individuals with Disabilities Education Act
IDEIA. *See* Individuals with Disabilities Education Improvement Act
Identification stage, risk management, 275-276
IEPs. *See* Individual Education Plans
IHAA. *See* Indiana High School Athletic Association
IHRSA Club Membership Standards, 287
Illegal per se activities, 626
ILP. *See Index to Legal Periodicals*
Image rights, 613-623
  common law misappropriation of, 615
  Federal Copyright Act and, 617-618
  Federal Trademark Act and, 616-617
  First Amendment defenses and, 618-619
  incidental use exception and, 618-619
  intellectual property provisions and, 616-619
  newsworthiness and, 618
  parody defense and, 619
  right of privacy and, 613-614
  right of publicity and, 613-616
  statutory protections of, 615-616
  transformative use defense, 619
Immunity, 88-104
  assault and battery and, 219
  charitable, 84, 89-90
  definition of, 88
  hazing and, 261-262
  legislation-based, 84
  negligence and, 45
  recreational user statutes and, 90
  sovereign/governmental, 53, 80, 88
  for sports instructors and officials, 69
  statutes, 69, 170
  transportation and, 181
  volunteer, 69, 90-97
Implied assumption of risk, 76
Implied consent, 218, 266
Implied contracts, 361
Implied warranty of fitness, 194
Implied warranty of merchantability, 194
Incentives, 375
Incidental use exception, 618-619
In-connection standard, 251
Indemnification agreements, 81-82
  corporate liability and, 57
Indemnification clauses, 278
Independent contractors, 56-57
  employment contracts and, 379-380
  insurance and, 344
  IRS checklist on, 379-380
  risk transfer and, 278
  for transportation, 179-180
  workers' compensation and, 349
Independent contracts for services, 82
Index to Legal Periodicals (ILP), 19
Indiana High School Athletic Association (IHAA), 468
Individual disparate treatment, 546-548
Individual Education Plans (IEPs), 503-504
Individual sports, 65-66
Individuals with Disabilities Education Act (IDEA), 503-504

Individuals with Disabilities Education Improvement Act (IDEIA), 503–504
Inference, 547
Informal recreational activities, 65–66
Informational signs, 335
Informed consent agreements, 80, 105, 116–120
    content of, 117
    definition of, 116
    documentation of, 120
    in human subject research, 116–117
    in medicine, 116
    minors and, 120
    in sport and fitness, 117–120
Infra hospitium doctrine, 201
Inherently dangerous activity exception, 279
Inherent relationships, 41, 149
Inherent risks, 43, 65–66, 75
    agreements related to, 116–128
    assumption of risk, 80, 124–125
    duty to warn of, 169–170
    informed consent agreements, 80, 105, 116–120
    skating statutes and, 101
Injunctions, 220, 367
    constitutional law and, 406–409
    judicial review of, 408–409
    permanent, 407–408
    preliminary, 406–407
Injunctive relief, 406–409
In loco parentis doctrine, 261, 449
In-service education program, 281
Inspections
    comprehensive, 303
    daily, 303–306
    in facility audits, 303–304
    obvious and hidden hazards and, 134
    periodic, 303–304
    risk reduction and, 280
Institute for Diversity and Ethics in Sport, 532
Institutional liability, 559
Instruction, proper, 169
Instructors, sports, negligence and, 67–70
Insurance, 278, 340–345
    accident, 341
    assault and battery and, 219
    automobile, 342
    business auto, 341
    crime, 341
    cyber risk, 341
    definition, 340
    employee benefits liability, 342
    employment practices liability, 341
    endorsements, 341
    equipment, 341
    general liability, 341
    key person, 341
    media coverage, 343
    motor vehicle, 342
    NCAA catastrophic injury, 352–353
    non-owned automobile, 342
    pollution liability, 341
    professional/malpractice, 342
    property, 341
    requiring of other parties, 343–344
    risk management plans and, 300
    selecting agents and carriers, 344–345
    sports insurance policies, 341
    umbrella liability, 341–342
    understanding policies, 340–341
    weather, 343
    worker's compensation, 343
Integration clauses, 111
Intellectual property law, 591–623
    copyright and patent, 592–600
    image rights, 613–623
    trademark law, 602–611
Intellectual property rights, 400
    alternative dispute resolution, 400
Intent, in assault and battery, 217
Intentional infliction of emotional distress, 213, 236, 241–242
Intentional torts, 54, 213–270
    assault and battery, 214–224
    breach of fiduciary duty, 213, 239–240
    defamation, 225–235
    defenses to, 218–219
    definition of, 213
    intentional infliction of emotional distress, 236, 241–242
    invasion of privacy, 236–239
    remedies for, 219–220
    tortious interference with contract, 213, 236, 240–241
    vicarious liability for, 220
Interactive websites, 204
Intermediate scrutiny, 435, 437–438
Internal Revenue Service, 379
International Association of Venue Managers (IAVM), 322
International Boxing Association, 399
International Council of Arbitration for Sport (ICAS), 398
International Health, Racquet & Sportsclub Association, 287

International Olympic Committee, 607
Internet
　copyright infringement and, 596
　crisis management resources, 321
　cybersquatters, 400, 607–608
　domain name trademarking, 400, 607
　freedom of expression and, 482
　legal research on, 20–21
　travel sales via, 204
Internet Corporation for Assigned Names and Numbers (ICANN), 608
Internet Reference Desk, 21
Interns, liability and, 55
Intervening act/intervening cause, 47
Intimate association, 514
Intoxicated patrons, 334
Invasion of privacy, 213, 236–239
　appropriation, 237–238
　false light intrusion, 239
　unreasonable disclosure of private facts, 238–239
　unreasonable intrusion on seclusion, 236
Involuntary servitude, 378
Iowa Libel Research Project, 229

J

Job Accommodation Network, 582, 584
John Jay High School, 214
Johnson-Klein, Stacy, 536
Joint and several liability doctrine, 55
Joint programming, 58
Joint ventures, 58
Jones, Marion, 399
Jordan, Michael, 365
Journal of Legal Aspects of Sport, 19
Journals, 19
Judgment proof, 220
Judicial branch, 3
Judicial review, 404–406, 467–471
Jumping, 469
Jurisdiction, 6–8, 106, 111
　in sponsorship contracts, 399–400
　in travel and tourism, 203–205
　in workers' compensation, 350
"Just cause" clauses, 376

K

Kennedy High School, 259
Key person insurance, 341
Knowledge of risk, 79

L

Labor disputes, 397–398
Labor exemption, antitrust law, 630

Labor law. *See also* Employment contracts
　antitrust law and, 629–630
　drug testing and, 494
　Fair Labor Standards Act, 647–649
　National Labor Relations Act, 3, 649–651, 664
　professional sport applications, 647–657
　Taft-Hartley Act, 651–653
Labor unions, 629–630
Laches, 605
Landowner-invitee theory, 261
Landowners, recreational use statutes and, 143, 144
Land use controls, 141–142
Lanham Act, 602–605, 616–617
Lausanne Declaration on Doping in Sport, 495
Law
　application of, 24
　case, 3
　common, 3
　definition of, 2
　identifying relevant, 24
　origins of, 2
　restatement of, 19
　sources of, 15
Law enforcement, 329
Law Journal EXTRA! Federal Courts, 21
Law Library Resource Xchange, 21
Law reviews, 19
Lawyer directories, 19
Layers of protection, 297
Leach, Mike, 249
Lease agreements, 388–389
Leasing facilities, 56, 81
Lectric Law Lexicon, 21
Legal audits, 296, 300–302
Legal authority, 29–33
Legal dictionaries, 19
Legal encyclopedias, 19
Legal indexes, 19
Legality of contracts, 363
Legal process, 7–13
Legal research, 15–27
　electronic and Web-based, 21–22
　resources for, 15–24
　summarizing cases and, 24–27
　techniques for, 23–24
Legal system, 2–13
　court system, 4–7
　law, origins of, 2–3
　legal process, 7–13
Legislation-based immunity, 84

Legislation, sport and, 521–669
    Age Discrimination in Employment Act, 569–578
    antitrust law, 626–645
    federal statutes and discrimination, 522–531
    gender equity in coaching and administration, 532–541
    labor law, 647–657
    sexual harassment, 556–567
    sport agent, 660–668
    Title VII, 515–516, 534–535, 543–546
Legislative branch, 2–3
Legitimate, nondiscriminatory reason, 547
Legitimate privacy expectation, 491
Lemon Test, 460
Lewd and indecent speech, 457
LEXIS, 20
LexisNexis Academic Universe, 20, 23
LHSAA. *See* Louisiana High School Athletic Association
Liability, 11, 12. *See also* Risk management
    business structure and, 31
    joint and several, 55
    limiting by contract, 56
    for negligence, 52–55
    premises, 129–138
    products, 190–199
    protecting employees, 342
    of sports participants, instructors, and officials, 63–70
    vicarious, 45, 54, 220
    waivers, 45, 105–115
Libel, 226
Liberty interests, 426–427
Licenses, 130, 606–607
Life coverage of participants, 343
Likelihood of occurrence, 249–250
    athletes participants, 249
    coaches, 249–250
    recreation participants, 249
Lilly Ledbetter Fair Pay Act of 2009, 536
Limited duty rule, 133–134, 242
Limited liability, 182
    statutes, 53
Limited liability companies (LLCs), 31
Limited liability partnership (LLP), 30
Limited partnerships, 30
Limited purpose public person, 228–229
Liquidated damages, 366–367, 377, 389
Litigious society, 2
LLCs. *See* Limited liability companies
LLP. *See* Limited liability partnership

Longevity, rules of, 472
Loss of consortium, 82
Louisiana High School Athletic Association (LHSAA), 467
Lystedt laws, 151

M

"Mailbox rule," 362
Maine Human Rights Act, 262
Maintenance programs, 280
Major League Baseball (MLB), 397, 494, 618–619, 648, 665
Major League Baseball Players Association (MLBPA), 619
Major League Soccer (MLS), 8, 628
Malice, actual, 225, 227–229
Malpractice insurance, 342
Managing the plan, 281
Mandatory arbitration, 396
Manuals, staff, 172
Manufacturing defects, 191
Maritime laws, 206. *See also* Admiralty law
Marketing, ambush, 390, 608
Marketing defects, 191–192
Married students, 404–405
Materazzi, Marco, 216
Media
    contact person for, 316, 320–321
    insurance coverage, 343
    news, 316, 319–320
    rights contracts, 388
    sponsorship and, 389
Mediation, 11, 109–110, 394, 397
Mediators, 397
Medicine, informed consent and, 116
Mens rea, 247–248
Mepham High School, 263–264
Mere rationality test, 435, 436
MHSAA. *See* Mississippi High School Athletic Association
Milutinovich, Diane, 536
Ministerial acts, 89
Minors
    capacity of to contract, 363
    informed consent and, 120
    supervising, 171
    waivers and, 107–110
Mismatching participants, 171–172, 298
Misrepresentation of warranty, 194
Mississippi High School Athletic Association (MHSAA), 259

Mitigate, duty to, 365
MLB. *See* Major League Baseball
MLBPA. *See* Major League Baseball Players Association
MLS. *See* Major League Soccer
Model Act, 142
Model Code of Professional Responsibility, 665
Model Penal Code, 248–250
Model State Act, 90, 96
Modified comparative fault, 83
Monopoly power, 637
Motions, 9
    to dismiss, 9
    to intervene, 405
    for judgment on the pleadings, 9
    for summary judgment, 9
Motor vehicle exception, 96
Motor vehicle insurance, 342
Municipal sports commission, 387
Music and performance, copyright and, 594–595
Mutual assent, 361
Mutual benefit corporations, 33
Mutual mistakes, 365

N

NAGAAA. *See* North American Gay Amateur Athletic Alliance
NAIA. *See* National Association of Intercollegiate Athletics
Napster, 596
National Association for Sport and Physical Education, 287
National Association of Intercollegiate Athletics (NAIA), 418
National Basketball Players Association, 650
National Center for State Courts, 21
National Collegiate Athletic Association (NCAA), 259, 467–469
    academic regulations, 471
    age rule, 472
    amateur status, 472
    antitrust law and, 638–640
    drug testing programs, 493
    gender equity and, 532
    image rights, 619
    Restitution Rule, 472–473
    search and seizure and, 447
    sport agents and, 663–664
    state action and, 418–419
    trademarks, 607
    transfer rules, 472

National Conference of Commissioners on Uniform State Laws (NCCUSL), 661
National Conference of State Legislatures, 182
National Federation of High Schools, 467
National Football League (NFL)
    age discrimination and, 570, 574
    behavior policies, 330–331
    collective bargaining agreements, 362, 397
    financial advisors and, 666
    sponsors of, 390
    sport agents and, 664, 665
    Standard Player contract, 397
National Highway Traffic Safety Administration (NHTSA), 183
National Intramural-Recreational Sports Association (NIRSA), 150, 151
National Junior College Athletic Association (NJCAA), 418
National Labor Relations Act (NLRA), 3, 649–651, 664
National Labor Relations Board (NLRB), 3, 649, 650
National origin, discrimination and, 545
National Parks and Recreation Association, 467
"National Special Security Events" (NSSE), 329
National Sports Law Institute of Marquette University Law School, 603
National Transportation Safety Board (NTSB), 180
Nature and immediacy of governmental concern, 492
NCAA. *See* National Collegiate Athletic Association
NCAA Catastrophic Injury Insurance Program, 352–353
NCCUSL. *See* National Conference of Commissioners on Uniform State Laws
Negative easements, 141
Negligence, 11, 40–212
    aggravated, 44
    assault and battery and, 216
    defenses against, 75–87
    definition of, 40
    fundamental concepts in, 40–48
    hazing and, 261
    hospitality and tourism law, 200–212
    liability and, 52–55
    medical, 116
    ordinary, risks arising from, 44
    per se, 42
    product liability and, 190–199
    risk management and, 275
    sport agents and, 663

Negligence *(Continued)*
  standard of care, 63–64, 66–67
  standards of practice and, 286
  supervision and, 165–177
  theory of, 40–48
  transportation and, 178–189
Negligence standard, 63–64, 69–70
Negligent conduct, 217
Negligent infliction of emotional distress (NIED), 242
Negotiation, 394, 396
Nelson, Don, 398
Neuheisel, Rick, 376
Neutral mediators, 397
Neutral reportage, 231
News media, 319–320
  communication with, 316
Newsworthiness doctrine, 618
Newton, Cam, 664
Nexus theory, 417
NFL. *See* National Football League
NHTSA. *See* National Highway Traffic Safety Administration
NIED. *See* Negligent infliction of emotional distress
NIRSA. *See* National Intramural-Recreational Sports Association
NJCAA. *See* National Junior College Athletic Association
NLRA. *See* National Labor Relations Act
NLRB. *See* National Labor Relations Board
Nominal damages, 366
Nonappearance insurance, 343
Nonbinding arbitration, 396
Non-compete clauses, 363
Noncompetitive recreational activities, 66–67
Non-contact recreational activities, 66–67
Non-contact sports, 65–66
Non-owned automobile endorsement, 342
Nonprofit corporations, 32–33
Nonprofit Risk Management Center, 322
Nonscholarship athletes, 352
Norris-La Guardia Act, 629
North American Gay Amateur Athletic Alliance (NAGAAA), 517
Notes of appreciation, 321
Notice of appeal, 11
Notice of claim, 84
NSSE. *See* "National Special Security Events"
NTSB. *See* National Transportation Safety Board
Nuisance law, 144–145

O

Objective test, 557
Obligations, 40, 143. *See also* Duty
Obscenity, 404
Observation, in risk management, 276
Occupational Safety and Health Administration (OSHA), 328
OCR. *See* Office for Civil Rights
Off-duty law enforcement, 329
Offers, in contract law, 361–362
Office for Civil Rights (OCR), 535, 559
Officials, sports, negligence and, 67–70
Ohio State University (OSU), 376
Oklahoma State University, 180
Older Workers Benefit Protection Act (OWBPA), 575
Olympic and Amateur Sports Act, 16
Olympic Games, 398, 399
  arbitration and, 400
  drug testing and, 494–495
  state action and, 419
  Ted Stevens Olympic and Amateur Sports Act and, 504
  trademarks, 607
Omnibus legislation, 102
"Open and obvious" dangers, 132–133
Opinion, expressions of, 229–230
Ordinances, 2
Ordinary negligence, 44
Organization for Economic Cooperation and Development, 602
Orientation program, 334
Osborne, Tom, 662
OSHA. *See* Occupational Safety and Health Administration
OSU. *See* Ohio State University
Outfitter and guide statutes, 101
Outside income provisions, 375
Outsourcing, 329
Overbooking, 201
Over inclusive classifications, 439–440
OWBPA. *See* Older Workers Benefit Protection Act

P

Paddle sports, 102
Pain and suffering, 47
Panel, 394
Paralympic athletes, 504, 581
Parcells, Bill, 379
Parental arbitration agreements, 109–110
Parental indemnity agreements, 109–110

Parental permission forms, 105
Parental waivers, 108–109
Parody
   image rights and, 619
   of trademarks, 605–606
Parol evidence rule, 364
Participant agreements, 110–111, 298
Participants. *See also* Gender discrimination
   coercion/threats against, 171–172
   criminal conduct by, 249
   with disabilities, 501–510
   evaluating physical and mental condition of, 170–172
   liability of, 64–67
   negligence and, 44–45, 66–67
   recklessness standard and, 68–69
   voluntary associations and eligibility of, 467
Parties to lawsuits, 8
Partnerships, 30–31
Passive websites, 204
Past consideration, 362
Patent law, 592–600
Pay equity, 533
Pearl, Bruce, 375
Peer-group security, 334
Peer sexual harassment, 560
Pennsylvania Interscholastic Athletic Association (PIAA) Attendance Rule, 470
Pennsylvania State University, 249
Periodic inspections, 303–304
Permanent injunctions, 407–408
Permissive subject, 650, 651
Per se rule, 638
Personal jurisdiction, 6
Personnel preparation, 316
Persuasive precedent, 3
Phelps, Carl, 157
Physical impairments, 47
Physical Security Measures, 329
PIAA Attendance Rule. *See* Pennsylvania Interscholastic Athletic Association Attendance Rule
PIPA. *See* Protect IP Act
Places of public accommodation, 514–515
Plaintiffs, 8, 9, 216
Planning
   for emergency care, 150–151
   legal research, 23–24
   in supervision, 168–169
Players' associations, 652, 664–665
Player statistics, ownership of, 618

Point shaving, 251
Policies and procedures, risk management and, 276, 290
   legal audits of, 300–302
   personnel, 297–298
   sexual harassment and, 558
Pollution liability insurance, 341
Post-concussive syndrome, 192
Precedent, 3
Pregnancy Discrimination Act of 1978, 536
Preliminary injunctions, 406–407
Premise-related injuries, 81
Premises liability, 129–138
   defect categories, 191–192
   duty of care and, 129–131
   emergency care and, 150
   factors affecting, 131–134
   legal obligations of facility managers and, 134–136
   reasonable care standard and, 131
Preponderance of the evidence, 215n3
Pretext for discrimination, 547, 574
Prima facie case, 547
Primary assumption of risk, 43, 76–79
Primary legal resources, 15–17
Principal–agent relationships, 181, 206–207
Principals, 206
Privacy
   crowd management searches and, 332
   definition of, 236
   drug testing and, 491–492
   of hotel guests, 202–203
   image rights and, 613–614
   invasion of, 213, 236–239
   legitimate expectation of, 491
   right of, 236
   search and seizure and, 446–453
Private carriers, 179
Private clubs, 513–519
   anti-discrimination legislation and, 514–517
   freedom of association, 513–514
Private figures, 229
Private nuisance, 144
Private *vs.* public facts, 238–239
Privilege, 219, 230, 469
Privity of contract, 193
Prize indemnity, 343
Probable cause, 492
Probable consequences rule, 47
Procedural due process, 426
Procedural noncompliance, 84

Products liability, 190–199
  causes of action and defenses in, 192–195
  definition of, 190
  warranty considerations and, 193–195
Professional associations, 543
Professional athletes
  labor law and, 652
  workers' compensation and, 350–351
Professional insurance, 342
Professional organizations, 286
Professional service contracts, 389
Professional sport teams and leagues, 157
  antitrust law and, 626–635
  sport agents and, 664–665
  state action and, 419
  trademarks, 606–607
Professionals, risk management, 275
Program sponsorship, 58
Promissory estoppel, 364
Proper instruction, 169
Property damage coverage, 343
Property exposures, 276
Property insurance, 341
Property interests, due process and, 427–429
Property law, 139–148
  nuisance, 144–145
  real property concept and, 139–142
  recreational user statutes, 142–144
Property, protection of guest, 201–202
Proportionality, 525–526
Proprietary functions, 89
Protected parties, 96
Protect IP Act (PIPA), 596
Proximate cause, 40, 46–47, 166
Public accommodation, places of, 505–506, 514–515
Public figures, 227–228
  invasion of privacy and, 238
  limited-purpose, 227–228
Public function theory, 416
Public health, safety, and welfare, crimes against, 251
Public invitee, 129
Publicity, right of, 238, 613–616
Public liability, 275
Publicly traded corporations, 32
Public nuisances, 144
Public officials, 227
Public performance restrictions, 595
Public policy, 105–106
Public trust doctrine, 141

Punitive damages, 45, 48, 219, 341, 366
Purchases of property, 139
Pure comparative fault, 83
Purposeful discrimination, 436
Pyle, Charles "Cash & Carry," 660

Q

Qualified individual with a disability, 582
Qualified privilege, 230
Questionnaires, risk management, 275
"Quick look" rule of reason, 638
Quid pro quo sexual harassment, 556

R

Race norming, 544
Racial discrimination, 439
Racial harassment, 545
Radio broadcasting, copyright and, 595
Rape, 560
Rapid eye examination (REE), 448
Rational basis review, 436–437
Real property, 139–142
  land use controls and, 141–142
  modes of acquisition of, 139–141
  rights of, 139
Reasonable accommodations, 503, 504, 546, 582–584
Reasonable care standard, 46, 131, 558
  defamation and, 229
  premises liability and, 135–136
Reasonable foreseeability, 166
Reasonable person test, 557
Reasonable precautions to protect from foreseeable dangers, 135
Reasonable suspicion, 447–448
Reasonably foreseeable defense, 250
Reason, rule of, 626, 638
Reassignment clauses, 374
Reckless conduct, 217
Reckless endangerment, 248–249
Reckless misconduct, 44
Recklessness, 248–249
Recklessness standard, 64–66, 68–69
  intentional infliction of emotional distress and, 241–242
Recommendations for Cardiovascular Screening, Staffing, and Emergency Policies at Health/Fitness Facilities, 287
Recovery, provisions precluding, 100
Recreational activities, non-competitive, noncontact, 66–67

Recreational users, 130–131
    immunity, 84
    statutes, 90, 131, 142–144
        analysis of applicability of, 143–144
        duty to supervise and, 165–167
Recreation and sport management
    crisis management, 299, 313–324
    crowd management, 327–338
    duty of care in, 129–131
    emergency care, 149–164
    facility audits, 302–308
    insurance in, 340–341
    legal audits, 300–302
    legal obligations of facility managers, 134–136
    premises liability and, 129–138
    products liability and, 190–199
    property law and, 139–148
    risk management and, 274–353
    standards of practice, 286–291
    state action and, 417–419
    supervision and, 165–167
    transportation and, 178–189
    workers' compensation, 348–353
Recreation and sport volunteer immunity statutes, 96
Recurring incident theory, 132
Redshirting, 470–471
Reduction of risks, 279, 304
REE. *See* Rapid eye examination
Regional reporters, 18
Regulations, 3, 15, 16
Rehabilitation Act of 1973, 376, 501–503
Releases, 105. *See also* Waivers
Religion, discrimination based on, 546
Religion, freedom of, 483–484
Remand, 12
Remuneration, 97
Rental agreements, 81, 388
Repair, keeping premises in safe, 134
Rescission, 367–368
Research, legal, 15–27
    electronic and Web-based, 21–22
    resources for, 15–23
    techniques for, 23–24
Research tools, 15
Residency classifications, 436
Respondeat superior, 45, 52, 54, 55
    assault and battery and, 220
    charitable immunity and, 89
    corporations and, 54–55
Restatement of Contracts, 19, 360

Restatement of law, 19
Restitution, 367–368
Restitution Rule, 472–473
Restorative justice (RJ), 397
Restraining orders, 220, 406
Restricted earnings coaches, 640
Restrictive covenants. *See* Non-compete clauses
Retaliation
    gender discrimination and, 535–540, 549–554
    for union activity, 650–651
Retention of risks, 279
Reversed decisions, 12
Reversed in part, 12
Reverse discrimination, 545
Revised Sexual Harassment Guidance, 559
Revised Uniform Arbitration Act, 395, 396
Ridge High School, 250
Right of publicity, 238
Right to discharge, 380
Right to privacy, 236, 237
    drug testing and, 491–492
    search and seizure and, 446–453
Right to terminate, 380
Risk
    allocation of, 77–78
    avoidance/elimination of, 277, 278
    categorization of, 275
    category matrix, 276
    classification of, 276
    in crisis management, 315
    elimination, 304
    express assumption of, 79
    identification of, 275–276
    implied primary assumption of, 79
    primary assumption of, 76–79
    reduction, 279, 304
    retention of, 279
    secondary assumption of, 79–80
    shared responsibility and statutory assumption of, 99–102
    supervisor warnings of, 169–170
    transfer of, 278
    treatment matrix, 277
    treatment of, 277–280, 302, 304, 306–307
    types of, 43–46, 76
Risk management, 274–353
    audits in, 296–310
    classification stage in, 276–277
    decision-making process for, 289–290
    definition of, 274
    D.I.M process in, 275–282

Risk management *(Continued)*
   evaluation of, 290
   identification stage in, 275–276
   insurance coverage in, 278
   insurance in, 300, 340–345
   standards of practice in, 286–291
   theory of, 273
Risk Management Manual, 150
Risk management plans, 296–302
   conduct of activities in, 298
   developing, 275–280
   D.I.M. process for, 275–282
   implementing, 280–281
   managing, 281–282
   organization description in, 297
   personnel in, 297–298
Risk managers, 281
Risk-utility balancing test, 192
RJ. *See* Restorative justice
Road races, 157
Roadworthiness of vehicles, 181
Rodeo, 102
Rollover provisions, 374
Rozelle Rule, 630
Rule of reason, 626, 638
Rules of longevity, 470
Rules of the game defense, 250

S

Saban, Nick, 376
Safe, Accountable, Flexible, Efficient Transportation Equity Act: A Legacy for Users, 183
Safe environment, 170
Safe facilities, 170
Safe harbor, 525
Safe repair, 134
Safety equipment, 170, 190
Safety in Student Transportation: A Resource Guide for Colleges and Universities, 180
Salary caps, 630
Sandusky, Jerry, 276
Save harmless agreements, 57
Scalping, 252
Schalley, Jeffrey, 400
School-based sports, emergency care and, 154
School buses, 181, 183–184
School coaches, 96
Schultz, Jeff, 374
S corporations, 32
Screeners/searchers, 333
Search and seizure, 446–453
   crowd management and, 331–333
   drug testing and, 490–492
   Fourth Amendment and, 446–448
   government interest and, 449
   privacy and, 448
Search engines, 20
SEC. *See* Security and Exchange Commission
Secondary assumption of risk, 79–80
Secondary meaning, 602
Secondary resources, 18–20
Secondary sources, 15, 21, 23
Security and Exchange Commission (SEC), 32
Security control, 299
Security, in crowd management, 329, 334
Self-insurance of risks, 279
Service marks, 603
Service personnel, 53
Settlement, 11
Severability, 110
Sex abuse/molestation claims, 341
Sex crimes, 263–264
Sexual harassment, 526, 545, 546, 548, 556–567
   behaviors in, 556
   in schools, 559–561
   state legislation on, 558
   totality of the circumstances in, 557–558
   in the workplace, 556–558
Sexual orientation, discrimination and, 517, 546
Sexual violence, 561
Shared responsibility statutes, 84, 99–102
Shepard's Citations, 19, 23–24
Sherman Antitrust Act, 626, 637–638
Shifting tests, 439
Signage, 335, 389
Simpson, O.J., 215
Single-entity status, 627–628
Skateboard parks, 101
Skating rinks, 157, 166
Skating statutes, 101
Skin color, discrimination and, 545
Ski operator immunity statutes, 100–101
Slander, 226
Smith de Bruin, Michelle, 494
Snowmobile statutes, 101
Social media, 318–319, 482
Sole proprietorship, 29
SOPA. *See* Stop Online Piracy Act
Sound training program, 281
Sovereign immunity, 53, 80
   definition of, 88
   school transportation and, 181, 375

SPARTA. *See* Sports Agent Responsibility and Trust Act
Spas, 156–157, 203
Special damages, 231
Special relationships, 165, 261
Specific performance, 220, 367, 407
Specific supervision, 167
Spectators, emergency care for, 157
Sphere of control, 203
SPK. *See* Standard player contract
Sponsorship contracts, 389–390
   endorsement, 390
   exclusive rights in, 389
   fees and expenses in, 388
   fundamental concepts of, 385–392
   intellectual property rights and, 400
   media issues in, 389
   professional service, 389
   venue concerns with, 389
Sport agents
   American Bar Association and, 665–666
   breach of fiduciary duty and, 239–240
   crimes by, 251
   financial advisors and, 666
   legislation on, 660–668
   national legislation on, 662–663
   state legislation on, 661
   Uniform Athlete Agent Act on, 661
Sport-related crimes
   crimes against government, 251–252
   crimes against persons, 248–251
   crimes against public health, safety, and welfare, 251
   defenses, 250–251
   gambling, 252
   hazing, 213, 249, 258–272
   likelihood of occurrence, 249–250
   point shaving, 251
   by sport agents, 251
   ticket scalping, 252
Sport safety acts, 99
Sports Agent Responsibility and Trust Act (SPARTA), 251, 662
Sports, definition of, 526
Sport shooting, 101
Sports instructors and officials, negligence and, 67–70
Sports liability insurance policies, 341
Sports Litigation Alerts, 20
Stand-alone document waivers, 110

Standard of care/duty, 286
Standard of proof, 215
Standard Operating Procedures, 324
Standard player contract (SPK), 396
Standards, 168
Standards of care
   aggravated negligence and, 46
   Good Samaritan statutes and, 97
   negligence, 63–64, 66–67
   reasonable care, 46
   recklessness, 64–66
   in sports, 64–65
Standards of conduct, 168
Standards of practice, 286–291
   changing law on, 289
   definition of, 286
   identifying and selecting, 289
   legal impact of, 286–287
   by professional organizations, 287
   proliferation of and inconsistency among, 288–289
   in risk management, 289–290
   terminology in, 288–289
Standing, 8, 405–406, 436
   constitutional law and, 405–406
State action, 416–425, 490
   college athletics and, 418–419
   definition of, 416
   high school athletic associations and, 418
   nexus/entanglement theory of, 417
   professional sports leagues and, 419
   public function theory of, 416
   recreational clubs/facilities and, 417–418
   search and seizure and, 447
   United States Olympic Committee and, 419
State actors, 468–469
   due process and, 426–430
   equal protection and, 435–436
   gender equity and, 522–523
State codes, transportation related, 182
State court systems, 5–7, 18
State high school athletic associations, 492
Statement of facts, 24, 229–230
Statement of issue/problem, 24
State reporters, 18
State tort claims acts, 84, 89, 181
Statistical evidence, 548
Statute of frauds, 364
Statute of limitations, 9, 84
Statutes, 2–3, 15, 16
   anti-discrimination, 517
   anti-hazing, 264–265

Statutes *(Continued)*
    duty and, 42
    emergency care and, 150
    on ticket scalping, 252
Statutory assumption of risk statutes, 84, 99–102
Statutory duty to supervise, 166
Statutory law, 2–3, 83–84
Steroids, 492–493
"Stigma plus" test, 427
Stinson, Jason, 250
St. Joseph's University, 259
Stop Online Piracy Act (SOPA), 596
Strasburg High School, 258
Strength and Conditioning Professional Standards and Guidelines, 287
Strict liability, 192, 348
Strict scrutiny, 435, 438–439
String cite, 17
Stringer, Korey, 157
Strip searches, 492
Subjective test, 557
Subject matter jurisdiction, 6
Substantial disruption exemption, 456
Substantial factor test, 47
Substantive due process, 426
Suggestive marks, 602
Summarizing cases, 15, 23–27
Summary judgment, 9
Summons, 8–9
Supervision, 165–177
    adhering to policies/standards and, 172
    attributes of proper, 167–168
    definition of, 165
    duty of, 165–167
    evaluating physical/mental condition of participants and, 170–172
    improper, 165
    lack of, 165
    primary duties of, 168–170
    risk management plans and, 299
    types of, 167
Supplemental income provisions, 375
Supreme Court Reporter, 17
Supreme courts, state, 5
Suspect classifications, 439
Suspended athletes, 629
Symbiotic relationships, 417
Syracuse University, 249
Systemic disparate treatment, 548, 572

T

Taft-Hartley Act of 1947, 651–653
Tagliabue, Paul, 377
Tampering, 240
Tangible employment actions, 556
Tariffs, 205
Tattle texting, 319
Tax Effect on School, 352
Team owners, 628–629
Team travel, 184
Ted Stevens Olympic and Amateur Sports Act, 504
Television broadcasting
    antitrust law and, 629, 639
    copyright and, 595
Temporary restraining orders, 406
Termination clauses, 375–377
Termination without cause, 376
Term of employment, 374
Terpstra, Mike, 545
Terrorism, 321–322
Texas Charitable Immunity and Liability Act, 182
Thirteenth Amendment, 378
Threats, 171–172
Ticket resale. *See* Ticket scalping
Ticket scalping, 252
Ticket takers, 333
Title II, 514–515
Title IX, 23, 24, 438, 483, 523–526
    enforcement of, 523–524
    gender equity and, 535–536
    requirements in, 524–526
    retaliation for speaking for gender equity and, 535–540
    sexual harassment and, 559–560
Title VII, 515–516, 534–535, 543–546
    administration of, 544
    classes protected under, 544–546
    defenses, 550
    Lilly Ledbetter Fair Pay Act and, 536
    on religion, 546
    remedies, 550
    retaliation claims, 549–550
    scope of, 543–544
    on sex discrimination, 545–546
    sexual harassment and, 556
    theories of liability and, 546–550
Tomlinson, Kathryn, 535
Tortfeasors, 216
Tortious interference, 213

Tortious interference with contract, 213, 236, 240–241
Torts
   federal and state tort claims acts, 84, 88, 181
   intentional, 54, 213–270
"Totality of the circumstances" test, 135, 557–558
Tour de France, 494, 495
Tour operators, 208
Trademark Dilution Revision Act, 604
Trademarks, 390, 400
   abandonment of, 605
   ambush marketing and, 608
   counterfeiting, 604
   defenses for, 605–608
   definition of, 602
   dilution of, 604
   disclaimers and, 606
   disparaging marks, 606
   doctrine of laches on, 605
   fair use/parody of, 605–606
   image rights and, 616–617
   infringement of, 603–604
   Internet domain names, 400, 607–608
   law on, 602–611
   licensing, 606–607
   unfair competition and false advertising and, 605
   use and registration of, 603
Trainees, liability and, 55
Training
   in emergency care, 153
   independent contractor *vs.* employee, 379
   in risk management, 280
Transfer of risk, 278
Transfer rules, 428, 469–470
Transformative use defense, 619
Transgender athletes, 438
Transgender people, 546
Transitional supervision, 167
Transportation, 178–189
   duty of care in, 178–179
   independent contractors and, 179–180
   in organization-owned vehicles, 180–181
   15-passenger van, 183–184
   policy recommendations, 184, 298
   in privately owned vehicles, 181–182
   tourism and, 205–206
Travel agents, 207–208
Treatises, 19
Trespasser, 130
Trial courts, 5
Trial phase, 8–11

Truth, as defense, 230
T-shirt security, 329, 334
Tyson, Mike, 216

U

UAA. *See* Uniform Arbitration Act of 1955
UAAA. *See* Uniform Athlete Agent Act
UCC. *See* Uniform Commercial Code
UDRP. *See* Uniform Dispute Resolution Process
Ultra vires acts, 54, 80, 180
Umbrella liability insurance, 341–342
Unauthorized use of names of likenesses, 236, 237
Unconstitutional conditions doctrine, 427
Under-inclusive classifications, 439–440
Understanding or risk, 79
Undue hardship, 546, 582–584
Unfair competition, 605
Unfair labor practices, 650–651
Uniform Arbitration Act of 1955 (UAA), 395
Uniform Athlete Agent Act (UAAA), 661
Uniform Commercial Code (UCC), 194, 360–361
Uniform contribution among joint tortfeasors, 55
Uniform Dispute Resolution Process (UDRP), 608
Uniformed/off-duty law enforcement, 329
Unilateral contracts, 361–362
Unilateral mistakes, 365
Uninsured/underinsured motorist coverage, 343
Unions, 651
United Nations Convention on the Rights of Persons with Disabilities, 585
United States Anti-Doping Agency (USADA), 490
United States Code (U.S.C), 16
United States Olympic Committee (USOC), 607
United States Soccer Federation (USSF), 570
United States Supreme Court (USSC), 4, 17
University athletes, liability and, 55
University of Georgia, 228
University of Pittsburgh, 227
University of San Diego (USD), 251
University of Toledo, 251
Unreasonable disclosure of private facts, 236, 238–239
Unreasonable intrusion on seclusion, 236–237
Unreasonable restraints of trade, 637
USADA. *See* United States Anti-Doping Agency
U.S.C. *See United States Code*
U.S. Court of Appeals, 17
USD. *See* University of San Diego
U.S. Department of Education, 322
Ushers, 333
USOC. *See* United States Olympic Committee

V

USSC. *See* United States Supreme Court
USSF. *See* United States Soccer Federation
U.S. Supreme Court Reports, 17

V

Validity of contracts, 361
Vans, 183–184
VARA. *See* Visual Artists Rights Act of 1990
Vehicles, hired, 342
Venue, 111, 389
Verdicts, 215
Vicarious liability, 45, 54
    assault and battery and, 220
    transportation and, 181
Violence, 400
Visual Artists Rights Act of 1990 (VARA), 593
Vivas, Lindy, 536
Void/Voidable contracts, 361
Voluntary arbitration, 396
Voluntary associations, 467–476
    definition of, 467
    fundamental concepts on, 467
    intercollegiate regulations and, 471–473
    judicial review and, 467–471
Voluntary assumption of duty, 41–42
    emergency care and, 149–150
    to supervise, 165–167
Voluntary consent, 79
Volunteer Protection Act (VPA), 55, 96–97, 182
Volunteers
    immunity, 69, 84, 90–97, 182
    liability and, 55
    workers' compensation and, 350
VPA. *See* Volunteer Protection Act

W

WADA. *See* World Anti-Doping Agency
Wage gap, 536
Waivers
    administering, 111
    admiralty law and, 106
    alternative dispute resolution and, 394
    corporate liability and, 57
    definition of, 105
    emergency care and, 156–157
    in equipment rental agreements, 81
    format of, 110–111
    liability, 45
    minors and, 107–110
    in negligence defense, 80, 81, 105–115
    requirements for valid, 106
    risk transfer with, 278
    tourism and, 208
Walters, Norby, 663
Warnings of risks, 169–170, 298
Warranty considerations, 193–195
Warren, Samuel, 613
Warsaw Convention, 205
Weather insurance, 343
Web-based research, 20
WESTLAW, 20
West's Key Number System, 23
West Virginia Secondary School Activities Commission (WVSSAC), 470
Where to Find Court Opinions, 21
White House Conference on Aging, 569
Willful acts, 54
Willful and wanton misconduct, 45
Wilson High School, 261
WIPO. *See* World Intellectual Property Organization
"Women in Intercollegiate Sport," 532
Woods, Tiger, 613
Woolf, Bob, 660
Workers' compensation, 343, 348–353, 437
    college athletes and, 351–353
    eligibility for, 348–349
    independent contractors, 349
    professional athletes and, 350–351
    small businesses and, 349
    transportation and, 183
    volunteers and, 350
Workers' Compensation Court, 6
World Anti-Doping Agency (WADA), 490, 495
World Anti-Doping Code, 399, 495
World Intellectual Property Organization (WIPO), 400, 608
Wright, Kirk, 666
Wrongful death, 156, 215
Wrongful termination, 535
WVSSAC. *See* West Virginia Secondary School Activities Commission

Y

Youth sports programs, 154–155

Z

Zidane, Zinedine, 216
Zoning, 141
Zoo Crew, 535